NORMAN RULE IN NORMANDY 911–1144

NORMAN RULE IN NORMANDY,

911–1144

Mark Hagger

THE BOYDELL PRESS

First published 2017
The Boydell Press, Woodbridge

ISBN 978 1 78327 214 3

The Boydell Press is an imprint of Boydell & Brewer Ltd
PO Box 9, Woodbridge, Suffolk IP12 3DF, UK
and of Boydell & Brewer Inc.
668 Mt Hope Avenue, Rochester, NY 14620–2731, USA
website: www.boydellandbrewer.com

A catalogue record for this book is available
from the British Library

The publisher has no responsibility for the continued existence or accuracy of URLs for
external or third-party internet websites referred to in this book, and does not guarantee
that any content on such websites is, or will remain, accurate or appropriate

Contents

Illustrations

The author and publishers are grateful to all the institutions and individuals listed for permission to reproduce the materials in which they hold copyright. Every effort has been made to trace the copyright holders; apologies are offered for any omission, and the publishers will be pleased to add any necessary acknowledgement in subsequent editions.

Acknowledgements

THE origins of this book lie in an AHRC-funded project to edit the charters and writs of Henry I, led by Professor Richard Sharpe in the Modern History Faculty at Oxford University. Work began (for me) in October 2003, and there followed three happy years of research and writing at the top of the old Indian Institute building, in the company of Richard and the other members of the project, Nicholas Karn and Hugh Doherty. Beginning with Saint-Evroult, I worked my way through most of the Norman archives that had preserved acts of King Henry, and thus began the work that would eventually lead, more than fourteen years later, to the publication of this book. One of the benefits of working on the project was access to a database of Anglo-Norman royal and ducal acts which, with some necessary additions and tweaks, has proven to be a very useful research tool. I should add that, following further funding and the employment of a new 'elf', completed files for a number of Henry I's beneficiaries have now appeared online (see < https://actswilliam2henry1.wordpress.com/ >).

Thanks are also due to a number of other people, who have helped me over the years in a number of different capacities. They include Christopher Trussel; Michael McMahon; Robert Bartlett; John Hudson; Lorna Walker; and Sally Roe. Professor Raimond Karl, while Head of the School of History, Welsh History, and Archaeology at Bangor, effectively extended my one-semester study leave across a whole academic year. The additional time allowed me to draft almost the whole of the book, and provided the essential momentum for its completion, which was slowed, if never actually halted, by the demands of a full teaching and administrative load.

I have also benefited enormously from the advice and knowledge of David Bates, whose new biography of William the Conqueror unfortunately emerged too late in the day to influence what follows; Bill Aird; Stephen Church; Elisabeth van Houts; and Nicholas Karn. Katy Dutton, Leonie Hicks, and Charles Insley deserve special mention, not just on account of their friendship, knowledge, and collegiality, but because they have read and commented on parts of this book. Indeed, Leonie deserves particular thanks for ploughing through the majority of the text and providing an in-depth critique of what she read – despite having to complete her own *A Short History of the Normans* at the same time. And last, but not least, I must thank Caroline Palmer of Boydell & Brewer both for her support and enthusiasm throughout, and, indeed, for her willingness to publish a rather long book.

I would also like to acknowledge the help of the staff of the various archives and centres that have furnished primary sources for this study: the archives départementales of Calvados, Eure, Orne, and Seine-Maritime (whose collection of diplomas and cartularies has been digitized and is available online, and provides a model of what could and should be achieved by other archives in France, the UK, and elsewhere); the Archives Nationales; the Bibliothèque nationale de France; the Bibliothèque municipal at Rouen; the British Library; and the Institut de Recherche et d'Histoire des Textes (whose BVMM website provides another model for such bodies to follow). The Scouloudi Foundation deserves thanks here, too, for their awards of funding to cover the costs of two research trips to France.

My biggest debt of gratitude, of course, is due to my wife Kate and my little boy, Daniel, who have had to live with me through the highs and lows that accompany writing, and finishing, a book. Their support and encouragement has been priceless. This book is dedicated to them.

Abbreviations

AAbps	*Acta Archiepiscoporum Rotomagensium: a study and edition*, ed. and trans. R. Allen, Tabularia, 'Documents', 9 (2009), 1–66
AD	Archives départementales, followed by the name of the département
AN	*Archives Nationale, Paris*
ANS	*Anglo-Norman Studies*, including its earlier incarnation, *The Proceedings of the Battle Conference on Anglo-Norman Studies*
ASChr	*Anglo-Saxon Chronicle*, followed by the manuscript version (C, D, E, etc.) and the year. I have used the translation by G. N. Garmonsway (see bibliography), and a reference to that work follows.
Bates, *Normandy*	D. Bates, *Normandy before 1066* (London, 1982)
Bessin, *Concilia*	G. Bessin, *Concilia Rotomagensis Provincia*, 2 vols (Rouen, 1717)
BL	British Library
BnF	Paris, Bibliothèque nationale de France
BSAN	*Bulletin de la société des antiquaires de normandie*
Chs. Jumièges	*Chartes de l'abbaye de Jumièges*, ed. J. J. Vernier, 2 vols (Rouen, 1916)
CDF	*Calendar of Documents preserved in France Illustrative of the History of Great Britain and Ireland. Vol I: AD 918–1206*, ed. J. H. Round (London, 1899)
Chanteux, *Recueil*	H. Chanteux, *Recueil des actes de Henri Ier Beauclerc*, 3 vols, thèse inédite de l'Ecole des Chartes, 1932
Constitutio	*Constitutio Domus Regis* in *Dialogus de Scaccario: The Dialogue of the Exchequer; Constitutio Domus Regis: The Establishment of the Royal Household*, ed. and trans. E. Amt and S. D. Church (Oxford, 2007)

Chs. Caen	*Charters and Custumals of the Abbey of Holy Trinity, Caen: Part 2. The French Estates*, ed. J. Walmsley, Records of Social and Economic History, new series 22 (Oxford, 1994)
Ctl. Beaumont-le-Roger	*Cartulaire de l'église de la Sainte-Trinité de Beaumont-le-Roger*, ed. E. Deville (Paris, 1912)
Ctl. Caen	Caen, AD Calvados, 1 J 41: cartulary of the abbey of Saint-Etienne of Caen
Ctl. Conches	*Le grand cartulaire de Conches et sa copie: transcription et analyse*, ed. Clare de Haas (2005)
Ctl. Grand-Beaulieu	*Cartulaire de la léproserie du Grand-Beaulieu*, eds. Merlet and Jusselin (Chartres, 1909)
Ctl. Montebourg	BnF, MS lat. 10087: cartulary of Montebourg abbey
Ctl. Mont-Saint-Michel	*The Cartulary of the Abbey of Mont-Saint-Michel*, ed. K. S. B. Keats-Rohan (Donnington, 2006)
Ctl. Normand	*Cartulaire Normand de Philippe-Auguste, Louis VIII, Saint Louis et Philippe-le-Hardi*, ed. L. Delisle (Caen, 1882)
Ctl. Perche	*Le zartulaire de l'abbaye de Marmoutier pour la Perche*, ed. P. Barret (Mortagne, 1894)
Ctl. Préaux	*Le cartulaire de l'abbaye bénédictine de Saint-Pierre-de-Préaux (1034–1227)*, ed. D. Rouet, Editions du Comité des travaux historiques et scientifiques (Paris, 2005)
Ctl. Rouen	Rouen, BM, MS 1193: cartulary of Rouen cathedral
Ctl. Saint-Père	*Cartulaire de l'abbaye de Saint-Père de Chartres*, ed. B. Guérard, 2 vols (Paris, 1840)
Ctl. Sées	Sées, bibliothèque de l'évêché de Sées, cartulaire de Saint-Martin de Sées
Ctl. Tiron	*Cartulaire de l'abbaye de la Sainte-Trinité de Tiron*, ed. M. L. Merlet, vol. 1 (Chartres, 1883)
Ctl. Troarn	BnF, MS lat. 10086 : cartulary of Troarn abbey
Ctl. Vendôme	*Cartulaire de l'abbaye cardinale de la Trinité du Vendôme*, ed. C. Métais, 5 vols (Paris, 1893–1904)
Dialogue	*Dialogus de Scaccario* in *Dialogus de Scaccario: The Dialogue of the Exchequer; Constitutio Domus Regis: The Establishment of the Royal Household*, ed. and trans. E. Amt and S. D. Church (Oxford, 2007)
Dudo	Dudonis Sancti Quintini, *De moribus et actis primorum Normanniae ducum*, ed. J. Lair, MSAN, 23 (1865)

Dudo | Dudo of Saint-Quentin, *History of the Normans: Translation with Introduction and Notes*, trans. E. Christiansen (Woodbridge, 1998)

Dunbabin, *France* | J. Dunbabin, *France in the Making 843–1180* (Oxford, 1991)

Eadmer, *HN* | Eadmer of Canterbury, *Historia novorum*, ed. M. Rule, rolls series (London, 1884). I have used the translation by G. Bosanquet, and a reference to that work follows where applicable

EHR | *English Historical Review*

EME | *Early Medieval Europe*

Etymologies | Isidore of Seville, *The Etymologies of Isidore of Seville*, trans. S. A. Barney, W. J. Lewis, J. A. Beach, and O. Berghof (Cambridge, 2006)

Flodoard | *Les annales de Flodoard*, ed. P. Lauer (Paris, 1905)

Flodoard | *The Annals of Flodoard of Reims 919–966*, ed. and trans. S. Fanning and B. Bachrach (Peterborough, Ontario and Plymouth, 2004)

Fulbert, *Letters* | Fulbert of Chartres, *The Letters and Poems of Fulbert of Chartres*, ed. and trans. F. Berends (Oxford, 1976)

Gaimar | Geffrei Gaimar, *Estoire des Engleis/History of the English*, ed. and trans. I. Short (Oxford, 2009)

GC | *Gallia Christiana in provincias ecclesiasticas distributa.: XI. De provincia Rotomagensi*, ed. D. Sammarthani et al. (Paris, 1759)

Glaber | Rodulfus Glaber, *Opera*, ed. and trans. J. France (Oxford, 1989)

GDB | Great Domesday Book, followed by a reference to the section/s in the Phillimore edition, edited by J. Morris.

Green, *Government* | J. A. Green, *The Government of England under Henry I* (Cambridge, 1986)

Green, *Henry* | J. A. Green, *Henry I King of England and Duke of Normandy* (Cambridge, 2006)

Heimskringla | Snorri Sturluson, *Heimskringla: A History of the Kings of Norway*, trans. L. M. Hollander (Austin, 1964)

Hollister, *Henry* | C. W. Hollister, *Henry I*, edited and completed by A. C. Frost (New Haven, CT and London, 2001)

HSJ | *Haskins Society Journal*

Huntingdon	Henry of Huntingdon, *Historia Anglorum: The History of the English People*, ed. and trans. D. Greenway (Oxford, 1996)
Hyde	*The Warenne (Hyde) Chronicle*, ed. and trans. E. M. C. van Houts (Oxford, 2013)
Inventio	*Inventio et miracula sancti Vulfrani*, ed. J. Laporte, Mélanges publiés par la Société de l'Histoire de Normandie (Rouen and Paris, 1938)
Inquisition	H. Navel, 'L'enquête de 1133 sur les fiefs de l'évêché de Bayeux', BSAN, 42 (1935), 5–80
JMH	*Journal of Medieval History*
Jumièges	William of Jumièges, Orderic Vitalis and Robert of Torigni, *The* Gesta Normannorum Ducum *of William of Jumièges, Orderic Vitalis, and Robert of Torigni*, ed. and trans. E. M. C. van Houts, 2 vols (Oxford, 1992–1995)
Letters of Lanfranc	*The Letters of Lanfranc, Archbishop of Canterbury*, ed. and trans. H. M. Clover and M. Gibson (Oxford, 1979)
Letters of St Anselm	*The Letters of St Anselm of Canterbury*, trans. W. Frölich, 3 vols (Kalamazoo, 1990–1994)
LHP	*Leges Henrici Primi*, ed. and trans. L. J. Downer (Oxford, 1972)
Life of Lanfranc	Milo Crispin, '*Life* of Lanfranc', *PL*, 150, cols. 29–58; trans. S. N. Vaughn, *The Abbey of Bec and the Anglo-Norman State* (Woodbridge, 1981)
Livre Noir	*Antiquus cartularius ecclesiæ Baiocensis (livre noir)*, ed. V. Bourienne, 2 vols (Rouen, 1902–3)
Louise, *Bellême*	G. Louise, *La seigneurie de Bellême X^e–XIIe siècles: devolution des pouvoirs territoriaux et construction d'une seigneurie de frontière aux confins de la Normandie et du Maine de la charnière de l'an mil*, La Pays Bas-Normand, 2 vols, 3 and 4 (1990) and 1 and 2 (1991)
Malmesbury, *GP*	William of Malmesbury, *Gesta Pontificum*, ed. and trans. M. Winterbottom, 2 vols (Oxford, 2007)
Malmesbury, *GR*	William of Malmesbury, *William of Malmesbury: Gesta Regum Anglorum*, ed. and trans. R. A. B. Mynors, R. M. Thomson, and M. Winterbotton, vol 1 (Oxford, 1998)
Malmesbury, *HN*	*Historia Novella: The Contemporary History*, ed. E. King, trans. K. R. Potter (Oxford, 1998)

Marchegay   M. P. Marchegay, *Chartes Normandes de l'abbaye de Saint-Florent près Saumur de 710 à 1200 environ*, Mémoires de la Société des Antiquaires de Normandie, 30 (1880)

MGH   *Monumenta Germaniae Historica*

MMI   C. W. Hollister, *Monarchy, Magnates and Institutions in the Anglo-Norman World* (London, 1986)

Monasticon   W. Dugdale and R. Dodsworth, *Monasticon Anglicanum*, ed. J. Caley *et al.*, 8 vols (London, 1817–30)

MSAN   Mémoires de la Société des Antiquaires de Normandie

NI   C. H. Haskins, *Norman Institutions* (Cambridge, MA, 1918)

Norman Pipe Rolls   *Pipe rolls for the Exchequer of Normandy for the Reign of Henry II: 1180 and 1184*, ed. V. Moss, Pipe Roll Society new series 53 (2004)

Normannia monastica   V. Gazeau, *Normannia monastica: prosopographie des abbés bénédictins (X^e–XIIe siècle)*, 2 vols (Caen, 2007)

Orderic   Orderic Vitalis, *Historia ecclesiastica*, ed. and trans. M. Chibnall, 6 vols (Oxford, 1969–80)

PL   *Patrologiae Latinae cursus completes, series Latina*, ed. J.-P. Migne, 221 vols (1844–1855)

Poitiers   William of Poitiers, *Gesta Guillelmi*, ed. and trans. R. H. C. Davis and M. Chibnall (Oxford, 1998)

PR 31 Henry I   *The Great Roll of the Pipe for the Thirty-First Year of the Reign of King Henry I, Michaelmas 1130 (Pipe Roll 1): A New Edition with a Translation and Images from the original in the Public Record Office/The National Archives*, ed. and trans. J. A. Green, Pipe Roll Society, new series 57 (London, 2012)

RADN   *Recueil des actes des ducs de Normandie de 911 à 1066*, ed. Marie Fauroux, Mémoires de la Société des Antiquaires de Normandie, 36 (Caen, 1961)

Recueil Henri II   *Recueil des actes d'Henri II, roi d'Angleterre et duc de Normandie concernant les provinces françaises et les affaires de France*, ed. L. Delisle and E. Berger, 3 vols (Paris, 1916–1927)

RHGF   *Recueil des Historiens des Gaules et de la France*, par Dom. M. Bouquet, nouvelle edition publiée sous la direction de M. L. Delisle, 24 vols (Paris, 1738–1904)

Regesta, i.	*Regesta regum Anglo-Normannorum 1066–1154, I. Regesta Willemi Conquestoris et Willelmi Rufi 1066–1100*, ed. H. W. C. Davis (Oxford, 1913)
Regesta, ii.	*Regesta regum Anglo-Normannorum 1066–1154, II. Regesta Henrici Primi, 1100–1135*, ed. C. Johnson and H. A. Cronne (Oxford, 1956)
Regesta, iii.	*Regesta regum Anglo-Normannorum, 1066–1154: III. Regesta regis Stephani ac Mathildis imperatricis ac Gaufridi et Henrici ducum Normannorum 1135–1154*, ed. H. A. Cronne and R. H. C. Davis (Oxford, 1968)
Regesta: William	*Regesta regum Anglo-Normannorum, the acta of William I (1066–1087)*, ed. D. Bates (Oxford, 1998)
Richer	Richer of Saint-Remi, *Histories*, ed. and trans. J. Lake, 2 vols (Cambridge, MA, 2011)
RT	Robert of Torigni, *Chronicle*, with the date of the annal and references to the editions by Léopold Delisle and Richard Howlett: 'The Chronicle of Robert of Torigni, Abbot of the Monastery of St. Michael in Peril of the Sea', in *Chronicles of the Reigns of Stephen, Henry II and Richard I*, ed. R. Howlett, vol 4 (London, 1889); and *Chronique de Robert de Torigni, abbé de Mont-Saint-Michel*, ed. L. Delisle, 2 vols (Rouen, 1872–3)
Searle, *PK*	E. Searle, *Predatory Kinship and the Formation of Norman Power* (Berkeley and London, 1988)
Tabuteau, *Transfers*	E. Z. Tabuteau, *Transfers of Property in Eleventh-Century Norman Law* (Chapel Hill, NC and London, 1988)
TAC	*Coutumiers de Normandie: textes critiques*, ed. E.-J. Tardif, vol 1 (Rouen, 1881)
Telma	Traitement électronique des manuscrits et des archives. Chartes originales antérieures à 1121 conservées en France: <http://www.cn-telma.fr/originaux/index/>
Van Houts, *Normans*	E. van Houts (ed. and trans.), *The Normans in Europe* (Manchester, 2000)
Wace	Wace, *The History of the Norman People: Wace's Roman de Rou*, trans. G. S. Burgess (Woodbridge, 2004)
Worcester	*The Chronicle of John of Worcester*, ed. and trans. P. McGurk, vol 3 (Oxford, 1998)

A Note on the Text

To provide a coherent and convincing explanation for the development and maintenance of the dukes' authority in the pages that follow, it is necessary to explore a number of different issues and influences. While all of these different factors reinforced each other, and consequently have to be understood in the round, nonetheless the need to marshal a coherent argument requires that they must be teased apart. Thus the various chapters of this book each explore one issue, or a small number of closely related issues, in some depth. The intentional result of this approach is that the book has been structured as a series of discrete but linked articles. Each section is designed to stand alone, while at the same time combining with the others to form a whole. The aim of this approach is to make the arguments advanced here more accessible, especially for those who want to pursue one thread in particular. Those who want to perceive the fuller picture will find cross-references in the footnotes, as well as comprehensive indices, which are intended to pull the contents back together again by acting as signposts to related discussions and topics.

The chapters themselves have been grouped into two parts. In broad terms, Part I forms an analytical narrative, which explores the politics of the creation of an autonomous, rather than an independent or separatist, Normandy. The first three chapters examine the development of the duchy, looking at the wars, diplomacy, and patronage that saw the dukes' rule first established and then maintained across a growing swathe of territory until, in the 1120s, Normandy at last reached its final form. While these chapters necessarily glance at the dukes' relationships with the Church and the kings of the French, their dealings and competition for authority with these two external powers are considered at greater length in Chapters 4 and 5, respectively. Part II comprises a thematic exploration and analysis of the structures, institutions, and psychologies that supported the dukes' rule within the duchy. It is concerned with the nature of the dukes' power, their courts, justice, revenues, and war machine.

These are the topics the book looks at directly. Other issues are explored only obliquely, or by implication, or not at all. For example, while government and institutions and authority necessarily impact society, and will in some ways reflect the shape of that society, too, this book does not look at Norman society explicitly in the pages that follow. I have not, for example, dwelt on the degree of Scandinavian settlement in what would become Normandy during the tenth and eleventh centuries, and I have not synthesized the large body of work that has explored place-name evidence, or the use of Scandinavian names and terms in the duchy, even if intermittent reference has been made to it.[1] That is also, in part, because of the inconclusive nature of such evidence. For example, the use of legal terms such as *ullac* and *hamfara* does little more than tell us what we know already – that Normandy was subject to a degree of Scandinavian settlement during its history and those settlers brought terms with them that for some reason were preferred to the equivalent Frankish ones.[2] The survival of such labels into the eleventh century does not necessarily tell us anything about eleventh-century Norman society, however, just as the modern legal profession's love of Latin maxims does not tell us much about the nature or language of the society of twenty-first-century England and Wales (other than that it continues to look to the past). As such a lawyer might say: *res ipsa loquitur*. Equally, as the discussion throughout focuses on the practicalities of the topics concerned – how they operated and how they worked to promote the dukes' rule – more theoretical concepts and questions have generally been omitted. Thus the discussion of justice focuses on jurisdiction and judgement, rather than on jurisprudence, while the exploration of the Norman Church looks at how Christianity might be used as a tool of government but has little to say about the ideology of the monastic revival in Normandy, or popular religion, or the cults of the saints and miracle collections (of which there are more than is commonly thought, and which are crying out to be studied in more detail). Yet more regrettably, there has also been no room for

---

[1] The thrust of the work done on this subject up to 1982 is conveniently summarized by Bates, *Normandy*, pp. 15–23 and there is a useful map illustrating the spread of Scandinavian place-names in L. Musset, 'Les scandinaves et l'ouest du contintent européen', in *Les Vikings: Les Scandinaves et l'Europe 800–1200*, ed. E. Roesdahl, J.-P. Mohen, and F.-X. Dillman (Paris, 1992), p. 92, Fig. 4. There are also recent related studies by A. N. Jaubert, G. Fellow-Jensen, A. K. H. Wagner, and E. Ridel in *Les fondations Scandinaves en occident et les débuts du duché de Normandie*, ed. P. Bauduin (Caen, 2005), pp. 209–71 inclusive.

[2] The words are found among the *consuetudines uicecomitatus* listed in *RADN*, no. 121; *Ctl. Préaux*, A161, A163. For a brief discussion of the *consuetudines* see J. Yver, 'Contribution à l'étude du développement de la compétence ducale en Normandie', *Annales de Normandie*, 8 (1958), 157–9; J. Yver, 'Les premières institutions du duché de Normandie', *I Normanni e la loro espansione in Europa*. Settimane di studio del centro Italiano sull'alto medioevo 16 (Spoleto, 1969), 345–7; and for a discussion of the Scandinavian origins of the term 'ullac' see L. Musset, 'Autour des modalités juridiques de l'expansion normande au XIe siècle: le droit d'exil', in *Autour du pouvoir ducal normand, Xe–XIIe siècles*, ed. L. Musset, J.-M. Bouvris, and J.-M. Maillefer (Caen, 1985), 45–59.

a consideration of the literary, artistic, and intellectual life of the duchy, except where the work and thought it produced also had a political dimension.

The arguments found in this book are built on the primary sources, principally the narratives and diplomas, writs, and charters that were produced in Normandy between 911 and 1144. Nonetheless, a great intellectual debt is owed to those historians who have worked on the duchy and its institutions previously, whose ideas sometimes challenged and sometimes supported, in whole or in part, the conclusions I had reached. They include Lucien Valin, Charles Homer Haskins, Jean-François Lemarignier, Lucien Musset, Jean Yver, John Le Patourel, David Bates, Eleanor Searle, and Pierre Bauduin. That earlier work has provided stimulation, understanding, and provocation (and sometimes all three), and its influence may be traced in the footnotes. But what follows has also been informed by work on Carolingian Francia, Anglo-Saxon England, and Norman Italy, which has provided some useful analogies and contrasts, and has sometimes helped to fill in the gaps in the Norman evidence as a result. However, although the net has been cast widely, some relevant work will no doubt have been missed (and I am particularly aware that the considerable historiography on rulership written in German is closed to me). But lines do have to be drawn somewhere, even if drawing them is a tricky and uncomfortable business, and the words of no less an authority than Quintilian on this subject are worth bearing in mind: 'to ferret out everything that has ever been said on the subject, even by the most worthless of writers, is a sign of tiresome pedantry or empty ostentation, and results in delaying and swamping the mind when it would be better employed on other themes'.[3]

---

[3] Quintilian, *Institutio Oratoria*, Bk. I.viii; ed. and trans. H. E. Butler (London, 1969), i. 154–5.

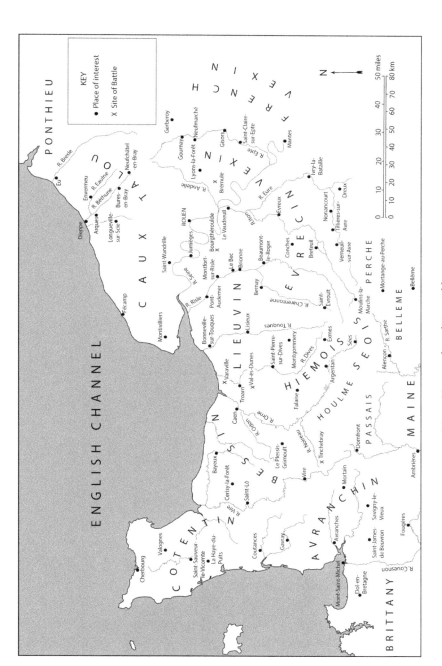

Map 1. Normandy and its neighbours

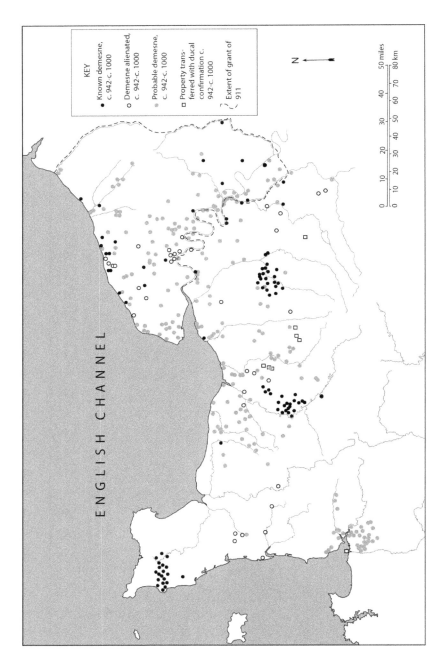

Map 2. The duke's demesne and property subject to ducal confirmation in Normandy, c. 942–c. 1000

KEY

- Known demesne, c. 942–c. 1000
○ Demesne alienated, c. 942–c. 1000
Probable demesne, c. 942–c. 1000
□ Property transferred with ducal confirmation c. 942–c. 1000
Extent of grant of 911

N

50 miles
80 km

ENGLISH CHANNEL

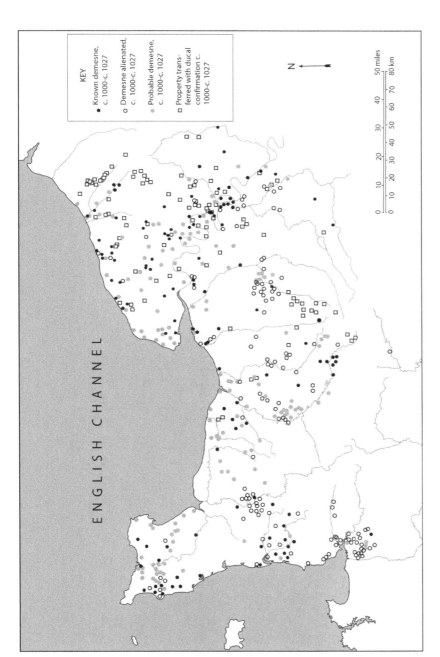

KEY

• Known demesne, c. 1000–c. 1027

○ Demesne alienated, c. 1000–c. 1027

● Probable demesne, c. 1000–c. 1027

□ Property transferred with ducal confirmation c. 1000–c. 1027

ENGLISH CHANNEL

N

0	10	20	30	40	50 miles
0	10 20	30 40	50 60	70	80 km

Map 3. The duke's demesne and property subject to ducal confirmation in Normandy, 996–1026

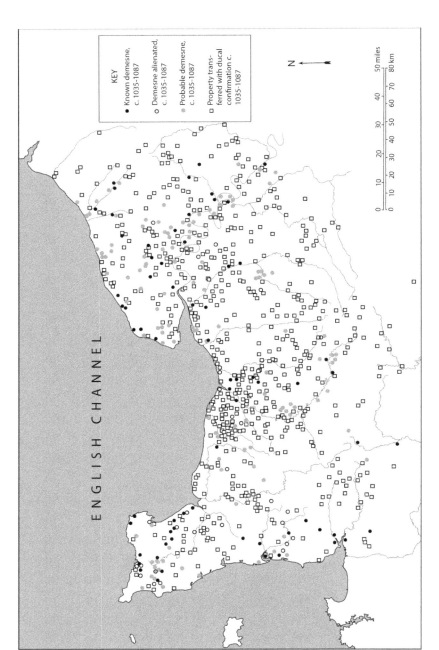

KEY

● Known demesne,
  c. 1035–1087

○ Demesne alienated,
  c. 1035–1087

● Probable demesne,
  c. 1035–1087

□ Property trans-
  ferred with ducal
  confirmation c.
  1035–1087

ENGLISH CHANNEL

N

| 0 | 10 | 20 | 30 | 40 | 50 miles |
| 0 | 10 | 20 | 30 | 40 | 50 | 60 | 70 | 80 km |

Map 4 The duke's demesne and property subject to ducal confirmation in Normandy, 1035–1087

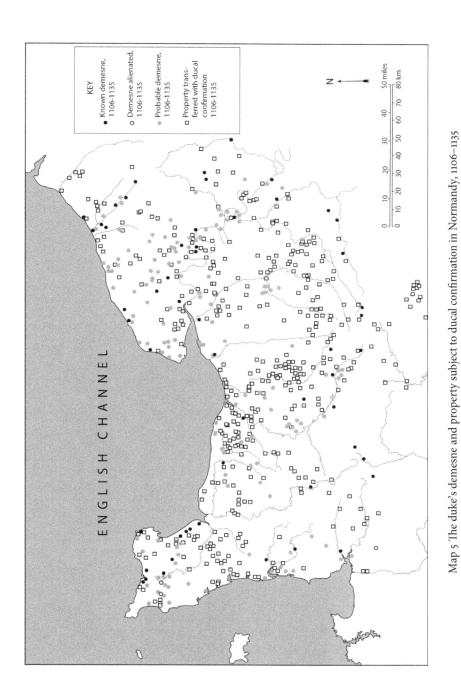

Map 5 The duke's demesne and property subject to ducal confirmation in Normandy, 1106–1135

KEY

● Known demesne, 1106–1135

○ Demesne alienated, 1106–1135

● Probable demesne, 1106–1135

□ Property trans-ferred with ducal confirmation 1106–1135

ENGLISH CHANNEL

N

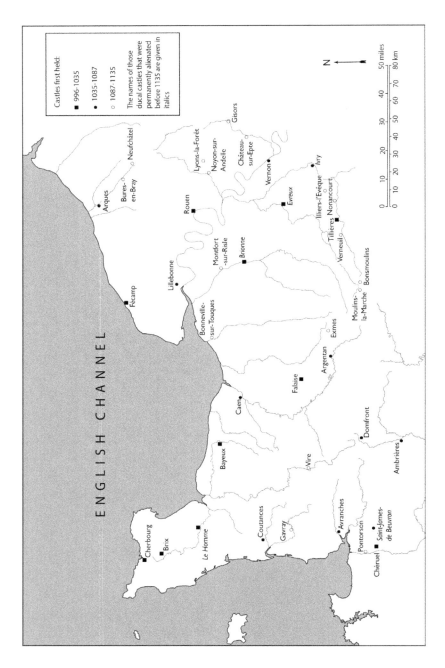

Castles first held:

■ 996–1035
● 1035–1087
○ 1087–1135

The names of those ducal castles that were permanently alienated before 1135 are given in italics

N

0   10   20   30   40   50 miles
0 10 20 30 40 50 60 70 80 km

ENGLISH CHANNEL

Arques
Bures-en-Bray
Neufchâtel
Lyons-la-Forêt
Noyon-sur-Andelle
Gisors
Château-sur-Epte
Rouen
Vernon
Ivry
Evreux
Illiers-l'Evêque
Nonancourt
Tillières
Verneuil
Montfort-sur-Risle
Brionne
Bonsmoulins
Fécamp
Lillebonne
Bonneville-sur-Touques
Moulins-la-Marche
Exmes
Argentan
Falaise
Caen
Bayeux
Domfront
Vire
Ambrières
Cherbourg
Brix
Le Homme
Coutances
Gavray
Avranches
Pontorson
Saint-James-de-Beuvron
Chéruel

Map 6. Ducal castles, 996–1135

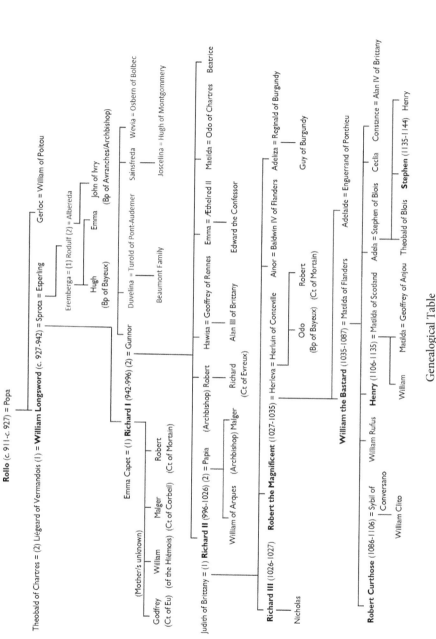

Genealogical Table

Introduction

THIS is a book about the creation, maintenance, rule, and governance of the duchy of Normandy and the power of the dukes who led that enterprise. It examines not only the structures that the dukes inherited or developed that allowed them to establish their authority across their territory, but also how the dukes won and then kept the loyalties of the lords who resided within their borders, how those lords manifested their loyalty to their ruler, and how they perceived and promoted it, too. In other words, this is a book that aims to look at the authority of the duke both as it was imposed from the top down *and* as it was recognized and strengthened from the bottom up.

Sources and approach

It is well known that contemporary sources for tenth-century Normandy are seriously lacking.[1] Some information is to be found in the *Annals* of Flodoard of Reims and rather less in the later, but still tenth-century, *Histories* of Richer of Reims. There is a brief mention of Rollo and his companions in an authentic act of Charles the Simple of 918 and of Richard I in an altogether more dubious diploma of Lothair V of 966. There are four authentic acts signed by Duke Richard, two of which record his gifts to his own foundations at Evreux and Fécamp, and to which might perhaps be added two eleventh-century acts that preserve grants that are said to have been made by tenth-century dukes.[2] This is not much to go on, and while it might be hoped that archaeological and place-name evidence might provide an additional foundation on which to build, that evidence is just as slight, ambiguous, and misleading as the written sources that purport to inform us of the relevant events.

One result of this absence of evidence is that while this book aims to look at the development of Normandy and of the dukes' authority from 911, many of the topics and trends explored in Chapters 4 through 11 can only be perceived, and still dimly at that, from the second decade of the eleventh century. That means

---

[1] See, for example, the earlier comments in Bates, *Normandy*, pp. xii–xiii.

[2] *RADN*, nos. 36, 53.

that the events, developments, and trends of the tenth century are often absent from this book. It also means that while we know, even if only approximately, what the Norman dukes had achieved by the first couple of decades of the eleventh century, we do not know how they got there. We certainly cannot assume a smooth or even logical progression from 911 to 1000. Indeed, what I hope will become clear from the following arguments is that the geographical growth of Normandy and the increase of the dukes' authority over that territory, as well as, for example, the Christianization of the Normans, was not at all smooth. There were reverses and advances, successes and failures, and while it might have been the case that Richard I had an idea about who should be encompassed within his *mouvance*, as indicated by the markers he set down during the 960s, there was no guarantee that his dream would become a reality.

In contrast to the tenth century, the eleventh saw the composition of a number of important narratives that were concerned with the birth and development of Normandy and which were written by men who lived, even if they had not been born, in the duchy. While letters, treatises, saints' *lives*, miracle collections, coins, and seals provide useful highlights and sidelights on the questions considered within these pages, it is the narratives and the ducal *acta* that provide the principal illumination. Both will consequently be discussed and critiqued throughout the book. As such, something needs to be said about who made them and when and why in order to gain a sense of their strengths and weaknesses before they are put to work, as well as to provide a context for that later analysis.

The more important of the Norman narratives for Norman history to 1144 are the *De moribus et actis primorum Normanniae ducum* or *Historia Normannorum* by Dudo of Saint-Quentin; the *Gesta Normannorum ducum* by William of Jumièges with later interpolations by Orderic Vitalis, Robert of Torigni, and unknown others; the *Gesta Guillelmi* of William of Poitiers; and the *Historia ecclesiastica* by Orderic Vitalis.[3] As Dudo's *De moribus* is the earliest of the four, we can begin there.

Dudo of Saint-Quentin and the De moribus

Dudo of Saint-Quentin's *De moribus*, although written at the beginning of the eleventh century, comprises a serial biography of the tenth-century dukes. It is

---

[3] All four are available in good modern translations, three of them in the Oxford Medieval Texts series with parallel Latin and English texts. The Latin text of Dudo's *De moribus*, however, is still only widely available in the edition made by Jules Lair in 1865. Publication details can be found in the Abbreviations, above, or the Bibliography, below.

likely that Dudo was born around 965 and educated perhaps at Liège or Reims. He first came to Normandy *c.* 987 as an ambassador for Count Albert I of the Vermandois. He remained and/or returned for some years, growing closer to the ageing Duke Richard I until, one day *c.* 994, the duke asked him to, 'describe the customs and deeds of the Norman land, nay, the rights which he established within the kingdom of his great-grandfather Rollo'.[4] That is what Dudo claimed, at least.

Part of Dudo's work might have been completed by 1001, when it was copied into the Fécamp chronicle, *if* we follow the argument of Matthieu Arnoux who concluded that the chronicle had been written by that date at the latest.[5] However, as the passage concerned was part of Dudo's description of the founding of Holy Trinity, Fécamp, which could quite easily have stood alone from the rest of his work,[6] it is not clear that the remainder of the *De moribus* must necessarily have also been written by that date, even if Arnoux is right. It is consequently safer to continue to suppose that Dudo's book was only completed *c.* 1015.[7]

Much of the recent scholarship on Dudo, which has saved him and his work from the oblivion into which it was thought they had fallen in 1982,[8] has focused on Dudo's sources and also on what his *De moribus* was intended to achieve. It

---

[4] *Dudo*, p. 6.

[5] M. Arnoux, 'Before the *Gesta Normannorum* and beyond Dudo: some evidence on early Norman historioraphy', *ANS*, 22 (1999), 45.

[6] *RADN*, no. 4.

[7] The work is dated to this period by, for example, L. Shopkow, 'The Carolingian world of Dudo of Saint-Quentin', *JMH*, 15 (1989), 33; P. Bauduin, *La première Normandie (X^e–XIe siècles). Sur les frontières de la Haute Normandie: Identité et construction d'une principauté* (Caen, 2004), p. 64; B. Pohl, *Dudo of Saint-Quentin's* Historia Normannorum: *Tradition, Innovation and Memory* (York, 2015), p. 3.

[8] See, for example, E. Searle, 'Fact and pattern in heroic history: Dudo of Saint-Quentin', *Viator*, 15 (1984), 119–37; L. Shopkow, 'The Carolingian world of Dudo of Saint-Quentin', 19–37; V. B. Jordan, 'The role of kingship in tenth-century Normandy: hagiography of Dudo of Saint-Quentin', *HSJ*, 3 (1991), 53–62; Shopkow, *History and Community: Norman Historical Writing in the Eleventh and Twelfth Centuries* (Washington, DC, 1997); Dudo of Saint-Quentin, *History of the Normans: Translation with an Introduction and Notes*, trans. E. Christiansen (Woodbridge, 1998); M. Arnoux, 'Before the *Gesta Normannorum* and beyond Dudo; some evidence on early Norman historiography', *Anglo-Norman Studies*, 22 (1999), 29–48; P. Bouet, 'Dudon de Saint-Quentin et le martyre de Guillaume Longue-Epée', in *Les Saints dans la Normandie Médiévale*, ed. P. Bouet and F. Neveux (Caen, 2000), 237–58; E. Albu, *The Normans in their Histories: Propaganda, Myth and Subversion* (Woodbridge, 2001), Ch. 1; B. S. Bachrach, 'Writing Latin history for a lay audience *c.* 1000: Dudo of Saint-Quentin at the Norman court', *HSJ*, 20 (2009), 58–77; Pohl, *Dudo of Saint-Quentin's* Historia Normannorum. See Bates, *Normandy*, pp. 10–11 for the judgement on Dudo's reputation now so completely overturned.

has consequently become clear that the *De moribus* owed much to the Classics, particularly Virgil's *Aeneid*, although Dudo also drew heavily on Eusebius's *Life of Constantine*, the *Life of St Lambert* (of Liège), and the *Life of St Germanus* (of Auxerre).[9] He knew the *Annals* composed by Flodoard of Reims, too, and perhaps also the nearly contemporary *Histories* of Richer of Reims. He wove these various sources together in a work that recognized and celebrated the Normans' Scandinavian origins (although he made Rollo a Dane rather than a Norwegian), that saw their desire to assimilate with the Franks first waver and then disappear as a result of a series of betrayals by Frankish counts and kings, and which emphasized that the settlers had become Christian Normans rather than remaining pagan Northmen, not least in a lengthy episode whereby Richard I insisted that his Scandinavian auxiliaries must convert to Christianity if they wanted to remain in the duchy under his rule.[10]

The nature of the events Dudo recorded, the speeches he put into his characters' mouths, and the asides to his audience(s) that he included in his poems, all suggest that he was writing a work of high politics, intended to resonate with a number of audiences simultaneously. He was, then, doing far more than indulging in a literary competition with Richer of Reims and Aimoin of Fleury and/ or providing a model of how to compose different styles of prose and poetry for young scholars in Frankish schools.[11] It is of course *possible* that the *De moribus* was in part a work of intellectual vanity or instruction, but the content and direction of his narrative suggests that Dudo was not principally working in an intellectual arena but a political one, and that the contents of his book were intended to be heard or read and digested and disseminated by the educated churchmen who attended Richard II's court. That might be to read far too much into Dudo's work and to credit him with more than his share of political nous, yet anyone working alongside Duke Richard II, especially one who stood close enough to the duke to describe himself as his chancellor,[12] would surely have been able to see that there was a need to address the duke's relations with his Breton, Frankish, and English neighbours, and a need also to promote a sense of unity among the duke's own subjects. And so I conclude that Dudo's *De moribus* should be seen as a pamphlet or manifesto intended to justify and legitimize Richard II's position vis-à-vis his neighbours and to help to create a stronger and more positive sense

---

[9] L. Shopkow, *History and Community*, pp. 151–2; *Dudo*, p. xxi; Pohl, *Dudo of Saint-Quentin's* Historia Normannorum, pp. 197–223.

[10] *Dudo*, pp. 156–62.

[11] As suggested by *Dudo*, pp. xx–xxi and L. B Mortensen, 'Stylistic choices in a reborn genre: the national histories of Widukind of Corvey and Dudo of St Quentin', in *Dudone di San Quintino*, ed. P. Gatti and A. Degl'Innocenti (Trent, 1995), pp. 100–1.

[12] *RADN*, no. 18 and see below, *infra*, pp. 31, 33.

of what it meant to be a Norman. The extent to which either Richard I or Richard II imposed this programme on Dudo is a separate question, and one which evades an answer, too.

Dudo's intentions, as outlined here, would have been achievable even if the book were only known to those present at Richard II's court, for they represented a wide constituency.[13] The duke himself was given a gallery of ruler portraits, some of which provided models for his edification and others of which warned him against the sort of behaviour considered unsuitable for a duke. William Longsword, for example, was portrayed as having become confused about the Christian behaviour appropriate for a ruler. Convinced that the monastic life was the only correct form of Christian life, he had to be cajoled into fighting for his duchy, fathering a son, and remaining duke at least until that son achieved his majority.[14] He was also depicted as having been too trusting and too peaceable, and to have paid the price with martyrdom/murder at the hands of the cronies of Count Arnulf of Flanders.[15] Richard I, in contrast, got the balance right. He lived according to the Beatitudes, but in a way that was appropriate for a ruler (who might also become a holy confessor).[16]

It is possible that Duke Richard II could have understood some of this for himself. In any event, and despite the ink that has been spilt on the question of whether the De moribus was directly accessible to Duke Richard and his courtiers or not, the fact remains that, even if they could not read it themselves, passages could still have been read aloud to them, with the various poems perhaps even sung, by way of entertainment at feasts or assemblies.[17] Elizabeth Tyler and Henry Bainton have discussed the oral performance of historical works at court in eleventh- and twelfth-century England, and it is entirely possible that such

---

[13] H. Prentout, *Essai sur les origines et fondation du duché de normandie* (Paris, 1911), pp. 139–41.

[14] *Dudo*, pp. 63, 67, 77–8, and see Shopkow, *History and Community*, pp. 73–4.

[15] *Dudo*, pp. 82–3 and see below, Chapter 1, pp. 59–60 and Chapter 4, pp. 198–201.

[16] See Shopkow, *History and Community*, pp. 75–8.

[17] The orality and aurality of narratives and *acta* seem often to have been forgotten or else dismissed by historians, who have consequently focused instead on the extent of literacy in Normandy and at the ducal court (Shopkow, *History and Community*, p. 184; Bachrach, 'Writing Latin history', 61–71). However, the absence of an explicit mention that the De moribus was read aloud in Latin and/or French does not allow the possibility to be dismissed outright, as Bachrach did. Indeed, the punctuation of the poems suggests that they were intended to be read aloud (Pohl, *Dudo of Saint-Quentin's* Historia Normannorum, pp. 18–19, 255–6; F. Lifshitz, [review of] 'Pohl, Benjamin. *Dudo of Saint-Quentin's* Historia Normannorum: *Tradition, Innovation and Memory*', *The Medieval Review*, 16 January 2015 <http://scholarworks.iu.edu/journals/index.php/tmr/article/view/20857/26863> accessed 6 February 2016).

performances took place in early eleventh-century Normandy, too.[18] Even if the allusions to classical and hagiographic models were (mostly) missed by a lay audience, there were still important and comprehensible messages in Dudo's work that would have been easily understood by the Norman *illiterati*. And that the work was intended for aural consumption is indicated by the fact that, 'more than half of the surviving medieval manuscripts of Dudo's prosimetrical work contain an "elaborate system of *positurae* used to punctuate the [book's] metrical poetry" to facilitate oral performance'.[19]

There were also messages for others at the duke's court. Edward (the future Confessor) and Alfred, Richard's nephews, might have been encouraged by the report of the support that Rollo had offered to English kings.[20] They might have gained consolation, too, from being informed that both Longsword and Richard I were saints who might support or supplant their own kinsman, Edward the Martyr.[21] Two more of Richard II's nephews, Alan and Odo of Brittany, might have been less delighted to hear of the grant of Brittany to Rollo and the subsequent oaths of fidelity sworn by Breton leaders to Norman dukes.[22] Richard II's *fidelis*, Nigel of the Cotentin, would similarly have learned of the service rendered to the dukes by the tenth-century lords of the Cotentin, while perhaps being flattered by the recollection of their martial vigour.[23] And the duke's half-brothers were informed why it was that Richard II ruled and they were mere counts.[24] Others of the duke's relatives and kinsmen through marriage found their lineage celebrated, not just by way of the sanctity of Richard I, but also by the pedigree and praise of Richard I's wife, Gunnor, albeit that she was not named in the earliest versions of the work.[25]

It is likely that Frankish prelates and lords also attended Richard II's court. King Robert was himself there in 1006, Richard's patronage of the canons and monks of Chartres would suggest that clergy from the Chartrain were at least occasionally present, while other clergymen might have been sent as ambassadors

---

[18]   E. M. Tyler, 'Talking about history in eleventh-century England: the *Encomium Emmae Reginae* and the court of Harthacnut', *EME*, 13 (2005), 364–7, 373; H. Bainton, 'Literate sociability and historical writing in later twelfth-century England', *ANS*, 34 (2012), 23–39, and see also Mortensen, 'Stylistic choice', pp. 95–9, although he did not think that the structure of Dudo's work lent itself to oral performance (p. 100).

[19]   Lifshitz, review of Pohl in *The Medieval Review* (see n. 17); Pohl, *Dudo of Saint-Quentin's Historia Normannorum*, pp. 18–19, 156–65, 255.

[20]   *Dudo*, pp. 30–2, 39–41.

[21]   See below, Chapter 2, p. 87 and Chapter 4, pp. 198–205.

[22]   *Dudo*, pp. 49, 60–3, 107, 139.

[23]   *Dudo*, pp. 80, 112, 115–16.

[24]   *Dudo*, p. 164.

[25]   Dudo, pp. 163–4, and see below, Chapter 1, pp. 67–9, 77.

to seek the duke's help and favour, just as Dudo had been *c.* 987. But Richard attended Frankish courts and joined in Frankish campaigns, too, and as Dudo was also associated with the college at Saint-Quentin, it is possible that he also publicized his book when resident in Picardy. That is suggested by the dedicatory letter to Adalbero of Laon, which would have provided another avenue by which the work could have become known to the French king and his court.[26] Leading figures in the Frankish political and religious hierarchies could thus have been informed about why Richard II acted as he did and, perhaps, refused to offer service in return for his duchy, and they would also have been impressed by the Normans' new-found respectability since 'the obvious, and indeed the only, route to historical respectability' in the Frankish world was to feature in a Latin history.[27] 'To have a history written in Latin was to emphasize one's Christianity and one's cultivation. To be the patron of such a work was to be princely; to have such a history written about one's territory was testimony to its importance.'[28]

Dudo's work, then, is complex and multi-layered and was almost certainly intended to speak to a number of different constituencies within and without Normandy at the same time. Its purpose was to reconcile all parties to the existence of an autonomous duchy of Normandy ruled by a line of Scandinavian dukes, whose attachment to Christianity was certain and who desired peace with their neighbours – but who could and would oppose and defeat any who attempted to destroy them. But above all, Dudo emphasized the right of Rollo's line to rule the duchy, the dukes' God-given mission to forge a united Christian *regnum* from the various peoples who lived within their territory, and the right of this Scandinavian-led enclave to remain free from the demands for homage and service usually rendered to the king of the Franks by other princes.

That claim to freedom from homage and service was a subject that most likely remained very much alive throughout the eleventh century, and which would become a cause of friction in the twelfth. It might help to explain the hiatus in the

---

[26] This suggestion is pursued below, Chapter 5, pp. 256–62. It has been made previously, although slightly elliptically, by Shopkow, 'The Carolingian world of Dudo of Saint-Quentin', p. 33. The idea was dismissed by Christiansen (*Dudo*, p. xxviii), but only on the grounds that if that had been the intention, Duke Richard could have approached King Robert directly. That summary dismissal consequently ignored the possibility that Adalbero might be used as an intercessor, like a saint, or like the French chancellor, Hugh of Champfleury, who had offered to act as an intermediary between Owain Gwynedd and King Louis VII in the 1160s (H. Pryce, 'Owain Gwynedd and Louis VII: the Franco-Welsh diplomacy of the first prince of Wales', *The Welsh History Review*, 19 (1998), 6).

[27] Bachrach, 'Writing Latin history', 59.

[28] Shopkow, *History and Community*, p. 185; Pohl, *Dudo of Saint-Quentin's* Historia Normannorum, pp. 44, 83, 106, 116, 119.

copying of the text that seems to have occupied Curthose's reign, since he brought his duchy into a close and essentially dependent relationship with King Philip of the Franks to which the sentiments in the *De moribus* were clearly opposed.[29] In contrast, Henry's determination to keep Louis VI at a political distance, despite the increasing pressure that the French king brought to bear in order to obtain his homage and service, might have given Dudo's defence of Norman autonomy a new lease of life. It would also in turn explain the production of an illustrated copy of the manuscript probably made during Henry's reign, which was presumably intended to act as a justification for the duke's claims to autonomy that could be understood by an illiterate, and therefore lay, audience as much as by a clerical or monastic one.[30]

The manuscript in question (Rouen, Bibliothèque Municipale, MS 1173), which was intended to be illustrated, was discovered by Leah Shopkow, but has subsequently been considered at much greater length by Ben Pohl who has also reconstructed the picture cycle that was to accompany Dudo's text.[31] His survey suggests that the majority of the images relate to the dukes' interactions with the Franks, and that the culmination of the cycle (if not quite the last image) was an illustration of the scene whereby Louis IV renewed his oath acknowledging Richard I as the rightful ruler of the duchy and granting that he should hold his territory free of any obligation to do homage or provide service.[32] It is this that suggests the manuscript was intended principally to speak to the threat to the duchy's autonomy posed by King Louis rather than, for example, to the sanctity of Longsword and Richard I. Although Pohl dated MS 1173 to *c.* 1075, Felice Lifshitz has pointed out

---

[29] Pohl, *Dudo of Saint-Quentin's* Historia Normannorum, p. 5 noted the hiatus, but explained it in relation to the novelty factor of the *Gesta Normannorum ducum*.

[30] Pohl appears to dismiss the possibility that the manuscript might have been intended to carry a political message, and sees it instead solely as a diplomatic gift or display copy (Pohl, *Dudo of Saint-Quentin's* Historia Normannorum, pp. 193–5). One of the remarks Lifshitz made during her review of Pohl's book is worth repeating here: 'By ignoring the specific political contexts that presumably conditioned the production of the extant manuscripts of the *HN*, Pohl has actually missed the chance fully to investigate the evolving significance and function of Dudo's *HN* during the decades when Normandy formed part of (what I will designate for convenience's sake) the Anglo-Norman realm and then the Angevin Empire' (Lifshitz, review of Pohl in *The Medieval Review* (see n. 17)).

[31] Shopkow, *History and Community*, pp. 220–1; Pohl, *Dudo of Saint-Quentin's* Historia Normannorum, pp. 173–97; Pohl, 'The illustrated archetype of the Historia Normannorum: did Dudo write a "chronicon pictum"?', *ANS*, 37 (2015), 221–51. It is not clear that Pohl was aware of Shopkow's earlier discovery, as he mistakenly claimed that the existence of this copy of the *De moribus* has been 'unrecognized in previous scholarship' (Pohl, *Dudo of Saint-Quentin's* Historia Normannorum, p. 195).

[32] *Dudo*, p. 121; Pohl, pp. 191–2.

that he used the same criterion to date another manuscript to the early twelfth century.[33] As such, the physical appearance of the manuscript need not speak against its production during Henry's reign. Dating the manuscript to the early twelfth century would also permit it to be seen as one of a number of examples of illustrated narratives produced at about the same time. Others include John of Worcester's *Chronicle*, with its images of Henry I's nightmares and his narrow escape from shipwreck, and the cartulary of Mont-Saint-Michel, made in the later 1140s, with its images that accompany the foundation narrative and some of the earliest acts preserved in it.[34] About the same time, *c.* 1139, Robert of Torigni would add back into his revision of the *Gesta Normannorum ducum* much of the material in Dudo's *De moribus* that William of Jumièges had excised when composing his work during the 1050s.[35] Torigni's revised *Gesta* thus emphasized in its text, as MS 1173 did in its images, the divinely ordained nature of autonomous Norman rule in Normandy at a time when it was coming under ever more serious threat.[36] Parts of Dudo's narrative thus remained highly relevant more than a century after he completed it and continued to attract copyists and an audience as a result.

William of Jumièges

In the middle of the eleventh century, William of Jumièges, a monk of that abbey, who apparently did not have any close connection to the ducal court, compiled a serial biography of all seven dukes of the Normans who had ruled the duchy from its inception in 911 to his own day. His work was called the *Gesta Normannorum ducum* (*The Deeds of the Dukes of the Normans*).

It is now, I think unanimously, accepted that the first version of the work was written and completed around 1057, with a second edition begun at some point after 1066 and completed by 1070.[37] There are no witnesses to this first version of the *Gesta*. Instead both identification and dating depend on a close reading of the earliest existing text and the recognition that there are some surprising omissions from the narrative, best explained by presuming that Jumièges had already stopped writing before the events in question took place. It seems unlikely that

---

[33] Lifshitz, review of Pohl in *The Medieval Review* (see n. 17).

[34] The dating of the cartulary has been revisited and revised by Katharine Keats-Rohan and Thomas Bisson, whose findings taken together suggest that the cartulary was composed between 1145 and 1150: *Ctl. Mont-Saint-Michel*, p. 13; T. N. Bisson, 'The "annuary" of Abbot Robert de Torigni (1155–1159)', *ANS*, 33 (2011), 65.

[35] The *Gesta Normannorum ducum* is discussed in the following section.

[36] Jumièges, i. lxxviii–lxxxii. Van Houts did not consider the political context when discussing the restoration of these passages.

[37] Jumièges, i. xxxii.

much was added to the existing material in the first seven books when Jumièges picked up his quill again, except perhaps some of the passages relating to the dukes' relationship with the kings of the English. So far as Normandy and Norman affairs are concerned, then, it may be presumed that the existing manuscripts more or less accurately reflect the text of this first edition up to and including the depiction of the battle of Varaville in 1057.

It is extremely unlikely that the work was originally commissioned by Duke William. As the following discussion will suggest, Jumièges wrote with the intention of reconciling Norman lords to the duke and vice versa, following the rebellions and invasions of the period between *c.* 1040 and 1157. That he was writing with these *two* objectives in mind would seem to eliminate the possibility of ducal patronage. It is, however, possible that the second edition of the work was commissioned by the new King William, in the hope that Jumièges could repeat his trick of reconciling two opposing factions with each other. In any event, there would certainly have been a different dedicatory letter at the beginning of the first edition of the work to that which survives as a preface to the second. How different that first letter was from the second in terms of its content is, of course, unknowable.

The first four books of William's work were based on Dudo of Saint-Quentin's *De moribus.* But Jumièges did not slavishly copy out this work. Instead, he abridged it, omitting some episodes altogether, such as those where the still-pagan Rollo, who would become the first duke of the Normans, received divinely inspired visions, interpreted in one instance by a Christian prisoner, that revealed his future rule over the future duchy to be the result of God's will.

These various changes have been remarked and discussed in earlier work on William, in particular by Elisabeth van Houts, Leah Shopkow, and Emily Albu. These commentators have attributed the cuts principally to the fact that William of Jumièges was a monk and was therefore unwilling to promote the story fabricated by Dudo, a secular canon, of pagan Vikings acting at God's bidding.[38] Thus Albu remarked, following the explanation found in the *existing* prefatory letter, that while William wanted to emphasize virtues he did not want to glorify the acts performed by men when they were pagans, and he did not want to describe in detail violent military actions for risk of glorifying them.[39] Others have suggested that his editing was instead the result of a chronological detachment from the events he described or 'dissimilarities in the two writers' educations and institutional affiliations'.[40]

---

[38] Jumièges, i. xxxv, xxxvii–xxxviii; Albu, *The Normans in their Histories*, p. 56; Pohl, *Dudo of Saint-Quentin's* Historia Normannorum, pp. 3, 130–2, 227.

[39] Albu, *The Normans in their Histories*, pp. 55–6.

[40] Pohl, *Dudo of Saint-Quentin's* Historia Normannorum, pp. 3–4.

These explanations miss the crucial point, however, which is that William had not just a different (monastic) viewpoint from Dudo, but also a different agenda. Dudo had intended to show *inter alia* that the Norman dukes were autonomous rulers of their duchy, who owed no service or homage to the kings of the French as a result of Frankish perfidy. To that end, he wrote of Rollo's princely status and defence of those Danes the king of the Danes had chosen to exile, of divinely inspired visions, and of saintly dukes. But Jumièges had an entirely different intention in mind, which related to internal rather than external political relationships, and which required him to revise and abridge Dudo's narrative.

Jumièges was consequently doing far more than taking the moral pruning shears to Dudo's earlier work. While that gave him a starting point for his attack on his predecessor, the complaints that William voiced about Dudo's methodology were themselves necessary if he was to achieve his objective, because, by the 1050s, Dudo's story had become established as the one and only formally sanctioned narrative of events.

Jumièges thus found ways to undermine, or at least nuance and qualify, Dudo's history. He began by attacking Dudo's methodology, stating that much of what his predecessor had written about the first duke, Rollo, was 'merely flattering'.[41] The implication was that Dudo's work had been inaccurate elsewhere, too, although Jumièges did not say this expressly.

Jumièges then emphasized the quality of his own work by baldly stating that he had made use of the eye-witness testimony of Richard I's half-brother, Count Rodulf. He did this at the end of Book IV, in other words at the close of the section of his work that covered the same ground as Dudo's earlier narrative: 'Thus far I have collected the facts as told by Count Rodulf, brother of the duke, a great and honest man.'[42] On one reading, he was doing nothing more than emphasizing the truthfulness of his own work by making reference to the original informant, whose testimony came to him *at second hand*, through the words written by Dudo of Saint-Quentin. But while he would acknowledge that Rodulf was *Dudo's* source of information in his (*later*) dedicatory letter,[43] he might not have done so originally and certainly did not do so here, and so those without the *De moribus* in front of them could easily have been fooled by William's sleight of hand into believing that he was making a claim for the veracity of his account *against* that found in the *De moribus*.[44] From Book V onwards, however, William of Jumièges

---

[41] Jumièges, i. 6.

[42] Jumièges, i. 134.

[43] Jumièges, i. 4.

[44] George Garnett's discussions of Richard I's death and succession suggest that even today this remark about the testimony of Count Rodulf can cause uncertainty, although the wording of the note in question is a little unclear: G. Garnett, '"Ducal" succession in

was on his own and did not have to worry about what earlier writers had said when shaping his arguments.

When he came to write his *Gesta*, Jumièges seems to have had two linked objectives in mind. One of them was identified by Leah Shopkow some years ago. She realized that Jumièges wanted to bring discontented Norman lords to accept William the Bastard's right to rule. She remarked that: 'William of Jumièges ... needed to justify William's succession by an appeal to contemporary ideas of authority. He had to accomplish this without overt reference to William the Bastard's illegitimacy, a point on which the duke was reportedly touchy. He rewrote Dudo's version of history to do this.'[45] In particular, Jumièges emphasized the right of the reigning duke to designate his successor, amending Dudo's *De moribus* to give each of them a much greater role in directing the succession to their chosen heir.[46] That made Duke Robert's establishment of his illegitimate son as his heir, recognized by the Norman *principes* through their oaths of fidelity and homage, binding. Jumièges returned to the importance of these oaths of fidelity when noting their breach by various rebels, allowing Shopkow to declare that: 'William emphasized fidelity to bolster the legitimacy of Norman rule.'[47]

Jumièges also undermined the criticism of Duke William's succession on the grounds of his illegitimate birth. In his *Gesta*, marriages *more Danico*, which to Christians were not marriages at all, were legitimate. This would have been an unusual view for a Benedictine monk to have held, were he not trying to make a political statement – although it is worth noting that the Burgundian writer Ralph Glaber, who knew Normandy quite well, had made this same point in the 1030s.[48] Moreover, William the Bastard's birth was implicitly compared with that of Duke Richard I, whose great deeds and triumphs were rehearsed by Jumièges in his Book IV. The point, clearly made, was that illegitimate birth did not preclude an extremely successful reign, and that similar circumstances would produce a similar result. In addition, what had become a problematic passage in Dudo's work that privileged Christian marriages over other 'forbidden' unions was quashed in Jumièges rewriting.[49] What all of this also suggests, of course, is

early Normandy', in *Law and Government in Medieval England and Normandy: Essays in Honour of Sir James Holt*, ed. G. Garnett and J. Hudson (Cambridge, 1994), pp. 89 and n. 46, 96 and n. 81; G. Garnett, *Conquered England: Kingship, Succession, and Tenure 1066–1166* (Oxford, 2007), pp. 144–5 and n. 71.

[45] Shopkow, *History and Community*, p. 83.

[46] See below, Chapter 6, pp. 312–17.

[47] Shopkow, *History and Community*, p. 86.

[48] Glaber, p. 204, and see below Chapter 6.

[49] For the suppression of the passage compare *Dudo*, pp. 163–4 and Jumièges, i. 128–30, where Richard's marriage with Gunnor is *more Christiano* from the outset. See also Shopkow,

that Orderic was not imposing the conventions of his own day on William's when emphasizing the problems that had been caused by the duke's illegitimate birth.[50]

To demonstrate that William the Bastard was the legitimate duke, and to suggest that his reign would be a success despite the problems he had faced during the period to *c.* 1057, Jumièges used episodes from earlier reigns to prefigure the events of William's day. He thus flattened time, which perhaps explains why, as Emily Albu remarked, 'with his indifference towards personalities, he ... allows the dukes to flow together in the reader's memory'.[51] So, for example, the beginning of Richard I's reign had been a time of danger for the duke and for his duchy, but eventually Richard had triumphed over King Louis IV as a result of the support of his guardians and *fideles*. The beginning of William the Bastard's reign was not so dissimilar, and the defeat of Louis IV on the banks of the Dives by Richard I's allies in 945 prefigured the defeat of King Henry I of the French on the banks of the same river in 1057. Similarly, Jumièges described the marriage of Richard I to Emma Capet in 960 in almost identical terms to the marriage of William to Matilda of Flanders *c.* 1049.[52]

Jumièges tells us that Richard I's successor, Richard II, had suffered the same sorts of danger as William during the first years of his rule. The peace was disturbed by a conspiracy of peasants, who colluded together. They were punished by Count Rodulf on the duke's behalf, who cut off the hands and feet of the peasants when they met at an assembly. Thus, too, were the townsmen of Alençon punished when they rebelled against William the Bastard *c.* 1052. Richard II had also been troubled by a long-lasting rebellion. His half-brother William rose against him in the Hiémois *c.* 1000. He was captured but then escaped and was finally forgiven and reinstated. Meanwhile, his supporters had continued the war in his absence. All was well that ended well, however; 'after the unrest had calmed down the land of Normandy rejoiced in peace under the duke.'[53] Anybody reading this passage after the revolts of 1047 and 1053 could, and probably would, have made the obvious comparisons with the rebellions of Guy of Burgundy (1046–7) and William of Arques (1053). Richard II subsequently became embroiled in a war with Odo II of Chartres, which was settled by King Robert the Pious. Afterwards, Richard II rode against the French king's enemies as part of his army. It is tempting to see this last episode as a justification of the assistance William the Bastard provided to King Henry I during his Mouliherne

History and Community, p. 84 and the discussion of the succession found in Chapter 6, as noted above.
[50] See for example, Jumièges, ii. 94–6; Orderic, iv. 82–4.
[51] Albu, *The Normans in their Histories*, p. 73.
[52] Noted by van Houts: Jumièges, i. lvi.
[53] Jumièges, ii. 10.

campaign *c.* 1048, after Henry had supported William against the Norman rebels at the battle of Val-ès-Dunes.[54]

There are, then, a number of echoes throughout the *Gesta* which seem intended to link together different events which took place at different times. Jumièges sometimes repeated words or phrases to make the comparisons clearer, although this was by no means always the case, or even common. For example, the descriptions of the punishments of the peasants who revolted against Richard II on the one hand, and the treatment of the defenders at Alençon on the other, have just three words in common: *manibus, pedibus,* and *paterentur.* But they would nonetheless have been noted by an audience used to thinking of history as comprising a set of repeating situations,[55] who would also have known that the later repetitions and echoes should be interpreted or judged in the same light as the earlier events. Indeed, the fact that the audience was given the satisfaction of being allowed to join the dots themselves would have given them an investment in the interpretation that Jumièges had steered them towards, making it stronger.

But there was more to the *Gesta* than this. The second objective was set out, or perhaps alluded to, by Jumièges himself. He wrote in the (later) dedicatory letter to King William that prefaces the second edition of his work that his *Gesta* had been written 'for the recollection of the exemplary deeds of your most pious predecessors in the most exalted of secular offices'. In other words, the book was intended as a mirror for princes and lords.

Leah Shopkow and Emily Albu both picked up on this comment, but neither thought that Jumièges had successfully achieved his aim. For Shopkow at least, this was because the *Gesta* is largely devoid of characterization and consequently fails to provide much in the way of moral guidance.[56] But that is to assume that Jumièges intended his mirror to reflect a full range of appropriate behaviours back at his readers. If his mirror was intended to show William the Bastard just two or three aspects of rulership – in this case the importance of pardon, reconciliation, and community – then he may be thought to have been considerably more successful.

And so, in the years that immediately followed William the Bastard's victory over King Henry of the French and Count Geoffrey Martel of Anjou at Varaville, Duke William was told that for Normandy to recover fully after the intermittent turmoil it had endured since his succession, he needed to forgive and forget, because Normandy was strongest when the duke worked in concert with his

---

[54] Jumièges, ii. 34–6.
[55] See on this Shopkow, *History and Community*, pp. 67–8 (and p. 67, n. 3), 84, 133–4.
[56] Shopkow, *History and Community*, p. 191.

subjects.[57] In this attempt at a reconciliation between a ruler and his subjects, the *Gesta Normannorum ducum* is comparable to two narratives written a century or so later. The first, the Hyde (Warenne) Chronicle, was composed with the intention of reminding Henry II of the help provided by the Warenne family to the Norman dukes and kings in the hope that Henry would be inspired to return that portion of the Warenne lands that he had taken into his own hands in Normandy to their rightful owner, William of Blois, King Stephen's son, who had inherited the Warenne honour through marriage.[58] Such at least is the view of the chronicle's most recent editor, Elisabeth van Houts. The second is Jordan Fantosme's verse chronicle about the Great War of 1173–4, which Matthew Strickland and Laura Ashe have told us was intended to reconcile Henry II with his son, Henry the young king, and others of the rebels who had fought against him.[59]

Jumièges went about this aspect of his work by ensuring that his dukes shared the limelight with their leading subjects. While the dukes remain the leaders and the figures who cause events to happen – this is after all the *Gesta Normannorum ducum* – they are not allowed to unbalance the narrative or entirely eclipse their loyal subjects. They were certainly not allowed to become the principal reason for Norman successes. Indeed, Jumièges ensured that the Normans as a people were always kept at the forefront of his account. 'At this time', he wrote, 'the Normans always used to put their enemies to flight, but fled before none of them (*Cuius tempore etatis semper fuerunt assueti hostes fugare Normanni, terga uertere nulli*)'.[60] This intention to emphasize community and concerted action was also reflected in his retelling of the story by which Rollo came to lead the Normans. Instead of Dudo's princely warrior with divine visions, the Rollo of the *Gesta Normannorum ducum* is simply one of a number of Viking warriors who became their leader as the result of the casting of lots. William the Bastard's ancestor, then, had been the first among equals who owed his position to chance. God had nothing to do with it.

In addition to underlining the need for community and concerted action, Jumièges also showed how earlier dukes had almost always reconciled with

---

[57] The Black Book of Saint-Ouen includes an eleventh- or twelfth-century list of the virtues and vices of different peoples. In this list, the Norman vice is rapacity and the virtue is *communio*: 'the ability to act together' (noted in Shopkow, *History and Community*, pp. 15–16).

[58] Hyde, p. xiii.

[59] See M. Strickland, 'Arms and the men: war, loyalty and lordship in Jordan Fantosme's Chronicle', *Medieval Knighthood IV. Papers from the Fifth Strawberry Hill Conference*, ed. C. Harper-Bill and R. Harvey (Woodbridge, 1992), pp. 187–220; L. Ashe, *Fiction and History in England, 1066–1200* (Cambridge, 2007), pp. 81–120.

[60] Jumièges, ii. 34.

those who had rebelled against them. In doing so, he was of course urging Duke William to reconcile with those who had rebelled against him. But at the time he was writing, those rebellions were still recent history and the wounds they had caused were still open. Jumièges thus trod carefully. He recognized that not all rebels had offended equally, and abandoned those who had committed especially heinous crimes to their fate.

This is most clearly seen in his division of those who had rebelled against William into two categories. First, there were those who had acted treacherously by calling on the king of the French for help in their revolts. Secondly, there were those who had simply defied the duke and relied on their own strength, even if in combination with others, when fighting against him. Jumièges seems to suggest that the two different types of rebel ought to be punished differently in accordance with the severity of their crimes.

So far as Jumièges was concerned, those few rebels in the former category, who included Thurstan Goz, *vicomte* of the Hiémois, and Count William of Arques, William's uncle and contemporary, might justly suffer permanent exile and for-feiture. His desire to make that point clearly led to a chronological problem when it came to writing up the events of William the Bastard's reign. Thurstan had rebelled *c.* 1043 and William of Arques *c.* 1053, but their two rebellions were separated by the domestic insurgency led by Guy of Burgundy. As a result, Jumièges was obliged to deal with the rebellion of Count William of Arques out of chronological order. This has been remarked upon in the past, for example by David Douglas and Elisabeth van Houts, but no convincing reason for it has been suggested.[61]

In contrast, the second category of rebel, those who had been more restrained and had not treacherously sought the aid of the French, could and should be forgiven. Jumièges provided models from previous reigns to make the point. Thus Richard II forgave his rebellious half-brother William, while Richard III forgave William the Bastard's own father, Robert. Duke Robert was made to recognize that he had been mistaken to attack Archbishop Robert of Rouen, having been misled by wicked men's advice. Jumièges added that after the two men had been reconciled they worked together for the remainder of Duke Robert's life.[62] William of Bellême, too, was forgiven after his revolt against Robert the Magnificent and restored to Alençon, even though it turned out to be an error. But still, he got his just deserts in the end, and at least the duke had given him a second chance.[63]

---

[61] The misplacing of the rebellion is noted in Jumièges, i. liii and D. C. Douglas, *William the Conqueror* (London, 1964), p. 66, n. 1, although no reason for it is suggested.

[62] Jumièges, ii. 48.

[63] Jumièges, ii. 50.

Even Bishop Hugh of Bayeux, despite the lack of justification for his revolt *c.* 1031, and despite the fact that he had employed French mercenaries to fight the duke (but had not turned to the French king), was restored to at least some of his possessions (if not to the duke's favour) after his rebellion had been defeated.

Hugh of Bayeux's rebellion in some ways parallels that of Thurstan Goz. And while Thurstan might himself have remained an exile, his son Richard would, by the time Jumièges wrote, have become *vicomte* of Avranches. He could consequently have been one of those Jumièges was referring to when he remarked that William had already reconciled with some former rebels and insurgents in a stage-whispered aside: 'I should have mentioned them by name, had I not wished to avoid their burning hatred. But yet, I shall whisper to all of you, surrounding me, that these are the very men who now claim to be most faithful, and have received so many honours from the duke.'[64] Another probable target for those words would have been Roger II of Montgommery, whose father had been no friend to either the young duke or the monks of Jumièges. That William delivered this comment as an aside was clearly not the result of any feeling of intimidation.[65] He would simply have remained silent if he had genuinely felt threatened. Instead, this touch – perhaps dramatized when the *Gesta* was read aloud – was almost certainly a comment on the injustice of pardoning some former rebels but continuing to punish others for similar offences.

That of course implies that Jumièges had a particular unforgiven rebel in mind, and it does seem that he was especially concerned to achieve a reconciliation between Duke William and Nigel II of the Cotentin – soon to be Nigel of Saint-Sauveur-le-Vicomte – who remained in exile after his part in the revolt of 1046–47 until *c.* 1060 – about three years after Jumièges completed his first edition of the *Gesta*. He was certainly still persona non grata in 1059 when he was to be found in the French army besieging Norman-held Thimert.[66] William's account of how Nigel's father, Nigel I, fought off an English attack designed to inflict shame and harm on Richard II *c.* 1008, as well as the record of how the same Nigel was given custody of the castles at Tillières and Chéruel, from both of which he successfully defended the duchy against foreign enemies, were no doubt intended to remind Duke William of the services rendered by Nigel's family in the past, and which would be rendered again in the future if only Nigel II were restored to his estates.[67]

Such arguments were thought to have been employed by others at a later date. Orderic reported that, in 1090, Roger of Beaumont sought to obtain the release

---

[64] Jumièges, ii. 92.
[65] Described as such by Garnett, *Conquered England*, p. 149.
[66] See below, Chapter 2, pp. 107–9, 111.
[67] Jumièges, ii. 12, 22–4, 58.

of his son from the duke's prison by reminding him that, 'I have remained at all times faithful to the dukes of Normandy. I have never deceived my lord; on the contrary I have borne much toil and peril for his sake ... From my childhood I have always chosen the path of loyalty; this is the inheritance that I received from my grandfather Turold and my father Humfrey and have treasured all my life long in adversity and prosperity.'[68] It may consequently be supposed that Jumièges and Orderic at least thought that such reminders of the loyal service rendered by predecessors might also be used as a promise of future loyalty.

And as it happened, Nigel II was recalled c. 1060, which is close enough to the completion of the first edition of the *Gesta Normannorum ducum* to be tempted to think that Jumièges had achieved his objective. In any event, Nigel II seems to have developed an affection for the monks of Jumièges after his return to Normandy, manifested most clearly in his refoundation of the college at Saint-Sauveur-le-Vicomte as an abbey staffed by monks from Jumièges. The foundation deed for the new monastery dates from c. 1080, but it is quite possible that the monks had been introduced some years earlier.

The hypothesis presented here explains why Jumièges abridged Dudo's work in the way he did; why he included the anecdote about Nigel of the Cotentin's defeat of Æthelred's English in the Cotentin c. 1008; the chronological misplacement of William of Arques's rebellion in the narrative; and the stage whispered aside, all of which have been remarked upon but not satisfactorily explained in the past. That the *Gesta Normannorum ducum* had this particular function did not of course prevent it from living on after William had been reconciled with the erstwhile rebels, for the spare narrative readily lent itself to addition, elaboration, and revision.

If the above hypothesis is correct, and Jumièges had helped to reconcile the Norman lords to their duke and vice versa, that would also explain why – as seems likely – the newly crowned William the Conqueror turned to this same monk after the Conquest and asked him to add to his existing work in order to promote a second reconciliation, this time between William and his new English subjects. Unfortunately, Jumièges would die before the work was completed, and his untimely demise meant that King William would be obliged to turn elsewhere for what he wanted. It is tempting to think that, during the dark days of 1070, the new king would have continued to believe that such a work was indeed necessary, and that he consequently turned to one of his own well-educated chaplains, William of Poitiers, to produce it. That would explain why Poitiers began his work only c. 1071. His approach, however, would be somewhat different from his predecessor's.

---

[68] Orderic, iv. 206.

William of Poitiers

Orderic tells us that William of Poitiers

> was a Norman by birth, a native of Préaux, and had a sister there who became abbess of the nunnery of Saint-Léger. We call him 'of Poitiers' because he drank deeply of the fountain of learning there. When he returned home he was conspicuous for his learning in his native parts, and as archdeacon helped the bishops of Lisieux, Hugh and Gilbert, in the administration of their diocese. He had been a brave soldier before entering the church, and had fought with warlike weapons for his earthly prince, so that he was all the better able to describe the battles he had seen through having himself some experience of the dire perils of war. In his old age he gave himself up to silence and prayer, and spent more time in composing narratives and verse than in discourse.[69]

Although, as suggested above, it is plausible that Poitiers was commissioned to write his *Gesta* by King William himself, Orderic reported only that he dedicated his work to the king, so it is possible that another might have been responsible.[70] Leah Shopkow tentatively put Bishop Hugh of Lisieux in the frame.[71] But it is equally possible that William wrote off his own bat to gain the new king's favour and thus perhaps to win an archdeaconry or bishopric.

A similar uncertainty also surrounds the intended audience. Poitiers might have intended, or hoped, that his *Gesta* would be heard by those attending William the Bastard's court, whether in England or in Normandy, not least because a number of the great and the good of the new Anglo-Norman *regnum* were lauded in its pages. At the same time, while Poitiers was good at building up to important and dramatic events, he almost always cut out the action itself, which might suggest he had a more literary and educated (and thus clerical) audience in mind.[72] Whether these churchmen were intended to be Normans or English is equally unclear. Both Leah Shopkow and Emily Albu apparently saw the work as written exclusively for Normans,[73] and Emily Winkler has followed their lead, albeit with some qualification,[74] but as the work is both a celebration of William's reign and victory

---

[69] Orderic, ii. 258.
[70] Orderic, ii. 78.
[71] Shopkow, *History and Community*, pp. 44, 227.
[72] Shopkow, *History and Community*, pp. 228–30.
[73] Shopkow, *History and Community*, pp. 195, 228; Albu, *The Normans in their Histories*, p. 87.
[74] E. A. Winkler, 'The Norman conquest of the classical past: William of Poitiers, language, and history', *JMH*, 42 (2016), 456–78.

and a justification of the conquest and Norman behaviour in its aftermath, it is perhaps more likely that it was intended principally for the consumption of the king's new subjects.

On one level, the *Gesta Guillelmi* of William of Poitiers comprises a portrait of an exemplary ruler who successfully fulfilled all the criteria of Christian ruler-ship.[75] The duke's people were protected by his peace, his justice was equitable, he protected and nurtured the Church and Christianity in his dominions, and his personal piety provided a moral compass for his subjects and ensured that God will look favourably on his endeavours.[76] Indeed, so favourable is the portrait, that many historians have found it more than a little sycophantic.[77] Nonetheless, what Poitiers tells us about William's rule in Normandy in Book I seems to be reliable. His flattery, then, might have led to hyperbole and superlatives, but he did at least stop short of outright fabrication.

The portrait of William as an ideal ruler was presumably intended to appeal to his new English subjects. Indeed, at one point Poitiers interrupted his narrative to make that appeal by way of authorial intervention: 'And you, too, you English land, would love him and hold him in the highest respect; you would gladly pros-trate yourself entirely at his feet, if putting aside your folly and wickedness you could judge more soundly the kind of man into whose power you had come.'[78] The Normans, it might be noted, were never so addressed. But an English audi-ence is also suggested because, as David Bates has plausibly noted, the *Gesta* seems to respond to a number of the criticisms being made by the English about the nature of their new foreign king's rule. These complaints are apparently reflected in the 'D' version of the Anglo-Saxon Chronicle, much of which is contemporary with events. Thus, 'Poitiers's statement about the limits placed on the collection of tax and tribute stands in direct opposition to 'D's mention of the imposition of a "severe tax". His praise of the quality of the custodians of castles likewise confronts 'D's criticisms directly … His need to state categorically that William's extensive generosity to churches in France was not a despoliation of the English Church looks like another reaction to an obvious criticism.'[79]

In addition, Poitiers addressed implied English criticisms about William's

---

[75] Shopkow, *History and Community*, p. 91.

[76] Shopkow, *History and Community*, pp. 92–3.

[77] Most famously John Gillingham: J. Gillingham, 'William the Bastard at War', in *Studies in Medieval History presented to R. Allen Brown*, ed. C. Harper-Bill et al. (Woodbridge, 1989), p. 141.

[78] Poitiers, p. 156.

[79] D. Bates, 'The Conqueror's earliest historians and the writing of his biography', in *Writing Medieval Biography: Essays in Honour of Frank Barlow*, ed. D. Bates, J. Crick, and S. Hamilton (Woodbridge, 2006), p. 132.

claim to the throne. His defence of the new king's actions was based on *English* law and custom, with William the recipient of a *post obitum* grant from Edward the Confessor, Harold a perjurer who should have refused the deathbed request in accordance with his former oath to the duke, and the coronation only proceeding after William had been made to observe a modesty topos by which the English leaders and then the non-Norman and therefore neutral Aimery of Thouars had begged William to take the crown.[80]

Poitiers also apparently attempted to reconcile William's new subjects to their new king through passages that compared and contrasted William with Julius Caesar and, to a lesser extent, Augustus, Aeneas, and Agamemnon.[81] The comparison with Julius Caesar might have begun with the story of William being snatched to safety and hidden away in lowly houses, which Orderic later embedded in the speech he put into William's mouth as he lay dying,[82] but within the surviving parts of the *Gesta* it can be traced through Poitiers's treatment of the siege of Alençon, in his remark that Caesar would have been terrified by the size of the army that King Henry of the French and Geoffrey of Anjou led into Normandy in 1054, and most obviously in the lengthy comparison of William's victory in 1066 with Caesar's less conclusive campaign.[83]

It may be supposed that the extended comparison/contrast with Caesar was designed to appease the English, first, by removing any sense of shame at being defeated by such a great general and, secondly, by inferring that just as Caesar had conquered England and thus civilized it, so William would reform the English Church, bring law and order to a dissolute country, and perhaps bring additional prestige to England as well by virtue of his power and reputation. The allusions to Aeneas and the *Aeneid* were employed for the same reason that they were used by Dudo: to portray William as the founder of a new dynasty that would unite the conquerors with the conquered to form a new and still stronger nation.

It is also possible, although not so clear, that Poitiers made these classical allusions in part to assert an 'imperial and civilized European identity' for William, as the anonymous author of the *Encomium Emmae reginae* had done for Cnut.[84] Although the comparison with Caesar seems too extended and too explicit for this purpose, even in the middle of the eleventh century the Normans were sometimes

---

[80] Poitiers, pp. 20, 70, 118–20 (Edward's gift of the kingdom to William and Harold's oath); 76–8, 118, 140 (perjury and deathbed bequest); 146–50 (election by English and Aimery of Thouars).

[81] See the detailed discussion in Winkler, 'The Norman conquest of the classical past', 461–75.

[82] Orderic, iv. 82.

[83] Poitiers, pp. 28, 46, 170–4, respectively.

[84] Tyler, 'Talking about history', 363.

seen as little better than Vikings,[85] so even if it were an unintended consequence it remains possible that the comparisons and allusions throughout the *Gesta Guillelmi* did help to make the Normans appear more civilized.

There is some evidence that the intention behind Poitiers' comparison would have been understood by an English audience, for the idea of Rome and its emperors remained vital into the eleventh century.[86] Thus two of the issues of pennies produced during the reign of Æthelred II depict the king as a Roman emperor, and were based on coins issued by the Emperor Maximian (286–310) and the usurper Magnentius (350–53).[87] Cnut went on pilgrimage to Rome in 1027 and attended the imperial coronation of Conrad II while he was there.[88] Moreover, his negotiations with the pope regarding English merchants and pilgrims indicate that more than a few Englishmen regularly made the journey to Rome and back.[89] A little later, the author of the *Encomium Emma Reginae* would equate Emma with Octavian, 'whose authoritative rule of the Roman Empire was legendary',[90] while the author of the *Vita Edwardi*, writing 1065–67, drew on Virgil's *Aeneid*, Lucan's *Civil War*, the *Thebaid* of Statius, and the poems of Ovid.[91] In both cases, there was apparently a presumption that 'a classicizing text could improve her situation at court'.[92] Poitiers, then, was writing in a tradition that had become established in England well before the Norman Conquest took place.

If Poitiers was addressing issues that were current in the years immediately following the conquest, and attempting to reconcile English prelates and lords with their Norman conquerors, then he most likely wrote his response *c.* 1071, soon after the monasteries had been 'sacked' and immediately after the death of Earl Edwin, which was the last thing he mentioned. It is unlikely that the work would have been begun much after that date, always supposing that it was indeed written for the reasons suggested here, because by 1075 there were almost no English bishops left, while the last English earl had by then been arrested and would be

---

85 *RADN*, no. 199.
86 Even if the idea of Rome as capital of empire seems to have lost some of its lustre after the end of the ninth century (N. Howe, *Writing the Map of Anglo-Saxon England: Essays in Cultural Geography* (New Haven, CT and London, 2008), Ch. 4, pp. 101–24).
87 M. M. Archibald, 'Anglo-Saxon coinage, Alfred to the Conquest', in *The Golden Age of Anglo-Saxon Art*, ed. J. Backhouse, D. H. Turner, and L. Webster (London, 1984), p. 178, nos. 202, 203.
88 K. K. Lawson, *Cnut: the Danes in England in the Early Eleventh Century* (Harlow, 1993), pp. 94, 99, 124, 127, 137.
89 Lawson, *Cnut*, p. 185.
90 Tyler, 'Talking about history', 381.
91 E. M. Tyler, 'The *Vita Ædwardi*: the politics of poetry at Wilton abbey', *ANS*, 31 (2009), 139–50.
92 Tyler, 'The *Vita Ædwardi*', 151–2, quotation at 151.

executed above Winchester in 1076.[93] In such a situation, there was no longer a need for a work of justification and reconciliation, and this might explain why Poitiers stopped work on his book before he had finished it. Orderic wrote that he was prevented from completing it by 'unfavourable circumstances (*aduersis casibus*)',[94] which, for a writer who maintained an English identity throughout his career, and lamented the death of Waltheof, might well have included the passing of the English earls and bishops. It would also explain why it was not much copied – although both William of Malmesbury and Orderic Vitalis did use it when constructing their own narratives.[95]

Orderic Vitalis

The *Ecclesiastical History* of Orderic Vitalis will loom large in the following pages. It is Orderic himself who tells us that he was born on 16 February 1075, probably within the parish of Atcham, on the Severn, a few miles from Shrewsbury.[96] He also tells us that his father, Odelerius of Orléans, was a chaplain of Roger II of Montgommery, earl of Shrewsbury, and the man who provided the impetus for the foundation of Shrewsbury abbey. He implies that his mother was English.[97] For ten years he lived in Shropshire, and during that time he would almost certainly have seen and perhaps met Earl Roger and his sons, including Robert of Bellême. It is even possible – although, of course, completely impossible to prove – that Orderic formed a personal dislike of Bellême at this early stage of his life. Be that as it may, when Orderic was ten years old, his father sent him to the abbey of Saint-Evroult in the Pays d'Ouche, where he remained for the rest of his life, albeit with occasional periods spent at the abbey's dependencies, and excursions to, for example, the abbey of Cluny, the council of Reims, and England.[98]

Orderic scattered autobiographical details throughout his *History*, but the fullest of those passages is found at the very conclusion of his work, perhaps as a deliberate echo of the autobiographical coda inserted by the Venerable Bede at the

---

[93] On the previous dating of the work see A. Gransden, *Historical Writing in England, c. 550–c. 1327* (London, 1974), p. 99 (who suggested the bulk of the work was written 1073–74); Poitiers, p. xx (with a wider date of 1071–77).

[94] Orderic, ii. 184.

[95] Orderic, ii. 258–60 (and see the various footnotes between p. 190 and p. 258 that refer to his use of Poitiers's text); R. M. Thomson, *William of Malmesbury*, revised edition (Woodbridge, 2003), pp. 69, 214.

[96] Orderic, iii. 6–8, vi. 552.

[97] Orderic, iii. 142, 146, 150.

[98] For Orderic's travels see most conveniently Orderic, i. 25–7; M. Chibnall, *The World of Orderic Vitalis: Norman Monks and Norman Knights* (Woodbridge, 1984), pp. 35–7.

end of his *Ecclesiastical History*.[99] Orderic's words are usually taken at face value, but it may be that he intended for them to be read allegorically. That is suggested by the several otherwise unexpected statements and coincidences found there, and elsewhere, in his *History*. Orderic does not say why he was sent to Saint-Evroult, but the abbey is unlikely to have been selected at random. Odelerius had a close connection with Roger II of Montgommery, but he did not send his son to one of Montgommery's foundations. Instead, he sent him to an abbey over which Montgommery had successfully extended his hegemony some fifteen years previously. It is therefore possible that Orderic went to Saint-Evroult to help to strengthen the links between the monastery and the house of Montgommery, and that his father hoped he would rise high in the abbey's administration as a result of his family connections. The monks' and the duke's subsequent conflicts with Robert of Bellême probably ensured that such hopes would be dashed.

As a result of those connections, when Orderic wrote of coming into Normandy 'as an exile, unknown to all, knowing no one' and, 'like Joseph in Egypt', hearing a language that he did not understand,[100] it seems unlikely that he was stating the literal truth. Norman French could not have been completely alien to him, given his father's background and the environment in which he had lived (even if he had been mostly brought up by his mother and schooled by an English priest). Equally, he might not have been personally known in Normandy, but he was not entirely without connections either. Not only did Montgommery's power encompass the abbey when he arrived, but it seems more likely than not that one of his relatives was part of the community. He was Geoffrey of Orléans, who was to become abbot of Crowland.[101] Some relationship to Orderic is suggested by his toponym, which suggests a kinship that Orderic obscured. It was not, after all, a popular toponym in Normandy. Nobody at all is said to be 'of Orléans' in Marie Fauroux's collection of ducal *acta* (except for the bishops of that place), or in the acts of William the Conqueror edited by David Bates, or those of Henry I, or even in Katherine Keats-Rohan's *Domesday Descendants*.[102] The chances of Odelerius and Geoffrey of Orléans having an entirely independent association with Saint-Evroult consequently seem rather slim. And then there is the fact that Orderic would later visit Abbot Geoffrey's relatively obscure monastery when he was in England but not, apparently, nearby Peterborough.[103]

[99] Orderic, vi. 552–6.

[100] Orderic, vi, 554.

[101] Orderic, ii. 346–8; D. Knowles, C. N. L. Brooke, V. London, *The Heads of Religious Houses England and Wales, 940–1216* (Cambridge, 1972), p. 42.

[102] K. S. B. Keats-Rohan, *Domesday Descendants: A Prosopography of Persons occurring in English Documents 1066–1166: II. Pipe Rolls to Cartae Baronum* (Woodbridge, 2002).

[103] Orderic tells us that he spent five weeks there (Orderic, ii. 324).

Orderic's interest in writing history first manifested itself in the interpolations he made to the *Gesta Normannorum ducum*. He did not begin work on his *Ecclesiastical History* until around 1117, however, and even then the work only began in earnest after Warin of Les Essarts became abbot in December 1122.[104] The work was initially conceived as a house chronicle, intended, at least in part, to record the properties given to the monks and thereby to help preserve them against any encroachments and alienations that might be attempted by their neighbours in the future. The initiative was thus perhaps related to the recovery of lands following the fall of Robert of Bellême, the confirmation of the monks' property in a charter issued by Henry I in 1113, and the subsequent *pancarte* of 1128 (which Orderic did not mention).[105] But Orderic was concerned about the precariousness of memory more generally, too, and included a variety of texts within his *History* to ensure that they should not be lost to posterity, along with the memories of some of his fellow monks and neighbours.[106]

The wider political narrative of events that Orderic set down might have been the result of this same concern to preserve the memory of past events. Aside from the *Gesta Normannorum ducum*, historical writing in Normandy seems to have been moribund when Orderic decided to take up his pen. The local annals that he might have come across (and he wrote part of the Annals of Saint-Evroult himself) must have seemed profoundly unsatisfactory to someone who had copied out Bede and who would himself produce a work of such prodigious length. Moreover, if those memories were to be saved, the work had to be started immediately. Those who could remember the events of Robert Curthose's reign were growing old. Curthose himself would die just a year after Orderic is thought to have begun Book VIII, which recounted his deeds.[107] Although we know that Orderic made some hasty notes on the *Life* of St William while the manuscript was at Saint-Evroult, it is not at all clear that he regularly made or relied on such aides-memoire at other times. Indeed we do not even know whether or not he had the opportunity to make such notes. It might well have been the case, then, that when he began finally to write Books VIII, X, XI, and perhaps even XII,

---

[104] Orderic, iii. 6.

[105] For this suggestion see Orderic, i. 32; Shopkow, *History and Community*, p. 47.

[106] Orderic made the point himself in his opening prologue to the *Ecclesiastical History* (Orderic, i. 130) as well as by his choice of content. Among the more precarious memories he preserved were his account of the court of Earl Hugh of Chester and work of Gerold of Avranches as remembered by his fellow monks (Orderic, iii. 216, 226–32); and the appearance of Hellequin's Hunt witnessed by the priest Walchelin (Orderic, iv. 236–50). See also Shopkow, *History and Community*, pp. 202–4.

[107] For the postulated dates of the composition of the various books of the *Ecclesiastical History* see Orderic, i. 47–8.

time was of the essence. And so the scope of the *Ecclesiastical History* widened considerably.

Orderic's original contribution covered the period from 1076 to 1141, and it is the period from 1087 until 1141 that constitutes the second, and more coherent, of the two distinct parts of the *Ecclesiastical History*.[108] In contrast to this basically chronological political narrative, Books I–VI comprise a universal chronicle that shades into a patchy political narrative of the creation and development of Normandy, although principally focused on the reign of William the Bastard, which is frequently interrupted (often at length) by a varied assemblage of texts, including a *Life* of St Guthlac and one of St Judoc, which then shades into a house history of Saint-Evroult and its dependencies.

The content and presentation of events in Orderic's *Ecclesiastical History* reflects its author's background and environment. Although his father was French, Orderic seems to have though of himself as English, even describing himself as Orderic or Vitalis 'the Englishman'.[109] This concern to speak up for the English can be seen particularly in his treatment of the changes and conflict that followed William the Bastard's victory at Hastings in 1066 and of his principal source for those events, the *Gesta Guillelmi* of William of Poitiers. Orderic's editing of that text speaks volumes.[110] As is well known, he omitted the sycophancy along with most of the classical allusions or explicit comparisons to classical figures in the text.[111] But he also corrected or added where he saw fit. Thus he asserted that the Malfosse incident during the battle of Hastings manifested the judgement of God on those who 'had been guilty of coveting the goods of other men contrary to the precept of the law'.[112] He remarked, in direct contradiction to Poitiers, that William fitz Osbern and Odo of Bayeux oppressed the English and protected their

---

[108] That is Books VII–XIII. Marjorie Chibnall and Leah Shopkow remarked upon the two distinct parts of Orderic's great work (Shopkow, *History and Community*, p. 163). James Bickford-Smith argued to the contrary that Orderic's work must be read as a whole if it is to be understood – although the fact that Books VII and VIII only survive as abridged copies means that is now impossible anyway (Orderic, iv. xiii–xviii; J. Bickford-Smith, 'Orderic Vitalis and Norman society c. 1035–1087' (unpublished D.Phil thesis, Oxford University, 2006), p. 62). Indeed, the arguments Bickford-Smith advanced regarding the interpretation of Orderic's work fail to convince, despite the enthusiastic reception of his thesis found in J. Hudson, review of *Robert Curthose, Duke of Normandy (c. 1050–1134)* by William. M. Aird (Woodbridge, 2008) in *History*, 95 (2010), 106).

[109] For example, Orderic, iii. 6, 168, 256; iv. 144.

[110] Orderic, ii. 168–208, with the text down to p. 258 said to have been based on the now missing part of his work.

[111] For example at Orderic, ii. 192.

[112] Orderic, ii. 178. He had earlier added this same interpolation to the *Gesta Normannorum ducum*: Jumièges, ii. 170.

followers who had been guilty of plunder and rape, causing the rebellion in Kent in 1067.[113] Poitiers had written that no Norman was given anything unjustly, but Orderic spent a great deal of time arguing that the reverse was true, including by putting a lengthy denunciation of the greed of Norman churchmen into the mouth of Guitmund of La Croix-Saint-Leufroy.[114] He also made it clear that the risings of 1068 and 1069 were due to a combination of Norman oppression and greed, and a resulting desire on behalf of the English to recover their lost liberty.[115] He responded to the Normans' condemnation of the English Church, too, noting that monasticism had been restored during the tenth century but then damaged by the Viking attacks of the later tenth and eleventh century. He included the explanation 'so that the patient reader may clearly understand why the Normans found the English a rustic and nearly illiterate people'.[116] That aside also answered Poitiers' criticism that the English had been illiterate barbarians before they were conquered, and inferred that it was actually the barbarians who had done the conquering. It was 'by the will of almighty God' that they had 'subdued a people that was greater, and wealthier than they were, with a longer history'.[117]

Aside from being English, Orderic was also a member of a community located in the south of Normandy, in an area populated by the successors and supplanters of his abbey's founders as well as its principal benefactors. He consequently saw events through that regional prism, perhaps because his (mostly unknown) sources of information tended to share the same local perspective, and/or because his interactions with local lords naturally highlighted their actions on the wider Anglo-Norman stage. Thus the families of Giroie, Grandmesnil, Courcy, Montpinçon, Pantulf, and Montgommery loom particularly large in the first half of his *History*, with Gilbert of L'Aigle and the notorious Robert of Bellême grabbing headlines during his portrayal of Curthose's reign, and Ralph the Red of Pont-Echanfray playing a prominent role in the battles fought during Henry I's reign. Equally, while Curthose presided over scandalous elections to the bishoprics of Lisieux and Bayeux, and while he was censored for them by churchmen within and without Normandy, including Pope Paschal II, in Orderic's work it was Bishop Serlo of Sées, driven from his see by the aggression of Robert of Bellême, who was allowed to speak for the whole of the Norman Church when he joined Henry's invasion force at Carentan in 1105.[118] On a wider stage, he drew

---

[113] Orderic, ii. 202.
[114] Orderic, ii. 270–8.
[115] Orderic, ii. 216, 222. See also on this subject Albu, *The Normans in their Histories*, pp. 196–8.
[116] Orderic, ii. 246.
[117] Orderic, ii. 268 and see Shopkow, *History and Community*, p. 206.
[118] Orderic, vi. 60–8 and see below, Chapter 3.

attention to the career of Robert of Grandmesnil in the south of Italy and noted the presence of members of the Grandmesnil family at the siege of Antioch.

Probably the greatest influence on Orderic's interpretation of events, however, was his assumption that God was directing them, and that he did so according to Christian values. That gave his *Ecclesiastical History* a typically monastic moral tinge, although it also allowed Orderic readily to explain the victories, reversals, and unexpected twists that he narrated. The manner of the death and burial of William the Bastard provides one well-known example of this, Henry's defeat of Curthose at Tinchebray in 1106 another (where God's will expressly trumped human customs), and the wreck of the *White Ship* a third (with the added implication that the *White Ship*'s captain paid for the sins of a father who had transported Duke William to England at the end of September 1066).[119] This moral complexion can also be seen in Orderic's use of scripture to understand or contextualize events,[120] and in the anecdotes that Orderic continued to add even to his more focused narrative, such as that concerning the vision of Hellequin's Hunt by the priest Walchelin.[121] Thus, for Orderic, History was not simply a guide to action but a means of understanding why things happened, not just in the past but also in the present and future.[122]

His approach, some at least of his content, and the length of his work suggests that his principal audience was always intended to be the monks of his own abbey and other interested ecclesiastical parties. He was not, therefore, trying to justify Henry I's accession for a secular audience. Indeed, as he wrote about Henry's reign after Henry had himself died, such justification was quite unnecessary. Equally, because he completed the books that deal with Curthose's reign just before Henry I died, and thus before Stephen's accession, and as he did not subsequently revise them to any great extent, it is unlikely that he was intending to emphasize the behaviour that Stephen should avoid if he were to defeat Geoffrey and Matilda and retain the duchy. (Although the comparisons between the two rulers are no less clear for that.) His *Ecclesiastical History*, then, was no mirror for princes. It was a moral lesson writ large for a monastic audience, who could come

---

[119] Orderic, iv. 106–8; vi. 88–92, 296–302.

[120] For example, Orderic, iii. 98, 112; iv. 8–10, 14, 42, 92, 108, 122, 128, 130, 132, 178, 190; v. 196, 214, 250, 252, 298; vi. 30, 74, 82, 184, 200. Note, however, that Orderic expressly stated that he was not interpreting the events he witnessed allegorically: 'I find many things in the pages of Scripture which, if they are subtly interpreted, seem to resemble the happenings of our own time. But I leave the allegorical implications and explanations appropriate to human customs to be interpreted by scholars' (Orderic, iv. 228).

[121] Orderic, iv. 236–50.

[122] Gransden, *Historical Writing in England*, pp. 154–5, 159–60; Shopkow, *History and Community*, pp. 203–5; A. J. Hingst, *The Written World: Past and Place in the Work of Orderic Vitalis* (Notre-Dame, 2009), pp. xii, xx.

closer to understanding God's workings on earth through the narrative of events, saints' *Lives*, visions, and prophecies that it included.[123]

Ducal acta

In addition to the Norman narratives, there are hundreds of Norman diplomas, charters, and writs that date from before 1144. These documents, particularly those acts issued or authenticated by the dukes, have proved fundamental to this study, and as such will be explored and discussed in depth in a number of the following chapters. Their importance means that, as with the narratives, some general remarks by way of introduction are necessary, even at risk of a little repetition.

There are in total 512 acts of the Norman dukes for the period 911–1144. Of these, 214 date from before 1066,[124] while 298 date from between 1066 and 1135. To some extent the surviving sample defies the upward trend that might be expected. There are 101 post-Conquest acts of King William for Normandy (4.8 per year) and 143 of King Henry I (4.9 per year). It may be that William's prestige helped to ensure that his acts would be well preserved. There are, however, far fewer surviving acts issued by those perceived by modern historians to have been weak dukes. Thus there are only thirty surviving acts of Robert Curthose for the period 1087–96 and 1100–06 (two per year that he was resident in the duchy with an additional six from the period when Rufus was lord of Normandy),[125] while Stephen, Matilda, and Geoffrey of Anjou between them issued a further seventeen acts

---

[123] In sum, the *Ecclesiastical History* embraces two chronicles, the lives of Christ and the apostles, an abbreviated *Liber pontificalis*, eight abbreviated saints' *Lives* (see Orderic, i. 61–2 for the complete list), an epitome of the *Translation of St Nicholas* by John of Bari, monastic histories of Saint-Evroult and Crowland, a history of the Normans and English after the Conquest, a history of the first crusade, a treatise on the new monastic orders, a few romance stories and moral exempla, more than thirty epitaphs and other sorts of verse, nineteen documents of various kinds including five sets of canons and eight charters, and assorted accounts of events in Germany, Italy, Ireland, England, Spain, and the Middle East (Shopkow, *History and Community*, p. 47).

[124] These break down between the reigns as follows: Richard I: 4; Richard II: 47; Richard III: 1; Robert the Magnificent: 27; William the Bastard: 135.

[125] Rufus's acts are: *NI*, p. 81, no. viii (Le Mans cathedral) and no. x (a lost act for Longueville); M. T. Clanchy, *From Memory to Written Record*, second edition (Oxford, 1993), pl. 1 (Facsimile); *Early Yorkshire Charters*, ed. C. T. Clay, vols 4–10, Yorkshire Archaeological Society, Record Series, extra series (1935–55), iii. no. 1483; R. Mortimer, 'Anglo-Norman Lay Charters, 1066–*c*. 1100: A Diplomatic Approach', *ANS*, 25 (2002), 157, n. 18 (Le Trinité-du-Mont); CDF, no. 116 (Saint-Florent of Saumur); *Regesta: William*, no. 281 (which includes a note that the act was confirmed by Rufus). There is also a writ for the monks of Montebourg which could have been issued by William I or William II, but has here been assigned to the former.

that encompassed lands within the duchy before the completion of Geoffrey's conquest of the duchy in 1144 (1.8 per year, although in reality almost all of these documents were issued by Stephen in 1137).[126]

It should be noted that the examination of the surviving original ducal *acta*, as well as later cartulary copies, has been made much easier by the high-quality digitization of the holdings of the Archives de la Seine-Maritime.[127] It must be hoped that the other Norman archives, particularly those of the Calvados, will follow suit in the near future. In addition, a number of Norman manuscripts found in the municipal libraries at Le Havre, Rouen, Lisieux, and elsewhere have been digitized in whole or in part by the Institut de recherche et d'histoire des textes on their bibliothèque virtuelle des manuscrits médiévaux website.[128] Finally, so far as electronic resources are concerned, the text of every original act preserved in France dating from before 1121 has been edited on the Telma database.[129] All of this is an enormous boon to scholars working on every aspect of Normandy in the Middle Ages.

The dukes' acts tell us a lot about the growing reach of their authority and about reactions to it. They also tell us a great deal about their revenues and the mechanisms that were in place to collect them on the ground. The full extent of their utility with regard to ducal finance, for example, has not perhaps always been recognized. Moreover, it seems clear that as the dukes' diplomas provided evidence of grants of particular sums, paid either in cash or in kind, these documents did not languish in ecclesiastical archives but were put to work and thereby travelled with representatives of the beneficiaries concerned to be produced as occasion demanded. In function, then, diplomas were probably not that different to some of the later writs, for example those granting exemption from toll and customs, even though they were very far from writs in terms of their diplomatic and (in most cases at least) appearance.[130]

But while they can tell us much about the dukes' power and administration, the ducal acts also tell us a lot about the reception of ducal power by the dukes'

---

[126]   *Regesta*, iii. nos. 67, 69, 70, 75, 111, 281, 282, 298, 594, 598, 608, 609, 727, 733 (1140 × 1154), 749, 774 (probably), 805.

[127]   Found at: < http://recherche.archivesdepartementales76.net/?id=recherche_guidee >.

[128]   Found at: < http://bvmm.irht.cnrs.fr/ >.

[129]   Found at: < http://www.cn-telma.fr/originaux/index/ >.

[130]   Writs of Henry I remained working documents into the fourteenth century. A *vidimus* of King Louis X of June 1315 states that the monks of Montebourg had sought the king's confirmation of four of Henry's acts because they were 'obliged to send them frequently to diverse places, on this side or the other of the sea, in order to defend their rights' and thus wished 'to avoid the accidental destruction of the originals' (*Registres du Trésor des Chartes*, ii. 39, no. 176). The acts in question included writs exempting the monks from tolls and customs, establishing their rights to timber, and prohibiting the taking of men or distress during the monks' markets (calendared at *Regesta*, ii. nos. 1949, 1950, 1951).

subjects and beneficiaries. That is because until the reign of Henry I, almost all ducal *acta* were drafted by scribes attached to the donor or beneficiary rather than by a duke's chaplains or scribes.[131] This is perhaps unexpected, for while there is no evidence for the existence of a chancery or writing office before 1066, except perhaps for a period during the reign of Richard II, the existence of a chapel and chaplains should have given the dukes a body of men who could have been put to work drafting an occasional diploma to be issued in their name.[132] That was the case in Anjou, where those of the counts' chaplains who staffed the chapel of Saint-Laud in the castle at Angers seem to have been responsible for drafting comital *acta* from the eleventh century.[133] And yet, while Dudo of Saint-Quentin styled himself 'chancellor', in an act he drafted in the name of Count Rodulf but at the command of Duke Richard, he is the only chaplain known to have done so, and even then there is no good reason to think that he held any formal office or that the duke would even have recognized him as his chancellor. That Dudo awarded himself the title might, therefore, simply have been a piece of self-aggrandizement rather than an accurate description of his role at the duke's court, or was perhaps intended only to reflect the fact that the duke had commanded him to write this single diploma.[134] No other ducal chaplain identified himself as the author of any ducal act, and when scribes are named in the acts they wrote it is not at all clear that they had any connection with the duke or his court.[135] Guy the notary, for example, who wrote an act of Richard II for the monks of Fécamp, could well have been in the employ of Robert the Pious who was at the

---

[131] 'The evidence overwhelmingly supports the view that William's Norman *acta* were written by their beneficiaries ... it is fair to say that charter production in Normandy after 1066 continues the pattern established before 1066' (*Regesta: William*, p. 10). Also *RADN*, p. 41; C. Potts, 'The early Norman charters: a new perspective on an old debate', in *England in the Eleventh Century*, ed. C. Hicks (Stamford, 1992), pp. 32–3.

[132] *RADN*, p. 42; Bates, *Normandy*, pp. 154–5; Potts, 'The early Norman charters', pp. 33, 36. Allen Brown used these few examples to argue for a longer-lived writing office (R. A. Brown, 'Some observations on Anglo-Norman charters', in *Tradition and Change: Essays in Honour of Marjorie Chibnall*, ed. D. Greenway, C. Holdsworth and J. Sayers (Cambridge, 1985), p. 161).

[133] K. Dutton, 'Angevin scribes and collaborative charter production, *c.* 1109–1151', paper read at the Leeds International Medieval Congress, 8 July 2014.

[134] *RADN*, no. 18. The lack of a ducal writing-office before 1066 is discussed below, *infra*, and also in Chapter 5, pp. 266–8, 275–9, 290 and Chapter 7, pp. 405–22. See also *RADN*, pp. 41–7; Bates, *Normandy*, pp. 154–5; R. A. Brown, 'Some observations', pp. 145–55; *Regesta: William*, p. 97. Ben Pohl has recently argued to the contrary, and asserted that Dudo did indeed act as chancellor (Pohl, *Dudo of Saint-Quentin's* Historia Normannorum, pp. 122–4, 126).

[135] *RADN*, nos. 9, 92, 15, 186, respectively. The point is also conceded by Brown ('Some observations', p. 152).

abbey at the time and perhaps issued his own confirmation during his stay.[136] In other cases, it is all but certain that the man named was a beneficiary scribe. They include Bernerius priest and monk for Saint-Ouen, Robert of Grandmesnil for Saint-Evroult, Paul the monk for Saint-Père of Chartres, and William the notary in an act of Count Richard of Evreux for Jumièges.[137] This last character has been discussed by Elisabeth van Houts, who has suggested that he should be identified as William of Jumièges, the author of the *Gesta Normannorum ducum*.[138]

The phrases and formulae employed in some of the Norman ducal *acta* seem to have been modelled on Carolingian usage.[139] The use of such elaborate wording has been seen as a demonstration of the revival of the monastic life of Normandy, but also as a looking back to a past that had disappeared when the Vikings first raided Neustria and then settled on the Seine. It has, in other words, become part of the argument about continuity or catastrophe. But the interpretation of the language used in such acts needs further nuance. The monks who staffed the refounded Norman abbeys were not Normans – at least not to begin with. The monks of Saint-Ouen of Rouen were Franks, who had perhaps returned from their self-imposed exile by 918.[140] The monks at Jumièges came from Saint-Cyprien at Poitiers.[141] Those established at Fécamp came with William of Volpiano from Dijon.[142] The monks who settled at Saint-Wandrille were from Ghent in Flanders.[143] These Frankish monks brought with them the forms with which they were familiar. Moreover, for them there had been no discontinuity. Their religious life had continued more or less without interruption outside what was quickly becoming Normandy, and it is not clear that their predecessors' exodus from the duchy had any lasting impact on their collective identity.[144]

The similarities in formulae found in acts for the same house, or even for dif-

---

[136] Telma, no. 2663. The surviving original is not authentic.

[137] *RADN*, nos. 42, 122, 147a, 92 respectively. Brown thought so, too ('Some observations', p. 151).

[138] E. M. C. van Houts, 'Une hypothèse sur l'identification de *Willelmus notarius* comme l'historien Guillaume de Jumièges', *Tabularia 'Etudes'*, 2 (2002) <http://www.unicaen.fr/mrsh/craham/revue/tabularia/print.php?dossier=dossier1&contribDebat=true&file=04vanhouts.xml> [accessed 7 April 2016].

[139] For example, *RADN*, p. 44; Brown, 'Some observations', pp. 150–2; Potts, 'The early Norman charters', p. 32.

[140] C. Potts, *Monastic Revival and Regional Identity in Early Normandy* (Woodbridge, 1997), pp. 21–2; *Normannia Monastica*, i. 8–9

[141] Potts, *Monastic Revival*, p. 18; *Normannia Monastica*, i. 9; ii. 143–4.

[142] Potts, *Monastic Revival*, pp. 28–9; *Normannia Monastica*, i. 10; ii. 101–5.

[143] Potts, *Monastic Revival*, p. 25; *Normannia Monastica*, i. 9; ii. 331–2.

[144] Just as the exodus of the monks of Lindisfarne and the odyssey that eventually took them to Durham helped to create a stronger sense of community and did not constitute a break in tradition or of the religious life.

ferent houses that were located in close proximity to each other, tend to support the view that they were written by scribes who were part of, or associated with, the communities concerned. Thus, two acts recording gifts by different donors for Mont-Saint-Michel look to have been drafted by a single scribe, and the same is true (on basis of both wording and appearance) of three acts for Saint-Ouen, and two for the cathedral at Bayeux.[145] Lucien Musset thought that the monks of Caen drafted acts for nuns of Holy Trinity, as well as for the monks of nearby Fontenay.[146] B.-M. Tock has examined the archive of originals from Jumièges and concluded similarly that, 'the monks of Jumièges wrote their acts themselves'.[147] Thus from the evidence at our disposal, it seems that it was almost always the beneficiary which drafted the acts made in its favour throughout the eleventh century. It is only during the reign of Henry I that we can see writing-office scribes drafting writs and charters for Norman beneficiaries in Normandy, but even then the royal duke's control over charter production was very far from complete.[148]

However, although there is no good reason to think that ducal chaplains wrote the text of ducal *acta*, it might be the case that they did draw the crosses at the bottom of the page, when these were not autograph, and/or labelled them so that the signer could be identified at a later date.[149] In most of the surviving authentic originals, it is certainly the case that the hand that added those labels is different from the hand that drafted the text.[150] Equally, the style attached to the duke's *signum* is often less inflated than that found within the text, and is also a little more consistent across the corpus of surviving acts, which might suggest a 'house-style' and thus, once again, the use of ducal scribes or chaplains for this work.[151] But even though the evidence points in this direction, there is still room for doubt. Dudo's involvement in writing ducal *acta*, limited though it was, is clear. He also named himself as a chaplain and chancellor. And yet even he did not add the names of the witnesses to the acts he wrote. Instead, he just left a blank space like any other beneficiary draftsman, and the names were subsequently added in different hands.

---

[145] *RADN*, nos. 16, 17 (Mont-Saint-Michel); *RADN*, nos. 39, 43, 45 (Saint-Ouen); *Regesta: William*, nos. 27 and 28 (Bayeux). See also Potts, 'The early Norman charters', p. 29.

[146] *Les actes de Guillaume le Conquérant et de la reine Mathilde pour les abbayes Caennaises*, ed. L. Musset, MSAN, 37 (1967), pp. 35–6.

[147] B.-M. Tock, 'Les chartes originales de l'abbaye de Jumièges jusqu'en 1120', *Tabularia 'Etudes'*, 2 (2002) <http://www.unicaen.fr/mrsh/craham/revue/tabularia/print.php?dossier=dossier1&file=04tock.xml> [accessed 7 April 2016].

[148] See below, Chapter 5, pp. 293–4.

[149] See in particular below, Chapter 5, pp. 277–9 and Chapter 7, pp. 419–21.

[150] See also Potts, 'The early Norman charters', pp. 32–3. But note the warning about this below, Chapter 5, p. 279.

[151] See below, Chapter 5, pp. 277–80 and Chapter 7, pp. 419–21.

As the acts produced by different beneficiaries, indeed even by the same beneficiary, can vary in wording and formulae, it can be quite difficult to detect
forgery, especially in those many cases where the original parchment does not
survive. It is also the case that where forgery has been exposed in Norman ducal
acta, it is often limited to a relatively minor interpolation related to an identified
or suspected dispute over property, rights, or freedoms.[152] In such cases, there
is no good reason to presume that the rest of the diploma was modified at the
same time. It seems much more likely that the surviving text accurately reflects
the original, authentic document. Similar problems arise with the compilation of
pancartes and cartularies, whereby it is possible that the original text was edited,
amended, or modernized (for example, Duke William became King William) as
it was copied down.[153]

In addition, two surviving original acts of William I from the Fécamp archive
demonstrate one important issue with regard to the appearance of genuine documents, and thus constitute a warning against dismissing as forgeries documents
that look wrong at first glance. The first was produced in the standard manner,
with the text in one hand, autograph crosses, and the names of the signers added
in a different hand. The second original is actually a copy of this diploma, apparently produced at the same time or immediately after the first one had been signed,
because the entire document, crosses and all, was written by the same scribe who
had added the names to the *signa* of that original version.[154] The existence of this
second contemporary copy raises some serious challenges to identifying forgeries
in Norman archives based on appearances alone. It is possible, for example, that
original acts from the archives of La Croix-Saint-Leufroy and Troarn were created
in the same way.[155] Clean copies of diplomata, with the entire text written in the

---

[152] For example, *RADN*, nos. 49 (abandonment of ducal and episcopal customs, and grant
of the right of doing justice on the men of the bourg, to the monks of Mont-Saint-
Michel with the consent of the pope); 122 (which lists military obligations that had most
likely not crystallized *c.* 1050 and a grant of free elections which was probably added
c. 1130. For a discussion see M. Chibnall, 'Military service in Normandy before 1066',
ANS, 5 (1983), pp. 69–72). Fauroux did not count no. 122 among the forged or interpolated documents, however (*RADN*, no. 122). Her list of false documents comprises
nos. 27, 56, 57, 62, 90*bis*, 90*ter*, 91, 127 (which is not, however, a ducal act), 136. Bates
identified only four Norman acts of King William that are forgeries: *Regesta: William*,
nos. 148, 245, 247, 258.

[153] See *Regesta: William*, p. 11.

[154] *Regesta: William*, no. 144, A¹ and A². Chaplais noted the existence of a second example,
in the form of an authentic original of Henry I for Cluny and a fair-copy of the same
document (P. Chaplais, 'The seals and original charters of Henry I', *EHR*, 75 (1960), 272,
n. 5).

[155] *Regesta: William*, nos. 65, 283, 284.

same hand, and without autograph *signa*, should not therefore automatically be written off as forgeries.

Where ducal *acta* can be certainly, or virtually certainly, identified as forgeries, they have generally been omitted from the discussion and any complementary tables or statistics. Where parts of ducal acts can be identified as later interpolations, those sections, too, have been discounted. Where there is merely suspicion of forgery, however, the acts and/or wording in question have been accepted and treated as if they were authentic (with due caveat).

It seems, then, that a duke's involvement in the drafting of his own diplomas was minimal. Where acts record a duke's own gift, it might have been limited to a dialogue between the duke and the beneficiary about what precisely the gift comprised, but in the vast majority of other cases it is not clear that there was any prior ducal involvement at all. Ducal *acta* style the duke in different ways, which suggests that there was no official line here.[156] The duke was almost certainly not involved in any decision about the inclusion or wording of *arengae* and anathema clauses. Indeed, as anathema clauses to some extent highlighted a duke's inability always to do justice on those who attached a church's property, their inclusion might be a positive indication of the duke's absence from the process.[157] In some cases, we have clear evidence of this absence of involvement. In 1080, for example, William the Bastard commanded the monks of Saint-Florent of Saumur to bring a previously written document to him so that he might add his sign to the page.[158] In 1113, Henry I commanded the monks of Saint-Evroult to draw up a confirmation which he would then issue in his name. They did so, but the act was written in Henry's absence and then presented to him as a finished product.[159] The presentation of previously written diplomas to the duke for authentication would also explain why so few scribes appear in witness lists or lists of signers. They were not there because their part in the proceedings was over already.

These same two documents of 1080 and 1113 also help to illustrate that the dukes' desire to confirm grants that had already been made by others was not motivated solely by a desire to protect a particular church. In 1080, the monks of Lonlay and Saint-Florent of Saumur brought a dispute over the church of Briouze before the royal duke. William the Bastard's authority in Houlme was probably still quite weak. The Montgommery family continued to dominate the region, as their predecessors, the lords of Bellême had done before them, and local ties of loyalty seem to have remained strong. Certainly, the monks of the monasteries

---

[156] See below, Chapter 5, pp. 266–9, 287–8.
[157] See below, Chapter 7, pp. 415–19.
[158] *Regesta: William*, no. 267.
[159] Orderic, vi. 174–6.

established within what had been the lordship of Bellême – Lonlay and Saint-Martin of Sées, in particular – did not see the need to seek confirmations of their possessions from the duke and did not generally seek his justice. William thus seized on the opportunity that had presented itself, not only to decide the dispute (if only after William of Briouze had surrendered his jurisdiction) but also to confirm the original grant by his own authority, as just noted. Thus he reinforced the imperative that had brought the monks of Saumur to his court in the first place and ensured their recognition of his authority over them and, by extension, the territory in which their churches stood.

Henry I's act for the monks of Saint-Evroult of 1113 was similarly presented as the result of a benign suggestion, made with the intention of protecting the monks' lands from their predatory neighbours. But there was almost certainly a political reason for Henry's generosity, too. Robert of Bellême had been arrested and imprisoned just four months previously. The area in which the abbey stood was experiencing strong ducal government for the first time. Henry was trying to establish his own power in the vacuum left behind by Bellême, which Bellême's son still hoped to fill himself. In such circumstances, Henry's confirmation would constitute evidence of the monks' acknowledgement of his authority and thus a demonstration of loyalty to his regime. It would also give Henry jurisdiction over any subsequent pleas involving the monks and their property, potentially allowing him to assert his authority in the region again in the future.[160]

More often, or so it may be supposed, beneficiaries decided to take their diplomas to the dukes for confirmation off their own bat. Their decision might still be political, and the document produced could still be a political weapon, but there is a qualitative difference in the evidence when it was created at the wish of the beneficiary rather than that of the duke. One example is provided by a diploma of 1053, which records a grant made by William of La Ferté-Macé to the monks of Saint-Julian at Tours. That an abbey in Angevin-held Tours was the beneficiary of his grant reveals that William, whose lands lay within the lordship of Bellême, had until very recently still looked south to Anjou and the Touraine rather than north to Normandy. His act thus reveals something of the political realignment caused by the imposition of Norman authority in the lordship of Bellême following the capture of Alençon and Domfront c. 1052. Further, the gift was said

---

[160] These two acts, then, were political weapons, not dissimilar to the records of lawsuits and diplomas discussed by Warren Brown and Geoffrey Koziol, intended to strengthen the duke's position and to undermine that of his provincial rivals (W. Brown, 'Charters as weapons: on the role played by early medieval dispute records in the disputes they record', *JMH*, 28 (2002), 227–48; G. Koziol, *The Politics of Memory and Identity in Carolingian Royal Diplomas: The West Frankish Kingdom (840–987)* (Turnhout, 2012), pp. 7, 39–42).

to have been made 'with the assent of my sons and their mother and of my lord Ivo, bishop of Sées (*Oxismorum*), from whom I hold the said customs of this church and the two subject to it as a benefice, and with the authority of William *princeps Normannorum* and of Roger my lord (*senior*)'.[161] William and the monks of Tours were aware of the political reality that they faced. They knew that the lords of Bellême were a spent force, and so they acknowledged the authority of Roger of Montgommery and Duke William. It is not clear that they had to do this. Indeed, the paucity of ducal acts for beneficiaries based in the lordship of Bellême (including those lands in the Séois, Houlme, and Passais which would become part of Normandy) suggests that they did not. But that just makes their decision all the more eloquent.

Other diplomas did not perhaps relate to matters of high politics to quite the same extent, but the fact that a beneficiary thought it worthwhile to travel to the duke's court says something about their perception of his power, and so, too, does the apparent replacement of anathema clauses with penalty clauses that specified fines to be paid to the duke should a grant be infringed. Together, they suggest a growth in the effectiveness of the duke's justice.[162] Beneficiaries also chose how to style the duke in the texts of their acts, which can give us a sense of how they defined the duke's functions or their power or their place in the political hierarchy. They decided whether or not to notice that he ruled thanks to the grace or clemency of God and/or his relationship to previous rulers, which might tell us something about views of a duke's legitimacy and his autonomy vis-à-vis the king of the Franks.[163] If not political weapons, then, such acts certainly constituted political comment, for they were the result of perception rather than propaganda. They provide views from the bottom up rather than the top down, from the early eleventh century until 1144, and their discordant voices tell us how that power was seen in different places at different times.

* * * * * *

This survey has, among other things, highlighted how many of the most important sources upon which this survey rests were constructed by authors and scribes working outside the court, even if for a courtly audience, for a specific reason or reasons. Thus Dudo of Saint-Quentin wrote to persuade those Normans, Franks, Bretons, and English who were to be found at the court of Richard II of the God-given place of the dukes at the head of an autonomous and powerful duchy.

---

[161] *RADN*, no. 131.
[162] See below, Chapter 7, pp. 415–19 for a discussion of the use of such formulae in ducal *acta*.
[163] See below, Chapter 5, pp. 259–60 and Chapter 6, pp. 320–1.

William of Jumièges wrote to reunite the duke with his subjects, stressing the need for unity and community after the divisions and attacks that had plagued William the Bastard's reign up to 1057. William of Poitiers strove to reconcile the English to their new Norman king. And Orderic Vitalis wrote to teach and inform the monk of his own monastery, and others, too, about the history of his abbey and the duchy in which it stood, while also providing a series of moral lessons. None of these authors intended to write history in the sense that it would be understood in the twenty-first century. They were instead political commentators, pundits, makers of opinion, and their works need to be read in that light.

It is worth noting explicitly, or repeating in the case of Dudo's *De moribus*, that I have assumed, on what I think is good evidence, that each of the first three of the narratives discussed above would have been heard and understood by those present at the dukes' court and other assemblies. While the straightforward Latin of the *Gesta Normannorum ducum* could perhaps have been understood by some of the laymen present, it is likely that they were all translated into the vernacular by whoever was reading and performing them. So even if the dukes had not commissioned these works directly, or had very little input regarding their content, they would still have been very much aware of the form and approach of the work as it was published, and so, too, would those who surrounded or visited them.

The diplomas produced in a duke's name or brought to him for authentication were also read out to those present at court. In most cases, their content was unexceptional, but even the recitation of a run-of-the-mill act still highlighted the role of a duke as the guarantor of the donation in question, even if he might have to share that role with God (by way of an anathema clause). More rarely, the wording of these acts might provide a rather fuller commentary on the perception of a duke's power or, more rarely still, might comprise a reprimand for his past behaviour or a guide to Christian rule. And because these acts were read and heard and understood, they made a contribution to the political culture of the duchy, reinforcing or challenging the foundations of the duke's power while furthering the cause of Christianity and the Church. They were a way for a duke's subjects to make their voices heard at the very top of the political hierarchy, while at the same time constituting an acknowledgement of the duke's power and the reach of his authority.

PART I

Conquest, Concession, Conversion, and Competition: Building the Duchy of Normandy

CHAPTER 1

Settlement and Survival: Normandy in the Tenth Century, 911–96

T HIS is the first of three chapters that explore and attempt to explain the creation, development, and ultimately the diminution of the territory that would
recognize the authority of the Norman dukes of the Normans between 911 and
1144. The discussion advances reign by reign, from Rollo to Stephen, and ends
with the completion of the conquest of the duchy by Geoffrey V of Anjou in 1144.
The use of this narrative structure is intended to foreground both continuity and
change over time, and the focus is on what might be described as state-building,
thus on conquest, coercion, diplomacy, marriages, fidelity, and the rewards or
bribes offered in return for service and support.

Narratives outlining the political history of the duchy are still scarce. Probably
the best to date are those written by Eleanor Searle, which ends in 1066, and
the equally scholarly but more 'popular' surveys by David Crouch and François
Neveux.[1] For Upper Normandy there is also Pierre Bauduin's excellent *La première Normandie*, which provides not only an in-depth examination of the establishment of ducal power in the region, but also a detailed look at the families who had
to be won over and their role in the continuing consolidation and operation of
ducal rule. While the debt owed to this earlier work must be acknowledged, the
outline provided here is based on a fresh look at the primary sources, and pays
more attention to the ducal *acta* than has generally been the case in the past. The
result is a story that, while not radically different from those which have gone
before, does offer different interpretations and emphases at a great many points
in the narrative. In particular, the duchy takes shape more slowly in the account
presented here than has been the case previously, and there is more emphasis on
the political fault lines that divided Norman lords even under a strong duke like
William the Bastard, manifested most obviously in the ambition and self-interest
of the Montgommery-Bellême family.

---

[1] Searle, *PK*, which, regardless of the validity of her arguments regarding kinship and
the pruning of the dukes' family tree, is in essence a political narrative of Normandy to
1066; D. Crouch, *The Normans: The History of a Dynasty* (London, 2002); F. Neveux,
A Brief History of the Normans: The Conquests that Changed the Face of Europe, trans.
H. Curtis (London, 2008).

That the contemporary sources for Norman history can be interpreted in so many different ways is a result of the intentions that lay behind their origins, discussed in the introduction. In particular, the agendas of their authors mean that the narratives that tell us about Normandy and its dukes distort and conceal as much as they reveal. Flodoard of Reims, a Frank writing a long way from Normandy, provided probably the most reliable account, as well as the most contemporary one, but his entries are also episodic, incomplete, and thus often cryptic. In their own way, Flodoard's *Annals* are as difficult to interpret as the altogether more constructed narrative of Richer of Reims, who knew Flodoard's work but recast and rewrote it to suit his own ends. That is not to say that everything Richer reports was fabricated, but it is clear that he liked to tell a story in a classical manner and was not averse to editing or supplementing his sources.[2] So, for example, while Flodoard wrote of a succession of three grants made *c*. 911 and in 924 and 933, which together comprised the concession of the territory that would become Normandy, Richer has just one grant that comprised the whole of the province of Rouen, in other words a grant that included all seven Norman bishoprics including those at Coutances and Avranches.[3] While Flodoard had his three grants made by King Charles and King Ralph to Rollo and Longsword, Richer had his single grant made by King Odo to Rollo's supposed father Ketil (Latinized as Catillus). He then had Ketil murdered immediately after his baptism because he 'would be the cause of future calamity' – a comment, or so it may be supposed, on the Normans of his own day.[4] Why Richer felt the need to rewrite Flodoard's account so dramatically is not clear, but the extent of the grant purportedly made to Ketil did accurately reflect the reach of the dukes' authority at the time Richer was writing, and in that sense he was reflecting, justifying, and excusing the situation of his own day.

Dudo of Saint-Quentin was likewise inclined to reflect the situation that pertained when he completed his work, *c*. 1015, rather than to provide an accurate account of the rise and fall and rise of tenth-century Normandy.[5] By the time Dudo arrived at Rouen in 987, Richard I had established a loose hold on the Bessin, Cotentin, and Avranchin. Before he completed his work, Richard II had gained hegemony over Brittany by virtue of acting as the guardian of his nephews,

---

[2] For Richer and his *Histories* see in particular J. Glenn, *Politics and History in the Tenth Century: The Work and World of Richer of Reims* (Cambridge, 2004), pp. 110–27, 171–214, 235–49; J. Lake, *Richer of Saint-Rémi: The Methods and Mentality of a Tenth-Century Historian* (Washington, DC, 2013).

[3] Richer, i. 16.

[4] Richer, i. 36. David Crouch thought Richer's story to be the most accurate regarding Rollo's parentage (Crouch, *The Normans*, pp. 1, 4, 299–300).

[5] For Dudo and his work, see above, Introduction, pp. 2–9.

Count Alan and his brother Odo, and had given refuge to King Æthelred II of the English. Dudo set about underpinning these recent developments, for example by remarking upon the assistance Rollo had given to King Æthelstan of the English when faced with civil war, and by asserting that the Cotentin and Avranchin had been granted to Rollo, with the rest of Normandy, in 911. Dudo must have been aware of the scale of Richard I's efforts to build his duchy, but he chose to conceal almost all of it, because only then could he write a grand justification of Norman rule both in Normandy and over Brittany.

Given these problems with the historical veracity of the narratives, the ducal *acta* must be used to gain a better understanding of how and when the dukes' authority expanded across what would come to be Normandy. That is not to say that the narrative elements of these diplomas are any more reliable than the annals and histories, but provided we can filter out the forgeries and interpolations the dispositions recorded do at least offer some indication of the extent of the dukes' demesne and rights across the duchy, so that plotting the location of the places concerned perhaps allows us to gain some idea about when and where their authority was recognized. To reach any conclusions, however, we must allow for rebuttable presumptions: first, that the appearance of a place in a ducal act means that the duke's authority *was* recognized there, at least by the beneficiary, and, secondly, that, to begin with at least, the dukes held the whole of every place found in their demesne. Equally, where individuals are said to hold, or to have held, land in particular vills from the duke, it cannot be assumed that these lands had once been demesne unless there is other evidence to support that view, for example, the duke can also be seen holding land there. They are consequently excluded from the survey.[6] The results are illustrated on Maps 2–5.

In common with the experiences of the kings of the French or the counts of Anjou and Brittany, it was generally the greater lords of the nascent duchy who were the most reticent about making their submission. Some were even strong enough to attempt to resist the dukes' demands that they should do so. And so, where powerful lords had to be subjugated and placated, the settlements made with them generally had to be especially attractive and honourable. The duke might therefore consider conferring land or office on such figures. A duke's ability to identify accurately the key players in the duchy and to reward them accordingly was vital here as there was only a limited amount of land that could be used in

---

[6] My thinking here is based in part on the coercive behaviour of the greater Norman lords that saw men within their dominion acknowledge, over time, that they held even their alods from them (see below, Chapter 11, pp. 662–3). Others have taken a different approach. Gérard Louise, for example, included as ducal demesne in the Hiémois lands that are not expressly said to have belonged to the duke (Louise, *Bellême*, i. 139–40).

this way. Local rivalries had also to be treated carefully and traditions of family power and independence had to be managed. The dukes could not afford to allow their greatest lords to develop a sense of injustice or to feel undervalued. This is one reason why the following discussion focuses on individuals, be they kinsmen or *fideles* or rivals or enemies, and attempts to establish when, why, and how they were brought into a duke's *mouvance* and how, or if, they were maintained there. For the same reason, this survey also pays much attention to the acquisition and alienation of the dukes' demesne (as plotted on the maps) and to their military successes or defeats.

In some cases, the duke might even offer erstwhile rivals or allies a chance to join the ruling dynasty through marriage. Marriages were, after all, intended to extend hegemony and so to usher in periods of peace by uniting warring peoples. Something of the process is perhaps revealed by Oddr Snorrason's *Saga of Olaf Tryggvason* – written in the late twelfth century but recalling or imagining the events of the tenth – which tells how King Olaf sailed to GulaÞingslǫg in Hǫrðaland. Hearing of his arrival, the most distinguished men of the region gathered together to discuss what to do. Their leader, Ǫlmóðr, spoke:

> You know that a powerful king is on his way to this region and this assembly. He will want to make us his subjects. The king pleases us in some ways but in other ways his practices displease us. We are pleased by his strength and eminence, and with respect to these qualities it would be a good thing to serve such a king. But his foreign customs displease us greatly. Therefore … let us not accept the practice that he urges on us unless he accommodates us in one major respect. I understand that he had a sister by the same mother, named Ástríðr … Now if the king is willing to marry Ástríðr to our kinsman Erlingr, who is standing here with us and who is commended by many good qualities and eminent lineage, then it would seem advisable to me to give his words a good reception, and his religion as well, which I believe to be a good one.[7]

This was done, and Olaf took control of the region.

Even if inaccurate, it is unlikely that this portrayal was anachronistic, and it may be supposed that similar discussions took place as Richard I sailed along the coast of Normandy or Richard II marched his armies to the Orne or as Henry I sought to secure support for his regime in the early twelfth century, for kinship

---

[7] Oddr Snorrason, *The Saga of Olaf Tryggvason*, trans. T. M. Andersson (Ithaca, NY and London, 2003), p. 79 and see also *Heimskringla*, pp. 197–8 for the same marriage as well as pp. 200–1, 224, 228–9 for some other examples, successful and otherwise, from Olaf Tryggvason's reign.

with the duke and his dynasty provided an honourable exchange for surrender. Marriage turned subjugation into a merger rather than a hostile takeover, although a later demerger was always a possibility. Patronage and office-holding, to continue the corporate metaphor, seem equivalent to corporate buyouts (or sell-outs, depending on your point of view) and golden hellos. But none of these mechanisms – kinship, office-holding, fidelity, patronage – was guaranteed to create permanent and immutable relationships. Kinsmen might remember their relationship with the dukes down through the generations, but that does not necessarily mean that the relationship between them was affective or effective. Such manoeuvres were a beginning, but they had to be maintained with a steady and continuing stream of patronage, respect, and success.

Rollo and Rouen, 911–28

Although Dudo of Saint-Quentin claimed that he was Danish, it is more likely that Rollo was the son of Earl Ragnvald of Møre in Norway and Hild the daughter of Rolf Nevja.[8] It is also likely that he had taken possession of Rouen and much of the region around it some years before Charles the Simple recognized and legitimized his lordship at Saint-Clair-sur-Epte c. 911.[9] Already by the time of the siege of Paris, 885–86, the lower Seine might well have been under the permanent control of the Northmen, and they might already have begun to establish themselves in villages that had been abandoned, even if only temporarily, by their previous inhabitants, as well as to clear some of the forest and create new settlements for themselves.[10] At the same time, it is unlikely that Rollo and his Vikings walked across an empty land. There are plenty of Frankish place names to be found in that country, and the tradition remembered at Saint-Wandrille in the middle of the eleventh century was that, 'few of the people he (Rollo) came up against fled, instead they were put under the auspicious yoke of his authority'.[11] Indeed, the very fact that the Vikings could remain on the Seine for so long is itself an indication that everyday life continued. As Eleanor Searle pointed out, somebody had to

[8] *Heimskringla*, pp. 78–9; Van Houts, *Normans*, p. 15; D. C. Douglas, 'Rollo of Normandy', *EHR*, 57 (1942), 417–23.
[9] For example, R. McKitterick, *The Frankish Kingdoms under the Carolingians 751–987* (London, 1983), p. 307, and see also the works by Jacques Le Maho and Pierre Bauduin cited below.
[10] See A. K. H. Wagner, 'Les noms de lieux issus de l'implantation Scandinave en Normandie: le case des noms en "-tuit"', in *Les fondations Scandinaves en occident et les débuts du duché de Normandie*, ed. P. Bauduin (Caen, 2005), 241–52 with a map at p. 244.
[11] *Inventio*, p. 26.

be producing the crops and keeping the livestock that fed the Vikings while they were there.[12]

There was continuity, too, in the operation of the archbishopric of Rouen and Pierre Bauduin has suggested that the Vikings of the Seine had established a modus vivendi with the archbishop and the city's population by the 890s.[13] This coexistence of Viking and archbishop, and the apparent stability at Rouen, stands against the assertion Flodoard made, probably from ignorance, that when Rollo was granted the city, Rouen and its district had been 'nearly destroyed (*pene deleverant*)', although in the context in which he was writing he might have meant only that the religious life of the area was in ruins, rather than that the buildings and infrastructure were falling apart.[14] The city was certainly still inhabited and it is likely that the majority of its population remained Frankish after 911. That would explain why the language of the Franks was commonly spoken there in Longsword's day.[15] It would also explain the survival of Frankish customs and administrative structures in Rouen, and Normandy more generally, after 911. As

---

[12] Searle, *PK*, p. 41.

[13] Bauduin, *Première Normandie*, pp. 110–12. In contrast, Jacques Le Maho thought that he saw evidence of a Frankish resurgence and reoccupation of Rouen at about this same time, when at least some Vikings left the Seine and raided the Cotentin and attacked Saint-Lô (see J. Le Maho, 'Les premières installations normandes dans la basse vallée de la Seine (fin du IX siècle)', in *La progression des Vikings; des raids à la colonisation*, ed. A.-M. Flambard-Héricher (Rouen, 2003), 162–7; J. Le Maho, 'Les normands de la Seine à la fin du IXᵉ siècle', in *Les fondations Scandinaves en occident et les débuts du duché de Normandie*, ed. P. Bauduin (Caen, 2005), p. 173; J. Le Maho, 'Fortifications et déplacements de populations en France au temps des invasions normandes (IXᵉ–Xᵉ siècle)', *Château Gaillard*, 22 (2006), 223–7) and see also *Recueil des actes de Charles III (le Simple)*, ed. P. Lauer, 2 vols (Paris, 1940–49), no. 51 which suggests a Frankish recovery of the area around Pîtres).

[14] Flodoard, *Flodoardi historia Remensis ecclesiæ*, ed. J. Heller and G. Waitz, *Monumenta Germaniae Historica, Scriptores* 13 (Hanover, 1881), p. 577. In his *Historia Novorum*, Eadmer put words into the mouth of Archbishop Anselm to the effect that the destruction of an abbey was caused not by the loss of material possessions but rather by a rupture in the observance of the Benedictine Rule brought about by a lack of an abbot (Eadmer, *HN*, p. 49). If Felice Lifshitz was right, however, then Flodoard was even more mistaken, as she has argued that the monastery at Jumièges had remained functioning throughout the ninth century (F. Lifshitz, *The Norman Conquest of Pious Neustria: Historiographic Discourse and Saintly Relics 684–1080* (Toronto, 1995), pp. 122–33).

[15] Historians have used Dudo's remark to infer that the Normans of Rouen had taken to speaking the Frankish language by this time. That is not what Dudo wrote, however. Dudo merely remarked that French was commonly spoken at Rouen and Dacian at Bayeux. That would fit with what we know of the history of the cities in this period. Rouen was subject to a peaceful takeover by Rollo and his men, probably from *c.* 876 while Bayeux received wave after wave of pagan immigrants. Dudo's comment thus tells us nothing about the assimilation of Normans into Frankish society.

discussed in more detail elsewhere, these survivals included royal rights over coinage and fortification,[16] as well as the boundaries of some demesne vills and some of the *pagi* or counties (the words are synonyms).[17]

When Rollo was granted Rouen and the maritime *pagi* that stood around it by King Charles, he was obliged in return to accept baptism and to swear fidelity to the king.[18] Dudo noted that as part of the settlement he was also to marry King Charles's daughter, Gisla. This was the first of several marriages made by Rollo's dynasty with members of the Frankish aristocracy that were designed to increase the dukes' prestige, legitimacy, and connections. Or at least it would have been had it actually taken place. Historians have not been at all convinced that Gisla existed outside Dudo's imagination, and although David Crouch and Pierre Bauduin have both noted that Witgar of Compiègne's geneaology of Count Arnulf of Flanders (compiled in the late 950s) does at least demonstrate that King Charles had a daughter of that name, Bauduin is likely correct to exclude her from consideration on the grounds of her age. She would have been only three or four in 911, and that is not at all how Dudo presented her.[19] Instead, the marriage of Rollo and Gisla seems to have been a deliberate echo of the marriage of the Dane Godfrid to Gisela, the illegitimate daughter of Lothair II, in 882.[20] In any event, William Longsword, Rollo's only known son, was the result of a different union, either with a lady called Popa, whose identity is debated and remains uncertain, or with an Irish lady whom Rollo met while in Orkney or Scotland and who was also the mother of a daughter called Kathleen.[21]

---

[16] See below, Chapter 8, pp. 442–3, 445–6 and Chapter 11, pp. 639–41.

[17] L. Musset, 'Les domaines de l'époque franque et les destinées du regime domanial du IXe au XIe siècle', *BSAN*, 49 (1942–45), 54.

[18] For more on these issues see below, Chapter 4, pp. 187–90 and Chapter 5, pp. 254–5.

[19] Those who see the marriage to Gisla as lying somewhere between uncertain and fictional include Bates, *Normandy*, p. 8; Searle, *PK*, pp. 43, 93; L. Shopkow, *History and Community*, pp. 127, 150; C. Potts, 'Normandy 911–1144', in *The Companion to the Anglo-Norman World*, ed. C. Harper-Bill and E. van Houts (Woodbridge, 2002), p. 21; J. Nelson, 'Normandy's early history since *Normandy before 1066*', in *Normandy and its Neighbours, 900–1250: Essays for David Bates*, ed. D. Crouch and K. Thompson (Turnhout, 2011), pp. 10–11. For Witgar of Compiègne see Crouch, *The Normans*, p. 321, n. 14; P. Bauduin, 'Chefs Normands et élites Franques, fin IXe–début Xe siècle', in *Les fondations Scandinaves en occident et les débuts du duché de Normandie*, ed. P. Bauduin (Caen, 2005), p. 183.

[20] S. Coupland, 'From poachers to gamekeepers: Scandinavian warlords and Carolingian kings', *EME*, 7 (1998), 109.

[21] On Popa see Bauduin, *Première Normandie*, pp. 129–32 and the summary in Nelson, 'Normandy's early history', pp. 11–12; on the anonymous Irish lady see E. van Houts, 'The *planctus* on the death of William Longsword (943) as a source for tenth-century culture in Normandy and Aquitaine', *ANS*, 36 (2014), 9.

By the beginning of the eleventh century, Rouen was clearly prosperous and was one of the keys to the dukes' power and influence. According to Orderic, it was 'a populous and wealthy city, thronged with merchants and a meeting place of trade routes. A fair city set among murmuring streams and smiling meadows, abounding in fruit and fish and all manner of produce, it stands surrounded by hills and woods, strongly encircled by walls and ramparts and battlements, and fair to behold with its mansions and houses and churches.'[22] Eleanor Searle described it as a goose that laid golden eggs.[23]

Rouen attracted merchants from far afield. *Deniers* minted at Rouen have been recovered from hoards buried in Scandinavia, Italy, and Poland, which attests to wide trading links, although Dudo focused principally on trade with England, Flanders, Francia, and Ireland when praising the city.[24] It is possible that some of the coins found in Scandinavia were the result of the agreement made between Richard II and King Swein of Denmark *c.* 1003 that allowed Viking ships to put in at Rouen and trade English booty there.[25] By the reign of Edward the Confessor, those links with England had become more regularized and the merchants of Rouen had their own wharf in London. The act that tells us of Edward's grant also reveals that, as late as 1150 × 1151, no boat should sail from Normandy for Ireland unless from Rouen and that no boat from Ireland should dock anywhere in Normandy except Rouen. The only exception was a single boat every year which could visit Cherbourg first.[26] As to commodities, the city was most famous, at least in Æthelred II's England, for its blubber fish and wine, and the appearance of wine cellars in the city by the end of the century would seem to confirm the importance of that trade.[27] There was also a slave market until perhaps as late as the 1020s, and there might also have been a

---

[22]   Orderic, iii. 36. The description of the city and its region that Orderic put into the mouth of the future Henry I to Conan, just before his precipitation in 1090, is similar (Orderic, iv. 224).

[23]   Searle, *PK*, p. 70.

[24]   See the catalogue of finds in F. Dumas, 'Les monnaies Normandes (Xᵉ–XIIᵉ siècles) avec un répertoire des trouvailles', *Révue Numismatique*, 21 (1979), 106–37 and also L. Musset, 'Les relations extérieures de la Normandie du IXᵉ au XIᵉ siècle', *Annales de Normandie*, 4 (1954), 31–8; reprinted in L. Musset, *Nordica et Normannica: Recueil d'études sur la Scandinavie ancienne et médiévale, les expéditions des Vikings et la fondation de la Normandie* (Paris, 1997), pp. 297–306; *Dudo*, pp. 100, 112.

[25]   Jumièges, ii.16–18.

[26]   *Regesta*, iii. no. 729.

[27]   Noted in D. Bates, 'Rouen from 900 to 1204: from Scandinavian settlement to Angevin "capital"', in *Medieval Art, Architecture, and Archaeology at Rouen*, ed. J. Stratford, The British Archaeological Association Conference Transactions for the Year 1986 (1993), p. 6.

trade in cloth, as Moriuht's wife, Glicerium, was found working at a loom in Le Vaudreuil upstream.[28]

The dukes were naturally keen to promote trade, not least because a flourishing trade would increase the revenues from tolls that flowed into their own coffers. Richard I or his son built the first bridge across the Seine, which would almost certainly have increased the amount of traffic coming into the city.[29] In addition, the dukes would have enjoyed revenues produced by the sale of licences for navigation and mooring charges, and they levied fees on the wine and merchandise stored in the warehouses on the Seine.[30] Then there were the rents that the dukes would receive from their tenants in the city, which must have increased considerably after it was extended to the west, *c.* 1000, arguably as part of a planned development – something that suggests the dukes' involvement – and arguably as a redevelopment of the commercial suburbs that Jacques Le Maho believed had existed in the ninth century.[31] In addition to such rights, the dukes held a great deal of property within the city. Duke Richard II, for example, granted to a variety of beneficiaries a total of two manses in the city, one of them the 'Tower of Alfred (*turris Alvredi*)' and one of them later recovered by exchange;[32] the churches of Saint-Gervase (next to the city), Saint-Laurent (in the suburbs), Saint-Amand (within the city), Saint-André (also in the suburbs),[33] and the chapels of Saint-Clement and Saint-Candé;[34] two mills outright; and the tithe of another eight

[28] Warner of Rouen, *Moriuht,* ed. and trans. C. J. McDonough (Ontario, 1995), pp. 5–6 (on dating), 76–6, 90–1 (for the implication of the slave market), 90–1 (for the loom). David Crouch, at least, saw this as a mill (Crouch, *The Normans*, p. 32). It might also be noted that fulling mills are known to have existed in Normandy by 1087, when one was given to the monks of Saint-Wandrille (F. Lot, *Études critiques sur l'abbaye de Saint-Wandrille* (Paris, 1913), pp. 96–7, noted in M. Arnoux, 'Border, trade route, or market? The Channel and the medieval European economy from the twelfth to the fifteenth century', *ANS*, 36 (2014), 40). The slave market is also discussed by L. Musset, 'La Seine normande et le commerce maritime du IIIe au XIe siècle', as reprinted in *Nordica et Normannica*, pp. 344–5.

[29] Suggested by an analogy with Saint-Lô, where the construction of a stone bridge by Bishop Geoffrey of Coutances resulted in a huge increase in the toll generated by the town from 15 *livres* to 220 *lives* ('De statu huius ecclesiae', *GC*, xi. Instr. Col. 219).

[30] See below, Chapter 10, pp. 581–5.

[31] B. Gauthiez, 'The urban development of Rouen, 989–1345', in *Society and Culture in Medieval Rouen, 911–1300*, ed. L. V. Hicks and E. Brenner (Turnhout, 2013), pp. 19–21; J. Le Maho, 'Rouen à l'époque des incursions vikings (841–911)', *Bulletin de la commission des antiquités de la Seine-Maritime*, 42 (1995), 143–202; Le Maho, 'Les normands de la Seine', p. 166.

[32] *RADN*, nos. 9 and 36. The manse with a chapel granted to the monks of Fécamp in 1006 might subsequently have been exchanged for Plein-Sève.

[33] *RADN*, nos. 34, 36, 52, 53.

[34] *RADN*, no. 6, 34 for Saint-Clement. For Saint-Candé see Gauthiez, 'The urban development of Rouen', pp. 21–2 (although the reference he provided appears to be erroneous).

mills on the Robec.[35] The farm due for the city in 1180 suggests that there was a lot left in the duke's hands despite this generosity.[36]

Upstream of Rouen, the duke's vill of Le Vaudreuil was developing as a port and urban centre, too. Moriuht was told: 'This port is not far distant from the city of your lady. Rather frequently it is full to bursting with the merchandise of wealth (supplied) by Vikings.'[37] That development is perhaps reflected by its division into five smaller vills during the early eleventh century, itself revealed by two diplomas for Fécamp. An act of May 1006 records that the monks of Fécamp were granted five churches at Le Vaudreuil, namely the churches of St Mary, St Stephen, St Cecilia, St Saturnin, and St Quentin, with the chapels that were subject to them and whatever arable land and meadow belonged to them.[38] Richard II's confirmation of this gift of August 1025, however, states that the monks' only possession in Le Vaudreuil was the church of St Mary 'and whatever belongs to it'. By then, the church of St Stephen was at Vauvray and the church of St Saturnin was in the appropriately named *Novilla*, while it is likely from the drafting of the act, and from the relevant dedications, that the churches at Poses (dedicated to St Quentin) and Portjoie (dedicated to St Cecilia) had also been included in the original grant but had now broken away to become the parish churches of these separate vills.[39] Similar divisions seem to have happened at Vascœuil and Longueville.

Rouen and the Seine were at the heart of Charles the Simple's grant to Rollo, and the wealth the city and the other ports on the Seine created was essential to the dukes' authority. But Rollo was also confirmed in possession of the city's hinterland. While no contemporary source spelt out precisely what was encompassed in King Charles's grant, Flodoard's reports of Norman raids into Francia and vice versa suggest that the Bresle comprised the north-eastern border at least by the 920s, while both Flodoard and Dudo tells us of a border on the Epte.[40] That frontier is also suggested by the tradition of early grants of land and property along the Epte, around Gasny, to the monks of Saint-Ouen and canons of the cathedral.[41] Across the Seine, Rollo gained at least part of the *pagus* of Madrie, probably the strip of land that lies between the Seine and the Eure. From the junction of the two rivers, it is likely that the Seine formed the boundary of the initial grant, although this can only be conjecture.[42]

---

[35] *RADN*, nos. 41, 53, 66.
[36] The farm was 3,000 *livres angevin* = £750 sterling (*Norman Pipe Rolls*, p. 50).
[37] Warner of Rouen, *Moriuht*, pp. 90–1.
[38] *RADN*, no. 9.
[39] *RADN*, no. 34. The church of Portjoie is now in the recently created town of Val-du-Reuil.
[40] *Flodoard*, pp. 9, 13–14; *Dudo*, pp. 49, 67.
[41] This had been alienated before 942 by Rollo and Longsword (*RADN*, nos. 53).
[42] See Searle, *PK*, pp. 71, 74–5; L. Musset, 'Considérations sur la genèse et la trace des

Table 1 Ducal grants to the ducal monasteries of Upper Normandy, 911–1026

Duke	Saint-Ouen	Jumièges	Fécamp	Saint-Wandrille
Rollo	14 + 2			
William Longsword	8 + 1	10 + 1		
Richard I	1 + 0	0 + 8	12 + 8	5 + 5
Richard II	1 + 3	2 + 12	10 + 35	1 + 19

While Rollo is said to have divided this land between his followers by rope,[43] he kept a lot of vills for himself, too. Some, like Pîtres, had once been part of the royal fisc. Some, like the large vill of Vascœuil on the right bank of the Andelle, had once belonged to the monasteries of the region, in this case that of Saint-Ouen. Some, such as Bliquetuit, might not have existed at all before the Vikings settled on the Seine.[44] Taken together, the dukes' demesne vills were concentrated on either bank of the meandering river Seine, from Harfleur at its mouth to Vernon in the Norman Vexin. There was another concentration of demesne along the coast of the Pays de Caux, which petered out east of Le Bourg-Dun. There was a scattering of estates in the interior of that county, too. But, so far as we can see, there was rather less demesne in the Vexin and in that part the Roumois away from the Seine.[45]

Something of the scale of the dukes' holdings in the Caux, Roumois, and Vexin is suggested by the grants made by the dukes from Rollo to Richard II to the abbeys that were founded or restored during the tenth century, which are shown for convenience in Table 1.

This amounts in sum to the complete alienation of sixty-four demesne vills (the first figure) over the course of a century, with grants of property and rights in another ninety-one (these partial alienations follow the '+' sign).[46] With many gifts comprising just a church, tithes, or even just a few *hôtes*, most of the real estate and rights in these demesne vills may be supposed to have been retained in the dukes' hands. The demesne, then, was not alienated prodigiously, but nonetheless

frontiers de la Normandie', as reprinted in *Nordica et Normannica*, pp. 404–5; Bauduin, *Première Normandie*, pp. 135–41.

[43] *Dudo*, p. 51.

[44] L. Musset, 'Ce qu'enseigne l'histoire d'un patrimoine monastique: Saint-Ouen de Rouen du IXe au XIe siècle', in *Aspects de la société et de l'économie dans la Normandie medieval (X^e–XIIIe siècles)*, ed. L. Musset, J.-M. Bouvris, and V. Gazeau (Caen, 1988), 115–29; Wagner, 'Les noms de lieux issus de l'implantation Scandinave en Normandie'.

[45] For the picture c. 1000 see Map 2, although note that it does not plot vills that had been alienated before 942.

[46] Figures from *RADN*, nos. 4, 9, 31, 34 (Fécamp); 36 (Jumièges); 52 (Saint-Wandrille); 53 (Saint-Ouen).

the scale of their patronage reveals the important role played by the ducal abbeys in promoting and maintaining the dukes' authority in Upper Normandy, as well as their desire to be seen as munificent patrons and good Christians.

Despite the density of the dukes' holdings in the Caux, only a very few places stand out as important ducal centres. Fécamp, on the coast, quickly became a favoured residence. Dudo noted that Sprota, William Longsword's wife *more Danico*, gave birth to the future Duke Richard I there, and that Richard I built a church in his castle which became one of the greatest abbeys of Normandy.[47] Further to the north-east, inland from Dieppe and on the very edge of the Pays de Caux, Arques-la-Bataille provided another centre. A fortress had been established there by 944, although it must have been dwarfed by William of Arques's castle when it was built *c.* 1050. By 1024 × 1026, Arques was the seat of a *vicomté*, and produced revenue from its tolls. In April 1033, Robert the Magnificent could describe it as 'a certain seat of ours' while augmenting the holdings of the monks of Saint-Wandrille there.[48] There was also the hunting lodge at Lyons-la-Forêt, where Longsword arranged the marriage of his sister, Gerloc, to Count William of Poitou and where Henry I would die.[49] Lillebonne had a few years of glory *c.* 1080, but the imperial Roman connotations that brought the place into the limelight during the second half of William the Bastard's reign might equally have caused it to fall back into the shadows during the altogether less august reign of Robert Curthose. Henry I or Stephen apparently gave it to Rabel of Tancarville.[50] Other ducal castles were constructed at Bures-en-Bray, and Neufchâtel, but neither of them seems to have been of great importance to the dukes other than as a strongpoint.

Although the grant of Rouen and its neighbouring *pagi* was intended to protect Francia from further Viking raids up the Seine, and seems to have succeeded in doing so, it did not result in an end to Norman attacks on northern France. Dudo of Saint-Quentin is all but silent about Rollo's later career, and Flodoard has very little, too, and it may well be that Rollo maintained the peace while King Charles remained on his throne. But in 923, the beleaguered king appealed to Rollo and his Normans for military assistance. Charles's enemies prevented their forces from uniting, but 923 nonetheless saw Norman raids on the *pagi* across the Oise, where they 'devastated the land, leading off flocks and herds, removing much of the portable wealth, and taking numerous prisoners'. In retaliation, King Ralph and Count Herbert of the Vermandois ravaged the *pagus* of Rouen later the same

[47] *Dudo*, pp. 68, 164–5; Jumièges, i. 78.
[48] *RADN*, nos. 9, 52, 69
[49] *Dudo*, p. 69; Jumièges, i. 80.
[50] Orderic, vi. 482.

year.[51] Eventually a peace was agreed, 'on the condition that the more spacious land beyond the Seine, which they (the Normans) had requested, would be given to them'. Early in 924, King Ralph ordered that the Normans should be paid a tribute in return for keeping the peace, and later the same year 'the Northmen' – it has been supposed that Flodoard meant the Normans of the Seine here, rather than those of the Loire, and the grant made to Longsword in 933 would not have made sense if this was not the case – were given Maine and the Bessin, presumably in fulfilment of the terms agreed the previous year.[52]

Despite this settlement, fighting between Franks and Normans flared up again in 925. A Norman camp on the Seine was besieged, although the Normans were able to break out and escape into a forest which concealed their movements.[53] Rollo's forces then attacked the *pagi* of Beauvais and Amiens. But Rollo also had to deal with a revolt of the men of the Bessin, which suggests that he had attempted to make a reality of the grant of the previous year, while Hugh the Great raided the *pagus* of Rouen and Count Herbert of the Vermandois led a successful attack on the Norman fort at Eu.[54] While it looks from these events as if Rollo and his Northmen were on the back foot, the next year they almost achieved a spectacular reversal when they came close to capturing King Ralph. They then plundered the forest region as far as the *pagus* of Porcien until they were paid a tribute to stop.[55]

Flodoard seems only ever to tell half the story, which further complicates the complex politics of these years, but it is possible that these conflicts were due to Rollo's continuing loyalty to King Charles, which would have pitted him against King Ralph, Hugh the Great, and Charles's gaoler Count Herbert.[56] It is notable that the grant of 924 was made in King Ralph's absence, albeit with his consent, and that Rollo is never said to have committed himself to him. Further, while

---

[51] *Flodoard*, p. 9. Quotation from Richer, i. 120.

[52] *Flodoard*, pp. 9–10; Richer noted only the collection and payment of the tribute, and had the Normans withdraw once they had received the money (Richer, i. 120). Musset thought that the grant of Maine did not include the later county of Maine, but rather some of the constituent parts of the larger duchy of Maine once held by Béranger, including the Hiémois. John Le Patourel suggested that Flodoard should be taken at face value, but that the Normans had been simply unable to gain control over Maine. Richard Barton was unsure that the grant could have been effective at all (see L. Musset, 'Naissance de la Normandie' in *L'Histoire de la Normandie*, ed. M. de Boüard (Toulouse, 1970), p. 98; J. Le Patourel, *The Norman Empire* (Oxford, 1976), p. 6; R. E. Barton, *Lordship in the County of Maine, c. 890–1160* (Woodbridge, 2004), pp. 29–30).

[53] *Flodoard*, p. 13.

[54] *Flodoard*, pp. 13–14. Richer of Reims implied that Rollo was one of the casualties of the attack on Eu (Richer, i. 124–6, 130).

[55] *Flodoard*, p. 15.

[56] A suggestion also made by Searle, *PK*, pp. 52–3.

Longsword did commit himself to Charles and reaffirm his friendship with Count Herbert at Eu in 927, Rollo seems not to have needed to do so.[57] And then in 928, Rollo refused to surrender Count Herbert's son, whom he was holding as a hostage, until Herbert had committed himself to King Charles whom he was using as his puppet.[58] Loyalty is not often associated with Vikings, and yet Rollo might well have remained faithful to his first patron long after others had deserted him.

William Longsword, c. 928–42

It is possible that Longsword's early association with Herbert of the Vermandois put him at odds with his father, and equally possible that Rollo's continuing loyalty to the lame-duck King Charles was seen as indicating that he was now out of touch with Frankish politics. It might also have been the case that Rollo faced discontent and revolt at the end of his reign due to his growing infirmity or even to the reverse he had suffered at Eu in 925.[59] Dudo's account of a ruler agreeing to abdicate in favour of his son might therefore be a very rosy picture of a rather more unfriendly exchange. Equally, while Dudo could suggest a smooth transfer of power from Rollo to Longsword when he was writing, it is possible that he was obliged to edit out a period of struggle to do so – as both the author of the *Planctus* and David Crouch suggest.[60] A period of insecurity is also suggested by the fact that it was only in 933 that Longsword made an otherwise surprisingly belated oath of fidelity to King Ralph. In return, he was given 'the land of the Bretons that was located along the sea coast'.[61] By then, Flodoard could describe him as *princeps* of the Normans, revealing that he had achieved ascendancy.

It is possible that the grant of 933 led to conflict with the Bretons. Dudo envisaged a campaign that resulted from the refusal of the Breton leaders to continue to recognize Longsword's overlordship.[62] It is difficult to establish the veracity of

---

[57] *Flodoard*, p. 17.

[58] *Flodoard*, p. 17.

[59] That Rollo suffered political fallout from his defeat at Eu was suggested by Crouch, *The Normans*, p. 9.

[60] Van Houts, *Planctus*, 3, 18; Crouch, *The Normans*, p. 9.

[61] *Flodoard*, p. 23. Although the belated oath of fidelity might simply have reflected the king's uncertain position, which resulted in Aquitainian lords delaying their acknowledgement of his rule for some years (McKitterick, *The Frankish Kingdoms*, p. 313). The grant of 933 is generally taken to have comprised the Cotentin and Avranchin, which is how it is interpreted here, but John Le Patourel wondered whether it actually comprised at least part of Brittany, too, and was intended to set the Vikings of the Seine at odds with those of the Loire (Le Patourel, *Norman Empire*, pp. 6–7).

[62] *Dudo*, pp. 62–3. Crouch similarly dated this campaign 933–34 (Crouch, *The Normans*, p. 14).

Dudo's account, however, because there is very little additional evidence either to support or to undermine his claims. The *Chronicle of Nantes*, a later compilation that is also of dubious accuracy, reports a raid on the coast of Brittany by Normans from Rouen in 919, and also notes that Alan Wrybeard drove Normans from Dol and Saint-Brieuc in 937 – which might be one of the attacks reported by Flodoard in his annal for the same year.[63] *If* the *Chronicle* provides an accurate record of events here, it may be that Dudo's story had its origins in a short-lived Norman occupation of Dol and the surrounding area. That would, of course, still fall far short of the sort of hegemony that Dudo envisaged, but it is at least plausible, and perhaps further supported by the tradition that Longsword granted a number of vills around the bay of Mont-Saint-Michel to the clergy living there, although it is not clear that this tradition was independent of Dudo's *De moribus*,[64] as well as the much-vaunted 'coin' that apparently describes William as 'dux Britonum' which was found somewhere on the Mont-Saint-Michel. While some historians have taken this object as evidence of short-lived Norman dominion, Eleanor Searle and Cassandra Potts in particular have been less impressed by it.[65] It is at best ambiguous, and at worst dubious, evidence, but while it was clearly not a product of the Norman mints, it *might* have been produced in Brittany, perhaps in Dol, by a Breton moneyer influenced by the English coins brought back to Brittany by Alan Barbe-Torte.[66]

---

[63] *La Chronique de Nantes (570–1049)*, ed. R. Merlet (Paris, 1896), p. 89; *Flodoard*, p. 30. Searle supposed that the Normans at Dol were Christians because the author of the *Chronicle of Nantes* noted that they were attacked while celebrating a wedding (Searle, *PK*, p. 32).

[64] *RADN*, no. 49. Pierre Bouet thought the act provided an accurate report: P. Bouet, 'Le Mont-Saint-Michel entre Bretagne et Normandie de 960 à 1060', in *Bretons et Normans au moyen âge: rivalités, malentendus, convergences*, ed. J. Quaghebeur and B. Merdrignac (Rennes, 2008), p. 173. Cassandra Potts was much less certain: Potts, *Monastic Revival*, pp. 97–8.

[65] Searle, *PK*, p. 53; Potts, *Monastic Revival*, p. 97, n. 90. Searle thought that this medal or coin 'is poor evidence of William's claim to a chieftainship'.

[66] The coin (see the image in M. Dolley and J. Yvon, 'A group of tenth-century coins found at Mont-Saint-Michel', *British Numismatic Journal*, 40 (1971), 1–12, with the coin discussed at pp. 7–11) and see also the drawing in N. S. Price, *The Vikings in Brittany* (London, 1989), p. 83/401) is based on an English prototype, as Dolley and Jens Moesgaard have noted (J. C. Moesgaard, 'A survey of coin production and currency in Normandy, 864–945', in *Silver Economy in the Viking Age*, ed. J. Graham-Campbell and G. Williams (Walnut Creek CA, 2007), pp. 99–121). It consequently looks very different from other Longsword coins minted in Normandy and it is also larger. The legend around the edge of the coin has been transcribed as: 'VVILEIM DU + IRB +', which, even if read correctly, spells William's name differently from his other coins, adds a title where none is found elsewhere, and reverses the direction of reading which does not occur on other Norman coins of his or any other reign. The reverse of the coin indicates

It was probably shortly after he had received the grant of the Cotentin and Avranchin from King Ralph that Longsword arranged the marriage of his sister, Gerloc, to Count William of Poitou.[67] This match perhaps constitutes evidence of the success of Longsword's attitude towards the other Frankish princes, as well as their recognition that his power had now become sufficiently extensive to make him a valuable ally. It might equally have been a pragmatic attempt on behalf of the Poitevins to use the Normans' continuing connections with the Scandinavian world to curb the continuing Viking raids into Poitou.[68] There is certainly some evidence that the Seine and Loire Vikings might still work together at this time, and the idea is supported by Adémar of Chabannes's later remark that it was only the intervention of Richard II, *c.* 1000, that freed Emma, *vicecomitessa* of Angoulême, from her lengthy captivity at the hands of Viking raiders, probably from Britain or Ireland.[69] What William gained from this alliance was less tangible but just as important: acceptance into the Frankish political community.

Longsword contracted his own marriage at about the same time. Probably within the period 933–39 he married Liégeard, the daughter of Count Herbert of the Vermandois.[70] Flodoard and Richer did not mention the union, but Dudo reported that:

> when Herbert saw that William of Rouen was growing strong and formidable … he gave his daughter to him by the counsel of duke Hugh the Great. Conveyed in a most seemly fashion, with wonderful 'Fescennine' displays, and with accoutrements of novel and inexpressible honour and dignity and

that it was struck by a moneyer called Rivallon, who may be taken to have been a Breton. It is likely that Breton moneyers were familiar with English coins struck during the reign of Æthelstan which had perhaps been brought to Brittany by the returning Alan Wrybeard in 936, but that familiarity might be a double-edged sword as the hoard of coins found at the Mont includes two imitations of pennies produced during the reign of Aethelstan. That does not inspire confidence in the authenticity of this particular *denier*.

[67] *Dudo*, p. 69; Jumièges, i. 80. The marriage had almost certainly occurred by 933 (see below, Chapter 4, pp. 191–2), a date to some extent reinforced by charter evidence noted by Elisabeth van Houts that suggests that the marriage had been made by 934 (Van Houts, '*Planctus*', 21).

[68] *Dudo*, p. 70 reports that the advance was made by the Poitevins rather than by Longsword. Dunbabin, *France*, p. 60; Van Houts, '*Planctus*', Appendix 2, 21–2.

[69] Adémar de Chabannes, *Chronique*, ed. J. Chavanon (Paris, 1897), pp. 166–7; translated in van Houts, *Normans*, p. 214. The origin of the raiders is suggested by the comment that Emma was held prisoner overseas.

[70] David Crouch dated the marriage more closely to *c.* 936–37 (Crouch, *The Normans*, p. 12). See also below, Chapter 4, pp. 191–2.

attended on the way on all sides by a crowd of matchless knights, he conducted her in splendour to the castle of the city of Rouen.[71]

The marriage seems to have solidified a relationship that Dudo had described as a
'fragile pact of amity', and brought William firmly into the *mouvance* of one of the
greatest Frankish magnates, whose lands marched along the north-eastern border
of his territory.[72] The *Annals* of Flodoard of Reims reveal that the two men had
supported each other in their intrigues from 927, but they did so increasingly from
939, often in alliance with Hugh, duke of the Franks, who would himself play an
important role during the minority of Longsword's son, Richard I.[73]

Although the precise details are lost, it is clear that William gave a sizeable
parcel of lands in the south of his county to his new wife as dower.[74] An act of 1012
records an exchange of property between the monks of Jumièges in Normandy
and those of Bourgueil in Poitou. As their part in this exchange, the monks of
Bourgueil gave a third of the vill of Longueville, by the 1020s known as Saint-
Pierre-d'Autils, on the Seine to the monks of Jumièges, recalling that

> the most noble William, count of the city of Rouen, had a wife called Liégeard
> to whom he gave as dower the vill which is called Longueville. Then that
> Liégeard had a certain daughter whose name was Emma, who was possessed
> of a third part of that land in the same vill. She gave her part of the vill to
> God in the place which is called Bourgueil … Therefore after this, in the
> time of Robert the most humble abbot of the holy convent of Jumièges and
> the venerable Abbot Bernard of the blessed monastery of Bourgueil, by their
> spontaneous wish and in free spirit they granted to St Peter in the monastery
> of Jumièges that land of that vill which is called Longueville.[75]

The Emma referred to in this act was not Longsword's daughter. She was the
child of Liégeard and her second husband, Count Theobald of Chartres.[76] In 1001,
this same Emma had given her foundation at Bourgueil the vill of Coudres in the

---

[71] *Dudo*, p. 70.
[72] *Dudo*, p. 64.
[73] *Flodoard*, pp. 17, 31, 32, 33, 36–7.
[74] It is generally agreed that Liégeard was the daughter of Count Herbert of Vermandois
mentioned by Dudo: L. Musset, 'Actes inédits du XIᵉ siècle III. Les plus anciens chartes
normandes de l'abbaye de Bourgueil', *BSAN*, 54 (1957–8), 16; Bates, *Normandy*, p. 12;
Bauduin, *Première Normandie*, p. 163; Van Houts, '*Planctus*', 2. Searle, *PK*, pp. 54–5 was
a little more hesitant in accepting this identification.
[75] *RADN*, no. 14*bis*, identified as Saint-Pierre-d'Autils in *RADN*, no. 36.
[76] Bauduin, *Première Normandie*, p. 163, n. 93.

Evrecin,[77] while in 983 × 985 a certain Avesgaud had given the church at Illiers-l'Evêque, which he had himself received from Countess Liégeard, to Notre-Dame of Chartres.[78] Both estates are likely to have comprised part of Liégeard's dower, too. Together these documents suggest that William had dowered his wife with a band of estates running from the Seine to the Avre.[79]

It was Longsword, then, who pushed Norman power south-west from Rouen into the Evrecin. Aside from those lands that later passed to Emma, there was a tradition, encapsulated in an act of 1025, that he granted Gauciel and Jouy-sur-Eure to the monks of Jumièges (which should be seen as a restitution of property held by the community under the Carolingians), while a second act, this time of 1028 × 1033, recorded that he had granted Saint-Germain-des-Angles to the chapter of Rouen.[80] Further evidence for the possession of Evreux under Longsword is provided by Flodoard, who reported that when the city was attacked by pagan Normans after Longsword's death, it was surrendered to Duke Hugh of the Franks by the 'Christian Northmen' who were holding the citadel against them.[81] It is the presence of Christian Northmen at Evreux that strongly suggests that the city had been under the authority of the duke before the end of 942.

Longsword seems often to have acted in alliance with Count Herbert and Duke Hugh the Great during the last years of his life. While he committed himself to Louis IV in 940, which might have seemed to put him at odds with those two princes, Flodoard's *Annals* imply that he had broken his oath before the end of the year when he was allied with Hugh and Herbert against Louis once again.[82] That was perhaps because Louis had subsequently confirmed Longsword only in possession of 'the land that his father Charles had conceded to the Northmen', which would seem to have excluded the two subsequent grants of 924 and 933.[83] Nonetheless, Longsword's support for Louis IV would be his undoing.

When, or soon after, William had commended himself to Louis, most likely

---

[77] L. Musset, 'Actes inédits III. Bourgueil', 48–9. Noted also in Potts, *Monastic Revival*, p. 65.

[78] Bauduin, *Première Normandie*, pp. 163, 171, 365–7 (no. 1) and Musset, 'Actes inédits III. Bourgueil'.

[79] See the discussion in P. Bauduin, 'Du bon usage de la dos dans la Normandie ducale (Xe–début XIIe siècle)', in *Dots et douaires dans le haut Moyen Age*, ed. F. Bougard, L. Feller, and R. Le Jan (Rome, 2002), p. 438 and Bauduin, *Première Normandie*, pp. 162–6.

[80] *RADN*, nos. 36, 66; L. Musset, 'Les destins de la propriété monastique durant les invasions normandes (IXe au XIe siècles). L'exemple de Jumièges', as reprinted in *Nordica et Normannica*, pp. 352, 355–6.

[81] *Flodoard*, p. 38.

[82] *Flodoard*, pp. 32, 36.

[83] *Flodoard*, p. 32.

during the king's visit to Rouen in 942,[84] he might have declared an intention 'that he would either restore the whole of the king's dominion to him in short order or else perish in the effort'. Both Richer and Dudo reported such a boast in their works, with Dudo indicating that it had irritated the Franks.[85] Such a speech suggests that Longsword saw himself as Louis's main support, and so he might have viewed the oaths of fidelity sworn to Louis by Hugh and Herbert later in 942 as a threat to his newly established position. That stance might explain the story, retailed by Richer of Reims, in which William is said to have forced his way into a meeting between Louis, Otto, Hugh the Great, and Arnulf of Flanders at Attigny and seated himself symbolically next to King Louis, offending King Otto in the process.[86] After the meeting, Otto complained to Hugh and Arnulf of William's behaviour, and stirred them up against him. Their deliberations again suggest that, so far as Richer was concerned, it was Longsword's assumption of the role of Louis's strong man that led to his death. The two princes 'debated what they should do about William. If they put him to the sword, then they would have more freedom to act as they wished. Moreover, with the duke gone, they would have an easier time bending the king to their will, since as long as Louis had William to rely on, he could never be coerced into doing anything.'[87]

According to Richer, Hugh and Arnulf came up with a plan to kill William at a meeting to which he would be summoned by Arnulf, but in a way that would allow Arnulf to escape (direct) blame. The narratives of both Richer and Dudo share common details of this final meeting, and the two authors might have derived their information from the *Planctus* or *Lament* written shortly after Longsword's murder. William met with Arnulf on an island in the Somme at Picquigny. 'When the sun went down and the innocent man returned in a rowing boat, three envoys shouted, "Wait! Wait! Thus far our lord's secret, which concerns you and him, has been kept hidden from you. Come here and it will be revealed". Thus they summoned him back. When William left the boat they, dressed in cloaks, embraced him. One of them, they say, struck the faithful man with a sword.'[88]

Although Dudo's account of this meeting at Picquigny is all but identical

---

[84] *Flodoard*, p. 36.
[85] Quotation from Richer, i. 208; *Dudo*, p. 75.
[86] Richer, i, 228–30. Flodoard's *Annals* indicate that in reality this meeting happened in 940 (*Flodoard*, p. 33), but Longsword's behaviour is not mentioned in his more contemporary account and it is likely that Flodoard dramatized the scene to suit his own purposes. As such, there is no need to suppose that his report need have any relationship to the genuine chronology. It might also be noted that Njal's wife Bergthora similarly demanded that Hallgerd move aside for another guest, which caused offence and a long-lasting feud (*Njal's Saga*, trans. R. Cook (London, 2001), p. 57).
[87] Richer, i. 232–4.
[88] Van Houts, '*Planctus*', 3, 19; Richer, i. 236–8; *Dudo*, pp. 81–4.

to Richer's, and although he makes it clear that the meeting at Visé and the favour bestowed on William by Louis IV led to plotting against William's life, he put more blame on William's deteriorating relationship with Count Arnulf of Flanders than did Flodoard or Richer. Although William and Arnulf were members of the same faction in 939 and 941,[89] relations between the two men were not always easy. In 939, William was excommunicated because he had attacked some of Arnulf's vills.[90] In that same year, he assisted Herluin of Montreuil to recover his castle from Arnulf, who then plotted his assassination, albeit with the encouragement of 'certain princes of the Frankish nation'.[91]

Longsword was assassinated, then, because he had attempted to integrate himself into Frankish politics and Frankish political society to the extent that he had trod on the toes of his better-established peers. That integration with Frankish politics, and Longsword's apparently sincere adoption of Christianity, the Franks' religion, had an effect within Normandy, too. Divisions emerged, perhaps during Longsword's reign and certainly immediately after it, which saw pagan Northmen, presumably opposed to greater assimilation with the Franks, pitted against Christian Normans, who presumably wanted the reverse. In December 942, with predatory Franks circling and the Scandinavian settlers of Rouen and its hinterland divided against each other, the future of Longsword's territory, not yet known as Normandy, was very much in the balance.

Richard I, 942–96

As a result of both the divisions among his subjects and his own youth (he was ten at the time of his succession), the first years of Richard I's reign saw the new duke struggle to retain his and his dynasty's hold on Rouen and the rapidly shrinking territory that he might claim to rule. Flodoard wrote that after William's death the Normans divided into factions. One, most likely the Normans based in Rouen and that part of the duchy that sat to the right of the Seine, swore fidelity to King Louis, while the other, probably the Normans of the Evrecin and the lands to the left of the Seine, committed themselves to Hugh the Great.[92] It is not at all clear that this division reflected the religious divide. It was probably owing to power politics alone.

During the first months of Richard's rule, King Louis helped to defeat a Viking fleet led by King Sihtric and a certain Turmold. Richer suggested that it was their

---

[89] *Flodoard*, pp. 32, 36.
[90] *Flodoard*, p. 31
[91] *Dudo*, pp. 81–4, quotation at p. 81.
[92] *Flodoard*, p. 40; Richer, i. 240.

intention to 'take over the whole area without a grant from the king, to convert the son of Duke William to the worship of idols, and to bring back pagan rites'. Flodoard's account, in contrast, indicates that they had already achieved those aims before the king arrived. Nonetheless, Louis routed the pagan army and killed Turmold in the process.[93] Rouen was then entrusted to Herluin of Montreuil and Richard was taken to Laon for education in Carolingian-style statecraft.

Dudo portrayed Richard's removal to Laon as captivity, and King Louis's subsequent defeat on the Dives at the hands of the Northmen of the Bessin and Cotentin as his just deserts for that act of perfidy. But Dudo's tale also allowed him to present Hugh the Great, duke of the Franks, as the young duke's ally. While Dudo's treatment of events might be deceptive, it seems nonetheless to have been the case that Duke Richard did form a strong alliance with Duke Hugh, and that the two men did support each other. Thus Richer of Reims had Louis IV assert that it was Duke Hugh who had engineered the skirmish on the Dives in 945 which saw the king's bodyguard overwhelmed by a much larger force under a Scandinavian chief called Harald who ruled Bayeux at the time. The aim had been to take Louis prisoner, and although he had escaped Harald's clutches he was subsequently arrested by Normans from Rouen, 'whom he thought to be faithful to him', and handed over to Hugh.[94] In 946, shortly after his release, King Louis attacked Duke Hugh's lands as well as those of his Normans allies.[95] In 948, a group of Normans fought alongside Hugh at Soissons and Roucy.[96] In 949, Normans again fought with Hugh, this time at Laon and at Soissons.[97] Peace was made in 950, and Hugh then acted to recover lands for the church of Rouen, ruled at the time by Archbishop Hugh who was almost certainly his own protégé.[98] In 954, 'Hugh duke of the Franks was in the *pagus* of the Cotentin with a large army, and overcame Harald the Northman', which must have helped Richard strengthen his position even if it had not been the primary aim of Hugh's action.[99] And at some point, Hugh had also betrothed his daughter, Emma, to the duke, although they would not marry until after Hugh's death in 956.

The relationship continued into the next generation, with Richard supporting

[93] Richer, i. 242–4; *Flodoard*, p. 38.

[94] *Flodoard*, p. 42; Richer, i. 268–72.

[95] Flodoard, p. 45. This seems to be the basis for Dudo's story of an attack on Rouen by King Otto, instigated by Arnulf of Flanders as a result of the engagement of Richard to Emma (*Dudo*, pp. 124–36).

[96] *Flodoard*, pp. 50–1; Richer, i. 350.

[97] *Flodoard*, p. 53.

[98] *Flodoard*, p. 55.

[99] Annales Nivernenses, *Annales Nivernenses*, ed. J. Heller and G. Waitz, *Monumenta Germaniae Historica, Scriptores* 13 (Hanover, 1881) , p. 89.

Hugh's son, Hugh Capet, who would become king of the Franks in 987. Dudo suggested that Richard acted as guardian of the young Hugh for the four years between his father's death and his majority in 960, and although that seems not to be true, it does at least indicate Dudo's awareness of the close ties between the two men. In 960 Richard finally married Emma.[100] On 18 March 968, Richard and his Capetian wife played host to an embassy of monks from Saint-Denis at Rouen and agreed to restore 'a certain power named Berneval, situated in the *pagus* of Talou, which once my predecessors, namely my grandfather and my father, William by name, had given in part to St Denis'. The diploma that recorded the restitution of this 'power' has Richard recognize Hugh Capet as his lord (*senior*).[101]

This diploma also reveals that the duke's authority had now been re-established in the county of Talou – the grant would have been pointless had it not been. In the eleventh and twelfth centuries, the dukes held a string of properties along the Béthune, from Dieppe and Arques-la-Bataille to Bures-en-Bray and Neufchâtel-en-Bray, as well as the forest of Aliermont located between the Béthune and Eaulne. The relative density of the demesne here suggests that this territory had been retained even after the retreat of Norman power that had followed Longsword's death.[102] That is also suggested by Flodoard's report that there were Norman guards stationed at Arques-la-Bataille in 944, which indicates that it was the first fortress west of the Norman border at that time.[103] The Eaulne was probably still the frontier *c.* 960, when Richard was summoned to a meeting with King Lothair there, which turned into an ambush and a defence of both the duke and duchy against the king's army.[104] But eight years later, Berneval had been recovered. And by that same time, or perhaps a few years later, it must also have been the case that the dukes had recovered Eu, as the town was granted to Richard II's half-brother Godfrey *c.* 1000 along with a small county that lay between the rivers Bresle and Yéres.[105]

The meeting-turned-ambush on the Eaulne *c.* 960 was the first clear indication of hostility between King Lothair and Duke Richard.[106] According to Flodoard, after Easter 961 Duke Richard sought to obstruct a meeting at Soissons attended

---

[100] *Flodoard*, pp. 64–5.

[101] *RADN*, no. 3.

[102] *Flodoard*, p. 14. Bauduin thought that Eu and the county of Talou had fallen under the control of the counts of Flanders in the interval (Bauduin, *Première Normandie*, p. 295).

[103] *Flodoard*, p. 40. That Arques marked the border in 944 was also implied by Searle, *PK*, p. 83.

[104] *Dudo*, pp. 145–6.

[105] S. Deck, 'Le comté d'Eu sous les ducs', *Annales de Normandie*, 4 (1954), 102. For the counts, see below, Chapter 9, pp. 560, 564–9.

[106] *Dudo*, pp. 145–6.

by King Lothair, Hugh Capet's brother Odo, and unnamed others. He clashed with the king's forces as he approached and, 'after a number of his own men were killed, Richard fled'.[107] Although Flodoard said nothing about the attempted ambush of the previous year, it is nonetheless likely that Richard was here paying the king back in kind, and had launched his attack with the intention of capturing the king and his chief counsellors. He was no more successful than Lothair had been.

It is tempting to speculate that Count Theobald of Chartres was among the unnamed others at Soissons, as he was almost certainly plotting against Richard at this time. Dudo reported that the count encouraged King Lothair to attack the Evrecin on his behalf, and that he was given the city of Evreux by the king after royal troops had taken it.[108] Shortly afterwards, the count launched an attack on Saint-Sever, across the Seine from Rouen, and was defeated by the duke's forces.[109] This is likely to have been what Flodoard was referring too when he remarked the defeat of 'a certain Theobald' at the hands of the Normans. If so, this skirmish took place in 962.[110]

Dudo thought that it was the jealousy and hatred aroused in Count Theobald of Chartres by Richard's marriage to Emma that caused him to plot against the duke.[111] The timing of his war against Richard certainly suggests that the marriage contributed to it, but it is just as likely to have been Richard's recovery of Evreux and the growth of his authority in the Evrecin that was the root cause of this conflict. Theobald, like Duke Richard, was one of Hugh Capet's *fideles*, but he had usurped some of Hugh's possessions and established his authority by force in Chartres and Châteaudun *c.* 960.[112] That made his wife's Norman dower lands all the more desirable, and it is possible that Theobald determined to take the city of Evreux to consolidate his hold in this region and to clip the wings of his Norman neighbour.[113]

---

[107] *Flodoard*, p. 65.

[108] *Dudo*, p. 147; Jumièges, i. 124; Bauduin, *Première Normandie*, pp. 167, 169–70 (which includes a discussion of whether Count Theobald is likely to have acted with Lothair's help or simply took Evreux as part of his campaign to subordinate the Chartrain to his rule).

[109] *Dudo*, pp. 148–50.

[110] *Flodoard*, p. 66.

[111] *Dudo*, p. 139.

[112] Y. Sassier, *Hugues Capet* (Paris, 1987), pp. 146–7.

[113] The presence of Bishop Guntard of Evreux at Chartres in the mid 950s might suggest that Theobald had established hegemony over the city for a time, but might equally have been the result of other factors, including the pagan backlash of the 940s. See Bauduin, *Première Normandie*, pp. 165–6 and n. 102. Fraser McNair's assertion, based on this same evidence, that Theobald had gained 'control' of the Evrecin looks like an

Peace was made with Count Theobald *c.* 965, not least because Richard had employed pagan auxiliaries from Denmark to ravage his lands.[114] Richard still failed to recover the property that had comprised Liégeard's dower, however,[115] but he did attempt to strengthen his hold on the remainder of the Evrecin in the years that followed, and to undermine the counts of Chartres where possible. Thus at some point between 966 and 996 he established the abbey of Saint-Taurin just outside Evreux and endowed it with a number of demesne possessions.[116] It is possible that Ivry-la-Bataille had been taken during the war with Count Theobald and was entrusted to Duke Richard's half-brother Rodulf, the son of Richard I's mother Sprota and an obscure individual named Esperling.[117] Richard might have given Rodulf Pacy-sur-Eure and some other properties in the north of the Evrecin at the same time so as to root him more securely on this frontier.[118] The duke most likely developed closer links with the Tosny family, too, whose first representative was Archbishop Hugh's brother, Ralph. He held estates based on Conches in the Evrecin as the result of the archbishop's patronage. The result was that in 991, two years after Hugh's death, Ralph was chosen to stand as security for the agreement between Æthelred II and Richard brokered by the pope.[119] A purported act of Count Walter of Dreux, dating from 965, would suggest – although obviously only in a qualified manner – that these moves meant that by then Duke Richard's authority was acknowledged even in the very south east of the Evrecin. The act records Richard's consent to the donation of the church of Saint-Georges-Motel to the monks of Saint-Père of Chartres. It was made 'in the county of Evreux', and Walter stated that the

overstatement (F. McNair, 'The politics of being Norman in the reign of Richard the Fearless, duke of Normandy (r. 942–996)', *EME*, 23 (2015), 314).

[114] For details of the war see below, Chapter 11, pp. 646–7.

[115] *Ctl. St-Père*, i. 65; Musset, 'Actes inédits III. Bourgueil', 48–9; Bauduin, *Première Normandie*, pp. 171–2).

[116] *RADN*, no. 5. The property granted to the monks was located in and around Evreux itself, and also in the more securely held north of the Evrecin at Elbeuf, Caudebec-les-Elbeuf, Louviers, and Pinterville.

[117] Jumièges, ii. 174.

[118] Rodulf made a gift to the monks of Saint-Ouen of, 'some places in the county of Evreux, namely Daubeuf-la-Campagne, Venon, Lignon, Quatremare' during the abbacy of Abbot Hildebert, *c.* 960–1006. Between 1006 and 1011 he added some mills and a fishery on the Eure and also 'the vill in the county of Rouen which is called Le Manoir … and the other vill which is called Chambray with Cocherel' (*RADN*, no. 13). Searle thought that the grant of Pacy-sur-Eure was made after Rodulf had taken Ivry (Searle, *PK*, p. 110).

[119] The text is in Malmesbury, *GR*, i. 278. See also L. Musset, 'Aux origines d'une classe dirigeante: Les Tosny, grands barons Normands du Xe au XIIIe siècle', *Francia*, 5 (1977), 48–9.

church was given 'as much by our hand as by that of Duke Richard in whose county it is seen to be'.[120]

The peace with the counts of Chartres was fragile, as is indicated by the fact that Richard fought against Count Theobald's son and successor, Count Odo I, in the French army that besieged Melun in 991. This action seems to have brought concerns about the relationship between the two men to a head.[121] A peace-weaving marriage was arranged shortly afterwards. Count Odo I's son, the future Odo II, wed Richard's daughter, Matilda. William of Jumièges, who dated the marriage to the reign of Richard II, wrote that, 'the duke gave him as dowry half the castle of Dreux with the adjacent land on the river Avre'.[122] As Odo had got hold of the castle of Dreux itself some time previously,[123] Jumièges's words may be taken to mean that Richard had promised to surrender his claims to the vills in Normandy north of the Avre that had formed part of Liégard's dower and which were by now being used to munition that castle. There is certainly no evidence that the duke had any claim to the region south of the river.[124]

While the war with Count Theobald in the 960s and the settlement made with his son centred on the Evrecin, the Normans achieved a more obvious advance in their power at the counts' expense further west. Although Longsword might have raided Brittany and occupied Dol, perhaps in the years between 933 and 937, as noted above, his campaign produced no lasting effect.[125] There is no evidence for Norman influence in Breton politics in the 940s, and when Alan Barbe-Torte and his son Drogo died in rapid succession c. 950 it was Count Theobald of Chartres and Count Fulk of Anjou who gained influence over Breton affairs, Count Theobald over Rennes and Count Fulk over Nantes. Count Conan of Rennes was thus to be found at the court of Odo of Chartres in 979, and was still seen as one of the count's men when he died in a battle against Count Fulk in 992.[126] But his brother and successor, Geoffrey, saw that the count of Chartres was unable to

---

[120] *RADN*, no. 2.

[121] Richer, ii. 364–6.

[122] Jumièges, ii. 22.

[123] Richer, ii. 276.

[124] On the meaning of Jumièges's words see Musset, 'Actes inédits III. Bourgueil', 44; Bauduin, *Première Normandie*, pp. 184–5. In addition, an act of William the Conqueror for the monks of Saint-Benoit-sur-Loire makes it clear that when an interest in a castle was transferred, in this case that at Saint-James-de-Beuvron, the grant might actually concern the surrounding territory dependent on the castle rather than the fortification itself (*Regesta: William*, no. 251).

[125] *Flodoard*, p. 30, and see above, *infra*, pp. 54–5.

[126] Richer, ii. 384, 394. The spheres of influence of the two counts, and the war that resulted from their competition, is remarked in Richer, ii. 370–4; Dunbabin, *France*, p. 196; J. Quaghebeur, 'Havoise, Constance et Mathilde, princesses de Normandie et duchesses

provide adequate support against Anjou and turned instead to Duke Richard II of the Normans.[127]

This was one result of Richard I's efforts to promote his authority in the west of the duchy which was manifested most dramatically in 966 when he appeared before Mont-Saint-Michel in the company of a community of monks whom he then established on the Mont under the rule of a Fleming, called Mainard, who had just restored the monastery at Saint-Wandrille on the Seine.[128] This might not have been Richard's first intervention on the Mont, however. Pierre Bouet has argued that only a few years before the duke installed Norman monks in the abbey he had established a body of canons there.[129] As that intervention would have acted to undermine Theobald's authority in Rennes, if it could be dated *c.* 960 it might have provided Count Theobald with a further reason to begin his war against the duke.

In the event, Duke Richard's reform of Mont-Saint-Michel did not have more than a passing influence on the community he established there. The monks of the Mont continued to look to Brittany and Maine, rather than Normandy, for support until the beginning of the eleventh century. Nonetheless, Richard I was probably more successful in expanding his influence in the Avranchin than the monks' disinterest in his patronage and vice versa would suggest. A series of grants made to the monks of Mont-Saint-Michel and the canons of Avranches by Richard II and Robert the Magnificent suggest that Richard I had seized a cluster of vills around the bay and along the river Sée, probably at about the same time he was seeking to gain hegemony over the Mont.[130] The acts that record the transfers of this property do not mention his campaigns or appropriations at all, but Richard I was the only figure who could have taken and retained lands in the Avranchin that could then have been passed on to his son Robert, established as the first count

de Bretagne', in *Bretons et Normans au moyen âge: rivalités, malentendus, convergences*, ed. J. Quaghebeur and B. Merdrignac (Rennes, 2008), pp. 146–7.

[127] Dunbabin, *France*, p. 197. That the expansion of Norman influence into Brittany was a cause of the war has also been suggested by Bauduin, *Première Normandie*, p. 169.

[128] *Inventio*, pp. 30, 34; Bouet, 'Le Mont-Saint-Michel entre Bretagne et Normandie', pp. 175–7. Bouet confirmed that Mainard was a Fleming, and connected with Saint-Wandrille, against Keat-Rohan's suggestion that he was from Maine.

[129] Bouet would push the date of the installation of the canons back before 960, as he thought that Richard began negotiations with the community over its manner of life at that date, as that was the year the Annals of Mont-Saint-Michel give for the inception of the monastic community (P. Bouet, 'Le Mont-Saint-Michel entre Bretagne et Normandie', p. 169). However, as suggested above, 960 would be a better date for the introduction of the canons themselves. The annalist might have wanted to avoid associating Richard with the canons that he so shortly afterwards marginalized.

[130] *RADN*, pp. 24, 26; no. 49

of Avranches-Mortain *c.* 1000; Richard II simply ruled too late to be the first to acquire them. That new county would form an isolated island of Norman influence in the Avranchin, but it spoke of a growth in Norman power nonetheless, especially when compared to the waning authority of the counts of Chartres.[131]

The end of the 960s saw another development that almost certainly enhanced Norman power in the west. After Emma's death after 968, Richard I began a liaison with a woman named Gunnor, whose family was very probably particularly powerful in the Cotentin.

The case for Gunnor's western origin rests on three bases. First, there is the diploma that records a donation made by her brother, Herfast, to the abbey of Saint-Père at Chartres *c.* 1022, which states that the property he gave to the monks in Le Ham and Barneville-sur-Mer in the *pagus* of the Cotentin was part of his inheritance (*res hereditatis meae*).[132] Secondly, Gunnor's sisters and nieces married into some of the greatest families of Upper Normandy, and in many cases their husbands' families can later be found holding lands in the Cotentin, which suggests they had comprised part of their wives' dowries. Thirdly, Gunnor had a Scandinavian name and to our knowledge her baptismal name, Alberada, was used only once, in a (lost) diploma.[133] The existence of a Scandinavian and a Frankish (baptismal) name for Gunnor strongly suggests that she was originally pagan – there was no need for a new name on cultural grounds here – which again indicates a western origin, as the Normans living in the east of the duchy had probably been Christian for decades.[134]

---

[131] Dunbabin, *France*, p. 197; Bauduin, *Première Normandie*, p. 180

[132] *Ctl. Saint-Père*, i. 108; D. C. Douglas, 'The ancestors of William fitz Osbern', *EHR*, 59 (1944), 67–8. Barneville later turns up as property of the count of Mortain (*Cartulaire Normand de Philippe-Auguste, Louis VIII, Saint Louis et Philippe-le-Hardi*, ed. L. Delisle (Caen, 1882), p. 66, no. 112), and had been almost certainly given to Count Robert by Duke William II. Lucien Musset thought that a final estate granted to the monks, at *Torgisuilla*, should be identified as Teurtheville-Hague (Musset, 'Les domaines de l'époque franque', 97) while Adigard des Gautries suggested Saint-Jean-de-la-Rivière near Barneville (noted in E. M. C. van Houts, 'Robert of Torigni as genealogist', in *Studies in Medieval History presented to R. Allen Brown*, ed. C. Harper-Bill, C. J. Holdsworth, and J. L. Nelson (Woodbridge, 1989), p. 230, n. 65).

[133] Van Houts, 'Robert of Torigni', p. 233 and n. 80. The lost act written at Saint-Ouen at Rouen is mentioned at *RADN*, p. 22. In contrast, Gunnor's sisters were known by Frankish, and thus Christian, names (Van Houts, 'Robert of Torigni', pp. 225 (for Duvelina), 233; 'Countess Gunnor of Normandy (*c.* 950–1031)', *Collegium Médiévale*, 12 (1999), 9).

[134] Although a – presumably twelfth-century – carving of Thor in the choir triforium of the church of Saint-Georges-de-Boscherville might suggest some lingering affection for the Nordic gods (see M. Baylé, 'Le décor sculpté de Saint-Georges-de-Boscherville: quelques questions de style et d'iconographie', *ANS*, 8 (1986), p. 36 and see below

Gunnor's leading role in the refoundation of the cathedral at Coutances *c.* 1026 suggests that she played some 'public' role in the west of the duchy, and it is possible that she was the first in a succession of ducal women who acted as the duke's representative or agent in the Cotentin. She can also be seen playing a central role at Rouen, particularly perhaps during the duke's absences or perhaps in her own right as a powerful patroness. Warner of Rouen pictured her presiding over a court (although not necessarily the duke's court). In his poem, Moriuht's wife had been enslaved by Viking raiders and taken to the market at Rouen where, it seems, Moriuht petitioned Gunnor for help. Her response was that he should: 'Go with speed throughout our realm and seek out your source of joy. When you have found her, be sure to report everything to me. If she happens to have been sold and is being kept in that service, I shall personally restore (her) to you, but I will give (her) back at a price.'[135] In addition, she was a relatively frequent witness of Richard II's acts, attesting ten of his diplomata.[136] Only Archbishop Robert of Rouen, Bishop Hugh of Bayeux, and her two grandsons witnessed more than her – although Archbishop Robert appears nearly three times as frequently.

Richard I's marriage to Gunnor would bring the dukes a swathe of property in the Cotentin, which they are most likely to have acquired in two phases. The first tranche probably came with the departure of Gunnor's brother, Herfast, for Chartres *c.* 1022, which perhaps left Duke Richard II with his possessions in the peninsula, either directly or by way of Herfast's nephew, Boselinus.[137] That would explain how Richard II could endow the cathedral at Coutances with estates in and around Saint-Lô and how Richard III came to possess property at Coutances, Esglandes, Moyon, Percy, Hambye, and elsewhere which he settled on his wife Adela.[138] It would also explain the lack of any ducal castles in this same area, in contrast to the position further north where Richard II had found it necessary to build forts at Cherbourg, Brix, and Le Homme. The second tranche would have been acquired when Gunnor herself died in 1030 or 1031.[139] Cerisy-la-

---

Chapter 4, pp. 209–12). Gunnor's origins are discussed at greater length in M. Hagger, 'How the west was won: the Norman dukes and the Cotentin, *c.* 987–*c.* 1087', *JMH*, 38 (2012), 27–9.

[135] Warner of Rouen, *Moriuht*, pp. 88–9.

[136] *RADN*, nos. 15, 16, 18, 19, 20, 21, 29, 32, 43, 47.

[137] *Ctl. Saint-Pere*, i. 108–9. Searle wrote that Herfast left Boselinus the rest of his estates in the Cotentin, but she was mistaken (Searle, *PK*, pp. 103, 115–16). Van Torhoudt accused Robert the Magnificent of driving him out of Normandy (E. van Torhoudt, 'Henri beauclerc, comte du Cotentin reconsidéré (1088–1101)', in *Tinchebray 1106–2006: actes du colloque de Tinchebray (28–30 Septembre 2006)*, ed. V. Gazeau and J. Green (Flers, 2009), p. 116), but the wording of the diploma does not support this view.

[138] *RADN*, nos. 58, 214, and see Map 3.

[139] RT, s.a. 1030; Delisle, i. 36; Howlett, p. 25. Howlett noted that the Annals of Rouen give

Forêt might have been one of the places concerned, while others are perhaps to be found among those donations to Coutances cathedral which, from their place in William the Bastard's diploma, were probably made by Robert the Magnificent or Duke William himself.[140]

If this reconstruction is right, it is almost certain that Duke Richard had wanted an alliance with Gunnor because of the power her family wielded in the Cotentin. It is likely that Gunnor's family could also see the advantage of a match with the duke. And it may be supposed that the most important factor in their calculations was that by the time Richard began his liaison with Gunnor he had expanded the reach of his authority throughout most, if not all, of the Lieuvin, and across much of the Bessin, too.

This authority need not have been recently acquired. It is possible that the north of the Lieuvin had been conquered or rendered tributary by Rollo and his *comites* even before his position had been legitimized by Charles the Simple *c.* 911, simply because as far west as the river Touques the county could be thought of as part of the Seine valley – as the concrete towers of the Pont de Normandie that now dominate the skyline looking north-east from Honfleur make very plain. At the same time, Dudo had the rebel Riulf suggest that Longsword had no control of the land between the Seine and the Risle, so it might be that the duke's authority over the county was imposed only after the mid 930s. Once established, however, it seems to have endured. Three years after Longsword's death, the frontier of the growing duchy had not retreated from the Dives, where Louis IV and his Norman allies met with Harald, the chief in control of Bayeux.

The location of the known ducal demesne in the county suggests that rivers had been crucial to the advance of that authority, whenever it occurred. The Lieuvin is divided, more or less north to south, by the wide but steep-sided valleys of the Risle, Charentonne, Orbiquet, Touques, Vie, and Dives. This geography in turn suggests that the county was conquered from north to south, rather than east to west, and the location of the demesne suggests a desire to ensure control of the mouths of these rivers, which provided not just harbours but also access to the interior.

There was a cluster of demesne vills at the mouth of the Risle (including at

the date as 1031, but there is no such entry in the edition by Holder-Egger presented under the heading 'Ex annalibus Normannicis' in *Monumenta Germaniae Historica: Scriptores* 26 (Hanover, 1882), pp. 488–500 at p. 498. Gunnor's death is, however, listed in the annal for 1031 in the *Annales Uticenses* edited by August le Prévost: *Orderici Vitalis ecclesiasticae historiae libri tredecim*, ed. A. le Prévost, Société de l'Histoire de France, 5 vols (Paris, 1838–55), v. 156 (although not in the version presented by Holder-Egger at op. cit, p. 498).

[140] *RADN*, no. 214.

Honfleur, Grestain, and Pont-Audemer), and another further south at the junction of the Risle and Charentonne, centred on Bernay, which would be given to Richard II's wife Judith as dower.[141] In between, lay the estates of Torf of Pont-Audemer, whose son Turold was to marry Gunnor's sister Duvelina.[142] From this marriage would spring the dynasty that would come to take their toponym from Beaumont-le-Roger and who would come to control the lower reaches of the Risle valley. Although the match was almost certainly made late in Richard I's reign, the sources are such that the first member of the family that we can see at the duke's court is Turold's son, Humfrey of Vieilles, who appears in a small number of acts that date from Richard II's and Robert the Magnificent's reigns.[143]

While to tell their story in detail is beyond the scope of this book, it should be stressed that while the Beaumonts might be numbered among the dukes' kinsmen, the bonds formed by that kinship were strengthened by a continuing trickle of patronage out of the demesne over the period down to 1144.[144] The family was also given more or less free licence to expand their own interests at the expense of local rivals. Bishop Hugh of Bayeux, for example, suffered losses at the hands of Humfrey of Vieilles;[145] the lords of Ferrières-Saint-Hilaire, apparently planted on the left bank of the river by Duke Richard II, would end up as *fideles* of Waleran of Meulan;[146] and the Beaumonts were also supported by the dukes in

---

[141]   *RADN*, no. 11.

[142]   Jumièges, ii. 268.

[143]   *RADN*, nos. 29, 32, 55, 88.

[144]   For Count Robert see below, Chapter 3, pp. 149, 154, 156 and Chapter 11, pp. 633–4. In 1035 × 1040, the young William the Bastard gave the fishery at Pont-Audemer to Humfrey's son, Roger of Beaumont, and the monks of Fécamp were compensated with property elsewhere (*RADN*, no. 94). Roger was also given property out of the ducal demesne at Martainville (*Regesta: William*, no. 158), Touques, and Dives-sur-Mer (*Regesta: William*, no. 284). By 1141, Roger's grandson Count Waleran of Meulan held 300 *livres* 'from the lord of Normandy' from the revenues of Pont-Audemer and it is likely that this was in origin another of Duke William's grants (*Ctl. Préaux*, B3).

[145]   Humfrey's appropriation of Bishop Hugh's property might have occurred during the bishop's time in exile. He seems to have acquired Hugh's possessions in the forest of Brotonne comprising *Nouus Boscus* (4 kilometres west of the forest of Vièvre, identified in the Saint-Léger *pancarte* as Incourt), Bois-Aubert, Mélimont, and Selles (See V. Gazeau, 'Le patrimoine d'Hughes de Bayeux (*c.* 1011–1049)', in *Les évêques normands du XIe siècle*, ed. P. Bouet and F. Neveux (Caen, 1995), pp. 139–47; *Regesta: William*, no. 217).

[146]   When the abbey at Bernay was founded in 1025, the endowment only partly overlapped with Judith's dower. Some places were, it may be supposed, retained by the duke. They included Broglie, Camfleur, Carentonne (although it might already have been subsumed into Bernay), Ferrières-Saint-Hilaire, and Menneval. It seems that some of these estates were instead used to endow the Ferrières family, who may be supposed to have been planted in the region in an effort to consolidate the duke's authority there. Aside from Ferrières-Saint-Hilaire, there is evidence that the family were granted property

their intermittent feud against the Tosny family which dragged on from the 1040s to 1139.[147] The family, then, were trusted supporters from the outset, and proved their fidelity time and again as the elderly Roger of Beaumont was to remind Robert Curthose *c.* 1090:

> From my childhood I have always chosen the path of loyalty; this is the inheritance that I received from my grandfather Turold and my father Humphrey, and have treasured all my life long in adversity and prosperity. God forbid that now, when I am grey with age, I should try my hand at deceits, which up to now I have loathed and have utterly shunned from my earliest years. And because your father found that I never turned from his side, but always stoutly persevered in loyalty and endured great misfortunes for his sake with manly courage, he always admitted me to his most intimate counsels before all his other magnates.[148]

The result was that, as with the Montgommery family, the Beaumonts were permitted to suborn their weaker neighbours and to achieve their ambitions, at least until Count Waleran of Meulan finally overstepped the mark in 1123–24 when he led a rebellion against Henry I.[149]

Across the Risle from Brionne and Pont-Authou, which had come under Richard's influence before his death, stood the forest of Vièvre. One of Robert of Torigni's interpolations into the *Gesta Normannorum ducum* comprises a story of how Richard I granted that forest to his half-brother Count Rodulf,[150] and the extent of Rodulf's possessions can be established in part by the estates that ended up in the hands of his sons, Bishop Hugh of Bayeux and John of Ivry, and his nephew, William fitz Osbern. Taken together, this evidence indicates that Rodulf had held a swathe of land that stretched from the banks of the Risle, past Cormeilles on the Calonne, to Fumichon and Firfol, almost on the right bank of the Touques.[151] In addition, and to jump ahead a little, Rodulf seems also to

---

in nearby Broglie as Henry II of Ferrières gave the monks of Lyre one *hôte* in the vill (Delisle *Recueil*, no. 65). Henry's son, Walchelin, subsequently confirmed the gift (AD Eure, J.-L. Lenoir, Collection du Marquis de Mathan, MS 23 (transcripts of acts for the monks of Lyre), no 78, where the *hôte* is described as a burgess).

[147] Jumièges, ii. 94–6 ; Orderic, ii. 40; iii. 88, 126–8; v. 300; vi. 330, 444–6, 456–8, 474, 514; D. Crouch, *The Beaumont Twins: The Roots and Branches of Power in the Twelfth Century* (Cambridge, 1986), pp. 38 and n. 47, 55.

[148] Orderic, iv. 206.

[149] See below, Chapter 3, pp. 175–7.

[150] Jumièges, ii. 174.

[151] For Rodulf's estates in the Lieuvin see: *RADN*, no. 229; *Regesta: William*, no. 166; *Ctl. Préaux*, A115; D. Bates, 'Notes sur l'aristocratie Normande', *Annales de Normandie*, 23

have had extensive possessions in the Bessin, where he apparently held Boulon and Laize-la-Ville and also, perhaps, the later honour of Le Plessis-Grimoult, which lay across the Orne from another cluster of vills given as dower to Judith by Richard II.[152] His possession of this lordship is suggested by the fact that it was later held from Bishop Hugh of Bayeux by Grimoult of Le Plessis-Grimoult and would return to the bishop after Grimoult's death in 1074.[153] How many of the other possessions later held by the bishops of Bayeux had first been conquered by Count Rodulf is not known, but a hint of the scale of his holdings in the Bessin might be provided by Orderic's description of him as count of Bayeux.[154]

We can return now to the Touques, where Richard I had probably acquired a string of properties on the right bank of the river from Hennequeville to Saint-Julien-sur-Calonne, including Touques and Bonneville-sur-Touques, which would later become the site of one of the dukes' palaces. To the south of these possessions lay the city of Lisieux. The first bishop to appear at a duke's court, so far as we know, was Bishop Roger who is mentioned in an act of 990, and who seems also to have attested the treaty made between Richard and Æthelred II in 991.[155] The bishop's acknowledgement of Duke Richard's authority, even if it might principally have been the result of the appointment of his brother Robert as archbishop of Rouen, gave Richard an ally with some influence in Lisieux and its hinterland.[156]

(1973), 14–15; Gazeau, 'Patrimoine', pp. 91, 141–3, 145 and the map on p. 144; Bauduin, *Première Normandie*, p. 201; *Normannia Monastica*, ii. 79; R. Allen, '"A proud and headstrong man": John of Ivry, bishop of Avranches and archbishop of Rouen, 1060–79', *Historical Research*, 83 (2010), 5.

[152] For Boulon and Laize-la-Ville see Ctl. Rouen, fos. 31r, 55v; *RADN*, no. 66; L. Musset, 'Actes inédits du XIᵉ siècle: V. Autour des origines de Saint-Etienne de Fontenay', *BSAN*, 56 (1963), 20–2; Bauduin, *Première Normandie*, p. 204. Bauduin's map suggests that he would add a number of other vills to Rodulf's possessions here.

[153] In 1074, William the Bastard granted the honour to his half-brother, Bishop Odo of Bayeux (*Regesta: William*, no. 27). The grant was couched as a restitution, and if that was the case then Grimoult must have held from Bishop Hugh.

[154] Orderic, ii. 200; iv. 290, though Bauduin thought this was due to confusion with Hugh of Bayeux's bishopric (*Première Normandie*, p. 200).

[155] *RADN*, no. 4; Malmesbury, *GR*, i. 278.

[156] The bishops were granted some property from the ducal demesne (*RADN*, nos. 48, 194), but an overarching view of their possessions is only possible from 1172. The survey of Normandy reveals that they owed the duke twenty knights, and had thirty enfeoffed on their estates, with another ten knights who ordinarily guarded the city of Lisieux. The survey commissioned by Philip Augustus in 1205 provides more detail, identifying subinfeudated estates at Piencourt, *Mesnil-Godoen*, Fontaine-le-Lovet, *Espreville*, Bonneville-le-Lovet, Glos, Courtonne-le-Meurdrac, *Malloc*, Mesnil-Eudes, Houblonnière, and Gonneville-Honfleur. In addition, the *leuga* of Lisieux encompassed the city and the seven neighbouring parishes of Saint-Germain-de-Livet, Saint-

Richard I had probably gained vills between Lisieux and the river Dives as he fought to make his power in the Lieuvin a reality. At the mouth of that river the dukes held another run of estates including Dives-sur-Mer, Bures-sur-Dives, and Troarn.[157] Further south, Richard had probably also acquired a cluster of estates based on Saint-Pierre-sur-Dives, which would later be transferred to his son, William, when he was given the county of the Hiémois in, or soon after, 996.[158] The tract known as the *Primordia abbatiae Sancti Petri super Diuam* suggests that William was also given the castle at Exmes, but this seems unlikely to have been in Norman hands before the second decade of the eleventh century.[159] There is certainly no strong evidence that the dukes had grabbed land any further south than Meulles and Lisores in that part of the Lieuvin by the turn of the century, although Richard I was thought to have granted the church at Saint-Aubert-sur-Orne to the monks of Saint-Bénigne of Dijon, even before William of Volpiano arrived in Normandy, and his son seems also to have held Bazoches-au-Houlme and Neuvy-au-Houlme, which would indicate that Richard had been able to take the whole of the south-west of the Lieuvin and then to make some inroads into the Hiémois.[160]

The rebellion over which William presided *c.* 1000, discussed below, reveals that even at that date some of the Frankish lords of the county resisted the advance of

Martin-de-la-Lieue, Saint-Hippolyte, Les Vaux, *Union*, Ouilly-le-Vicomte, Beuvillers, and Roques (H. de Formeville, *Histoire de l'ancien évêché-comté de Lisieux* (Lisieux, 1873), p. cxxxviii).

[157] *RADN*, nos. 34, 36; *Regesta: William*, no. 158 (Risle); *RADN*, nos. 11 (Bernay); 15, 34 (Touques); 34, 94, 231; *Regesta: William*, nos. 45, 52, 53, 54, 59, 62, 271, 280, 281 (all versions) (Dives).

[158] For William, see below Chapter 2, p. 79 and Chapter 6, pp. 324–5. The *Primordia abbatiae Sancti Petri super Diuam* states that Saint-Pierre-sur-Dives had been the location of one of the count's houses which had passed to his wife Lecelina 'by right of dower (*ex iure dotali*)' (*GC*, xi. Instr. 153). It is likely that the surrounding vills had also been given to the count by his father and so had once formed part of the ducal demesne, too.

[159] *GC*, xi. Instr. 153.

[160] Meulles was given to the monks of Saint-Taurin by Richard I (*RADN*, no. 5), while Lisores, near both Montgommery and Vimoutiers, first appears in a duke's hands in 1035 when half the vill was given to the nuns of Montivilliers (*RADN*, no. 90). For Saint-Aubin see *RADN*, no. 86, and for Bazoches and Neuvy see AD Calvados, H 7031(5) = *Regesta*, ii. no. 1569. In addition, the recent excavations at Falaise have indicated that the earliest work there might date from the very end of the tenth century (F. Fichet de Clairfontaine, J. Mastrolorenzo, and R. Brown, 'Le château de Falaise (Calvados): état des connaissances sur l'évolution du site castral du dixième au treizième siècles', in *Castles and the Anglo-Norman World: Proceedings of a Conference held at Norwich Castle in 2012*, ed. J. A. Davies, A. Riley, J.-M. Levesque, and C. Lapiche (Oxford, 2016), pp. 232–4 and also Figs. 15.5–7, pp. 236–7).

Norman power and sought to cling to their independence and identity.[161] Others, however, had already made a show of loyalty to the new regime before Richard I's death by giving some of their property to the abbeys associated with their new lord. The evidence for this is found in an act for the monks of Jumièges of 1025, which records the existence of an earlier 'little charter (*cartulis*)' of Richard I which outlined, apparently rather vaguely, the possessions that had been granted to the monks in the Lieuvin by a number of lords who were resident there.[162] The relevant part of the act records that the duke had confirmed grants at and around Vimoutiers and at Le Renouard and Crouttes nearby, all located in the very south of the county, as well as at Ouézy, Vieux-Fumé, and Condé-sur-Ifs in the Bessin. The lands around Vimoutiers had been conceded by Osmund Gelth, Walter, and some unnamed others; those to the west of the Dives by Everard, Albinus, and Theodmar. None of these men seems to have been of the first rank, socially speaking, and they also seem to have been of both Frankish and Scandinavian origins. And while their appearance in this act reveals something of how the expansion of the dukes' authority might manifest itself, it tells us nothing about how it was achieved.

In the Bessin, the dukes acquired property along or close to the Orne and the Odon, suggesting that, as with the Lieuvin, ducal power had flowed into the county up the rivers. The dukes' possessions here included Caen, just a village in the tenth century but one which would eventually develop into their principal centre in Lower Normandy, with a scattering of estates around it including Ouistreham to the north;[163] Mondeville, Janville, and Argences to the east;[164] and Bretteville-sur-Odon,[165] Carpiquet,[166] Verson,[167] Mondrainville,[168] Cheux,[169] Le Mesnil-Patry,[170] and Rots to the west.[171] To the south of Caen, on the right bank of the Orne, another cluster of thirty-one demesne vills (with fifteen churches and fifteen mills) was found, 'in the hilly region southeast of Thury-Harcourt, plus that strategically important site, and in the Cinglais forest nearby'.[172] These would be

---

[161]   See below, Chapter 6, p. 324.

[162]   *RADN*, no. 36.

[163]   *Regesta: William,* no. 59.

[164]   *RADN*, nos. 4, 34.

[165]   *RADN*, no. 17. Bretteville had been given to Gunnor as part of her dower, as the act states.

[166]   *RADN*, no. 231; *Regesta: William,* nos. 53, 59, 61, 62, 281 (II).

[167]   *RADN*, nos. 47, 48.

[168]   *RADN*, no. 49.

[169]   *Regesta: William,* nos. 45, 50, 52, 53, 54, 57.

[170]   *RADN*, no. 52.

[171]   *RADN*, no. 44. Rots had belonged to Saint-Ouen in the Carolingian period: Musset, 'Saint-Ouen de Rouen', 117.

[172]   *RADN*, no. 11; *PK*, p. 129.

given to Richard II's first wife Judith as part of her dower *c.* 1000. As the dukes do not seem to have had the opportunity to acquire property in the Bessin on this scale after the beginning of the eleventh century, it is likely that all the demesne that appears in the hands of later dukes had been acquired by Richard I when he was fighting to assert and consolidate his power here.

In Richard I's day Bayeux was the most important city in the county. Dudo insisted that both Rollo and Longsword had authority over it, but we only have his word for it. But even if Longsword had established his authority over the city, it was lost in the aftermath of his assassination. By 945, the city was under the control of a chieftain called Harald, and he might still have exercised power over the Cotentin in 954.[173] It was only thirty years later, around 989, that the city, and much of the county, too, was under Richard's control.[174] This should probably be seen as another milestone in the expansion of ducal authority over Lower Normandy, but the fact that Richard I had to build a tower in the city to root himself there suggests that it was not achieved without a fight. That is also suggested by the chronicle written by Hariulf of Saint-Riquier, who remembered that around 987 the relics of St Vigor had been taken from Bayeux to Ponthieu by Avitianus, the master of works of the cathedral, who despaired of the ruin of the county which had been wasted by a relentless enemy.[175] That enemy had probably been Richard I fighting to take control of it.

Bayeux was, at least up to the middle of the eleventh century, the second city of Normandy. Serlo of Bayeux wrote that in 1105 there was a population of some 3,000 people, most of whom were involved in trade. That commerce might account for the presence of a ducal mint in the city in the 1090s, which was the only one in Normandy outside Rouen. There were suburbs, one of them established around the monastery of St Vigor that Bishop Odo had founded and which had subsequently become a dependency of Saint-Bénigne at Dijon. Serlo remarked, too, on the number of churches, Odo's decorated hall, 'the famous house of Conan', and the duke's castle, located in the south-west corner of the city.[176]

---

[173] Flodoard, pp. 94, 98; *Flodoard*, pp. 40, 42; Annales Niverneses, *MGH, Scriptores* 13, p. 89, noted in Bates, *Normandy*, p. 14 and P. Bauduin, 'Du bon usage de la dos', pp. 429–65 at p. 440.

[174] The recovery is dated with reference to the translation of the relics of Saint-Ouen ('Variae translationes sacri corporis', in *Acta Sanctorum* 38 (August IV) (Paris, 1867), pp. 823–4), which is also thought to have occurred in 989. That looks about right, although the evidence is such that any conclusion must remain uncertain.

[175] Hariulf, *Chronique de l'abbaye de Saint-Riquier (Ve siècle au 1104)*, ed. F. Lot (Paris, 1894), p. 163; noted in S. Herrick, *Imagining the Sacred Past: Hagiography and Power in Early Normandy* (Cambridge, MA and London, 2007), pp. 91–2.

[176] Serlo of Bayeux, 'Versus Serlonis capta Baiocensium ciuitate', in *Anglo-Latin Satirical Poets and Epigrammatists of the Twelfth Century: 2. Minor Anglo-Latin Satirists and*

It is not clear how far west of Bayeux Richard I had managed to push his authority by the time of his death. Gunnor was given Domjean as part of her dower, which might suggest that Richard had established his dominion almost to the river Vire south of Saint-Lô, but it is equally possible that the place had been acquired during a smash-and-grab campaign, designed to impress on Gunnor's family the threat that he now posed to their own security. Indeed, it might even have been taken from Gunnor's family to make the point still more forcefully, to be returned when the marriage took place.[177] In any event, Domjean seems to have been an isolated possession. There is nothing else to suggest that Richard had pushed his power so far west in the Bessin.

Nonetheless, even though he had not yet brought the whole of the Bessin under his sway, it is almost certain that Richard I had already begun the process of establishing ducal power in the Cotentin before his death. By c. 1000, Richard II was able to give his wife a cluster of demesne vills in the so-called *vicaria* of 'Kelgenas'.[178] These lands were located in the far north-west of the peninsula, in a band stretching from Brix in the east to the sea in the west.[179] Thirty-seven places are named,[180] with seventeen churches (even at this time when the conversion of pagan Scandinavian settlers was still ongoing). It may be supposed that these had been taken during a raid, perhaps even as part of Hugh the Great's attack on the Cotentin of 954. They formed an island of ducal power, surrounded by as yet untamed and independent lords, but they constituted a bridgehead from which further gains, in terms of both land and souls, might be made in the future.

With Richard so strong, and growing stronger all the time, it is no wonder that Gunnor's family was willing to agree to her marriage to Richard. They had perhaps also been encouraged to make the match by Richard's own political views vis-à-

Epigrammatists of the Twelfth Century, ed. T. Wright, Rolls Series (London, 1872), p. 246. An English translation is now provided in E. van Houts, 'The fate of priest's sons in Normandy with special reference to Serlo of Bayeux', *HSJ*, 25 (2014), 86–105. The cathedral in particular was also praised by Rodulf Tortarius at the end of the eleventh century (Rodulfus Tortarius, *Carmina*, ed. M. B. Ogle and D. M. Schullian (Rome, 1933), p. 39 (ll. 291–9) (Epistula IX: Ad Roberti).

177 See also the brief discussion of Richard II's treatment of Alençon c. 1025, which Jumièges implied was taken from William of Bellême but then restored to him to be held from then on as a benefice (see below, Chapter 2, p. 93).

178 Musset thought this region to be one and the same as the *pagus* of *Helgenes* mentioned in Adela's dower agreement of 1026 (*RADN*, no. 58, and see *RADN*, p. 82, n. 1 and p. 180, n. 2 for Musset's identification of the *vicaria* of *Kelgenas* with the *pagus* of *Helgenes*).

179 Searle wrote that 'all are key possessions, all show a keen strategical sense of geography' (Searle, *PK*, p. 129), but this is somewhat exaggerated.

180 Bauduin calculated that there are forty-seven 'domaines', and Musset counted forty-three, but both count some twice (Bauduin, 'Du bon usage de la dos', p. 439; L. Musset, 'Actes inédits du XIᵉ siècle III. Bourgueil', 32).

vis the Franks. As will be examined in more detail in Chapters 4 and 5, Richard's reign marked a shift away from the policy of assimilation and amity with the Franks pursued under his father to an altogether more independent stance. The marriage of Richard and Gunnor was indicative of that departure, and its role in realigning Normandy away from Francia and towards its Scandinavian heritage was emphasized by Dudo's treatment of the match in his *De moribus*. In his narrative, every betrayal by the Franks made Richard and the Normans become more Scandinavian, with the result that the story of Rollo's dynasty becomes less and less like the union of two peoples portrayed in the *Aeneid* that had provided a model for the opening books of Dudo's work.[181] That trajectory was made particularly clear in the way that Dudo dealt with the marriages his three dukes made. Rollo took a Frankish wife and had also had a Frankish mistress. That made Longsword half-Frankish, which might be why Dudo was rather coy about suggesting an ethnic origin for Sprota.[182] He perhaps did not want to remind his audience that Richard I's Scandinavian blood had been diluted still further on his mother's side. Although Richard's first wife was Emma, the daughter of Hugh the Great, the diplomatic triumph the marriage represented was downplayed by Dudo. Even as he recorded the happy event, he composed a poem that remarked the couple's lack of children and looked ahead to, and praised, the marriage that Richard would subsequently contract with Gunnor. That marriage took place only after the final act of Frankish betrayal and the resulting creation of the autonomous 'kingdom' of Normandy. In particular, Dudo lauded Gunnor's noble Scandinavian descent, and made it clear that her children's claims to the succession would be preferred to those of the sons produced by earlier liaisons with, presumably, Frankish women. The Norman dukes, then, were to be Scandinavian chiefs once again. Seen in this light, Richard I might not have been at all concerned to be styled *dux pyratarum* by Richer of Reims at the end of his reign (or just after his death). Indeed, he might have approved of it.

[181] Shopkow, *History and Community*, pp. 150–1.
[182] *Dudo*, p. 63.

CHAPTER 2

Expansion: Normandy and its Dukes in the Eleventh Century, 996–1087

Richard II, 996–1026

ALTHOUGH the evidence can be interpreted in different ways, the interpretation offered in the previous chapter would have Richard I expand the reach
of his authority to cover an area that stretched from the Bresle to the Drome, and
from the Channel coast to the very south of the Lieuvin and perhaps even into
Houlme. He had also grabbed one isolated pocket of demesne, and thus influence,
in the north-west of the Cotentin between Les Pieux and Brix, and another in
the Avranchin, where he held a cluster of vills along the coast from Saint-Jean-
le-Thomas to Mont-Saint-Michel (see Maps 2 and 3). These pockets of Norman
influence in the west, which almost certainly owed their origin to seaborne raids,
had become loosely joined to the bulk of Richard's dominions as a result of his
marriage to Gunnor, which brought a great swathe of the central and southern
Cotentin under his (indirect) sway. This expansion of the duke's authority, as
well as the appearance of all seven bishops of the province of Rouen at Richard's
court in 990, allowed Richer of Reims to write of a grant to Ketil of the whole
area covered by the province of Rouen in the second half of the 990s, although he
thereby implied that the duke's authority ran evenly across the whole of this area,
which was very far from being the case.

Such expansion was bound to cause resistance, and so it was that when the
long-lived and well-established Richard I died, the metal of his untried son was
tested almost immediately. Assuming that the story was not inserted into the
Gesta Normannorum ducum solely to provide a precedent for the treatment of
the burgesses of Alençon *c.* 1052, it seems that a 'peasants' revolt' broke out in
unspecified regions of the duchy *c.* 1000. 'Throughout every part of Normandy
the peasants unanimously formed many assemblies and decided to live according
to their own wishes, such that in respect both of short cuts through the woods
and of the traffic of the rivers with no bar of previously established right in their
way, they might follow laws of their own.'[1] The rebels, then, seem to have been

---

[1] Jumièges, ii. 8. The revolt has recently been usefully discussed by Bernard Gowers,
although Count Rodulf's area of operation is too narrowly drawn (pp. 88–9) which

dissatisfied with the new tolls and forest customs that they had to observe. Their grumblings in turn suggest that the smack of firm ducal government had now enveloped areas that previously had been out of reach and had perhaps also silenced the political voice that farmers had in both Frankish and Scandinavian society.[2] Count Rodulf was dispatched to put the rebels down. He did so with an uncompromising demonstration of power that would have been horrific to suffer and to witness, so it is not surprising that 'having seen this the peasants hurriedly dissolved their assemblies and returned to their ploughs'. Such was the coercive force employed to subjugate peasants to the duke's rule.

At about the same time, there was a rebellion in the Hiémois. At the beginning of Richard's reign, his half-brother, William, 'received the county (*comitatum*) of the Hiémois as a gift' from the duke.[3] The lands that William subsequently held in the Lieuvin and the Hiémois, which were centred on his house at Saint-Pierre-sur-Dives, may consequently be supposed to have been part of the ducal demesne prior to that point, as suggested above.[4] William might have been successful in pushing Norman authority forward, or at least in consolidating what must have been a precarious hold on Falaise and the nearby Bazoches-au-Houlme and Neuvy-au-Houlme. His successes seem to have made him over-ambitious, however, and he rebelled against his half-brother intending to gain independent rule in the region. He was supported, it seems, by a number of local lords, some of whom might well have been Franks, who saw in William a chance to escape coming still more securely under ducal authority. It took a lot of fighting to convince them otherwise.[5]

It is possible that the rebels had been encouraged to revolt by Richard's grant of Bernay and its members to his wife Judith *c.* 1000 which might have made ducal authority in the Lieuvin appear more remote. In any event, when she died in 1017, Richard acted to establish his authority more strongly in the valley of the Charentonne. Having recovered her dower to the demesne, he used some of it to plant the family of Ferrières on the left bank of the river.[6] A few years later, Bernay and some of its dependent vills that had previously been granted to Judith, as well

affects the discussion of the area encompassed by the revolt (B. Gowers, '996 and all that: the Norman peasants' revolt reconsidered', *EME*, 21 (2013), 71–98).

[2] The role of non-elite members of society in political assemblies is noted by Gowers, pp. 88–9.

[3] Jumièges, ii. 8. David Douglas was of the view that although he received the county, he did not become count of the Hiémois (D. C. Douglas, 'The earliest Norman counts', *EHR*, 61 (1946), 135–7).

[4] *GC*, xi. Instr. 153–4; Bauduin, *Première Normandie*, pp. 296–7.

[5] See below, Chapter 6, p. 324.

[6] See above, Chapter 1, n. 146.

as some of the other (previously unrecorded) demesne vills in the vicinity, were used to endow the duke's new foundation at Bernay which was given to the monks of Fécamp as a dependency.

Even more important in establishing Richard's rule in the Lieuvin, however, was the negotiation of a marriage between Hugh of Montgommery and Joscelina, one of Gunnor's nieces (her mother was Sainsfreda).[7] That Duke Richard was prepared to broker a marriage involving one of his cousins strongly suggests that the Montgommery family was already important in the south of the Lieuvin before Richard's authority came up against theirs.[8] It is also possible that the family was Frankish rather than Scandinavian. First, there was an apparent lack of Scandinavian settlement in the region; secondly, Hugh's name was Frankish (notwithstanding the appearance of a Hugh the Dane c. 980); and, thirdly, Gunnor's niece took a Frankish name, Joscelina, after her marriage to Hugh. If this hypothesis is correct, it was Joscelina's Scandinavian blood that allowed Roger II of Montgommery so famously to claim that he was 'a Norman of Norman stock' during William the Bastard's reign.[9] Hugh was also given some of the ducal demesne by way of dowry. The grant probably included the three vills in the Cotentin and the two vills on the lower reaches of the Dives that were found in the possession of Roger II of Montgommery in the middle of the eleventh century. These last two, Janville and Bures-sur-Dives, were also part of the dukes' demesne, and it is this which suggests that Richard II had granted Hugh or his successors their interest in them.[10] We also know that Roger I of Montgommery

---

[7] Jumièges, ii. 264–6 and n. 1. Ivo of Chartres identified Joscelina's mother (*RHGF*, xv. 167–8). Kathleen Thompson noted that Torigni apparently skipped a generation in his genealogy: K. Thompson, 'The Norman aristocracy before 1066: the example of the Montgomerys', *Historical Research*, 60 (1987), 254. The tombstone that is thought to have covered Hugh's grave is now preserved in the parish church in Troarn.

[8] See in addition the conclusions in Thompson, 'The Norman aristocracy', 251–2 (who kept an open mind) and Louise, *Bellême*, i. 207–8 (who thought that Roger I was given Montgommery by Duke Robert c. 1033).

[9] *Regesta: William*, no. 281. It is a lack of Scandinavian place names – admittedly mendacious evidence (Bates, *Normandy*, p. 17 and also the Note on the Text, p. xvii and n.1) – that suggests a lack of Scandinavian settlement here. See the maps in: L. Musset, 'Les Scandinaves et l'ouest du continent européan', p. 92; G. Fellows-Jensen, 'Les relations entre la Normandie et les colonies scandinaves', in *Les fondations Scandinaves en occident et les débuts du duché de Normandie*, ed. P. Bauduin (Caen, 2005), p. 228. Gérard Louise also questioned the Montgommery family's Scandinavian origins (Louise, *Bellême*, i. 217–22). Thompson had earlier argued that the Montgommery 'were descendants of the earliest Scandinavian colonists of central Normandy' (Thompson, 'The Norman aristocracy', 252). For two coins minted in the name of Hugh the Dane, see Dumas, 'Les monnaies Normandes', 107.

[10] Orderic, iii. 136; *Regesta: William*, nos. 280, 281.I.

was given half of Bernay between 1025 and 1027 by the custodian Thierry, who is said to have been his kinsman (providing another indication of this family's Frankish origins).[11] It is possible that Thierry also engineered grants of Troarn and Almenèches to Roger I, lands which the monks had themselves only recently been granted by the duke, so that Roger's acquisition of this property after 1025 should not necessarily be seen as despoliation.[12]

Richard II thus laid foundations in the Lieuvin and Hiémois on which he would successfully have built by the end of his reign. Further west, however, he was able to enjoy the fruit of his father's work much earlier. Around the year 1000, Count Geoffrey of Rennes paid Duke Richard a visit. 'When Count Geoffrey of the Bretons observed that Duke Richard prospered in all he undertook, and how from day to day he accumulated more power and wealth, he concluded that his own safety and strength would grow if he sought his friendship and assistance.' Geoffrey thus visited Richard's court and was impressed. He thus, 'reasoned with himself that a marriage to the duke's sister Hawisa would strengthen their bond even more ... Therefore, after pacts of friendship had been concluded, he eagerly proposed to marry her.'[13] By 1008, as noted already, Duke Richard had in turn married Count Geoffrey's sister, Judith. The marriage took place at Mont-Saint-Michel (or at least Richard met his bride there), which might indicate that the abbey was thought to stand in Norman territory by that date.[14] Richard certainly seems to have thought that the abbey should have been under his control, and was given the opportunity to make that clear when Abbot Mainard resigned in 1009. Although he was replaced by Hildebert, who had been a monk at the Mont and who was not clearly any more pro-Norman than his predecessor, Mainard's resignation allowed Duke Richard to be portrayed both as sanctioning the election of the new abbot and as doing so as a result of the petition of the community. The record of the election thus acknowledged and promoted the legitimacy of his rule, while perhaps alleviating the fears of the community about what Norman dominion might mean for them.[15]

Norman control over the abbey resulted in Norman patronage of the monks.

[11] The Latin is Theodericus: Robert of Torigni, 'Des ordres monastiques', ed. Delisle, ii. 194. Robert of Torigni, 'Des ordres monastiques', in *Chronique de Robert de Torigni, abbé de Mont-Saint-Michel*, ed. L. Delisle, 2 vols (Rouen, 1872–73), ii. 194.

[12] *RADN*, no. 34. For a more detailed and more complete discussion of the Montgommery family's estates see Thompson, 'The Norman aristocracy', 251–63 and Louise, *Bellême*, i. 389–91.

[13] Jumièges, ii. 14.

[14] This belief is suggested by a comparison with the arrangements made for the reception of Matilda of Flanders *c.* 1049, but the evidence is uncertain and Joëlle Quaghebeur thought otherwise: 'Havoise, Constance et Mathilde', p. 152.

[15] *RADN*, no. 12.

Count Robert of Avranches-Mortain and Duchess Gunnor both made donations to them *c.* 1015.[16] Duke Richard subsequently granted the community property in Verson in the Bessin, giving them an interest in a region much more firmly under his control and thus helping to tie them to his duchy. He also restored a string of properties around the bay to the monks, which were said in the diploma to have been first given to them by William Longsword.[17] In addition, Richard II was a patron of the bishop and canons of Avranches, and his success in building links with the cathedral and its community is perhaps revealed by the presence of bishops Norgod and Mangis (the latter's name suggests that he was a Breton) in a number of the witness lists of his acts from *c.* 1015.[18]

The two marriages with the Breton comital house were owing to the policies and campaigns of Richard I. They led in turn, although rather more unexpectedly, to an opportunity to establish Norman hegemony over Brittany. According to William of Jumièges, when Count Geoffrey decided to go on pilgrimage in 1008 he left his two sons, Alan and Odo, and Brittany, too, in the care of his wife and her brother, Duke Richard.[19] But Geoffrey died while returning from his pilgrimage, and the temporary arrangements that he had made for the administration of his county in his absence became rather more long-lived than he had intended. Moreover, the long minority of Geoffrey's sons gave Duke Richard an opportunity to stamp his authority on the Avranchin without the diversions that conflict with Brittany would have caused, and to shore up the border with the counts of Chartres and the emerging lords of Bellême with the help of Breton troops.

One further consequence of Richard's wardship of Geoffrey's heirs was Dudo's inclusion in his *De moribus* of the story of Charles the Simple's grant to Rollo of Brittany to provide the Normans with sustenance and service while Normandy was returned to cultivation, and of the oaths of fidelity later sworn to Longsword by the Bretons' leaders. It may be supposed that these stories were intended to legitimize Richard's claim to lordship over Brittany.[20] And although it is unlikely that many living in the county of Rennes ever got to hear Dudo's words, it is almost certain that the young Alan III and his brother were made aware of this

---

[16] *RADN*, no. 16.

[17] *RADN*, no. 49 and see also above, Chapter 1, pp. 55, 66–7.

[18] *RADN*, nos. 16, 17, 31, 35, 36, 47, 49. As none of these acts survive as an authentic original, it cannot be assumed that the bishop was present at the ducal court simply because his name appears in the witness lists. It could have been added later (see below, Chapter 7, pp. 372–4 for a discussion).

[19] Jumièges, ii. 28; Potts, *Monastic Revival*, p. 96; Quaghebeur, 'Havoise, Constance et Mathilde', pp. 147–8.

[20] Dudo, p. 168; *Dudo*, p. 49. See the Introduction, p. 6 above. The suggestion has previously been made by Cassandra Potts: Potts, *Monastic Revival*, p. 96.

propaganda while they were resident at their uncle's court in Rouen. That Bretons had been sent to help Richard in his war against Odo of Chartres *c.* 1013 would no doubt have come readily to the minds of those listening to Dudo's story, and would have demonstrated the reality of the claims he advanced.[21]

The opportunities for the further expansion and consolidation of his authority in the west of the duchy presented to Richard II by Geoffrey's (un)timely demise might have led him to focus his energies there for the next few years. His presence in the Cotentin at this time might have been noted across the Channel, too, as it was probably in 1008 that Æthelred II of the English launched an attack against the peninsula that was intended to 'inflict shame and harm' on Richard by devastating the land and taking him captive. William of Jumièges, the only authority for this tale, tells us that the plan was foiled when a certain Nigel 'gathered the knights of the Cotentin together with a multitude of common people' and defeated the English raiders.[22]

If this story is true, it would be Nigel's first appearance as a supporter of the duke. He was certainly the chief supporter of ducal authority in the north of the Cotentin during Richard II's reign. Nigel attested seven of Richard II's fifty surviving acts.[23] Although these documents do not have place-dates, and although his name *could* have been added to some of them later, it is likely that Nigel went to Upper Normandy to sign them.[24] One diploma for Marmoutier was probably issued at Rouen (in part because the bishop of Coutances attested it), while diplomata for Fécamp and Bernay were probably signed at the August court of 1025 held at Fécamp. Although many of these acts cannot be closely dated, Nigel's attestations seem to become more common from 1020. Indeed, none of the acts that he signed as *vicomte* must date from before that decade.

The importance of gaining Nigel's fidelity is suggested by the patronage that he received to win and/or maintain it. Aside from being awarded the office of *vicomte*, and with it the opportunity to administer the duke's demesne in the county, Nigel was given land. Six or seven of the thirty-seven vills in the *vicaria* of *Kelgenas* granted to Judith in dower later turn up in the hands of Nigel II and his successors, which constitutes an unusually large grant out of the demesne. Given

---

[21] Jumièges, ii. 22.

[22] Jumièges, ii. 10–12.

[23] *RADN*, nos. 23 (1013 × 1027), 31 (1017 × 1025), 33 (c. 1025), 34 (August 1025), 35 (1035), 49 (1022 × 1026), 55 (1025 × 1026). 'Nigel', without a title, attests another three: nos. 16 (1015), 17 (1015), and 43 (1015 × 1026).

[24] For the most part, however, there is no clear reason why his name should have been added to these acts later as most of them did not involve beneficiaries or lands in the west. The surviving originals (a number of them actually pseudo-originals) provide no grounds for thinking otherwise.

the later history of the family, it is almost certain that they had been granted to this first Nigel before his death *c.* 1042 rather than to his son.[25] Richard was also concerned to give Nigel a stake in the wider political community – and thus to make yet more certain of his loyalty – and so gave him, with Ralph of Tosny and his son Roger, custody of the castle at Tillières, on the southern frontier of the duchy, *c.* 1013.[26] It may be supposed that this patronage, his standing at court, and the figure that it allowed him to cut in the Cotentin were enough to keep him loyal to the duke. But while the grant of custody of Tillières suggests that Richard trusted Nigel to uphold his authority, it also had the advantage of removing Nigel from the Cotentin which might have given Richard the opportunity to establish his own authority there.

The construction of the castle at Tillières marked the last stage of a brief war with Count Odo II of Chartres. It is possible that Odo's marriage to Richard I's daughter Matilda *c.* 991 ushered in a period of cordial relations to begin with. This is suggested by the fact that in 995, despite their competition for influence over Brittany, Odo I had called on the Normans for help while fighting Fulk Nerra of Anjou.[27] But unfortunately the marriage ultimately reopened old wounds rather than healed them. Both Richard I and Odo I died in 996. Richard was succeeded by his son, Richard II, Odo I by his son, Odo II. Matilda died *c.* 1005 without children. Richard II, by then well established in his duchy, demanded the return of the southern part of the Evrecin from Odo. That was not something that the count was prepared to allow. War was the outcome, 'whereupon the duke, having brought together Breton and Norman forces, made a foray to the river Avre and built a stronghold (*castrum*) there called Tillières-sur-Avre'.[28] As just noted, Nigel of the Cotentin and Ralph of Tosny were given custody of the fortification and they subsequently fended off an attack by Odo and his allies from this new base.[29]

Richard, following the pattern laid down by his father, then called in Scandinavian allies as reinforcements. These men were not apparently put in the field, but the threat was such that the warring parties were brought to peace by

---

[25]   These are Tréauville, Flamanville, Benoistville, Neuville, Grosville, and Bricqueboscq (probably including Psalmonville). See M. Hagger, 'How the west was won: the Norman dukes and the Cotentin, *c.* 987–*c.* 1087', *JMH*, 38 (2012), Appendix, 48–55 for the descent of these vills to Nigel.

[26]   Jumièges, ii. 22. For the date of the foundation I rely on Bauduin, *Première Normandie*, p. 237.

[27]   Richer, ii. 390–2; Bauduin, *Première Normandie*, p. 184.

[28]   Jumièges, ii. 22.

[29]   His first attestation of a ducal act comes in 1014 when he signed Richard's diploma for Notre-Dame of Chartres (*RADN*, no. 15).

King Robert at Coudres, probably chosen as the location of this meeting because it was itself one of the places in dispute. By the agreement, Count Odo kept Dreux and its territory, although not for long, and Richard kept Tillières and 'the land he had seized with the stronghold'.[30] Tillières and its surrounding lordship, which were later given to the Crispin family, thus provides an example of how demesne vills might be acquired through conquest during military campaigns – something that can only be conjectured for much of the ducal demesne found along the Channel coast.

The agreement with Odo seems to be reflected in two grants made to the monks of Saint-Père of Chartres. The first was a grant of the church of Breteuil, now in the commune of Saint-Georges-Motel, which probably dates to the years before *c.* 1013.[31] The church is there said to be situated in the county of Evreux, as was the case with Walter of Dreux's earlier (and perhaps fabricated) grant of the same church.[32] A few years later, between 1021 and 1025, Richard II gave – perhaps more properly restored – to the monks of Chartres the church of Saint-Georges-Motel. It may be supposed that it had been lost in the fighting. There, in contrast to the wording of the two earlier acts, the church is said to have been in the Dreugesin.[33] It would appear from this that Richard II had accepted the terms of the agreement made with Odo, perhaps because he, too, had gained something in the war. But in this same act he also gave the monks of Chartres a stake in Normandy, granting them property in the Cotentin and at Caen, fisheries on the Seine and in the Lieuvin, and an exemption from paying tolls in all the markets of the duchy.[34]

Duke Richard thus used his demesne to give the monks of Chartres a vested interest in the maintenance of the peace between Normandy and Chartres. But he did not rely on their self-interest alone. Rather, Richard strengthened the defences of this section of the frontier shortly after the war with Count Odo by giving his brother, Archbishop Robert, the city of Evreux, and presumably the other ducal demesne in the county, along with a comital title.[35] His new county together with

[30] Jumièges, ii. 26. Odo lost Dreux to King Robert between 1015 and 1025 (Dunbabin, *France*, p. 195; Bauduin, *Première Normandie*, p. 186).
[31] *RADN*, no. 29. Fauroux dated the act 1015 × 1025 on the basis of the witness list. As the act does not survive as an original there is no reason to follow her here (see below, Chapter 7, pp. 372–5). If the argument advanced above is right, the act could not have been made later than *c.* 1013, given the agreement made at Coudres. The Breteuil of the act is now in the commune of Saint-Georges-Motel and should not be confused with the better known Breteuil-sur-Iton.
[32] *RADN*, no. 2.
[33] *RADN*, no. 32. Fauroux dated the act 1021 × 1025.
[34] *RADN*, no. 32.
[35] This transferred demesne probably included Gravigny as it was the subject of a later dispute. Duke Robert the Magnificent had given the church there to the monks of La

his archiepiscopal estates sandwiched the lordship dependent on Ivry-la-Bataille held by the ageing Count Rodulf, which would shortly pass to his son, Bishop Hugh of Bayeux. It is possible that the ambiguity created by handing these two bishops strategically important castles and secular lordships was intended further to defend the frontier, by implying that an attack on these lands would constitute an attack on ecclesiastical property.

A few years after the war with Count Odo, Richard's attention seems to have turned from his southern borders to his northern ones. The principal cause of this refocusing was probably Cnut's succession as king of the English in 1017. It might be supposed that Duke Richard would have welcomed this turn of events. The Normans and their dukes were still very much a part of the Scandinavian world in the tenth and early eleventh centuries.[36] That was why the beleaguered English king, Æthelred II, had made a treaty with Richard I in 991, by which the duke and king swore not to aid each other's enemies.[37] Immediately after Richard I's death, however, Viking raids on England began again. In 1000, Richard II, not long on his throne, welcomed a Viking fleet which had been raiding England into his 'kingdom'.[38] Soon afterwards, Æthelred responded by proposing a marriage to Richard's sister Emma. Which of the parties had sought the match is not revealed by the sources, but it was perhaps the English king who had the most to gain from it. The wedding took place in 1002, not long after Æthelred had been obliged to pay a Danegeld of £24,000, and it is likely that the marriage was 'designed to cut off Danish armies from Norman harbours'.[39] But Æthelred then undermined the advantages of his alliance with the Normans by his actions on St Brice's Day (13 November) that same year, when he commanded 'all the Danish people who were in England to be slain'.[40] William of Jumièges reported the repugnance felt in Normandy about the massacre, which led directly to a new agreement with the Danish King Swein whereby Rouen was opened as a refuge and a market for the sale of English plunder.[41] And then c. 1008, as noted above, Æthelred raided

---

Trinité-du-Mont but it was then claimed by Count Richard. The count subsequently restored it to the monks (*RADN*, no. 201).

[36] See L. W. Breese, 'The persistence of Scandinavian connections in Normandy in the tenth and early eleventh centuries', *Viator*, 8 (1977), 47–61, and below, Chapter 4, pp. 211–12.

[37] Malmesbury, *GR*, i. 278.

[38] *ASChr*, 'E', s.a. 1000; trans. Garmonsway, p. 133.

[39] *ASChr*, 'E', s.a. 1002; trans. Garmonsway, p. 133; P. Stafford, *Queen Emma and Queen Edith: Queenship and Women's Power in Eleventh-Century England* (Oxford, 1997), p. 220, quoted with approval by A. Williams, *Æthelred the Unready: The Ill-Counselled King* (London, 2003), p. 55.

[40] *ASChr*, 'E', s.a. 1002; trans. Garmonsway, p. 135.

[41] Jumièges, ii. 14–18.

the Cotentin in the hope of capturing Richard, presumably motivated by a desire for vengeance.

But as King Swein and his son Cnut gained ground against Æthelred, so Richard seems to have become more concerned about the detrimental effects that a neighbouring Danish kingdom might have on his duchy. In 1013, he welcomed the English king, his wife, their sons, and a daughter – his own sister, nephews, and niece – to Rouen. The boys would remain there for the rest of his reign. Æthelred, however, returned to England, possibly with Norman support, in 1014. It is at least likely that Dudo's passages concerning the assistance that Rollo gave to the beleaguered King Æthelstan was intended to suggest a parallel with the contemporary situation and thus acted as an encouragement for Edward and Alfred (who would almost certainly have heard the story at court) and a warning to Swein and Cnut (who might not have heard it at all), and the portrayal of Longsword and Richard I as saints might also have been intended as a riposte to Cnut's promotion of the cult of Edward the Martyr.[42] Portraying Rollo as a Dane forced into exile by the Danish king would also have put clear water between Richard and Cnut. That there *was* tension is indicated by Ralph Glaber who remarked that Cnut 'made a peace with Richard by which he married the duke's sister, Æthelred's widow'.[43] The marriage restored some of Richard's lost prestige, and would therefore have helped to reduce the tension, while for Cnut, as Michael Lawson suggested, it reduced the likelihood that Richard II would offer military support to his nephews (and adopted sons) Edward and Alfred who continued to live at his court.[44]

Another factor that might have turned the duke's attention to his northern border at this time was the growing influence of the count of Flanders on those regions that lay to the right of the river Bresle, and which thus marched with the north-eastern border of the duchy. While King Robert had gained control over Montreuil in 989 when he married the widow of Count Arnulf II of Flanders, and had retained the castle even when he repudiated her two or three years later, he was apparently not seen as a threat to ducal ambitions. Richard II hosted the king at Rouen in 1006 and fought with him against Baldwin IV of Flanders the same year.[45] He probably did so because, in contrast to the king, Baldwin *was* seen as

---

[42] See above, Chapter 1, p. 43 and below, Chapter 4, pp. 198–205.

[43] Glaber, p. 54. The author of the *Inventio* also noted Cnut's negotiations with Richard (*Inventio*, p. 36).

[44] Lawson, *Cnut*, pp. 85–6. Glaber's work suggests that relations did subsequently improve (see below, Chapter 11, p. 648).

[45] *Gesta pontificum Camaracensium*, ed. L. C. Bethmann, in *Monumenta Germaniae Historica, Scriptores 7* (Hanover, 1846), p. 414; E. A. Freeman, *The History of the Norman Conquest of England, its Causes and its Results*, vol. 1 (Oxford, 1873), p. 306; Bates, *Normandy*, p. 66.

a potential danger. He was the sort of aggressive and expansionist count likely to rekindle memories of the enmity of Arnulf of Flanders and its results, which would be highlighted by Dudo of Saint-Quentin *c.* 1015, at precisely the time that King Robert had changed political direction and was courting the count's goodwill. In 1019, Baldwin then seized the Ternois, a move that brought Flemish power almost to the borders of Ponthieu, although it was soon pushed back north a little.[46]

Just as the threat posed by Cnut had been neutralized by marriage, so too was that posed by the expansionist count of Flanders. Richard married one of his daughters to Count Baldwin IV. George Beech identified her as the Ainor who was to marry Vicomte Geoffrey of Thouars sometime after Baldwin's death in 1035.[47] Moreover, most likely in 1024, Godgifu, Richard II's niece and adopted daughter, was married to Count Drogo of the Vexin.[48] It is likely that this union was related to this same threat to Normandy's north-eastern frontier, for Drogo's lands in the Amienois and the Vexin made him a useful ally against Flanders. He would have been an equally useful ally against Odo II of Chartres, and perhaps the lords of Bellême. Indeed, a role against this last lord would explain why the dowry he received with Godgifu included the recently acquired Chambois on the Dives.[49]

At about the same time Godgifu married Drogo, Richard took a second wife. She was called Papia, and her family's estates lay in the Pays de Talou and Pays de Bray.[50] The marriage thus looks to have spoken to Richard's concerns about the vulnerability of his position in Upper Normandy once again. Richard would of course have been well informed about his bride, and there is some indication that he was already developing his relationship with the lords of Talou from *c.* 1010 when he had made a judgement on the composition of the lordship of Douvrend

[46] For the above see H. Tanner, *Families, Friends and Allies: Boulogne and Politics in Northern France and England c. 879–1160* (Leiden, 2004), pp. 74–8; Dunbabin, *France*, p. 217; Bauduin, *Première Normandie*, p. 286.

[47] Bauduin, *Première Normandie*, p. 305, who opined that the marriage to Baldwin was made after 1030; G. Beech, 'The participation of Aquitainians in the conquest of England, 1066–1100', *ANS*, 9 (1987), 8–9; noted Jumièges, ii. 29, n. 5.

[48] E. M. C. van Houts, 'Edward and Normandy', in *Edward the Confessor: The Man and the Legend*, ed. R. Mortimer (Woodbridge, 2009), p. 66.

[49] Torigni stated that he was also given Elbeuf on the Seine upstream from Rouen and that both places were given to Drogo in return for his permission to allow the Norman army to march over his lands on the way to Burgundy. It is much more likely to have been part of the dowry he received when he married Godgifu, however. Elisabeth van Houts dated the marriage to 7 April 1024 (RT, s.a. 1024; Delisle, i. 33; E. M. C. van Houts, 'Edward and Normandy', in *Edward the Confessor: The Man and the Legend*, ed. R. Mortimer (Woodbridge, 2009), pp. 65–6.

[50] Torigni dated the marriage to 1024 (RT, s.a. 1024; Delisle, i. 32; Howlett, p. 23).

and had sent representatives – Goscelin fitz Heddo, Richard the *vicomte* the son of Tescelin, Ralph the bishop's son, and Osbern of Auge – to dine with the archbishop in a wood publicly to display his lordship over it. They had been joined there by a number of other local figures including, at the head of the list, Walter and Wacelin of Envermeu.[51] It is possible that these two brothers were Papia's kinsmen, because she is known to have held land at Envermeu herself. But our knowledge of her and her family is too scanty for us to join up the various dots convincingly. We do know, however, that her mother was called Richildis, which was a Frankish name like hers, but that her two known brothers were called Osbern and Ansfrid, which are Scandinavian names. This choice of names might suggest that Papia's generation of the family was the product of a mixed Scandinavian-Frankish marriage, or else that the family had decided that one strategy to retain their power over the next generation was to adopt Scandinavian names to help their male children merge with the predominantly Scandinavian lords of Upper Normandy. Be that as it may, just as Herfast, Gunnor's brother, had waived his right to his family's estates by becoming a monk at Chartres, so Papia's brothers volunteered, or were convinced, to surrender their own rights in favour of their sister and to become monks at the abbey of Saint-Wandrille.[52] Papia was dowered with estates that included Perrièrs-sur-Andelle. That is revealed, first, by Richard II's grant of the church there to Saint-Ouen,[53] and, secondly, by the subsequent gift of the rest of the vill and its dependencies from Count William of Arques and his brother Malger, Papia's sons, in 1037 × 1048, which was said to be in conformity with her wishes.[54]

Other marriages made at about this same time further consolidated Richard's authority in the Caux and Talou. That is not to say that the lords of Upper Normandy had been entirely ignored previously – it was almost certainly during Richard I's reign that Osbern of Bolbec had been given Gunnor's sister Wevia as a wife – but we can perhaps see a new focus on developing relationships with them after *c.* 1020.[55] Thus Rodulf of Warenne, father of William of Warenne,

---

[51] *RADN*, no. 10.

[52] *RADN*, nos. 46, 46*bis*, 67 and see Bauduin, *Première Normandie*, p. 289. *RADN*, no. 46 concerns Montérolier, which was given to Saint-Wandrille when her brothers became monks there. *RADN*, no. 46*bis* adds more, recording grants at Carcuit and Gonneville-sur-Scie as well as that at Montérolier. *RADN*, no. 67 mentions the gift of Envermeu by Richeldis and her daughter Papia, which was given with the consent of Duke Richard II. On the marriage see also Searle, *PK*, pp. 141–2.

[53] *RADN*, no. 53.

[54] *RADN*, no. 112. It may originally have been part of Vascœuil (Musset, 'Saint-Ouen de Rouen', p. 121).

[55] Jumièges, ii. 268. The couple's children were the progenitors of the Giffard and Tancarville families.

married Beatrice, one of Gunnor's nieces, almost certainly during Richard's reign.[56] Much later, Rodulf and Beatrice made a gift to the monks of Saint-Pierre at Préaux of 'whatever he had in the same land, namely Vascœuil, in open land, in water, in wood'.[57] As Vascœuil was part of the ducal demesne, and as the gift was made jointly with Beatrice, it is likely that Rodulf's apparently substantial possessions here comprised part of his wife's dowry. It is possible that her dowry had also included part of Motteville. Rodulf gave the church here to the monks of La Trinité-du-Mont, while Duke William still held at least a third of the vill in demesne in 1060 × 1066.[58] Rodulf, and his family's tenants, can be found holding other estates to the east of Rouen and scattered across the Pays de Caux and Talou, as far east as the valley of the Yéres.[59] Their centre, it may be supposed, was at Varenne. The duke thereby acknowledged the role that might be played by the Warennes in upholding his authority in Upper Normandy.

Another of Gunnor's nieces married Richard *vicomte* of Rouen. We know very little of Richard himself, but he was the father of Lambert of Saint-Saëns who was in turn the father of Helias, the long-time protector of William Clito, and himself the husband of Robert Curthose's illegitimate daughter.[60] As Richard held his office from *c.* 1010 until *c.* 1030, it is likely that the marriage was made during the first two decades of Richard II's reign and that the *vicomté* was given to him as a result.

Once these marriages had been made, the lords concerned naturally brought their own *fideles* to recognize the duke's authority. For example, a certain Yves, who is described as Richard's faithful knight, is very likely to have had some pre-existing relationship with Papia's family. His lands neighboured theirs and he, too, chose to become a monk at Saint-Wandrille.[61] There was also a certain Rainald, who is the first known *vicomte* of Arques. Rainald's subsequent gifts to the monks of Fécamp comprised a public acknowledgement of his recognition of ducal authority, and reveal that he held lands close to Envermeu. Here, then, it seems we have another individual with a likely association with Papia's family,

---

[56] Jumièges, ii. 272. Robert of Torigni, in contrast, claimed that Walter of Saint-Martin was the father of Roger Mortemer and William of Warenne (Robert of Torigni, 'Des ordres monastiques', ed. Delise, ii. 204).

[57] *Ctl. Préaux*, A162.

[58] *Ctl. Trinité-du-Mont*, no. 29; also printed as *RADN*, no. 143. William's act is *RADN*, no. 220.

[59] The family held estates at Blosseville, Lescure, Emanville, Anglesqueville, and Flamanville (*Ctl. Trinité-du-Mont*, nos. 28–9; the latter is also printed as *RADN*, no. 143). Tenants held fiefs at Cailly, Chesney, Grandcourt, Pierrepont, Rosay-sur-Lieure, and Wanchy (C. P. Lewis, 'Warenne, William (I) de, first earl of Surrey', *Oxford Dictionary of National Biography*, vol. 57 (Oxford, 2003), p. 404).

[60] Jumièges, ii. 274 and n. 3.

[61] *RADN*, no. 30.

rewarded with high office, and who acknowledged the duke's authority through his gifts to a ducal abbey.[62]

Although Richard appears to have concentrated on building up his power in Upper Normandy for a period *c.* 1020, and Map 3 reveals that he did achieve some measure of success, he did not allow the situation elsewhere to stagnate. In particular, Richard seems to have pushed his authority south to the Dives, acquiring demesne at Exmes (with nearby Chauffour and Villebadin), Chambois, and Fel in the process.[63]

This advance of the duke's authority across the Lieuvin and into the Hiémois was recognized by the lords who were already established in the area concerned, as well as by Richard's neighbour to the south of that frontier, William of Bellême. That acknowledgement is evidenced by a story relating to Giroie, the progenitor of one of the founders of Saint-Evroult, which was retailed by Orderic in his *Ecclesiastical History*. The duke's estates around Bernay lay to the north of those belonging to a warrior called Heugon. Towards the end of his life, Heugon married his daughter to Giroie. Of Breton origin, Giroie lived during the reigns of Hugh Capet (987–96) and Robert the Pious (996–1031), and was a *fidelis* of William of Bellême. According to Orderic:

A powerful Norman knight named Heugon offered his only daughter in marriage to Giroie, with Montreuil-l'Argillé and Echauffour and all the land

[62] *RADN*, no. 54. The act reveals that Rainald held property in Saint-Aubin-sur-Scie, 'Appasilva', Tourville-la-Chapelle, and Saintigny (cne. Freulleville), as well as in Arques. Rainald first appears in an act recording a judgement made by Richard II concerning Douvrend. Fauroux dated the act 996 × 1007, but J.-M. Bouvris suggested that those dates should apply only to the first part of the act, and that the judgment of Richard's court mentioned in it was made between 1010 and 1026 (*RADN*, no. 10; J.-M. Bouvris, 'Contribution à une étude de l'institution vicomtale en Normandie au XIe siècle. L'exemple de la partie orientale du duché: les vicomtes de Rouen et de Fécamp', in *Autour du pouvoir ducal normand, X^e–XIIe siècles*, ed. L. Musset, J.-M. Bouvris, and J.-M. Maillefer (Caen, 1985), p. 157, n. 42). If Rainald's appointment was related to Richard's marriage to Papia, then the judgement could be even more closely dated *c.* 1024 × 1026. These arguments for redating this part of the act, however, depend on the reference found within the report to the property being held for thirty years or more as a reference to a legal rule rather than a reflection of reality. Otherwise, the plea must date from no later than 1007 – thirty years before Archbishop Robert's death.

[63] Chambois was given to Drogo of the Vexin, probably in 1024, as noted above p. 88 and n. 49. For Exmes see Jumièges, ii. 274; Orderic, ii. 46–8; iii. 268, 310–12; vi. 32–6; RT, s.a. 1123, 1135; Delisle, i. 165, 199; Howlett, pp. 107, 128; J, Yver, 'Les châteaux forts en Normandie jusqu'au milieu du XIIe siècles', *BSAN*, 53 (1955), 35; A. Renoux, 'Châteaux et residences fortifiées des ducs de Normandie aux Xe et XIe siècles', in *Les Mondes Normands (XIIIe–XIIe siècle)*, ed. H. Galinié (Caen, 1989), 114; *RADN*, no. 231; *Regesta: William*, nos. 59, 61.

dependent on them as her dower. When Heugon died a little while afterwards, Giroie entered into possession of all his fiefs, but his betrothed died an
untimely death before the marriage. To legalize this William of Bellême took
Giroie to Richard duke of the Normans at Rouen, and the generous duke,
recognizing his valour, received him favourably and granted him all the land
of Heugon by hereditary tenure.[64]

Bellême's suggestion that Giroie should seek the duke's permission to inherit
these lands, and Giroie's willingness to do so, reveals that both men recognized
that Richard had jurisdiction here, or at least that without his permission to
inherit Giroie could not be certain that he would be able to hold on to these
estates. That recognition reveals that Richard's power was thought to be effective
even at the very periphery of his duchy, affirms that Normandy was created lordship by lordship, and indicates that there was a border that could be identified,
even if it might comprise a zone rather than a line. The new political reality was
also reflected in Giroie's decision to move Heugon's erstwhile estates out of the
diocese of Sées and into that of Lisieux. The former was a possession of the house
of Bellême, while the latter was in Norman hands.[65]

   But Richard was not content to limit his authority to the north of the Dives.
Later in his reign, most likely c. 1020, he pushed through the forest of Gouffern
to the river Orne, grabbing Almenèches, Argentan (with members at Chiffreville,
Coulandon, Mauvaisville, and Sarceaux),[66] and nearby Ecouché.[67] These vills had
all been gained by 1025, and Almenèches at least had been taken from William,
lord of Bellême.[68] After Richard's campaigns, Bellême marched with Normandy
along the river Orne as far north as its junction with the Noireau, turning south-
west just south of that latter river, and then following the indeterminate edge
of the county of Mortain.[69] Evidence that the lordship had once been larger is

---

[64] Orderic, ii. 22. For a more detailed inventory of Heugon's lands see *RADN*, no. 122;
   Orderic, ii. 22–4, 34–6. They are included among the lands transferred with duke's
   permission on Map 3.

[65] Orderic, ii. 26. Orderic's explanation for the boundary change was probably misin-
   formed or deceptive.

[66] *RADN*, no. 52.

[67] *Regesta: William*, no. 59; Orderic, iv. 184–6.

[68] G. H. White, 'The first house of Bellême', *Transactions of the Royal Historical Society*,
   22 (1940), 68–80; K. Thompson, 'Family and influence to the south of Normandy in
   the eleventh century: the lordship of Bellême', *JMH*, 11 (1985), 215–17; Louise, *Bellême*, i.
   114–17.

[69] It is the foundation deed of the abbey that William of Bellême founded at Lonlay-
   l'Abbaye between 1015 and 1025 that notes a 'commarchia' with Mortain, which might
   have comprised the forests of Lande-Purrie and Sylve Drue and which also reveals just

provided by the fact that William of Bellême still held some property north of the Orne *c.* 1025.[70] Duke Richard was even able to stage at least one raid as far south as the Sarthe during which he took the town of Alençon.

Bellême was seriously, if perhaps only temporarily, weakened by Richard's aggression. He lost possession of the bishopric of Sées, allowing the installation of the Norman Radbod Fleitel as bishop.[71] He was also required to make restoration of various properties to the new Norman bishop, which are listed in a diploma William made *c.* 1025. That diploma was attested by both King Robert and Duke Richard. Kathleen Thompson interpreted this double corroboration as suggesting that 'William [was] uncertain which power could effectively guarantee his act',[72] but it is more likely to reveal the new political reality that Bellême faced. Some of the restored properties lay south of the Orne and so were theoretically held from the king, but Chailloué north of the Orne at least was now seen to be within Normandy, so that the duke's assent was also required. In addition, although Alençon was restored to Bellême – Richard could hardly have held such an isolated outpost in the face of Bellême's hostility – William was obliged to acknowledge that he held it from the duke as a *beneficium*.[73]

The circumstances surrounding the transfer of Heugon's lands, the double attestation (by king and duke) of William of Bellême's act for Sées, and the need to redraw a diocesan boundary indicate that Normandy had become a recognized and recognizable territory by the end of Richard II's reign. That was also reflected in the acts and narratives produced from the 1020s. Normandy first appears by that name in ducal *acta* only at that date, while Adémar of Chabannes, writing *c.* 1034, remarked that what had once been known as the march between Francia and Brittany was now a corner of Normandy.[74]

That growing sense of identity was perhaps also reflected in the increasing number of donations that lords both great and small were making to the ducal abbeys of Upper Normandy, and by their efforts to enjoy the good will of the communities that they patronized. Among them was Emma of Ponchardon, who

how far east the counts of Avranches-Mortain had by then driven their power (AD Orne, H 462, cited in Louise, *Bellême*, i. 299, 306). The possible location of the border is also discussed at length in Louise, *Bellême*, i. 305–10. In sum, the lordship may have covered between 2,500 and 3,500 km² (Louise, *Bellême*, i. 336).

[70] For a map of known Bellême property within the *pagus* of Sées, both north and south of the Orne, see Louise, *Bellême*, i. 319.

[71] Radbod was bishop from *c.* 1025 until *c.* 1045 (D. S. Spear, *The Personnel of the Norman Cathedrals during the Ducal Period, 911–1204* (London, 2006), pp. 271–2).

[72] *RADN*, no. 33; Thompson, 'Family and influence', 216.

[73] Implied by the report of the events of Robert's reign: Jumièges, ii. 50.

[74] Adémar de Chabannes, *Chronique*, ed. J. Chavanon (Paris, 1897), p. 148; translation in van Houts, *Normans*, p. 212. See also below, Chapter 5, p. 286.

gave property in Breuil-en-Auge, on the Touques to the north of Lisieux, and Ticheville, on the same river south of that city, to the monks of Saint-Wandrille in 1025 × 1026.[75] Her toponym, if accurately reported by the monk who wrote the later *Inventio et miracula sancti Vulfrani*, suggests that her influence would have been strongest at the southern limit of the Lieuvin. The author also added the gift of an estate at La Croisille and noted that Emma's donations were made for the reconstruction of the monks' dormitory. He recorded, too, that she 'replaced with silver what had previously been made of wood', which presumably means that she provided the monks with precious vessels for their services, or at least the cash with which to have them made. She died as a nun close to the abbey in 1036, and was buried in the chapel in which she had lived.[76] Here, then, was a native of the Lieuvin who bought into the idea, and the religious life, of Normandy. The dukes of the Normans were therefore not just winning battles for territory, but also the more important one for the hearts and minds of their new subjects.

Richard III and Robert the Magnificent, 1026–35

Richard III ruled for just a single year before an untimely death that later writers put down to poisoning. In that year he defeated a rebellion instigated by his brother from Falaise in the Hiémois, which seems to have lacked general support and was quickly put down, and married a lady called Adela. Adela has often been supposed to have been a daughter of King Robert the Pious.[77] There is no strong evidence to support this view, however. The basis for the supposition seems to rest on two planks. First, there was the pope's hostility to the marriage of William the Bastard and Matilda of Flanders, which, *if* based on consanguinity, might be explained in this way.[78] Secondly, there is the survival of seventeenth-century transcripts of the document setting out Adela's dower in at least two cartularies (both lost) from the college of Saint-Pierre d'Aire-sur-la-Lys, which was founded by Count Baldwin V, Adela's husband. In the absence of the manuscripts, however, the copies could have been added to the cartularies at any time before their seventeenth-century transcription, in the same mistaken belief that Baldwin's wife had previously been married to Richard. The evidence in favour of the identification of Richard's bride with the king's daughter is thus weak. Moreover, William of Jumièges provided good evidence against it when he wrote

---

[75] *RADN*, no. 55.
[76] *Inventio*, pp. 43–4.
[77] For example by Musset, 'Actes inédits III. Bourgueil', 33; Bauduin, 'Du bon usage de la dos dans la Normandie ducale', p. 432; Neveux, *A Brief History of the Normans*, pp. 98, 107; Crouch, *The Normans*, p. 46.
[78] Crouch, *The Normans*, pp. 71–2.

that Adela was still in the cradle when she was betrothed to Baldwin.[79] It may be supposed that he made that comment not because she had earlier been married to Richard but rather to remind his readers that William the Bastard's wife, Matilda, was a kinswoman of the reigning French king.

The dower settled on Adela suggests something of the developments that had taken place in the Cotentin during Richard II's reign with regard to the advance of that duke's authority and the location and organization of his demesne. Richard endowed her with a sweep of property and rights located almost exclusively in the peninsula.[80] She was given the city and county of Coutances, except for the land of Archbishop Robert (which was probably at Varreville and Saint-Marcouf); the castles that had been built at Cherbourg, Le Homme, and Brix;[81] the estate centres (*curtes*) at Ver, Cérences, Agon, Valognes, Esglandes, Percy, Moyon, and Hambye and their districts (*pagi*); the abbey at Portbail; and the vill of Caen in the Bessin with all its appurtenances.

The three castles were all in the peninsula proper. Le Homme was situated in the marshes, while Cherbourg and Brix were at the northern tip of the Cotentin. The fact that Richard II had built these castles suggests that he had faced some resistance to the imposition of his authority there, perhaps even from his *fidelis*, Nigel. Their absence further south indicates that domination had been effected more peaceably in that area (as might be expected as this was Gunnor's family's area of influence). The settlement also implies that ducal control had now been imposed across the Cotentin as a whole, and although the terminology employed in the settlement is unusual, and not always correctly used, it seems to reveal the existence of ducal estate centres across the county.[82]

Richard still had the resources for the location of Adela's dower to have been the result of a choice.[83] That choice suggests that Adela was to act as Richard's representative in the Cotentin. Gunnor's career provided a ready model for Richard III and Adela to follow, and as Gunnor was an old woman in 1026 it may be

---

[79] Elisabeth van Houts reached the same conclusion: Jumièges, ii. 52 and p. 53, n. 2.

[80] *RADN*, no. 58. For a discussion of the composition of the dower see Searle, *PK*, pp. 129–30; Musset, 'Les domaines de l'époque franque', 96–7; Bates, *Normandy*, pp. 152–3; Bauduin, 'Du bon usage de la dos', pp. 438–9.

[81] There is no evidence that the dukes constructed the castle at La Roche, further south, or that it was in existence at this date (E. van Torhoudt, 'Les sieges du pouvoir des Néels, vicomtes dans le Cotentin', in *Les lieux de pouvoir au Moyen Age en Normandie et sur ses marges*, ed. A.-M. Flambard Héricher (Caen, 2006), pp. 15–24).

[82] These are discussed below, Chapter 10, pp. 593–6. For the use of Carolingian terms to demonstrate the (possible) continuity of Carolingian administrative traditions see, for example, Brown, 'Some observations, pp. 145–63; Bates, *Normandy*, pp. 12–13, 32; and Tabuteau, *Transfers*, p. 5 and n. 36 (pp. 273–4).

[83] See Hagger, 'How the west was won', 30–1.

supposed that the grant of Coutances – apparently her base of operations when out of Rouen – did not cause much or any resentment.[84] With no other close kin to turn to – his brother Robert was already established in the Hiémois – Adela was Duke Richard's only option for a close family agent in the county of Coutances, and if she had not been intended to serve as his representative, then why surrender (even if only for her lifetime) his immediate authority over all this land to her?[85] It gave her the incentive and authority to strengthen ducal authority there, in the same way that the Norman counts had been given the ducal demesne in their counties to strengthen and defend Norman rule in them. It is easy to interpret the alienation of demesne as signalling a retreat or increasing, rather than shrinking, the distance of the duke from the peripheries of his duchy, but lordship was lordship over men (and women), not land . The presence of powerful, loyal supporters in Eu, Evreux, Mortain, and now Coutances would thus have brought ducal rule closer to, and made it more effective in, those zones.

When Richard died he was succeeded by his brother Robert rather than his illegitimate son, Nicholas.[86] The account in the *Gesta Normannorum ducum* reveals that Robert was elected, presumably by a majority and presumably in preference to Richard III's young illegitimate son, Nicholas. Archbishop Robert of Rouen seems to have thrown his weight behind Robert, and might have carried the day for him. But the archbishop was quickly to become disillusioned by his successful candidate's behaviour, not least because in 1027 or 1028 Duke Robert besieged him at Evreux and forced him into exile in France. Fulbert of Chartres sent a letter

---

[84] Simon MacLean suggested that certain places were associated with queenship (S. MacLean, 'Making a difference in tenth-century politics: Athelstan's sisters and Frankish queenship', in *Frankland: the Franks and the world of the early middle ages. Essays in honour of Dame Jinty Nelson*, ed. P. Fouracre and D. Ganz (Manchester, 2008), pp. 187–8), so that possession of Coutances *might* have been necessary to demonstrate Adela's power in the Cotentin in the mid eleventh century. Wedmore in Somerset might similarly have been a possession of English queens (see the note to *Regesta: William*, no. 289).

[85] It is not clear how much control Richard would have had over these lands during Adela's lifetime. Absolute rights over dower might no longer have accrued to the wife after the early eleventh century, although Bauduin's discussion of Adela's case assumes that she was the daughter of King Robert (see n. 77 above). It seems that any attempt permanently to alienate the land would have required the consent of her heirs, as was the case with Gunnor's gift to Mont-Saint-Michel (Bauduin, 'Du bon usage de la dos', pp. 445–8). That, however, would still leave Adela with direct control over these estates and rights during her lifetime. It might be noted, by way of comparison, that in England the scribe compiling Domesday Book kept Queen Edith's dower lands separate from the rest of the royal demesne, suggesting that she had enjoyed complete control over the property until her death in 1075 (Stafford, *Queen Emma and Queen Edith*, pp. 123–7).

[86] See below, Chapter 6, pp. 317–19.

to the archbishop, offering his sympathy 'over the injuries with which you have been unjustly afflicted ... from one who owed himself and his all to your good faith'.[87] It is his words that imply the archbishop's leading role in Robert's succession. The archbishop subsequently placed Normandy under an interdict, which only Bishop Hugh of Avranches seems to have been prepared to break,[88] with the result that Duke Robert 'not long afterwards recalled him from France, restored his former honour to him, and ... thereafter sought his advice and for the rest of his life remained faithful to him'.[89]

What precisely led to this breach is not known. The most likely cause was that Duke Robert had already embarked on the widespread despoliation of Church property that would be remembered and condemned by the communities who had suffered from it, and that he failed to prevent his *fideles* from following his lead. But that does not mean that Robert's actions were necessarily entirely wanton. What was later presented as youthful folly could have equally been a real need to find lands with which to reward and maintain his supporters. His act of restitution for the monks of Fécamp implies that all the lands he returned had been used to endow knights, while Ticheville, donated to the monks of Saint-Wandrille by Emma of Pontchardon as noted above, had been given to one of the duke's knights called Haimo.[90] In this case, too, the grant seems to have been strategic. Ticheville was on the left bank of the Touques, at the very south of the Lieuvin, and Haimo might have been given it because there was no alienable demesne closer to the border with Bellême at Sées (some 24 miles away). But it was also close to the lands now held by Giroie, who might have been seen as a potential fifth-columnist, and those held by Roger I of Montgommery, who remained something of a loose cannon.

Indeed, Montgommery was one of those who was said to have taken advantage of the atmosphere of the first years of Duke Robert's reign to seize lands and usurp

---

[87] Fulbert, *Letters*, no. 126.

[88] Bishop Hugh blessed Abbot John as abbot of Fécamp in 1028 (*Normannia Monastica*, ii. 105–10). That the pontiffs of sees located closer to the abbey did not do so might indicate that they were not prepared to break the interdict, which might in turn suggest that the bishop of Avranches could still claim to preside over a see not entirely located within the duchy.

[89] Jumièges, ii. 48. There is no suggestion in the *Deeds of the Archbishops of Rouen* that Archbishop Robert was permitted to return only on condition that he renounced his worldly lifestyle, despite the assertion to that effect made by Lifshitz, *Pious Neustria*, p. 187.

[90] Fécamp lost Argences, Heudebouville, Maromme, 'Wasa', and a house in Caen, and two churches that had belonged to the monastery of Montivilliers, which had not yet been refounded as a nunnery (*RADN*, nos. 70). Saint-Wandrille temporarily lost both of Emma's earlier gifts, Le Breuil-an-Auge (*RADN*, no. 85) and Ticheville (*RADN*, no. 95).

rights from monasteries for his own benefit. It is possible, although not certain, that he took lands from the monks of Fécamp at Troarn and Almèneches,[91] and his subsequent foundations of monastic houses on these sites might support that view, especially as his house at Troarn followed Fécamp's liturgical practices. He certainly destroyed the market at Vimoutiers that had been given to the monks of Jumièges by Richard II, replacing it with his own at Montgommery a few miles down the valley of the Vie. Duke Robert was obliged to intervene to uphold family honour and to maintain the strength of his rule, and Montgommery subsequently agreed to restore the market at Vimoutiers to the monks and to pay them a rent in order to retain his own market.[92]

Perhaps because he had spent his early career in the Hiémois, or perhaps because the south and south-west of the duchy were those areas where ducal power remained weakest, Robert concentrated on building up his authority there. William of Jumièges cast the lords of Bellême as his archenemies. Even more than the Bretons, they were the target of his aggression. Robert's principal objective thus seems to have been to control William of Bellême, who appears to have been unwilling to accept the strengthening of the duke's control around Alençon. Indeed, such was William's resentment that

> at the fortress of Alençon which he held by right as a benefice, he rashly started a rebellion and made great effort to cast off the yoke of service from his obstinate neck. In order to curb William's fierce insolence, the duke immediately hastened to Alençon with a large force of soldiers and besieged him in the stronghold which supported his rebellion until finally he came out on bare feet asking forgiveness while by way of expiation he carried his horse's saddle on his shoulders.[93]

His ritual humiliation in the Frankish manner speaks loudly of the cultural differences between Franks and Normans and thus the political position of the lordship of Bellême.[94] But Duke Robert had made his point, and so William of Bellême was

---

[91]   See above, *infra*, p. 81.

[92]   *RADN*, no. 74.

[93]   Jumièges, ii. 50.

[94]   Jim Bradbury seems to suggest that the knights carried their saddles because their horses had died during the siege (J. Bradbury, *The Medieval Siege* (Woodbridge, 1992), p. 65). This is possible, but in Francia the carrying of saddles was symbolic of surrender, and a ritual sign of submission, known as *harmiscara*. See, for example, M. DeJong, 'Power and humility in Carolingian society: the public penance of Louis the Pious', *Early Medieval Europe*, 1 (1992), 45–50 and J. Hemming, '*Sellan gestare*: saddle-bearing punishments of medieval Europe and the case of Rhinnon', *Viator*, 28 (1997), 45–64.

forgiven and the castle was restored to him. Robert, it seems, recognized that he, like his father, could not hold these places himself in the face of Bellême's hostility, and so hoped to rule as his overlord.

Bellême remained restive, however, and shortly afterwards he and his sons raided Normandy. They were defeated by the duke's household troops at Blavou. One of William's sons died in the fighting. William himself is said to have died shortly after hearing the news. Duke Robert, on the other hand, had demonstrated his own strength by defeating his local rival. The loyalty of those men living north of Alençon who had once supported the Bellême family must now have begun to waver. Robert strengthened his authority by displaying it, planting his supporters in the region. Perhaps the most important of them was Gerard Fleitel. Originally from Upper Normandy, he apparently had some connection with Papia's family, and his brother Radbod had been bishop of Sées since *c.* 1025.[95] Duke Robert gave Gerard his demesne manors at Ecouché and Gacé, perhaps before the two men went on pilgrimage to Jerusalem together, although Chambois and, most likely, neighbouring Fel could only have been added in 1035 between the deaths of Count Drogo of the Vexin, who had held Chambois since 1024, and that of Duke Robert himself.[96] It is worth stressing that the Fleitel brothers were the principal *fideles* of Duke Robert in the southern Hiémois. It was only during the reign of William the Bastard that the Montgommery family would become pre-eminent here.

Jumièges wrote expressly that it was while Robert was engaged in his campaigns against Bellême that Bishop Hugh of Bayeux rebelled against him. By the time of Richard II's death in 1026, the duke's cousin was no longer the only anchor of the duke's authority in the Bessin, despite the likelihood that he still dominated the county. Ralph Taisson, originally from Anjou, had been planted on at least some of Judith's old dower in the Cinglais by Richard II.[97] In addition, other local men appeared at the duke's court during Robert's reign. Ansketil of Briquessart,

---

[95] The relationship with Papia's family is suggested by the location of Gerard's estates in Upper Normandy, by the fact that he retired to become a monk at Saint-Wandrille (*RADN*, no. 108), and by the fact that some of his lands were later held from Count William of Arques (AD Seine-Maritime, 16H14, fo. 319r (Ctl. Saint-Wandrille); D. Bates, 'The Conqueror's adolescence', *ANS*, 25 (2003), 11). Radbod's son, William, would later become abbot of Saint-Etienne of Caen and then archbishop of Rouen and that, too, suggests a link with the duke's family. One of Gerard's sons, William, became bishop of Lisieux *c.* 1046 (Orderic, ii. 78; Spear, *The Personnel of the Norman Cathedrals during the Ducal Period, 911–1204* (London, 2006), p. 133).

[96] This attractive suggestion is made by van Houts, 'Edward and Normandy', p. 67.

[97] See L. Musset, 'Actes inédits du XIᵉ siècle: V. Autour des origines de Saint-Etienne de Fontenay', *BSAN*, 56 (1963), 11–41. The vills in question certainly included Thury-Harcourt, Esson, Caumont-sur-Orne, Saint-Rémi, Cingal (now cne. Moulines), Fresney-le-Vieux, and Saint-Aignan-de-Crasmesnil.

the first known *vicomte* of the Bessin, attested four of Duke Robert's acts, while Richard of Creully attested two.[98] Nonetheless, Bishop Hugh remained the single most important figure in the Bessin, and so it must have seemed contrary to all reason to him that the duke should disregard his advice. His rebellion, however, centred not on Bayeux but on his castle at Ivry on the river Eure, which was easier to defend and to which outside help could more quickly come. And so Hugh 'by cunning and trickery amply fortified the castle of Ivry with arms and food. After installing a garrison there he left for France to hire soldiers to help him defend it stoutly.'[99] He did not succeed. Duke Robert quickly took the castle and retained it in his own hands. And while Bishop Hugh did return to his diocese, it is not clear that he recovered the influence at court that he had once had. He *seems* to have attested far fewer ducal acts than had previously been the case, although the frequent omission of the name of a bishop's see from witness lists means that it is not always possible to tell which of the Bishop Hughs is witnessing which act.[100] Moreover, the agreement that Hugh made with the monks of Fécamp for a life lease of Argences was so one-sided, and the cost so punitive, that it speaks of a smouldering resentment, on the duke's part at least.[101] No wonder Hugh did not attempt to seek the restoration of property lost during his exile until after Robert's death.[102]

Between 1030 and 1032, Bishop Hugh's influence in the Bessin was further undermined by the establishment of an outpost of ducal authority in the form of the abbey of Cerisy-la-Forêt.[103] This was one of the more important events of Robert the Magnificent's reign so far as Lower Normandy was concerned. The location of the abbey, as well as the lands given to it,[104] reveals that the duke's power had now been established in the west of the county as far as the marshes of the Cotentin, although it is possible that this was a very recent development,

---

[98]   *RADN*, nos. 65, 69, 76, 80 (Ansketil); 65, 72 (Richard of Creully).

[99]   Jumièges, ii. 52.

[100] The position of Bishop Hugh at Robert's court is obscured by the frequent omission of bishops' dioceses from their attestations and the existence of more than one bishop named Hugh in Robert's Normandy. If, as seems likely, 'Bishop Hugh' should be identified as Hugh of Bayeux, then he actually attested more of Robert's *acta* than any individual save Archbishop Robert of Rouen and Goscelin the *vicomte*. 'Bishop Hugh of Bayeux', however, attests just three times.

[101] *RADN*, no. 71.

[102] *Livre Noir*, i. 27–9 (no. 21); L. Delisle, *Histoire du château et des sires de Saint-Sauveur –le-Vicomte, suivi des pièces justificatives* (Paris, 1867), preuves, pp. 13–16 (no. 13).

[103] *RADN*, no. 64. The date of the foundation is discussed in Potts, *Monastic Revival*, pp. 31–2 and V. Gazeau, *Normannia monastica: prosopographie des abbés bénédictins (X^e–XIIe siècle)*, 2 vols (Caen, 2007), ii. 59 and n. 1.

[104] *RADN*, no. 64.

and that Cerisy had only come into Robert's possession after Gunnor's death in the previous year or so. The first, short-lived, abbot of Cerisy was a monk of Saint-Ouen in Rouen, whose monastery also housed the only relic in Normandy of St Vigor, Cerisy's patron saint.[105] He was replaced *c.* 1033 by Aumode, previously abbot of Mont-Saint-Michel.

Further west, Robert had given his demesne at La Croix-Avranchin, a vill most likely first taken by Richard I, to a knight called Adelelm.[106] This was close to the increasingly 'hot' frontier with Brittany. Trouble had been brewing from around 1025, when Alan III gained his majority and began to rule Brittany in his own right. He distanced himself from the dukes, supporting a rival candidate for the abbacy of Mont-Saint-Michel and marrying Bertha, the daughter of Odo II of Chartres, in 1029. The result was that Robert the Magnificent led at least two campaigns against him. The first occurred *c.* 1030. Robert built a castle at Chéruel on the Couesnon, 'in order to fortify the Norman frontier and to curb the arrogance of this most presumptuous man'. The campaign thus provides further evidence that selected vills might be seized during campaigns and then added to the demesne – there is no evidence that Chéruel had been in the demesne before Robert built his castle there. Duke Robert then invaded Brittany, ravaged the area around Dol, and returned home. 'Alan, wishing to avenge the injury inflicted upon him, instantly set out after him with a large army in order to devastate the county of Avranches. There he was met by Nigel and Alured, called the Giant, guardians of the fortress, with their men in battle.' The Normans won the day.[107]

Robert's second Breton campaign seems to have happened almost by accident. Almost twenty years after Cnut's coronation as king of the English, it must have been becoming clear that the dukes had little to fear from their neighbour across the Channel after all. Indeed, Robert's lack of concern about the ageing king was such that he was not afraid to insult him. Ralph Glaber reported that: 'as is well known, he had married a sister of Cnut, king of the English, but he so disliked the woman that he divorced her.'[108] It is likely that the marriage had been intended by Cnut to maintain Norman neutrality on the matter of the English throne, which suggests that while the duke's fears had been alleviated the king's had not – perhaps because he was growing concerned about his succession. And Cnut was right to be worried. William of Jumièges reported that *c.* 1032 Robert, acting on behalf of Edward and Alfred, 'sent envoys to King Cnut with the request that since their exile had been sufficiently long he should be merciful and return to them,

---

[105] Herrick, *Imagining the Sacred Past*, pp. 43–4 and see below, Chapter 4, pp. 209–11.
[106] *RADN*, no. 110.
[107] Jumièges, ii. 56–8.
[108] Glaber, p. 204.

however late, what was theirs for love of him. King Cnut rejected these sound warnings and sent the envoys back empty handed.' His refusal led, we are told, to the preparation of an invasion fleet, and while there is some corroborating evidence for this plan, in the event the fleet was used to attack the Bretons instead.[109]

> The duke ordered one part of the fleet to go to Brittany to lay it waste by sword and fire. He himself gathered an army of mounted soldiers and prepared to attack by land. Aware of this serious threat from two sides, Alan sent envoys to his and the duke's uncle, Robert, archbishop of the Normans, requesting him to come immediately. When Alan had told him about the terrible destruction in Brittany and the ruthless expedition of the aggressive duke, the archbishop acted as a mediator and took him to Mont-Saint-Michel imploring the duke, who was about to invade Brittany, to be merciful.[110]

The result of the two campaigns was not just an acknowledgement by Count Alan of his subservience, but also the ending of a related dispute at Mont-Saint-Michel that had begun in 1023 and which had seen Count Alan support the Manceau Abbot Aumode against the claims of the would-be Norman abbot, Thierry. After the campaign, Aumode was removed, although not disgraced. Perhaps unexpectedly, and as noted above, he found himself made abbot of the duke's recently founded abbey at Cerisy-la-Forêt. It is likely, however, that some force had been applied to obtain Aumode's surrender. An act of Duke Robert speaks of lands being returned, rather than confirmed, to the monks following the campaign.[111] This might reveal no more than the losses and disruption perpetrated by Duke Robert's army as it marched to the border, but it might equally suggest a show of strength intended to bend the monks to the duke's will. In any event, Count Alan seems not to have borne a grudge, and the renewal of cordial relations between Brittany and Normandy is clearly revealed by the count's position in the minority administration that Robert left behind when he went on pilgrimage to Jerusalem in 1035. Indeed, Alan would meet his death defending ducal interests against the insurgent Roger I of Montgommery c. 1040.[112]

The campaigns against both the lord of Bellême and the count of Brittany seem principally to have been intended to consolidate the achievements of Richard II,

---

[109] Jumièges, ii. 76; Lawson, *Cnut*, pp. 86–7, 110; S. Keynes, 'The Æthelings in Normandy', *ANS*, 13 (1991), 193–4. The date of these events is uncertain, but 1032 is supported by the style of *marchio* awarded to Duke Robert in his foundation charter for Cerisy (see also below, Chapter 5, p. 272).

[110] Jumièges, ii. 78.

[111] *RADN*, no. 65.

[112] Orderic, iv. 76.

rather than to conquer new land or gain new submission. But there were some related gains. Chéruel has been mentioned already, but in addition the second campaign against Brittany seems to have brought the Channel Islands under Robert's control. The only mention of any land in the islands in ducal *acta* before Robert's reign comprises a confirmation of some property on Jersey which had been given to the monks of Mont-Saint-Michel by Peter the monk, and which does not therefore indicate that the duke had gained effective control over the island.[113] Duke Robert, however, granted half of Guernsey to the monks of Mont-Saint-Michel, almost certainly between 1033 and 1035.[114] Contrary to Robert's usual reputation, the grant constituted the despoliation of a layman in favour of a monastery. The property transferred to the monks seems previously to have been granted to Ansketil of Briquessart, *vicomte* of the Bessin. The other half of the island was given to Nigel of the Cotentin, who was thus given a further incentive to remain loyal to the duke.[115] Jersey, in contrast, was retained in demesne.

And there were diplomatic successes further afield, too. The marriage between Baldwin IV and Robert's sister Ainor seems to have ensured good relations between the duke and the count for the duration of Robert's reign. Certainly when Baldwin IV of Flanders sought refuge in Normandy *c.* 1030, after he had been chased from his county by his son, the future Baldwin V, he received both succour and aid. Robert subsequently left Normandy on his brother-in-law's behalf, 'like a fearsome whirlwind', ravaged Flanders, and arrived before the castle at Chocques which was burned down around the garrison. The rebellion collapsed and Baldwin IV was restored.[116]

Then, in 1033, in another diplomatic coup, Robert provided a haven for King Henry I of the French, who had been driven from his lands by 'the stepmother-like hatred of his mother Constance' who had made an effort to dethrone Henry in favour of his younger brother, and her son, Robert, duke of Burgundy. The duke sent the king to his uncle, Count Malger of Corbeil, whose attacks on the rebels slowly wore them down and led to the king's restoration.[117] As a reward, so Orderic tells us, Robert was given the French Vexin, with the approval of Count Drogo, who would subsequently join Robert on his pilgrimage to Jerusalem.[118]

---

[113] *RADN*, no. 49.

[114] *RADN*, no. 73.

[115] Ranulf's portion was restored to him *c.* 1047 (*RADN*, no. 111), although the monks portrayed this as despoliation (*Ctl. Mont-Saint-Michel*, pp. 180–4, no. 115). See also J. Everard and J. C. Holt, *Jersey 1204: The Forging of an Island Community* (London, 2004), pp. 42–5 and below, *infra*, p. 110.

[116] Jumièges, ii. 52–4.

[117] Jumièges, ii. 54–6. *RADN*, no. 69 also reveals the king's presence at the duke's court.

[118] Orderic, iv. 74–6.

Kinship played key roles in these last campaigns, with the duke both answering calls for help from his kinsmen, and calling on his relatives for their support, too. That is not to say that Robert was a selfless supporter of his extended family. He acted as he did because there was also some political capital to be made. He helped Edward and Alfred, for example, because of the potential rewards that might be gained if the duke helped them to win the English throne. In the event, of course, the reward was even greater than Robert probably hoped. Even smaller-scale acts of apparent generosity had benefits. Duke Robert's sister, Adeliza, who had married Reginald of Burgundy, returned to Normandy during his reign and was allowed to purchase the castle and vill of Le Homme – except for those rights already given to the canons of Coutances by Richard II.[119] That gave the duke a reliable set of eyes and ears in the Cotentin, an agent who might work to advance his authority in this remote region. At the other end of the duchy, Robert's aunt Beatrice was made the first abbess of his foundation at Montivilliers.[120] The abbey was richly endowed with property in the west of the county of the Caux including the port of Le Havre, which meant that the abbess was to some extent the first line of defence of the Seine estuary, an important lord of the Pays de Caux, and a means to salvation. A close member of Robert's family thus made an ideal candidate for the job.

Family, then, was still at the heart of the duke's regime in 1035, although it could hardly be otherwise, as Robert's predecessors had ensured that the leading families of the duchy were joined to their own through marriages, as we have seen. The network of great lords who were also kinsmen that had been created is revealed by the composition of the regency council established to safeguard Normandy and the seven-year-old William the Bastard while Robert was on pilgrimage. This council included Archbishop Robert of Rouen (Robert's uncle), Count Gilbert of Eu (his cousin), Count Alan of Brittany (another cousin), Osbern the Steward (his first cousin once removed), and a little later Ralph of Gacé (his cousin). But while kinsmen dominated, there were also some affective and effective relationships outside the extended family. Nigel of the Cotentin might have been a welcome face when he joined the court, and was apparently close enough to the ruling clique to be a part of the ruling council after 1035. And such was the authority of

---

[119] *Regesta: William*, no. 58. She seems to have entrusted custody of the castle to the first Nigel of the Cotentin, and his son apparently inherited that position, holding the castle as her official. See also E. M. C. van Houts, 'Les femmes dans l'histoire du duché de Normandie', *Tabularia: sources écrites de la Normandie médiévale: Études*, 2(2002), 21 (available online at <http://www.unicaen.fr/mrsh/craham/revue/tabularia/dossier2/textes/03vanhouts.pdf>) <accessed 7 April 2016>.

[120] *RADN*, no. 90. The word used to describe her, 'amita', reveals her to have been one of his father's sisters.

these men that Normandy seems to have remained largely at peace despite the minority until their deaths ushered in a period of insecurity which would first shake, but ultimately strengthen, the duchy.

William the Bastard, 1035–87

Between 1035 and 1041, then, the succession of the seven-year-old William the Bastard seems not to have had a detrimental effect on the political life of the duchy. Archbishop Robert and then Count Gilbert apparently maintained the peace and did justice.[121] Yet while Normandy did hold together as a polity during the early years of the reign, the competition for power and influence between families that only a strong duke could hold in check manifested itself in violent if localized warfare.

Before 1046, however, William had more to fear from external rivals rather than internal disorder. In particular, c. 1042, King Henry of the French attacked Tillières on Normandy's southern border. He then burned the duke's town of Argentan, which was also still a frontier outpost at the time. On his way back to France, he returned to Tillières and rebuilt and garrisoned the castle in breach of the terms of surrender agreed with William.[122] King Henry's actions were probably intended to strengthen his hold on Dreux and perhaps also to assist the lord of Bellême, who had taken the opportunity offered by William's minority to recover control of the region north of Alençon.[123] It may also be supposed that King Henry knew of the recent deaths of Count Gilbert and Osbern the Steward, and also of the exile of Roger I of Montgommery c. 1040, which had deprived this stretch of the frontier of those best able to protect it.[124]

Montgommery, exiled for an insurrection that had affected the country around Vimoutiers, had been replaced as *vicomte* of the Hiémois by Thurstan Goz. He seems not to have had strong connections with the county before then, instead having lands in the Lieuvin.[125] His background might hint that Count Gilbert,

---

[121] Orderic, iv. 82; Malmesbury, *GR*, i. 426. See also Bates, 'Adolescence', 6–7.

[122] Jumièges, ii. 100. David Crouch suggested that King Henry's attack on Argentan was intended to support Thurstan Goz, who rebelled against the duke from Falaise (Crouch, *The Normans*, p. 62). This is as likely as the alternative course of events suggested here.

[123] The identity of the lord of Alençon at this time is not clear. It might have been Robert I of Bellême or William Talvas. Moreover Domfront might have been under the control of their older brother Warin (see the family tree at Louise, *Bellême*, ii. 157).

[124] Roger's exile was related to his usurpation of lands around Vimoutiers (again). Duke William subsequently restored property to the monks of Jumièges that Roger had taken by force (*Regesta: William*, no. 164).

[125] L. Musset, 'Les origines et le patrimoine de l'abbaye de Saint-Sever', in *La Normandie Bénédictine au temps de Guillaume le Conquérant (Xe siècle)* (Lille, 1967), pp. 357–73;

who held lands in both the Lieuvin and the Evrecin (at Meulles, close to the border with the Hiémois), had been instrumental in his appointment to the office. If so, it is likely that Thurstan saw Count Gilbert's murder *c.* 1041 and King Henry's attack on Argentan as fundamentally changing the political landscape of his *vicomté*, which included that town. In the absence of any evidence that Duke William was still capable of protecting the Hiémois, and with rival powers at his gates, Thurstan bowed to what looked like the inevitable, accepted that it was the king's authority that was effective in his county, and thus recognized his right to enter his castle.[126] That would explain both his actions and the motives that William of Jumièges imputed to him (which *might* have been portrayed so as to emphasize the similarities between Thurstan's rebellion and that perpetrated by Bishop Hugh of Bayeux against Robert the Magnificent):

> When Thurstan, *vicomte* of the Hiémois, observed that the young duke had made several concessions to the king and that like a beaten man he had endured any amount of oppression at the latter's hands, he became inspired by treacherous zeal. He hired royal soldiers as mercenaries whom he welcomed as his accomplices for the defence of the fortress at Falaise, because he did not wish to serve the duke. As soon as the duke heard of the plans of this spiteful character he summoned troops of Normans from all over the country and swiftly laid siege to him. There the excited soldiers fought with such bravery that at one moment they even demolished part of the walls, and if the night had not put an end to the battle they would no doubt eagerly have destroyed the whole place.[127]

Thurstan was thus proved wrong. William the Bastard's lieutenants had demonstrated that his power was still effective in the Hiémois after all. Thurstan Goz was consequently forced into exile, leaving the way clear for Roger II of Montgommery, who seems already to have established himself at court, to recover his father's place in the Hiémois.[128]

Duke William's minority probably ended around the time of Thurstan's defeat,[129] and he quickly built up a ruling clique, the members of which included

'Une famille vicomtale: les Goz', *Documents de l'histoire de Normandie* (Toulouse, 1972), pp. 94–8.

[126] Bates suggested, in a similar vein, that Thurstan Goz had been concerned about the disorder around Bellême and Alençon and did not believe that William or his supporters were capable of helping him (Bates, 'Adolescence', 9).

[127] Jumièges, ii. 102.

[128] *RADN*, no. 99.

[129] Bates, 'Adolescence', 3–4.

his uncles (and contemporaries) Archbishop Malger of Rouen and Count William of Arques, Roger II of Montgommery, William fitz Osbern (the son of Osbern the Steward), Roger of Beaumont, and Ralph Taisson. William's cousin, Guy of Burgundy, was apparently excluded from his group of close counsellors, however. He thus determined on rebellion.[130]

Guy was to be joined by another disaffected lord, Nigel II of the Cotentin. When his father died *c.* 1042, Nigel II inherited his office of *vicomte* of the Cotentin but not his position in the duke's counsels. He attests few ducal *acta* and he was no longer the principal link between the Cotentin and the duke. In particular, an act of 1042, which records a transfer of some revenues produced by the *vicomtés* of the Cotentin, Coutances, and Gavray, was not attested by Nigel, despite the fact that he was one of the relevant *vicomtes*, but by Roger of Montgommery and William fitz Osbern, already so prominent in the duke's counsels that they might be described as his henchmen, and by Alured the Giant and Thurstan Haldup.[131]

Alured the Giant had been one of the men entrusted with the castle of Chéruel. Thurstan (or Richard) Haldup seems to have been an even greater figure. While he had perhaps recognized ducal authority during the reign of Richard II – and was perhaps baptized by the duke's efforts – he only now seems to have become part of the ruling elite. He was lord of Le Plessis and Créances in the Cotentin, but married into an unidentified family with lands around Argentan, some of which he later gave to the monks of Cerisy.[132] It is likely that his developing interest in the Hiémois was the reason behind the marriage, recorded by Orderic Vitalis, of his daughter Emma to Arnold of Echauffour.[133] Orderic noted at the same time that Thurstan's son, Eudo, was 'one of the wealthiest and most powerful of the Norman nobles in the Cotentin'. It is a comment supported by the foundation diploma for Lessay abbey which reveals the family as important landholders in the peninsula.[134]

Thurstan's support was acquired and maintained by grants made out of the ducal demesne in the Bessin.[135] In addition, Thurstan's son, Eudo, was given

---

[130] See below, Chapter 6, p. 326.

[131] *RADN*, no. 99.

[132] He gave Marcei, Le Val, Cordey, and Flaugny (*RADN*, no. 167). The act states that these were 'ex uxoria hereditate'.

[133] Orderic, ii. 124–6.

[134] *Regesta: William*, no. 175.

[135] Revealed by a ducal diploma for La Trinité, Caen, which records that: 'Adelaide, a nun of this church, the daughter of Thurstan Haldup, begged the permission (*misericordia*) of Count William that she might give those lands which her father had given to her as dowry, and which she at that time held from that count, to the Holy Trinity' (*RADN*, no. 231 at p. 445). Later acts of confirmation to Holy Trinity state that the lands were granted with the consent of Adelaide's brother, and Thurstan's son, Eudo, and Ranulf of the Bessin (*Regesta: William*, nos. 59 and 61).

property at Héauville[136] and the church of St Mary at Portbail (previously part of Adela's settlement), both of which he gave to his foundation at Lessay – the first abbey founded in the Cotentin, which was staffed by monks from the all-but-ducal abbey at Le Bec.[137] Eudo also received property in Baupte, which he gave to Saint-Etienne of Caen,[138] and probably also at Pouppeville, which appears in the hands of his heir, Robert of La Haye-du-Puits.[139] It is possible that Henry I gave Robert this directly, but the identity of Robert's tenant – Humfrey of Aubigny – suggests that it had belonged to Eudo first, as the link between the Haldup and the Aubigny families seems to have been close.[140] Most important of all, Eudo married Muriel, Duke William's half-sister.[141] Eleanor Searle said almost nothing about this alliance,[142] which is odd as it gave the duke a kinsman in the Cotentin for the first time, and must have altered the political landscape of the region.

Nigel II's influence, then, was being diminished. Others were taking the patronage that Nigel might have thought was due to him. And so he rebelled, just as Bishop Hugh of Bayeux had rebelled against Duke Robert and just as Earl Roger of Hereford would rebel against King William in 1075 because they did not enjoy

---

[136] He gave his share of the church and land there to Marmoutier in *c.* 1070 × 1083: *Regesta: William*, no. 206; L. Couppey, *Encore Héauville: supplément aux notes historiques sur le prieur, conventuel d'Héauville la Hague*, Revue catholique de Normandie, 10 (1900–01), pp. 7–9.

[137] *Regesta*, ii. 353–4 (no. clxxvii). The gift is not in *Regesta: William*, no. 175, suggesting it was made after 1080; R. Herval, 'L'abbaye de Lessay', in *La Normandie bénédictine au temps de Guillaume le Conquérant (XIe siècle)*, ed. D. Gaillard and J. Daoust (Lille, 1967), pp. 289–92; *Normannia monastica*, ii. 171–2.

[138] *Regesta: William*, no. 49. A second act, *Regesta: William*, no. 45, reveals that Baupte had been in the ducal demesne. The other half seems to have been granted to Bishop Odo of Bayeux who subsequently enfeoffed Rainald of Orval with it. The abbey's holdings in and around Baupte were administered by a priory. See J.-M. Bouvris, *Dans le marais du Cotentin à la fin du XIe siècle. Autour de la fondation du prieuré de Baupte, dépendance de l'abbaye de Saint-Etienne de Caen*, MSAN, 43 (2009).

[139] Ctl. Montebourg, p. 113, no. 307.

[140] The Aubigny family were donors to Lessay, and one member of the family, Richard, was a monk there before becoming abbot of St Albans (*Regesta: William*, no. 175; L. C. Loyd, 'The origins of the family of Aubigny of Cainhoe', *Bedfordshire Historical Record Society*, 19 (1937), 102–6). Moreover, there seems to have been a tenurial relationship between the two families. In an act of Henry II, William and Roger of Aubigny are said to have given the abbey the church of Feugères (Delisle, *Recueil*, no. 679). In Henry I's earlier confirmation, however, it is said to have been a gift from their contemporaries Thurstan Haldup and Eudo (*Regesta*, ii. 353–4, no. clxxvii).

[141] *GC*, xi. instr. 228 names Eudo's wife as Muriel. Wace, p. 158, provides her name and also her relationship to the duke. She was, he says, the daughter of Herleva and Herluin (of Conteville).

[142] Searle, *PK*, p. 202.

the place in the duke's counsels that they thought they deserved.[143] But this was no good reason for rebellion, and Nigel might consequently have wavered before taking the plunge. Count Guy was thus obliged to purchase his support by giving him the castle of Le Homme, although he had to take it from his mother first.[144]

The other two leading rebels named by William of Poitiers, Ranulf of Bayeux and Haimo 'the Toothy', seem to have had rather different, and altogether conventional, reasons for rebellion. It seems that Ranulf's father had been unjustly deprived of lands on Guernsey by Robert the Magnificent, and that these had not been justly restored.[145] Haimo probably rebelled because he had been frustrated in his attempts to reconcile the duke with his kinsman, Thurstan Goz, by more peaceful means.[146] The motives that brought Grimoult of Le Plessis-Grimoult to rebel, in contrast, are entirely obscure.

The rebels suffered a variety of fates after William defeated them, with the help of King Henry, at the battle of Val-ès-Dunes in 1047. Count Guy, the leader and instigator of the revolt, retreated to his castle at Brionne – on an island in the river, and not on the hill where the later ruins stand today – where he was besieged for another three years until he surrendered. He was then kept under house arrest at the duke's court for some time until finally he was permitted to return to Burgundy.[147] His castles and lands were recovered to the duke's demesne, with some at least given into the custody of William fitz Osbern.[148]

Grimoult of Le Plessis-Grimoult was imprisoned in irons until his death. His

[143] It seems unlikely that Nigel II was simply too young to hold the office as Eric van Torhoudt suggested (Van Torhoudt, 'Les sieges du pouvoir des Néels', p. 14). Nigel 'the young' attested without his father in or before 1041 (*RADN*, no. 73), which suggests that he had reached his majority some years before 1047. For Bishop Hugh's rebellion see above, *infra*, pp. 99–100 and below, Chapter 6, p. 325 and Chapter 11, p. 648. For Roger of Hereford's rebellion see Orderic, ii. 310–18; *Letters of Lanfranc*, pp. 118–22 (nos. 31–33B); and, for example, D. Bates, *William the Conqueror* (London, 1989), p. 155; A. Williams, *The English and the Norman Conquest* (Woodbridge, 1995), p. 60.

[144] See *Regesta: William*, no. 58.

[145] It *might* have been the case that Grimoult of Le Plessis-Grimoult rebelled for a similar reason. Robert the Magnificent had granted the monks of his foundation at Cerisy-la-Forêt seven acres of land at Montpinçon (*RADN*, no. 64), a place which seems to have lain inside Grimoult's honour if the boundaries set out in 1074 were also those that applied in the 1030s (*Regesta: William*, no. 27 and plotted by E. Zadora-Rio, 'L'enceinte fortifiée du Plessis-Grimoult (Calvados). Contribution à l'étude historique et archéologique de l'habitat seigneurial au XIe siècle', *Archéologie Médiévale*, 3–4 (1973–4), 114). The honour was held from Bishop Hugh of Bayeux, who was almost certainly in disgrace at this time (see above, *infra*, pp. 99–100 and n. 153, below).

[146] For their kinship see Hagger, 'How the west was won', 39 and n. 129.

[147] Poitiers, pp. 8–10; Jumièges, ii. 120–2; *RADN*, nos. 131 (1053), 194 (1050 × 1066).

[148] *RADN*, no. 189 and see also below, *infra*, pp. 133–4.

extraordinary punishment reflected the extraordinary gravity of his crimes. He was, claimed Wace, guilty of an attempt on the duke's life. The inquisition on the bishopric of Bayeux of 1133 provides some support for this claim: 'King William gave Odo his brother, the bishop of Bayeux, the whole fee of Grimoult of Le-Plessis for the increase of the church of Bayeux, after the death of Grimoult, who died in the king's prison at Rouen and was buried in the cemetery of Saint-Gervase outside the town, still having his legs in iron shackles as a sign of the treason of which he was accused by that king.' As his honour only reverted to the bishop of Bayeux in 1074,[149] it may be that the duke had held it while Grimoult lived, which would explain how Queen Matilda could make a grant of a ploughland at Cauville to La Trinité of Caen and how Ralph Taisson could hold the church of that same vill.[150]

Haimo 'the Toothy' was killed in the battle, although he had fought so valiantly that he was given a splendid funeral by his erstwhile enemies. He was succeeded by his son, also Haimo, who apparently gained possession of all his father's lands, and would pass them on to his own son, Robert, in turn. After the conquest of England, Haimo would receive additional estates in Kent and Essex from the king and also serve as sheriff of Kent from 1077.[151] Moreover, by 1054 the Goz family had been restored to favour and had been appointed *vicomtes* of the Avranchin.

Ranulf, *vicomte* of the Bessin, perhaps because he also had just reason to rebel, also seems to have escaped without punishment. Indeed, his half of Guernsey was restored to him. He also married a daughter of Richard III called Aeliz, and he and his family continued to serve as *vicomtes* of the Bessin for decades to come.[152]

Grimoult, Haimo, and Ranulf had all been tenants of Bishop Hugh of Bayeux, which suggests that he had lost his energy during the last few years of his life, or his ability to shape or control events in the Bessin, or had supported the rebels.[153]

---

[149] *Regesta: William*, no. 27.

[150] *Regesta: William*, nos. 59, 149.

[151] GDB, fos. 2r, 14r; Kent, § C1, 12; LDB, fos. 54v–56v; Essex § 28; J. A. Green, *English Sheriffs to 1154* (London, 1990), p. 50.

[152] The marriage was noted by Robert of Torigni (RT, s.a. 1026; Delisle, i. 34; Howlett, p. 24).

[153] Bishop Hugh died in 1049, after attending the council of Reims. Grimoult is revealed to have been a tenant by *Regesta: William*, no. 27, although the Inquisition of 1133 treats the grant as a gift rather than restitution (*Inquisition*, p. 16). Haimo Dentatus almost certainly held the honour of Evrecy from Bishop Hugh, just as Haimo's successor Robert of Gloucester held it from the bishop in 1133 (*Inquisition*, p. 15). The relationship with the *vicomtes* of the Bessin and Ranulf is also established by the inquisition of 1133 (*Inquisition*, p. 16) but also by an earlier document establishing mutual obligations between Odo of Bayeux and Ranulf I of Briquessart: *Livre Noir*, i. 95–7 (no. 76).

Any or all of these reasons would have emphasized the importance of the bishop of Bayeux with regard to the enforcement of ducal authority in the Bessin. And so when Bishop Hugh died in 1049, William the Bastard filled the vacancy immediately. The importance of the position meant that only a close kinsman would suffice as bishop. He thus had the canons elect his own half-brother, Odo. The fact that Odo was well under the canonical age to be elected a bishop reveals just how important it was to the duke to have the right man established in the office.[154]

The biggest loser from the rebellion, with the exception of Grimoult, was Nigel II of the Cotentin. Eleanor Searle downplayed what happened to him after his defeat: 'Rumour put him in brief exile in Brittany, and evidently gifts to Marmoutier are to be connected with penance for his unfortunate choice. But that was all.'[155] But Wace made it clear that this was no light punishment. Writing of the immediate aftermath of the rebellion, he stated that: 'No reconciliation with Nigel was possible and he did not dare dwell in that country; he was in Brittany for a long time before he made peace.'[156] And we do not have to rely solely on Wace's later testimony. In a diploma for Marmoutier, Nigel revealed that he was in exile and uncertain of his future – he will give the monks property on Guernsey '*if* my lord shall call me back to my honour (*si me dominus in honorem meum reuocaverit*)'.[157] Nigel was thus removed from the Cotentin by exile, and that exile was not 'brief'. He moved from Brittany to the court of Count Geoffrey Martel of Anjou *c.* 1056 and then joined King Henry of the French at the siege of Thimert in 1059.[158] In the meantime, his estates were carved up into two or three distinct honours.

---

[154] Bates suggested that Odo was elected in 1049 or 1050, at which point he would have been nineteen at best (D. Bates, 'The character and career of Odo, bishop of Bayeux (1049/50–1097)', *Speculum*, 50 (1975), 1–2).

[155] Searle, *PK*, p. 216.

[156] Wace, p. 137. Poitiers wrote, in apparent contrast, that Nigel was exiled 'at another time (*in alio tempore*)' (Poitiers, p. 12). However, as he had just claimed that William had pardoned those who deserved death, his comment appears to be disingenuous. This is especially the case if the following phrase, 'since he had offended seriously (*quoniam improbe offensabat*)', was intended to refer back to the rebellion. In any event, exile and rebellion were almost certainly linked, even if there might have been a short gap during which time William worked out how he could remove Nigel without danger to himself.

[157] Delisle, *Histoire de Saint-Sauveur-le-Vicomte*, preuves, p. 25, no. 21.

[158] *Cartulaire de Saint-Aubin d'Angers*, ed. Le Comte B. de Brousillon, 3 vols (Paris, 1903), ii. 171–4 (no. 677) at p. 173; *Catalogue des actes d'Henri I, roi de France*, ed. F. Soehnée (Paris, 1907), p. 17 (no. 116); and see the notes in H. Guillotel, *Actes des ducs de Bretagne (944–1148)*, ed. P. Charon, P. Guigon, C. Henry, M. Jones, K. Keats-Rohan, and J.-C. Meuret (Rennes, 2014), p. 301 (no. 55). I would like to thank David Bates for pointing out this last reference.

When Nigel was allowed to return from his exile *c.* 1060, he was permitted to take one of them, based on Saint-Sauveur-le-Vicomte and La Colombe.[159] A second lordship, based on Néhou, almost certainly Nigel's original seat, had been given to Richard of Reviers by 1060.[160] Reviers was an outsider, taking his toponym from a place in the Bessin, a few miles to the north-west of Caen. The (probable) third honour was based on Bricquebec and was given to Robert Bertram,[161] lord of Honfleur and Beaumont-en-Auge in the Lieuvin.[162] As he subsequently founded a priory at Beaumont-en-Auge, rather than at Bricquebec,[163] it might be that Robert continued to see himself as an outsider in the Cotentin. Perhaps that stance made him all the more dependable in Duke William's eyes, as he was *vicomte* of the Cotentin in 1080 and had probably held the office since 1060.[164]

Between 1055 and 1068, William's wife Matilda was also given land in the

[159]   As indicated by the donations Nigel II made to the abbey at Saint-Sauveur-le-Vicomte (*Regesta: William*, no. 260; Delisle, *Histoire de Saint-Sauveur-le-Vicomte*, pp. 50–5, no. 45).

[160]   The name means 'Nigel's residence'. The earliest evidence for Richard of Reviers's possession of Néhou dates from 1100 × 1107 (*Charters of the Redvers family*, ed. Bearman, pp. 55–7 (no. 4)), but it is likely that he was given it in the immediate aftermath of the battle (see also Van Tourhoudt, 'Les sieges du pouvoir des Néels', p. 30). Delacampagne states that the honour of Néhou comprised property in 29 vills (Delacampagne, 'Seigneurs, fiefs et mottes du Cotentin (X^e–XIIe siècles): étude historique et topographique', *Archéologie Médiévale*, 12 (1982), 182).

[161]   Although a seventeenth-century tradition links the Bertram family with Anslech, one of Richard I's supporters (*Dudo*, p. 101; Jumièges, i. 100), and the supposed builder of Bricquebec castle (see, for example, C. de Gerville, 'Mémoire sur les anciens châteaux du département de la Manche', *Mémoires de la Société des Antiquaires de Normandie*, 1 (1825), 247–8), there is no evidence to support such a conjectural relationship, and no evidence at all to suggest that Robert Bertram had been established in the Cotentin before Val-ès-Dunes.

[162]   *RADN*, no. 205. In the Cotentin Robert granted the churches at Magneville, Vrétot, Surtainville, and Bricquebec, a plough at *Fontenait*, and also a fief at Barneville-le-Bertrand. Most of these possessions were confirmed to the priory in 1221 (*Les cartulaires de la baronnie de Bricquebec*, ed. L. Delisle (Saint-Lô, 1894), p. 7; *Cartulaires de Saint-Ymer-en-Auge et de Bricquebec, publiés avec notices par Charles Bréard* (Rouen, 1908), pp. 205–7, no. 19).

[163]   *Normannia monastica*, i.15, n. 70.

[164]   *Regesta: William*, no. 202 and see below. As Bertram acted as *vicomte* in the Cotentin, there is no reason at all to think that he was *vicomte* of the pays d'Auge (see Van Torhoudt, 'Les sieges du pouvoir des Néels', p. 27). On the role of the *vicomtes* see below, Chapter 7, pp. 592–6 and M. Hagger, 'The Norman *vicomte c.* 1035–1135: what did he do?', *ANS*, 29 (2007), 65–83. It is the pattern of attestations of ducal acts by Robert Bertram, Eudo Haldup, and Nigel II that suggests Robert was *vicomte* from around 1060 to 1080, when he died.

Cotentin, including at Quettehou.[165] Her estates here might not have formed part of her dower, in which case they could have been intended to compensate her for the loss of Kent, which seems to have been promised to her in 1066, but which was actually given to Bishop Odo of Bayeux.[166] Alternatively, it may be that the conquest of England, and the resulting absences of Bishop Geoffrey and Count Robert, caused William to insert Matilda as an additional (or replacement) prop for his regime there in case of attack from Ireland or Brittany or even, perhaps, from Denmark. In any event, Matilda's authority in the peninsula is revealed by a letter from the monks of Saint-Florent near Saumur who wrote to Matilda asking her to assist them in recovering property at Barneville and elsewhere that had once belonged to the abbey but had been lost.[167] The monks stated that the Cotentin was in Matilda's power – without reference to Duke William – and styled her 'marchioness'.[168] Matilda also acted alone when Countess Adeliza of Burgundy granted the castle at Le Homme to Sainte-Trinité of Caen,[169] and in confirming a settlement made between Mont-Saint-Michel and William Paynel concerning the services William would provide to the abbey for lands in the Cotentin.[170] There are also two post-Conquest mandates that William sent her which are concerned particularly with the Cotentin. In 1080, Matilda was commanded to ensure that property at Héauville that the *vicomte* had usurped was restored to the abbey of Marmoutier, which she did while resident at Cherbourg. Perhaps in the same year, William sent her a letter informing her of a grant of the church of Les Pieux, in the north of the peninsula, to Marmoutier and ordering her to 'make all the land of St Martin that is within Normandy absolved and quit from all collectors of *grauarium* and foresters, as is right. And specifically you shall command Hugolin of Cherbourg not to interfere further therein.'[171] Her leading role in the area might also be

---

[165] Her possession is revealed by a grant to Sainte-Trinité, Caen (*Regesta: William*, no. 63).

[166] E. M. C. van Houts, 'The ship list of William the Conqueror', *ANS*, 10 (1988), 159, 166, 173–4.

[167] The mid-thirteenth-century polyptique of Coutances notes the existence of a church dedicated to St. Florent at Barneville, which might support the monks' claim (*RHGF*, xxiii. 517).

[168] Marchegay, pp. 666–8 (no. 2), at p. 667. He dated the act to between the marriage of William and Matilda and the Conquest of England in 1066, on the grounds (it may be inferred) that Matilda was styled 'marchioness of the Normans'. Matilda, however, was not crowned until 1068 and, as there is no reference at all to William in the act, might thus have been so styled until that year.

[169] *Regesta: William*, no. 58.

[170] *Ctl. Mont-Saint-Michel*, pp. 166–7, no. 90.

[171] *Regesta: William*, no. 202. Bates dated the act '1066 × 1083, and perhaps *c*. 27 December 1080'.

indicated by the trouble taken to add her *signum* to the bottom of her husband's act of 1042 for the monks of Cerisy.[172]

In addition to this plantation of his secular supporters in the north of the peninsula, William founded an abbey at Montebourg *c.* 1080, to act as a bastion of his rule – just as Robert the Magnificent had established the abbey at Cerisy-la-Forêt and William himself had earlier established two monasteries at Caen. It is possible, but on balance unlikely, that the abbey was endowed with estates that the duke had earlier taken from Nigel's honour and retained in his demesne. It is more likely that the property in question had been part of the demesne since the reign of Richard II.[173] In any event, the duke's new foundation also attracted donations from a number of minor local families, or those with minor interests in the region, such as William Broc (tenants of the *vicomtes* of the Bessin), Richard of Lestre (a tenant of the count of Mortain), Richard of Angerville (related to Richard of Reviers through marriage, and a justice in the time of King Henry I), William of Tancarville, and William of Beaumont (both of whom held land in the Cotentin perhaps through their ancestors' marriages to Gunnor's sisters, as noted above).[174] It may be supposed that their support was intended to act as a public display of their loyalty to the duke, and if so then it is apparent that William had won over to his side lords from lower down the social spectrum than had previously been the case – at least so far as we can see. If the archive of Henry I's writs is anything to go by, ducal power would have been further underpinned by a steady stream of traffic to and from William's court, with the monks of Montebourg requesting exemptions from toll, the right to take wood from the ducal forests, and the protection of their property.[175]

And it was not just the monks of Montebourg who beat a path to William's door. The monks of Marmoutier had been given land in the north of the Cotentin by Richard II in 1017 × 1020, and they were to receive more there and in the

[172] *RADN*, no. 99.
[173] Although Orderic Vitalis claimed that the abbey was founded by Richard of Reviers (Orderic, iv. 220, vi. 144–6), a confirmation issued by Richard and signed by Henry I reveals that the real founder was King William (Ctl. Montebourg, p. 65 (no. 141); *Charters of the Redvers family*, ed. Bearman, pp. 57–9 (no. 5)). Robert of Torigni's suggestion that Baldwin of Reviers was the founder (Jumièges, ii. 134) can probably be discounted altogether. For a different view see E. van Torhoudt, 'L' "énigme" des origines de l'abbaye de Montebourg: une question de méthode?', pp. 331–46, particularly pp. 339–46. By way of comparison, Judith Green noted that Henry I was probably inclined to patronize the Augustinian house at Nostell because it acted as a counterbalance to Hugh of Laval at nearby Pontefract (J. A. Green, 'William Rufus, Henry I and the royal demesne', *History*, 64 (1979), 343).
[174] *Charters of the Redvers family*, ed. Bearman, pp. 57–9 (no. 5).
[175] For some of the writs see *NI*, pp. 101–3.

Channel Islands from later dukes and local lords. A priory had been established at Héauville to administer those possessions before 1066.[176] These monks crossed the Channel to request William's assistance against his *vicomte* in 1080,[177] drafted a letter from William to Matilda exempting them from tolls and *grauarium*, and pleaded in his court before Bishop Geoffrey of Coutances, Bishop Michael of Avranches, Bishop Gilbert of Lisieux, and Eudo the *vicomte* (the son of Thurstan Haldup) over their rights at Saint-Georges-de-Bohon.[178] Thus we see ducal justice exercised in the Cotentin because the monks of Marmoutier had demanded it. And it may be that William welcomed such approaches, which allowed him to expand the reach of his authority outside areas that were already firmly under his control.[179] The monastic houses established in the peninsula thus gave the duke the opportunity to intervene in local affairs and to throw his protection over monasteries, even if they were not ducal foundations. In short, they helped to make the theory of his overlordship a reality.[180]

Duke William thus established a variety of outsiders in the north of the Cotentin after his victory in 1047. They owed their position to him, and had no local sympathies or sympathizers – at least to begin with. But the rebellion of 1046–47 seems to have caused Duke William to rethink and reform the political and tenurial landscape of the whole western third of Normandy, not just the north of the Cotentin peninsula. In the middle and south of the Cotentin, all the estate centres that had been settled on Adela in 1026 were given to the duke's supporters. The greatest of these was William's half-brother, Robert, who had been made count of Mortain by 1063 and who was also given Cérences.[181] Hambye was given to William Paynel, whose original caput had probably been at Les Moutiers-Hubert in the Lieuvin.[182] Duke William also gave him some property in the south

---

[176] L. Couppey, *Notes historiques sur le prieuré conventuel d'Héauville de la Hague* (Evreux, 1898), pp. 13–16.

[177] *Regesta: William*, no. 200.

[178] *Regesta: William*, no. 201.

[179] Louis VI was to employ the same tactic: G. Duby, *France in the Middle Ages 987–1460: from Hugh Capet to Joan of Arc*, trans. J. Vale (Oxford, 1991), pp. 129–32; E. M. Hallam and J. Everard, *Capetian France 987–1328*, second edition (London, 2001), pp. 173, 220.

[180] See on this Potts, *Monastic Revival*, pp. 114–15.

[181] B. Golding, 'Robert of Mortain', *ANS*, 13 (1991), 120 and see below, *infra*, p. 117.

[182] *Early Yorkshire Charters*, ed. C. T. Clay, vols 4–10, Yorkshire Archaeological Society, record series, extra series (1935–55), vi. 1–2; *Orderici Vitalis ecclesiasticae historiae libri tredecim*, ed. le Prévost, iii. 259; L. C. Loyd, *The origins of some Anglo-Norman families*, Publications of the Harleian Society, 103 (Leeds, 1951), p. 77; and, most recently, M. Guilmin, 'Un exemple de réseau relationnel de l'aristocratie anglo-normande, les Paynel et leur entourage (milieu du XIe siècle–début du XIIe siècle', in *Tinchebray 1106–2006: actes du colloque de Tinchebray (28–30 Septembre 2006)*, ed. V. Gazeau and J. Green (Flers, 1998), pp. 221–34.

west of the Cotentin that belonged to the monks of Mont-Saint-Michel when he found him a wife, perhaps in around 1048 when relations between William and the abbey were strained.[183] Percy was given, at least in part, to Ralph Taisson, who may consequently be supposed not to have acted so dubiously in 1047 as Wace later asserted.[184] Some of the vill was retained in Ralph's own hands, but by the end of the century he had enfeoffed at least two men there as well.[185] Moyon was given to a man called Alured, who was succeeded by William. As the name Alured was quite unusual – there are only eight individuals with it in Fauroux's *Recueil* – it is remarkable that Alured the Giant also had an heir called William (his brother, if Wace is to be believed).[186] One thus wonders if the two Alureds were actually one man, and whether Alured the Giant, custodian of Chéruel, was later established as a supporter in the Cotentin by a grant out of the ducal demesne.[187]

Even after this redistribution of the demesne, Duke William might have remained concerned about the imbalances in the power and wealth of the lords of the Cotentin. As a result, he used the huge bank of land provided by his conquest of England to put the various lords of the peninsula on a more equal footing. While William's cronies – Count Robert of Mortain, Hugh of Avranches, and Bishop Geoffrey of Coutances – did very well out of the Conquest, the greatest lords of the northern Cotentin, Eudo Haldup, Richard of Reviers, William Bertram, and the only recently restored Nigel II, gained nothing or virtually nothing.[188] In contrast, William gave Nigel of Aubigny – whose family was closely allied with the Haldups, as well as with the rebel Grimoult of Le Plessis-Grimoult – an honour based on Cainhoe (Bedfordshire), while William of Moyon received the honour of Dunster (Somerset), Peter of Valognes became lord of the honour

---

[183] *Ctl. Mont-Saint-Michel*, pp. 166–7 (no. 90). The act states that William held Longueville-la-Val and La Lande from the abbey. Relations between Duke William and the abbey at this time are touched on in Potts, *Monastic Revival*, p. 101–2. The construction of an honour from a variety of sources, as here, can also be seen in Yorkshire (Green, 'William Rufus, Henry I and the royal demesne', 344; *Charters of the Honour of Mowbray 1107–1191*, ed. D. Greenway, Records of Social and Economic History, new series 1 (London, 1972), pp. xix–xxv.

[184] Wace, pp. 134, 136.

[185] L. Musset, 'Actes inédits du XIe siècle: V. Fontenay', 17, 29, n. 59, 33–7.

[186] *RADN*, no. 231; *Regesta: William*, no 59. Wace, pp. 130–1.

[187] Alured has not been considered before because, although Elisabeth van Houts linked him with Gavray (Jumièges, ii. 58–9, n. 1), the evidence she cited does not support this association. The location of the property that Alured gave to the abbey of Cerisy, which he granted with hereditary right and with the consent of his heir, suggests that he was actually from the west of the Bessin (*RADN*, no. 95).

[188] The second Richard of Reviers was given Mosterton in Dorset (GDB, fo. 83r; Dorset, § 54.5) while William Bertram, probably Robert's son, held Polhampton in Hampshire (GDB, fo. 47r; Hampshire § 31.1).

of Benington (Hertfordshire), and Ralph Paynel was given lands in six counties.[189] By enriching these selected men, William both tied them to his regime and made them the equals of their neighbours in the Cotentin. He thus fragmented political power in the peninsula still further, and packed the county with men beholden to him. It suggests he adopted a policy of isolating, dividing, and thus conquering the aristocracy of the region.

The all-encompassing changes in personnel and land-holding continued still further south, in the counties of Avranches and Mortain. Probably in the md-1050s, William Werlenc, count of Mortain, was forfeited and exiled on the basis of a rather ephemeral rumour that he was planning to rebel against Duke William, which travelled by way of Roger Bigod and Richard Goz to William's ear.[190] The story is late, however, and it might well be that Orderic felt the need to find some justification for the apparently arbitrary forfeiture of Werlenc at a time when to be a count was no longer seen as an office but as an inheritance.[191] He was replaced by the duke's half-brother, Robert, who did not, however, obtain all the lands held by his predecessor. The city of Avranches and some vills in the Avranchin including Vains and Saint-James-de-Beuvron were subtracted from the county and recovered to the ducal demesne. As compensation, William granted Count Robert his vill of Cérences, as noted above, as well as property in Muneville-sur-Mer, Coutances, Baupte, Barfleur, and Helleville in the Cotentin.[192] Robert was permitted to inherit his father's honour based on Conteville and Grestain in the Lieuvin, too, which gave him geographically widespread interests, perhaps to ensure that he would not strive to gain too much independence in the west.

With Avranches now in the duke's hands, and with at least some of the vills that used to belong to the counts added to what had previously been a somewhat

---

[189] Aubigny: GDB, fos. 59v, 151v, 214r–v; Berks, §12; Bucks, § 39, Beds, §24; I. J. Sanders, *English Baronies: A Study of their Origin and Descent 1086–1327* (Oxford, 1960), pp. 26–7; Loyd, 'The origins of the family of Aubigny of Cainhoe', 101–10. Moyon: GDB, fos. 72r, 81v–82r, 95v–96v, 110r; Wilts, § 34; Dorset, § 36; Somerset, § 25; Devon, § 18; Sanders, *English baronies*, p. 114; J. A. Green, *The Aristocracy of Norman England* (Cambridge, 1997), p. 66. Valognes: GDB, fos. 140v–141v, 201v, 368v; Herts, § 36; Cambs, § 31[33]; Lincs, § 60; LDB, fos, 78r–79v, 256r–258v, 420v–421v; Essex, § 36; Norf, § 34; Suff, § 37; Sanders, *English Baronies*, pp. 12–13. Paynel: *Early Yorkshire Charters*, ed. Clay, vi. 56–65; Guilmin, 'Un exemple de réseau relationnel de l'aristocratie anglo-normande, les Paynel et leur entourage (milieu du XIe siècle–début du XIIe siècle', p. 226.

[190] Jumièges, ii. 126.

[191] See below, Chapter 9, pp. 568–9.

[192] The lands that comprised the county of Mortain are listed in *Cartulaire Normand de Philippe-Auguste, Louis VIII, Saint Louis et Philippe-le-Hardi*, ed. L. Delisle (Caen, 1882), p. 66, no. 112. From Count Robert's own day there is *Regesta: William*, no. 215 and see also J. Boussard, 'Le comté de Mortain au XIe siècle', *Moyen Age*, 58 (1952), 271.

limited demesne, there was a need for a *vicomte* of Avranches – apparently for the first time. The man chosen was Richard Goz, son of that Thurstan Goz who had revolted at Falaise *c.* 1043, and whose continued exile had perhaps caused Haimo the Toothy to rebel in 1046–47. Richard had been appointed by 1054, perhaps earlier.[193] Lucien Musset suggested that the lands in the Avranchin that subsequently appeared in the hands of Richard Goz and his son Hugh had been acquired only after Richard was made *vicomte*, but it is possible that he held these lands already and that it was his association with the Avranchin that qualified him for office. The evidence is so poor that no firm conclusion can be reached either way, but it is at least clear that Richard Goz and his son came to hold lands in the Lieuvin, Bessin, Hiémois, and Avranchin, while Hugh was hugely enriched with possessions in England before 1086.[194] The Goz family thus came to be thoroughly invested in Duke William's regime, and might consequently be relied upon to support him against Bretons, Angevins, and, indeed, anyone else.

Secular land-holding in the west of Normandy was, then, thoroughly reformed and transformed by William the Bastard during the decades following his victory at Val-ès-Dunes. And in addition to establishing loyal lay supporters in the region, he ensured that the bishoprics would be in safe hands, too. In 1048 or 1049, at almost exactly the same time that Odo was elected to Bayeux, Geoffrey of Montbray was given the bishopric of Coutances. The Montbray family could be described as 'noble' by the author of the *De statu huius ecclesiae*, but it does not seem to have

---

[193] David Douglas suggested that Richard Goz was in office by 1046 (*RADN*, no. 110; Douglas, *William the Conqueror*, p. 93), but while a Richard the *vicomte* did attest the act in question, he is not further identified in the witness list. Indeed, the Richard fitz Thurstan who also signed this diploma is more likely to have been Richard Goz. The timing of the appointment, of course, helps to date the fall of William Werlenc.

[194] In 1068, Richard had interests at Tailleville and Rucqueville in the Bessin, while a cadet branch of the family held property at Eterville and Colomby-sur-Thaon (Musset, 'Saint-Sever', pp. 358–60). The endowment of the abbey of Saint-Sever reveals further lands in the county at Mesnil-Auzouf, Saint-Denis-Maisoncelles, Les Loges, Chovain, Vaux-sur-Aure, Mosles, Vierville-sur-Mer. Just across the Dives, the Goz also held at Ranville. Some of these might have been lands held from the bishop of Bayeux in 1133 (Musset, 'Saint-Sever', p. 365). In the Hiémois, the family had possessions at Champaubert, Sainte-Anastasie-de-la-Briquetière, Ginai, Cisay-Saint-Aubin, and in a number of unidentified places, too (Musset, 'Saint-Sever', p. 363). These have been supposed to have been a legacy from Thurstan's time as *vicomte* of the Hiémois (Musset, 'Saint-Sever', p. 365). In the Avranchin, the family held lands around Saint-Sever itself (a few kilometres west of Vire) as well as at Martilly, Tallevande, and Sainte-Marie-Laumont in the Val-de-Vire (Musset, 'Saint-Sever', pp. 361–2). In the Avranchin, the Goz endowed their abbey with the tithe of Saint-James-de-Beuvron, which they held of the duke, and at Lucerne, Monteil, Bouillon, and the unidentified 'Campus Botri' (Musset, 'Saint-Sever', p. 362).

been especially powerful, and the fact that Nigel II of the Cotentin was apparently one of Geoffrey's kinsmen might well have been thought a disadvantage in the year of his election. That he obtained the see is thus a little surprising, and it may be that we do not have all the evidence necessary to understand why William chose him. But as it happened, his appointment was a triumph. He was very well remembered by his canons. John Le Patourel remarked that the *De statu* approaches hagiography when reporting his career.[195] Duke William was obviously pleased, too, as Geoffrey was given vast estates in England after the Conquest.[196]

It took William a little longer to put his own candidate into the bishopric of Avranches, although there is no reason to doubt the loyalty of the bishop, Hugh, who had been elected during his father's reign and who apparently appeared quite regularly at William's court. We do not know when Hugh died. It could have been as early as 1055, although it seems unlikely that William would have kept the bishopric vacant for five years. He was succeeded as bishop by John of Ivry, the younger son of Count Rodulf, and by the time of his appointment in 1060 a relatively old man. As he seems to have lived the secular life up to this point, it may be that he was pressed into the role as a result of William's need for an unwaveringly loyal supporter in a county where ducal control seems still to have been remote and thus weak. The monks of Mont-Saint-Michel had certainly failed to fulfil the role of promoters and respecters of ducal supporters that was played by the monks of the Upper Norman abbeys at Fécamp, Jumièges, Saint-Ouen, and Saint-Wandrille. Abbot Suppo's term of office (*c.* 1033–48) even saw the monks divided into factions: one that supported Norman influence, led by their Fécampois abbot, and one that feared what that influence might mean for the abbey's well-established liberties. Faced with this bitter opposition, Abbot Suppo resigned his office. He was replaced by Ralph of Beaumont, whose kinship with one of the greatest and most powerful of Norman families ensured that tensions would remain high. He died in 1053, while on pilgrimage, and Duke William then left the abbey vacant for two years until he permitted Ranulf of Bayeux to succeed as abbot. He had been elected by the monks, but was also clearly from Normandy and probably a Norman, and thus constituted a compromise candidate.[197] He ruled the abbey when Bishop John came to Avranches, and it was he who submitted to John as the bishop worked to impose clear lines of authority that led, ultimately, to Rouen.[198]

---

[195] J. Le Patourel, 'Geoffrey of Montbray, bishop of Coutances, 1049–93', *EHR*, 59 (1944), 130.

[196] Le Patourel, 'Geoffrey of Montbray', 152.

[197] Potts, *Monastic Revival*, pp. 101–2.

[198] In particular, he regularized the relationship between the bishop and abbot of Mont-Saint-Michel, putting limits on the abbot's autonomy and requiring the abbot, two

These moves could strengthen Duke William's authority in the west of his duchy, but the Bretons across the border still posed a threat to his security. And so William reached out to a select few Breton lords and offered them his patronage, too. Maino of Fougères was thus given land in Normandy in the 1050s,[199] while Rivallon of Dol seems to have enjoyed friendly relations with the duke in the 1060s and might even have sworn fidelity to William in order to gain a firm hold on Céaux.[200] Nonetheless, not every dangerous Breton lord benefited from such patronage, and so William still found himself facing the threat of an invasion of Normandy led by Conan, the son of Alan III, *c*. 1064. Given that Alan III had attacked the Norman frontier in the 1030s, William was obliged to respond. That response comprised the construction of the castle at Saint-James-de-Beuvron as well as a military campaign.[201] Taking his army past Mont-Saint-Michel, Duke William attacked Dol, which Conan had been besieging, Rennes, and Dinan. Conan fled and sought the aid of Count Geoffrey of Anjou. But although the two counts subsequently led a combined force against Duke William, the two sides failed to engage. William of Poitiers saw this as a Norman victory, but it was at best a psychological one as the campaign lacked any tangible outcome.

In the absence of better options, William continued to patronize select Bretons after his victory at Hastings in 1066, rewarding them with lands in England. The greatest of them were Alan the Red, who became the lord of Richmond in North Yorkshire (with land in twelve other counties), who was the brother of Alan Fergant and Alan the Black of Penthièvre and was thus William's cousin;[202] Ralph of Fougères, who was given lands in Buckinghamshire, Devon, Surrey, Suffolk,

---

canons, and the priests to attend the episcopal synods twice a year and the monks to process to the cathedral on the fifth day of Pentecost: *Ctl. Mont-Saint-Michel*, Appendix II, no. 9; R. Allen, '"A proud and headstrong man"', 9–10.

[199] *RADN*, no. 162; Bates, *Normandy*, p. 83. His holdings included Savigny-le-Vieux, which had almost certainly once comprised a part of the county of Mortain. It may be supposed that Duke William had taken this vill into his demesne after the forfeiture of William Werlenc, and had given it to Maino before creating his half-brother Robert count.

[200] *RADN*, no. 159 (1060 × 1066); Marchegay, pp. 16–18; K. S. B. Keats-Rohan, 'William I and the Breton contingent in the non-Norman conquest 1060–1087', *ANS*, 13 (1991), 164–6.

[201] *Regesta: William*, no. 251; Jumièges, ii. 208; Poitiers, p. 72. Katharine Keats-Rohan argued that the campaign was in fact the result of Norman aggression, designed to cow Conan and thus to gain an oath of fidelity from him so as to clear the ground for his attempt on the English throne (Keats-Rohan, 'The Breton contingent', 166)

[202] GDB, fos. 309r–313r; Yorks § 6N; P. Dalton, *Conquest, Anarchy and Lordship: Yorkshire 1066–1154* (Cambridge, 1994), pp. 39–47.

and Norfolk;[203] Wihenoc and Baderon of Le Boussac near Dol, who became the lords of Monmouth;[204] and Aubrey of Vern (Vere), who has been shown to have been a Breton by Katharine Keats-Rohan.[205] In addition, Ralph of Gael was made earl of East Anglia, although his links with William and Normandy were perhaps less important than had been the case with the others, as his father had served Edward the Confessor.[206]

William would have good cause to regret his generosity to this last figure. In 1075, Ralph of Gael masterminded the so-called rebellion of the three earls at the feast held to celebrate his marriage to the daughter of Earl Roger of Hereford. Although the rebellion failed swiftly and utterly in England, Ralph of Gael evaded William's clutches and returned to his Breton estates.[207] He then took the castle at Dol and garrisoned it with the help of Angevin troops. William was obliged to respond and settled down to besiege Ralph. But in the meantime, King Philip of the French began to construct a party against him. He sought the help of Duke Guy Geoffrey of Aquitaine while at Poitou in 1076, apparently unsuccessfully, but led a force to the relief of Dol regardless. William was forced to retire in some haste, abandoning his siege train in the process.[208] David Douglas emphasized the scale and importance of this reverse which he thought brought the Norman juggernaut finally to a standstill.

In 1077, Duke William made peace with King Philip. He also attempted to rebuild his bridges with the Bretons by diplomatic means. According to Orderic, 'the statesman king, recognizing that he could not conquer the Bretons by force ... made a treaty of friendship with Alan Fergant and gave him his daughter Constance in marriage.'[209] As Orderic claimed that the two had been married for fifteen years it is possible that they were betrothed as part of this treaty of friendship,[210] but they were only married at Caen or Bayeux between

---

[203] GDB, fos. 36v, 113v, 151v; Surrey § 32; Devon § 34; Bucks § 37; LDB, fos. 263r, 432r–v; Norfolk § 41; Suffolk § 50.

[204] These lands were held by William fitz Baderon in 1086: GDB, fos. 48v, 167r, 180v, 185v; Hants § 50; Glos §§ 32, E35; Hereford § 15.

[205] Keats-Rohan, 'The Breton contingent', 170–1 and for some of the Breton sub-tenants of these Breton lords see 169–72; Douglas, *William the Conqueror*, p. 231.

[206] F. Barlow, *Edward the Confessor* (London, 1970), p. 165.

[207] *ASChr*, 'D', s.a. 1076, 'E', s.a. 1075; trans. Garmonsway, pp. 210–11; Orderic, ii. 310–18; Worcester, iii. 24–6; Douglas, *William the Conqueror*, pp. 231–3.

[208] Orderic, ii. 350–2. On the siege see also Douglas, *William the Conqueror*, pp. 234–6 and W. S. Jesse, *Robert the Burgundian and the Counts of Anjou, ca. 1025–1098* (Washington DC, 2000), pp. 118–20.

[209] Orderic, ii. 352.

[210] Chibnall noted this theory, first suggested by Stapleton (Orderic, ii. 352–3, n. 4). While there is indeed no evidence to support it, it would explain Orderic's comments and certainly does not offend against common sense.

July and December 1086.[211] Less than a year before his death, then, William might have thought that he had finally established a permanent peace on his western frontier.

Having considered the changes and developments that occurred in the west of the duchy during William's reign, we need now to rewind to the 1050s and to consider what was happening further east. Soon after his suppression of Guy of Burgundy's rebellion, Duke William was obliged to begin manoeuvres to deal with a further challenge. While Richard II's marriage to Papia had brought the duke's authority to the Pays de Talou and Bray, it also resulted in a second ducal family and two children, William and Malger, with claims to the duchy. This was an unusual and dangerous development, as Searle pointed out.[212] The two brothers would rise to great heights during the reign of their young nephew, William the Bastard, the former being granted the castle and county of Arques c. 1037, and the latter being elected archbishop of Rouen at about the same time. They both seem to have been ambitious, and both apparently bridled under the rule of a boy whose claim, or so it seemed to them, should not have been preferred to their own, especially as Robert the Magnificent had succeeded his brother in preference to that brother's illegitimate son. Indeed, their sense of rivalry might have been increased by the closeness in age of all three men. Robert of Torigni thought that Richard had married Papia in 1024.[213] If he was right, and if William of Arques had been born the next year, he would have been only two years older than his nephew. Even if Richard had remarried immediately after Judith's death in 1017, his son could only have been nine years older than his nephew at most. Malger was even younger, and was probably very close in age to Duke William, as he was described as being in his boyhood (*in pueritia*) when made archbishop of Rouen in 1037.[214] These men, then, were contemporaries. They had almost certainly been brought up together, and that is likely to have sharpened their rivalry and – eventually – contempt.

Count William of Arques set about increasing his own power in Upper Normandy by marrying the daughter of Count Enguerrand of Ponthieu sometime before 1047.[215] His machinations probably forced Duke William to continue his

---

[211] Douglas, *William the Conqueror*, pp. 393–5.

[212] Searle, *PK*, pp. 214–16.

[213] RT, s.a. 1024; Delisle, i. 32; Howlett, p. 23.

[214] *Acts of the Archbishops*, pp. 38, 52. Boyhood continued until the fourteenth year (*Etymologies*, p. 241; also noted in Bates, 'Adolescence', 3, n. 12).

[215] Jumièges, ii. 104 and ns. 2 and 3 (p. 105); Lot, *Saint-Wandrille*, no. 15 (the act is dated 1035 × 1047 and as it is signed by Walter the count's son, and also mentions the souls of his sons in the plural, it reveals that the marriage must have taken place some years

grandfather's policy of building up alliances to the east of his duchy. First, William attempted to disarm the count's ability to draw on support from Ponthieu by marrying his own sister, Adelaide, to Count Enguerrand himself.[216] Then around 1049, William negotiated a marriage with Matilda, the daughter of Baldwin V of Flanders.[217] As Heather Tanner has remarked, the marriage gave William 'both prestige and the potential to reassert his power in the Pays de Caux ... Renewed ducal power would threaten William of Arques's influence and the effectiveness of the English-Boulonnais-Picard alliance'.[218] And when Duke William was promised the English throne by Edward the Confessor in 1051, he must have thought that he had now gained diplomatic victory and that his position in Upper Normandy had become unassailable.[219]

But although Duke William had apparently stymied the efforts of Count William of Arques to build up an independent power base in the county of Talou, concern about his loyalty probably remained. Count William was thus obliged to serve in the army that the duke took to besiege Domfront in 1052 – a campaign discussed below. But the count did not remain in the army for long. Perhaps believing that the siege would occupy Duke William for some time, Count William seized what he thought was his chance. He returned home without leave and took to arms. 'Haughty because of his noble birth, William built the stronghold of Arques on top of that hill, and assuming arbitrary power ... he dared to instigate a rebellion against the duke.'[220]

Count William ravaged Talou, and was obliged to do so because he was not entirely unopposed there. Gulbert of Auffay, who had married one of Richard III's daughters, stood against him.[221] He was joined by Geoffrey of Neuf-Marché, who had married Gulbert's sister, and Geoffrey's brother, Hugh of Morimont. Their

---

previously); Douglas, *William the Conqueror*, p. 63; Bauduin, *Première Normandie*, p. 306; H. J. Tanner, *Family, Friends and Allies*, pp. 89–90.

[216] Searle, *PK*, p. 324, n. 20; Bauduin, *Première Normandie*, pp. 306–7 and ns; K. Thompson, 'Being the ducal sister: the role of Adelaide of Aumale', in *Normandy and its Neighbours, 900–1250: Essays for David Bates*, ed. D. Crouch and K. Thompson (Turnhout, 2011), pp. 65–6.

[217] Jumièges, ii. 128–30; Poitiers, p. 32. The couple had been betrothed before the council of Reims 1049 as the marriage was discussed there. The date of the marriage itself is less clear. Douglas preferred 1052 (Douglas, *William the Conqueror*, p. 76) while Bates thought 1050 or 1051 (Bates, *William the Conqueror*, p. 32).

[218] Tanner, *Families, Friends and Allies*, pp. 88, 90–1.

[219] This is of course controversial, although Douglas, *William the Conqueror*, p.169 thought that there was no reasonable doubt that the promise had been made.

[220] Jumièges, ii. 102. See also Poitiers, pp. 32–42. For more on this rebellion see below, Chapter 6, pp. 326–7.

[221] Orderic, iii. 252–4.

father Turketil had been one of William's guardians, which also helps to explain their loyalty to the duke. But Gulbert and his allies seem not to have been able to make headway, and their failure to confine Count William might explain why they gained no benefit from the duke in return for their loyalty. Indeed, Geoffrey of Neuf-Marché would be disinherited by Duke William *c.* 1060, apparently as a result of his ineffectiveness in another theatre.[222]

Duke William responded swiftly in person and besieged Count William in his castle at Arques. Faced with this display of ducal power in his own heartland, Count William petitioned King Henry of the French for aid. Henry responded favourably and invaded Normandy. This was the first sign that relations between King Henry and Duke William had broken down.[223] Others might also have attempted to help Count William. Milo Crispin noted in his tract *Miraculum quo Beata Maria subuenit Guillelmo Crispino Seniori* that Count Walter of Amiens-Vexin attacked Normandy at around this same time. Duke William consequently reorganized this stretch of the frontier, handing the castle at Neaufles to William Crispin and appointing him *vicomte* of the Vexin, most likely in 1052.[224] William was a cadet of the family that had been established at Tillières before *c.* 1042 and was re-established there again after 1060, but he does not seem to had any prior connection with the Norman Vexin.[225] It is also the case that Neaufles was not William's to give. The vill was a possession of the archbishop of Rouen, and had been acknowledged as such by Robert the Magnificent, but such niceties seem to have been brushed aside at this time when William needed effective commanders in such strategic forts.[226]

William of Poitiers noted expressly that Guitmand of Moulins-la-Marche had handed his large border castle to King Henry during the rebellion, and implied that the two events were linked.[227] It is not at all clear that Guitmand would have seen his actions as comprising rebellion, however, as it is not at all clear that any part of his lordship had been part of Normandy to that date. It was only between 1040 and 1053, and most probably 1050 × 1053, that the duke's authority was recognized as encompassing any part of the lordship. This was the date at which

---

[222] Orderic, ii. 130; Bauduin, *Première Normandie*, p. 274. For Geoffrey's forfeiture, see below, *infra*, p. 135.

[223] For the relationship between king and duke see below, Chapter 5, pp. 262–3.

[224] J. A. Green, 'Lords of the Norman Vexin', in *War and Government in the Middle Ages: Essays in Honour of J. O. Prestwich*, ed. J. Gillingham and J. C. Holt (Woodbridge, 1984), pp. 49–50; Bauduin, *Première Normandie*, pp. 61, 276–8. I follow Pierre Bauduin with regard to the date.

[225] *PL*, 150, col. 737; translation in Van Houts, *Normans*, pp. 85–6.

[226] *RADN*, nos. 66, 67.

[227] Poitiers, p. 42.

Guitmund and his wife Emma gave the monks of Chartres the vill of Planches, as well as tithes at Moulins-la-Marche, with the consent of 'my lord Count William, from whose benefice I am seen to hold it'.[228] Guitmund, then, recognized Duke William's authority over his lordship, but was also happy to go along with the monks' decision to describe Normandy as a *beneficium* – presumably held from King Henry. This choice indicates a Frankish point of view, as does Guitmund's decision to make a gift to the 'foreign' monks of Chartres rather than to a Norman house. The diploma thus implies that Duke William was still in the process of bringing Guitmund's lands under his authority, and so it is possible and plausible that his appeal to the king of France in 1053 was the act of a lord whose independence and loyalties were under threat – perhaps as much from Roger of Montgommery as from Duke William himself. That might also be why he was not forfeited after his rebellion, despite handing his castle to the king of the French in a manner comparable with the actions of Thurstan Goz.[229]

Despite the support he received from King Henry and others, Count William was soon defeated and exiled. Arques and at least some of the other lands that William had been given when created count were subsequently recovered to the ducal demesne and a *vicomte* appointed to administer them.[230] Other lands that had belonged to Count William were redistributed. Walter Giffard was given a new honour centred on Longueville-sur-Scie, which seems previously to have belonged to the count.[231] Twelve years later he was to cross to England with William and to fight with him at Hastings. He was rewarded with a vast honour based on Long Crendon in Buckinghamshire.[232] Those English resources far outweighed his estates in Normandy, part of which were now held by a younger brother, and they would come to undermine Walter II Giffard's loyalty to a duke who was not also king. For the rest of William's reign, however, this patronage ensured that this well-established and well-connected family of the Pays de Caux would remain unshakeably loyal to the duke.

The last act in the rebellion-turned-war came in the form of a second French

[228] *RADN*, no. 117.
[229] Emily Tabuteau discussed the question of forfeiture, although not the loyalties of the lords of Moulins-la-Marche or the situation of their lordship (E. Z. Tabuteau, 'The family of Moulins-la-Marche in the eleventh century', *Medieval Prosopography*, 13 (1992), 49–51).
[230] A letter from the monks of Fécamp to William, written after 1066, reveals the existence of this *vicomte* (*PL*, 147, col. 476; Bates, *Normandy*, p. 206).
[231] J. Le Maho, 'L'apparition des seigneuries chatelaines dans le Grand Caux a l'époque ducale', *Archéologie Médiévale*, 6 (1976), 31–46.
[232] GDB, fos. 60r, 71v, 95r, 147r–148r, 157v, 196r, 205v, 211r–v: Berks 20; Wilts 31; Somerset 23; Bucks 14; Oxon, 20; Cambs 27[17]; Hunts 12; Beds 16; LDB, fos. 240v–243r, 430r; Norfolk § 25; Suffolk § 45.

invasion of Normandy. A Norman force met the French at Mortemer, even as they were 'totally preoccupied with arson and rape of women'.[233] The battle, if such it could be called, lasted from dawn to noon and resulted in the defeat of the French. Aside from ending the hostilities, it had three further political benefits. Firstly, Count Guy of Ponthieu was captured, to be released only after spending two years in captivity. He was obliged to do homage to the duke, and was sufficiently threatened to maintain that fidelity into the 1060s, surrendering Harold Godwinsson when ordered to do so, and allowing Duke William's invasion fleet to harbour on the Somme in the autumn of 1066. Secondly, as a result of Ralph of Mortimer's treachery during the battle, William of Warenne was given the castle of Mortemer and the vill of Bellencombre on the Varenne. The Warenne holdings in the county of Talou were thus augmented, and William would be still further enriched after the conquest of England, being granted the rape of Lewes and wide estates in Norfolk and elsewhere before 1086.[234] Thirdly, the French defeat at Mortemer seems to have spelled the end for Archbishop Malger of Rouen.

It is possible that Malger was never forgiven for his attempt to undermine William's marriage to Matilda. William of Malmesbury was later to report: 'some say that there was a secret reason for his deposition: Matilda, whom William had taken as his wife, was a near relation, and in his zeal for the Christian faith Malger found it intolerable that two blood relations should share the marriage bed, and had aimed the weapon of excommunication against his nephew and that nephew's consort.'[235] Archbishop Malger does seem to have enjoyed pronouncing anathema, as an act for the monks of Saint-Ouen makes plain.[236] Moreover, it is almost impossible to believe that he stayed entirely clear of his older brother's revolt, and again a denunciation of the marriage to Matilda would certainly have suited their own political ends. The official explanation for his deposition in 1054 or 1055, however, was that Malger had alienated the property of his archbishopric and behaved childishly. Yet Malger was a reformer, and had held a council at Rouen in the 1040s that had legislated against such things as the purchase of ordination, the usurpation of office, and the alienation of a church's property.[237] It is

---

[233] Jumièges, ii. 144.

[234] See most conveniently, Lewis, 'Warenne, William (I) de, first earl of Surrey', p. 404.

[235] Malmesbury, *GR*, i. 494. Malmesbury is the only writer to suggest this was the cause of Malger's deposition. His account was otherwise based on that provided by Poitiers, who provided the details about Malger's inappropriate lifestyle (Poitiers, pp. 86–8). Jumièges wrote that 'at that time Malger, archbishop of Rouen, began to behave foolishly and inspired by folly gave back the archbishopric to the duke' (Jumièges, ii. 130).

[236] AD S-M, 14 H 189. The anathema clause is not printed in Fauroux's edition of the act (*RADN*, no. 112). See below, Chapter 7, pp. 416–17 and Fig. 7.

[237] Bessin, *Concilia*, i. 40–2. For the possible date of the council, see M. de Boüard, 'Notes et hypothèses sur Maurille, moine de Fécamp', in *L'abbaye bénédictine de Fécamp*.

consequently difficult to escape the conclusion that the duke pushed for his depo-sition for political reasons, be it the result of his condemnation of the marriage or simply the potential for a hostile archbishop – especially one who failed to secure the return of his brother from exile – to undermine William's rule. So William took the trouble to ensure that Malger's deposition was well above board and, once it had been effected, acted to blacken his name.[238] He ended up portrayed as a pagan warlock.[239] He was replaced as archbishop by a well-educated and experienced monk of Fécamp called Maurillius, whom it is nonetheless possible to describe as a political nonentity.[240]

Even before all this had come to pass, Duke William had begun to look to the security of his southern frontier. Robert the Magnificent had held William of Bellême in check, and even the campaigns of 1042 and 1043 seem to have done little to turn the tide, except perhaps from providing the conditions to permit William Talvas, William of Bellême's successor, to recover independent posses-sion of Alençon. This was not enough to prevent Talvas's *fideles* from being drawn into the duke's orbit as Norman power recovered from the later 1040s, however. The members of the Giroie family, for example, were beginning to look on the duke of the Normans as their lord for the lands they held to the south of the Sarthe, not just those within the Lieuvin that Giroie had inherited from Heugon. Indeed, when William fitz Giroie was mutilated by William Talvas *c.* 1048, it was perhaps as a result of this perceived disloyalty.[241] The act, however, simply alien-ated the Giroie still further. And so in 1050 William fitz Giroie and other members of his family sought Duke William's confirmation of the donations they had made to their foundation at Saint-Evroult which included properties located in this disputed border region.[242] The lord of Alençon was not asked to do likewise.

By 1050, then, Duke William's power had advanced into the county of Maine. That awoke the concerns of a much more powerful lord than William Talvas,

---

Ouvrage scientifique du XIIIe centenaire (658–1958) (Fécamp, 1959), i. 89–92 (who argued for 1055); R. Foreville, 'The synod of the province of Rouen in the eleventh and twelfth centuries', in *Church and Government in the Middle Ages*, ed. C. N. L. Brooke, D. E. Luscombe, G. H. Martin, and D. Owen (Cambridge, 1976), pp. 22 and ns. a and b, 27 (who argued for 1054).

[238] For a similar view of Malger see M. Gibson, *Lanfranc of Bec* (Oxford, 1978), pp. 106–7.

[239] Wace wrote that after his self-imposed exile on the Channel Islands 'he had a devil as a familiar. I do not know whether or not it was a type of goblin' (Wace, p. 142).

[240] Lifshitz, *Pious Neustria*, p. 200.

[241] Thompson, on the other hand, thought that William's actions were the result of Giroie's allegiance becoming divided between himself and Geoffrey of Mayenne (Thompson, 'Family and influence', 219). The ideas are not mutually exclusive; they simply require a different emphasis.

[242] *RADN*, no. 122; Orderic, ii. 32–8.

and so, *c.* 1052, Count Geoffrey Martel of Anjou took control of Talvas's towns of Alençon and Domfront.[243] Duke William responded swiftly and in person:

> William, well able to defend the inheritance of his father and ancestors, and even to extend it further, arrived with his army *on Angevin territory*, intending as a reprisal to take Domfront from Geoffrey before capturing Alençon.[244]

He was successful. Alençon and Domfront fell to Duke William, who now gained a real hold on all the territory north of the Sarthe as well as in the Passais.[245] This was the first significant advance in Norman power since the reign of Richard II. William subsequently retained Domfront in his demesne, and seems to have attempted to settle his *fideles* on lands round about. Roger of Beaumont was given Annebecq, where he had already built a castle *c.* 1053.[246] It may be supposed that it was Roger who had constructed the church dedicated to Saint Vulfran there that is referred to in one of the miracle stories found in the *Inventio et miracula sancti Vulfrani*, thereby linking his frontier castle with one of the principal saints of Upper Normandy.[247] Gérard Louise thought that the Patry family were planted in Houlme at around this time, too.[248] He argued that this was also true of the lords of Briouze, but here the evidence is more ambiguous. They were perhaps more likely to have been local lords who were now, and slowly, brought into the duke's *mouvance*. That is suggested by the fact that William of Briouze named his son Philip, indicating that the family had previously been in the French king's orbit, and by his grants of the church at Briouze first to the monks of Bellême's abbey of Lonlay and then to the Angevin monks of Saumur. It is consequently less surprising than would otherwise be the case that it was only *c.* 1075, after the lords of Briouze had demonstrated their loyalty to the duke over a period of some twenty years, that William of Briouze was finally rewarded by a grant of the lordship of Bramber in Sussex, necessitating a rejigging of the existing rapes in the process.[249]

---

[243] The dating of this episode follows Douglas, *William the Conqueror*, pp. 385–8. Others, such as Pierre Bauduin, *Première Normandie*, pp. 309–10, have suggested that these events took place in 1049.

[244] Poitiers, p. 22 (my italics).

[245] Jumèges, ii. 122–4; Poitiers, p. 28.

[246] Louise, *Bellême*, i. 381–2.

[247] *Inventio*, pp. 70–1; Van Houts, *Normans*, pp. 78–9.

[248] Louise, *Bellême*, i. 377–8. The family probably settled in the Bessin first, especially if Musset was right in his suggestion that they had come to Normandy from Ireland (L. Musset, 'Participation de Vikings venus des pays celtes à la colonisation scandinave de la Normandie', *Cahiers du Centre de recherches sur les pays du Nord et du Nord Ouest*, 1 (1979), 107–17, as reprinted in *Nordica et Normannica*, pp. 286–7).

[249] Bramber is thought to have been created later than the neighbouring rapes of Lewes

While Duke William retained Domfront after the campaign, Alençon was given to Roger of Montgommery who then sought to establish his control over the rest of Talvas's estates, legitimizing his position through his marriage to Mabel of Bellême, William's daughter and ultimately heiress of both her father and her uncle, Ivo of Bellême, bishop of Sées.[250] One hint about the advance of this process may be found in a diploma of William of La Ferté-Macé, who sought a ducal confirmation of his grants to Saint-Julien of Tours in 1053, just as Duke William was asserting his authority in the region in person. It is perhaps worthy of note that even in an act that was confirmed by the duke, it was Roger and Bishop Ivo who were described as his lords (seniores).[251] A second hint is provided by Orderic's account of the rebellions of Robert fitz Giroie and Arnold of Echauffour, which took place about six years later. Orderic reported that Robert fitz Giroie, who held the castle at Saint-Céneri on the Sarthe a little south-west of Alençon, had been married to one of Duke William's kinswomen (consobrina). It may be supposed that the duke intended to win his loyalty as a result. However, Robert fortified his castle at Saint-Céneri against the duke c. 1059 and called on Angevin aid. He died during the subsequent siege, Orderic alleged by poison. His nephew and heir, Arnold of Echauffour, continued the revolt but then submitted to the duke who confirmed him in possession of Saint-Céneri and the rest of his paternal inheritance in return for his fidelity.[252] The duke, then, had gained overlordship of Saint-Céneri. But this was very close to Montgommery's centre of operations at Alençon, and so while these arrangements must have been highly satisfactory to Duke William, they were not at all acceptable to Montgommery who seems to have wanted Arnold's castle and lordship for himself. So Roger of Montgommery undermined the rapprochement for his own benefit. Orderic noted that 'serious troubles broke out between William duke of Normandy and his magnates. For one would try through jealousy to oust another from his position ... Then Roger of Montgommery and Mabel his wife made the most of the disorders of the time, flattered the duke into taking their part, and cunningly incited him to anger against their neighbours.'[253] That anger saw Arnold of Echauffour, Hugh of Grandmesnil, and Ralph of Tosny exiled from Normandy. According to Orderic, Mabel of Bellême subsequently had Arnold poisoned. Roger of Montgommery then ensured that his lands passed to him.[254]

and Arundel (T. P. Hudson, 'Bramber Rape', in A History of the County of Sussex, Vol VI, Part 1: Bramber Rape (Southern Part), ed. T. P. Hudson (London, 1980), p. 3.

[250] Jumièges, ii. 118; Orderic, ii. 46–8.
[251] RADN, no. 131 and see Louise, Bellême, i. 315.
[252] Orderic, ii. 78–80.
[253] Orderic, ii. 90.
[254] Orderic, iii. 134.

The conclusion of this struggle suggests its cause. Robert fitz Giroie discovered that his kinship to the duke could not protect him from Roger of Montgommery's attempts to establish his own hegemony over him and his lands. So he rebelled. Montgommery then ensured that the Giroie lands came to him. Throughout, he acted to extend his own undisputed authority over the land and men of the lordship of Bellême, even to the extent of undermining the duke's efforts to establish his own authority in the region.

It is likely that Montgommery's growing power in the area around Alençon also acted to diminish Angevin influence there, already in retreat after the events of 1052, still further. The result was that Geoffrey Martel sought a new alliance with King Henry in 1057. The two men then led an army into Normandy through the Hiémois, and burned and ravaged their way through that county and into Bessin.[255] The area they apparently chose to attack suggests that the real target of this campaign was Geoffrey's rival, Roger of Montgommery, rather than the duke. There was very little ducal demesne in the Hiémois, and an attack on any of the duke's three principal possessions, Exmes, Argentan, and Falaise, would surely have been mentioned by the chroniclers had it happened. Montgommery's estates, however, were concentrated in this area. The lack of comment in any of the narratives might therefore reflect their focus on the duke's tribulations and successes, and their disinterest in those that impacted even one of his greatest lords. But in any event, the campaign signally failed to gain any benefit for king and count, and saw instead the destruction of the rearguard of the royal army by the duke's forces at the battle of Varaville.[256] Count Geoffrey's influence to the south of Alençon thus continued to wane, its retreat underlined by the appearance of Bishop Ivo of Sées, a long-time ally of the Angevin, at Duke William's court in 1059.[257] And William's victory seems also to have marked the beginning of a new phase in William's career, indicated by William of Jumièges's decision that the time had come to reconcile restless Norman lords with William's regime, and William with his defeated opponents.

It is just possible that the intended target of the 1057 campaign had been Caen – and Wace's later testimony actually has the French troops capture the undefended

---

[255] Poitiers, p. 54; Malmesbury says that King Henry invaded by way of Exmes (Malmesbury, *GR*, i. 434).

[256] Jumièges, ii. 150–2; Poitiers, pp. 54–6.

[257] Thompson, 'Family and influence', p. 223. Ivo attested an act for the monks of Saint-Ouen, recording a grant of land by Hugh of La Ferté-en-Bray. The act probably dates from 1046, but it is not clear that Ivo had been present at William's court when the act was made, as his *signum* is in a different ink and in a different hand from that of Duke William (AD Seine-Maritime, 14 H 829: *RADN*, no. 102). In contrast see Bates, 'Adolescence', 9.

town – which was already the principal ducal centre in Lower Normandy.[258] It was Duke Richard II who had first seen the potential of the place. It was a Gallo-Roman site not far from the sea, at the junction of the rivers Odon and Orne,[259] and set on the Roman road from Rouen to Cherbourg, just east of the junction with the Roman road to Sées, Le Mans, and Tours. In addition, much of the duke's demesne in the Bessin was scattered around the vill, which must have made it an obvious centre for the administration of those estates, and ensured it could be well-provisioned during those intermittent and brief occasions when the duke, his household, and his *familia* were in residence. Richard II thus began the development of the town in the 1020s, and the moment that it moved from vill to *bourg* is perhaps revealed by two of his acts. The first, dating from 1021 × 1025, records a grant to the monks of Saint-Père at Chartres of a house at Caen, a place which was then described as a 'villa'.[260] By August 1025, however, Richard II had given the monks of Fécamp the tithe of the toll of the *bourg* of Caen and an *hôte*.[261]

William the Bastard might have been encouraged to develop Caen further as a result of the rebellion of 1046–47 and the failure of the bishop of Bayeux to prevent it or combat it. Those events had revealed the need for a strong ducal centre in Lower Normandy. He perhaps signalled that intention by holding a council in the *bourg* immediately after his victory, apparently *before* he had begun to build the place up. Work on the abbeys, and presumably on the castle, too, began soon afterwards. By 1066, a *prévôt* had been appointed to administer the *bourg* for the duke, and 100 *sous* from the revenues had been given to the nuns of Montivilliers.[262] Those revenues were principally derived from trade. The Orne was navigable as far as Caen, and by the end of the eleventh century the town had 'a large port from which she sends ships to the sea'. It was Rodulf Tortarius who remarked upon the port, and he observed, too, the bustling markets of Caen, which sold merchandise brought from England and diverse other places and included vegetables, wools, linens, soft silks, spices such as cinnamon and pepper, incense, apples, honey, bristly swine, woolly sheep, cattle, and the skins of wild animals.[263]

---

[258] Wace, p. 148. This is probably an exaggeration, born of an attempt to understand why the king and count attacked this part of the duchy. None of the contemporary or near-contemporary accounts suggest that the French army crossed the Orne.

[259] For some early history see J. Decaëns, 'Le premier château, de Guillaume le Conquérant à Richard Cœur de Lion (XIe–XIIe siècles)', in *Mémoires du Château de Caen*, ed. J.-Y. Marin and J.-M. Levesque (Caen, 2000), pp. 15–16.

[260] *RADN*, no. 32.

[261] *RADN*, no. 34.

[262] *RADN*, no. 172.

[263] Rodulfus Tortarius, *Carmina*, pp. 324, 327 (Epistula IX: Ad Roberti).

The *prévôt* almost certainly operated out of the castle that William built on a rock that stood to the north of the town, which was provided with a small palace next to the entrance.[264] A suburb quickly grew up around the abbey of Saint-Etienne, located on the main road to Bayeux, which William raised into a *bourg* in its own right in 1066 × 1077 and gave to the monks. That gift led to a dispute with the nuns of La Sainte-Trinité, who held the churches of Saint-Etienne-le-Vieux and Saint-Martin, which were now within the monk's *bourg*. The resulting settlement informs us that the *bourg* was populated by five cobblers, two fullers, an iron-worker, and a leather-worker.[265] The royal duke surrendered to his monks all his customs in that *bourg*, with the exception of the tolls levied on merchants coming from outside to sell at the Monday market, and on those who were transporting goods to the officials of the greater *bourg* (who probably enjoyed an exemption that he did not want the monks to abolish). The monks were also to have one piece of wood from every cart that came to Caen to sell wood.[266] Finally, William endowed his abbey with a modest collection of relics: an ampoule of St Stephen's blood and a fragment of one of the rocks with which he had been stoned; some of his hairs with a piece of skull; some oil of St Catherine; a finger of St Nicholas; and some blood of St George.[267]

William resided only occasionally at Caen, but the castle and his abbeys stood as permanent monuments to his authority, and even though he was almost always absent his rule was maintained and promoted by his abbots and monks, as well as by Ranulf the *vicomte*, and Roger of Montgommery, his kinsmen, and a variety of other lords, both great and small, whose patronage of the duke's monasteries can be taken as a token of their support for his regime.[268] By the 1080s, then, William had much more direct control over the Bessin than he had enjoyed in the period 1046–47, and much more control over the bishop's men, too, not least because of the lands that they held in England both directly and indirectly from him. That control only increased after Bishop Odo's imprisonment *c.* 1083, in part because William used the bishop's estates to patronize his own supporters. Ranulf the *vicomte*, for example, was given property that had belonged to the bishopric while William 'was ill at Coutances'.[269] William also seems to have taken some of the bishop's property for himself. In 1089 while at Vernon, Robert Curthose restored a number of possessions to Bishop Odo,

---

[264] See below, Chapter 10, pp. 592–3.
[265] *Les actes de Guillaume le Conquérant et de la reine Mathilde pour les abbayes Caennaises*, ed. L. Musset, MSAN, 37 (1967), no. 17*bis*; noted in Bates, *Normandy*, pp. 131.
[266] *Regesta: William*, no. 54.
[267] *Actes Caenaises*, pp. 16, 18, 141 (no. 29).
[268] See *Regesta: William*, nos. 49, 50)
[269] *Livre Noir*, i. 95 (no. 76); *CDF*, no. 1435.

which had been either retained in demesne by William or granted to other churches in the interval.[270]

The Varaville campaign resulted in a tit-for-tat advance by William across his southern frontier. The ground work for this had been prepared some years earlier when, after the battle of Mortemer, 'opposite the castle of Tillières, which earlier on the king had taken away from him, the duke built another one, not less strong, to this day called Breteuil, which he entrusted to William fitz Osbern to guard against his enemies'.[271] It is possible that Breteuil was among the possessions that fitz Osbern had inherited via his grandmother from Count Rodulf and Bishop Hugh of Bayeux – his lands around Cormeilles certainly were. If so, the fact that the castle was entrusted to William fitz Osbern would have been only right. Nonetheless, it should also be seen as a sign of favour, as Duke William was not averse to taking castles away from those whom he thought unable to hold them.[272] Fitz Osbern recognized that the defences of his lordship might be strengthened by the development of a town next to the castle as much as the fortification itself, and sought to recruit settlers to, and develop the economy of, his new borough by a grant of generous laws which would provide a model for the later laws of, for example, Hereford, Rhuddlan, and Verneuil.[273]

As would be expected, given William fitz Osbern's place in the duke's counsels and, it may be supposed, affections, the castle at Breteuil was not the only piece of patronage he received from Duke William's hands. He had already been given part of the lordship of Brionne after the defeat of Guy of Burgundy, revealed by an act of c. 1050 × 1066 which records that Duke William gave the monks of Le Bec part of the forest of Brionne that had formerly been given to Robert fitz Ricucio by Guy. The gift was 'witnessed and praised by William fitz Osbern who held that benefice and returned it to the count, accepting 20 livres from Abbot Herluin'.[274] Around the time Breteuil was rebuilt, in 1054 × 1066, a certain Alured gave the monks of Préaux 'whatever he held at Bonneville-sur-Touques, namely in fields and salt-works with the consent of William fitz Osbern from whom he held it as a

---

[270] *Livre Noir*, i. 6–8 (no. 4).

[271] Jumièges, ii. 146.

[272] Fitz Osbern had inherited lands in the Lieuvin originally held from Rodulf, including Cormeilles, Firfol, Fumichon, Saint-Aubin-de-Scellon, and la Chapelle-Bayvel (Gazeau, 'Patrimoine', pp. 142–3). There is, however, no clear evidence that the lands that now were formed into the honour of Breteuil, lying within the triangle formed by Breteuil, Lyre, and Glos-la-Ferrière had been held by Rodulf (Crouch, *Beaumont Twins*, pp. 102–14; Bauduin, *Première Normandie*, pp. 221–3).

[273] See M. Bateson, 'The Laws of Breteuil', *EHR*, 15 (1900), 73–8, 302–18, 496–523, 754–7; 16 (1901), 92–110, 332–45; A. Ballard, 'The Law of Breteuil', *EHR*, 30 (1915), 646–58.

[274] *RADN*, no. 189.

benefice'.[275] This last, at least, seems to have been a grant made directly from the duke's demesne.

With Breteuil in safe hands and with this place established as a forward base, William advanced to, and then crossed, the Avre in 1058 and marched his army to Thimert, just a few miles from Châteauneuf-en-Thymerais, which he captured. His troops, led at one stage by Richard of Reviers, then held it against King Henry and his allies, who included Count Ralph of Valois, Waleran of Meulan, and Simon of Montfort-l'Amaury, from the beginning of the summer of that year until after the king's death in August 1060.[276] Duke William seems also to have attempted to recover those lands that had made up Liégeard's dower around Coudres and Saint-André-de-l'Eure. His presence at Evreux in 1059 and his attestation of Richard of Revier's grant to the monks of Saint-Pére of Chartres at Courdemanche (probably one of the places concerned) in 1060 provides some evidence of this.[277] Duke William failed in his attempt, however. Liégeard's dower lands in the south of the Evrecin remained outside Norman control, and would continue to do so until Henry' I's reign. Nonetheless, the complexities of the political and geographical situation were recognized by contemporaries. When Gaston of Châteauneuf-en-Thymerais founded a priory of Marmoutiers at Croth near Saint-André-de-l'Eure in 1060, he did so with the consent of his lord, Hugh Bardulf, and with the confirmation of King Philip I. But that did not stop the monks of Marmoutier from describing Croth as located 'in Normandy, in the territory of Evreux'.[278]

Duke William's campaign against Thimert gave rise to enmities which would work against him in the future. This was first to become apparent in the case of Count Ralph of Valois, who had been among those at the siege of Thimert and who soon afterwards began launching his own raids across the Norman border. As that warfare was associated with his inheritance of the county of the Vexin in 1063, those attacks focused on the frontier that ran along the Epte. Duke William seems to have been unhappy with the local response, as he acted to shore up his defences:

---

[275] *Ctl. Préaux*, A19.

[276] Douglas, *William the Conqueror*, p. 74; Bauduin, *Première Normandie*, p. 191; A. Lemoine-Descourtieux, *La frontière normande de l'Avre: de la foundation de la Normandie à sa réunion au domaine royal (911–1204)* (Mont-Saint-Aignan, 2011), p. 36. That Richard led William's troops is revealed by *RADN*, no. 147, which records his deathbed request and bequest to the monks of Chartres.

[277] Orderic, ii. 74; *RADN*, no. 147; Lemoine-Descourtieux, *Le frontière normande de l'Avre*, p. 173.

[278] *Recueil des actes de Philippe Ier roi de France (1059–1108)*, ed. M. Prou (Paris, 1907), p. 24 (no. 2), noted by Lemoine-Descourtieux, *La frontière normande de l'Avre*, p. 42.

William the renowned marquis of Normandy, in the course of defending his frontiers against the ravages of the men of Beauvais expelled Geoffrey the natural heir of the castle of Neuf-Marché for some trivial offence and entrusted the defence of the castle to several of his barons; but scarcely one of them could defend it for as much as a year against the attacks of the men of Milli and Gerberoy and other frontier regions. Finally the great duke granted half the town to Hugh of Grandmesnil, a man of outstanding bravery and courtesy, and entrusted the defence of it to him and Gerald the Steward.[279]

William, then, once again dispossessed the rightful lord of a border castle in order to strengthen the defences of his duchy, providing another indication of the arbitrary way in which the ducal demesne might be augmented. Hugh, we are told, subsequently fought valiantly against Count Ralph, even if he did not always triumph. He also made a marriage with the Beaumont family from the neighbouring Beauvaisis, presumably in the hope of strengthening his position against Ralph.[280]

Perhaps because of the greater resistance he now faced, but more likely because he was bribed to do so by a life-grant of Gisors from Archbishop Maurilius of Rouen, Count Ralph had come to terms with Duke William by 1066. It is unlikely that Duke William trusted Ralph to keep the peace, however, as he was required to hand over his son, Simon, as a surety. Simon was subsequently brought up in William's household, and the two men seem to have developed a genuine and close friendship, which boded well for the future security of this stretch of the frontier.[281] Or it would have done had Simon not decided, three years after he had succeeded to his father's counties, and on his wedding night, to declare his intention to become a monk. And so in 1077, King Philip seized his county. As William had just been defeated before the gates of Dol, he was in no position to resist.

King Philip's possession of the Vexin constituted a threat to Norman security to a much greater extent than had been the case under Count Ralph, as he would demonstrate just a few months after acquiring it, as both he and another of the enemies that William had made in the course of his Thimert campaign, Hugh of Châteauneuf-en-Thymerais, would play a supporting role in the first of the two rebellions of Robert Curthose.

---

[279] Orderic, ii. 130.

[280] Douglas, *William the Conqueror*, p. 137 and Searle, *PK*, p. 188 misidentified Hugh's bride as coming from the important Norman family of Beaumont-le-Roger.

[281] See D. Bates, 'Lord Sudeley's ancestors: the family of the counts of Amiens, Valois and the Vexin in France and England during the 11th century', in *The Sudeley – Lords of Toddington* (Thetford, 1987), pp. 34–48 and M. Hagger, 'Kinship and identity in eleventh-century Normandy: the case of Hugh de Grandmesnil, c. 1040–1098', *JMH*, 32 (2006), pp. 212–30.

This rebellion broke out in late 1077 or 1078, and seems to have been provoked by William's continued refusal to surrender any authority in either Normandy or Maine to his son. Its timing might also have been a result of William's defeat at Dol.[282] The rebellion revealed divisions within Normandy and within Norman families, albeit ones that would not usually have operated to undermine ducal power or Norman solidarity in the case of external threats. Those divisions are revealed by the support that Curthose could muster against his father.

The most important of those who sided with Curthose was probably Robert of Bellême.[283] He should not, perhaps, be seen simply as Roger of Montgommery's son, nor necessarily as seeking independence from his father, as he had most likely inherited the lordship of Bellême in his own right on his mother's death c. 1077.[284] Bellême might have hoped that any settlement would see Curthose given more authority in Maine, where his own influence might then grow to resemble that exercised by his maternal grandfather. He might even have been given promises to that effect. But whatever he was offered it would have seemed worth it to Curthose, as Bellême's support seems to have been crucial. Firstly, his lordship gave him the ability to bankroll Curthose's revolt. Secondly, he was the brother-in-law of Hugh of Châteauneuf-en-Thymerais, and although Hugh had his own axe to grind with Duke William, it might have been Bellême's presence among Curthose's supporters that persuaded Hugh to hand over his castles at Rémalard, Sorel, and Châteauneuf-en-Thymerais to the rebels so that they might raid across the borders of the duchy. Thirdly, it is possible that others were convinced to follow Curthose because of the support offered to him by Bellême. William of Moulins-la-Marche, for example, seems to have inherited the view of his prede-cessors that his lordship lay in France and within the *mouvance* of the lords of Bellême. Joel, the son of Alured the Giant, might have joined the revolt as a result of his family's connection with the lords of Bellême, too.[285] Even Ivo and Aubrey

---

[282] *ASChr*, 'E', s.a. 1077; trans. Garmonsway, p. 213. That reason for the rebellion is also suggested by the letter Pope Gregory VII sent to Robert after peace had been made in 1080: *The Register of Pope Gregory VII 1073–1085. An English Translation*, trans. H. E. J. Cowdrey (Oxford, 2002), pp. 358–9 (no. 7.27).

[283] Orderic, ii. 358; iii. 100.

[284] Louise, *Bellême*, i. 388. Louise dated Mabel's death c. 1079, but Chibnall preferred c. 1077 (Orderic, iii. 136–7, n. 1; iv. 132, n. 4) and her view is followed here. That would mean that Bellême was almost certainly in control of his mother's lordship when Curthose rebelled. We know that Roger had delegated authority over his Norman lands to his son because it was Robert of Bellême who turned about when hearing the news of William the Bastard's death and drove the ducal garrisons from his castles (Orderic, iv. 112–14), and also because Roger of Montgommery sent his son a writ about them (Ctl. Sées, fo. 95r).

[285] For their presence among Robert's followers see Orderic, iii. 100.

of Grandmesnil, probably the fourth and fifth sons of Hugh of Grandmesnil at this stage of their careers (their eldest brother would die during their father's lifetime but was still alive when Curthose revolted), are most likely to have joined the rebellion as a result of Bellême's involvement. The Montgommery's lands marched with their own in the Pays d'Auge, and they might have hoped to win the affection of their powerful neighbour and thereby supplant their brothers should Robert succeed in extending his lordship over their family's estates in the future.

William of Breteuil was the next most important of those who followed Curthose into rebellion. Like Bellême, he was an established lord, having inherited Breteuil, Pacy-sur-l'Eure, and Cormeilles on his father's death in 1071. He was thus another in a position to help finance the revolt, if only in its early stages as his lands were likely confiscated by King William once the revolt had broken out.[286] It may be supposed that William rebelled in the hope of winning the freedom of his brother, Earl Roger of Hereford, who had languished in William's prison since 1075, but he might equally have already developed the close friendship with Curthose that would be later manifested in his support for the absent duke's claim to the English throne in 1100. It is possible that William of Breteuil's decision to rebel also brought Ralph II of Tosny, another established lord in the Evrecin and on the Seine, into the conspiracy, as he was William's father-in-law.[287] He was, however, also the husband of Isabella of Montfort-l'Amaury, and it might equally have been that French connection that caused Ralph to rebel.[288]

Curthose was thus able to take advantage of ambition and injustice when prosecuting his complaint against his father, but they were not enough to give him a strong base within either Normandy or Maine. So he established himself at Rémalard just across the Avre frontier instead. The royal duke responded by attacking Curthose's castles and allies across his border. But first he purchased peace with Rotrou of Mortagne, in whose fee Rémalard lay, probably to ensure that any strike against that castle would not be seen as an act of war against Rotrou as well as the rebels.[289] The castle was then besieged. Aymer of Villeray was killed in a skirmish. His son made peace. And Curthose seems to have recognized that he had now outstayed his welcome.

So Curthose approached King Philip for help. The king sent him to the castle of

---

[286] Orderic, iii. 100. William's confiscation of the rebels' estates was remarked upon by Orderic (Orderic ii. 358).

[287] Orderic, ii. 358.

[288] See L. Musset, 'Aux origines d'une classe dirigeante: Les Tosny, grands barons Normands du Xᵉ au XIIIᵉ siècle', *Francia*, 5 (1977), 56–61.

[289] Orderic, ii. 360. As Chibnall noted, Orderic's remark that William made peace with Rotrou has been taken to mean that he was previously fighting him (as with Douglas, *William the Conqueror*, p. 238), but there is no evidence for this belief.

Gerberoy, in the Vexin, across the Epte from Gournay-en-Bray. King William fortified his frontiers, putting garrisons in his castles to prevent Robert and his allies
from raiding across the border. But he was unable to tolerate the presence of his
enemies so close to his frontier for very long. And so, towards the end of 1078, he
raised an army and marched against his errant son and his allies. His luck deserted
him once again. Robert's forces sallied out of the castle and joined battle. Robert
attacked his own father and wounded his hand or arm. William's horse was killed
beneath him. According to John of Worcester, it was only then that Robert realized just whom he was fighting. 'As soon as Robert recognized William's voice,
he quickly dismounted, and ordered his father to mount his horse, and in this
way allowed him to leave.' The 'D' version of the *Anglo-Saxon Chronicle* tells a
different story. According to the chronicler, an Englishman, Toki son of Wigod
of Wallingford, brought up another horse for William only to be killed by a
crossbow bolt for his trouble.[290] Orderic, on the other hand, failed to mention
the episode altogether. William made peace with his son soon afterwards, but the
issues between them remained largely unresolved.

The fighting of 1077–79, and the identity of the principal enemies that William
had faced during those campaigns, were together responsible for the two strategic marriages of the last years of William's reign. The first was the marriage
of Constance to Alan of Brittany, noted above. The second was the marriage
of William's daughter Adela to Count Stephen of Blois-Chartres. Around 1083,
'Stephen, count palatine of Blois, anxious to strengthen the bonds of friendship
with King William, sought the hand of his daughter Adela in marriage. By the
counsel of his advisers her father gave his consent, and she was united to him
with due ceremonial. They were betrothed at Breteuil and honourably married
at Chartres.'[291] William thus gained an ally against both the French king and the
lords of Châteauneuf-en-Thymerais – and at precisely the time that Curthose
began his second rebellion. But Orderic's report suggests that Duke William was
not the only one with something to gain from the alliance. Stephen had inherited
his family's long-standing hostility to the Angevins, and an alliance with the
Normans against this common enemy was probably what made the marriage
so desirable from his point of view, especially as the earlier disputes with the
Normans over Dreux and Tillières were now a thing of the past.[292] A new marriage, then, was a viable prospect and one likely to achieve its aim of joining the

[290]   *ASChr*, 'D', s.a. 1079; trans. Garmonsway, p. 214; Malmesbury, *GR*, i. 476; Worcester, iii.
        32.
[291]   Orderic, iii. 116.
[292]   See also the discussion in K. LoPrete, *Adela of Blois: Countess and Lord (c. 1067–1137)*
        (Dublin, 2006), pp. 34–5, 39, 55–60.

two houses in amity rather than dividing them once again. And indeed, the marriage did achieve a strong and long-lasting alliance, which bore its fruit during the reign of William's son, Henry I.

The final episode of William's life indicates how the enmity and rivalry of the French king, his possession of the French Vexin and Dreux, and the growth of royal influence in the surrounding lordships had by then made that region the focus of friction and the stage for the two kings' shows of strength. During the royal duke's absence in England in 1086, King Philip had taken the opportunity to attack the diocese of Evreux, ravage the lands of William of Breteuil and Roger of Ivry around Pacy-sur-Eure, and drive away herds of cattle and prisoners. His actions roused King William to anger. He demanded that the whole of the Vexin, including Pontoise, Mantes, and Chaumont should be restored to him, basing his claim on a purported grant to Robert the Magnificent,[293] and he uttered dire threats about what he would do should Philip not bow to his will. It took some time for William to make good his threats, however, because he fell ill and took to his bed at Rouen. King Philip of France, making fun of William's corpulence, joked that the king of the English was keeping to his bed 'like a woman who has just had her baby'. This personal insult drove William to still further fury. He led an army into the Vexin and attacked Mantes. But during the fighting he received an internal injury, perhaps because 'his horse, in jumping a steep ditch, ruptured its rider's internal organs because his stomach projected over the forward part of the saddle'.[294] He retired to Rouen, and it was there that he died on 9 September 1087.

[293] Orderic, iv. 74–6.

[294] Malmesbury, *GR*, i. 510. Orderic, in contrast, blamed exhaustion and the heat of the flames: Orderic, iv. 78.

CHAPTER 3

Sibling Rivalry: Normandy under the Conqueror's Heirs, 1087–1144

Robert Curthose, 1087–1106 (with the Norman rule of William Rufus, 1096–1100)

IT is difficult to gain a clear picture of Robert Curthose as either a man or a ruler. Almost all the writers that wrote about his reign did so after he had lost his duchy, and that coloured their portraits of him. As God had chosen to punish Curthose and to promote Henry I, the monastic chroniclers in particular were left to find suitable explanations for these divine actions. They found them in Curthose's ineptitude and/or his failure to protect the Church, or else in his refusal to take the throne of Jerusalem when it was offered to him at the end of the First Crusade. Thus Orderic Vitalis, who wrote by far the fullest account of the reign, criticized Curthose's sloth, his prodigality, and lack of foresight, and remarked upon the duke's inability to garrison his subjects' castles, uphold the Truce of God, and do justice in accordance with the obligations of Christian rulership and, more specifically, with the lists of ducal rights laid down in the *Consuetudines et iusticie* of 1091 or 1096.[1] Orderic's condemnation of Curthose's rule was thus carefully constructed and intended to chime with contemporaries' expectations of ducal power – especially after their long experience of Henry I's effective government. But some secular writers took a different tack and criticized the infidelity of Robert's supporters. Thus Serlo of Bayeux, writing immediately after Henry I's siege of Bayeux in 1105, condemned the defenders of the city for their failure to protect the city, but did not condemn Curthose in any way.[2] Wace, writing in the 1170s, went even further. He portrayed Henry I as an unjustified usurper – although precisely why he did so may be obscured by the fact that his poem stops in its tracks at this point.[3] Not everyone remembered Curthose as a

---

[1] See below, Chapter 8, pp. 445–8.

[2] Serlo of Bayeux, 'The Capture of Bayeux', ed. and trans. M. Arbabzadah in E. van Houts, 'The fate of priests' sons in Normandy with special reference to Serlo of Bayeux', *HSJ*, 25 (2014), 86–105.

[3] Wace, pp. 218–20. For his dismissal see M. Aurell, *The Plantagenet Empire, 1154–1224*, trans. D. Crouch (London, 2007), pp. 138–9 and C. Urbanski, *Writing History for the King: Henry II and the Politics of Vernacular Historiography* (Ithaca, NY and London,

poor ruler, then. To some, he was a victim of treachery and his brother's over-weening ambition.[4]

Nineteenth- and early-twentieth-century historians who first sketched out the shape of the reign were more inclined to follow Orderic than those quieter voices who defended Curthose's record. His portrayal of the reign consequently set the tone for the negative views of the duke found in, for example, the studies by Charles Homer Haskins and Charles Wendell David, who were persuaded that Orderic could be trusted by the small number of Curthose's surviving acts; the apparent reluctance of litigants to seek justice in his court; the preservation in muniments and cartularies of records attesting to widespread alienations and usurpations during the reign; and letters, such as that condemning Curthose's treatment of the bishopric of Lisieux.[5] More recent accounts have reconsidered the evidence and found it less damning.[6] And while the ambiguities in the sources mean that any attempts to revise our perception of the reign cannot entirely convince, any more than the older view to the contrary can, they are at least the result of the more nuanced appreciation of the materials we have at our disposal – which is only to be expected after a century's worth of academic investigation into medieval writing, of course – and of the other factors that impacted Curthose's ability to rule.

Even the most negative of sources reveals that Curthose faced a number of problems that his predecessors had not had to deal with. Firstly, the area ruled by the duke of the Normans ceased to expand for the first time after 1087. Indeed, it shrank as Curthose inherited Normandy but not England. As a result, the sense

2013), pp. 108–47. Although this is not the place for a full discussion of Wace's intentions, if he were writing after the Great War of 1173–74 it would certainly have been quite difficult for him to paint Henry I in glowing colours without implying that the Young King had also had just cause for his own rebellion.

[4] See below, Chapter 5, pp. 295–8. It is likely that Henry eschewed the ducal title until *c.* 1115 to quieten the opposition he faced.

[5] See *NI*, pp. 62–4 ('it is a dreary tale of private war, murder, and pillage, of perjury, disloyalty, and revolt'). Haskins did recognize that Orderic's account was 'largely local and episodic', and so based his account on the documentary sources, only to conclude that they supported Orderic's gloomy view (*NI*, pp. 65–72, 76–8). See also Hollister, *Henry*, at, for example, pp. 55, 98, 132, 185, 217. Green acknowledged that the list from La Sainte-Trinité could not be 'totally discounted' as evidence of Curthose's weak rule (J. A. Green, 'Robert Curthose reassessed', *ANS*, 22 (2000), 115). She, and others, have omitted mention of a similar list in the cartulary of Mont-Saint-Michel, although that usefully reveals how monastic losses might actually be the result of right justice (see above, p. Chapter 2, pp. 103, 109, 110).

[6] See in particular: Green, 'Robert Curthose reassessed', 95–116; W. M. Aird, *Robert Curthose, Duke of Normandy (c. 1050–1134)* (Woodbridge, 2008); K. Lack, 'Robert Curthose: ineffectual duke or victim of spin?', *HSJ*, 20 (2009), 110–40.

of common purpose, success, momentum, and enrichment that had kept the Normans together since William the Bastard had achieved his majority was lost. In such circumstances, Norman lords necessarily began to compete with each other for the much more limited amount of patronage now on offer, and here Curthose was hampered by the fact that his greatest subjects, including Count Robert of Mortain, Earl Roger of Shrewsbury, and Earl Hugh of Chester, could have been only a little less wealthy than he was.[7]

Curthose's relative lack of wealth was of course the result of the division of the Anglo-Norman *regnum* in 1087, which affected the duke but not his *fideles*. William the Bastard must have known that Curthose would face serious problems as a result of the partition, and it might well have given him much consolation when it became clear that he would be obliged to pass the duchy on to his eldest son despite his own feelings on the matter. In addition, the Norman king of the English could not help but be seen as a rival or even as an alternative to the reigning duke. Too many lords had interests on both sides of the Channel for that not to have been the case, and although Orderic thought that the Normans would have liked to see Curthose take the kingdom from his brother in 1088, and apparently preferred the weak rule that he would offer to the stronger authority of his brother, his failure to seize the opportunity, Rufus's retaliatory moves, and the king's reputation for generosity and wealth turned the tables from 1089.

It is to Curthose's credit that he was not submerged by the flood of English silver that Rufus poured into the pockets of his mercenaries and allies. He seems also to have been able to manage the aggressive ambition of Robert of Bellême, at least before his return from the crusade in 1100, and to have held his brother Henry in check, too. Together these three principal competitors for power troubled the whole of the duchy. Rufus's interest focused on Upper Normandy, where he established his power in the counties of Eu, Talou, part of the Roumois, and part of the Evrecin. Bellême operated in central Normandy, in an area that corresponded roughly to that granted to Rollo in 924. Henry was based in the Avranchin and Cotentin, in the region granted to William Longsword in 933. Curthose's reign thus seems to emphasize the survival of those divisions which had remained just under the surface of the united duchy forged so recently by William the Bastard. Moreover, as Bellême and Henry were the very men that Curthose would have

---

[7] Roger of Montgommery's English lands were worth £2,078 in 1086, of which land to the value of £1,031 had been retained in demesne. On Domesday evidence, William of Mortain's English honours were worth £2,100, William of Warenne's £1,165, and Earl Hugh of Chester's £800. The values of their Norman estates can only be guessed at. The revenue that flowed into the ducal coffers from the farms of the various *vicomtés* and *prévôtés* in 1180, on the evidence of the Norman pipe roll of that year, equates to around £4,160 sterling.

relied on to uphold his authority in mid and western Normandy, Curthose found himself fighting their ambition with one hand tied behind his back.

We can start with Henry. Curthose's decision to establish his brother in the west of Normandy was perhaps related to his need for cash. His father had, after all, been fighting a war when he died and it might have been the case that ready funds were running low at a time when Curthose needed to win supporters to his side through his patronage. And so, at the very beginning of his reign

> when his treasure was exhausted he asked his brother Henry to give him some of his wealth, which Henry flatly refused to do. The duke then offered to sell him a portion of his land if he would like to buy it. This was precisely what Henry desired, and as soon as he heard his brother's offer he accepted it … Henry provided the duke with three thousand pounds in silver, and received from him the whole of the Cotentin, which is a third part of Normandy. In this way Henry first acquired Avranches and Coutances and Mont-Saint-Michel in peril of the sea, and the whole fee which Hugh, earl of Chester, held in Normandy.[8]

The deal that Curthose negotiated with his brother made good sense for both men. Like his predecessors, Curthose needed a representative in the west of the duchy, and if that representative was also a member of the ducal dynasty then so much the better. And that Henry *was* intended to act as such is indicated by the fact that he was made count of the Cotentin.[9] The idea was as sensible in Curthose's day as it had been during the reigns of Richard I and Richard II, and Henry did prove to be both a competent count and, until Curthose alienated him by his own actions, a loyal supporter of his brother's regime.[10] Indeed, even when Henry broke from his brother there is no sense that he wanted to make his county independent of ducal rule in a way comparable with the Bellêmois or the Perche, for example. He simply wanted the autonomy enjoyed by the other Norman counts.

Although Henry was driven from the duchy by his brothers in 1091, his exile was short-lived. Henry was back by invitation the next year.

> In the year of our Lord 1092 … King William's son Henry gained possession of the fortified town of Domfront with the help of God and the support of his

---

[8] Orderic, iv. 118–20. Orderic's story should probably be preferred to that offered by Malmesbury: Malmesbury, *GR*, i. 710–12.

[9] For the Norman counts, see below, Chapter 9, pp. 559–69.

[10] Firstly, Curthose arrested and incarcerated Henry in 1088 when he returned from England (Orderic, iv. 148). Secondly, he deprived him of some of the property in the Cotentin that he had earlier sold him in the treaty of Rouen of 1091 (Worcester, iii. 58; *ASChr*, 'E', s.a. 1091; trans. Garmonsway, p. 226).

friends, and from there made a bold claim for his inheritance ... [By] God's will the men of Domfront took pity on the misfortunes of the noble exile, and sending for him from France ... received him with honour. Throwing off the rule of Robert of Bellême, by whom they had been sorely oppressed for many years, they made Henry their lord. He took up arms energetically against Robert, duke of Normandy, avenging the injustice of his banishment with fire and plunder, and capturing and imprisoning many men.[11]

Henry thus took possession of the town and castle of Domfront, and his acquisition of the Domfrontois might explain why the abbot of Lonlay had second thoughts about bringing a plea before the duke the next year.[12] He used his new base as a bridgehead from which to recover possession of the western Avranchin and the Cotentin, apparently in defiance of his brother. Henry, with 'the support of Richard of Reviers and Roger of Magneville immediately regained the lordship over the greater part of the Cotentin ... In this as well as in many other cases Earl Hugh of Chester had shown himself a loyal supporter and therefore Henry granted him the whole town of Saint-James-de-Beuvron, where until that moment the earl had held not more than the custody of the castle of the town.'[13] Earl Hugh had been a long-standing supporter of Henry. Roger of Magneville might have been a more recent recruit. He had previously been a *fidelis* of the count of Mortain, but would become a power in his own right under Henry. Similarly, Thomas of Saint-Jean-le-Thomas, to whom Henry was to entrust the siege castle at Tinchebray in 1106, was previously only a tenant of the abbot of Mont-Saint-Michel. Some lords who saw their men falling into Henry's orbit might have taken it badly, and Kerrith Davies has suggested that the hostility between Henry and Count William, which came to a head in England in 1104, probably originated in their struggle for dominance in the Cotentin at a time when they shared comital status.[14]

Curthose's lack of response to Henry's reinstatement was perhaps because he was planning a campaign against Maine in the company of King William when he returned to the duchy, and he might anyway have preferred to see Domfront in Henry's hands rather than Bellême's. Conditions in the Cotentin were such that Henry might even have been the duke's best option for stability there, too. Indeed, it should perhaps be borne in mind that Curthose had only moved against Henry in the first place for Rufus's benefit, and his prosecution of the siege of

---

[11] Orderic, iv. 256–8.

[12] Marchegay, pp. 684–5 (no. 16). The abbot's *volte-face* might also have been due to the opposition, on similar grounds, of Robert of Bellême.

[13] Jumièges, ii.208.

[14] K. Davies, 'The count of the Cotentin: western Normandy, William of Mortain, and the career of Henry I', *HSJ*, 22 (2012), 123–40.

Mont-Saint-Michel was such as to suggest that he was not entirely committed to the aggrandizement of the English king's power in his duchy. Moreover, Henry was now needed even more than before in the west, as the other great lords of the county were ageing and, it may be supposed, increasingly ineffective. Nigel II of the Cotentin died in 1092, Bishop Geoffrey of Coutances in 1093, and Count Robert of Mortain in 1095.[15] So, in practice, and whatever his feelings about it, Curthose probably had little choice but to accept his brother's fait accompli and to hope that Henry would provide him with support should the need arise. And indeed, with the exception of the short spell in 1092, Henry did not openly oppose his brother while he built up his power in the Cotentin and Avranchin – at least so so far as we know.

That was not the case with the figure whom Orderic depicted as Curthose's nemesis: Robert of Bellême. His ambition for greater independence was clear from the outset of Curthose's reign when, on learning of William the Bastard's death, he had thrown the ducal garrisons out of his castles.[16] Even before his father's death in July 1094 Bellême dominated the lands that lay from the Orne in the west to the Dives and the Vie in the east, and from the sea to the Sarthe, and he had ruled Bellême in his own right since his mother's death c. 1077.[17] That lordship was still seen to lie outside the duchy, and as a result Bellême had done homage for it to King Philip of the French.[18] What made this situation worse, so far as Robert Curthose was concerned, was that there was very little ducal demesne in the Hiémois and Houlme. His power consequently relied on the loyalty and support of the Montgommery family, and the result was that local loyalties were owed to that family rather than to the dukes.

Robert's chosen toponym indicates that he was more his mother's heir than his father's. We can imagine that he was told stories by Mabel of the past greatness of her house, and that he was perhaps encouraged by her and her men to reflect on their once-independent lordship and how that independence might, and should, be restored. Attempts have been made by Kathleen Thompson and Judith Green to revise the black picture painted by Orderic, who lived far too near to Bellême's area of operations to have seen him as anything other than the devil incarnate, but they have not entirely convinced because they have missed, or

---

[15] The date of Count Robert's death has been established by Jean-Michel Bouvris and Brian Golding: 'J.-M. Bouvris, 'Aux origines du prieuré de Vains', *Revue de l'Avranchin et du pays de Granville*, 64 (1987), 74; B. Golding, 'Robert of Mortain', 122.

[16] Orderic, iv. 112–14.

[17] For the date of Mabel's death see above, Chapter 2, p. 136, n. 284.

[18] *Recueil des actes de Philippe Ier roi de France (1059–1108)*, ed. M. Prou (Paris, 1907), no. 129 describes him as a 'vassalus'. Henry I was to acknowledge that Bellême was held from the French king in 1113 (Orderic, vi. 180: and see below, *infra*, pp. 168–9 and Chapter 5, pp. 296–8).

denied, the crucial point.[19] This is that Robert of Bellême should not be seen as a rebel, but rather as the would-be restorer of the fortunes of the house of Bellême. Orderic, who arrived in Normandy in 1085, fourteen years after the death of Ivo of Bellême and many years since the Norman conquest of Houlme and the Passais, did not fully understand this. He thought that Bellême's attempt to take Houlme went beyond the rights enjoyed by his predecessors.[20] But he was almost certainly wrong. Orderic did, however, provide some clues that reveal that he, and perhaps others, understood that Robert of Bellême was not truly a Norman lord. The most significant of these is that he wrote that Curthose summoned the army of Normandy against Robert. It is significant because in the pages of Orderic's *Ecclesiastical History* the 'army of Normandy' was deployed only against external threats.[21]

Although Curthose campaigned against Bellême in 1088 and c. 1092,[22] and although he demonstrated to an audience that would have included Bellême's own men that he had the capability to strike at the very heart of Bellême's lands and to do justice within them, he struggled to prevent the erosion of his own authority in the Hiémois. To some extent, this retreat of ducal authority was the result of factors over which Curthose had no control. William the Bastard had permitted Roger II of Montgommery to win an almost-autonomous lordship that straddled the borders of Normandy and Maine, and had then enriched him with huge estates in England. That bought Roger's loyalty for the duration of William's reign, but it also made him and his son a serious threat to a duke who was not also a king, who held very litte demesne in the region they dominated, and who had lost control of Maine. Moreover, the division of the Montgommery-Bellême lands that was effective from c. 1077, which saw Roger more or less permanently based in England and Robert holding Bellême in his own right and administering his father's Norman estates as *his agent*, made it impossible for Curthose to impose any serious penalty on Robert even when he did have him in his power. He could not, for example, move to forfeit Bellême's Norman lands in either 1088 or 1092 because they were not his but his father's. Moreover, when Curthose imprisoned Bellême in 1088, Roger of Montgommery crossed the Channel and fortified his Norman castles in protest. Curthose thus lost the advantage he might otherwise have gained by imprisoning the leading lord in the Hiémois, simply because another man, who was of even greater standing and had committed no offence

---

[19]   In contrast to the view here, Thompson rejected the idea that Bellême was attempting to reassert the independence of his house against the dukes of the Normans (K. Thompson, 'Robert of Bellême reconsidered', *ANS*, 13 (1991), 285).

[20]   Orderic, iv. 228.

[21]   On this see below, Chapter 11, pp. 659–60.

[22]   Orderic, iv. 158, 294 and again see below, Chapter 11, p. 660.

against the duke, could simply step into his place and force his release. It was only after Roger II's death in July 1094 that Curthose could even attempt to forfeit Bellême's Norman lands, but his vast estates in England would always remain out of Curthose's reach because he had no authority there at all.

Curthose thus had little choice but to do what William the Bastard had done before him, which was to allow the lord of Montgommery and Bellême free rein to impose his authority on his neighbours. Unlike his father, however, Curthose did not have the safety net that rule over both Normandy and England had given his father. Moreover, he lacked the authority to insist that ducal garrisons should be put into Bellême's castles, as his father had done, and was thus unable to ensure the security of his own position and possessions.

The predictable result was that Bellême made no distinction between the ducal demesne and the property of his other neighbours. As early as early 1090, Bellême attacked the duke's castle at Exmes which was held by Gilbert of L'Aigle. He was rebuffed.[23] But having found that castle and frontier held against him, he simply turned his attention to the west of the county instead, built unlicenced castles at Fourches and Château-Gontier, and used them to bring Houlme more securely under his control.[24] Curthose's response to such moves was to make concessions to Bellême, perhaps in the hope that he would thereby purchase his loyalty. Indeed, in January 1091 he joined Bellême at the siege of Courcy in the Hiémois, which was held against him by Richard of Courcy and his men with the help of Hugh of Grandmesnil, both of whom were resisting Bellême's attempt to impose his authority over them. Curthose's presence clearly hindered the defence of the castle – Hugh of Grandmesnil asked him to withdraw for a day as a result – until the news of Rufus's return to Normandy drew both men away and saved the garrison from defeat.[25]

Rufus constituted the third, and perhaps most serious, threat to Curthose's authority. He had probably been motivated to act against his brother as a result of Curthose's own attempt to take his throne in 1088, although he might also have claimed to be acting in defence of the Church.[26] As early as 1089 he began to construct a a party based in Upper Normandy that included Walter of Saint-Valéry-en-Caux, Stephen of Aumale, Count Robert of Eu, Gerard of Gournay, Walter Giffard, and Ralph of Mortemer.[27] Curthose responded rapidly and successfully to the threat. By the end of August he had successfully besieged the castle at Eu,

---

[23] Orderic, iv. 200.
[24] Orderic, iv. 228.
[25] Orderic, iv. 230–6.
[26] Orderic, iv. 178–80.
[27] Orderic, iv. 178–82; F. Barlow, *William Rufus* (London, 1988), p. 273.

and an act that he issued during the siege reveals that he had in his camp a number of important lords from across his duchy: Count William of Evreux; William of Breteuil; William Crispin, *vicomte* of the Vexin; William of Moulins-la-Marche; Engelran fitz Gilbert of L'Aigle; Hugh of Vernon; Robert of Montfort; William Bertram, Montfort's neighbour and kinsman and the only one to hold an honour in the west of the duchy; and Richard of Courcy.[28] The witness list of this act, then, indicates that Curthose could rely on the support of important lords from central Normandy during this first royal invasion, even if the Count of Evreux was the only one of them to hold significant estates in the Pays de Caux or Talou.

Although Curthose defeated Rufus and his allies at Eu, the king's party did not collapse. And so, Orderic tells us, 'Duke Robert, to put up a barrier against his numerous enemies, gave his daughter by a concubine in marriage to Helias, the son of Lambert of Saint-Saëns, and provided Arques and Bures and the adjoining province as her marriage portion, so that Helias would resist his enemies and defend the county of Talou.'[29] Curthose, then, turned to the senior representative of a well-established family in his time of need, albeit one that had been eclipsed by the rise of the Giffards and Warennes, and secured his loyalty in the time-honoured way: by a marriage to a member of the duke's close family and by a grant of demense property. And the fact that Curthose was still in control of the ducal demesne in the Pays de Talou itself reveals that the defection of the power-ful families of the region had not yet undermined the duke's control of his own possessions there.

Curthose used more of the ducal demesne to gain and maintain the support of other important *fideles* and friends elsewhere. Early in 1089, the Norman hold on Maine looked insecure. Duke Robert approached Count Fulk, his overlord, for help in averting rebellion against his rule. In return for that help, Count Fulk demanded Bertrada of Montfort as a wife. Bertrada was the niece of Count William of Evreux and was in his wardship, and before he would agree to the match he demanded justice – the return of the estates of Robert of Gacé that had been, in his eyes, unjustly retained by Duke William since around 1050. As Curthose needed the marriage to go ahead, and as Count William was one of his principal supporters, he surrendered what had previously been his demesne at Bavent, Noyon-sur-Andelle, Gacé, Gravenchon, and Ecouché along with 'the other estates of my uncle Ralph (who was nicknamed Tête d'Ane in jest because of his huge head and shaggy hair)'. In addition, he agreed to restore to William of Breteuil, Count William's nephew, 'Le Pont-Saint-Pierre

---

[28] *Livre Noir*, 10–13 (no. 6) = *Regesta*, i. no. 310.
[29] Orderic, iv. 182. As these words suggest, this seems to have comprised a grant of the county of Arques (Orderic, vi. 92) although without the title of count.

and other properties which we can reasonably and lawfully prove to be ours by hereditary right'.[30]

Those 'other properties' likely included the castle at Ivry, which had certainly been restored to William of Breteuil by 1089. That restitution naturally resulted in the dismissal of the duke's custodian, Roger of Beaumont, who was compensated with custody of the duke's castle at Brionne. But Roger's son, Count Robert of Meulan, complained about the loss of Ivry, which he had come to regard as his inheritance, in an offensive manner. Ivry would have been a very useful possession for a count of Meulan who also held lands in Normandy, so his disappointment is perhaps understandable. He was arrested and imprisoned. As had been the case after the arrest of Robert of Bellême in 1088, Count Robert's father then intervened to obtain his release, and also succeeded in recovering Brionne into the bargain, which had been given to another custodian in the interval. Although there was no reason for Roger of Beaumont to support William Rufus, given his lack of property in England, the English king's continuing attempts to undermine Curthose's rule almost certainly strengthened Roger's hand during his negotiations with the duke.

Unfortunately, the new custodian, Robert of Meulles, saw Brionne as his own inheritance and refused to surrender the castle to the duke just so that it could be given to another lord. Brionne was thus besieged in June 1090 until the tiny garrison surrendered. Robert of Meulles was not punished for his defiance, but was instead compensated with the lordship of Le Hommet in the Cotentin, which he also claimed as his inheritance, most likely in 1091 when Henry had been driven into his brief exile.

The grant of Ivry thus turned out to be expensive, for it led directly to the loss of Brionne and the lordship of Le Hommet – although the latter might already have been lost to the demesne anyway. And while Curthose's actions look at first glance to have been just and necessary if he were to retain the support of Breteuil and Beaumont, he still made mistakes in his handling of the situation. For example, if Curthose had foreseen that he would end up restoring custody of Brionne to Roger of Beaumont, then he would have been better advised not to entrust the castle in the meantime to a man with his own claim to it. If he had not intended to restore Brionne to the Beaumonts, then he should have adopted a stronger position when he agreed to release Count Robert of Meulan. Restoring his freedom was, after all, patronage in itself. And although Robert of Meulles was related to the Clare family, it is not clear that he carried sufficient weight in the duchy to be able to demand such rich compensation for the loss of his custodianship of the duke's castle, especially as he had defied the duke when doing so. We

---

[30] Orderic, iv. 184.

might not have all the necessary information, but Curthose's handling of this bout of frustrated ambition gives the impression that he was not very good at thinking through the likely outcomes of his actions.

Curthose had little time to rest after sorting out the trouble over Brionne, as in November 1090 his brother's allies in Upper Normandy, including one of the leading burgesses of Rouen called Conan, sought to wrest that city from his control. They failed, but it seems that Rufus had now determined to oust his brother from his duchy, and he returned to Normandy in person to do just that in February 1091.[31] As noted above, Duke Robert abandoned the siege of Courcy to meet him, but in the event there does not seem to have been any fighting and before the month was out Rufus and Robert had come to terms. Their agreement was embodied in the so-called Treaty of Rouen. The terms agreed indicate that Curthose had by then reconciled himself to the loss of the fidelity of the lords of Upper Normandy, consoled no doubt by the compensation he received in return: 'Duke Robert then received great gifts from the king, and granted him the county of Eu with Aumale and the whole territory of Gerard of Gournay and Ralph of Conches, with all the castles held by them or their vassals.'[32] John of Worcester added some extra details: 'under its terms the duke would with good will surrender to the king the county of Eu, the abbey of Fécamp, the abbey at Mont-Saint-Michel, Cherbourg, and the castles which had abandoned the duke.'[33] It is likely that John of Worcester's additions were well founded, because the grant of Mont-Saint-Michel and Cherbourg provided a reason for the campaign against Henry in the Cotentin pursued later in the year, mentioned above. In any event, as Curthose could not rely on the loyalty of the count of Eu – although neither could Rufus as it turned out – and these other lords, his agreement to surrender their fidelity to Rufus was not necessarily foolish. Equally, as the duke had no demesne in Eu, Aumale, the Pays de Bray, or the south of the Evrecin, and as Henry ruled in the west, the transfer of these lordships and castles to William Rufus is unlikely to have further reduced the revenues that Curthose's officials collected on his behalf.[34] He might also have expected his brother to rein these lords in, thereby re-establishing peace in Upper Normandy.

The Treaty of Rouen lasted only until 1094, when the sureties declared that Rufus had failed to satisfy his side of the bargain – he had been required to help Curthose restore Norman rule over Maine.[35] When that verdict was announced,

---

[31] Worcester, iii. 56–8.

[32] Orderic, iv. 236.

[33] Worcester, iii. 58. The *Anglo-Saxon Chronicle* also reported the surrender of Fécamp and Cherbourg (*ASChr*, 'E', s.a. 1091; trans. Garmonsway, p. 226).

[34] The Norman pipe roll of 1180 seems to confirm this view.

[35] Worcester, iii. 68.

Rufus angrily left for Eu and hostilities between the brothers were renewed. The castle that Robert had given to Helias of Saint-Saëns at Bures-en-Bray was attacked and taken. 'Forced by extreme need, Robert brought his lord, Philip, king of the Franks, with an army into Normandy.'[36] But while the castles at Argentan and 'Houlme' fell to Curthose and the king, no real headway was made. As Rufus remained in England during 1095, where he had to put down a rebellion, the next time he returned to the duchy he would come to take possession of it for the duration of Curthose's absence on the First Crusade.

Curthose might have been relieved to exchange bickering with his brother over Upper Normandy and walking the political tightrope with lords such as Robert of Bellême for the single-minded aim of the crusade. But there is no need to see his part in that great enterprise as in some way saving his duchy from falling into the clutches of his rivals. Robert did not leave Normandy a cowed duke. The campaign of 1094 had seen Rufus, not Curthose, on the defensive. The duke could still summon his army when it was required, and he could apparently depend on a number of important *fideles* to fight for him. He retained the support of Count William of Evreux, Count Robert of Meulan, Robert of Montfort, and William of Breteuil, perhaps because they did not hold lands in England, right up to the time that he left on crusade. Indeed, Breteuil would speak up for Curthose in opposition to Henry's claim to the throne in August 1100.[37] His loyalty reveals that the grant of the castle of Ivry, though expensive, had been demesne well spent.[38] Moreover, while Curthose could not do justice to Ralph of Tosny against Count William of Evreux, that was more likely a result of his dependence on the count rather than weakness per se.[39] He had certainly been able to rein in Bellême on more than one occasion, and also to frustrate his plans by guile if not by force.[40]

In 1096, then, Curthose was no lame-duck duke, at least not when looking from the top down. The view from the bottom up – which is where Orderic was observing events from – might have been rather different, however. Curthose's dependence on his *fideles* allowed them to exert a more onerous control over their men and neighbours, which made the duke look weak, and his inability to take a strong stand against his supporters would also have made it pointless for lesser lords, including the abbots of the duchy, to seek justice and redress

---

[36] Worcester, iii. 70–2.

[37] Orderic, v. 290.

[38] See in contrast, S. Mooers Christelow, '"Backers and stabbers": problems of loyalty in Robert Curthose's entourage', *Journal of British Studies*, 21 (1981), 3.

[39] Orderic, iv. 214.

[40] Here I agree with Bill Aird who has pointed in particular to the siege of Courcy and also the attack on Montaigu in 1093 as examples of this guile (Aird, *Robert Curthose*, pp. 139, 147).

at Curthose's court. The state of Normandy under Curthose would thus have appeared strikingly different from these two vantage points, hence the apparent mismatch between Orderic's narrative of the reign up to 1096 and a view of events informed by the full range of the evidence at our disposal.

The four years that Rufus spent as lord of Normandy were dominated by his wars in Maine and the Vexin, the details of which do not concern us here. Those wars did, however, help to reunite the Norman lords under their undisputed, if temporary, ruler. Among those who fought in the Vexin campaign of 1097, for example, were Rufus's younger brother Henry, Robert of Bellême, Count William of Evreux, Earl Hugh of Chester, Walter Giffard, and many others.[41] These men represented all of the factions that had existed in Normandy from at least 1092, but now they fought alongside each other in a common enterprise. Count Robert of Meulan, too, who had consistently sided with Curthose in the contest with Rufus, gave the king access to his French castles. In addition, William constructed the castle at Gisors to a design drawn up by Robert of Bellême to strengthen the frontier still further.[42] As was so often the case in this frontier region, the castle was constructed on land that belonged to another lord, in this case King Philip of the French, who had been given the vill by Curthose, who had himself had to take it from the archbishop of Rouen in order to do so.[43]

But while Rufus restored unity to the duchy, he also did perhaps three things that would help to undermine Curthose's rule still further when he returned in 1100. Firstly, he helped to strengthen Robert of Bellême by giving him a leading role in his campaign in Maine and by allowing him to build up his authority in the Hiémois where he had ruled his family's lands in his own right since his father's death. Moreover, in 1100 he became count of Ponthieu in right of his wife as a result of a marriage arranged for him long before by William the Bastard.[44]

Secondly, Rufus gave his brother Henry control of the Bessin, although he kept Bayeux and Caen for himself. Henry was needed there to fill the gap left by Bishop Odo, who had probably ruled the county on Duke Robert's behalf, and who had gone with him on the crusade. Orderic wrote that Odo had become 'a close counsellor of his nephew the duke' after his release from prison in 1087, and that he sought 'supreme power in Normandy, since Duke Robert was weak and ineffectual'.[45] That was an overstatement, but it does offer a sense of the bishop's prominence in the duchy and so, too, do the grants by which Robert confirmed,

[41] Orderic, v. 214

[42] Orderic, v. 214–16.

[43] *Regesta: William*, no. 229; *RHGF*, xiv. 68; Orderic, v. 308; Barlow, *William Rufus*, p. 273.

[44] Bauduin, *Première Normandie*, p. 312.

[45] Orderic, iv. 114, 146.

granted, or restored to Odo and his cathedral a considerable amount of property.[46] As a result, Henry established his authority in the county over the next four
years and took the opportunity to recruit new supporters to his side. Among
them was Ranulf le Meschin, *vicomte* of the Bessin, who would command one of
the wings of Henry's army at the battle of Tinchebray in 1106. By 1101, as a result
of Henry's patronage, Ranulf had married Lucy, daughter and heiress of Thorold
of Lincoln, and had acquired through her large estates in Lincolnshire and on
the frontier in Cumberland, with centres at Carlisle and Appleby.[47] Robert fitz
Haimo, who held estates based on Torigni, Evrecy, and Creully, also supported
Henry during his wars against Curthose after 1100, and it is likely that he, too, had
come over to Henry's side after 1096. Such was the bond between the two men that
Robert's capture by the garrison of Bayeux in 1104 led directly to Henry's destruc-
tive campaign of 1105.[48]

Thirdly, soon after news of Odo's death reached the duchy, Rufus appointed a
new but inappropriate bishop of Bayeux. The man chosen was Turold of Envermeu,
who had served as one of Rufus's chaplains and who, perhaps, was also related to
Papia's family – although that is only suggested by his toponym. Turold's election
would be opposed by the clergy and people of Bayeux, and perhaps had been from
the beginning, and although he had managed to gain possession of his bishopric
by 1101, he had only been able to do so by force.

The matter was still pending when Curthose returned to the duchy in 1100,
but rather than disown his brother's candidate, Curthose continued to support
him. Indeed, it is possible that Turold's belated establishment at Bayeux was
related to the visit that Curthose made to the Bessin in that year. In any event,
his diploma for the monks of Caen, which recorded his grant of a market at
Cheux, was attested by 'the bishop of Bayeux'.[49] Indeed, the witness list to this
diploma – which is the last of his surviving acts – reveals something of the breadth
of support that Curthose continued to enjoy in the months following his return
to Normandy. The witnesses include William of Warenne, Robert of Montfort,
Gilbert of L'Aigle, Rainald of Orval, William of Ferrières, Ralph Taisson, Robert
Marmion, and Robert of Grandmesnil. Some, but not all, of these same men
would have moved into Henry's camp by 1106 which suggests that they were only
alienated by his actions after his return from the crusade.

Curthose's handling of the Bayeux election was out of step with the spirit of

---

[46] *Livre Noir*, i. 6–8 (no. 4).
[47] R. Sharpe, *Norman rule in Cumbria*, Cumberland and Westmorland Antiquarian and
Archaeological Society, Tract Series 21 (2006), pp. 44–6.
[48] Orderic, vi. 60.
[49] *NI*, Appendix E, no. 3.

reform and ecclesiastical liberty which had swept Latin Europe, and which even Henry I's England would prove unable to resist. It is possible that Curthose was lured into a false sense of security in his (mis)handling of the Norman Church as a result of the problems that Henry I was facing at the same time in England, where the recently returned Archbishop Anselm had refused to consecrate the bishops that Henry had elected in his absence. But although Henry faced excommunication as a result of his reluctance to concede anything of his customary rights over elections to churches, his candidates were at least respectable and all, in the end, were invested with their bishoprics. In contrast, the men Curthose allowed to be installed as bishops outraged ecclesiastical, and perhaps even popular, opinion.

Bayeux comprised one such problem, but it was one that Curthose had inherited. The controversial elections to the bishopric of Lisieux, in contrast, were of his own making. In 1100, Ranulf Flambard escaped from his imprisonment in the Tower of London and sought sanctuary in Normandy. His arrival probably helped to strengthen the duke's administration, and might also have given it more purpose and direction. But such benefits came at a cost. When the bishopric of Lisieux fell vacant on the death of Gilbert Maminot in 1101, Flambard ensured that his illiterate brother Fulcher was elected. When Fulcher died soon afterwards, Flambard then had the duke agree to install his twelve-year-old son, Thomas, as bishop in his place, and even gained the duke's agreement that should Thomas die another of Flambard's still younger sons would be elected.[50] In the meantime, Flambard governed Lisieux as the bishop's guardian, plundering its possessions in the process.

By 1105, news of what had happened had reached the ears of Bishop Ivo of Chartres, who expressed his outrage in letters addressed to the Norman bishops. His threat to expose the scandal led to the deposition of Thomas from the bishopric. William, archdeacon of Evreux, was elected in his place. That should have resolved the issue, but Archbishop William of Rouen was suspended as a result of his opposition to the archbishop of Lyon's claims to primacy over Rouen.[51] As a result, there was a delay while William of Evreux sought to obtain consecration, and that delay allowed Flambard to hoist another of his cronies into the bishopric, paying a great sum of money to the duke to do so. Bishop Ivo, more outraged than ever, then informed the pope of the whole sorry story. He also wrote to Count Robert of Meulan and urged him to use his influence on Henry I so that he might liberate the oppressed Norman Church.[52] It need hardly be said that Henry

---

[50] Orderic, v. 322.

[51] See below, Chapter 4, pp. 234, 241, 246.

[52] *PL*, 162, cols. 157–8 (letter cliv, to Count Robert), 162–3 (letter clvii, to the pope); C. W. David, *Robert Curthose, Duke of Normandy* (Cambridge MA, 1920), pp. 151–3; Aird, *Robert Curthose*, pp. 211–12, who downplays the affair.

took up that particular call with enthusiasm, but it should be highlighted that the initiative in this case came not from Paschal II but from a vocal and influential neighbouring prelate, whose reputation gave him almost the same moral authority as the altogether more distant pope.

Curthose's failure to protect the Norman Church was also evidenced, or so his political enemies would have it, by his surrender to Robert of Bellême of 'the bishopric of Sées, the stronghold of Argentan, and the forest of Gouffern' soon after his return to the duchy in 1100.[53] That the duke was prepared to expend so much of his nugatory demesne in the Hiémois to maintain Bellême's support indicates how important it was to him, but it was Bellême's treatment of the Church that probably caused most damage to Curthose, as once the bishopric had been handed over to Robert, he began to oppress Bishop Serlo as well as his archdeacon, John, and Abbot Ralph of Sées, to the extent that all three churchmen fled into exile.[54] Serlo would, of course, become the first of the Norman bishops to rally to Henry's side against Curthose, appearing at Henry's court at Carentan in 1105 where he preached a famous sermon that condemned the duke's failure to protect the Church or to restrain Bellême.[55] Orderic's *Ecclesiastical History* thus reveals that, at least so far as he was concerned, the grant of Sées to Robert of Bellême was the final plank in the ecclesiastical coffin that Curthose made for himself.

That end was still not quite foreseeable when, in 1102, Curthose took to arms against this most important of allies. He did so because Henry I had insisted that he should, under the terms of the Treaty of Alton that they had made the previous year. It would seem that Curthose felt he had more to fear from Henry than Bellême at that point. But, perhaps because he was under an obligation, Curthose seems to have acted without first gaining a consensus among his own barons. As a result, his army suffered from internal divisions, and those divisions led directly to the failure of his siege of Bellême's castle at Vignats.[56] This failure had disastrous consequences, because it demonstrated Curthose's weakness and emboldened Bellême accordingly. The next year he defeated the duke's army close to Exmes and then seized the duke's castle there.[57] 'From that day he held the duke in contempt and attempted to bring the whole of Normandy under his sway.'[58] Two years later, having been unable to hold back the tide, Curthose recognized his impotence in the Hiémois and Séois in the face of Bellême's hostility, and in an effort to maintain the integrity of his duchy came to terms with him. 'When the

---

[53] Orderic, v. 308.
[54] Orderic, vi. 46, 142–4.
[55] Orderic, vi. 60–8.
[56] Orderic, vi. 24.
[57] Orderic, vi. 32–6.
[58] Orderic, vi. 34.

idle duke saw that his country was being utterly wasted and that he was power-less to defend the territory of his duchy against Robert of Bellême, he broke the treaty he had made with the king and … made peace with Robert and granted him his father's lordships which consisted of the bishopric of Sées and other things already mentioned.'[59] It is likely that Duke Robert knew that making peace with Bellême would give Henry the excuse he was looking for to invade Normandy, but he had probably also come to appreciate that Henry intended to attack him no matter what he did. Much better, then, to go into battle with the troops that Robert of Bellême could bring to the fray than without them.

There were several reasons why Duke Robert could have divined Henry's intentions by 1104. Firstly, his own experiences with Rufus would have suggested that after his own failed invasion of England in 1101 Henry would at some point attemt a tit-for-tat invasion of Normandy. Secondly, by 1104 it was obvious that Henry was successfully building up his own body of supporters across the duchy. Already in 1100 he could rely on the friends and *fideles* he had accumulated while he ruled the Avranchin, Cotentin, and Bessin. As Count Robert of Meulan and his brother Earl Henry of Warwick had played a key role in having Henry crowned, it may be supposed that Henry knew he could also rely on the Beaumonts and their satellites should he attempt to take the duchy.[60] That was especially the case after 1101 when Count Robert had gained control of Ivo of Grandmesnil's estates in the English Midlands. Although Ivo had only mortgaged them to him, the count was allowed to enjoy those lands for the rest of his life, and thereby acquired estates in England sufficiently wide to see him created earl of Leicester.[61] Property in England was used to recruit and reward others, too. Thus Ralph of Tosny had been allowed to inherit his father's English lands in 1102, and was given as a wife Adeliza, one of the co-heiresses of Countess Judith, whose estates had been valued at just over £600 in 1086; Robert of La Haye-du-Puits, still the steward of Count William of Mortain at the time, was given the honour of Halnaker in Sussex after Robert of Bellême's banishment; and Gilbert of L'Aigle was given the honour of Pevensey shortly after Count William of Mortain had forfeited it in 1104. Others beside were brought into Henry's party, through both grants of lands and marriages, including Eustace, lord of Breteuil.

---

[59] Orderic, vi. 46.

[60] Malmesbury noted only the efforts of Henry of Warwick (Malmesbury, *GR*, i. 714), but Orderic reported that Robert of Meulan accompanied Henry to Westmnster (Orderic, v. 290, 294).

[61] Orderic, vi. 18–20. For more on Robert of Meulan see below, Chapter 11, p. 633. Stephanie Mooers did not acknowledge that Count Robert of Meulan had been a frequent signatory to Curthose's acts and so concealed his *volte-face c.* 1100 (Mooers, "'Backers and stabbers'", 4, 7).

Mention of Eustace takes us to the third point. Henry's ambitions were clear by 1104 because he had already begun to intervene in Norman affairs in a noticeably high-handed manner. In particular, Count Robert of Meulan was dispatched to Normandy in 1103 on Henry's behalf to settle the dispute over the inheritance of the honour of Breteuil. Reginald of Grancey had claimed the honour as his inheritance and was supported by Count William of Evreux, Ralph of Tosny, Ascelin Goel, and Amaury of Montfort-l'Amaury, Count William's nephew. The men of the honour, however, preferred to have William of Breteuil's illegitimate son, Eustace, as their lord, and they were supported by Henry, who arranged the marriage of Eustace to one of his own illegitimate daughters, Juliana.[62] It is not clear that Henry acted in open opposition to Duke Robert in this matter, but he certainly seems to have attempted to usurp his brother's place, not just by assuming that his intervention would settle the dispute, but also when he subsequently 'commanded Duke Robert and the other magnates to spare his son-in-law and take up arms against his enemies, unless they wished to feel the weight of the royal anger'.[63]

As Curthose must have known it would – unless he was still unable to see where his actions would lead – his reconciliation with Bellême in 1104 gave Henry the excuse he needed to move against him. He crossed the Channel and progressed through Normandy, meeting his supporters. Orderic listed the magnates who had by then gone over to him, many of whom had estates on both sides of the Channel: Count Robert of Meulan, Earl Richard of Chester, Count Stephen of Aumale, Count Henry of Eu, Eustace of Breteuil, Ralph of Conches, Robert fitz Haimo, Robert of Montfort, and Ralph of Mortemer.[64] The young Walter III Giffard could probably be added to the list. Here was a body of support that covered the whole of the duchy from east to west, and it may be supposed that the geographical extent of Henry's party made him a much more dangerous rival than Rufus had been. Having rallied his supporters, Henry summoned his brother 'and accused him of breaking the treaty they had made in England by failing to consult the king and making peace with Robert of Bellême, a traitor to both of them, and giving him his father's dominions contrary to right and ordinance'.[65]

Until this point, Curthose might not have realized just how strong Henry's support was. He certainly seems to have been caught on the back foot, because his reaction looks to have been defensive and intended to buy time. Rather than moving to arrest his brother, as Henry had done to him in 1103, Curthose bought

[62] Orderic, vi. 40.
[63] Orderic, vi. 44.
[64] Orderic, vi. 56.
[65] Orderic, vi. 56.

him off by offering up the fidelity of Count William of Evreux.[66] As the count had been one of the mainstays of Curthose's regime since 1088, and as his strength had been called on more than once in the past, the offer seems foolish. It might be that Henry's interventions in Breteuil, and the support that he now enjoyed from Beaumont and Tosny, had made Count William waver in his allegiance to the duke, and that Curthose had realized he could no longer rely on the count. But Curthose's willingness to give away Count William, 'like a horse or ox', could not have gone down well with his other *fideles*. His position was seriously weakened by the loss of the count's support. They might have wondered both whether they, too, would be jettisoned in due course, and whether they had backed the wrong horse. As Bill Aird remarked, 'the political calculations of the Norman barons dominate the period between 1100 and 1106. Their priority was to retain land and political influence, and personal loyalties were weighed against those goals.'[67] In such an environment, appearances mattered, and Curthose looked like a man who was running out of time.

Nonetheless, the duke was not yet friendless. The enmities and rivalries among the Norman aristocracy ensured that Curthose would retain some support. Henry I himself had made important enemies in the duchy both before and after his coronation in 1100. He had taken Domfront from Robert of Bellême in 1092 and driven him from England ten years later. If it came to a showdown against Henry, Curthose could rely on Bellême, despite their uneven relationship. Count William of Mortain had lost influence and men to Henry in the Avranchin and Cotentin before 1100, and he had also lost his English estates to the king in 1104. He, too, was certain to oppose Henry should he attempt to conquer the duchy. Lower down the social scale, Robert of Etoutteville, the commander of Robert's troops in the Caux, was perhaps keen to resist the advancing power of Henry's ally, Walter Giffard,[68] to the extent that he was prepared to put his English estates in jeopardy.[69] Similarly, Gunter of Aunay-sur-Odon, constable of Bayeux *c.* 1105, may be supposed to have supported Curthose in the hope that he would be able to count on the duke's help against the ambitions of his greater neighbours, Robert fitz Haimo and Ranulf le Meschin, both of them Henry's allies and high in his favour.

Such concerns seem to be particularly clear in the case of William of Ferrières, who was to remain faithful to Curthose until the bitter end. From the middle of

---

[66]   Orderic, vi. 58.

[67]   Aird, *Robert Curthose*, p. 223.

[68]   Orderic, vi. 72.

[69]   After his capture at Tinchebray and imprisonment, his estates were forfeited and later given to Nigel of Aubigny (*Charters of the Honour of Mowbray 1107–1191*, ed. D. Greenway, Records of Social and Economic History, new series 1 (London, 1972), pp. xxi–xxii).

the eleventh century, the lordship and independence of the Ferrières's family had been menaced by the ambitions of the neighbouring houses of Beaumont and Montfort. Walchelin of Ferrières died fighting Hugh of Montfort during William the Bastard's minority.[70] His successor, Henry of Ferrières, might have tried to protect himself by becoming a *fidelis* of the count of Eu, whose estates in the Lieuvin were not so far away. That is suggested by the fact that when Henry founded an abbey next to his seat at Tutbury *c.* 1080, it was staffed by monks from Saint-Pierre-sur-Dives.[71] By the beginning of the twelfth century, both the Beaumont and Montfort families were allies of Henry I, and so too was the count of Eu. But by then William of Ferrières might also have struck up a genuine friendship with the duke, whom he had followed to Jerusalem. He was with Curthose when the duke granted a market to the monks of Caen, probably in 1101 and certainly at Saint-Pierre-sur-Dives, and his fidelity was of such strength even in September 1106 that Curthose had arranged that the castle at Falaise should be surrendered to no one other than himself and William.[72]

Not unsurprisingly, Henry I's victory over Curthose in 1106 seems to have had the effect that William of Ferrières had been trying to avoid, even if we can see very little of the timing or means by which the Beaumonts established their sway over him. But by Stephen's reign, William's successor Henry II of Ferrières was clearly within the *mouvance* of Waleran of Meulan. He raided Exmes with Waleran in 1136, went with the count to Paris in 1138, and joined with Waleran in alienating the lands of the nearby abbey of Bernay.[73] He also attested the act by which Waleran of Meulan turned the college at Beaumont-le-Roger into a priory of Le Bec, and made a donation of his own – albeit on a small scale – to Robert of Leicester's abbey at Lyre.[74]

Still, in 1105, the odds had not shifted perceptaby against Curthose. Henry certainly gained ground in that year, but those gains need to be seen in perspective. Henry was already master of the Cotentin and Bessin. His capture of Bayeux and Caen was significant, but perhaps not unexpected.[75] Like West Berlin in the days of the DDR, these were ducal enclaves surrounded by the men and lands of a rival power. Without any equivalent of the Berlin airlift, they fell swiftly to that

[70] Jumièges, ii. 92.

[71] *The Cartulary of Tutbury Priory*, ed. A. Saltman, Historical Manuscripts Commission (London, 1962), pp. 3–15.

[72] *NI*, Appendix E, no. 3; *Regesta*, ii. 313 (no. xxxvi) = no. 764; Orderic, vi. 90.

[73] Orderic, vi. 424–6; Crouch, *Beaumont Twins*, pp. 34–5.

[74] *Ctl. Beaumont-le-Roger*, no. 4 (at p. 16); *Recueil Henri II*, no. 65.

[75] For the taking of Bayeux and Caen see Serlo of Bayeux, 'The Capture of Bayeux', 86–105; *ASChr*, 'E' s.a. 1105; trans. Garmonsway, p. 239; Orderic, vi. 78; Worcester, iii. 106. There is also Wace's rather later account: Wace, pp. 214–19.

rival when he determined to take them. But elsewhere, even just across the border of the Bessin, Curthose's power remained more effective than Henry's. The castle of Falaise, for example, did not yield to Henry when he attacked it later in 1105.[76]

So Henry adopted a new tactic in 1106. Rather than attack his brother's demesne possessions, he targeted the county of Mortain, perhaps because it was almost surrounded by those parts of Normandy most securely under Henry's control. Henry thus laid siege to the castle of Tinchebray, which was located at the north-east corner of the county, and thus accessible from the Bessin and Cotentin. A siege castle was constructed and placed in the custody of Thomas of Saint-Jean-le-Thomas from the Avranchin. He failed to achieve anything against the count, however, both because his men outnumbered Henry's garrison and because of the well-established regional loyalties that worked against the English king. Henry's response was to muster a larger force and lead it against Tinchebray in person. Count William appealed to the duke for assistance. And the two sides came together at Tinchebray at the end of September.

Even now, as the duke and the king mustered their armies for battle, the two sides were fairly evenly matched, as even Orderic had to admit, and neither brother had gained a clear advantage over the other. And just as the ducal family was divided, so too were the families of their supporters. As Orderic noted this conflict was, under the definition set out by Isidore of Seville, 'a worse than civil war'.[77] And this is why, in the aftermath of his God-given triumph over his brother, Henry still had to justify his rule in Normandy and the imprisonment of his brother, and seems to have hesitated for some years before adopting a ducal style.[78] There must have been many who were disappointed by the result, who thought it unjust, and who consequently had to be won over with diplomacy, smooth words, and good government.

---

[76] Orderic, vi. 78–80. Henry had already been required to besiege the castle before Count Helias of Maine left his army at the request of the Normans. Helias's motives have been discussed by Hollister, *Henry*, pp. 189–91 and R. E. Barton, 'Henry I, Count Helias of Maine, and the battle of Tinchebray', in *Henry I and the Anglo-Norman World: Studies in Memory of C. Warren Hollister*, ed. D. Fleming and J. M. Pope (Woodbridge, 2007), p. 88. Barton's comment, that Helias was asked to leave in order to avoid upsetting an agreement for peace brokered by both sides, is convincing.

[77] Orderic, vi. 84. Marjorie Chibnall and Bill Aird thought that this was a reference to Lucan's *Pharsalia* (Orderic, vi. 84, n. 3; Aird, *Robert Curthose*, p. 239), but it is more likely to have been a technical use of the term in accordance with Isidore: *Etymologies*, p. 359.

[78] See below, Chapter 5, pp. 294–8.

Henry I, 1106–35

According to Orderic, soon after his conquest of the duchy, Henry declared that all the grants Curthose had made from the demesne were void – which probably explains why so few of Curthose's acts have survived. Helias of Saint-Saëns would thus have ceased to enjoy custody of Arques and Bures-en-Bray (if he had recovered the latter after its loss to Rufus in 1094), and there does seem to have been a *vicomte* already established at Arques before Helias fled the duchy and forfeited his lands *c.* 1110. Robert of Bellême was similarly required to return Argentan and all the other ducal demesne that he had usurped, including no doubt the castle at Exmes.[79] But in other cases, even if Henry did rescind Curthose's grants, he seems to have made them again in his own name shortly afterwards. Count Robert of Meulan continued to enjoy custody of the castle and lordship of Brionne. The monks of Caen continued to hold the market at Cheux, 'just as Robert my brother granted and signed by his hand at Saint-Pierre-sur-Dives'.[80] Duke Robert's grants were declared void, then, not because Henry needed to recover the lost property, but because he wanted to deprive Curthose's supporters of his patronage, which they might have used against him, and to gain the gratitude of those who were permitted to retain their gifts.

Orderic also remarked that Henry had declared that he would restore good government to the duchy. While this declaration might have owed something to the benefit of hindsight, effective government was clearly in place by 1107. The earliest surviving original Norman writ dates from that year, and is concerned with doing justice for the abbot of Jumièges. Henry also did justice for the Church more generally. At Lisieux, Flambard's son was deposed and replaced by John, previously archdeacon of Sées, in 1107.[81] Bishop Turold gave up his fight for the bishopric of Bayeux the same year and retired to the abbey of Le Bec. He was replaced by Richard fitz Samson (or Richard of Douvres), son of the bishop of Worcester, and a respected clergyman whose intellectual abilities earned him the affections of Ivo of Chartres and Adelard of Bath.[82]

Richard of Douvres was not to enjoy the same pre-eminence in the Bessin as his predecessors Hugh and Odo, as a result of both his background and circumstances. He was not a member of the ducal family, and so could not claim the fidelity of his subjects by right in the way that they had done. Moreover, Henry

---

[79] Orderic, vi. 94–8.
[80] *Regesta*, ii. 313 (no. xxxvi) = no. 764.
[81] Orderic, vi. 142.
[82] The year depends on Orderic's comment, made when recording the bishop's death at Easter 1133, that he had held the see for twenty-six years (Orderic, v. 210, vi. 428).

had made personal connections and established his authority in the county before he became duke to an extent that his predecessors had not. The royal duke's power in the Bessin was thus mediated through a number of figures whom he knew personally, not just the bishop. One of them was Ranulf le Meschin, *vicomte* of the Bessin. As noted above, the king had enriched Ranulf with lands in England even before he had completed the conquest of the duchy. That patronage was to continue. After the death of Richard, earl of Chester, in the wreck of the *White Ship* in 1120, Ranulf would be allowed to succeed to the majority of Richard's English estates and to his Norman lands, too.[83]

Robert, the king's oldest illegitimate son, was, or would become, an even greater figure in the Bessin. He was created earl of Gloucester *c*. 1121, but before then, although possibly not much before then, he had married Mabel, the daughter of his father's erstwhile ally, Robert fitz Haimo.[84] 'The culmination of the honour which Robert acquired in this way was the town of Torigni on the border of the counties of the Bessin and the Cotentin ... Once he had taken possession of this town, Robert, the king's son, fortified it against all hostile attacks with high towers, strong walls, and deep ditches hewn out of the rocky hill.'[85] Robert also gained his deceased father-in-law's possessions at Evrecy and Saint-Scholasse-sur-Sarthe and, it may be supposed, at Creully, too.[86]

Robert's kinship to Henry, his loyalty, and his wealth were to make him the leading power in the Bessin – indeed, from *c*. 1120 Robert was probably also the leading layman in his father's Norman administration.[87] His standing is perhaps reflected in his custody of the important castle at Caen, which is first remarked in 1135, but which Robert is likely to have held for some years previously, possibly in right of his wife.[88] By the end of Henry's reign Robert also had custody of the castle at Falaise, along with the treasure held there, which he surrendered to Stephen in 1135.[89] Even Robert's liaisons seem to have been intended to consolidate his authority in the Bessin. He took as a mistress Isabella of Douvres, Bishop Richard's sister, which probably gave him more control over the bishop and his possessions than vice versa. And when Bishop Richard died in 1133, he was suc-

---

[83] Hollister, *Henry*, p. 293; Green, *Henry*, p. 173.

[84] Jumièges, ii. 248. David Crouch thought that the marriage was celebrated in 1120. See also D. Crouch, 'Robert, earl of Gloucester', *Oxford Dictionary of National Biography*, vol. 47 (Oxford, 2003), p. 94.

[85] Jumièges, ii. 248.

[86] Patterson, *Earldom of Gloucester Charters*, p. 3; Crouch, 'Robert, earl of Gloucester', p. 94.

[87] See below, Chapter 6, pp. 354–5.

[88] Orderic, vi. 516. Wace wrote that Henry had 'granted Robert fitz Haimo the wardenship of Caen as a fief ... as soon as he could get possession of it' (Wace, p. 218).

[89] RT, s.a. 1135; Delisle, i. 200–1; Howlett, p. 129.

ceeded by Earl Robert's illegitimate son by Isabella, also named Richard.[90] His investiture, which was delayed by Archbishop Hugh of Rouen's concerns about his birth, almost certainly gave Earl Robert the opportunity to appropriate the cathedral's property on a grand scale, to the extent that Bishop Philip of Harcourt later complained that the earl had 'taken for himself the greatest part of the goods of the church of Bayeux'.[91]

Henry did not abandon the Bessin entirely to his son and *fideles*, however. The royal duke was occasionally resident at Caen himself, as is revealed by the fifteen of his authentic *acta* that were place-dated there.[92] He also stopped at Bayeux at least once after he had burned it in 1105,[93] and he stayed at Arganchy, too, which was a possession of the bishop, located just to the south of his cathedral city.[94] Aside from Bishop Richard and Earl Robert, Henry was attended on these occasions by a number of men with lands in, or close to, the Bessin. They included William of Aubigny, who held lands of the bishop at Danvou-la-Ferrière and Bougy and from the monks of Caen at Etavaux;[95] Nigel of Aubigny, William's brother, who had inherited the Montbray fee in right of his wife;[96] Geoffrey fitz Payn; William Peverel of Douvres; and Haimo of Saint-Clair-sur-Elle, who had once been a tenant of Eudo Dapifer and who was given lands in England at Eaton Socon and Walkern by Henry I.[97] Some of these men, William and Nigel of Aubigny in particular, were prominent in Henry's administration in both Normandy and England. Henry could thus count on the support of local men of the second rank as well as the great regional magnates, the abbot of Saint-Etienne, and the abbess of La Trinité of Caen. Indeed, for part of Henry's reign the abbess was none other than Henry's older sister Cecilia. She had been given as an oblate to the nuns in June 1066 and succeeded the first abbess, Matilda, in 1112 – although, as Matilda had wanted to give up the burden of her office owing to age and infirmity as early as 1103, it is possible that Cecilia had been in de facto control of the abbey even before Henry conquered the duchy.[98]

[90] Orderic, vi. 442.
[91] *Livre Noir*, i. 237–8, no. 190.
[92] See below, Chapter 9, pp. 512–13.
[93] *Regesta*, ii. no. 1212.
[94] *Regesta*, ii. nos. 1224, 1589, 1592, 1898, 1899, 1899n.
[95] *Inquisition*, p. 20; Chanteux, *Recueil*, ii. 258–70 (no. 79); *NI*, pp. 94–6; *Regesta*, ii. no. 1215.
[96] *Mowbray Charters*, pp. xvii–xxvi.
[97] W. Farrer, *Honors and Knights Fees. Volume 3: Arundel, Eudes the Sewer, Warenne* (Manchester, 1925), pp. 287–91; Sanders, *English Baronies*, pp. 40, 92; Loyd, *Origins*, pp. 88–9; Green, *Government*, pp. 272–3; N. Vincent, 'Warin and Henry fitz Gerald, the king's chamberlains: the origins of the FitzGeralds revisited', *ANS*, 21 (1999), 243, n. 64.
[98] *Letters of St Anselm*, no. 298.

Henry could thus count on a lot of support in the Cotentin and Bessin, where he had been able to recruit men to his side since 1087. His authority in the Cotentin could only have increased after 1106 when the count of Mortain was imprisoned and his county forfeited into Henry's hands. The royal duke would continue to hold Mortain until around 1113 when it was given to Stephen of Blois,[99] and Henry must have found his possession of it extremely useful in keeping Robert of Bellême under control. The county Stephen eventually received was a little less extensive than that held by his predecessors, however, as in the interval Henry had hived off some of its castles and vills and given them to others. Vire, most likely previously part of the county, was divided between Henry and Earl Richard of Chester. Henry built a castle in the town, the keep of which still stands, and property there was granted to the monks of Troarn jointly by Henry and Earl Richard of Chester, probably between 1112 and 1119.[100] Henry also gave the castle of La Haye-du-Puits and its dependent lands, located in the Cotentin, to Robert of La Haye-du-Puits as an independent lordship. His power in the Cotentin had already increased enormously as a result of his succession to the lordships of Le Plessis and Créances on the death of Eudo, Thurstan Haldup's son, c. 1105, and he had been further enriched by Henry's grant to him of lands in Sussex at about the same time.[101] That he received such favour is probably a reflection of his central role in Henry's administration, where he seems to have been second only to Bishop John of Liseux until the 1120s.[102]

The depth of support that Henry had in the Bessin and Cotentin perhaps explains why those counties seem to have remained at peace throughout his reign. Elsewhere, along the southern border of the Hiémois and then east along the Avre, Epte, and Bresle, the situation was considerably more fraught. Here, Henry faced a variety of threats: Robert of Bellême; Count Fulk of Anjou; Hugh and Gervase of Châteauneuf-en-Thymerais; Amaury of Montfort-l'Amaury; the counts of Flanders; and King Louis VI of the French. That many of these lords would be hostile to Henry was eminently foreseeable, and so it is not surprising that Henry had begun to construct a party of supporters to use against them even before he had taken Normandy from his brother.

As early as 1103, as noted above, Henry had married one illegitimate daughter, Juliana, to Eustace of Breteuil. Another, Matilda, was married to Rotrou of the Perche. In addition, Henry 'built up [Rotrou's] power by greatly augmenting

---

[99] E. King, *King Stephen* (New Haven, CT and London, 2010), pp. 12–13.

[100] *NI*, p. 304 (no. 15); *Regesta*, ii. 327–8 (no. lxxix).

[101] Revealed by Robert's foundation deed for Boxgrove priory: *GC*, xi. Instr. 233; 'The Chartulary of the Priory of Boxgrove', ed. L. Fleming, *Sussex Record Society*, 59 (1901), 16–17 (no. 4).

[102] See below, Chapter 6, p. 354.

his estates and wealth in England'.[103] Both men might be useful in any hostilities against the lords of Châteauneuf-en-Thymerais, and Rotrou would also be an ideal ally in a fight against Robert of Bellême, not least because Rotrou's father had quarrelled with Robert over the partition of the Bellême inheritance and the argument had never been resolved.[104] This was no doubt why Rotrou was rewarded with the grant of the lordship of Bellême following Robert's arrest, imprisonment, and forfeiture in 1112.[105] Indeed, the lordship might have been promised to him in anticipation of its forfeiture when the marriage was first discussed. A third illegitimate daughter, Mabel, was married to William Gouet, a lord of the Perche who also had a history of hostility towards Robert of Bellême.[106] A fourth daughter, Constance, was married to Roscelin of Beaumont-sur-Sarthe in Maine. Although Kathleen Thompson proposed that the marriage took place in the 1120s, it could have been made earlier. The location of Roscelin's estates at least implies a connection to Henry's dispute with Bellême.[107]

Henry had attempted to defuse the tensions he had inherited with the family of Châteauneuf-en-Thymerais that were the result of the disputed possession of those lands in the south-eastern angle of Normandy that had once comprised Liégearde's dower, including Illiers-l'Evêque and Nonancourt-sur-Avre.[108] Henry had proposed the marriage of one of his illegitimate daughters to Hugh fitz Gervase of Châteauneuf-en-Thymerais, most likely *c.* 1110, but the plan was scuppered on the ground of consanguinity, probably by Hugh himself – suggested by the fact that it was Hugh's own relations who proved consanguinity before Bishop Ivo of Chartres.[109] If Hugh did use his kinship with Henry (by way of Roger of Montgommery and Gunnor) to manoeuvre himself out of an uncongenial marriage, he might have regretted it. Henry was concerned about this stretch of the frontier, and in particular by the existence of lordships on Norman soil that were

---

[103] Orderic, vi. 398.
[104] See below; Orderic, vi. 40; K. Thompson, *Power and Border Lordship in Medieval France: The County of the Perche, 1000–1226* (Woodbridge, 2002), p. 55. She would die in the wreck of the *White Ship* in 1120.
[105] Orderic, vi. 180–2.
[106] K. Thompson, 'Affairs of state: the illegitimate children of Henry I', *JMH*, 29 (2003), 148.
[107] Thompson, 'Affairs of state', 135, 148.
[108] Astrid Lemoine-Descourtieux noted that the people of Coudres petitioned to be incuded within the commune of Nonancourt, and took it to suggest a long-standing link between the two places that might indicate that Nonancourt had also been part of Liégeard's dowry (Lemoine-Descourtieux, *Le frontière Normande de l'Avre*, p. 174).
[109] *RHGF*, xv. 167–8 (a letter of Ivo of Chartres to Henry I condemning the planned marriage); Thompson, 'Affairs of state', 139; Crouch, *The Normans*, pp. 288–9. Crouch included a translation of part of Bishop Ivo's letter.

in the hands of Frenchmen such as Hugh. And now that he had failed to gain oversight of the Châteauneuf family's castles and towns by diplomatic means, Henry seems to have decided to win them by force.

By 1109, Henry had already recovered the castle of Gisors from King Louis VI.[110] By 1111, he had made an alliance with Count Theobald of Blois, his nephew, who fought against Louis at the siege of Le Puiset and then contended for possession of Corbeil. Henry sent Theobald troops, five hundred of whom fought with him at the siege of Toury.[111] It is likely that Henry hoped that Theobald's campaign would keep Louis's attention away from his own southern border where he was busy building a new tower in the castle at Evreux, presumably with the intention of strengthening its defences before launching a campaign to recover those lands north of the Avre that remained outside his control. Count William of Evreux, who was closely allied to those French lords who would be his targets during the campaign, objected to the building, demolished Henry's work, and was exiled for his trouble.[112]

With King Louis and Count William both off the scene, Henry moved against his enemies. Around 1112, he took Illiers-l'Evêque from Aseclin Goel and Nonancourt-sur-Avre probably from Gervase of Châteauneuf-en-Thymerais, and constructed (or strengthened) castles in both places against Gervase.[113] A third castle at Sorel was also fortified against him.[114] Both Nonancourt and Illiers were subsequently retained in demesne, and a fair was soon established at the former to help make it economically viable and to give the burgesses a reason to remain loyal to Henry's rule.[115]

[110] Suger of Saint-Denis, *Suger: the Deeds of Louis the Fat*, trans. R. Cusimano and J. Moorhead (Washington, DC, 1992), pp. 77–80.

[111] Orderic, vi. 160–2, 176–8; Suger, *Deeds of Louis the Fat*, pp. 94, 100–1.

[112] Torigni dated the exile to 1112: RT, s.a. 1112; Delisle, i. 142; Howlett, p. 93. It is not clear that his dating is reliable, however. The kinship network that linked the counts of Evreux to the families of Montfort-l'Amaury, Tosny, and others is also remarked by D. Power, *The Norman Frontier in the Twelfth and Early-Thirteenth Centuries* (Cambridge, 2004), pp. 380–1.

[113] Ascelin's possession of Illiers is revealed by his grant of the chapel within the castle to the monks of Saint-Taurin of Evreux. The act can only be dated 1112 × 1118, but as it is argued here that Ascelin lost Illiers in 1112, the act should be dated to that year: *Cartulaire de Louviers: documents historiques originaux du Xᵉ au XVIIIᵉ siècle, la plupart inédits, extraits des chroniques, et des manuscrits des bibliothèques et des archives publiques de la France et d'Angleterre*, ed. T. Bonnin, vol. 1 (Evreux, 1870), p. 64 (in a *pancarte* of 1195); Lemoine-Descourtieux, *Le frontière Normande de l'Avre*, p. 169. In contrast, Lemoine-Descourtieux thought that Ascelin gained possession of Illiers only after Henry had taken it.

[114] Orderic, vi. 176.

[115] *Regesta*, ii. 347 (no. clvii a) = no. 1356.

Having had his possessions at Nonancourt taken from him by force, it may be supposed that Gervase laid a complaint before his lord and king, Louis VI. The requirements of good lordship, as well as Louis's own public image, required that he act to restore Gervase to his property. Thus, he agreed to make representations on Gervase's behalf at Henry's court. The man chosen for this delicate mission was none other than Robert of Bellême, whose kinship with Gervase would have made him an appropriate envoy but for the fact that he was already openly opposing the royal duke – perhaps as a result of this same campaign against Gervase. Robert was sent as Louis's envoy nonetheless, and would have walked into Henry's court at Bonneville-sur-Touques thinking himself under a safe conduct and ready to lay out his case and his demands.[116] He was wrong. He was arrested without warning and charged with a number of offences:

> why he had acted against his lord's interests, why he had failed to come to his court after being summoned three times, why he had not rendered account as the king's *vicomte* and officer for the royal revenues pertaining to the *vicomtés* of Argentan and Exmes and Falaise, and also for other misdeeds. By a just judgement of the royal court he was sentenced to close imprisonment in fetters for the many shocking crimes which he was unable to deny he had committed both against God and against the king.[117]

Robert was first taken to Cherbourg and from there to the castle at 'Wareham' – presumably Corfe[118] – and that was apparently where he remained until his death. While a payment in the pipe roll reveals that he lived until after Michaelmas 1129, the date of his death is unknown. Contemporaries did not know when he died either. Henry of Huntingdon noted: 'this wicked man ... was placed in perpetual imprisonment by King Henry and perished after lengthy torments. While he lived in prison – he whom fame had so greatly cherished – it was not known whether he was alive or dead. Silence and ignorance surrounded the day of his death.'[119] Meanwhile, Henry moved to take Bellême's lands for himself, attacking Alençon which quickly surrendered to him.[120]

---

[116] Orderic stated that Bellême had acted as Louis's envoy when recounting that king's complaint against Henry at the council of Reims in 1119 (Orderic, vi. 256–8).

[117] Orderic, vi. 178.

[118] Worcester, iii.132–4; Huntingdon, p. 458; RT, s.a. 1113; ed. Delisle, i. 144; ed. Howlett, p. 95.

[119] *Pipe Roll 31 Henry I*, p. 10 (the entry is found under Wiltshire and Dorset, which suggests that Bellême was still at Corfe); Huntingdon, p. 604).

[120] Orderic, vi. 180.

Louis might have been irritated by Henry's actions, but he could do little about them, not least because Henry had manoeuvred to build a powerful coalition against him, too. Henry of Huntingdon reported that it was in 1109 that, 'envoys remarkable for their massive physique and magnificent apparel were sent by Henry, the Roman emperor, to ask for the king's daughter in marriage'.[121] Although the prestige of a marriage with the emperor was not to be sniffed at, Henry must also have calculated that the marriage was to his political advantage in his cold war with Louis – even more so when it finally took place in 1114.[122] Furthermore, as noted above, Henry had also encouraged his nephew, Count Theobald of Blois, to attack Louis's possessions in the Ile de France in 1111 and had supported his efforts with his own troops and money. Louis had taken to the field against Theobald, but despite Suger's best efforts to laud his actions, it is clear that the French king had struggled to maintain his authority. After February 1113, Louis would have found it even harder to begin hostilities against Henry because he had already made peace with a number of Louis's potential allies, most notably Count Fulk of Anjou, who had met with Henry at Alençon and negotiated a settlement that also reconciled Henry with Amaury of Montfort-l'Amaury and Count William of Evreux.[123] And so, despite Henry's outrageous behaviour in November 1112, Louis came to terms with him at a meeting at Gisors at the end of March 1113 and confirmed him in possession of Maine, Bellême, and Brittany.[124] The agreement also implicitly acknowledged Henry as the legitimate ruler of Normandy, despite the claims of William Clito and Louis's supposed support for him at this time.[125]

The grant of Brittany probably reflected Henry's continued good relations with the counts rather than an achievable political reality. It is likely that Henry had been on friendly terms with Count Alan IV of Brittany, even after he took as his second wife a daughter of the count of Anjou. That is probably why Henry had sought sanctuary in Brittany after his expulsion from Mont-Saint-Michel in 1091. Alan was subsequently to fight on Henry's side at the battle of Tinchebray in 1106, but as he seems to have retired between 1112 and 1116, it was perhaps his

---

[121]   Huntingdon, p. 456.
[122]   M. Chibnall, *The Empress Matilda: Queen Consort, Queen Mother, and Lady of the English* (Oxford, 1991), pp. 22–6 and see below, *infra*, p. 177.
[123]   Orderic, vi. 180.
[124]   Orderic, vi. 180. See also below, Chapter 5, pp. 296–7.
[125]   The Hyde chronicler claimed that Louis would not accept the homage of William Adelin for Normandy in 1114 because he had promised to support Clito's claim (Hyde, pp. 58–60, 82). For more on the recognition of Henry as duke see below, Chapter 5, pp. 296–8.

son, Conan, who was party to the agreement at Gisors.[126] Conan might have been betrothed to one of Henry's illegitimate daughters, Matilda, at this same time and as part of the renegotiation of the relationship between the two princes. The marriage itself probably went ahead only after another few years, however. Joëlle Quaghebeur noted that it had been made by October 1118, but Henry was mired in a rebellion at that time, making that an unlikely date for either the betrothal or the wedding. Orderic described the marriage as having been made 'recently' in Book IV of his *Ecclesiastical History*, which is thought to have been written around 1125, so it is more likely that the marriage was celebrated sometime after Henry's victory over the rebels in 1119.[127]

Quaghebeur saw Henry's moves as revealing a change in the attitude of the Norman dukes to the Bretons, and one that would be reflected in the reign of Henry II.[128] Instead of a policy of rapprochement, she argued, from Henry I's reign on the dukes would attempt to establish hegemony over Brittany and would use marriages to make good their claims. In the light of the full sweep of the relations between Bretons and Normans, however, that argument seems overstated. Henry's actions were not materially different from those of Richard II, who had attempted to achieve the same dynastic and seigniorial ends at the beginning of the eleventh century by the same means, subsequently supported by Dudo's propaganda. The campaigns led by his son *c.* 1030 had the same intention. Rather than change, then, it is the continuity here that is remarkable.

After Bellême's arrest and imprisonment, Henry attempted to forfeit his lands. Bellême itself, given to Henry by Louis VI, was given in turn to Count Rotrou of the Perche. The towns of Sées and Alençon, previously part of the lordship of Bellême but now firmly within Normandy, were granted to Count Theobald of Blois. Theobald passed them on to his younger brother, Stephen,[129] who had already been given Bellême's former estates at Almenèches and La Roche-Mabile in his own right, and would shortly be created count of Mortain, too.[130]

It may be supposed, in the absence of evidence to the contrary, that Henry retained the remainder of Bellême's lands and castles in the Hiémois and Lieuvin in his own hands. While he could maintain his grasp on them, this dubious acquisition of Vignats, Fourches, Trun, Montgommery, Bures-sur-Dives, and more would have increased the extent of the royal duke's demesne in this part of Normandy enormously. And with the land came jurisdiction. As discussed more

[126] Quaghebeur, 'Havoise, Constance et Mathilde', p. 149; Guillotel, *Actes des ducs de Bretagne*, pp. 422–5, no. 115.
[127] Quaghebeur, 'Havoise, Constance et Mathilde', pp. 155–6; Orderic, ii. 352.
[128] Quaghebeur, 'Havoise, Constance et Mathilde', p. 161.
[129] Orderic, vi. 194–6.
[130] See above, *infra*, p. 164.

fully below, between *c.* 1110 and 1118, and almost certainly between 1112 and 1118, Henry heard a plea between the monks of Troarn and Robert of Ussy over land in the Hiémois. We know of the plea, and the result, because Henry sent a writ-charter to Bishop Richard of Bayeux and the men of the county informing them of it. This is Henry's only writ-charter addressed to the men of the Hiémois, and so was almost certainly issued during this brief period when Henry had gained control of Bellême's honour.[131]

Local loyalties to the Montgommery family remained strong, however, and William Talvas was not tarred with the same brush as his father by his men and neighbours. Local sensitivities were further offended when Stephen of Blois mishandled what was already a delicate situation by imposing novel exactions on the men of Alençon.[132] The result was an uprising in 1118 which saw Arnulf of Montgommery, Robert of Bellême's brother, take control of the town – possibly because William Talvas himself was in his county of Ponthieu at the time. Further north, just inside the Lieuvin and not far from the castle at Montgommery, Reginald of Bailleul, who had defied Henry to his face, was besieged at his castle of Le Renouard. The men of Exmes and Courcy, places which had fallen under the authority of Robert of Bellême, as well as those of Grandmesnil and Montpinçon nearby, waited for the right time to revolt, too.[133] Henry's attempt to forfeit Bellême's heir thus seriously misfired, with the flames of insurrection no doubt fanned by Count Fulk of Anjou who was still attempting to establish his own authority in Maine.

Henry was faced with war and rebellion elsewhere along his frontiers at this same time, and may be thought to have rapidly concluded that he would have to allow William Talvas to succeed to his father's Norman lands after all. And so when Count Fulk approached him in 1119 to seek terms, Henry pardoned Talvas for his rebellion and restored his Norman lands to him. Henry did, however, maintain his own garrisons in the castles at Alençon, Almenèches, Vignats, and elsewhere, as was his right.[134] He also seems to have withheld the office of *vicomte* of the Hiémois, which Talvas's father, grandfather, and great-grandfather had held. Talvas would also be unable to prevent Henry from exercising justice over his Norman lordships on occasion.[135] In short, Henry ensured that ducal power

---

[131] *NI*, p. 90 and see below, Chapter 8, p. 473.

[132] Orderic, vi. 204–6.

[133] Orderic, vi. 214–16.

[134] Orderic, vi. 224, and see below Chapter 11, pp. 639–41. Bellême remained in the hands of Count Rotrou of the Perche, of course (K. Thompson, 'William Talvas, count of Ponthieu, and the politics of the Anglo-Norman realm', in *England and Normandy in the Middle Ages*, ed. D. Bates and A. Curry (London, 1994), p. 173).

[135] See below, Chapter 8, pp. 473–4. Noted also by Thompson, 'William Talvas', p. 174.

here was as effective and secure as it had been in his father's day, but while Roger of Montgommery had been part of the ruling clique, Talvas was not fully restored to favour, and Henry seems never entirely to have trusted him.

Fulk of Anjou had twice taken the lead in seeking peace with Henry, and had twice obtained his aim, at least in part because he had recognized Henry's authority on the Sarthe frontier and in Maine. But although Fulk seems to have treated Henry with respect, Anjou remained a clear rival for power in this border region. Henry's responses included making alliances with some Manceaux, which gave him some control over some of the castles located just south of the Norman frontier with Maine.[136] But they paled in importance beside Henry's great diplomatic triumph: the marriage of his sole legitimate son, William, to Fulk's daughter, Matilda. They had been betrothed as early as 1113,[137] but the marriage was only finally celebrated in 1119.

> In May Prince William, the king's son, crossed from England to Normandy and his father, delighted at his coming, then revealed the plan he had previously kept secret. He sent envoys of peace to Fulk, count of Anjou, and, after agreeing to satisfactory terms of peace with him, graciously invited him to his court. In June, Prince William married the count's daughter at Lisieux. The union of these noble families pleased many people who hoped for peace. Although it lasted only a short while, for fate soon cut the thread of the young husband's life in the deep sea, still for the present it gave a much-needed breathing space to the hostile people.[138]

The terms of peace that Orderic noted but did not spell out included a large, undisclosed sum of money paid by Henry to Fulk, which is why Suger could complain that Fulk 'now put greed before fidelity' to his French allies, and a dowry consisting of the disputed county of Maine and the border town of Alençon (which, it should be noted, was not Fulk's to give).[139]

Suger complained of Fulk's behaviour because the war/rebellion that Henry faced in the Hiémois in 1118–19 was associated with a war that threatened the

---

[136] The marriage of one of Henry's illegitimate daughters to Roscelin of Beaumont-sur-Sarthe has been noted above. In addition, Henry made an exchange with Hamelin of Mayene, by which he was given lands in Devon and Henry obtained his castles at Ambrières and Gorron (*Book of Fees*, i. 86 noted in Hollister, *Henry*, p. 229 and ns. 100 and 101).

[137] Orderic, vi. 180.

[138] Orderic, vi. 224.

[139] Malmesbury, *GR*, i. 758; Worcester, iii. 144; Suger, *Deeds of Louis the Fat*, p. 116 (translation slightly altered).

eastern borders of the duchy that was purportedly raised in support of William Clito's claim to the duchy. Despite the fact that King Louis had recognized Henry's right to Normandy in 1113, he had come to see the advantages of supporting Henry's young rival. Clito was the son of Robert Curthose. He had been taken into custody when Henry took Falaise, immediately after his victory at Tinchebray, and entrusted to the care of Helias of Saint-Saëns. He was almost four years old at the time. Around 1110, when Henry was beginning to campaign against the French lords across the Avre, he seems to have decided that Clito posed too much of a risk to be allowed to remain at large any longer. So he sent the *vicomte* of Arques, Robert of Beauchamp, to Saint-Saëns to arrest the boy. But he was not there. And when Helias got wind of what had transpired he and his charge fled into exile. The *vicomte* of Arques then took Helias's property into the royal duke's hand 'and afterwards the king gave it to his kinsman, William of Warenne, to secure his loyal support and resolute defence against enemy attacks'.[140] Thus Orderic expressly spelt out the intention behind the grant.

But while Clito constituted a stick with which to beat Henry for King Louis and Norman rebels alike until his death in 1128, the rebellion that broke out in eastern Normandy in 1118 was not really about his claim to rule Normandy at all. It was caused instead by Louis's desire to expand the reach of his own authority as well as by the diverse claims of the various rebels to what they saw as their own inheritances and Henry's unjust refusal to let them enjoy them. And the real leader of the rebellion was neither Louis nor Clito, but Amaury of Montfort-l'Amaury, whose claim to the county of Evreux had been denied by Henry.

Amaury was Count William of Evreux's nephew and closest heir. When the count died on 18 April, Amaury might well have been expected to succeed to his county. However, he was French, had fought against Henry in 1112, and had encouraged Count Fulk of Anjou (his nephew) to attack the duchy into the bargain. With such a track record, Henry did not look favourably on his claim. There might have been a point of principle at work, too, as it looks as if Henry's settled policy at this point was the elimination of French lords from Norman soil. Eustace of Breteuil's claim to Breteuil had been supported in preference to that of a French claimant, even before Henry had gained the duchy. Gervase of Châteauneuf's interests had been pushed back. The Avre frontier had been strengthened. The French lordship of Bellême had been split from the Montgommery family's Norman estates. If Amaury of Montfort were to inherit the county of Evreux, Henry's work would be stopped in its tracks. So he refused to allow Amaury's claim, perhaps arguing that there was no established right for a nephew to succeed an uncle and that the county was anyway an office held at the duke's pleasure. While Henry's line was

[140] Orderic, vi. 164.

probably still defensible, Amaury naturally thought otherwise and 'raised a major rebellion, stirring up almost the whole of Gaul against Henry'.[141]

Amaury was an intelligent and astute operator, who succeeded in bringing together a number of discontented lords under William Clito's banner. His allies included King Louis; Count Baldwin of Flanders, who attacked Arques in September 1118 and received a mortal wound for his trouble;[142] Hugh of Gournay who, with Robert Haget, Gerard of Fécamp, Enguerrand of Vascœuil, Anceaume and Gilbert of Cressy, ravaged Talou and Caux;[143] Eustace of Breteuil, who claimed Ivry which his father had held, but which Curthose or Henry had recovered to the demesne after his death; William Crispin, who had a personal dislike of the royal duke; Count Fulk of Anjou; and William Talvas, whose county of Ponthieu gave Count Baldwin access to the Norman border. It is notable that none of the Norman lords involved held lands in England, and that Richer of L'Aigle broke with his fellow conspirators the moment that he was promised the English inheritance he had claimed. This is hardly surprising. Support for William Clito and possession of cross-Channel holdings were, politically speaking, mutually exclusive.

Despite the extent of the opposition he faced, and despite a plot to assassinate him fomented by one of his own chamberlains, Henry triumphed. He defeated King Louis in battle at Brémule in 1119, and each of his other enemies in a combination of sieges and skirmishes. Orderic's list of those who fought for Henry at the battle, which is supported by the witness lists of those few acts that can be dated to 1119, included men who had benefitted from Henry's patronage and who held lands in both England and Normandy. They included William of Warenne, Walter Giffard, Roger fitz Richard of Clare, William of Roumare, Nigel of Aubigny, William of Tancarville, and Count Henry of Eu. This last had initially opposed Henry in 1118, but had been brought to his senses as the result of his brief and unexpected imprisonment and/or by the death of the count of Flanders, which deprived him and the other Norman rebels based in the north east of the duchy of their principal support. Indeed, that may be why Hugh of Gournay and Stephen of Aumale did not fight for either side; they were waiting to see what transpired.[144]

But although victorious against his enemies, Henry probably reasoned that his troubles would continue unless he pacified Amaury of Montfort. And so he allowed him to inherit the county of Evreux in 1119, although he also insisted on

---

[141] Orderic, vi. 188.
[142] Orderic, vi. 190. He died in 1119: RT, s.a. 1119; Delisle, i. 158; Howlett, p. 103.
[143] Orderic, vi. 192–4.
[144] See also Hollister, *Henry*, p. 264.

retaining the keeps of the count's castles in his own hands.[145] This was a compromise, and one that Amaury had not been willing to accept when it was first offered in 1118.[146] But the very fact that Henry had made the offer comprised an acknowledgement that his plan to keep French lords out of Normandy had failed. And once Henry had admitted that, he moved to restore other French lords to border lordships. So, despite the fact that Henry had taken Illiers-l'Evêque from Ascelin Goel c. 1112, he gave the castle of Ivry to Ascelin's son, Robert Goel, in 1118.[147] Then, after his victory at Brémule, he gave Breteuil to Ralph of Gael. He, however, quickly surrendered the lordship to his daughter Amice who was betrothed to Richard, Henry I's illegitimate son.[148] Unfortunately, Richard died in the wreck of the *White Ship* before the marriage could take place,[149] and so Amice was married to Robert of Leicester, Waleran of Meulan's twin brother, in 1121 instead.[150]

That does not mean that Henry reconciled with all the French lords across his border, however, and so about a year after the end of the war, c. 1120, Henry would establish a new forward base on the Avre when he seized Verneuil-sur-Avre. It is likely that he took the place from Hugh of Châteauneuf-en-Thymerais, who had opposed him in the rebellion of 1118–19 and would do so again, probably as a result, in 1123–24.[151] This move finally brought all the land to the north of the Avre under Henry's control, thereby establishing a natural Norman frontier that ran along the river – although it is possible that the Crispin lords of Tillières had previously enjoyed a degree of influence over the town.[152] In any event, Henry built a new castle in Verneuil, which he retained in his own demesne, and established a borough alongside it which had been given its own laws, broadly similar to those of Breteuil, by 1126.[153] That grant of laws and liberties to the burgesses might have been intended to assure the royal duke of their loyalty. The actions of the burgesses of Breteuil in 1118 would certainly have made it clear how decisive intervention by townsmen might be.[154] The churches at Verneuil were subsequently given to the bishop of Evreux, although it seems that Henry overrode the existing claims of the monks of Saint-Evroult and Saint-Laumer of Blois when making his grant.[155]

[145] Orderic, vi. 278.
[146] Orderic, vi. 220.
[147] Orderic, vi. 228.
[148] Orderic, vi. 278, 294.
[149] Orderic, vi. 304.
[150] Orderic, vi. 330.
[151] Orderic, vi. 198, 346.
[152] Lemoine-Descourtieux, *Le frontière Normande de l'Avre*, p. 175.
[153] A comparison of the two codes is provided by A. Ballard, 'The law of Breteuil', 646–58.
[154] Suggested by Lemoine-Descourtieux, *Le frontière Normande de l'Avre*, p. 175.
[155] *Regesta*, ii. 361 (no. ccviii) = no. 1554; *Regesta*, ii. 373 (no. cclii) = no. 1700. Pope Innocent

It should be noted that the claims of the monks of Blois to property in Verneuil indicates that the town had once been held by the counts of Blois-Chartres, and so had almost certainly been among the lands disputed between Odo II and Richard II before it had passed into the possession of the Châteauneuf family.

In November 1120, Henry lost his only legitimate son, and established heir, in the wreck of the *White Ship*. This was a personal tragedy for Henry, and it both reopened the question of the succession and dissolved the alliance with Anjou. But it is not clear that it significantly weakened Henry or that it contributed substantively to the rebellion that he faced in 1123–24. Instead, it is likely that this rebellion was the result of Henry's continuing warfare on the Avre.

So far as the fighting was concerned, Orderic gave the leading role in this rebellion to Waleran of Meulan, who had only recently achieved his majority.[156] Waleran might have been piqued by the recent grant of the honour of Breteuil to his twin brother who, it should be noticed, remained loyal to Henry throughout. Waleran had not received such patronage himself and he might not have wanted his brother to develop Norman interests to rival his own. That jealousy would also explain why he failed to defend Breteuil in 1141 at a time when he was in charge of the defence of the duchy.[157] Secondly, Waleran's possession of Meulan seems to have played a central role in his decision to rebel. David Crouch suggested that the rebellion was intended to promote his position in Meulan and increase his standing among his French neighbours, and there is certainly support for this view in the marriages that Waleran orchestrated for his three sisters. One was married to Hugh of Montfort-sur-Risle, whose estates divided the Beaumont possessions at Pont-Audemer from those at Brionne, a second was matched with William Louvel, who was the son of Ascelin Goel and by then held both Ivry and the lordship of Bréval across the Eure in France, and the third wed Hugh fitz Gervase of Châteauneuf-en-Thymerais.[158] Thirdly, Waleran's castles were garrisoned with French knights.[159] This French connection is emphasized still further by the fact that, while Waleran led the rebellion on the ground, it was orchestrated by Amaury of Montfort. Orderic tells us that Amaury of Montfort had been unable to bear the demands of Henry's tax collectors and officials, and it is certainly unlikely that any such customs had been due under, or paid by, the previous counts.[160] But he, too, would have wanted to ensure that the border between Normandy and France

II confirmed the grant in 1142 (*Papsturkunden in Frankreich. II. Normandie*, ed. J. Ramackers (Göttingen, 1937), pp. 72–4, no. 16).
[156] Orderic, vi. 332. David Crouch concurred: Crouch, *Beaumont Twins*, pp. 15–24.
[157] Crouch, *Beaumont Twins*, p. 55.
[158] Orderic, vi. 332; Crouch, *Beaumont Twins*, pp. 15–17.
[159] Orderic, vi. 340, 342 identified some of the French knights in these garrisons.
[160] See below, Chapter 9, pp. 564–5.

that ran along the Avre remained permeable while limiting Henry's opportunities to build up his own authority to the south of the river. These lords with one foot in Normandy and one foot in France did not want to find that all of their estates had suddenly been absorbed into Henry's *regnum*. They had more influence if Henry and Louis continued to fight for their loyalty, and had more independence if neither king could claim overarching authority over them.

In this game, Hugh of Montfort was the odd man out, and that is probably why Henry chose to ambush him at his court in October 1123. Face-to-face with his sovereign, Hugh had no option but to agree to surrender his castle at Montfort to the royal duke, but as he was leading Henry's men there, Hugh used his local knowledge to escape from his escort and to warn both his wife and his co-conspirators that they were discovered.[161] Henry was thus forced to fight against the rebels, who legitimized their actions by once again claiming that they had revolted in favour of William Clito. They were also supported, although from a distance, by King Louis. Henry was successful against almost all of his enemies. Only William of Roumare, who had rebelled not in favour of Clito but over what he saw as Henry's unjust refusal to allow him to inherit his mother's lands in England (which Ranulf le Meschin had surrendered to Henry in return for the grant of the earldom of Chester in 1120), withstood the onslaught and obliged the royal duke to come to terms.[162] The castle at Montfort fell within a month; Waleran's stronghold at Pont-Audemer after a siege of six or seven weeks.[163] In the meantime, Henry's justices seized the county of Evreux and as many of the estates of the other rebels as they could and annexed them to the ducal demesne.[164]

After a truce over the winter, Henry resumed his campaign in Lent 1124 and won a swift victory in absentia at Bourgthéroulde, where his household knights, led by William of Tancarville and Odo Borleng, captured Count Waleran, Hugh of Montfort, Hugh of Châteauneuf, and some others.[165] Amaury of Montfort, who had counselled against giving battle, escaped thanks to the sympathy and assistance of William of Grandcourt, while William Louvel escaped his pursuers by disguising himself and using his possessions as bribes. It was money well spent, as Henry inflicted harsh judgements on those he captured, to encourage those who still persisted in their rebellion to surrender. Despite initial intransigence

---

[161]   Orderic, vi. 334.

[162]   Orderic, vi. 332–4.

[163]   Orderic, vi. 336; Simeon of Durham, *Symeonis monachi opera omnia*, ed. T. Arnold, Rolls Series, 2 vols (London, 1882–5), ii. 274. For the events around Le Bec see also *Life of Abbot William*, pp. 124–5.

[164]   Orderic, vi. 344.

[165]   Orderic gave the leading role to Odo Borleng, but Robert of Torigni said that Henry's army was led by William of Tancarville (RT, s.a. 1124; Delisle, i. 166; Howlett, p. 107).

by Waleran's steward, Morin of Le Pin, the castle at Brionne surrendered shorty afterwards. So, too, did the castle at Vatteville. Waleran was then obliged to order his garrison at Beaumont to surrender, thereby ending the rebellion.[166] He, along with Hugh of Montfort and Hugh of Châteauneuf, was taken to England and kept in prison – Waleran and Hugh of Châteauneuf until 1129 and Hugh of Montfort until at least 1136.[167] Their lands were absorbed into the ducal demesne for the duration of their imprisonment, which gave Henry enormously extended posses- sions along the Risle valley for that period.

King Louis did not in the end enter the conflict because Henry had engineered a diversion for him. It was the marriage of Henry's daughter, Matilda, to the Emperor Henry V that finally paid dividends here. In July or August in 1124, the emperor led his forces against Reims, with the counsel of his father-in-law. And while the emperor turned back without a fight when he saw the forces that Louis had gathered against him, for the royal duke the campaign, and the build up to it, had been a triumph because it had done what he had hoped it would, which was prevent the French king from joining in the rebellion against him.[168]

At the same time, Henry had also striven to ensure that William Clito should not gain any advantage by a marriage to Fulk of Anjou's daughter by making a timely complaint to the papal curia that the planned match was within the prohib- ited degrees. His case was strengthened by the condemnation of such marriages as 'infamous and abominable' at the first Lateran council held just the year before. By 26 August, at about the same time that the emperor was leading his army to the French border, a total of four legates had been won over and a papal bull had been issued that annulled the marriage and imposed an interdict on any territory that Clito visited unless he was separated from his wife within a given time.[169] Count Fulk was so angry at this outcome that he threw the papal envoys into prison, singed their beards and burned their papers. He was excommunicated as a result and an interdict was placed on his lands. He submitted quickly, perhaps because his sights were already fixed on the throne of Jerusalem. In return, Henry allowed the papal legate, John of Crema, to hold a legatine council in England.

Although Henry had defeated the rebels in 1124, William Clito remained a threat. Indeed, that threat was growing for Clito had not only gained the backing of Louis VI, he had gained his patronage, too. He was first given the county of the Vexin in January 1127 but then, after the murder of Count Charles the Good on 2 March of that same year, the king had him elected as count of Flanders instead. Fortunately

---

[166] Orderic, vi. 354–6.
[167] Orderic, vi. 356.
[168] Suger, *The Deeds of Louis the Fat*, pp. 127–32.
[169] See the discussion in Hollister, *Henry*, pp. 304–5.

for Henry, the politics of the French court meant that he could now count Amaury of Montfort as an ally rather than a rebel, while the death of the Emperor Henry V in 1125 meant that his widow, Henry's legitimate daughter Matilda, could be remarried in order to forge a new alliance. And this was precisely what happened. In 1127, Matilda was betrothed to Geofrey le Bel, the son of Count Fulk of Anjou, in a move that would secure peace on Henry's southern frontier at a time when he needed to concentrate on his borders with Ponthieu and the Vexin. But Henry was not so vulnerable or desperate that he was prepared to commit his daughter to the marriage without certain safeguards. As Judith Green has observed, Henry firstly required Count Fulk to leave Anjou to become king of Jerusalem and, secondly, to make arrangements that would ensure that Geoffrey's brother, Helias, would have no claim to any part of Anjou. To ensure that would be the case, Helias was married to Phillippa, the daughter and heiress of Rotrou of the Perche and Henry's illegitimate daughter Matilda. Geoffrey le Bel was thus the reigning and undisputed count of Anjou when he married Matilda on 17 June 1128. A month later, William Clito died of a wound to his hand at the siege of Aalst.[170]

Henry was by now about sixty years old. He might have been reminded of his mortality by the deaths of some of those who had helped him to govern his cross-Channel *regnum*. William of Tancarville died in 1128. Nigel of Aubigny died in 1129, and so did Ranulf le Meschin. When the oaths were made regarding Matilda's succession it was the coming generation who swore first: Henry's nephew Stephen of Blois and the king's illegitimate son Robert of Gloucester. Henry was increasingly surrounded by younger faces. That must have been clear to Geoffrey and Matilda, and might have been of some concern to them, for Henry had not released Matilda's dowry into their hands and, as such, there was nothing to back up the oaths sworn by Henry's *fideles* as to her succession.[171] And so Geoffrey and Matilda demanded that Henry surrender the castles at Domfront, Argentan, and Exmes to them. Henry, aware that surrendering these castles would leave his southern frontier wide open, refused to do so. And so Geoffrey attacked Henry's son-in-law Roscelin the *vicomte* of Maine and lord of Beaumont-sur-Sarthe.

Henry seems to have considered Geoffrey's actions as tantamount to war and took action against those suspected of sympathizing with the Angevin.[172] He put

---

[170]   Clito died on 27 or 28 July (Orderic, vi. 376 and n. 1). For the arrangements made concerning the marriage see J. A. Green, 'Henry I and the origins of the civil war', in *King Stephen's Reign 1135–1154*, ed. P. Dalton and G. J. White (Woodbridge, 2008), p. 17; Green, *Henry*, pp. 198, 200–2.

[171]   On the oaths, see also below, Chapter 6, pp. 332–4.

[172]   Marjorie Chibnall also described these hostilities as a war: Chibnall, *Matilda*, p. 61–2, 64.

a garrison into Roger of Tosny's castle at Conches, and he summoned William Talvas to his court. Not surprisingly, given how Henry had treated his father in 1112, Talvas did not go. And so, in September 1135, Henry disseised him of his whole honour. He then took Alençon and Almenèches into his hands and strengthened his own castle at Argentan.[173] Finally, at the end of November he removed to Lyons-la-Forêt to hunt, and it was there that he fell ill and died on 1 December 1135.

The end of Norman rule in Normandy: Stephen of Blois and Geoffrey of Anjou, 1135–44

When Henry I died, he was effectively at war with Count Geoffrey and Matilda, and it may be that the oaths taken to Matilda regarding the succession fell away as a result.[174] In any event, when Henry died Stephen was advantageously placed, as a result of Henry's patronage to him and his brother and his possession of the county of Boulogne in right of his wife, and succeeded in winning the English throne. Once he had done that, the Anglo-Norman magnates whose cross-Channel holdings had made them such loyal supporters of Henry I, ensured that he would also become duke of the Normans. But Matilda was not abandoned entirely. Wigan the Marshall surrendered the castles at Exmes, Domfront, and Argentan to Matilda 'as his natural lady (*naturam dominam*)'.[175] Matilda also gained possession of the castles at Châtillon-sur-Colmont, Gorron, and Ambrières, and granted them to Juhel of Mayenne in order to gain his support.[176] Geoffrey and Matilda also enjoyed the support of William Talvas, who was now able to leave his refuge in Anjou and was restored to his own estates without opposition.[177]

There is no reason to think that Talvas did not recover all his Norman estates swiftly. As noted previously, the local loyalties to him and his family were strong, and his lands had only been out of his control for less than a year. As such, the fact that Geoffrey and Matilda could rely on the support of William Talvas opened up a huge swathe of Normandy to their influence. This has been downplayed in much of the recent historiography, although it has been given due emphasis by Katy Dutton.[178] Although the lordship of Bellême remained outside his control, Talvas

---

[173] Orderic, vi. 446.
[174] See below, Chapter 6, p. 333.
[175] Orderic, vi. 454.
[176] RT, s.a. 1135; Delisle, i. 199–200; Howlett, p. 128.
[177] RT, s.a. 1135; Delisle, i. 200; Howlett, p. 128.
[178] K. A. Dutton, 'Geoffrey, Count of Anjou and Duke of Normandy, 1129–51' (unpublished Ph.D. thesis, University of Glasgow, 2011), pp. 185–9. His importance was downplayed by Chibnall, *Matilda* and his role ignored by King, *King Stephen*.

held a number of important fortresses, including those at Alençon, Vignats, and Bures-sur-Dives, which together gave Geoffrey and Matilda indirect control over a slice of central Normandy that stretched from its southern border almost to the Channel coast. The importance of Talvas's estates to Geoffrey's ambitions is revealed by his initial campaigns, which attempted to encourage those living around the edges of Talvas's lands – at Carrouges, Annebecq, Ecouché, and Le Sap – to join the Angevin party. Even Geoffrey's principal objective in 1136, the city of Lisieux, lay only a few miles north of Talvas's castle at Montgommery.

Stephen recognized the importance of Talvas to Geoffrey's cause, too. In an effort to build up his own support on the southern frontier of the duchy, he handed the castles at Moulins-la-Marche and Bonsmoulins to Rotrou of the Perche and Richer of L'Aigle, respectively.[179] As he was himself count of Mortain, it is likely that he garrisoned his own castles against the threat the Angevins posed to his rule – something implicit in John of Marmoutier's report that Alexander of Bohon and his brother frequently attacked the county on Matilda's behalf.[180] Moreover, Stephen's 1137 campaign against Geoffrey in Normandy was actually aimed at Talvas's lands – or at least the route chosen would take the army across them – and it is perhaps suspicious that Stephen's force broke up at Livarot, just as it was about to enter his territory.

Stephen's wife, Matilda of Boulogne, seems to have played no role in the duchy, although she was of course vital to Stephen's survival in England. Instead, Stephen relied on a series of male aristocratic deputies, with Waleran of Meulan perhaps the most important of them. Stephen attempted to assure himself of Waleran's support by granting him the castle at Montfort-sur-Risle, which gave him control of the entire stretch of the Risle from Pont-Audemer to Beaumont-le-Roger. By 1138, he had also given him one of his daughters as a wife, and the earldom of Worcester as a dowry, thereby providing the cross-Channel dimension to Waleran's interests that would have given him a vested interest in maintaining Stephen's rule in the duchy.[181] But he also allowed Waleran to gain a political ascendancy in England that must have hindered his ability and desire to act as Stephen's deputy in Normandy.[182]

In contrast, although the Empress Matilda was largely absent from the administration of Anjou,[183] in those parts of Normandy that recognized her succession

[179] Orderic, vi. 484. The grants were made in 1137.
[180] John of Marmoutier, 'Historia Gaufredi ducis Normannorum et comitis Andegavorum', *Chroniques des comtes d'Anjou et des seigneurs d'Amboise*, ed. L. Halphen and R. Poupardin (Paris, 1913), p. 225; Dutton, 'Geoffrey', p. 180.
[181] Crouch, *Beaumont Twins*, pp. 30, 39–40.
[182] Crouch, *Beaumont Twins*, pp. 36–7.
[183] Dutton, 'Geoffrey', pp. 98–100.

she was as much in evidence as her husband Duke Geoffrey, both before and after his conquest of the duchy in 1144. She was of course an abnormal case, in that she was the heiress (even if not an undisputed one) of Normandy rather than a run-of-the-mill consort. Surviving writs reveal that in 1135 × 1139 she commanded the foresters of Tinchebray – part of King Stephen's county of Mortain throughout the possible date range – to allow the monks of Savigny to have their forge;[184] in 1148 × 1151 she commanded the constable of Cherbourg to restore to the canons of St Mary of Cherbourg the alms land in Beaumont-Hague that they had deraigned;[185] and in 1151 × 1153 she gave the monks of Saint-André-en-Gouffern relief from *grauarium*, amounting to 46s. 6d. annually, from the vill of *Mons-Guaralfus* in the vicinity of Argentan.[186] Robert of Gloucester's restoration of various Norman properties to Bayeux cathedral, made at Devizes in 1146 before Matilda, also made no provision for Geoffrey's involvement.[187] This was not the patronage of a noble woman, or even the patronage of a duchess, for not all of the places concerned were part of the demesne. Indeed, it is surprising that Tinchebray was under Matilda's control at all. This, then, was government. Matilda's commands were sent to the local officials who would put them into effect, just as her father's writs had been.[188] Matilda also had her own military household, giving her further independence. In 1138, Alexander of Bohon was said to be 'foremost among the countess's military retinue' in an act for the men of Saumur, and it seems that she also retained the service of Guy of Sablé who held the castle at Gacé for her (which belonged to the ageing Count Amaury of Evreux) in 1136.[189] Matilda's men also captured Ralph of Esson, from the Cinglais, most likely in 1138, which gave her control of his castles which may be supposed to have stood on or near the right bank of the Orne south of Caen.[190]

That does not necessarily mean, however, that Matilda was seen as wielding a power that was the equal of her husband's. It might have been the case that Matilda issued acts only when Geoffrey was absent from Normandy.[191] That is suggested most strongly by the fact that two acts for the inmates of the Grand Beaulieu outside Chartres were made in the name of both Matilda and Duke

[184] *Regesta*, iii. no. 805.
[185] *Regesta*, iii. no. 168.
[186] *Regesta*, iii. no. 748.
[187] *Regesta*, iii. no. 58.
[188] Chibnall perhaps understated Matilda's role in Normandy in the period before 1139, although the evidence is certainly thin (Chibnall, *Matilda*, pp. 70–1).
[189] *Recueil Henri II*, i. 4–6 (no. 1); Chibnall, *Matilda*, p. 71 (Alexander of Bohon); Dutton, 'Geoffrey', p. 187 (Guy of Sablé).
[190] Orderic, vi. 512–14.
[191] See also Chibnall, *Matilda*, pp. 158–61.

Henry, as well as by Henry's confirmation of one of Matilda's acts for the monks of Sillé.[192] Moreover, it was Geoffrey, not Matilda, who was recognized as duke by the Normans in 1144 and by King Louis in 1151. It was Geoffrey, too, who nominated bishops to Lisieux, Bayeux, and Avranches even before his investiture as duke.[193] Matilda's role in Normandy, then, should not be taken too far, but at the same time it should be acknowledged that her freedom of action appears to have been far greater than that enjoyed by previous duchesses. In particular, Matilda seems to have been able to act on her own initiative, even if her acts might still be subject to her husband's confirmation.

In 1137, Geoffrey raided well into the Bessin, appearing before Argences, and Caen, as well as at Saint-Pierre-sur-Dives in the Lieuvin. The next year, 1138, Robert of Gloucester defected to Geoffrey's side as a result of discontent with Stephen's rule, a residual loyalty to his sister, and, perhaps, because he was concerned that his own estates were now threatened by Geoffrey's raiding. His defection brought Geoffrey the town of Caen, the city of Bayeux, and 'numerous Norman strongholds', presumably including Robert's own castles at Creully, Evrecy, Torigni-sur-Vire, and Saint-Scholasse-sur-Sarthe.[194] But while Robert was pushed into Geoffrey's camp by this combination of factors, he was pulled there, too, with a mixture of pleas and promises of an unspecified nature. It is plausible, for example, that Robert was given permission to retain those lands that he had already alienated from the bishop of Bayeux, and given free licence further to prey on his neighbours.[195]

But even with Robert of Gloucester as an ally, Count Geoffrey still failed to make much progress in Normandy. As late as 1140, Robert Marmion continued to hold the castle of Falaise against him, with the result that Geoffrey razed Marmion's castle at Fontenay-la-Marmion.[196] It was only after Stephen's capture at the battle of Lincoln on 2 February 1141 that Geoffrey began to make significant progress. Perhaps in March, Verneuil and Nonancourt surrendered to the count. In April, Lisieux was surrendered to him by the elderly Bishop John. Robert of Torigni wrote that Count Waleran of Meulan abandoned Stephen at about the same time, a move caused not only by the threat now posed to his Norman estates, but also because the battle had destroyed the hegemony he had built up in England.[197] As access over his lands would open up the east of Normandy to

[192] *Regesta*, iii. nos. 71, 72, 824, respectively.
[193] See Dutton, 'Geoffrey', pp. 198–205.
[194] Orderic, vi. 516; RT, s.a. 1138; Delisle, i. 213; Howlett, p. 136.
[195] See *Regesta*, iii. no. 58 and the discussion in Dutton, 'Geoffrey', pp. 193–5
[196] Orderic, vi. 526; RT, s.a. 1140 (although the date is omitted in Torigni's own MS); Delisle, i. 219; Howlett, p. 139.
[197] Orderic, vi. 546–8; Crouch, *Beaumont Twins*, p. 49.

Geoffrey's power, it is no surprise that Geoffrey was willing to secure Waleran's support with a confirmation of his possession of Montfort-sur-Risle.[198] Moreover, in 1143, Bishop Richard of Bayeux died and was succeeded by Philip of Harcourt, from a family that was a satellite of the Beaumonts. Indeed, Geoffrey even promised to do justice to Philip and the canons of Bayeux, thereby providing himself with the opportunity to exercise justice in the Bessin – in other words to act as duke even before the conquest of Normandy was complete. By that point, the Bessin belonged to Geoffrey and Earl Robert of Gloucester's support was no longer required. Waleran's support, however, was essential if Rouen were to fall to the count of the Angevins.

Waleran's support brought the Roumois up to the Seine under Geoffrey's control. Falaise, too, finally surrendered to the count. But Geoffrey decided to let Rouen stew. In 1142, he pushed west, not east. He took Aunay-sur-Orne and then the castles of Stephen's own county of Mortain. By the end of the year the Avranchin, and most of the Cotentin were under his control.[199] Only the castle at Cherbourg held out against him into 1143.[200] That same year, Geoffrey finally moved to take the east of the duchy, receiving the surrender of Le Vaudreuil on the Seine, not far upstream from Rouen. The men of the Caux, led by Walter Giffard, also submitted.[201] During January 1144, Geoffrey crossed the Seine at Vernon with a great army and settled down to besiege Rouen, establishing his headquarters in the abbey of La Trinité-du-Mont. He did not have to wait long. The citizens opened their gates the very next day, 20 January. The castle, however, was a harder nut to crack. The garrison under Earl William of Warenne held out against him until their supplies failed. Only then did Geoffrey become duke of the Normans.[202] Once Rouen had fallen, there was only a little mopping up left to do. The castles at Neufchâtel-en-Bray and Lyons-la-Forêt soon fell to the new duke, and by the new year only the castle at Arques continued to hold out against him.[203] It fell during the summer of 1145 when its commander, William the Monk, was accidentally killed by an arrow.[204] Thus ended Norman rule in Normandy.

* * * * * *

If the argument developed in these first three chapters is right, it took a long time for Normandy to reach its full extent; certainly longer than previous studies

---

[198] RT, s.a. 1141; Delisle, i. 224–5; Howlett, p. 142.
[199] RT, s.a. 1142; Delisle, i. 226–7; Howlett, p. 143.
[200] RT, s.a. 1143; Delisle, i. 229; Howlett, p. 145.
[201] RT, s.a. 1143; Delisle, i. 229; Howlett, p. 145.
[202] RT, s.a. 1144; Delisle, i. 233–4; Howlett, pp. 147–8.
[203] RT, s.a. 1144; Delisle, i. 235; Howlett, p. 148–9.
[204] RT, s.a. 1145; Delisle, i. 237; Howlett, p. 150.

have suggested. While Rollo was established at Rouen *c.* 911, the assassination of William Longsword and the losses of men and territory that occurred during the minority of his son Richard I means that the growth of ducal power only really began *c.* 945, when Richard I's allies defeated King Louis on the Dives and reversed the decline that had begun to threaten the continued existence of the duchy. That power continued to grow, in fits and starts, until *c.* 1120, when Henry I finally completed the process with his recovery, or acquisition, of Verneuil-sur-Avre.[205] And so while Rollo might have been the founding father of the duchy, it was Richard I who was to make Normandy a viable political entity, and he did so by making alliances, as well as by cajoling and coercing his neighbours to recognize his greater authority.

This is a reminder that Normandy was composed of individual lords, who placed themselves and their lands under the duke's protection and power because they saw an advantage in doing so. If ducal authority was to be maintained, they and their successors had to continue to believe that it was in their best interests to remain within the dukes' *mouvance*. Some were not convinced that it was. Their own powerbases, alliances, and ambitions led them to break with the duke, or even just to attempt to maintain their independence in the face of an intensification of ducal lordship. Some might succeed for a time – the lords of Bellême and of Moulins-la-Marche come to mind – but others were quickly crushed.

There were rewards to be had for recognizing a duke's overlordship. The regional chiefs were brought into the dukes' family by way of marriages, and enriched with grants made out of the ducal demesne, thereby gaining a vested interest in the dynasty's continued success. The dukes' growing control over the ambitions of these regional powers offered those living there greater stability and some protection from the arbitrary behaviour of their powerful neighbours. When these chiefs were Scandinavian, the dukes' demands that they should convert to Christianity as part of the bargain struck between them provided greater unity as well as greater security for the Christian communities established in the duchy. Thus the monks of the abbeys that were in, or had lands within, the duchy sought the dukes' confirmation of their properties in order to hold them more securely. Some of his *fideles*, both great and small, made grants to those same monasteries, and showed their fidelity by bringing, or allowing, those donations to be confirmed by the dukes.

Christianity would thus play a role in uniting Normandy under the dukes' rule,

---

[205] Henry's achievement in this region has not generally been recognized in previous scholarship (see, for example, Hollister, *Henry*, pp. 225–7; Green, *Henry*, pp. 124–5), but allowing it to take its proper place gives Henry's reign a different emphasis and trajectory.

but only after the dukes had gained control of this Frankish religion. For while Christianity was identified with the Franks, it was more likely to divide the people of Normandy than to unite them. It was therefore only from 989, when Richard I's second son, Robert, became archbishop of Rouen, that the dukes began actively to promote the Christianization of their duchy, to reform it in their own image, and to begin to construct barriers against those who might threaten their control. From the middle of the eleventh century that meant, in particular, the popes and their legates. How the dukes did this will be traced in the following chapter.

CHAPTER 4

Holier than Thou: The Dukes and the Church

CHRISTIANITY was the Franks' religion. When Rollo was given Rouen and its hinterland by Charles the Simple he was obliged to convert and conform. Rouen was worth a Mass, but Rollo's authority was now subject to a religion he did not control but by which he would be judged. This was a new problem for a Scandinavian lord. The kings of Denmark and Norway had still to convert their people to Christianity in 911, and in the meantime there was no institutionalized religion in those countries, and thus no central control of it. But while the Danes and Norwegians did not have control over religion, it is also the case that they did not live with a religion that operated within their territory but which was under the control of someone else. The potential for disunity that such a rival authority brought with it must have become clear to the new duke very quickly. Fortunately for Rollo, the disruption brought by the Viking raiding of the ninth century ensured that it would be some time before the Church was in a position to be used against him or his successors. Indeed, it was only in 990 that the scribe of a ducal act could remark on the simultaneous existence of bishops for all seven of the dioceses of the province of Rouen. And by then the Franks were no longer in control. Instead, Richard I and his brother, Archbishop Robert of Rouen, stood at the helm of the Norman Church, even if their authority would not be undisputed.

Chief among their, and their successors', rivals were the popes. The advent of the so-called reform papacy in the middle of the eleventh century, and with it a greater desire to unify and oversee religious practices, led to a greater interference by the popes in Norman affairs. This was not always welcome. The dukes might on occasion seek the pope's help when they were preparing the diplomatic ground work for, by way of example, the deposition of Archbishop Malger in 1054 or 1055 or the transfer of Bishop John of Avranches to the archbishopric of Rouen c. 1066, but they opposed appeals to papal authority by their subjects when those appeals infringed their own authority and freedom of action. Nonetheless, by the reign of William the Bastard, the dukes had become less able to control traffic to and from the papal curia, and the popes and their legates were consequently beginning to intervene in Normandy when they had not been asked to do so by the duke. Moreover, while the French kings were never approached to confirm the Norman possessions of Norman churches before 1144, the popes occasionally were.

Of course, as the dukes also maintained almost complete control over the elections to the bishoprics of the duchy, and over the councils convened by the archbishops of Rouen, the potential for serious competition was kept to a minimum anyway. And as will also be discussed below, the opportunity for outside voices to gain influence in Normandy and England was further reduced by what looks like a calculated indifference to the supranational reformed monastic orders. The dukes, then, could benefit from the prayers and processions of the Church, as well as the supportive canons issued by Norman Church councils, without having to worry overmuch about competition or contradiction. And for the most part they would continue to do so throughout the period under discussion, or at least until 1135, because they usually took the trouble to behave as Christian rulers should, and to protect their Church, thereby providing few opportunities for internal discontent and resulting appeals to outside rival authorities.

This chapter begins by exploring the dukes' relationship with Christianity and the conversion of the Normans during the tenth century. It then moves on to consider how Dudo of Saint-Quentin and later writers highlighted the dukes' piety – Dudo to the extent of attempting to turn Longsword and Richard I into saints. There follow a further exploration of the conversion and Christianization of Normandy during the eleventh century and a discussion of how the Church could support the duke's rule through its liturgy and legislation. The chapter ends with a look at the dukes' relationship with the popes and the popes' representatives, which was itself influenced and supported by a wider distrust of papal authority on the part of secular – if not regular – Norman clergy.

The tenth century

The conversion of the Normans to Christianity began with the baptism of Rollo by the archbishop of Rouen.[1] According to Dudo of Saint-Quentin, his baptism took place in the 912th year since the incarnation, in other words in 911. Charles the Simple stood as sponsor, while Robert of Neustria acted as his godfather – which

---

[1] The assumption here is that conversion began with the baptism of the acknowledged leader. Thus the conversion of Clovis was seen to represent the conversion of the Franks as a people. The conversions of King Æthelbert and King Edwin were, similarly, the first steps in the conversion of those who were subject to their rule (S. Coviaux, 'Baptême et conversion des chefs scandinaves du IXe au XIe siècle', in *Les fondations Scandinaves en occident et les duts du duché de Normandie*, ed. P. Bauduin (Caen, 2005), p. 72). Guthrum, too, had been baptized by Alfred with thirty of his followers, and had then remained with the king for twelve days while he was instructed in his new religion (Asser, *Alfred the Greast: Asser's Life of King Alfred and other Contemporary Sources*, trans. S. Keynes and M. Lapidge (Harmondsworth, 1983), p. 85; *ASChr*, 'A' and 'E', s.a. 878; trans. Garmonsway, pp. 76–7).

is why Rollo adopted the baptismal name Robert. Dudo wrote that during the days after his baptism, Rollo granted lands to the greatest churches in Normandy, as well as to the abbey of Saint-Denis. His story might be corroborated by one later act for the monks of Saint-Ouen that included grants supposedly made by Rollo. However, as the act dates from after the publication of Dudo's *De moribus* it is not an independent witness, and it may be that Dudo was in any case more concerned that his work should reflect the deeds of the Emperor Constantine than reality.[2] In any event, so far as we can tell, contemporaries seem not to have doubted the sincerity of Rollo's conversion, and the fact that Longsword faced a pagan reaction on his father's death suggests that he had attempted to force Christianity on his people, too.[3]

That pagan reaction reveals that Rollo's adoption of the Frankish religion by no means guaranteed that all his subjects would follow his lead. While some would convert as a demonstration of loyalty and perhaps in the hope that it would give them some advantage in their new world, others might not have thought that such a gesture was necessary. After all, even at the end of the tenth century, Christians and pagans might ally together to achieve a particular objective. In 994 the Christian King Swein of Denmark fought alongside the pagan Olaf Tryggvasson against the Christian king of the English. In 1000, King Swein fought alongside the Christian Olaf Ericsson and the pagan Earl Eric against the by then Christian Olaf Tryggvason.[4] Although they were separated by their religion, they were nonetheless on the same side and from the same background. Dukes Richard I and Richard II did something similar when they recruited pagan Scandinavians to fight against the Franks *c.* 962 and *c.* 1013.

However, it would become clear that temporary military alliances and political expediency were not at all the same as permanent residence by pagans within the territory of a Christian ruler. That was because it would have been almost impossible to construct a united and viable duchy if its people followed two mutually exclusive religions. The best and most well-known example is provided by Iceland where, *c.* 1000, such divisions were tearing the country apart. Many Icelanders remained pagans, but by that date Christianity had gained a significant following, not least as a result of missions sponsored by the Norwegian king Olaf Tryggvason. Finally, at one of the annual meetings of the Thing (the Icelanders' national assembly), the differences between the two sides reached a head. The Christians and the pagans of the island declared that they were no longer bound

---

[2] *Dudo*, pp. 50–1; *RADN*, no. 53; Shopkow, *History and Community*, p. 127.

[3] E. M. C. van Houts, '*Planctus*', 3, 18.

[4] A. Winroth, *The Conversion of Scandinavia: Vikings, Merchants and Missionaries in the Remaking of Northern Europe* (New Haven, CT and London, 2012), p. 118.

by law to each other. This sparked a debate and the consequent realization that a binding decision about whether or not to adopt Christianity would have to be made. The Christians chose one of their own as their law-speaker, but he asked a pagan, Thorgeir the Godi of Ljosavatn, to declare the law in his place. Thorgeir opened with a statement of common sense: 'It appears to me that our affairs will reach an impasse if we don't all have the same law, for if the law is split asunder, so also will peace be split asunder, and we cannot live with that.' Then, once he had gained assurances that his judgement would be respected, he declared that 'all men in this land are to be Christians ... and give up all worship of false idols, the exposure of children, and the eating of horse meat'. Iceland thus adopted Christianity – at least in public.[5] The Normans would do the same, but over a much longer period, not least because Richard I seems to have been lukewarm towards the religion until the last few years of his reign, as we shall see.

Of course, the earliest efforts to convert the pagan Scandinavian settlers of Normandy depended not only on the dukes and their *principes*, perhaps new converts themselves, but also on the efforts of the established institutionalized Church of Francia, principally in the form of the archbishop of Rouen and his clergy. Richer of Reims went into some detail regarding the practicalities of the initial conversion:

> When the issue of their baptism arose, the duke (Hugh the Great) entrusted Archbishop Witto of Rouen with the task of ministering to them. Witto, however, not wishing to act alone, sent a letter to Hervé of Reims inquiring about the appropriate procedure and method for incorporating a formerly heathen people into the Church. Desiring to be scrupulous in attending to these matters, Archbishop Hervé convened a council of bishops so that the question might be properly submitted to a collective decision.[6]

Archbishop Hervé of Reims subsequently sent Witto an anthology on conversion in the hope that it would bolster his morale and provide guidance. He also wrote to Pope John X to tell him that the pagan Scandinavian converts were not doing well. Hervé wrote that they sought and received baptism on more than one occasion, contrary to the canons, and that they anyway continued to live like pagans, playing indecent pagan games and practising abominable rites. They killed Christians, too, he added. The pope, perhaps with Gregory the Great's letters to St

---

[5] *Njal's Saga*, trans. R. Cook, p. 181.
[6] Richer, pp. 86–7 and see also the discussion in O. Guillot, 'La conversion des Normands peu après 911: des refets contemporains à l'historiographie ultiérieure (Xᵉ–XIᵉ siècles)', *Cahiers de civilisation médiévale*, 24 (1981), 182–8 and Bates, *Normandy*, pp. 11–12.

Augustine in mind, wrote a tolerant response in which he expressed his satisfaction that the pagans had at least begun their journey towards the Christian faith.[7] But he did acknowledge that more would have to be done. There should be no more casting of lots, or making sacrifices, or interpreting omens. In addition, converts should know the basics of their new religion, such as the Lord's Prayer, and they should hand over tithes and other dues to their ecclesiastical holders.[8]

This correspondence suggests that those involved realized that the conversion of the Normans would be a long and drawn-out process. Indeed, it is likely that it continued well into the eleventh century. That was in part because the authority of the dukes based at Rouen took decades to encompass the whole of what would become Normandy, as discussed at length above. Moreover, where Scandinavian settlement had been relatively dense, as in the Cotentin, and where new waves of pagan settlers from Norway and Ireland probably continued to arrive over some decades, the advance of the dukes' religion would have been held back by that incoming tide. It is also possible that Christianity had also to overcome its association with the Franks before it could be sincerely embraced by all the Normans of Normandy, and that would not happen until the middle of the century at the earliest.

It is possible that Rollo, while he embraced his role as a *fidelis* of Charles the Simple, was less than sincere in his conversion to Christianity. Indeed, it is not even clear that Rollo had brought his children up as Christians, simply because of the names they were given and when they were given them. Thus the first time William Longsword was mentioned by Flodoard of Reims, in his annal for 927, he was not given a name at all. He was simply 'Rollo's son'.[9] Flodoard first called him William only in his annal for 933, written only a few years at most after that year. This delay and the very fact that Longsword was called William at all deserve a little more attention than they are usually given, firstly because William was a name previously taken *exclusively* by the dukes of Aquitaine and their family and, secondly, because Longsword's adoption of the name consequently raises the question of *when* precisely he was baptized.

The author of the *Planctus* or *Lament* on the death of William Longsword who wrote *c.* 943, just after Longword's assassination, made it clear that he had been born before Rollo's baptism.[10] He was, however, silent as to when he had been baptized. Sixty years or so later, Dudo strongly implied that this had happened

---

[7] Guillot, 'La conversion des Normands', 186–7.
[8] For a discussion of the appearance of tithes and ecclesiastical customs in Normandy, see below, *infra*, pp. 214–17.
[9] *Flodoard*, p. 17, s.a. 927.
[10] Van Houts, '*Planctus*', 3, 18.

while Longsword was still a child (*puer*).[11] Adémar of Chabannes made it explicit: 'when Rollo died his son William took his place. He had been baptized as a child (*a puericia baptizatus*) and the whole throng of Normans who lived next to France accepted the Christian faith, put aside their pagan language and got used to speaking romance.'[12] It is not clear, however, that these later assertions can be trusted, and it is possible to suggest an alternative course of events.

Stanza fifteen of the *Planctus* states: 'There were two noblemen of the world / O William, called by the same name, / You were one of them, called "of Rouen"; / and the other still shines at Poitou.'[13] As noted above, William was a name that had been unique to the dukes of Aquitaine before Longsword adopted it. That Longsword was named William therefore strongly suggests that his godfather was Duke William of Aquitaine – he who still shone at Poitou *c.* 943. Rollo is not known to have had an especially close connection with the dukes of Aquitaine, and his reign thus provides no obvious occasion for the transfer of the name to his heir. In contrast, Longsword's own reign saw the marriage of his sister Gerloc to William Towhead of Aquitaine in around 933 (give or take a couple of years), and it seems likely that his baptism was in some way associated with that marriage.[14]

Gerloc is a Scandinavian name, but after her marriage to Duke William she became known as Adela.[15] That *might* suggest it was the name she adopted when she was baptized, although she could equally have taken a Frankish name to conform to the expectations of the Frankish cultural milieu in which she then lived.[16] Be that as it may, she had a Scandinavian name first, and if she had

---

[11] Dudo, p. 179; *Dudo*, p. 57.

[12] Adémar, *Chronique*, p. 148, trans in van Houts, *Normans*, p. 213. See also Lifshitz, *Pious Neustria*, p. 172.

[13] Van Houts, '*Planctus*', p. 20; Van Houts, *Normans*, p. 41.

[14] Van Houts, '*Planctus*', pp. 2, 21–2. The marriage is itself dated by reference to Riulf's rebellion, which is thought to have taken place in 932. The dating, however, is necessarily conjecture built on Dudo's all-too-symbolic assertion that Richard I was born on the day of the battle and on Orderic's statement that he was ten when his father died (see *Dudo*, p. 200, n. 243; Orderic, ii. 8; iii. 80). In any event, Longsword's baptism had occurred by the time Flodoard wrote his annal for 933, when he called him William, and before 939 when he was excommunicated as a result of attacking some vills belonging to Count Arnulf of Flanders (Flodoard, pp. 23, 31). It would have been pointless to excommunicate him *before* his conversion, of course.

[15] Adhémar, pp. 143–4; and see Jumièges, i. 80, n. 6.

[16] As evidenced, for example, by the cases of Emma of Normandy, who became Ælfgifu when she married Æthelred II (Stafford, *Queen Emma and Queen Edith*, pp. ix, 89–90). Similarly, Godgifu became Emma when she married Drogo of the Vexin (*RADN*, no. 63; van Houts, 'Edward and Normandy', pp. 65–6), the Welsh Nest became Agnes when she married Bernard of Neuf-Marché, lord of Brecon (Gerald of Wales, *Itinerario Cambresis*, in *Giraldi Cambresensis Opera*, ed. J. S. Brewer, J. F. Dimock, and G. F.

one it is highly likely that her brother had one, too. If that is right, and he subsequently changed his name to William, then that change cannot similarly be explained away on cultural grounds. Men changed their names only when they went through religious ceremonies such as baptism or ordination.[17] And so it may be presumed that Longsword only became William at his baptism, and that his baptism occurred only at about the time his sister married Duke William.

Although Longsword might therefore have been baptized as an adult rather than as a child, there seems little reason to doubt the sincerity of his conversion once it had happened. His piety was praised by the author of the *Planctus*, who wrote that William had lived a virtuous life, fulfilling the requirements of a good ruler, and that after his death he enjoyed the rewards of heaven: 'O William, bringer and lover of peace, / consoler and defender of the poor, / supporter of widows and orphans, / now joyfully joined to heaven.' There is no good reason to doubt his involvement in the refoundation of the abbey at Jumièges, especially as it involved monks brought from Aquitaine. It is also plausible that he entertained thoughts of becoming a monk there later in life, as both the author of the *Planctus* and Dudo claimed, just as Rollo had resigned his leadership of the Normans before his own death.

Moreover, William also seems to have ensured that his son, Richard I, was baptized. Yet the sincerity of Richard I's belief, at least during his adult years, is more open to question than Longsword's. The pagan reaction he had faced on his father's death, and his subsequent discovery that Christianity provided no security from the hostility and opportunism of his Frankish neighbours, might have turned him against what was probably still seen as the Frankish religion for some years.[18]

The best evidence for thinking that tenth-century Normans linked Christianity with the Franks is found in the *Life* of St Romain written at Jumièges by a monk called Fulbert *c.* 940.[19] Fulbert wrote at a time when the Normans at Rouen were supporters of the Frankish kings, and when they faced opposition from pagan settlers like Riulf (if he actually existed), who resisted the adoption of Frankish

---

Warner, Rolls Series, 8 vols (London, 1861–91), bk. I, ch. 2; *The Journey through Wales*, trans. L. Thorpe (London, 1978), pp. 88–9), and the Scottish Edith became Matilda when she married Henry I (L. L. Huneycutt, *Matilda of Scotland: A Study in Medieval Queenship* (Woodbridge, 2003), p. 26).

[17] Rollo and Guthrum both provide examples of this practice. For Guthrum see *ASChr*, 'A' and 'E', s.a. 890; trans. Garmonsway, pp. 82–3. On changes of name on ordination or investiture see R. Bartlett, *The Making of Europe: Conquest, Colonization and Cultural Change 950–1350* (London, 1993), p. 278.

[18] For these events see above, Chapter 1, pp. 60–6.

[19] Lifshitz, *Pious Neustria*, p. 178, and see also p. 164, n. 67.

mores and the Frankish religion.[20] The result was that in Fulbert's hands, Romain was portrayed as a militant saint who evidenced his power by saving Rouen from the pagan Vikings led by Rollo. That demonstration of God's power made all the more effective the speeches that Fulbert put into the saint's mouth in which he called on the people of Rouen to pull down their pagan temples and reject the worship of idols. Fulbert thus told his audience of the great benefits that had accrued to the Franks as a result of their conversion to Christianity, and implied that such practical benefits would also accrue to those Normans who embraced the Franks' religion and, indeed, their king. Fulbert, then, did not shy away from associating Christianity with the Franks and with the Frankish political hierarchy. For him, conversion was assimilation. In sum, his *Life* was intended 'to convince the Normans that the Providential Plan of Sacred History required them to choose, at this moment, the "Christian-Frankish" side. "Demons" (that is, "pagan" deities) were to be shunned, Frankish royalty was to be embraced.'[21]

The violent reaction against Christianity that beset Rouen and Evreux immediately after Longsword's death in 942 indicates that the approach reflected in Fulbert's *Life* had not been entirely successful. The subsequent duplicity of the Frankish king, his capture at the skirmish on the Dives in 945, and the growing tensions between Richard and his Frankish neighbours that would come to a head *c.* 960 together ensured that the sentiment reflected in Fulbert's *Life* would alienate rather than attract potential Norman converts from then on. If the Normans were to adopt Christianity, then, the dukes and those churchmen engaged in their conversion would have to find a way to separate Christianity from the Franks and thus to stop it being seen as the religion of the enemy.[22]

The first attempts to do this were already in hand by the middle of the tenth century. Most likely in the 950s, Gerard of Brogne rewrote Fulbert's *Life* of St Romain.[23] That reworking saw 'the systematic expunging of the central theme of the royal majesty' from the work.[24] Thus the French kings were written out of the picture soon after Richard's triumph over Louis IV and just a few years before the opening of hostilities with Lothair V, at a time when the duke had already adopted the position – or so we are led to believe by Dudo – that Normandy was held from God and not from the king.[25]

The events of the earlier decades of his reign, up to the middle of the 960s,

---

[20] For Riulf, see below, *infra* p. 197 and Chapter 6, pp. 323–4.

[21] Lifshitz, *Pious Neustria*, p. 178.

[22] For this issue see also R. Bartlett, 'The conversion of a pagan society', *History*, 70 (1985), 190–1.

[23] Lifshitz, *Pious Neustria*, pp. 159–66.

[24] Lifshitz, *Pious Neustria*, p. 166.

[25] Lifshitz, *Pious Neustria*, p. 167.

certainly suggest that Richard wore his Christianity lightly and was happy to shrug it off altogether if he could gain a political advantage by doing so. Before 959, Richard presided over a court that saw his barely Christian warlords refuse point blank to return lands to the would-be abbot of Saint-Wandrille, Gerard of Brogne.[26] From *c.* 960 to *c.* 965, he had been prepared to unleash Viking mercenaries on the neighbouring provinces of Francia.[27] A little later he made a marriage *more Danico* with Gunnor, which was only Christianized at the end of the 980s. She felt no obligation to use her baptismal name in her husband's *acta*, and seems to have been unenthusiastic about the Church herself.[28] Richard's restoration of Mont-Saint-Michel in 966, his restitution of Berneval to the monks to Saint-Denis in 968, and his foundation of the abbey of Saint-Taurin just outside Evreux between 966 and 996, even his role in the translation of St Ouen, if it really took place under Archbishop Hugh, were all political acts rather than religious ones. And while his coins carried a cross and his name by around 980, they were the products of the moneyers established at Rouen, and the extent of the duke's input, if any, is unknown.[29] In contrast, his grants to the monks of Jumièges and Saint-Ouen, which seem more likely to have been motivated by his faith, need not have been made before 990. Hariulf of Saint-Riquier remarked on the fighting around Bayeux and the removal of the relics of St Vigor *c.* 987, and while his work indicates that the cathedral there was still operating, it is perhaps telling that even at that date the relics did not stop at Rouen but were deposited at Saint-Riquier instead.[30]

It was, then, probably only during the last decade or so of his career that Richard (re)discovered his faith – or at least saw the benefit in acting more overtly as a Christian ruler. Evidence of a new or renewed Christian conviction is best provided by the foundation of the college of canons at Fécamp by 990, which would become a Benedictine monastery under Richard II – although even then the monks seem later to have felt the need to inflate the number of possessions given to them by their founder.[31] The following year, Richard welcomed at Rouen

[26] *Inventio*, p. 30. Laporte dated the refusal between 944 and 953, assuming that a young Richard I would not have been able to force his own will on his lords. If the argument set out here is accepted, the date might be considerably later.

[27] *Dudo*, pp. 150–6, and see above, Chapter 1, p. 64, and below, Chapter 11, pp. 646–7.

[28] See above, Chapter 1, pp. 67–8.

[29] It might be that the moneyers worked independently, or that the cross was permitted by Richard for political reasons, or that it was Archbishop Hugh who exercised de facto control over the mints and their activities – suggested by the existence of numerous coins bearing Hugh's monogram (Dumas, 'Les monnaies Normandes', 89–91).

[30] Hariulf, *Chronique de l'abbaye de Saint-Riquier*, p. 163; noted in Herrick, *Imagining the Sacred Past*, pp. 91–2. See also above, Chapter 1, p. 75.

[31] The long confirmation issued by Richard II in 1025 includes a number of gifts which are

the papal chancellor and some representatives of King Æthelred II who came to him to conclude a treaty whereby each swore not to harbour the enemies of the other. Their mission was sponsored by Pope John XV, and their reception by the duke suggests that he was now recognized as a Christian ruler and willing to portray himself as one, too.[32]

It is tempting to suppose that this belated interest in the religion was linked to the appointment of Richard I's son, Robert, as archbishop of Rouen c. 989, although he was almost certainly well under the canonical age when elected. His predecessor, Hugh, had been a Frankish monk from Saint-Denis, who seems to have remained at least as much under the influence of Duke Hugh of the Franks as Duke Richard of the Normans. His grants to his brother, Ralph of Tosny, effectively increased Frankish influence on the borders of the duchy at the duke's expense, until Richard brought him within his *mouvance c.* 991. The poor reputation Archbishop Hugh enjoyed at the end of the eleventh century might have been the result of such actions and sympathies, as much as the retrospective application of reforming ideals to his career.[33] His death finally allowed Richard I to take control of the Church in the duchy, and gave him the opportunity to use it to advance ducal authority without any fear of divided loyalties. If Christianity was useful to kings and chieftains only if they had control over the personnel who would put its teachings and rites into effect, then the reluctance of Richard I fully to support the religion while a Frankish archbishop was at the helm in Rouen is entirely understandable on a political level.[34]

Once the dukes had established control over the Norman Church, they ensured that they retained it. Archbishop Robert continued in office throughout the reign of his brother, Richard II, and his nephews, Richard III and Robert the Magnificent. He died two years into the reign of his great nephew, William the Bastard. Under Richard II, the religious life of Normandy flowered. According to William of Jumièges, he 'made the Norman fatherland an almost united church of Christ'. The duke patronized the Norman abbeys – all of them still ducal abbeys at this point – to an even greater extent than his predecessors, and was remembered accordingly as 'the most devout father of monks and clerks'.[35] Fécamp became an abbey during his reign, and was placed under the authority of the reforming William of Volpiano. This was probably not just the result of religious conviction.

there said to have been made by Richard I but which are not evidenced by Richard I's own act of 990 or which had been said to have been made by Richard II in an act of 1017 × 1025. They include properties in Dun and Eletot (*RADN*, nos. 4, 31, 34).
[32] Malmesbury, *GR*, i. 278, and see also above, Chapter 2, p. 86.
[33] *AAbps*, pp. 38, 51–2; Orderic, iii. 80, 82.
[34] See, for example, Winroth, *Conversion of Scandinavia*, pp. 145–6, 160, 163.
[35] Jumièges, ii. 6, 38, respectively.

Duke Richard might here have been emulating the activities of Count Arnulf of Flanders, who had

> established a model for princely authority based on Charlemage himself. Without denying his theoretical obedience to the West Frankish king, and without allowing any whisper of claimed innovation, he started to behave in his territory in an imperial fashion. He began by reconstructing the Flemish church, relying particularly on the old monasteries of the area. With the partnership between Louis the Pious and Benedict of Aniane in mind, he invited the distinguished monastic reformer Gerard of Brogne to restore St Peter's, Ghent, as a strict Benedictine foundation.[36]

But while Richard might have been promoting his own rule, as much as saving his soul, his actions also put the duchy on the Frankish ecclesiastical map by linking the Norman Church to a reformer of European renown. The reformed Fécamp received a large number of new grants from both the duke and his subjects, as did the monks of Jumièges. In addition, Saint-Wandrille had been re-established by 1006, while a new abbey, placed under the auspices of Fécamp, was established at Bernay c. 1025. The bishoprics, too, were restored and developed during Richard II's reign. The bishop of Lisieux received at least one grant from the duke; the bishopric of Bayeux was handed to Hugh of Ivry, the duke's cousin, and its endowment was inflated by the acquisition of some or all of Count Rodulf's estates in the Bessin; and by the very end of Richard's reign, the bishop of Coutances had finally returned to his cathedral city.

The cult of the ruler: the dukes and Christianity

Although Gerard of Brogne's *Life* of St Romain took some important first steps in the separation of Frankishness and Christianity, it was Dudo in his *De moribus* who took this separation to a higher level. Among the multifarious intentions behind this work was a concern to rebrand Christianity. Rollo and his Northmen were turned into instruments of the divine will. Their successes were evidence of divine support. But more than this the martyrdom of Longsword and the career of the holy confessor Richard turned the Normans into Christians *par excellence* and left the deceitful, treacherous, vice-ridden Franks as the enemies of their own religion, doing the devil's work for him.[37] By the time a reader has finished

---

[36] Dunbabin, *France*, p. 71.
[37] For example, Count Arnulf is said to act with 'devilish deceit (*diabolicae fraudis*)' (Dudo, p. 205; *Dudo*, p. 81) and the assassins act with 'diabolical inspiration (*diabolicoque spiritu exagitati*)' (Dudo, p. 208; *Dudo*, p. 83).

Dudo's work, there is no doubt that Christianity belonged to the Normans, not to the Franks.

One of the ideas that influenced Dudo's work was that of the *translatio imperii*, the transfer of authority from one people to another.[38] But he also worked hard to show that the Christian religion had been similarly handed over by God from the Franks to the Normans. One result of this is that while the skirmishes and battles Dudo depicted saw the Norman dukes pitted against pagan rebels or Franks, they also saw Norman virtues fighting against their enemies' vices. Thus the dukes fought alongside the cardinal virtues – fortitude, prudence, temperance, and justice – while their various enemies were motivated by the cardinal vices. The *De moribus*, then, is to a small extent a psychomachia, with the battle ending with justice for the Norman dukes; they retained their duchy and gained no small degree of autonomy from the Frankish kings.

The most well-known list of the cardinal vices is found in Gregory of Great's *Moralia in Job*. They resulted from pride (*superbia*) and comprised vanity (*inanis gloria*), envy (*inuidia*), anger (*ira*), sadness (*tristitia*), avarice (*auaritia*), gluttony (*uentris ingluuies*), and lust (*luxuria*).[39] With these vices in mind, Dudo's description of the rebel Riulf as guilty of treason (*perfidia*) and envy (*inuidia*), suffering from vice (*uitius*) and pride (*superbia*), opposing God's will, and driven wild by the furies is illustrative of his approach, even if the words employed do not always precisely reflect those found in Gregory's famous book. At the end of the poem in which this description appears, Riulf's 'proud airs' are seen to be defeated by 'meek humility'.[40] Riulf, enveloped in vice, is thus defeated by virtues. Another of Longsword's greatest enemies, Arnulf of Flanders, was 'infected with deceitful and nefarious envy (*nefarie dolositatis liuore infectus*)',[41] while 'a satrap by the name of Theobald, who was rich in possessions and very well supplied with knights, was inflamed by malevolent rage, and by jealousy and hatred, and began to connive against him by means of numerous slanders (*nouercalibus furiis, zeloque et odio succensus, coepit insidiari ei multis subsannationibus*), and to raise a quarrel against him' – the 'him' in this case being Duke Richard I.[42] A little later, 'being infected with the poison of jealousy (*uenonoque*

---

[38] Shopkow, *History and Community*, pp. 112–13, understood that Dudo's work could be read as including such a *translatio*, but thought that he had largely downplayed it.

[39] Gregory the Great, *Morals in the Book of Job*, trans. J. H. Parker, 3 vols (London, 1844–50), iii. 489–91 (Bk. 31, Cseveralighted.nse – it" sure I;d s sure Id'hs. 87–89); B. H. Rosenwein, *Emotional Communities in the Early Middle Ages* (Ithaca, NY and London, 2006), p. 48.

[40] Dudo, p. 188; *Dudo*, p. 66.

[41] Dudo, p. 207; *Dudo*, p. 82.

[42] Dudo, p. 265; *Dudo*, p. 139.

liuoris infectus)',[43] Theobald urged the young King Lothair to take action against the duke. As a result of his words, the queen, too, became 'sad and angry (*tristis et commota*)'.[44] In a poem addressed to Count Theobald, Dudo wrote: 'Alas, why still do you rage, blazing with hatred and treason, / Too much afflicted and wracked by the fires of envy (*quid adhuc furis ardescens odio perfidiaque / Invidiae nimium afflictus tædis et laniatus*)?'[45] His anger was the result of pride and envy – bad anger – and the result of his vice was failure, loss, and disgrace.[46]

Here, then, was a portrait of Normandy and its relations with the Franks that was designed to unsettle an external audience by turning assumptions on their head. This was not a tale of Christian Franks defeating pagan pirates. Rather it was the Franks who were the aggressors, deceivers, and betrayers, who sought to foil God's own plan for this corner of Francia. In this scheme, even the use of Viking auxiliaries *c.* 965 could be justified. They were the scourge of God, used to punish the Franks for their sins, who were afterwards brought to the faith by the efforts of Richard I himself.

But there was more than this. The Franks were not only attacking God's plan, they were attacking his saints. According to Dudo, William Longsword 'consecrated to Jesus Christ' his youthful years and 'strove to submit himself entirely to things divine'.[47] Even at this early age 'he longed to leave this tottering world and become a monk at Jumièges. He reflected on this again and again, and kept thinking of it resolutely and often … Therefore did he brood earnestly and tearfully and austerely stopped his body from taking food … Fired with this violent desire he vowed that he would abandon the world and become a monk.'[48] It is worth noting that according to the *Planctus* Jumièges had not been founded yet, but this was irrelevant to Dudo's programme. Knowledge of William's chastity – another sign of his holiness – was spread abroad, and his continence was such that he had to be forced to take a wife by his magnates so that he could produce a legitimate heir. Later on we are told that 'holiness and prudence radiated from him, and his equity and justice shone forth without ceasing … He would lead pagans and unbelievers by gifts and words to worship the True Faith.'[49] Thus William acted

---

[43]   Dudo, p. 265; *Dudo*, p. 139.

[44]   Dudo, p. 265; *Dudo*, p. 140.

[45]   Dudo, p. 266; *Dudo*, p. 140.

[46]   For 'bad anger' see R. E. Barton, '"Zealous anger" and the renegotiation of aristocratic relationships in eleventh- and twelfth-century France', in *Anger's Past: The Social Uses of an Emotion in the Middle Ages*, ed. B. H. Rosenwein (Ithaca, NY 1998), pp. 153–70, and below, Chapter 7, pp. 422–32.

[47]   *Dudo*, p. 57.

[48]   *Dudo*, p. 58.

[49]   *Dudo*, p. 70.

as a confessor and evangelist. William's desire to become a monk arose again in his later life, but he was persuaded to remain duke until his son, Richard, was old enough to replace him. And when William was assassinated at the hands of four knights of Arnulf of Flanders, Dudo described his murder as a martyrdom and declared that William 'lives in Christ and wears the blessed crown'.[50] Indeed, Dudo continued to describe William as a martyr as he narrated the life of his son Richard. According to Pierre Bouet, he used the word only eleven times in total, and on six of these occasions he used it to describe Longsword.[51] The message still comes across loud and clear.

'Murder by fellow Christians for secular motives may seem to us an improbable qualification for sanctity', but that seems not to have been the case for contemporaries.[52] Bouet argued that William could be depicted as a martyr because his assassination was the last stage in a life dedicated to Christ, and because his death was caused by his overriding desire for peace. Further, Arnulf and his companions were made to act at the instigation of Satan, so that Longsword died as a result of his faith, a victim of the Devil's enmity.[53] Alternatively or additionally, Susan Ridyard, in her study of Anglo-Saxon royal saints, has suggested that a requirement for male royal saints was either that the saint in question should have achieved martyrdom through royal duty (just the sort of desire to make peace with his enemies for the benefit of his subjects that led to William's death) or that he should have been a martyred innocent.[54] Dudo ensured that William Longsword satisfied both of these conditions, too. But it might simply be the case that 'contemporaries did not hesitate to bestow the name of martyr upon victims of political violence'.[55]

Longsword was not the only, or indeed the first, ruler to have enjoyed a reputation for sanctity, of course. Although they were not common in France,[56] royal cults had become prominent in England. For example, Oswald – killed in battle

---

[50] *Dudo*, p. 84. Death at the hands of the agents of those who sought to murder a rival is a common theme in English royal saints' *Lives* (D. W. Rollason, 'Cults of murdered royal saints', *Anglo-Saxon England*, 11 (1982), 13).

[51] P. Bouet, 'Dudon de Saint-Quentin et le martyre de Guillaume Longue-Epée', in *Les Saints dans la Normandie médiévale*, ed. P. Bouet and F. Neveux (Caen, 2000), p. 247.

[52] Rollason, 'Cults of murdered royal saints', 1.

[53] Bouet, 'Dudon de Saint-Quentin et le martyre de Guillaume Longue-Epée', pp. 247–8.

[54] S. J. Ridyard, *The Royal Saints of Anglo-Saxon England* (Cambridge, 1988), pp. 92–5.

[55] C. Cubitt, 'Sites and sanctity: revisiting the cult of murdered and martyred Anglo-Saxon royal saints', *EME*, 9 (2000), 59. Cubitt was discussing Bede's depiction of Oswald as a martyr when she made this comment, but there seems no good reason to think that those living in the eleventh century and later saw things differently (as indicated at p. 66).

[56] Rollason, 'Cults of murdered royal saints', 14.

against pagans – and Ceolwulf of Northumbria – who ended his days as a monk – were both commemorated as saints. Furthermore, there seems to have been an increasing interest in these English royal saints' cults at precisely the time that Dudo was writing. Around the end of the tenth and the beginning of the eleventh centuries, the murdered Kentish princes, Æthelberht and Æthelred, were translated to Ramsey. The cult of St Kenelm (king of Mercia, murdered by his sister c. 821) was flourishing at Winchcombe at about this same time, and the cult of Wigstan (briefly king of Mercia, murdered 849 by his godfather and successor) was revived in King Cnut's reign (1016–35) when his relics were translated from Repton to Evesham, a house that had been revitalized by monastic reformers.

More important than all these, however, was the cult of King Edward the Martyr, who was murdered in 978 or 979 by the retainers of his half-brother Æthelred who consequently became King Æthelred II. Æthelred, who was not implicated in the murder by contemporaries, promoted Edward's cult. Ridyard suggested that he did this because he hoped that it would both enhance his own prestige and act to condemn the crime of regicide.[57] Cnut, on the other hand, might have promoted the cult after his conquest of England to blacken his predecessor's name as well as those of his sons, Alfred and Edward, who had taken shelter in Normandy and were threats to his position.[58]

The English cults, and Edward's in particular, might have acted as models and motivation for Dudo when he was writing, not least because in 1002 King Æthelred II had married Emma, Richard II's sister. Dudo might have reacted to news of the nascent cult of Edward the Martyr by attempting to cast Longsword in a similar light, and for similar political reasons. The martyrdom emphasized still more strongly the Normans' Christianity and helped to turn the Franks, especially Arnulf of Flanders, into agents of the Devil. It thus attacked their prestige while promoting the duke's. It suggested, too, that the Norman dynasty and their duchy now had a saintly protector, which might have been intended to warn off their Frankish rivals and enemies. It might also have been a warning to Cnut, whose promotion of the cult of Edward the Martyr now received a riposte, in part because his conquest of England menaced the Norman dukes at the time Dudo was writing.[59] Indeed, Dudo's attempt to canonize Longsword (and Richard I) might also have been intended to give the Æthelings some hope that the reigning dukes would be able to restore them to their lost English throne. They now had a saint on the maternal side of the family, to counter the paternal one that Cnut had usurped for his own use.

[57] Ridyard, *Royal Saints*, pp. 156–69.
[58] Rollason, 'Cults of murdered royal saints', 18, and see above, Chapter 2, pp. 87, 101–2.
[59] See above, Chapter 2, pp. 86–7.

Despite the advantages it might have brought the Normans and the Æthelings, the cult of William Longsword did not catch on. Pierre Bouet has suggested that this was because William had failed to perform any miracles.[60] But King Robert the Pious was credited with miracles in the 1030s and his cult failed to ignite anyway, so there was perhaps more to it than that. To begin with, it was rather late in the day for Dudo to turn Longsword into a saint. There is no evidence that he had been acclaimed as such after his death or at any point in the intervening period.[61] There is also no evidence that anyone had any interest in seeing Longsword belatedly canonized. Equally, while relations with Flanders might have been tense around the time that Dudo wrote, so that his portrait of Longsword's murder provided a timely reminder of the threat that the counts of Flanders might pose to the dukes, they improved a few years later with the marriage of Richard's daughter, Ainor, to Count Baldwin IV.[62] That would have made it impolitic for him to promote the cult any further. Archbishop Robert of Rouen does not seem to have supported the cult of Longsword either, even though he was the only individual other than Richard II related to him in the direct male line, perhaps because he was concerned that it would give his brother, and subsequent dukes, too much influence over his church. The archbishops concentrated their energies instead on St Romain.[63] And so the case for Longsword's sanctity was quietly dropped in the years that followed the publication of Dudo's work. William of Jumièges certainly removed all talk of William being a martyr from his *Gesta Normannorum ducum*. Indeed, the claim only cropped up again in the late-twelfth-century *History of the Dukes of Normandy*, written by Benedict of Sainte-Maure.[64]

But all was not lost, as Longsword was not the only duke that Dudo sought to canonize. While he portrayed Longsword as a martyr, he depicted Richard I as a holy confessor.[65] Once again, Dudo gave Richard the necessary qualities to qualify for the role. Born of a soon-to-be martyr and a 'sainted mother', he loved good and hated evil in his youth, acted as a good ruler should, overcame

[60] Bouet, 'Dudon de Saint-Quentin et le martyre de Guillaume Longue-Epée', 250.

[61] In contrast, Cubitt has highlighted the importance of spontaneous lay acclamation of the Anglo-Saxon royal saints in the making of their cults (Cubitt, 'Revisiting the cult of murdered royal saints', particularly 77–80).

[62] See above, Chapter 2, p. 88.

[63] See Orderic, iii. 22–4; Lifshitz, *Pious Neustria*, pp. 189–206.

[64] Benedict of Sainte-Maure, *Chronique des ducs de Normandie par Benoit*, ed. F. Michel, vol. 1 (Paris, 1836), l. 12,255, p. 504; ll. 12453–5, p. 511; l. 12593, p. 516.

[65] On Richard's sanctity see also Jordan, 'The role of kingship in tenth-century Normandy', 53–62 and, more generally, R. Bartlett, *Why Can the Dead Do Such Great Things? Saints and Worshippers from the Martyrs to the Reformation* (Princeton and Woodstock, 2013), pp. 211–16.

dramatic conflicts with unjust and proud enemies, as St Martin had done,[66] and acted as the evangelist of the heathen Danes he had used to crush his Frankish enemies in the 960s.[67] While the whole portrait is shot through with poetic assertions of Richard's sanctity and evidence of his piety,[68] it is in the section where Dudo reveals how Richard's life had reflected the Beatitudes that the argument for his sanctity is most strongly made.[69] Here, Richard is described as a confessor who lived his life *in imitatio Christi*, who remained humble and gentle, who prostrated himself and wept when he thought of the depravities of the monks and canons of the duchy as well as his own failings, a doer of justice, pure in heart, a peacemaker, and so on. And finally, the day after Richard's funeral, when Count Rodulf came to his tomb with the Norman bishops, 'they pulled aside the lid of the tomb and ... found all his limbs as if they were those of a live man; and from them spread an odour sweeter than the fragrance of turpentine and balsam, wafting to their senses.'[70] Here, then, was the very odour of sanctity.

Dudo was a little ahead of his time, here. While living up to the values of Christian rulership would come to be a basis for canonization, that development 'was first recognized with the canonization in 1083 of the Hungarian king Stephen (997–1038)'.[71] But while it is true that Richard was not established formally as a saint, nonetheless the idea of Richard's sanctity lived on outside of Dudo's pages. To begin with, William of Jumièges did not entirely expurgate the passages that depicted the duke as a holy man. Indeed, there is even a faint echo of Dudo's Beatitude passage in his *Gesta Normannorum ducum*:

> Duke Richard flourished more and more by virtue of his happy reign, for whenever he heard that any of his men were in conflict, he set out to restore the peace ... according to the scripture 'Blessed are the feet that bring peace'. He was ... a very devout patron of monks, and a wise protector of clerks; he despised the haughty but loved the humble, he sustained the poor

[66] P. Brown, *The Cult of the Saints: Its Rise and Function in Latin Christianity* (Chicago, 1981), p. 101.

[67] The evangelization of the Danes is found at *Dudo*, pp. 157–60, 162–3.

[68] For the poems, see, for example, *Dudo*, pp. 96, 97, 100, 117, 122, 129–30, 133, 137. And for other evidence see *Dudo*, pp. 99, 105, 122, 136–7, 143, 164–5, 166.

[69] *Dudo*, pp. 167–70.

[70] *Dudo*, p. 173. Edward the Confessor would be portrayed in a similar way: R. Mortimer, 'Edward the Confessor: the man and the legend', in *Edward the Confessor: The Man and the Legend*, ed. R. Mortimer (Woodbridge, 2009), pp. 36–7 and see also E. Bozoky, 'The sanctity and canonization of Edward the Confessor', in *Edward the Confessor: The Man and the Legend*, p. 175.

[71] Bozoky, 'The sanctity and canonization of Edward the Confessor', p. 175.

and was a guardian of orphans, a defender of widows, and a redeemer of captives.[72]

He also wrote of Richard I as 'this precious stone of Christ dressed in the habit of a layman'.[73] Given Jumièges's sparse narrative and his unwillingness to mark one duke out from another, his inclusion of such comments is remarkable, and implies that such views had both wide currency and political value.

A number of twelfth-century narratives also included a marvel or two involving Richard I. Guibert of Nogent included one in his autobiography, written c. 1115, that saw the soul of a monk, who had abandoned his abbey for one with a stricter observance, argued over by 'accusing spirits who tried to condemn him by arguing that he had broken his original vow' and 'the spirits of light, who based themselves on the testimony of his good actions'. The question was brought before St Peter himself, but he deferred judgement to Duke Richard, who had been 'an extraordinarily powerful man in his earthly possessions, but he was even more powerful for the quality of his sense of equity and justice'.[74] Henry of Huntingdon had another story, or rather a reference to one: 'And lest it should seem enough to have conquered men, he himself overcame the Devil in the flesh, wrestling with him and overthrowing him, and binding his hands behind his back, and as victor of angels left him defeated.'[75] Richard I continued to appear in the company of deceased souls and demons into the 1170s. Wace's *Roman de Rou*, written a little after Richard I and Richard II had been translated into their new tomb (or shrine) at Fécamp, includes two more marvellous – if not quite miraculous – stories. In the first, Richard fought the Devil who had occupied a dead man's body in a church. The second saw Richard judge the soul of a monk of Saint-Ouen who had died as the result of a fall while on his way to meet with a lady he had fallen in love with. In a similar way to the earlier story told by Guibert, the monk's soul was contested by an angel and a demon, so the two parties presented themselves before Richard and asked him to make a judgement, which he did.[76] When Wace's work was taken up by his replacement, Benedict of Sainte-Maure, in the 1180s, he highlighted Richard's role as an evangelist and his piety, charity, and devotion to the welfare of his people and claimed that Richard's dealings with angels and demons were marvels sent by God.[77]

---

[72] Jumièges, i. 132–4.
[73] Jumièges, i. 134.
[74] Guibert of Nogent, *A Monk's Confession: The Memoirs of Guibert of Nogent*, trans. P. J. Archambault (Philadelphia, 1996), pp. 204–5.
[75] Huntingdon, p. 26.
[76] Wace, pp. 92–7.
[77] Benedict of Sainte-Maure, *Chronique des ducs de Normandie*, ll. 24,976–25,941, pp. 325–62; N. Cazauran, 'Richard sans peur: un personnage en quête d'auteur', *Travaux de*

Richard I's claims to sanctity thus took root, perhaps because elements of the portrait were believable. These claims were made almost immediately after his death, and were given added credibility, or so it may be supposed, by the public memory of his achievements and good works. For example, during his reign both Frankish and Scandinavian lords had come to recognize the authority of the duke of the Normans and it is likely that some of the latter had been obliged to convert to Christianity as part of this process. In other words, Richard could be painted as an evangelist and confessor with some degree of accuracy. In addition, a number of the most important lords of Normandy could claim kinship with Richard I through their marriages to Gunnor's sisters and nieces. There was thus a wide vested interest in his sanctity and the prestige attached to it.[78] Indeed, even the French king, Robert the Pious, might look more favourably on a duke who was the son of such a man – and perhaps might gain some prestige himself as his aunt had been married to him.

But it is likely that there was also a political need for Richard's canonization. Outside the duchy, the counts of Chartres and Flanders remained threats to Norman security. They might be deterred from attacking if they were warned that the man who had defeated their predecessors in life continued to defend his duchy and people even after his death.[79] And the issues around Cnut, discussed above with regard to Longsword's cult, were equally relevant to Richard's. Inside the duchy, the apparent rivalries between saints such as Ouen, Romain, Nicaise, and Taurin, and the localized nature of such cults, too, did not help to promote a spirit of unity or a sense of Norman identity. A cult of Richard I or Longsword, however, might have done just that, by giving the people of the duchy a 'national' saint. The canonized dukes' Scandinavian origins might have encouraged the pagan settlers to convert, simply by making Christianity appear more Norman and less Frankish, while the Franks – including the bishops of Evreux, Sées, and Avranches – who found themselves brought under Norman rule might have found some consolation in the conspicuous Christianity of the ducal dynasty. Normans of all backgrounds would perhaps also have been encouraged to undertake pilgrimages to the dukes' centre at Fécamp, thereby helping to develop a sense of

---

Littérature, 4 (1991), 26. Martin Aurell thought that Wace had been commissioned to write the *Roman de Rou* by Henry II with the intention that he should highlight the sanctity of the dukes – particularly Richard I. His failure to do this adequately was one of the reasons for his dismissal (M. Aurell, *The Plantagenet Empire 1154–1224*, trans. D. Crouch (London, 2007), pp. 138–9).

[78] The prestige that a canonized predecessor might provide is illustrated by Bartlett, *Why Can the Dead do Such Great Things?*, p. 228.

[79] Compare Margaret of Scotland who rushed from her shrine to defend Scotland from Norwegian attack in 1263: Bartlett, *Why Can the Dead do Such Great Things?*, p. 228.

the duchy as a single polity.[80] Even those not yet under the dukes' lordship, might have been brought to submission more willingly as a result of such cults for 'we read that the goodness of the king [here read duke] is the prosperity of the whole people, the victory of the army, the pleasantness of the air, the abundance of the soil, the blessing of sons, the health of the populace. It is a great thing to rule a whole people.'[81] Thus, 'when the emperor Henry IV died in 1106, eager crowds attempted to touch his funeral bier, "believing that they sanctified themselves by doing so", while others sought fertility for their crops: "many people scraped up earth from his grave with their nails and scattered it on their own fields and homes as a blessing; others placed last year's corn on his bier, and … sowed it, hoping in this way to secure for themselves an abundant harvest".'[82]

In addition to its other audiences, the piety exhibited by Longsword and Richard I in the pages of Dudo's work was perhaps intended to provide a model for Richard II to emulate. The duke would have been informed of the importance of protecting those unable to protect themselves, of doing justice, and of confronting internal and external threats without fear, but also warned against abandoning his people and seeking erroneous paths to salvation: a duke should not become a monk – at least, not until he had a viable successor. Living up to these standards was not perhaps essential, but it was certainly advisable, especially in the case of the Norman dukes who were still struggling to shuffle off a reputation as pagan 'pirates' no better than their Viking forebears at the beginning of the eleventh century. Moreover, piety protected kingdoms, whereas a lack of it would lead to divine punishment, as the Franks had discovered.

Not surprisingly, the importance of a duke's piety was also recognized by William of Jumièges and, at greater length, by William of Poitiers. In Book I of his *Gesta Guillelmi*, Poitiers praised at length Duke William's piety and care for the Church in his duchy.

He was accustomed to lend an eager ear to readings from Holy Writ and to savour their sweetness; he found in them a feast for the soul, for he wished to be delighted, corrected, and edified by them. He received and honoured with seemly reverence the Host of salvation, the blood of our Lord, holding in strong faith to that which true doctrine has ordained, that the bread and wine which are placed on the altar and consecrated by the word and hand

---

[80] See, for example, R. Bartlett, *Why Can the Dead do Such Great Things?*, pp. 227–33 and Bozoky, 'The sanctity and canonization of Edward the Confessor', p. 180.

[81] Alcuin, *Epistolae*, ed. E. Dümmler, *MGH, Epistolae*, 4 (*Karolini aevi* 2) (Berlin, 1895), p. 51 (no. 18), quoted in Bartlett, *Why Can the Dead do Such Great Things?*, p. 213.

[82] Bartlett, *Why Can the Dead do Such Great Things?*, pp. 213–14.

of the priest according to the holy canon, are the true flesh and blood of the Redeemer. It is certainly not unknown with what zeal he pursued and endeavoured to drive out of his land the wicked error of those who thought otherwise. From a tender age he took part devoutly in religious services, often joining in the celebration of them in the company of a religious community of clerks or monks. To old men this youth shone as a fine example for the daily assiduity with which he attended the sacred mysteries. Likewise his children learnt Christian piety from infancy, thanks to the careful provision he made for them.[83]

William, then, was orthodox in his belief and indeed Poitiers goes on to say that he punished heretics living in the duchy. This was almost certainly a reference to the controversy that had focused on Berengar of Tours, whose doctrines had been publicly refuted at the council of Brionne in 1050 and again at Rouen in 1055.[84]

Although the *Gesta Guillelmi* could have been used as a mirror for princes, too, it is likely that Poitiers wrote with other considerations in mind. Poitiers could have made these comments about Duke William's piety more succinctly, and the fact that he dwelt on them – perhaps even laboured them – suggests that he was responding to specific concerns or criticisms. Why, for example, write that William ensured that his children were brought up as Christians unless there was some doubt about the Normans' Christian credentials? That this was the case, at least in some quarters, is indicated by an act drafted by the monks of Saint-Florent of Saumur in 1050 × 1066 – perhaps only six years or so before Poitiers wrote. The text implies that the monks were not quite sure that Duke William and his companions knew how alms should be given. 'For the monks when saying that alms ought to be given pure, that man, as a most prudent man, responded: "although we are Normans, still we know well how it ought to be done, and so, if it shall please God, we will do it".'[85] And if there was doubt about the Normans' beliefs on the continent, that was probably even more the case in England. As the *Gesta Guillelmi* was almost certainly principally intended for the consumption of William's new English subjects, it may be supposed that they needed to be convinced that their new king and the Normans more generally were not just Vikings

---

[83] Poitiers, pp. 80–2.
[84] The re-dating of Maurilius's confession to 1055 means that he did not hold a council against Berengar's doctrine in 1063, as was once thought (see *AAbps*, p. 16, although Allen's conclusion is subsequently qualified by the table on p. 31). On the Berengar controversy, see also: Bessin, *Concilia*, i. 45–6, 49; Gibson, *Lanfranc*, pp. 66–97; Bates, *Normandy*, pp. 202–4; H. E. G. Cowdrey, *Lanfranc: Scholar, Monk, and Archbishop* (Oxford, 2003), pp. 59–74.
[85] *RADN*, no. 199.

by a different name, but shared English cultural and religious values.[86] There is, then, an overlap between Dudo's motivations for writing his *De moribus* and Poitiers's intentions for his *Gesta Guillelmi*. Both wanted to legitimize their rulers particularly in the eyes of churchmen and recently subjugated peoples, and both realized that this could be attempted only by stressing their common religious beliefs and their success in living up to the values and obligations of Christian kingship.

But it was not enough just to say that a ruler was thoroughly Christian and a defender of the poor and weak. A duke had to behave in a way that evidenced those Christian credentials. After all, outside appearances were held to be a true reflection of invisible inside emotions and beliefs. Moreover, a failure to live up to Christian values or to protect the Church could result in disaster. Duke Robert the Magnificent's early differences with his uncle, Archbishop Robert of Rouen, saw Normandy put under interdict. Bishop Fulbert of Chartres wrote to the archbishop expressing his sympathy, indicating that the affair had come to the attention of the French clergy and perhaps also the French king.[87] But although Duke Robert flirted with disaster, he saw the need to make peace with his uncle and the Church and ruled securely from then on.

In contrast, his namesake, Robert Curthose, followed his grandfather in his quest to use the Church and its property to satisfy the demands of his lay supporters, but seems to have failed to recognize that such actions were not sustainable. As discussed above, Curthose's capricious treatment of the Church in his duchy led to the pope's complaint that he was treating the Church as a servant rather than a spouse, handing her over to be ruled by usurping enemies,[88] and to Bishop Ivo of Chartres's appeal to Henry I by way of Robert of Meulan to come to its aid.[89] Such well-publicized criticism gave Henry I all the justification he needed to take the duchy from his brother and to legitimize his actions by claiming they revealed God's will.[90] His letter to Archbishop Anselm makes the point:

> Robert, duke of Normandy ... fought with me furiously before the walls of Tinchebray and in the end by the mercy of God the victory was ours ... The mercy of God has delivered into our hands the duke of Normandy, the count of Mortain, William Crispin, William of Ferrières, the elder Robert of

---

[86] See above, Introduction, pp. 20–2.
[87] See above, Chapter 2, pp. 96–7.
[88] *Papsturkunden in Frankreich. II. Normandie*, ed. J. Ramackers (Göttingen, 1937), pp. 56–8 (no. 4).
[89] *PL*, 162, cols. 157–8 (no. cliv).
[90] See above, Chapter 3, pp. 153–5 and also below, *infra*, pp. 221–2.

Etoutteville … and Normandy itself … The result I do not count to my own glory or pride nor to my own power but as a gift of God who so disposed it.[91]

When Orderic came to write his account of the fall of Curthose *c.* 1137, he took up this theme with enthusiasm, often employing elaborate and lengthy speeches to set out the reasons for Curthose's defeat. At various points in his narrative, he portrayed Henry as responding to cries for help from the Norman Church rather than acting from his own ambition.[92] Before the battle of Tinchebray, Orderic had the king commend himself to God in such a way that the battle would decide if he should rule Normandy: 'I beg him who is our maker, from the depths of my heart, to give the victory in this day's conflict to him through whom he wishes to give protection and tranquillity to his people.'[93] Both points were subsequently repeated in the speech put into the mouth of Helias of Maine to justify Henry's takeover: 'It is by the just judgement of God that victory has been bestowed by heaven on the friend of peace and justice, and the opposing party utterly destroyed.'[94] In Orderic's *Ecclesiastical History*, then, a failure to live up to the requirements of Christian rulership was made to provide grounds for deposition.[95] But what Orderic obscured was that this had happened because the reigning duke had lost control over the Norman Church.

The Norman Church in the eleventh century

Dudo's work made a very clear link between Christianity and Rouen – with Fécamp playing a supporting role. That link did not exist only in Dudo's imagination. Rouen was the duke's capital, the seat of the archbishop, and home to the great abbey of Saint-Ouen. The conversion of the duchy was planned from Rouen and, in the absence of fully operational dioceses and parish priests, required monks from the ducal abbeys of Upper Normandy. Those monks set about the conversion of the people and the reconstruction of churches and parishes, and the monks of Fécamp at least were rewarded for their efforts by a grant of the right to ordain priests to the churches they held.[96] From the outset, some of those

---

[91]   *Letters of St Anselm*, no. 401.
[92]   For example, Orderic, vi. 86.
[93]   Orderic, vi. 88.
[94]   Orderic, vi. 94–6. Also vi. 284–6.
[95]   As it had with Louis the Pious, who was deposed in 833 as a result of his failure to live up to the ministry of kingship as it had been defined by capitularies and church councils in the first half of his reign (M. De Jong, *The Penitential State: Authority and Atonement in the Age of Louis the Pious, 814–840* (Cambridge, 2009), pp. 238–41).
[96]   *RADN*, nos. 9, 34; Bates, *Normandy*, p. 193.

churches were located a long way from the abbey, for already by 990 the monks had been given the duke's demesne vills at Argences and Mondeville in that part of the Bessin that lay east of the Orne. In addition, by the last years of Richard II's reign, the monks of Saint-Ouen had the church at Rots, west of Caen, those of Saint-Wandrille held churches and chapels around Argentan, and the monks of Jumièges held property around Vimoutiers. Thus the ducal abbeys of Upper Normandy were apparently given zones within which they 'were responsible for the reform of the local clergy'.[97]

The involvement of the monks of Fécamp in the process of conversion perhaps accounts for one of the miracles recorded in the Fécamp chronicle. In the miracle, a priest called Isaac, who served the church of Saint-Maclou-le-Brière, discovers a morsel of the flesh of Christ soaked in blood at the bottom of his communion chalice. Matthieu Arnoux concluded that the miracle was included in the chronicle because of 'a Norman sensitiveness to the theology of the Eucharist, even before the beginning of the controversey with Berengar of Tours'.[98] However, it might equally have been intended to provide new converts with a vivid illustration of the meaning of the Eucharist. The concluding lines of the story are certainly open to that interpretation: 'And the duke, full of joy, gave thanks to God who had deigned to reveal to mortals such a mystery, so that henceforth no one should be in doubt about the body and the blood of God.'[99]

The involvement of monks from Upper Normandy in the conversion of Lower Normandy continued even after the bishoprics had been revived and brought under ducal control, and even after some reconstruction of the ecclesiastical infrastructure had occurred. The most likely reason for this is that the dukes remained concerned to ensure that Christianity should be linked with Rouen and thus with them. That would also explain both the dukes' desire to bring the monks of Mont-Saint-Michel firmly under their hegemony and the Mont's apparent lack of engagement with the process of conversion. Thus, when Robert the Magnificent founded an abbey at Cerisy-la-Forêt in the Bessin in 1032, it was staffed by monks from the abbey of Saint-Ouen.

Saint-Ouen was chosen to provide the first inmates not only because it was an important ducal abbey, located just outside Rouen's city wall, but also because it was home to a relic of St Vigor, to whom the new foundation was dedicated. Vigor was of local importance. He was a sixth century, or earlier, bishop of Bayeux, and his cult had been established at Bayeux from the ninth century.[100] As noted above,

[97] Bates, *Normandy*, p. 194.
[98] Arnoux, 'Before the *Gesta Normannorum*', 34.
[99] Arnoux, 'Before the *Gesta Normannorum*', 46.
[100] Herrick, *Imagining the Sacred Past*, p. 41.

the disturbed state of the Bessin resulted in the transfer of his relics from Bayeux to Saint-Riquier around 987, and that was where they remained.[101] The monks of Saint-Ouen, however, claimed to possess Vigor's chin bone. That was enough to provide a living connection between the new abbey's patron and the founder's capital and ensured that monks from Saint-Ouen would be chosen to serve the new abbey.[102]

The importance of Saint-Ouen's possession of that relic is emphasized by events that happened just a few years later. At some point before 1045, Abbot Angelramnus of Saint-Riquier visited Rouen and stunned the monks of Saint-Ouen by claiming that *his* abbey held the *whole* body of St Vigor, chin bone and all. The monks of Saint-Ouen disputed his assertion. Angelramnus was brought round to their point of view in return for a copy of the *Vita* that had recently been composed by an unknown monk at the abbey.[103] In 1048, William the Bastard seized the opportunity to acquire an additional relic of the saint for the monks of Cerisy. Abbot Gervin of Saint-Riquier came to Normandy to seek the duke's confirmation of the church at Equemauville, possession of which was disputed by the abbess of Montivilliers. The abbot believed that Duke William preferred the abbess's claim – she was after all his great aunt and her abbey was also within his duchy – and so he surrendered the relic of Vigor that he had brought with him to William when the duke asked for it.[104] The abbot subsequently won his case.

The eleventh-century *Life* of St Vigor, a copy of which went to Saint-Riquier with Abbot Angelramnus, was intended for an eleventh-century audience and so may be supposed to offer an indication of the conditions pertaining in the Bessin during the 1030s when it was written. It emphasized Vigor's role in the conversion of the Bessin, which was probably intended to mirror the effort being put into conversion by Vigor's monks at the time of composition.[105] The *Life* showed how conversion might be unwelcome and achieved only through coercion by the secular power.[106] That suggests that there was also some coercion in eleventh-century Normandy. That was certainly the case in Norway under St Olaf, and as he had been baptized by Archbishop Robert of Rouen *c.* 1013, and perhaps took Norman clergy back to Norway with him, it is possible that his actions reflect

[101] See above, Chapter 1, p. 75.

[102] Herrick also suggested that the dedication was due in part to friendly relations between Ponthieu and Normandy (Herrick, *Imagining the Sacred Past*, pp. 41–3).

[103] Herrick, *Imagining the Sacred Past*, p. 43.

[104] Hariulf, *Chronique de l'abbaye de Saint-Riquier*, iv. 19, p. 236; Herrick, *Imagining the Sacred Past*, p. 130, exaggerated the degree of William's threat a little. William's confirmation, preserved by Hariulf in his Chronicle, may also be found at *RADN*, no. 115.

[105] Herrick, *Imagining the Sacred Past*, p. 74

[106] Herrick, *Imagining the Sacred Past*, pp. 86–7.

those experienced in the duchy. In any event, the *Heimskringla* reveals that St Olaf would force his subjects to convert where they were unwilling to do so of their own volition, remarking how he travelled into the remote parts of the kingdom where 'he investigated how Christianity was being kept, and when he considered that there was need of improvement, he taught them the right faith. And … if he found anyone who did not want to abandon heathendom, he drove him out of the land. Some he had maimed, having their hands or feet lopped off or their eyes gouged out, others he had hanged or beheaded, but left no one unchastized who refused to serve God.'[107]

Some support for the persistence of pagan beliefs in the Bessin during the eleventh century is provided by a piece of sculpture in the church at Rots, which belonged to the monks of Saint-Ouen from 1017 × 1024 (see Fig. 1).[108] While the present church dates from the second quarter of the twelfth century, the sculpture in question, which is found in the east wall of the south transept, is most likely earlier – perhaps dating from the later eleventh century. It seems to depict Thor, with his hammer, attempting to make off with someone under his cloak. As his head is not carved fully in profile, he seems to glance back at the figure of a bishop, one of whose hands is raised in blessing while the other holds a crozier. The halo around his head and the ownership of the church together suggest that this figure is St Ouen. The image looks like a warning against allowing the old gods to run off with souls that could be saved through conversion. And while Christianity had almost certainly been well-established in the Bessin by the time the stone was carved, its manufacture does suggest that the old religion still exerted a pull that needed to be addressed.[109]

The attempt to link Christianity with the dukes at Rouen, while at the same time distancing it from the Franks, probably helped to push the conversion of the Scandinavian settlers of Normandy forward, but it still took decades and was not easily achieved. Coercion could take the process only so far.[110] Hearts and minds

---

[107] *Heimskringla*, p. 309. The theological ground for conversion by coercion is provided by Luke 14:23, and was identified as such by Theodericus Monachus in his *Historia Norwegiae* (noted in Winroth, *Conversion of Scandinavia*, pp. 126–7).

[108] *RADN*, no. 44.

[109] There is an image of Thor at Boscherville, too, which probably dates from the first quarter of the twelfth century (see Baylé, 'Le décor sculpté de Saint-Georges-de-Boscherville', 37, pl. 11). Earlier evidence of Thor's cult in Normandy is perhaps provided by a Thor's hammer, dating from 'the Viking age', that was found at a hillfort above the Seine at L'Anerie (J. Callas, 'A Thor's hammer found in Normandy', in *Viking Trade and Settlement in Continental Western Europe*, ed. I. S. Klæsøe (Copenhagen, 2010), pp. 145–7).

[110] As also noted, in an English context, by Leslie Abrams, 'Conversion and assimilation', in *Cultures in Contact: Scandinavian Settlement in England in the Ninth and Tenth Centuries*, ed. D. M. Hadley and J. D. Richards (Turnhout, 2000), p. 136.

Fig. 1 Image of Thor and a bishop, possibly St Ouen, in the church at Rots (Author)

needed to be won, and that was achieved only with the passing of generations. Something of the process, at least in overview, is provided by the maps found in the first three chapters of this book. They plot not only the location of the ducal demesne, but gifts that were subject to the dukes' confirmation. They thus reveal when and where the dukes' subjects were making grants to churches, and they consequently provide supporting evidence for the slow spread of Christianity across the duchy. And if our knowledge of the process is perhaps stunted by the lack of monasteries in the west of the duchy, that perhaps says something about the Normans' commitment to the new religion, too.

The Christianization of the people of Normandy was paralleled by an 'institutional conversion' of the duchy.[111] The two went together, because they were mutually dependent. For the people to be baptized and instructed in the new religion, and for the sacraments to be administered, there had to be a body of educated priests who might then be used to staff the parish churches that existed, or would come to be built, in the duchy. Indeed, while we know that there were churches on the duke's demesne (if not elsewhere) in the Cotentin *c.* 1000, it is not quite so clear that there were priests officiating in them. At least, it might be unwise to make the assumption that there were without more evidence. And so this institutional conversion was about establishing the infrastructure that was necessary for the spread and practice of Christianity and those rights and/

---

[111] For this idea see Winroth, *Conversion of Scandinavia*, p. 104.

or obligations that went with it: the construction of churches; the education and provision of clergy; the restoration of the bishoprics and the return of Norman bishops to their cathedral cities; the creation of archdeaconries; the holding of synods and making of visitations; and the payment of tithes.

Fécamp's involvement in missionary activities, remarked upon above, resulted in the foundation of a school. At the beginning of the eleventh century William of Volpiano, seeing that 'the science of reading and singing psalms had greatly declined and was becoming extinct, especially amongst the common people, founded schools in the holy ministry for clerics which brethren learned in that office were to attend assiduously for the love of God. Here indeed the benefit of teaching was to be freely bestowed on all those who converged on the monasteries entrusted to his charge.'[112] It is not clear, however, that such provision was established anywhere outside Fécamp until the school at Le Bec took root at the end of the 1040s.[113] But even so, provision across the duchy as a whole seems to have remained inadequate. The poor standard of the clergy generally *c.* 1034 was remarked by Gilbert Crispin in his *Life* of Herluin: 'It was rare in Normandy at that time to find anyone who could point out or blaze the right path. Priests and great bishops married freely and carried arms, just like laymen. They all still lived in the manner of the old Danes.'[114] Orderic, too, made similar (and in some cases anachronistic) criticisms:

> For indeed in Normandy after the coming of the Normans the practice of celibacy among the clergy was so relaxed that not only priests but even bishops freely shared the beds of concubines and openly boasted of their numerous progeny of sons and daughters. This custom took root in the time of the converts who were baptized with Rollo, who had forcibly invaded the depopulated province and were trained in arms but not in letters. From that time barely literate priests of Danish stock held parishes and, bearing arms, held their lay fees by military service.[115]

[112] Glaber, p. 272.

[113] There might have been a school at Avranches, but the evidence for this is slight and ambiguous (Gibson, *Lanfranc*, pp. 20–1; Cowdrey, *Lanfranc*, p. 10; R. Allen, 'The Norman Episcopate 989–1110', (unpublished Ph.D. thesis, University of Glasgow, 2009), pp. 55–7).

[114] Gilbert Crispin, *Life of Lord Herluin, Abbot of Bec*, trans. S. N. Vaughn, in *The Abbey of Bec and the Anglo-Norman State* (Woodbridge, 1981), p. 69. Note that the *Life* of Bernard of Tiron also talks about the poor quality of practice in the west of the duchy with married priests, but in a very reform-minded way. The issues complained about, married priests, inheritance of churches, and so on, was not limited to Normandy – hence papal edicts on the issue (see Geoffrey Grossus, *The Life of Blessed Bernard of Tiron*, trans. R. H. Cline (Washington, DC, 2009), pp. 56–7).

[115] Orderic, iii. 120.

The implication of both Crispin's and Orderic's comments is that times had changed, although the continued prohibition on priests taking wives or mistresses set out in the canons of the councils of the province of Rouen into the twelfth century indicates that there was still room for improvement.[116]

But despite the problems that missionaries and clergy faced, the structures and institutions of the Church did make headway from the end of the tenth century. Ducal and episcopal *acta* in particular reveal either the establishment of such institutions across the duchy or else the dukes' and bishops' success in gaining control of existing structures and rights that had previously escaped them. The collection of tithes, for example, which appears to have been possible only across a limited geographical area at the beginning of the eleventh century, was commonplace across the duchy by the middle of it – although, of course, the wording of the documents that appear to reveal this process are open to more than one interpretation. Thus while Duke Richard I granted the monks of his foundation of Saint-Taurin tithes in the Evrecin, they were given only men and land in the Cotentin and the Lieuvin, with no mention of either churches or tithes in those counties;[117] an act for the monks of Jumièges of 1025 includes grants of property from both William Longsword and Richard I, but tithes are only found among the gifts made by Richard II;[118] in 996 × 1006, the monks of Saint-Wandrille were given Livry in the Bessin with the churches and other things belonging to it, but there was no specific mention of tithes;[119] in 1006, the monks of Fécamp were given churches in the Scandinavian-settled Pays de Caux 'with whatever pertains to them', but again there was no explicit mention of tithes;[120] in 1014, the canons of Chartres were given tithes in the Evrecin, but in the Lieuvin they were given only churches;[121] a grant to the monks of Marmoutier of 1013 × 1020 saw them receive Helleville in the Cotentin, but without any mention of churches or tithes;[122] and the foundation deed for Bernay abbey of 1025, which concerns only property around that place in the Lieuvin, makes occasional mention of churches and mills, but does not include tithes.[123]

These acts perhaps provide some support for the view, presented above, that Richard I had not embraced Christianity until the last decade or so of his reign. Even where the ducal demesne was concerned, it seems only to have been possible

---

[116] As with the canons of the council held at Rouen in 1128: Orderic, vi. 388.
[117] *RADN*, no. 5.
[118] *RADN*, no. 36.
[119] *RADN*, no. 7.
[120] RADN, no. 9.
[121] *RADN*, no. 15.
[122] *RADN*, no. 23.
[123] *RADN*, no. 35.

for the dukes to grant tithes in certain places – particularly in the Evrecin where Frankish traditions seem to have survived well. For whatever reason, be it Richard I's unenthusiastic stance, a lack of personnel or churches, or even an abiding resistance to the more onerous demands of Christianity on behalf of the general population, the necessary infrastructure had not been established or maintained elsewhere. The combination of causes might, of course, vary from place to place. They might also have lasted for some considerable time. There is, for example, a late hint about continuing resistance to the payment of tithes in the Bessin in a transfer of the vill of Trungy brokered by William the Bastard in 1035 × 1040. Abbot John of Fécamp gave the vill to Hugh the son of Hugh the *vicomte*, but retained in his own hand the tithes of the churches along with a 'guest' to protect those tithes.[124] The evidence is ambiguous, but on one reading the arrangements suggest that even at the beginning of William the Bastard's reign tithes could not be collected or retained in this region without some protection.

It took a similar amount of time to restore the bishoprics of the province of Rouen either to a functioning state or else to their obedience to their Norman archbishop. The ambiguity is once again a result of the nature of the evidence. Viking raiding and Frankish ravaging together led to the disruption of the bishoprics of the province, evidenced by their bishops' absence from ducal acts or gaps in episcopal lists.[125] But even when we know that there were bishops in particular sees, as in 990, it does not necessarily follow that they acknowledged the authority of the duke of the Normans over them or their bishoprics. The bishops of Evreux, for example, seem to have taken refuge with the counts of Chartres into the second decade of the eleventh century,[126] while the bishopric of Sées was, with the exception of the pontificate of Radbod Fleitel (*c.* 1025–*c.* 1035), who almost certainly gained his diocese as a direct result of Richard II's campaigns against William of Bellême, outside Norman control until 1071.[127]

The restoration of the Norman bishoprics occurred at different times for different sees, as would be expected, with Coutances, which was probably the last to be put back on a firm footing, only fully operational from the middle of the eleventh century. It may be supposed that different bishops reasserted their rights over their clergy at different times, too. The archbishops of Rouen had episcopal customs in churches in the Pays de Caux as early as 990,[128] but as the archbishopric had not experienced the dislocation caused by the Viking invasions elsewhere,

---

[124] *RADN*, no. 93.
[125] See, for example, Potts, *Monastic Revival*, pp. 16–17.
[126] Bauduin, *Première Normandie*, pp. 165–6 and n. 102.
[127] See above, Chapter 2, pp. 91–3.
[128] *RADN*, no. 4 and also *RADN*, no. 90 of January 1035.

it does not present a typical case. Unfortunately, the situation outside the archdiocese is obscured by the lack of monasteries in Lower Normandy until the middle of the eleventh century. That being the case it is perhaps significant that we first learn about the progress achieved by the bishops of Lisieux not from a diploma but from a letter of Bishop Fulbert of Chartres and another from the canons of his cathedral that date from 1014 × 1022. In his letter, Fulbert complained that:

> The priests who serve the churches which belong to our canons in your diocese came and told us that you prohibited them from exercising their office because they did not pay you the synodal dues for these churches. We are well aware that the law requires these to be paid to you, but Tetoldus our provost and your servant did not understand it as he was misled by the fact that none of the churches which our canons possess in our own diocese is obliged to pay them since they were remitted to them by my predecessors out of their generosity and devotion. [129]

He went on to say that they would pay them from then on, unless 'it should please you in your charity to follow the example of my holy predecessors and to remit them'.

Apparently, it did not please Bishop Roger to remit any of the dues owed to him, so his successor Bishop Herbert received a second letter from the canons c. 1022 on a similar subject:

> You order us, your excellency, to pay you the visitation dues for our churches which lie in your diocese. But we wish to inform your eminence … that the bishops of holy memory in whose diocese we have churches have always shown their loving and reverent devotion to our most holy Lady by not exacting from us … the payment that you demand. So we beg you … to follow in the honourable footsteps of the holy fathers and not to make us pay these dues for fear that you might be blamed as the one who was first responsible for the loss that this causes us. [130]

By the 1020s, then, the bishops of Lisieux were able to demand the customary payments of synod and visitation that were levied across Francia – and presumably not just from the canons of Chartres. [131] By 1032, unspecified ecclesiastical customs

---

[129] Fulbert, *Letters*, no. 39.
[130] Fulbert, *Letters*, no. 66.
[131] David Bates remarked that while there are numerous references to *synoda* and *circada* (synods and visitations) in Francia, such terms are not seen in Normandy much before 1080 (Bates, *Normandy*, pp. 211–12). Fulbert's letters – which were noted by Bates, *Normandy*, p. 212 – clearly qualify this comment.

(*consuetudine ecclesiastica*) belonged to the archbishop of Rouen and the bishop of Bayeux in the Bessin.[132] An act of 1053 mentions episcopal customs, including visitation and synod as well as the forfeitures due from sacrilege, theft, and the violation of cemeteries, in the diocese of Sées – still largely outside ducal control at this time[133] – while an act of 1055 × 1066 mentions episcopal customs held by the bishop of Evreux.[134]

Both tithes and episcopal customs thus seem only to have become institutionalized around the middle of the eleventh century, which is also when Archbishop Malger held the first known provincial council since 911. The canons of that council suggest, as should by now be expected, that the ecclesiastical institutions of the province were still forming. Bishops were thus commanded not to usurp the possessions of other bishops; archdeacons and priests were commanded to do the same. As a result of this and later evidence, David Bates suggested that it was only from 1072 that the Norman Church could take its basic organization for granted.[135] This is unlikely to be very far off the mark, and even if we want to push the date back to *c.* 1060 it would still be the case that institutional conversion had only been achieved some thirty or forty years after the Normans themselves may be thought finally to have become a Christian people.

The dukes and the Church

According to Dudo, when Rollo arrived at Rouen at the end of the ninth century it was the archbishop who came out of the city to negotiate with him. He did so because of his status and standing. That same status gave weight to the archbishop's pronouncements more generally, while the churches that were still operational would have given the archbishop access to the ears and hearts of both the urban and the rural populations of his diocese and province. In addition, his archives preserved legislation and registers that could be of use to the new secular administration and which could give it a sense of continuity with the previous Carolingian regime. The Church in Normandy, then, even before it was revitalized during the eleventh century, could give the duke access to his subjects in a way no other institution could. Indeed, even in the twelfth century the bishop of Evreux's diocesan court acted as the local public forum, as the county court was in the hands of the count of Evreux.[136]

---

[132] *RADN*, no. 64 and see also no. 99.
[133] *RADN*, no. 131.
[134] *RADN*, no. 208.
[135] Bates, *Normandy*, p. 204.
[136] Orderic, vi. 288; *Regesta*, ii. no. 1578; and see below, Chapter 9, p. 566.

The support that the Church provided to the duke might thus manifest itself in a number of different ways. In addition to those means just noted, that support might comprise prayers for the security of the duke and the duchy. That activity had a practical value as much as a spiritual one, for such prayers could act as a demonstration of fidelity to a ruler and support for him and his rule. It should be noted in this respect that saying prayers for the Carolingian ruler was a litmus test of loyalty in Lombardy after Charlemagne's conquest.[137] It could bring people together and be used to direct 'national' sympathy and action. For example, when, in Dudo's *De moribus*, the Normans of Rouen are told that the young Duke Richard is being held captive by King Louis, 'they send to every church in Normandy and Brittany to ask the priests to celebrate masses devoutly for him; and the clergy are to sing psalms, and the people to go barefoot and fasting in sackcloth. And when the Norman and Breton bishops hear the news … they ordain a three-day fast for the people every month, and beseech the Lord God in supplication, with the outpouring of prayers, and the giving of alms to the poor, that He will return Richard to them.'[138] The result was that, 'as time passed, the lord who is the King of Kings was placated by the continual prayers and fasting most devoutly engaged in by the Normans and Bretons, and He snatched Richard, the boy of inestimable promise, from the king's hands'.[139] Even relatively mundane events might be used to demonstrate loyalty and support like this. When the recently crowned William the Bastard returned to England in December 1067, for example, he 'made a good crossing and reached the harbour of Winchelsea on the opposite shore next morning. The wintry season made the sea rough; but the church of God was celebrating the feast of St. Nicholas, bishop of Myra, and all over Normandy prayers were offered for the good duke.'[140]

The Church could further promote the duke's authority by bathing the duke's person in ecclesiastical splendour and public acclaim. There were the *Laudes*, sung at the feasts held during the great religious festivals of the year which 'graphically set out current ideas of order and hierarchy in a comparatively unitary society';[141] the organization of an *aduentus* when the duke visited an abbey or the town in which an abbey was located, complete with procession and singing choir;[142] and

[137] J. Nelson, 'Kingship and royal government', in *The New Cambridge Medieval History: II. c. 700–c. 900*, ed. R. McKitterick (Cambridge, 1995) p. 391.

[138] *Dudo*, p. 105, echoed at Jumièges, i. 104.

[139] *Dudo*, p. 105.

[140] Orderic, ii. 208. William's crossing was probably deliberately timed to coincide with the feast of St Nicholas, as he was the patron saint of sailors/sea-farers (D. H. Farmer, *The Oxford Dictionary of Saints*, third edition (Oxford, 1992), p. 355.

[141] Cowdrey, *Lanfranc*, p. 28.

[142] See below, Chapter 9, pp. 520–3.

the duke's presence at the dedication of an important church or the translation of a saint's relics, which allowed the duke to be seen as standing at the pinnacle of the ecclesiastical hierarchy in the duchy and fully involved in the spiritual life of his subjects. What there was not, however, was ecclesiastical involvement at the installation of a new duke. That did happen, but only from the end of the twelfth century, or so it seems.[143]

In addition to its prayers, chants, and liturgies, the canons produced by the provincial councils could also help to support ducal authority.[144] At the council held at Caen in the aftermath of the battle of Val-ès-Dunes, for example, the lords of Normandy swore their oaths to uphold Duke William's rule and the peace which he instituted there on the relics of Saint-Ouen.[145] In 1080, the clergy present at the council held at Lillebonne made William the Bastard the guarantor of the Norman Truce of God:

> All who refuse to observe [the Truce of God] or break it in any way shall receive just sentence from the bishops according to the ordinance already established. If anyone then disobeys his bishop, the bishop shall make them known to the lord on whose land he lives, and the lord shall compel him to submit to episcopal justice. But if the lord refuses to do this, the king's *vicomte*, on being requested by the bishop, shall act without prevarication.[146]

The 1096 council of Rouen decreed, among other things, that 'all churches and their churchyards, all monks, clerks, nuns, women, pilgrims, and merchants, and their households, and oxen and horses at the plough … shall be in peace at all times'.[147] The penalty for an infringement of this canon was excommunication, which was also the punishment meted out to 'counterfeiters and brigands and purchasers of booty, and all who congregate in castles for the purposes of plundering, and lords who retain such men in their castles in future'.[148] These provisions

---

[143] Roger of Howden, *Chronica magistri Rogeri de Houedene*, ed. W. Stubbs, Rolls Series, vol 3 (London, 1870), p. 3; *The Benedictional of Archbishop Robert*, ed. H. A. Wilson, Henry Bradshaw Society 24 (1903), pp. 157–9; L. Valin, *Le duc de Normandie et sa cour (912–1204): étude d'histoire juridique* (Paris, 1910), pp. 43–5.

[144] On the councils held in Normandy, see also below, *infra*, pp. 225–6, 237–9.

[145] See *Acta Sanctorum, August Vol. IV*, pp. 834–5. In England, to provide an example from across the Channel, the council of Winchester of 1072 declared that every priest in England was to say three masses for the king's health, and that anyone who committed treason should be excommunicated (see, most conveniently, F. Barlow, *The English Church 1066–1154*, (London, 1979), p. 125).

[146] Orderic, iii. 26–34.

[147] Orderic, v. 20.

[148] Orderic, v. 22.

overlap, or seem to overlap, with ducal legislation protecting the plough, in force by *c.* 1015, and also clauses 11, 12, 13, and 14 of the *Consuetudines et iusticie* that were recorded in 1091 or 1096.[149] This in turn suggests not only that the duke's peace overlapped significantly with the Truce of God, but that the duke and the Church might in such cases reinforce each other's authority.[150]

That reinforcement can again be seen in the practicalities of doing justice. The re-establishment of the Christian Church across Normandy allowed the dukes to do justice in a new and more efficient way. Dudo included the story of the peasant of Longpaon in his *De moribus*, and probably did so to emphasize how the dukes would be able to find out all those who offended against their laws now that God was on their side.[151] In pagan times, offenders established their innocence through compurgation or by the decisions of panels of arbitrators,[152] but after conversion the Christian ordeal provided an alternative way to establish guilt or innocence. It had the advantage of removing the need to involve members of the community when doing so, but it also required a formal process over which the duke, through the bishops, had some control. The ordeal could thus be used to emphasize and promote the duke's right to do justice, and might also have the advantage of bringing pleas into his courts which would previously have been dealt with without his involvement.[153] The dukes thus gained a psychological and practical benefit here, but only because they had embraced the Church, for without the Church there was no ordeal.

The churches of Normandy were also important landowners, not least as a result of the generosity of Richard I and Richard II to the ducal abbeys of Upper Normandy. Those grants should not be seen as outright losses to the demesne, however, for, as argued here, the Church was vital for the functioning of the state.[154] Janet Nelson remarked that under the Carolingians, the grant of demesne lands to churches should be seen as devolution not disengagement, because those churches were firmly under royal protection, and hence still open to royal influ-

---

[149] *NI*, Appendix D, pp. 281–4.
[150] On the overlap between the dukes' peace and the Truce of God see also below, Chapter 8, pp. 442–5.
[151] *Dudo*, pp. 52–3.
[152] See, for example, W. I. Miller, 'Ordeal in Iceland', *Scandinavian Studies*, 60 (1988), 192–3 (Miller noted that there was a pre-Christian ordeal in Iceland known as the ordeal of turf); E. Christiansen, *The Norsemen in the Viking Age* (Oxford, 2002), pp. 256–9; S. Bagge, *From Viking Stronghold to Christian Kingdom: State Formation in Norway, c. 900–1350* (Copenhagen, 2010), pp. 189–90.
[153] Following the examples of Iceland or Norway, see the previous note as well as Bagge, *Viking Stronghold*, pp. 187–8.
[154] A point also made by Janet Nelson, 'Kingship and royal government', p. 392.

ence and intervention.[155] The same was true in Normandy, where as noted in earlier chapters, ducal abbeys helped to plant and consolidate the dukes' authority across the duchy, including in the Pays de Caux. The abbots of those abbeys were thus not just the heads of their monasteries but also important local agents who could speak up for the duke in local assemblies and whose men could, if necessary, fight to support him against both internal and external enemies.[156] Moreover, while a church might endure forever, the bishop or abbot who administered the estates and collected the wealth they produced did not. Dukes might consequently expect to appoint their own prelates to at least some of the greater churches of Normandy during every generation, so that many ecclesiastics were beholden to the current duke for their office and could therefore be expected to support him.

Richard I's apparent reluctance to promote the Church in Normandy before his son became archbishop c. 989 indicates his awareness that the Church could seriously undermine ducal rule. If the dukes failed to maintain control of elections to bishoprics or lost their ability to determine Church policy, either by accident or design, the Church might oppose the dukes when making further appointments, or when they were attempting to gain support for wars against foreign threats, or even by preventing them from collecting taxes and imposts from ecclesiastical lands or personnel. And because the Church was a supranational body, such contests could quickly become international incidents, to be taken up and used by hostile counts and kings and bishops and popes against the dukes.

Sometimes, such ecclesiastical opprobrium had no effect whatsoever. King Philip of France, for example, lived under excommunication for years without amending his ways.[157] He was strong enough to weather the storm, and even his prelates were not unanimous in their condemnation of his actions. William Rufus was likewise strong enough to ignore ecclesiastical censure, as Archbishop Anselm knew only too well, not least because Rufus was defending the secular fashions and practices he shared with his *principes*.[158] In contrast, a ruler with well-placed enemies might be more seriously inconvenienced, especially if the point at issue was not seen to benefit a wide enough pool of support. Robert Curthose was one such, of course. His mishandling of the Norman Church, and the clamour that ensued as a result of his dealings with the bishoprics of Lisieux

[155] Nelson, 'Kingship and royal government', pp. 389–90.
[156] On the composition of ducal armies, and the size of some of the contingents supplied by Norman churches, see below, Chapter 11, pp. 668–73.
[157] E. M. Hallam and J. Everard, *Capetian France 987–1328*, second edition (London, 2001), pp. 138–9.
[158] 'I have been told by my friends who are under that king that my excommunication, if pronounced, would be scorned by him and turned into ridicule': *Letters of St Anselm*, no. 210.

and Bayeux, as well as the abbacy of Saint-Pierre-sur-Dives, would lead directly to his defeat and imprisonment at the hands of his brother, Henry.[159]

Most bones of contention could be avoided, however, if the duke's leading churchmen were sympathetic to the needs and scope of the secular power, and if the duke demonstrated a willingness to acknowledge at least something of the ecclesiastical agenda, including by his choice of candidates. The background of the bishops before the reign of William the Bastard is often obscure, however, which also means that it is difficult to gain any sense of the criteria for selection employed by the duke and, indeed, anything of the role that he played in proceedings. Nonetheless, some trends can be observed from the beginning of the eleventh century, which have become clearer as a result of the recent publication of a number of lists of Norman bishops and their backgrounds for the whole period under discussion.[160] In addition, there has also been some commentary and analysis of the appointments that William the Bastard, Curthose, and Henry I made, both individually and in the round.[161]

Kinship with the dukes seems to have been important, especially with regard to the earlier appointments to the archbishopric of Rouen and the bishopric of Bayeux. We can guess that Robert was Richard I's clear choice for the archbishopric c. 989 because he was his son. We might also suspect that the appointment of Hugh of Ivry to Bayeux c. 1011 was at least in part the result of his kinship to Richard II. In Hugh's case, however, it is possible that the appointment was also strategic. It gave Hugh the status befitting Count Rodulf's eldest son while at the same time ensuring that he would not threaten Richard's rule and would not have direct heirs of his own.

There are perhaps four examples of the appointment of kinsmen to the episcopal bench under William the Bastard. Two of them concerned Rouen. Malger was made archbishop c. 1037, only to be deposed in 1054 or 1055, while John of Ivry, Count Rodulf's eldest son by his second wife, was elected archbishop in 1067 having served as bishop of Avranches from 1060. Malger was only a boy when appointed, and John had to be transferred from the bishopric of Avranches, which required the pope's approval. That Duke William was prepared to overcome these obstacles to have these men as his archbishops suggests that their kinship was

---

[159] See above, Chapter 3, pp. 153–5.

[160] P. Bouet and M. Dosdat, 'Les évêques normands de 985 à 1150', in *Les évêques normands du XIe siècle*, ed. P. Bouet and F. Neveux (Caen, 1995), pp. 19–37; Spear, *Personnel of the Norman Cathedrals*; Allen, 'The Norman Episcopate 989–1110'.

[161] For example, Douglas, *William the Conqueror*, pp. 118–22; Bates, *Normandy*, pp. 209–12; L. Musset, 'Les évêques normands envisagés dans le cadre européen (Xe–XIIe siècles', in *Les évêques normands du XIe siècle*, pp. 53–65; Allen, *The Norman Episcopate 989–1110*.

their essential qualification for the job. The same is probably true of the appointment of Duke William's half-brother Odo to the bishopric of Bayeux in 1049, as Odo, like Malger, was under the canonical age for appointment to a bishopric at the time. Finally, Hugh of Eu was appointed to the bishopric of Lisieux, probably in the later 1040s. He was the son of Richard II's half-brother Count William of Eu and Lescelina, and thus the brother of Count Robert of Eu. But although Bishop Hugh was another of the duke's kinsmen – something, incidentally, which might explain why Lisieux was chosen to host the council that deposed Archbishop Malger – the counts of Eu held extensive possessions in the Lieuvin so that Hugh's appointment both helped to consolidate his family's power in the county and gave Duke William a strong bishop in a diocese that was, or had been, at the centre of the rebellion led by Guy of Burgundy.

Although the pool of kinsmen that Curthose and Rufus might dip into in order to find bishops was significantly diminished, that was not the case under Henry I who fathered plenty of illegitimate sons who could have been given ecclesiastical positions – and he did make one of his illegitimate daughters abbess of Montivilliers.[162] So it is remarkable that so few kinsmen were appointed to bishoprics in either England or Normandy by that royal duke. The one notable exception is Henry of Blois, Henry I's nephew, who was elected abbot of Glastonbury in 1126 and bishop of Winchester in 1129. As Martin Brett noted, his promotion was more to do with Henry's alliance with the house of Blois on the continent than with the Church in England.[163] The only other example is provided by the election of Richard, the illegitimate son of Henry's eldest illegitimate son, Robert of Gloucester, to the bishopric of Bayeux c. 1133. His mother was Isabella of Douvres, the deceased Bishop Richard's sister. That appointment was made in 1133, but he was not invested until 1135, a delay owing, at least in part, to Archbishop Hugh of Rouen's reluctance to consecrate him without the pope's approval.[164] But although that appointment established one of the royal duke's grandsons in that diocese, it was Robert of Gloucester who was far more likely to reap any reward from that election – which is exactly what happened. The appointment was thus as much about patronage as kinship, and comparable to William the Bastard's appointment of Hugh of Eu to Lisieux.

When kinsmen were lacking, or else unwanted, the dukes turned to churchmen whose characters and qualities they had come to know either because they

---

[162] Chibnall, *The Empress Matilda*, p. 186; K. Thompson, 'Affairs of state', 136, 149; V. Gazeau, 'Femmes en religion, personnes d'autorité: les abbesses normandes (XIe–XIIIe siècles)', *ANS*, 35 (2013), 25.

[163] M. Brett, *The English Church under Henry I* (Oxford, 1975), p. 5.

[164] Orderic, vi. 442.

had previously served as chaplains in their household or because they had been established in ducal abbeys before they were made bishops. John of Ivry's successor at Rouen was William Bona Anima, who may be supposed to have recommended himself by his existing association with the duke – like Lanfranc before him he was abbot of the ducal abbey of Saint-Etienne at Caen at the time of his election. The next but one archbishop was Hugh of Amiens, a Cluniac monk who had been prior of Lewes and then abbot of Henry I's foundation at Reading. In addition, Bishop Baldwin of Evreux (appointed 1066); Michael of Avranches (1067); Gilbert of Lisieux (1077); John of Lisieux (1107); Ouen of Evreux (1113); and Richard of Avranches (1133) were all ducal chaplains, while Bishop Roger of Coutances (*c.* 1112) was the father of one of Henry I's chaplains.

As was the case with their *vicomtes*,[165] the dukes seem to have appreciated the value of experience, and a number of these candidates might have recommended themselves by their previous employment. William Bona Anima and Hugh of Amiens had ruled ducal abbeys, Ouen of Evreux had been a royal scribe and a canon of St Paul's, London,[166] and Richard of Beaufou had been archdeacon of Norwich. In addition, Bishop Algar of Coutances had been procurator of the Augustinian house at Bodmin.[167]

In some cases, the premium on experience led to the creation of episcopal dynasties. Radbod Fleitel was made bishop of Sées around 1025. Between 1037 and 1046, William Fleitel, Radbod's brother, was appointed bishop of Evreux, and Radbod's son, William Bona Anima, became archbishop of Rouen in 1079. When Turold of Envermeu, the would-be bishop of Bayeux, retired to Le Bec in 1107, the bishopric was given to Richard the son of Bishop Samson of Worcester, William of Malmesbury's 'Great Maw', who was himself the son of the first Archbishop Thomas of York and father of the second (who was therefore Richard's brother).[168] John, archdeacon of Sées, was made bishop of Lisieux in 1107. In 1123, his nephew, John fitz Haduin, succeeded Serlo of Orgères as bishop of Sées. It should also perhaps be noted that Bishop Ouen of Evreux and Archbishop Thurstan of York were brothers.

Regardless of precisely why they were appointed, there is little doubt that all these men were Henry's appointees, which reveals that it was *his* concerns that were paramount when an election was made and that he had retained as much control over the composition of the bench as his father had enjoyed. The only exception across Henry's dominions as a whole seems to have been the arch-

[165] See below, Chapter 9, pp. 555–6.
[166] See also Orderic, vi. 530.
[167] Brett, *English Church*, p. 9.
[168] Malmesbury, *GP*, i. 438–40.

bishopric of Canterbury, where the views of Henry's lords, the English bishops, and the monks of the cathedral priory were all taken on board before a choice was made.[169] In practical terms, then, the reform papacy's attempts to gain free elections to bishoprics by denying the duke's right to invest bishops with the ring and staff had stalled, despite the scandals over Curthose's appointments to Lisieux and Bayeux and Henry I's own troubled relationships with Archbishop Anselm and Pope Paschal II during the first years of his reign. As is well known, although Henry formally surrendered the right to invest bishops with the ring and staff in 1107, in an agreement made in England but which may be supposed to have been observed in Normandy, too, he was permitted to be present at elections and to take the homage of the new prelate in return for the temporalities of his see. The result, arguably, was that Henry lost very little other than a degree of prestige. As Hugh the Chanter pointed out: 'he did at length give up investitures because of the prohibition and anathema of the Roman church; a concession which cost him little or nothing, a little, perhaps, of his royal dignity, but nothing at all of his power to enthrone anyone he pleased.'[170] That view certainly seems to have been borne out by the lack of impact on the degree of control that Henry exercised over subsequent elections.

The dukes thus retained the ability to nominate bishops to the Norman sees throughout the period to 1144, which helped to ensure, in general terms, that the Norman Church remained an ally rather than an opponent. In addition, the dukes would also maintain their presidency of Church councils and oversight of the canons they produced. At the beginning of the twelfth century, Eadmer of Canterbury noted that, among other things, William the Bastard 'would not let the primate of his kingdom, by which I mean the archbishop of Canterbury ... if he were presiding over a general council of bishops, lay down any ordinance or prohibition unless these were agreeable to the king's wishes and had been first settled by him'.[171] Eadmer explained that this was a right that William had imported from Normandy, and his words are supported by a similar comment provided by William of Poitiers in his *Gesta Guillelmi*, who 'commented with admiration upon the duke's employment of councils to keep the higher clergy up to the mark':[172]

As the source of authority, though a layman, he used to give subtle advice to abbots and bishops on ecclesiastical discipline, encouraging firmly and

[169] Brett, *English Church*, pp. 73–5.
[170] Hugh the Chanter, *The History of the Church of York 1066–1127*, ed. and trans. C. Johnson revised by M. Brett, C. N. L. Brooke, and M. Winterbottom (Oxford, 1990), pp. 22–4.
[171] Eadmer, *HN*, pp. 9–10; trans Bosanquet, pp. 9–10.
[172] Cowdrey, *Lanfranc*, p. 30.

punishing severely. Whenever at his command and by his encouragement the prelates, metropolitan and suffragans assembled to deal with the state of religion of clerks, monks, and laymen, he endeavoured not to miss being an arbiter at these synods, so that by his presence he might add zeal to the zealous and circumspection to the provident, and finally, so that he did not need to learn from the testimony of another how things had been done, when he wished all to be done in a reasonable, orderly, and holy way.[173]

During William the Bastard's reign, such councils were held quite frequently. Archbishop Malger held a council *c.* 1045 (and might have held an earlier one in 1042 as well), and this was followed by councils at Brionne in 1050, Lisieux in 1054 or 1055, Caen in 1061, Rouen in 1063, Lisieux in 1064, Rouen in 1069, 1070, 1072, 1073, 1074, and 1078, Lillebonne in 1080, and Oissel in 1082. There were two councils held during Curthose's reign, in 1091 and 1096, both of them at Rouen. The latter saw the duke take control of the prohibition on clerical marriage, as the bishops had been too lax. Four councils were held during Henry I's reign: at Lisieux in 1106, Rouen in 1118, Lisieux in 1119, and Rouen again in 1128.[174]

The dukes' desire to maintain their undisputed control over the Norman Church could only be achieved in part by determining elections and censoring the canons produced by Norman Church councils. It was also essential to silence dissenting voices from outside the duchy. That is probably why the Norman councils were usually closed to outside clergy, which was not the practice elsewhere in France.[175] Furthermore, the dukes from William the Bastard onwards attempted to control communications with the papacy, as Eadmer noted: 'now it was the policy of King William to maintain in England the usages and laws which he and his fathers before him were accustomed to have in Normandy ... He would not, for instance, allow anyone in all his dominion, except on his instructions, to recognize the established pontiff of the city of Rome as pope, or under any circumstance to accept a letter from him if it had not first been submitted to the king himself.'[176]

---

[173] Poitiers, p. 82.
[174] Some of these councils dealt with only very limited business. The councils at Brionne in 1050 and Rouen in 1063, for example, related to the heresy of Berengar of Tours. The former was almost certainly the direct result of Lanfranc's visit to Rouen from the end of 1049 to clear himself of sharing in Berengar's beliefs. The council at Lisieux in 1054 or 1055 was summoned apparently exclusively for the purpose of deposing Archbishop Malger (see Foreville, 'The synod of the province of Rouen', pp. 19–39, with a useful tabular breakdown at p. 22).
[175] Foreville, 'The synod of the province of Rouen', pp. 34–5.
[176] Eadmer, *HN*, pp. 9–10; trans Bosanquet, pp. 9–10.

The reformed monastic orders, such as the Cluniacs and Cistercians, whose monks remained closely tied to their mother houses in Burgundy, would have seriously weakened the dukes' control over communications with the outside ecclesiastical world, and that may be why they seem to have been so unenthusiastic about establishing those orders on Norman soil. There was just one Cluniac priory in the duchy, at Longueville, founded by Walter Giffard in 1093, but it was never important. And while Henry did found a very important Cluniac house at Reading in 1121, which would serve as his mausoleum, it was very quickly elevated from a priory to an independent abbey.[177] However, while Henry seems not to have promoted the foundation of Cluniac houses in his duchy, he did maintain very good relations with Cluny itself. According to a petition presented to King Henry VI in 1457, which recounted the benefactions of that king's predecessors, Henry I had provided much-needed funds to Abbot Hugh in 1101 so that work on the abbey church (Cluny III) could continue. He was also remembered as having contributed 100 marks per year to the abbey, although that gift is also recorded in the royal duke's surviving *acta*.[178] So great was Henry's generosity to Cluny that Peter the Venerable wrote that 'among all the kings of the Latin west who for the last three hundred years have testified their affection for the church of Cluny … Henry, king of the English and duke of the Normans, has surpassed all others in his gifts and has shown more than an ordinary share of love and attachment to [Cluny]. It was he who perfected that grand basilica, commenced under the auspices and donations of Alfonso king of Spain, exceeding all other known churches in the Christian world in its construction and beauty.'[179] Christopher Brooke thought that Henry's interest in Cluny was 'connected with the presence there of one of his favourite nephews, his namesake Henry of Blois, son of the count of Blois and of Henry's sister Adela, and brother of the other favourite nephew, Count, later King Stephen',[180] but it is just as likely that Henry saw the political benefit in supporting this great abbey, and of being fêted by its abbot in return. Henry needed to be seen as a friend of the Church if his efforts to keep control

[177] See *Reading Abbey Cartularies: I. General Documents and those relating to English Counties other than Berkshire*, ed. B. R. Kemp, Camden Society, fourth series 31 (London, 1986), pp. 14–15; Hollister, *Henry*, pp. 434–41 and especially p. 437.

[178] *Regesta*, ii. nos. 1691, 1713.

[179] *Recueil des chartes de l'abbaye de Cluny*, v. 532–4 (no. 4183), cited in Hollister, *Henry*, p. 413. Henry's involvement in the project was also noted by Robert of Torigni and by Walter Map, who also credited the king with its construction: Walter Map, *De nugis curialium: Courtiers' Trifles*, ed. and trans. M. R. James, revised by C. N. L. Brooke, and R. A. B. Mynors (Oxford, 1983), pp. 436–8.

[180] C. N. L. Brooke, 'Princes and kings as patrons of monasteries', *Il monachesmo e la riforma ecclesiastica (1049–1122)*, Miscellanea del Centro di Studi Medioevali, 6 (Milan, 1971), 138.

of it in his duchy were not to be looked at askance. Supporting the Burgundian abbey, indeed providing the funds for its construction, was an easy way to do this without it costing anything other than money.

Cluny's great rival, Cîteaux, was a different proposition, however. The wave of enthusiasm for the Cistercians felt across much of Latin Europe broke at the borders of the Anglo-Norman *regum*. The first Cistercian house in England, at Waverley in Surrey, was founded only in 1128. Those at Tintern, Rievaulx, and Fountains followed in 1131 and 1132, after Henry I had met with Innocent II at Chartres and Rouen and thus after his Anglo-Norman *familiares* had met Bernard of Clairvaux face-to-face. But there was no Cistercian house in Normandy, for either men or women, until 1137, when the monks of the abbey at Mortemer chose to bring themselves into that order.[181] Henry I had not known that would happen when he gave the monks land in Beauficel-en-Lyons for the construction of a grange, as well as freedom and immunity from all custom throughout his whole land 'on this side of the sea and on the other', and all his profits in the Forêt de Lyons.[182] His patronage of the Cistercians was otherwise limited to grants of exemption from toll and custom, granted to the monks of the order generally and also specifically to the community at Pontigny.[183] But that was the extent of the royal duke's patronage, almost certainly because the Cistercian abbots gathered at Cîteaux for the annual general chapter, where Henry I had no influence, and because they were effectively led by the extremely vocal and influential Abbot Bernard, who could not be relied upon to be sympathetic to Henry's policies and ambitions. It is likely that Henry's failure to patronize the Templars to any extent was caused by the same concerns. In contrast, Henry did support the the Savignacs, a home-grown reformed monastic order that provided a real alternative to the Cistercians, and also the Tironensians, from just across the border in the county of the Perche.[184]

---

[181] For Savignac and Cistercian nunneries see B. L. Venarde, *Women's Monasticism and Medieval Society: Nunneries in France and England, 890–1215* (Ithaca, NY and London, 1997), pp. 71–6; L. Grant, *Architecture and Society in Normandy 1120–1270* (New Haven, CT and London, 2005), pp. 223; L. V. Hicks, *Religious Life in Normandy, 1050–1300: Space, Gender and Social Pressure* (Woodbridge, 2007), Appendix A and Appendix B.

[182] *RHGF*, xiv. 510

[183] *Le premier cartulaire de l'abbaye cistercienne de Pontigny (XIIe–XIIIe siècles)* ed. M. Garrigues (Paris, 1981), 86 (no. 3). The date-range is 1114 × 1131, but it should almost certainly be dated January 1130 × August 1131; *Regesta*, ii. no. 1720 is for the Order generally.

[184] *Regesta*, ii. nos. 1003, 1015, 1016, 1212 (Savigny); 1169, 1236 (Tiron). The Savignac nunnery at Villers-Canivet, founded 1127, also received a grant of exemption from toll and custom (*NI*, p. 308 (no. 23) = *Regesta*, ii. no. 1919).

Henry's promotion of those orders once again meant that he could portray himself as a supporter of ecclesiastical reform without his having to worry about any loss of control over the Church in the duchy.

Nonetheless, despite the dukes' desire to maintain control over the Norman Church, there were times when they themselves resorted to the popes to legitimize otherwise controversial actions that they wanted to take, thereby acknowledging that it was the popes, and not them, who were supreme in such matters. Their lead was followed, on occasion, by Norman prelates. There was, then, a chink in the armour that the dukes had constructed around their control of the Church. And as papal reform gathered ground, and papal legates were dispatched across Latin Europe to promulgate and uphold the reforming canons and prohibitions those popes produced at legatine councils, so the dukes' would find their all-but-absolute control of the Church increasingly under threat.

The dukes, the popes, and the contest for supremacy over the Norman Church

While the archbishop of Reims and the bishop of Chartres became involved in Norman affairs in the course of the tenth century, the pope intervened only in 991, when legates of John XV brokered a peace treaty between Richard I of the Normans and Æthelred II of the English by which the king and duke promised not to aid each other's enemies.[185] It is virtually certain that this involvement was the result of a petition by the English king, and it may be that Richard I was rather bemused by the appearance of a papal legate at his court. The English king's timing, however, was opportune. Richard I's brother, Robert, had become archbishop of Rouen c. 989 following the death of the Frankish Hugh of Cavelcamp. With no rival for control over the church in the province of Rouen, Richard could afford to be generous and thus to give the papal legates what they wanted, and might have welcomed the chance to appear as a faithful son of the Church as a result.

John XV's intervention in Norman affairs was the last by a pope for more than fifty years. After the middle of the eleventh century, however, the dukes would begin to petition the popes in order to legitimize some of the actions they wished to take, both at home and abroad. Their petitions reveal that they thought the popes had the right to intervene in such matters, and that it was to their advantage to gain papal support for them. But they also seem to have been limited to matters where the dukes would have expected that support to be forthcoming. As Cowdrey has noted, there was an 'expectation that popes would act in response

---

[185] Malmesbury, *GR*, i, 278.

to ducal needs and to fulfil ducal requirements; papal authority ... must not challenge that of the duke in his duchy.'[186]

The earliest example dates from 1054 or 1055, when Archbishop Malger was removed from office with the support of Pope Leo IX. The *Acts of the Archbishops of Rouen* records that William, 'with the authority of Pope Leo, and in the presence of the papal legate Ermenfrid, bishop of Sion, and the other bishops of the province, relieved him of the episcopate in the church of Lisieux'.[187]

William also appealed to Pope Alexander II for his support regarding several issues. Firstly, when it became clear that Archbishop Maurilius was coming to the end of his life, probably in the summer of 1066, Duke William determined to replace him with John, who was also his kinsman. John was already bishop of Avranches, however, and so would need to be transferred from that see to the archbishopric. For that to happen, papal approval was thought necessary. And so to 'ensure that the translation should be canonical [Lanfranc] went to Rome to obtain licence for John's consecration from Pope Alexander, and with the licence brought back the sacred pallium, giving himself and all Normandy alike just cause for congratulation'.[188] Alexander sent a letter, too, which implicitly acknowledged that the choice of archbishop lay with William: 'We learned, by the report of the bishop of Sion and Abbot Lanfranc that, with the church of Rouen being deprived of a pastor, our most dear son William, king of the English, your prince, had promoted you in consideration of your integrity and your morality to this vacant seat, provided that you have the assent of the apostolic see, which by the authority of God we occupy.'[189]

It is possible that Alexander supported William's claim to the English throne, manifested by his gift of a papal banner.[190] If so, it would have been the first occasion on which the pope was asked to support a succession that itself relied on an oath – an oath falling under ecclesiastical jurisdiction. It would not be the last. Around 1101, before embarking on his invasion of England, Robert Curthose had written to Paschal II complaining that his brother Henry had violated the oath he had sworn to him in assuming the English crown. Once again, it was the broken oath, rather than any jurisdiction over the succession per se, that gave the pope jurisdiction. Paschal's response, at least as it survives in a letter to Archbishop Anselm, was to send legates to mediate between the two brothers 'if peace has not

---

[186] Cowdrey, *Lanfranc*, p. 31.
[187] *AAbps*, pp. 38–9, 52.
[188] Orderic, ii. 200.
[189] *AAbps*, pp. 40–1, 54; 'Epistolae et diplomata Alexandri II papae', *PL*, 146, col. 1339 (no. 56).
[190] Poitiers, p. 104.

yet been agreed between them', which, in the event, it had.[191] Given his exploits during the crusade, Curthose might have found this response disappointing, and it is possible that it soured relations between the duke and the papacy and the Church in general, which were not especially good over the remaining five years of his reign.

The contested succession of 1135 saw Stephen of Blois follow in his predecessors' footsteps and seek the pope's help with regard to his claim. One of Stephen's acts, perhaps best described as his second coronation charter, which dates from 1136, states expressly that he was king as a result of his election by his people, his consecration by Archbishop William of Canterbury, and the confirmation of Pope Innocent.[192] Innocent II's confirmation of Stephen's kingship was itself confirmed in 1139, in the face of an embassy sent to the curia to argue the case for Geoffrey and Matilda, once again on the basis of broken oaths.[193]

Henry I seems not to have sought the pope's support for his conquest of Normandy in 1106, presumably because no oath had been broken. Indeed, it seems that Henry made his first petition to the pope only in 1124, when he undermined plans to marry William Clito to Sibyl, Count Fulk of Anjou's daughter.[194] Around nine years later, Henry petitioned the pope again, this time to gain permission for the consecration of his illegitimate grandson Richard to the bishopric of Bayeux. At about the same time, Henry made a third complaint. He wrote to Pope Innocent II about the behaviour of Archbishop Hugh of Rouen, who had been attempting to gain professions of obedience from the abbots of Le Bec, Saint-Wandrille, Jumièges, and Saint-Ouen of Rouen. These demands, Henry claimed, went 'against the honour, customs and dignities of my *regnum* and my duchy', and he warned the pope that if Hugh was not corrected then he would be compelled 'to leave the love and fealty and service of you and yours on account of these unusual innovations and similar causes of harm'.[195] The royal duke was perhaps especially concerned by the divided loyalties that such professions might cause, so his stand against professions of obedience which monastic writers found so appealing was probably no more than self-interest. The pope, too, supported

---

[191] *Letters of St Anselm*, no. 213, discussed in David, *Robert Curthose*, pp. 153–4.

[192] *Regesta*, iii. no. 271; *English Historical Documents II, 1042–1189*, ed. and trans. D. C. Douglas and G. W. Greenaway (London, 1953), p. 403. The pope had been sent testimonials on Stephen's behalf by Louis VI and Count Theobald. See also King, *King Stephen*, pp. 62–3.

[193] John of Salisbury remarked that he had also been 'willing to accept papal judgement when the count [Geoffrey] had despoiled him of the duchy and part of the kingdom' (John of Salisbury, *Historia pontificalis*, ed. and trans. M. Chibnall (Oxford, 1956), p. 44).

[194] See above, Chapter 3, p. 177 and the discussion in Hollister, *Henry*, pp. 304–5.

[195] 'Epistoloae variorum ad Innocentium', *PL*, 179, cols. 669–70.

the monasteries' independence. He, along with Bernard of Clairvaux and Peter the Venerable, urged Hugh to moderation and patience. Innocent might then have followed up this counsel with a distraction. In another letter, he wrote to Archbishop Hugh complaining of the abuses committed within the province of Rouen, noting in particular that archdeacons were being promoted by laymen without having acted as deacons first, and that churches were being treated as the hereditary possessions of priestly dynasties, despite repeated canons prohibiting clerical marriage and the ordinations of the sons of priests. Such complaints were typical, and reflected in the canons of the councils held at Rouen during Henry's reign, but the timing of Innocent's letter is such as to raise the possibility that he was reminding Hugh that there were more important issues to attend to than obtaining written professions of obedience from abbots.[196]

Of course, others made petitions to the popes, too, and for similar reasons. As such, the dukes of the Normans sometimes found their own actions, ambitions, or alliances threatened by complaints or appeals lodged by other parties. The earliest example of such a threat hung over the betrothal of William the Bastard to Matilda of Flanders *c.* 1049. The complaint, aired at the council of Reims in 1049, was almost certainly a diplomatic move, perhaps designed to end the alliance between Normandy and Flanders which could have impacted imperial politics – Leo IX was after all an imperial appointee – or perhaps intended to put pressure on Duke William to intervene in southern Italian affairs where the Normans were becoming a threat to the security of the papal city of Benevento and had made themselves cordially hated across the peninsula.[197] The issue seems to have been resolved quickly, however. While it was once thought that the controversy over William's marriage lasted some years, David Bates argued in 1982 that this view depends solely on Milo Crispin's *Vita Lanfranci*, written *c.* 1140, which is contradicted by better and more contemporary evidence on key points.[198] Duke William's use of papal legates to depose Malger in 1054 or 1055 would certainly suggest that the dispute had been resolved by that date, but we remain in ignorance of the arguments presented to Pope Leo in order to achieve that resolution.

Another council of Reims, this one held in 1119, raised questions about the legitimacy of Henry I's rule in Normandy because Louis VI, defeated at Brémule earlier that same year, used it as an opportunity to denounce Henry's actions – the

---

[196]   AD Seine-Maritime, G 1116; Ctl. Rouen, fos. 41v–43r.

[197]   See Douglas, *William the Conqueror*, p. 78; Tanner, *Families, Friend and Allies*, p. 87; G. A. Loud, *The Age of Robert Guiscard: Southern Italy and the Norman Conquest* (Harlow, 2000), pp. 114–16.

[198]   Bates, *Normandy*, pp. 199–201 followed by Cowdrey, *Lanfranc*, pp. 35–7. The authorship of the *Life*, which is not certain, and the date of its composition are discussed by Gibson, *Lanfranc*, pp. 195–225.

imprisonment of Robert Curthose and the disinheritance of William Clito, as well as his part in the rebellions of Count Theobald of Blois – and asked for Calixtus II's counsel (not judgement) in the matter.[199] Fortunately for Henry, Archbishop Thurstan of York arranged a meeting with the pope, using the legate Cardinal Cuno of Palestrina as an intermediary, so that Henry was able to justify his position to the pope's satisfaction.[200] Eadmer wrote that Henry also took the opportunity to ask Calixtus to concede him all the rights that his father had enjoyed in both England and Normandy, which does not suggest that he felt he was on the back foot during the interview.[201] Nonetheless, that some sort of response to Louis's complaint was felt necessary reveals that Henry thought it was important to ensure that Calixtus's eventual pronouncement should take account of both sides of the argument, and that in turn suggests it could have been influential or damaging. Indeed, Henry would have known from his own experience just how damaging any ecclesiastical condemnation of his actions might turn out to be.

As the reforming popes grew stronger, in part because of recourse to their curia by the kings and princes of Europe, and in part because of the creation of a system of legates who brought papal power into the provinces of Latin Europe,[202] so they began to intervene more and more often in the ecclesiastical affairs of the duchy of Normandy and elsewhere. In other words, popes began to bring their own complaints against the rulers of Latin Europe, rather than waiting for petitions to be brought to them. They were concerned, for the most part, with the organization of the Church, the quality of its personnel, and with the reforming agenda. Such concerns could act to undermine the duke's ability to appoint his candidates to bishoprics or abbacies, although when they did so it was because there were wider political issues involved or else the choice of candidate had been a poor one.

In 1077, for example, Pope Gregory VII undermined William the Bastard's authority in Brittany – itself damaged by his precipitate retreat from Dol the previous year – by deposing William's candidate for the bishopric of Dol, Juhel, and electing in his place Evenus. That decision was probably as much the result of his desire to recruit the Bretons as allies against Count Fulk of Anjou, as of Juhel's 'most corrupt life'.[203] William protested, and although he would not succeed in

---

[199] 'Ad hanc' inquit, 'sanctam concionem pro inuestigando consilio cum baronibus meis uenio, domine papa et uos O seniores audite me obsecro' (Orderic, vi. 256–8 with the quotation at p. 256).

[200] Orderic, vi. 282–90.

[201] Eadmer, *HN*, p. 258; Brett, *English Church*, p. 40.

[202] I. Robinson, *The Papacy, 1073–1198: Continuity and Innovation* (Cambridge, 1990), pp. 146ff.

[203] *The Register of Pope Gregory VII 1073–1085. An English Translation*, trans. H. E. J. Cowdrey (Oxford, 2002), pp. 227–8.

reversing the pope's decision, Gregory still went out of his way to allow the case to be heard in Brittany before papal legates and to ensure that William's views should be represented in that forum.[204]

There was also the controversy that surrounded the primacy of the archbishops of Lyon over the provinces of Lyon, Tours, Rouen, and Sens.[205] The grant, made by Gregory VII to Archbishop Gebuin in 1079, was seen by David Douglas as part of a three-pronged attack on 'the barriers which William set up around the Anglo-Norman church', made between 1079 and 1081.[206] That was probably not the intention, however, and Rouen was, of course, not singled out by the grant itself. In any event, no political or religious realignment resulted from this reordering. The province of Rouen and duchy of Normandy remained more or less coterminous, and the authority of the absent archbishops of Lyon was no stronger than that of absent popes. But the grant of the primacy did nonetheless act seriously to undermine a duke, in this case Robert Curthose, as a result of an unforeseen combination of factors. Although the grant of 1079 seems to have been ineffectual so far as Normandy was concerned, it was confirmed by Pope Urban II during the council at Clermont in 1095. By then, the primacy was openly resisted by the archbishops of Rouen and Sens. Indeed, the pope was obliged to threaten to place the two provinces under interdicts unless the archbishops submitted. In the event, Urban did not follow through on that threat, but Archbishop William was suspended from his office by Paschal II from 1101 to 1106 as a result of his continuing disobedience. The result of that suspension was the archbishop's inability to consecrate William of Evreux as the new bishop of Lisieux. That allowed Ranulf Flambard to impose another of his own candidates on the see, which led to Ivo of Chartres complaining to the pope and appealing to Henry I to liberate the Norman Church, and thus to Curthose's defeat at Tinchebray.[207] Of course, there were other factors that combined to see Henry take Normandy from his brother, but the scandal over Lisieux, which gave Henry the chance to justify his hostile actions, only reached the point it did because of the popes' grants of the primacy to Lyon.

These actions concerned the dukes of the Normans, and affected the reach of their authority, but they did not relate directly to the duchy. When the popes did attempt to intervene in the duchy itself, as they did in 1078 when Gregory VII sent his legate Hubert to investigate the severity of Archbishop John of Rouen's incapacity,[208] or in 1079 when Gregory questioned William Bona Anima's elec-

---

[204] *Register of Pope Gregory VII*, pp. 271–3.
[205] *Register of Pope Gregory VII*, pp. 315–16.
[206] Douglas, *William the Conqueror*, p. 338–9.
[207] As discussed above, Chapter 3, pp. 153–5 and *infra*, pp. 221–2.
[208] *Register of Pope Gregory VII*, pp. 268–9.

tion to Rouen,[209] their interventions were ineffective. According to the *Acts of the Archbishops of Rouen*, it was Duke William not Hubert who insisted that Archbishop John surrender his office,[210] while Archbishop William was not deposed despite being the son of a priest.

That Gregory VII did not always seek to impose his authority on the duke was the result of his high regard for William, his gratitude for the duke's support for his papacy, and his promotion of the reforming agenda.[211] Indeed, 'for no contemporary ruler did [Gregory] profess a higher regard during his lifetime than for William, duke of Normandy from 1035 and king of England from 1066 until his death in 1087'.[212] Alexander II had earlier been similarly impressed. He had written to William in October 1071, remarking that 'we learn at this time of your outstanding reputation for piety among the rulers and princes of this world and we receive unmistakable evidence of your support for the Church'.[213] Such words might have inspired William of Poitiers in his fulsome praise of William's piety, the political benefits of which are clearly revealed by this relationship.[214] Gregory's willingness to allow the duke to guide the Church in Normandy, and his desire not to provoke William's hostility, is encapsulated in a letter he sent to his legates Hugh of Die and Amatus of Oloron in 1081: 'it has been reported to us that your religious selves have suspended all the Norman pontiffs, except the archbishop of Rouen and the abbot of La Couture whom we have restored, who were summoned to a council. However, as it has been intimated to us, they have withdrawn not out of disobedience but out of fear of the king of France, in other words because they could not come safely.'[215] He commanded them to undo the remaining suspensions, and told them that they were not to act against William in future without his prior agreement: 'for it seems to us that he may be much better and more readily won for God and stimulated to a perpetual love of blessed Peter by the charm of gentleness and by a display of reason than by severity or the rigour of righteousness.'[216] Henry I enjoyed a similarly good reputation in both England and Normandy, at least once the controversy over investitures had been concluded. Like his father, he perhaps also benefited from the disputes between

---

[209] *Register of Pope Gregory VII*, pp. 324–5.
[210] *AAbps*, pp. 45, 60.
[211] *Register of Pope Gregory VII*, pp. 405.
[212] *Register of Pope Gregory VII*, p. 459.
[213] *Letters of Lanfranc*, no. 7; *PL*, 146, cols. 1365–6.
[214] See above, *infra*, p. 230.
[215] *Register of Pope Gregory VII*, pp. 405–6.
[216] *Register of Pope Gregory VII*, p. 406. The comment is similar to one attributed to Lanfranc by William of Malmesbury, who said that William could be won round by humour rather than argument (Malmesbury, *GP*, i. 90).

the emperors and the popes, especially between 1109 and 1125 when the emperor was also Henry's son-in-law.

Papal interventions in Normandy might also have been limited by the dukes' control of communications to and from the papal curia. Letters could not be sent or received without undergoing the dukes' censorship. The dukes seem also to have regulated journeys to the curia. Gregory VII, who seems to have realized this, suggested to Archbishop Lanfranc that it was fear of the king that had prevented him visiting Rome.[217] Lanfranc later remarked that he did not see the need for personal visits,[218] and was subsequently threatened with suspension in May or June 1082 should he continue to absent himself from Rome.[219] Lanfranc remained unmoved, perhaps because the threat seemed empty after the legates had reversed the suspensions they had imposed on Norman prelates the previous year at the pope's command (as noted above). Lanfranc was not the only Norman prelate to attract Gregory's disapproval. In the letter which also reveals the complete absence of Norman bishops from the curia between 1073 and 1081,[220] Gregory reprimanded Archbishop William of Rouen for his own continued failure to collect his *pallium* from Rome, and forbade him from ordaining priests or consecrating churches until he had collected it, although that prohibition seems not to have taken effect. Curthose was strong enough to ensure that the Norman prelates should not travel to the curia during his reign either. Only Bishop Turold of Bayeux is known to have travelled to the curia during his reign, and he did so in answer to a second summons to defend his election before Paschal II. Visits to the curia remained equally rare during Henry I's reign, although Pope Innocent's tour of France in 1130–31 gave Norman clergy the chance to obtain bulls for their churches, without having to make the long journey to Italy and without risk of incurring Henry's displeasure, because he was with them – at Chartres, at least.

In addition, the dukes were very reluctant to allow Norman churchmen to attend councils held outside the duchy. After all, the canons produced by those councils might run counter to the dukes' interests – as Henry I was to find out after Anselm returned from his first exile in 1100.[221] Likewise, Norman prelates might bring pleas against their fellows while a council was in progress, thus avoiding the dukes' own jurisdiction and allowing another to exercise lordship within the confines of the duchy. The dukes could only be certain of retaining control of the Church in Normandy, therefore, if they prohibited attendance at Church

[217] *Register of Pope Gregory VII*, pp. 312–13.
[218] *Letters of Lanfranc*, no. 38.
[219] *Register of Pope Gregory VII*, pp. 419–20.
[220] *Register of Pope Gregory VII*, p. 398.
[221] For example, R. Southern, *Saint Anselm: A Portrait in a Landscape* (Cambridge, 1990), pp. 291–4; Hollister, *Henry*, pp. 118–20; Green, *Henry*, pp. 52–3, 66.

councils held outside the duchy, which explains why they so frequently did so. But there was, it seems, one exception to this rule; the dukes seem to have permitted attendance by at least a representative body of Norman prelates at councils presided over by the popes themselves when they were held in France. Thus Norman churchmen attended the council of Reims in 1049,[222] the council of Clermont of 1095,[223] and the council of Reims of 1119. In contrast, they were usually prohibited from attending legatine councils held in France – or at least did not generally attend them whether prohibited or not.

This absenteeism became a cause of friction with popes and papal legates, who saw in it an obstacle to the promulgation of reforming decrees in the province of Rouen as well as a barrier to developing relationships with Norman clergy. They were not always prepared to tolerate such obstacles. In September 1079, Gregory VII ended a letter sent to his legate Hubert with an injunction that at least two bishops from the province of Rouen as well as the two English archbishops should go to the Roman synod that he planned for Lent 1080. His command was ignored.[224] Instead, William responded by holding a council of his own at Lillebonne at Pentecost 1080, soon after he had come to terms with his rebellious son. The next year, as noted above, the legates Hugh of Die and Amatus of Oloron suspended almost the whole Norman bench for their failure to attend a council they had summoned. In 1115, Cardinal Cuno of Palestrina, the formidable papal legate for France, similarly suspended the Norman bishops for failing to attend his council at Chalons-sur-Marne that July – which was the third time that they had failed to attend one of his legatine councils. Henry regarded this as a flagrant breach of his customary rights and sent envoys to Cuno to make his displeasure clear.[225] As there is no evidence for their continued suspension it may be supposed that some settlement was quickly reached, perhaps because Pope Paschal needed to retain Henry's support during this time of friction with the Emperor Henry V.[226] There was some attempt at a compromise a few years later, however. Cuno was invited to attend the ecclesiastical council that Henry had summoned

---

[222] Five of the seven bishops of the province of Rouen attended this council (Cowdrey, *Lanfranc*, p. 31.

[223] Archbishop William or Rouen and Abbot Gontard of Jumièges as well as other unnamed Norman bishops and abbots attended the council (Orderic, ii. 294).

[224] Cowdrey, *Register of Pope Gregory VII*, pp. 324–5 and see also H. E. J. Cowdrey, *Pope Gregory VII, 1073–1085* (Oxford, 1998), pp. 466–7 and Douglas, *William the Conqueror*, p. 338.

[225] Eadmer, *HN*, p. 234; Malmesbury, *GP*, i. 206; Brett, *English Church*, p. 37.

[226] Hollister noted that we do not know the outcome, (*Henry*, p. 241). See also Robinson, *The Papacy*, pp. 157–8 for a discussion of Cuno's career. The legate had just returned from the empire, where he had attempted to raise rebellion against Henry V, which would have given Paschal a good reason not to push the point too hard at this time.

to Rouen in October 1118. His presence would have revealed to the legate both Henry's desire for reform and his mastery of the Norman Church. It is also possible that Cuno was asked to attend because Henry hoped that his presence would both help to secure peace with his rebellious lords and make any settlement concluded all the more binding.[227] In the event, no such moves were made, but the meeting still allowed Cuno to address the Norman bishops on the subject of the emperor and his anti-pope.

After the council of Reims of 1119, Cuno continued to act as legate for France and Normandy and in 1120 summoned a further council to Beauvais. Henry now reverted to previous form, probably because it was not the pope who would preside over the council, or perhaps because of the political embarrassments of the previous year. And so, once again, the archbishop of Rouen and the other Norman bishops and abbots did not attend. The council decided that they should be excommunicated as a result, but the intervention of Archbishop Thurstan of York resulted in the sentence being reduced. Henry then met with Cuno. Their first interview was stormy. A second, which took place at Gisors just before Henry crossed to England, was friendlier. Henry thanked the legate for coming,

> and after a long conversation about God, Holy Church, and matters of busi-
> ness and mirth, commended to him his bishops and abbots. He also gave pre-
> sents to him and almost all who were with him. The legate hinted, intimated,
> and urged that [Henry] should act in the archbishop's case in such a way as
> to secure the pope's gratitude. When he had promised to do so, the legate
> blessed him, commended him to God for his coming crossing, and with a kiss
> of friendship departed.[228]

Henry thus placated the legate, proving that it was possible to get away with frustrating his attempts to make Norman prelates attend the councils he held.

But Cuno *had* been allowed to address a council in Normandy, albeit one held under Henry's auspices. The same courtesy was extended to his successor, Matthew of Albano. He presided over a council held in October 1128 at Rouen, the timing owing in part to the lengthy illness of Archbishop Geoffrey of Rouen (who would die a month later), which had prevented the archbishop holding councils on his own initiative – or so at least Orderic wrote. But the timing of the council might also have owed something to the untimely demise of William Clito, which would prevent any further possibility of Henry's claim to the duchy being questioned by the French bishops who attended with the cardinal. Orderic

---

[227] Suggested by Green, *Henry*, p. 144.
[228] Orderic, vi. 162.

also explicitly stated that the council was assembled 'by the king's command', so it would have provided a further demonstration of the royal duke's place at the head of the ecclesiastical hierarchy in Normandy to the legate and the others present with him. Orderic tells us that they included 'Geoffrey, bishop of Chartres, Joscelin the Red, bishop of Soissons, and all the bishops of Normandy: Richard of Bayeux, Ouen of Evreux, Turgis of Avranches, John of Lisieux, Richard of Coutances, and John of Sées. Many abbots also were present: Roger of Fécamp, William of Jumièges, Rainfrid of Saint-Ouen, Warin of Saint-Evroult, Philip of Saint-Taurin, Alan, abbot elect of Saint-Wandrille, and a number of others.' The assembled body heard the reforming decrees promulgated by Pope Honorius on clerical marriage, pluralism, and other matters, but none of these issues was novel, and none threatened Henry's position. There might also have been some attempt by the Norman bishops to impose additional burdens on the Norman abbots, or else Orderic had been concerned that would be the case, as he remarked that 'King Henry was present as their protector, and did not allow any burdens to be imposed on them by the bishops'.[229]

Nonetheless, despite this apparently effective control, some Norman or Anglo-Norman prelates did break the duke's embargo and, worse, petition the pope for help against their own prince. When this happened, which it did only very rarely, the churchman concerned met with a hostile response. Thus, in around 1060 Robert of Grandmesnil, abbot of Saint-Evroult, was exiled from Normandy. We are told by Orderic Vitalis that he had made scurrilous remarks about the duke to his prior (and thus committed *lèse majesté*), that the prior had informed the duke, and that William had taken offence. Robert was deposed and a new abbot was installed at the duke's command.[230] Robert, having heard this news, travelled to Rome to set his complaint before the pope and received a favourable hearing. He then returned to Normandy with papal letters and in the company of two papal legates, and set out for the duke's court which was apparently meeting at Lillebonne.

When the duke heard that Abbot Robert was approaching in the company of papal legates to claim the abbacy of Saint-Evroult and charge the duke's candidate, Osbern, with usurpation of his rights, he flew into a violent rage, declaring that he was ready to receive legates of the pope, their common father, in matters touching the Christian faith, but that if any monk from his duchy dared to bring a plea against him he would ignore his cloth and hang him by his cowl from the top of the highest oak tree in the wood nearby.[231]

[229] Orderic, vi. 388–90; Hollister, *Henry*, p. 446.
[230] Orderic, ii. 90–2.
[231] Orderic, ii. 200; Bates, *Normandy*, p. 202.

Abbot Robert was advised by his friends at court to beat a hasty retreat, and he did so. It may be supposed that the legates retreated with him. But they did not then excommunicate William for his rejection of their mission, and there seems to have been no backlash. That was perhaps because in 1060 the pope needed the Normans of southern Italy as allies, but it might also have been because there was little that the pope could do against a strong duke when dealing with a minor cause like this one.

That was to remain the case throughout William's reign, but circumstances had changed by the time Henry I came to the throne. In 1100, Archbishop Anselm, freshly returned from exile, refused to consecrate the bishops that Henry had elected to fill vacant English dioceses as a result of the papal prohibition on lay investiture. He was subsequently exiled, went to the curia, and set the issues before the pope. He returned to the north of France in 1105, but this time when word of his coming reached Henry, the king did not threaten the archbishop with corporal punishment, but rather reopened negotiations and found a way to settle the issues in dispute.[232] Henry's willingness to compromise might have been due to the delicate political situation at the time, except for the fact that he backed down again when faced with a similar threat in 1121. This was the last act in a drama that concerned the primacy of Canterbury over York. Archbishop Thurstan of York had refused to acknowledge this primacy, and despite Henry's prohibition had referred the matter to Pope Paschal. He had then allowed himself to be consecrated by Pope Calixtus II at Reims in 1119, which again Henry had expressly prohibited.[233] When Henry heard of Thurstan's disobedience, he refused to allow him to return to York. Henry's meeting with the pope after the council did not end with a settlement so far as this matter was concerned, and nor did the efforts of Archbishop Geoffrey of Rouen who acted as a papal judge delegate in 1119–20.[234] Moreover, after Henry returned to England in November 1120 he confiscated Thurstan's archiepiscopal estates. It was only at the beginning of 1121 that Thurstan was recalled. The cessation of hostilities was perhaps due to Thurstan's work at the curia on Henry's behalf in the interval, but it might also have been the result of the pope's threat to place England under an interdict should Thurstan's exile continue.[235]

---

[232] Southern, *Saint Anselm*, pp. 302–4; Hollister, *Henry*, pp. 191–8; Green, *Henry*, pp. 81, 86, 87–8.

[233] Henry had also forbidden the bishops from bringing any litigation before the pope: Eadmer, *HN*, p. 257; Hugh the Chanter, *The History of the Church of York*, pp. 118–20; Orderic, vi. 252.

[234] D. Spear, 'The double display of St Romanus of Rouen in 1124', in *Henry I and the Anglo-Norman World: Studies in Memory of C. Warren Hollister*, ed. D. F. Fleming and J. M. Pope (Woodbridge, 2007), p. 125.

[235] Hugh the Chanter, *The History of the Church of York*, pp. 172–4; Hollister, *Henry*, p. 272; Green, *Henry*, pp. 160–1.

The dukes thus reacted sternly against those who ignored their prohibition on unlicensed communication with the papacy, especially if they challenged or disobeyed their own decisions or commands, even if Henry I at least seems to have been prepared to back down rather than face serious ecclesiastical sanctions. But the dukes were not the only parties whose authority was threatened by papal interventions in the duchy. The archbishops of Canterbury saw such interventions, particularly the appointment of legates for England, as an infringement of their authority,[236] and it is likely that the archbishops of Rouen thought similarly where Normandy was concerned – hence Archbishop William's opposition to the primacy of Lyon. Moreover, Norman clergymen do not seem to have been especially keen to travel to Rome to petition the pope, perhaps because of the risk of harassment as they travelled through both France and Italy.[237] And even if they did go, appeals to the curia were still 'faltering and experimental', with hearings muddled by litigants' economies with the truth and the popes' own ignorance of local circumstances.[238] There could be no guarantee in such circumstances of obtaining the 'right' decision.

Table 2 lists all known (by me) appeals, petitions, and privileges made to, or obtained from, the popes by Norman beneficiaries from c. 1000 down to 1144. Several of them have been mentioned already, in part because the number of examples is limited, but when looking at them in the round some additional points suggest themselves. First, churchmen were more likely to seek a papal privilege if the pope was nearby. Geoffrey of Coutances, Lanfranc, and Odo of Bayeux were all on other business in Italy when they gained their privileges for Coutances, Caen, and Bayeux, respectively. Bishop Ouen of Evreux gained his privilege in 1126 when he was at Rome in the company of his brother Archbishop Thurstan, who had gone there as part of his continuing battle over Canterbury's primacy.[239] The three privileges obtained in 1131 were all acquired while the pope was in the north of France, during or shortly after his meetings with Henry I at Chartres and Rouen. The opportunity provided by the pope's proximity was thus seized by some, particularly those responsible for newly founded convents.

Secondly, a number of the privileges that were obtained seem to have been

[236] *Letters of St Anselm*, no. 214; Malmesbury, *GP*, i. 204–6; Brett, *English Church*, pp. 35–6, 39–40, 42.
[237] Gregory VII had noted that the Norman bishops had blamed their absences from legatine councils on their fear of travelling through France (Cowdrey, *Register of Pope Gregory VII*, pp. 405–6), while c. 1050 Abbot John of Fécamp could remark how dangerous it was for Normans to cross Italy (*PL*. 143, cols. 797–80).
[238] Brett, *English Church*, p. 56.
[239] Hugh the Chanter, *The History of the Church of York*, p. 208, also noted in Spear, 'The double display of St Romanus', p. 125.

Table 2 Papal interventions in Normandy, 1000–1144

Date	Petitioner/beneficiary	Reason
1016 (perhaps)	Monks of Fécamp	To obtain a privilege that placed the abbey under apostolic protection and reserved cases of excommunication to the Holy See. Possibly inauthentic.[a]
1023	Monks of Saint-Vaast and/or monks of Jumièges	Papal confirmation of an exchange of lands between the two houses, also confirmed by Duke Richard II.[b]
1050	Geoffrey of Coutances	Privilege allowing the transfer of canons from Rouen to Coutances, most likely obtained during his attendance at the Roman synod of 1050, probably on the way to or from his fund-raising trip around southern Italy.[c]
c. 1050	Abbot John of Fécamp	Unknown, but seems to have subsequently acted as a papal legate in southern Italy.[d]
c. 1066	Lanfranc	Privilege for Saint-Etienne of Caen exempting the abbey from the jurisdiction of the bishops of Bayeux.[e]
1090	Monks of Fécamp	Appeal to the pope claiming an exemption from the interdict that Archbishop William of Rouen had imposed on the duchy following Robert Curthose's seizure of his castle at Gisors. The claim was based on the purported privilege of 1016, which was subsequently confirmed in 1103.[f]
1090	Abbot Anselm of Le Bec	Request to Urban II (by letter) to place Le Bec under his protection.[g]
1092	Abbot Fulk of Saint-Pierre-sur-Dives (unjustly deposed)	Goes to Rome as an exile, presumably to appeal his deposition, remains a monk at Montecassino until his return with papal letters c. 1099 and recovered his abbey.[h]

Notes

[a] *Regesta pontificum Romanorum*, ed. P. Jaffé and G. Wattenbach (Leipzig, 1885–88), no. 4056; discussed by J.-F. Lemarignier, *Étude sur les privileges d'exemption et de juridiction ecclésiastique des abbayes normandes depuis les origines jusqu'en 1140* (Paris, 1937), pp. 37–8 and ns. 37–38, p. 192.

[b] *Acta pontificum Romanorum inedita*, ed. J. von Pflugk-Harttung (Tübingen and Stuttgart, 1881–86), i. 10–11 (no. 13) with the duke's assent to the transfer at *RADN*, no. 26.

[c] *GC*, xi. Instr. cols. 219–20.

[d] *PL*. 143, cols. 797–80. The letter is partly translated in Loud, *The Age of Robert Guiscard*, p. 115. See also Cowdrey, *Lanfranc*, p. 31.

[e] *PL*, 146, cols. 1339–41. The text has no date. Gregory VII referred to the privilege in a letter of 1074 (Cowdrey, *Register of Pope Gregory VII*, p. 74). It is discussed in Lemarignier, *Privileges*, pp. 143–6.

[f] See David, *Robert Curthose*, pp. 82, 88–9; Lemarignier, *Privileges*, pp. 193–6; *Acta inedita*, pp. 75–6, no. 83.

[g] *Letters of St Anselm*, no. 126.

[h] Orderic, iii. 168 and n. 3; v. 212 and n. 3.

Date	Petitioner/beneficiary	Reason
1096	Bishop Odo of Bayeux	Protection for the possessions of the cathedral at Bayeux under penalty of papal anathema.[i]
1103 at Rome	Clergy and people of Bayeux	Appeal against the election and imposition of Turold of Envermeu.
1126 at Rome	Bishop Ouen of Evreux	Confirmation to St Mary of Evreux (the cathedral) of all its possessions including specifically ecclesiastical property at Vernon and Nonancourt.[j]
1127 at Le Mans	Monks of Marmoutier at Bellême	Bishop Gerard of Angoulême, the papal legate, confirms a settlement between the monks and Bishop John of Sées.[k]
1131 at Chartres	Augustinian canons of Sainte-Barbe-en-Auge	Confirmation of and protection for the possessions given to the canons by Bishop John of Lisieux and Henry I, whether in England or Normandy, under penalty of excommunication.
1131 at Etampes	Notre-Dame-du-Désert	Confirmation of property in Normandy.[l]
1131 at Blois	Archbishop Hugh of Rouen	Confirmation of archiepiscopal rights.[m]
1132	Hospital of St John Falaise	Letters from Innocent II corroborating grants to the hospital are noted in Henry I's confirmation.[n] They were most probably obtained during the papal meetings of 1131.
1137 at Viterbo	Bishop John of Sées	Confirmation of an agreement made by King Henry I, with the monks of Sées and William Talvas.[o]
1139	Monks of Eu	Confirmation of property in Normandy.[p]
1140 at Rome	Monks of Fécamp	Confirmation of freedom from archbishop and restatement of its subjection to Rome alone.[q]
1140 × 1143	Monks of Le Bec at Beaumont-le-Roger	Confirmation of property in Normandy.
1142 at Rome	Archbishop Hugh of Rouen and Bishop Philip of Bayeux	Licence to excommunicate oppressors of the church of Bayeux.[r]

[i] *Papsturkunden*, pp. 55–6 (no. 3).
[j] *Papsturkunden*, pp. 60–1 (no. 6).
[k] *Papsturkunden*, no. 7. The dispute related to a series of suits that involved William the Bastard and Henry I and which are discussed below, Chapter 8, pp. 470–3.
[l] *Papsturkunden*, pp. 65–6 (no. 9).
[m] AD Seine-Maritime, G 1115; Ctl. Rouen, fos. 32r–33v (no. xix).
[n] *Regesta*, ii. 376–7 (no. cclxvi) = no. 1742.
[o] *Papsturkunden*, pp. 67–9 (no. 12).
[p] AD Seine-Maritime, 6 H 4; *Acta inedita*, no. 178.
[q] *Papsturkunden*, pp. 69–70 (no. 13).
[r] *Papsturkunden*, pp. 70–1 (no. 14).

Date	Petitioner/beneficiary	Reason
1142 at Rome	Monks of Mortemer	Confirmation of property in Normandy.[s]
1142 at Rome	Bishop Rotrou of Evreux	Confirmation to St Mary of Evreux (the cathedral) of all its possessions including specifically ecclesiastical property at Vernon, Nonancourt, and Verneuil.[t] And also a privilege regarding the reconstruction of the cathedral, most likely obtained at this same time.[u]
1142 at Rome	Monks of Saint-Wandrille	Confirmation of property in Normandy.[v]
1143 at Rome	Monks of Le Bec	Confirmation of Beaumont-le-Roger and its possessions to the monks of Le Bec.[w]
1144 at Rome	Monks of Fécamp	Protection regarding rights of ordination and over dependencies.[x]
1144 at Rome	Monks of Le Bec	Confirmation and protection of lands in Normandy and England.[y]

[s] *Papsturkunden*, pp. 71–2 (no. 15)
[t] *Papsturkunden*, pp. 72–4 (no. 16).
[u] *Papsturkunden*, p. 79 (no. 18).
[v] *Papsturkunden*, pp. 74–9 (no. 17); Lot, *Saint-Wandrille*, no. 72.
[w] *Ctl. Beaumont-le-Roger*, no. 49.
[x] *Papsturkunden*, pp. 80–2 (no. 21).
[y] *Papsturkunden*, p. 82 (no. 22).

concerned to address a particular issue that could not be otherwise dealt with, even by a strong duke. Thus the bulls acquired by the monks of Fécamp, Caen, and Bellême were about establishing exemptions from episcopal jurisdiction, which the dukes could not provide, even though they might be seen as the principal line of defence against such demands.[240] Similarly, while Henry I might grant property at Vernon, Nonancourt, and Verneuil to the bishops of Evreux, and while both the royal duke and the bishop would expect those acts to guarantee possession if it were disputed within the duchy, neither could have been quite so sure that Henry's grant and seal would be respected by the French lords across the Avre, especially the lords of Châteauneuf-en-Thymerais, from whom Nonancourt and

---

[240] The anonymous writer of *De libertate Beccensi abbatie* saw Henry I as the defender of the abbey's liberties against the claims of the bishop of Lisieux and archbishop of Rouen. As noted above, Henry had also stepped in to defend four abbeys from the demands of Archbishop Hugh of Rouen in 1131. Equally, while the duke could not grant such exemptions, his court could find that they already existed, as with the dispute between the canons of Bellême and the bishop of Sées c. 1070 × 1079 (*Regesta: William*, no. 29, and see below, Chapter 8, p. 470).

Verneuil had been taken. Across the Avre, then, the property concerned was better protected by a papal privilege. In such cases, therefore, the papal privileges did not supplement Henry's acts, but complemented them.

It was only after 1135 that Norman prelates began to obtain papal protections and confirmations that do seem to have overlapped with the duke's authority. It is possible that the trend was foreshadowed by the protections for Le Bec and Bayeux acquired during the 1090s, although the latter at least was more likely acquired as a result of Bishop Odo's proximity to the pope as he travelled with Curthose to Sicily, and because of the hostility between Bishop Odo and William Rufus, at that time ruling Normandy in his brother's place, which might have caused Odo to fear what might happen to his church's possessions in his absence. Stephen's reign thus appears to be something of a turning point, when Norman prelates, concerned about a lack of ducal protection and justice, turned to the pope to fill the vacuum. That scenario is certainly suggested by the significant increase in petitions for papal protections made after Henry's death in 1135, and particularly after Stephen's imprisonment in 1141, including a licence to excommunicate those who had oppressed the church of Bayeux which was obtained in 1142.

There was to be no looking back. Stephen's reign coincided with an increase in the reach of the pope's authority and even Henry II could not turn back the clock, although even then it is difficult to maintain that traffic to and from Rome had become a matter of routine. The first papal bull procured by the monks of Montebourg was apparently obtained from Adrian IV, with subsequent privileges from Innocent III and Alexander IV. The monks of Jumièges seem not to have approached a pope between 1023 and 1147, when they obtained a privilege from Eugenius III which was followed by another from Adrian IV in 1156.[241] Only the archbishops of Rouen seem to have reached out to the popes on anything like a regular basis. The first papal confirmation for Rouen preserved in cartulary, which also survives in the original, was issued by Innocent II in 1131.[242] This was followed by a privilege issued by Eugenius III and one by Adrian IV.[243] Privileges from subsequent popes, Alexander III, Celestine III, and Innocent III, for example, survive in greater number. This general picture for Normandy stands in contrast with that presented, for example, by the activities of the monks of La Sainte-Trinité at Vendôme. The cartulary of that house preserves a run of papal privileges beginning with documents issued by Pope Clement II in the middle of the eleventh century.[244] That does not mean that Normans did not recognize the authority

---

[241] *Jumièges*, nos. 68 and 77.

[242] AD Seine-Maritime, G 1115; Ctl. Rouen, fos. 32r–33v (no. xix).

[243] Ctl. Rouen, fos. 33v–36v (nos. xx, xxi).

[244] For example, *Ctl. Vendôme*, i. 61–70 (no. 36), 139–45 (no. 76), 193–4 (no. 106), 194–200

of the papacy. For Orderic, when he wrote *c.* 1130 of the arrest of Bishop Odo of Bayeux, to be pope was 'to have authority … over the Latins and all the peoples of the earth'.[245] It was simply that, for the most part, Norman prelates had no need of the popes. The duke could give them what they wanted without the need to travel to and from the distant curia, at risk of incurring ducal displeasure or of coming away empty-handed.

This picture also suggests that it was likely, rather than merely possible, that the view of the popes advanced by the writer known as the Norman Anonymous was one that was widely recognized and widely held in the duchy at the beginning of the twelfth century.[246] It is Tract 28, most likely written between 1102 and 1107, that most clearly reveals the Anonymous's views about, and reception of, papal demands and policies. He complained about the popes' demands that the archbishops travel to Rome to attend the curia. He bewailed the popes' grants of privileges exempting monasteries from episcopal authority. A bishop should be permitted to govern the abbots within his diocese and take a profession from them, so that the abbeys should not then rise up against their father.[247] He complained, too, about the unjust excommunication of bishops and developed a theory which established all bishops as equals, all of them deriving their power

---

(no. 107), 250–2 (no. 144), 255–9 (no. 146), 284–90 (no. 164), 290–2 (no. 165, 310–11 (no. 180), 377–9 (no. 238), 398–402 (no. 252).

[245] Orderic, iv. 40. Book VII is dated at p. xix.

[246] In total, the Norman Anonymous wrote thirty-one tracts, of varying length, on a number of issues that were relevant to him and his ideas regarding the functioning of the Church. They included a tract on the question of whether the pope should be judged (Tract 1), one which undermined Rome's claims for supremacy in the Church (Tract 12), and one which listed papal abuses (Tract 28). There is a tract that relates to the authority of the archbishops of Rouen and constitutes a defence to the claims of Lyon, and another that defended Archbishop William from accusations of disobedience which was probably related to the lifting of his suspension by Archbishop Anselm in 1106 (Tracts 2 and 4). There is also a piece aimed against the monks of Fécamp who sought exemption from archiepiscopal authority, as noted above (Tract 27). The supposed bull of 1016, also mentioned above, was probably fabricated as part of this campaign. He also discussed such issues as the proper punishments to be delivered in ecclesiastical courts, clerical marriage, and the defrocking of priests. For the Norman Anonymous see G. Williams, *The Norman Anonymous: Towards the Identification and Evaluation of the So-Called Anonymous of York* (Cambridge, MA, 1951). The Latin text of the various tracts that make up the Anonymous's work, as well as a detailed commentary on each, are now available online at <http://normananonymous.org/ENAP/>. Parts of three of the tracts have been translated into English in *English Historical Documents, II. 1042–1189*, ed. and trans. D. C. Douglas and G. W. Greenaway (London, 1953), pp. 675–7 (no. 113) and Barlow, *The English Church 1066–1154*, p. 294.

[247] Williams, *Anonymous*, pp. 136–7; J. R. Ginther, 'Between *plena caritas* and *plenitudo legis*: the ecclesiology of the Norman Anonymous', *HSJ*, 22 (2012), 157.

from Peter and thus from Christ.[248] Warming to his theme, he argued that bishops must live an apostolic life, and thus act with humility and charity,[249] which led him to attack the wealth and judicial presumption of the papacy and to put limits on the pope's authority: 'only insofar as he is Christ-like in his injunctions is the pope authoritative, and only as he refrains from giving instructions is he Apostolic!'[250] As a result, when a pope sought to judge the world, he went beyond his powers and thus became a sinner and a member of Satan and should not be obeyed.[251] Indeed, as long as a bishop obeyed Christ, he need not fear the pope. Then, finally, he returned to the theme of an earlier piece, Tract 24.

Tract 24 constitutes an investigation into Christian kingship and effectively a defence of the rights of kings against the papacy. Through their anointing, kings became another Christ and, through grace, took on part of the character of Christ himself. They became Christ the king, which the Norman Anonymous likened to Christ's divine nature. In contrast, priests were members of Christ's priesthood, which was linked with his human nature. The Anonymous argued that as a result kings held a superior position to anointed priests within the Christian community, using authorities from both Old and New Testaments as well as the prayers used when bishops and kings were consecrated.[252] He went on to argue that it was consequently not improper for a king to call and preside over Church councils, or to give the bishops the ring and staff that symbolized their rule. In addition, he argued that the exclusion of the king from the government of the Church would lead to division, desolation, and lack of protection.[253]

* * * * * *

The Church was a double-edged sword. It had the potential to unite the duchy under the dukes' rule, but also to undermine that rule and to cause divisions among the dukes' subjects that could well tear the duchy apart. To ensure that they gained the benefits but did not suffer the penalties, the dukes had to overcome – or be made to appear to have overcome – what must have looked like insuperable obstacles. Firstly, they had to ensure that they acted in accordance with Christian concepts of rulership, preferably to a greater degree than the Frankish lords who surrounded them. Secondly, they had to convince the Scandinavian element of

---

[248] Williams, *Anonymous*, pp. 132–3.
[249] Williams, *Anonymous*, pp. 134–5, 140.
[250] Williams, *Anonymous*, p. 140.
[251] Williams, *Anonymous*, pp. 137, 141.
[252] Williams, *Anonymous*, p. 132.
[253] Hugh a monk of Benoit-sur-Loire wrote in a similar vein, and addressed his treatise to Henry. He wrote that he had composed his treatise in answer to those who sought to separate royal and priestly dignity (Green, *Henry*, p. 257).

the population to be baptized and to live in an ostensibly Christian manner. To achieve that, the dukes had to find a way to take Christianity out of the hands of the Franks by making their predecessors both the benefactors of a divine plan and the paragons of Christian virtue. Fortunately for Richard II, he could call on the services of Dudo of Saint-Quentin whose work demonstrated that God had acted to support the Normans and to defeat the Franks who opposed them at every turn, thereby providing incontrovertible evidence that ownership of Christianity had been transferred from the perfidious Franks to the virtuous Normans. No wonder that the Norman battle cry dispensed with an appeal to a saintly intercessor and went straight to the top: 'God's help', rather than 'Saint Denis'! Of course, it helped that by the time Dudo wrote, Norman ownership of Christianity was manifested in the person of Archbishop Robert of Rouen, whose wealth and splendour revealed just what God could do for those who subscribed to His teachings.[254] But still, the conversion of the Scandinavian settlers took time, and the reconstruction of the institutions of the Norman Church took even longer, so that it was not until the beginning of the second half of the eleventh century that the duchy was fully part of the Latin Church once again. That did not, of course, prevent the Normans, with all the zealotry of the recently converted, from criticizing the practices of Anglo-Saxon England or, worse, those found in Wales after the Conquest of 1066.

With the Church under their control, the Norman dukes gained an institution that could add lustre and prestige to their persons and office. The bishops and priests would pray for the duke, and for his safety and salvation. Their *laudes*, liturgies, and sermons saw the dukes exalted, and their ambitions praised and promulgated. Spiritual weapons such as interdict and excommunication could be launched against their enemies, while even those who silently opposed the dukes might be made to fear damnation for their offence. It was not the case, then, that 'the Norman community was the warrior class alone', whether in the 1040s or at any time after 989.[255] The Norman Church and its personnel were also responsible for the creation and maintenance of that community. But to ensure that the dukes and their prelates all sang from the same hymn sheet, and thus that the community remained united, the dukes had to ensure that they gained and maintained control over elections. And this they did, by ensuring that they chose good-quality candidates, sometimes of international renown. Where such candidates were chosen, the dukes got their way, even after the prohibition on investiture. Only when Robert Curthose supported highly contentious nominations was there a backlash.

---

[254] See also the reception of Otto of Bamberg by the Pomeranians in the 1120s: Bartlett, 'The conversion of a pagan society', 198–9.
[255] Searle, *PK*, p. 207.

The ostentatious piety of the dukes, evidenced in their patronage of monasteries within and without their duchy, including Marmoutier and Cluny, as well as the strength of their rule and justice within Normandy, allowed them to withstand the attempts of popes and papal legates to gain a foothold in their dominions – at least until *c.* 1141. Despite the clamour produced by the investiture contest, and despite the growing bureaucracy that surrounded the popes and which attempted to put their will into effect, papal interventions in Normandy were few and far between. They occurred because, on occasion, the dukes needed the pope to legitimize their actions, or because foreign rivals saw an opportunity to cause diplomatic embarrassment, or simply because the dukes' power was not unlimited – as the dukes themselves acknowledged. Even more rarely, papal interventions undermined the dukes' authority, but that does not seem to have been the intention. With the contest between empire and papacy between 1074 and 1122, the presence of Normans in Apulia and Sicily, and the schism of 1130, the popes did not want to alienate the dukes any more than the dukes wanted to earn the hostility of the popes. Both sides generally compromised, even if it meant disappointing the papal legates who had promoted or defended papal ideals the most vociferously. But the popes had still not developed their power to its full potential, and besides, as was the case with the French kings, Norman prelates did not need to appeal to the pope for protection and liberty. The power of the dukes in their duchy was such that they could do more for the Church than the popes could, and as they had a better command of the facts, their justice was not only more effective but also more just. And so, before the reign of Stephen, the popes made little headway in Normandy and, despite their strictures and prohibitions, the dukes enjoyed unrivalled control of their Church.

CHAPTER 5

Sovereigns, Styles, and Scribes

ALTHOUGH Duke Richard I acknowledged Hugh Capet as his lord (*senior*) in 968, and although Hugh's father had supported Richard's rule during the 940s and 950s, all the sources at our disposal indicate that from *c.* 945 until 1144 the dukes ruled Normandy without reference to the kings of the French. But although they did not recognize the kings' authority within their duchy, the dukes did not deny that Normandy lay within their kingdom. Indeed, the dukes seem often to have involved the kings in the arrangements made for their successions, presumably to make them more secure, which in itself was an acknowledgement of royal authority over their land. Furthermore, on occasion, as during the reign of Richard II, they sent contingents to serve in royal armies. As such actions tended to promote the dukes' power and prestige to a wide Frankish audience, they might have performed them simply to enhance their standing among their peers, but it is equally possible that such service was an obligation that resulted from the oaths of fidelity (not necessarily homage) that the dukes continued to swear to successive French monarchs down to the 1060s – although both Dudo of Saint-Quentin and the anonymous author of the *Breuis relatio* argued that this was not the case.

A king's ability to demand service, or to take jurisdiction over a lawsuit, was not the automatic result of a tenth-, eleventh-, or early-twelfth-century oath of fidelity, however. To some extent, it depended on whether the land was held as a benefice or fief or owned as an alod.[1] That is why Dudo was so keen to imagine that Normandy was given to Rollo, after some negotiations, as an alod, and that is why the nature of the relationship established between Rollo and Charles the Simple at Saint-Clair-sur-Epte in 911 has been considered so often in histories of Normandy – although as we are entirely reliant on Dudo of Saint-Quentin's account of this meeting the conclusions that have been reached are necessarily tenuous and have depended on each historian's view of Dudo's reliability and intentions. The question is reconsidered below, in the first section of this chapter, where the focus is necessarily once again on Dudo's narrative and the trajectory of Franco-Norman relations depicted in it. The section then considers what we

---

[1] For a discussion of these terms, see below, Chapter 11, pp. 661–5.

know of the relationship between the kings of the French and the dukes up to and including the pre-Conquest rule of William the Bastard.

The diverse and divergent hints about the nature of those relationships found in the narratives have resulted in an equally diverse number of arguments and conclusions about them. But the different characterizations of a duke's relationship with his contemporary kings of the French need not be the result of the different agendas of the writers concerned, or of the different times in which they lived. With regard to relations between Henry I and William the Bastard, for example, their comments, whether intentionally or not, to some extent reflected the fact that William's relationship with that king changed throughout his reign. Oaths of fidelity were not immutable. They could be dissolved and then remade as circumstances suggested and for so long as both of the parties were willing to allow it. Flodoard's *Annals* reveal Frankish lords breaking their oaths of fidelity on a regular basis, seemingly without garnering much in the way of opprobrium, although there were rules that men were supposed to follow when acting thus. For example, Charlemagne stated that a man should not abandon his lord unless his lord sought to kill him; or assaulted him with a stave; or debauched his wife and daughter; or took away his alodial inheritance.[2] The so-called capitulary concerning freemen and vassals also set out a number of eventualities that would absolve a vassal from his fidelity to his lord:

in the first place, if the lord has wished to reduce him unjustly into servitude; in the second place, if he has taken counsel against his life; in the third place, if the lord has committed adultery with the wife of his vassal; in the fourth place, if he has wilfully attacked him with a drawn sword; in the fifth place, if the lord has been able to bring defence to his vassal after he has commended his hands to him and has not done so, it is allowed to the vassal to leave him.[3]

Fulbert of Chartres considered that the obligations of a *fidelis* were also those of a lord, so that he should protect and maintain his men.[4] If he failed to do so he would 'rightly be considered unfaithful', although what that would entail is not clear. In Raoul of Cambrai, the honest Bernier remains faithful to Raoul even though he is 'more villainous than Judas', because he had sworn fidelity to him. It is only after Raoul has murdered Bernier's mother and strikes him until he bleeds that he defies him.[5] But that was fiction, and in reality most vassals would have defied their lords long before that point had been reached.

---

[2] Nelson, 'Kingship and royal government', p. 425.
[3] *MGH, Capitularia*, i. 215 (ch. 8).
[4] Fulbert, *Letters*, pp. 90–2.
[5] Noted in C. B. Bouchard, *Strong of Body, Brave and Noble: Chivalry and Society in Medieval France* (London, 1998), p. 44.

Men certainly abandoned lords who failed to protect them. Herluin of Montreuil sought the assistance of Hugh the Great against Arnulf of Flanders, and when it was not forthcoming stated: 'Since you are not in the least eager to assist me in my need, as would be proper, it is right that you should not take offence if anyone else should come to my aid.'[6] That 'anyone else' was William Longsword, who assisted Herluin to recover his castle and then promised that he would strengthen it, provide men and supplies, and bring help should Arnulf attack again.[7] Around 1052, Geoffrey of Anjou told Geoffrey of Mayenne that he might 'renounce my lordship completely, as that of a vile and dishonoured lord' should he fail to come to his aid.[8] In 1091, Ralph of Tosny sought Robert Curthose's help against Count William of Evreux. The duke was unable to help him. His failure to protect his *fidelis* led to the loss of his fidelity as Ralph then turned to Curthose's rival, William Rufus, who *was* able to provide aid, sending Count Stephen of Aumale and Gerard of Gournay and others to lend Ralph their support and garrison his castles.[9] Such failures thus broke the bonds of fidelity, so that a man might terminate his allegiance, or transfer it to another, apparently without the need to take any formal action.[10] Such breaches occurred on a number of occasions during Duke William's reign.

But just because the dukes, sometimes intermittently, swore fidelity to the kings of the French, it did not follow that they would allow them to intervene in their duchy. Furthermore, that stance was effectively supported by the behaviour of the dukes' subjects and others who held land within the duchy. While they might obtain a ducal diploma for the property they held within Normandy, and while they might seek his justice, even 'foreign' beneficiaries such as the monks of Marmoutier or Chartres did not ask the kings of the French to do likewise. The role of beneficiary scribes and chroniclers in promoting the dukes' authority is particularly noticeable when it comes to the styles they deployed when addressing or describing them. Previously, historians have argued that the dukes adopted titles with the intention of emphasizing their own authority or of taking a particular place in the political hierarchy. For example, when discussing the use of the title 'dux' by Richard II, David Bates suggested that his 'assumption of the new title must be regarded as an attempt to push himself into a small elite of French territorial rulers'.[11] But Richard II did not so much assume the style 'dux' as have

---

[6] *Dudo*, p. 80.

[7] *Dudo*, p. 80.

[8] Poitiers, p. 52.

[9] Orderic, iv. 214.

[10] Tabuteau, *Transfers*, p. 55. See also Galbert of Bruges, *The Murder of Charles the Good*, trans. J. B. Ross (New York, 1959, reprinted 2005) p. 281.

[11] Bates, *Normandy*, p. 149.

it thrust upon him by the beneficiaries of his donations and confirmations. And those beneficiaries might also write of the dukes' 'regnum', or their rule over a people, or claim that they had been established as dukes by the grace of God rather than by the benevolence of the kings of the Franks. As these documents were only presented to the duke for authentication after they had been written, the dukes had little or no control over the use of any of the politically charged styles or statements contained in the text (it might have been a little different with regard to subscriptions, however). Down to 1106, at least, these were, 'individual utterances by individual minds'.[12] Nonetheless, such utterances say something about how a duke's subjects perceived his power. That is why they are discussed at length in the second part of this chapter.

The assumption that the dukes took titles for themselves, and that those titles were intended to reflect a particular rank in society, is one reason why historians such as John Le Patourel and C. Warren Hollister argued about whether the use of the style 'rex Anglorum' alone in the post-Conquest acts of William the Bastard and post-Tinchebray acts of Henry I reflected a qualitative change in the nature of the royal dukes' power over their duchy, and whether it was intended to suggest that they intended to make their duchy independent from the kingdom of France.[13] But while the styles adopted by, or awarded to, William the Bastard and Henry I can certainly help to untangle this knotty problem, they have to be used with caution. The conventions of the day have to be given due consideration; we must be wary of allowing individual voices to be drowned out by the roar of the royal writing office; and we must allow, too, for the effect of the mass of documents produced by that writing office on the practices of Norman beneficiary scribes. Nonetheless, there are some hints and clues about the relationship between the royal dukes and the French kings after 1066 in the wording of the ducal *acta*, and more, too, in the narratives and in the actions of the key players that they record. The examination of this issue comprises the third and last part of this chapter, which also offers a new view of the timing of Henry I's adoption of the title 'dux Normannorum'.

---

[12] T. Reuter, 'Whose race, whose ethnicity? Recent medievalists' discussions of identity', in *Medieval Polities and Modern Mentalities*, ed. J. L. Nelson (Cambridge, 2006), p. 101.

[13] C. W. Hollister, 'Normandy, France and the Anglo-Norman *regnum*', *Speculum*, 51 (1976), 202–42, reprinted in *MMI*, pp. 17–57; Le Patourel, *Norman Empire*; Le Patourel, 'Norman kings or Norman "king-dukes"?', in *Droit privé et institutions régionales: études historiques offertes à Jean Yver* (Paris, 1976), pp. 469–79. See also the response to these arguments found in D. Bates, 'Normandy and England after 1066', *EHR*, 104 (1989), 851–80.

Fideles *or* Vassals? *Monarchs and Myths, 911–1066*

The relationship between the dukes and the kings is likely to have begun with the acknowledgement by Rollo that he held Rouen and its hinterland by the gift of Charles the Simple. Dudo wrote that in 911, at Saint-Clair-sur-Epte, Rollo 'put his hands between the hands of the king (*manus suas misit inter manus regis*), which neither his father, nor his grandfather, nor his great-grandfather had done for any man. And so the king gave him his daughter, Gisla by name, to be the wife of that same duke, and he gave the specified territory from the river Epte to the sea as an alod and property (*alodum et fundum*).'[14]

Despite the fact that Dudo was not an eyewitness and was not writing his *De moribus* with the intention of recording what had actually happened, this passage has led to a great deal of debate. Jacques Flach argued strongly that it did not provide proof that Rollo had done homage to Charles the Simple in 911, and nor did it support the contention that Normandy had been conceded to him as a fief by King Charles. Ferdinand Lot, Auguste Dumas, and Henri Prentout lined up against him, arguing to the contrary that Rollo *was* a vassal, that he *had* performed homage on the banks of the Epte, and that he had in turn received Normandy as a fief.[15] In 1945, Jean-François Lemarignier picked over the evidence again and, noting the emphasis placed on peace by the chroniclers, concluded that Rollo and his successors had performed a *hommage de paix*.[16] This was a species of homage that had developed by the thirteenth century and which was intended to restore lord and man to peace after, for example, a murder or feud.[17] But this form of homage, at least as set out in the *Très ancien coutumier*, did not provide a template for international relations.[18] Furthermore, the act of homage was still required, providing a sense of hierarchy which is entirely lacking from the narratives (and, indeed, from Lemarignier's own interpretation of *hommage de paix*). Nonetheless, as some of the forms of such homage (although not the Norman one) made a clear distinction between it and the more usual *hommage vassalique*, Lemarignier could argue that, although the dukes of the Normans did homage to the kings of the Franks, their homage did not constitute 'the clear-cut subordina-

---

[14] Dudo, p. 169; *Dudo*, p. 49. See above, Chapter 1, p. 47.

[15] Summed up by J.-F. Lemarignier, *Recherches sur l'hommage en marche et les frontières féodales* (Lille, 1945), pp. 79–80.

[16] Lemarignier, *Hommage en marche*, pp. 79–85.

[17] Lemarignier, *Hommage en marche*, p. 82.

[18] The form of the oath required a man to place his hands within those of his lord and to say 'I become your man, and bring to you faith against all others, saving fidelity to the duke of Normandy' (*TAC*, ii. 94–5 (ch. 27); cited by Lemarignier, *Hommage en marche*, p. 82, n. 34).

tion or the full range of feudal obligations that were involved in the more common *hommage vassalique*.[19] Lemarignier's anachronistic view has continued to hold sway,[20] although it has become increasingly fragile as a result of our developing understanding of the sorts of medieval rites and symbolism that Dudo employed in his narrative. For example, Susan Reynolds has noted that Fulk IV of Anjou 'did not intend to make himself the vassal – in any sense – of the abbot of Holy Trinity, Vendôme, when he swore faith to him, putting his hands in the abbot's hands, as secular custom required. He was simply making peace and promising not to bully the abbey anymore.'[21] That remark clearly impacts any interpretation of what Dudo had Rollo perform at Saint-Clair-sur-Epte. Reynold's view of the matter was that Dudo's narrative was simply intended to demonstrate that Rollo understood that his lands lay within Charles's kingdom.[22]

Of course, the nature of Rollo's oath does not really matter, at least so far as Normandy is concerned. Dudo's mise en scène was intended simply to show that Rollo did whatever his contemporaries would have expected the recipient of a royal grant to do, albeit that he had Rollo baulk when it came to kissing the royal foot. He also knew that, no matter how he depicted them – and, indeed, no matter how they were depicted in Flodoard's *Annals* – Rollo's actions, and those of his successor William Longsword, too, would not set a precedent for his successors to follow. William Longsword might have committed himself (*se commisit*) to Louis IV on a number of occasions, and might even have forged a close personal relationship with the monarch, but that did not matter either. For by the time Dudo was writing *c.* 1015 the oaths they had sworn, and the relationship they symbolized, were history. By then, the kings of the Franks had acknowledged, at least in Dudo's book, that the dukes of the Normans owed neither homage nor service for the duchy which they owned, rather than held, as an alod and by right of inheritance. Indeed, the *De moribus* was most likely written in part to explain and justify why that was the case.

As discussed above, Richard I's minority saw factions form within Normandy.

---

[19] As paraphrased by Hollister, '*Regnum*', pp. 18–19. See also ns. 5 and 6 for references to relevant parts of Lemarignier's *Hommage en marche*.

[20] As noted by J. Gillingham, 'Doing homage to the king of France', in *Henry II: New Interpretations*, ed. C. Harper-Bill and N. Vincent (Woodbridge, 2007), p. 65 and citing G. Koziol, *Begging Pardon and Favor: Ritual and Political Order in Early Medieval France* (Ithaca, NY and London, 1992), pp. 6, 155. It should be noted that, although he was right about the nature of the alliances created, Lemarignier's decision to see them as early examples of *hommage de paix* was anachronistic and ill-founded, as discussed below, *infra*, p. 265.

[21] S. Reynolds, *Fiefs and Vassals: The Medieval Evidence Reinterpreted* (Oxford, 1994), p. 128 and n. 41.

[22] Reynolds, *Fiefs*, p. 137.

Flodoard of Reims noted that some Normans sided with Louis while others allied with Duke Hugh. There were other divisions, too. Flodoard reported that there was a pagan reaction in 942, from which Richard had to be saved by both the king and Hugh the Great.[23] Dudo mentioned none of this. Instead, he had Richard abducted from Normandy by the king and held hostage at Laon, only to be smuggled to the safety of Coucy by his tutor. The king's bad faith led directly to the first dénoument of Dudo's story. In 945, King Louis and his Frankified Northmen from Rouen came face-to-face with the 'Dacian' Harold and his less-well-assimilated forces on the banks of the river Dives. Louis was captured after the unscheduled skirmish that ensued, and the relationship between the king and the teenage duke was transformed.[24]

Louis's captivity, which Dudo saw as the result of his double-dealing and his complicity in the murder of William Longsword, was followed by his release into the custody of Hugh the Great, accompanied by a staged scene of reconciliation on the banks of the river Epte. There, Louis 'placed his hand over the casket with the relics, and he guaranteed to the boy Richard in his own words the kingdom (*regnum*) which Rollo had won for himself by might and power, and by arms and battles. He himself, and all the venerable bishops, counts and abbots and the princes of Francia's realm, [gave it] to the innocent boy Richard to have and to hold, and he and his successors are to render service to none but God.'[25] The king, however, also promised that he would help Richard to defend his 'kingdom (*regnum*)'. Thus Richard was to hold Normandy without service, and with some considerable degree of autonomy, as a result of the king's own duplicity.

Dudo repeated what may be taken to have been the Norman position – the defence of which was one of the intentions behind his work – on several occasions. He wrote of Richard, 'governing the realm of Normandy like a king subject to none but God alone'.[26] Lothair writes to him: 'Will you never bow the neck to anyone? Will you not recognise me as king of the Franks?'[27] Jumièges made the same point here, but in a way that once again condensed and clarified Dudo's work: 'Duke, how long are you going to refuse to pay the service you owe me? Do you not know that I am the king of the Franks, to whom you should give military service and whose orders and decisions you should never contravene?'[28] Later,

---

[23] *Flodoard*, p. 38.

[24] *Flodoard*, p. 42; *Dudo*, pp. 115–19.

[25] *Dudo*, p. 121. Henry of Huntingdon elaborated the terms of the treaty, stating that the dukes should come armed to their meetings with the French kings, but that the kings were not allowed to have even a small knife on them (Huntingdon, p. 390).

[26] *Dudo*, p. 124.

[27] *Dudo*, p. 144.

[28] Jumièges, ii. 122.

Dudo had Count Theobald of Chartres ask King Lothair, 'Is [Richard] to hold the Norman kingdom without your generous permission?'[29]

According to Dudo, Theobald's scheming led directly to the king's invasion of the duchy and capture of Evreux, in breach of the agreement sworn in 945, and to Richard's use of pagan Northmen to ravage France.[30] The hostilities were finally ended at another meeting on the Epte where the king and his magnates 'swore the Norman realm to Richard and to his posterity so that neither himself nor anyone with his encouragement would do the least damage to that realm. And when the peace-making assembly had been concluded and the king and Duke Richard had been allied (*fœderatisque rege et duce Ricardo*), and each had been copiously enriched by gifts from the other, each rode home to his own country in safety.'[31] This is the sort of horizontal relationship of *amicitia* that Rollo had concluded with King Æthelstan.[32] As Geoffrey Koziol has noted, such pacts suggest equality between the two parties concerned.[33] The report of this meeting certainly does not imply that Richard once again commended himself to the king – that was not at all a part of Dudo's agenda – and with Richard's pagan Northmen still apparently in the duchy it may be supposed that Lothair was not in a position to command that he do so. But still, none of this suggests that Richard I or Dudo was attempting to claim that Normandy lay outside France. Indeed, Dudo's own narrative warned against taking that stance.[34] Instead, the point was that it lay outside the control of the king of the French.

The duke of the Normans, then, did not hold his lands from the king of the French, did not do him homage, and did not owe him service. The duke was instead an autonomous ruler. And perhaps in an attempt to make that point as forcefully as possible, Dudo described the duchy of Normandy as a kingdom (*regnum*). The appearance of a Norman *regnum* in an act of 968 recording the restoration of Berneval to the abbey of Saint-Denis[35] might have provided Dudo with a precedent, but the use of the word there, in an act signed by Hugh Capet,

---

[29] *Dudo*, p. 147.

[30] See also above, Chapter 1, pp. 63–4 and below, Chapter 11, pp. 646–7.

[31] Dudo, p. 287; *Dudo*, p. 162.

[32] Dudo, p. 148; *Dudo*, p. 32.

[33] Koziol, *Begging Pardon*, p. 111.

[34] 'It is certainly not the custom of Francia that any prince or duke so numerously attended by so many knights should remain thus within the lordship under his jurisdiction all his days, without rising up against the emperor, king or duke, either under the sway of his own will or compelled by force and power; and if he should happen to persist in his audacious rashness, he will not voluntarily serve anyone owing to the superabundant richness of his own resources; and it most usually comes about that quarrels and divisions and occasions of inestimable loss are apt to befall him' (*Dudo*, pp. 124–5).

[35] *RADN*, no. 3.

was most likely much less politically loaded than were its appearances in Dudo's *De moribus* and in some eleventh-century ducal *acta*.[36] Graham Loud described Dudo's choice of word as revealing 'staggering ambition ... necessary though it was if the Normans were to assert their independence from the French king'.[37] More recent considerations of the meaning of the word, however, have had the effect of toning down Dudo's message a little. Thus Nick Webber has remarked: 'whereas, at one time, to be one of those *regna* within the *regnum Francorum* was to support the superior status of the *rex Francorum* ... by the eleventh century things had changed. As well as territorial definition, "regnum" implied power, and a *certain amount* of independence from the monarch.'[38] Susan Reynolds glossed the word a little differently but to similar effect. Those who ruled *regna* 'were king-like in their authority – rather more king-like than the king of France was at the time'.[39]

Dudo's use of the word, then, underlined the dukes' autonomous authority, but probably did not go much further than that, as is also indicated by his assertion that Richard I ruled 'like' a king. He made the same point implicitly by his repeated use of the phrase 'praesit et prosit' when referring to the function of the dukes, too. The words were taken from Hincmar's Ordo for the coronation of Charles the Bald, subsequently copied into the Annals of Saint-Bertin.[40] As the eleventh century progressed, however, others were prepared to go further than Dudo had done, although probably only to emphasize the reigning duke's power and prestige rather than to suggest that they saw Normandy as a sovereign state in its own right. Thus Richard II was styled 'King Richard' on the tombstone sup-

---

[36] In 1028 × 1033, for example, Rouen was described as 'the caput and metropolis of our kingdom (*regni nostri*)' (*RADN*, no. 67). Two acts for Jumièges speak of a 'monarchy of the kingdom of the Normans', with the later, dated 1038, recording the time 'at which time William, the son of Count Robert, obtained the monarchy of the kingdom of the Normans' (*RADN*, nos. 74, 92). Finally, an act of 1063 for the abbey of Saint-Ouen notes that Robert Curthose had been elected 'to the government of the kingdom after [Duke William's] death' (*RADN*, no. 158).

[37] G. A. Loud, 'The *gens Normannorum*—myth or reality?', *ANS*, 4 (1982), 110.

[38] N. Webber, *The Evolution of Norman Identity, 911–1154* (Woodbridge, 2005), p. 29 (my italics).

[39] Reynolds, *Fiefs*, p. 140. Reynolds had earlier suggested that the word might be intended to reflect the good government of Normandy and other areas where the title was used. She cited Flanders (S. Reynolds, *Kingdoms and Communities in Western Europe, 900–1300* (Oxford, 1984), p. 260), but as the word was also used of Aquitaine, never a well-governed territory, not everyone used it like that.

[40] *PL*, 125, cols. 803–8 at col. 804. The words were also found in the *Orationes in synodo Metis coadunate in ecclesia sancti Stephani habitae* (*PL*, 121, col. 1149) and in the Annals of Saint-Bertin (*The Annals of St-Bertin*, trans. J. L. Nelson (Manchester, 1991), p. 158, s.a. 869). It seems most likely that Dudo found them in this last source.

posed to be that of Hugh of Montgommery now to be found in the parish church in Troarn,[41] while, in 1055, one monk of Marmoutier went so far as to describe William the Bastard as 'king of all his land'.[42]

Dudo had also claimed, as noted above, that Richard I held Normandy directly from God. Some of the scribes who wrote the ducal *acta* subsequently repeated that claim. It has been suggested that 'in the 850s–860s, the formula "gratia Dei" began to indicate a special blessing of a ruler to a certain extent connected with the ritual of anointment; henceforth, his authority was mainly based on divine grace and liturgical proximity to God, and less on ties with his *gens* or a Roman imperial legacy.'[43] The dukes could not claim to have been anointed, and again employment of this formula should not be taken to imply an attempt at independence, but the inconsistent employment of similar forms of words in beneficiary-drafted diplomas could have acted to support the dukes' claims to autonomy. Arnulf of Flanders had been styled 'marquis by the aid of God's mercy' in 941,[44] but such wording first appears in Norman *acta* only in 1009 when a monk of Mont-Saint-Michel styled Richard II, 'Richard by the disposition of God "princeps" and "marchio" of the whole of the province of Normandy'.[45] By 1015, Dudo of Saint-Quentin styled Richard II 'Richard, the son of the most happy Count Richard, and permitted to be called, by the grace of the highest and indivisible and sacred Trinity, unworthy duke and patrician of the Northmen' in one of the diplomata he wrote.[46] In 1010 × 1017, the monks of Saint-Riquier adopted the similar 'by divine grace's consent' duke of the Normans[47] – the first time a beneficiary based outside Normandy had used such words. In 1017 × 1026, the monks of Mont-Saint-Michel styled Richard II 'gratia Dei' duke of the Normans, which was the first time that formulation was used in the surviving acts.[48] By the reign of Richard II, then, it is possible that at least some of the beneficiaries of ducal gifts saw the dukes as appointed to their office by the grace of God, rather than as a result of the permission (as Dudo put it) of the kings of the French.[49] Given the inconsistency in the ducal *acta*, and the variety of meanings and interpretations that might be applied to such formulae, it would be unwise to push this argument very far, but

---

[41] Van Houts, *Normans*, p. 21. The relevant words on the stone read: 'Hugo miles Ricardi reg(is) Normandorum.'

[42] *RADN*, no. 137.

[43] I. H. Garipzanov, 'Communication of authority in Carolingian titles', *Viator*, 36 (2005), 66.

[44] Dunbabin, *France*, p. 48.

[45] *RADN*, no. 12.

[46] *RADN*, no. 18.

[47] *RADN*, no. 20

[48] *RADN*, no. 47.

[49] *Dudo*, p. 147.

such a view would fit with the broader pattern discerned by Elizabeth Hallam, Jean Dunbabin, and Geoffrey Koziol.[50]

Beneficiary draftsmen promoted the dukes' authority against that of the kings of the French in other ways, too. Fines for breaches of the protection offered by ducal confirmations were to be paid both to the duke and to the king of the Franks in acts produced at the beginning of the eleventh century,[51] but to the dukes' fisc alone from the end of the reign of Richard II.[52] Royal confirmations were not sought for grants of lands within Normandy (and also only very infrequently by Norman monks for lands outside Normandy).[53] It was, perhaps, the beneficiaries who chose not to date acts with reference to French regnal years. And, to move away from charter diplomatic for a moment, *if* it was really the case that it was from Richard II's reign that a blood relationship with the duke, often by way of Gunnor's family, became the principal foundation of noble status, rather than kinship with the Carolingians which was the *sine qua non* elsewhere,[54] then that, too, was a development driven by the dukes' subjects (especially, no doubt, those who counted themselves among the dukes' kin).

The king-like complexion of ducal rule, reflected and promoted in the words and

[50]   E. M. Hallam, 'The kings and the princes in eleventh-century France', *Bulletin of the Institute of Historical Research*, 53 (1980), 151; Dunbabin, *France*, p. 48; Koziol, *Begging Pardon*, pp. 27–30, 33, 109. Koziol warned that the adoption of the phrase does not necessarily suggest the usurpation of regalian prerogative as a result of the weakening of royal authority in the tenth century, but that does not affect the suggestion made here.

[51]   *RADN*, nos. 13, 18 (both written by Dudo).

[52]   For payments to both king and duke see *RADN*, nos. 13, 18. For payments to the duke alone: *RADN*, nos. 34, 35, 36, 45, 53, 69, 70, 102, 109, 162, 188, 219, 225. The rarity of such clauses and the inconsistencies in the amount of the fine between them indicate beneficiary drafting/formulation. Indeed, some set such a ridiculously high penalty that the duke could not have been consulted. See also below, Chapter 7, p. 416.

[53]   When King Lothair confirmed Richard I's refoundation of Mont-Saint-Michel in 966, the abbey was not situated within Normandy. Equally, when King Robert confirmed some Norman possessions of the monks of Fécamp in 1006, it is extremely unlikely that his confirmation was sought. It was more likely forced on the monks by the king who was present at the abbey when Richard II made the grants that the king subsequently confirmed (Fécamp, Musée de la Bénédictine, no. 2; Telma, no. 2663. It should be noted that the surviving original is of doubtful authenticity). Hollister noted correctly that 'not a single extant act of King Philip I relates in any way whatever to Norman lands or customs' (Hollister, '*Regnum*', p. 19). The same is also true for the surviving acts of Louis VI collected in *Recueil des actes de Louis VI roi de France (1108–1137)*, ed. R.-H. Bautier and J. Dufour, 4 vols (Paris, 1992–4). There is no evidence that the duke could, or wanted to, close his borders to those who wanted to attend the French king's court.

[54]   Hallam, 'The kings and the princes', pp.146–7. Hallam cited Le Patourel (*Norman Empire*, p. 289), who did not quite say what she said he did. Moreover, the evidence for such a trend dates mostly from the twelfth century rather than the eleventh.

Fig. 2 Twelfth-century Norman coin, probably issued under Henry I, bearing the legend 'Normannia' (Author)

phrases of these acts, was not entirely in the imagination of the beneficiaries who wrote them of course. It rested in part on the dukes' practical usurpation of some regalian rights within their duchy. Thus William Longsword and Richard I broke the royal monopoly on coinage when they minted their own coins with their own names on them, and while the wording on the coinage was replaced by simple shapes from *c.* 1026 until the end of the eleventh century, the use of the word 'Normannia' from that point speaks just as strongly of a unified duchy under the rule of a single duke.[55] From 989, the dukes appointed their own bishops to the dioceses in their duchy. In addition, the *Consuetudines et iusticie* of 1091 or 1096 reveal that the dukes had later usurped the royal right to enter their subjects' castles, and that the dukes' wars were seen as public wars.[56] Eadmer tells us that the dukes had already begun to preside over church councils before the Conquest. William certainly did so at Lillebonne in 1080.[57] The kings' jurisdiction was thus ousted from within the duchy of Normandy, their rights, and some of the symbols used to promote their power fell to the dukes. The French kings themselves were either not strong enough or did not care to win their rights back. Thus Norman autonomy grew.

[55] Dumas, 'Les monnaies Normandes', 87–8 (Longsword), 93 (for 'Normannia'). See also below, *infra*, pp. 282–4, 285–6.

[56] *Consuetudines et iusticie*, clauses 2 and 4.

[57] Eadmer, *HN*, p. 10; trans. Bosanquet, p. 10; Orderic, iii. 26–34.

During the reigns of Richard II and Robert the Magnificent, relations between the dukes and the kings of the Franks seem generally to have been good. Richard II, described as a *fidelis* of Robert the Pious by Fulbert of Chartres,[58] assisted his king at Auxerre in 1003 and *c.* 1005.[59] The king was at Richard's court at Fécamp in May 1006, before the two marched against Baldwin IV of Flanders.[60] King Robert arbitrated the dispute between Odo of Chartres and Richard II in 1013–14,[61] while in 1023 Richard attempted to return the favour, setting up an 'independent enquiry' to investigate the dispute between the king and the same Count Odo, although in the event it did not meet.[62] Friendly relations continued into the reign of Robert the Magnificent, who, in 1033, provided refuge for King Henry I at Fécamp, 'where he asked for the duke's assistance according to the faith Robert owed him'. This was forthcoming, so that Norman writers at least could credit Robert with restoring Henry to his throne.[63]

The relationship between William the Bastard and the kings of the French is harder to establish, however, not least because it is difficult to find a single tune among the cacophony of voices singing about it from different eleventh- and twelfth-century hymn sheets. But perhaps that is the point. The relationship between William and Kings Henry and Philip was not immutable. It changed and developed, moving from periods of friendship to periods of enmity and back again, and the chroniclers reflected these changes.

We may begin by supposing that the seven-year-old Duke William had sworn fidelity to, or been allied with, King Henry in 1035. But if so, the king's attack on Normandy *c.* 1042 may be supposed to have broken the bond between them.[64] That breach, however, was healed by 1047 at the latest. In that year, William was 'forced by necessity' to seek the aid of King Henry, who came to his assistance not on the grounds that William was his man, but perhaps because he remembered the support given to him by Robert the Magnificent, or – and less likely – because

---

[58] Fulbert, *Letters*, no. 86. See also Reynolds, *Fiefs*, pp. 23 and 127 for the definition.

[59] Jumièges, ii. 32–4, and pp. 33, n. 3, 34–5, n. 4; Hugh of Flavigny, *RHGF*, x. 221 (dating the campaign to 1003). In addition, William of Jumièges described Richard helping King Robert against Count Odo, where the king appealed to Richard's loyalty (*fidelitas*), although this passage apparently relates to the siege of Melun in 991, which occurred, of course, before Richard was duke. See also Jumièges, ii. 34–6; Le Patourel, *Norman Empire*, p. 218.

[60] *RADN*, no. 9; Telma, no. 2663; Sigibert of Gembloux, *MGH, Scriptores* 6, p. 354 (s.a. 1006); *Gesta episcoporum Camaracensium*, ed. Pertz, *MGH, Scriptores* 7 (1846), p. 414.

[61] Bates, *Normandy*, p. 65.

[62] Fulbert, *Letters*, p. 152. The description is from Bates, *Normandy*, p. 66.

[63] Jumièges, ii. 54–6; Orderic, iv. 76; *RADN*, no. 69. Ralph Glaber gave the credit to Fulk of Anjou (Glaber, *Opera*, p. 158).

[64] See above, Chapter 2, p. 105.

he was the twenty-year-old William's guardian (*tutor*).[65] His principal motivation, however, was a need to counter the growing threat posed by Count Geoffrey Martel of Anjou.[66]

In 1047, Henry helped William to defeat Count Guy and his allies at Val-ès-Dunes. The assistance he offered seems to have ushered in a second period of amity, during which William might have been knighted by the king. Then, in May 1048, William attended King Henry's court at Senlis, and he was present in the army that marched against the count of Anjou the same year or in 1049.[67] It is entirely possible, given both his knighting and the royal support that was given to him, that William had commended himself to Henry for a second time. We hear nothing about it, however, as any new oath of fidelity was soon voided by the king's subsequent actions.

In 1052–53, the king came to the aid of the rebellious Count William of Arques.[68] It was at this point in his narrative – after the siege of Arques and before the battle at Mortemer – that William of Poitiers described William's relationship with King Henry in the clearest of terms: 'The king bore it ill and considered it an affront very greatly to be avenged, that while he had the Roman emperor as a friend ... and while he presided over many powerful provinces of which the lord and rulers commanded troops in his army, Count William was neither his friend nor his knight, but his enemy; and that Normandy, which had been under the kings of the Franks from the earliest times, had now been raised almost to a kingdom.'[69] And so in 1054 King Henry led an army into Normandy, part of which was defeated at Mortemer. In 1057 he attacked again, this time to watch the tail end of his army defeated at Varaville – although it is noteworthy that William only attacked when Henry could not join battle against him and so when William could not be accused of attacking the king.[70] The hostility between king and duke endured until King Henry's death in 1060, at a time when the French were still besieging William's garrison inside the fortress at Thimert. Thus William had almost certainly not been bound by any oath of fidelity to the king for at least the last eight years of Henry's reign.

[65] Jumièges, ii. 120; Malmesbury, *GR*, i. 428.
[66] Hallam and Everard, *Capetian France*, second edition (London, 2001), p. 97.
[67] *RADN*, no. 114. The Mouliherne campaign is reported by Malmesbury, *GR*, i. 428. William's movements are noted in Bates, 'Adolescence', 15.
[68] Jumièges, ii. 102.
[69] Poitiers, p. 44.
[70] This may be compared with Henry II's refusal to fight against Louis VII at Toulouse in 1159. See also M. Strickland, 'Against the Lord's anointed: aspects of warfare and baronial rebellion in England and Normandy, 1075–1265', in *Law and Government in Medieval England and Normandy: Essays in Honour of Sir James Holt*, ed. G. Garnett and J. Hudson (Cambridge, 1994), pp. 56–79.

The coronation of the young Philip I led to a third period of friendly relations. William of Poitiers tells us that Duke William was encouraged to establish a 'firm peace and calm friendship' with the young King Philip *c.* 1060.[71] Put like this, the arrangement does not sound much like the performance of homage or commendation to the new king, rather the creation of another alliance between equal parties. The statement in the 'D' version of the *Anglo-Saxon Chronicle*, repeated by John of Worcester, goes a little further. These English sources remark that Robert Curthose had been recognized as heir to the duchy of Normandy by the young King Philip, in 1063 and/or just before the Hastings campaign in 1066.[72] If William had asked the boy king to recognize his son as the rightful heir to Normandy, that would imply that he, not yet a king, had also recognized Philip's superior standing, perhaps even his overlordship. That would also explain how William of Malmesbury could describe William as having been Philip's man (*homo*) and how Orderic could describe Philip as William's lord (*dominus*)[73] – although they might both have been reflecting twelfth-century expectations.

Once again, however, events arose that would have allowed William to treat any oath that he had sworn to Philip as broken. In 1076, the grown-up King Philip relieved the siege of Dol, after travelling to Poitiers in an unsuccessful attempt to win the support of the duke of Aquitaine. In 1077 or 1078 Robert Curthose rebelled and received the support of the French king. Such actions would once again have voided William's oath of fidelity, and there is no reason to think that William ever renewed his fealty to King Philip after the quarrel with his son had been patched up in 1080.

The depiction of these events, albeit by different chroniclers and at different times, highlights one constant theme in the relationship between dukes and kings. Normandy, or Duke Richard I, was attacked by the king of the Franks (in person or by proxy) in 943, *c.* 959, and 960. Normandy, or Duke William, was attacked by the kings of the French *c.* 1042 and *c.* 1043, and in 1053, 1054, 1057, 1076, and 1087. So far as we can see, on no occasion did the dukes make the first hostile move against a king of the French. Even when attacked, William the Bastard seems to have been concerned to show the respect due to the monarch. He did not fight against King Henry at Mortemer. When the duke encountered the king's army at Varaville in 1057, he waited until King Henry was out of harm's way before engaging with his rearguard. In 1076, William retreated from Dol before the king

---

[71]   Poitiers, p. 56.

[72]   *ASChr*, D, s.a. 1079; trans. Garmonsway, p. 214; Worcester, iii. 30. Aird judged that Curthose was designated William's successor before the Hastings campaign (Aird, *Robert Curthose*, pp. 58–9, 63). I follow his lead.

[73]   Malmesbury, *GR*, i. 476; Orderic, iv. 78.

arrived. In 1087, he attacked Mantes as a result of King Philip's own attacks, but in the king's absence. He allowed Philip to negotiate an end to the quarrel with Curthose. He allowed monks to date their acts by Henry's or Philip's reigns, no matter the state of the relationship between them.[74] In all of this, then, there was deference to, and an acknowledgement of, the king's rank and role.

William seems also to have been keen to normalize relations – in other words to convince or force the king to accept his renewed fidelity – as soon as possible after peace was restored between them. It may be supposed that his motives for doing so were the same as those that had led his tenth-century predecessors, and twelfth-century successors, to swear their own oaths to their kings. As Dudo tells us, Duke Richard I swore fidelity to King Louis in the hope that he would protect the duchy from attack, and was allied with Hugh the Great for the same reason.[75] Such patterns of behaviour suggest that, as John Gillingham suggested for a later period, it was the dukes rather than the kings who gained most from swearing fidelity, and it was consequently the dukes rather than the kings who sought to make the oaths.[76]

Those oaths of fidelity need not have been sworn on the frontiers of the duchy, however. Just as there is no evidence for the existence of a *hommage de paix* at this time, so there is no evidence for the existence of a concept of *hommage en marche* either.[77] Indeed, Lemarignier's argument depended on a rather selective reading of the narratives. He noted that William Longsword commended himself to Charles at Eu in 927, but omitted to mention his meeting with representatives of King Ralph in 933 at an unknown location, and then claimed that the *pagus* of Amiens comprised a frontier territory. He mentioned the meeting between Richard and Louis on the Epte in 945, but that was not an occasion on which an oath of fidelity was sworn. Louis's visits to Rouen in 942 and 943 were ignored, as were Richard II's meetings with King Robert at Fécamp in 1006 and Compiègne in 1017, Richard III's visit to Senlis in 1027, and William the Bastard's possible visit to Paris in 1046. It is by no means clear, then, that the kings and dukes habitually met on the borders of their respective *regna* in this period, even though they did do so on occasion. Things were not so tidy in the tenth, eleventh, and early twelfth centuries as they would become later.

---

[74] As, for example, with *RADN*, nos. 99, 132. On the dating of Norman ducal acts see also L. Musset, 'Sur la datation des actes par le nom du prince en Normandie (XIᵉ–XIIᵉ siècles), in *Autour du pouvoir ducal normand, Xᵉ–XIIᵉ siècles*, ed. L. Musset, J.-M. Bouvris, and J.-M. Maillefer (Caen, 1985), 5–17.

[75] *Dudo*, pp. 102, 124–5.

[76] As discussed above, and see also Gillingham, 'Doing homage to the king of France', pp. 67–9, 77.

[77] See also Reynolds, *Fiefs*, p. 128.

Doing it in styles: the use of titles in Norman narratives and acta, 968–1066

As the titles used to style the duke have featured so prominently in earlier attempts to perceive the political relationships between the dukes of the Normans and kings of the French, they must be explored in some detail before moving on to reconsider the relationship that existed between those dukes who were also kings of the English, following William the Bastard's coronation on Christmas Day 1066. As previously noted, pre-Conquest ducal *acta* were drafted by beneficiaries or donors, not by scribes working for the dukes. So rather than tell us about how the dukes saw their roles or powers, they actually reveal how a duke's power was seen and promoted by his subjects. Likewise, Dudo of Saint-Quentin, William of Jumièges, and William of Poitiers might have written their works with the intention of presenting them to their dukes, but the styles and phrases they used to describe their office and authority were chosen at their own discretion, rather than being imposed by their patrons – at least there is nothing to suggest that this was not the case.

Those who wrote these narratives and *acta* used a variety of styles to describe their rulers. As the various sources that tell us about Normandy and its dukes were written by both Franks and Normans at a variety of different times, and with a variety of viewpoints, it is hardly surprising that they are, as a body, inconsistent in the choice of title that they apply to the dukes. They referred to them as 'dux', and their territory as a 'ducatus', but they used other terms, too, so that Normandy might also be described as a 'comitatus' or a 'principatus' or a 'regnum', while the duke might also be styled 'comes' or 'marchio' or 'princeps' or 'rector'. All of these words reveal subtle variations in the way that the dukes and their territory were seen by those over whom they ruled or who sought their favour.

Thus, Dudo of Saint-Quentin used titles and styles to reflect his subjects' various functions, and appears at first glance to be inconsistent in his use of designators as a result. He styled the leader of the Normans 'dux', but he also employed 'marchio', 'patricius', and 'comes', often all four at the same time.[78] Other writers seem to have used titles and styles without any attempt at precision, and without any discernible reference to an agenda. The Burgundian Ralph Glaber, writing in the 1030s and 1040s, changed his mind about styles as he wrote his *Five Books of Histories*. He entitled Richard I and Richard II either count or duke 'of the men of Rouen' in his first two books, but by Book IV he was styling Robert the Magnificent 'duke of the Normans'.[79] This was perhaps the result of a greater familiarity with

---

[78]   For example, *Dudo*, pp. 86, 87, 88, 107, 122, 128, 129, 132, 136, 137, 142.
[79]   Glaber, pp. 36, 54, 76, 162, 202–4, 270–2 (duke); 78, 96 (count). For the dating see p. xlv.

Normandy following the marriage of Robert's sister to Duke Reginald and his composition of the *Life* of William of Volpiano. However, it might equally have been because Ralph did not use titles technically or precisely. William of Jumièges used 'dux' consistently in his *Gesta Normannorum ducum*, and it is possible that his unusually single-minded usage influenced those who knew his work. In the 1070s, William of Poitiers employed a limited range of designators to describe William before his coronation, namely 'dux', apparently his preferred title (used sixty-two times),[80] 'princeps' (used fourteen times),[81] 'comes' (used ten times),[82] and, just once, 'dominus Normannie'.[83] After William's coronation, however, he used 'rex' exclusively, unless providing retrospectives or comparisons.[84] Orderic Vitalis almost always used 'dux',[85] but scattered other titles across his narrative, too: 'princeps';[86] 'marchio';[87] 'consul';[88] and 'comes'.[89] William of Malmesbury, writing in England c. 1125, tended to prefer 'comes',[90] although he used 'dux' occasionally, and apparently with regard to status rather than function.[91]

Ducal *acta* were written by a diverse body of scribes from different houses and with different backgrounds. It is consequently no surprise that the documents they produced lack any consistency with regard to the ducal style, not only when examined as a body, but also between different acts produced by the same house, and sometimes even within the same diploma. In some cases, it looks as if dukes were styled in a particular way simply because that was how they had been styled in the models used by the scribes.[92] The monks of Saint-Père of Chartres could mix titles with an ease that suggests they were not using them carefully:

---

[80] Poitiers, pp. 6, 8, 10, 12, 24, 26, 34, 40, 42, 46, 48, 50, 58, 64, 68, 70, 74, 76, 100, 102, 104, 106, 110, 112, 116, 118, 122, 124, 128, 134, 138, 140, 142, 144, 146, 150, 170.

[81] Poitiers, pp. 108, 118, 130.

[82] Poitiers, pp. 12, 14, 16, 18, 44, 56, 68, 118, 132.

[83] Poitiers, p. 96.

[84] Poitiers, pp. 154, 158, 160, 166, 174, 178, 180, 182, 184, 186.

[85] For example, Orderic, iii. 80, 82, 84, 88, 90, 106, 128, 214, 250, 252, 304, 306, 310, 314, 328, 346; iv. 74, 76, 80, 98, 106, 110, 112, 114, 118, 122, 124, 126, 146, 148, 150, 152, 164, 182, 198, 200, 204 , 210, 214, 220, 222, 224, 236, 250, 252, 268, 286, 288, 292, 296, 300, 302, 306; vi. 12, 14, 16, 22, 36, 38, 44, 88, 90, 92, 162, 164, 166, 168.

[86] For example, Orderic, ii. 118, 144; iii. 26, 104, 112 (interestingly used here when William was king), 132, 248, 254; iv. 102, 104, 106, 146, 154, 162, 180.

[87] Orderic, ii. 130, 144.

[88] Orderic, ii. 170.

[89] Orderic, ii.172; iii. 84, 250; iv. 106, 258.

[90] For example, Malmesbury, *GR*, i. 444, 446, 454, 548, 552, 562, 628, 702, 704, 712, 714, 722.

[91] For example, Malmesbury, *GR*, i. 304, 432, 450. William is styled *comes* while leading his army on the Hastings campaign. See below, *infra*, pp. 270, 272–3.

[92] For example, *RADN*, nos. 69 and 102 ; 65 and **73** (with, in addition, the style for Richard II based on that in nos. 47 and 49).

Table 3 Styles in pre-Conquest ducal *acta*

Duke	Princeps	Dux	Marchio	Comes
Richard I (4 acts in total, 3 with style in text, 3 witnessed)	2 S. 1	1 S. 1	1 S. 1	1 S. 0
Richard II (47 acts in total, 41 with style in text, 33 witnessed)	7 (17%) s. 1 (3%)	17 (41%) s. 8 (24%)	5 (12%) s. 3 (9%)	20 (49%) s. 21 (64%)
Robert the Magnificent (27 acts in total, 22 with style in text, 18 witnessed)	7 (32%) s. 3 (17%)	14 (64%) s. 4 (22%)	1 (4%) s. 1 (6%)	8 (36%) s. 10 (56%)
William the Bastard (135 acts in total, 109 with style in text, 110 witnessed)	20 (18%) s. 12 (11%)	39 (36%) s. 28 (25%)	4 (4%) s. 0 (0%)	64 (59%) s. 70 (64%)

'as much by our hand as by that of *Duke* Richard, in whose *county* it is seen to be.'[93] The one point of consistency is that the various scribes who wrote Norman ducal *acta* overwhelmingly used the same limited number of titles as Dudo and Oderic: 'comes' (which Marie Fauroux thought the most ancient), 'dux' (which she thought, following Ferdinand Lot, was first used by Dudo of Saint-Quentin), 'princeps', 'marchio', and 'consul', as well as, although rarely, 'patronus' and 'rector'.

Something of the variety and inconsistency can be seen in Table 3 which illustrates the use of the most important titles given to the dukes in the surviving *acta*, separating out those found in the body of the text and those employed as labels to the *signa*.[94] The percentages have been adjusted, to reflect the fact that not all diplomas mention the duke in the text, or include his subscription.

Of course, not all of these acts survive as originals, and there is a danger that later copies might change the ducal style to reflect the current fashion.[95] Table 4 thus provides the same breakdown for the styles applied in the text and to *signa* in the surviving authentic originals for Richard II and William the Bastard. The numbers seem to confirm that the broader picture is tolerably accurate.

This 'bewildering randomness'[96] has been the subject of comment in the past. For Karl Werner, in an article published in 1976, the titles adopted by the rulers of

---

[93] *RADN*, no. 2. The act is dubious, but the point remains regardless.

[94] One result of this, which may be worth noting to avoid confusion, is that the figures do not match those found in Bates, *Normandy*, p. 149.

[95] See Bates, *Normandy*, p. 148. The surviving originals are *RADN*, nos. 9, 13, 14*bis*, 15, 16 (until 1944), 18, 19, 21, 23, 25, 26 (destroyed 1915), 30, 31, 32, 37, 39, 41, 42, 43, 44, 45, 52, 55, 73 (destroyed 1944), 74, 85, 92, 100, 103, 107, 111 (with 73), 112, 113, 114, 124, 126, 133, 134, 140 (destroyed 1944), 158, 159, 161, 162 (destroyed), 188, 191, 193, 199, 204, 205, 210, 218, 223, 225. It should be noted that in this section of this chapter, originals are highlighted in bold font in the footnotes.

[96] Bates, *Normandy*, p. 149.

Table 4 Styles in original pre-Conquest *acta*. No title or are provided in six originals[a]

Duke	Princeps	Dux	Marchio	Comes
Richard II (23 acts, 17 with style in text, 14 witnessed)	2 (12%) s. 1 (7%)	6 (35%) s. 2 (14%)	3 (18%) s. 1 (7%)	11 (65%) s. 10 (71%)
William (28 acts, 19 with style in text, witnessed 27)	4 (21%) s. 3 (11%)	6 (32%) s. 7 (26%)	1 (5%) s. 0	10 (53%) s. 18 (67%)

Notes

[a] *RADN*, nos. 18, 25, 52 ; 41, 42, 225.

the Normans reflected the opportunity to scramble up the Carolingian hierarchy provided by the concurrent political advances made by their neighbours.[97] He argued that Rollo became count of Rouen in 911 by virtue of the grant of the city and its region to him by Charles the Simple. As counts, the Rollonids (as they have been termed) were *fideles* of the Robertine 'marchiones' until *c.* 960, when the Robertines became 'duces' thus allowing the Rollonids to take the title of 'marchio' for themselves. When the Robertines, now Capetians, took the throne in 987, the Rollonids could become 'duces' in turn. The Rollonids might nonetheless continue to use their earlier lesser titles, but the appearance in diplomata of titles before their due time had to be explained away as the result of forgery or later interpolation.

Robert Helmerichs reconsidered this question in 1997, looking at the designators used for Rollo, Longsword, and Richard I. Werner, he argued, had approached matters of intitulation too legalistically. The titles adopted by the Rollonids did not have to reflect an official view of their position in Frankish society, and, indeed, they did not do so. There was 'no clear evidence that the Rollonids were duly appointed "comites", exercising specific powers over a specific territory by royal grant'.[98] Helmerichs also demonstrated that there was no sense of progression in the adoption of these titles (what he called the 'promotion theory'), pointing out that the title 'dux' was already being used to style the dukes by 965,[99] and that 'each mention of Richard I as "comes" occurs after the Rollonids' supposed "promotion" to "marchio", while at least one occurrence of "dux" is long before their ducal "promotion"'.[100] Helmerichs also remarked that Richard I or William the Bastard were often given two or more titles in the

---

[97] K.-F. Werner, 'Quelques observations au sujets des débuts du "duché" de normandie', in *Droit privé et institutions régionales: etudes historiques offertes à Jean Yver* (Paris, 1976), pp. 691–709.

[98] R. Helmerichs, '*Princeps, comes, dux Normannorum*: early Rollonid designators and their significance', *HSJ*, 9 (2001), 69.

[99] *RADN*, no. 2.

[100] Helmerichs, 'Rollonid designators', 63.

same document. His conclusion: 'the issue of what the Rollonids were called is much more important to modern historians than it was to the Rollonids themselves.'[101]

Helmerichs observed that the title 'dux' could be used in the Carolingian period simply to mean the leader of a war-band,[102] which offers a hint that function might have been as important as status when applying these designators to rulers or leaders. Unfortunately, he did not pursue this avenue of enquiry, and neither did David Crouch, although he noted the use scribes made of the list of ranks (with definitions) found in Isidore of Seville's *Etymologies*.[103]

It is likely that Isidore's *Etymologies* provides a key to understanding the use of different titles to style the Norman dukes. According to the definition provided in that work, a 'dux' 'is so called because he is the commander of an army. But not everyone who is a prince or a general can immediately be called a king. Moreover in wartime it is better to be titled a general than a king, for the former title signifies one in command in battle.'[104] The use of that style for Richard I in Count Walter of Dreux's act for Chartres in 965 is thus highly appropriate, as Richard had been embroiled in conflict with Count Theobald of Chartres in the area concerned from *c.* 960.[105] Dudo, too, seems to have used 'dux' with that function in mind, and thus to have been aware that it was particularly appropriate at particular points in a ruler's career. He wrote that Richard I was: 'Marquis and holy patrician, / Now a duke also, magnanimous and brave.'[106] The reason why Richard I was 'now a duke' is that the passage is found at the point in the narrative where King Otto determines to attack Rouen. Consequently, Richard was now a general, and the additional title was necessary.

But the word 'dux' was not only used to describe a function. It was also a recognized title which represented an established step on the social ladder.[107] In the secular hierarchy of the tenth to twelfth centuries a duke stood just one step below a king. Used like this, its application to a ruler was prestigious. It would both reflect and confer honour on the man to whom it was applied. A usurpation of the title might, therefore, be contentious, which is why the monks of Fécamp forged

---

[101] Helmerichs, 'Rollonid designators', 64.

[102] Helmerichs, 'Rollonid designators', 61–2, 69–70.

[103] D. Crouch, *The Image of Aristocracy in Britain, 1000–1300* (London, 1992), pp. 28–9, 43.

[104] *Etymologies*, p. 201. Some have noted that a *dux* was simply a man who ruled over a number of counts, but that meaning, even if accurate, seems irrelevant here (*Dudo*, p. xxiv; Bouchard, *Strong of Body, Brave and Noble*, pp. 8–9).

[105] *RADN*, no. 2 and see above, Chapter 1, pp. 63–5.

[106] *Dudo*, p. 129.

[107] McKitterick noted that a *ducatus* was in the eighth and ninth centuries 'a command temporarily entrusted to a person who had under him a number of counts, and whose functions were primarily military' (McKitterick, *The Frankish Kingdoms*, p. 87).

a papal bull at the end of the eleventh century when Richard II was incidentally granted the title by Pope Benedict VIII.[108] But which scribes intended the word to be interpreted as relating to function, and which as relating to honour, is not clear – an ambiguity that the scribes might have found useful.

On the next rung down the political hierarchy was found the 'marchio', a title that was used just ten times in acts dating from before 1066, and not at all subsequently.[109] This title is not found in Isidore's *Etymologies*, but Dudo himself tells us that the title meant 'keeper of the march',[110] a definition that appears just before he tells us that Richard was keeping the 'kingship of the Normans and Bretons (*regnum Northmannicae Britannicaeque regionis*)'.[111] The title first appears in a ducal act in 968,[112] when Richard I restored property in Berneval to the monks of Saint-Denis, although Richard was also given that title in the probably or partly forged diploma of King Lothair recording his refoundation of the monastery of Mont-Saint-Michel in 966.[113] This usage again seems apt. The monks of Saint-Denis would have been aware that Normandy was part of the Neustrian March, and the (belated) defence provided by the Normans against pagan Scandinavians would also have been fresh in the memory given the raiding and destruction of Richard I's Viking allies during the war with Theobald of Chartres. The monks of Mont-Saint-Michel would have been sensitive to the duchy's border with Brittany, but also to the hegemony exercised by the duke over the Bretons. It was probably the latter that suggested the title, as later uses of 'marchio' to describe the duke suggest that its employment was linked to political events rather than geography. Thus Richard II was styled 'marchio' for the first time in an act of 1009 which recorded his replacement of the ageing

---

[108] *Acta inedita*, i. 10–11 (no. 13), noted in Bates, *Normandy*, p. 150 and n. 12, p. 182.

[109] The monks of Saint-Pierre of Préaux, however, regularly used it in their dating clauses as in, for example, *Ctl. Préaux*, nos. A2, A9, A40, A67, A74, A79, A85.

[110] *Dudo*, p. 137. Bates wrote that the title simply meant someone who ruled over other counts (Bates, *Normandy*, pp. 26–7). Nelson suggested that 'several counts could be responsible for a single frontier area … and were called *marchiones*', although the word came to denote a powerful count (Nelson, 'Kingship and royal government', pp. 411–12). Dunbabin noted that the title had, by the tenth century, lost all association with a border region and was conferred by the kings of the French as an honorific related to their own kingship. She noted, too, that others might not have seen the title in the same way, remarking that the monks of Saint-Bertin styled Count Baldwin II *marchisus* well before he obtained chancery recognition of that title. Rather than reflecting an official title, however, it seems likely that the monks of Saint-Bertin were recognizing his achievement in bringing the whole Flemish seaboard under his dominion (Dunbabin, *France*, p. 47).

[111] Dudo, p. 263; *Dudo*, p. 137.

[112] *RADN*, no. 3.

[113] *Ctl. Mont-St-Michel*, p. 75.

Abbot Mainard of Mont-Saint-Michel with Hildebert.[114] A clutch of four other acts, dating from 1011, probably 1012, 1014, and 1012 × 1026 give him the same title.[115] All thus either certainly, or most probably, date from the period when Count Geoffrey had died and Richard was attempting to bring Brittany under his authority.[116] Robert the Magnificent was described as 'marchio' (and 'comes') in his foundation deed for Cerisy-la-Forêt of November 1032. It may be that he had launched his expedition against the Bretons in that year,[117] so that the title was to the fore of the monastic draftsman's mind at the time the act was made. Equally, William the Bastard was styled 'marchio' in three acts, all of which date from the period between 1059 and 1066, which might thus be more closely dated to the period of his Breton campaign in 1064.

'Comes' was, as has been seen, apparently the preferred title of the dukes of the Normans until the conquest of England in 1066, at least if the labels to the *signa* more accurately reflect the official line than the superscriptions and texts of ducal acts. A count had been a Carolingian official, although the office had developed from one established during the later Roman Empire. It had been a civilian post, associated with the government of a city and its surrounding county. Under the Carolingians, counts were the conduit by which the kings and emperors transmitted their will to the regions of their kingdom. They summoned men to the royal host, organized and supervised judicial assemblies, received dues and tolls, and maintained the roads, bridges, and public buildings.[118] Dudo can be seen to use the title in this way. He so often links together duke, patrician, count, and 'marchio' that when he uses other phrases in the place of some of these styles, they act as implied definitions of the absent terms. Thus in one poem 'marchio' and 'dux' are followed by 'Protector of the clergy and laity's fosterer' which stands for 'patrician', and 'governor of the people, just and benignant' which stands here for 'count'.[119] Thus for Dudo, the count was someone who did justice and who

---

[114] *RADN*, no. 12.

[115] *RADN*, nos. **13**, 14, **15**, **41**.

[116] Jumièges, ii. 28; Bates, *Normandy*, p. 70 and n. 67, p. 90; J. Quaghebeur, 'Havoise, Constance et Mathilde', pp. 147–8.

[117] The campaign is dated only by a series of acts that relate to it, which can be dated to 1033 but which do not have to belong to that year. Thus in 1982, David Bates had dated the campaign only to the 1030s (Bates, *Normandy*, p. 70). Pushing the campaign back to 1032 thus does no damage either to the evidence or to the argument set out by Keynes, who placed Edward the Confessor's grant to Mont-Saint-Michel in 1033 *after* the expedition (Keynes, 'The Æthelings in Normandy', 194).

[118] McKitterick, *The Frankish Kingdoms*, p. 88; R. E. Barton, *Lordship in the County of Maine, c. 890–1160* (Woodbridge, 2004), pp. 21–2; J. L. Nelson, 'Kingship and royal government', pp. 410–11.

[119] *Dudo*, p. 148.

governed his people, functions that Richard I can be seen performing throughout Book IV of his *De moribus*.

Other writers might have used the title in order to suggest that the dukes held a legitimate place in the Frankish hierarchy, as suggested by Lot, Douglas, Bates, and others.[120] It might even have celebrated the dukes' achievement in being so recognized, as the first use of the style 'count of Rouen' for any of the Norman dukes comes only between 942 and 963 in the *Planctus* of William Longsword, written by an Aquitainian author either in Poitou or in Normandy, probably at the request of Longsword's sister.[121] Even then, the style was not awarded to the dukes in any of the surviving *acta* until the reign of Richard II.

Still other writers might have used the style to indicate a duke's status, without intending in any way to suggest a dependency on the king of the Franks. Fulk Nerra's refusal to accept that he held his county from the king shows how the title might confer a prestige that was independent of royal service even before the end of the tenth century, and by the eleventh century those styled counts included men who had usurped the title for themselves, or were awarded it by their subjects, as a result of ruling over a city or a castle. Thus, when the Norman garrison surrendered Le Mans to Helias of Maine they are also made to say that 'we choose to serve you and ... proclaim you count of Maine'.[122] Rodulf of Ivry was, according to Robert of Torigni, a count simply because he held the castle at Ivry.[123] The situation was not dissimilar with regard to the counts of Meulan.[124] With Rouen the clear focus for Norman power and wealth, to describe its Norman ruler as a count might have seemed appropriate, even if the dukes did neither homage nor service to the king of the Franks for their territory from Richard I's reign at the latest.

All of this suggests that titles were not, or not only, about establishing 'constitutional precision'.[125] Indeed, not all the titles used to describe and honour

---

[120] F. Lot, *Fidèles ou vassaux? Essai sur la nature juridique du lien qui unissait les grands vassaux à la royauté depuis le milieu du IXᵉ siècle jusqu'a l fin du XIIᵉ siècle* (Paris, 1904), pp. 177–85; Douglas, *William the Conqueror*, p. 24; Bates, *Normandy*, pp. 10–11, 149–50.

[121] Elisabeth van Houts has recently concluded that the author of the poem was Anno, second abbot of Jumièges. Originally from Poitiers, he would have known Longsword's sister, and probably composed his lament shortly after arriving in Normandy (Van Houts, 'Planctus', 7–9). For her previous views on the subject see: Jumièges, i. xxix; Van Houts, *Normans*, p. 41

[122] Orderic, v. 306.

[123] 'Moreover, the duke gave him the fortress of Ivry; because of this fact he is called count (*unde uocatus est comes*)' (Jumièges, ii. 174).

[124] Jumièges, ii. 32 (*Milidunensis castri comes*).

[125] Bates, *Normandy*, p. 149.

the dukes reflected an established rank in the secular hierarchy. Some were simply honorifics. The most widely used of these was 'princeps'. This title was usefully vague in the tenth and early eleventh centuries as it conferred honour but was ambiguous in its meaning.[126] In the plural, the style could be used simply to describe the greatest men in a political community, as when Dudo imagines a dialogue between Bernard the Dane and William Longsword before the 'other *principes*' at Rouen during Riulf's rebellion.[127] 'Other *principes*' can also be found in an act of 1035 × 1047 for La Trinité-du-Mont outside Rouen, and Norman 'principes' are mentioned in an act for the monks of Chartres of 1063 × 1066.[128] In the singular, however, its value increased. Its use by emperors (Augustus was the first to adopt the style) and kings associated it with sovereignty. Perhaps because it had no official place in the Frankish hierarchy it was the only title that Flodoard was prepared to give the dukes (although he did use it of Frankish magnates, too).[129] Later Norman writers such as William of Poitiers and Orderic also used the style (inconsistently), as did Abbot Osbern of Saint-Evroult in the letter that he sent to the pope *c*. 1063, which survives in Orderic's *Ecclesiastical History*.[130]

From the middle of the eleventh century, it is possible that 'princeps' was beginning to be used by some scribes to suggest a more elevated form of rulership, and one that encompassed a territory. An act for the monks of Jumièges drafted *c*. 1030 states that Richard III had inherited a 'principatus', and although this might simply be translated as 'rule' or 'governance', William of Jumièges, who seems to have had sight of this act, rephrased 'principatus' as 'comitatus' in his *Gesta Normannorum ducum*, while Orderic, writing even later, used the word to mean 'principality' far more than anything else.[131] This was the only time the style was used in ducal *acta* before 1066, but the act does survive as an original and its use, especially as it was partnered by the phrase 'monarchiam regni Normannorum', might infer a meaning close to 'principality', thereby making a 'princeps' a prince.[132]

---

[126] The definition found in Isidore's *Etymologies* borders on the meaningless: 'the term *princeps* derives from the sense of taking because he first takes, just as one speaks of a citizen of a municipality because he takes office' (*Etymologies*, p. 201).

[127] Dudo, p. 190; *Dudo*, p. 67.

[128] *RADN*, nos. 104, **225**, respectively.

[129] Such as Henry of Germany, Ragenold the Northman, William of Aquitaine, Hugh the Great, Arnulf of Flanders, and others.

[130] Orderic, ii. 110.

[131] *RADN*, no. **74**; Jumièges, ii. 46. William's use of the act is suggested by Garnett, '"Ducal" succession in early Normandy', p. 105. See Orderic, i. 351. *Principatus* was also used to describe the principality of Antioch by William of Malmesbury at *GR*. i. 694.

[132] It is only in the 1160s, however, that we can see the word clearly used in that way. Thus in 1163, Henry II was offended by Owain Gwynedd's adoption of the title since

Other honorifics most likely made similar allusion to the Roman past. 'Consul', for example, was used eight times in ducal *acta* before 1066.[133] Although the word might have been used as a synonym for count, or even as 'literary affectation', it was perhaps more likely intended to add to a ruler's prestige by making an allusion to the Roman Republic and to a title that Caesar had held before becoming emperor.[134] Another distinctly Roman honorific, 'patritius', was used in three *acta* of Duke Richard II, two of them written by Dudo of Saint-Quentin, who also styled the dukes thus in his *De moribus*.[135] The dignity was another of those defined by Isidore in his *Etymologies*: 'The patricians are so-called because, as fathers watch over their children, so they watch over the state.'[136] Similarly, Richard II and William the Bastard were styled 'the father of the country (*pater patrie*)' by William of Jumièges, Orderic Vitalis, and by Robert of Torigni,[137] with Richard II alone given the accolade in the *Breuis relatio*.[138] The style was first conferred on Cicero in 63 bc, on Caesar after the end of the civil wars, and subsequently on other emperors including Augustus, Marcus Aurelius, and Constantine. It is perhaps worthy of note that Orderic also used it of Count Gilbert of Eu,[139] whose death was seen as ushering in the worst period of anarchy during William the Bastard's minority. It may be supposed that the title recognized his achievement in holding the duchy together after Archbishop Robert's death in 1037.

These styles, then, were awarded to the dukes of the Normans by authors such

---

it, 'implied that Owain, not Henry, was the chief ruler of Wales' (H. Pryce, 'Owain Gwynedd and Louis VII', 4–5, 21–2; quotation from p. 22).

[133] *RADN*, nos. 4, 69, 102, 130, 143, 148, 196, 214, **218**, 224. *RADN*, no. 102 for Saint-Wandrille borrows its wording, including the style, from the related but earlier *RADN*, no. 69. The two acts were both for Saint-Wandrille, and William's act confirmed the grant made by his father.

[134] Crouch, *Image of Aristocracy*, p. 43 (as a synonym); N. Karn, 'Nigel, bishop of Ely, and the restoration of the exchequer after the 'anarchy' of King Stephen's reign', *Historical Research*, 80 (2007), 306, n. 45 (as affectation); B. S. Bachrach, *Fulk Nerra the Neo-Roman Consul, 987–1040: A Political Biography of the Angevin count* (Berkeley and London, 1993), p. 153 (ancient Rome). Bachrach thought that the impetus to employ the style came not from Isidore but from Livy, whose work was known in the late tenth and early eleventh centuries by, for example, Fulbert of Chartres (Bachrach, *Fulk Nerra*, p. 152).

[135] *RADN*, nos. **9, 13, 18**. Dudo, pp. 86, 87, 88, 107, 122, 128, 129, 132, 136, 137, 142. He also used the word to describe Archbishop Robert of Rouen and Count Theobald the Trickster: pp. 12, 140, respectively.

[136] *Etymologies*, p. 201.

[137] Jumièges, ii.132, 286; Orderic, iv. 100.

[138] 'The Breuis relatio de Guillelmo nobilissimo comite Normannorum, written by a monk of Battle Abbey', ed. E. M. C. van Houts, *Camden Society Miscellany*, 34 (1997), p. 45.

[139] Orderic, iv. 82.

as Dudo of Saint-Quentin and William of Jumièges, as well as by the variety of beneficiary draftsmen, who were searching for ways to describe their subjects, or to flatter or reassure them, free from ducal oversight and without being constrained by the sort of conventions that characterize the employment of such styles today. That lack of central control could be found in even the greatest of Western regimes. In 871, Louis II had rejected a request from the Byzantines to command his people not to call him emperor, on the dubious ground that it was not appropriate to instruct others on what they should call him. He also indicated that he had not commanded his subjects to style him emperor in their letters.[140]

This lack of control is something that tends to be forgotten. Helmerichs, for example, suggested that the Rollonids were themselves responsible for the style given to them in the diplomata they authenticated. He wrote that William the Conqueror 'had a strong, if not overwhelming, preference for "comes" over "dux" or "princeps"', and that 'the Rollonids'' use of designators was precise, rational, and based on their relationship to the Robertines.[141] In this he followed David Bates, whose comments in 1982 on this issue included 'it remains undeniable that Rollo, in assuming the title of count of Rouen, was identifying himself and the province that he ruled with Frankish forms' and that 'from 966 [Richard I] began to refer to himself as a marquis (*marchisus* or *marchio*), inferring, within the contemporary meaning of the term, that he was someone who ruled over other counts'. He went so far as to accuse the dukes of a 'preoccupation with titles and status'.[142] Hollister, too, had written in a similar vein that before the Conquest William, 'usually styled himself in his charters "dux Normannorum"'.[143] However, we do not know what Rollo and his successors called themselves, because the dukes of the Normans did not draft these documents. Instead, both before and after 1066, 'there are usually compellingly strong reasons to believe that the vast majority, if not all, of William's *acta* (here, specifically, that means diplomas) were written by scribes employed by their beneficiaries'.[144] As such, if anyone had a preoccupation with

---

[140] Garipzanov, 'Communication of authority', 42.

[141] Helmerichs, 'Rollonid designators', 64, 70.

[142] Bates, *Normandy*, pp. 23, 26–7 and 28, respectively. He also writes of 'the practice by which its rulers sometimes described themselves as "counts" or "dukes" of "Normandy" as opposed to the more usual title of "count/duke of the Normans" (pp. 56–7). For additional examples see pp. 148–9.

[143] Hollister, '*Regnum*', 202–42, reprinted in *MMI*, pp. 17–57 at p. 22. Christiansen, among others, also falls into the same trap: *Dudo*, p. xxiv.

[144] *Regesta: William*, p. 11 and see the Introduction, p. 30–3, 35–7. It should be added that Eleanor Searle also recognized this, and remarked that it means that, 'styles tell us nothing about how [the duke] and his warleaders described him, and little more about his powers' (Searle, *PK*, p. 125).

the ducal style it was beneficiaries and writers such as William of Jumièges and William of Poitiers.

Nonetheless, and as hinted already, it might be possible to get a little closer to what the dukes thought they should be called as a result of the way that ducal *acta* were created. English diplomas were written throughout in one hand and in the same ink.[145] As will by now have become clear, Norman diplomas were not. They were instead drafted by their beneficiaries away from the court. Or rather, the proem, superscription, and dispositive clauses were. A diploma could not be signed by the duke and his court, however, until it had been presented to him there. Thus one clear indication that a diploma is authentic is provided by its appearance, as the text of a single sheet authenticated at the ducal court will almost always be written in a hand that is different to that which added the labels to the *signa*. Pre-Conquest examples survive in the archives of Saint-Ouen, Saint-Wandrille, Jumièges, and the cathedral at Chartres.[146] Indeed, this last was signed by an 'Everard the *signum*-writer (*signatoris*)'. Equally, for William the Conqueror's reign after 1066, there survive nine original Norman diplomas.[147] In all three from Saint-Etienne, Caen, the body of the text and the names of the witnesses were written by two different scribes (or at least in a different hand).[148] The same is true of the single surviving original for the cathedral at Rouen,[149] and the two originals for Saint-Ouen,[150] one of which has similar drafting to an act for La Trinité-du-Mont[151] and may have been written in the same scriptorium. Had

---

[145] S. Keynes, *The Diplomas of King Æthelred 'the Unready' 978–1016: A Study in Their Use as Historical Evidence* (Cambridge, 1980), p. 35. The five reasons that Simon Keynes put forward to support his theory of an English writing office before 1066 are consequently unconvincing in a Norman context (Keynes, *Diplomas*, p. 39). The five reasons are as follows: (1) The prominent religious element in the diplomas reflected the circumstances in which they were first drawn up in the seventh century; (2) ecclesiastical interest is detectable, but it accounts for their preservation rather than their creation; (3) secular considerations would not always have been compatible with the production of diplomas in ecclesiastical *scriptoria*; (4) the production of royal diplomas would have to be controlled in the interests of king and beneficiary alike, and so could not have been drafted by beneficiaries; (5) diplomas were produced on the occasion of a witenagemot and so needed to be made at the time and not sent to a scriptorium in advance of, or after, the event.

[146] For example, AD Seine-Maritime, 9 H 30(2); 9 H 30(3) (Jumièges); 14 H 915(3); 14 H 145(3); 14 H 327(2) (Saint-Ouen); BL, Add. Ch. 75743 (Chartres).

[147] Bates counted eleven (*Regesta: William*, p. 12), but the two for Fécamp (both of them versions of no. 144) concern property in England alone.

[148] *Regesta: William*, nos. 46, 47, 51.

[149] *Regesta: William*, no. 229.

[150] *Regesta: William*, no. 246.

[151] *Regesta: William*, no. 236.

it survived as an original, an act of 1080 for the monks of Saumur would no doubt have shared these characteristics. It includes a note that 'Primaldus, chaplain of the same William of Briouze, dictated and spread (*linivit*) this writing', which comes at the end of the witness list added in William of Briouze's court, but before the names of the witnesses who confirmed the document at the royal duke's court.[152] The same processes are equally apparent in Henry I's reign. A *notitia* for Le Bec, which if it had not survived in the original would have looked like a summary of an earlier grant, has King Henry's autograph *signum* at the bottom of the sheet, with his name added in a different hand from that which drafted the text. Its appearance was so unexpected that T. A. M. Bishop thought that it was not authentic, but there is no reason to agree with that conclusion.[153] There is an act, too, for the abbey of Saint-Etienne of Caen which likewise has autograph *signa* added at the bottom of the sheet, with the crosses identified in a chancery hand which is again different from that of the draftsman.[154]

With the *signa* only added at court, probably by a scribe employed for the purpose by the duke (and thus probably one of the duke's chaplains), it is likely that the styles attached to *signa* are more likely to reflect an 'official' position than those found in the preambles and bodies of the texts. There is certainly a noticeable difference in the way that these styles were awarded in the text on the one hand and subscription on the other. As Marie Fauroux noted in the introduction of her edition of ducal *acta*, 'The titles borne by the duke vary, not only from one act to another, but also between the superscription and the subscription and the body of the text of the same act. As a general rule, the titlature appears more complex and more detailed in the superscription than in the subscription; this readily associates several titles and rarely omits to mention the people over which the duke exercises his jurisdiction.'[155] It is likely that this can be explained by a presumption that the titles found in subscriptions were attached to names and *signa* while the witnesses, scribes, and parchment were at the court, perhaps even as the names of the signatories were spoken aloud, and perhaps according to dictation by a court official. The differences between those styles and the ones used to describe the dukes within the body of the act *might* thus provide some insights

---

[152] *Regesta: William*, no. 266 (II). His words come at the end of the local witness list and before that drawn up at the duke's court.

[153] AD Eure, H 28; T. A. M. Bishop, *Scriptores Regis: Facsimiles to Identify the Hands of Royal Scribes in Original Charters of Henry I, Stephen and Henry II* (Oxford, 1961), no. 204.

[154] New York, Morgan Library, MA1217. Reported as untraced Bishop, *Scriptores*, no. 776. Such criteria for authenticity were also observed by Pierre Chaplais, 'The seals and original charters of Henry I', *EHR*, 75 (1960), 270–1.

[155] *RADN*, p. 49.

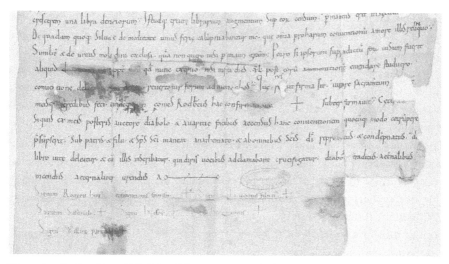

Fig. 3   Act for Jumièges (AD Seine-Maritime, 9H30/1) showing beneficiary drafting and later ducal *signum*

into the nature and promotion of ducal power (and that is why they have been separated in Tables 3 and 4).

Of course, there are cases which complicate this picture. There were no doubt times when the scribe who added the *signa* was not one of the duke's chaplains and thus not familiar with, or unconstrained by, the preferred style. An example is provided by one of the versions of William the Bastard's confirmation for the monks of Saint-Evroult of 1050 which was written and then signed by Robert, probably Robert of Grandmesnil, who may be supposed to have added the unusual style to the duke's sign, too.[156] Another issue is exemplified by the famous act of *c.* 1030 by which Roger of Montgommery restored the market at Vimoutiers to the monks of Jumièges (Fig. 3).[157] At first sight, we have an act written by one scribe, with the labels attached to the non-autograph *signa* written by another. However, the first scribe knew that this act would be taken to the court to be confirmed by Duke Robert, and so when he wrote it, he added the subscription clause for the duke and left a space for his cross. Here, then, the style was chosen by the beneficiary scribe rather than reflecting the words spoken at court.

Despite the possible complications and idiosyncrasies, Tables 3 and 4 suggest that the differences between the style employed by the beneficiary when drafting the text of the diploma on one hand, and the (probably) more official labelling of

[156]   *RADN*, no. 122. William's *signum* was labelled: 'The sign of William the great prince of Normandy.'
[157]   *RADN*, no. **74**.

the *signa* on the other, are significant, if not always drastic. Across the board, the 'official' style is more modest. Even on the eve of the Conquest, the sign of William the Bastard was usually labelled 'the sign of Count William'. Perhaps the most important conclusion to be drawn from this – assuming that a scribe intended titles such as 'dux' and 'comes' to represent ranks in the secular hierarchy – is that the use of titles to promote ducal power was driven from the bottom up. It was beneficiary scribes and authors such as William of Jumièges who employed the more prestigious styles, not the duke. Indeed, it is possible that it was the widespread reception of the *Gesta Normannorum ducum* that led to the near universal use of 'dux' as *the* ducal style by the beginning of the twelfth century – although the title had also been used on some of the coins minted in Normandy during William the Bastard's reign.[158]

But there was more to the ducal style than the use of the words 'dux', 'comes', 'marchio', and so on. Often, although by no means always, these words were paired with an adjective, and that adjective added a further dimension to the intended meaning of the chosen style. In Carolingian and French *acta*, 'comites' were usually associated with a city or a territory. It is an assumption that permeates at least some capitularies[159] and hundreds of Frankish *acta*. The Telma database contains the texts of every original or pseudo-original act preserved in France that dates from before 1121. In the vast majority of cases, when counts were described as more than simply 'comes' they were counts of cities or territories or, very rarely, counts of the people of a city.[160] This can be seen, sometimes, with regard to the dukes of the Normans. For example, the Poitevin author of the *Planctus* that lamented the death of William Longsword, who wrote c. 943, styled his son and successor the 'count of Rouen'. So, too, did the author of an original act recording an exchange of land between the monks of Jumièges and Bourgueil in the Touraine, as well as the Aquitainian chronicler Adémar of Chabannes.[161] All these writers, it should be noted, were Franks.

But there were some notable exceptions to this general rule. The style 'comes Pictauorum' was in use from 854, and there are ten original *acta* from before 1066 which employ the style. 'Comites Andegauorum' can also be found in original *acta* from 1005. The style 'comes Flandrensium' appears in an original act for the

---

[158] Dumas, 'Monnaies', 93.

[159] Edict of Pîtres, in *RHGF*, vii. 658; see also pp. 670, 686, 702.

[160] For example, Telma, nos. 1580, 156, 2490, 3672, 1826, 1416, 2918, 2066, 2067, 2064, 3683, 1209, 813, 2079, 3420, 'Hugo, Caenomannicus comes' (act of 1046 × 1047; Telma, no. 1555), 4171, 4180, 2083, 2701, 3112, 4616, 1692.

[161] *RADN*, no. **14bis**; Adémar, *Chronique*, p. 166, with an English translation in van Houts, *Normans*, p. 214.

Table 5 Styles and adjectives before 1066

Style	Richard II	Robert the Magnificent	William the Bastard
Princeps	1	0	3
		s. 2	s. 4
Princeps Normannorum	5	6	16
	s. 1	s. 1	s. 11
Princeps Normannie	1	1	1
			s. 3
Dux	1	0	3
	s. 1	s. 0	s. 6
Dux Normannorum	17	14	33
	s. 5	s. 4	s. 22
Dux Normannie	1	0	3
Comes	14	4	24
	s. 20	s. 8	s. 46
Comes Normannorum	6	4	24
	s. 1	s. 2	s. 19
Comes Normannie	0	0	14
			s. 6

first time in 1066.[162] These styles were not used consistently, but such variations are noteworthy simply because they were unusual.

The Norman tradition is also inconsistent, but has the same notable variations on the typical model. More often than not, when the duke signed an act as 'comes' there was no adjective supplied. That was typical of Frankish practice generally. However, when ducal *acta* do include an adjective, it is usually 'Normannorum'. The combination of 'comes' with the name of a *gens* was not created in Normandy, as has been seen, and indeed the earliest original act to include the style was drafted by the monks of Saint-Père at Chartres,[163] but the style is found in an unusually high number of Norman acts. There are eleven of them, dating from between 1025 and 1066. The same adjective was also regularly paired with both 'princeps' and 'dux', and although that was more in accordance with contemporary practice there were still alternatives that might have been used instead.

It is worth looking in more detail at the use of the adjective *Normannorum* in Norman *acta*, especially, but not only, when used with 'comes', because the variations in the style given to the duke reveal that scribes had a choice. That choice may be supposed to have meant something to the writer concerned.

[162] *Pictavorum*: Telma, nos. 1060, 1088, 1095, 1107, 1448, 1415, 19, 2666, 774, 2846; *Andegavorum*: Telma, no. 1551 and also 27; *Flandrensium*: Telma, no. 380.
[163] Telma, no. 1889; *RADN*, no. **32**.

One possible reason for the use of the style 'comes Normannorum' in particular was the need to find a way to maintain an appropriate hierarchy. Norman sources make a distinction between the count of the Normans on the one hand, and other counts based within or without Normandy on the other. Almost invariably, the counts who held counties within Normandy are described by reference to their chief cities or their territories. Thus we find the count of Evreux, the count of Eu, and the count of Mortain.[164] Richard II's brother William, and Richard III's brother Robert, were both for a time apparently counts of the Hiémois,[165] William the Bastard's uncle was count of Arques,[166] his cousin was perhaps the count of Brionne,[167] while his youngest son, Henry, was the count of the Cotentin.[168] They were all, then, counts of places, not peoples. As Normans, they all fell under the authority of the count of the Normans, whose title thus reflected his superior position in the hierarchy.

A second possibility is that, as the adjective 'Normannorum' describes a people, the style 'comes', 'dux', or 'princeps Normannorum' was intended to suggest a distinct identity for the people that the dukes ruled.[169] Frankish sources of the ninth and tenth centuries certainly make it clear that the Normans were not seen as Franks. They were different. They were invaders and outsiders.[170] These sources also used the word 'Normanni' or 'Danii' in a generic way for all the Scandinavian groups that ravaged or settled in Francia, and indeed for everyone who lived within Normandy regardless of their ethnic origin. Some Franks, then, might have used the style 'dux Normannorum' in a disparaging way, not dissimilar to Richer of Reims's 'pyratarum dux'.[171] In any event, it was a label applied

---

[164]   For example: *RADN*, nos. 201, 202; Jumièges, ii. 98, 232 (Evreux); *RADN*, nos. 96, 123, **191**, 200, 208; Jumièges, ii. 10, 128, 132 (Eu); *RADN*, nos. **16**, 190; Jumièges, ii. 186 (Mortain).

[165]   Jumièges, ii. 8, 40. Douglas thought that William did not have the title even though he presided over a county. He was, however, less concerned about Robert's possession of the comital title (Douglas, 'The earliest Norman counts', 136, 145–6).

[166]   *RADN*, no. **100** (*comes territorii quod Talohu nuncupatur*), 108, 113, 131.

[167]   *RADN*, no. 131.

[168]   Orderic, iv. 148.

[169]   On this subject see the important paper by Timothy Reuter, 'Whose race, whose ethnicity?', pp. 100–8 and also Loud, 'The *gens Normannorum* – myth or reality?', 104–16. Much of the second and third chapters of Webber's *The Evolution of Norman Identity* deal with this issue, too, although the emphasis there is different to that presented here.

[170]   For example, *The Annals of Saint-Bertin*, trans. Nelson; Abbo of Saint-Germain-des-Prés, *Bella parisiacae urbis*, ed. and trans. N. Dass (Paris, Lieuvin, Dudley MA, 2007); Richer of Saint-Rémi, *Histories*, ed. and trans. J. Lake, 2 vols (Cambridge, MA and London, 2011). This tradition continued into the twelfth century: Suger, *Deeds of Louis the Fat*, p. 70 and Hyde, p. 2.

[171]   Richer, ii. 436. Although, as noted above, it is possible that Richard I did not feel

to another group of people without much regard for their actual background.[172] Norman writers could use such labels of others just as easily, of course. William of Jumièges wrote of Count Geoffrey of the Bretons and Count Geoffry of the Angevins,[173] recognizing these peoples as distinct from other Franks, and thereby providing the heroes of his story with more peoples whom they might overcome. He ensured that a suitable hierarchy was maintained, despite the use of these adjectives, by styling the Norman rulers 'dukes' and not 'counts' throughout.

The adjective was not just used *of* the Normans, however, it was used *by* them, too. An act of Duke William has the duke declare that, 'although we are Normans, still we know well how it ought to be done, and so, if it shall please God, we will do it'.[174] Roger of Montgommery was famously described as 'a Norman of Norman stock'.[175] But although Rollo was quite clearly a Norman, and although Roger of Montgommery was apparently equally sure of his own racial identity (most likely inherited from his grandmother), others living within Normandy might have needed to be told that they were Normans now. The style, then, might not simply recognize a political community; it might also be used as part of an attempt to create one. Dudo of Saint-Quentin, a Frank but writing in part for a domestic audience, was at the forefront of this attempt. Rollo's dreams speak of the creation of a united community under the future duke. These people were Normans, led by a 'dux Northmannorum'.[176] It was a theme taken up by the author of the *Inventio et miracula sancti Vulfrani*.[177] The mention of 'the customs of Normandy' or 'the customs of the patria' in a few ducal *acta* was probably also intended to suggest a unity, since according to William of Apulia, once the Normans in the south of Italy received 'any malefactor from the neighbourhood' into their community, 'they taught their own language and customs to those who joined them, creating

---

himself disparaged but pleased, regardless of Richer's intention (see above, Chapter 1, p. 77).

[172] Webber, *The Evolution of Norman Identity*, pp. 40–7. See also Christiansen, *Norsemen in the Viking Age*, pp. 118–21, who noted, *inter alia*, that to outside sources 'Danes' were Northmen in general; members of the armies that troubled Francia in the ninth and tenth centuries; Normans; the inhabitants of Dublin (but only after 986); the inhabitants of the English Danelaw, regardless of their true origin; or the inhabitants of Denmark.

[173] Jumièges, ii.14, 28, 42, 122.

[174] *RADN*, no. **199**.

[175] *Regesta: William*, no. 281.I.

[176] *Dudo*, pp. 124, 125, 141. Emily Albu, discussing the defence of Normandy during the minority of Richard I remarks: 'Here at last, in Dudo's account, the Normans possess all the elements of a distinctive ethnic community' (Albu, *The Normans in their Histories*, p. 34).

[177] *Inventio*, p. 21.

a single, seemingly united, people'.[178] In the hands of some writers, then, the use of the style 'Normannorum' was about the construction of a group identity that included not only the descendants of the Scandinavian conquerors and settlers but also the Franks, Angevins, and Bretons living in the territory that had been brought under the dukes' authority.[179] Whether an individual 'Norman' would have recognized, or could have been convinced, that he was indeed Norman remains open to question, although the members of the Tosny family at least seem to have bought into this construct, and turned their founding father from a Frank into a Viking in the process.[180]

Thirdly, the increasing use of the adjective 'Normannorum' alongside 'comes' and even 'princeps' or 'dux' is a further example of the usurpation of words associated with royalty, with the intention of emphasizing the duke's power and highlighting the autonomy of his rule. When kings were styled anything other than simply 'rex', they were kings of peoples.[181] Thus from his takeover of the kingdom of Lotharingia in 911, the scribes of Charles the Simple's writing office styled him 'king of the Franks', perhaps to claim that he, and not the king of the Germans, was the true successor of Charlemagne. The kings of Wessex became 'reges Anglorum' from the reign of Æthelstan, although even before that they had still been kings of peoples. Otto III became 'imperator Romanorum' in 996.[182] The point is made implicitly by John of Salisbury who, when drafting a letter for Archbishop Theobald of Canterbury c. 1161, styled Henry II 'king of the English, duke of Normandy and Aquitaine and count of Anjou'.[183] The adjectival change from a people to go with 'king' to a territory for 'duke' and 'count' is telling. So in the cases of 'dux' or 'princeps' – and perhaps even 'comes' given that counts were 'the kings' nearest neighbours in dignity'[184] – the addition of 'Normannorum' might have been intended to imply near-sovereign rule.

The use of a *gens* style thus suggested a high degree of autonomy as a result

---

[178] William of Apulia, *La Geste de Robert Guiscard*, ed. M. Mathieu (Palermo, 1961), i. 108 (ll. 165–8); translation by Loud, *The Age of Robert Guiscard*, p. 83. More generally, Susan Reynolds noted that law and custom was one of the ways of creating a people (Reynolds, *Kingdoms and Communities*, pp. 256–61). In contrast, Webber has suggested that customs should be seen as the product, and not the cause, of an ethnic identity (*The Evolution of Norman Identity*, p. 22).

[179] See also Reuter, 'Whose race, whose ethnicity?', pp. 102–4;

[180] Musset, 'Aux origines d'une classe dirigeante', 48–50.

[181] On this point generally, see Reynolds, *Kingdoms and Communities*, ch. 8, especially p. 250.

[182] G. Althoff, *Otto III*, trans. P. G. Jestice (Pennsylvania, 2003), p. 60.

[183] *The Letters of John of Salisbury, Vol 1. The Early Letters (1153–1161)*, ed. and trans. W. J. Millor, H. E. Butler, and C. N. L. Brooke (Oxford, 1986), no. 135.

[184] Crouch, *Image of Aristocracy*, pp. 60–1.

of its association with kingship. William the Great of Aquitaine, who succeeded in 990, was 'more like a king than a duke' according to the flattering Adémar of Chabannes, and was described with imperial superlatives by Fulbert of Chartres.[185] The use of the title 'count of the Poitevins' by some of the beneficiaries of his *acta* might have been intended to reflect his standing. Geoffrey Greymantle of Anjou might have recognized that he held his county from the French king, but Fulk Nerra did not, and the use of the style 'comes Andegavorum' should perhaps be seen as an acknowledgement or promotion of his increased independence which can also be seen in the reign of Geoffrey Martel, whom Jean Dunbabin described as 'acting in the manner of a king or an emperor, not of a mere count'.[186]

As Norman ducal *acta* only survive from the 960s, it is not possible to see if the adoption of the adjective 'Normannorum' coincided with the agreements made with King Louis in 945 or Lothair *c.* 965.[187] However, some evidence for the Normans' use of a *gens* adjective to make a claim for autonomy might be found in the later eleventh century. After William the Bastard conquered Maine in 1063, Norman *acta* – particularly the diplomas produced by the monks of Saint-Etienne of Caen – style William, inter alia, '*princeps* of the Manceaux' rather than 'count of Le Mans' or 'the men of Le Mans' as had been the practice previously.[188] The change seems unnecessary if it was not also intended to make a point.

Although less often used than 'Nomannorum', the style 'count of Normandy' or 'duke of Normandy' is also interesting, especially in light of the decision made by, or under, King Richard the Lionheart to change his style to 'king of England, duke of Normandy and Aquitaine and count of Anjou'. 'Normandy' appears as a province in 1012 and 1015.[189] The style 'marquis of Normandy' appears in 1014;[190] 'duke of Normandy' in an original drafted by Dudo in 1015;[191] and 'count of Normandy' from around 1040. In contrast to Frankish practice, the style 'count of Normandy' is both unusual and late, although quite widely used as it appears in texts produced by five Norman houses (including one original) and three French

---

[185] Dunbabin, *France*, pp. 173–4, and also p. 48.
[186] Dunbabin, *France*, pp. 185, 187.
[187] See above, *infra*, pp. 256–7.
[188] For example, *RADN*, no. 229 (the first use of *Cenomannorum* in an original act); *Regesta: William*, nos. 45, 46, 48, 49, 50, 51, 52, 54, 57. For previous usage, and some later examples, too, see Telma, nos. 625, 1553, 1555, 1919. I disagree here with Barton, *Maine*, p. 58.
[189] *RADN*, nos. 14, **18**. The text that records Richard I's foundation and endowment of the abbey of Saint-Taurin (*RADN*, no. 5) styles him 'Richard the son of William duke of Normandy', but the surviving text does not necessarily represent the style used in Richard's own day.
[190] *RADN*, no. **15**.
[191] *RADN*, no. **18**.

ones (including another original).[192] For the Frankish scribes, the employment of the adjective might have been intended to suggest that Normandy was now just another Frankish province. For others, however, the use of the word 'Normandy' might have said something about the establishment of a distinctive territory,[193] or the increasingly cosmopolitan society that lived under the dukes' rule. The latter is suggested by the change in the nature of rebellions from the 1040s, discussed below, and also by the later decisions made by the chancery of Roger II of Sicily. At a time when other kings remained kings of peoples, Roger was styled 'king of Sicily, of the duchy of Apulia, and the principality of Calabria'.[194] This decision was probably taken because of the inconvenience of describing Roger as king of all the different peoples who made up his kingdom. An adequately encompassing title would have made him something like 'king of the Normans, Franks, Lombards, Greeks, and Arabs of the kingdom of Sicily, duchy of Apulia and principality of Capua'. It was far easier, and less intellectually difficult or politically divisive, to make him king of the territories he ruled. The dukes of the Normans were now also ruling over French, Bretons, Manceaux, and Angevins. Some scribes – and notably ones from the borders of Normandy or outside it – might have felt that this was better reflected in a territorial style rather than one suggesting lordship over only one element of this population. But they were, and remained, in a minority.

One noteworthy use of the adjective 'Normandy' saw it twinned with 'dominus'. The style, Lord of Normandy, was used only rarely, but it was apparently significant nonetheless. The word 'dominus' was ambiguous, and that was probably the point, for the phrase seems to have been used in particular when there was more than one possible figure who might hold lordship over the duchy although, perhaps, not necessarily the fidelity of its men (hence the territorial adjective). The clearest example of this usage is found in the *Consuetudines et iusticie* of 1091 or 1096. These customs were found by the barons of Normandy at the instruction of Robert Curthose and William Rufus. Although the former was duke, Rufus had an interest in the matter either because of the terms of the Treaty of Rouen of 1091 or because he was about to gain control over the duchy while his brother was away on crusade. With two possible rulers, it was impossible for the barons to find that the customs they identified were to be held, effectively personally, by the 'duke of the Normans'. By associating the customs with the 'lord of Normandy', that is the

---

[192] Jumièges, Saint-Wandrille, Mont-Saint-Michel, Trinité-du-Mont, and Le Bec. Marmoutier, Lehon and Saint-Père of Chartres.

[193] Adémar of Chabannes seems to have used the word in this way: Adémar, *Chronique*, p. 148; translation in van Houts, *Normans*, p. 212.

[194] H. Houben, *Roger II of Sicily: A Ruler between East and West*, trans. G. A. Loud and D. Milburn (Cambridge, 2002), p. 132.

person who was actually exercising lordship over the duchy, ducal rights could be held by someone who was not the duke.[195]

The phrase was not new in the 1090s. William of Poitiers had employed it once in his *Gesta Guillelmi*, and it is tempting to see that appearance as somehow related to the contemporary discussions about the role of Robert Curthose in Normandy and the style he might take.[196] As his father was duke, and unlikely to yield the title, another was required for the man who might exercise control over the duchy in his father's place.

Such usage perhaps bears comparison with the style afforded to Cnut's widow, Emma, in the 'D' version of the *Anglo-Saxon Chronicle*, where she is consistently described as 'the Lady'. That might suggest that the author of that version of the chronicle found a logical difficulty in describing a woman who was no longer the wife of a king as a queen, although not all of his contemporaries thought likewise, perhaps holding the view that a woman who had been consecrated a queen would always be a queen.[197] Similarly, the Empress Matilda was styled Lady of the English in 1141, perhaps because she had not yet been crowned, or perhaps because it was not intended that Geoffrey of Anjou should be crowned king, or perhaps because there was a queen already in the form of Stephen's wife, Matilda.[198] For any or all of these reasons, Matilda had to be content with the style 'Lady', although Malmesbury was also happy to style her 'Lady of the Angevins', suggesting that the word was also used more straightforwardly to identify someone who held lordship (albeit in this case over a people).[199]

The styles employed to describe the dukes of the Normans, then, meant different things to different people. To some they were about function, to others they were about status. The differing views, and thus the same ambiguity in use and interpretation, remained equally prominent after 1066, when the conquest of England allowed William the Bastard and Henry I to adopt the style 'rex' and to use it in acts that would take effect in Normandy. The dukes' and royal dukes' own views on the matter are not at all clear, as Eleanor Searle recognized,[200] but it is interesting that they did not apparently seek to promote their authority before 1066 by taking the more prestigious titles available to them, for the styles found

[195] For a detailed discussion of the *Consuetudines* see below, Chapter 8, pp. 441–8.

[196] Poitiers, p. 22 and see below, Chapter 6, pp. 327–8, 344–7.

[197] *ASChr*, C, D, s.a. 1035; D, s.a. 1043; trans Garmonsway, pp. 158, 159, 163. Those contemporaries included the author of the 'C' version of the *Anglo-Saxon Chronicle* and the author of the *Encomium Emmae Reginae*.

[198] Malmesbury, *HN*, pp. 88, 92. Malmesbury describes Stephen's wife as queen at *HN*, p. 96.

[199] Malmesbury, *HN*, p. 110.

[200] Searle, *PK*, p. 125.

in subscription clauses, which are perhaps as close as we can come to the 'official' view, are generally less prestigious than those found in the superscriptions and texts of the diplomata. The promotion of the dukes' authority through titles was thus apparently driven from the bottom up. This might have been because Norman scribes and churchmen, because they were educated, were concerned to find a way to underpin intellectually the dukes' autonomous rule over Normandy, but it might equally have been down to flattery, or the intention to suggest that the dukes were primarily warriors rather than administrators.

A clash of kings, 1066–1144

The conquest of England in 1066 turned Duke William into a king, as Guy of Amiens observed. William of Poitiers implicitly agreed. Once William had been crowned, Poitiers styled him only as king, no matter what side of the Channel he was on. Other writers such as Orderic Vitalis also referred to both William and Henry I as kings when they were resident in the duchy, and those writers, as well as the beneficiaries of William's and Henry's grants and confirmations, might write of their having acted through their royal authority (or similar) while they were there, too.[201]

These formulations, as well as the elegant but ambiguous simplicity of the style used by the scribes of the royal writing office, 'rex Anglorum',[202] which owed much to tradition and very little to political reality, have tempted some historians to question whether William, and Henry I for that matter, remained content to rule over Normandy as a duke, or whether he had sought to annex the duchy to

[201] To take a few examples from many more: Orderic tells us that William I 'assembled the nobles of Normandy and Maine and used all his royal powers of persuasion to move them to peace and just government' (Orderic, ii. 284); that the council of Lillebonne of 1080 'was held in a royal village (*in uico regali*) by the Seine' (Orderic, iii. 34); and that 'King William ruled the English and the Normans' (Orderic, iv. 38). A general confirmation to the nuns of the Holy Trinity of Caen of 1082 ends with the statement that William was 'establishing the privilege by royal majesty (*privilegium regie maestatis imponens*)' (*Regesta: William*, no. 59). An early-twelfth-century act for the abbey of Troarn, which was not authenticated by the king, includes a grant made by King William of the 'royal customs' in Falaise (*Regesta: William*, no. 281 (III).Also nos. 245, 282, 284 for royal authority). For lawsuits see, for example, *Regesta: William*, nos. 29, 235.

[202] The evidence for a writing office and for the employment of scribes in a writing office during William's reign is both disputed and sketchy, and has most recently been summed up at *Regesta: William*, pp. 96–102. As noted in the Introduction (above, p. 33), it may be supposed that the chancellor or a chaplain or clerk would be called on to add *signa* and that, as before the Conquest, the words chosen reflected a more official view of the king's preferred style than that of the beneficiary's draftsman.

his English kingdom and thus to remove it once and for all from the authority of the kings of the French. That supposes, of course, that the dukes of the Normans had ever wanted their duchy to be entirely independent of the French kings in the first place, and the preceding discussion has suggested strongly that they had not, but C. Warren Hollister, at least, was certain that they had.

Hollister published his argument in 1976. As it happened, John Le Patourel published both a stand-alone article on the same subject, as well as his *The Norman Empire* in the same year.[203] Both historians were interested in the nature of the dukes' authority within Normandy after 1066, and in particular whether they had henceforth ruled the duchy as kings or had continued to rule as dukes. Le Patourel's arguments on the subject were careful and qualified. He pushed for 'assimilation' but nonetheless held back from making extreme and unsubstantiated assertions. Hollister was much more bullish. Despite counselling caution on a number of occasions, he often treated his evidence in the most literal way. So far as he was concerned, if the Norman acts of William I and Henry I styled them kings, then that accurately reflected the nature of their rule in Normandy. If they used their royal authority there, they had acted as kings in the duchy. Alternative explanations were dismissed. And so Hollister's conclusion for the period between 1066 and 1087 as a whole was that: 'The evidence from William the Conqueror's time, varied and ambiguous though it is, demonstrates Normandy's gradual drift from the fitful French suzerainty of earlier days toward complete independence and, after the Conquest, toward a kind of half-conscious absorption into the larger kingdom.'[204] Moving on to consider Henry I's reign in Normandy after 1106, Hollister's assumptions about the use of titles and the role of the writing office led him to argue that, 'in order to sever the ancient tie between France and Normandy, Henry I quite consciously eschewed the ducal title altogether and ruled simply as "rex Anglorum"'.[205] Again, alternative interpretations were dismissed. And even when Henry did adopt the ducal title, that adoption was 'half-hearted'.[206]

Hollister's arguments cannot stand. Indeed, they were seriously undermined by David Bates as long ago as 1989. His long-established views will often be echoed in what follows.[207] Another blow has more recently been struck as a result of the redating of the Hyde (Warenne) Chronicle, which consequently can no longer

[203] Le Patourel, *Norman Empire*, pp. 232–43; Le Patourel, 'Norman kings or Norman "king-dukes"?', pp. 469–79; Hollister, '*Regnum*', 202–42, reprinted in *MMI*, pp. 17–57.
[204] Hollister, '*Regnum*', 27.
[205] Hollister, '*Regnum*', 29.
[206] Hollister, '*Regnum*', 46.
[207] Bates, 'Normandy and England after 1066', 851–80.

be thought to tell us anything about the political ideas circulating in the 1120s.[208] Nonetheless, it is worth re-examining the evidence for and against the nature of the Norman kings' rule in Normandy, not just because there is still a little more to say about it, but also because one related detail – the date of Henry I's assumption of the duchy, as reflected in the styles found on his seal and in his *acta* – might be in need of revision.

William arguably inherited a nascent writing office from his English predecessors, which produced documents according to a more or less standard set of formulae. As a result, we have a lot of acts that look similar to each other, employ a number of more or less identical phrases, and which all style William as either 'king' or 'king of the English'. The royal seal was attached to all of these acts, on a tag cut along their bottom edge. As the writing office was an English 'institution', staffed at least to begin with by English scribes, whose acts were intended to take effect in England, it may be supposed that the seal made for William in the immediate aftermath of his coronation was designed for an English audience. That is probably why it describes William as 'patron' of the Normans, for in England he was their protector and not their duke. While these documents were of course issued for Norman lords in England, allowing Norman beneficiaries to become familiar with the forms and diplomatic of these English documents, only two or three of them found their way to Normandy. That was because in the duchy beneficiary drafting was still the norm. And it would continue to be so until towards the end of Henry I's reign.

Those of William's Norman acts produced by their beneficiaries provide no strong evidence that William was understood to have ruled over Normandy by virtue of being king of the English. There are eighty-nine such Norman acts which include a reference to William either in the address clause or within the body of the act. Fifty-two of them style William king *and* duke, 'princeps', or count of the Normans – although 'comes', which had been the most commonly used style before 1066, quickly fell out of favour, perhaps because the powers of a count were but the delegated powers of a king, so that it was now superfluous, or perhaps because the occasional use of 'comes' as a title for William's children had devalued it.[209]

Among those who differentiated William's rulership for his different dominions were the monks of William's own foundation of Saint-Etienne at Caen, who consistently styled him, 'rex Anglorum et princeps Normannorum et Cenomannorum'. Moreover, when William's authority was invoked in their acts,

---

[208]   Hyde, pp. xviii–xx.
[209]   *Regesta: William*, pp. 94–6.

the adjective 'royal' was omitted.[210] The canons of Rouen dated one of their acts 'in the 41st year of William's rule over the duchy and the tenth over the kingdom'.[211] One monk of Saint-Ouen took a stridently Normanocentric stance: 'This was enacted at Rouen on the altar of Saint-Ouen, when the said William, strenuous duke of the Normans, was ruling (*imperante*) the English, in the year 1080 from the incarnation of the Lord.' Although the title *'rex'* had been used earlier in the act, it was not employed at this point when the quality of William's rule was in focus, and the gift was also made by William's 'authority', without the inclusion of the adjective 'royal', just as had been the case with pre-Conquest *acta*.[212] Something similar can be seen in one of William's confirmations for the monks of Troarn, too. The scribe began his act with a statement as to the context: 'These are the possessions of St Martin of Troarn that Earl Roger wanted written down in letters, and which were presented for corroboration into the hand of King William.' But when it came to executive power, William was given an appropriately fuller title. The *pancarte* includes one of William's own acts which begins: 'And I William, duke of the Normans, by the grace of God, and king of the English, grant and confirm all the above written alms.' He signed this same act simply as king. Then, at the end, we have: 'This confirmation was made by William king of the English and "princeps" of the Normans in year from the incarnation of the Lord 1068.'[213] The monks of Saint-Wandrille found a different way through this morass of terminology. Recognizing the personal foundation of William's power, they had him corroborate a general confirmation through 'the authority of my name (*auctoritate niminis mei corroboro*)'.[214]

In these cases, there is no suggestion that William ruled Normandy as a king. The remaining thirty-seven acts which style William king alone do nothing to qualify that view,[215] not least because thirty-two of them mention William only within the body of the text and by way of a comment, explanation, or narrative.

---

[210] *Regesta: William*, nos. 46, 49, 53. Similarly, when Orderic reported the succession of Robert Curthose in 1087, he gave him his full style: 'Normannorum dux et Cenomannorum princeps' (Orderic, iv. 110). On later occasions, however, his Manceau style was omitted (for example, Orderic, vi. 154, 156, 184, 192).

[211] *Regesta: William*, no. 229.

[212] *Regesta: William*, no. 248. The act survives as an original. For pre-Conquest examples see, for example, *RADN*, nos. 86, 90, 164, 195, 200.

[213] *Regesta: William*, no. 280.

[214] *Regesta: William*, no. 261. For other examples of confirmations by William's 'authority' without a reference to his royalty see *Regesta: William*, nos. 64(II), 142, 147, 199, 248, 281.

[215] *Regesta: William*, nos. 27, 29 (I, II), 56, 63, 89, 90, 92, 93, 94, 95, 97, 161, 163, 179, 197, 198, 200, 201, 202, 209, 211, 213 (I and II), 231, 235, 236, 237, 239, 240, 242, 246, 260, 266 (I, II, III), 267 (I, II), 279, 281 (II, III), 282, 284.

Thus, something was done 'in the time of King William', or 'King William gave his consent to this gift', or 'this complaint was brought before King William'. Such words have nothing to do with the quality of William's rule in the duchy; they are about respect and convention. That leaves just five acts in which William, styled king, commanded that something should be done in Normandy. Three were probably produced by the writing office, and two by their beneficiaries,[216] but all concern either grants that were being made out of the ducal demesne or else exemptions from, or grants of, ducal rights – in these cases an exemption from customs and the right to hold a market.

Again, the style given to William in these acts did not speak to the nature of his rule. Instead it was the result of convention, and the same convention can also be seen in acts issued in the name of King David of Scots after 1124 that relate to the earldom of Huntingdon. This material was used by Hollister to support his argument that Henry I ruled Normandy as king rather than duke,[217] but it actually does quite the reverse. David had been earl of Huntingdon since 1113, but after his coronation in 1124 he ruled over his English lands as king, not earl.[218] This cannot suggest that he was trying to break free from the jurisdiction of another king, but rather that he was content to have his lesser title omitted from the acts issued by his writing office. David witnessed four of Henry I's acts after his coronation, too, and was styled king in all of them.[219] The only time he was not given that title was in an address to a charter of Henry I that he witnessed as king. There he was simply 'the earl of Huntingdon'.[220] As the act had a general address, and would have been intended to bind subsequent earls, it is likely that David was styled in this way simply to ensure that the document could be re-used after his death. But the change is telling. It reveals that he ruled Huntingdon as earl. Contemporaries, of course, would never have thought otherwise, despite the royal style he regularly received or used. John of Worcester and William of Malmesbury, incidentally, likewise referred to David as king of Scots in their narratives, and omitted his comital title, even when he was in England conducting purely English business.[221] There is, then, good reason to think that there was a protocol about styles that was reflected in the drafting of English and Norman writs and writ-charters. As

---

[216] *Regesta: William*, nos. 161, 202, 209, 240, 242.

[217] Hollister, 'Regnum', 221.

[218] *The Charters of David I: The Written Acts of David I King of Scots, 1124–53, and of His Son Henry, Earl of Northumberland, 1139–52*, ed. G. W. S. Barrow (Woodbridge, 1999), nos. 23–8, 40, 45–7, 105–6, 111–12. Hollister noticed this, but overlooked it when discussing the use of titles in royal *acta*.

[219] *Regesta*, ii. nos. 1451, 1639, 1654, 1659.

[220] *Regesta*, ii. no. 1659.

[221] Worcester, iii. 178; Malmesbury, *HN*, pp. 8, 30, 98; Orderic, vi. 518.

Table 6 Styles in post-Conquest Norman *acta*

	Rex	*Dux*	*Princeps*	*Comes*
William I (101 acts), mentioned	89 (100%)	25 (28%)	33 (37%)	3 (3%)
in 89, witnessed 80	s. 80 (100%)	s. 5 (4%)	s. 10 (10%)	s. 1 (1%)
Robert Curthose (31 acts),		13 (59%)	5 (26%)	8 (36%)
mentioned in 22, witnessed 22	×	s. 4 (3%)		s. 18 (82%)
Henry I (143 acts), mentioned	140 (100%)	35 (25%)	1 (1%)	2 (1%)
in 140, witnessed 32	S. 32 (100%)	S. 1 (3%)	S. 1 (3%)	S. 0

Richard of Poitiers observed when writing about Henry II in the later twelfth century (in a passage dismissed by Hollister), 'he is seen to possess many peoples under his dominion, from his father, or from his mother, or from his wife ... but in consideration of the honour and reverence of the royal name he is called king of the English'.[222]

All of this explains why William (and Henry I) might be styled 'king' alone in Norman acts, or when active in the duchy. But something needs also to be said about references to their exercise of 'royal authority' in Normandy. The most likely stimulus for the use of such wording was simply the personal nature of kingship. A king was 'anointed with chrism and heralded at his coronation as a quasi-sacral figure, a "sharer in the ministry" of bishops, the *auctor ac stabilator* of a Christian kingdom'.[223] Just as men were reborn by baptism, so kings were reborn by their anointing. They became something new, raised above their subjects by their closer relationship with God. That was not something that could be thrown off by kings when they left their kingdom, and it was not something that another could deprive them of. Even imprisoned kings remained kings – as was the case with Louis IV and Stephen.[224] And that is why William and Henry I are said to have acted with 'royal authority' when in Normandy after 1066 and 1106. They ruled there as dukes, but their royalty was of a higher order, and made their actions something more than they would otherwise have been.

Many of the comments made above about William's acts and authority of

---

[222] Richard of Poitiers, *RHGF*, xii. 417, echoed by Barlow, *William Rufus*, p. 52; Bates, 'Normandy and England after 1066', 863. Hollister's dismissal is at 'Regnum', 209.

[223] Koziol, *Begging Pardon*, p. 109 and see also pp. 84, 131. See also Green, *Henry I*, pp. 256–7 who highlighted the contemporary views of the Norman Anonymous and Hugh of Fleury. In fairness, it should be noted that Hollister, too, remarked on this at the beginning of his article, but did not then take it into consideration when formulating his argument ('Regnum', 207–8).

[224] *Flodoard*, pp. 42, 44; McKitterick, *The Frankish Kingdoms*, p. 316; Stephen was referred to as king throughout his captivity, and was not re-crowned on his release (*Gesta Stephani*, ed. and trans. K. R. Potter with a new introduction and notes by R. H. C. Davis (Oxford, 1976), pp. 136–8; Malmesbury, *HN*, pp. 118–22).

course apply to Henry I, too. While the proportion of acts that style him both king and duke (or 'princeps' or 'count') is smaller than under his father, that is due to the impact on the surviving sample of the diplomatic practices of the English writing office. Thus, of Henry I's fifty-seven Norman charters (most of them beneficiary productions), twenty-two style him 'dux' or 'princeps' in addition to 'rex'. Half of his twenty-four Norman diplomas do so, too. In contrast, only one of Henry's forty-six Norman writs and writ-charters – documents which were produced almost exclusively by the royal duke's writing office[225] – styles Henry 'rex' *and* 'dux Normannorum'. The rest style him 'rex' alone.

As these statistics suggest, the conventions and uniformity of writing-office productions should not be allowed to muffle the message found in such a large proportion of the beneficiary productions, namely that to the scribes concerned Henry ruled in Normandy not as king but in some other capacity, be it as duke or 'princeps'. Henry, too, was well aware that he ruled over both a duchy and a kingdom. When he wrote to Pope Innocent II *c.* 1133 about the trouble Archbishop Hugh was causing in Normandy, he wrote of his 'regnum' *and* his 'ducatus'.[226] Henry's so-called fourth seal made effectively the same point. On one side he was portrayed as 'rex Anglorum' and on the other as 'dux Normannorum'. It should be noted, incidentally, that the writing-office scribes continued to style Henry as 'rex' alone after the introduction of the new seal, apparently oblivious to, or unconcerned about, the mismatch between the style in the text and on the seal that now resulted. That would have been very odd, had the style been anything other than convention.

It was probably the introduction of the wording on the fourth seal that was at the root of Hollister's mistaken claim that, 'in order to sever the ancient tie between France and Normandy, Henry I quite consciously eschewed the ducal title altogether and ruled simply as "rex Anglorum"'.[227] Henry's earlier seals did not bear the words 'dux Normannorum'. On those seals, Henry was instead styled 'rex Anglorum' on both faces. In 1960, Pierre Chaplais reconsidered the impressions of Henry's various great seals.[228] In doing so, he declared that the first seal was a forgery. He also noted that the first use of the so-called fourth seal could be dated to 1121. Chaplais, not surprisingly, supposed that a change in the wording of the seal reflected political change. He suggested that Henry had taken the title 'dux Normannorum' following the death of his son and designated heir, William Adelin, in the wreck of the *White Ship* in November 1120.

---

[225] M. Hagger, 'The earliest Norman writs revisited', *Historical Research*, 82 (2009), 188.

[226] *PL*, 179, cols. 669–70.

[227] Hollister, '*Regnum*', **29**, the idea is repeated at p. 31. Bates has previously criticised Hollister's position here: Bates, 'England and Normandy after 1066', 864–5.

[228] Chaplais, 'The seals and original charters of Henry I', 260–75.

But while the wreck of the *White Ship* looks at first glance to constitute the most obvious reason for Henry's decision to adopt the ducal title, other just as plausible causes can be identified. Indeed, the evidence suggests that Henry's decision first to eschew and then to adopt the ducal style had nothing to do with the events of 1120. Instead, it was quite possibly the result of the manner by which Henry had gained control of Normandy, and his concern to appease domestic opinion and opposition. That Henry did not formally take the ducal title during the first years of his reign in Normandy thus had nothing to do with his relationship with the kings of the French, and everything to do with quietening the residual opposition to his rule found within the duchy.

Henry's difficulties here stemmed from the fact that when he defeated his brother, he took Normandy from the reigning duke whom he then imprisoned. Even an incarcerated duke was still a duke, however, just as the imprisoned Stephen and Richard I were still kings. Furthermore, Curthose need not have been as unpopular as Orderic Vitalis would have us believe, and Henry's victory might not have seemed so just as Henry himself, and Orderic, too, portrayed it. Henry, as a wise and cautious ruler, might consequently have decided that adopting the ducal title could only put the spotlight on his imprisoned brother and open up questions about the basis of his rule over the duchy. A cautious silence on the matter was thus maintained, and prominent individuals, such as Anselm, who sought to bestow the ducal title on Henry in letters that were read aloud in court, were quietly told to desist from doing so.[229]

Chaplais argued that the last use of the third seal dated from between 1114, when it was appended to an act issued for the new archbishop of Canterbury and his monks,[230] and 1118, when Henry confirmed to the monks of Tiron a grant of land in Wales made by Robert fitz Martin.[231] But Chaplais himself recognized that the act for Tiron might have been issued as early as 1114, and it could even have been made before that. It was place-dated at Mortain, and as Henry had occupied Alençon in 1112, led further campaigns against the lordship of Bellême in 1113, and granted the county of Mortain to Stephen in or around the same year,[232] it is possible that it was made during one of those visits. If so, that would make the act for Tiron earlier than that for Canterbury. Thus the fourth seal might actually have been introduced at any point after 1114 (the date of the Canterbury act). This

---

[229] *Letters of St Anselm*, nos. 401, 402, 404, 424, 462. The point was also made by Hollister, 'Regnum', p. **31**, but to a different end.

[230] *Regesta*, ii.no. 1055.

[231] *Ctl. Tiron*, i. 42 (no. xxvi); *Regesta*, ii.no. 1187; Chaplais, 'The seals and original charters of Henry I', 265. Chaplais dated the act 1114 × 1118 but it could have been made as early as 1107.

[232] King, *King Stephen*, pp. 11–12.

fits very well with what we know of the acknowledgement of Henry's rule over Normandy by his neighbours and subjects.

We can begin at the end. In 1120, Henry's possession of Normandy was so secure that he was able to ensure that his only legitimate son, William Adelin, would succeed him there as well as in England. William thus did homage to Louis VI or his son Philip for the duchy in that year.[233] Although both Malmesbury and John of Worcester wrote of the grant of Normandy to William in a way that suggests they saw it as comprising an immediate gift from the French king in return for William's homage, Hugh the Chanter made it clear that, like his predecessors, William Adelin would have to wait until his father died before he gained authority over the duchy, styling him 'rex et dux designatus'.[234] In the meantime, Henry continued to rule Normandy himself. The Anglo-Saxon chronicler remarked that after the reconciliation with Louis, Henry made arrangements for 'the administration of his castles and his land in Normandy' before returning to England.[235] At Barfleur, even as the royal household was about to sail for England, it was Henry who confirmed the *pancarte* presented to him by the monks of Cerisy-la-Forêt.[236] William Adelin was not even among the witnesses.

But if William was to succeed Henry, even if only in the future, then Henry's own claim to, and hold on, Normandy must have been acknowledged by the majority of the Normans, too. William's right could hardly have been plucked out of thin air. The homage of 1120 should therefore be seen as the final move in a game that had been playing out for some years previously. Henry had won domestic support to his side by Christmas 1114, or early 1115, when he presented William to the Norman lords and they did homage to him.[237] Again, this must have been homage in anticipation of his succession, because it was Henry who continued to rule in Normandy, as Books XI and XII of Orderic's *Ecclesiastical History* and several ducal *acta* that can be dated to the period between 1106 and 1120 make abundantly clear.[238]

But even before William received the homage of his future subjects, Henry had

[233] Malmesbury, *GR*, i. 734, 758; Worcester, iii. 144. Orderic does not mention the homage to Louis, and he also says, when recording William's death, that he was the 'lawful heir of the English realm', pointedly omitting all mention of Normandy (Orderic, vi. 300).

[234] Hugh the Chanter, *The History of the Church of York*, p. 98.

[235] *ASChr*, E, s.a. 1120; trans. Garmonsway, p. 249.

[236] *Monasticon*, vi². 1073–5 = *Regesta*, ii. no. 1233.

[237] Malmesbury, *GR*, i. 758; ; *ASChr*, E, s.a. 1115; trans. Garmonsway, p. 246. It should be noted that the English lords did homage to William in 1116, which does not suggest that William would be ruling Normandy as king (Worcester, iii. 138, noted by Le Patourel, *Norman Empire*, p. 90).

[238] Books 11 and 12 are printed in Orderic, vi. See also the acts calendared at, for example, *Regesta*, ii. nos. 764, 792, 794, 842, 912, 1074, 1186, 1216.

himself been recognized as duke of the Normans by his neighbours and rivals. In February 1113, Fulk of Anjou had come to Alençon to do fealty to Henry in return for the county of Maine. Implicit in his act was the acknowledgement that Henry was the rightful duke of the Normans.[239] At the end of March, Henry met with Louis VI near Gisors. 'Louis then granted Bellême and the county of Maine and the whole of Brittany to Henry.'[240] For Louis to have done that, he must also have recognized that Henry was the legitimate ruler of Normandy.[241] Indeed, Suger of Saint-Denis said as much when recording a meeting of the two kings in 1109 at Neaufles-Saint-Martin: 'your efforts have gained for you the duchy of Normandy by the noble leave of the lord king of the French.'[242] Suger might not have been exaggerating, even though he was writing with the benefit of hindsight. Both William of Malmesbury and the slightly later Chronicle of Morigny suggest that Louis had encouraged Henry to take Normandy from his brother while his father Philip I was still alive.[243]

Putting all this together, it is possible to suggest a new interpretation of events leading up to the creation of the fourth seal and the adoption of the ducal style. In 1106, Henry took Normandy with the tacit support of the future Louis VI and imprisoned his brother. The young William Clito was left in the care of Helias of Saint-Saëns. In the interval, Henry deliberately eschewed the ducal title and worked to consolidate his position and win over his domestic opponents. By c. 1110, Henry was strong enough to move against William Clito, and sought to arrest him. He failed, and Clito fled into exile.[244] From then on he was a focus of rebellion, which made the recognition of Henry's right to the duchy a matter of loyalty and the reverse, treason. In 1113, at the very latest, and from a position of strength, Henry was recognized as duke of the Normans by Louis VI and Fulk of Anjou – interestingly, the first dateable application of the style 'dux Normannorum' to Henry after 1107 dates from 2 March of that year.[245] At the end of 1114 or in 1115, Henry had his own son acknowledged as his successor by the Normans, but continued to rule the duchy himself, as his predecessors had done. Now that his rule was acknowledged by the king of the Franks, the count

---

[239] Orderic, vi. 180.

[240] Orderic, vi. 180.

[241] The grant would mean in turn that the later Hyde chronicler was mistaken when he wrote that Louis insisted on recognizing Clito's right to the duchy in 1114 (Hyde, p. 82).

[242] Suger, *Deeds of Louis the Fat*, p. 72.

[243] Malmesbury, *GR*, i. 732; *La chronique de Morigny (1095–1152)*, ed. L. Mirot, second edition (Paris, 1912), p. 21. Book 2 of the chronicle was written in the second quarter of the twelfth century (p. iv).

[244] Orderic, vi. 164.

[245] An original act for Savigny (now lost): *Neustria pia seu de omnibus et singulis abbatis et prioratibus totiis Normanniae, ed. A du Monstier (1663)*, p. 760 = *Regesta*, ii. no. 1015.

of Anjou, and all the freemen of Normandy over twelve years old, Henry could take the title 'dux Normannorum' without fear of political repercussions. He thus changed his seal to reflect that fact. With William Clito providing a focus for revolt by c. 1110, his actions also ensured that Clito could not take the title for himself before William Adelin's anticipated succession – although as his father was still alive, Clito might have felt unable to do so anyway.

Henry was thus both a king and a duke in Normandy. From about 1115, both titles were emblazoned on his seal, which was attached to almost every document that he authenticated. The presence of those two titles on his seal and in some of his *acta* – perhaps including the letter he sent to Bishop Lambert of Arras that must have been written before the bishop's death in 1115 – indicate that he ruled in Normandy as a duke, albeit a royal duke, and not as a king.[246] Furthermore, the fourth seal also highlighted the fact that Henry ruled over two distinct peoples and, by extension, two territories.[247]

This fact was increasingly reflected in Henry's acts. In 1115, one scribe from the west of Normandy had dated an act for the monks of Lessay 'in the year of the Lord 1115, during the rule of Henry as king in England and as "princeps" in Normandy'.[248] The first of two acts for the Hospital of St John at Falaise, dating from 1132, styles Henry 'rex Anglorum' but refers to his 'kingdom of England and duchy of Normandy (*regnum meum Anglie et ducatus Normannie*)'.[249] An act of 1135 saw King Henry granting 10 *livres* of Rouen to the lepers of the Grand Beaulieu each year for the security of 'my kingdom of England and my duchy of Normandy (*regni mei Anglie et ducatus mei Normannie*)', which gift was also confirmed by Henry's royal authority.[250] But Normans of all kinds would have been reminded that Normandy and England were different in all sorts of ways, and from well before 1115. The general addresses used in Henry I's charters were different if an act was to apply only in England or only in Normandy. Exemptions from custom and toll might be limited to one side of the Channel or the other, or might encompass the whole of Henry's dominions.[251] The English coinage was distinct from the Norman coinage, and although English pennies seem not to have circulated widely in the duchy – perhaps because most of them were melted down when they arrived at Rouen for the silver to be debased and minted into Norman *deniers* – when they were seen and weighed the differences between them

---

[246] *PL*, 162, col. 684.
[247] For a similar view see Hallam and Everard, *Capetian France*, p. 64.
[248] Chanteux, *Recueil*, ii. 71–4 (no. 17). Henry signed as *rex*.
[249] *Regesta*, ii. 376–7 (no. cclxvi).
[250] *NI*, pp. 106–7 (no. 17).
[251] *Regesta*, ii. nos. 1750,1258, 1674 (for England only); *NI*, p. 308; *Regesta*, ii. no. 1919 (for Normandy only); *Regesta*, ii. no. 1925, 1555, 1682 (for both England and Normandy).

and the native Norman *deniers* would have been immediately apparent, even before Henry's reform of the English coinage in 1124.[252] Customs and laws were distinct, too, as reflected, for example, in the wording of documents transferring property from one person to another and the fact that bernage and *grauarium* were collected in Normandy but not in England.[253]

In sum, then, Henry ruled England as king and Normandy as duke. England and Normandy remained separate entities, even though they might have been 'associated' under Henry's rule.[254] There was no attempt to create a single Anglo-Norman *regnum*, independent of the king of the Franks, as Hollister proposed.

---

[252] Some English coins did circulate in Normandy. Robert of Torigni famously reported the grumbling of Henry's household knights about the quality of the English coins that were paid out to them in Normandy in 1124, while the pipe roll of 1130 records a shipment of coins to the duchy (where they might, of course, have been melted down) (Jumièges, ii. 238; *PR 31 Henry I*, p. 63; for the suggestion that English pennies were recoined when they reached Normandy see D. Bates, *The Normans and Empire: The Ford Lectures delivered in the University of Oxford during Hilary Term 2010* (Oxford, 2013), p. 118). The dukes of the Normans were not the first to melt down English pennies to satisfy their own need for silver. A single penny of King Offa found at Dorestad is thought to be the sole survivor of a batch that was melted down to make Carolingian deniers (S. Coupland, 'Trading places: Quentovich and Dorestad reassessed', *EME*, 11 (2002), 221). That relatively few English pennies circulated is suggested by the composition of the hoards found within Normandy. Thus a small hoard found at Sébecourt (Eure) comprised six Norman *deniers* and two English pennies of William the Conqueror's last issue (Dumas, 'Les monnaies Normandes', p. 121), while a hoard discovered at Ferrières-sur-Risle, thought to have been buried in the first years of twelfth century, was made up almost exclusively of Norman *deniers* (Dumas, 'Les monnaies Normandes', p. 127). There were just five Norman *deniers* among the 2,200 coins buried just across the border at Montfort-l'Amaury *c.* 1120, but no English pennies at all (Dumas, 'Les monnaies Normandes', pp. 127–8). In contrast, it should be noted that the Pimprez hoard, unearthed in 2002 near Beauvais, comprised 569 coins in total, of which 374 were English pennies of Henry I and 72 were English pennies of King Stephen. There were 123 continental pennies or bracteates, too, and twelve silver ingots, but there was no example of a Norman *denier* (or indeed of French royal coinage). The vill belonged to the Templars, so the large quantity of English pennies suggests something of the order's international reach and need for good quality coin, and also suggests that the coins had not reached this place by way of the duchy.

[253] There was, for example, no 'sake and soke, toll and team' in Norman acts (see Hagger, 'The earliest Norman writs revisited', 195). For bernage and *grauarium* see below, Chapter 10, pp. 585–7.

[254] The *Chronicle of Morigny* reports that when Henry defeated his brother he 'associated that man's county with his kingdom (*comitatum illius regno suo sociauit*)': *Chronique de Morigny*, p. 21. Orderic made the same point, recording the conspiracy to make Curthose 'the prince of both England and Normandy so as to preserve the unity of both *regna*' in 1088 (Orderic, iv. 124). His words are a useful reminder that the *regnum* referred to in Henry's Norman acts could be Normandy.

For that to have happened, the French king's lordship would have to have been denied in Normandy, and not simply sidelined. That did not happen. As John Le Patourel remarked: 'in the time of William the Conqueror and his sons … Normandy was traditionally a part of the kingdom of which Henry I (of France), Philip I, and Louis VI were kings.'[255]

Indeed, if anything the ties between Normandy and France grew closer rather than more distant during Henry's reign, although that could not have been foreseen in 1106 when Henry took the duchy as, unlike his predecessors, Henry had not sworn fidelity to the king of the French. He seems to have maintained the freedom that state of affairs gave him for most, if not all, of his reign. Indeed, a report in the chronicle written at Saint-Pierre-le-Vif of Sens claims that Henry, along with the dukes of Aquitaine and Burgundy, actively resisted the newly crowned Louis VI's demand for his homage in 1108.[256] The meeting of Henry and Louis at Gisors in March 1113 saw the two kings take a step closer to each other, however, as they were there 'bound in an alliance of friendship (*amoris uinculo complexati sunt*)' with Henry's right to Normandy apparently recognized.[257] This restored the sort of relationship that had pertained under Richard II, Robert the Magnificent, and William the Bastard (at intervals before 1076). But, as was all too predictable, the compact did not last for long. When Henry I met with Pope Calixtus in 1119, he is said to have spoken to the same pope of this same *pactum amiciciæ* but to have declared that Louis had broken it.[258]

A significant break with the past was made in 1120. Then, as noted above, 'the homage which he himself (that is, Henry) as a sovereign prince was too proud to pay' was performed by his son. As William of Malmesbury reported it, 'William, our king's son, did homage to the king of the French for Normandy, acknowledging that he would hold the province from him by legal right'.[259] Hollister

255   Le Patourel, *Norman Empire*, p. 218 and see also p. 221.
256   *Chronique de Saint-Pierre-le-Vif de Sens, dite de Clarius*, ed. and trans. R.-H. Bautier and M. Giles (Paris, 1979), pp. 148–9, cited in Bates, 'Normandy and England after 1066', 864.
257   Orderic, vi. 180. See above, *infra*, p. 297.
258   Orderic, vi. 288. Orderic talks about such pacts made between others, too. For example, Henry I and Curthose made at Alton in 1101 (Orderic, v. 318–20), which was described as a *feodera* in 1103 (Orderic, vi. 14). This had been broken by the duke's actions in 1102 and was then broken for a second time by Gunter of Aunay (Orderic, vi. 60). There was a second *foederus* between Henry and Fulk of Anjou (Orderic, vi. 224). In addition, there was a peace treaty between Stephen and Louis, which followed the form of the relationship between Louis and Henry (Orderic, vi. 482).
259   Malmesbury, *GR*, i. 759 and 734, respectively. William's homage is also noted by Suger: *Deeds of Louis the Fat*, p. 75 and Worcester, iii. 144, in similar terms. The later Hyde chronicler thought that William received the duchy from Louis's son, Philip, and did

concluded that 'the … 1120 homage … bound the king of France to Henry's succession plan without binding the lord of Normandy to the king of France'.[260] Nonetheless, although Henry might have maintained his own freedom of action, the principle had been established that the dukes did homage for Normandy. Moreover, that homage was clearly linked to the succession.

It is worth remarking that one response to these changing circumstances might have been a renewed interest in Dudo's work with its central message of Norman autonomy from the king of the French. No fewer than five of the surviving manuscripts might have been written between *c.* 1120 and the end of Henry's reign.[261] The narrative known as the *Breuis relatio*, written *c.* 1114–20 in England, although apparently by a writer with a foot on both sides of the Channel, might also have been composed as a response to this same event (or the negotiations leading up to it).[262] In it, Dudo's account of the agreement made on the banks of the Epte in 945 was revised and reinterpreted: 'It was also agreed in this pact that the count of Normandy should not render any service to the king of France for Normandy or otherwise perform service, unless the king of France should grant him a fief in France for which he would owe service. Therefore the count of Normandy renders nothing to the king of France except homage for Normandy and fealty during his lifetime and for his earthly honour.'[263] Thus, so far as the unknown author was concerned, although homage and fealty were now due for Normandy, Dudo's venerable assertion that the dukes owed no service for the duchy remained inviolate.

By 1133, even this had been given up. Or rather, by then Henry had agreed to render service from Normandy to the French king, even if it is not clear that this obligation was linked to the tenure of, or succession to, the duchy. But whatever the precise foundation and nature of the service, the inquisition on the lands of

homage to him for it, too, as Louis did not want to break his promise to uphold Clito's claim (Hyde, p. 82; Gillingham, 'Doing homage to the king of France', p. 69. Louis's son, Philip, would have been two years old at the time).

[260] Hollister, *Henry*, p. 276, and see also p. 274 and n. 160.

[261] Pohl, *Dudo of Saint-Quentin's* Historia Normannorum, p. 263, Appendix 2. The date of MS R should probably be revised to 1100–1125 in accordance with the remarks made by Felice Lifshitz (F. Lifshitz, [review of] 'Pohl, Benjamin. *Dudo of Saint-Quentin's* Historia Normannorum: *Tradition, Innovation and Memory*', The Medieval Review, 16 January 2015 <http://scholarworks.iu.edu/journals/index.php/tmr/article/view/20857/26863> accessed 6 February 2016, and see the Introduction, pp. 8–9).

[262] See Hollister, '*Regnum*', pp. 44–6, whose interpretation of the passage does not hold up when it is compared to Dudo's account. Van Houts, *Normans*, pp. 199–200 suggests that the passage was a response to growing uncertainty about the relationship with the king of the French.

[263] *Breuis relatio*, ed. and trans. E. M. C. van Houts in *History and Family Traditions in England and the Continent, 1000–1200* (Aldershot, 1999), p. 45.

the bishop of Bayeux held in that year states unequivocally that 'the bishop of Bayeux owed to the lord of Normandy ten knights for the service of the king of the French'.[264] Indeed, it may be supposed that the appearance of a Norman contingent in the army that Louis VI led to the Auvergne in 1126 reveals that the concession had been made by that point.[265] If so, it is likely that it was made in the hope that it would undermine Louis's support for William Clito's rival claim to the duchy, at a time when Henry had lost the potential support of his son-in-law, the Emperor Henry V, which had proved so useful in 1124.[266]

Alternatively, it may be that a Norman contingent was in the army of 1126 because Henry had finally been obliged to respect a long-standing obligation that he had previously been able to avoid, about which the author of the *Breuis relatio* was understandably ignorant. David Bates, Elizabeth Hallam, and John Gillingham have all argued that the dukes had owed military service to the kings of the French since William the Conqueror's reign.[267] As the only evidence for this view is the presence of a small Norman contingent in the army that King Philip mustered against Robert the Frisian in 1071 which was defeated at the battle of Cassel, the argument is not entirely convincing. Moreover, 1071 seems an odd time for William to have agreed to perform military service to the French king. If the concession does date from the reign of William the Bastard, it is more likely that the service was first demanded and provided *c.* 1048 when William joined King Henry of the French on the Mouliherne campaign in the immediate aftermath of the battle of Val-ès-Dunes. Fragile support might be provided for this hypothesis by the concern evidenced by William of Jumièges to demonstrate that earlier dukes had served the French kings in the field, too, which implies a criticism of a newly conceded obligation.[268] Of course, William, like Richard II before him, might well have been providing this service as a result only of the personal bond of fidelity that made him the French king's man.[269] There is no reason to suppose that the obligation to provide such service had anything to do with the way that Normandy was held.

In any event, these agreements and concessions had very little impact on

---

[264] *Inquisition*, p. 14.

[265] *The Deeds of Louis the Fat*, p. 135. Gillingham, 'Doing homage', p. 75, n. 2 thought that the obligation to provide knights to the French king was reflected in Suger's description of the Norman contingent as 'exercitus tributarius'. Cusimano and Moorhead, however, translate this passage as: 'a host from Normandy that owed tribute to the English king Henry.'

[266] See above, Chapter 3, p. 177.

[267] Ordeirc, ii. 282; Bates, 'Normandy and England after 1066', 865; Hallam and Everard, *Capetian France*, p. 125; Gillingham, 'Doing homage', p. 75, n. 1.

[268] See above, Introduction, pp. 13–14.

[269] Jumièges, ii. 32–4.

Henry's power within the duchy. The agreement to provide Louis VI with military service did not open up the duchy to his jurisdiction, even if the homage of 1120 had given him a theoretical right to intervene in its internal affairs, not least because Henry's subjects continued to treat him as the ultimate authority in the duchy. They did not seek Louis's justice or his confirmations of their Norman possessions, because the peace and security Henry offered could not have been improved upon. That left warfare as the only avenue by which Louis might try to enhance his power over Normandy, but he had tried that on several occasions and had consistently come off the worst. So Normandy remained autonomous for the rest of Henry's reign, and even under Stephen the French king did not make inroads. Nonetheless, Louis was laying foundations on which his successors would successfully build. And, as we know, Normandy would eventually fall to a French king sixty years after it fell to the Angevins.

* * * * * *

At the very end of the period covered by this book, Stephen of Blois felt obliged to defend his seizure of the English throne *and* the duchy of the Normans at the papal curia, with the help of the testimonial provided by Louis VI.[270] He had likewise to turn to Louis in 1137 to have his son, Eustace, recognized as his successor in the duchy. Henry of Huntingdon reported this as follows: 'Eustace … was made the French king's man for Normandy, which belongs to French overlordship.'[271] While Huntingdon would have been unlikely to make his point so strongly before c. 1120, his view did no more than reflect a long-standing truth. French overlordship was only expressly acknowledged when it suited the dukes to do so, but it was implied by the dating clauses of some ducal *acta*, and by the Norman form of the *Laudes Regiae*. Such evidence helps to underscore the point that the dukes had never, not even in Dudo's *De moribus*, denied that Normandy was in France or that the French kings were their overlords. Rather, they were concerned to ensure that the French kings should have no rights within Normandy itself, and no opportunity to impose them either. In that ambition, as the complete absence of royal confirmations for property in Normandy, and the total lack of Norman lawsuits in French royal courts reveal, they were entirely successful.

---

[270] *Recueil des actes de Louis VI*, ii. 331 (no. 396).
[271] Huntingdon, p. 708. Gervase of Canterbury turned this into homage in 1140 (Gillingham, 'Doing homage', pp. 66–7).

PART II

The Minister of God

Let every soul be subject unto the higher powers. For there is no power but of God: the powers that be are ordained of God. Whosoever therefore resisteth the power, resisteth the ordinance of God: and they that resist shall receive to themselves damnation. For rulers are not a terror to good works, but to the evil. Wilt thou then not be afraid of the power? Do that which is good, and thou shalt have praise of the same: for he is the minister of God to thee for good. But if thou do that which is evil, be afraid: for he beareth not the sword in vain: for he is the minister of God, a revenger to execute wrath upon him that doeth evil.

Romans, 13:1–4

CHAPTER 6

Lonely at the Top: The Duke and his Executive Authority

Pᴀᴜʟ's letter to the Romans provided one foundation for medieval theories about secular power. God had established the terrestrial powers that ruled on earth. He had delegated a part of his power to kings and other secular rulers so that they might guide His people to do right, and punish them for their transgressions. Dudo of Saint Quentin developed this idea of divinely delegated authority further with the intention of legitimizing the rule of the dukes of the Normans. He had Rollo chosen by God to establish a dynasty to rule over Normandy. His foundation of a principality based on Rouen was the fulfilment of a divine plan.[1] If God's will were to continue to be done, then the rule of members of Rollo's line had to be maintained. Nonetheless, even when there was a clear heir, Dudo of Saint-Quentin suggested that an assembly might take the lead in demanding the designation of a successor, even if the right to nominate belonged to the duke, and even if the *principes* always accepted that nomination, and that might have kept the idea of an elective principle alive in the duchy until at least the end of the tenth century.

For the reasons discussed above, William of Jumièges amended Dudo's story in a way that allowed him to dispense with much of Dudo's myth-making, while joining with him in emphasizing the right of Rollo's heirs to rule the duchy.[2] The Christian God is largely absent from his account. Instead, he had Rollo chosen by lot (*sorte eligentes*) after the arrival of the Viking army at Rouen.[3] According to Rimbert's *Life of St Anskar*, Danes and Swedes used lots to seek the opinion of the gods on particular matters,[4] but it does not seem to be the case that Jumièges intended his readers to understand that the Norse gods had selected a leader from among the Viking chiefs. Rather, he stated explicitly that this was how those chiefs

---

[1] Searle, *PK*, p. 65; Shopkow, *History and Community*, pp. 38, 79, 82.

[2] See the Introduction, pp. 14–18.

[3] Jumièges, i. 52.

[4] Rimbert, *Anskar: The Apostle of the North. 801–865. Translated from the Vita Anskarii by Bishop Rimbert, his Fellow Missionary and Successor*, trans. C. H. Robinson (London, 1921), pp. 60, 67–8, 91; E. Roesdahl, *The Vikings*, trans. S. M. Margeson and K. Williams, second edition (London, 1998), p. 69; Christiansen, *Norsemen in the Viking Age*, pp. 288–9.

themselves had chosen or elected Rollo as their leader, adding later that he had been 'appointed' as such.[5] The manner of Rollo's election as leader is important, not just because it removed any sense that Rollo and his successors ruled as the result of divine appointment and emphasized the sense of community and cooperation that bound the Normans together. It also suggested that where there was no clear leader or successor, one should be chosen by the community.

There were other issues relating to the succession, too, which would have occupied the thoughts of those involved in the establishment and recognition of the heir, and which emerge clearly in Dudo's work as well as in more recent discussions about the succession of 1087. And as these issues are relevant to much of the content of this chapter, it seems most appropriate to set them out here.

The first issue, emphasized by John Le Patourel and George Garnett, is that rule over and the territory of Normandy were considered indivisible. While the demesne might be shared with, or alienated to, the duke's brothers, as was the case with the counts, the office of duke and the geographic extent of the duke's rule had to be preserved intact. Garnett thought that this ran counter to Norman inheritance customs, but Normans were well aware that other offices, such as that of bishop or *vicomte* or *prévôt*, and the rights and responsibilities that went with them, could only be held or inherited by one person at a time.[6] Indeed, from the tenth century at least, rule over the west Frankish kingdom as well as the duchy of Aquitaine and the counties of Blois, Anjou, and Flanders was also indivisible. This principle, then, was not something peculiar to Normandy.[7] The result, in the duchy as elsewhere, was that counts, dukes, or kings might have to console disappointed sons or siblings with lands and lesser titles, and that occasionally this was not enough to prevent rebellion.[8] The Frankish experience suggests that there need have been no influence from other traditions to cause such disturbances, but it is possible that a duke's disappointed younger sons were aware of the Norwegian custom whereby more than one member of the ruling dynasty might be elected king at the same time (until 1163).[9]

---

[5] Jumièges, i. 52.

[6] Garnett, '"Ducal" succession', pp. 88, 101.

[7] Garnett suggests the reverse: '"Ducal" succession', 86; Garnett, *Conquered England*, pp. 142, 146.

[8] Le Patourel, 'The Norman succession 996–1135', *EHR*, 86 (1971)', 237–40; Garnett, '"Ducal" succession', 80–110.

[9] Bagge, *Viking Stronghold*, pp. 40–1, 166. That was not the case with Denmark where there were four co-kings c. 819. Although they had been replaced by just one king, Horik, c. 827, towards the end of his reign he was forced to share power with two nephews (Bagge, *Viking Stronghold*, pp. 208, 211). It was Harald Gormsson (Bluetooth) who finally created a united Denmark under one king (N. Lund, 'Scandinavia, c. 700–1066', in *The New Cambridge Medieval History: II. c. 700–c. 900*, ed. R. McKitterick (Cambridge, 1995), pp. 208, 215–16).

A second issue concerns the position or role of the designated successor. Ralph Davis was of the view that when Robert Curthose was designated William the Bastard's heir in 1063 and 1066, he was associated in the rule of the duchy, and did in fact rule as duke during William's absences in England between 1068 and 1071. That probably goes too far. Curthose might have acted as his father's lieutenant in Normandy, but the limited role played by Matilda during William's absences, the duke's subsequent behaviour, and Robert's rebellions all indicate that he was not associated in his father's rule over the duchy at all. Garnett's view that the designated heir did not share power with the reigning duke is therefore probably to be preferred. The succession, then, was anticipatory, not associative.[10]

A third point which has been made repeatedly is that the designated heir's succession was assured. Emily Zack Tabuteau, following John Beckerman, made a strong case that the designation of Curthose as the heir to Normandy in 1063 and 1066, with the associated doing of homage by the Norman lords, constituted a *post obitum* grant 'and such a gift could not be cancelled by any subsequent disposition'.[11] While it was in all probability the renewed oaths sworn to Curthose *c.* 1080, rather than those of the 1060s, that ensured his succession to the duchy, it was nonetheless the case that William was thus forced to divide his *regnum* in 1087 because, in this instance, the principles which he and his predecessors had nurtured to ensure that the succession passed to their own sons prevented him from changing his mind after the relevant arrangements had been put in place. But as those oaths almost certainly included a saving clause, privileging the fidelity previously sworn to Duke William, it was also important that Curthose did not render those oaths void by his own actions.[12]

The indivisibility of the ducal office was necessary if a single figure was to wield power without competition or significant opposition across the whole of the territory that would become Normandy. It is consequently not surprising that the dukes should have insisted that the powers that God had delegated to them should not be delegated to anyone else. But while this generally strengthened ducal rule, it might also lead disappointed contenders to rebellion. In 1106, one such rebellion unseated the reigning duke, Robert Curthose, and established his brother, already King Henry I of the English, in his place. Nine years after Henry's death, a second conqueror, Geoffrey of Anjou, gained control of the duchy. These two conquests,

[10] Garnett, '"Ducal" succession', pp. 91–5.
[11] J. Beckerman, 'Succession in Normandy, 1087, and in England, 1066: the role of testamentary custom', *Speculum*, 47 (1972), 258–60; E. Z. Tabuteau, 'The role of law in the succession to Normandy and England, 1087', *HSJ*, 3 (1991), 141–69, especially here p. 152; and see also G. Garnett, 'Robert Curthose: the duke who lost his trousers', *ANS*, 35 (2013), 229–31.
[12] See above, Chapter 5, pp. 251–2 and below, *infra*, pp. 332–4.

like the rebellions more generally, tell us a great deal about the fragile unity of the duchy, the conditions that would-be dukes had to satisfy if they were to achieve their ambition to rule, and the power of the aristocracy to influence the succession (from a limited range of candidates). They are considered in the second section of this chapter.

Having discussed the succession and the related rebellions, the chapter concludes with a consideration of the monopoly on executive power that the dukes maintained in their hands. The two minorities of 942–c. 948 and 1035–c. 1043 were occasions when the dukes' hold on power slackened, but the blood that was shed to gain control over the boys reveals just how important the person of the duke remained with regard to rule over Normandy. The conspirators did not want to harm the children, they wanted to influence them. And that means that their unedifying behaviour was just another of the several elements that acknowledged, highlighted, and thus ultimately strengthened the dukes' power. The limited capabilities of ducal officials and the willingness of Norman beneficiaries to track down the duke even if he was in England indicates the absence of anything like a viceroy who might act as the duke's substitute in his absence, and reveals that the dukes did not delegate their executive power, thereby ensuring their grip on the duchy remained uncontested and paramount.

Legitimacy and succession

As discussed above, Rollo had probably been ruling at Rouen for some years before his possession of the city and its hinterland was recognized by King Charles the Simple, perhaps at Saint-Clair-sur-Epte, and perhaps in 911.[13] He continued to lead the Normans of Rouen until *c.* 927. At that point, the question arose as to his successor. In both Scandinavia and Francia, there was an expectation that sons would inherit their parents' property, and Normandy provided no exception to this rule. Neither Flodoard nor Richer raised eyebrows at the succession of William Longsword, whom both explicitly identified as Rollo's son. They therefore seem implicitly to have accepted that Normandy was the hereditary possession of Rollo's family, although Dudo was the first to assert, *c.* 1015, that Rouen and Normandy were held as an inheritance and an alod to be passed down to Rollo's heirs.[14]

At the same time, when it came to making both Scandinavian and French kings there was a second principle that came into play: election. John Le Patourel observed in 1971 that 'the relative strength of each principle at any one time

---

[13]   See above, Chapter 1, pp. 45–6.
[14]   *Dudo*, p. 49.

depended very much upon personal and political circumstances. When the king was strong, as the early Carolingians were strong, he could designate his successor or successors and thus render the elective principle ineffective .... when the king was weak, as the later Carolingians were weak, the elective principle revived and on occasion it was decisive.'[15] Le Patourel's argument was based on work that was seriously undermined in 1978, and the role of election in the succession to the west Frankish throne, or to other west Frankish principalities, has been downplayed ever since.[16] Heredity and election were much more equal partners in parts of Scandinavia, however, and those traditions might have influenced Norman practice into the eleventh century.[17]

The role of election might also have been highlighted in the duchy by the fact that successive dukes could only succeed their fathers in those areas that their fathers had ruled. But Normandy was not at its fullest extent in 927, 942, 996, or even 1026. As described above, during Richard I's reign, the duchy grew to encompass the Lieuvin, the northern part of the Hiémois, the Bessin at least as far west as Bayeux, the tip of the Cotentin, and part of the Avranchin.[18] Here, Richard did not succeed his father. Instead, he was acknowledged – elected – as duke by the men or communities living there, just as he may be supposed to have been chosen as their leader by those of his Viking allies who decided to settle in Normandy c. 965.[19] In some places, such recognition might have been the result of military force. Elsewhere it might have been the result of local debate.[20] But, however it happened, lords brought themselves and their lordships under the rule of the dukes. Thus during Richard II's reign, figures such as Giroie or Emma of Ponchardon acknowledged his lordship over at least some of their lands,[21] while in the 1050s William of La Ferté-Macé came to call Roger of Montgommery his lord and William the Bastard his duke.[22] At such times, it is almost certain that these individuals or communities would have sworn oaths of fidelity to the duke, just as those who had already lived under their rule had done at, or soon after, their succession. Such negotiations and the making of such oaths may be supposed to

---

[15] Le Patourel, 'Norman succession', 236–7. See also J. L. Nelson, 'The Lord's anointed and the people's choice: Carolingian royal ritual', in *Ritual and Royalty: Power and Ceremonial in Traditional Societies*, ed. D. Cannadine and S. Price (Cambridge, 1987), pp. 140, 146, 157–8, 163–4.

[16] By A. W. Lewis, 'Anticipatory association of the heir in early Capetian France', *American Historical Review*, 83 (1978), 906–27.

[17] Roesdahl, *The Vikings*, p. 66; Bagge, *Viking Stronghold*, pp. 40–1 58–60, 166–9.

[18] See above, Chapter 1, pp. 66–7, 69–75.

[19] *Dudo*, pp. 160, 162; Searle, *PK*, p. 87.

[20] See above, Chapter 1, pp. 43–5.

[21] Orderic, ii. 22. See also above, Chapter 2, pp. 91–2, 93–4.

[22] *RADN*, no. 131, and see above, Chapter 2, p. 129.

have kept alive a sense that ducal rule was not solely about inheritance, because they represented 'ratification by the lesser district chiefs'.[23] It certainly ensured that up until the 1060s the recognition of the duke's power and right to rule was not a once-in-a-lifetime event. Instead, it was, to some extent at least, a continuing process and one which tended to highlight choice/election rather than inheritance in the making of the duke.[24] In any event, there were occasions when the succession did not pass from father to son, at which point the *seniores* of Normandy either implicitly or explicitly elected the next duke. Once or twice, there is even a suggestion that the burgesses of Rouen might have had a role to play in acclaiming a new duke – although their rights seem to have been much more limited than those exercised by the citizens of Bruges and Ghent in 1127 or London in 1135.[25]

The earliest accounts of ducal successions are found in Dudo of Saint-Quentin's *De moribus*.[26] Dudo's book was intended, inter alia, to demonstrate that the rule of Rollo and his successors was ordained by God, so it is not surprising that he should emphasize the role of inheritance in the succession. At the same time, he either needed or wanted to show that the dukes also ruled as a result of consensus and election. Both factors are clearly visible in Dudo's account of the negotiations that took place when the time came to choose a successor to the elderly Rollo. Dudo first had unnamed Norman *principes* confer together: 'We would inquire from him whom he would choose as his heir to the kingdom he has won in battles, and whom he would present to us as suitable. For he has a son, begotten from a most noble lineage of the Franks, who is both supremely well-formed … and extremely knowledgeable in mind. With his father's approval, we would prefer him to be our duke, and our patrician and count.'[27] These Norman lords thus acknowledged that it was for Rollo to nominate his heir, but they also took the lead in opening up the question of a successor and expressed their own preference as to his identity in colloquy. They then approached Rollo, who likewise suggested his son but made it clear that the Normans had a choice in the matter: 'choose

---

[23] Searle, *PK*, p. 73

[24] It is likely that such oaths were also sworn over several days and in a number of different places, which is likely to have heightened the sense of election still further. A comparison might be provided by William Clito's investiture as count of Flanders in 1127 as recorded by Galbert of Bruges (Galbert of Bruges, *The Murder of Charles the Good*, pp. 206–7).

[25] Galbert of Bruges, *The Murder of Charles the Good*, pp. 206–7; *Gesta Stephani*, pp. 4–6.

[26] Flodoard and Richer noted successions, but did not describe the processes involved.

[27] *Dudo*, p. 59. The *Plaintsong* might suggest otherwise, as suggested by Douglas, 'Rollo of Normandy', 422. For present purposes, the true identity of the mother does not matter but, as Neveux implies, the words of the *Plaintsong* and the account by Dudo are not necessarily mutually exclusive (Neveux, *A Brief History of the Normans*, p. 62).

that one, I beg you, to be your duke.'[28] Each side, then, had a role in the process of choosing a successor, but there were limits. In this case, those limits resulted in the Normans having no choice at all. The next duke had to be a son of the ruling duke: 'this one will be the right *hereditary* duke (*dux haereditarius*) for us.'[29] As Rollo had only the one son, his successor had to be William Longsword.[30] Immediately after the choice had been made, oaths were sworn to the heir in anticipation of his succession. That would usually have created a *post obitum* gift, but in this case, at least as Dudo presented it, Rollo seems to have resigned the duchy to his son with immediate effect.[31]

Forty years later, William of Jumièges presented Longsword's succession a little differently from Dudo. His tweaks reflected the custom and assumption that sons would inherit their father's lands and offices that had developed by the middle of the 1050s, but they were also intended to reveal that the dukes had the right to direct the succession without contradiction when they had a clear heir. And so, in his account, it was Rollo who summoned the lords of Normandy along with two Breton leaders and presented William Longsword to them. He then 'ordered them to choose him as their lord and to accept him as the leader of their army. He spoke: "it is my duty to withdraw in favour of my son; it is yours to follow him faithfully". He won them all with smooth persuasive speeches and then compelled them to swear an oath of fealty to his son.'[32] Despite the initial appearances, this was not a unilateral decision on Rollo's part, but the starting point for a discussion which saw him *persuade* them to do what he wanted. Nonetheless, the Norman lords play a subordinate role in Jumièges's account, and do what they are told.

Neither writer expressed any concern about Longsword's right to succeed his father. All parties, including the Franks, apparently recognized him as Rollo's undoubted heir. Dudo had described Rollo and Popa, William's mother, as married (*eamque sibi connubio ascivit*), and as he made no reference to this union when discussing the arrangements for Rollo's marriage to Gisla, his readers are left to infer that she had died before 911.[33] He was more circumspect about the

---

[28] *Dudo*, p. 59.

[29] Dudo, p. 181; *Dudo*, p. 59 (my italics).

[30] Eleanor Searle implied that Rollo and Longsword might have had more than one son, but that they were simply not acknowledged (Searle, *PK*, pp. 93–7). Garnett noted that this is possible, but that there is no proof to support the contention (Garnett, '"Ducal" succession', p. 86).

[31] *Dudo*, p. 60. The oath might itself have constituted part of the process of election (Garnett, *Conquered England*, p. 3), as well as establishing the *post-obitum*, and thus binding, gift (Beckerman, 'Succession in Normandy', 258–60; Tabuteau, *Transfers*, pp. 24–7; Tabuteau, 'The role of law', 152).

[32] Jumièges, i. 72.

[33] *Dudo*, pp. 38–9. For reasons which are not clear, Jumièges had Rollo reunited with Popa

relationship between Longsword and Sprota. The two were joined (*connexuit*), but no more was said.[34] As Dudo was writing long after Richard I's death, at a time when Longsword's grandson was well-established as duke, his reticence on the issue is unlikely to have related to concern about undermining the legitimacy of the ducal line. It might instead have been because he did not want to highlight the further dilution of the duke's Scandinavian blood through a liaison with a Breton, or because she was not of noble birth, or simply because he did not want to offend Sprota's son, Count Rodulf, who was still very much alive and powerful when Dudo wrote.

William of Jumièges seems to have been a little more concerned about the standing of these same marriages. That was because he was looking at them, not just in a mid-eleventh-century context, but in circumstances where the product of just such a union had only recently defeated rebels and enemies who had almost certainly used his illegitimate birth to undermine the legitimacy of his rule. So he emphasized the acceptability of these unions in a Scandinavian context, creating the phrase *more Danico* to describe both Rollo's liaison with Popa and Longsword's relationship with Sprota.[35] He thereby informed his readers that such unions 'had a long and very respectable tradition behind them, even if, in the 1050s they might well be becoming less acceptable in the eyes of churchmen'.[36] The phrase Jumièges employed strongly suggests that it was his Frankish audience that needed convincing, and that is also indicated by an insult that he added to his account of Richard I's reign. To the Franks, Richard I was 'the son of a whore who had seduced another woman's husband'.[37]

William of Jumièges was not a lone voice on this issue. Those Franks who knew Normandy and its Scandinavian traditions would have recognized his concerns and justifications. Ralph Glaber, for example, had earlier remarked that 'this had been the custom of this people since it first appeared in Gaul, as we noted earlier, to take as *principes* offspring born of similar unions with concubines'. He then went on to comment that this should not be thought of as an abomination nor as an impediment to rule, as the sons of Jacob were born of concubines and so, too, was the Emperor Constantine.[38] It is tempting to think that Glaber wrote those

after Gisla's death, even though Longsword had been born before 911 (Jumièges, i. 72. Van Houts's note is misleading here).

[34] Dudo, p. 185; *Dudo*, p. 63.

[35] Jumièges, i. 78, 88.

[36] Bates, 'Adolescence', 6.

[37] Jumièges, i. 102. In contrast to the view set out above (Introduction, pp. 12–13), Emily Albu thought that this insult was inserted because it reflected William's own disapproval of such marriages (Albu, *The Normans in their Histories*, pp. 69–70).

[38] Glaber, p. 204. In addition, Adam of Bremen, writing *c.* 1076, wrote of the Swedes

words in the knowledge of the problems that William the Bastard's birth were causing him, as he is believed to have composed Book IV of his *Histories*, where they are found, between *c*. 1036 and *c*. 1041.[39] Indeed, illegitimacy might be overlooked in Normandy even after 1100, if other considerations came into play. Thus the men of the honour of Breteuil accepted Eustace of Breteuil as their lord in 1103 'because they chose to be ruled by a compatriot who was a bastard rather than by a legitimate Breton or Burgundian'.[40]

Although he made no comment one way or the other on his birth, Dudo stressed Richard I's right to succeed by emphasizing the importance of hereditary succession at this point in his narrative: 'every kingdom that lacks a hereditary lord is laid waste and divided up, and much dissension, and unappeasable grievances, and unheard-of conflicts are generated in great numbers. And so, with your consent, this little boy shall be made heir to myself, and successor to the authority of our dukedom.'[41] But if Richard's right to inherit was stressed by Dudo, so too was the need for that right to be recognized by the *principes* in attendance. Longsword had already been made to address the Norman chiefs to this effect: 'I implore you to look favourably on my designs and, whatsoever fate may attend human affairs, you will elect (*eligatis*) for yourselves as duke my son Richard.'[42] Once again, then, Dudo preserved the idea of an elective element in the succession.

William of Jumièges adapted Dudo's account a little for his own purposes, changing the verbs and with them the balance of power, so that once again the duke took a clearer lead in proceedings. Shocked by Longsword's admission that he wanted to become a monk, the Norman *principes* asked the duke why he wished to abandon them and who would replace him. 'The duke answered: "I have a son called Richard. Now I beg you, if ever you felt any love towards me, show it to me now with a calm mind and set him over yourselves in my place" … Unable to resist his wish, though full of grief, they gave their common consent.'[43] Passive consent is not active election, however, and a demand that the *principes* should show their love for their leader by doing what he wanted removed still more of

that 'a man according to his means has two or three or more wives at one time, rich men and princes an unlimited number. And they also consider the sons born of such unions legitimate' (Adam of Bremen, *History of the Archbishops of Hamburg-Bremen*, trans. F. J. Tschan with new introduction by T. Reuter (New York, 2002) p. 203; cited in Roesdahl, *The Vikings*, p. 61 and see also E. Eames, 'Mariage et concubinage légal en Norvège à l'époque des Vikings', *Annales de Normandie*, 2 (1952), 195–208).

[39] Glaber, p. xlv.

[40] Orderic, vi. 40, and see above, Chapter 3, p. 157, and below, *infra*, pp. 335–6.

[41] *Dudo*, p. 96.

[42] *Dudo*, p. 78. The point is repeated throughout Book IV at, for example, pp. 102, 123.

[43] Jumièges, i. 88.

their freedom to choose.[44] Of course, Jumièges was concerned to demonstrate the importance of ducal direction in the succession and probably exaggerated its force accordingly.

According to Dudo, although Richard I failed to have children by his first wife, Emma, he did produce two sons, Godfrey (later count of Eu) and William (later lord of the Hiémois and then count of Eu), by mistresses (*ex concubinis*).[45] Subsequently, Richard 'connected himself to a young woman of radiant majesty, sprung from the most famous stock of Dacian nobles'.[46] This woman was Gunnor, who is not named in the earliest manuscripts of Dudo's work. When Richard I died in 996, there was, as a result, and for the first time, more than one possible heir to the duchy. Moreover, it was not the eldest son who succeeded.[47]

Dudo thus had to justify why Richard's eldest son by Gunnor had a better right to the duchy than his older half-siblings. He did so, first, by emphasizing Gunnor's blood: 'we think that the providence of the highest Godhead has tied you to this Dacian-born woman whom you now cherish, so that an heir to this land might be born to a Dacian father and mother, and be a most valiant defender and protector of it.'[48] By the time he recounted this succession, then, in terms of both the political reality and the schema of his work, the best heir would be one with Scandinavian blood from both parents running through his veins, rather than one of his half-brothers from one of the duke's earlier liaisons who, it must be inferred, would have been more than half-Frankish. It was the Norman lords who made this point, and who thus effectively elected the next duke even before his birth, and they did so when demanding that Richard should legitimize his union with Gunnor through a Christian marriage. Dudo thus also made it clear

---

[44] Here, the requirements of love seem analogous to the duties of friendship discussed by Koziol, *Begging Pardon*, pp. 55–6.

[45] *Dudo*, p. 163.

[46] *Dudo*, p. 163.

[47] Emily Tabuteau remarked that the dukes always designated their eldest sons as their successors (Tabuteau, 'The role of law', p. 150 and see also Garnett, *Conquered England*, p. 44) but if Dudo's account is accurate that was not the case here. Searle would disagree (Searle, *PK*, p. 132). In 1103, Fulk IV of Anjou made a similar decision to designate his second son, but the eldest by his second wife Bertrada of Montfort, as his heir. His eldest son, Geoffrey Martel, subsequently rebelled and forced his father to associate him in the government of Anjou until his premature death in 1106 (Lewis, 'Anticipatory association', pp. 916–17; J. Martindale, 'Succession and politics in the Romance-speaking world, c. 1000–1140', in *England and Her Neighbours 1066–1453: Essays in Honour of Pierre Chaplais*, ed. M. Jones and M. Vale (London, 1989), pp. 33–4; K. A. Dutton, 'Geoffrey, Count of Anjou and Duke of Normandy, 1129–51' (unpublished Ph.D. thesis, University of Glasgow, 2011), p. 24 and n. 113).

[48] *Dudo*, p. 164.

that a son produced by a Christian marriage would have a better right to succeed than a son produced by 'a forbidden union', in other words a marriage *more Danico*.[49] Dudo then went on to give a very strong impression that Richard II and his siblings were born only after the marriage had taken place, making them unquestionably legitimate heirs.[50] In this passage, Dudo appealed to two, often mutually exclusive, but equally important, constituencies within Normandy, and he did so at a time when the memory of the rebellion of one of the duke's half-brothers, William, would have been fresh in his readers' minds. Hence this portrayal of the succession and also his statement that 'honourable provision' had been made for the disappointed contenders.

When William of Jumièges revised this story four decades later, he once again placed the emphasis firmly on inheritance and ducal direction. It was Richard who opened the negotiations regarding his successor, and Richard who chose his heir. Indeed, Count Rodulf was made expressly to acknowledge that 'it is your duty to decide the country's destiny'.[51] In addition, Jumièges omitted mention of all of Richard I's earlier liaisons and their offspring, so that the duke's illegitimate son, William, who is only mentioned in his next book, had to become one of two unnamed 'others' whom he had fathered with Gunnor.[52] That distortion was necessary, given the circumstances in which he was writing and the intention behind his work.[53] He also had Richard married to Gunnor *Christiano more* from the outset, thereby removing any need to suggest that Christian marriage was somehow better than marriage *more Danico*, as Dudo had done, which would also have been problematic at the time he was writing.

William of Jumièges went on to deal with the succession to Richard II in much the same way as he had dealt with the tenth-century examples, as was required by his agenda. Richard II, 'summoned his son Richard, and with the advice of his wise men he set him over his duchy and his brother Robert over the county of the Hiémois, in such manner that Robert owed obedience to Richard'.[54] Although the *principes* were asked to give counsel, there is only the slightest implication that a consensus was being sought and an election made here.

The succession of Robert the Magnificent in 1027 was a little more problematic, however, and William's handling of it reveals his own concern to mark it out as different. Here, brother succeeded brother despite the existence of a young

---

[49]   *Dudo*, p. 164. See also the discussion above, Introduction, p. 61 and Chapter 1, p. 77.
[50]   It was Robert of Torigni who later remarked that Richard and Gunnor legitimized their union only *after* the birth of their sons Richard and Robert (Jumièges, i. 130, ii. 266–8).
[51]   Jumièges, i. 134.
[52]   Jumièges, i. 130.
[53]   See above, Introduction, pp. 9–18.
[54]   Jumièges, ii. 40.

illegitimate son.[55] In these unusual circumstances, and with his eye on the succession of 1035, Jumièges subtly highlighted the role of election. He first stated matter-of-factly that when Richard III died he left 'his brother as his heir to his duchy'. This more or less repeated the supposed model for this passage, an act of Roger of Montgommery of c. 1030, which says only that Richard III, 'surprised by swift death … relinquished it by hereditary right to his brother Robert'.[56] But there is no record of an assembly or of the swearing of fidelity in anticipation of Robert's succession as had been the case elsewhere, and Richard's sudden death makes it unlikely that such an assembly had taken place. As such, for the first time, the reigning duke had not designated his successor. And so Jumièges supplemented his model at the beginning of his next chapter, noting tha, 'when Duke Richard left the worldly pinnacle of princely rule and, as we believe, ascended to the heavenly kingdom, his brother Robert was elected (subrogatur) in his place to the rulership (monarchie) of the whole county'.[57] The verb he employed to describe the election was also used in his account of the election of Hugh Capet, perhaps to suggest that such elections were normal in the absence of a clear heir. His addition suggests that he was concerned to highlight the uncertainty – and thus the need for consensus – that was the result of a lack of ducal direction when a choice would have to be made between an adult brother and a young illegitimate son.

   William of Jumièges made these points about the succession of 1027 not because he doubted the legitimacy of Duke Robert's rule,[58] but because he needed to show how it was different from the similarly debatable succession in 1035, which saw William the Bastard become duke. William was, of course, the illegitimate son of the previous duke. But although Duke Robert left no legitimate heir, there was another contender for the duchy, the soon-to-be Count William of Arques. He was Duke Robert's much younger half-brother, and he was also of

---

55 William of Jumièges omitted all reference to Nicholas (Jumièges, ii. 46). Douglas, *William the Conqueror*, p. 32 argued that Nicholas (whom he thought was a legitimate son) was 'relegated' to the monastic life on Robert's accession. Likewise, Lifshitz, *Pious Neustria*, p. 193 thought that Nicholas was cheated of ducal rule in 1027 (and also in 1035), and Gazeau, *Normannia Monastica*, i. 102, 139, 168, 187–9, 247 also believed that Nicholas was placed in monastic orders only after 1027. It does seem unlikely that Richard III would have allowed his only son, legitimate or not, to become a monk. Orderic, who was the first to provide any details, certainly thought that Robert had become duke before Nicholas was professed: 'He was compelled by his uncle, Duke Robert, to become an oblate monk in the abbey of Fécamp under Abbot John' (Orderic, iv. 396).

56 *RADN*, no. 74.

57 Jumièges, ii. 46, perhaps based on *RADN*, no. 74 as suggested by Elisabeth van Houts (Jumièges, i. xl).

58 Jumièges, i. lii.

legitimate birth. If the succession of 1027 had been seen as providing a precedent, William of Arques would have become duke. But he did not. Instead, while the duke's illegitimate son lost out to the duke's brother in 1027, the duke's brother lost out to the duke's illegitimate son in 1035.

William of Jumièges was keen to point out why this should have been the case. In a lengthy scene, he records how Duke Robert had obliged his *fideles* to swear an oath of fidelity to his son when he left on pilgrimage for Jerusalem. We are told that he summoned Archbishop Robert of Rouen, his uncle, and the other great men of his duchy to his court and, 'presented them with his only son, William, and earnestly besought them to choose him as their lord in his place and to accept him as military leader'. This must be understood to have been agreed, because the next part of the passage sees William's succession presented as a fait accompli, indeed as a demand, to the wider constituency of Normans living within the capital city: 'In spite of the boy's tender years *everyone in the town* rejoiced in his encouragement and in accordance with *the duke's decree* readily and unanimously acclaimed him their prince and lord and pledged him their fealty with inviolable oaths'.[59] This is all very unusual, at least so far as the record of successions in the narratives is concerned. And it meant that when Robert died on his pilgrimage, William the Bastard would be duke because he had been selected by his predecessor, elected by the *principes*, and acclaimed by the citizens of Rouen. Jumièges was clearly concerned to ensure that no-one could doubt the legitimacy of his succession, and thus emphasized that just as the whole political community of Normandy had decided the succession in one way in 1027, so they had decided it in another in 1035. Their involvement made their decision binding.

As discussed above, Jumièges made these points as part of his attempt to reconcile the duke and his various opponents after the rebellions and wars of the period to 1057.[60] William the Bastard's succession had clearly not pleased everyone, and it is likely that his illegitimacy was a concern in 1035 and for some years afterwards in a way it would not have been had William been the only possibly claimant to the duchy, as had been the case in 927 and 942. The election of 1027 might not have helped here, especially if Robert the Magnificent had made an argument for his own succession based on the illegitimacy of his young rival, Nicholas. There are certainly clues in the *Gesta Normannorum ducum* that suggest William's bastardy provided a ground for concern, even if it did not constitute a fundamental flaw to his succession.

---

[59] Jumièges, ii. 80 (my italics). It is possible that the burgesses of Rouen claimed a right to a say in the succession, as the burgesses of London did (Jumièges ii. 170; *ASChr*, D, s.a. 1066; trans. Garmonsway, p. 200; *Gesta Stephani*, pp. 4–6).

[60] See above, Introduction, pp. 9–18.

If ducal *acta* have so far been remote from this discussion, that is because they say far less about the succession than the narratives. Indeed, for the most part they do no more than remark the reigning duke's kinship with his predecessor, presumably to stress his right to make the grant. Thus in 962 × 996, Richard I was described as 'Richard the son of William duke of Normandy'.[61] Similarly, Richard II was variously 'the son of the most happy Count Richard'; 'duke and *princeps* of the Normans, the son of the elder Richard'; and 'Richard, duke of the Normans, the son of the first Richard, the best duke'.[62] Richard II's act of 1025 for Jumièges makes mention of the gifts of earlier dukes, and associates Richard with them: 'these are the things that my grandfather William restored to this place … To him succeeded my father.'[63] Furthermore, Richard III and Robert are described as sons and heirs of Richard II in his great confirmations for Bernay and Saint-Ouen of 1025.[64] Robert the Magnificent's lineage is set out in an act of Roger of Montgommery for Jumièges,[65] and in addition he is said to have been 'the son of the great Richard' in acts for Mont-Saint-Michel,[66] and 'the son of the second Richard, by the grace of God duke of the Normans and himself by the grace of God duke and *princeps* of the Normans'.[67] William the Bastard was named as Robert's successor apparently as early as 1030 in an act for Sainte-Trinité-du-Mont,[68] and later appears as 'count of the Normans, the son of Count Robert' and 'by the grace of God count of the Normans, the son of Robert once the most noble count of the Normans'.[69]

These statements acknowledged facts or expectations, but they are unlikely to have influenced the choice of a successor, not least because almost all of them were written after the succession had occurred. They were included in an act because a beneficiary's scribe thought that there was some advantage to be had by making them. So, for example, such pedigrees might tell us that a man was known to take pride in his ancestry – something which is especially clear in the acts of Count William of Arques, a number of which stress that he was the son of Richard II – and that beneficiaries realized it was wise to pander to such donors.[70] They

---

[61]   *RADN*, no. 5.
[62]   *RADN*, nos. 18, 24, 44, respectively (*RADN*, no. 30 repeats no. 24).
[63]   *RADN*, no. 36.
[64]   *RADN*, nos. 35 and 53.
[65]   *RADN*, no. 74.
[66]   *RADN*, nos. 65, 73.
[67]   *RADN*, no. 85.
[68]   *RADN*, no. 60.
[69]   *RADN*, nos. 73, 94.
[70]   Editions of Count William's acts can be found at: *RADN*, nos. 100, 112 and D. Bates and P. Bauduin, 'Autour de l'année 1047: un acte de Guillaume, comte d'Arques, pour Fécamp (18 Juillet 1047)', in *De part et d'autre de la normandie médiévale: recueil d'études*

show that the duke's pedigree might be used to underline his right to make the grant.[71] Further, if dynastic longevity strengthened ducal authority, then it was in the beneficiary's interest to remark on those ties as they would also strengthen the duke's ability to protect the grant. Finally, although a duke might not care a fig for this or that church, he might be concerned to uphold family honour by protecting the grants that he was informed had been made or confirmed by his predecessors. Robert the Magnificent's insistence that Roger of Montgommery should restore the market that his father had granted to the monks of Jumièges at Vimoutiers is probably an example of this.[72] As such, while these phrases might tell us something about how power, succession, and inheritance affected the strength of a gift, they tell us rather less about any principles relating to the succession to the duchy.

Despite these general rules, it is an act of 1063 that provides perhaps the best account of Robert Curthose's election to the duchy. It notes the presence at court of William and Matilda and of 'Robert their son, whom they elected to the governance of the realm after his death (*quem elegerant ad gubernandum regnum post suum obitum*)'.[73] Here, 'they' seems to mean William and Matilda rather than the *principes* of Normandy, so that the duke's right to nominate his heir seems by now to have merged with the *principes'* right to choose him. Jumièges did not mention Robert's succession to the duchy until recording the events of 1067, but at that point he stated that William granted (*tradidit*) Robert dominion over the duchy.[74] This, too, suggests that William had a right to dispose of his property as he wished without the need to take the counsel of his subjects. The 'D' version of the *Anglo-Saxon Chronicle* seems to support the idea that William was able to direct the succession unilaterally as it reports that Robert left Normandy for Flanders because 'his father would not let him govern his earldom in Normandy which he himself and also King Philip with his consent had given him'.[75] The speech that Orderic put into William's mouth on his deathbed, although written from a

---

en hommage à François Neveux, ed. P. Bouet, C. Bougy, B. Garnuier, and C. Maneuvrier (Caen, 2009), pp. 49–52.

[71] See J. C. Holt, 'Feudal society and the family in early Medieval England: II. Notions of patrimony', *Transactions of the Royal Historical Society*, fifth series 33 (1983), 204.

[72] *RADN*, no. 74. Similarly, in 1145, Geoffrey, count of the Angevins and duke of the Normans, arbitrated a dispute between the monks of Saint-Julien of Tours and La Trinité of Vendôme that concerned three chapels in Anjou. The agreement notes that Geoffrey encouraged his son Henry to fulfil his duties as protector of the abbey, which had been founded by Geoffrey's ancestors (Delisle, *Recueil*, no. 2).

[73] *RADN*, no. 158 of 29 June 1063; Aird, *Robert Curthose*, p. 47. Garnett warns that the act does not necessarily record a formal designation ceremony, with pledging of oaths (Garnett, *Conquered England*, p. 155).

[74] Jumièges, ii. 178.

[75] *ASChr*, D, s.a. 1079; trans. Garmonsway, p. 214.

twelfth-century viewpoint, further reinforces this conclusion: 'I invested my son Robert with the duchy of Normandy before I fought against Harold on the heath of Senlac; because he is my first born and has received the homage of almost all the barons of the country the honour then granted cannot be taken from him.'[76]

These accounts all imply that the requirement for election by the Norman *principes* became a step more distant in the 1060s. Although Orderic's focus on primogeniture might stem from the concerns of his own time rather than reflecting the mindset of the mid eleventh century, William the Bastard seems nonetheless to have treated Normandy as his own personal property.[77] The accounts give the impression that Robert's future subjects did homage to him apparently without complaint about the sidelining of their rights. With all lords concerned to establish the hereditary principle for their own lands and secular titles, turning *beneficia* into alods at all levels of society and at about this same time, it is perhaps no surprise that William's actions seem not to have been controversial. Times and expectations had changed, at least where there was a son who might succeed his father.[78]

Where there was no legitimate son, however, there was still a role for the Norman *principes* to play a role in the negotiations that would lead to the identification of an heir. Thus in 1091, the *Anglo-Saxon Chronicle* states that King William Rufus and Duke Robert reconciled and made each other their heir: 'If the duke should pass away without son by lawful wedlock, the king was to be heir of all Normandy. By this same treaty, if the king should die, the duke was to be heir of all England. This treaty was ratified by twelve of the noblest men on the king's behalf, and twelve on the duke's, and yet did not remain inviolate for long.'[79] The same terms were reached between Robert and Henry I in 1101, again with twelve men from each side ratifying the agreement.[80] The duke and his *principes* together thus sought to ensure that the rights and obligations of the ducal office passed intact from one sibling to the other, in the absence of any legitimate sons to succeed them. These treaties thus established more firmly the rule that had been laid down in 1027 (but overturned in 1035), that where there was no legitimate

---

[76] Orderic, iv. 92. Orderic seems here to be referring to the re-grant made by William in 1080, which was presumably followed by a renewal of the oaths of fealty previously sworn to Curthose (Orderic, iii. 112) rather than the original homage of 1063 or 1066 (see below, pp. 332–3).

[77] See Orderic, ii. xxxvi–xxxvii, noted in Holt, 'Notions of patrimony', 215, and also Le Patourel, 'Norman succession', 237–40.

[78] See also the discussion of the heritability of *vicomtés* and counties below, Chapter 9, pp. 550–4, 568–9.

[79] *ASChr*, E, s.a. 1091; trans. Garmonsway, p. 226.

[80] *ASChr*, E, s.a. 1101; trans. Garmonsway, p. 237.

son, a brother took precedence over an illegitimate son. Even so, these agreements included the names of twenty-four men who had, it may be supposed, been involved in negotiating the terms of these successions, and who had therefore effectively elected the heir to the duchy in advance of his birth (like the Norman lords in Dudo's account of the succession of 996). These men were named to ensure that the agreement stuck. They were living evidence of the consensus of the political community and the guarantors of it.[81] And while they were bound to its terms as a result, they would also have to defend the arrangement against any who spoke against it.

In the event, Henry I did indeed succeed his brother in Normandy, but not because of the terms of the Treaty of Alton. Henry succeeded by right of conquest, either as a foreign rival or as a rebel, depending on the point of view. He was not the first member of Rollo's line to rebel against the established duke, but he was the first to succeed in removing and replacing him. The two dukes who ruled after Henry followed him not just chronologically but in the way in which they gained the duchy. Like him, they did not so much succeed to it as seize it from other equally legitimate candidates. These rebellions and contested successions form the subject of the next section of this chapter.

Contesting the right to rule

The authority of Rollo and his duly established successors over what would become Normandy was not always uncontested. In some cases, what later chroniclers portrayed as rebellion was in reality a desperate struggle on behalf of established settlers or Frankish lords to maintain their independence and/or traditional religion in the face of the duke's military might and demands for conversion to Christianity. Theirs were not rebellions aimed at dividing the duchy or overthrowing the reigning duke, but rather wars waged in the hope that they would prevent the duke's power from encompassing them and their lordships. This seems to have been the nature of most of the 'rebellions' faced by the dukes down to the 1020s, not least because it was only after that decade that Normandy could really be said to have become an established and recognized territory.[82]

According to Dudo, William Longsword faced a 'rebellion' led by a certain Riulf which was motivated by resentment about, and a rejection of, Longsword's

---

[81] This can be seen in the *Anglo-Saxon Chronicle* s.a. 1094, where it is said that 'afterwards they [Curthose and Rufus] met together with the same guarantors who had originally made the treaty and ratified it, who laid the entire responsibility for the breach of the treaty on the king, but he would not accept their verdict, nor indeed keep the covenant' (*ASChr*, E, s.a. 1094; trans. Garmonsway, p. 229).

[82] See above, Chapter 2, p. 93.

Frankish or Frankified counsellors. But Riulf and his allies did not contend the succession, at least not to begin with. They were concerned instead with cession.[83] Flodoard reported that on Richard I's succession in 942, a civil war broke out in Normandy. Richard himself was forced to renounce Christianity by Viking invaders before he was saved by King Louis and Duke Hugh.[84] But although he remained in control of Rouen, it seems that the Bessin slipped from his grasp as a result of his youth and, it may be supposed, the latent desire for independence of the settlers there. According to William of Jumièges, Richard II faced a 'peasants' revolt' *c.* 1000. That uprising was almost certainly the result of his father's recovery of the Bessin and expansion into the Hiémois, so that the loss of liberty against which the peasants were rebelling was in fact the result of the dukes' imposition of their own authority manifested in their demands for tolls and other tribute from the previously free settlers of those areas.[85]

Dudo of Saint-Quentin must have lived through the earliest of the uprisings purportedly led by one of the dukes' kinsmen. As he ended his story in 996 he did not have to acknowledge it, but his account of Richard II's succession with its stress on his greater right to the duchy, and his earlier comments concerning the need for unity under one ruler, does seem to have been related to it. William of Jumièges could not avoid the issue, however, and so recorded the trouble that might arise when one of the potential claimants to the duchy decided that the honourable provision made for them was not honourable enough. This first rebel was William, a half-brother of Richard II, who had sworn fealty to the new duke and had been given the Hiémois in the hope that it would prove sufficient consolation. According to Jumièges, William was encouraged to rebel by 'the insolence of some wicked men', which suggests that they used him as their puppet to give their actions greater legitimacy and weight. That interpretation seems to receive support from the report that some of his partisans (*satellitum*) continued their uprising despite defeat in successive battles even after William himself had been captured and imprisoned.[86] So again, then, this uprising was an attempt by the lords of the Hiémois to hold back the advance of ducal power and to retain their independence.

Regardless of whether William took the lead or not, he was the first rebel who is known previously to have sworn fidelity to the duke and to have recognized the reach of his authority. It is possible, but unlikely, that William's rebellion was justified in some way. He was forgiven only after he had been confined at

---

[83] *Dudo*, pp. 64–5; Searle, *PK*, pp. 74–5.
[84] *Flodoard*, p. 38.
[85] Jumièges, ii. 8.
[86] Jumièges, ii. 8–10, and see above, Chapter 2, p. 79.

Rouen for five years, and perhaps only because he does not seem to have aimed to overthrow his half-brother and to take the whole duchy for himself. Like his followers, he seems to have aimed only at independent rule over the Hiémois. That seems also to have been true of the next rebellious scion of the ducal house, the future Robert the Magnificent. Robert had been given the Hiémois by his father *c.* 1026, and subsequently rebelled against his brother, most likely with the intention of setting himself up as an independent ruler in his county rather than taking Normandy for himself.[87] Unlike his half-uncle, Robert seems to have rebelled on his own initiative, and he was apparently unable to construct a party to support his claim. As such he was no threat to Duke Richard, and so he was allowed to remain at Falaise after his rebellion had ended, a defeated and no doubt derided figure.[88] These two revolts, then, happened because of the continuing uncertainty about where Normandy ended and because of the principle that the ducal office was indivisible. Some of the dukes' siblings consequently took advantage of their chance to carve out an independent lordship for themselves which they might have seen as their right by birth, and might have been especially moved to do so when they were not given a comital title along with their lands.

After he became duke, Robert the Magnificent faced defiance from his kinsman Bishop Hugh of Bayeux. According to William of Jumièges, 'Hugh, bishop of Bayeux and son of Count Rodulf, observing that the duke wished to follow the advice of wise men and disregarded his, by cunning and trickery amply fortified the castle of Ivry with arms and food. After installing a garrison there he left for France to hire soldiers to help him defend it stoutly.'[89] This rebellion, then, was not about any rival claim to the duchy, but was rather the result of pique at his exclusion from the duke's inner circle. Given the extent of Hugh's authority in the Bessin, he might have had some grounds for feeling ill-used, although his rebellion was nevertheless unjustified.[90] The result of his revolt was a period spent in exile, during which some of Hugh's lands seem to have been grabbed by his neighbours.[91] Although he seems to have recovered most of them after his return, he lost the castle at Ivry to the duke, along with any chance of recovering his place in the duke's counsels.

William the Bastard was not so fortunate as his predecessors. In the early years of his reign, he suffered a series of rebellions headed by disgruntled kinsmen. The chroniclers seem to have realized that the nature of these rebellions was qualitatively different from those which had gone before. For the first time, the reports speak of

---

[87] Jumièges provided no reason to think that Robert sought to overthrow his brother, but see in contrast Garnett, '"Ducal" succession', p. 109; Garnett, *Conquered England*, p. 152.

[88] Jumièges, ii. 44. See Searle, *PK*, p. 150 for a similar view.

[89] Jumièges, ii. 52.

[90] See above, Chapter 2, pp. 99–100.

[91] Gazeau, 'Patrimoine', 139–47.

rebels attempting to take or divide the duchy, perhaps also revealing that Normandy was now a much more coherent political and territorial unit. The first of these rebellions occurred in 1046–47, when Guy of Burgundy, a legitimate descendant of Richard II in the female line, made an attempt on the duchy. William of Jumièges wrote that William feared that he would be 'thrown down from the summit of his ducal power and replaced by a rival',[92] Poitiers that Guy 'desired to get either the *principatus* or the greater part of Normandy'.[93] If Guy really intended to overthrow William, then he was unusually ambitious – a point that Poitiers perhaps recognized in the second part of that sentence. His aims, then, are not entirely clear. Neither are his motives. Guy might have rebelled simply because he felt himself sidelined at court, or he might have considered himself the better heir.[94] Another feature of Guy's rebellion was that it took the form of a conspiracy. Guy constructed a party that would support his claim, and for the first time we know who some of those conspirators were, so that we can see that they had their own grievances but needed a figurehead – a rival to William with a clear relationship to Rollo's line – to legitimize their actions.[95] Guy and his allies were defeated at Val-ès-Dunes, although it took Duke William three years to reduce Guy's castle at Brionne. Guy was not immediately driven from Normandy as a result of his crime, however. William of Jumièges wrote that Guy was held under house arrest,[96] which William of Poitiers reshaped into a statement that Duke William 'allowed Guy to remain at his court', perhaps for some years after his defeat.[97] As a result of his rebellion, Guy lost his castles, but as he had held them from the duke as a benefice, that was only to be expected. It seems to go too far to call this 'disinheritance' as Guy had inherited nothing.[98]

In 1053, the duke's uncle and near contemporary Count William of Arques rebelled. Like Guy, he was a proud scion of the ducal line, which William of Poitiers thought was at the root of his revolt.[99] He might have believed that the

[92] Jumièges, ii. 120.

[93] Poitiers, p. 8.

[94] Hagger, 'How the west was won', 37 and see also above, Chapter 2, p. 107, which takes the former view.

[95] Hagger, 'How the west was won', 37–40 and see above, Chapter 2, p. 107–9.

[96] Jumièges, ii. 122.

[97] Poitiers, p. 12, supported by *RADN*, nos. 131, 142, 194. Bates thought that nos. 131 and 142 were suspect (*Normandy*, pp. 91, n. 88, 256), although James Holt thought no. 131 at least was authentic (J. C. Holt, 'What's in a name?', Stenton Lecture (Reading, 1982), p. 19, n. 80). See also above, Chapter 2, p. 109 and below, Chapter 7, pp. 401–2.

[98] Garnett, '"Ducal" succession', p. 102 suggested that after Robert's rebellion of 1027 all subsequent rebels were disinherited as punishment for rebellion.

[99] Poitiers, pp. 32–4, 40. The monks of Jumièges also recognized the pride that he took in his ancestry and so styled him: 'the son of the great Richard, duke of the Normans, by the grace of the eternal king, count of the territory which is called Talou' (*RADN*, no. 100). See also Bates, 'Adolesence', 12.

election of 1027 provided a precedent that should have been followed in 1035, which would have resulted in him becoming duke, even if for a time he felt adequately compensated by the grant of the county of Arques, c. 1037, and his leading place at court. But as Duke William leaned more and more heavily on the counsel of others, so Count William became more and more alienated from him, until finally, at about the age of thirty, he rebelled. It seems that his aim was to divide Normandy. This aim is not made explicit in the accounts, but it is nonetheless implied by Poitiers's statement that 'for a long time he had promoted many disturbances, endeavouring to increase his own lands against the might of his lord, whom he had attempted to bar from entry, not only to the castle of Arques, but to all the adjacent part of Normandy on this side of the river Seine'.[100] In a novel step that would henceforth become a hallmark of major rebellions, Count William appealed to King Henry of the French for aid. But despite the king's support the count was defeated. He was exiled, but allowed to retain at least part of his inheritance.[101] His probable co-conspirators received contrasting punishments. William Busac, count of Eu, was forfeited,[102] but Guitmund of Moulins-la-Marche was apparently forgiven – perhaps because he was not really a rebel at all, but a French lord clinging desperately to his independence.[103]

Later in his reign, William became the first duke to face a rebellion raised by a designated heir to the duchy when his son, Robert Curthose, rose against him. The first of his two revolts took place between c. 1077 and 1080 and the second began sometime after 1083 and continued until 1087.[104] Both rebellions were caused by his father's refusal to give him either land or authority, despite his designation as heir and perhaps investiture as duke in 1063 and 1066. William of Jumièges had thought that Curthose would rule in his father's place, now that William had become king, and Orderic suggested the likely arrangement that Curthose would rule as duke under William's overarching authority as king.[105] Probably because

---

[100] Poitiers, p. 34. Jumièges states that he assumed 'arbitrary power' with the support of King Henry of the French (Jumièges, ii. 102), which apparently supports Poitiers's position.

[101] Jumièges, ii. 104; Poitiers, p. 42. Poitiers says that Count William was allowed to keep his patrimony (actually lands inherited from his mother, Papia). However, the lands granted to him by the duke, including Arques, were recovered to the demesne (see above, Chapter 2, p. 125).

[102] Jumièges, ii. 128 said that the count 'wished to claim the duchy for himself', which assertion was followed by Orderic. It is more likely, however, that Busac's rebellion should be associated with that of his neighbour rather than seen as an independent insurgency.

[103] See above, Chapter 2, pp. 124–5.

[104] See Lack, 'Robert Curthose', 129–31 for a discussion of the date of the second rebellion.

[105] Orderic, iii. 98. On Curthose's rebellions, see also above, Chapter 2, pp. 136–8.

he was the designated heir, Robert's aims seem to have been more ambitious than those of any other rebel to this date. His intention was, it seems, to take control of the whole of Normandy, albeit leaving William with England.[106] This, then, was the first rebellion that aimed to overthrow the reigning duke. In the event, Curthose did not make headway against his father, but he was not disinherited either – or at least not entirely. He would succeed to the undivided duchy in 1087, and Maine, too, but not his father's kingdom of the English.

Curthose's own reign was famously disturbed. First he faced war with his younger brother, William Rufus, who used his wealth, and their divided loyalties, to turn some of Robert's own lords against him. While he did not make as much progress as might be expected, the Treaty of Rouen agreed between Curthose and Rufus in 1091 undermined the idea, developed from the tenth century, that Normandy was indivisible and should be united under the rule of a single duke. According to the detailed account found in the *Anglo-Saxon Chronicle*, 'the duke surrendered Fécamp to [Rufus], with the county of Eu, and Cherbourg. Furthermore, the king's men were to be left unmolested in the castles which they had won from the duke against his will.'[107] Orderic added that William held more than twenty castles in Normandy, and that he maintained the support of Count Robert of Eu, Stephen of Aumale, Gerard of Gournay, Ralph of Conches, Count Robert of Meulan, Walter Giffard, Philip of Briouze, Richard of Courcy, and many others.[108] There is no sense here that William held these possessions from the duke, and no sense either that the fidelity William had previously sworn to his brother could have survived the war between them. He thus held these lands independently of him, while those who had commended themselves to the king were released from their obligations to the duke – as was Count William of Evreux when his fidelity was transferred to King Henry I in 1104.[109] This was a seismic change where the idea of the unity of Normandy was concerned, but it has received little comment in the past, perhaps because the agreement was in the event so short-lived.

The capricious but magnanimous Rufus was an entirely different proposition from his brother, Henry. Frustrated by Duke Robert's alliance with his own greatest enemies, Robert of Bellême and Count William of Mortain,[110] King Henry at

---

[106]   Orderic, ii. 356; iii. 96.

[107]   *ASChr*, 'E'.s.a. 1091; trans. Garmonsway, p. 226.

[108]   Orderic, v. 26.

[109]   In contrast, Frank Barlow thought that Rufus had acquired an appanage from Curthose in 1091, and held it as a feudal benefice (Barlow, *William Rufus*, pp. 281–3), although he also supposed that William's oath of fidelity to Robert had survived intact. For the transfer of the fidelity of the count of Evreux, see Orderic, vi. 58.

[110]   The *Anglo-Saxon Chronicle* makes the point explicitly, at least with regard to Bellême: *ASChr*, E, s.a. 1104; trans. Garmonsway, p. 239.

first attempted to divide Normandy. His intention, if Orderic recorded it accurately, was to divide the demesne in half but to take the undivided government of the duchy for himself, allowing his brother to enjoy his share of the revenues in peace.[111] In some ways, this reflected the pattern of succession and provision before the Conquest, although it should be noted that Henry claimed for himself the rights that traditionally belonged to the eldest son and offered Robert the provision made for a cadet. Robert refused the offer. The result was that he became the first duke of the Normans to be overthrown by his rival when he risked battle against his brother at Tinchebray and lost.

This was the first time that a man who might be classed as a rebel had succeeded in overthrowing the reigning duke, the first time that succession to the whole duchy was the result of military conquest, and the first time that a 'foreign' king had added the duchy to his *regnum*. Some might have been unhappy about this state of affairs, and for a variety of reasons. Orderic put a speech into Robert of Bellême's mouth after the battle which made some of these clear: 'the world is upside down. A younger brother has rebelled against an elder, a servant has conquered his master in war and thrown him into chains. Moreover he has robbed him of his ancestral inheritance and, as a perjured vassal, has taken his lord's rights into his own hand.'[112] Orderic might have seen some strength in this argument, because when he had Count Helias of Maine respond to Bellême he did not dwell on these points. Helias was made to confine himself to remarking that a man 'ought also to make it his business not to raise anyone higher than he deserves or allow any man who does not know how to rule himself to have authority over others'.[113] Elsewhere, however, Orderic did make brief claims for Henry's right to inherit. For example, he wrote that 'in the spring of the same year, King Henry crossed to Normandy … and laid claim to the heritage of his fathers'.[114] Robert of Torigni, in his additions to the *Gesta Normannorum ducum*, was equally reticent. He wrote only that Henry was so 'very angry that his brother so squandered the paternal inheritance, namely the duchy of Normandy' that he invaded it in 1105.[115] In addition, a handful of ducal *acta* include phrases such as 'just as it was in the year when my father was alive and dead',[116] and 'in the time of William my father duke of the Normans, afterwards king of England',[117] and confirm the

---

[111] Orderic, vi. 86.
[112] Orderic, vi. 94.
[113] Orderic, vi. 94.
[114] Orderic, vi. 78.
[115] Jumièges, ii. 220.
[116] *Regesta*, ii. nos.1022, 1962.
[117] *Regesta*, ii. 364–5 (no. ccxvi).

gifts 'that King William my father' made of lands and right within the duchy.[118] These phrases stressed Henry's hereditary right, but without a strong emphasis, and moreover were perhaps inserted in the hope that it would make Henry more enthusiastic about protecting or recognizing the grants in question. But even if contemporaries recognized the relative weakness of Henry's claim to inherit, it was only Wace who was prepared to make it explicit – and he paid the price for what could still be seen as undermining Henry II's right to rule.[119]

Henry seems principally to have legitimized his actions by claiming his victory revealed God's will.[120] It is unlikely that every Norman was convinced by the propaganda put out on Henry's behalf, however, and it is not clear that Henry believed it himself.[121] He certainly did not rely on it. Rather he had built up a network of allies across Normandy – not just in the Cotentin – since 1100. The resources of his kingdom helped him enormously, and allowed him to gain the loyalty of lords who feared to lose their estates there. Orderic noted that a number of Norman magnates 'held great estates from Henry in England, had already gone over to his side in Normandy with their vassals, and were ready and eager to fight with him against all the world'.[122]

The Beaumonts numbered among them. Count Robert of Meulan was sent across the Channel 'to put down the civil disturbances in Normandy' that had been caused by Eustace of Breteuil's succession to that honour in 1103 – some three years before Henry took the duchy.[123] Robert fitz Haimo, lord of Creully, Evrecy, and Torigni in the Bessin raided around Caen on Henry's behalf in 1105.[124] As had been the case with Ralph of Tosny in 1091, those with complaints that Curthose could not or would not address turned to his rival for help. They included in their number Robert of Grandmesnil, whose lands were under threat from Robert of Bellême.[125] The Warenne family, whose estates lay in the Pays de Caux, were won round in stages, firstly when Henry restored the family's English lands to William of Warenne in 1103, secondly when Henry released Reginald of Warenne on the eve of the battle of Tinchebray, and thirdly when Henry invested William with the

---

[118]   Chanteux, *Recueil*, iii. 403–6 (no. 115) = *Regesta*, ii. no. 1948; *Monasticon*, vii. 1071 = *Regesta*, ii. no. 1575; *Regesta*, ii. 353 (no. clxxvi).

[119]   Wace, pp. 212–14, 216–18, 220; C. Urbanski, 'Apology, protest, and suppression: interpreting the surrender of Caen (1105), *HSJ*, 19 (2008), 138–9, 142–7, 150–3.

[120]   As in the letter he sent to Anselm announcing his victory (*Letters of St Anselm*, no. 401).

[121]   See above, Chapters 3, pp. 160–1 and 5, pp. 295–8.

[122]   Orderic, vi. 56.

[123]   Orderic, vi. 44. See also Le Patourel, *Norman Empire*, pp. 347–8.

[124]   Wace, p. 216; Green, *Henry* p. 82.

[125]   Orderic, vi. 84.

castle of Saint-Saëns *c.* 1110.[126] Henry thus ensured that he had enough support to hold Normandy before he gained the victory at Tinchebray, and in some ways this should be seen as the equivalent of election, even if the result of that election could only be imposed by force.

But although Henry had six out of the eight greatest Norman lords in his army in 1106,[127] he did not win over everybody, and those who had complaints or a grudge were able to turn to Curthose's son, William Clito, when they wanted to force Henry's hand. The rebellion of 1118–19 was principally the result of Henry's resistance to the claims of Amaury of Montfort to the county of Evreux, but Amaury and those others who also felt that they had been treated unjustly by Henry could legitimize their actions and bring greater pressure to bear against Henry by claiming to act in support of Clito's claim. It is clear that such support might be superficial and self-serving, as Richer of L'Aigle's actions reveal very clearly,[128] but Henry nonetheless recognized that the customs concerning hereditary succession meant that Clito presented a grave threat to his power and was forced to fight and negotiate to nullify that threat. Although his victory at Brémule was important, Henry's pragmatism played just as great a role here. Indeed, far from disinheriting rebels, Henry was obliged to allow Amaury of Montfort to inherit the county of Evreux and William Talvas to recover his father's lands in Normandy.[129] Even Eustace of Breteuil, who lost all of his estates except for Pacy, was compensated with a pension.

A second rebellion in 1123–24, again purportedly in favour of Clito's claim, but more likely to do with Henry's successes on the Avre frontier, seems to have posed less of a threat. That was in part because it did not attract such widespread support as had the earlier revolt, and in part because Henry ensured that Louis VI would be occupied elsewhere. Of the leaders, only Hugh of Montfort lost his lands permanently, although Count Waleran of Meulan was imprisoned for five years and some of the lesser rebels were punished by mutilation or death.[130]

But the claims of inheritance worked in Henry's favour, too. Once Clito was dead, Henry's position was secure. Only a member of Rollo's line might hold the duchy, and Henry was the last man standing, at least in the direct male line. To an extent that was the result of Henry's awareness of the conflict that could be

---

[126] Orderic, vi. 14, 84, 88, 164; C. W. Hollister, 'The taming of a turbulent earl: Henry I and William of Warenne', *Réflexions Historiques*, 3 (1976), 83–91, reprinted in *MMI*, pp. 137–44 at pp. 142–3; Hollister, *Henry*, pp. 182, 340–1; Green, *Henry*, pp. 76, 90–1, 122.

[127] Hollister, *Henry*, p. 200.

[128] Orderic, vi. 196–8.

[129] See above, Chapter 3, pp. 169–71, 172–4.

[130] Orderic, vi. 356. For the rebellion see above, Chapter 3, pp. 175–7, and for the punishment of the rebels see below, Chapter 8, pp. 493, 494.

caused by having too many close kinsmen, and the action he took to mitigate that problem. Searle remarked approvingly that Henry 'practised the manipulation of family and wealth with consummate ability, producing twenty-one noble bastards on whom he and his successor might rely, while limiting his legitimate family to two boys and a girl'.[131] But what Searle did not say is that Henry's manipulation of family and wealth ultimately left him with only one legitimate daughter to succeed him. His attempts to ensure her succession have left us with more evidence about the procedures and mechanisms that might be used to achieve the desired result than usual, but the unique circumstances mean that it is unclear whether such elaborate steps had always been taken to secure the succession of a designated heir, or whether they were a response to this specific 'crisis'.

Although we are not so well informed about them, the arrangements made for the succession of Robert Curthose seem to bear comparison with the better-known ones made for Matilda, so the differences between the two might be instructive. In both cases, oaths of fidelity were taken on at least two occasions. Curthose received the homage of the *principes* in, perhaps, 1063, 1066, and 1080, and also seems to have been acknowledged as William's heir by King Philip.[132] Matilda received oaths in 1127 and again in 1131.[133] The second oath-swearing was probably due to her marriage to Geoffrey of Anjou, and was required because the marriage had changed her status and identity.[134] Yet the oath did not bind the *principes* of Normandy as intended. To gain an insight into why these oaths failed to create an inviolable *post obitum* gift, it is necessary to turn again to the example of Robert Curthose.

When Curthose rebelled in 1077 or 1078, it is likely that his actions voided the grant made by his father and the homage done to him by the Norman *principes*, which presumably included a clause privileging the homage they had already done to William. As a result, William the Bastard had to re-grant Normandy to his son following their reconciliation in 1080. Orderic recorded the re-grant but was silent about the renewal of homage.[135] He might not have thought that he

[131] Searle, *PK*, p. 249. The identity of the second boy is not clear, but presumably Searle meant Stephen of Blois (even though that would mean ignoring his elder brother Theobald).

[132] *ASChr*, 'D', s.a. 1079; trans. Garmonsway, p. 214.

[133] Malmesbury, *HN*, pp. 6–10, 18–20; Worcester, iii. 166, 176–82.

[134] This is suggested by Malmesbury's comment that Roger of Salisbury claimed to have been released from his oath by virtue of the marriage, and that 'In saying this, I would not wish it to be thought that I accepted the word of a man who knew how to adapt himself to any occasion … I merely, like a faithful historian, add to my narrative what was thought by people in my part of the country' (Malmesbury, *HN*, p. 10).

[135] Orderic, iii. 112. The speech he later put into William's mouth does not conflict with this

needed to spell it out, however, as a re-grant would necessarily be followed by a renewal of homage. When Curthose rebelled for a second time he did not take up arms against his father. He simply exiled himself from the duchy. That was a canny move, because it ensured that the re-grant and associated homage of 1080 remained intact, so that the *post obitum* grant had to be respected in 1087, regardless of William's own wishes at that time. In contrast, when Geoffrey and Matilda took up arms against Henry I in 1135, it is likely that the oaths sworn to Matilda by the Anglo-Norman lords (which presumably saved their loyalty to King Henry) were voided. Henry's death before the parties had been reconciled, and without the necessary third oath-swearing, allowed Stephen to seize the throne of England, and Normandy with it. Furthermore, as King Louis seems not to have acknowledged either Matilda or Geoffrey as Henry's heir, he was also free to support Stephen's accession.

The chief problem with this tidy picture is that no chronicler mentions it. But that was because it got in the way of the arguments that they did choose to present. The author of the *Gesta Stephani* concentrated instead on the more fundamental issue of Henry's 'forcible imposition of the oath on his barons' and the acknowledgement that it was consequently 'impossible for the breaking of that oath to constitute a perjury'.[136] If the oaths had never been lawful, there was no need to argue that they had been broken. The *Liber Eliensis*, written towards the end of the twelfth century but perhaps based on an earlier source here, omitted all mention of the oaths sworn to Matilda (perhaps because they had been voided by her actions in 1135) and instead wrote of Henry's deathbed designation of Stephen as his heir, with the story supported on oath by Hugh Bigod.[137] This claim was also made by Arnulf of Lisieux on Stephen's behalf at the papal curia. Arnulf's principal line of attack, however, was to suggest that Matilda was illegitimate, and thus not a lawful heir, as her mother had been a professed nun. Although his approach meant he did not consider the oath in detail, Arnulf is reported to have added that Henry had taken advantage of the conditional nature of the oath to

interpretation. The statement that the duchy was given to Robert before the Hastings campaign is accurate. The punctuation suggests a break in the sentence before William adds that he should (also) inherit because he was the first-born son and because he had received the homage of the *barones* of the county (Orderic, iv. 92). Chibnall noted the possible relationship of Orderic's words to the crisis of the 1130s ('The statement attributed to William I, that he could not take back Normandy from Robert because Robert was his eldest son and had received the homage of almost all the Norman lords, may have been coloured by the knowledge of the fealty sworn to Henry's daughter Matilda': Orderic, iv. xix–xx).

[136] *Gesta Stephani*, p. 12.

[137] *Liber Eliensis*, p. 348. Edmund King (*King Stephen*, p. 49) suggested that the account found in the *Liber Eliensis* was based on an 'official newsletter' and was 'official history'.

declare that it was no longer binding, and although it is clear that the condition in question had not been satisfied – Henry still had no legitimate male heir in 1135 – this does at least hint that something had happened that allowed Henry to declare the oath void.[138] Orderic omitted almost all mention of the oath sworn to Matilda, noting only that it might have motivated King David of Scots to attack Carlisle.[139] His omissions, like that of the *Liber Eliensis*, might have been due to a belief that the oaths had been invalidated by Geoffrey and Matilda's actions before 1135 and so were irrelevant to the question of the succession, although they might also have been due to his dislike of the Angevins. William of Malmesbury, writing for Earl Robert of Gloucester, described at length the oath-swearings of 1127 and 1131 and treated them as though they remained in force. However, he also omitted all mention of the hostilities that broke out between the king and Geoffrey and Matilda in 1135, writing only that Geoffrey (not Matilda) 'had vexed the king by not a few threats and insults'. He thus suppressed any reason for thinking that the oaths had been invalidated, and shored up his argument by having Henry assign all his lands to Matilda on his deathbed.[140] John of Worcester likewise thought all those who had taken the oath guilty of perjury, although he seems to have been hesitant to say so, and did not mention the oaths at all when discussing Stephen's accession.[141]

I venture, then, to propose that this is why Robert Curthose succeeded to Normandy and why Matilda and Geoffrey did not, even though much must be implied from silence. Perhaps the circumstances surrounding Stephen's succession reveal only that, as with the events of 1027, where there were no clear rules about who should be preferred the *principes* might make their own choice and find excuses to justify themselves later. In 1027, the choice had been between an illegitimate boy and a grown brother. In 1135, the choice was between a daughter and her foreign husband on the one hand and a nephew on the other. Given the divisions that followed, that choice was not apparently so clear-cut as the choice between Robert and Nicholas had been – or perhaps this was simply the result of chronicles being written before the issues had been resolved.[142]

Some accepted Stephen's claim, influenced no doubt by factors such as his

---

[138] John of Salisbury, *Historia pontificalis*, pp. 83–4; C. P. Schriber, *The Dilemma of Arnulf of Lisieux: New Ideas versus Old Ideals* (Bloomington and Indianapolis, 1990), pp. 16–17; Garnett, *Conquered England*, pp. 232–4.

[139] Orderic, vi. 518 and 519, n. 10.

[140] Malmesbury, *HN*, pp. 22–4.

[141] Worcester, iii. 180–2.

[142] On the ability of a woman to succeed to an office see Martindale, 'Succession and politics', p. 27 and on the transfer of counties or duchies through (but not to) women, pp. 32–6.

pliable character and his ability to encourage the cross-Channel trade between London and Boulogne. Orderic, writing in the 1130s, made it clear that the Anglo-Norman aristocracy did not much like the idea of a division between England and Normandy, and so Stephen's bold move on the English throne brought him the duchy as well. He pictured a small assembly, convened with the purpose of choosing a successor in the absence of a son, thereby following the established practice of the duchy. 'The Normans ... who met together at Neubourg wished to have [Stephen's] brother Theobald as their ruler, but at that meeting they heard ... that all the English had accepted Stephen and wished to obey him and make him their king. All the barons immediately determined, with Theobald's consent, to serve under one lord on account of the honours that they held in both provinces.'[143] Robert of Gloucester was, it seems, one of those who had preferred Theobald, but who was now faced by a fait accompli that established another man as duke.

Although Earl Robert recognized Stephen for the time being, others did not. For some at least, the oaths taken to Matilda and the sense that she was Henry's nearest heir remained of paramount importance. On the news of Henry's death, Wigan the Marshal had surrendered the castles at Exmes, Argentan, and Domfront into the hands of Geoffrey and Matilda, the latter of whom he recognized as his 'natural lord'.[144] Geoffrey and Matilda were recognized, too, by the men of Sées and also by the vassals of William Talvas. That gave Geoffrey control of much of central Normandy, even before Robert of Gloucester's defection in 1138. Orderic did his best to conceal this, and that deception may be supposed to have stemmed from his own preference for Stephen, which is further indicated by his attempts to blacken the reputation of the Angevins in general and to ridicule Geoffrey in particular. They 'committed outrages, violated churches and cemeteries, oppressed their peasants, and repaid those who had received them kindly with many injuries and wrongs'.[145] Geoffrey received a javelin in his foot at Le Sap, and had to be taken back to Maine in a litter, losing his chamberlain and baggage in an ambush on the way.[146] Matilda herself is described disparagingly as 'the countess'.[147]

Although he continued to paint a positive picture of Stephen's rule until the end of his work, it is not clear that Orderic had much sympathy for him either. He might have preferred him to Geoffrey, but there is the briefest of hints in his *Ecclesiastical History* that he would much rather have had Robert of Gloucester as duke than anyone else. When Eustace of Breteuil succeeded to Breteuil it

---

[143] Orderic, vi. 454.
[144] Orderic, vi. 454.
[145] Orderic, vi. 454 and also p. 470.
[146] Orderic, vi. 472–4.
[147] Orderic, vi. 512.

was because the men of the honour 'chose to be ruled by a compatriot who was a bastard rather than by a legitimate Breton or Burgundian'.[148] Those words were probably written in 1136–37, at which time Orderic might have expected his readers readily to substitute 'Blésois' and 'Angevin' for 'Breton' and 'Burgundian'.

Geoffrey's eventual victory in 1144 owed little to inheritance but much to the new duke's own political acumen. There is only one act issued by Geoffrey before his conquest of the duchy, which was made for the monks of Saint-Evroult. In it, Geoffrey was styled 'count of the Angevins, the son of King Fulk of Jerusalem of good memory', but his grant to the monks says that they should have all their possessions as freely and quitly as they held them 'in the time of King Henry my *antecessor*'.[149] Fifteen of Geoffrey's post-Conquest acts make similar reference to Henry I as Geoffrey's *antecessor* or else to Henry's reign. Such wording might have been an attempt to expunge Stephen's reign from the tenurial record, but it also suggests that Geoffrey was aware that his grip on Normandy could be strengthened by reminding beneficiaries that he was Henry's legitimate successor. His emphasis on inheritance, however, was slight indeed when compared to that of his wife. Matilda's scribes consistently adopted the style 'Matilda, the empress, daughter of King Henry' in her Norman acts, both before and after her husband's conquest of the duchy.[150] *Pro anima* clauses, such as that found in her gift to the Hospitallers of 100 *sous* from the rents of Argentan, further reinforced this foundation of her claim.[151]

The focus on kinship to Henry, as well as Geoffrey's willingness to associate his son Henry in the rule of Normandy, helped to legitimize Geoffrey's conquest because they helped Normans to forget that Geoffrey had won Normandy by conquest and patronage. But Katy Dutton has shown how 'defection was a fundamental dynamic of conquest' and also how that defection was the result of Geoffrey's willingness to win supporters through a liberal use of patronage.[152] For example, Geoffrey won Robert of Gloucester to his side by allowing him to retain the lands and rights that he had usurped from the bishop of Bayeux and from the bishop's tenants, while Reginald of Saint-Valéry was granted the port of Dieppe out of the ducal demesne.[153] His approach was not so different from that of Henry I in the years before 1106. It was equally successful.

---

[148] Orderic, vi. 40.

[149] *Regesta*, iii. no. 774.

[150] *Regesta*, iii. nos. 20, 168, 432, 567 (this act should be redated 1138 × 1139, as Chibnall showed), 748, 805, 824, 826, 899).

[151] *Regesta*, iii. no. 409.

[152] Dutton, 'Geoffrey', pp. 177–8.

[153] Dutton, 'Geoffrey', pp. 192–5 (Robert of Gloucester); *Regesta*, iii. no. 329; Dutton, 'Geoffrey', p. 192 (Reginald of Saint-Valéry). See also King, *King Stephen*, pp. 200–2.

The succession to the duchy of Normandy, then, was not simply a matter of inheritance. In the period between 911 and 1144, there were six regular successions, where Normandy was passed from father to son, and four irregular successions where the duchy passed to a brother, nephew, and son-in-law of the previous duke. In other words, 40 per cent of the time – and all the time from 1106 – the succession was not handed down from father to son. Where the succession was straightforward the hereditary principle applied, and it is likely that this concept was strongly imbedded in the Frankish and Norman psyches from the inception of Norman rule. In such cases the *principes* of Normandy appear to have acted simply as a rubber stamp, giving their consent to the choice of successor made by the reigning duke. As they wanted the right to direct the inheritance to their own estates in a similar way, their actions are not surprising. Only if dukes changed their minds – and that only happened in the case of Curthose – did the principles that they struggled so hard to build work against them. But when the succession was not straightforward, the *principes* of the duchy played a more active role. The details are lost, but they arbitrated the competing claims of Robert the Magnificent and the young Nicholas in 1027, probably those of William the Bastard and William of Arques in 1035, Robert Curthose and Henry I in 1106, Stephen and Matilda in 1135, and Geoffrey and Stephen in 1141–44. Jumièges no doubt simplified what happened in 1027, so it might be unwise to conclude that there was anything so formal as an assembly during which the claims were discussed and a decision made, but the later cases, beginning with Henry I, were certainly not so tidy. These 'elections' involved the would-be duke in political manoeuvrings some months, if not years, before the final blow was struck. Henry I could march into Rouen in 1106 because he had already laid the groundwork for his takeover, although the presence of a highly compliant duke must have helped. Stephen might have acted spontaneously in 1135, but he must have known what his friends and supporters thought about the oaths to Matilda, the level of support for her and her foreign husband, and what sort of reception he might expect. As Richard of York discovered to his cost in 1460, discontent alone was not enough to gain a kingdom.[154] Geoffrey of Anjou, like Henry I, won allies and built up support before taking Rouen in 1144. These twelfth-century dukes ruled because the political community agreed that it should be so, often for their own purposes. And so even as rules on heredity were hardening, so the succession to Normandy fell more regularly into the lap of the magnates, and though the dukes might claim that they ruled by inheritance, they actually gained power by cutting deals, arguing their case, and winning battles.

[154] C. Ross, *Edward IV* (London, 1974), p. 28.

The delegation of power: minorities, absences, and the question of the justiciar

One point will by now have become clear: only one man could be duke of the Normans at any one time. The dukes might divide their estates between their sons, but rulership over the duchy was indivisible, as Dudo of Saint-Quentin made clear c. 1015 and despite the hiccup of Robert Curthose's reign.[155] Heirs might have been designated in their father's lifetimes, but that did not make them co-rulers. And to make that point, the dukes ensured that executive power remained in their hands alone.[156] Others might help with the day-to-day running of the duchy, supervising and accounting for the collection of revenues, but if a decision needed to be made or a gift confirmed, they could not act for the duke in his absence.

Nonetheless, there was a time when the dukes could not exercise their powers independently, and that was when they were minors. There were only two minorities in the period between 911 and 1144, and although both were kept as short as possible they reveal the continuing importance of the person and authority of the duke even when he was himself unable to exercise power independently of his guardians.[157] Richard I was ten years old when he succeeded his murdered father, and probably sixteen when he began to rule in his own right, a step marked by the dismissal of Ralph Torta.[158] William the Bastard was a minor for perhaps eight years after his succession. In the interval, someone had to act for him when military leadership was called for and if battle was met. But in times of peace, William ruled as if he were an adult. He was likely to be swayed by the advice of his guardians, however, and that was what made influence over the mind and person of the young duke something that was worth fighting for. It also meant that the choice of guardian was important and sensitive, which in turn might explain why there was always more than one of them.

It is not clear if Longsword had made arrangements for a minority administration before his assassination in 942, even though Dudo tells us that he had been planning to become a monk at Jumièges. William of Jumièges wrote that Botho, Longsword's military leader, was appointed as Richard's guardian,[159] but when Louis IV arrived at Rouen in 942 or 943 there was apparently a triumvirate in

---

[155] *Dudo*, p. 96; see also Le Patourel, 'Norman succession', 235–8, 240; Garnett, '"Ducal" succession', pp. 88–91.

[156] Garnett, '"Ducal" succession', pp. 91–3.

[157] It has been suggested that Richard II was a minor when he succeeded in 996 (Neveux, *A Brief History of the Normans*, p. 74), but Jumièges described him as *in sue iuventutis* at the beginning of his reign, which does not imply a minority (Jumièges, ii. 8).

[158] Orderic, ii. 8.

[159] Jumièges, i. 88.

control: 'Ralph, Bernard and Anslech, guardians of the whole duchy of Normandy (*totius Normannici ducatus tutores*), welcomed him with royal honour as befitting such a great king, submitted themselves to his service and swore fealty on behalf of their little lord.'[160] These three men then seem to have been replaced as Richard's (or the duchy's) guardians by the king himself. Richard was surrendered to King Louis, and was taken to Evreux and Laon, 'so that he should be educated in king-craft and courtly eloquence'.[161] Norman writers beginning with Dudo saw this as an abduction, but Louis might well have had Richard's best interests at heart because Normandy was by no means united at this time. Richard might well have been safer with the king, outside the duchy, than he would have been if allowed to remain at Rouen.[162]

Louis now seems to have established his own administration in the duchy. Bernard the Dane apparently remained as 'leader of the Norman army (*princeps northmannici exercitus*)'. The civilian administration, however, fell into the hands of Ralph Torta. According to Jumièges, 'after a short stay at Rouen the king appointed as governor of the duchy (*perfectum comitatui*) Ralph, surnamed Torta, who was to raise annual revenues from his subjects and to administer all matters of law and all other business in the province'.[163] His regime survived the return of Richard to Rouen and the defeat and imprisonment of King Louis in 945 – but not for long. According to Dudo,

> at that time there was one Ralph, known by the nick-name of Twist, and after the death of William he won for himself the chief position throughout Normandy, higher than the rest of his peers; and he improperly arrogated to himself the property that belonged to the ruler. Every day, he used to distribute to the worthy boy Richard and the young knights daily allowances of eighteen deniers. And his retainers in the household were humiliated, and disgracefully pinched with hunger.[164]

Richard now set about undermining the network of patronage and alliances that Ralph had created to buttress his position, and gained oaths of loyalty from his knights and the burgesses of Rouen. Once he was strong enough, and had obliged Ralph's men to recognize his own lordship, Richard banished Ralph from the duchy and his independent rule could begin. His minority thus ended because he

---

[160] Jumieges, i. 100.
[161] *Dudo*, pp. 101, 102–3.
[162] See above, Chapter 1, pp. 60–1.
[163] Jumièges, i. 108.
[164] *Dudo*, p. 122; Jumièges, i. 114 repeated the story but reduced the sum to 12 *deniers*. See also below, Chapter 11, pp. 626, 627.

had demonstrated through his own actions that he was capable of wielding power for himself.

The second minority began in 1035, although no one knew that it would be a minority at the time. In that year, Robert the Magnificent declared to his assembled lords that he was going on pilgrimage to Jerusalem. His son William was then designated as his heir.[165] Robert died on his way back from Jerusalem, and arrangements that should have lasted for just a few months suddenly had to hold for some years.

Robert's speech, as reported by William of Jumièges, set out two of the functions of the duke. He was lord and military leader. But although William the Bastard might be recognized as such, he could not act as a military leader in his own right until he had been knighted, and that did not happen until c. 1044. And so it seems that Count Gilbert of Brionne acted as the duke's principal guardian and military leader until his death c. 1041. At that point he was replaced by his murderer, Ralph of Gacé, the son of Archbishop Robert of Rouen, who fought for the duke against the rebel Thurstan Goz at Falaise c. 1043. Others of William's guardians, who included Archbishop Robert of Rouen, Count Alan of Brittany, and Osbern the Steward, may have been more concerned with keeping the peace, doing justice, and attempting to protect ducal lands from the encroachments of opportunistic lords such as Roger I of Montgommery. It is also likely that they acted as a council rather than independently, so that power – even if simply in the form of custody of the duke – did not devolve to any one individual.[166]

Orderic claimed that, for fear of his kinsmen and to save him from discovery by traitors who sought his death, William would be smuggled secretly out of his chamber in the castle at night by his uncle Walter (one of Herleva's brothers) and taken to the cottages and hiding places of the poor.[167] It is a dramatic image, but although some historians have been swayed by it, it is not clear that it has any basis in reality.[168] Indeed, it might have been intended to echo the uncertain youth of Julius Caesar, as told by the Roman writer Suetonius.[169] William of Jumièges, who

[165] Jumièges, ii. 80, and see above, *infra*, pp. 318-19.
[166] In contrast, Godwin acted as military leader for the young Harthacnut, while Emma took care of Wessex from Winchester on behalf of her son (*in opus filii sui*): Huntingdon, p. 368.
[167] Orderic, iv. 82.
[168] Douglas, *William the Conqueror*, p. 44 (it is indeed a matter of some wonder that the young duke survived the troubles of his minority'); D. Bates, 'William I (1027/8–1087)', *Oxford Dictionary of National Biography*, online edition, [http://o-www.oxforddnb.com.unicat.bangor.ac.uk/view/article/29448, accessed 3 June 2010]
[169] Suetonius, *The Twelve Caesars*, trans. R. Graves, revised by J. B. Rives (London, 2007), p. 1.

was much closer to events than Orderic, did not mention that the young duke was personally in danger at any point.[170]

What the dramatic events of the minority do highlight, however, is that the person of the duke was important. They suggest that William, even though a minor, still had real power over his subjects. Although that is not apparent from the record of a plea of 1037, whereby Bishop Hugh of Bayeux recovered properties lost following the death of Richard II, William can be seen making permanent donations to a number of Norman beneficiaries in this same period.[171] In 1037 × 1040, for example, the boy (*puer*) William was persuaded to restore Ticheville to Saint-Wandrille, although he was allowed up to three years to make the restoration, a delay apparently intended to give the duke the opportunity to find a new benefice to give to his knight Haimo.[172] In 1040, William gave the church of Boulleville, part of his demesne, to Saint-Pierre of Préaux.[173] In April 1042, he gave the monks of his father's foundation of Cerisy-la-Forêt various tithes from demesne rights or properties in the Cotentin. An anathema clause protected the gifts and established the grant in perpetuity.[174] There is no sense here, then, that William's grant would last only until he came of age, and the same is true of the other grants that he made or might have made while he was still a minor – a position that may be contrasted with that pertaining during the minority of Henry III.[175] Furthermore, donors and their beneficiaries continued to attend William's court in order to gain confirmations of the gifts made by, or to, them. The monks of Jumièges were there in 1038.[176] Those of Fécamp also attended, and while he was in attendance Abbot John was 'begged, indeed compelled' to make a grant of Trungy to Hugh of Montfort.[177] The duke, then, might still be able to exercise coercive lordship, despite the fact that he was a boy of between seven and ten years of age at the time.

William seems also to have been present on campaign, even if he were not able to take charge in any fighting. When the Normans agreed to surrender the castle at Tillières to the French *c.* 1042, Gilbert Crispin refused to carry out those orders until the fourteen-year-old William appeared in person and commanded him

---

[170] Jumièges, ii. 94. See also Bates, 'Adolescence', 7–8.

[171] The judges are named as Archbishop Robert, Count Odo, and Nigel the *vicomte*, and there is no reference at all to the young Duke William (*Livre Noir*, i. 27–9, no. 21).

[172] *RADN*, no. 95. A second grant from the demesne to the same monks that might also date from the minority is found at *RADN*, no. 102.

[173] *RADN*, no. 97.

[174] *RADN*, no. 99. For anathema clauses, see below, Chapter 7, pp. 415–19.

[175] *RADN*, nos. 92–7, 99, 100–5, 110, 112–13; D. Carpenter, *The Minority of Henry III* (London, 1990), pp. 18–19, 95.

[176] *RADN*, no. 92.

[177] *RADN*, no. 93.

to do so.[178] By the time Thurstan Goz rebelled *c.* 1043, William might have been leading the army himself: 'As soon as the duke heard of the plans of this spiteful character he summoned troops of Normans from all over the country and swiftly laid siege to him … When Thurstan saw that he was unable to withstand any longer such a forceful attack, he sought to abandon the place to the duke.'[179] But although William might have moved from boyhood to adolescence by that point, he was almost certainly still to be knighted. Orderic's later interpolation here – 'at that time Ralph of Gacé was the leader of the army and supported his duke with all means' – might, therefore, be right.[180] But even if Jumièges had been trying to push William prematurely to the fore, that would only underline the importance of the duke's leadership of the army in time of war.

Beneath the high-profile activities of making war and confirming grants there was the largely mechanical tedium of routine administrative business. Judith Green has remarked that 'medieval kings had little time, even if they had the inclination or capacity, for routine administrative matters: kingship was about much more than totting up accounts.'[181] The same was true of the dukes. Thus, from the very beginning they had to create structures that did not require their constant attention to enable them to rule their duchy efficiently. Those structures were staffed by men who would travel with the duke, who would receive their orders from him, and who would thus be closely involved in many of the decisions made. After 1066, some of those men found themselves criss-crossing the Channel in the duke's wake. Others, however, would have stayed behind in Normandy and would have found their communication with the duke detrimentally affected by his drastically extended movements. For those at the centre of government, then, the Conquest made a difference. Their job remained the same, but their ability to do it may have been affected – even if only because they had to wait longer for the royal duke's orders to reach them. On the other hand – and this is a point to which we shall return in Chapter 9 – those officials who were based in the localities, the *vicomtes* and the *prévôts*, as well as the mass of the duke's subjects, would have been largely unaffected by the Conquest. For most of them, the duke had always been remote, except for those rare occasions when his itinerary took him through their neighbourhood. Indeed, for some Normans, it might well have been easier to reach the new king at Winchester than to track him down in the Forêt de Lyons.[182]

The chief problem that faced William the Conqueror after 1066, then, was not

---

178 Jumièges, ii. 100.
179 Jumièges, ii. 102. See also above, Chapter 2, pp. 105–6.
180 Jumièges, ii.
181 Green, *Government*, p. 1.
182 For the dukes' itineraries see below, Chapter 9, pp. 506–24.

to ensure the continued administration of the duchy – he already had officials in place to deal with that – but rather the increased delays in corresponding with his administrators, which in time of invasion might well have a detrimental impact on the duchy's security. Moreover, whomever was left in charge would have to be able to rally the duke's troops around them on his behalf. That the defence of Normandy during his absences was what concerned William most was indicated by William of Poitiers when he noted the arrangements made for the security of the duchy during the Hastings campaign; 'No less wisely did he determine who should govern and protect Normandy during his absence', he wrote,[183] adding more detail later:

> For its government (*gubernaculo*) had been carried on smoothly by our lady Matilda, already commonly known by the title of queen, though as yet uncrowned. Men of great experience had added their counsel to her wisdom; among them the first in dignity was Roger of Beaumont (son of the illustrious Humfrey), who on account of his mature age was more suitable for home affairs, and had handed over military duties to his more youthful son ... But in truth the fact that neighbours had not dared to make any attack though they knew the land to be almost emptied of knights, must, we think, be attributed primarily to the king himself, whose return they feared.[184]

So government, whatever that might mean, continued, but more importantly the land remained secure despite the absence of the duke and the fact that the duchy was denuded of knights because of William's reputation. The same emphasis on protection is also found in Orderic's limited comments on the subject, which were perhaps taken from the lost sections of Poitiers's work. Thus, in 1068, 'King William sent his beloved wife Matilda back to Normandy so that she might give up her time to religious devotions in peace ... and together with the boy Robert could keep the duchy secure'.[185] In 1071, 'King William sent William fitz Osbern to Normandy to act as protector of the province (*tueretur provinciam*) with Queen Matilda'.[186] Those who were left to manage and protect the duchy thus included Matilda, Robert Curthose, Roger of Beaumont, William fitz Osbern, and also Roger of Montgommery.[187] As with earlier dukes, William was using members of his family to support his rule, as well as a number of his closest allies and friends.

---

[183] Poitiers, p. 102. Orderic follows him (Orderic, ii. 208), noting that the role of Matilda, Curthose, and the others was to 'protect the province'.
[184] Poitiers, p. 178.
[185] Orderic, ii. 222.
[186] Orderic, ii. 280.
[187] In addition to the notes above, see also Orderic, ii. 210.

The role of Matilda and Roger of Beaumont, and indeed what Poitiers meant by 'government', may be reflected in an act of Count Simon of the Vexin, which was made in the presence of Matilda and Roger and also Archbishop John – although the latter was the beneficiary of the gift.[188] It suggests that they presided over the court in William's absence. Lords made gifts to religious houses in their presence; administrators might have reported problems to them and requested their advice. Perhaps they received embassies and visitors, other than Count Simon, on the duke's behalf. It is unlikely, however, that they were able to issue commands or to hear lawsuits or to direct policy without William's instructions. They were representatives, not proxies, and there is no evidence that they could supply an authority equivalent to William's own.[189]

William, then, remained in control, even when absent. Mention has been made of Matilda's role in restoring customs at Héauville to the monks of Marmoutier in 1080, but the monks had not approached Matilda directly. Instead, Gauzelin the monk 'for this thing crossed the sea, and made a claim to the king, who angrily sent back the said monk with his chaplain Bernard fitz Ospac, to the queen, commanding her to do justice to St Martin … and restore the said gift'.[190] This does not suggest that judicial authority resided in Matilda when William was absent in England. And so while William might not always have been present at hearings, the judges who did justice on his behalf only acted on his mandate, never independently.

While it is clear that Matilda acted as William's eyes and ears in Normandy during his absences, the role of Robert Curthose is less clear. As discussed above, he had been designated heir before the Hastings campaign as a precautionary measure, just as Robert the Magnificent had established William as his heir when he went on pilgrimage to Jerusalem. But whereas Duke Robert died at Nicaea on the return leg of his trip, William survived the battle of Hastings and returned to his duchy. Contemporaries might not have been sure what would happen next, and the situation might have been confused by Robert acting as William's lieutenant in Normandy between 1067 and 1071.[191] Orderic suggested that he acted in the same capacity as Matilda, but William of Jumièges seems to have been clear in his own mind that Curthose was acting as duke at this time. He wrote that William 'granted lordship over the duchy of the Normans (*Normannici ducatus dominium tradidit*) to his son Robert, who was blossoming in the flower of his youth', and added that in 1070 the Normans were rejoicing in Robert as their 'duke and

---

[188] *Regesta: William*, no. 229.
[189] For a contrary view, see F. West, *The Justiciarship in England 1066–1232* (Cambridge, 1966), p. 3, where he argues that Matilda 'certainly acted as regent in Normandy', and D. Bates, 'The origins of the justiciarship', *ANS*, 4 (1982), p. 8.
[190] *Regesta: William*, no. 200. See also above, Chapter 2, pp. 112–14.
[191] Jumièges, ii. 178.

advocate (*dux et aduocatus*)'.[192] The scribe who wrote an act for the nuns of Saint-Désir outside Lisieux seems to have thought similarly. In 1068, he dated an act 'during the reign of Philip in France, of the most noble King William in England, and during the principate of his son Robert in Normandy and Maine (*regnante Philippo in Francia, Guilelmo regum nobilissimo apud Anglos, Rotberto filio eius principante apud Normannos et Cenomannos*)'.[193] It is possible that William of Jumièges and the scribe writing for Saint-Désir exaggerated Curthose's role in Normandy because they expected him to take control of his inheritance now that he was a knight and William was an absent king.[194] In other words, they saw what they expected to see. Alternatively, they might have been carried away by the fact that, with Matilda's departure for her coronation, Curthose was left as his father's sole lieutenant for the first time. Matilda's return to Normandy later in 1068, might not have clearly reversed his position, and if so the limited nature of Robert's rule would only have become apparent when William returned to Normandy in 1071 and continued to exercise full authority there. As William of Jumièges had completed his work in 1070, and is presumed to have died soon after, he was unable to revise his wording.[195] Equally, there is no indication that the *pancarte* for Saint-Désir was ever presented to King William for authentication, and the same is also true of the acts of 1068 and 1076 found in it. The dating clauses it includes do not therefore carry any official weight. Indeed, it is possible that the charter was not presented to the duke because it had become clear that Curthose would not be ruling in either Normandy or Maine after all.[196]

Other evidence for Curthose ruling Normandy in association with his father is slight, although it is possible that he did have some authority in Maine after 1073.[197] The monks of Caen liked to style Robert *comes*, but they styled his brother

---

[192] Jumièges, ii. 178, 184.

[193] *Regesta: William*, no. 179. This act is found in a late-eleventh-century *pancarte* which survived until 1944. The texts are all in one hand, although the *signa*, which belong to the first act, were added at the bottom of the collected acts by a different scribe. The document is also discussed by Garnett, *Conquered England*, pp. 160–1 and remarked by Lack, 'Robert Curthose', 122).

[194] Aird, *Robert Curthose*, p. 57. Aird goes on to suggest that Curthose might have been knighted in 1066 when King Philip recognized his designation (pp. 58–9), which seems equally plausible.

[195] Jumièges, i. xxxv.

[196] It should be noted that while Katherine Lack has asserted that 'Curthose was sometimes styled "duke" in the Conqueror's *acta*', she provided no evidence in support of that claim. The description of Robert Curthose as the 'second Robert' is also taken out of context (Lack, 'Robert Curthose', 122).

[197] *Regesta: William*, nos. 172, 173; Aird, *Robert Curthose*, p. 68 and n. 52 and 53. For a more negative view of Robert's role see Garnett, *Conquered England*, pp. 161–2.

William *comes*, too.[198] Three acts, all of them dating to 1082, apparently style Robert *comes Normannorum* in the witness lists, but none of them survive as an original or even in an early copy.[199] Any implication that Robert was exercising authority in Normandy is thus somewhat tenuous, and it is by no means clear that any weight can be placed on this evidence. Furthermore, Orderic, William of Malmesbury, and John of Worcester were certain that it was Curthose's frustrated ambition that led him to rebel against his father in 1077 or 1078.[200] Orderic pictures a stand-up row over the subject. William told Robert, at great length, not to press his demands and to be patient. He responded:

> 'My lord king, I did not come here to listen to a lecture, for I have had more than enough of these from my schoolmasters and am surfeited with them. Give me instead a satisfactory answer about the honour due to me, which I am awaiting so that I may know what kind of life I may live. On one thing I am unshakeably resolved and wish all to know: that I will no longer fight for anyone in Normandy with the hopeless status of a hired dependant'. On hearing this the king exclaimed in anger, 'I have already told you plainly enough and have no scruples in telling you again even more plainly that I will never agree as long as I live to relax my grip on my native land of Normandy. Moreover, I do not choose to divide the kingdom of England, which I won with such great pains, in my lifetime … Let no one doubt this for one moment: as long as I live I will surrender my duchy to no one, and will allow no living man to share my kingdom with me.'[201]

Although Orderic dramatized the scene, his evidence is thought to be reliable, so it does seem that Curthose rebelled because he was denied any power despite his designation as heir.[202] Moreover, Orderic's view appears to be supported by the contents of a letter sent to Robert in 1080 by Pope Gregory VII: 'we counsel and in a fatherly way beseech that it may ever be graven on your mind that whatever your father may possess with so strong a hand and with such widespread renown he seized from the mouth of his enemies, knowing, however, that he would not live forever but so manfully pressing forward with this in mind; that he would pass it on to some heir of his own.'[203]

---

[198] *Regesta: William*, nos. 46, 52, 53, 54, and also 280 (for Troarn).
[199] *Regesta: William*, nos. 158, 204, 205. One copy of this last act omits the word 'Normannorum', throwing doubt on whether it was there at all in the lost original document. See also the brief discussion by Garnett, *Conquered England*, p. 159.
[200] Orderic, iii. 98–100; Malmesbury, *GR*, i. 502; Worcester, iii. 30 (s.a. 1077).
[201] Orderic, iii. 100.
[202] Garnett, *Conquered England*, pp. 153–4, 165–6, and see above, Chapter 2, p. 136.
[203] *The Register of Pope Gregory VII*, p. 358 (no. 7.27).

Although Curthose seems to have been entrusted with a little more responsibility in 1080, albeit in England rather than in the duchy, there is no sense that the reconciliation with his father in that year saw Robert associated in the rule of Normandy. The letter of Gregory VII argues against it, and so too does Robert's second exile *c.* 1084.[204] Two acts drafted in 1096 by the monks of Dijon, which count the years of Robert's reign from 1077, might reveal something of the Frankish view of events, leavened by the yeast of hindsight, but they do not seem to reflect the reality of Robert's situation at all.[205]

When reporting the row with Curthose, Orderic had William declare that he would not surrender Normandy nor share England. A number of narratives, however, appear to suggest that certain individuals had much more responsibility in England than was the case in Normandy. Lanfranc is said, in the *Life* composed by Milo Crispin, to have been '*princeps* and guardian of England, with all the nobles subject to him and giving their help in matters concerning the defence and management or the peace of the kingdom'.[206] Although the *Life* is a late witness, this seems a fair description of Lanfranc's position in 1075, especially because it does not require Lanfranc to have been given any real independence of action.

More impressive, or so it seems, was the position that Odo of Bayeux held in England before his fall in 1082 or 1083. When reporting his arrest, Orderic had King William say: 'I condemn neither a clerk nor a bishop but arrest my earl, whom I had put in my place in my kingdom (*meo uice mea proposui regno*), desiring to hear an account of the stewardship entrusted to him.'[207] In the deathbed speech composed by Orderic, William describes Odo as 'rector'.[208] These words do not bear technical, precise meanings. Orderic wrote only that Odo acted in William's place – that does not necessarily mean he could act without his order

---

[204] Aird, *Robert Curthose*, pp. 95–8. This period of self-imposed exile might be compared to the future Henry II's actions in 1153, whereby he left England for Normandy after being recognized as heir, probably to reduce the possibility for discord with Stephen (E. King, 'The accession of Henry II', in *Henry II: New Interpretations*, ed. C. Harper-Bill and N. Vincent (Woodbridge, 2007), pp. 38–9.

[205] This view was also taken by Garnett: 'the 1096 charters represent nothing more than a retrospective interpretation of the significance of Curthose's first rebellion. This appears to bear no relation to Norman tradition, or to other assessments of his status during that period' (Garnett, *Conquered England*, pp. 162–3). It might also be set against a dating clause of an act for Bayeux cathedral: 'Anno igitur ab incarnatione domini millesimo octogesimo nono ... principatus Roberti comitis anno secundo' (*Livre Noir*, i. 6–8, no. 4).

[206] *Life of Lanfranc*, p. 109.

[207] Orderic, iv. 42 and see Luke 16: 2 for the requirement that the steward should account for his stewardship.

[208] Orderic, iv. 98.

to do something. An act of Henry I for Saint-Pierre-sur-Dives, dating from 1121 ×
1128, uses a similar phrase to describe the justiciar of Normandy, and that official
certainly had no independence of action, as will be seen below.[209] All the other
evidence for Odo's activities is equally ambiguous, regardless of the words that
Orderic or Malmesbury used to describe him or his position. That men were said
to hold land by the seal of Odo, for example, does not mean that his seal was the
best warrant.[210] It might suggest instead that the land in question was held on a
temporary basis, pending the king's confirmation. It is also not clear if Odo acted
only because he had received a command to do so, or indeed if he was acting ultra
vires. The fact that Odo's involvement was specifically recorded might in itself
indicate the dubious character of the grant. Furthermore, although place-dates
are unusual on William's *acta*, there are examples that reveal that the monks
of St Augustine's Canterbury crossed to Normandy to obtain writs for English
affairs, which suggests that Odo could not give them what they wanted.[211] The
evidence, then, is ambiguous, and can be explained without the need to make
Odo a viceroy.

When Curthose succeeded to Normandy in 1087, he did not also succeed to his
father's kingdom, and so although Orderic tells us how reliant the duke was on
the advice of Bishop Odo, Edgar Ætheling, Robert of Bellême, William of Arques,
and Ranulf Flambard,[212] these men were not routinely left to administer the duchy
in his absence. His reign does, however, provide one insight as to the continuing
personal importance of the duke of the Normans to affairs in the duchy. In 1091,
the monks of Saint-Evroult elected a new abbot, Roger of Le Sap.

Then Herman, the prior, and Arnold of le Tilleul, and several others took
him to the duke's court, but they could not find the duke in Normandy. Both
brothers had been roused by the sudden news of secret plots which threatened
the English kingdom, and had caused general surprise by suddenly crossing
from Normandy into England. So Herman returned to Saint-Evroult to take
charge of the house, and Arnold and the abbot elect followed the princes
of the realm across the sea. Reaching the royal residence at Windsor, they
showed the duke the record of the election by the convent with the authority of the bishop of Sées and three abbots. He readily gave his assent and

---

[209] See below, pp. 350–2 and also Chapter 8, p. 476.
[210] West, *Justiciarship*, pp. 4–6; D. Bates, 'The origins of the justiciarship', *ANS*, 4 (1982),
       3–4.
[211] *Regesta: William*, nos. 83 (made at Bayeux in 1077), 88 (made at Rouen in 1080 × 1087).
[212] Orderic, iv. 186. For Odo see also: iv. 114, 146–54. William the monk of Arques was a
       regular witness of Robert's *acta*, attesting, for example, *Regesta*, i. nos. 299, 308, 310; *NI*,
       Appendix E, no. 4a.

committed the temporal charge of the monastery to Roger by handing him the pastoral staff, as was customary at that time, and sent letters to the bishop of Lisieux instructing him to admit him fully according to the canons.[213]

In contrast with the situation in 1122, discussed below, the monks of Saint-Evroult seem not to have sought, nor to have received, permission to leave the duchy. This may have been because of the precipitate nature of Curthose's departure, but it also suggests that there was no administrative machinery in place to supervise Channel crossings in Curthose's reign, as might have been expected given his lack of control over England. That was to change under Henry I. It is, however, clear that the need for the monks to have the election confirmed by their duke was as important and as pressing as it was to be thirty years later, perhaps even more so as they would have wanted to ensure that Robert of Bellême should be denied any opportunity to ratify the election in the duke's absence. And it is quite clear from their actions that there was no one in Normandy who could act in the duke's name in his absence.

Orderic's account of the election also reveals that Robert Curthose might act as duke of the Normans while he was in England. William Rufus might equally act as a king in Normandy.[214] There is no reason to suppose that either could do this only by special concession of his brother. In 1106, Henry I crossed to Normandy and summoned Robert to appear before him to answer for his incompetence, holding what seems to have been a formal trial.[215] He could only have been acting as king, but he was acting outside England, within his brother's jurisdiction, but certainly without the duke's permission. Equally, Henry I issued an act for the nuns of Fontevraud, which survives as an original written by Robert de Sigillo, while in the jurisdiction of Theobald of Blois at Chartres in January 1131.[216] Even without these examples, it would be unlikely that there was a convention that 'sovereigns did not attest and did not seal acts in their name when they were resident in the jurisdiction of another'.[217] A king like William the Conqueror or Henry I would have refused to accept that their power over their own kingdom had any geographical limits. Apart from the fact that it would have made visits to the courts of other rulers impossible, royal power was personal. A king's quasi-sacral

---

[213] Orderic, iv. 254.

[214] Orderic, iv. 250.

[215] Orderic, vi. 56.

[216] *Regesta*, ii. no. 1687. Orderic wrote that Henry lodged with Helisende the *vidamesse* for three days (Orderic, vi. 420).

[217] H. Doherty, 'La bataille de Tinchebray et les actes d'Henri Ier', in *Tinchebray 1106–2006: actes du colloque de Tinchebray (28–30 Septembre 2006)*, ed. V. Gazeau and J. Green (Flers, 2009), p. 183.

persona and authority could hardly be shuffled off the moment the king crossed a political frontier, and his people left to fend for themselves.[218]

In August 1131, perhaps while at Tosny, Henry, king of the English and duke of the Normans, declared that he was leaving France for England.[219] The fact that Henry's crossing had commenced was reflected in the place-dates of most of the acts issued at this time, which note that they were made *in transitu* or 'during the crossing'. This seems to indicate – perhaps misleadingly – that something had changed. The earliest of the documents issued as Henry progressed to the coast was addressed in particular to the men who worked the administrative machinery that allowed ducal government to function, the archbishop of Rouen, Bishop John of Lisieux, and Robert of La Haye-du-Puits.[220] By the time Henry had reached Arques, Bishop John had caught up with him, and either he or Robert of La Haye witness, but are not addressed by, the remaining acts.[221]

These documents comprise some of the handful of Norman writs and charters, that is *acta* intended to take effect in the duchy, that have survived from Henry's reign.[222] The survival of these documents is haphazard, but they are nonetheless the most useful source of information for the activities of Henry's administration in Normandy, and the identities of the men who staffed the machinery of government. That is because some were addressed to specific individuals and officials who presumably had some interest in the business they contained, and because they generally ordered that action should be taken or, indeed, desisted from, thus revealing something of the addressees' responsibilities. Such documents do not exist from William the Bastard's day. Also in contrast to those issued by his predecessors, the bulk of Henry's *acta* also have place-dates, and these can help to establish the extent to which he retained power in his own hands even when absent from Normandy.

The importance of Henry's *acta* for this subject was recognized by Charles Homer Haskins at the beginning of the twentieth century. He wrote: 'what means were provided for maintaining the government during the king's absence is a question which we cannot answer from the chroniclers … The charters, however, tell us before 1108 of ducal justices in the Cotentin, and before 1109 of a chief

---

[218] As discussed above, Chapter 5, pp. 292–3.

[219] Much of the following discussion is an English translation of a paper delivered at Cerisy-la-Salle in 2011 and published as M. Hagger, 'Le gouvernement *in absentia*: la Normandie sous Henri Beauclerc, 1106–1135', in *Penser les mondes normandes médiévaux (911–2011)*, ed. D. Bates and P. Bauduin (Caen, 2017).

[220] *Regesta*, ii. no. 1699.

[221] *Regesta*, ii. nos. 1694, 1695, 1697, 1698.

[222] For the Norman writs see Hagger, 'The earliest Norman writs revisited', 181–205 and D. Bates, 'The earliest Norman writs', *EHR*, 100 (1985), 266–84.

justiciar.'[223] Haskins's excitement about the mention of justiciars and justices in Norman acts, and his assumption that they maintained government in Henry's absence, was due to his knowledge of the work of Maitland and Stubbs who saw the justiciar as a viceroy.[224] The appearance of a *iusticiarius* in Normandy thus appeared to demonstrate a parallel development in the duchy, and led Haskins to conclude that Bishop John of Lisieux was the Norman equivalent of Bishop Roger of Salisbury, Henry's supposed viceroy during his absences from England.[225] Fifty years or so later, Francis West found it much more difficult to see such a figure in the Anglo-Norman period, but was at least clearer about what he was looking for. 'The justiciar', he wrote, 'was the king's *alter ego* whose office met the need for an extension of the king's person and power' and that 'royal power had to be delegated at the highest level if government was to operate smoothly and not in fits and starts'.[226] Despite West's caution, historians have continued to see the justiciars as equivalent to viceroys, and to perceive such officials operating during the reigns of William the Conqueror and Henry I.[227] In contrast, when the twelfth-century chronicler William of Malmesbury commented on Roger of Salisbury's role in the English administration, he wrote that Henry 'entrusted to his judgement the administration of justice throughout the realm, *whether he were himself in England or detained in Normandy*'.[228] Quite what he meant by this is not entirely clear, but the emphasis on continuity – a sense of which has often been lacking in the later historiography and which was expressly excluded by Stubbs – is important as it would seem to make it impossible to see Roger as a viceroy.

The first thing to do, then, is to consider briefly whether the role of a *justiciarius* was equivalent to that of a viceroy. Justiciars did justice, so much is clear from Henry's *acta* and the reports of Norman pleas, which employ the word as a synonym for *justicia*, or 'a justice'. It might have been chosen to avoid confusion between the ducal official and the abstract virtue. Orderic occasionally used the word to mean a just ruler, but more often it was, as with the other sources, simply

---

[223] *NI*, p. 87. The 'chief justiciar' is, in fact, only found in an inauthentic act for Beaubec.

[224] W. Stubbs, *The Constitutional History of England in its Origin and Development*, vol. 1, sixth edition (Oxford, 1913), pp. 374–5.

[225] *NI*, pp. 87, 99. For the description of Roger as *iusticiarius tocius Anglie* see Huntingdon, p. 470.

[226] West, *Justiciarship*, p. 1.

[227] See, for example, Bates, 'Justiciarship' (as discussed above); W. L. Warren, *The Governance of Norman and Angevin England 1086–1272* (London, 1987), p. 80; C. W. Hollister and J. W. Baldwin, 'The rise of administrative kingship', *American Historical Review*, 83 (1978), reprinted in *MMI*, pp. 228–231, repeated in Hollister, *Henry*, pp. 364–7.

[228] Malmesbury, *GR*, i. 738 (para. 408) (my italics).

someone who did justice (the two are not exclusive, of course).[229] This usage indicates that justiciars had a limited function, and even though doing justice was one of the principal functions of a medieval ruler, that function alone was not enough to create a viceroy (or several of them), especially as they seem to have done justice only on the royal duke's order.[230] Moreover, those men who appear to have had a leading role in Henry's administration are never anywhere styled justiciar, while the existence of a chief justice or a justice of Normandy need indicate only that there were at least two tiers of justices – something Haskins recognized – with some exercising a judicial or juridical function in the regions, and others being possessed of an authority that covered the whole of the duchy.[231] They did not, then, have the independence of action, or the wide-ranging responsibilities, required to make them viceregal figures.

Looking at the role of the justiciars, then, does not help establish how Henry governed his duchy when he was not resident in it. An alternative approach is to follow the careers of at least some of the individuals named in the addresses of Henry's *acta* to see what they did and if that helps to establish the scope of their office. Henry's wife Matilda was not one of those involved, and nor was his son William. Indeed, an examination of those Henry placed at the head of his administration in Normandy seems to highlight a significant change from the picture under his father. As discussed, William had appointed his family and his closest and most loyal friends to act as his representatives in Normandy during his absences. In contrast, Henry turned to lesser men, even if they were not exactly raised from the dust. The most prominent was Bishop John of Lisieux, whom Haskins long ago identified as the head, 'or at least an important member', of the Norman administration from Henry's earliest years.[232] John was regularly employed as a justice, both when Henry was present at court and when he was not.[233] When Henry was in the duchy, Bishop John was treated as a general

---

[229] Orderic, ii. 316; iv. 102; vi. 74, 76, 356, 468, 494. Orderic hinted at a wider responsibility when he wrote that justiciars had entered the county of Evreux, following Amaury of Montfort's second rebellion in 1123, and annexed it to the royal demesne (Orderic, vi. 344). But quite how this was achieved in practice is unclear, and it might have been as much a judicial as an administrative process.

[230] For Henry's justices, see also Chapter 8, pp. 475–86.

[231] These might have been the successors of the judges that William I appointed in the localities of Normandy after the Conquest (Orderic, ii. 208). Green noted that the 'justice of all England' was similarly a justice whose jurisdiction was not geographically circumscribed (Green, *Government*, p. 48).

[232] *NI*, p. 88.

[233] *NI*, pp. 95–6. One of the cases at Caen was heard in the king's absence, and one in his presence. The first of the *emptiones* printed by Haskins shows that Bishop John and his associated were also judges at Argentan in Henry's presence.

dogsbody. He was sent to Argentan from Saint-Evroult to deliver salted hogs and wheat to the monks in 1113, and dispatched from Pont-Audemer by the king to conduct the funeral of Bishop Serlo of Sées in 1123.[234] He was consulted by Henry on the marriage of Matilda to Geoffrey of Anjou (if that does not confuse counsel and office). When Henry was away, it seems to have been John's job to keep tabs on those who crossed the Channel – thus he gave Warin the Bald permission to cross to England in the winter of 1122.[235] However, although Bishop John seems to have been the most *prominent* of Henry's Norman bureaucrats, he was not *pre-eminent* – unlike Bishop Roger of Salisbury in England.[236] The contemporary Norman chronicler, Orderic Vitalis, had plenty of opportunities to inform his readers of Bishop John's position. He provided a brief biography when recounting John's election to the see of Lisieux in 1107, and noted his death and his 'long experience' at the close of his *History*.[237] But Orderic never gave any indication that John was the Norman equivalent of Bishop Roger of Salisbury, whom he described in contrast as entrusted with 'the government of the whole English kingdom' by Henry I and Stephen,[238] and whom he wrote had 'enjoyed authority over all England during the whole lifetime of King Henry'.[239] Orderic might have been disinclined to celebrate John's role in the administration as a result of his activities as his diocesan, which he was equally at pains to conceal.[240] The same may also be true of Milo Crispin and another anonymous writer at Le Bec, both of whom failed to describe John's role in Henry's administration, while nonetheless making it clear that he was close to the king. Instead, they highlighted the bishop's hostility to the monks due to Abbot Boso's refusal to do homage to Henry.[241] In any event, there is no evidence that John raised taxes like Roger in 1123–24, or changed the way that the *vicomtes* held their office as Roger had altered the sheriffs' terms, or increased the reach of royal justice.[242] It cannot even be said that he 'pleaded the cases, controlled the expenditure himself, kept the treasure himself' as Malmesbury could claim for the bishop of Salisbury.[243]

---

[234] Orderic, vi. 176 and 340, respectively.

[235] Orderic, vi. 324. See also below, Chapter 7, pp. 366–70.

[236] West, *Justiciarship*, p. 23.

[237] Orderic, vi. 142–4; 550.

[238] Orderic, vi. 462.

[239] Orderic, vi. 530.

[240] It should be noted, however, that Marjorie Chibnall thought that relations between Bishop John and the abbey of Saint-Evroult were generally good (Orderic, i. 74, 90).

[241] 'The Life of the Venerable Boso, known as the wise, fourth abbot of Bec' and 'On the Liberty of the Abbey of Bec', in S. N. Vaughn, *The Abbey of Bec and the Anglo-Norman State 1034–1136* (Woodbridge, 1981), pp. 129, 140–1.

[242] Green, *Henry*, p. 183.

[243] Malmesbury, *HN*, p. 66.

Instead, the *acta* indicate that Bishop John was just one of several men who helped to administer Normandy for King Henry, apparently without an established title or formal role. Notable among these others is Robert of La Haye-du-Puits, who was identified as the leading layman in the administration by Haskins.[244] His importance is certainly clear. He acted as a justice with Bishop John and was addressed in four of Henry's writs and writ-charters. But Haskins went a little too far in making his case. Perhaps because Stubbs had noted that a later steward of Normandy had acted as justiciar, Haskins attempted to make Robert a ducal *dapifer*, too. However, Robert did not describe himself as such in his foundation deed for Boxgrove priory, issued in 1105, or in the three acts that evidence his gifts to the abbey at Montebourg, and there is no evidence at all that he was a ducal steward before 1131 (although his father at least was a steward of the count of Mortain).[245] Furthermore, the three royal acts that give him this title are all a little suspect, and in any event describe him only as steward and not as 'steward of Normandy' which is the title accorded to Robert of Courcy in 1129 × 1130.[246] Equally, it is not the case, as Haskins claimed, that Robert's name 'always heads the list of laymen both in the address and in the testing clause of Henry's charters except when he is preceded by someone of the rank of count'.[247] The names of, for example, Brien fitz Count, Robert of Vern, and Humfrey of Bohon can all be found before his in the witness lists of Henry's *acta*.[248] This is not to suggest that Robert of La Haye was not important in Henry's administration – clearly he was – but he may not have been the leading layman, at least not for the whole reign and especially as Robert can also be found acting in an unknown capacity in Lincolnshire where he had inherited the honour held before 1066 by Kolswein when he married Muriel, the heiress of Kolswein's successor, Picot.[249]

The address clauses of Henry's Norman writ-charters suggest that Count Stephen of Mortain had a central role in the Norman administration during the 1120s, but there is not enough evidence to be certain of what that role was or for how long he played it.[250] Earl Robert of Gloucester, however, was certainly a leading

---

[244] *NI*, p. 99. Followed by Hollister, *Henry*, p. 364.

[245] 'The Chartulary of the Priory of Boxgrove', ed. L. Fleming, Sussex Record Society, 59 (1901), 16–17 (no. 4); Ctl. Montebourg, p. 113, nos. 305–7.

[246] *NI*, p. 299 (no. 10) = *Regesta*, i. no. 1688; Ctl. *Beaumont-le-Roger*, pp. 7–10 (no. 3) = *Regesta*, ii. no. 1693; *NI*, pp. 300–2 (no. 11) = *Regesta*, ii. no.1698. Bernard's suit against Serlo the Dumb is calendared at *Regesta*, ii. no. 1585. This record dates from 1129 × 1130, but Robert of Courcy lived on after 1135 and there is no reason to believe that he was deprived of his title before his death.

[247] *NI*, p. 99.

[248] For example, the acts calendered at *Regesta*, ii. nos. 1215, 1427, 1581, 1680, 1690.

[249] *Monasticon*, viii. 1275, no. xlv = *Regesta*, ii. no. 1154, dated 1115 × 1120.

[250] Orderic, vi. 354 = *Regesta*, no. 1337; *Regesta*, ii. p.347 (no. clviia) = no. 1356.

figure in the administration during the last decade or so of Henry's reign. He was sent to Normandy in 1123 with Ranulf le Meschin, earl of Chester, to reinforce Henry's garrisons there, and this may help to narrow the date of the act addressed to Bishop John, Earl Robert, Earl Ranulf, and Robert of La Haye-du-Puits that was issued sometime between 1122 and 1131 when Henry was at Arques or Arganchy.[251] Earl Robert played a broader role in the Norman administration, too, holding the castles at Caen, Bayeux, and Falaise and also being responsible for the treasure stored at this last stronghold – one of Roger of Salisbury's functions, too, according to William of Malmesbury.[252] Further, he was one of three men – the others were Bishop John and Brien fitz Count – who were involved in negotiations for the marriage of Geoffrey of Anjou to Matilda. He was also commissioned to carry out the inquisition on the lands of the bishop of Bayeux in 1133, and he was party to the discussions that led to Henry's edict on homicide during the periods covered by the Truce of God of 1135.[253] The earl was also sole witness to a number of writs that might also reveal his official capacity, as they deal with the sort of business it is likely that Henry's administrators would need to know about. John Le Patourel had thought that Count Stephen and Earl Robert had no role in Normandy, but the evidence suggests that, in fact, Earl Robert had become the leading layman in the Norman administration by c. 1130.[254] Nonetheless, he was hardly a viceroy.

Something else of the role and responsibilities of these men can be seen if Henry's Norman writs and writ-charters are examined collectively. In general, the six authentic acts addressed to Bishop John and his colleagues were instructions or notifications to do with the extent or limitation of ducal justice and rights. The first commanded that Bishop Richard of Bayeux was to have justice over his diocese and tenants (thus removing them from the duke's jurisdiction);[255] the second commanded that the bishop of Evreux was to share the profits of the fair held at Nonancourt with the king (as that money would have to be handed over to the bishop by the relevant ducal officials);[256] the third evidenced the appointment of Warin as abbot of Saint-Evroult (as the property of the church would have to be released from the duke's custody);[257] the fourth commanded Bishop John and

---

[251] *Livre Noir,* i. 41–2 (no. 34) = *Regesta,* ii. no. 1589. The act may be dated 1122 × 1129.

[252] Orderic, vi. 448, 516.

[253] Malmesbury, *HN,* p. 10 (marriage); *RHGF,* xiii. 699–702; *TAC,* i. 65–8 (ch. 71) (edict on the Truce).

[254] Le Patourel, *Norman Empire,* p. 143.

[255] *Livre Noir,* i. 36 (no. 29) = *Regesta,* ii. no. 951.

[256] *Regesta,* ii. 347 (no. clviia) = no. 1356.

[257] Orderic, vi. 354 = *Regesta,* ii. no. 1337. The next act in the *Regesta* has proved deceptive. It has been taken by Hollister to show that Bishop John was at York in December 1122, despite the contradiction provided by Orderic's narrative, and has been seen by King as 'suspicious' as a result (King, *King Stephen,* p. 19, n. 114). However, the place date should

Roger of Magneville to do right to the abbey of Saint-Etienne of Caen over the water of Vains (thus commanding ducal justice to be done);[258] the fifth, place-dated at Arques or Arganchy, commanded that the canons of Bayeux should hold their lands and prebends well and honourably (perhaps best seen as a grant of ducal protection, and thus potential jurisdiction);[259] and the sixth was one of the acts of August 1131, mentioned above, which notified Bishop John and his colleagues that the college of Beaumont-le-Roger had been confirmed in its possessions at Bourneville.[260] This may simply have been of general interest. These documents, then, informed Bishop John and his colleagues about decisions Henry had already made that needed to be recorded and observed. There was no invitation for them to act on their own initiative.

Moreover, Bishop John and his associates were not, it seems, told about every decision Henry had made. A small number of writs issued in England seem to have bypassed Henry's central administrators completely. In 1107, for example, William of Tancarville and Gilbert of L'Aigle were commanded to do justice to the abbot of Jumièges regarding a 'fat fish' caught at Quillebeuf when the king was at Westminster.[261] A second writ, this one datable 1106 × 1129 and issued at London, instructed Algar of Sainte-Mère-Eglise and the other justices of the Cotentin to allow Prior Rinald of Héauville to have 'the fish newly caught in the land of the blessed Martin and they shall possess whatever pertains to the same house as much in lands as in tithes in peace and quitly since my father gave them in alms'.[262] A third writ of 1107 × 1123, issued in Cirencester and addressed to Bishop Richard of Bayeux, commanded that Godfrey the Priest should have his church of Saint-Sauveur at Caen.[263] Such acts are a reminder that Bishop John and his colleagues were not all-powerful deputies, that others were involved in the administration of the duchy, and that they had their own rights and jurisdictions.

almost certainly be read as *Ebroicas* rather than *Eboracum*, a mistake due to the natural tendency of a fourteenth-century Chancery scribe to assume that York was intended.

[258]   *Regesta*, ii. 370 (no. ccxlii) = no. 1672.

[259]   *Livre Noir*, i. 41–2 (no. 34) = *Regesta*, ii. no. 1589. 'Archenc' might be identified as Arques, following Bourienne, or as Arganchy, following the editors of the *Regesta*.

[260]   *Ctl. Beaumont-le-Roger*, p. 22 (no. 13) = *Regesta*, ii. no. 1699. It should be noted that although *Regesta*, no. 1587 for Sainte-Barbe-en-Auge also seems to have been addressed to Bishop John and others, this address seems erroneous, especially as he also witnessed the document, and is probably the result of later forgery.

[261]   *Chs. Jumièges*, i. 134–5 (no. 47) = *Regesta*, ii. no. 842.

[262]   L. Couppey, *Encore Héauville: supplément aux notes historiques sur le prieur, conventuel d'Héauville la Hague*, Revue catholique de Normandie, 10 (1900–01), p. 350.

[263]   *Livre Noir*, i. 44 (no. 38) = *Regesta*, ii. no. 819. Roger of Salisbury might be circumvented too, as Kealey briefly noted (E. J. Kealey, *Roger of Salisbury, Viceroy of England* (Berkeley, Los Angeles, and London, 1972), p. 34).

There was a plethora of ducal officials, from Bishop John down to the *vicomtes*, *prévôts*, and collectors of tolls and customs, and all of them held their positions whether the king were in England or Normandy. All might consequently be addressed in Henry's Norman writs no matter where they were issued, whether in England or the duchy. They were addressed because they were not at the king's side, and they were absent from court because they were doing their job administering the regions of Normandy in Henry's name and on his behalf. Thus, while he was resident in the duchy, Henry addressed writs to, among others, the justices and foresters of the Cotentin,[264] the officials of Saint-Marcouf and Varreville,[265] and the *prévôt* of Argentan.[266] Bishop John of Lisieux and his colleagues, too, were addressed in writs on those occasions when they were not at the king's side in Normandy – hence the acts addressed to the bishop and his associates which are place-dated at Tosny and either Arques or Arganchy.[267]

What we see here, then, is continuity in Henry's Norman administration. There is nothing in the documents addressed to the bishop and his colleagues that in any way suggests that they took on a different role during Henry's absences from Normandy. They do *not* provide any evidence for a viceregal administration that swung into action only when Henry left the duchy. Furthermore, government was never delegated at the highest level to any of these men. There is no evidence to support a conjecture that Henry's justices initiated pleas without the king's writ commanding them to do so – indeed, the writ for Caen concerning the water of Vains, noted above, provides some against it. Henry did not ask, or allow, Bishop John, or Robert of La Haye-du-Puits, or the other individuals addressed to make decisions on his behalf. It was Henry alone who could command that justice be done, or that the profits of one of his fairs be shared with another lord, or make appointments to vacant churches. That is why when Abbot Roger of Le Sap of Saint-Evroult decided that he wanted to resign his abbacy, he sent a letter to Henry in England asking for his permission to do so, and to hold an election to find a successor. This the king allowed. But even then, he did not delegate the approval of the duly elected successor to Bishop John or any other of his officials. Instead, the abbot-elect, Warin the Bald, was obliged to seek Bishop John's permission (given on the king's behalf) to leave Normandy, and to journey to York to have his election confirmed by the king in person and to receive the writ that would give him possession of his monastery and its property.[268]

---

[264] *NI*, p. 102 = *Regesta*, ii. no. 1951.

[265] *NI*, p. 101 = *Regesta*, ii. no. 1950; Chanteax, *Recueil*, no. 155.

[266] *NI*, p. 306 = *Regesta*, ii. no. 1946.

[267] *Livre Noir*, i. 41–2 (no. 34) = *Regesta*, ii. no. 1589; *Ctl. Beaumont-le-Roger*, p. 22 (no. 13) = *Regesta*, ii. no. 1699.

[268] Orderic, ii. 324; vi. 354 = *Regesta*, ii. no. 1337.

Warin's case is instructive, if only because it acts as a reminder that writs and charters were not issued spontaneously by the king or duke, but rather were requested, usually in person, by the prospective beneficiary, sometimes after a lengthy journey. The place-dates of royal *acta* do not reveal only Henry's itinerary, which has tended to be what they have been used for,[269] and which has tended to highlight his absences from particular places and regions and thus apparently to emphasize the need for a viceroy if government was to continue. Place-dates also tell us where beneficiaries took themselves in order to make the king present. They show the lengths to which beneficiaries would go to get the documents they needed. By extension, they demonstrate that only Henry was able to give them what they wanted, and thus that his power was not delegated at any point to his officials.

Petitioners were prepared to make such journeys because it was a fact of political life that Henry was almost always absent. Even before 1066, it would have been apparent that the duke could not be everywhere in his duchy at the same time. Indeed, the dukes seem to have been based in the region around Rouen and Fécamp until the reign of William the Conqueror. Henry I stopped in particular at Rouen, Caen, and Argentan, and was apparently rarely seen outside that triangle. Across the Channel, the English kings seldom ventured to the North. William of Malmesbury could consequently remark that 'the kings, once English now Norman … spend more time in the south than in the north. In our parts, the king himself makes do with a squad of household troops; but when he is visiting *those* parts of his realm he always takes with him a large company of auxiliaries.'[270] For those based in the peripheral areas to which the king or duke rarely came, Henry might as well not have been in the country at all. His Channel crossings are unlikely to have made much difference to them, which may account for the almost universal omission of news of them from the Norman chronicles.[271]

The geographic limitations of Henry's itinerary within Normandy were just as much of a problem for those who needed his support as his absences across the Channel. The archive for the abbey of Montebourg in the Cotentin comprises the largest single assemblage of Henry I's writs for a Norman beneficiary. It can thus

---

[269] For example, W. Farrer, 'An Outline Itinerary of King Henry I', *EHR*, 34 (1919), 303–82, 505–79; S. Mooers Christelow, 'A moveable feast? Itineration and the centralization of government under Henry I', *Albion*, 28 (1996), 187–228; H. Tanner, 'Henry I's administrative legacy: the significance of place-date distribution in the *acta* of King Stephen', in *Henry I and the Anglo-Norman World: Studies in Memory of C. Warren Hollister*, ed. D. F. Fleming and J. M. Pope (Woodbridge, 2007), pp. 183–99.

[270] Malmesbury, *GP*, ii. 326.

[271] Although the Chronicle of Rouen does note Henry's arrival in the duchy in 1133, and that he did not return to England until after his death (*RHGF*, xii. 785). In contrast, English narratives, especially the *Anglo-Saxon Chronicle* and the other histories based on it, are much more prone to notice the king's comings and goings.

give us a clearer picture of the strategies employed by the monks than the single writ for Saint-Evroult – even if that document does highlight to the extreme the lengths to which beneficiaries might go when they had business that needed to be concluded. The monks of Montebourg were active in seeking Henry out when they wanted writs to deal with problematic ducal officials. They did not generally venture overseas, however, although they did travel to London to obtain a writ commanding that they should hold their lands and customs in peace.[272] Instead, they sought out Henry in other parts of Normandy, at, for example, Rouen (137 miles from their abbey by land),[273] and La Croix-Saint-Leufroy (150 miles away).[274] Sometimes they used agents to obtain documents on their behalf; Robert of La Haye-du-Puits, for example, and William of Glastonbury.[275] But in no case could the monks simply stay at home and wait for the king to come to them, and unless they went to his court he did not intervene in their affairs in person.

English and French beneficiaries did the same in reverse, of course, making trips to Normandy to obtain writs and confirmations. During his various visits to Rouen, for example, Henry was approached by the monks of Battle, Bermondsey, Bruton, Bury St Edmunds, Canterbury, Chartres, Durham, Marmoutier, Pontigny, St Albans, St Osyth, Westminster, and Winchester,[276] and by canons from Carlisle, Colchester, Kenilworth, Lincoln, and Nostell.[277] In 1125, Henry even appointed new bishops to Chichester, Worcester, and Rochester while he was in Normandy.[278] It seems that even Roger of Salisbury could not wrest the royal prerogative from Henry. No wonder the monks of Bury St Edmunds found it expedient to obtain some property in the city.[279]

The importance of the king's person and presence is perhaps best illustrated

---

[272] *Regesta*, ii. 334 (no. cviii) = no. 1155.

[273] *NI*, p. 101 = *Regesta*, ii. no. 1950; *NI*, p. 102 = *Regesta*, ii. no. 1953.

[274] *Calendar of the Charter Rolls*, 6 vols (London, 1903–27), iv. 157 = *Regesta*, ii. no. 1682.

[275] *NI*, p. 102 = *Regesta*, ii. no. 1951; *Regesta*, ii. 334 (no. cviii) = no. 1155, respectively. There is no evidence that William of Glastonbury was part of the 'regency', just a justice (cf. Hollister, *Henry*, p. 364) and the same is true of Robert of Courcy.

[276] *Regesta*, ii. nos. 1225 (Battle); 1021 (Bermondsey); 1925(Bruton); 1430, 1597, 1598, 1599 (Bury St Edmunds); 1232, 1417 (Canterbury); 1931 (Chartres); 1563, 1705 (Durham); 1948 (Marmoutier); 1203 (St Albans); 1209 (St Osyth); 1987 (Westminster); 1425 (Hyde abbey, Winchester); *Le premier cartulaire de l'abbaye cistercienne de Pontigny (XIIe–XIIIe siècles)*, ed. M. Garrigues (Paris, 1981), 86 (no. 3) (Pontigny).

[277] *Regesta*, ii. nos. 1431 (Carlisle); 1205 (St John, Colchester); 1445 (Kenilworth); 1707, 1911 (Lincoln); 1207 (Nostell).

[278] Worcester, iii. 158 (Worcester and Rochester); Huntingdon, p. 472 (Chichester and Rochester).

[279] D. C. Douglas, *Feudal Documents from the Abbey of Bury St Edmunds* (Oxford, 1932), p. 79 (no. 56) = *Regesta*, ii. no. 1913. For the importance of Rouen as a capital see below, Chapter 9, pp. 506–24.

with reference to justice. Henry was not always present at lawsuits, and this may be supposed to have been because he was out of the duchy at the time. However, those pleas that were heard in Henry's absence seem not always to have been as conclusive as they should have been. One plea held at Caen saw the justices taking surety from the defendant, perhaps in an attempt to ensure that he abided by their judgement.[280] But it was not always enough. Godfrey the priest of Caen seems to have risked having his case heard at Rouen in the king's absence. Although the decision went in his favour, the fact that the king had not confirmed the verdict seems to have given the bishop of Bayeux some hope that the unfavourable judgment might be avoided. He was wrong, but Godfrey had to journey to England, and there had to be an implied exchange of letters between the king and his justices in Normandy, before the priest was finally issued with a writ which supported his claim.[281] The same is true in the celebrated case of Bernard the Scribe, who had a judgement made in his favour at Caen by Bishop John and Robert of la Haye, but who had to appeal to the king later to have this judgment enforced in the face of his recalcitrant opponent. Only once the king had confirmed these judgements could they be made effective.[282]

Stephen's reign demonstrates that although Henry I had set up an efficient, smoothly functioning administration that could cope with his absences from the duchy for a few months at a time, ducal power could not be maintained through appointed representatives in the face of a hostile and rebellious aristocracy. Henry himself had not allowed his administration to be tested in this way, ensuring that he was in the duchy shortly after a rebellion occurred or even before it, as was the case in 1123 when Henry seems to have had advance warning. Stephen, however, was almost entirely absent from Normandy between 1135 and 1144, with just one visit in 1137 which did little to revive his authority. He was thus entirely dependent on trusted men to administer the duchy in his name. As Roger of Salisbury retained his role in England until 1139, it might be expected that Bishop John of Lisieux would have continued to stand at the head of Stephen's Norman administration until his death in 1141. There is virtually no evidence to support this supposition, however. There is just one act for the abbey of St John at Falaise which records that a claim had been settled in Bishop John's presence,[283] and two other attestations, which place the bishop with the king at Rouen and Evreux but which tell us nothing about his role in Normandy as both acts concerned

[280]   *NI*, p. 95.
[281]   *Livre Noir*, i. 44 (no. 38) = *Regesta*, ii. no. 819.
[282]   *NI*, p. 88, n. 18 = *Regesta*, ii. no. 1548.
[283]   *Regesta*, iii. no. 298.

English revenues or properties.[284] Further, Robert of Torigni's note that Bishop John surrendered Lisieux to Geoffrey in 1141 does not suggest that the bishop had any wider role at that time. Indeed, the absence of individual addressees in all but one of Stephen's Norman writs and charters makes the identification of his administrators almost impossible to establish, and while Waleran of Meulan is prominent in the witness lists, his activities in Normandy in 1136–38 seem to have been military rather than administrative.[285]

There is reason to doubt that the king was able to collect revenues or do justice across the whole of the duchy by 1137. It is likely that effective power had quickly devolved into the hands of the greater lords, especially when they were either biding their time or openly supporting Geoffrey of Anjou, as was the case with Earl Robert of Gloucester and William Talvas. Stephen's response was, perhaps by necessity, limited. Just before leaving Normandy in 1137 'he appointed William of Roumare and Roger the *vicomte* and various others as justiciars in Normandy, instructing them to do what he himself had failed to do in person: namely, to mete out justice to the malcontents and ensure peace for the helpless populace.'[286] But although Stephen might have recognized the need for justice, he did nothing to stop the administrative rot.[287] 'Beyond this point, no regular administration of the duchy can be traced.'[288] Thus when Normandy fell to Geoffrey it fell lordship by lordship and town by town. By 1141 the indivisible duchy had become completely fragmented.

There were, then, occasions when the dukes of the Normans entrusted named individuals with the protection of the duchy during their absence. Orderic, apparently much more prepared to comment on past rather than present arrangements, perhaps because he was borrowing from Poitiers when doing so, tells us that Matilda of Flanders, Robert Curthose, Roger of Montgommery, and William fitz Osbern were on occasion entrusted with the duchy during the reign of William I, even if they had no formal role.[289] Such ad hoc arrangements were temporary, however, and even Queen Matilda's powers were limited so that litigants like the

---

[284] *Regesta*, iii. nos. 327, 843.

[285] *Regesta*, iii. nos. 75, 281, 282, 327, 594, 598, 608, 749; Orderic, vi. 458, 464, 468, 494, 516. Torigni notes Waleran's pre-eminence in lands and castles, but does not suggest that he had any official role in the duchy (s.a. 1141). See also Crouch, *Beaumont Twins*, pp. 31, 37–8. Crouch also comments that Normans placed themselves under Waleran's protection at this time, perhaps providing further evidence of the lack of any ducal government (*Beaumont Twins*, pp. 35–6).

[286] Orderic, vi. 494.

[287] Given the limited role of justiciars, discussed above, Haskins was mistaken to suggest that 'Stephen left the government of Normandy' in their hands (*NI*, p. 127).

[288] *NI*, p. 127.

[289] Orderic, ii. 208, 210, 222, 280.

monks of Marmoutier and Saint-Florent of Saumur took themselves to the king in England when they had disputes to prosecute.[290] There is, then, no sense of the development of a 'justiciarship' either in William's reign or during that of his son Henry I. Nonetheless, historians such as Francis West and John Le Patourel were keen to find an emergent justiciar or viceroy in both England and Normandy under Henry in particular because they saw the king's itinerary, revealed above all in the place-dates of his *acta*, as creating absence, and thus a vacuum at the heart of government. Something had to fill the gap, they thought, if the administration were not to collapse the moment William or Henry left Normandy. But this over-looks the efficiency of the administrative structures established in the regions of the duchy. Henry, like his father and the other dukes before them, governed the regions through a variety of officials who held their office continuously and who came to the court or were sent letters or, later, writs as the need arose. There was, of course, also a need for officials at court. The chancellor and chaplains drafted Henry's *acta* and went with him as he crossed and re-crossed the Channel, but in Normandy, as in England, Henry's court was also home to a number of adminis-trators who were based on one side of the Channel, who kept an eye on Henry's finances and rights and were notified of any changes to their scope, and who were trusted to do justice in his name – should he command them to do so. Today they would be high-ranking civil servants or judges. But they would not be, and never were, ministers. They were not part of the executive. They did not make decisions. They had no independence of action. They were not, then, extensions of the king's person or viceroys.

Instead, Henry retained sole control of all executive decisions, as had his father – hence his clashes with Robert Curthose.[291] And so all of his subjects were obliged to seek him out, no matter where he was, if they wanted justice done, or their appointment confirmed, or an exemption from toll and custom granted. It is not the case that petitioners *could* approach the king. All of them *had* to do so. Every one of Henry's Norman *acta* is the result of a direct approach by the beneficiary in person or by proxy. Thus every one of Henry's acts actually reveals the duke's presence, so far as that beneficiary was concerned, as well as the lengths that his subjects would go to in order to make their duke present. Such journeys were acceptable, because *impétrants* only came to Henry when they needed him to do something for them, and that need arose infrequently. For them, and most likely for Henry I as well, executive and judicial action in fits and starts was perfectly adequate.

---

[290] *Regesta: William*, no. 200; Marchegay, 675 (no. 11).
[291] Orderic, iii. 98–100.

CHAPTER 7

The Duke and the Court: The Display and Experience of Power

THE dukes' power – their ability to make people do what they wanted, regardless of any resistance – was grounded in legitimacy and inheritance, and reinforced by their success in establishing autonomous rule and hegemony over the people living within the confines of the duchy.[1] The recognition of the dukes' position was also the result of physical strength and diplomacy – carrot and stick – as well as a decision on the part of his greater subjects that there was more to be gained by siding with the duke than going against him. But it was also the result of appearances and environment.[2] The duke *was* successful and powerful in part at least because he *looked* successful and powerful. A man surrounded by warriors and bishops, who could eat from gold and silver vessels, and pass such objects to his followers as rewards, was a man who deserved respect and who should not be crossed. That respect required a show of deference and submission, appropriate behaviour, and bearing. A failure to perform as required might smack of rebellion and result in a demonstration of anger and coercive force. At that point the protagonists would discover whether appearances were deceptive. But up to that point the mirage of power remained intact.

The previous chapter explored the duke: the succession to the duchy, questions of competition and legitimacy, and the executive authority that the duke wielded. This chapter goes on to look at the court, defined by Stuart Airlie as the king (here the duke), his family, and the personnel around them together with the institutions (such as the chapel) and buildings that housed and served them.[3] In

---

[1] 'Power' is defined in *Etymologies*, Bk. 10, Ch. 208; p. 226. See also R. E. Barton, 'Emotions and power in Orderic Vitalis', *ANS*, 33 (2011), 42–3.

[2] Otto of Bamberg's predecessor in Pomerania, Bernhardt, failed to convert the people of Wollin to Christianity because of his humble appearance. While this was de rigueur for the pious churchmen of long-Christian France and Germany, it suggested to the people of Pomerania that God did not bother to reward his own. His appearance, then, discouraged conversion in spite of his intention (Ebo and Herbordus, *The Life of Otto the Apostle of Pomerania, 1060–1139*, trans. C. H. Robinson (London, 1920), pp. 19–22).

[3] S. Airlie, 'The palace of memory: the Carolingian court as political centre', in *Courts and Regions in Medieval Europe*, ed. S. Rees Jones, R. Marks, and A. J. Minnis (York, 2000), p. 3.

particular, it is concerned with how the dukes could use the court to broadcast and maintain their authority over the duchy as a whole.

The discussion begins with a consideration of the settings for the dukes' courts, before moving on to explore who went to them, and what they saw and heard when they got there, through an examination (separately) of the ducal *acta* and the narratives. As has been discussed above, and will be considered further below, the *acta* in particular do not perhaps tell us what we expect them to. They tell us rather less about ducal power than might be thought and rather more about beneficiaries' views of it and their resulting concerns about the security of the gifts they received. Moreover, all the sources tell us not what the dukes did but what those who were present remembered or thought was important – in the case of the narratives almost always at second hand. That selectivity is itself useful, as it highlights what contemporaries thought actually mattered. But at the same time, it opens up a gap between reality and record which becomes a gulf when we try to establish the emotional reactions of the dukes and their subjects to slights and threats.

Nonetheless, to the extent that it is possible to do so from the evidence at our disposal, the intention here is to establish how the dukes could manifest power in ways that would influence men to follow and obey them, not least through the manipulation of their emotions through the theatrical revelation of authority and wealth.

Attendance at court

'The court was at once the setting for the king's daily life and the principal instrument of his rule over England and Normandy.'[4] In the domestic management of his court and household, the duke was not unlike the other lords of the duchy. He and his guests were sustained by a household staff of cooks, bakers, men who looked after the table linen, the duke's bed, and his tapestries, a turn-spit superintendent, a water-bearer (who might also dry the duke's clothes), dishwashers, huntsmen, a bow-man, and so on.[5] One difference, however, was that the greater officials of the duke's household – the steward, butler, and master chamberlains, in particular – were often among the greater men of Normandy. Osbern the duke's steward

---

[4] Green, *Henry*, p. 284.
[5] We know little about these persons until their duties and stipends were recorded in the *Constitutio domus regis*, compiled sometime in Henry I's reign but reaching its final form only after his death (*Constitutio*, pp. xxxviii–xxxix). As that document, and the allowances it records, seem to have begun life only after 1108, however, it is not possible to project these backwards, although it seems likely that most of these positions had existed since the tenth century.

was the son of Herfast, Gunnor's brother. His son was William fitz Osbern. These men, like their successors Gerald, Ralph of Montpinçon, and Humfrey of Bohon, were 'energetically in charge of providing food and drink', presumably in association with the butlers, who included in their number William of Aubigny.[6] Later evidence would suggest that at the greater gatherings, they would even perform such offices in person.[7] The chamberlains, originally custodians of the chamber and treasure, included in their number Rotselin, Ralph of Tancarville, and William Mauduit.[8] In addition, the duke generally travelled with those officials who would put his will into effect. When in Normandy, Henry I was therefore likely to have been joined frequently by Bishop John of Lisieux and Robert of La Haye-du-Puits, who ran the Norman administration both when he was resident in the duchy and when he was not.[9] But there were also the men who travelled with the king and can be found with him on both sides of the Channel. These figures included the various chancellors who served under William and Henry,[10] as well as the keeper of the seal, the chaplains, and the duke's most important counsellors.

Aside from the household officials and servants, the court was attended by messengers bringing news or petitions. Family and friends – among them the greatest lords of the duchy – would have come and gone. Important visitors and embassies arrived to transact their business. William of Jumièges recorded an apparently unheralded visit to the court of Richard II by Count Geoffrey of the Bretons, for example.[11] Similarly, 'the bishops and counts of Francia, Burgundy, and of even more distant provinces, frequented the court of the lord of Normandy; some to receive advice, others in search of benefices, most to bask in his favour.'[12] One lawsuit of 1080 was judged by, among others, Archbishop Richard of Bourges, Archbishop Warmund of Vienne, and Count Guy of Ponthieu.[13]

---

[6] Worcester, iii. 148.

[7] See in particular Walter Map's tales about William of Tancarville, chamberlain, and William of Aubigny, butler (Walter Map, *De nugis curialium*, pp. 488–94.

[8] See below, Chapter 10, pp. 606–7.

[9] See above, Chapter 6, pp. 352–5.

[10] *Regesta: William*, pp. 98–102 and no. 73. The existence of a chancellor in Normandy has been much debated in the past (see, for example, *RADN*, pp. 41–7; Douglas, *William the Conqueror*, pp. 147–8; Bates, *Normandy*, pp. 154–5; Pohl, *Dudo of Saint-Quentin's Historia Normannorum*, pp. 120–4). It seems that such a figure appeared briefly at the end of the reign of Richard II, perhaps created by or at the suggestion of Dudo of Saint-Quentin and thus on the Frankish model. In any event, the troubles of the early years of Robert the Magnificent's reign seem to have undone this precarious work, and no chancellor appears again until after, and as a result of, the Conquest of England.

[11] Jumieges, ii. 14.

[12] Poitiers, p. 96.

[13] *Regesta: William*, no. 235.

The extent to which courtiers, *fideles*, or visitors declared their intention to attend the court in advance is not clear. The fact that the monks of Boscherville had their monastery's property confirmed by Henry I before their patron Rabel of Tancarville arrived might suggest that no one knew he was on his way, however.[14] Others may be supposed to have signalled that they would be attending so as to ensure that they received a suitable welcome, or perhaps to discover where the duke proposed to be resident when they expected to arrive, as it is not clear that the dukes generally publicized their intended movements.[15]

When it was made, such notification gave the dukes an opportunity to put off potential visitors. For example, there survives a letter sent by Geoffrey, abbot of Vendôme, to Henry I that indicates that Henry had dissuaded him from making an intended journey to Normandy.[16] But such advance notification may have been *obligatory* only when men who might have otherwise been classed as enemies were making the trip.[17] Thus, in order to end the state of war that had existed between them for the last few years, Theobald of Chartres sought permission from Richard I to attend his court and to make peace *c.* 965.[18] In contrast, in 1088 the future Henry I received permission to depart from William II's court in England but thought it unnecessary to gain Robert Curthose's permission to return to Normandy. He was arrested on arrival because he appeared to be entering the duchy as an enemy.[19] Robert Curthose was treated the same way when he arrived in England in 1103.[20]

Some would not have signalled their intention to attend, however, simply because they had been summoned to the court. Charlemagne had required his estate managers to come to the court three times each year and to present accounts, and the Norman dukes may be supposed to have required their *vicomtes* and *prévôts* to do similarly.[21] William the Bastard is also known to have summoned

---

[14] See below, *infra*, p. 377–8.

[15] That seems to be as true of Henry I – despite what Walter Map said – as for his predecessors (Walter Map, *De nugis curialium*, p. 438). For the dukes' movements, see below Chapter 9, pp. 506–24.

[16] *PL*, 157, col. 200 (no. 252). Noted in Green, *Henry*, p. 293. In the mid ninth century, Lupus of Ferrières had also signalled his intention to attend by letter, not least so as to be told where the court would be meeting ('The letters of Lupus of Ferrières', in P. E. Dutton (ed. and trans.), *Carolingian Civilization: A Reader* (Peterborough, Ontario, and Plymouth, 2004), p. 462 (no. 3).

[17] Contrast here to Green, *Henry*, p. 293: 'arrivals and departures from court involved seeking permission.'

[18] Jumièges, i. 128.

[19] Orderic, iv. 148.

[20] Orderic, v. 316–18.

[21] Nelson, 'Kingship and royal government', p. 410; D. Campbell, 'The *Capitulaire de uillis*,

his men to his court to ensure that attendance would be sufficient to impress the foreign envoys and embassies who might also be present: 'all great men of whatever walk of life were summoned to them by royal edict, so that envoys from other nations might admire the large and brilliant company and the splendid luxury of the feast.'[22] Similarly, the prelates and magnates of Normandy were summoned to Lillebonne in 1080, or so Orderic thought, so as to ensure that the important council there was suitably well attended.[23]

The variety of those in attendance, in terms of both status and function, is indicative of the importance of the court as an instrument of rule. As will be discussed below, it was a focus for the magnificent display of the duke's person and power, demonstrated in this setting by the ostentatious show of wealth and the number of men in attendance. It was home to at least some of the dukes' household knights. It was a forum in which lawsuits were concluded.[24] In addition, the court was where important embassies or refugees would be received and entertained,[25] where questions of succession or marriage were discussed and decided,[26] and where campaigns were commanded.[27] Dudo tells us that William Longsword gained approval for his campaign against the Bretons in his court c. 927.[28] In 1066, when informed of Harold's accession to the English throne, William the Bastard 'called together the Norman nobles for a public discussion of what ought to be done in an affair of such moment … All these men came together at the duke's command to find a common course of action, and of hearing of this tremendous enterprise expressed as many different opinions as there were different kinds of men.' Indeed, the divisions were such that William sent an embassy to Rome to get the pope's view on the matter.[29] The court was also an assembly that the duke could use to discover what was happening in Normandy as a whole, just as he did in England. There, Eadmer stated that 'the king, anxious to make enquiry into

---

the *Breuium exempla*, and the Carolingian court at Aachen', *EME*, 18 (2010), 247. See also below, Chapter 10, pp. 592–6, 597–603.

[22] Malmesbury, *GR*, i. 508.

[23] Orderic, iii. 24.

[24] For example, *RADN*, nos. 3, 115, 148, 157, 209, 229; *Regesta: William*, nos. 29, 64, 142, 143, 214, 235, 262, 267; Orderic, ii. 208, iii. 18, vi. 178, 352. For ducal justice see also below, Chapter 8.

[25] For example, *Dudo*, pp. 60–3; Jumièges, ii. 14, 16–18; Poitiers, pp. 68–70, 96, 178–80; Orderic, ii. 196–8; *Regesta: William*, no. 229.

[26] For example, *Dudo*, pp. 54, 59–60; Jumièges, i. 72; ii. 38–40, 80, 128 (succession); *Dudo*, pp. 69–70, 164; Jumièges, i. 58–60, 64, 90, 100; ii. 14; Poitiers, pp. 30–2 (marriages).

[27] For example, the campaigns of 1033 (Jumièges, ii. 76) and 1066 (Poitiers, pp. 100–2; Orderic, ii. 140).

[28] *Dudo*, pp. 61–2.

[29] Orderic, ii. 140–2.

the state of the kingdom, assembled together by authority of his writ the bishops, abbots, and all the chief persons of his realm'.[30]

The court was also a place where laws were made. After his victory at Val-ès-Dunes, William held a council at Caen, where he commanded that the Truce of God should be respected in Normandy.[31] Equally, in the weeks that followed his victory at Tinchebray in September 1106, King Henry I held a council at Lisieux and there 'he decreed by royal authority that peace should be firmly established throughout Normandy, that all robbery and plundering should be wholly suppressed, that all churches should hold their possessions as they had held them on the day his father had died, and that all lawful heirs should likewise hold their inheritances'.[32] All this black-letter legislation has been lost. Indeed, while some of Henry's English laws survive in the writs that promulgated it, there is no Norman text from before 1135. That text is found in a charter, and in it Henry laid down the procedure to be followed if a man who accused another of committing murder during the period covered by the Truce of God chose to prove the charge by trial by battle. The change was relatively minor, and so suggests that Henry made laws or tweaked existing ones routinely. Moreover, the act reveals that this particular change was made in a council attended by five of the seven bishops of Normandy and a number of important lay magnates.[33]

Those travelling to or from the court enjoyed the duke's protection. The opening clause of the *Consuetudines et iusticie* of 1091 or 1096 states that:

This is the justice of the lord of Normandy, that in his court, or going to court or returning from court, no man shall have to protect himself from his enemy. And if anyone shall make forfeit from his enemy on the road of the court or in court, in the knowledge that he has done him ill on his way to the court or returning from it, the lord of Normandy shall be able, the proof having been made, to take his moveable goods and his person for the doing of justice. And the guilty shall lose their lands, so that neither he nor any of his relatives shall be able to reclaim it. And if he shall be able to prove that he had not done this

30 Eadmer, *HN*, p. 83.
31 Michel de Boüard, 'Sur les origines de la trêve de Dieu en Normandie', *Annales de Normandie*, 9 (1958), 169–89 at 172–4; Bates, *Normandy*, pp. 163–4. For a more general study see H. E. J. Cowdrey, 'The Peace and the Truce of God in the eleventh century', *Past and Present* 46 (1970), 42–67. Wace also noted that the duke imposed the Truce of God on Normandy, but he appeared to suggest that the council was held after the battle of Varaville in 1157 (Wace, pp. 150–1). The council is also mentioned in a *pancarte* for the abbey of Saint-Pierre of Préaux dating from 1078 × 1079 (*Ctl. Préaux*, A1 at p. 7).
32 Orderic, vi. 92–4.
33 See M. Hagger, 'Secular law and custom in ducal Normandy, *c.* 1000–1144', *Speculum*, 85 (2010), 840–5.

in such knowledge, his moveable goods shall be at the mercy of the lord of Normandy, but he will retain his land.[34]

A deliberate attack on a man's person or property while he was going to, staying at, or returning from court was thus punished harshly. To command a man's presence, the duke had to have such a deterrent available, just as the Church could only recruit for the crusades if similar protection was provided by ecclesiastical sanction. The dukes were also obliged to abide by that same rule, and seem almost always to have done so. Nonetheless, on occasion, they might break the peace that was supposed to protect all those who attended their court in order to arrest political enemies, as Robert of Bellême was to discover to his cost at Bonneville in 1112.[35] Henry could have claimed in his defence that Bellême was belatedly answering a summons, as had also been the case with Roger of Hereford in 1075, but that seems not to have been true of Count Henry of Eu and Hugh of Gournay, who were both 'unexpectedly … seized in his court and … thrown into prison' in 1118.[36]

Although arrival at court seems to have been uncontrolled, departure was more formalized. Before 1008, Count Geoffrey of Brittany married Richard II's sister. 'Not long after the wedding, [Richard] lavishly bestowed gifts upon them and allowed them joyfully to leave (*abire permisit*).'[37] The duke might himself observe the same etiquette. Richard II is said to have served the abbot of Fécamp the first course of his dinner. 'Having performed this in great humility, he came up before the abbot who gave him permission to leave.'[38]

As leave-taking was a mark of respect, departure without reason and before the conclusion of business might consequently cause outrage. Thus, Robert Curthose was angry (*iratus est*) when he learned that Abbot Ranulf of Lonlay had left his

---

[34] *NI*, Appendix D, pp. 281–2. These customs are considered at length in the next chapter. Orderic noted that Emperor Henry IV would attack men when they were on the way to his court, when they thought themselves safe, which suggests that a similar rule existed in the Empire, too (Orderic, iv. 8). David Rollason has provided an interesting, related discussion about whether the protection of the hall related to the building itself (like the sanctuary of a church), or whether it depended on who was using it, or whether the protection applied specifically to times when it was being used for the consumption of alcoholic drink (D. Rollason, 'Protection and the mead-hall', in *Peace and Protection in the Middle Ages*, ed. T. B. Lambert and D. Rollason (Toronto, 2009), pp. 19–35.

[35] Orderic, vi. 178. Stephen did the same to Roger of Salisbury, but at least took the trouble to arrange a pretext (Malmesbury, *HN*, pp. 46–8; *Gesta Stephani*, pp. 76–8).

[36] Orderic, ii. 318; *Letters of Lanfranc*, p. 122 (nos. 33A and 33B). For Count Henry and Hugh of Gournay see Hyde, pp. 66–8; Orderic, vi. 190.

[37] Jumièges, ii. 14.

[38] Jumièges, ii. 288.

court before concluding his plea, which was seen as evidencing derision (*tanta derisione*) and which also prevented Curthose from being seen to do justice on a guilty party.[39] In other cases, the anger caused by unheralded departures was most likely related to the loss of a man's (potential) service. That would explain why a visiting smith might depart from Robert the Magnificent's court without leave and not be punished for it, while a lord's or knight's unexpected departure might be interpreted as a sign of defiance.[40] Thus, William of Poitiers wrote that during the siege of Domfront *c.* 1052, Count William of Arques 'slipped away furtively, like a deserter, without asking permission'.[41] As a result, the duke seized his castle at Arques, although it was later restored to the count by the disloyal garrison and his rebellion then had to be suppressed by force. Robert Curthose likewise left L'Aigle without leave *c.* 1078, marking the outbreak of his first rebellion against his father.[42] Baudry fitz Nicholas lost his lands because he had abandoned William's service – in other words he had left Normandy without leave – to go to fight in Spain.[43] Ducal displeasure at unheralded departures and the consequent loss of a man's service might also explain the enigmatic arrest of Bishop Odo of Bayeux in 1082 or 1083, although Odo seems also to have been in correspondence with the Roman curia despite King William's prohibition.[44]

The court and the charters: the evidence of the witness lists

As Walter Map complained during Henry II's reign, the composition of the court was constantly changing.[45] That is also suggested by the lists of witnesses or signers found at the end of the ducal *acta*.[46] Those lists have been mined time and again for what they can tell us about the identities of those who attended the court and their place in the secular hierarchy, and almost as frequently warnings

---

[39] *Regesta: William*, no. 267.II.

[40] Jumièges, ii. 58–60 (for the smith); S. B. D. Brown, 'Leavetaking: lordship and mobility in England and Normandy in the twelfth century', *History*, 79 (1994), 211.

[41] Poitiers, p. 34.

[42] Orderic, ii. 358.

[43] Orderic, iv. 100.

[44] The prohibition on unlicensed communication with the papal curia is noted by Eadmer, *HN*, p. 10; trans. Bosanquet, p. 10, and see above, Chapter 4, pp. 236–41.

[45] Walter Map, *De nugis curialium*, p. 2.

[46] I have throughout this section treated signers and witnesses as equivalents, as did the monks of La Trinité-du-Mont *c.* 1091. The same is true of witness lists and the lists of signatures appended to diplomata. While that might be mistaken if examining the legal distinction between these modes of assurance (Tabuteau, *Transfers*, pp. 146–63), it seems largely unproblematic to do so in this more relaxed context.

have been sounded about their treacherousness, which is especially mendacious where originals do not survive. As a result it is now generally acknowledged that while a survey of these lists *might* provide a general idea about who was most frequently with the duke, even this is to build on the most unstable of foundations. At best, the names that can be harvested from the witness lists constitute an incomplete and selective sample, and so are entirely unsuitable for scientific statistical analysis.[47] Moreover, until the reign of Robert the Magnificent it is all but impossible to identify the vast majority of those who attested ducal acts simply because most laymen were identified by their first name alone, constituting 'those lists of unidentifiable Norse-Germanic names of men said to have been present on some occasion when a charter is said to have been shown to Richard II'.[48] But even when toponyms become more common, and we can begin to track individuals in the witness lists, it is by no means clear that the witnesses of any particular act truly reflected the composition of the court at the time it was made.

One major problem is that we do not know why particular witnesses were selected while others were considered unnecessary. The witness list of an act made on Easter Wednesday at Fécamp between 1051 and 1066 would suggest that no bishops were present at the time. This seems unlikely.[49] Perhaps the bishops were preparing for a service during the short period of time required for the signing of the act in question. Perhaps they were present, but the monks of Saint-Florent outside Saumur were simply not concerned to gain the signature of Norman bishops when their act had been witnessed by the duke, his family, and the most important of his *fideles*, especially if the relevant bishop, Geoffrey of Coutances, was in Italy at the time.

[47] On witness lists in ducal *acta* generally see Bates, *Normandy*, pp. 158–60; idem, 'The prosopographical study of Anglo-Norman royal charters', in *Family Trees and the Roots of Politics: The Prosopography of Britain and France from the Tenth to the Twelfth Century*, ed. K. S. B. Keats-Rohan (Woodbridge, 1997), pp. 91–6, 101–2. Warren Hollister responded to these points in the appendix to his *Henry I*, pp. 499–506, but did not convincingly dismiss the issues. The insuperable problems include the loss of an unknown number of *acta*, the largely unknown rationale behind the choice of witnesses, and the fact that multiple acts might be made on one occasion skewing the analysis (as with a series of grants to Marmoutier in 1050 × 1064: *RADN*, nos. 160, 161, 162. The proposed end date of 1064 is too late, as Count William Werlenc attests no. 162 and he was deposed before that date and Richard fitz Thurstan is not yet said to be *vicomte*, which he was *c.* 1054).

[48] Searle, *PK*, p. 127.

[49] *RADN*, no. 199. On bishops, and the suggestion that they remained important at court, see D. Bates, 'Le rôle des évêques dans l'élaboration des actes ducaux et royaux entre 1066 et 1087', in *Les évêques normands du XIᵉ siècle*, ed. P. Bouet and F. Neveux (Caen, 1995), pp. 109–11 and Bates, 'The prosopographical study of Anglo-Norman royal charters', p. 95.

Witness lists, then, do not provide a complete record of the names of those at court at any given moment. Rather it may be supposed they were the names of the men and women who were thought to have been in the best position to support the donation should a claim be made against it at a later date. Among them would have been some (but not necessarily all) of those *curiales* who would have been found frequently at the duke's court – it would have been pointless to add their name to the lists if they were largely absent from it, as they could not then have supported the donation if it was challenged. But others of the witnesses would have been men brought by the beneficiary to the court, or even men whose names were added to the diploma concerned at a later date.[50]

The addition of names outside the court, or at different courts, is particularly problematic and often impossible to detect. An act of 1025 for the monks of Bernay provides an extreme example of this practice. This document is remarkable for the fact that it is attested by a total of 127 witnesses, 101 of whom are effectively anonymous, and 118 of whom do not appear in the other two acts made, it is believed, at the same court.[51] David Bates suggested that this revealed how large the gathering had been, but that fails to explain why so many of these individuals did not attest the other acts. The most likely explanation for the disparity is that these men were not present when the act was issued by the duke. Instead, these additional witnesses were probably men from the area around Bernay, whose names were added to the foot of the parchment on later occasions, perhaps at times when the act was read aloud to local audiences, in the hope that they would maintain the grants if they were threatened. The appearance of the act would certainly suggest that this was the case, with names added by one or two different hands, albeit in very similar inks.[52]

---

50   For example, the monks of La Trinité-du-Mont outside Rouen, whose abbey held estates mostly in Caux, Talou, and on the Seine near Vernon, and whose patron was also based in the county of Talou, routinely had their *acta* attested by the duke, the donors and their family, but also by a body of men described as being 'from our side', almost always among whom were Richard the seneschal and Bernard the cook (*RADN*, nos. 60, 61, 81–4, 96, 101, 104, 118, 119, 123, 130, 135, 138, 143, 200–2, 206, 221, 233; *Regesta: William*, nos. 231, 233–6; *Norman Charters from English Sources*, ed. N. Vincent, Pipe Roll Society, new series 59 (2013), p. 108 (no. 1). For some comments on the use of cooks ('the extent to which cooks witnessed is startling') and other artisans or tradesmen as witnesses see, Tabuteau, *Tranfers*, pp. 152, 155–6). The production or selection of witnesses on a similar basis can be found in many other ducal acts, for example: *RADN*, nos. 122, 230, 232; *Regesta: William*, no. 149; *Ctl. Beaumont-le-Roger*, pp. 7–10 (no. 3) = *Regesta*, ii. 1693.

51   *RADN*, nos. 35 (the Bernay act), 34 and 36. A fourth act for the monks of Saint-Ouen was likely issued at the same time, but the witness list has been cut from the surviving copies (*RADN*, no. 53).

52   Despite the note in Fauroux's *Recueil*, and its absence from the Telma database, this act for the monks of Bernay survives as an original among the muniments of the Palais de Bénédictine at Fécamp.

The industry of the community of Bernay does not help to establish who was present at the duke's court in 1025, but it does say a lot about their concern for their property throughout the remainder of the 1020s – but probably not much later as none of the witnesses has toponyms – and also about the role that local men might have in upholding the monks' title. Such anxiety was justified. Bernay itself seems to have been divided between the Montgommery and Beaumont families just after the abbey was founded, perhaps with the connivance of its custodian, Thierry, while the monks' property at Beaumont and Vieilles also passed into the hands of the latter family.[53] The same concerns most likely motivated all beneficiaries. The use of local witnesses, often with some relationship to the beneficiary, and even if not often on the same scale, was almost certainly intended to prevent disputes arising. If challenges were made regardless, then the local witnesses could be called forward in the local seigniorial courts, thereby ending disputes swiftly. That spared the parties an expensive journey back to the duke's court, but if necessary they could return there and prevail on the duke to uphold his act supported by the testimony of the other, curial witnesses.[54]

The practical purpose behind the addition of witnesses to existing acts means that the monks of Bernay were not alone in doing it. As is now well known, the monks of Lessay similarly updated the *pancarte* that was issued for them by William I, adding names into the twelfth century, at least twenty-seven years after the act was first issued.[55] Less extreme examples include the addition of the name of Bishop Hugh of Bayeux to an act of Duke Richard II for the monks of Chartres, with a second copy of the same act being attested by Bishop Hugh of Avranches and Bishop Fulk of Amiens,[56] and the addition of Robert of Montfort's name to an act previously issued for the monks of Le Bec by Robert Curthose in February 1092.[57]

Two other acts were made at the court of 1025 at which the act for the monks of Bernay was first issued. One of them is a diploma for the monks of Fécamp which survives only as a pseudo-original. Nonetheless, the layout suggests that the original list of signers was supplemented at some later date with some additional names. Those added were Richard fitz Gulbert, Nigel the *vicomte*, Hugh the chancellor who, if he wrote and subscribed anything, wrote only these additional *signa*, and Thurstan the *vicomte*. The additional witnesses

---

[53] See Bates, *Normandy*, p. 100 and above, Chapter 2, pp. 80–1.

[54] See below, Chapter 8, pp. 464–9, 497–8 and also Tabuteau, *Transfers*, pp. 148–52.

[55] Bates, *Normandy*, p. 158. The Lessay *pancarte* is discussed by Bates at length at *Regesta: William*, no. 175.

[56] BL, Add. Ch. 17473 (for the addition of Bishop Hugh of Bayeux); *RADN*, no. 15, commentary at p. 94.

[57] AD Seine-Maritime, 20 HP 5; *NI*, p. 68, no. 7.

are, of course, nowhere near as numerous as those marshalled by the monks of Bernay, but they perhaps speak of a similar concern that the act should remain firm at a time when some of the earlier witnesses had died. Richard fitz Gulbert, for example, was almost certainly the lord of Heugleville and Auffay mentioned by Orderic, who was active from the time of Robert the Magnificent into the 1050s.[58] Thurstan the *vicomte* was perhaps Thurstan Goz, who seems to have held that office only between *c.* 1040 and *c.* 1043. Nigel the *vicomte* was active from Richard II's reign until *c.* 1042. The presence of Hugh the chancellor, who did not claim responsibility for the other acts drawn up in 1025, suggests a formal reconfirmation of the act, but as we do not know when he was active, or whose chancellor he was, we do not know when this was happened. Any hope of precision rests on the uncertain identification of Thurstan the *vicomte* with Thurstan Goz, but if that is correct then it looks as though the monks gathered a small body of men together during William the Bastard's minority to replace the original witnesses and thereby to give their confirmation the human support it would need to remain effective.

A third act thought to have been made at this court, this one for the monks of Jumièges, is attested by only seven men. These same seven men come at the head of the witnesses to the two acts for the monks of Bernay and Fécamp just discussed, which suggests that it was only these seven men who witnessed all three acts when they were first issued. Aside from the duke, they were his sons, the future Richard III and Robert the Magnificent, Archbishop Robert of Rouen, Bishop Mangis of Avranches, Bishop Hugh of Bayeux, and Bishop Hugh of Evreux. The emphasis on the duke's family found here is repeated on the larger canvas provided by the whole corpus of Richard's acts. The pattern might suggest that the duke's family was still central to ducal power even at the end of Richard II's reign, but it is most likely better interpreted as the result of a widespread perception among beneficiaries that certain members of the duke's family were powerful *and* likely to be found at court regularly *and* would consequently be better guarantors of their donations than other lords.[59] Such grounds for selection might explain why Countess Gunnor did not sign any of these three acts. She was among the most frequent witnesses of Richard's surviving *acta*, but by 1025 she would have been

---

[58] Orderic, iii. 252-4.

[59] The same conclusion was reached by Bates, *Normandy*, pp. 158-9. He noted that 'the documents from Richard II's reign are attested almost exclusively by the "official" classes; immediate family, the counts, the bishops, the *vicomtes*, and household familiars. Sometimes the witness lists are very much family affairs of wife, mother, sons, Archbishop Robert of Rouen, and Bishop Hugh of Bayeux.' It should perhaps be remarked that there was some considerable overlap between immediate family on one hand and the counts and bishops on the other.

old, at least by the standards of the time, and she or the monks might not have thought it worth her while signing the documents as a result.[60]

A second portrait of the duke's court, this time with a longer exposure, is provided by a series of seven acts that were probably made between April and July 1066. While the sequence is not entirely certain, they may be supposed to begin with an act made at the Easter court at Fécamp, and end with one made during a halt at Troarn, most likely as William was on his way to Dives-sur-Mer to rendezvous with his invasion force. It should be noted that the order and date of the last two acts is suggested in part by problematic references to John of Ivry as archbishop of Rouen. Fortunately, as his appearances are not essential to the sequence suggested here, they are also not fatal to it.[61] As a group, these acts reveal that those who waited on the duke (almost) throughout included men whom we would expect to see with him, especially during this critical year, on the evidence of our sources as a whole: Roger of Beaumont, William fitz Osbern, and Roger

---

[60] It is perhaps notable in this respect that Gunnor did not attest any of Robert the Magnificent's acts even though she lived on until c. 1030 and despite the fact that Warner of Rouen put her at Rouen c. 1027.

[61] *RADN*, nos. 230 (dated 13 April 1066 at Fécamp), 228 (dated 1066 at Rouen), 232 (dated 1066 – Fauroux suggested after 27 May), 231 (dated 18 June 1066), 229 (dated 1066, and the act also refers to a council the day after the dedication of the church of Holy Trinity, Caen), 227 (Fauroux suggested 1066 on the basis of the appearance of Count Eustace among the witnesses – although probably at Rouen rather than Bayeux), 222 (which probably dates to 1066 because of the transfer of the college to the custody of Roger of Montgommery who would be remaining in the duchy on William's departure). The presence of Archbishop John and Bishop Michael of Avranches among the witnesses to this act is problematic, as John is generally thought not to have been promoted to the archbishopric until June 1067. Yet William is still styled duke in the same act, and John's appearance as archbishop cannot simply be a later addition to the witness list as he is also styled archbishop within the text. There are similar problems with the inclusion of Bishop Michael of Avranches among the witnesses to no. 222 as well as another act dated to 1066 (*Ctl. Mont-Saint-Michel*, no. 73). The evidence provided by the narratives is similarly ambiguous or suspect. Both the *Gesta Normannorum ducum*, here composed c. 1070, and the Annals of Jumièges, which were composed later as they stand, are often a year in advance at this time. It is possible that they mistakenly date the accession of Archbishop Maurilius to 1055, for example, when he might have become archbishop in 1054, and so it might be the case that the date 1067 for John's election should be revised to 1066. It is consequently *possible* that William of Jumièges's date for the dedication of the abbey church at Jumièges is also unsafe. For some discussion of the point see E. Vacandard, 'Un essai d'histoire des archevêques de Rouen au XIe siècle', *Revue catholique de Normandie*, 3 (1893), 117–27, at p. 117, n. 1. The issue was not reconsidered by Spear, *Personnel of the Norman Cathedrals* nor by Allen, '"A proud and headstrong man"'. It might be possible to reconcile the contradictory evidence to some extent if plans to promote John to the archbishopric were put into motion some months before Archbishop Maurilius actually died.

of Montgommery.[62] They also included John, bishop of Avranches/archbishop of Rouen, and Bishop Hugh of Lisieux, both of them the duke's kinsmen as well as prelates. It is surprising, though, that Count Robert of Mortain and Roger of Beaumont were both with the duke as he made his way to Caen for the dedication of the abbey church of La Sainte-Trinité on 18 June, and were with him again the day after, and yet missed the big day itself. It may be supposed that the witness lists deceive us here, suggesting a discontinuity that was the opposite of the reality. Perhaps they had fallen ill, perhaps they were obliged to receive an unexpected guest, perhaps there was pressing business that they were asked to take care of, or perhaps William allowed them to sleep through the whole occasion so that he could joke about it at their expense later.[63]

A witness list thus apparently deceives us here, although the details as to precisely how and why escape us. In other cases, the picture seems to be more accurate. For example, Richard *vicomte* of the Avranchin and Robert Bertram apparently did not follow William from Caen back to Rouen. Their departure from the court at that juncture would be explicable on the basis that their estates were concentrated in the west of the duchy. In contrast, Walter Giffard and William of Warenne seem only to have appeared at court after William had returned to Rouen from Caen, as did Eustace of Boulogne, which may be supposed to have been because their lands were located in Upper Normandy (or beyond its eastern border). This pattern perhaps suggests that distance was an adequate excuse for absence from even a particularly solemn court. It also indicates that many of the greater lords of Normandy did not feel obliged to remain at the court for long, but would come to 'touch base' with the duke when it was convenient for them to do so and then return to their own estates.

Other lords were apparently absent throughout proceedings, even though their lands lay close to places the duke stopped at. The diploma for the nuns of Holy Trinity Caen, for example, was witnessed by some of the greatest lords of the Bessin and some middling ones, too: Ranulf of Briquessart, Ralph Taisson, and Fulk of Alnou. But others such as Robert fitz Haimo, Hubert of Ryes, and Robert fitz Erneis were absent, as were some who had given gifts to the nuns, such as Roger of Montbray. Equally, the diploma was witnessed by a number of abbots such as John of Fécamp, Herluin of Le Bec, and Warin of Cerisy-la-Forêt, but it was not witnessed by the abbots of Troarn, Fontenay, or Saint-Pierre-sur-Dives

---

[62] Their importance to William is made clear not only by the number of *acta* they attested across his reign as a whole, but also by the narratives of Jumièges, Poitiers, and Orderic, and also (excepting here Roger of Beaumont) by their enrichment with vast estates in England after the Conquest.

[63] On William's humour see M. Hagger, *William: King and Conqueror* (London, 2012), pp. 137–8.

– Abbot Lanfranc of Caen was, of course, absent in Rome at the time, obtaining a papal banner for the duke. What this tells us is not clear. It may simply be that there was no obligation even for local lords to attend the court. Perhaps they were not summoned because they held only a little land directly from the duke, and so did not rank among *his* greatest lords – this is perhaps the most likely explanation. Perhaps it was felt that there were already enough witnesses to these acts, and that these witnesses were of such standing, to ensure that the donations would be safe. That would in turn suggest that witnessing was not something that highlighted an individual's status at court or in the political community more generally, for otherwise the missing abbots and lords would perhaps have insisted that they should be allowed to make their mark, too.[64]

The third case study dates from August 1131, as Henry was winding up Norman business before crossing to England from Dieppe.[65] These seven acts have been discussed above in the light of what they can tell us about how Henry governed Normandy *in absentia*, but they are also of interest with regard to what they can tell us about the composition of the court. One of the most notable things about them is that they suggest that the greatest Norman lords were absent.[66] Waleran of Meulan attested two of them, but they were both issued in favour of his own foundation at Beaumont-le-Roger. Rabel of Tancarville, William of Warenne, and Walter Giffard were in attendance, too, but witnessed only one of the acts: the deed of foundation for Beaumont-le-Roger. It is consequently difficult to escape the conclusion that they only did so because they were pressed into service either as a sop to Waleran of Meulan's pride or because Henry was obliged to react to the presence of five of Waleran's own men among the witnesses by inflating the status and number of witnesses from his own entourage. Instead, the witnesses were principally members of the household (for example Robert de Sigillo, William fitz Odo, and Humfrey of Bohon) and Henry's Norman administrators (Bishop John of Lisieux, Earl Robert of Gloucester, Robert of La Haye-du-Puits, and Brien fitz Count). Indeed, these men were among the most frequent witnesses to Henry's acts generally. The impression given by this clutch of documents, then, is that witnessing acts had become the purview of administrators or justices, the men who needed to know that grants had been made in order to adjust the collection of revenue or to judge disputes. Indeed, the relevant *vicomtes* also appeared as witnesses, although only in the act that related to their *vicomté*, and even though

---

[64] This conclusion is in agreement with the line of argument advanced by Bates, *Normandy*, p. 159.

[65] See also above, Chapter 6, p. 350.

[66] BnF, MS lat. 10058, fo. 7; *Ctl. Beaumont-le-Roger*, pp. 7–10 (no. 3), 22 (no. 13); *Regesta*, ii. 370 (no. ccl); G.-A. de la Roque, *Histoire Généalogique de la maison de Harcourt*, 4 vols (Paris, 1662), iii. 149; Lot, *Saint-Wandrille*, p. 118 (no. 64); *NI*, pp. 300–2 (no. 11).

it may be supposed that the *vicomte* of Arques was present at the court throughout Henry's sojourn at the seat of his county.

This all suggests that by the reign of Henry I witness lists are not at all likely to reveal who was at court and when. Certainly the disparity between the witness lists and the assertions made in the narratives is wider than at any previous point. For example, William of Tancarville appears quite regularly among the witnesses of Henry I's acts, but not so regularly as to support Orderic's assertion that he was one of Henry's closest counsellors. His son, Rabel, was apparently just as prominent. The not unprejudiced author of the *Chronicle of Sainte-Barbe-en-Auge* went so far as to say that his counsel dominated almost the whole of the royal court at that time ('cuius consilio tota fere regalis curia tunc temporis incombebat').[67] Yet Rabel attested just six Norman acts (and only nine of Henry's acts in total), two of them for houses of which he was patron.[68] Count Robert of Meulan was 'Henry's chief adviser, his most frequent lay attester, his alter ego', but while he might have been most of these things on both sides of the Channel, he attested few of Henry's Norman acts and therefore seems to have been generally absent from the court when Henry was in the duchy.[69] He witnessed a total of nine Norman acts, two of them in England, although he also witnessed an additional two English acts while at Rouen and Caen.[70] Stephen of Blois, Henry's nephew and ultimate successor, and the recipient of a great deal of royal patronage was very rarely at court if the evidence of the charter witness lists is to be believed. He witnessed just four Norman acts, one of them while in England, although he attested an additional two English acts in Normandy. The place-dates put him exclusively in the south of the duchy, at Argentan, Sées, and Evreux.[71] Finally, Ranulf le Meschin must have known Henry well before he became duke to have sided with him at Tinchebray. He was given lands in Westmorland by Henry, and was permitted to inherit the earldom of Chester and *vicomté* of the Avranchin after the death of Earl Richard in the wreck of the *White Ship* (apparently without having to pay the due relief).[72] In 1123, he took charge of the defence of the duchy in advance of Henry's own Channel crossing, and as a member of Henry's household played a leading role in

---

[67] *La chronique de Sainte-Barbe-en-Auge*, ed. R. N. Sauvage, Mémoires de l'académie nationale des sciences, arts, et belles-lettres de Caen (1906), pp. 21–2.

[68] *Regesta*, ii. nos. 1012, 1587, 1687, 1688, 1693, 1698.

[69] Hollister, *Henry*, p. 345.

[70] *Regesta*, ii. nos. 764, 792, 826, 829, 842, 1019, 1022, 1074, 1200. The English acts are nos. 911 and 1181.

[71] *Regesta*, ii. nos. 1338, 1588, 1830, 1932, 1934, 1941.

[72] R. Sharpe, *Norman rule in Cumbria*, Cumberland and Westmorland Antiquarian and Archaeological Society, Tract Series 21 (2006), pp. 43–52; Hollister, *Henry*, pp. 342–3.

the defence of the duchy after the royal duke had arrived.[73] Yet he witnessed just two of Henry's Norman acts, both dating from before 1121.[74]

The discrepancy between those whose names appear in the witness lists and the great lords who gathered around Henry and were trusted and favoured by him was noted by Warren Hollister in his biography of the royal duke. 'One must bear in mind a distinction between administrators and counsellors', he wrote, adding a little later that, 'although Henry's chief administrators might give him advice and although his greatest cross-Channel counsellors had the wits to adapt the latest royal administrative innovations to their own honorial uses, the distinction between them remains useful'.[75] The witness lists of Henry's Norman acts certainly seem to reflect this division. They inform us about the court, but they identify the semi-professional administrator class rather than the great lords who came and went and whose functions made them increasingly less useful as witnesses than their fathers had been. In other words, they show us the men who put the counsel of the great lords into effect, rather than the ruling clique themselves.

All this being the case, it is difficult to know what to make of the changing witnessing profiles of the Norman bishops from the reign of Richard II to that of Henry I. The presence of 'phalanxes' of bishops at Richard II's court and their notable absence from around 1035 has been remarked upon and discussed in the past by Marie Fauroux, David Bates, Geoffrey Koziol, and others. Fauroux noted that 'the bishops are often represented at the bottom of the acts of Richard II and Robert, while in the acts of William the Bastard, to the contrary, it is the lay element of the ducal court that predominates'.[76] She did not develop the implications of her observation, but Bates suggested that even though bishops regularly witnessed acts during the second half of the eleventh century 'nothing can erase the generally secular character of the court of William the Conqueror in Normandy after 1066'.[77] Koziol further suggested that the relative lack of episcopal attestations after 1035 reflected a 'significant change in ducal government', whereby formal assemblies became, 'less and less common in William's reign, at least as a forum for issuing charters', with the result that the issue of ducal *acta* was, 'no longer part of a celebration of political order' but had become a 'private matter'.[78]

---

[73]   Simeon of Durham, *Historia ecclesiae Dunelmensis*, in *Symeonis monachi opera omnia*, ii. 267–8; Orderic, vi. 346–8.

[74]   *Regesta*, ii. nos. 829, 1233.

[75]   Hollister, *Henry*, pp. 366–7.

[76]   *RADN*, p. 58; Bates, 'Le rôle des évêques', p. 109; Bates, 'The prosopographical study of Anglo-Norman royal charters', p. 95; Koziol, *Begging Pardon*, p. 274.

[77]   Bates, 'Le rôle des évêques', p. 111.

[78]   Koziol, *Begging Pardon*, p. 274.

Such conclusions assume that the absence of bishops from acts accurately reflects their absence from court. As the preceding discussion has illustrated, it is by no means clear that is the case. The absence of phalanxes of bishops from acts issued during William the Bastard's reign might reflect only a change in the nature or requirements of attestation, whereby ducal *acta* were increasingly witnessed either by those who might best support the gift in case of challenge or by those who needed to know about it in their 'official' capacity as administrators or justices.[79] Of course, some of those figures – Bishop John of Lisieux springs to mind – were themselves bishops.

As witness lists do not accurately reflect the composition of the court, there are also grounds for questioning the 'significant change' that Koziol observed, whereby after 1035 ducal acts were more often issued during informal courts. Furthermore, even if we limit ourselves to what we can see in the documents themselves, it is by no means clear that all of Richard II's acts were issued during the large, formal gatherings that punctuated the year, particularly at Christmas and Easter, but which we can see at other times, too. Some of the duke's acts have no witnesses at all.[80] Thirteen others were signed by members of Richard's close family and a few others, a number of whom seem to have been connected with the beneficiaries.[81] None of these needed to have been issued at formal courts. And again, if we discount episcopal kinsmen, these acts were not witnessed by bishops in any number, or at all. If this seems more common after 1035, that is because the number of beneficiaries grew significantly in the years after William's succession. Norman monasteries multiplied, but houses such as Marmoutier and Saint-Florent of Saumur also began to gain property in the duchy. Again, then, it may be that beneficiaries had always approached the duke at a time of their own choosing to have their donations confirmed, rather than being obliged to wait for a formal court.

That raises a further issue related to the atmosphere of the court. If William's court is considered to have been secular in its atmosphere, especially after 1066, that can only be because of an assumption that the presence of bishops at court gave those occasions a religious flavour. Such an assumption rests on uncertain foundations, however. As remarked already, from Richard II's day until the reign of William the Bastard, the Norman bishops included in their number the dukes' close kinsmen, and it is not clear whether Archbishop Robert, Bishop Hugh of

---

[79]   This overlaps with David Bates's conclusion that bishops did not sign ducal acts in number after 1035 because the changing form of the documents rendered their attestations unnecessary (Bates, 'Le rôle des évêques', p. 109; Bates, 'The prosopographical study of Anglo-Norman royal charters', p. 95).

[80]   For example, *RADN*, nos. 11, 12.

[81]   *RADN*, nos. 20, 23, 25, 26, 29, 37, 38, 39, 40, 41, 44, 45, 46.

Bayeux, or, later, Archbishop Malger and Bishop Odo of Bayeux attended in their capacity as bishops or as family. If it were the latter, the courts of both Richard II and Robert the Magnificent would look much more secular. All three prelates also held large estates – Robert and Odo even came to have comital status – and this, too, makes it uncertain that their attendance would have helped to make the court an ecclesiastical affair. Then there was Bishop Gilbert Maminot of Lisieux who 'gave himself up to secular interests and activities all his life', or the jocular Ivo of Sées, who was also lord of Bellême, neither of whom were noted for their clerical aura.[82] Bishop John of Lisieux, likewise, while concerned for the spiritual life of his diocese, was at court because he was an administrator. His opposite number in England, Roger of Salisbury, is said to have recommended himself to the king because he could say mass more quickly than anyone else. The liturgical atmosphere of the court, then, did not necessarily wax and wane as bishops came and went. The reality was far more complex and ambiguous.

The political theatre of landscape and buildings

These courts were held in the dukes' houses, palaces, and castles which were spread across Normandy, although not all of them remained in their hands at all times. Their existence could proclaim a duke's authority even in his absence – and they still do so today. Even the most basic earth-and-timber fortification might make a political statement. It revealed that the duke had the strength, and thus the coercive force, to oblige some of the (presumably) more lowly of his subjects to pile up the earth and to cut and set the timber. Moreover, at the most basic level, a castle literally planted the duke's authority in his duchy. Orderic's well-known comments on the construction of castles in England after 1066 make that point very clearly indeed.[83] For those who bridled under the duke's authority even these basic fortifications were a symbol of oppression and a deterrent to action. For the loyalist majority they were a consolation and a reminder of the duke's ability to defend them against their enemies. They might also provide a refuge for that population in times of trouble – and could thus allow the duke to act as a good lord should. Stone towers and palaces made these points still more clearly.[84]

---

[82] Orderic, iii. 20 (Gilbert); ii. 46 (Ivo).

[83] Orderic, ii. 218. See also *Brut y Tywysogion*, ed. T. Jones (Cardiff, 1955), p. 19 (s.a. 1093); *A Prince of Medieval Wales: The Life of Gruffydd ap Cynan*, trans. D. S. Evans (Llanerch, 1990), p. 70; *The Song of Dermot and the Earl: An Old French Poem from the Carew Manuscript No. 596 in the Archiepiscopal Library at Lambeth Palace*, ed. and trans. G. H. Orpen (Oxford, 1892), p. 233 (ll. 3202–7).

[84] For discussion of the functions of the great towers/keeps/donjons in particular see, for example, P. Dixon, 'The myth of the keep' and P. Marshall, 'The great tower as

But the dukes' houses, palaces, and castles were about more than defence and security. A swathe of recent work on castles, in particular, and the landscapes in which they were/are situated has focused on their part in the theatre of political ritual. They were, of course, the stage on which such rituals were enacted. Indeed, some great towers may have been intended to act principally as a series of reception rooms rather than as a residence, fortification, or treasury.[85] It is those functions and that work that provide the focus and comparisons for the following discussion.

Given the commonplace association of Normans and castles, it is worth remarking that we know surprisingly little about the palaces and castles built by the dukes, and Normans generally, during the period covered in this book. There were Frankish fortifications within what would become Normandy when the Normans arrived, and some of these would later be utilized by the dukes. They included the Carolingian fortifications at Rouen and perhaps also Eu and

residence', both in *The Seigneurial Residence in Western Europe AD c.800–1600*, ed. G. Meiron-Jones, E. Impey, and M. Jones (Oxford, 2002). On monumentality and decoration as an expression of power see, for example, R. McKitterick, *Charlemagne: The Formation of a European Identity* (Cambridge, 2008), pp. 162–71; J. L. Nelson, 'Aachen as a place of power', in *Topographies of Power in the Early Middle Ages*, ed. M de Jong and F. Theuws with C. van Rhijn (Leiden, 2001), pp. 219–22.

[85] Much work has been done on castles and their various functions in the last twenty years or so, with the result that these buildings, and their surroundings, are now seen in a much more nuanced manner. The following is a selection: C. Coulson, 'Cultural realities and reappraisals in English castle-study', *JMH*, 22 (1996), 171–208; C. Coulson, 'Peaceable power in English castles', *ANS*, 23 (2001), 69–95; O. Creighton, *Early European Castles: Aristocracy and Authority, AD800–1200* (London, 2012) (with thanks to Leonie Hicks for this reference); P. Dixon, 'Design in castle-building: the controlling of access to the lord', *Château Gaillard*, 18 (1998), 47–57; P. Dixon, 'The myth of the keep', in *The Seigneurial Residence in Western Europe*, pp. 9–13; P. Dixon, 'The influence of the White Tower on the great towers of the twelfth century', in *The White Tower*, ed. E. Impey (New Haven, CT and London, 2008), pp. 243–75; P. Dixon and P. Marshall, 'Norwich castle and its analogues', in *The Seigneurial Residence in Western Europe*, pp. 235–43; L. V. Hicks, 'Magnificent entrances and undignified exits: chronicling the symbolism of castle space in Normandy', *JMH*, 35 (2009), 52–69; R. Liddiard, 'Castle Rising, Norfolk: a "landscape of lordship"?' *ANS*, 22 (2000), 169–86; P. Marshall, 'The ceremonial function of the donjon in the twelfth century', *Château Gaillard*, 20 (2000), 141–51; P. Marshall, 'The great tower as residence', in *The Seigneurial Residence in Western Europe*, pp. 27–44; A. Renoux, 'Les fondements architecturaux du pouvoir princier en France (fin IXᵉ–début XIIIᵉ siècle)', in *Les princes et le pouvoir au Moyen Age*, ed. M. Balard (Paris, 1993), pp. 167–94; A. Renoux, '*Palatium* et *castrum* en France du Nord (fin IXᵉ–début XIIIᵉ siècle)', in *The Seigneurial Residence in Western Europe*, pp. 15–25; J. M. Steane, *The Archaeology of Power: England and Northern Europe AD800–1600* (Stroud, 2001).

Exmes.[86] The impressive earthworks of this last fortification survive, and form a triangular enclosure to the north of the village (visible along Place Couloy), but in the absence of excavations we know nothing of its likely appearance or layout. The Normans themselves established fortified camps at, for example, Jeufosse, but this has disappeared. The earliest of the permanent residential halls known to have been founded by the dukes after the grant to Rollo was at Fécamp. The earliest work uncovered by excavations has been dated to the reign of William Longsword. His wooden-walled, Scandinavian-style hall was replaced in stone by Richard I, who added at least one wooden chamber, with the whole surrounded by a ditch and an earth bank. These defences were in turn further strengthened by Richard II.[87]

Richard I may also have been responsible for constructing the tower at Rouen, in the south-east of the city. Previously, the dukes had resided in the old palace in the south-west which had been inherited from the Carolingian counts. Robert of Torigni certainly thought that the stone tower at Rouen was built by him, which would make it a very early example of such a building. He suggested that it was no less tall than Henry I's keep at Caen, which from the surviving seventeenth-, eighteenth-, and nineteenth-century views seems to have had at least three floors.[88] The remains of the tower at Ivry-la-Bataille and the slightly later examples at Beaugency on the Loire and Loches also indicate what might be achieved around this date,[89] but there were other towers, too, that have since been demolished, including one at Laon that Richard would have seen as a boy.[90] Although Bernard Gauthiez has argued that the tower was more likely constructed by Richard II

---

[86] For Rouen see below. Although Flodoard refers to a *castrum* at Eu, he seems to use that word to refer to what he also calls an *oppidum*; in other words a fortified town. However, he also mentions a *munitio*, which may be supposed to mean a smaller strongpoint (*Flodoard*, p. 38). Orderic says that the fortification at Exmes dated to the Carolingian period (Orderic, iii. 268, 310–12), but Renoux is less sure (A. Renoux, 'Châteaux et residences fortifiées', p. 114.

[87] A. Renoux, *Fécamp: du palais ducal au palaise de dieu* (Paris, 1991), pp. 343–86.

[88] For example, see in *Mémoires du château de Caen*, ed. J.-V. Marin and J.-M. Levesque (Caen, 2000): BnF, *Veüe du château de Caën dessiné du coté d'une hauteur en dehors de la ville, vis à vis*, collection Gaignières, 1702 (front cover); Caen, Musée de Normandie, *Le donjon de Caen*, by Jolimont (1825), p. 25; Caen, BM, *Le château de Caen*, by Gilet (eighteenth century), p. 27; Vincennes, 'Vue cavalière du château de Caen', *Atlas Louis XIII* (*c.* 1650), p. 128.

[89] RT, s.a. 1123; Delisle, i. 164; Howlett, p. 106. For Ivry see E. Impey, 'The *turris famosa* at Ivry-la-Bataille, Normandy', in *The Seigneurial Residence in Western Europe*, pp. 189–210; for Beaugency and Loches see E. Impey, 'The ancestry of the White Tower', in *The White Tower*, p. 230 and also p. 235.

[90] The influence of the tower at Laon on the duke is suggested by Renoux, 'Châteaux et residences fortifiées', p. 122.

than Richard I, his argument was based on the assumptions that Richard II gave the chapel of Saint-Clement to the abbot of Fécamp immediately after he moved out of the old Carolingian palace located in the south-west angle of the city wall, and that the chapel of Saint-Candé by the tower was granted to the bishop of Lisieux the moment that it was in use.[91] As neither of these things *must* have happened, it remains possible that Richard I did build the tower as Torigni reported. If so, the new building was not just a statement of Richard's power. The transfer of the castle from the south-west corner of the city to the south-east was a visual statement of Richard's sense of alienation from the French king, and a declaration of his autonomy. His principal seat and residence now faced towards Paris, and would protect his city from any further attacks launched by the king of the Franks or his other enemies in the future.[92] Furthermore, the relocation of the castle and its tower placed it next to the cathedral, allowing Richard to exploit his association with the Church.[93]

The fortress at Rouen is lost, and the images on the Bayeux Tapestry, if they depict the tower at Rouen at all, are unlikely to provide an accurate portrait of the buildings. Nonetheless, even the Tapestry provides some attempt to reveal power through buildings and environment.[94] In scene 12, the building before which Duke William sits is made of stone, has a defensible wall patrolled by sentries, two stone towers, and a central arcaded and domed building that looks as though it is based on a Byzantine and thus imperial model. In scene 14, which depicts Harold's meeting with Duke William following his liberation from Guy of Ponthieu, the men are found in an arcaded hall, which again looks to have been built of stone, and there are peacocks on the roof – birds which the capitulary *De Villis* stated should be present as ornaments (or on account of dignity).[95] Duke William is seated on a

---

[91] B. Gautiez, 'Hypothèses sur la fortification de Rouen au onzième siècle: le donjon, la tour de Richard I et l'enceinte de Guillaume', *ANS*, 14 (1992), 68; Gauthiez, 'The urban development of Rouen', pp. 21–2.

[92] Edward Impey suggested that the tower at Rouen likely provided 'the essential private, "public" and liturgical accommodation associated with the seigneurial residence', probably over three floors (Impey, 'The ancestry of the White Tower', pp. 234, 239). For Rouen as capital, see below, Chapter 9, pp. 506–24.

[93] Impey, 'The ancestry of the White Tower', p. 236, with reference to J. Le Maho, 'Autour d'un millénaire: l'oeuvre architecturale à Rouen de Richard Ier, duc de Normandie (d. 996)', *Bulletin des amis des monuments Rouennais* (1996), 63–83.

[94] See also: W. Grape, *The Bayeux Tapestry* (Munich, London, and New York, 1994), p. 27; C. Hart, 'The Bayeux Tapestry and schools of illumination at Canterbury', *ANS*, 22 (2000), 117–67, especially 129–33; E. C. Pastan, 'Building stories: the representation of architecture in the Bayeux embroidery', *ANS*, 33 (2011), 150–85.

[95] *Capitularia Regum Francorum*, 2, ed. A Boreti and V. Krause, *MGH, Leges* (Hanover, 1897), p. 88; Dutton, *Carolingian Civilization*, p. 88.

cushioned throne with his feet on a foot stool, a sentry behind him, and a sheathed sword representing his temporal authority in his hand. These details suggest the parts that cost, wealth, ornament, and luxury might play in the construction of power – and we shall meet all of them again in the next section of this chapter.

It is likely that the masonry, decoration, and height of the tower at Rouen were all intended as manifestations of ducal power. It is possible that the arrangement of doors, passages, rooms, and staircases within would also have been planned with the same intention. And it is equally clear that the tower was a public building, not just from the narratives, but from the note that one act was made at Rouen 'in the hall of the tower (*in aula turris*)'.[96] Analogies drawn with other keeps suggest how this might have been achieved. So, for example, Pamela Marshall has argued that at Loches (built *c.* 1020) the door to the great hall could not be barred if the keep were attacked because it opened outwards. Although that conclusion is open to question, the point remains that this decision had perhaps been taken to ensure that opening the door did not obstruct a visitor's first view of the hall. Here, then, defence came second to making the right first impression. Furthermore, as the kitchen servants were kept out of sight by their use of a passage, they did not clutter the stairway or the grand entrance through the forebuilding, again allowing clear views of the architecture. The rooms in the keep were probably arranged hierarchically, too, with the most public at the bottom and the most private at the top, while the climb was made by way of staircases that ran through the thickness of the wall, providing a more dignified assent – perhaps – than a spiral stair.[97]

Another example is provided by Philip Dixon's examination of the mid-twelfth-century keep at Castle Rising. He suggested that it was designed with the intention of emphasizing the importance of its lord, William of Aubigny, earl of Arundel, and the lesser standing of those who visited him. A visitor would be faced with the decorated forebuilding, which highlighted the earl's wealth, before passing through the gate, with more decoration above, and climbing the impressive flight of stairs to an antechamber. There, he or she would have stood before an elaborate multi-ordered door, lit by large windows. The level of this room was some feet below the floor of the hall, so that the visitor would be at the waist level of the person who opened this inner door and would have to walk up into the room, requiring them to walk slowly and formally as they gained entry. Once in the hall, the lord would have been on a dais, in an alcove behind them, lit by a large window.[98] This might have caused a sense of disorientation, putting them still more on the back foot.

---

[96] *Regesta: William*, no. 26.
[97] Marshall, 'The ceremonial function of the donjon'; Marshall, 'The great tower', p. 29.
[98] Dixon, 'Design in castle-building', 47–57.

Towers, then, could be used to display power and reinforce hierarchies in a number of ways. Further, Richard I's tower at Rouen also provided a panoramic view over the city, river, and the surrounding countryside, and that view could be used to reveal the dukes' power, too. Orderic recognized this when depicting the last minutes of the rebel Conan in 1090. The future King Henry I took him to a window and said:

> admire, Conan, the beauty of the country you tried to conquer. Away to the south there is a delightful hunting region, wooded and well-stocked with beasts of the chase. See how the river Seine, full of fishes, laps the wall of Rouen and daily brings in ships laden with merchandise of many kinds. On the other side, see the fair and populous city, with its ramparts and churches and town buildings, which has rightly been the capital of Normandy from the earliest days.[99]

This is to see a view as a boast. If power could be represented by trade, food, and deer parks, then the dukes of the Normans were very wealthy indeed.

The new tower at Rouen was not Richard I's only politically important building. The twelfth-century *Translatio secunda sancti Audoeni* states that he also built a tower (*arx*) and palace at Bayeux, probably in 989,[100] which must have made it very clear to his new Scandinavian subjects that Richard was, and intended to remain, their lord. Other castles were subsequently constructed by Richard II and his successors, for example at Brionne (where the stone hall with its shingle roof might have looked similar to that constructed at Chepstow by Brionne's one-time custodian, William fitz Osbern) and Tillières.[101]

One of the most important of these later ducal fortifications was the castle that William the Bastard built at Caen, the form of which was recovered by excavations carried out by Michel du Boüard from 1947, but particularly between 1955 and 1966.[102] William was responsible for enclosing the outcrop on which the castle stands first with a wooden palisade and then with a stone wall. This probably had wooden hoards running along the parapet but no mural towers. There was a gate tower to the north, however, similar to the later examples at Richmond or Ludlow, which formed the principal strong point at this time. Inside the enclosure, which covers some 5 hectares, there was a palace comprising a hall

---

[99] Orderic, iv. 224.
[100] 'Variae translationes sacri corporis', in *Acta Sanctorum* 38 (August IV) (Paris, 1867), p. 823. Lucien Musset suggested the date, noted in Yver, 'Château forts', 33–4, n. 20. The Bayeux Tapestry suggests that the *arx* included a motte topped by a tower (scene 22).
[101] See above, Chapter 2, pp. 84, 95, 101, 109, 120, 131, 133, and below, Chapter 11, pp. 634–9.
[102] Best approached through M. du Boüard, *Le château de Caen* (Caen, 1979).

Fig. 4 William's palace within the castle at Caen (Author)

(16 metres by 8 metres), a chapel of about the same size, and some chambers. It is worth noting that, with an internal space of around 128 square metres, the hall would nowadays be thought suitable for seating around 90 guests for dinner, with perhaps a capacity of 150 if those present were standing.[103] There must also have been a kitchen and other domestic offices, but these have not been found. These seem to have been free-standing buildings, all of them apparently equally accessible, although the reality is likely to have been more hierarchical. Henry I later added a keep to the ensemble, as well, perhaps, as the hall known as the *salle d'echiquier*.[104]

In addition to the buildings, it is still possible to see how the castle at Caen was designed – or at least could have been used – as part of a managed landscape.[105] Those arriving in Caen from any direction apart from the north would most likely have found themselves passing through the town, and thus within view of one or both of the two abbeys that William and his wife had founded there. Dominating the scene, however, was the château. Even today, a traveller arriving from the railway station can see the castle's walls long before they arrive before it, and the

---

[103] These figures are derived from an informal trawl of hotel and convention centre websites.

[104] RT, s.a. 1123; Delisle, i. 164–5; Howlett, p. 106.

[105] As at the later Castle Rising in Norfolk, discussed by Liddiard, 'Castle Rising, Norfolk', 169–86.

Fig. 5 The view over Caen to the abbey of Sainte-Etienne from the castle (Author)

impact must have been all the greater in the eleventh and twelfth centuries. This is unlikely to have been an accident. Twelfth- and thirteenth-century romances make play with distant views of important buildings, and similar considerations can be seen in ninth-century Norway, too.[106] With Henry's keep standing sentinel, the view must have been all the more impressive, and all the more dominant.

Supposing that a visitor did indeed approach through the town, he or she would have had to pass around the walls of the castle to reach the principal entrance through the gate tower on the north side. If allowed entry, the visitor would then have been treated to a view of the compact palace complex to the right, with the roof of the hall rising behind the other domestic buildings. A visitor standing in front of the hall could then, as now, have seen the towers of Saint-Etienne, and a walk to the rampart would have provided a view over the town of Caen below. Thus, the castle bailey acted as a balcony, offering a sweeping view over the duke's town – just like the tower at Rouen.[107]

As Fig. 4 shows, only the footings of William's work at Caen now survive,

---

[106] Discussed by Liddiard, 'Castle Rising, Norfolk', 184. The Norwegian example I have in mind is the great hall at Borg in Vestvågøy, discussed in A. Pedersen, 'Power and aristocracy', in Vikings: Life and Legend, ed. G. Williams, P. Pentz, and M. Wemhoff (London, 2014), pp. 125–6. It might be noted in passing that the hall of this house covered about the same area as William's hall at Caen.

[107] See also M. Johnson, Behind the Castle Gate: From Medieval to Renaissance (London, 2002), p. 77; Hicks, 'Magnificent entrances', 59.

but something of its lost grandeur might be seen in the same duke's work – if it was indeed William's work – at Lillebonne.[108] This, too, has been lost, but it stood, albeit in ruinous condition, until its demolition in 1832 by the new owner, the industrialist Pierre-Abraham Lévesque, so there are drawings which convey something of its appearance. The eleventh-century residential buildings made an 'L'-shape at the south and west of the castle bailey, with the chamber surviving to its full height until demolition. This was the subject of well-known drawings by Cotman from 1822, and less well-known ones by Truchet, Fragonard, and others, which depict a building with a blind arcade of five or six round arches at ground level, and seven round-headed two-light windows above. The chamber communicated directly with the great hall, which formed most of the west side of the bailey. Like the chamber, this had an arcade at ground level, and there was a large window in the south gable wall at first-floor level – drawn in the 1820s by Jules Dumas and Louis-François Le Sage.[109] It is likely that the hall occupied this upper level, with storage rooms below. The kitchen was located on the ground floor of a building found on the north side of the bailey, with the chapel and the priest's room above. By the eleventh century there was a church within the enceinte, St Mary in the castle (*in castello*), which was given to the nuns of Montivilliers.[110]

At Lillebonne, the upper (principal) floor of the chamber block was perhaps divided into three rooms, identified by Jean Mesqui as the lord's private chamber, a *chambre de retrait* (for more private meetings), and a waiting room closest to the

---

[108] The building has generally been considered the work of William's reign (see, for example, M. W. Thomson, *The Rise of the Castle* (Cambridge, 1991), p. 29 and E. Impey, 'La demeure seigneuriale en Normandie entre 1125 et 1225 et la tradition Anglo-Normande', in *L'Architecture Normande au moyen age*, ed. M. Baylé (Caen, 2001), i. 238). Annie Renoux implied that the building dated from Henry I's reign (A. Renoux, 'Résidences et châteaux ducaux Normans au XIIᵉ siècle', in *L'Architecture Normande au moyen age*, i. 214), which would be possible. In 2008, however, Jean Mesqui argued that the chamber dated from the middle of the twelfth century, based on a drawing of a volute capital from one of the chamber's windows, which he compared to an example of *c.* 1160 from the chapel later dedicated to St Thomas Becket at Gisors, and the door of the hall at Angers, which he compared to the arches of the ground-floor arcade (J. Mesqui, *Le château de Lillebonne des ducs de Normandie aux ducs d'Harcourt*, MSAN, 42 (Caen, 2008), pp. 90–1). This is slight and ambiguous evidence, not least because the door at Angers does not have an abacus, unlike those found at Lillebonne. A better comparison would be the doors at the church of Notre-Dame-sur-l'Eau at Domfront, which date from 1090 to 1100 or those in the palace at Rouen as depicted in the Bayeux Tapestry (scenes 12 and 14). On architectural grounds alone, then, the traditional attribution of these buildings to William I's reign seems better, although they might date from Henry I's reign at a push.

[109] Mesqui, *Le château de Lillebonne*, p. 71, Fig. 34.

[110] *Regesta: William*, no. 212.

hall and communicating with it. These rooms were all smaller than the hall, and that alone made them more exclusive. Furthermore, it may be that entry to the chamber was restricted to the closest of the king's counsellors and friends, thus establishing and reinforcing hierarchies.[111]

But the hall at Lillebonne might have been intended to act in a more symbolic way, too. The hall connected with the chamber block at the south end. It may therefore be supposed that the dais was at the south end, too. If that were the case, then the large window in the south gable wall of the hall would have backlit those on the dais for some hours every day, illuminating the duke and making it very difficult to look upon him or to see his expression. This would have put the observer at a disadvantage. One is reminded here of the words of King David, linking light to rulership: 'He that ruleth over men must be just, ruling in fear of God. And he shall be as the light of the morning, when the sun riseth, even a morning without clouds.'[112] Light, in this case glittering from gold and gems, was also the foundation for the joke made by the Conqueror's jester: 'I see God!' Light, then, could be used to suggest power, for both religious and psychological reasons. It may be that the large windows on the principal floors at Domfront and in the Beaumont keep at Brionne performed a similar function, even if that is by no means clear from what survives.[113]

Furthermore, although it was a ducal possession by 1025,[114] there is no evidence that Lillebonne was used as a ducal residence before the Conquest – Malmesbury's depiction of a council held here in 1066 was written much too late to suggest otherwise.[115] It is therefore interesting that a decision was apparently made to build a new palace just above the prominent ruins of a Roman amphitheatre at that time. Much was being made of Roman imperial imagery and symbolism in Normandy after William's conquest of England. William of Poitiers used Roman authors, particularly Sallust, Virgil, and Caesar in the composition of his

---

[111] Hicks, 'Magnificent entrances', 62–3.

[112] 2 Samuel 23:3–4. It is possible, but less likely, that the employment of light in these buildings was related to the *Celestial Hierarchy* by the Pseudo-Dionysius. Although there was a copy of this work at Le Bec by the middle of the twelfth century (*PL*, 150, col. 777), the use to which that work was put by Suger of Saint-Denis was apparently both novel and limited, and was based on the identification of the author with St Denis, the dedicatee and patron of his abbey and of the kings of the French. Suger's work is discussed in Dunbabin, *France*, pp. 257–8 and L. Grant, *Abbot Suger of Saint-Denis: Church and State in Early Twelfth-Century France* (London, 1998), pp. 23–4. A translation of the *Celestial Hierarchy* is available in: *Pseudo-Dionysius: The Complete Works*, trans. C. Luibheid (New York and Mahwah, 1987), pp. 145–91.

[113] See also Hicks, 'Magnificent entrances', 61–2.

[114] *RADN*, no. 36.

[115] Malmesbury, *GR*, i. 448.

Gesta Guillelmi, made an extended comparison of William with Julius Caesar, and described the new king's counsellors as another Roman senate.[116] The poem *Plus tibi fama*, written as early as 1070, claimed that William was greater than Caesar, too, and Elisabeth van Houts has pointed out that 'one of the main themes of the poems dedicated to William in the aftermath of the Conquest held out the possibility of him as emperor'.[117] The Bayeux Tapestry might have been intended to echo Roman friezes such as those on Trajan's Column.[118] And so it is possible that the design of the hall and chamber blocks at Lillebonne was intended to reflect the architecture of the neighbouring ruins and thus to promote William's new-found, almost imperial authority, in a similar way to these literary or artistic products.[119] The location almost certainly was.

Impressive as these buildings were, William's work was outdone by that paid for by his son, Henry I. Robert of Torigni, in his additions to the *Gesta Normannorum ducum*, wrote:

King Henry built many fortresses in his kingdom as well as in the duchy. He also restored almost all the fortified places built by his predecessors, not only the strongholds but also the old towns. The names of the fortresses in Normandy on the frontier of the duchy and the neighbouring provinces are: Drincourt; Châteauneuf-sur-Epte; Verneuil; Nonancourt; Bonsmoulins; Colmont; Pontorson; and others which I shall pass by in order not to delay the narrative.[120]

---

[116] Poitiers, pp. xix, 168–74.

[117] E. M. C. van Houts, 'Latin poetry and the Norman court 1066–1135: the *Carmen de Hastingae Proelio*', *JMH*, 15 (1989), 42; 'Rouen as another Rome in the twelfth century', in *Society and Culture in Medieval Rouen, 911–1300*, ed. L. V. Hicks and E. Brenner (Turnhout, 2013), p. 105.

[118] O. K. Werkmeister, 'The Political Ideology of the Bayeux Tapestry', *Studi Medievali*, third series, 17 (1976), 535–95; Bachrach, *Fulk Nerra*, p. 134; G. Owen-Crocker, 'Stylistic Variation and Roman Influence in the Bayeux Tapestry', *Peregrinations*, 9 (2009), 51–96.

[119] William or his Norman designers would not have been alone in doing so. Charlemagne's palace at Aachen combined a hall perhaps based on the Roman basilica at Trier with a chapel probably based on Justinian's San Vitale (K. J. Conant, *Carolingian and Romanesque Architecture, 800–1200*, second integrated edition (London, 1978), pp. 46–51; Steane, *The Archaeology of Power*, p. 23). The Carolingian tower at Mayenne of *c.* 900 reused masonry from the Roman site at Jublains, and 'the replication of Roman features, it is tempting to suppose, was a symbolic reference to Roman order and Roman power' (Steane, *The Archaeology of Power*, p. 26). Fulk Nerra had a frieze at his foundation of 'Belli Locus' near Loches *c.* 1011 that also echoed Roman models (Bachrach, *Fulk Nerra*, pp. 131–4).

[120] Jumièges, ii. 250.

He added to this information in his *Chronicle*:

> King Henry surrounded the tower of Rouen, which the first Richard, the duke
> of the Normans, had built as his palace, with a high and broad turreted wall,
> within which he erected such buildings as were fitting for a royal residence.
> And to the town he added such new defences as were required ... Besides this,
> he erected a very lofty tower in the castle at Caen, and carried up to a greater
> height the wall of that fortress, which had been built by his father. But the
> wall with which his father had surrounded the entire town he left untouched,
> just as it had been finished by his father. He strengthened the castle called
> Arques with a tower and walls in a wonderful manner, and he did the same
> for the castles at Gisors, Falaise, Argentan, Exmes, Domfront, Ambrières and
> the castle of Vire and Gavray (*Wavrai*). The same may be said of the tower of
> Vernon.[121]

There are trends here, as Torigni made plain, and perhaps a new emphasis.
William's buildings were defended palaces that fitted into conservative Carolingian
and Scandinavian traditions, and which perhaps made allusions to Rome and a
use of light for political purposes.[122] Henry's buildings seem principally to have
been intended to impress by their bulk, solidity, and height. In particular, Henry
was a builder of tower keeps.[123] A number of his towers survive in various states
of preservation: Arques (20.2 metres by 20.2 metres, with walls between 3.5 and
2.2 metres thick and sporting large buttresses on the north and east walls, measur-
ing 3 metres by 3 metres); Caen (27.4 metres by 24 metres, with walls 4.4 metres
thick); Domfront (26.3 metres by 22.4 metres, with walls 4 metres thick at the
base); Falaise (26.6 metres by 22.8 metres, with walls about 3.5 metres thick); and
Vire (14 metres by 14 metres, with walls 2.3 metres thick).[124] With the exception of
Vire, these are among the larger examples of their kind and they were all visually
impressive, as eighteenth- and nineteenth-century views reveal. In contrast, if the
surviving work at Argentan dates from Henry I's reign, and this has been rejected
in some more recent work on the castle, he was responsible for an ambitious
shell keep there. The existing motte was encased in masonry, creating a polygonal

---

[121]   RT, s.a. 1123; Delisle, i. 164–5 ; Howlett, pp. 106–7.

[122]   Renoux, 'Châteaux et residences fortifiées', p. 121.

[123]   In contrast, Judith Green sees him as a builder of halls, in the image of his father,
        although she does also note that he built large keeps (Green, *Henry*, pp. 303–4).

[124]   For the keeps at Arques, Caen, Domfront, and Falaise see the articles in *L'architecture
        normande au moyen âge*, ed. M. Balylé, second edition (Caen, 2001), ii. 312–14, 298–301,
        288–90, 305–9, respectively.

enclosure which rises to a height of some 15 metres, and which looks rather like the work (*c*. 1180) at Farnham (Hampshire).[125]

At one level, much of Henry's building was utilitarian. He was concerned to defend his frontiers, and his new towers were built at places which were vulnerable to attack. That is true as much for Falaise, which stood in the midst of lands dominated by the Montgommery-Bellême family, as for the more obviously frontier castles at Verneuil and Nonancourt. Even so, his building operations were no doubt meant to impress those who saw them as much as to provide strong points – although the two uses overlap, of course. Equally, if Rufus's hall at Westminster was designed to awe, then so, too, was Henry's admittedly smaller hall at Caen. Contemporaries were certainly aware that castle-building might have such a function. Orderic talks of the Basset castle at Montreuil-au-Houlme being intended to do just that: 'Richard Basset, who had enjoyed great power in England as chief justice (*capitalis iusticiarii*) during King Henry's lifetime and was swollen with the wealth of England, had made a show of superiority to all his peers and fellow countrymen by the magnificence of his building in the little fief he had inherited from his parents in Normandy. He had therefore built a very well-fortified castle of ashlar blocks.'[126]

Establishing how Henry I's buildings worked in practice is hampered by the fact that so many of them have been lost, and that those which survive are in a ruined or reconstructed state. Falaise, for example, may appear to present Henry's work, but much of the keep was reconstructed in the mid nineteenth century and again in the late twentieth century. Nonetheless, the plan suggested by Philip Dixon and Pamela Marshall would have a hall at first floor level, entered at the north-east, with three two-light windows with interlace capitals. To the west, screened off from the hall, there was a side chamber which might have acted as a waiting room, and which had at least one garderobe attached to it. From there, a visitor moved south into a smaller antechamber, although this was probably not vaulted as they suggested.[127] From there, they would finally be admitted into a chamber, which stood on the other side of the spine wall from the hall and which had a chapel attached.[128] The window nearest the fireplace in this room has a capital depicting a man holding two hounds by leashes (Fig. 6), and

---

[125] I. Chave, C. Corvisier, and J. Desloges, 'Le château d'Argentan (XIe–XVe siècle): du castrum Roman à la residence princière', in *Argentan et ses environs au Moyen Age*, ed. M.-A. Moulin et al. (Caen, 2008), pp. 127–43.

[126] Orderic, vi. 468.

[127] The surviving masonry is too low in the wall and would have provided very cramped and very low vaults. It does not look as though it belongs in its current location.

[128] See Dixon and Marshall, 'Norwich castle and its analogues', p. 238 with the plan (based on that drawn by R. E. Doranlo) at p. 243.

Fig. 6 Capital in the chamber at Falaise, depicting a man holding two hounds on leashes (Author)

it is very tempting to see this as an allegorical representation of Henry's control over his two *regna*. The plan is open to question – the waiting room might actually have been a kitchen (it has a chimney), for example – but *if* it is right the anticlockwise progression around the first floor would have been intended to heighten anticipation, while the diminution of room size might have emphasized the increasingly intimate nature of the visit. Furthermore, only the anteroom and chamber were positioned to enjoy direct sunlight, so that light itself might again have been used in an allegorical and/or theatrical way. That said, it is not clear that the keep was intended for public display at all. Dixon has suggested that 'this tower may well … have been conceived as a set of apartments for the king's private use' making the keep 'an early example of the type sometimes described as a "solar keep"'.[129]

The buildings erected by the dukes thus spoke on a number of different levels about their authority. They were a tangible manifestation of their power which might further be made to reflect the God-given foundation of their authority or their imperial aspirations; they reflected and reinforced political hierarchies. They were not just the stage for their courts, then; they were part of the staging, too. The next section of this chapter considers how those stages were furnished and dressed, and how the duke and the other actors strode upon them.

[129] Dixon, 'The influence of the White Tower', pp. 254–5.

The court and the chroniclers

Despite the fact that the narratives were written, like the acts, by chaplains, canons, and monks – and Dudo of Saint-Quentin, of course, wrote both – the chronicles focus much more on the secular side of the court than do the *acta*. They tell us of the great assemblies and feasts that promoted the duke's wealth, and thus his power, that took place in his castles and palaces, in buildings that were designed to impress and also to stress hierarchy and community. Here the duke would appear splendidly dressed, and preside over an ostentatious display of wealth, manifested in the food and drink on offer, the vessels from which it was taken, and the dress of the servants who pandered to the needs of the diners.

Such conspicuous displays of wealth had a serious point. They reminded those in attendance of the power of the duke. A man who could provide such a feast in such a sumptuous setting was rich in cash and land and so could pay for castles and mercenaries, bribe enemies to make peace, and thus emerge victorious. Bede had recognized this in the eighth century when he expressed his concern that the foundation of monasteries in Northumbria was depriving the king of the landed resources with which to reward 'the sons of noblemen and veteran warriors'. If the king lacked the land necessary to reward his warriors, then they would go elsewhere.[130] Asser noted how Alfred attracted men to his court through his reputation for generosity and concomitant ability to reward them.[131] The author of the *Encomium Emmae Reginae* asserted that 'display instils loyalty and projects royal dignity, military might and imperial ambition'.[132] By the time this last author was writing, the link between wealth and power seems to have become closer

---

[130] Bede, 'Letter to Egbert', ch. 11. This is most readily available in *The Ecclesiastical History of the English People*, trans. L. Shirley-Price, revised by L. E. Latham, with the translation of the minor works, new introduction, and notes by D. H. Farmer (London, 1990), p. 345.

[131] Asser, *Life of King Alfred*, ch. 76, most easily found in *Alfred the Great: Asser's Life of King Alfred and Other Contemporary Sources*, trans. S. Keynes and M. Lapidge (London, 1983), p. 91. See also R. Abels, 'Household men, mercenaries and Vikings in Anglo-Saxon England', in *Mercenaries and Paid Men: The Mercenary Identity in the Middle Ages*, ed. J. France (Leiden, 2008), pp. 150–4.

[132] E. M. Tyler, '"The eyes of the beholders were dazzled": treasure and artifice in the *Encomium Emmae Reginae*', *EME*, 8 (1999), 268, also noted in C. Insley, 'Where did all the charters go? Anglo-Saxon charters and the new politics of the eleventh century', *ANS*, 24 (2002), 124). Alexander of Telese remarked, in a similar vein, that Roger II's coronation at Palermo in 1130 was so splendid, and so revealing of the wealth of the king, that 'it caused great wonder and deep stupefaction – so great indeed that it instilled not a little fear in all those who had come from so far away' (Alexander of Telese, 'The History of the Most Serene Roger, First King of Sicily', in *Roger II and the Creation of the Kingdom of Sicily*, ed. and trans. G. A. Loud (Manchester, 2012), p. 79.

than it had been previously, reflected by the fact that from the last decades of the tenth century the Old English word *rice* had changed its equivalent meaning in Latin from simply *potens* ('powerful') to both 'powerful' *and* 'wealthy'(previously *welig*).[133] Thus by the eleventh century the distinguishing characteristic of those with authority were their conspicuous wealth, demonstrated by what they ate and how they ate it, how they dressed and what they dressed in, and their buildings, too.[134]

At the centre of this political drama was the duke, so we may begin with a consideration of the pains the dukes took with their appearance and presentation. Unfortunately, there is not much to go on until after the dukes became kings. Dudo of Saint-Quentin seems to have been largely unconcerned with appearance. He does lead us to believe, however, that the scorn that the Saxons directed at William Longsword was the result of his failure to look suitably splendid: 'He comes without the display and magnificence appropriate to such an occasion.'[135] Their view was changed only when they had experienced the strength of William's following, seen the quality of his outsize sword, and learned of the obedience that he commanded in his men. Dudo was perhaps making a point. Geoffrey Koziol has remarked that 'a king could lack power, but without dignity he was nothing'.[136] Dudo might have been pricking this bubble by pointing out that the reverse was true. The duke might not have looked as splendid as his rivals, but he was more powerful than they were. In contrast, the king's display was empty; he knew how to keep up appearances but could marshal no real power.

Dudo provided a partial pen-portrait of Richard I as he knew him in his later years, but while there seem to be echoes of some of the portraits found in Suetonius's *Twelve Caesars*, it deals in the splendour of Richard's physical form as an externalization of his interior virtues: 'His outward appearance was wreathed about with a marvellously appropriate beauty, and "glory shone out of his countenance" as if with the brightness of the sun ... Most lovely to look upon, bristling with brilliant white hair, brilliant in eyebrows and the pupil of the eye, resplendent of nostril and cheek, honoured for a thick, long beard, lofty of stature.'[137] This portrait, then, was about character, not about display or presentation. The depictions of Duke William in the Bayeux Tapestry are similarly limited

---

[133] M. Godden, 'Money, power and morality in late Anglo-Saxon England', *ASE*, 19 (1990), 42–55.

[134] See R. Fleming, 'The new wealth, the new rich, and the new political style', *ANS*, 23 (2001), 1–22. On wealth and display as a means of recruitment, see also below, Chapter 11, pp. 619–20, 626–7.

[135] Shopkow, *History and Community*, p. 73.

[136] Koziol, *Begging Pardon*, p. 125.

[137] *Dudo*, p. 166.

to establishing William's place in the hierarchy through stock iconography. Duke William is presented as the focus of his court. He sits on a throne, with his feet on a footstool, sheathed sword in hand or over his shoulder, wearing a cloak. This is the ruler portrait suitable for a figure who was not a king. Count Guy of Ponthieu is presented in an almost identical manner.

The post-Conquest narratives provide more detail, not least because the royal duke's appearance was a personification of the wealth of his kingdom. During the great feasts over which they presided, and perhaps during the greater assemblies and councils, too, the royal dukes were gloriously arrayed. Solomon provided the biblical model, with his throne of ivory and drinking vessels of gold: 'so King Solomon exceeded all the kings of the earth for riches and wisdom.'[138] The emperor Diocletian had also helped to create the requirement for elaborate outfits and an increase in court ceremonial, by dressing in a diadem, purple robes, and jewelled shoes.[139] The Norman kings, like their peers, were obliged to follow suit.

And so when William the Bastard held his triumphal court at Fécamp at Easter 1067, all those in attendance, 'as they looked at the clothes of the king and his courtiers, woven and encrusted with gold, … considered whatever they had seen before to be of little worth. Similarly they marvelled at the vessels of silver and gold, of whose number and beauty incredible things could truthfully be told … But they recognized that far more distinguished and memorable than these things was the splendour of the king himself.'[140]

The unbeatable splendour of William's appearance was also recognized by William's jester in a well-known passage in Milo Crispin's Life of Lanfranc. The incident happened while King William was at one of these feasts, sitting next to his archbishop of Canterbury, Lanfranc.

> It was one of those three great festivals on which the king, wearing his crown, is accustomed to hold his court. On the day of the festival, when the king was seated at table adorned in crown and royal robes, and Lanfranc beside him, a certain jester, seeing the king resplendent in gold and jewels, cried out in the hall in great tones of adulation: 'Behold I see God! Behold I see God!' Lanfranc turned to the king and said, 'don't allow such things to be said of you. These things are not for man but for God. Order that fellow to be severely flogged so that he won't ever dare to say such things again.'[141]

[138] 1 Kings 10: 18–23.

[139] F. Oakley, Kingship: The Politics of Enchantment (Oxford, 2006), p. 69; S. Corcoran, 'Before Constantine', in The Cambridge Companion to the Age of Constantine, ed. N. Lenski (Cambridge, 2005), p. 43.

[140] Poitiers, pp. 178–80.

[141] The Life of Lanfranc is translated by S. Vaughn, The Abbey of Bec and the Anglo-Norman

Geoffrey Koziol has suggested that the jester was beaten because 'he had revealed William for what he really was: a bastard count who was assuming too many airs for his own good.'[142] It seems more likely, however, that the jester was making a joke at the royal duke's expense – that he might try to emulate the splendour of God but could never attain his aim – which at the same time emphasized the magnificence of his appearance. His comment, of course, smacked a little too much of blasphemy for Lanfranc's liking. A similar comment was later made about Henry I by Henry of Huntingdon. His 'crowned head had sparkled with gold and the finest jewels, like the splendour of God, whose hands had shone with sceptres, while the rest of his body had been dressed in gorgeous cloth of gold and his mouth had always fed on the most delicious and choice foods, for whom everyone would rise to their feet, whom everyone feared, with whom everyone rejoiced, and whom everyone admired'.[143] His son, William, was likewise 'gleaming in an almost heavenly glory'.[144]

While the gloriously arrayed duke presided over these gatherings, it was essential that the feasts held during such assemblies should also be costly and ostentatious. As men symbolized power and authority, William the Bastard, and all the other dukes, too, hoped to awe their guests by the size of the company attending their courts. The types of food and drink on offer, and the plates and vessels from which they were consumed, were equally important.[145]

Here, Dudo does provide some details. He reported a meeting of William Longsword, Count Herbert of the Vermandois, Hugh the Great, and Count William of Poitou, who assembled at Lyons-la-Forêt. Dudo wrote that 'William was jubilant at their coming, and he received them respectfully with a large attendance; and in order to keep them with him as long as the good hunting lasted, he held a magnificent banquet of kingly opulence.'[146] William, then, although a humble duke, was as rich as a king. Later, when Dudo had Longsword ride with the king of the French to treat with King Henry of the lands across the Rhine, Duke Cono of the Saxons said to the king that: 'There is no king, other than you, and no duke nor count as magnificent as William. Surrounded by a zealous crowd of great men and young warriors, he feasts in splendour from golden vessels

State (Woodbridge, 1981), pp. 87–111 with the passage in question at p. 107. The translation here, however, follows (for the most part) J. A. Nelson, 'The rites of the Conqueror', ANS, 4 (1981), 131.

[142] Koziol, Begging Pardon, pp. 290–1.

[143] Huntingdon, p. 702.

[144] Huntingdon, p. 592.

[145] For more on this see M. Hagger, 'Lordship and lunching: interpretations of eating and food in the Anglo-Norman world, 1050-1200, with reference to the Bayeux Tapestry', in The English and Their Legacy, 900-1200. Essays in Honour of Ann Williams, ed. D. Roffe (Woodbridge, 2012), pp. 229–44, and in particular, pp. 233–4.

[146] Dudo, p. 69.

and cups; hedged about by a multifarious gathering of servants, both noble and unfree.'[147] It would seem that Longsword, like his Viking forebears, was thus surrounded when possible with 'glittering splendour'.[148]

William of Jumièges remarked other occasions when the duke welcomed and entertained guests with magnificence and splendour. When Count Geoffrey of the Bretons came to Richard II to seek his friendship 'the duke welcomed him honourably ... [and] kept the count with him for a while, through his enormous wealth revealing to the count the greatness of his wealth as he chose'. The subsequent wedding of the count to Hawisa, Richard's sister, was 'celebrated with extravagant honour' and gifts were 'lavishly bestowed' upon them.[149] When Swein of Denmark visited Richard II at Rouen 'the duke entertained him magnificently for some time'.[150] King Æthelred II, driven from England by Swein, was in turn welcomed to Rouen by Richard 'with a great display of splendour'.[151] The presence of important guests, then, required that a show be put on for them, not only to demonstrate due respect, but also to advertise the wealth of the duke to this potential threat or ally.

Formal courts might also be associated with translations of saints' relics or the dedications of cathedral and abbey churches, which linked the duke to the life of the duchy and to its patron saints. The association with the duke and Church – and the duke's control over the latter – might be further highlighted by holding a Church council after the court was over, as at Lillebonne in 1080.[152] The greatest occasions, however, or so it seems, were the great banquets that were held at the three principal feasts of the Christian calendar, Christmas, Easter and Pentecost, during which the royal dukes might have worn their crowns in the duchy (as they did when in England). According to William of Malmesbury,

> the dinners in which [William the Bastard] took part on the major festivals were costly and splendid ... all great men of whatever walk of life were summoned to them by royal edict, so that envoys from other nations might admire the large and brilliant company, and the splendid luxury of the feast. Nor was he at any other season so courteous or so ready to oblige, so that foreign visitors might carry a lively report to every country of the generosity that matched his wealth.[153]

---

[147] *Dudo*, p. 72. Dudo mentioned William's gold and silver vessels again later (*Dudo*, p. 80).

[148] Roesdahl, *The Vikings*, p. 67.

[149] Jumièges, ii. 14.

[150] Jumièges, ii. 16.

[151] Jumièges, ii. 18.

[152] See also above, Chapter 4, pp. 219–20, 225–6, 237.

[153] Malmesbury, *GR*, i. 508.

According to Michael Dietler, 'feasts are, in fact, ritualized social events in which food and drink constitute the medium of expression in the performance of ... "politico-symbolic drama". As public ritual events, in contrast to daily activity, feasts provide an arena for the highly condensed symbolic representation of social relations.'[154] Although he wrote these words in an article about prehistoric societies, they are equally germane to the Middle Ages, although it is perhaps the case that any form of communal eating, including even mealtime in a monastic refectory, could create an appropriate arena for representing social relations. Thus feasts provided the personnel involved in them with the opportunity to reinforce their place in the hierarchy.

The hierarchical social relationships that the dukes and their contemporaries wanted to demonstrate and reinforce at feasts are illustrated in Gaimar's description of the feast (*feste*) staged by William Rufus in his new hall at Westminster in 1099:

> Numerous kings, earls and dukes were present, and at the doors stood three hundred ushers, each one wearing a cloak lined either with grey and white miniver (squirrel) or with fine imported silk brocade. Their task was to keep back the rabble ... Or again in the case of those who had to bring in the different courses, both food and drink, from the kitchen or offices, these same ushers would escort them to prevent any greedy lout from upsetting, damaging or breaking the silver serving dishes.[155]

The scale and richness of clothing and food demonstrated William's power and influence; the ushers keeping out the rabble emphasized the exclusive nature of the feast and thus the sense of community of those invited to it. The lords who attended and ate formed an exclusive club and were celebrated – and celebrated themselves – as the best men of the duchy. Such self-congratulation strengthened ducal authority by cementing loyalties and building new friendships.[156]

The restraint imposed on the diners, who were prevented from helping themselves to the dishes by the ushers, was a further powerful display of the king's control over their persons and hunger. The importance of bodily self-restraint in front of one's lord is also one of the themes in the *Urbanus*, written by Daniel of Beccles during the reign of Henry II, and the sorts of thing mentioned there – not picking off fleas in the lord's presence, for example – would also have stressed the

---

[154] Dietler, 'Feasts and commensal politics in the political economy', p. 89.
[155] Gaimar, p. 324.
[156] See, for example, G. Althoff, *Family, Friends and Followers: Political and Social Bonds in Early Medieval Europe*, trans. C. Carroll (Cambridge, 2004), pp. 152–9.

duke's authority in his own hall.[157] But the dukes' ability to control their subjects' attitudes and appetites was not limited to the dinner table. Such control was also exercised over those who came to court seeking pardon or favour. Although the posture of those seeking grants is not recorded, the narratives suggest that those seeking justice or forgiveness for their part in war or rebellion were required, or chose, to adopt attitudes of humility when supplicating the duke – the narratives tend not to notice petitions for the more mundane business of grants or restitutions of land and so tend not to overlap with the *acta*.[158] Dudo of Saint-Quentin recorded that an ambassador from King Æthelstan approached Rollo, then besieging Paris, 'with humble mien' and told him that the king 'beseeches you, with your mighty power over all things, to come to help him with all speed'.[159] Dudo also reported that King Louis IV came before William Longsword and 'begged that he help and defend him against the rebel Franks'. In an associated poem, Dudo imagined that the king 'lies prone in entreaty, / Humbly beseeches you to grant him protection'.[160] When Longsword's troops broke down the billets in which King Henry's troops were staying, Duke Cono rushed up to the duke and proclaimed: 'I beseech you, bowing to the very ground, not to let such things happen.'[161] Herluin, seeking Longsword's help in recovering Montreuil, 'threw himself at [William's] feet'.[162] Soon afterwards, envoys sent by Arnulf of Flanders lured William into a trap, persuading him to make a treaty of friendship with Arnulf, 'with downcast eyes and submissive voice, in words of supplication and peace'.[163] William of Jumièges provided further examples. After spending five years in prison in the tower at Rouen as the result of his insurgency in the Hiémois, Richard II's brother, William, escaped, happened on his brother in the valley of Vernon and 'threw himself on the ground at his feet, and miserably asked for forgiveness for his misdeeds'.[164] At the end of the siege of Brionne *c.* 1050, Count Guy 'was compelled by his friends to seek the duke's clemency as suppliant and penitent. The duke, having taken counsel, took pity on his misery and treated him mercifully.'[165]

---

[157] R. Bartlett, *England under the Norman and Angevin Kings 1075–1225* (Oxford, 2000), p. 585.

[158] There are, of course, exceptions. The Chronicle of Sainte-Barbe-en-Auge notes that Prior William, a man who was almost part of the court, had petitioned Henry I for a grant (*La Chronique de Sainte-Barbe-en-Auge*, ed. Sauvage, p. 25).

[159] *Dudo*, p. 39.

[160] *Dudo*, p. 71.

[161] *Dudo*, p. 74.

[162] *Dudo*, p. 80.

[163] *Dudo*, p. 81.

[164] Jumièges, ii. 10. For his actions, see above, Chapters 2, p. 79 and 6, pp. 324–5.

[165] Jumièges, ii. 122. See also Poitiers, p. 12 for a similar account and above, Chapters 2, pp. 107–9 and 6, p. 326.

Incidentally, Guy seems to have been kept under 'house arrest' at William's court following his submission. It may be supposed that his presence was intended as a deterrent to would-be rebels, and a reminder of the duke's power.[166] Similarly, Count Hugh of Châlons, defeated by the future Duke Richard III in Burgundy between 1017 and 1026, 'promised by an oath that he would give satisfaction to Duke Richard at Rouen',[167] and the greatest English lords were paraded before the assembled Franks and Normans at Fécamp at Easter 1067.[168] Thus the defeat of a foreign foe outside the duchy could be recognized publicly, before a domestic audience, through their public submission at court.

As might be expected, the narratives indicate that such petitions continued to be made into the later eleventh and twelfth centuries. Orderic, for example, tells us that in 1079, during Robert Curthose's first rebellion, the Norman *proceres* tried to make peace between father and son. He put a speech into their mouths: 'we humbly approach your mighty presence, great king, begging you to lend a propitious ear to our entreaties.' They begged for his mercy and asked him to pardon his son.[169] In 1087, Count Robert of Mortain petitioned the dying King William for his brother's release from captivity. He 'begged for mercy for his brother in person and through his friends, and wearied the dying man with his entreaties'.[170] In 1091, Orderic tells us that Robert of Bellême, unable to defeat his neighbours alone, 'placated the duke of the Normans with promises, and humbly entreated and begged him to come to his aid against his rivals'.[171] After Henry I's victory at Tinchebray, Ranulf Flambard, who held Lisieux at that time, 'sent messengers hurrying to the king when he was elated by his recent victory, to sue humbly for peace'.[172] Henry pardoned Ranulf, and the city of Lisieux was surrendered to him. In contrast, Henry remained implacable to Count William of Mortain, Robert of Etoutteville, and others, 'and although many persons tried to temper his severity with petitions and promises and gifts he could never be persuaded to relent'.[173] Following the death of William Clito in 1128, Henry 'received the rebels who renounced their rash defiance and humbly sought his mercy, and with shrewd graciousness agreed to be reconciled with them'.[174] Orderic's narrative, then,

---

[166]   Some evidence for his presence at court into the 1050s is found in *RADN*, nos. 107, 113, 131. A further act of *c.* 1059 is a forgery (*RADN*, no. 142).

[167]   Jumièges, ii. 38. For the date of the campaign see p. 39, n. 1.

[168]   Poitiers, pp. 178–80; Orderic, ii. 196–8.

[169]   Orderic, iii. 110.

[170]   Orderic, iv. 98.

[171]   Orderic, iv. 232.

[172]   Orderic, vi. 142.

[173]   Orderic, vi. 94.

[174]   Orderic, vi. 378–80.

would suggest that even in the middle of the twelfth century men still petitioned the dukes, and indeed their own lords, too, when they wanted patronage, justice, or forgiveness, and did so in a far more elaborate manner than those who wanted only confirmations of their charters. That was perhaps appropriate. The humility of the petition was fitted to the request. Pardon for political sins, or a large favour, naturally required greater humility and deference than a request that the duke should confirm a gift to a Church.

Charters and competition at the dukes' courts

As the preceding review indicates, the narratives tend to depict the duke very much at the centre of his court, in absolute uncontested control of proceedings, dispensing patronage, making laws, and doing justice with his subjects' counsel and consent, rarely opposed but on those occasions when it happened always winning the argument. In contrast, the ducal *acta* paint a much more nuanced picture, and one that includes a lot more in the way of a subtle competition for credit and sometimes even power waged between the duke, the beneficiary, the donor, and attendant prelates.

The duke did begin with some advantages, however. The imperative to journey to the court revealed that the duke's confirmation was felt to be important to the beneficiary, and thus also said something about their perception of the effectiveness of ducal authority.[175] Gifts needed to be protected from rapacious *milites* or heirs discontented at the diminution of their inheritance, and the best guarantee was the duke's sign at the foot of the parchment recording the donation. As one act for the monks of La Trinité-du-Mont put it, 'so that no one should be able to contradict this sale, and so that no challenge should be able to exist, it was corroborated by the sign and authority of William *princeps* of the Normans'.[176] Similarly, an act of Herbert fitz Geoffrey for the monks of Troarn recorded all his donations, 'all of which I wished to be written down together in this charter and according to the custom to be made firm by the authority of the aforesaid king and to be strengthened by the subscription of my lords and other faithful men, so that by this our donation of the aforesaid things should be stable and settled and safe from and undisturbed by the assault of faithless men'.[177] But in this case, although Herbert had made the journey to the royal duke's court to obtain his sign, William's authority nonetheless openly competed with that of Herbert's lords, who no doubt included Roger of Montgommery.

[175] See also above, Chapter 6, pp. 341, 358–62.
[176] *RADN*, no. 200.
[177] *Regesta: William*, no. 282; Tabuteau, *Transfers*, p. 157.

The sign was what counted. Where it was applied was much less important. Beneficiaries wanted these documents at their own convenience and by the 1060s they were not prepared to wait. The monks of Marmoutier could not even wait until William had reached his lodgings for the night. Most likely in the autumn of 1081 they had him sign their charter while he was halted in the open air at Bénouville.[178] The duke was thus deprived of a formal occasion on which to act as a patron of one of the greatest monasteries in Francia. But, still, the monks had to cover a lot of ground to arrive at the duke's carpet, and the distance that beneficiaries were prepared to travel highlighted the importance of obtaining the duke's confirmation to the beneficiary and also to those who had been asked to travel with its representative. That sense of importance could only have been increased if the need to find the duke took beneficiaries and their witnesses into the middle of a war zone, regardless of the relative informality of the courts held in such circumstances.

Furthermore, the presence of saddle-sore, weary, hungry, thirsty, inconvenienced beneficiaries at the court would have reminded those already there of the duke's position as fount of patronage and justice, and of the geographical extent of his authority and connections. That would have been the case even in small and informal courts, making them suitable venues for the celebration of the political order, despite Koziol's suggestion to the contrary. Those who had travelled to the court as escorts or to act as witnesses, and who were not regular attendees at such gatherings, would have noted their lord's deference to the duke, the size of the duke's court, the importance of those in attendance, and the number of household knights. This was a chance, then, for the duke to awe rear-vassals and local men who would otherwise have remained entirely outside his direct experience – especially if he did not itinerate much or widely.[179] As Orderic's account of the siege of Shrewsbury in 1102 suggests, it was men like these, who stood a step or two below the great lords, who might have had the most sympathy with the dukes' attempts to maintain order in the duchy, especially if that meant curbing the arbitrary power of those greater lords.[180] They were, then, an important constituency, whose support might prove to be vital if the chips ever went down.

However, while we see beneficiaries from across the duchy, and indeed from

[178] *Regesta: William*, no. 201.

[179] For a discussion of the dukes' itineraries, and the dominant place of Rouen, see below, Chapter 9, pp. 506–24.

[180] Orderic, vi. 26. The capitulary *De Villis* noted, in a similar vein, that *maiores* should be chosen from among the middling ranks of men and not from the *potentiores*, as they 'are faithful' (*De Villis*, ch. 60, printed in *Capitularia Regum Francorum*, 2, ed. Boreti and Krause, *MGH, Leges*, p. 88; noted in Nelson, 'Kingship and royal government', p. 410).

outside it, approaching the duke, they did not come from *everywhere*. Some local loyalties and local ties resisted the attempts of every duke to establish their supremacy. For example, if we look at those who brought their charters and complaints before Henry I, whose rule went wider and deeper than even his father's had done, they tend overwhelmingly to be the bishops and canons of the Norman cathedrals and the monks of the royal duke's own abbeys. On occasion, monks who had temporarily come under his sway, or had been offered a confirmation they couldn't refuse, appeared at his court, too. But there were many who apparently never bothered to go, and their absence from the record cannot always be put down to the destruction of the relevant archives. Such absentees included the monks of Saint-Martin of Sées (at least for their Norman lands); Saint-Sever-Calvados; Saint-Sauveur-le-Vicomte; Fontenay; La Croix-Saint-Leufroy; Cormeilles; Grestain; Foucarmont; Eu; and Le Tréport. Getting beneficiaries to court in the first place, then, was more of a struggle for the dukes than might be expected. Not only did a duke have to compete with the desires of patrons and beneficiaries to promote their authority and deeds at his expense, he also had to contend with local loyalties and the limits placed on his practical authority by the vested interests of the great families of his duchy.

Unlike in England, where diplomas and writs would be drawn up by royal scribes at court, Norman and Frankish would-be beneficiaries generally came to the dukes' courts armed with prepared acts, that wanted only the duke's *signum* and those of the other witnesses, throughout the eleventh century. That began to change during the reign of Henry I, when some charters were drafted by the scribes of the royal duke's writing office, but beneficiary production did not die out altogether in the duchy until after 1144. Many of these soon-to-be ducal acts – a significant proportion of them before 1026, and the great majority of them after that date – were brief and business-like documents. Their brevity infers a confidence in the duke, his power, and his ability to ensure that the gifts in question remained secure. They also suggest that writing was a matter of routine, with charters comprising a collection of boilerplate formulations, uncluttered in style and practical in function. Their quiet message is important, and should not be forgotten during the following discussion which will focus not on these typical acts but on the untypical minority.

The scribes who wrote these atypical acts were, by their more elaborate formulations, making comments on the nature and effectiveness of the duke's power, on contemporary Norman society, and on the work of their abbots, patrons, and protectors. These acts, then, reveal something of the competition for credit and reward that took place at the court in the sight and hearing of all those who would witness the act in question. And many acts do make it clear that the contents had been seen and heard by their witnesses. Indeed, even at Bénouville, when the

Table 7 *Arenga*, petitions to the dukes, and anathema clauses found in ducal *acta*, 996–1135

	Richard II	Robert	William pre-1066	William post-1066	Robert Curthose	Henry I
Arenga	25 (49%)	5 (16%)	22 (16%)	12 (12%)	2 (6%)	7 (5%)
Petition	10 (20%)	6 (19%)	26 (19%)	5 (5%)	2 (6%)	10 (7%)
Anathema	19 (37%)	14 (45%)	38 (28%)	11 (11%)	4 (13%)	5 (3%)

monks of Marmoutier importuned William the Bastard for his confirmation of a document, 'while he was sitting on his carpet between the forester's house and the church', the witnesses 'saw' the act in question.[181]

The following discussion will concentrate on three elements found in these *acta* that do not relate directly to the property being transferred, the addition of which may consequently be supposed to have been the result of a choice made by the person who composed the document. First, some acts begin with an *arenga*, a short homily that might provide information about the history of a dispute concerning the land in question or outline the spiritual motivation for making the gift. Second, and as has been noted already, there might occasionally be a reference to a petition made to the duke. Thirdly, an anathema clause might call down divine punishment on any who violated the grant. Some of these clauses were elaborately worded, and must have provided a dramatic conclusion to the recitation of these documents. These three elements can tell us about the actions of beneficiaries and donors, the tone of the court, and way that acts might be used there and in the regions to promote the duke's rule or justify his actions. But they also offer something of a political commentary on perceptions of the duke's power, and the weaknesses that beneficiaries felt obliged to make up for in other ways.

As Table 7 illustrates, 49 per cent of Richard II's surviving *acta* have an *arenga* compared to 16 per cent of Robert the Magnificent's and those that William the Bastard issued before 1066.[182] After the Conquest, only 12 per cent of William's Norman acts had an *arenga*, and only 5 per cent of Henry I's. It is also the case that the *arengae* of Richard II's acts are generally longer than those found in later ones. Those whose careers spanned the reigns of Richard II and Robert the Magnificent might thus have noticed a difference in the atmosphere at court when ducal *acta* were recited. At the same time, they would have been as hard pressed as we are to observe or perceive general trends, as some beneficiaries, such as the monks

---

[181] *Regesta: William*, no. 201.1

[182] My figures disagree with those provided by Koziol, *Begging Pardon*, pp. 139–40 because he omitted subscriptions and *notitia*. My interpretation of these documents is for the most part also at variance with that found in Koziol's book.

of Saint-Ouen, La Trinité-du-Mont, or Caen had rarely added *arengae* to their acts at any time, whereas the monks of other houses such as Saint-Wandrille or Marmoutier did so frequently, even into the 1060s. It is likely that the succinct and secular model provided by acts drafted by the English writing office had some effect on the wording of beneficiary-produced Norman *acta* after 1066, but there might have been other influences acting to this same end, too, even if they evade detection for now.

For the most part the passages that introduce the duke's grants or the gifts that he confirmed were similar to those found at the head of acts recording the grants of even quite lowly knights. For the most part they noted the spiritual benefits that would be awarded to those who made donations to churches, or else remarked that the gift was being committed to writing to preserve an accurate record in case of future dispute.[183]

Such wording was included for the beneficiary's benefit. It is likely that the inclusion of *arengae* that spoke of the spiritual benefits to be gained by making a gift to a church, or that reminded laymen of their responsibility to protect the Church and its possessions, was intended to remind potential claimants that a later dispute over the property would imperil both the donor's and the challenger's souls. Where such *arengae* head the long diplomas confirming the grants that the dukes had made, for example, to the monks of Fécamp or Jumièges, it may be that they were inserted not only to remind the duke of his obligation to maintain the grant, but also to remind the duke's *fideles* of the spiritual benefits that accrued, perhaps in the hope that it would stave off complaints that the duke should have used those lands to reward them instead.[184] Wording about the need to commit the donation to writing not only justified the creation of the charter, but also undermined the testimony of witnesses who might attempt to limit or reverse the donation in the future. Clearly, that was to the beneficiary's advantage, too.[185]

The fact that Norman ducal diplomas were almost always drafted by their beneficiaries means that the *arengae* do not usually set out an ideology of rulership or a justification for actions past or present as was the case, in contrast, with the diplomas of the Emperor Henry IV, the Norman kings of Sicily, and the Anglo-Saxon kings of the English.[186] Only three of the surviving examples, all of them

[183] See, for example, *RADN*, nos. 13, 16, 17, 18, 29, 32, 43, 44, 45, 47, 85.
[184] For example, *RADN*, nos. 4, 9, 31, 34, 36.
[185] For a discussion of this wording see Tabuteau, *Transfers*, pp. 212–19.
[186] I. S. Robinson, *Henry IV of Germany, 1056–1106* (Cambridge, 1999), p. 12; H. Enzensberger, 'Chanceries, charters and administration in Norman Italy', in *The Society of Norman Italy*, ed. G. A. Loud and A. Metcalfe (Leiden, 2002), pp. 141–5; C. Insley, 'Where did all the charters go? Anglo-Saxon charters and the new politics of the eleventh century', *ANS*, 24 (2002), 111–20.

found in acts that must have been produced at the duke's behest, relate to what today would be labelled 'policy'. Two of them are the acts establishing the dower for Judith and Adela, both of which begin with *arengae* that wax lyrical about the virtues of Christian marriage.[187] This might have been especially relevant at a time when Normans still took wives *more Danico*, as the dukes concerned might have needed to explain their actions to some of their influential subjects. Dudo's account of the succession of Richard II, discussed above, also suggests that this was the case.[188] At the same time, it is likely that the ecclesiastical draftsman would have wanted to take the opportunity to promote this sacrament, too. The third exception is found in Richard II's act recording the resignation of Abbot Mainard of Mont-Saint-Michel in 1009. This document begins with a statement concerning the care of the Church, which might have been intended to stave off any suggestion – probably from members of the local audience in the Avranchin rather than those at Richard's court – that his actions were politically motivated, or to prevent a hostile reception of the new abbot.[189] These examples suggest that the duke needed to convince at least some of his subjects that he was taking the right course of action and that he was, therefore, on the defensive.

In other cases, beneficiary drafting ensured that the few politically motivated *arenga* did not celebrate the duke's power so much as reprimand him (sometimes posthumously) for his inappropriate rapaciousness and injustice, or excuse and explain what some of his subjects might have seen as mistaken actions. The monastic scribes might even go so far as to take the opportunity to teach the dukes about what was expected of a Christian ruler. For example, Robert the Magnificent was not averse to alienating the possessions of the monasteries of his duchy and giving them to his knights. When these were recovered, the successful community might publicly reprimand him for his actions. The *arenga* of one such act, drafted by the monks of Fécamp, runs:

> I Robert by the grace of God duke of the Normans wish it to be known to our *fideles* as much of the present as of the future that, persuaded by certain of our counsellors, who were not justly looking after the Church of God, I had

---

[187] *RADN*, nos. 11 and 58.
[188] See above, Chapter 6, pp. 316–17.
[189] *RADN*, no. 12. The *arenga* constitutes one enormous sentence in Fauroux's edition. The sort of reception Hildebert might have hoped to avoid met Abbot Osbern when he was elected to Saint-Evroult in place of the exiled Abbot Robert of Grandmesnil (Orderic ii. 90–8). In the event, the words of the *arenga*, as well as Richard's power, apparently saved him from the problems that a later imposed abbot, Suppo, suffered. His alienation of the abbey's property attracted the hostility of his monks and he resigned his abbacy in 1048 (Potts, *Monastic Revival*, p. 101 and n. 112).

transferred to certain of our knights possessions of the monastery of the Holy Trinity. But touched, truly, by respect for God, when I entered the period of young manhood, with His mercy operating in me, the understanding of my mind soon realized that I had not done well, and so I have restored to the aforesaid church entirely those villages that they stole, and I decree them with all authority to have been restored in perpetuity.[190]

Another example is provided by the act for the monks of Jumièges that records Roger of Montgommery's restitution of their market at Vimoutiers:

Rule over the realm of the Normans, with the aid of the clemency of Christ, was manfully wielded by the great Duke Richard ... And he, as we believe, rising to the heavenly kingdom, his son of the same name, Richard, obtained the principality. But surprised by swift death, he relinquished it by hereditary right to his brother Robert, who by the counsel of perverse men, did not worship with love the Church of God as his father had done. And certainly I, Roger, perceiving this and exceeding the malice of all evildoers, instigated by the Devil against God, myself showered on <the monks> of St Peter of Jumièges innumerable ills, taking away by force their goods. Among the other things that I took from them, I destroyed the market that was at Vimoutiers, and I established my own at Montgommery. But afterwards this same count, touched by the piety of God and penitent of his evil works, removed it and restored the market in its original place.[191]

These *arengae* set the scene for the transfer or restitution of property recorded in the act, but they were a reminder of the obligations of good rulership, and the lesson was provided in the hope that it would prevent the same problem from arising in the future. Æthelred II of the English wanted to cry when he was reprimanded for his youthful follies in a similar fashion.[192] Robert's reactions are not recorded – the acts had already been written so there was no opportunity to record his response – but the atmosphere might have become tense as these words were read. Perhaps that was a calculated manipulation of emotions by the monks.

---

[190] *RADN*, no. 70.

[191] *RADN*, no. 74.

[192] The point is made expressly by L. Roach, 'Penitential discourse in the diplomas of King Æthelred "the Unready"', *Journal of Ecclesiastical History*, 64 (2013), 262–3. This series of restitutions made by Æthelred is most recently discussed by Roach, and also by Keynes, *Diplomas*, pp. 176–86; P. Stafford, 'Political ideas in late tenth-century England: charters as evidence', in *Law, Laity and Solidarities: Essays in Honour of Susan Reynolds*, ed. P. Stafford, J. L Nelson, and J. Martindale (Manchester, 2001), pp. 68–82.

The hope that the grants would remain intact from that time on rested, in part, on the duke remembering his discomfiture as he was harangued before his greatest subjects by those same monks who sought his confirmation.

That brings us to the second element to be discussed, namely the record of petitions found in the dukes' acts. Geoffrey Koziol's study of the petitions found in Frankish *acta* led him to observe that 'the arabesque phrases of condescension of princely diplomas ... were most pronounced in the early stages of the process by which a given dynasty established its power, since it was then that its members most needed to cloak their authority in an aura of majesty'.[193] His discussion of the petitionary language found in a selection of the Norman ducal *acta* issued between 996 and 1066 linked the use of such language with a recognition of the legitimacy of Richard II – 'the first count of Rouen ... to be taken seriously by the Franks as something more than a pirate' – and the 'political fragmentation' of the duchy that he saw occurring during the reign of Robert the Magnificent and minority of William the Bastard.[194] He concluded that the record of such petitions reflected the political situation pertaining at the time each act was made. Thus, their resurgence during the rule of Robert the Magnificent suggested 'that the duke was falling back on an image of authority as the legitimacy of his rule was being questioned and the reality of power was being stripped from him'.[195]

In fact, if all the ducal *acta* are considered, the proportion of them including words that recalled the petitions, humble or otherwise, of a donor or beneficiary that resulted in the ducal confirmation of their grant by the duke slowly fell over the years to 1066, from 20 per cent under Richard II to 16 per cent under William the Bastard before 1066. After the Conquest, however, it plummeted to just 5 per cent for the period 1066–87 and 6 per cent for the period 1106–35. The large drop in the proportion of petitions recorded in post-Conquest acts is unexpected. As William's new status enhanced both his power and his prestige, it is surprising that beneficiaries did not put on record more visible displays of deference. Instead, we have fewer.

Koziol's conclusions thus need rethinking, at least so far as Normandy is concerned. To begin with, there is a striking absence of elaborate petitions in Norman ducal *acta*, and only one could be said to have utilized arabesque phrases. This one is Dudo of Saint-Quentin's autobiographical account of his requests for Richard II's patronage:

---

[193] Koziol, *Begging Pardon*, p. 50.
[194] Koziol, *Begging Pardon*, p. 271.
[195] Koziol, *Begging Pardon*, p. 273. This view of Robert's reign is somewhat different from the one presented here, see above, Chapter 2, pp. 96–105.

Wherefore let it be known to all present and future men of Normandy and to my successors that Dudo, canon of Saint-Quentin, the precious martyr of Christ, and our *fidelis*, came to me who am called Richard, son of the glorious Count Richard, and, though unworthy, by the grace of the supreme, divine and undivided Trinity duke and patrician of the Normans, beseeching through Count Rodulf, my uncle, and with many and repeated supplications of his own, that I would grant the churches which my abovesaid father gave him as a benefice to the precious martyr of Christ Quentin for the salvation of my father's soul and of mine. Approving and assenting to his most humble petitions and sincere requests I grant to the above written martyr Quentin those same churches located in the county of Caux.[196]

For the most part, records of petitions are more restrained in their language and omit mention of the duke's majesty or clemency and of the petitioner's humility. They could certainly not be described as liturgical entreaties. One act of 1017 × 1023 reads as follows: 'I Richard, duke and *princeps* of the Normans, son of the elder Richard, at the request of certain of my knights, namely Gunduin and Rotscelin his brother, grant to St Ouen and his servants that which they possessed in Auzouville-sur-Ry and the little villages roundabout by right of inheritance.'[197] Similarly, an act dating from 1061 has: 'I William, by the grace of God duke of the whole of Normandy, asked in many ways by Abbot Ranulf of the monastery of the blessed Archangel Michael, which is on the mount which was of old called Tumba, grant to the same place the mill of the vill called Vains.'[198] The abbess of Montivilliers is said simply to have begged (*deprecatione*) William to confirm her abbey's possessions in 1068 × 1076.[199] This brevity is much more typical of Norman ducal *acta* than Dudo's obsequious language or the phrases employed by the monks of Saint-Wandrille or Fleury.[200]

Petitions were made to the duke before the diploma or charter was authenticated. If petitions had been made after that point and subsequently recorded, they would have to have been added in a different hand or a different ink below the body of the text, and with one or two exceptions this is not what we see where

---

[196]   *RADN*, no. 18.
[197]   *RADN*, no. 24.
[198]   *RADN*, no. 148.
[199]   *Regesta: William*, no. 212.
[200]   *RADN*, no. 69 (Saint-Wandrille); *Regesta: William*, no. 251. These two acts include probably the second and third most elaborate petitions found in Norman ducal *acta*. It is likely that the act for Saint-Wandrille was based on an earlier Carolingian model, as its wording to some extent echoes that of an act of Louis the Pious for the Carolingian community (Lot, *Saint-Wandrille*, no. 4).

originals survive.[201] At small informal gatherings, those making petitions would have been remarked upon and observed. The monks of Marmoutier importuned William the Bastard not just at Bémouville but also while he was at dinner with two other people at La Hougue.[202] The duke's fellow diners, at least, were clearly aware of what was happening. They are said to have heard the grant, and one who spoke up against the gift was silenced only when the duke threatened – probably jokingly – to strike him with a pig's shoulder blade that was to hand. If a petition were made at a full court, however, it is possible that the humble entreaties of supplicants would have been missed by almost all of those present. The humble attitude adopted – head bowed and arms outstretched – if anything more than a *topos*, might have been easily overlooked in a court full of men making obeisance to the duke.[203] We know nothing about court etiquette, but it must be supposed that if petitioners really did act out their supplication, protocols were in place whereby they were announced and then enacted their petition before the assembled throng. The *Inventio et miracula sancti Vulfrani* recounts such a petition being made before Richard I and his *fideles*, but as the process shaded into a form of lawsuit it might not have been typical.[204] The Bayeux Tapestry perhaps suggests such a protocol, too, albeit in scenes unrelated to the granting of lands or rights to religious communities.[205] Orderic also provided an account of how Abbot Mainer, his prior, and William Pantulf (a donor) went to Roger of Montgommery 'and humbly requested him to confirm his knight's gifts with his charter. And since he was just and generous he favoured their lawful request and granted what they asked in the presence of all who were assembled in his court at that time to transact various kinds of business.'[206] If this is a reference to the petition rather than to the subsequent issue of the act, Orderic's words provide some evidence to

---

[201] In addition, it seems to have been unusual enough to warrant comment even in acts that survive only as copies. Thus an act for the monks of Saint-Florent concerning lands in Wales and England notes the addition of a gift that had not been discussed with the king in advance (*Regesta: William*, no. 268).

[202] Jumièges, ii. 10; *RADN*, no. 151 and *Regesta: William*, no. 200; *Regesta: William*, no. 201, respectively.

[203] Koziol, *Begging Pardon*, p. 60. That this was a stereotypical attitude of supplication is suggested by the Bayeux Tapestry (scenes 12 and 25) and also by the appearance of Muslims submitting to Robert Guiscard in a similar way, with heads bowed and arms crossed (Amatus of Montecassino, *The History of the Normans by Amatus of Montecassino*, trans. P. N. Dunbar and revised by G. A. Loud (Woodbridge, 2004), p. 141). The widespread use of this or similar postures suggests an ideal, and raises the possibility of a disconnection from reality.

[204] *Inventio*, p. 30.

[205] Bayeux Tapestry, scenes 9, 12, 25.

[206] Orderic, iii. 158.

support the suggestion that petitions were indeed heard and answered before an attentive audience, rather than lost amid the hubbub of the court.

In any event, it is clear that ducal acts frequently omit to mention petitions when they had been made. Indeed, every ducal confirmation must have been organized in advance, even if only by a few minutes, which would have necessitated a petition of some sort, even if limited to something along the lines of 'please will you authenticate this act for us?' In a few instances, we can see that this is precisely what happened, that a petition was made but that all mention of it was omitted from the act in question. For example, in 1113, King Henry I commanded the monks of Saint-Evroult to draw up a general confirmation of all their property, which he subsequently authenticated at Rouen. There is no mention of a petition being made in the text of the act, but Orderic tells us that it was Robert of Meulan who suggested to Henry that the monks should be told to draw up a charter listing their possessions for confirmation, in other words that he made a petition on their behalf.[207] This was of course all the more likely to occur once the writing office scribes began to draft Norman acts. Thus, some years earlier, in England, the monks of Abingdon had petitioned William Rufus for the grant of property at Sutton, and had paid £20 for the grant. William's act, however, reveals none of this. The writ-charter itself states only that the king had 'given to the church of St Mary at Abingdon and to Abbot Rainald and his monks the church of Sutton with its lands and tithes and customs as the foresaid church well had them in my father's time'.[208]

Norman draftsmen thus made a choice about whether or not to include a reference to a petition in an act. That such a record was not included as a matter of course suggests that, when they did include them, draftsmen were not primarily motivated by a desire to show deference to the duke. Reference to a petition thus served a different function.[209] A clue as to the actual intention is provided by an act that records a gift to the monks of Saint-Ouen made by a certain Emma. It survives as an original. The text is written in one hand. The *signa*, which include that

---

[207] Orderic, vi. 174.

[208] *Historia Ecclesie Abbendonensis: The History of the Church of Abingdon*, ed. and trans. J. Hudson, 2 vols (Oxford, 2002–07), ii. 36.

[209] Geoffrey Koziol argued that: 'petitioners beseeched the count's intervention with all the humility that was fitting for God's protector of earthly order. As for the count, as a ruler by the grace of God he had to fulfil his own obligations to God. Most prominent among them was his duty to use his authority in the service of the divine institutions he protected, insofar as they showed due respect by petitioning acts from him' (Koziol, *Begging Pardon*, p. 55 and also, p. 103). I would not disagree with the main thrust of this argument – that dukes were required to act as good lords by protecting and promoting the Church in their duchy – but my view on *why* petitions were recorded in *acta* is thus diametrically opposed to his.

of Richard II, are added in a second hand in a much lighter ink. Under the *signa*, a third hand added the following wording: 'And all of these abovesaid things for the remedy of his soul, and for that of my husband and for the absolution of my soul, the aforesaid count Richard, at my humble prayer, gave to the monks of the saints Peter the apostle of God and his glorious confessor Ouen, namely on the condition that you monks, as much of the present as of the future, shall have our memory continually in their prayers.'[210] The layout of the act suggests that Emma had made her grant and obtained the duke's confirmation of it before taking the act to the monks at Saint-Ouen. The final addition to Emma's act looks as though it is a more or less verbatim record of her delivery of the act to the monks (suggested also by the 'my husband' and the 'you monks'). As Duke Richard never saw or heard this record of her petition, it was clearly not written down for his benefit. Instead, it was recorded so that Emma's role in making the gift and obtaining the duke's consent to it could be highlighted, applauded, and rewarded.

A second example is found in an act by which William the Bastard augmented the possessions of the monks of Saint-Père of Chartres in Brullemail in 1050 × 1060.

> I William, count of Normandy, make known to everybody living in my county the act that I, thinking it might be lost, have narrated in the below-written account. There is in our parts a certain vill which is called Brullemail, given of old to the founders of the monastery of St Peter the apostle of Chartres, which monastery of St Peter is situated in the suburb of the city of Chartres. From this place, then, a certain monk called Geoffrey, coming to us, asked me to give to St Peter the judicial power of the said vill, which I, through the gift of God, had among other things hitherto possessed there through the luck of inheritance. Hoping therefore that a relaxation of my sins would be due to me as a result, through the power granted to St Peter by the redeemer, I consented to the petitions of Landric, abbot of that monastery, and of all the brethren, which the said monk had told us about at their command.[211]

Again, the petition was recorded not to highlight the duke's role or favour, but rather to celebrate the work of Abbot Landric and his community.[212] There is no sense of deference or humility here. William was fortunate to be count, and owed

---

[210] *RADN*, no. 43. Note that Fauroux privileged a later version of this act, making this witness 'Abis'. As such, the text is found in the apparatus rather than in the edition m.

[211] *RADN*, no. 146.

[212] And it should be remembered that this is the sort of behaviour celebrated in the *Gesta abbatum* produced at, for example, Saint-Benoit-sur-Loire (*Vita Gauzelini*), Saint-Wandrille (*Inventio*), and St Albans (*Gesta abbatum monasterii sancti Albani*).

his position to the gift of God. The draftsman has made it seem that he was all but obliged to grant the request, even though he did so as part of a *quid pro quo*.

And this, it seems, was the purpose of recording petitions. They were there to celebrate the hard work of an abbot who had recovered property for his abbey, or to show the concern of a donor to secure the transfer of property that he or she had arranged for the benefit of his or her soul, which might be useful if a dispute about the donor's intentions should later arise. Any acknowledgement of, or deference to, ducal power was of secondary importance.

An additional practice of indirectly recording petitions had developed by Henry I's reign. A number of Henry's Norman and English acts end with a clause that reads, for example, 'through (*per*) William of Glastonbury'. Stephanie Mooers Christelow suggested that the formula revealed that 'a message came from the king through (*per*) a trusted individual'.[213] It is equally plausible, however, that such wording recorded a petition for a writ or a charter made by a man – usually someone associated with Henry's household or administration – on behalf of the beneficiary. The name follows on from those of the witnesses because the figure concerned was in a position to act as an additional witness. It is likely that his name was also recorded for financial reasons. It may be that if the beneficiary failed to hand over the money due for the writ, then the person named in the *per* clause became liable for the sum, just as a surety would become liable to pay bail if an accused man failed to appear at court.

So much for petitions. We now turn to the third element to be considered. As with *arengae* and petitions, anathema clauses do not appear in a majority of the ducal *acta* surviving from any reign. The pattern of such clauses in ducal acts suggests that their insertion was related to the willingness or ability of the dukes to do justice.[214] Where the secular power was weak, or where dukes could not be

---

[213] Mooers Christelow, 'A moveable feast?, 190.

[214] Tabuteau, *Transfers*, p. 207 reached the same conclusion. For example, Bishop Geoffrey of Coutances issued a charter just before his death in 1093 which included an anathema clause and 'often had it recited in his presence, and in that of the bishops and abbots who came to visit him while still living'. That suggests that such clauses were felt to be more effective than reliance on ducal justice during the reign of Robert Curthose ('De statu huius ecclesiae', *GC*, xi. Instr. 223–4; Tabuteau, *Transfers*, pp. 206–7). The monks of Mont-Saint-Michel prayed to God for his vengeance to be visited on Thomas of Saint-Jean-le-Thomas, who was close to Henry I, but who had alienated some of their property (*Ctl. Mont-Saint-Michel*, p. 94 (no. 16); Green, *Henry*, p. 239). A contemporary case of 1120 × 1128 saw Robert fitz Bernard, who had burned four houses at Moult (perhaps – the Latin name is 'Meul' or 'Moul') belonging to the abbey of Saint-Etienne of Caen, as well as a grape press and all the grapes during the grape harvest, excommunicated by the abbot and monks. He was thus brought to make a settlement before the bishop of Bayeux (*Ctl. Caen*, fos. 53v–54r). But excommunication did not always work.

relied upon to protect the churches of their duchy, ecclesiastical beneficiaries were more likely to resort to the pronouncement of spiritual punishments on those who might seek to take away the land granted to them. That most likely explains why they reached a peak during the reign of Robert the Magnificent, not because he was a weak duke but because he was an unreliable protector of ecclesiastical property. It also explains why the compiler of the cartulary of Christ Church Canterbury was so free with them in the years around 1080.[215] Where the secular power was stronger and willing to protect church property, beneficiaries might either omit such clauses altogether or add additional wording which linked a secular financial penalty to the ecclesiastical sanction.[216]

With regard to performance and atmosphere, it must have been the case that, when they were included, such ritual pronouncements of anathema and excommunication provided the most liturgical and dramatic aspect of the ceremony by which grants were made or confirmed. On 13 April 1033, for example, the monks of Saint-Wandrille were given the church at Arques-la-Bataille and its dependencies by Robert the Magnificent. The gift was witnessed by a relatively large number of men who were representative of the political community of the whole of the duchy, as well as by King Henry I of the French who had sought refuge at Rouen at the time. After the grant was confirmed, Archbishop Robert of Rouen threatened excommunication on any who attempted to usurp the duke's gift.[217] Archbishop Malger likewise added a lengthy malediction to an act recording a gift that he and his brother, Count William of Arques, had made to the monks of Saint-Ouen (see Fig. 7). As it was written by the same scribe who wrote down the names of the witnesses and not by the scribe who had drawn up the diploma, it would seem that he recorded verbatim the curse that was spoken by Malger when the gift was authenticated, and thus before the assembled witnesses, probably using the parchment that the archbishop had himself read from:

I Malger by the grace of God archbishop, with the authority of holy mother Church which I govern by the wish of God, desire that this description should

The monks of Mont-Saint-Michel excommunicated one individual many times before he finally made a quit-claim with them (*Ctl. Mont-Saint-Michel*, no. 116). For a discussion of anathema clauses more generally see L. K. Little, *Benedictine Maledictions: Liturgical Cursing in Romanesque France* (Ithaca, NY and London, 1993), pp. 30–44.

[215] R. Fleming, 'Christ Church Canterbury's Anglo-Norman cartulary', in *Anglo-Norman Political Culture and the Twelfth-Century Renaissance*, ed. C. W. Hollister (Woodbridge, 1997), pp. 91, 96, 102–3.

[216] *RADN*, nos. 18, 35, 53, 147, 162, 188; *Regesta: William*, nos. 148, 198 (in both of these cases, the clauses do not include true anathemas, but rather warnings about incurring the anger of God).

[217] *RADN*, no. 69.

be ratified in every way, and also by the sign of the holy cross that I write below, and I command that my name and those of our faithful men should be imprinted on it. And so that this grant shall remain firm and inviolate through severity, that if anyone shall take away anything from this donation – and, we believe, even if it shall have been only minimal opposition to it – he shall be subject to this curse which is set out below: He shall be cursed by all the power of God; by the curse by which the Devil and his angels are cursed into eternal fire. The holy Mary the Mother of God curses him; that he shall have no share with the elect placed to the right of God, but with justice he shall be placed to the left. St Michael curses him, with all the orders of angels. St John the Baptist curses him, and all the patriarchs and prophets. St Peter curses him with the other apostles. St Stephen curses him with the other martyrs. St Ouen curses him with all the confessors of Christ. St Agnes curses him with all the virgins. All the curses with which one can be cursed shall come upon him, with Cain, Dathan and Abiron, Antiochus, Herod, Pontius Pilate, Judas the betrayer of the Lord, Nero, Simon Magus, Diocletian, Maximian, and Decius. He shall have his share with those of all iniquity in the inferno below, where the fire does not go out and the heat does not die. The days shall do to him dread and evil. And … he shall appear before the eyes of men as the worst and basest. And in the future his light shall be extinguished and his name shall be deleted from the book of life. Amen. Amen. Fiat.[218]

The pronouncement of this lengthy curse must have been very dramatic. Indeed, it probably stole the show, leaving the duke's own previous confirmation rather in the shade.

That Duke William at least saw such liturgical drama as undermining his own position is suggested by his subsequent interventions. At Christmas 1054, in the cathedral at Rouen, 'Count William made the said bishops pronounce excommunication before the altar of St Mary on those who should prepare to violate this donation, or who wished to take from the monks of St Michael any part of this gift, or to molest the possessions of St Michael on account of this gift'.[219] At some time between 1066 and 1077, William confirmed a gift to the monks of Saint-Ouen at Rouen. The text ends with a report that 'at our request and at the command of King William, Lord Maurilius and Bishop Hugh of Lisieux damned such robbers with the sentence of anathema'.[220] Here, then, even if God's curse was called down

---

[218] AD S-M, 14 H 189. The anathema clause is not printed in Fauroux's edition of the act (*RADN*, no. 112) which she dated to between 1037 and 1048.

[219] *RADN*, no. 133.

[220] *Regesta: William*, no. 244.

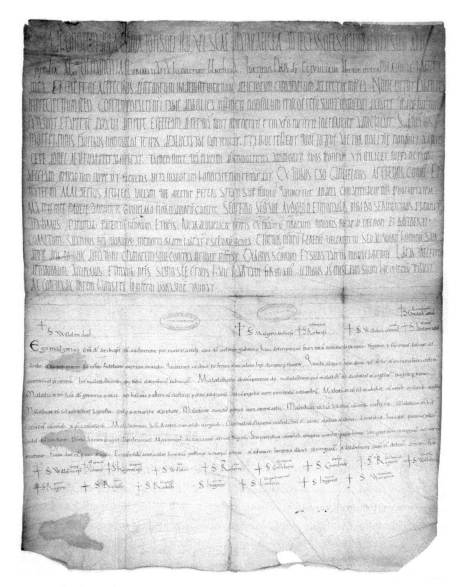

Fig. 7 Malger's anathema, added to the foot of his brother's donation to Saint-
Wandrille, itself confirmed by Duke William (AD Seine-Maritime, 14H189)
(© AD Seine-Maritime)

on those who attacked the donation, Duke William had ensured that there was
still room for him to play a role by commanding the anathema to be declared.
Such commands suggested that the Church acted at William's order and thereby
upheld his God-given authority, rather than diminishing or replacing it. Such

commands were thus a way to take ownership of such clauses in a manner that benefited the duke as much as the beneficiary.[221]

William's post-Conquest acts include far fewer anathema clauses than his pre-Conquest ones, probably reflecting his enhanced status and greater authority as king and the correspondingly increased confidence in the strength of his commands and protection. Henry I's Norman acts include an anathema clause even more rarely. Such clauses were replaced by formulae which made play with the corroborative power of William's and Henry's royal authority, apparently at the expense of a divine sanction.[222] That perhaps reflected the enhanced status and greater authority of a duke who was also a king, although it is equally possible that Norman and French beneficiaries were influenced by wider trends. Perhaps because of the 'Gregorian' reform, perhaps because of the practices of the English writing office, perhaps because of developing ideas about law, justice, and the evidentiary value of charters,[223] or perhaps for other reasons entirely, anathema clauses seem to have been becoming less common across Europe generally. This trend was noted by Arthur Giry as long ago as 1894, and can be seen in Catalonian and Portuguese acts as well as Norman ones.[224] That does not mean to say that Norman religious would not excommunicate or curse those who invaded or destroyed their property in the twelfth century, only that they resorted to such sanction only *after* the event and only *after* ducal justice had failed to remedy it.

So far as the strength of the duke's power was concerned, this discussion suggests that less was more in ducal acts. The absence of an *arenga*, petitionary language, and an anathema clause revealed the duke's authority, simply because the draftsman was unconcerned to employ alternative and additional methods of assurance. The duke's corroboration was enough. But even where these clauses were included, and the duke's authority was therefore in competition with divine sanction and protection, he was placed at centre stage when the time came to corroborate and sign (or seal) the act, regardless of the words in the act, or the venue, or the number of witnesses present.

Even in the most informal of settings, there might have been some performance in the handing over of the act to highlight the transfer from donor or beneficiary to duke. One of Roger of Montgommery's acts, for example, states that he 'put his charter into the hands of the duke', which suggests that he literally handed over the document, symbolizing the transfer of the responsibility for protection of

---

[221] See also Tabuteau, *Transfers*, pp. 206–7 and also below, Chapter 8, pp. 502–3.

[222] For example, *Regesta: William*, nos. 245, 282, 284; *NI*, p. 307 (no. 22); *Regesta*, ii. 360–1 (no. ccvi); 378 (no. cclxx); *Monasticon*, vi¹. 1113.

[223] See below, Chapter 8, pp. 464–7, 497–500.

[224] Little, *Benedictine Maledictions*, pp. 54–5.

the gift to the duke.[225] Before the witnesses, who had perhaps already been mar-shalled into a hierarchical order by this stage in the proceedings, the duke stepped forward to add his cross to the foot of the parchment. It may be that this crucial moment was extended or that the duke took the opportunity to utter some words. While he sometimes added a cross by his own hand, at other times he may simply have made a sign of the cross in the air. This action might then be reflected in the non-autograph crosses that end so many apparently authentic single sheets. The words spoken at this time, which made the purpose of the duke's actions clear, might have reflected the wording commonly found in diplomas, which state that the duke had made his sign with his own hand so that the gift should remain firm in perpetuity, although these were written before the event and so do not provide a verbatim record of what was actually said.

The application of a ring or seal would have provided another opportunity for political theatre. Indeed, by the reign of Henry I it would have been the highlight of the ritual, especially when, as was often the case, the royal duke did not sign or witness an act himself.[226] We have two acts of Robert the Magnificent which state that he had authenticated them by the impression of his ring (*anulus*).[227] Around 1040, William the Bastard corroborated an act for La Trinité-du-Mont 'by his own hand with his seal (*sigillo*)', which might indicate a similar practice, but probably means that he made his *signum* on the parchment.[228] This is indicated by another act for the monks of La Trinité-du-Mont, this time of 1060 × 1066, which states that each of the witnesses 'sigillum subscripserunt' on the altar.[229] If they were 'writing' their seal, then the word can only have been used as a synonym for *signum*. That further explains why a donor such as Landric Aculeus, well below the social level of a man who might be expected to have had a seal in this period, might be said to have had a *sigillum*.[230] It is not, then, clear that the dukes had a seal before 1066, and the most recent work on the subject would concur with that conclusion.[231] And although it is likely that William the Bastard did use his seal in

---

[225] *RADN*, no. 227.

[226] See above, Chapter 5, p. 293, Table 6.

[227] *RADN*, nos. 61, 90. According to Fauroux, the Carolingian chancery used the word to describe a seal (*RADN*, p. 55). I would hesitate to allow that meaning here. It is more likely that the ring was just that, a signet ring, as used by English and European rulers in stories and sagas (M. Lupoi, *The Origins of the European Legal Order* (Cambridge, 2000), p. 313).

[228] *RADN*, no. 96.

[229] *RADN*, no. 221.

[230] *RADN*, no. 139. Tabuteau also noticed the way that *sigillum* and *signum* might be used as synonyms, but did not reach the conclusions found here (Tabuteau, *Transfers*, p. 221).

[231] See J.-F. Nieus, 'Early aristocratic seals: an Anglo-Norman success story', *ANS*, 38

the duchy after 1066, the evidence is ambiguous, in terms of both the appearance of the surviving originals and the wording of copies.[232] None of William's diplomas appear to have been sealed, and nor does his one likely surviving Norman writ or his sole beneficiary-drafted executive letter. One of his Norman acts does state that it had been signed with his ring,[233] but this seems not to have been a reference to the double-sided great seal that he used when in England. As such, it was only under Henry I that the use of the seal in Normandy became routine, replacing the royal duke's *signum* or name altogether in many cases.

The duke's corroboration, signing, or sealing of the act was the culmination of the process that saw ducal *acta* – as they had now become – authenticated or confirmed. But that was not the end of the matter. Others now also signed or witnessed the document so that the gifts recorded within should become yet more stable, producing the lists discussed above. Cassandra Potts saw these additional signers as evidence for an important change. During the reign of Richard II, the duke's sign alone had been enough to corroborate and secure an act. Under Robert and William, however, the witnesses were required to add their signs, too. Potts interpreted this development as evidence for a weakening of ducal authority, although that argument necessarily sidelines other acts where Richard II had not been the only signer to add a cross, and makes a distinction between the appearance of a cross and the use of a large 'S' for other witnesses.[234] But even if her argument is allowed to stand, another interpretation is possible. As discussed above, developments in the drafting of ducal acts reflected a growth in ducal authority. The additional subscriptions can also be interpreted as part of this same trend. With an increasing reliance on the secular authority of the duke and the other great lords of the duchy to maintain donations, religious houses needed to record the names of guarantees and witnesses to whom they might turn should the grant be challenged in court. Indeed, it is at least arguable that contemporaries saw the grants recorded in ducal acts as henceforth under his protection, and thus under

---

(2016), 101. Crouch, *The Normans*, p. 323 (without reference) stated the contrary view. See also the discussion in *RADN*, at pp. 45–7.

[232] Herman of Tournai had seen it, which might suggest that it was appended to Norman acts, although perhaps he had seen simply seen the original acts for the monks of Ghent that concerned their English possessions (Herman of Tournai, *The Restoration of the Monastery of Saint-Martin of Tournai*, trans. L. H. Nelson (Washington, DC, 1996), p. 29). See on this *Regesta: William*, pp. 102–5.

[233] *Regesta: William*, no. 212: '+ annulus Willelmi ducis Normannorum regis Anglorum.'

[234] Potts, 'The early Norman charters', pp. 31–2, 34, 38. She noted that Richard II's cross was the only one added to *RADN*, nos. 9, 15, 19, 21, 32, 37, 41, 44, and also 23. This is true, but an initial 'S' is placed before the names of the other signers in nos. 15, 19, 21, 32, 37, 44, so that only 9 and 41 truly support her argument. Others besides the duke made the sign of a cross in, for example, *RADN*, no. 43.

his jurisdiction, as will be discussed further in the next chapter.[235] Those who broke the terms of the diploma might therefore find themselves hauled up before the duke in court, and with their name and sign at the bottom of the sheet would be hard-pressed to defend their actions. So the use of witnesses might actually be more coercive than it first appears. They were bound to uphold the duke's grant, whether they wanted to or not, and it may be that some lords tried very hard not to witness acts which confirmed grants they disputed as a result.

The political use of emotions

The atmosphere at court was manipulated by the dukes to their own advantage. The clothes they wore, the feasts that they held, the buildings in which they held them, their generosity to petitioners, and the display of defeated rivals were intended to promote their power. It was an exercise to win hearts and minds. But such displays might excite fear or envy as much as love and joy. Whatever the reaction, emotions of one kind or another lay at the heart of the matter for 'emotions were conductors and manipulators of power'.[236] As such, this final section of the chapter focuses on how the dukes *might* have attempted to use their own emotions, or indeed emotionlessness, to further their power – not least by causing emotional responses in others.

It must be highlighted at the outset of this discussion that it is all but impossible to establish whether the emotions and emotional responses attributed to individuals by eleventh- and twelfth-century narratives had any basis in reality. The work of Gerd Althoff, Richard Barton, Barbara Rosenwein, and others has demonstrated that the emotional responses ascribed to the dukes and other rulers were constructed by men who had not witnessed events at first hand and who wrote about what *should* have happened, rather than what *did* happen, in the light of their Christian or classical learning. They reflected conventions rather than reality, and so do not necessarily provide any evidence whatsoever that an individual actually reacted as we are told that they did, or felt what we are told they felt.[237] Instead, these conventions seem to have resulted in a conventional use of emotional responses to a given situation. When lords were dishonoured, for example, they were made to show grief or anger. Where they failed to show anger at an appropriate point – whether in reality or in the story as it was told –

---

[235] See below, Chapter 8, pp. 464–9.
[236] Barton, 'Emotions and power', 56.
[237] The likely conventions are discussed by S. White, 'The politics of anger', in *Anger's Past: Social Uses of an Emotion in the Middle Ages*, ed. B. H. Rosenwein (Ithaca, NY and London, 1998), pp. 137–9.

then they might be derided for it, or otherwise brought to anger by their friends. If help were required, then a man would approach his own lord or ally dolefully, effectively shaming him into action. Anger would end when peace was made or honour restored. At that stage, a man might even show joy. Joy was thus linked to honour, just as shame was linked with dishonour.[238] Furthermore, as this outline suggests, medieval writers used only a limited range of emotions which tend to comprise anger, grief, shame, love, hatred or enmity, fear, and joy.[239] While the mix of emotions might change depending on contemporary conventions, it is likely that it remained detached from reality.

To gain a better sense of the rules surrounding the use of emotions and emotional responses, and thus of the artificiality of the portraits produced, we can look in a little more detail at the use of anger in our narratives.[240] As anger might also be a vice, the manner in which chroniclers or (rarely in Normandy) draftsmen wrote about that emotion in their narratives or diplomas was necessarily influenced by, and conformed to, the views of writers such as Gregory the Great in his *Moralia in Job*,[241] Alcuin in his *Liber de uirtutibus et uitiis*, or perhaps even Prudentius in his *Psychomachia* – although that work seems not to have been

---

[238] White, 'The politics of anger', pp. 142–4. Orderic followed this pattern, at least in part: see Barton, 'Emotions and power', 52. Barton noted that Orderic did not describe Henry as satisfying his anger when punishing Luke of La Barre, but that was probably because Orderic could not depict Henry as angry here, for fear that it might undermine the justice of the punishment (Barton, 'Emotions and power', 52–3).

[239] White, 'The politics of anger', p. 134; Barton, 'Emotions and power', 47–8.

[240] On anger see, for example, C. S. Jaeger, *The Origins of Courtliness: Civilizing Trends and the Formation of Courtly Ideals, 939–1210* (Philadelphia, 1985); the papers (particularly by by Althoff, White, and Barton) in *Anger's Past*, ed. Rosenwein; the debate between Rosenwein, Airlie, and others in *EME*, 10 (2001); Rosenwein, *Emotional Communities*; Barton, 'Emotions and power', 41–59. On humour see in particular D. Ganz, 'Humour as history in Notker's *Gesta Karoli Magni*' in *Monks, Nuns and Friars in Medieval Society*, ed. E. B. King, J. T. Schaefer, and W. B. Wadley (Sewanee, TN, 1989), pp. 171–83, and the articles found in G. Halsall (ed.), *Humour, History and Politics in Late Antiquity and the Early Middle Ages* (Cambridge, 2002).

[241] The following quotation gives a flavour: 'By Anger wisdom is parted with, so that we are left wholly in ignorance what to do, and in what order to do it; as it is written, 'Anger resteth in the bosom of a fool' [Ecc. 7, 9]; in this way, that it withdraws the light of understanding, while by agitating it troubles the mind. By Anger life is lost, even though wisdom seem to be retained; as it is written, 'Anger destroyeth even the wise' [Prov. 15, 1. LXX]. For in truth the mind being in a state of confusion never puts it in execution, even if it has power to discern anything with good judgment. By Anger righteousness is abandoned, as it is written, 'The wrath of man worketh not the righeousness of God' [Jam. 1, 20]' (Gregory the Great, *Moralia in Job*, Bk. 5, Ch. 78; *Morals in the Book of Job*, trans. Parker, i. 303).

available in Normandy in this period.[242] Those rules meant that good kings could not be angry at particular times because they would have appeared to succumb to vice, to have lost reason, and thus to have acted not as kings but as tyrants. Indeed, Gerd Althoff has argued that from the Carolingian period into the twelfth century, anger was not a kingly virtue, but a sign of weakness, or even the very antithesis of kingship. The result was that in contemporary narratives, kings were moved to grief rather than anger when confronted with injustice or infidelity. From the twelfth century, however, Althoff discerned the development of the idea of just anger which now became more important than clemency in ruler portraits.[243] Kings, therefore, might now get angry, although that royal anger had to be the right type of anger. It had to be zealous anger. This was a distinction again learned from Gregory the Great: 'we must bear in mind with nice discernment that the anger which hastiness of temper stirs is one thing, while that which zeal gives its character to is another. The first is engendered of evil, the second of good.'[244] This is the same sort of anger that Richard Barton has found in the works of Alcuin and Hincmar of Reims, much earlier than Althoff found it, exemplified by God's destruction of Sodom and Gomorrah or Christ's expulsion of the money lenders from the Temple.[245] It is also found in the speech that Orderic put into the mouth of Bishop Serlo of Sées at Carentan in 1105, when the bishop told King Henry to 'be angry to some purpose and, as David, prophet and king, teaches, sin not by taking up arms not for lust for earthly power but the defence of your country'.[246]

As if all of this were not problematic enough, emotional responses might also

[242] See R. Newhauser, *The Treatise on Vices and Virtues in Latin and the Vernacular* (Turnhout, 1993), pp. 97–122, and Rosenwein, *Emotional Communities*, pp. 32–56 for some of the classical texts that influenced medieval writers; G. Nortier, *Les bibliothèques médiévales des abbayes Bénédictines de Normandie* (Paris, 1971), p. 226. In the *Psychomachia*, Anger or Wrath (*Ira*) is found among the vices, as are Pride, Vaunting Ambition, Deceit, and Abusive Speech (pp. 232–3). As the vices and virtues battle with each other, Anger (*Ira*) shows her teeth and foams at the mouth, eyes shot with blood and gall. She fails to kill Long Suffering, who simply waits for Anger to perish by her own violence. She gets so annoyed by her inability to kill her opponent that she kills herself. The moral: 'fury is its own enemy' (p. 289). There is evidence in the poem for a concept of zealous anger, however. The virtue, Good Works, is allowed to grow angry and to dash around in anger to help the other virtues (pp. 318–19). Justice would also be roused to a righteous wrath (p. 63).

[243] G. Althoff, '*Ira regis*: prolegomena to a history of royal anger', in *Anger's Past: The Social Uses of an Emotion in the Middle Ages*, ed. B. Rosenwein (Ithaca, NY and London, 1998), p. 70.

[244] Gregory the Great, *Moralia in Job*, Bk. 5, Ch. 82; *Morals in the Book of Job*, trans. Parker, i. 307.

[245] Barton, '"Zealous anger"', pp. 156–9.

[246] Orderic, vi. 62, echoing Psalms 4:5, 4.

incorporate references or allusions to precedents that the uneducated might miss. For example, Thietmer of Merseburg's description of the tears of Otto III might have been intended to remind his readers of Chapter 6 of Matthew's Gospel, and knowledge of that reference would have recast the emperor's actions in an unflattering light.[247] Here is another demonstration of how the way in which emotions are recorded in the text is likely to say more about the author than the actor.

Dudo of Saint-Quentin's use of anger in his *De moribus* is entirely in accordance with these rules. Although he rarely allowed his dukes to display anger, when they did it was always justified. Their responses were appropriate according to the conventions of his time. Thus they avoid falling into the vice, which would have clouded their reactions. For example, Rollo, informed that French knights were staying with his wife without his knowledge, grew angry (*ira commotus*), arrested the hidden men, and executed them in the marketplace.[248] Their actions caused ridicule and smacked of treason. Rollo's response was thus appropriate. When William Longsword had defeated the Bretons in battle, they sent envoys to him to obtain peace. While making their petition, Dudo has them say, 'may your anger be turned aside from your servants (*auertatur furor tuus a seruis tuis*), and grant us the multifarious blessings of peace'. Their words seem to echo passages from either the Book of Numbers or, less likely, Jeremiah.[249] This echo was probably intended to highlight the righteousness of this ducal anger as well, perhaps, as William's power. Finally, at some date after 945, Ralph Torta found himself the target of Duke Richard I's anger. According to Dudo, Ralph's friends informed him that the duke was increasingly angry and hostile as a result of the financial straits that Ralph had imposed on him and his household.[250] Ralph consequently sent knights to Richard and sought through them to clear his name. In other words, he responded to what he interpreted as a threat and a danger. He was right to be concerned, as Richard did not listen to his excuses but exiled him from Normandy. The Norman lords saw how Richard had banished Ralph Torta 'and they "feared him mightily"' as a result.[251] Dudo, then, thought that the duke's anger could be used to create fear. That fear could be used to influence men to give up their nefarious activities and to seek pardon. Thus (zealous) anger could be used as a tool of rule.

---

[247] S. Airlie, 'The history of emotions and emotional history', *EME*, 10 (2001), 237–8.

[248] Dudo, p. 173; *Dudo*, p. 53.

[249] Dudo, p. 185; *Dudo*, p. 63; '… take all the heads of the people and hang them up before the Lord against the sun, that the fierce anger of the Lord may be moved away from Israel (*ut avertatur furor meus ab Israhel*)': Numbers 25:4. The alternative is: '… because I am innocent, surely his anger shall turn from me': Jeremiah 2:35.

[250] *Dudo*, p. 122. See also Jumièges, i. 114.

[251] *Dudo*, p. 124.

For the most part, however, Dudo preferred not to allow his dukes to show any emotion at all. Richard I 'was always calm with a most merry heart', but it was the calmness rather than the cheer that Dudo chose to emphasize.[252] Indeed, Richard was generally not allowed to display emotion at all. Dudo seems to have thought it better that his dukes should follow in the steps of the stoics, as represented in his day by Cicero, Jerome, and John Cassian.[253] Alternatively, he might have been picking up on imperial models. While discussing the straight-faced and straight-laced reaction of Louis the Pious to the entertainers who made his subjects laugh during his feasts, at least as portrayed by Thegan, Matthew Innes noted that the late-antique Roman emperors, and ninth-century Byzantine emperors, 'adopted a statuesque, static persona, demonstrating an unruffled self-control'.[254] And so, for either or both of these reasons, rather than react emotionally both Longsword and Richard I stared into the distance as they absorbed and digested the information or insult that they had just received. Thus, when Richard was warned by two of Count Theobald's men that he was in danger he 'was "lost in a gaze at one object" (*in uno obtutu defixo*), speechless with amazement, and gave them no word in reply ... However, when he had examined the meaning of the proposal that had been made, and had grasped it inwardly', then he made reply.[255] Richard, then, was in control of his emotions and his reactions– rational and unruffled; in short he was imperial.

The same lack of emotion can be seen when the French attempted to ambush Richard I when he had come to a parley on the river Eaulne. Richard's scouts discovered the plot. One of them rushed back to tell the duke of the planned treachery:

'O my lord, O most powerful lord duke, get away or you will be undone by an outrageous attack. For all your enemies are collected together with the king, and they are longing either to capture you and your men, or to slaughter them.'

When he heard this, the unperturbed Duke Richard rose up, and said to his assembled followers: 'See a meal has been prepared for us before we leave. Let us have a taste of that first, in the name of the Lord. And so we will be

[252] *Dudo*, p. 136.
[253] Rosenwein, *Emotional Communities*, pp. 39–49; Barton, 'Emotions and power', 48–50.
[254] M. Innes, '"He never even allowed his white teeth to be bared in laughter": the politics of humour in the Carolingian renaissance', in *Humour, History and Politics in Late Antiquity and the Early Middle Ages*, ed. G. Halsall (Cambridge, 2002), pp. 140–2.
[255] *Dudo*, p. 141. Dudo seems to echo Virgil, *Æneid*, i. 495 here: '... obtutuque haeret defixus in uno ...'

protected beforehand by the standard of the holy cross, and then let us face
the enemy squadrons unafraid ... Do not let the onset of those masses of
wicked men put you in a panic; but let the memory of your forebears, who
were undaunted in the face of every adversity, make you strong.'[256]

It was only when the French actually appeared, and charged the duke's table,
that Richard finally abandoned his meal, and withdrew across the Béthune. Such
equanimity in the face of danger could inspire a lord's followers and boost morale
– although the apparent reference to Psalm 23 also allowed Dudo to make parallels with King David and to highlight Richard's faith. For Dudo, then, shows
of emotion and shows of a lack of emotion could both be used to manipulate a
political situation, to make rivals back down or to boost the morale of supporters. Which he chose might have depended on whether it was the duke taking the
action (anger) or responding to it (impassiveness). That does at least appear to be
one pattern.

It has been argued above that Dudo's work was intended for the public consumption of Richard II's court.[257] If so, then those treated to the performance
of extracts from the work would have learned of these responses. And if the De
moribus were intended in part to be a mirror for princes, then Richard II would
also have been taught how to behave in particular situations. We might consequently wonder whether these constructed emotional responses both influenced
actual behaviour and reflected it, and thus whether this is a case of life imitating
art imitating life. And so while Richard I might not have acted as Dudo portrayed
him, it is possible that Richard II did. At least the possibility that he did so cannot
be dismissed entirely out of hand.

Not surprisingly, given the established conventions, other writers used
emotion and/or a lack of emotion in similar ways. For example, on the night of
28 September 1066, William the Bastard's ship, the Mora, outstripped the rest
of his fleet so that as the new day dawned the lookout reported that he could see
no other vessels. According to William of Poitiers, the anchor was dropped and,
so that fear and grief might not trouble his companions, 'the mettlesome duke
partook of an abundant meal, accompanied by spiced wine, as if he were in his
hall at home, asserting with remarkable cheerfulness that all the others would
arrive before long'.[258] In this situation, William's ability to dine as though he were
at home revealed his calmness, cheer, and confidence and put heart back into the
crew. The depiction in the Bayeux Tapestry of the Norman army taking lunch at

---

[256] Dudo, p. 145.
[257] See the Introduction, pp. 5–7, and also Chapter 2, pp. 82–3, 87.
[258] Poitiers, p. 112.

Pevensey shortly after landing might have been intended to show, in a similar manner, that the Normans felt entirely unthreatened by Harold and his English in the days before the battle of Hastings.[259] It is possible that both things really happened. It is equally possible that they are fictions that drew on convention and precedent and which were intended to suggest an appropriate state of mind for the soon-to-be-victorious Norman duke and his men.

While William of Malmesbury and Orderic Vitalis might portray emotional responses in a conventional way, both writers also ventured beyond those established bounds and seem to have attempted to give a flavour of the character and personality of these figures. It is the unconventional approach, albeit perhaps influenced by the writings of Suetonius and Einhard, that hints at an attempt to portray the actual behaviour of the person concerned. Thus, although there is evidence for his courage and also for his sense of humour,[260] William the Bastard was more often portrayed as using anger to manipulate situations to his advantage. William of Malmesbury, writing c. 1125, included an anecdote in his *Gesta regum Anglorum* which reveals something of this practice. When the royal duke was informed of a joke that Philip of France had made at his expense, 'William retorted: "When I go to Mass after my lying-in, I will offer a hundred thousand candles on his behalf", and confirmed that with, "by the resurrection and glory of God"! For it was his practice deliberately to use such oaths, so that the mere roar from his open mouth might somehow strike terror into the minds of his audience.'[261]

Writing around 1120, Orderic Vitalis, in this case most likely drawing on the memory of his own monastic community, provided an example of how William the Bastard had manipulated a potentially embarrassing situation to his advantage through the use of his anger. In 1061, Robert of Grandmesnil, abbot of Saint-Evroult, fled Normandy rather than face the duke at court, because he had been warned by friends that 'the duke was raging against him and all his kindred, and was out for their blood, and [was] warned by his friends that the duke's fury would not stop short of violence to him'.[262] When the abbot later returned to Normandy in the company of papal legates with the intention of demanding justice, Orderic tells us that William

flew into a violent rage (*uehementer iratus*), declaring that he was ready to receive legates of the pope, their common father, in matters touching the

---

[259] For more on this see Hagger, 'Lordship and lunching', 238–40.
[260] See above, *infra*, p. 376 and ns.
[261] Malmesbury, *GR*, i. 510.
[262] Orderic, ii. 90. For Robert see M. Hagger, 'Kinship and identity', 212–30 and especially 218.

Christian faith, but that if any monk from his duchy dared to bring a plea against him he would ignore his cloth and hang him by his cowl from the top of the highest oak tree in the wood nearby. On hearing this, Bishop Hugh sent warning to Robert and advised him not to come within sight of the raging prince (*furibundi principis*).[263]

Orderic's depiction of a furious duke goes beyond the conventional portrayal of zealous anger, even though William would have thought his reaction to be justified. As such, it is possible that we see here a memory, perhaps exaggerated in the retelling, of how Duke William might use emotions to manipulate a situation to his own advantage.[264]

Malmesbury provided a pen-portrait of Rufus, too, and reported or imagined that 'abroad, and in the gatherings of men, his aspect was haughty and unbending. He would fix the man before him with a threatening gaze, and with assumed severity and harsh voice overbear those with whom he spoke.'[265] That was a public face for formal meetings. In smaller conferences, he apparently adopted a different attitude: 'at home and in the chamber, with his private friends, he was all mildness and complaisance, and relied much on jest to carry a point, being in particular a merry critic of his own mistakes, so as to reduce the unpopularity they caused.'[266] Rufus thus employed a different persona, and different emotions and emotional responses, in different settings, although always to the same end – so that he could get his way.

In contrast, of course, Malmesbury portrayed Curthose as friendly, affable, and compliant even during formal gatherings, to which might then be added his indolence, sloth, imprudence, and prodigality. In sum, 'he was, then, a man with no memory for wrongs done to him, and forgave offences beyond what was right … By this gentleness of character, a man who ought to have been praised for it, and

[263] Orderic, ii. 94.
[264] Other examples of William's use of anger at court – or at least of Orderic's view that anger would have been an appropriate response – can be found in his reaction to Robert Curthose's attempt to seize the castle at Rouen *c.* 1078 and to Matilda's dispatch of money to her rebellious son (Orderic, ii. 306, 358; iii. 104). Matilda's support for her son is also noted by Malmesbury who retails a story, that he did not himself believe, that William beat her to death as a result (Malmesbury, *GR*, i. 500–2). A later example is provided by Robert of Torigni, writing of Henry's invasion of Normandy in 1105: Jumièges, ii. 220.
[265] Malmesbury, *GR*, i. 554.
[266] Malmesbury, *GR*, i. 556. In contrast, Alexander of Telese wrote that Roger II of Sicily 'was both in public and private restrained in familiarity, affability, and mirth, so that he never ceased to be feared' (Alexander of Telese, in *Roger II and the Creation of the Norman Kingdom of Sicily*, p. 122).

to have won the affection of his subjects, goaded the Normans into such contempt that they thought him of no account at all.'[267] The result of these character flaws was that Curthose lost his authority, power, and duchy.[268]

When discussing Henry I, both Malmesbury and Orderic deployed emotions in a conventional way. Thus when Orderic reported on Curthose's invasion of England in 1101, he wrote that: 'On hearing of this the king became very angry and asked his attendants and close counsellors, "what should be done to my enemies, when they presume to descend on me and invade my kingdom without my permission?"'[269] Here is a rare example of Orderic allowing Henry to become angry, although he had good reason to react like this for his land had been invaded by a rival and, as noted above, anger was an appropriate way of manifesting displeasure at an action or threat. Furthermore, the conventions employed by the chroniclers gave anger predictable consequences. Orderic wrote that 'it is the way of prudence for a powerful man to hide his feelings where his power alone cannot satisfy his appetites'.[270] Thus Henry's anger also revealed his future success. Furthermore, by ascribing anger to Henry, Orderic could also show the appropriate effect on Curthose: 'The duke, thoroughly alarmed, dissembled his fear with forced cheerfulness, and the king likewise concealed his smouldering wrath under a smiling face.'[271]

But although such conventional usage of emotion more likely conceals rather than reveals a genuine response, there are still occasions where Orderic and other writers explored Henry's character in a more rounded way and thus suggest something of how his use of emotions was remembered and the atmosphere he could

---

[267] Malmesbury, *GR*, i. 704. See also Eadmer, *HN*, p. 176. For a brief discussion of the relevance of charisma to medieval lordship, see Barton, 'Emotions and power', 46–7 and Barton, *Lordship in the County of Maine*, pp. 7–8, 77–111.

[268] See also Barton, 'Emotions and power', 46.

[269] Orderic, vi. 12–14.

[270] Orderic, v. 46 and see also Malmesbury, *GR,* i. 716 where Henry must remain silent as he cannot satisfy his ire. Barton noted that in satisfying their anger, Orderic showed the power of men like Henry I who could act in the face of the opposition and win (Barton, 'Emotions and power', 53). Such portraits can also be found outside the Anglo-Norman *regnum*. For example, Alexander of Telese, a contemporary of Orderic, in his *History of King Roger* discussed Roger's defeat by rebels at the battle of Nocera in 1132. Afterwards, King Roger is said to have 'remained at Salerno with a joyful face, showing himself to be resolute in mind, knowing for certain that this setback would be replaced by God's gift by some happier outcome' (Alexander of Telese, 'History of King Roger', trans. Loud, p. 89). In contrast, Geoffrey Malaterra described Count Roger I of Sicily as angry before the walls of Iato, despite the fact that he was, at that time, unable to take the city (Geoffrey Malaterra, *The Deeds of Count Roger of Calabria and Sicily and of his Brother Duke Robert Guiscard*, trans. K. B. Wolf (Ann Arbor, 2005), p. 150).

[271] Orderic, vi. 14.

create at court. Orderic noted that, in 1101, Henry concealed his wrath under a smiling face, and this seems to have been Henry's usual *modus operandi*. As such, it seems that he did not manipulate his subjects through the use of emotion. Rather William of Malmesbury, Orderic Vitalis, and Henry of Huntingdon all suggest that Henry I manipulated his subjects by an impassiveness that seems to have created an even deeper climate of fear than his anger did – and this despite the fact that Malmesbury did at one point report that Henry was prone to 'great fits of rage'.[272]

While that might itself suggest that the chroniclers simply preferred to follow the stoic/Prudentian convention about emotional responses, the accuracy of the portrait is supported by Henry's intelligence network, his willingness to wait for the right moment to strike against his enemies, and his determination to get the job done once he had made his move. Orderic wrote that Henry was: 'a diligent investigator, he inquired into everything … He was thoroughly familiar with all secrets and things done surreptitiously, so that their perpetrators could not imagine how the king could be aware of their most secret plots.'[273] He provided some examples, too. Henry, he wrote, had a file on Robert of Bellême ready for use in 1102.[274] He also knew that there would be a rebellion in 1123 and that Hugh of Montfort was implicated.[275] The result was that he was able to defeat even the greatest of lords. Orderic made the point when discussing the siege at Shrewsbury in 1102: 'If the king defeats a mighty earl by force, and carries his enmity to the point of disinheriting him, as he is now striving to do, he will from that moment trample on us like helpless slave-girls.'[276] The result, according to Malmesbury, was 'his power of keeping rebellion in check by the fear of his name'.[277] Henry's subjects were simply scared of him, and for good reason.

This was, then, a different type of psychological manipulation than that found in his father's day. Instead of open anger, Henry hid his feelings until the moment to strike had come. Robert Bloet, who knew Henry's ways well, grew alarmed when he heard that the king had praised him: 'he sighed and said, "the king only praises one of his men when he has decided to destroy him utterly". For King

---

[272] Malmesbury, *GR*, i. 742.

[273] Orderic, vi. 10. Orderic notes fear of Henry at, for example, Orderic, vi. 18, 78, 216, 330, 356, 442. John of Worcester provides a reference to fear of Henry, too (Worcester, iii. 200), although his quotation was intended to suggest wicked rule over poor people, reflecting the first of Henry's dreams which he had just recounted.

[274] Orderic, vi. 20.

[275] Orderic, vi. 334.

[276] Orderic, vi. 26.

[277] Malmesbury, *GR*, i. 740.

Henry … was a man of the utmost animosity, whose purpose was inscrutable.'[278]
Such a duke, apparently unpredictable and capricious, would have been fearful
indeed.

* * * * * *

A duke's court was at the heart of his power. It was his stage, designed and dressed
at his command. The approaches to the castles at Rouen and Caen took visitors
through the most important centres of ducal power, revealing the dukes' wealth
and command over nature. Rouen, Caen – and Fécamp, too – impressed by their
proximity to important and massive churches; Lillebonne by the neighbouring
Roman ruins; Falaise and Arques by the power of their settings. Within their
buildings, the dukes displayed themselves to their subjects, visitors, and rivals to
best effect, especially during the banquets attached to the great annual festivals of
Christmas, Easter, and perhaps Pentecost, as well as to councils. There they sat
on their thrones, richly attired, bejewelled, divinely splendid, served by almost
equally richly attired servants, in control of their subjects' ability to satisfy their
appetites, fawned upon, inscrutable but often magnanimous. Surrounded by their
men, summoned to attend and thereby to demonstrate their loyalty, they embodied secular power.

    And yet even here in their homes and in their presence, the dukes were not
all-powerful and their power was not uncontested. Those who came to the court
to gain charters, confirmations, or justice recognized the dukes' authority – they
would not have bothered to make the journey otherwise – but they recognized
other powers and other agents, too. Christianity was always a rival, and while the
dukes recognized that they derived their power from God and might even have
welcomed His support and affirmation of their actions, the spectacle of bishops
self-importantly pronouncing solemn anathema might have proved irksome, not
least as it tended to suggest that the dukes' protection of any gift alone was not
sufficient. Petitioners, too, might have sought the dukes' clemency, but they were
just as willing to berate a duke for his past misdeeds and also to take the credit
for his confirmation for themselves – even if the duke did not always get to hear
about it. Equally, while the duke signed the act before the assembled witnesses and
witnessed the application of their own *signa* to what was now his act, beneficiaries might later brandish those documents before other lords, outside the duke's
court, to gain the benefit of their partisanship, too. The duke's protection was all
very well, but if local witnesses could save a lengthy and costly and dangerous
journey back to the court, then so much the better.

    Slowly, the dukes won this competition. Anathema clauses in particular were

---

[278] Huntingdon, p. 588.

employed less and less often; additional witnesses were no longer added to exist-ing acts. The growing rift between ecclesiastical and secular power that was the result of the ideology of the reform papacy might have played a role here. So, too, might the Normans' growing familiarity with the succinct and secular formula-tions of the English writing office, and indeed the increasing use of the royal duke's writing office to draft Norman acts. The royal duke's seal might have carried his personal authority into the darkest corners of his duchy, too.[279] But it is likely that of at least equal importance was the duke's ability to protect his grants and to carry out effective justice on those who attempted to undermine them. This was recognized by the monks of Marmoutier as early as 1055:

> For which thing the lord Abbot Albert, then presiding over Marmoutier, since he knew not otherwise how this donation could remain stable, went to William, *princeps* of the Normans, and duke, and, to speak more accurately, king of his *whole* land, which is difficult to find elsewhere, and, presuming on several others familiar and dear to him, exhorted him that he should approve and authorize the said donation.[280]

The ability of the dukes to punish those who would undermine their grants and thus their authority was therefore vital. It allowed them to build their authority, and was essential to its maintenance. The dukes consequently worked hard to establish their jurisdiction and then to expand its reach, not just because their clerical counsellors emphasized the importance of peace and justice as the central elements of Christian rulership, but also because they recognized that justice lay at the very heart of their power – especially in peacetime. And so it is to this aspect of the dukes' authority that we now turn.

---

[279] As has been suggested for Carolingian seals: Koziol, *Politics of Memory and Identity*, p. 36.

[280] *RADN*, no. 137. Reynolds translated this passage similarly as: 'William, prince and duke of the Normans and, to say plainly what you might otherwise discover with difficulty, king of all his land' (Reynolds, *Fiefs*, p. 147).

CHAPTER 8

The Chief Purpose of our Government: The Dukes and Justice

Since, by a disposition of the divine clemency, we have received from Christ
... the charge of an earthly kingdom for the affirmation of peace and justice,
which is the chief purpose of our government, we have the need to work with
all our zeal and with all our force to protect the innocent by the protection of
goods and to bring before justice the audacity of the malicious.[1]

FOR the monks of Le Bec, as the above quotation shows, the requirement that
a ruler should bring peace and do justice was paramount. In that sentiment,
they were entirely in accord with the mainstream of medieval thought. Isidore of
Seville had highlighted the need for kings to do justice, as had Alcuin, Wipo, and
Fulbert of Chartres who, about a century before the monks of Le Bec wrote their
act, had opined that the position of the king 'makes him the fountain-head of
justice'.[2] Good rulers were supposed to bring peace and justice to their subjects,
and those who were characterized as good rulers were made to perform that role
by those who wrote about them. Thus, William of Poitiers might remark that 'at
last a most joyful day dawned splendidly for all who desired and eagerly awaited
peace and justice. Our duke ... was armed as a knight.'[3] Conversely, the construction of a negative image of Robert Curthose required that he should be unable to
do justice, even though his military ability could be acknowledged.[4]

The purpose of this chapter is to establish how the dukes went about maintaining the peace in their duchy and doing justice on those who broke it – ambitions
which constitute two sides of the same coin. To pursue this objective, the chapter
has been broken down into sections that divide justice into offences on one hand

---

[1] BnF, MS lat. 13905, fo. 9r–v, printed in A. Porée, *Histoire de l'abbaye du Bec*, 2 vols
(Evreux, 1901), i. 658 = *Regesta*, ii. no. 1900.
[2] Fulbert, *Letters*, no. 7. For a discussion of Thietmar of Merseberg's concerns with justice
see S. Bagge, *Kings, Politics, and the Right Order of the World in German Historiography,
c. 950–1150* (Leiden, 2002), pp. 133, 150–1, 182. Bagge also discussed the importance of
justice in Wipo's *Gesta Chuonradi* at pp. 194, 217–20.
[3] Poitiers, p. 6.
[4] For example, Orderic, iv. 114; vi. 96.

and disputes over property on the other.[5] That division is not intended to suggest that contemporaries thought in more modern terms of criminal law and civil law, nor that the duke was supposed to act in one sphere but not the other. William of Poitiers, for one, made it clear that the duke was to do justice regarding all sorts of trespasses: 'By his strict discipline (i.e. justice) and by his laws robbers, homicides, and evil-doers have been driven out of Normandy.' But he went on to remark that he judged justly so that 'no one, however powerful or close to him, dared to move the boundary of a weaker neighbour's field or take anything from him'.[6] Nonetheless, Poitiers does here make an implicit distinction between offences on the one hand and disputes over property on the other, and this perhaps reveals his awareness that the nature of causes, jurisdictions, and penalties was so different that the duke's success in these two spheres needed, at the very least, to be highlighted in separate sentences. Rolling an examination of offences and 'civil' pleas together, then, is just as likely to result in anachronism as keeping them apart.

The sources for this examination of peace and justice in Normandy are limited. Bringing the evidence found in narrative sources, *acta*, and the records of pleas together, there is information about some 180 complaints and pleas, some of them mentioned in only the most cursory fashion. Only sixteen of them concern offences.[7] The evidence is also uneven chronologically, with the fullest evidence dating from the reign of William the Bastard. Although there are some detailed

---

[5] I have preferred to use the word 'offence' rather than 'crime' in the discussion that follows, although they are occasionally treated as synonyms. For present purposes, and following John Hudson and Paul Hyams, an offence may be defined as a misdeed subject primarily to ducal punishment (J. Hudson, *The Formation of the English Common Law: Law and Society in England from the Norman Conquest to Magna Carta* (London, 1996), p. 56; P. Hyams, *Rancor and Reconciliation in Medieval England* (Ithaca, NY 2003), pp. 13, 220–4). 'Crime' is a problematic concept in the Anglo-Norman world before the end of the twelfth century. Although the English word derives from the Latin *crimen*, Isidore of Seville made it clear that a *crimen* was an offence such as 'theft, deceit, and other actions that do not kill but cause disgrace'. A second category of offence was covered by the word *facinus*, which comprised an offence involving 'doing evil that harms another' (*Etymologies*, p. 122). Given the importance of the *Etymologies* in contemporary education, it is likely that many educated Normans thought in these terms. In a recent article, T. B. Lambert has argued that Anglo-Saxon kings saw a different distinction – one which differentiated between offences that were prohibited by law, such as theft, and those which breached royal protection, such as a homicide on the king's highway or the killing of one of his officials (T. B. Lambert, 'Theft, homicide and crime in late Anglo-Saxon law', *Past and Present*, 214 (2012), 16–43).

[6] Poitiers, p. 80.

[7] The situation is similar with the records of Carolingian pleas heard before 814. Of the 276 cases, only fourteen concern homicides and five assaults. Noted in L. Oliver, 'Protecting the body in early medieval law', in *Peace and Protection in the Middle Ages*, ed. T. B. Lambert and D. Rollason (Toronto, 2009), pp. 68–9.

records from the reign of Henry I, too, an increasing number of records of judgements or settlements made in that duke's court take the form of writs notifying individuals or assemblies about the outcome of a dispute rather than the procedures or arguments involved, which limits their usefulness so far as the following discussion is concerned.

Overwhelmingly, these records were written or preserved by the winners.[8] They are consequently one-sided, and paint the opponent's case as weak and unjust. As it was the result that mattered, few provide much information about process or argument. Indeed, only about half of the reports (ninety-four) provide any detail as to the procedures employed when bringing a case to court and when pleading it. For the most part such details are not relevant to the present investigation, but it might nonetheless be useful to note that only nine of the surviving records provide details about the use of witnesses, only seven mention the swearing of oaths, and there are only four cases where the dispute was decided by use of the ordeal. Instead an author's emphasis was on the number of witnesses who supported the victorious party and the complete absence of justification for the other side's claims, or sometimes on the role of the patron of a house in defending its position. Indeed, as well as functioning as muniments, *placita* should often be seen as narratives recounting and memorializing the part played by patrons and abbots and God in favour of a particular church.[9]

Before embarking on an examination of the dukes' role in maintaining peace and justice it is worth pausing to establish what contemporaries meant by those words. Bede had celebrated the peace of King Edwin's reign when he remarked that 'even if a woman with a recently born child wanted to walk across the whole island, from sea to sea, she could do so without anyone harming her'.[10] But, as Paul Kershaw has observed, that does not set the bar at a very high level. It also implies that even these limited aspirations were not always achieved; that it was not always possible for women, or men for that matter, to travel along the public roads in safety without the protection of arms.[11] Norman writers wrote about peace in similar terms. Dudo of Saint-Quentin remarked that the bishop

---

[8] Two exceptions are provided by the lists of losses preserved by the monks of Mont-Saint-Michel and the nuns of Sainte-Trinité, Caen: *Ctl. Mont-Saint-Michel*, pp. 180–4 (no. 115); *Chs. Caen*, pp. 125–8 (no. 15).

[9] See, for example, E. van Torhoudt, 'L'écrit et la justice au Mont-Saint-Michel: les notices narratives (vers 1060–1150), *Tabularia*, Etudes, 7 (2007), 122–3.

[10] Bede, *Historia Ecclesiastica*, Ch. 2, Bk. 16; *Bede's Ecclesiastical History of the English People*, ed. and trans. B. Colgrave and R. A. B. Mynors, revised edition (Oxford, 1992), p. 192.

[11] P. J. E. Kershaw, *Peaceful Kings: Peace, Power, and the Early Medieval Political Imagination* (Oxford, 2011), pp. 31–2.

of Chartres, coming to Normandy to discuss peace with Richard I *c.* 965, found 'the peasants of this land secure from enemies. They are not afraid of any sudden misfortune. I noticed that shrines and churches were respectfully attended by the inhabitants and the mystery of the Holy Office solemnly celebrated.' In contrast, he added, 'we are worn down by robberies and burning, and also by sudden death in the night'.[12] William of Poitiers, writing *c.* 1071, celebrated the peace that Normandy enjoyed under William the Bastard at various points throughout his *Gesta Guillelmi*. He wrote that 'the Church rejoiced, because it was possible to celebrate the divine mystery in peace; the merchant rejoiced at being able to go where he would in safety; the farmer gave thanks for being able to plough the fields and scatter seed, instead of hiding from the sight of soldiers'; that 'a man who was weak or unarmed could ride singing on his horse wherever he wished, without trembling at the sight of squadrons of knights'; and that 'strangers, seeing that in our country horsemen go to and fro unarmed, and that the road is safe for every traveller, have often wished to have a similar blessing in their regions; this is the peace and distinction that the virtue of William has bestowed on his country.'[13]

Poitiers had earlier lamented what happened when the peace was broken: 'that the goods of churches, the labours of country people, and the profits of merchants were unjustly made the booty of men-at-arms.'[14] Orderic's descriptions of the suffering of the duchy under Curthose echo these same themes. The Church suffered; crops were destroyed; innocent people were butchered.[15] The duke's task was to prevent such destruction, to allow his people to enjoy their property and to be productive, and to protect trade. By allowing farmers to grow and harvest their produce, and by ensuring that merchants could freely move around the duchy, the food supply was assured – and it was, of course, one function of a lord to feed his people. By prohibiting attacks on pilgrims, and by protecting churchmen and their property, the sins of his people might be assuaged and the shrines could receive offerings. The dukes, then, policed their people for the good of the economic and spiritual life – and thus the stability and well-being – of the duchy, and so it is not surprising that they used the concept of their peace to increase the reach of their jurisdiction.[16]

The link between peace and royal or ducal protection has been clearly made

[12] *Dudo*, p. 152.
[13] Poitiers, pp. 12, 102–4, 96, respectively.
[14] Poitiers, p. 36.
[15] For example, Orderic, vi. 60–2, 86, 96.
[16] As did the kings of the English: P. Stafford, 'King and kin, lord and community: England in the tenth and eleventh centuries', in P. Stafford, *Gender, Family, and the Legitimation of Power: England from the Ninth to Early Twelfth Century* (Aldershot, 2006), VIII. 23.

and illustrated by Tom Lambert, who has remarked, too, on the necessity of taking swift and forceful action against those who broke the peace: 'the protector must make sure that the violator is publicly and severely punished or the deterrent effect of his protection will be diminished.'[17] Peace, then, required the threat or application of punishment. And that was where justice came in. The Normans of the tenth to twelfth centuries had inherited a great deal of thought on the subject of justice. It had been long established, for example, that justice, fortitude, temperance, and prudence together comprised the four cardinal virtues. This idea seems to have originated with Plato, although in the absence of the *Republic*, Plato's ideas on this subject reached tenth- to twelfth-century audiences through the Bible, Cicero, or St Augustine's *De ciuitate Dei* (which paraphrases or employs quotations from the works of both Plato and Cicero).[18] In his *Moralia in Job*, Gregory the Great argued that all four virtues had to be used together: 'one virtue without another is either none at all or but imperfect ... For neither is it real prudence which has not justice, temperance, fortitude ... nor genuine justice which has not prudence, fortitude, and temperance.'[19] Gregory went on to point out that temperance and mercy in moderation might be required to mitigate the harshness of justice: 'we, in following out the straight line of justice, generally leave mercy behind; and in aiming to observe mercy, we deviate from the straight line of justice.'[20] Isidore of Seville, writing about twenty years after Gregory, opined that 'the royal virtues are these two especially: justice and mercy – but mercy is more praised in kings, because justice in itself is harsh.'[21]

The recognition that justice required some, but not too much,[22] dilution with

---

[17] T. B. Lambert, 'Introduction: some approaches to peace and protection', in *Peace and Protection in the Middle Ages*, ed. T. B. Lambert and D. Rollason (Toronto, 2009), pp. 1–16 at p. 3.

[18] See, for example, Wisdom of Solomon, 8:7; Cicero, *De officiis*, Bk. 1, Ch. 20, trans. P. G. Walsh, p. 9; Augustine, *De ciuitate Dei*, Bk. 4, Ch. 20. Although Plato's *Phaedo* was probably known in Normandy in this period (Orderic, i. 22), the *Timaeus* might have only reached the duchy in the fourth decade of the twelfth century. The monks at Le Bec were given a copy by Philip of Harcourt after he became bishop of Bayeux *c.* 1142 ('Catalogus librorum abbatiae Beccensis circa saeculum duodecimum', *PL*, vol. 150, cols. 781; noted in G. Nortier, *Les bibliothèques médiévales des abbayes bénédictines de Normandie: Fécamp, le Bec, le Mont Saint-Michel, Saint-Evroul, Lyre, Jumièges, Saint-Wandrille, Saint-Ouen* (Paris, 1971), p. 225). In any event, Plato's ideas about the cardinal virtues are not clearly spelt out in these texts, and that is why these later works have been privileged here.

[19] Gregory the Great, *Moralia in Job*, Bk. 22, Ch. 2.

[20] *Moralia in Job*, Bk. 1, Ch. 16.

[21] *Etymologies*, p. 200.

[22] Geoffrey Malaterra asserted that 'justice must sometimes be withheld lest justice be administered with too much indulgence and vice grow too strong' (Geoffrey Malaterra,

mercy or temperance reveals that it was not simply an abstract virtue, but something that was related to, and had a real impact on, the physical world. Both classical and medieval works make it clear that this impact took a number of different, but interlocking, forms. Briefly, and thus at risk of oversimplification, justice was, first, about allowing others the peaceful enjoyment of their property and rights.[23] Justice, then, would act against those who tried to take away property through theft or robbery (offences committed secretly or with violence). It would be brought into play where ownership was openly contested. It would also act against those who tried to overreach their God-given place in society, because to rise too far would be to deprive another with more right to it of that place.[24] Secondly, justice was about taking action against someone who sought to deprive another of their property or rights.[25] Justice, then, was both active and passive. Thirdly, and the logical result of the other two requirements, justice was about the punishment of those who had acted unjustly or unlawfully in seeking to deprive others of their property or rights (including attacks on their person).[26] This in turn meant that justice, as well as being tempered by mercy, had to be fair. God was the 'just judge', treating all men fairly according to their just deserts. Men had to do the same, irrespective of the rank or condition of the accused. In its opening verse, the Book of Wisdom urges judges to be fair: 'love righteousness (*iusticia*), ye that be judges of the earth.' It goes on to say that man should 'order the world according to equity and righteousness (*iusticia*), and execute judgement with an upright heart.'[27]

The Deeds of Count Roger of Calabria and Sicily and of his Brother Duke Robert Guiscard, trans. K. B. Wolf (Ann Arbor, 2005), p. 166).

[23] Plato, *The Republic*, para. 433; *De ciuitate Dei*, 19: 21, p. 951; Augustine, *Letters*, no. 155: Augustine to Macedonius, in *Political Writings*, ed. E. M. Atkins and R. J. Dodaro, Cambridge Texts in the History of Political Thought (Cambridge, 2001), p. 95; *Etymologies*, p. 79. The idea was also taken up by Ulpian, perhaps from the stoics, and thus became important in the development of legal studies during the twelfth-century renaissance (I. P. Bejczy, 'Law and ethics: twelfth-century jurists on the virtue of justice', *Viator*, 36 (2005), 204–6). Unsurprisingly, given the rediscovery of Roman law that had reinforced the existing understanding, John of Salisbury's *Policraticus* of 1159 made the same point (John of Salisbury, *Policraticus*, Bk. 4, chs. 2, 12; *Policraticus: Of the Frivolities of Courtiers and the Footprints of Philosophers*, ed. and trans. C. J. Nederman (Cambridge, 1990), pp. 30, 62).

[24] For example, Orderic, ii. 302–4; vi. 94 (this last being effectively Orderic's argument in favour of Henry I's conquest of Normandy).

[25] Cicero, *De officiis*, Bk. 1, Chs. 20, 23, trans. Walsh, pp. 9–10; Martin of Braga, *Formula honestae vitae*, ch. 5 (Latin text available online at < http://www.thelatinlibrary.com/martinbraga/formula.shtml > accessed 2 January 2016.)

[26] Revelation, 20:13;

[27] Wisdom, 1:1, 9:3.

As the Normans of the tenth to twelfth centuries had ready access to the Bible, *De Officiis*, *De ciuitate Dei*, *Moralia in Job*, and the *Etymologiae*, they were well aware of what justice was and how it should be put into practice. They could have found everything that has been set out in the preceding paragraphs in those works.[28] It is not surprising, then, that the principal Norman chroniclers, Dudo of Saint-Quentin, William of Jumièges, William of Poitiers, and Orderic Vitalis, do seem to have taken these ideas on board and to have reflected them in their narratives.[29]

How justice was to be put into practice had also been set out by the same ancient authorities. Justice (*iusticia*) was closely tied to right (*ius*).[30] Cicero had written that: 'the origin of justice must be derived from law. For law is a force of nature, the intelligence and reason of a wise man, and the criterion of justice and injustice.'[31] St Augustine had remarked in a similar vein that 'where … there is no justice (*iusticia*) there can be no right (*ius*). For that which is done according to right is inevitably a just act, whereas nothing that is done unjustly can be done according to right.'[32] Isidore of Seville brought these ideas together: 'all right (*ius*) consists of laws and customs. A law is a written statute. A custom is usage tested

---

28 Poitiers certainly knew *De officiis* as he quoted from it in his *Gesta Guillelmi* (Poitiers, p. 18). He also knew *De ciuitate Dei* (p. 189). Orderic used all of these works except Cicero's.

29 For example: Enjoyment of property: *Dudo*, pp. 119, 131; Jumièges, ii. 32, 106; Poitiers, pp. 58, 118; Orderic, ii. 208, 302–4, 310, iii. 136, iv. 284, 130; Punishment and equity: *Dudo*, pp. 117, 142; Jumièges, ii. 94, 170, 178; Poitiers, pp. 8, 80, 84, 158; *LHP*, p. 80, para. 3.1; Orderic, ii. 320, iv. 242, 262–4. These writers were not, of course, alone. Anselm of Le Bec considered justice as fitting punishment in his *Proslogion* (*Proslogion*, in *The Prayers and Meditations of St Anselm with the Proslogion*, trans. B. Ward (London, 1973), pp. 250 (where he seems to follow St Augustine, *De ciuitate Dei*, 20:2, pp. 967–8), 252). The author of the *Leges Henrici Primi* followed suit, noting that true justice in particular required the punishment of thieves, although mercy might be extended to first-time offenders (*LHP*, para. 59.20).

30 As an aside, it should be noted that Norman and Anglo-Norman writers used *ius* or *iusticia* on the one hand and *rectum* on the other as synonyms – as does Du Cange where 'rectum' is defined 'ius'. See for example, Poitiers, pp. 24, 158, 174; *Regesta: William*, nos. 18, 42, 43, 88, 125, 162, 267.II, 310; *Livre Noir*, i. 36 (no. 29) = *Regesta*, ii. no. 951; *Regesta*, ii. 370 (no. ccxlii) = no. 1672. Two Norman writs of Henry I even use both words, perhaps to ensure that there should be no confusion: 'Et nisi feceris iusticia mea faciat, ne inde amplius clamorem audiam pro penuria plene iusticie uel recti' (*NI*, p. 102 (no. 13) = *Regesta*, ii. no. 1684) and 'Precipio quod iuste faciatis habere Reginaldo filio Roberti Nep' decimam suam … sicut illam dirationauit in curia mea, ne audiam inde clamorem pro penuria iusticie et recti' (*Livre Noir*, i. 43–4 (no. 37) = *Regesta*, ii. no. 1898). Even in the thirteenth century, despite the language employed by Bracton, *Fleta* could still say that 'what in written law is called "ius" is said in English law to be "rectum"' (*Fleta*, Bk. 6, Ch. 1; *Fleta*, Vol. 4, ed. and trans. G. O. Sayles, Selden Society, 99 (1984), p. 107).

31 Cicero, *De legibus*, 1: 19; trans. Rudd, p. 103.

32 *De ciuitate Dei*, 19:21, p. 950.

by age, or unwritten law, for law is named from reading because it is written.'[33] Thus justice was done by following the laws and customs recognized at any one time by a given society.

The Consuetudines et iusticie *and jurisdiction over offences*

Some of the customs recognized in Normandy at the end of the eleventh century were set down in a document known as the *Consuetudines et iusticie* (its title providing an example of the contemporary use of 'iusticia' to mean 'jurisdiction') made by 'the bishops and barons of Caen' in 1091 or 1096.[34] This document begins with a declaration: 'Here are the rights which King William who acquired the kingdom of England had in Normandy.' It goes on to provide the first, albeit non-exhaustive, survey of the extent of ducal jurisdiction, overlapping, so far as offences were concerned, with the much briefer extent of ducal jurisdiction and/ or rights found in the *consuetudines uicecomitatus* given to the monks of Préaux c. 1050.[35] The *Consuetudines et iusticie*, then, perhaps provide an insight into what the political community thought the duke was and was not for, as the choice of customs to record and which to omit may be supposed to indicate what Normans considered he needed to do his job, and also suggests limits on what the duke was supposed to do and what his peace was intended to cover.

---

[33] *Etymologies*, p. 117 (5:3) and also p. 73 (2:10). This definition is very similar to the statement set out in the *Leges Henrici Primi*, written in England in the twelfth century by a Norman or Frenchman, and recognized as having been based on the *Etymologies* by its most recent editor (*LHP*, para. 4.3a, p. 82 and see Hagger, 'Secular law and custom', 831–3).

[34] *NI*, Appendix D, pp. 281–4. The date of 1091 was suggested by Haskins. Bill Aird has recently suggested that 1096 fits better with events (Aird, *Robert Curthose*, pp. 141, 163–4). The introductory wording is of interest. Three of the four medieval manuscripts that contain the text state that the customs were found by the barons not *at* Caen but *of* Caen (*Cadomi*). The use of the genitive might suggest that the precursor to the Norman Exchequer – in terms of its function as a court rather than an auditing body – was already in existence by the end of the eleventh century. Alternatively, and perhaps more likely, the introductory wording was added in the twelfth century when the exchequer had become established.

[35] That the list is incomplete is revealed by a second statement explaining why the document had been made: 'And these which have been said above have been written down since they are particularly necessary. But there remain many things outside this writing concerning the justice of money and the other justice of Normandy. And although this has not been written down, Count Robert and King William shall lose nothing of the justice which their father had, and nor shall the barons lose what they had in the time of King William.' The *consuetudines uicecomitatus* are found at *RADN*, no. 121; *Ctl. Préaux*, A161, A163.

The *Consuetudines* insist that the 'Lord of Normandy', who was usually but not always the duke, had rights that included jurisdiction over: a breach of the peace against an individual going to, attending, and departing from the duke's court (§1); a breach of the peace over an individual serving in the duke's army, and for eight days before and after the period of service (§2); unlicensed castle-building, and a failure to surrender a castle to the duke at his will (§4); an individual who had burned a house or a mill, made waste, or taken prey for a claim over land (§6); an individual who had assaulted or ambushed a man in his forest (§7); an individual who had sought out their enemy, or made distraint, with hauberk and standard and sounding their horn, and over those who had condemned a person to loss of limb unless they had been caught in the act of committing an offence for which that was the lawful punishment and had been justly judged in court (§8); an individual who had committed housebreaking, arson, rape, or made distraint (unless that distraint had been announced at the house of the relevant person), with the recognition that other lords might have an interest in the punishment of the offender (§9 and §10); an individual who had disturbed a merchant unless he owed a debt to him or was surety for a debt owed to him (§11); an individual who had disturbed a pilgrim (§12); an individual who had minted coins outside the duke's mints at Rouen and Bayeux, or made false money inside them, or who had allowed these things to be done (§13);[36] and those who took or ransomed men or took arms and horses through war (§14). In addition, the *Consuetudines* state that the duke had the right to take a hostage from his barons, provided the hostage was not (yet) a knight (§5). A breach of any of the customs listed here constituted an offence against the 'Lord of Normandy'.

These customs seem to have been brought together in the years before 1087 from disparate origins. Previous work on the *Consuetudines*, particularly by Jean

---

[36] There is almost no overlap here with the later list of pleas pertaining to the duke found in Part I of the so-called *Très ancien coutumier* of c. 1200. This records that the dukes had jurisdiction over 'possessions of the Church, infractions on the roads and insults to the peace, house-breaking and insults while at the plough, disseisin and all recognitions' (*TAC*, i. 43, ch. 53). In contrast, there is much greater similarity with the duke's jurisdiction as set out in Part II. Here the duke is said to have the right to hear: 'homicide, when it is done secretly, which the Dacian tongue calls murder ... similarly the severance of members of their breaking; similarly of things taken away by force which by the vulgar is called robbery; similarly of waste made by force; similarly of rape namely of women raped by force; similarly of arson, that is the burning of houses or crops; similarly of premeditated assault due to an old hatred; similarly of assault within the four corners of a house; similarly of assault at the plough; similarly of assault on the king's road which leads from city to city or to a royal castle; similarly of assault while travelling to the king's court; similarly of a truce given before royal justices; similarly all justice of the army or coinage pertains to the duke alone' (*TAC*, i. 64–5, ch. 70).

Yver, has shown that some of them had their origins in Carolingian legislation. The edict of Pitres was plausibly the origin of the customs concerning the dukes' monopoly on minting coins (§ 13).[37] The dukes' claims to jurisdiction over assaults on travellers and pilgrims might have originated in Carolingian jurisdiction over public roads.[38] The right to garrison subjects' castles was also inherited from the dukes' Carolingian predecessors, and had survived across much of France. For example, it appears in a set of complaints drawn up by or for Hugh of Lusignan in the 1020s, in which he acknowledged Duke William V of Aquitaine's right to enter his castle at Gençay.[39] The homage given by the count of Foix to the bishop of Gerona and Carcassonne in 1034 provides another example, as the count swore not to withhold the defences of the castles at Foix, Queille, and Saissac from the bishop. (The castle at Montpellier, on the other hand, was not rendible, but the count swore instead to guarantee it innocuous.) Equally, in 1119, Louis VI claimed the right to take possession of Cluny's castles should it be necessary for him to do so.[40]

Some of these same customs, however, and others, too, might also have been related to the safeguards enshrined in some of the oaths relating to the Truce of God formulated from the 1020s to 1050s.[41] H. E. J. Cowdrey hinted at this in his article on the Truce of 1970.[42] He did so because he had perused the text of the supposed Norman Truce printed in Guillaume Bessin's *Concilia*, which included a protection for merchants and 'all men who from other regions are crossing yours'.[43]

Bessin thought that the text he printed was the Truce promulgated by William the Bastard after his victory at Val-ès-Dunes in 1047, because that was what one thirteenth-century copy of the text told him it was. After a close inspection of all the surviving manuscripts in which this text – or ones very like it – appear, Michel de Boüard was not so sure.[44] David Douglas, following his lead, noted in 1964 that 'the exact nature of the Truce which was … proclaimed can only be considered by reference to texts which were compiled at a later date.[45] Certainly, the text

---

[37] Yver, 'Contribution à l'étude du développement', 144–5; Yver, 'Premières institutions', p. 303.

[38] Yver, 'Premières institutions', p. 303; Bates, *Normandy*, p. 163.

[39] Cited in Reynolds, *Fiefs*, pp. 125–6.

[40] See C. L. H. Coulson, 'Rendability and castellation in medieval France', *Château Gaillard*, 6 (1973), 59–69.

[41] Though some of these clauses seem also to have origins in Carolingian legislation; for example, clause 17 of Herstal of 779 protected travellers going to the court or elsewhere.

[42] Cowdrey, 'Peace and the Truce of God', *Past and Present*, 46 (1970), 61.

[43] Bessin, *Concilia*, p. 39.

[44] De Boüard, 'Sur les origines de la trêve de Dieu', *Annales de Normandie*, 9 (1959), 176–89.

[45] Douglas, *William the Conqueror*, p. 51.

printed by Bessin was known in Normandy. It is found in two early- to mid-twelfth-century manuscripts, one from Fécamp and the other from Jumièges.[46] But that does not mean it originated in Normandy. There is also a thirteenth-century manuscript, of unknown provenance but now in the Vatican Library, that contains this text of the Truce as well as the canons of the council of Lillebonne and the *Consuetudines et iusticie*.[47] It is this manuscript, and only this one, which declares that the text was that issued by William the Bastard in 1047.

One thirteenth-century heading is not enough to convince, especially when the earlier Norman manuscripts do not make such a claim. Moreover, Bessin's text is not particularly convincing as a Norman Truce. First, the act begins: 'Dearest brothers in the Lord, during the peace which the vulgar call the Truce of God and which begins as the sun sets on Wednesday and ends when the sun rises on Monday, you ought to observe those things which I write for you'. That is not ducal legislation, even taking into account beneficiary drafting. Second, Bessin's text relaxes the terms of the Truce should a man ride with either the king or, 'the count of this country' on cavalcade or during hostilities. This, even in the aftermath of Val-ès-Dunes, seems rather unlikely in a Norman document of the mid-eleventh century. Third, the Truce is explicitly stated to be limited to 'this bishopric' which is unexpected in a document supposedly promulgated during an assembly that brought together the whole political community of Normandy at Caen.

There are, then, problems with accepting Bessin's text as William's Truce but as a version of this document was published by the bishop of Cambrai in 1036 it might still have *influenced* the Norman Truce and thus the *Consuetudines*. The same might be said of the text of the Truce produced by Bishop Warin of Beauvais in 1023, which he presented to King Robert the Pious. This text includes prohibitions and promises not found in Bessin's text but which seem to be relevant here:

> I will not seize villeins of either sex or sergeants or merchants or their coins or hold them for ransom or ruin them with exactions on account of their lord's war ... I will not burn or destroy houses unless I find an enemy horseman or a thief within, and unless they are joined to a real castle ... I will not destroy a mill or seize the grain that is in it, unless I am on a cavalcade or with the host, or it is on my land ... I will not attack merchants or pilgrims or take their possessions unless they commit crimes.[48]

---

[46] BnF, MS lat. 1928 and Rouen, BM, MS 1383, respectively.

[47] The manuscript in question is Vatican, MS Regin. Latin, no. 596.

[48] 'Peace oath proposed by Bishop Warin of Beauvais to King Robert the Pious (1023)', trans. R. Landes, in T. Head and R. Landes (ed.), *The Peace of God: Social Violence and*

Normandy's proximity to Beauvais, Bishop Warin's presence at Richard II's court in January 1024,[49] and Duke Richard II's generally good relations with King Robert, suggest that Richard might at least have perused a text of Bishop Warin's Truce. Even though it was not implemented in the duchy, a copy might have remained to hand.

And so it is possible that the prohibitions found in clauses 11, 12, and 14 of the *Consuetudines* – which were concerned with the protection of merchants and pilgrims, and the capture of men and their possessions during war – were ultimately derived from one form of Truce or another. The same might also be the case with clauses 6, 7, and 8 – which prohibited arson and destruction of property, assaults in the forests, and distraint. But these three clauses might equally have been the result of a more specific concern to limit the damage that might arise during disputes over property and feuds.[50]

There is some evidence that the dukes' rights of jurisdiction as set out in the *Consuetudines* were respected and enforced. The dukes were certainly determined to establish their right to enter and garrison their subjects' castles at need, and can be seen doing so from 1053 up to 1135, as will be discussed below.[51] The right to licence castles, and to demolish unlicensed ones, also found in clause 4 of the *Consuetudines*, is evidenced in the narrative sources, too. For example, Poitiers says that after Val-ès-Dunes the erstwhile rebels, 'hastened at [Duke William's] command to destroy utterly all the new fortifications which they had constructed in their eagerness for change'.[52] Equally, after Henry I's victory at Tinchebray he, 'demolished the unlicensed castles (*adulterina castella*) that Robert [of Bellême] and the factious lords had built'.[53]

Orderic's depiction of the failings and injustices of Robert Curthose's rule implies that the dukes had previously exercised, and would later do so again, others of the rights listed in the *Consuetudines*. He recorded, for example, that Robert of Bellême was responsible for a breach of clause 2 of the *Consuetudines*. Both he and Robert fitz Giroie had been serving in the duke's army. Bellême was returning from the campaign when he attacked Robert fitz Giroie's castle of Saint-Céneri. Orderic made it clear that this took place within the period

---

Religious Response in France around the Year 1000 (Ithaca, NY and London, 1992), pp. 332–4.

[49] *RADN*, no. 26.

[50] See below, *infra*, pp. 451–2.

[51] See below, Chapter 11, pp. 639–41.

[52] Poitiers, p. 12. William of Jumièges noted this, too, but less clearly: 'And thus after the fortresses had been destroyed everywhere no rebel dared to rise against him any more' (Jumièges, ii. 122).

[53] Orderic, vi. 98.

covered by the duke's peace: 'The garrison, thinking that Robert was sharing in the general military service with the duke, had left the castle and were scattered about the countryside where they pleased, believing themselves secure'.[54] This breach went unpunished, although Robert of Bellême was obliged to hand the castle back to Robert fitz Giroie in 1094 as the unexpected result of a campaign that Bellême had himself demanded in the hope that the duke would demolish the castle at Montaigu which Giroie had built without licence. In this instance, the unlicensed castle was duly demolished, too.[55] The duke's success here might have been unusual. Orderic wrote bluntly that during his reign, 'unlicensed castles were built in many places'.[56]

Orderic noted a number of other breaches of the *Consuetudines*, too. Houses and mills were burned and property laid waste as a result of disputes over property, in breach of clause 6: 'They [the lords of Normandy] found pretexts for quarrelling so that they might overrun the surrounding settlements in their conflicts with each other, and be free to plunder and burn without respect for anyone'.[57] A specific example of such a practice might be found in a notice in the cartulary of Saint-Etienne of Caen which records that a certain Robert fitz Bernard burned four houses and a wine press along with all the vessels containing wine during the grape-harvest at Moult one year between 1101 and 1107.[58] The prohibition on open warfare was also frequently ignored. There were open wars between William of Breteuil and Ascelin Goel over the castle of Ivry;[59] Ralph of Tosny was attacked by Count William of Evreux, apparently due to some slighting remarks Ralph's wife had made to William's;[60] and Richard of Courcy and Robert of Bellême also fought each other, this time due to the latter's ambition.[61] Writing of the period after Curthose's return to Normandy in 1100, Orderic remarked that, 'some rebels waged open war against their loyal neighbours and stained the fertile soil with ravages, conflagrations, and bloody slaughter'.[62] As all of these likely involved riding out with hauberk and standard, they may all be supposed to have breached clause 8 of the *Consuetudines*.

Orderic seems also to have noted the lack of enforcement of clause 9. He

---

[54] Orderic, iv. 292.

[55] Orderic, iv. 294.

[56] Orderic, iv. 146. In particular he may have had in mind the castles built by Robert of Bellême at Fourches and Château-Gontier (Orderic, iv. 228).

[57] Orderic, iv. 146–8.

[58] Ctl. Caen, fos. 53v–54r. The dates are the limits of Abbot Robert's rule over the monastery (*Normannia Monastica*, ii. 47–8).

[59] Orderic, iv. 198, 202.

[60] Orderic, iv. 212–14.

[61] Orderic, iv. 230.

[62] Orderic, v. 310.

certainly appears to have focused on the offences covered by that section in particular, even if he did not give them exclusive attention. He reported that: 'Daily they did arson, rape and homicide',[63] and that 'arson and rapine devastated the whole province',[64] although he also wrote that 'theft and rapine were daily occurrences'.[65] In 1105 at Carentan, Bishop Serlo told Henry I that

> this very year, Robert of Bellême burnt the church of Tournai in my own diocese, and destroyed forty-five men and women inside it. I recall these things with sorrow in the sight of God; I address them too, my lord king, to your ears, so that your spirit may be kindled by the zeal of God to imitate Phineas and Mattathias and his sons. Rise up boldly in the name of God, win the heritage of your fathers with the sword of justice, and rescue your ancestral land and the people of God from the hands of reprobates.

There is no sense in Orderic's *History* that these offenders were punished by Curthose, of course. Indeed he made the point that the duke was unable to do anything about any of them.

Orderic, then, suggested that Curthose was unable to enforce clauses 2, 4, 6, 8, and 9 of the *Consuetudines*, albeit that he rarely supported his claims with examples, and even when he did they were not numerous. Still, it is significant that he used what was evidently a well-known list of ducal rights to make the point that Curthose had lost control of Normandy. Indeed, in addition to the customs on Orderic's implied list, it is possible that Curthose lost control of the coinage, too, although the evidence for this is ambiguous.[66] Indications of Curthose's increasing ineffectiveness might also be found in the unusually high number of settlements and the unusually low number of ducal judgements, made during his rule, and the list of losses suffered by the nuns of Caen which covered Curthose's reign but not those of his father or brother (unlike the similar list compiled by the monks of Mont-Saint-Michel). Indeed, the nuns also complained

---

[63] Orderic, iv. 146.

[64] Orderic, v. 24.

[65] Orderic, v. 302.

[66] This evidence takes the form of an issue of coins bearing the legend 'ROBERTUS COM' instead of 'NORMANNIA' as was usual at this period (Dumas, 'Les monnaies Normandes', 128; F. Dumas, 'Un denier normand au nom de Robert, comte', *Bulletin de la société françoise de numismatique*, 35 (1980), 669–70; F. Dumas and J. Pilet-Lemière, 'La monnaie normand – X^e–Xe siècles: Le point de la recherche en 1987', in *Les mondes normands (VIIIe–XIIe siècles)* (Caen, 1989), p. 127. The coins date to around the beginning of the twelfth century, and it has been suggested that rather than Curthose the count concerned is Robert of Eu, Robert of Meulan, or Robert of Mortain.

of men wounded and beaten during the period covered by the Truce of God.[67] As a good ruler by definition did justice and kept the peace, it is hardly surprising that Orderic should portray Curthose as such a failure (especially as he wrote with the benefit of hindsight), or that he should lament, in light of the duke's apparent inability to uphold and enforce the customs enjoyed by his father, that, 'all that had been achieved by the activity and zeal of the far-sighted lord and his support-ers and preserved in Normandy for a long time past was ruined by the inactivity of the slothful duke'.[68]

The *Consuetudines et iusticie*, then, established a list of offences over which the duke had jurisdiction. We can see that the dukes had inherited some of the rights enjoyed by Carolingian kings, for example concerning the minting of coins and the construction of castles and possibly protection of travellers, as well as some of the protections elsewhere found in the Truce of God, and perhaps some additional rights related to a desire to limit the disorder that might be caused by the feud. The list was avowedly incomplete, but it may be supposed that it reflected what the political community thought was most important. It is therefore interesting that economic concerns seem to have been so prominent. The duke was responsible for the production of a reliable and stable coinage, and thus might punish those who undermined this work. Merchants, too, were protected. Property – houses and mills and the land itself – was protected from destruction related to minor disputes, which not only established peace but also protected the food supply. There were political concerns, too. Those going to or from the duke's court, some of whom would have to travel very long distances, were protected. So were those who went to fight in the army. The safety of these individuals was paramount to the working of the duchy, and as they were on the duke's business, it was only right that they should be enveloped by his protection. In contrast, conventional offences are remote from the *Consuetudines*. Only arson, rape, and housebreak-ing are explicitly mentioned, although the impression is that the duke would usually be expected to have jurisdiction over them. Other offences, however, were omitted from the list altogether.

In some cases, the omissions may be readily explained. Theft and robbery, for example, could be left out because they had been the subject of ducal legisla-tion. Dudo of Saint-Quentin was able to picture Rollo issuing 'a law within the boundaries of Normandy that no one should take part in any robbery',[69] and although Rollo himself is unlikely really to have legislated in this manner, Dudo

---

[67] For settlements see Table 8. *Chs. Holy Trinity*, pp. 125–8 (no. 15), *NI*, pp. 63–4, with an English abstract in *CDF*, no. 424; *Ctl. Mont-Saint-Michel*, pp. 180–4 (no. 115).

[68] Orderic, iv. 148.

[69] *Dudo*, p. 52; Jumièges, i. 68.

was writing for Duke Richard II, and *he* might have done so. After all, Dudo is unlikely to have said something that appeared ridiculous to his contemporaries. William of Poitiers could remark that 'in Normandy the robber and brigand were hated, that both of them were punished by a just custom, and that neither could purchase pardon cheaply'.[70] Orderic noted that, in 1067, 'William remained in Normandy, giving all his thoughts to establishing an enduring peace in the country. With the advice of discerning men he laid down just laws ... He sent out heralds to proclaim peace for all men, denizens and foreigners alike, and threatened thieves, rebels, and all disturbers of the peace with severe but just judgements.'[71] In all probability, then, there was no need to resort to custom for such matters, as law was not lacking. Moreover, there may have been a presumption that lords would have jurisdiction over thieves who were either their men or found on their land. The monks of Saint-Evroult tried one of their tenants for theft, for example, and the monks of Saint-Pierre-sur-Dives were given jurisdiction over thieves by their founders.[72] The much later *Très ancien coutumier* gives a sense of how widespread this right was by the beginning of the thirteenth century when it states that 'each lord shall have his pleas, and theft'. Although the evidence is late, it does seem unlikely that this state of affairs had only come about under Angevin rule.[73]

The complete omission of all mention of homicide from the *Consuetudines* most likely reflects the fact that prosecution of that offence was not a ducal monopoly. It was often pursued by way of the feud instead.[74] On the basis of the six or seven homicides reported for eleventh-century Normandy (although not necessarily by eleventh-century writers), Emily Zack Tabuteau has argued that 'the prescribed method of pursuing homicide, whether deliberate or accidental, seems to have been the feud'.[75] Orderic provided a useful example of how a feud might arise and be pursued. He wrote that, in 1077, Hugh Bunel broke into the castle at Bures-sur-Dives, found Countess Mabel of Bellême relaxing in bed after a

<hr/>

[70] Poitiers, pp. 24–6.
[71] Orderic, ii. 208.
[72] Orderic, ii. 60–4. For Saint-Pierre-sur-Dives, and also the example of Count Robert of Meulan, see below, pp. 456–9.
[73] *TAC*, i. 50 (ch. 59).
[74] The idea of the feud is usefully discussed in W. I. Miller, *Bloodtaking and Peacemaking: Feud, Law, and Society in Saga Iceland* (Chicago and London, 1990), pp. 179–82 and Hyams, *Rancor and Reconciliation*, pp. 4–16. Both English and Carolingian monarchs had been reticent in making laws about homicide: see the discussion in Lambert, 'Theft, homicide and crime', 9–10, 15–16, 20–25.
[75] E. Z. Tabuteau, 'Punishments in eleventh-century Normandy, in *Conflict in Medieval Europe: Changing Perspectives on Society and Culture*, ed. W. C. Brown and P. Górecki (Aldershot, 2003), p. 136.

bath, and cut off her head with his sword.[76] The attack was not unprovoked. Mabel had unjustly deprived Hugh of his paternal inheritance comprising the castle of La Roche-Mabile near Alençon, which had driven him to a frenzy of grief. 'When the murder of this terrible lady had been accomplished', he added, '… the authors of the crime fled to Apulia. Hugh of Montgommery was in the same place with sixteen knights; but although on learning of his mother's death he pursued the fugitive homicides he could not capture them.'[77]

Just a short time after the murder, William Pantulf returned to Normandy from Italy. His timing was unfortunate. As William had also suffered at the hands of his lady, Mabel of Bellême, losing the castle of Peray to her, 'a suspicion arose that she had perished by his scheming, especially as Hugh and William were close friends and in frequent communication with one another'. William thus fled to sanctuary at Saint-Evroult with his wife and sons until it was agreed that he might prove his innocence by the ordeal of hot iron. 'He carried the glowing iron in his bare hand, and by the will of God remained unscorched … His enemies, eager for his blood, stood looking on ready armed, so that if the accused were found guilty by the ordeal of fire they might forthwith punish him by cutting off his guilty head.'[78]

Orderic made it clear that members of the Montgommery family took the lead in the hunt for Mabel's killers. Hugh of Montgommery chased Hugh Bunel and his brothers as they fled. The agents of Mabel's sons pursued Hugh to Apulia, Sicily, and Byzantium. The family stood waiting with drawn swords at William Pantulf's trial. It was, then, the victim's family which took the lead in attempting to bring the killers to justice and punishment.

By the time Mabel was murdered, William the Bastard had already legislated to reduce the disruptive effects of the feud. In 1075, he introduced a rule forbidding the prosecution of a feud by anyone other than the son or father of the victim.[79] Some of the clauses found in the *Consuetudines* also seem to have been concerned with – or would have had the effect of – limiting the feud still further. For example, after the fictional and eponymous Raoul of Cambrai had been killed, his kinsman gathered their relatives and friends and went to the Vermandois, where 'they have set up their ambush in a copse'.[80] This would have been forbidden in Normandy

---

[76] It has been noted that this may be a reference to the murder of Agamemnon and thus not accurate.

[77] Orderic, iii. 136.

[78] Orderic, iii. 160–2.

[79] 'Annales Uticensis', in *Orderici Vitalis ecclesiasticae historiae libri tredecim*, ed. Le Prévost, p. 158; *RHGF*, xi. 379 (s.a. 1074); noted in *NI*, Appendix D, p. 278 and n. 9 and in Bates, *Normandy*, pp. 164, 185 n. 69.

[80] Quoted in S. D. White, 'Feuding and peace-making in the Touraine around the year

under clause 7. Equally, the prohibition on arson and wasting for a plea over property prevented the use of violence in negotiations that were intended to lead to settlements. Elsewhere in France, according to Stephen White, such violence might be used as an element in legal strategy: 'even where the violence escalated to the point where litigants damaged a mill or a vineyard, cut down trees, attacked people, or killed animals or people, its relationship to a claim is clear.'[81] If the dukes were strong enough to do it, preventing such activities made it more likely that an accommodation would be reached by the parties, limited the likelihood that a new feud (or feuds) would be created, and – most important of all – allowed the duke to bring more cases into his own court.

The *Consuetudines*, however, failed to acknowledge an innovation that William the Bastard had made in order to trump the claims of families to prosecute the feud and to bring more cases of homicide into his court. That innovation is revealed by Orderic's report of the murder of Mabel of Bellême and its aftermath, which reveals that the Montgommery family did not act alone in their attempts to bring Mabel's killers to justice. Hugh Bunel was pursued across Europe by the spies and agents not just of Roger of Montgommery but of King William, too. Equally, when William Pantulf returned to Normandy he was accused not of murder but of treason ('nam crimen ei proditionis impingebatur'),[82] and although Roger of Montgommery seized his lands (as his lord) and demanded his death, Pantulf's case was heard in the royal duke's court.

King William's actions here suggest an attempt to bring cases of homicide more completely under his own jurisdiction. Clearly, the right of the victim's family to prosecute a feud remained intact, but William could gain jurisdiction over Pantulf's case by claiming that the homicide was treason, presumably because it breached his peace (although in this case the offence might also have been characterized as housebreaking).[83] Orderic's representation of the charge

---

1100', *Traditio*, 42 (1986), 262–3, reprinted in S. D. White, *Feuding and Peace-Making in Eleventh-Century France* (Aldershot, 2005), Ch. I.

[81] S. D. White, 'The "feudal revolution" comment', *Past and Present*, 152 (1996), 212–13, reprinted in S. D. White, *Feuding and Peace-Making in Eleventh-Century France* (Aldershot, 2005), Ch. II.

[82] Orderic, iii. 160.

[83] This is similar to an idea expounded by Patrick Wormald, who argued that 'conventional offences' such as theft were a breach of the oath of fidelity sworn to the English kings: P. Wormald, 'Frederic William Maitland and the Earliest English law', in his *Legal Culture in the Early Medieval West: Law as Text, Image and Experience* (London, 1999), pp. 62–3. Lambert found that royal intervention in homicide arose as a result of breaches of the kings' protection. Where such breaches were absent, kings were not involved (Lambert, 'Theft, homicide and crime', 34). Alice Taylor has argued that homicides in Scotland might also have resulted in breaches of a lord's protection that would

is supported by the terminology used in the record of another homicide found in the cartulary of the abbey of Mont-Saint-Michel. The report states that a certain Roger had come across the monks' swine at Potrel and wickedly killed the swine-herd. Abbot Ranulf immediately appealed to Duke William who banished Roger from the duchy because of his crime of *lèse majesté* (the Latin term *maiestas* is, unusually, used here).[84] It may be supposed that here, too, the treason took the form of a breach of the duke's peace. That is a conclusion supported by the English *Leges Henrici Primi*, which announces that some pleas cannot be compensated for with money, including 'violation of ... the protection of the king through the commission of homicide'.[85] Thus it seems that the dukes could bring cases of homicide, otherwise dealt with by a 'private' feud, into their courts by developing the law of treason. The fact that the *Consuetudines et iusticie* makes no mention of this recent development might indicate that it had not yet become firmly estab-lished or that the Norman lords opposed the extension of the duke's jurisdiction or peace in this way. And in any event, the feud continued in Normandy, and might still be pursued even at the end of the twelfth century, when these same dual interests in homicides seem to be reflected in the *Très ancien coutumier*. Among the clauses of this enigmatic customary is one which states that a fugitive for homicide could not have peace until he had made a compact with both the duke *and* the relatives of the victim.[86]

At the very end of his reign, Henry I took his jurisdiction over homicide a step further, although building on the same foundation. After his victory at Val-ès-Dunes in 1047, Duke William had commanded that the Truce of God should be respected in Normandy.[87] The dukes had continued to oversee the enforcement of the Truce, which thus comprised part of the duke's peace even though it was

require compensation: A. Taylor, 'Crime without punishment: medieval Scottish law in comparative perspective', *ANS*, 35 (2013), 296–300.

[84] See Hagger, 'Secular law and custom', 835–7. The term was also used by Thietmar of Merseberg, who wrote *c.* 1009–18 and Lampert of Herfeld, who wrote *c.* 1080, following its introduction into German law by Henry III: Bagge, *Kings, Politics, and the Right Order of the World*, pp. 146, 244–5, 259; T. Reuter, *Germany in the Early Middle Ages, c. 800–1056* (London, 1991), pp. 322–5.

[85] *LHP*, para. 12.1a.

[86] *TAC*, i. 31, Ch. 36.4. On the other side of the Channel, the anonymous author of the *Leges Henrici Primi* seems also to have been concerned to promote Henry I's posi-tion as 'dominant regulator of feud arrangements' (Hyams, *Rancor and Reconciliation*, pp. 138–9).

[87] De Boüard, 'Sur les origines de la trêve de Dieu en Normandie', 172–4; Bates, *Normandy*, pp. 163–4. Wace also noted that the duke imposed the Truce of God on Normandy, but apparently suggested that the council was held after the battle of Varaville in 1157 (Wace, pp. 150–1). The council is also mentioned in a *pancarte* for the abbey of Saint-Pierre of Préaux dating from 1078 × 1079 (*Ctl. Préaux*, A1 at p. 7).

largely administered by the Church. In 1135, Henry issued an edict concerning 'killers who kill men during the Truce and in the peace of the Church and infringe the Truce'. The edict then established: 'if someone shall wish to challenge that killer to a duel, that duel shall be held in my court, and, if he shall be convicted by it, that bishop in whose diocese this deed was done shall have the fine by the hand of my justice.'[88] Thus Henry extended his jurisdiction to cover an additional, albeit select, species of homicide.

If the dukes came to characterize homicide as a breach of their peace, and sought to gain jurisdiction over a greater proportion of cases as a result, then it may be supposed that they would also hope to extend their jurisdiction over as many other serious offences as they could. Indeed, the *Consuetudines et iusticie* itself provides some evidence of the dukes' attempts to trump, or to gain oversight of, offences that would otherwise fall to the jurisdiction of their barons. If a lord had jurisdiction over arson, for example, that jurisdiction would have been lost if the offence was related to a plea over land. Even jurisdiction over conventional offences such as assault would be lost if the assault was on an individual going to or coming from the duke's court, or serving in the duke's army, or if he was a merchant or a pilgrim, or if it had happened in a forest. Furthermore, the dukes could legislate, and thereby set out a procedure to be followed in certain situations or oblige lords to enforce particular punishments on those they convicted. In this regard, it may be significant that after Rollo is said to have legislated to extend his protection to all ploughs, the peasant of Longpaon brought his case before the duke.[89]

But although the dukes might attempt to enlarge their jurisdiction, it is clear that they did not need a monopoly on the judgement of offenders to be lauded for their peace and justice. The comments of William of Jumièges and William of Poitiers regarding the peace that Normandy enjoyed under William the Bastard, and those of Orderic and others on Henry I, suggest that they at least retained enough control over the punishment of offenders to ensure that they

---

[88] The earliest copy is Evreux, AD Eure, G122 (s. xiii–xiv, cartulary of the cathedral chapter), fol. 40v. The text is printed in *TAC*, 1.65–8 (ch. 71), and see also p. 65, n. 7 for Tardif's view that the part of the cartulary that contains the text was written early in the thirteenth century. A summary is printed at *CDF*, no. 290. The act is discussed by R. C. Van Caenegem, 'Public prosecution of crime in twelfth-century England', in *Church and Government in the Middle Ages: Essays presented to C. R. Cheney on his 70th Birthday*, ed. C. N. L. Brooke, D. E. Luscombe, G. H. Martin, and D. Owen (Cambridge, 1976), p. 66 and by Hagger, 'Secular law and custom', 840–5. See also above, Chapter 7, p. 368.

[89] *Dudo*, p. 52; Jumièges, i. 68. Robert of Torigny believed that the duke concerned was Richard II (Jumièges, ii. 286–8). For the story of the peasant of Longpaon see also below, *infra*, pp. 487–8.

gained their plaudits and their duchy enjoyed what contemporaries thought of as peace.[90]

It is nonetheless worth reconsidering what the evidence – which is somewhat limited – can tell us about the extent of seigniorial jurisdiction over offenders, not least because it brings into question the widely accepted view that Norman lords enjoyed greater rights of jurisdiction than English ones.[91]

Clauses 8 and 10 of the *Consuetudines et iusticie* illustrate well the difficulty of the evidence where it exists. Clause 8 reads:

> It was not permitted, while looking for an enemy or taking a surety, [for anyone] to carry a standard or hauberk or to sound their horn, nor to send a body of men to set an ambush, nor to condemn a man to loss of members without judgment unless, however, he was discovered in such act or offence (*forisfacto*) for which he ought to lose members, and unless by judgement of the court of the lord of Normandy of this which pertains to him or by the judgment of the court of the barons (*iudicio curie baronum*) for this which pertains to the barons.

Given the function of the *Consuetudines*, this clause is principally about the duke's jurisdiction rather than that of his barons. Nonetheless, it implies that some lords had the right to sentence an offender who had been caught in a particular act to the loss of members, provided they held a trial before doing so (there was no right to summary punishment in such cases, it seems). But the clause does not elaborate on baronial rights, and what was written suggests those rights were limited. For example, even if they had caught the offender red-handed, lords had no right to inflict a capital penalty on him/her.[92] Those English lords who had the right to hang thieves caught red-handed, and there were many of them, thus enjoyed a greater liberty than was implied here. Instead, the clause is evidence that the political community of Normandy acknowledged the lord of Normandy's right to supervise even quite mundane 'criminal' justice, and that lords who overstepped the mark should be punished.

---

[90] For example, see Poitiers, p. 80.

[91] David Douglas opined that 'many of the greatest magnates in Normandy ... such as Roger of Beaumont or the count of Evreux, certainly exercised very wide judicial rights' (Douglas, *William the Conqueror*, pp. 151–2). His failure to name others is probably telling. Judith Green thought that 'Norman lords probably enjoyed much wider powers of justice on their continental estates than in England' (Green, *Government*, p. 116). David Crouch agreed (D. Crouch, *The English Aristocracy, 1066–1272: A Social Transformation* (New Haven, CT and London, 2011), p. 182). In both cases, this suggestion was made without any proof or authority being offered.

[92] Haskins thought otherwise: 'the forfeiture of life and limb in baronial courts is presupposed in the inquest of 1091' (*NI*, p. 29).

Clauses 9 and 10, in contrast, concern serious offences. They read:

9. It was not permitted in Normandy to do *hamfara* or arson or rape of wives or to take distraint, unless a claim about it was made at the house of the person who ought to have the claim about it.[93]

10. And if these things have been done, the lord of Normandy shall have concerning it what he ought to have in those places where he ought to have it, and the barons shall have concerning it that which pertains to them in those places in which they ought to have it (*barones inde habuerunt quod ad eos pertinuit in illis locis in quibus habere debuerunt*).

Haskins wrote that these two clauses revealed a division of 'jurisdiction' which 'belongs in some places to the duke and in others to his barons', but that is not what the clause says at all.[94] Before offering an alternative interpretation, however, some context is required. Let us imagine that a man holds his property from two lords, a bishop and an abbot. This man lives in the outer sanctuary of a church. He commissions a theft. He is caught in the act. He is judged before the duke who orders him to be hanged. The bishop and the abbot recover the lands that he held from them, as is their right. The canons made at the council of Lillebonne in 1080 provided that in such a case the bishop was also entitled to a fine.[95] Clause 10 of the *Consuetudines*, then, need not be about jurisdiction. It might simply comprise an acknowledgement that some barons had an interest in the punishment of those who had commissioned the listed offences, in the form of forfeitures and fines. Further, clause 10 reveals that seigniorial interests might be limited to particular places rather than encompassing their entire honours.

   In part because he was to some extent misled by an interpolated act for the monks of Mont-Saint-Michel, Haskins also argued that grants of 'criminal' jurisdiction were revealed by the gifts of ducal customs found in acts for the monks of Bernay, Jumièges, and Mont-Saint-Michel: 'we may say provisionally that when the duke wished to convey jurisdiction, he made a grant of the ducal *consuetudines*.'[96] In interpreting that word in this way, he almost certainly

---

[93] The *Leges Henrici Primi* state in a similar vein that 'no one may distrain another without judgment or permission' (*LHP*, p. 166, para 51.3). The clause is discussed in J. Hudson, *Land, Law, and Lordship in Anglo-Norman England* (Oxford, 1994), pp. 27–29.

[94] *NI*, pp. 28–9. Fauroux believed that part of the act for the monks of Mont-Saint-Michel on which Haskins relied to have been a later interpolation (*RADN*, no. 49).

[95] Orderic, iii. 32.

[96] *NI*, pp. 27, 29. Haskins may also have been too reliant on Wace's translation of earlier grants of *consuetudines* to the monks of Cerisy-la-Forêt. Wace said that Duke Robert gave his monks 'the same jurisdiction the duke had in his land, covering murder, theft, kidnap, homicide and arson' (Wace, p. 117; *NI*, p. 279, n. 15), but does not state his source. There may have been intervening documents, now lost.

conjured seigniorial jurisdictions over offences out of thin air. Instead, there is no good reason to think that a grant of *consuetudines* comprised anything more than a grant of the income arising from the specified pleas or revenues. The records relating to the grant of the *consuetudines vicecomitatus* to the monks of Préaux;[97] the use of the word in the canons of the council of Lillebonne and in relation to episcopal customs more generally;[98] the twelfth-century title of the *Consuetudines et iusticie*; the context of such wording in ducal *acta*;[99] the failure of later confirmations to elaborate on earlier vague wording;[100] and near contemporary usage in England where, according to Bruce O'Brien, grants of *grithbrce, hamsocn*, wreck, and so on were actually grants of the fines arising from such pleas, or perhaps freedom from the consequences of particular events or actions, not jurisdiction over them,[101] all reinforce this interpretation.

Occasionally, the evidence is full enough and precise enough to reveal that a Norman lord *did* enjoy jurisdiction over important offences. These lords certainly included in their number the counts of Eu, and although the evidence is less good for the other Norman counties, the fact that the counts of Evreux and Mortain employed justices in the twelfth century implies that they, too, enjoyed wide-ranging franchises.[102] Countess Lecelina of Eu's deed of foundation for the monks of her abbey of Saint-Pierre-sur-Dives, originally made *c.* 1046, was confirmed by

---

[97] *RADN*, no. 121; *Ctl. Préaux*, A161, A163. This is because those customs included the revenue produced by bernage, which was a tax (see below, Chapter 10, pp. 585–6).

[98] Orderic, iii. 26–34. The episcopal *consuetudines* recorded at Lillebonne in 1080 were generally concerned with revenues in the form of fines rather than with jurisdiction over offences – as is further suggested by a clause that expressly states: 'where the crimes of the inhabitants of a diocese are subject by custom to the bishop they shall be judged by the bishop.' Notably, the grants of justice over 'criminal sins' to the monks of Caen were not described as comprising 'customs' (*Regesta: William*, no. 57).

[99] For example *NI*, p. 101 for Montebourg: 'Precipio quod abbatia de Monteburgo teneat … elemosinam meam terram de Foucaruilla liberam et quietam de teloneo et de uerec et de omnibus consuetudinibus et de omnibus querelis.' Freedom from wreck would probably allow an individual to recover beached ships and the cargo that would otherwise have been lost to the duke or the local franchise holder.

[100] The relevant part of the act for Bernay reads: 'I grant also in the vill of Bernay the market through each week of the year and the annual fairs and all customs which from these things, as much as from all the aforesaid vills, pertain to us' (*RADN*, no. 35). The monks of Jumièges received: 'all the customs which I held by right in all the lands of that place in the county' (*RADN*, no. 36). Henry's later confirmations for Bernay and Jumièges may be found at *Recueil Henri II*, nos. 95, 527.

[101] B. R. O'Brien, *God's Peace and King's Peace: The Laws of Edward the Confessor* (Philadelphia, 1999), pp. 74–7.

[102] For more on the Norman counts, see below, Chapter 9, pp. 564–5.

Henry I in 1121 × 1128.[103] According to this diploma, which survives as an authentic original, the monks were to hold their estates

> free and absolved and quit from all exactions and secular customs … and services, except army-service, and my aids, and pleas of money and of my army. Such pleas, if they arise, shall be held in the abbot's court just as they were in Count William's court. And not only this, but all other pleas of all complaints of their men shall be held in the abbot's court, except war (*bellum*), if it should arise. Of pleas of money, the same shall be judged in the abbot's court but they shall be concluded at the treasury (ar*cham monete*). And none of my justices (*iusticiariorum*) shall presume violently to force the abbot to pleadings outside his court unless they are such pleas as ought to be concluded in my presence. Also no one shall presume to disturb the abbey with seizures And if a claim is made to the abbot and that man (i.e. the abbot) does not wish to do justice and right, then my own justice (*iusticiarius*) shall be required to do it, who above all others in my place holds justice. Of arson, truly, and rape and murder, should anyone be convicted, the abbot shall have all their goods … That if a thief is taken within the *centenaria*, he shall be returned to the abbot. And if duel (*bellum*) should arise from whatever cause or complaint, it shall be held in the abbot's court, and the fine and forfeiture shall be his, just as they were Count William's.[104]

Pleas over money, that is counterfeit coins, and of the army were two of the customs held by the duke in the *Consuetudines et iusticie*. These pleas, jurisdiction over which must have been transferred to Count William before he gave them to the monks, were heard in the abbot's court, although pleas over the coinage had still to be terminated at the duke's treasury (although, strictly speaking, there was no treasury yet).[105] Jurisdiction over the pleas 'of all complaints' of the abbey's men – but only the abbey's men – was also held by the abbot. Their 'complaints (*querelis*)', presumably relating to both 'criminal' and 'civil' matters,[106] would previously have been heard by the count, of course. That jurisdiction included cases of arson, rape, and murder, and the diploma excluded the claims of other parties to a convicted man's chattels and thus to any fines that might otherwise have accrued. The prosecution of thieves who were taken within the abbey's *banlieu* also fell to

[103] *Normannia monastica*, ii. 295, 299.
[104] Caen, AD Calvados, H 7031(5) = *Regesta*, ii. no. 1569.
[105] For a discussion of the treasury, see below, Chapter 10, pp. 607–9.
[106] *Querela* could relate to offences or crimes as well as pleas over property (see, for example, Malmesbury, *GP*, i. 184).

the abbot's jurisdiction. This would be expected given the relatively widespread right to try this category of offender, but it is possible that mention is made of a *centenaria* here because the abbot's jurisdiction covered all thieves taken within this *banlieu*, rather than only thieves who were also his men. The abbot *might* also hold duels to settle cases in his court, although it is possible that the diploma contradicts itself on this point, perhaps because it was updated but not revised owing to concerns about the shedding of blood in a monastic forum.[107] Here, then, there is excellent evidence for the existence of a wide-ranging jurisdiction, now divided between the count and the abbot of Saint-Pierre-sur-Dives. The counts continued to enjoy these wide-ranging rights, by then expressly said to have included the pleas of the sword, until the thirteenth century.[108]

The jurisdiction enjoyed by the Beaumont family, lords of Pont-Audemer and Beaumont-le-Roger and also counts of Meulan in France from 1080,[109] is less clear, owing to the ambiguous nature of the evidence. In its ambiguity it is much more typical of the materials that must be used to estimate the extent of seigniorial jurisdiction in Normandy. For that reason alone, the wording of a notice found in the cartulary of Saint-Pierre of Préaux recording a grant made by Count Robert of Meulan in 1106 is worth giving in full, although the document also sheds light on the apprehension of robbers and thieves as well as the division of the revenues that would accrue when an offender was convicted:

> In the year of the incarnation 1106, Robert, count of Meulan, sitting in the chapter of the blessed Peter of Préaux, in the presence of Abbot Richard of Bayeux, and with the convent sitting around them, granted to the abbot his liberty of earthly possessions and the customs of judicial power, saving the order of the monks, just as the count has them in his own lands. This is: that the same abbot shall have his forfeitures which he had following human laws from homicides and thieves and others convicted by capital sentence as required by the custom of the country. That if a member of the count's household should perhaps find a robber (*latronus*) in the land of the abbot, he shall take him immediately and entrust him to the abbot's *procurator* or,

---

[107] Such a concern may be seen in the record of a dispute of 1074 (*Regesta: William*, no. 262 and see below, *infra*, p. 463).

[108] In 1219, when Philip restored the county to Countess Alice, he reserved to himself the pleas of the sword in the county (D. Power, *The Norman Frontier in the Twelfth and Early Thirteenth Centuries* (Cambridge, 2004), p. 56).

[109] D. Crouch, 'Robert of Beaumont, count of Meulan and Leicester: his lands, his acts, and his self-image', in *Henry I and the Anglo-Norman World: Studies in Memory of C. Warren Hollister*, ed. D. F. Fleming and J. M. Pope (Woodbridge, 2007), p. 92 and the references at n. 3.

giving pledges, he shall be retained in the same land until the matter should be brought to the ears of the abbot. Then whatever he [i.e. the count] has in a robber thus caught in his [land] the same abbot shall have in his. Moreover, if any thief (*fur*) of the land of the abbot shall be taken in the land of the count, the abbot shall give pledges for him, if he wishes to have him, and afterwards the charge will be heard in the court of the count. And if he shall be convicted, the power shall remain with the count and everything that shall be found on the land of St Peter will be handed over to the said abbot.

Again, he bestowed on his abbey a *banlieu* and *ullac* and *hamfara* and arson. And the bounds of this *banlieu* shall be from Saint-Germain up to the lazar-house and up to Pont-Guéroult, and up to Foutelaie.[110]

The notice reveals that Count Robert held the right to the forfeitures of those robbers and other offenders who were his men and who were sentenced to the death penalty, although it is not clear that he had the right to convict or sentence such offenders himself. He did have the right to try thieves, however, and he might have had the right to sentence them to death. It is not clear that he would otherwise have had the right to take their chattels. The creation of a *banlieu* implies a grant of jurisdiction over the offences mentioned. An issue here, however, is that *ullac* comprised outlawry and was thus a punishment rather than an offence,[111] and that might in turn suggest that the abbot was entitled only to the forfeitures left by outlawed men and those convicted of arson and housebreaking rather than comprising a grant of jurisdiction over such offenders. The *banlieu* itself was also limited, comprising a suburb of Pont-Audemer. While it may be supposed that Count Robert continued to hold these rights outside the abbot's *banlieu*, his own jurisdiction or rights might not have covered more than the rest of the town.[112] The act thus provides only ambiguous evidence for the extent of the jurisdictions of both abbot and count, which could have included the right to judge serious offences, but might equally have comprised only the right to take some of the profits of justice.

The possibility that a lord's jurisdiction over serious offences might be limited to a single town or vill, as suggested above, should not be excluded from consideration, not least because that is what we see in each of the four surviving grants in which the dukes handed over a wide-ranging jurisdiction over offences to their

---

[110] *Ctl. Préaux*, A69.
[111] L. Musset, 'Autour des modalités juridiques', 45–59.
[112] David Crouch noted jurisdiction over property pleas (Crouch, *Beaumont Twins*, pp. 158–62) but not offences.

beneficiaries. As these grants were made over the 166 years between 968 and 1134, the consistent parsimony that they reveal may say something about the dukes' continuing determination to concentrate and maintain jurisdiction over offences in their own hands.

The first of these grants dates from 968, when Richard I restored Berneval to the French abbey of Saint-Denis. He granted the monks all the lordship (*potestas*) exercised at Berneval in his name by the count, the *vicomte*, the *vicarius*, the *centenarius*,[113] and all holders of judicial power.[114] Such words would seem to encompass rights of justice there. In 1050 × 1060, William the Bastard granted to the monks of Saint-Père of Chartres judicial power (*potestatem iudiciariam*) in Brullemail on the southern frontier.[115] In 1115 × 1129, Henry I granted the monks of Boscherville 'full power and freedom … of justice of its men and of wreck no matter who's possession it is' in the port of Bruneval.[116] In 1134, as noted previously, King Henry I granted to the monks of Le Bec 'that they shall have in the whole of the parish of Le Bec all royal liberties, murder, death of men, pleas of mayhem, blood, water and fire … and all other royal liberties except rape alone, which it is better for honest secular men rather than monks to judge'.[117] It is perhaps significant that in two of the four acts the jurisdiction over offenders covered ports, where those commissioning offences might not be natives of the towns in question and could also quickly escape the scene of the crime. The dukes might have hoped that by delegating justice to a local power, more offenders would be apprehended and caught than would otherwise have been the case.

Although other examples could be examined, the limitations and ambiguities of the evidence are such that the piling up of case studies does not help to clarify the picture in a meaningful way. Although it is virtually certain that some lords in addition to the counts of Eu and monks of Saint-Pierre-sur-Dives enjoyed jurisdiction over the serious offences that would later be termed the pleas of the sword, their number is unknown and so, too, is the geographical extent of their jurisdiction. What does seem clear, however, is that fewer lords held such franchises than has previously been thought to be the case. Indeed, even the right to hang a thief caught red-handed seems not to have been widely held in the duchy – so far

---

[113] The *centenarius* was a Carolingian official who had jurisdiction over the prosecution of offences that did not incur the death penalty (M. Bloch, *Feudal Society*, Volume 2, trans. L. A. Manyon (London, 1961), 364–5).

[114] *RADN*, no. 3.

[115] *RADN*, no. 146.

[116] *Regesta*, ii. pp. 365–6 (no. 219).

[117] BnF, MS lat. 13905, fo. 9v, printed in Porée, *Histoire de l'abbaye du Bec*, i. 659 = *Regesta*, ii. nos. 1434 and 1901. *CDF*, 125 (no. 375) constitutes a reasonably full English translation of the act as a whole, albeit not of the section noted here.

as we can tell. But, and perhaps more importantly, the *Consuetudines et iusticie* demonstrate that even when lords did have jurisdiction over offences, the dukes were concerned to oversee the justice done in their courts (and did so with regard to pleas over property, too). Moreover, on at least one occasion, Henry I reserved the right to step in should a lord fail to do justice over offenders.[118] Indeed, when Henry granted the right to do justice in Le Bec to the monks of the abbey there, he did so as a result of 'the too great leniency of the lords ... and also ... the inveterate insolence of the inhabitants' which had brought the parish of Le Bec into 'indiscipline and disorder'. The failure of the local lords to do justice on offenders thus provoked a strong response from the royal duke, who removed their jurisdiction and handed it to the monks of Le Bec instead. It would seem, then, that the dukes were generally concerned to ensure that offenders were punished so that they should not be accused – as Curthose was – of having 'abandoned all Normandy to thieves and robbers'.[119]

Jurisdiction over property

If the dukes may be supposed generally to have retained jurisdiction over important offences (the later pleas of the sword) in their hands, they faced much more competition where disputes over property were concerned. Each lord had his own court where he might judge pleas pertaining to the lands held from him or concerning the men who lived on them – including some of the offences they commissioned – and records survive to show the operation of the courts, for example, of the monks of Caen, Sées, Saint-Evroult, and Mont-Saint-Michel, as well as those of William of Breteuil, Robert of Bellême, Gilbert Crispin, and others.[120]

---

[118] See above, *infra*, p. 457. For a brief discussion of a general trend here see Bloch, *Feudal Society*, ii. 373.

[119] Orderic, vi. 56.

[120] For the general point regarding the jurisdiction of lords over the property disputes of their men, see Bloch, *Feudal Society*, ii. 367; Hudson, *The Formation of the English Common Law: Law and Society in England from the Norman Conquest to Magna Carta* (London, 1996), pp. 40–7. For specific examples, see: Ctl. Caen, fos. 27r–v (no. 97), 28r (no. 99), 35r–v (no. 118), 37v–38r (no. 122), 39v–40r (no. 129), 42v (no. 137), 53v–54r (no. 159), 54r–v (no. 160), 56r (no. 164), 56v (no. 166); *Regesta: William*, no. 53; Chanteux, *Recueil*, no. 79 (Caen); Ctl. Sées, fos. 87v, 91v, 95r (Sées); Orderic, ii. 60–4, 120 (Saint-Evroult); *Ctl. Mont-Saint-Michel*, pp. 93–7 (no. 16), with a full English translation at *CDF*, no. 724; Tabuteau, *Transfers*, p. 198 (Mont-Saint-Michel); Orderic, iv. 286 (Breteuil); L. Musset, 'Administration et justice dans une grande baronnie normande au XIe siècle: les terres des Bellême sous Roger II et Robert', in *Autour du pouvoir ducal normand X^e–XIIe siècles*, ed. L. Musset, J.-M. Bouvris, and J.-M. Maillefer (Caen, 1985), 131–6; Ctl. Troarn, fos. 180r–v, 182; Ctl. Sées, fo. 34r–v (calendared at *CDF*, no. 654), *Chs. Jumièges*, i. 110–13, no. 34 (Bellême); *Chs. Jumièges*, i. 142–4 (no. 53) (Crispin).

To deprive their subjects of their jurisdiction would, of course, be unjust unless the dukes could establish a rival interest in a dispute. But while both dukes and potential litigants do seem to have acknowledged some general principles that would have allowed the dukes justly to claim jurisdiction over pleas involving the men of other lords, or lands outside the demesne, these seem to have had very little effect. For the most part, the dukes settled or judged the 'civil' pleas only of their own men and the monks of their abbeys. Others preferred to settle their own disputes or else to resort to the courts of their immediate lords. Thus, a survey of the surviving records of disputes reveals that those who sought the dukes' brokerage or confirmation of settlements between 968 and 1144 comprised the prelates and canons of the Norman cathedrals,[121] the abbots and monks of ducal abbeys or of abbeys that were in the dukes' hands at the time the dispute arose,[122] a handful of the dukes' *fideles*,[123] and monks from French houses with property in the duchy who would naturally have looked to the dukes for justice when there were disputes over their Norman possessions.[124] Those who appealed to the dukes for judgement in more intractable disputes comprised the same groups,[125] with

---

[121] Avranches (*RADN*, nos. 145, 229); Coutances (*Regesta*, ii. no. 1902), Rouen (*Regesta: William*, no. 230.

[122] Cerisy-la-Forêt (Lot, *Saint-Wandrille*, p. 115, no. 60); Holy Trinity of Caen (*Regesta: William*, no. 64); Saint-Etienne of Caen (*NI*, pp. 95–6; Chanteux, *Recueil*, no. 27); Fécamp (*RADN*, nos. 72, 145; *Regesta: William*, nos. 142, 143, 145); Jumièges (*RADN*, no. 74), Mont-Saint-Michel (*Ctl. Mont-Saint-Michel*, no. 16, English translation at *CDF*, no. 724); Troarn (*NI*, p. 90, (no. 2) = *Regesta*, ii. no. 1200); Saint-Wandrille (*Regesta: William*, no. 262); Savigny (Chanteux, *Receuil*, no. 27).

[123] Roger of Montgommery (*RADN*, no. 233; *Regesta: William*, no. 29); Waleran fitz Ranulf (*Regesta: William*, no. 143); Count William of Evreux, although perhaps unwillingly (*Regesta: William*, no. 262); Orderic, iv. 184–6); Walter Giffard (*Regesta: William*, no. 230); Gulbert of Auffay (*Regesta: William*, no. 145).

[124] *RADN*, no. 157 (Marmoutier); *RADN*, no. 230 (Coulombs).

[125] Prelates: Rouen (*RADN*, nos. 66, 67); Bayeux (*Livre Noir*, no. 21); Evreux (*Regesta: William*, no. 235); the canons of Lisieux and the nuns of Saint-Désir (Orderic, iii. 18); Monks: Bec (*NI*, p. 296 (no. 5); *Life of the venerable William, third abbot of Bec*, in Vaughn, *The Abbey of Bec*, pp. 121–2); Saint-Etienne of Caen (*NI*, pp. 95–6); Fécamp (*GC*, xi. Instr. 127-8; *Regesta*, ii. nos. 1579, 1698); Jumièges (*Regesta: William*, no. 162; *Chs. Jumièges*, i. 157-61, no. 61); Lonlay (*Regesta: William*, no. 267); Mont-Saint-Michel (*RADN*, nos. 148, 232; *Regesta: William*, no. 214); Préaux (*Ctl. Préaux*, A111); Saint-Amand, Rouen (*Regesta*, ii. no. 819); Saint-Wandrille (*RADN*, no. 95; *Regesta: William*, no. 264); Troarn (*NI*, pp. 98 (no. 6), 304 (no. 15); Sauvage, *Troarn*, p. 368); *Fideles*: Count Gilbert (Crispin, *Life of Lord of Herluin*, p. 70); Bernard the scribe (*Regesta*, ii. no. 1584); Reginald fitz Robert (*Regesta*, ii. no. 1898); Humfrey of Bohon (*PR 31 Henry I*, p. 18); French monks: St Peters, Ghent (*Inventio*, pp. 29–30); Saint-Denis (*RADN*, no. 3; R. Barroux, 'L'anniversaire de la mort de Dagobert à Saint-Denis au XIIᵉ siècle', *Bulletin philologique et historique du comité des travaux historiques et scientifiques* (1942–43), 148–51); Saint-Riquier (*RADN*, no. 115); Saint-Magloire de Lehon (*RADN*, no. 209);

the addition of two individuals who felt that they had been, or would be, denied justice elsewhere.[126]

However, although it is clear that the dukes' *fideles* (including the bishops) and monks might sometimes have asked the duke to settle or judge their disputes, they did not always do so. The monks of Saint-Etienne of Caen, for example, concluded twelve out of seventeen disputes outside the dukes' court.[127] As the dukes' authority was not undermined when their men and monks made agreements with third parties, the dukes were usually content to allow them to make their own arrangements. Where the dukes had concerns about the way disputes were being dealt with, however, they would intervene – even when the parties concerned had not asked them to.[128] (Although there were other occasions when they were not so keen to take jurisdiction over disputes, as we shall see.) Thus, in 1074, the count of Evreux and abbot of Saint-Wandrille were quarrelling over the abbey's right to customs in the forests of Caudebec and Gauville. The two parties had agreed to settle their difference by judicial duel, but Duke William stepped in as he did not want 'a cause of the Church to be determined by human blood (*ne causa ecclesie determinaretur humano sanguine*)'. The two sides were then brought to a settlement in his court.[129] In 1080, Bishop Gilbert of Evreux had made a claim to the island of Oissel, which had been held for some fifty years by the abbey of La Trinité-du-Mont. News of this dispute 'found its way to the king's hall (*que usque ad regiam aulam peruenit*)'. William then commanded the parties to appear before him.[130]

The dukes, then, did not require their men to bring their disputes and settlements before their courts. They were equally willing to uphold the jurisdictions of their subjects, even when they were asked to intervene. For example, in 1080, Abbot Hugh of Lonlay came to Duke William's court at Caen to demand justice over the church of Briouze. The church had been given to the monks of Saint-Florent by William of Briouze. When Abbot Hugh and his monks heard this,

Marmoutier (*RADN*, no. 159; *Regesta: William*, nos. 200, 201; *Ctl. Perche*, nos. 23, 25); Saint-Florent of Saumur (*Regesta: William*, no. 267).
[126] Godfrey the priest (*Regesta*, ii. no. 819); monks of Lonlay (*Regesta: William*, no. 267).
[127] Those concluded outside the duke's court may be found at Ctl. Caen, fos. 27r–v (no. 97), 28r (no. 99), 35r–v (no. 118), 37v–38r (no. 122), 39v–40r (no. 129), 42v (no. 137), 53v–54r (no. 159), 54r–v (no. 160), 56r (no. 164), 56v (no. 166); *Regesta: William*, no. 53; Chanteux, *Recueil*, no. 79.
[128] Similarly, during the first years of his reign at least, Henry II was content to issue writs and to allow others to do the justice required, but he was concerned 'to improve judicial procedures in other courts' (G. J. White, *Restoration and Reform 1153–1165: Recovery from Civil War in England* (Cambridge, 2000), p. 177.
[129] *Regesta: William*, no. 262.
[130] *Regesta: William*, no. 235. See also below, *infra*, pp. 464, 474, 501.

'burning with great envy, they now tried to claim the said church, ringing the ears of the great king of the English with their *clamor* … The king hearing this claim, believing that a real complaint had been brought, commanded William of Briouze to do right to the monks of Lonlay in his court. Hearing this, William came to the court, namely at Caen, to do right to the monks in the presence of the king.'[131] In other words, Duke William did not bring the case under his own jurisdiction, but simply commanded William of Briouze to do justice justly, and to be seen to do so, in his court. It was Briouze himself who surrendered jurisdiction over the plea to the duke, perhaps because he could not act as both witness and judge.[132] In 1107 × 1123, Godfrey the priest of Caen brought a plea before Henry I at Cirencester. Henry sent a writ to the bishop of Bayeux and his chapter instructing them that 'Godfrey the priest deraigned his church of Saint-Sauveur which is in the market at Caen in my court before my bishops and my clergy … And see that he is not henceforth disseised without the correct judgment.'[133] Although Henry and his court had apparently been convinced by Godfrey's claim, the writ suggests that he had not taken jurisdiction over Godfrey's plea. Instead, Henry commanded the bishop to do justice correctly. In both cases, the dukes' actions reveal their respect for another's jurisdiction, but also demonstrate their willingness to oversee and direct seigniorial justice.

There is some suggestion that William the Bastard *might* have acted differently had he confirmed the donation before the dispute had arisen. Around 1055, 'Abbot Albert, then presiding over Marmoutier, since he knew not otherwise how this donation could remain stable, went to William *princeps* of the Normans and duke and, to speak more accurately, king of his whole land, which is difficult to find elsewhere, and, presuming on several others familiar and dear to him, exhorted him that he should approve and authorize the said donation'.[134] It is likely that the stability provided by the duke's sign was due

---

[131] *Regesta: William*, no. 267.II.
[132] See also *Regesta: William*, no. 235, mentioned above. In this case, King William had ordered that the case should be judged by a number of important men, one of whom was William of Arques. During the arguments, however, 'this said William, in the judgement of the plea, to make satisfaction to the bishop and to make an end to the dissension, put himself forward as a witness to his grandfather's gift'. At this point, it is likely that William waived his right to act as a judge. That would have been the case in England where, according to the *Leges Henrici Primi*: 'In all causes, ecclesiastical and secular, which are to be tried properly and according to the law, some are accusers, some defendants, some witnesses and some judges, persons who in every legal hearing are to be of appropriate integrity and who are not at the same time, in any lawsuit, to perform any other function' (*LHP*, para 5.1).
[133] *Livre Noir*, i. 44 (no. 38) = *Regesta*, ii. no. 819.
[134] *RADN*, no. 137.

to it having established the duke's protection over the gift and thus placed subsequent disputes about it under his jurisdiction unless, and this seems unlikely, the power of his name alone was thought to be sufficient. In 1080, William issued an act for the monks of Saint-Florent of Saumur, following the dispute over the church of Briouze noted above. The act states that William of Briouze had made his donation to Saint-Florent for the good of the souls of King William and Queen Matilda, 'in order that they themselves should consent to these alms and, if anyone should wish to commit an injustice therein, they should hold him to right'.[135] The wording suggests that had the king confirmed the gift, he would also have had a right to jurisdiction over any subsequent dispute. The inclusion of these words further indicates that the monks of Saint-Florent wanted to have their disputes heard before the duke in future. And, indeed, three years later, when a new dispute arose, they acted to put that preference into effect:

> the gift of Céaux, which John of Dol gave to Saint-Florent and King William of the English granted, was claimed by the monks of Mont-Saint-Michel. Thanks to this matter, two of the monks of Saint-Florent, David and Wihenoc, were crossing to the king, so that either he should acquit the gift that he had granted or have the plea himself (*ut aut donum concesserat adquietaret, aut illud sibi haberet*). While they were passing the Mont, the monks of the Mont, hearing of the reason for their journey, took counsel and, thanks to charity, demised all their claim against the said monks.[136]

Here, then, the monks already had King William's confirmation of the gift that was now in dispute, and so determined to bring their plea before his court. The response of the monks of Mont-Saint-Michel suggests that they, too, recognized that the king's confirmation would indeed give him a right to claim jurisdiction, even though their reasoning is not spelled out in this brief report.

As Emily Zack Tabuteau has remarked, 'one or two references to ducal consent may imply that consent conveyed jurisdictional responsibility, but too little is known of the court system of eleventh-century Normandy to permit this speculation to be carried very far'.[137] The attitude of monks from Anjou, who had

---

[135] *Regesta: William*, no. 266; translation from Tabuteau, *Transfers*, p. 185. Although the act was 'dictated and lined' by Primaldus the chaplain of William of Briouze, the survival of a draft copy of the act (no. 266.I) suggests that much of it had been prepared in advance by the monks of Saint-Florent and thus reflected their views of what a confirmation should allow.

[136] Marchegay, no. 11. William's grant is at *Regesta: William*, no. 269.

[137] Tabuteau, *Transfers*, p. 195.

no powerful patron in Normandy except for the duke, was not necessarily typical. Nonetheless, by the twelfth century there does seem to have been an established link between the duke's confirmation of the donations written into a charter and his protection and thus his jurisdiction. These links can also be discerned by reference to the early history of the abbey of Saint-Evroult which was written down by Orderic *c*. 1120. He asserted that the founders of the abbey voluntarily placed their foundation under the duke's protection *c*. 1050:

> to prevent any harm being inflicted on [the monks] at the instigation of the devil, let us entrust the monastery to the duke of all Normandy in return for his protection against us, our posterity, and other mortals. So that if we by force demand any service or gift, save this spiritual benefice, ducal authority will immediately check us and against our will we will refrain from any molestation of Christ's soldiers.[138]

By the time Orderic was writing, then, if a monastery was placed under the duke's protection, and thus peace, the duke gained the right to prosecute and punish those who offended against him by breaking it.

The surviving text of Duke William's confirmation of the monks' possessions – which may suffer from later interpolation here – goes on explicitly to spell out that the duke's protection extended to the gifts recorded therein, too:

> the possessions which Robert and Hugh his brother, Wiliam and his brothers and sons, and other faithful men of Christ granted, or will grant, to the same house from the possessions of their inheritances … I command, by the authority of our privilege, to remain firm and unshaken, and if anyone coming as an adversary shall be tempted to plot to do damage to the said monastery, whether large or small, and if they shall be tempted to violate the charter of this our privilege, he knows himself to be guilty of treason (*maiestas*) against us, and that all his patrimony will be added to our demesne possessions.[139]

Even if a later addition, the views are not outrageous for the period before 1144 and the use of *maiestas* does not go beyond the use of the word in the *Etymologies*.[140] The wording may certainly be taken to indicate how some beneficiaries might have thought ducal confirmations operated, and that a breach of the duke's protection might turn a dispute over property into a serious offence

---

[138] Jumièges, ii. 140.
[139] *RADN*, no. 122.
[140] See the discussion in Hagger, 'Secular law and custom', 835–7.

resulting in forfeiture to the duke (apparently rather than to a man's existing lord).[141]

The same idea is found in essence in the deathbed speech that Orderic put into the mouth of William the Conqueror: 'by my royal authority I freely confirmed the charters preserving these gifts against all who might covet or attack them.'[142] If Orderic thought that a charter preserved a gift against would-be attackers, that can only have been because the royal duke's confirmation provided protection against them (just as a lord's gift was protected from a change of heart by his own *signum*). That protection was explicitly established by the formulas that appear at the end of a very many ducal acts: 'and so that this donation shall be stable in perpetuity by the support of letters I have commanded a notice about it to be written, and truly corroborated by the sign of the cross and my name.'[143]

It appears that the inclusion of such wording acted as a 'promise to guarantee titles, apparently in court'.[144] That might also have been the case with regard to statements that beneficiaries should hold their property 'in peace (*in pace*)' – often found in association with other terms such as 'freely'. Those words are present in only five of the authentic acts of William the Bastard (although none of them were to take effect in Normandy), and only six authentic acts of William Rufus.[145] But they are found in hundreds of the acts issued by Henry I.[146] *Prima facie* that would appear to suggest that Henry attempted to extend his opportunities for intervention in lawsuits by equating an appropriation of the gifts listed in his acts with a violation of his peace – something that might also be related to the decline in anathema clauses discussed in Chapter 7.[147] The same encroachment on seigniorial jurisdiction can also be seen, although to a much lesser extent, in the employment of wording expressly stating that the duke had brought a monastery or a particular donation under his protection. Such wording is apparently found

---

[141] This was also the case with a failure to apprehend fugitives, at least by the end of the twelfth century: see below, *infra*, p. 492.

[142] Orderic, iv. 92.

[143] *RADN*, no. 15, and see above, Chapter 7, pp. 419–22.

[144] Reynolds, *Fiefs*, p. 132.

[145] *Regesta: William*, nos. 42, 116, 188, 191, 314 (William I); *Regesta*, i. lxvi = no. 396; *Regesta*, i. xcii = no. 481; V. H. Galbraith, 'Royal Charters to Winchester', *EHR*, 35 (1920), 382–400 (no. xii) = *Regesta*, ii. errata 483a; *Early Charters of St Paul's*, no. 17 = *Regesta*, ii. errata 429b; *Early Charters of the Cathedral Church of St Paul, London*, ed. M. Gibbs, Camden Society, third series, 58 (1939), no. 14 = *Regesta*, ii. errata 444a; *Early Yorkshire Charters: Vols 4–10*, ed. C. T. Clay, no. 930 = *Regesta*, i. no. 412.

[146] For example, for Montebourg (*Regesta*, ii. no. 1953), Robert and Hamelin the royal duke's *loricarii* (*Regesta*, ii. no. 1946), Jumièges (*Regesta*, ii. no. 912), Le Bec (*Regesta*, ii. no. 1186 and see a little below), and Troarn (*Regesta*, ii. no. 1200).

[147] See above, Chapter 7, p. 419.

in ducal *acta* only after 1066. William the Bastard brought the monks of Ely, Evesham, and Troarn under his protection after the Conquest,[148] and his example was followed by Count Robert of Mortain and Earl Roger of Montgommery who extended their own protection over some of the grants made to their own foundations in the duchy.[149] Most of the examples of the use of the words *protectio* and *defensio* in the surviving corpus of William's *acta*, however, are found in mid-twelfth-century forgeries.[150] So once again, it is Henry I's reign that is highlighted as a time when the royal duke was seeking to establish jurisdiction (particularly in England). Authentic acts of Henry I extended his protection (*defensio*) over eight individuals, although none of them were in Normandy. But his protection (*protectio*) *was* extended to two Norman houses: Notre-Dame-du-Désert in 1130 and the hospital at Falaise in 1132 and 1133.[151] In this last case at least, the act was drafted by one of Henry's own scribes, albeit one with a somewhat idiosyncratic style.[152]

Another variation on this same theme can be found in three more of Henry I's Norman acts. His general confirmation for the monks of Saint-Evroult, issued at Rouen late in 1113, 'forbade anyone to implead the monks for any of the properties he had confirmed by his royal charter anywhere except by an action in the king's court'.[153] An almost identical provision was added to a contemporary act for the monks of Lyre: 'and I command that no one shall take away any of these under-written possessions, of which the abbey is now seised, and neither shall there be a plea about them except in my court (*nec inde sit placitum nisi in mea curia*).'[154] The close links between the two houses might explain the shared wording, but it is perhaps more likely that the formula was added at the royal duke's command as there are also similarities with the third act, a writ of 1107 × 1120, by which Henry I instructed Hugh of Montfort to reseise the abbot of Le Bec with 20 acres of land belonging to the church of Saint-Philbert. His writ concluded: 'I do not wish that

---

[148] *Regesta: William*, nos. 114, 118, 134, 280.

[149] *Regesta: William*, nos. 215 (Mortain), 281.II (Montgommery's protection covered just one of the gifts made to the monks of Troarn, at p. 851).

[150] *Regesta: William*, nos. 108, 111, 220, 290, 305, 306, 324 (*defensio*); 109, 110, 111 (*protectio*).

[151] Chanteux, *Recueil*, no. 72 = *Regesta*, ii. no. 1680 (Désert); *Regesta*, ii. 376–7 (no. cclxvi) = no. 1742; 378 (no. cclxx) = no. 1764 (Falaise). The abbey at Beaubec might also have been placed under Henry's protection, but the act betrays evidence of later interpolation, so it is difficult to be certain (*Recueil Henri II*, no. 314 = *Regesta*, ii. no. 1270).

[152] See N. Karn, 'Robert de Sigillo: an unruly head of the royal scriptorium in the 1120s and 1130s', *EHR*, 123 (2008), 539–53.

[153] Orderic vi. 176; Orderici Vitalis, *Historiæ Ecclesiasticæ*, ed. le Prévost, Société de l'Histoire de France, vol. 5 (Paris, 1855), 196–199. The relevant wording reads: 'Et precipio quatinus ex istis subscriptis quibus nunc sasitata est nullus aliquid surripiat nec inde sit placitum nisi in mea curia.'

[154] Chanteux, *Recueil*, no. 13.

anyone should implead him about anything of which he was seised on the day I gave you the honour of Montfort unless before me (*Nolo enim ut quis eum placitet de aliqua re unde fuit saisitus die qua dedi tibi honorem de Monfort nisi coram mei*).'[155] In all three cases, the words of the acts should probably be interpreted to allow for a dispute being heard before a ducal justice in a seigniorial court as well as before the duke in person, but in any event none of these ouster clauses seem to have had any practical effect whatsoever.

The absence from the great majority of ducal *acta* of a formula establishing, in one form or another, the duke's protection suggests that across the whole period covered by this book beneficiaries saw no advantage to obtaining such a grant. That might perhaps have been because such wording was often too specific to have as much practical value as the dukes or their beneficiaries had intended. What if, for example, the dispute was not about the land listed in a charter but rather the service due from it? When faced with this problem, the abbot of Saint-Evroult chose to devise his own remedy rather than to seek Duke William's help, even though the lands in question had been included in his confirmation. Baudri and Vigor of Bocqu had refused to render to the monks the service due from their lands *c.* 1060 and so Abbot Robert of Grandmesnil transferred the services due from them to his kinsman Arnold of Echauffour for Arnold's lifetime. He made their lives so difficult that they soon begged to be restored to the abbot's service and promised to fulfil their obligations from then on.[156] The only time that the monks of Saint-Evroult resorted to the duke's justice – at a time when the duchy was in the hands of William Rufus – was to conclude a dispute with the bishop of Lisieux that concerned the bishop's demand to a profession from the abbot.[157] They did so because there was no other way for them to obtain justice against such a powerful figure, and it may be supposed that they waited until Curthose had left on crusade because they did not believe that he would be able to enforce his will against Bishop Gilbert.

Where pleas over property were concerned, then, litigants brought their claims to the duke only when they saw an advantage in doing so. The initiative lay with them. Some of the various factors that impacted their decision to resolve the dispute themselves or to bring it before the duke can be examined by reference to the lordships held by Roger of Montgommery and his son Robert of Bellême before the latter's forfeiture in November 1112. Henry's subsequent grant of the

---

[155] *NI*, p. 296, no. 5. The wording can also be found in dubious acts for Beaubec (*Recueil Henri II*, no. 314 = *Regesta*, ii. no. 1270. Robert of Bellême had earlier attempted to oust any other's jurisdiction, too: see below and note 159).

[156] Orderic, ii. 80–2.

[157] Orderic, v. 262.

lordship of Bellême to Count Rotrou of the Perche, and his refusal to restore the rump of his father's lands in the Hiémois to William Talvas until 1119, had a dramatic effect on the political landscape of the two regions. The existing loyalties to the long-established ruling family were broken. Men, monks, and churches lost a lord and patron whose well-entrenched power could not be ignored. A new lord was parachuted into Bellême, who could not hope to exercise the authority that his predecessor had wielded in the short term, especially as he did not also control the region north of the Sarthe, and particularly that around Sées. And while Talvas would eventually be restored to his lordships in the Hiémois, and would be able to reclaim the affection and loyalty of his family's men and the monks of his houses at Troarn and Sées, he could no longer hope to keep the interests and officials of the royal duke at arm's length.

The first dispute in a series that would plague relations between the canons, later monks, of Saint-Léonard of Bellême and the bishops of Sées arose between 1070 and 1079. The dispute, which concerned the bishop's right to the offerings made by the congregation at Bellême, was heard before William the Bastard. The case was brought not by the canons of the church, but rather by their lord, Roger of Montgommery, who had complained about the bishop's behaviour (he had excommunicated the canons after they had resisted his attempts to take the money) to the archbishop of Rouen. His actions suggest that he was prepared to recognize the archbishop's right to hear cases concerning ecclesiastical issues in his province. Roger had not approached the royal duke, however, and while that might simply have been on the grounds that this was an ecclesiastical case, it might equally have been because Roger did not wish to recognize William's authority over the lordship of Bellême which was inside the province of Rouen but outside Normandy. It is possible, then, that the case was heard in William's court because he insisted that it should be, effectively snatching jurisdiction from the archbishop. If there was a quiet tussle for jurisdiction, however, the canons of Bellême were not inclined to report it. In their record of the plea they were concerned only with the quality of their case and its resolution, which was that the royal duke's court found that the church of Saint-Léonard was free from all episcopal customs.[158]

In January 1091, Bishop Gerard of Sées claimed episcopal rights in the church of Saint-Léonard equivalent to those which he had in other churches in his diocese – in other words he extended, and so indirectly reopened, the dispute settled by King William by 1079. By the time the dispute was heard, the canons of Bellême had been replaced by monks from Marmoutier, who had been given their priory by Robert of Bellême. The newly installed monks quickly forged a charter

---

[158] *Regesta: William*, no. 29.

of William of Bellême, and a new record of the lawsuit of 1070 × 1079 heard in King William's court, to provide proof that their church had been made free by William of Bellême, King Robert of France, and Duke Richard II of Normandy. A brief record of the plea was made, and this reported that the monks had again triumphed over the bishop, this time in the bishop's own court:

> we came to Sées for the plea and there Lord Robert of Bellême, who gave it to us, showed through the privileges and precepts of that church, and by the authority of those who had made it free and quit, that the bishop had nothing in it. Similarly of the church of Saint-Martin-du-Vieux-Bellême in which he had claimed blood and *infracturam*, that it was determined that he had nothing in it besides a rent and one pound of pepper and one pound of frankincense, and this by charity and not by custom.[159]

Robert of Bellême had no desire to recognize anyone else's authority over his lordship. He had made this clear in the deed by which he gave the church of Saint-Léonard of Bellême to the monks of Marmoutier. This included a clause preventing the monks from appealing to any authority other than himself: 'Robert did not wish that they should seek any justice except his own. And if they did so, and if they did not cease to do so after he had demonstrated it to the abbot and chapter of Marmoutier, whatever he had given to them they would lose.'[160] That clause could not prevent the bishop of Sées from impleading the monks, but it did make it impossible for them to appeal to the duke. That might not have mattered. Robert Curthose was in no position to demand that the case should be referred to him. He was losing control over the lordship of Bellême and would have been unable to enforce any judgement that his court reached.[161] Moreover, obtaining justice in the court of their adversary might not have been as problematic for the monks as it might at first sight seem. Bellême's power over the bishopric of Sées was increasing in the last decade of the eleventh century,[162] so the monks could have their case heard in the 'correct' forum and still expect to win as a result of the coercive power of their patron and the documents they had concocted. Indeed,

[159] *Ctl. Perche*, pp. 27–8, no. 15.
[160] AD Orne, H 2152; *Ctl. Perche*, pp. 23–6 (no. 13).
[161] 'In those days', wrote Orderic, 'ducal censure could not touch him' (Orderic, iv. 298). When the monks of Marmoutier forged a confirmation of Bellême's diploma for Saint-Léonard c. 1092, they drafted it in the name of King Philip of France rather than Robert Curthose (*Ctl. Perche*, pp. 26–7 (no. 14); Thompson, 'Robert of Bellême reconsidered', p. 285). The breach is noted by Orderic, iv. 228. Curthose's inability to do justice in the duchy is discussed at greater length above, *infra*, pp. 445–8 and below, *infra*, pp. 501–2.
[162] Orderic, iv. 296–8; Louise, *Bellême*, i. 396.

Bellême's presence at the court as a witness for the monks must have made that coercive power seem very real and very dangerous so far as the bishop and the judges were concerned. The monks thus won their case hands down, a verdict which highlighted Robert of Bellême's effective lordship.

After Bellême's arrest, things started to change. Around 1117, Fulk the archdeacon claimed the offerings from a third of the cemetery of the church of Saint-Martin-du-Vieux-Bellême. The monks of Marmoutier said that the cemetery was entirely theirs. The case was again heard in the court of the bishop of Sées. As the monks were respondents, they had not chosen the venue, although it was anyway the correct forum. And on this occasion, the monks would have found themselves without a patron. In 1117, Robert of Bellême was in King Henry's prison and effective lordship over Bellême was probably disputed between Rotrou of the Perche and Bellême's brother Arnulf of Montgommery who was certainly active around Alençon in 1118.[163] Moreover, Rotrou's lordship ended at the Sarthe, so that he could not have posed a threat to the bishop of Sées' interests in the way that Robert of Bellême had done. The lack of a strong lord in Bellême as well as King Henry's influence over the bishop of Sées together made his justice appear more attractive than it had in the past. The monks of Bellême seem consequently to have asked him to take oversight of the case. This invitation is indicated by the presence of two members of his court, Ranulf the chancellor and Grimbald the physician, at the head of the witnesses to the settlement made between the bishop and the monks. The two men had perhaps presided over the negotiations, just as ducal justices might have done had the agreement been made a few years later. The loss of the partisan support of Robert of Bellême, and the more balanced view brought to bear by Henry's envoys, may be supposed to have forced the monks to adopt a more conciliatory tone on this occasion. They agreed to compensate the bishop for his loss of rights (and thus revenue) by payments of pepper, now due as an annual rent rather than from the monks' charity as had been the case in 1092.[164]

By 1126, the monks seem to have decided that the only way to silence the claims of the bishop of Sées once and for all was to bring their case before Henry's court. This time, the dispute with the bishop concerned the provision of priests in the churches of Saint-Martin of Vieille-Bellême and Dancé. The report of the plea, which comprises a deceptive and defective record, notes that it was held in Henry's court which met near Rouen. Henry, then, made the parties come to him, which had last happened in his father's day and which likely reveals a significant change in the balance of power and influence in the lordship of Bellême. 'The king at length established and commanded that the bishop henceforth should quit his

---

[163] Orderic, vi. 206, 214.
[164] AD Orne, H 2157; *Ctl. Perche*, pp. 31–2 (no. 19).

complaint.'[165] No other local power could have terminated the dispute in such terms, which was, of course, why he had been asked to intercede in the first place.

It was, however, only in 1127 that Bishop John of Sées finally came to a lasting agreement with Abbot Odo of Marmoutier, and even then only with the counsel of the king and archbishop of Rouen. By this time, the dispute between bishop and monks had expanded to encompass the fines due from the cemetery at Saint-Martin, the bishops' rights in various of the possessions of Saint-Léonard, offerings for private masses, confessions in the church of Saint-Sauveur of Bellême, and attendance at synods. Henry's jurisdiction was already established by this point, but he was even stronger in 1127 than he had been the year before. The threat posed by the count of Anjou to the south of the duchy had just been neutralized by the betrothal of his daughter to Geoffrey of Anjou. It is perhaps significant that the record is dated by this event.[166] And although the papacy had by then become involved, too, with a further judgement against the bishop of Sées made before the papal legate at Le Mans in the same year, it was the agreement brokered by Henry I that was confirmed by Pope Innocent in 1137.[167]

Robert of Bellême had also been the patron of the monks of Troarn, whose abbey stood above the marshes of the Dives in the Bessin. The monks had been impleaded in William the Bastard's court by the community of Fécamp in 1067 × 1083,[168] but had not brought any claims before that duke themselves. They did bring a plea to Robert of Bellême's court in 1101, however, which was judged in their favour.[169] As noted, after Bellême's arrest in November 1112, Henry forfeited his estates into his own hands. That gave him the chance to extend his jurisdiction over the monks. His success in doing so was probably signalled by a writ by which Henry announced to 'Bishop Richard of Bayeux and all his barons and sworn men of the Hiémois' that he had 'granted to God and St Martin and the monks of Troarn ... the whole of Le Marais about which there was a plea in my court between the said monks and Robert of Ussy'.[170] In 1115 ×1135, and perhaps before 1118, Henry heard a second plea, this time concerning the church of Vire, and again found in favour of the monks of Troarn.[171] Even after Bellême's lordships in the Hiémois had been restored to William Talvas, Henry ensured that he did not

---

[165] *Ctl. Perche*, pp. 36–8 (no. 23).

[166] AD Orne, H 2159(3); *Ctl. Perche*, pp. 40–3 (no. 25); Green, *Henry I*, p. 199.

[167] AD Orne, H 2159(11); *Papsturkunden*, pp. 61–3 (no. 7), 67–9 (no. 12), respectively.

[168] *Regesta: William*, no. 142.

[169] Ctl. Troarn, fos. 180r–v, 182v.

[170] AD Calvados, H 7752; *NI*, p. 90 (no. 2) = *Regesta*, ii. no. 1200. The writ could date from as early as 1108 when Bishop Richard of Bayeux took office, but it is not later than 1118 as it was witnessed by Count Robert of Meulan.

[171] *NI*, p. 304 (no. 15) = *Regesta*, ii. no. 1982.

entirely lose his grip on his new-found jurisdiction. At Pentecost 1129, William Talvas spoke for the monks during a suit heard at Falaise in Henry's court.[172] Then, in 1133, Henry was given further opportunity to intervene in the abbey's affairs when claims were brought against the abbot on behalf of Fulk fitz Fulk, a minor, by his guardian – whom Henry had appointed. The duke's justices became involved, overseeing due process. William Talvas became involved, too, questioning the guardian and apparently bringing him to a settlement. He may have done so in an attempt to limit the erosion of his own jurisdiction.[173]

A beneficiary, then, might be influenced by a variety of factors, including the existing local networks and loyalties, the attitude of their own lord, the cost and time involved, and the likely effectiveness of the settlement or judgement made. As the above examples show, the interplay of these various factors could change over time for a variety of reasons. But even when an individual did make the decision to take their dispute to the duke, there was no guarantee that he would agree to hear it. There were times when a duke might be reluctant, or might even refuse, to take cognizance of a claim. This reluctance might be owing to their knowledge that they would need to break established norms if a case was heard. For example, when word of Bishop Gilbert of Evreux's claim to Oissel reached William the Bastard's hall in 1080, the duke was initially unhappy to hear a plea arising after the monks of La Trinité-du-Mont had enjoyed so many years of undisturbed possession, 'but on account of his reverence for the bishop's person he admitted the plea (*placitum dedit*), and decreed that it should be done in his court'.[174] More typically, when the dukes refused – or may be supposed to have refused – to hear a plea altogether, their decision was the result of a combination of factors such as: a desire to prevent individual lords amassing extensive honours in England and Normandy; a determination to prevent a particular individual from obtaining the land in question; and the need to use that land for other purposes. The political dimension of jurisdiction is once again clear here, and not just in the reasons for the duke's refusal to hear the plea. The narratives suggest that when justice was denied to a lord, he might rebel, often lining up behind a rival for the duchy in order to give his continuing demand for justice greater weight.[175]

These refusals to do justice should not be seen as foolhardy or capricious. Orderic criticized Robert Curthose for his handling of the claims to the castles of Brionne and Ivry and suggested that dukes should say 'no' when there were

---

[172]   AD Calvados, H 7758(1); Sauvage, *Troarn*, p. 368.
[173]   Ctl. Troarn, fo. 35v; Valin, *Le duc et sa cour*, pp. 62–3 (no. 8); *NI*, p. 98.
[174]   *Regesta: William*, no. 235.
[175]   See the discussion of the revolts of Ranulf of Briquessart (1046–7), Amaury of Montfort (1118–19), and Richer of L'Aigle (1118) discussed above, Chapter 2, pp. 109–10 and Chapter 3, pp. 172–3, for example.

good political reasons for doing so, regardless of the justice of the claim put forward:

> Through his wish to please all men he either gave or promised or granted whatever anyone asked. He diminished his inheritance daily by his foolish prodigality, giving away to everyone whatever was sought; and as he impoverished himself he strengthened the hands of others against him. To William of Breteuil he gave Ivry, where the almost impregnable fortress built by his great-grandmother Aubrey stands; and to Roger of Beaumont who had been appointed castellan of Ivry by King William he granted Brionne, a well-fortified castle in the heart of the duchy.[176]

Orderic wrote those words despite the fact that he thought Ascelin Goel had 'feloniously' taken the castle of Ivry from William of Breteuil. As Ascelin had then surrendered the castle to Duke Robert, the duke's possession of it could hardly have been thought to be just. As such, Orderic's complaint can only have been founded on the greater injustice subsequently suffered by those living around Ivry. Restoring the castle to William resulted in a 'prolonged war between [William and Ascelin], and the entire neighbourhood was troubled by plundering, burning and slaughter'.[177] So while a failure to do justice might lead in some circumstances to rebellion, there were sometimes reasons to refuse to restore to lords even those lands and possessions that they justly demanded.

The ducal justices

Henry I's interest in overseeing the justice done in seigniorial courts has been touched on already. The abbot of Saint-Pierre-sur-Dives was threatened with the loss of his jurisdiction to the official known as the justice of Normandy if he refused to do justice in his court. One of Henry's justices oversaw due process in the court of the abbot of Troarn in 1133. As these examples demonstrate, it was the official known as the justice that allowed Henry both to monitor seigniorial courts and to take action against lords who were seen to be behaving unjustly. Indeed, their role came to encompass all aspects of justice in Normandy, making their institutionalization one of the most important developments of Henry I's reign.

Charles Homer Haskins surveyed Henry's achievement in this field in 1909:

[176] Orderic, iv. 114.
[177] Orderic, iv. 200. The monk added a shorter version of the story, omitting all mention of Curthose's grant, to the *Gesta Normannorum ducum*: Jumièges, ii. 228.

The existence of a regular body of Norman justices is plain, first of all from their enumeration with the other ducal officers in the addresses of his general charters, and is clearly seen from the writs directed *iusticiis suis Normannie* and from the clause … *nisi feceris iusticia mea faciat.* The duke's justices are mentioned as early as 1108 in a charter for Montebourg, and about the same time … we find a chief justiciar, *meus proprius iusticiarius … qui super omnes alios in uice mea iusticiam tenet.*[178]

While Haskins' discussion of the justices still provides a solid starting point for any consideration of them and their functions, he was mistaken about the date at which they appeared in Henry's Norman writs. The justice first appeared between 1111 and 1116, not 1108.[179] Equally, the so-called chief justiciar, who might be better styled 'the justice of Normandy', does not appear in 1108 or 1109 at all, but rather in an act of 1121 × 1128.[180] When they appear, the justices might be termed *iusticiarius* or *iusticia*, apparently without any difference in meaning, and tend to be listed just before or just after the *vicomtes* in the address clauses of Henry's Norman acts that mention both officials.

As Haskins also noted, these acts also make it clear that there were two types, or tiers, of justices, as seems to have been the case in England, too.[181] The senior was known as the 'justice of Normandy', although there seems to have been more than one such official at any one time.[182] It is likely that this figure should be identified with the justiciar, 'who above any other holds justice in my place', referred to in the authentic diploma for Saint-Pierre-sur-Dives of 1121 × 1128.[183]

---

[178] C. H. Haskins, 'The administration of Normandy under Henry I', *EHR*, 24 (1909), 213–14, repeated at *NI*, p. 93.

[179] The year 1111 is the last date at which we have a record of a plea heard without any reference to justices (*Chs. Jumièges*, i. 157–61, no. 61). April 1116 is the last possible date for the issue of an act for the abbey of Montebourg that includes the justices in its address (*Regesta*, ii. no. 1155). Together they seem to provide the narrowest date range for the introduction of justices into Normandy.

[180] Caen, AD Calvados, H 7031(5) = *Regesta*, ii. no. 1569. The purported act of Henry I that Haskins used is based on this document, but has interpolations (in particular a reference to *bailliis*) that date its fabrication to after 1144. See also Chapter 6, pp. 350–2 above.

[181] Green, *Government*, p. 107, with suitable warning as to the difficulties of distinguishing between the different types of justice.

[182] Writs for Montebourg and Bayeux are addressed to 'iustitiis Normannie' or 'iustic(iis) suis Norm(annie)' in the plural (*Regesta*, ii. 334 (no. cviii) = no. 1155; *Livre Noir*, i. 14 (no. 8) = *Regesta*, ii. no. 1897). Also both John and Robert appear together on occasion, as in the *Emptiones Eudonis* (see below). Similarly, the *magister iusticiarius* of the kingdom of Sicily, an office created in 1156, was always held by two men acting together (H. Enzensberger, 'Chanceries, charters and administration', p. 130).

[183] Caen, AD Calvados, H 7031(5) = *Regesta*, ii. no. 1569. See also above, Chapter 6, pp. 350–2.

Under the justices of Normandy were a number of local justices. These officials are revealed chiefly by the address clauses of a number of Henry I's Norman writs. Thus we can see the justices of the Cotentin,[184] the justices of Saint-Marcouf and Varreville (assuming that this address was not simply a more specific way of referring to the same justices of the Cotentin),[185] and the justices and custodians of the bishopric of Bayeux.[186] That these justices are said to be justices of specific places rather than 'of Normandy' suggests their inferior standing, and this is more firmly established by the wording of this last writ, which states that should the justices of the bishopric not allow Reginald fitz Robert the tithe that he had deraigned in the *curia regis*, then the justice of Normandy would do it (*Et nisi feceritis, iusticia Normannica faciat fieri*).

The identity of some of the justices, as well as how they heard pleas both in the king's presence and in his absence, is revealed by the document known as the *Emptiones Eudonis*, a list of purchases, gifts, and disputes made by Abbot Eudo of Caen between 1107 and 1131.[187] The *Emptiones* describe a number of pleas before King Henry and/or his justices, including the two following examples:

> Roger the son of Peter of Fontenay-le-Pesnel, in the castle of Caen in the presence of the whole of the justice (*presentia tocius iusticię*), returned to St Stephen that land and all those tithes which that saint had had from Geoffrey, that man's uncle, and from his father, and granted them to the same saint firmly holding them from then on in perpetuity. And since that Roger had often vexed the abbot and monks for the same tithes, from the consideration of the justice Geoffrey of Subles he swore his oath that he would never more make contrary injury and toil about them but would maintain them and leave them in peace. And so that St Stephen should hold all these things in most firm and indissoluble bonds, the abbot and the monks granted to that man the society in the monastery which his predecessors had had, and in addition they had given him 40 *sous* out of their charity and one horse. Witnesses that justice (*testes ipsa iusticia*): John bishop of Lisieux, Robert of La Haye-du-Puits, Hugh of Montfort, Geoffrey of Subles, Roger Marmion.

---

[184] *NI*, p. 102 = *Regesta*, ii. no. 1951.

[185] *NI*, p. 101 = *Regesta*, ii. no. 1950.

[186] *Livre Noir*, i. 43–4 (no. 37) = *Regesta*, ii. no. 1898.

[187] Caen, AD Calvados, H 1834, edited in Chanteux, *Recueil*, no. 79 and with some (relevant) passages printed in *NI*, pp. 95–6. The surviving document seems not to be an authentic original, although there is no reason to suppose that the contents are not authentic. Eudo became abbot in 1107 and the act was made before the death of Bishop Richard of Coutances on 18 November 1131.

Herbert, a certain clerk, complaining in all kinds of ways that St Stephen had managed to take away the church of this vill (Secqueville-en-Bessin) from him, which St Stephen had held of old in great peace, thoroughly vexed the abbot and the monks. King Henry, determining to put an end to these vexations, set a day for the pleadings of both parties before him in the castle of Caen. Therefore on the appointed day the abbot and the monks with everything that was necessary to them brought their plea to the king and the justices. And Herbert, there in the presence of the king and all the justices and barons, failed, so that the judgment of the king and the justices was that St Stephen should remain seised of the said church, from then on answering to no one about it. Witnesses to these things King Henry himself and the justice (*iustitia*) namely John, bishop of Lisieux, Robert of La Haye-du-Puits, Geoffrey of Subles, and the barons Ralph Taisson, Roger Marmion, William Patrick, Robert Charcoal-burner.

The identities of the men who judged these lawsuits suggest that the bench included representatives from both tiers of justices. Bishop John of Lisieux and Robert of La Haye-du-Puits, who judged both cases, would seem to be justices of Normandy – they were certainly men with a wide-ranging authority who stood close to Henry at the centre of affairs who would be expected to hold that position.[188] The others, Geoffrey of Subles, Roger Marmion, and Hugh of Montfort, may have been local justices. Geoffrey of Subles, who was also addressed in one of Henry's writs for the canons of Bayeux cathedral,[189] took his name from Subles (Calvados) on the road between Caen and Bayeux. He probably continued to serve as a justice into the reign of Duke Geoffrey.[190] Roger Marmion, who was dead by 1130,[191] was based to the south of Caen at Fontenay-le-Marmion (Calvados), and it may be relevant that he, along with Bishop John of Lisieux, attested an act of King Henry for Savigny at Argentan in 1114 × 1120 following a plea concerning unspecified alms at Caen.[192] Hugh of Montfort had his seat at Montfort-sur-Risle, but also

---

[188] See above, Chapter 6, pp. 352–4.

[189] Caen, AD Calvados, H 1834; *NI*, pp. 95–6; *Regesta*, ii. 1897. Geoffrey is clearly differentiated from the justices of Normandy in this address, supporting the idea that he was a local justice.

[190] *Regesta*, iii. no. 55. The editors of the *Regesta* mis-expanded the initial G. as Guy rather than Geoffrey, but it is likely that this 'G. de Sableio', who is addressed in the act and named as a justice, was actually the same Geoffrey of Subles who had been active during Henry I's reign. He has also been confused with Geoffrey of Sablé who was active on the Avre frontier during Stephen's reign and who came from Maine (Power, *The Norman Frontier*, pp. 393, 501; Dutton, 'Geoffrey', p. 187).

[191] *PR 31 Henry I*, p. 88.

[192] *Regesta*, ii. no. 1183.

held lands around Saint-Hymer in the Lieuvin and a fee of eight knights from the bishop of Bayeux.[193] The location of his estates and his relative importance mean it is unclear whether he acted as a local justice or as a justice of Normandy before his rebellion in 1123.

In addition to those men named as justices in the *Emptiones Eudonis*, William Tanetin was named as such when he intervened in, and observed, a lawsuit involving the monks of Troarn against Fulk fitz Fulk and his guardian in 1133.[194] He, too, was clearly a man with local interests. Indeed, he was both a patron of Troarn abbey and a vassal of its lord, William Talvas. In 1129, he had given the monks a third of the mill of Saint-Sylvain (Calvados), the land that the monks had previously given him there to make a house, and four acres of land at *Rainerii Masnil*.[195] In 1135, he went to the abbey and gave his nephew, Roger, to the community.[196] William was also a benefactor of the nuns at Vignats, another foundation of the Montgommery-Bellême family, and the knights of the Temple.[197] He was, then, an important local figure, if not one who stood on the top rung of aristocratic society, and his local connections, standing, and knowledge may be supposed to have given him the tools he needed to do his job effectively.

The records of the pleas in the *Emptiones Eudonis* reveal that one of the things that justices did was justice. First and foremost they heard pleas in the dukes' courts. As they did so in the dukes' absence, it may be that one of the reasons for establishing a bench of justices was to ensure that the dukes' courts could continue to dispense justice in their name even when the duke was personally absent. In addition, they were Henry's main resource in his drive to ensure that justice was done in seigniorial courts, as noted above. Henry had responded to just such a perceived lack of justice when he demanded that the bishop of Bayeux should not disseise Godfrey the priest of Caen of his church without right judgement.[198] He also made provision for potential failures to do justice in some of his Norman acts. The abbot of Saint-Pierre-sur-Dives, for example, had jurisdiction, including over serious offences, but 'if a claim is made to the abbot, and that man (i.e. the abbot) does not wish to do justice and right, then my own justice (*iusticiarius*) shall be required to do it, who above all

---

[193] *Inquisition*, p. 16.

[194] Ctl. Troarn, fo. 35v; Valin, *Le duc et sa cour*, pp. 62–3 (no. 8); *NI*, p. 98.

[195] Ctl. Troarn, fo. 31r.

[196] Ctl. Troarn, fo. 31r.

[197] *Regesta*, ii. no. 1909 (Vignats); Ctl. Troarn, fol. 31r–v (Temple). The gift to Vignats provides the evidence for William holding land from William Talvas. An act of a Roger Tanetin of 1092 reveals that he and his brothers held property from Roger II of Montgommery (Ctl. Troarn, fo. 86v). It is likely that this Roger was William's father.

[198] Noted above, infra, p. 464.

others in my place holds justice'.[199] They might also supervise or observe pleas held in seigniorial courts when there was a possibility that justice there might be prejudiced by a lord's self-interest.[200] Aside from William Tanetin's involvement in the dispute just mentioned, ducal justices were present at the court of Nigel of Saint-Sauveur-le-Vicomte at some point during Henry I's reign, to observe a plea brought against Nigel and his men by the monks of Saint-Sauveur-le-Vicomte.[201] In these cases, a lord was involved in a plea heard in his own court against one of his own men. In England, c. 1130, royal justices also attended seigniorial courts as a matter of course when the plea involved 'men of other barons'.[202] There is no evidence that they did so in Normandy, too, but on balance it seems likely that they did.

By the 1120s, Henry or his officials had also developed a clause, known as a *nisi feceris* clause, which allowed ducal justices to seize jurisdiction and to enforce a decision or judgement should the lord concerned fail to do so in his court. One is found at the end of the writ for Reginald fitz Robert, as noted above. Another example is provided by a writ for the abbey of Montebourg, dating perhaps from 1129 to 1135. This commanded William of Aubigny to allow the monks to 'hold of my alms its land of Morsalines … And unless you do it my justice shall do right so that I do not hear more of this for want of full justice or right.'[203]

The *nisi feceris* clause was not among Henry's innovations. One appears in an English writ of King William II for the abbey of Saints Serge and Bach of Angers made at Rouen.[204] There were other precedents, too. In 1102, Pope Paschal II sent a letter to Bishop Osbern of Exeter which commanded him to allow the monks of Battle at St Nicholas in Exeter to have a cemetery for their dead. The letter concludes with what is to all intents and purposes a *nisi feceris* clause: 'if anyone attempts to oppose this decision, we have instructed our venerable brother and fellow bishop Anselm to carry out the punishment of apostolic discipline against whoever despises the Apostolic See.'[205] But although Henry (or one of his administrators or clerks) did not invent the clause, its potential was certainly developed during his reign, although even then they appear in only thirty-two English writs (out of 571) and four Norman ones (out of forty-two).[206] Two of the Norman writs with the phrase certainly date from after 1129. The other two are harder to pin

---

[199] Caen, AD Calvados, H 7031(5) = *Regesta*, ii. no. 1569.
[200] As noted above, pp. 457, 469, 474.
[201] BL Add. Ch. 15281, quoted in *NI*, pp. 103–4.
[202] *Leges Edwardi*, 9.2, in O'Brien, *God's Peace and King's Peace*, p. 167.
[203] *NI*, p. 102; *Regesta*, ii. no. 1684.
[204] *Regesta*, ii. 411 (no. lxixa).
[205] *Letters of St Anselm*, no. 226.
[206] *Regesta*, ii. nos. 1684, 1898, 1962; Chanteux, *Recueil*, no. 155.

down but one of them at least most likely dates from no earlier than the 1120s. The use of this clause in Normandy thus seems to relate to the institutionalization of the office of justice, although this might be deceptive.

Julia Boorman has discussed how *nisi feceris* clauses worked during the reign of Henry II. She recited a story found in the *Gesta abbatum monasterii sancti Albani* by which Roger of Valognes obtained writs from the king with *nisi feceris* clauses. The abbot of St Albans did not put Roger in possession of the land he had claimed, so Roger took his writ to Earl Robert of Leicester, the chief justiciar, who actioned it as commanded by the *nisi feceris* clause of writ itself.[207] Although two of the four Norman writs make it clear that they were issued following a plea, there are no narratives that can confirm, or otherwise, whether the procedure that could be invoked when a beneficiary had a writ with a *nisi feceris* clause was the same in Normandy as it was in England. It may be noted, however, that all four Norman *nisi feceris* clauses state that the justices should act if the addressees failed to do so, with one of them also adding the archbishop of Rouen and another Robert of La Haye (who also served as a justice of Normandy).[208] In contrast, English writs provided for a variety of men and officials to take the necessary action. Walter the arbalester of York, the bishops of Lincoln and Norwich, sheriffs, and justices were commanded to take action should the addressee fail to do so.[209] English writs even provide for the victims to take distraint on livestock of the malefactor's fee should the wrong not be put right in accordance with the king's command.[210] The Norman writs, therefore, hint that the procedure to be followed in Normandy was different from that found in England. They also seem to confirm that the justice had a near monopoly in the administration of Norman justice in the duke's absence.

The development of the *nisi feceris* clause also reveals a desire to make ducal

---

[207] Thomas of Walsingham, *Gesta abbatum monasterii sancti Albani*, ed. H. T. Riley, Rolls Series, vol. 1 (London, 1867), pp. 159–66; J. Boorman, '*Nisi feceris* under Henry II', *ANS*, 24 (2002), 85–97, with the story at 86–7.

[208] *Regesta*, ii. no. 1962; Chanteux, *Recueil*, no. 155. This is also the case with the approximately twenty-five Norman writs of Henry II that have a *nisi feceris* clause (N. Vincent, 'Regional variations in the charters of King Henry II', in *Charters and Charter Scholarship in Britain and Ireland*, ed. M. T. Flanagan and J. A. Green (Basingstoke, 2005), p. 89).

[209] *Regesta*, ii. nos. 642 (Walter the arbalester), 1837 (bishop of Lincoln), 1712 (bishop of Norwich), 1115, 1669 (sheriffs), 1533, 1541 (justices), 1566 (sheriff and justice). Nicholas Vincent noted that sheriffs, bishops, and local justices are only referred to in the *nisi feceris* clauses of Henry II's writs after 1172, and apparently suggested that this was a new development (Vincent, 'Regional variations in the charters of King Henry II', p. 88). These writs of Henry I would suggest otherwise.

[210] For example, *Regesta*, ii. nos. 533, 1860a.

justice more efficient and thus cheaper and more attractive. It is likely that before the justices were instituted, claimants would have had to find the duke before they could commence their plea. That might have entailed a journey to England and back, as was the case with the monks of Marmoutier in 1080, and perhaps a delay while awaiting the duke's return to the duchy, as with the plea between the monks of Mont-Saint-Michel and William Paynel.[211] Cases could become drawn out. In 1108, Suger of Saint-Denis had problems obtaining justice over a fish-render at Berneval and, although this is not expressly stated in the report of the proceedings, the delays and uncertainties might have been the result of a need for those officials handling the plea to correspond with the king before moving to the next stage in proceedings, leading to pointless hearings and numerous deferments.[212] It is likely that the institution of an established bench of justices, thereby creating the Norman exchequer court, was intended to make justice more efficient. Henry I's writ concerning Vains suggests that while he might have to set the wheels in motion, once the process had been started it moved quite quickly.[213] Equally, the use of the *nisi feceris* clause meant that the enforcement of a verdict could not be delayed and so allowed ducal justice to appear more swift and efficient when it really counted. It is likely that in these developments Henry was, again, trying to find ways to attract his subjects to his court.

As the *nisi feceris* clauses suggest, justices carried out the administrative work necessary to put judicial decisions into effect. This can be seen from the thirteen (of forty-two) authentic Norman writs of Henry I that are addressed to these officials. The business is more varied than that in the acts addressed to *vicomtes*, but most of them relate to the rightful or undisturbed possession of property, with occasional revelations about judicial procedure. Thus, three of the acts command that beneficiaries should have possession of property following lawsuits;[214] three writs command that the beneficiary should hold its property in peace;[215] and one commands that property should be held well and freely – which suggests that such words relate to undisturbed possession.[216] Others are concerned with more specific events. In 1106 × 1129, for example, Henry I sent a writ to Algar of

[211] *Regesta: William*, no. 200 (Marmoutier); *Ctl. Mont-Saint-Michel*, pp. 166–7 (no. 90), with an English translation at Tabuteau, *Transfers*, pp. 56–7 (Mont-Saint-Michel).

[212] Barroux, 'L'anniversaire de la mort de Dagobert à Saint-Denis', 131–51 at 148–51; Grant, *Abbot Suger of Saint-Denis*, p. 53.

[213] *Regesta*, ii. 370 (no. ccxlii) = no. 1672.

[214] *NI*, p. 93, n. 30 = *Regesta* ii. no. 1216; *Livre Noir*, i. 43–4 (no. 37) = *Regesta* ii. no. 1898; *NI*, p. 102 (no. 14) = *Regesta* ii. no. 1952.

[215] *Regesta* ii. 334 (no. cviii) = no. 1155, *Livre Noir*, i. 14 (no. 8) = *Regesta* ii. no. 1897; *NI*, p. 102 = *Regesta* ii. no. 1953.

[216] *NI*, p. 101 (no. 9) = *Regesta*, ii. no. 1950.

Sainte-Mère-Eglise 'and his other justices of the Cotentin' commanding them to allow Rinald, prior of Heauville, 'to have the fish newly caught in the land of the blessed Martin'.[217] A writ for the abbey at Montebourg commanded that the monks should have 'as many trees from the forest of Brix as there are weeks in the year', and that 'the foresters shall be quit in my pleas of so many trees for which the monks shall guarantee them by their tallies'.[218] The writ thus provides evidence of the existence of forest pleas in Henry's Normandy, and reveals that these pleadings were presided over by the justices (this is why they were addressed).

Henry I's reign certainly saw important developments in the way that justice was done in Normandy. But while he should be credited with the introduction of the exchequer court and the increasingly routine use of the *nisi feceris* clause, the introduction of the word 'justice' to describe an official probably obscures their earlier if less institutionalized existence of such an official. It is highly likely that there were men who did the work of justices before the office was institutionalized. This is suggested by a report in the *Emptiones Eudonis* of an earlier plea that took place at Argentan:

> Abbot Eudo bought from William of the chapel the mill of Crocy next to the Dives for 22 *livres* in the first purchase. Disseised of this mill by Robert Frellam, the said abbot gave the said William another 22 *livres* that he would deraign that mill against the said Robert and quit it to St Stephen. Which deraignment and quittance was made at Argentan before King Henry, and there in the presence of that king and of the whole court that mill was recognized to be of the fee of the king. Of this thing the witness is the king himself and his barons, namely John bishop of Lisieux, Robert of Courcy, William of Tancarville, William Peverel, Rainald of Argentan.

If the barons were also the judges, as seems likely, then the bench was very similar to those found in the pleas concerning Fontenay-le-Pesnel and Secqueville-en-Bessin. But whereas the bishop and his colleagues were there described as justices, a few years earlier (or so it may be supposed) they were simply Henry's barons and a part of his court.

Men were certainly doing the job that the justices would later do, albeit without the title, from the beginning of Henry's rule over Normandy. In 1107, Henry sent a writ to William of Tancarville and Gilbert of L'Aigle, commanding that

---

[217] Couppey, *Encore Héauville!*, p. 350. Unusually, the writ seems to have been drafted by the beneficiary. Were it not for the monks of Marmoutier, whose practices consistently defied the usual conventions, this would suggest forgery.

[218] *NI*, p. 102 (no. 11) = *Regesta* ii. no. 1951.

the monks of Jumièges be allowed to enjoy the 'fat fish' that was washed up at nearby Quillebeuf. It goes on to command these men – and this is why they must have been equivalent to justices – to 'do to the abbot right concerning these men who have had the same unjustly'.[219] Roger of Magneville was addressed in two Norman writs of Henry I. In the first, dating from 1107 × 1130, he and Bishop John of Lisieux were commanded to 'hold full right for the abbot of Caen of the water of Vains, just as that water belonged to the manor in the time of my father, so that I do not hear more claim about it'.[220] Again, these men were not described as justices, but their function was clearly that which the justices would later perform. In 1108 × 1122, Roger of Magneville, Bishop John, and William fitz Ansger were ordered to 'let Richard, bishop of Bayeux, have justice over his bishopric and his men just as Bishop Odo his predecessor well and freely once had them … And whoever hinders him or his ministers you shall do full justice to them' – this last sentence looks like an early form of *nisi feceris* clause.[221] There is also a writ for the monks of Saint-Père, Chartres, made 1106 × 1120, which commanded Wiger of Sainte-Mère-Eglise to hold right (in other words, hold a plea) for the monks of Saint-Père concerning their land.[222] Ranulf the chancellor and Grimbald the physician might have been present at Sées in 1117 effectively as justices, to oversee the judgement made there.[223] Eudo of Bayeux and William of Glastonbury seem also to have numbered among the justices before 1135, while Robert of Courcy was a justice in the first of the pleas reported in the *Emptiones* and continued to function as such into the reign of Duke Geoffrey.[224]

It is impossible that William of Tancarville, Gilbert of L'Aigle, and the other individuals addressed in these writs did not hold some office at the royal duke's pleasure. How else would a writing-office scribe have known who to address the writ to? If they were not royal officials, how could William or Gilbert have

---

[219] *Chs. Jumièges*, i. 134–5 (no. 47) = *Regesta*, ii. no. 842. The writ is similar in content to that addressed to Algar and the other justices of the Cotentin, making the comparison all the more telling.

[220] *Regesta*, ii. 370 (no. ccxlii) = no. 1672.

[221] *Livre Noir*, i. 36 (no. 29) = *Regesta*, ii. no. 951.

[222] *NI*, p. 223 = *Regesta*, ii. no. 1229. In addition to the writs discussed here, there is also a writ for Saint-Père, Chartres, giving it the right to any new tithes it acquired in Moulins-la-Marche and Bonsmoulins. The justices seem here to have been addressed as part of the generality of Normandy (*Ctl. Saint-Père*, ii. 640–1 (no. 25) (with errors) = *Regesta*, ii. no. 1932). There are also four writs granting exemption from toll, passage, and custom (*Foedera*, ix. 350 = *Regesta*, ii. no. 1573; *Cal. Chart R.*, iv. 157 = *Regesta* ii. no. 1682; *NI*, p. 308 (no. 23) = *Regesta*, ii. no. 1919; *Ctl. Grand-Beaulieu*, p. 2 (no. 2), omitted from *Regesta*).

[223] *Ctl. Perche*, pp. 31–2 (no. 19) and see above, *infra*, p. 472.

[224] *Regesta*, iii. no. 56.

acted upon the order they received? This being the case, it is possible, indeed likely, that men who performed similar functions as the later justices, but who were not called by that name, had operated in Normandy for years, perhaps decades, previously. Orderic noted that, on his return to Normandy in 1067, William the Bastard 'appointed the best possible men as judges and officials (*iudices et rectores*) in the provinces of Normandy'.[225] It seems unlikely that the role of these apparently permanently established officials was much different from that of the local justices of Henry I's reign.[226] The development of permanently established justices of Normandy might have taken longer, however. Two cases decided in William the Bastard's reign were judged by small panel of judges, and in another case, an agreement was to be made before Gerald the king's steward,[227] but the duke apparently delegated authority to them only on a one-off basis.[228]

It seems almost certain, then, that there had been men who had carried out the duties of the later local justices from the 1060s, even if the 'justices of Normandy' might only have developed under Henry I. But even then the label seems to have been created some years after men began to perform that role. The creation of this new term was itself necessitated, perhaps, not by the role itself but rather by a wider trend that saw a move from the particular to the general during Henry's reign. Among the most important and relevant of these was the move away from the writ-charter, which began with an address naming the current bishop and *vicomte* for each county (in England the earl, bishop, and/or sheriff), to the charter, which began with a hierarchical but unspecific general address that could encompass all people at all times. As beneficiaries began to see that writs could be used like diplomas or charters to record and enforce rights, so they wanted to ensure that they could be reused on later occasions should the need arise. As documents addressed to named individuals might have become void after the addressee left office, it was important to find a way of ensuring their permanence.[229] That meant

[225] Orderic, ii. 208.

[226] Bruce O'Brien wondered, similarly, whether the use of local justices in England under Henry I differed significantly from Edgar's, Cnut's, and Edward the Confessor's use of royal agents whose principal tasks were judicial (O'Brien, *God's Peace and King's Peace*, p. 70).

[227] *NI*, p. 56, n. 270.

[228] *Regesta: William*, nos. 214 and 201, respectively.

[229] Richard Sharpe has argued that, in England, writ-charters became invalid once the beneficiary or grantor died. The result was a succession of writs or writ-charters dealing with the same matter in near-identical terms (R. Sharpe, 'The use of writs in the eleventh century: a hypothesis based on the archive of Bury St Edmunds', *Anglo-Saxon England*, 32 (2003), 283–91). On that basis, an address that named a deceased bishop, or a defunct official, might equally have been rendered useless. That in turn is likely to

coining a name for the office that the individuals held. And so the office of justice was created, with Henry's writs addressed to the current holder of the position and the 'other justices' of the region concerned – by which it was probably meant the successors rather than partners of the man named in it.

Doing justice on offenders: obstacles and outcomes

To do justice on offenders, the dukes had to know that they had commissioned, or were accused of commissioning, offences. The offender had to be apprehended and then had to appear before the duke's court. Only then could his or her guilt or innocence be ascertained and a just judgement handed down.

Most offences were probably brought to the duke's attention by the victim. Complaints might be brought directly to the duke even by the very humble, as had been the case in Carolingian times.[230] For example, Dudo tells us that when he thought his plough had been stolen, the peasant of Longpaon approached Duke Rollo directly.[231] Similarly, even though he stood on a much higher social rung, Abbot Ranulf of Mont-Saint-Michel complained directly to Duke William of the murder of his swineherd in 1066.[232]

Where the victim did not or could not bring an accusation him or herself, it might be brought by members of the local community. The oath of the hundredmen taken in 853 in West Francia reveals that there was at that time a general obligation on all free men to report and pursue offenders.[233] This obligation seems to have continued into the twelfth century. King Henry I's grant of jurisdiction to the monks of Le Bec of 1134, for example, makes it clear that the monks' men – presumably all the freemen of the parish of Le Bec – were required to apprehend malefactors: 'if the abbot's men shall see anyone … offending and shall not arrest him, they shall either prove in the abbot's court that they could not, or shall pay, each of them, 18 *sous*.'[234] Count Robert of Meulan's 1106 grant to the monks of Préaux foresaw the possibility that one of his men would come

---

have been one of the principal causes of the move to the general address which would never go out of date. See also Hagger, 'The earliest Norman writs revisited', 195–6.

[230] Nelson, 'Kingship and royal government', p. 417.

[231] *Dudo*, p. 52; Jumièges, i. 68. Longpaon might have been a demesne vill at the time. It seems later to have been held from William fitz Osbern by Hugh of *Nirei* (*RADN*, no. 212).

[232] *Ctl. Mont-Saint-Michel*, pp. 148–9 (no. 70). The *Leges Henrici Primi* note that accusations of theft, robbery, or offences of that type might be brought before justices in England (*LHP*, para. 59.27), but there is no evidence for this in Normandy.

[233] Cited in Nelson, 'Kingship and royal government', p. 421.

[234] BnF, MS lat. 13905, fo. 9r–v, printed in Porée, *Histoire de l'Abbaye du Bec*, i. 658 = *Regesta*, ii. no. 1900.

across a robber and that he would then arrest him, implying an obligation or duty so to act.[235]

Whether the duke himself had officials in place who would actively seek out offenders is not clear, however. Henry I *might* have had them. Orderic tells us that, after the rebellion of 1123–24, 'sworn allies lay low, in great fear of being denounced before justices and lawmen (*iusticiariis et iurisperitis*) for bring privy to treason',[236] although those doing the denouncing need not have been ducal officials, of course. There is no unambiguous evidence, however, for a Norman equivalent to men such as Robert Malarteis, who 'seemed to have no function except to catch men out',[237] although we may suspect that they did operate in the duchy. It is possible that the *vicomtes* played a role here, too. Certainly, they had such a role in the thirteenth century. The so-called *Très ancien coutumier* makes very little mention of *vicomtes*, but in the chapter dealing with 'how assizes should be held' it states that 'the *vicomtes* of the duke shall inquire, or their sergeants, of the evil or worst that has occurred in their balliwicks against the innocent'.[238] Assizes and balliwicks were introduced into Normandy after the death of Henry I, but the function performed here *may* reflect what the *vicomtes* had been doing before 1144. Similarly, the less ancient *Ancienne Coutume de Normandie* relates that the *vicomte* should enquire 'diligently and in secret about malefactors concerning murders and arsons and the deflowering of virgins and other criminal actions. And those that are found culpable on the oath of several faithful men, who are not suspect, he ought to hold in prison while they await the common inquest or else that they shall be freed by the law of the country.'[239]

Once an offence had been reported or discovered, but where the identity of the perpetrator was unknown, the duke would have to establish who had commissioned it. Thus, once the peasant of Longpaon had reported the theft of his plough, Rollo (or Richard II) attempted to uncover the thief:

> [Rollo] immediately summoned one of his *prévôts* and said to him: 'Give five *sous* to this peasant so he can buy what he has lost. You go to the vill with all speed, and inquire who was responsible for the theft by the judgment of fire.'

> And the *prévôt* examined all the inhabitants of the vill by fire, and found none of them guilty of the theft, and reported back to Duke Rollo. He summoned

---

[235] *Ctl. Préaux*, A69, quoted above, *infra*, pp. 458–9.

[236] Orderic, vi. 356.

[237] Orderic, iii. 348.

[238] *TAC*, i. 44 (ch. 55).

[239] *L'Ancienne Coutume de Normandie*, ed. W. L. de Grunchy (St Helier 1881), pp. 16–17. The text was written between 1270 and 1314 (p. viii). For more on the role and responsibilities of the *vicomtes* see below, Chapter 9, pp. 542–50 and Chapter 10, pp. 592–4.

Archbishop Franco and said: 'If the God of the Christians in whose name I have been baptised knows all things, I am amazed that he has not indicated the one guilty of theft when tried by fire in His name.'

And Franco replied: 'The fire has not yet touched the guilty one.'

And [Rollo] said to the *prévôt*: 'Go again, and examine the inhabitants of the neighbouring villages by the process of fire in the name of Jesus Christ.'

He carried out the duke's orders and told him that he had not found anyone guilty.

It was only then that the peasant was summoned to the court, and his guilt and that of his wife was revealed.[240]

Where they *were* known, offenders would have to be apprehended if they had not been caught in the act. A writ of Henry I for the monks of Montebourg suggests that officials might lay in wait for their man or woman on market days, perhaps because the suspect hoped to hide among the crowd or perhaps because that was a time when they would have money on them.[241] In any event, such activities were likely to damage the market, and those whose market it was might consequently try to stop it:

Henry king of the English to the *vicomtes* and *prévôts* and his officials of all the Cotentin greeting. I command that you do not apprehend any men or take distress on any occasion in the market of Montebourg on the days when the market is held, if you are able to take it on another day and in another place in my land. Since I do not will that the market, which is my alms, should be destroyed by the opportunity.[242]

---

[240] *Dudo*, p. 52; Jumièges, i. 68, ii. 286–8. Although there are some differences, the process employed by the duke bears comparison with that laid down in the Capitulary of Quierzy of 873 which ordered that bondsmen suspected of crimes should be brought before the count, 'and if no-one wishes to accuse them let them nevertheless clear their ill fame through the ordeal' (quoted in R. Bartlett, *Trial by Fire and Water: The Medieval Judicial Ordeal* (Oxford, 1986), p. 29, n. 63. The Assize of Clarendon of 1166 set out similar rules: W. Stubbs, *Select Charters and other Illustrations of English Constitutional History from the Earliest Times to the Reign of Edward the First*, ninth edition (Oxford, 1913), p. 170; translated in *English Historical Documents II, 1042–1189*, ed. and trans. D. C. Douglas and G. W. Greenaway (London, 1953) p. 408).

[241] See also the apparently related provision in *TAC*, i. 32, ch. 37.2 noted below (p. 491).

[242] *NI*, p. 101 = *Regesta*, ii. no. 1949.

The laws of Breteuil similarly forbade summonses to be made on market days, as did an act for Préaux, presumably for the same reasons.[243]

In addition, the first canon of the Council of Lillebonne of 1080 provided that:

> The peace commonly known as the Truce of God shall be steadfastly observed as it was when it was first established by Duke William himself … All who refuse to observe it or break it in any way shall receive just sentence from the bishops according to the ordinance already established. If anyone then disobeys his bishop, the bishop shall make this known to the lord on whose land he lives, and the lord shall compel him to submit to episcopal justice. But if the lord refuses to do this, the king's *vicomte*, on being requested by the bishop, shall act without prevarication.[244]

The evidence, such as it is, would suggest that the *vicomtes* and *prévôts* had a leading role in arresting and holding offenders so that they might be brought to trial.

If an offender could not be taken, they could not be tried for the offence he or she had commissioned. The same was true, of course, if an offender simply refused to attend the duke's court. It is likely that this happened in 1091. Ralph of Tosny's lands had been attacked by Count William of Evreux. 'Ralph went to Duke Robert to complain to him of the injuries inflicted by his fellow countrymen and ask him as his liege lord for help; but he wasted his time, for nothing was done. Therefore he looked elsewhere, since he had to seek effective patronage. He sent envoys to describe his misfortunes to the king of England and promised to submit himself and all he owned to William if help were forthcoming.'[245] Even though Count William had almost certainly breached clause 8 of the *Consuetudines et iusticie*, it seems that Duke Robert was unwilling or unable to bring him to justice. In contrast, Rufus responded favourably, and although he could not bring the count to trial, he could and did help Ralph to garrison his castles and to protect his estates. The result of Curthose's weakness, then, was the loss of a supporter to his brother.

The sources tend to gloss over incidents like this, but it is clear that they did occur. It is also clear that it was not a problem experienced only by weak dukes of the Normans. Fulbert of Chartres had all but begged Count Fulk of Anjou to submit to royal justice in 1008.[246] William the Bastard, hearing of Count William

---

[243] Ballard, 'Law of Breteuil', p. 652; *Ctl. Préaux*, A114.

[244] Orderic, III, 26.

[245] Orderic, iv. 214. Ralph of Tosny was subsequently listed among those loyal to Rufus (Orderic, vi. 56).

[246] Fulbert, *Letters*, no. 13.

of Arques's incipient rebellion, 'sought to turn him from his madness and summoned him, by way of messengers, to come in order to show his allegiance. In great confidence, however, having scorned the embassy, he fortified himself ready for rebellion.'[247] The various offences that Robert of Bellême commissioned against Robert Curthose similarly went unpunished. Even when Curthose rode in force into his lordship to do justice there in person, he could right only two of Bellême's multifarious wrongs.[248] Even Henry I was unable to do anything about Bellême's offences until 1112, and only then because he broke the peace that protected visitors to his court (under clause 1 of the *Consuetudines et iusticie*). Indeed, one of the offences Bellême was charged with was his failure to attend court 'after being summoned three times'.[249]

Reputations for weakness or injustice were problematic. They resulted in a loss of prestige and honour, the loss of *fideles* such as Ralph of Tosny and thus of knights and strength, and might even end in rebellions which could result in the total loss of their duchy. Dukes sought to avoid such issues or to ensure that they did not endure, even if it meant breaching the protection offered to those who attended their court, allowing an individual to inherit land despite having previously offered the strongest opposition to their claim, or in the last resort taking up arms against them. It is consequently no surprise that the dukes were concerned to ensure that those who were not strong enough to oppose them did not then avoid their justice by running away.

How many fled from justice in Normandy is not known, but it is certain that some did attempt to do so. Amatus of Montecassino recounted a story – corroborated or merely repeated by Orderic – of how Gilbert Buatre murdered William Repostellus who was a ducal *vicomte*. Count Richard II 'was very angry at William's death and ordered the execution of the one who had done the murder, for if this offence went unpunished, it would seem that it gave licence to anyone to kill a *vicomte*'.[250] The guilty man escaped punishment by fleeing to self-imposed exile in Italy. The same was true of Serlo of Hauteville, who fled Normandy during the reign of Robert the Magnificent after having killed a 'certain powerful man'.[251]

By the reign of William the Bastard at least, such flagrant attempts to escape

---

[247] Jumièges, ii. 102. Similarly, Roger I of Sicily sought to prevent the citizens of Iato from revolting through a combination of flattery and threats, but was ultimately unsuccessful and had to bring them to heel by fighting them (Malaterra, *The Deeds of Count Roger*, p. 150).

[248] Orderic, iv. 294.

[249] Orderic, vi. 178.

[250] Amatus of Montecassino, *History of the Normans*, pp. 50–1; Orderic, ii. 56; Jumièges, ii. 154.

[251] Geoffrey Malaterra, *The Deeds of Count Roger*, p. 75.

ducal justice resulted in a very public pursuit of the fugitive. As noted above, Hugh Bunel, who murdered Mabel of Bellême, found himself pursued for years. Orderic tells us that Hugh fled first to Apulia, then to Sicily, and from there to the service of the Byzantine emperor Alexios Comnenos. But wherever Hugh went he was pursued by the threats and bribes of King William and Mabel's sons, who 'promised rewards and gifts to any spies who could kill the exiled assassin in whatever land they might find him'.[252] And so Hugh left Christendom altogether and lived among the Saracens for twenty years until, during the First Crusade, he appeared before Robert Curthose at the siege of Jerusalem and offered him his help and service in counsel and battle. There is no suggestion, however, that Hugh recovered his possessions in Normandy as a result of his aid, and they were not anyway in the duke's gift, but it was perhaps enough for Hugh that he could now, at last, stop running.

There was, then, some attempt to recapture those who had fled, although more details are only available for the second half of the twelfth century. Thus, at some time between 1156 and 1163 Henry II granted that 'all who shall come to the Holy Trinity fair at Fécamp between Palm Sunday and Trinity Sunday each year shall have my firm peace and guardianship and they shall be safe and secure going and returning through my whole land … unless they are fugitives of my land for murder or theft or some other crime'. And by the end of the twelfth century – apparently by 1180 – discrete laws and/or customs applying specifically to fugitives had developed. These are set out in the *Très ancien coutumier*, and include the following provision:

> if anyone for any crime (*crimen*) shall flee and shall not dare to come to three assizes or to the markets of the country … all his chattels shall be taken and rendered to the exchequer and his name shall be written in the duke's roll and his house shall be burned down if it is in a village. And if his house shall be established in a town or a city, it shall be torn down and taken outside the town and shall be burned in the middle of the day. This is done so that all and each can see the lawful justice of the duke and they shall fear this danger to run to themselves.[253]

In addition, those harbouring fugitives were to be subject to loss of chattels and death or mutilation, and captured fugitives would be mutilated or executed.

---

[252] Orderic, v. 158.

[253] *TAC*, i. 32, ch. 37.2. These customs may be supposed to have been in place by 1180, as we can see the duke's officers accounting for the chattels of fugitives in the Norman pipe roll for that year (see, for example, *Norman Pipe Rolls*, pp. 3, 7–8, 11, 16, 18, 20, 24).

Further, the rules on fugitives in the *Coutumier* had an impact on the rights usually enjoyed by other lords. The *Consuetudines et iusticie*, it will be remembered, allowed that lords might have some right in the punishment of offenders when they had committed housebreaking, rape, or arson, or had made distraint without following due process. In such cases, it may be supposed that they would have a right to the profits produced by the sale of the chattels of those found guilty. But here, the chattels of *all* who fled and for *any* crime belonged to the duke. Where a man escaped, then, a lord with rights to fines and forfeitures would lose out. As this custom penalized not just the fugitive, but also the lord who had perhaps allowed him to flee, it should perhaps be seen as a financial penalty imposed on those who had failed to see justice done and an incentive to prevent it from happening.

If the duke could apprehend a wrong-doer and bring him to court, he would be tried and, if convicted, sentenced. We know very little about the procedure or arguments involved. The role of the *vicomtes* and justices in processing 'low justice', for example, is very obscure. The county court seems not to have been used as a forum for hearing pleas,[254] but it may be that the hundred courts of the Carolingian era had continued to function at some level.[255] There are hints that they had, most obviously in the reference to a *centenaria* around Saint-Pierre-sur-Dives. The *curtes* found in the dower agreement made for Adela in 1026, which acted as estate centres and depots for the produce of the ducal demesne and ducal revenues, *might* also have been the venues for courts. In any event, we are unlikely to go too far wrong if we suppose that the greater vills of the ducal demesne provided the venue for such trials.

Orderic Vitalis provided some evidence of the procedure followed at trial in a few celebrated cases. His narrative suggests that high-status offenders at least were judged before a panel of judges. In 1088, Robert Curthose commanded the blinding of Robert Quarrel, the castellan of Saint-Céneri-le-Gérei, and 'many others, too, who had contumaciously resisted the prince of Normandy there were mutilated by the *sentence of the court*'.[256] On 4 November 1112, Robert of Bellême appeared before Henry I at Bonneville-sur-Touques. Bellême was, according to Orderic, required to answer as to why he had acted against his lord's interests; why he had failed to come to the court after being summoned three times; why he had not rendered account as the king's *vicomte* and officer for the revenues pertaining to the *vicomtés* of Exmes, Argentan, and Falaise; and for other misdeeds. 'By just

---

[254] On the county courts and their likely function see M. Hagger, 'The Norman *vicomte*: what did he do?', *ANS*, 29 (2007), 75–6 and Hagger, 'The earliest Norman writs revisited', *Historical Research*, 191–4. Note that the second paragraph on p. 193 should be expunged, in accordance with the erratum published in the next volume.

[255] Bloch, *Feudal Society*, ii. 363–5.

[256] Orderic, iv. 154 (my italics).

judgment of the royal court he was sentenced to close imprisonment in fetters for the many shocking crimes he had been unable to deny he had committed against God and the king.'[257] That the judgement is said to have been that of the 'royal court' indicates that this, too, was a verdict reached by at least some of the men in attendance, and not solely by the king, against whom Bellême had offended. After Henry had defeated the rebels of 1123–24, he took an active part in handing out judgement. But, again, he did not act alone. 'After Easter the king sat in judgment on the rebels who had been captured. There he had Geoffrey of Tourville and Odard of Le Pin blinded for the crime of treason. He also commanded that Luke of La Barre should have his eyes put out as a punishment for his scurrilous songs and rash escapades.'[258] When Henry pronounced his verdict on Luke, Count Charles of Flanders spoke up and argued that what the king was doing was 'contrary to our customs in punishing by mutilation knights captured in war in the service of their lord'. Count Charles's intervention reveals that Henry was not acting in isolation, but that others were joining in his judgements, even if those others were not in this case bold enough to object to the king's intended sentence. This view is confirmed by the fact that Henry did not sweep the count's objections aside, but answered them so that 'when he heard this the duke of Flanders made no reply, for he had no reasonable argument to advance against it'.[259]

When doing justice on offenders, then, the duke presided over the court and took the lead in making the judgement himself. He did not make that judgement alone, however. Others helped to find it and joined in it, thereby ensuring that the duke could not be accused of injustice. This was perhaps why the dukes, with the probable exception of Robert Curthose, do not seem to have experienced difficulties enforcing the sentences that they handed down. Even the greatest lords were apparently unable to resist their decisions. Richard II imprisoned his brother William for five years (at which point he escaped) as a result of his rebellion in the Hiémois.[260] He also sent Count Richard of Avranches into exile.[261] William the Bastard exiled Thurstan Goz, Nigel II of the Cotentin, Count William of Eu, and William Werlenc. And he arrested his half-brother Odo of Bayeux c. 1083 and held him in captivity for the rest of his reign.[262] Henry I imprisoned his brother,

---

[257] Orderic, vi. 178.

[258] Orderic, vi. 352.

[259] Orderic, vi. 354.

[260] Jumièges, ii. 8–10.

[261] André de Fleury, *Vie de Gauzlin, Abbé de Fleury: Vita Gauzelini abbatis Floriacensis monasterii*, ed. R.-H. Bautier and G. Labory (Paris, 1969), pp. 48–51.

[262] Jumièges, ii. 102 (Goz); L. Delisle, *Histoire de Saint-Sauveur-le-Vicomte*, p. 25, no. 21; Wace, p. 137 (Nigel); Jumièges, ii. 128 (Eu); Jumièges, ii. 146 (Werlenc); Orderic, iv. 40–2 (Odo).

Robert Curthose, after his victory at Tinchebray and held him in captivity until his death in 1134.[263] That was also the case for Count William of Mortain, although he seems in addition to have been blinded – a rare example of the mutilation of a Norman magnate.[264] He exiled the count and countess of Evreux when they demolished the tower he had built in their castle at Evreux, and they returned to the duchy only when Henry permitted them to do so.[265] Robert of Bellême might have been able to evade Henry's justice for some years, but when he did finally appear at court he was imprisoned for the rest of his life.[266] As discussed above, the various rebels of 1123–24 were also punished. Count Waleran of Meulan and Hugh of Montfort were imprisoned.[267] Morin of Le Pin was driven into exile.[268] Geoffrey of Tourville and Odard of Le Pin were blinded for their treason.[269] Count Amaury of Evreux, William Louvel, and some others escaped punishment, however, because, 'at length, humbling themselves, they placated the king, were restored to his favour with a pardon for past crimes, and recovered their former honours'.[270]

In the absence of evidence for the punishment of thieves, robbers, rapists, and others at any level, it is impossible to assess whether the dukes were typically able to overcome the obstacles to doing justice on such offenders. The Norman pipe rolls of Henry II's reign suggest that many, about whom we know nothing else, fled from the duke's justice, saving their person if not their property. Nonetheless, the reputations of William the Bastard and Henry I, and the generalizations lauding their success in prosecuting offenders and keeping the peace, as recorded by Jumièges, Poitiers, Orderic, and Abbot Suger, suggest that they were effective enough to be considered successful. Suger, who had reasons of his own to celebrate Henry I's justice, wrote in his *Deeds of Louis the Fat* that 'to those who plundered he promised nothing but the ripping out of their eyes and the swing of the gibbet; and the swift enforcement of these and like promises astounded them, for "anyone can be rich in promises" but the "land grew silent in his sight".'[271]

---

[263] Orderic, vi. 98.
[264] Huntingdon, 698–700 and see also the discussion in K. Davies, 'The count of the Cotentin', 123–40.
[265] Orderic, vi. 148.
[266] Orderic, vi. 178.
[267] Orderic, vi. 356.
[268] Orderic, vi. 356.
[269] Orderic, vi. 352.
[270] Orderic, vi. 358. Amaury was lucky. He had been captured at Bourgthéroulde, but William of Grandcourt, a member of Henry's household and the son of the count of Eu, had allowed him to escape back to France as he knew that Henry would imprison him for the rest of his life (Orderic, vi. 350–2).
[271] Suger, *Deeds of Louis the Fat*, p. 70.

The lack of specifics for these lesser offenders contrasts with the glare of publicity that illuminates the offences commissioned by the great lords of the duchy. That might itself be significant. The way that Orderic made his case against Curthose and in favour of Henry I suggests that, for him at least, it was the dukes' ability to bring the greatest of their lords to book that was of paramount concern to their subjects. Communities could perhaps police themselves, but they could do little against predatory lords. That is why the *Consuetudines et iusticie* were concerned above all with the duke's peace and protection, rather than with his jurisdiction over the petty crimes and petty criminals of the duchy. And that is why Orderic was at pains to record the dukes' successes, or failures, in restraining and punishing their greatest subjects.

Concluding disputes over property

Disputes over property were heard and concluded rather differently from actions involving offences, perhaps because their treatment did not so closely display the duke's power and were not encompassed within his responsibility to curb wrong-doing. Jurisdiction over property disputes was also much more divided, as has been discussed already. It is clear that many claims were settled outside court, with the parties agreeing to come together to resolve the issues in contention between them. In such cases, the only trace that there had even been a dispute is the briefest of references to it in an act granting the land in question to a church or abbey with, perhaps, an account of any counter-gift or payment provided. When disputes were brought to a court, many of them were settled, rather than judged, there, too. As Emily Tabuteau remarked, 'relatively few court cases are reported from eleventh-century Normandy... and most of them ended in a compromise, a quitclaim, or a default. Indeed, compromises were probably preferred to decisions.'[272] This preference for settlement rather than judgement was in accordance with the ideals of the time. The author of the *Leges Henrici Primi*, for example, recorded a principle whereby lawsuits were 'preferably to be settled by friendly concord'.[273] And, for many, the settlements they made were apparently sufficient. The general absence of later records referring to the same issue suggests that settlements voluntarily made between parties were usually effective, even if not always.[274]

---

[272] Tabuteau, *Transfers*, p. 228 and see Bates, *Normandy*, p. 160.

[273] *LHP*, pp. 80–1, para. 3.1.

[274] See for example *Ctl. Préaux*, A84 which records the recurring claim of Ralph Lutrel to a meadow. Abbot Richard of Conteville made a final agreement with him in 1125 × 1146, paying him 15 *sous* and a cartload of hay for his consent which he had received from the monk Nicholas. Then Robert of Aincourt said ironically: 'when these pennies have

Table 8 Judgements and settlements in Norman property disputes, 1066–1135

Date range	Judged by the duke's court	Settled before duke	Judged in a seigniorial court	Settled outside the duke's court	Total
1066–1087	10 (25%)	8 (20%)	5 (13%)	17 (43%)	40
1087–1106	4 (1) (15%)	1 (3%)	5 (15%)	22 (67%)	33
1106–1135	21 (37%)	8 (14%)	11 (19%)	17 (30%)	57
Total	36 (28%)	17 (13%)	21 (16%)	56 (43%)	130

The majority of Norman settlements were made outside the dukes' courts, as Table 8 illustrates. As noted above, many disputes that did come before the duke likely did so because the litigants could see no other way to resolve the issues between them, although one incentive to reaching an agreement might have been the threat of taking a dispute before the duke should one not emerge. Indeed, it is possible that a failure to reach a settlement would have been held against the respondent in any action.[275] Moreover, if a settlement had been reached and was then broken, it is possible that the duke or a justice would readily have stepped in to enforce its terms. While this does not seem to have happened in practice, the possibility would explain the history of one dispute recorded in the cartulary of Mont-Saint-Michel. This reports that Peter of Saint-Hilaire-du-Harcouët had claimed and then taken the vill of La Croix-Avranchin from the monks of Mont-Saint-Michel. They excommunicated him on numerous occasions, but to no effect. Finally, Peter went to the abbey and surrendered his claim, making an oath about it on the altar and also on the arm of St Aubert. The terms of his quit-claim were not recorded, but it seems that the agreement favoured the monks too much, because although Peter continued to observe this oath while King Henry lived, he broke it after his death in 1135. It took perhaps another five years for the monks finally to bring him to renounce possession of the vill for a second time. This time, we are told, the settlement was made willingly, perhaps because Peter was given 10 *livres* of Le Mans as a counter-gift.[276] It is the reference to Henry I that is of interest here. There is no evidence that the royal duke had played any part in the proceedings by which this agreement was made, yet Peter continued to observe an apparently one-sided quit-claim until Henry's death created the conditions that would allow him to break it with impunity. This comment might have been made with the benefit of hindsight, but it does hint that Henry's reputa-

been spent, you'll reclaim the meadow again, just as you always do'. I am grateful to Dr Kate Hammond for alerting me to this example.

[275] Archbishop John of Rouen was fined in part for his inability to come to a settlement with the monks of Saint-Ouen in the aftermath of the riot of 1072 (*AAbps*, p. 58)

[276] *Ctl. Mont-Saint-Michel*, no. 116.

tion had been sufficient to give even those settlements brokered without his direct involvement a greater strength than they would otherwise have possessed, and that was presumably because he or his justice would have enforced the terms of a settlement that both parties had agreed to, willingly or not.

In other cases, the parties concerned brought the agreement that they had hammered out themselves to the duke for confirmation. For example, around 1120 Abbot Hugh of Cerisy-la-Forêt wrote to Abbot Gerard of Saint-Wandrille with the intention of settling a dispute between their two monasteries over the tithe of Saint-Marcouf de l'Isle in the Cotentin.

> You know that we and our brothers William of Aunay and Durand, have already spoken of a common agreement regarding our possessions at Saint-Marcouf, over which we both of us have suffered great loss. Should you praise and grant this, we shall divide the whole tithes, both yours and ours, in half. And if you agree this with us, we will give to you a place for a grange in our land located where ours used to be, and 4 burgesses – Robert fitz Sifred, Robert Babuisel, William Freelde, Erueus Gusbart – in the same vill along with what they hold and eight acres of suitable land and a salt-pan.[277]

An agreement was subsequently drawn up between the two parties – both of them the communities of ducal abbeys – that reflected these terms, albeit with one minor change (a wood was substituted for the salt-pan). But an additional step was then taken. The monks assembled before King Henry at Rouen, some 108 miles from Cerisy-la-Forêt, and read their agreement to him. And words were added to the end of the concord recording that this had been done: 'And this was done at Rouen before Henry the venerable king of the English with the witness of Ralph archbishop of the church of Canterbury, Ranulf bishop of Durham, Nigel of Aubigny.'[278] Henry's role here was simply to rubber-stamp a done deal. But in doing so he put the weight of his own authority behind it, and it must be supposed that the monks thought that would make it more stable, just as if he had confirmed the monks' possessions. Indeed, it is difficult to see much of a difference in practice between these two species of documents so far as future disputes were concerned. Abbot Hugh was so concerned that the agreement should endure that he also obtained the confirmation of his diocesan when Bishop Richard of Bayeux visited his abbey, perhaps hoping to save himself a return trip to Rouen should anything upset the settlement, or perhaps because he was concerned that the witnesses who had been found at court would often be absent from the duchy should the agreement be challenged in future.

---

[277] Lot, *Saint-Wandrille*, pp. 114–15 (no. 59).
[278] Lot, *Saint-Wandrille*, p. 115 (no. 60).

The duke's confirmation of a settlement or judgement turned it, in some respects, into *his* settlement, just as a confirmation turned the gifts in it into the duke's gifts and placed them under his protection – as argued above. When a settlement was reached in his court, however, words might be added to the record that were intended to bring the agreement still more firmly under the duke's protection. Such words generally exaggerated the duke's role, taking him as close to the heart of the settlement as possible, and perhaps also blurred what modern writers at least might see as the distinction between a settlement and a judgement. For example, a dispute between the abbot and monks of Saint-Wandrille and the count of Evreux over the customs of the forests of Caudebec and Gauville was ended by a settlement in 1074. Duke William had brought the case into his court and then made peace between the two parties on the advice of his leading men (*principium*). It was expressly recorded that both parties would acknowledge this settlement as having been established by William's authority, rather than by the gift of one or the other of the parties.[279] In 1083, there was a dispute over property at Martin-Eglise between Archbishop William of Rouen on the one hand and Walter II Giffard and William fitz Godfrey on the other. The land, said to have been an ancient possession of the church of Rouen, had been alienated to laymen by Archbishop Robert (d. 1037). Walter Giffard and William fitz Godfrey had initially claimed that the land was within their lordships, but reached a settlement in the king's court at Fécamp whereby they would hold the land during their lifetime and do service for it. On their deaths, their respective halves would revert to the church of Rouen. The settlement was described as both a 'concord' and an 'ordinance' – this last the same word for the canons of the council of Lillebonne, suggesting that the agreement had the force of ducal legislation.[280] A third example dates from 1085. Gulbert of Auffay and the abbot of Fécamp reached an agreement before King William concerning the claims that Gulbert had advanced to the wood of Les Canadas and to some vacant land in that wood. Although the dispute was concluded with a settlement, in which both sides conceding something, the outcome is said to have been judged.[281] In all three cases, the duke was placed at the heart of proceedings, with the settlements established by his authority and as a result of his judgement.

The treatment of the settlements found in these acts also indicates what factors might turn a settlement into a judgement. The difference between the two seems to have been that the former was reached by the parties alone, while the latter was the result of the intervention of third parties. It may be supposed that the duke

[279]   *Regesta: William*, no. 262.
[280]   *Regesta: William*, no. 230.
[281]   *Regesta: William*, no. 145.

would attempt to bring litigants to terms first, and that only if this proved unfruit-
ful would he appoint judges who would then hand down a judgement. The nature
of the outcome to a plea was seriously and significantly altered at that point. When
disputes over property went to a final judgement in the duke's court, it was usually
the case that the loser lost everything – in contrast to the situation elsewhere in
France.[282] For example, when the church of Equemauville was recovered by the
abbot of Saint-Riquier, the nuns of Montivilliers received nothing to help make
the loss easier to swallow.[283] The same was true for Hugh fitz Warin, who gave up
his claim to the church of Saint-Cyr to the monks of Lehon after judgement;[284]
the bishop of Sées who lost his claim to customs against the canons of Bellême
in 1070 × 1079;[285] John fitz Richard who lost the mill on the water of Vains to
the monks of Mont-Saint-Michel;[286] the monks of Lonlay, in 1080, who lost the
church of Briouze to the monks of Saint-Florent;[287] Bishop Gilbert of Evreux who
comprehensively lost his claim to the island of Oissel to the monks of La Trinité-
du-Mont;[288] and Herbert the clerk who lost the church of Secqueville-en-Bessin to
the monks of Saint-Etienne of Caen.[289]

There is only perhaps one counter-example, where a case judged in the duke's
court concluded with both sides getting something. In 1134, ownership of the
church of St Mary on Alderney was disputed between the bishop of Coutances
and the canons of Cherbourg. The report of the plea, which is drafted as an act of
King Henry I, reads as follows:

> Know that in my presence, and in the hearing of all the subscribers, the
> canons of Cherbourg and especially Humfrey of Ansgerville returned the
> church of blessed Mary of Alderney with 4 virgates of land to the church of
> Coutances and to Bishop Algar and his successors quit and absolved from

---

[282]   See, for example, S. D. White, '"*Pactum ... legem uincit et amor iudicium*": the settlement of disputes by compromise in eleventh-century France', *American Journal of
Legal History*, 22 (1978), 281–308, reprinted in S. D. White, *Feuding and Peace-Making
in Eleventh-Century France* (Aldershot, 2005), Ch. 5. White did acknowledge, however,
that the counts of Vendôme and Blois *could* make judgements that gave everything
to one side in a dispute (White, 'The settlement of disputes', 286–8); H. Teunis, *The
Appeal to the Original Status: Social Justice in Anjou in the Eleventh Century* (2006),
pp. 64, 139.

[283]   *RADN*, no. 115.

[284]   *RADN*, no. 209.

[285]   *Regesta: William*, no. 29.

[286]   *Regesta: William*, no. 214.

[287]   *Regesta: William*, 267.

[288]   *Regesta: William*, no. 235.

[289]   AD Calvados, H 1834 (*Emptiones Eudonis*); *NI*, pp. 95–6.

all claim of the church of Cherbourg and of that Humfrey, who in that time unjustly held it which was of the church of Coutances by ancient right, just as the charter of my father which he had contested has it. And also those canons of Cherbourg placed their charter in public for the common consideration of my court and of those who were present and it was quashed and false. And so I will and firmly command that that church with everything that pertains to it shall remain quit to the church of Coutances and the bishop for all eternity. And with the advice of my bishops, the holy Algar grants to the said Humfrey that church with its alms, holding of the bishop and church of Coutances for his life unless he is receives the habit of religion.[290]

The record does not explain what made the diploma produced by the canons of Coutances more convincing than the one proffered by the canons of Cherbourg, even though it seems likely that both documents were examined and evaluated by those present. There may have been good reason for keeping quiet about this, however, as the decision seems to have been a convenient fudge. The reality of the matter was that Duke William had granted the church to both Coutances *and* Cherbourg, so that the court here silently gave priority to the earlier grant for the church of Coutances while at the same time maintaining the appearance of efficient justice. That would explain why the judgement here was so generous to Humfrey, who was allowed to hold the church for life unless he became a monk. Had the canons of Cherbourg really produced a forged charter, it is likely that Humfrey would have lost everything including, perhaps, his liberty.

So far as we can see, the judgements made in the dukes' courts were respected and observed, even if one of the parties was dissatisfied about the way the judgement had been reached. In the mid 1060s, for example, the monks of Marmoutier were pitted against those of La Couture in a dispute about a parcel of land in Laval.[291] The dispute arose because, as Guy of Laval admitted, he had granted the same land to both the parties at different times and on different terms. He also stated that in his view the claim of the monks of Marmoutier was the better of the two. The judges at the initial hearing concluded that Guy should prove his story with an oath and an ordeal. Guy resisted, saying that in his view an ordeal was not appropriate in this case. The judges, in Richard Barton's words, 'scratched their heads and admitted they weren't sure'. A second meeting of the court did not produce greater clarity. So the case was then brought to the court of Duke William by the monks of Marmoutier. The duke's judges, however, discovered 'not one judgement, but rather many' and became mired in disagreement. So William

[290] *Regesta*, ii. 1902.
[291] *RADN*, no. 159, discussed by Barton, *Maine*, pp. 215–18.

heard the case for a second time at his castle at Domfront. He then decided the dispute himself, 'undoubtedly based more on his military and political competence than on a satisfactory legal decision'. But this was precisely why the dispute had been brought before William in the first place. In the court of the lord of Laval, as Barton highlighted, the suit had to be concluded to the satisfaction of all.[292] Such concerns hampered the operation of justice thereby making it impossible for Guy to overcome an impasse. In contrast, Duke William was unfettered by any considerations of community or personal relationships and because none could stand against his power he could impose his own judgement. Moreover, he carried the majority with him. The monks of La Couture might have complained, but the monks of Marmoutier and Guy, too, were satisfied with the outcome. There was, then, consensus as well as strength. Both were required.

In 1080, Bishop Gilbert of Evreux claimed the island of Oissel, which belonged to the monks of La Trinité-du-Mont outside Rouen. William of Arques, who was the grandson and heir of Goscelin the *vicomte* who had founded the abbey, in order to give satisfaction and to end the dispute completely, put himself forward as a witness to his grandfather's gift and said that he was prepared to confirm it on oath. 'Then, as the bishop was not willing to receive the oath, by the order and authority of the king it was confirmed, and by all those judges who were present … that Abbot Walter and the monks of Holy Trinity would hold from then on and for all time freely and absolutely the said island of Oissel.'[293] Here again, King William simply overrode the objections of the losing party and made a judgement against him regardless. And while the bishop might have grumbled about it, he does not seem to have attempted to overturn or evade the judgement.

Duke William's ability to win a consensus and thus to make his judgements effective most likely explains why, in contrast to other regions of France, so many lawsuits were ended by a judgement in the duke's court in Normandy. Even though some individuals did not bring their disputes before the duke, Table 8 reveals that William the Bastard judged 25 per cent and settled 20 per cent of all known property pleas that arose between 1066 and 1087. Henry I, judged 37 per cent of those disputes that arose between 1106 and 1135 and settled 14 per cent of them. His was the only reign where the duke heard the majority of known disputes in his court, which suggests that Henry was successful in making his justice more attractive to his subjects than it had been previously. In fact, Henry more than repaired the damage done to the duke's prestige during the reign of Robert Curthose. That reign stands out as a time when individuals apparently deserted

---

[292] The counts of Maine, for example, were obliged to work through their allies and local connections (Barton, *Maine*, p. 213).

[293] *Regesta: William*, no. 235.

the duke's court in numbers. His inability to do justice over offenders has already been remarked upon, especially with reference to the offences covered by the *Consuetudines et iusticie*, but it can also be seen with regard to the behaviour of litigants during his reign. Only 15 per cent of the pleas that arose during the period 1087–1106 were judged in his court, and only 3 per cent were settled there. In contrast, litigants either settled their disputes themselves or took them to seigniorial courts to be judged or settled in those fora. This was the only time – for which we have sufficient evidence – that the picture in Normandy looks similar to that seen outside the duchy where, for example, the monks of Marmoutier settled about two-thirds of their eleventh-century disputes outside court.[294]

Curthose's reign, moreover, was the only period during which earlier judgements were questioned or reopened. In 1091, as we have seen, Bishop Gerard of Sées brought a claim against the monks of Bellême which concerned his rights in their churches. That effectively challenged the judgement made in Duke William's court in 1070 × 1079. In 1093, Abbot Ranulf of Lonlay expressly reopened the case against the monks of Saumur that had been concluded in 1080. Robert Curthose's weakness is evidenced by his willingness to agree to hear the plea, and the fact that in the event Abbot Ranulf failed to appear in court on the day set to hear the case – offending against the duke in the process – could not have repaired the damage done.

No harm came to Bishop Gerard or Abbot Ranulf as a result of their actions. In William the Bastard's day, they might have been punished for questioning the duke's judgement in this manner, and not just by the duke. Orderic reported a dispute over the right to the body of Bishop Hugh of Lisieux, which concluded with the duke's judgement that the prelate should be buried in the church of the abbey of Saint-Désir, which he had founded, rather than in the cathedral. And so, the duke

> sent for Archbishop John and commanded him to go at once to Lisieux and have the bishop's body honourably buried in the church of St Mary. But since John was a proud and headstrong man, who had harboured hatred of the bishop in his heart for many years, he contemptuously ignored the royal command, and took no steps to bury his fellow bishop. As he was returning home from the king's court, riding on his mule through the city, and haughtily speaking of the business in hand, he suddenly suffered a stroke, by God's

[294] Stephen White has argued that that the monks of Marmoutier settled their suits so often because the lords of north-west France were 'probably unable to enforce such decisions with enough regularity to deter losing parties from continuing to vex the monks' (White, 'The settlement of disputes', 292, 300).

will, and fell from his mount in the sight of the crowd. He lived for two years afterwards, but never recovered his speech.[295]

The archbishop, then, was swiftly struck down by God for his contempt for the royal duke's judgement. The story was clearly still circulating *c.* 1127 when Orderic wrote it down and said much about the quality and finality of the duke's justice in the contemporary imagination.[296]

* * * * * *

While Jumièges and Orderic repeatedly highlighted the turbulence of the Norman lords, most of the troubles that impacted the minority of William the Bastard, the reign of Robert Curthose, and the years 1118–19 and 1123–24 were about legitimate disputes over property and rights acted out in a way that contemporaries outside Normandy would not have found surprising but which Norman churchmen were unable to countenance. That in itself says much about the general efficacy of ducal justice in Normandy in the period to 1144. It also suggests that there was generally a sense of a shared interest in peace and prosperity, revealed by the recognition of the ducal rights enshrined in the *Consuetudines et iusticie*, which were intended to give the 'Lord of Normandy' the tools he needed to look after the well-being of his people.

There was, of course, an expectation on a Christian ruler to do just that, albeit mitigated and mediated by the recognition that in some areas the dukes could not have total control or responsibility for injustices that might arise in their duchy. Jurisdiction over property disputes, for example, was complex owing to the right of lords to hear the pleas of their men over the lands held from them, but this was understood. Orderic Vitalis, for example, praised Abbot Robert of Grandmesnil's self-help and lamented the inability of later abbots to satisfy the heirs of Vitot, but he did not blame the duke for the problems they faced. They were matters between lord and tenant. The duke's function here was simply to ensure that the claims of his own *fideles* did not result in the loss or destruction of other people's property. So long as he brought the rapacious lords of the duchy to account, which for Orderic principally meant curbing the would-be autonomy of the lord of Bellême, that was enough.

It was on offenders, then, that the dukes' justice had to fall hardest. And the dukes took up the challenge to do justice and to protect their subjects from such malefactors, no doubt because it tended to highlight their place at the pinnacle of

---

[295] Orderic, iii. 18. For the dating of this part of Book V see Orderic, iii. xiv–xv.
[296] See also the discussion of William's intervention in the pronouncement of anathema clauses above, Chapter 7, pp. 417–19.

Norman society and reinforced their authority. As early as *c*. 1015, Dudo had his dukes seeking out offenders and punishing them according to their just deserts, while both William the Bastard and Henry I sought both to legislate and to develop mechanisms that would allow them to effect both 'criminal' and 'civil' justice with greater efficiency and success and to expand the reach of their own jurisdiction, particularly over homicides. William's legislation against robbers and regarding the feud may also have been intended to help keep the duchy peaceful during the royal duke's absences following his conquest of England. In addition, the year after his victory at Hastings, he instituted the forerunners of local justices in the regions of his duchy – or so it would seem from Orderic's comments. Henry I did still more. His edict tweaking jurisdiction over the Truce of God increased the reach of his courts over homicide. The employment of formula in chancery-produced *acta* concerning the duke's peace and protection that *could* be used to claim jurisdiction over disputes, and which turned 'civil' pleas into offences in the process, seems to have grown strikingly during Henry's reign, while the development of the justices allowed his courts to remain in session even when Henry was not there (although decisions made in the royal duke's absence, as noted above, seem to have carried less weight than those made in his presence). Such developments seem to have had some practical effect. Henry apparently attracted more pleas to his court than his predecessors had done, although it was to take the genius of Henry II and his possessionary assizes to really undermine traditional seigniorial jurisdictions. Henry's justices also gave him eyes and ears in seigniorial courts, where they were employed to supervise procedure in disputes where there was a risk of injustice. In 1134, Henry was even able to deprive unnamed lords – almost certainly including Waleran of Meulan – of their jurisdiction over offences in the parish of Le Bec owing to their leniency. No wonder that Henry was remembered as the 'lion of justice'.

CHAPTER 9

Movements, Messengers, Mandates, and Minions

I T was concluded in Chapter 6 that the duke retained executive power over his duchy in his own hands at all times.[1] That power might wax and wane across his dominions as a whole, but in theory at least the duke stood at the top of the Norman political hierarchy, and was the principal point of contact with the French king, the pope and his legates, and other outside powers and visitors. All of this provided a strong incentive for petitoners and beneficiaries to visit his court. These visitors, it was hoped, would be awed by the political theatre of the buildings, the furniture and utensils and servants found in them, and by the appearance and aspect of the dukes themselves.[2]

But it was essential that ducal government and power should be more than just a show. Petitioners and would-be beneficiaries wanted effective government. They wanted to know that a duke's confirmation of their possessions was worth the parchment it was written on – and the cost of the ink used to write on it and that of the journey to the court and back. The belt and braces of an anathema clause and a fine provided a degree of insurance, but as Church reform and ducal power grew the anathema slowly gave way to the forfeiture clause, making God less central where secular matters were concerned.[3] Ducal justice, too, was shown to be effective and efficient, even though existing ties of lordship and local loyalties might obstruct the dukes' attempts to bring the whole of the duchy under their jurisdiction.[4] The dukes, then, proved their worth to their subejcts, and their subjects kept coming to the court for help, justice, and confirmations as a result.

This, then, was a symbiotic relationship. A duke needed his subjects to come to them, and a duke's subjects needed his aid and protection against their aggressive, sometimes stronger, sometimes socially superior, neighbours. And so they sought him out wherever he was. More often than not, that would have been Rouen, or so the first section of this chapter will argue, for the dukes seem to have operated what historians have termed a palace government, that is one that

---

[1] See above, Chapter 6, pp. 338–62.
[2] See above, Chapter 7, *passim*.
[3] See above, Chapter 7, pp. 415–19.
[4] See above, Chapter 8, pp. 464–9, 470–4.

remained largely static in a capital city or palace (or at least in a very few of them), rather than an itinerant government that moved regularly between a number of different centres. If that was the case, and the dukes *were* largely based at Rouen, mechanisms had to be developed that would allow the dukes to rule their duchy remotely and effectively. It is the exploration of those mechanisms – the use of messengers and writs and the establishment of the various officials who put the duke's will into practice and represented his interests in the localities, including the Norman counts – that is the purpose of the rest of this chapter.[5]

Rouen: the dukes' capital city

Emperors, kings, dukes, and counts moved around their territories for a variety of reasons. It has been supposed that in some cases at least one of those reasons was to make their government work effectively.[6] It now seems virtually certain that the Salian and Staufen kings of the Germans spent about half their time on the road, staying in any one place typically only for a few days.[7] It is supposed, on less certain evidence, that the kings of the English also itinerated on a regular basis, with the post-Conquest crown-wearings providing some evidence of an annual

---

[5] See Douglas, 'The earliest Norman counts', 152. Others have been hesitant to see the counts as agents of ducal authority, although the idea that they were charged with the defence of a section of the frontier remains fairly strong. See, for example, Yver, 'Premières institutions', 324–5; Le Patourel, *Norman Empire*, pp. 258–9; Bates, *Normandy*, p. 156; Bauduin, *Première Normandie*, pp. 193–4.

[6] John Bernhardt argued that 'itinerant kingship existed throughout all of Europe during most of the Middle Ages' (J. W. Bernhardt, *Itinerant Kingship and Royal Monasteries in Early Medieval Germany, c. 936–1075* (Cambridge, 1993), p. 45). His definition of itineration was so wide, however, that this is not surprising. He included rulers who travelled either periodically or constantly, and rulers who either ventured out of (and returned to) a more-or-less established capital or who had no clear capital at all (Bernhardt, *Itinerant Kingship*, pp. 45–7). While Bernhardt did go on to recognize that different practices might reveal important differences in the way that kingdoms were structured, such a wide definition is likely to obscure important distinctions by being too inclusive. Indeed, his definition of itinerant kingship or rulership could be made to encompass every head of state of the twenty-first century. Even before he wrote, however, itineration was seen as an important aspect of medieval kingship. See, for example, Green, *Government*, p. 5 (although see more recently her 'King Henry I and northern England', *Transactions of the Royal Historical Society*, 17 (2007), 35–55, which recognizes the important role played by local agents); R. Fletcher, *Bloodfeud: Murder and Revenge in Anglo-Saxon England* (London, 2003), pp. 26–8; P. Heather, *Empires and Barbarians: Migration, Development and the Birth of Europe* (London, 2010), pp. 529–30; K. Randsborg, *The Viking Age in Denmark: The Formation of a State* (London, 1980), pp. 75–80. A useful and critical discussion of the subject may be found in McKitterick, *Charlemagne*, pp. 171–86.

[7] Bernhardt, *Itinerant Kingship*, p. 48.

cycle.[8] On the other hand, Charlemagne is believed to have spent much of the last decade or so of his reign at Aachen.[9] Nor was he the only member of his dynasty to rule largely from one principal palace. His son, Louis the Pious, ruled from three main areas: Aachen, which was his most important residence near which he established an abbey for his leading religious adviser Benedict of Aniane; the Seine-Oise region; and the Middle Rhine. He maintained his authority by sending his *missi* out to the regions of the empire and by summoning great assemblies to his court. His son Louis the German ruled his kingdom from Frankfurt and Regensburg, with the former described as 'the chief seat of the kingdom'.[10] These men ruled over much wider lands than did the dukes of the Normans, but even so they might remain largely stationary, with one palace in particular associated with their rule.[11]

It has been supposed, principally by anglophone historians, that the Norman dukes should be fitted into the first, and more English, of these two models.[12] But this seems to confuse mere movement with a *necessarily* itinerant government. The dukes were the sole executive power in Normandy. As they moved so their executive power moved with them. But that is not at all the same as holding that their government *had* to be itinerant in order to be effective. In fact, the dukes seem better to fit the second model, and to have operated a palace-style government in the Carolingian mould, remaining at Rouen unless hunting,[13] or the

---

[8] See, for example, M. Biddle, 'Seasonal festivals and residence: Winchester, Westminster and Gloucester in the tenth to twelfth centuries', *ANS*, 8 (1986), 51–72; Mooers Christelow, 'A moveable feast?', 187–228.

[9] Rosamund McKitterick has suggested that he spent around sixty per cent of his time there (McKitterick, *Charlemagne*, p. 161).

[10] M. Costambeys, M. Innes, and S. MacLean, *The Carolingian World* (Cambridge, 2011), pp. 174–5, 409–11; Nelson, 'Aachen as a place of power', p. 219.

[11] See the very full and useful discussion in McKitterick, *Charlemagne*, pp. 171–213.

[12] See, for example, *NI*, pp. 118–19 and Appendix G; Le Patourel, *Norman Empire*, pp. 123–31; C. W. Hollister and J. W. Baldwin, 'The rise of administrative kingship', *American Historical Review*, 83 (1978), 869, 870; Bates, *Normandy*, pp. 151–2. In contrast, and more in line with the view presented here, see Bouvris, 'Contribution à une étude', 153.

[13] Dudo of Saint-Quentin wrote that William Longsword removed to Lyons-la-Forêt from Rouen for the hunting, and remained there for so long as the hunting remained good (*Dudo*, p. 69). William of Jumièges added a hunting trip to Jumièges to Longsword's itinerary (Jumièges, i. 86), and also had Richard II hunting around Vernon (Jumièges, ii. 10). The dukes were not alone. For example, after Easter 831, Louis the Pious moved from Ingelheim to the district of Remiremont, 'and there indulged in fishing and hunting as long as it was agreeable to him' (*Son of Charlemagne: A Contemporary Life of Louis the Pious*, trans. A. Cabaniss (Clinton, MA, 1961), p. 93). The correlation between the place-dates of the English *acta* of the Norman kings and the royal forests is also remarkable, and implies that leisure activities were the cause of many of the royal dukes' movements when in England, too.

dedication of an important church,[14] or diplomacy, or the threat of war caused
them to move elsewhere.

While some indication of the dukes' movements is provided by the place-dates
appended to their *acta* and by the narratives, it should be stressed at the outset
that this evidence is limited. Indeed, the details we have for the movements of the
earliest of the dukes are so thin that historians have evidently, and rightly, considered it pointless to produce itineraries for them. For example, when William
of Jumièges reported on Richard II's thirty-year reign he recorded just one campaign in the Hiémois, an expedition to Tillières and the related war with Odo of
Chartres, his attendance at assemblies at Coudres and Fécamp, and his hunting
around Vernon.[15] Jumièges gives the impression that between times Richard
was based at Rouen, and his implication is supported by Richard's acts, as these
are place-dated exclusively at Rouen and Fécamp, where the dukes traditionally
held their Easter court.[16] Now, it is impossible to believe that his travels were as
restricted as the evidence suggests. His construction of castles in the Cotentin at
Cherbourg, Le Homme, and perhaps Brix, for example, suggests that he spent
some time campaigning there, and as Caen became a *bourg* during his reign it
is likely that he spent some time there, too. Fortunately, these conjectures, and
others that might be added, would not undermine the argument ventured below
as they were not the result of a need to move in order to make domestic government effective. In any case, there seems to have been no annual pattern to his
movements, or those of any other duke, with the possible exception of the Easter
excursion to Fécamp which most likely began during the reign of Richard II and
continued at least until the reign of William the Bastard.

The evidence becomes a little fuller after 1066, and as it has been anglophone
historians who have been concerned with the construction of itineraries, it is no
surprise that they have been produced only for the period when the dukes of the
Normans were also kings of the English. In 1913, H. W. C. Davis attempted to
construct a post-Conquest itinerary for William I, sensibly restricting himself to
those occasions when William is known through the narratives and statements

---

[14] For example, William the Bastard attended the dedications of the churches at Saint-
Pierre-sur-Dives and Jumièges in 1067 (Jumièges, ii. 172; Orderic, ii. 198), and at Caen,
Bayeux, and Evreux in 1077 (Orderic, iii. 10–12). Robert Curthose was at Bayeux when
the monastery of Saint-Vigor was granted to Abbot Gerento of Dijon (*NI*, Appendix E,
no. 3). Henry I attended the dedication of the cathedral at Sées in 1126 (Orderic, vi. 366).

[15] Jumièges, ii.10 (Hiémois and Vernon), 22 (Tillières), 26 (Coudres), 38 (Fécamp).

[16] *RADN*, nos. 12, 13, 15, 18, 20, 25, 26 are place-dated at Rouen. *RADN*, nos. 34, 35, 36 are
place-dated at Fécamp, although all three apparently relate to one court in 1025. This
may be the occasion referred to by Jumièges: ii. 38.

in his *acta* to have been in a particular place at a particular time.[17] Nonetheless, despite his careful approach, the discovery of new *acta*, as well as the rejection as forgeries of acts for the monks of Durham and Westminster, means that the itinerary constructed by David Bates in 1998 'differs considerably' from that produced by Davis.[18] In fact, Bates produced not one but two itineraries. The first was based exclusively on precisely dated acts and precisely dated events noted in the narratives. The second was compiled using 'chronicle accounts of William's activities and by *acta* which date his movements by month or by year. This provides a much fuller picture of the Conqueror's itinerary, which should be read in conjunction with the exact dates ... which are normally not repeated.'[19] In order to establish a complete itinerary, then, a reader must integrate the two itineraries him- or herself. Naturally, some points remain matters for argument,[20] and some apparently exact dates might not be quite as exact as they seem,[21] but Bates's work has made it clear that William crossed the Channel more often than was previously thought, and might stay in the duchy only for short periods of time. Even now, though, we have a seriously incomplete record of William's travels and little sense of how long he spent where. The following, then, is only one interpretation of this uncertain evidence.

The limited number of place-dates appended to William's Norman *acta* hint – they can do no more – that he was most often at Rouen (eight acts) before 1066,[22] although three each were place-dated at Fécamp and Bonneville-sur-Touques.[23] Other places, including Lyons-la-Forêt, Caen, and Brionne, appear among the place-dates just once.[24] For the period after 1066, there are a further eight acts place-dated at Rouen,[25] with four place-dated at Bonneville-sur-Touques (although issued on only two occasions),[26] three at Oissel (but evidencing only

---

[17] *Regesta*, i. xxi–xxii.

[18] *Regesta: William*, p. 75.

[19] *Regesta: William*, p. 78.

[20] For example, the suggestion that William crossed to Normandy in 1068 is not supported by the acts cited (p. 78). Nonetheless, an act for the monks of the priory of Saint-Gabriel (*Regesta: William*, no. 256) reveals that William almost certainly crossed to Normandy at some point during 1069 – a trip missed by Davis.

[21] For example, the dedication of the abbey church at Saint-Pierre-sur-Dives is said to have occurred on 1 May by Orderic and is included in the appropriate place by Davis. Bates, in contrast, relegated this to his second table (Orderic, ii. 198: *Regesta: William*, p. 78).

[22] *RADN*, nos. 123, 130, 133, 139, 148, 180, 213, 228.

[23] *RADN*, nos. 7, 199, 230 (Fécamp); 142, 152, 232 (Bonneville).

[24] *RADN*, nos. 122 (Lyons-la-Forêt), 231 (Caen), 181 (Brionne).

[25] *Regesta: William*, nos. 26, 29, 88, 163, 179a, 229, 248, 261.

[26] *Regesta: William*, nos. 173, 175, 274, 275.

two stays),[27] two at Lillebonne,[28] two revealing the royal duke's presence at Caen,[29] and one place-dated at each of Bayeux, Bénouville, Fécamp, Le Vaudreuil, Lyons-la-Forêt, Saint-Georges de Boscherville, and Valognes.[30]

Several of these place-dates are linked to one-off events; others were most likely places that Duke William stopped at while on the way to somewhere else. For example, in 1067 he spent Easter at Fécamp, as was the custom. At some point in April he was at Le Vaudreuil, almost certainly en route to the dedication of the abbey church at Saint-Pierre-sur-Dives on 1 May. He was at Lyons-la-Forêt in June, it may be supposed, because he was hunting. He was then at Jumièges for the dedication of the abbey church on 1 July. There then follows a five-month gap in the evidence before William returned to England, and it *might* have been the case that he spent all of that time at Rouen. Thirteen years later, William began 1080 at Caen, moving to Rouen via Boscherville by the end of January. Bates preferred to think that William spent Easter at Rouen, but it is possible that he moved to Fécamp for the festival. On 31 May he was at Lillebonne for the great ecclesiastical council held there in that year. Then in July he was at Bonneville-sur-Touques, almost certainly because he intended to cross from Touques to England (although we do not know when he made the crossing).[31]

William thus moved for specific reasons, related to government, but more to highlight his central role in the religious life of his duchy than because he needed to move to make it effective. Moreover, the place-dates to William's acts need not indicate a lengthy stay at any of the places noted. Indeed, in a number of cases it is very likely that the stay was very brief. For example, the sole act of William the Bastard that is place-dated at Valognes, which dates from 1069, was probably issued while the king spent the night there at the end of a stage of a journey to or from the port at Cherbourg or Barfleur.[32] William was at Bayeux on 14 July 1077 for the dedication of the cathedral, but his stay in the city might have been very short indeed, as Orderic put him back in Rouen just a few days after the event.[33] In 1080 × 1081, William was at Bénouville (between Ouistreham and Caen) when he was importuned by a monk of Marmoutier to authenticate an act, which he did while sitting on his carpet between the church and the forester's house.[34] It is

---

[27] *Regesta: William*, nos. 204, 205, 264.

[28] *Regesta: William*, nos. 147, 262.

[29] *Regesta: William*, nos. 46, 267.

[30] *Regesta: William*, nos. 83 (Bayeux), 201 (Bénouville), 230 (Fécamp), 251 (Le Vaudreuil), 196 (Lyons-la-Forêt), 266 (Boscherville), 256 (Valognes).

[31] Rufus crossed to Touques in 1099 (Orderic, v. 256).

[32] *Regesta: William*, no. 256, and see the itinerary at pp. 78–9.

[33] *Regesta: William*, no. 83 and p. 80 for the itinerary; Orderic, iii. 18.

[34] *Regesta: William*, no. 201.

unlikely that William stayed at Bénouville for more than an hour or two. This act in particular stands as testimony to the fact that acts did not have to be issued at courts. They were issued at the convenience of the beneficiary.[35]

Probably because Robert Curthose was not king of the English, no attempt has been made to construct an itinerary for him, although the information is anyway too meagre to make the attempt worthwhile. But Charles Homer Haskins did publish a Norman itinerary for his brother and successor Henry I in his *Norman Institutions* in 1918.[36] The next year, William Farrer published his fuller 'outline itinerary' for Henry I in the *English Historical Review*. His efforts were followed, with little change, by Charles Johnson and H. A. Cronne in their volume of the *Regesta Regum Anglo-Normannorum*, published in 1956.[37] Both Farrer's outline and the itinerary in the *Regesta* were made using only the evidence that allowed the king to be located at particular places at given times (and indicated where that was not the case). In 1996, Stephanie Mooers Christelow reconsidered Henry's itinerary. She supplemented the *Regesta* with a number of additional Norman acts found among those collected by Henri Chanteux and from other sources, too, and added *acta* apparently dated to a month of a particular year, but not to a specific day, to the dataset.[38]

Unfortunately, however, some of the acts employed are not so exactly dated as the editors of the *Regesta*, and Mooers Christelow in turn, thought. For example, an act for Vitalis the hermit of Savigny which is dated '1112, *c*. Nov. 4' might actually date from any time between 1112 and 1120; acts for Le Bec and Savigny which the editors of *Regesta* decided were issued in 1113, are dated 1112; and an act, again for Savigny, dated '? October 1118' might actually have been issued at any time between September 1114–July 1115 and April 1116–November 1120. Furthermore, Henry's seal was probably attached to this last act at Argentan rather than Arganchy.[39] In addition, there seems also to have been an assumption that all Henry's *acta* were issued during a court. That assumption is unfounded, as noted already. Place-dates are just as likely to reveal the location of the stages of Henry's journeys as the holding of a court, just as was the case under his father.[40]

It might, therefore, be better to think about the general picture rather than

---

[35] See above, Chapter 7, p. 404.
[36] *NI*, Appendix G, pp. 309–20.
[37] W. Farrer, 'An outline itinerary for Henry I', *EHR*, 34 (1919), 303–82, 505–79; *Regesta*, ii. xxix–xxxi.
[38] Mooers Christelow, 'A moveable feast?', 187–228.
[39] *Regesta*, ii. nos. 1003 (Vitalis); 1013 and 1015 (Le Bec and Savigny); 1183 (Savigny; the place-date reads 'Argenteium'); Mooers Christelow, 'A moveable feast?', 218–21. Some references, incidentally, are omitted on pp. 220–1.
[40] Mooers Christelow, 'A moveable feast?', 193, 199–200.

attempt to create an itinerary based on so little certain evidence. Taken together, the place-dates of Henry's acts, especially when viewed in conjunction with what we know of his movements from the narratives and the identity of the beneficiary, support the conclusion that Henry resided in Rouen for most of the time he was in the duchy.

No fewer than ninety-nine of Henry I's acts are place-dated at Rouen – although it is possible that not all of them are authentic even where the place-date is concerned.[41] Aside from these, the present corpus of Henry's acts was issued at another thirty-one places in the duchy, but none of them approached the position occupied by Rouen. So far as I am aware, there are sixteen acts place-dated at Argentan;[42] fifteen at Caen;[43] eight at Falaise;[44] seven at Arques (half of which probably date from August 1131);[45] six at Arganchy near Bayeux;[46] four at Dieppe, Evreux, and Le Vaudreuil;[47] three at Bonneville-sur-Touques, Sainte-Vaubourg, and Perriers-sur-Andelle;[48] two at Avranches (both for Savigny) and La Croix-Saint-Leufroy (probably made on the same occasion), Lyons-la-Forêt, Oissel, Saint-Pierre-sur-Dives (made on a single occasion), Sées, and Touques (also made on a single occasion);[49] and one at each of Aumale, Barfleur, Elbeuf, L'Aigle,

---

41   *Regesta*, ii. nos. 791, 809 (but a forgery), 911, 1021, 1022, 1024, 1025, 1074, 1085, 1086, 1186, 1200, 1203, 1204, 1204a, 1205, 1207, 1209, 1213, 1214, 1221, 1225, 1226, 1227, 1232, 1234, 1235, 1237, 1417, 1425, 1426, 1430, 1431, 1445, 1446, 1447, 1528, 1529, 1547, 1552, 1553, 1563, 1574, 1576, 1578, 1579, 1580, 1583, 1585, 1596, 1597, 1598, 1599, 1599a, 1602, 1680, 1683, 1685, 1688, 1689, 1690, 1703, 1704, 1705, 1706, 1707, 1708, 1709, 1892, 1896, 1900, 1902, 1908, 1910, 1911, 1917, 1921, 1922, 1924, 1925, 1927, 1931, 1948, 1950, 1951, 1952, 1953, 1955, 1956, 1962, 1963, 1964, 1965 (although a forgery), 1987; *Recueil de Henri II*, i. 304 (no. 173); *Le premier cartulaire de l'abbaye cistercienne de Pontigny*, ed. Garrigues, p. 86 (no. 3); Rouen, AD Seine-Maritime, 55 H 8 (a diploma-form conversion of no. 1221, which should perhaps not be counted separately); Chanteux, *Recueil*, no. 13; *Norman Charters from English Sources*, ed. Vincent, p. 108 (no. 1).

42   *Regesta*, ii. nos. 1183, 1419, 1420, 1421, 1556, 1557, 1899, 1899n, 1916, 1934, 1938, 1941, 1946, 1949, 1960, 1982.

43   *Regesta*, ii. nos. 688, 912, 1087, 1181, 1215, 1229, 1230, 1231, 1236, 1575, 1595, 1897, 1909, 1983; Chanteux, *Recueil*, no. 155.

44   *Regesta*, ii. nos. 1571, 1572, 1913, 1914, 1915, 1919, 1942; Ctl. Montebourg, p. 7 (no. 7).

45   *Regesta*, ii. nos. 795, 1692, 1693, 1694, 1696, 1898; G. A. de la Roque, *Histoire généalogique*, iii. 149.

46   *Regesta*, ii. nos. 1224, 1589, 1590, 1592, 1899, 1899n.

47   *Regesta*, ii. nos. 1443, 1444, 1697, 1698 (Dieppe); 1338, 1429, 1432, 1433 (Evreux); 1550, 1551, 1700, Ctl. *Grand-Beaulieu*, p. 2 (no. 2) (Le Vaudreuil).

48   *Regesta*, ii. nos. 1216, 1217, 1686 (Bonneville); 1222, 1223, 1440 (Sainte-Vaubourg); 1418, 1912; Ctl. *Mont-Saint-Michel*, p. 177 (Perrièrs-sur-Andelle).

49   *Regesta*, ii. nos. 1015, 1016 (Avranches); 1681, 1682 (La Croix-Saint-Leufroy); 676, 1586 (Lyons-la-Forêt); 1010, 1573 (Oissel); 1542, 1543 (Saint-Pierre-sur-Dives); 1932, 1974 (Sées); 1554, 1555 (Touques).

Lillebonne, Montfort-sur-Risle, Mortain, Nonant, Pont de l'Arche, Sainte-Mère-Eglise, Saint-Wandrille, Tosny, and Verneuil.[50]

The possible date ranges for many of these acts, as well as the place-dates themselves, fit with what we know of Henry's movements from Orderic's *Ecclesiastical History* and other narratives. The three made at Sainte-Vaubourg, for example, could all have been made when Henry was campaigning against nearby Neubourg in 1118.[51] We know from Orderic, the record of a lawsuit, and the date range of an act for Villers-Canivet that Henry was at Falaise on four occasions,[52] and all of the eight acts place-dated there *might* have been issued during those visits. The two acts made at Avranches both related to the foundation of the abbey of Savigny, which was formalized in March 1112. Richard of Chester would have reached his majority around that time, too, and Henry's trip to Avranches might also have been related to that milestone. A third reason for his presence in the city was provided by the division of the old county of Mortain between Henry and his *fideles* (Earl Richard, for example, was apparently given a share of Vire). In other words, the place-dates of Henry I's Norman acts do not undermine the view that he remained largely static at Rouen except for short periods when he was obliged to campaign against rivals or rebels or when he attended the dedications of cathedrals and other major churches.

This picture of palace-style government from Rouen seems also to be corroborated by the behaviour of the Norman beneficiaries of Henry's *acta*. Those who wanted to obtain diplomas or writs from him were prepared to travel to get them, and those based far from Rouen had to do so because he came so infrequently to the peripheries of Normandy. The acts of William the Bastard for his foundation at Caen seem to have been made in large assemblies that may well have taken place at the town. In contrast, and despite his building works there, Henry I seems not to have resided at Caen very often. It is consequently not surprising that the monks of Caen were prepared to travel at least a short distance to find him. They went to Argentan to have a plea tried in Henry's presence, but also crossed the Channel and travelled to Cannock.[53] Equally, rather than wait in or around the town for Henry I to pass by, Godfrey the priest of Caen crossed the Channel to have him confirm the judgement in his favour passed down by Henry's justices

---

[50] *Regesta*, ii. nos. 1904 (Aumale); 1233 (Barfleur); 1973 (Elbeuf); Winchester Cathedral MS xxb, 183 (L'Aigle); *Regesta*, ii. nos. 807 (Lillebonne); 1947 (Montfort-sur-Risle); 1187 (Mortain); 1185 (Nonant); 789 (Pont de l'Arche); 1018 (Sainte-Mère-Eglise); 1971 (Saint-Wandrille); 1699 (Tosny); 1895 (Verneuil).

[51] Orderic, vi. 200.

[52] Orderic, vi. 136 (in 1107), 214 (in 1119); *Regesta*, ii. 1570 (in 1129).

[53] *Regesta*, ii. no. 764. Not all the acts for the monks of Saint-Etienne of Caen have place-dates, and it is possible that they went to England for acts on other occasions, too.

in Normandy.[54] The bishop of Bayeux went to Stamford to obtain a writ granting him justice over his bishopric,[55] although his canons were apparently prepared to wait to obtain documents until Henry should pass closer to home. The monks of Montebourg travelled to Caen, Falaise, Argentan, La-Croix-Saint-Leufroy, Sainte-Mère-Eglise (although which of the two possible locations is not known), Rouen, and England on their business.[56] The bishop of Coutances took his lawsuit against the canons of Cherbourg to the royal duke's court at Rouen in 1134.[57]

In contrast, when the archbishop and canons of Rouen had Norman business that needed the royal duke's attention, they popped into the castle to see him there.[58] The single act for the nuns of Fécamp resident at Saint-Paul – the contents of which, at least, are fabricated – was place-dated at Rouen.[59] So were Henry's authentic acts for the nuns of Saint-Amand and the monks of Le Bec at Notre-Dame-du-Pré.[60] The monks of Saint-Ouen were prepared on occasion to travel so far as the island of Oissel a little upstream, where Henry had a house and an official, Roland, who kept his bedding ready for his apparently infrequent visits,[61] while the cordwainers of Rouen were obliged to traipse to Arques for their act, although they might have started their business before the royal duke headed for the coast.[62] So, those individuals based in the metropolitan city, and those based nearby such as the monks of Boscherville,[63] did not go far from home when they wanted to obtain acts relating to their Norman holdings. Thus the place-dates of Norman ducal *acta* when considered alongside the location of their

[54] *Regesta*, ii. no. 819.
[55] *Regesta*, ii. no. 951.
[56] Chanteux, *Recueil*, no. 155 (Caen); Ctl. Montebourg, p. 7 (Falaise); *Regesta*, ii. nos. 1684, 1949 (Argentan); 1682 (La-Croix-Saint-Leufroy); 1018 (Sainte-Mère-Eglise); 1950, 1951, 1952, 1953, 1683, 1708 (Rouen); 1155 (London).
[57] *Regesta*, ii. no. 1902.
[58] *Regesta*, ii. nos. 1234, 1963.
[59] *Regesta*, ii. no. 1965.
[60] Saint-Amand: *Regesta*, ii. nos. 1221, 1962; Notre-Dame-du-Pré: *Regesta*, ii. no. 1964.
[61] *Regesta*, ii. nos. 1010, 1573. It is notable in this regard that during Stephen's rule, the monks were obliged to cross to England (*Regesta*, iii. no. 733). Henry's steward, Roland of Oissel, and something of his duties, may be found in *Ctl. Normand*, no. 2 = *Regesta*, ii. no. 1087.
[62] *Regesta*, ii. no. 1695. The situation here might reflect the experience of the monks of Saint-Evroult. Henry I suggested that they draft an act while he stayed with them, but they were then obliged to take it to Rouen to have it authenticated. Alternatively, the actions of the cordwainers might be compared to those of the burgesses of Saumur in 1138, who travelled to Carrouges in Normandy to obtain the confirmation of the Empress Matilda to a grant of freedom from the vinage of Saumur, despite the fact that Geoffrey and his wife were often resident in their own town (*Recueil Henri II*, i. 1).
[63] *Regesta*, ii. nos. 1694 (Arques); 1440 (Sainte-Vaubourg); 1596 (Rouen).

beneficiaries help to reinforce the picture of a largely static duke based for most of the time at Rouen.

The Norman place-dates on Henry's acts for English beneficiaries might provide further support for this conclusion. Norman beneficiaries knew that the royal duke was most often to be found at Rouen and often went to find him there.[64] English beneficiaries, driven across the Channel by the need to get their business done, did not want to wait for Henry to return to Rouen if he was not there and were more active in tracking him down as a result. French beneficiaries were likewise concerned to transact their business, and to end expensive and hazardous journeys, as quickly as possible. It is consequently no surprise that the beneficiaries whose acts were place-dated at the smaller palaces and staging posts were principally from England and France. For example, the eight acts issued at Falaise were for Bury St Edmunds (one of them an act that granted the abbot of Bury St Edmunds a plot for a house in Rouen next to the plot that Henry had already granted to Geoffrey fitz Payn, which itself provides further evidence for the importance of that city and which might even have been the result of a complaint about the traipse across Normandy to find the royal duke); St Augustine's, Canterbury; Leeds; and Ramsey, as well as the nuns of nearby Villers-Canivet and the Norman monks of Saint-Evroult and Montebourg.[65] The two acts place-dated at Lyons-la-Forêt were for the monks of Abingdon and Durham.[66] The single act place-dated at L'Aigle was for the canons of Huntingdon; that place-dated at Lillebonne was for the canons of York Minster;[67] and that place-dated at Nonant was for the monks of Winchester cathedral priory.[68] The evidence is not unambiguous. It overlaps a little with the needs and experiences of Norman beneficiaries based some distance away from Rouen who might have been in just as much of a hurry to get their business done for the same reasons. But the overall pattern indicates that it was only those who were pressed for time, or were visitors to the duchy, that went to find the duke at somewhere other than Rouen.

The dominance of Rouen throughout the period 911–1144 can also be seen in the narratives, where the city is treated differently from other places in the

---

[64] Apparently implied by Orderic when recounting the election of Roger of Le Sap as abbot of Saint-Evroult (Orderic, iv. 254).

[65] *Regesta*, ii. nos. 1913, 1914 (Bury); 1571 (Canterbury); 1942 (Leeds); 1915 (Ramsey). It is perhaps worth noting, with regard to the grant to the abbot of Bury, that Einhard had a house at Aachen during the reign of Charlemagne (Nelson, 'Aachen as a place of power', p. 224). Robert Curthose had earlier granted the abbot of Mont-Saint-Michel a site for the construction of a house in the city, too (*Ctl. Mont-Saint-Michel*, pp. 147–8 (no. 69)).

[66] *Regesta*, ii. nos. 676, 1586.

[67] *Regesta*, ii. no. 807.

[68] *Regesta*, ii. no. 1185 (1111 × 1126).

duchy. Dudo of Saint-Quentin put William Longsword and Richard I at Rouen far more than anywhere else in Normandy.[69] Messengers and campaigns set out from there. The young Richard I was sent away from the court at Rouen to Bayeux to learn the Dacian tongue, Dudo's words suggesting that it was not a city to which Longsword ventured at all frequently. Moreover, Dudo wrote of William and Richard I 'returning (*regresso, reuersus est, redire, repetiit*)' to Rouen, which suggests that it was their base – indeed Dudo does also refer to it as their seat (*sedes*).[70] References to other places in the duchy lack that sense of familiarity or precedence. Thus, Richard I simply 'came one day to the walled residence of Fécamp' and, at the end of his life, 'withdrew from the district of Bayeux to the hall of his Fécamp residence'.[71] Furthermore, a number of Dudo's poems identifies the dukes with Rouen, and the city with the duchy and its government. That again suggests a very frequent residence in the city, but it also reveals how Rouen, the duke, and his rule all merged into one another. The sentiment bears comparison with Walahfrid Strabo's identification of Aachen with the regime of Louis the Pious when writing of the political tensions of 829.[72] In addition, the coins minted in the names of William Longsword and Richard I bear their names on the obverse, while the reverse reads only 'Rouen (*Rotomacius, Rotomagus*)', without naming a moneyer (see Fig. 8). That is because the coins are apparently identifying the dukes with their capital city – this is not the name of the mint as in England – and emphasizing that this was the place from which they took their title and power.

In the 1030s, Ralph Glaber felt able to describe the Rouen as the capital (*metropolis*) of the duchy during Richard's reign, and wrote that 'each year monks came to Rouen … and took back with them many presents of gold and silver for their communities'.[73] The comment reveals an expectation that Rouen was where the duke would be found. The later domestic narratives written by William of Jumièges, William of Poitiers, and Orderic provide further evidence that Rouen

---

[69] *Dudo*, pp. 57, 59, 61, 63, 65–8, 70, 71, 76, 81, 99–100, 121, 127–35, 139, 142, 146, 148, 150, 153.

[70] Dudo, pp. 185, 205, 267, 276; *Dudo*, pp. 63, 81, 142, 150 (for returnings); Dudo, p. 194; *Dudo*, p. 71 (for the statement that it was their seat). Janet Nelson remarked that when the *Annales regni Francorum* record that Charlemagne 'returned home' to Aachen from Saxony the phrase 'assumes a more or less fixed capital' (Nelson, 'Aachen as a place of power', p. 231).

[71] *Dudo*, pp. 164, 171.

[72] *Dudo*, pp. 76, 100, 103, 122, 147, 150; Costambeys, Innes, and MacLean, *The Carolingian World*, p. 178. For this symbolic importance of Rouen see also E. van Houts, 'Rouen as another Rome', pp. 101–24 and L. V. Hicks, 'Through the city streets: movement and space as seen by the Norman chroniclers' in *Society and Culture in Medieval Rouen, 911–1300*, ed. L. V. Hicks and E. Brenner (Turnhout, 2013), pp. 125–49.

[73] Adémar de Chabannes, *Chronique*, p. 167; Glaber, p. 36; both also found in van Houts, *Normans*, pp. 214–15, 218.

Fig. 8 *Denier* of Richard I (Author)

was the dukes' principal residence and centre of government.[74] So prominent is Rouen in the *Gesta Normannorum ducum*, that it looks like William of Jumièges saw it as the dukes' default place of residence.[75] William of Poitiers described Rouen as 'the chief city of [the] principality (*urbem sui principatus caput*)'.[76] Orderic also described it as the metropolis of the duchy, and it may be supposed that he meant that literally.[77] His choice of word might have been influenced by the issue of a new coinage, if it could be securely dated *c.* 1135, that included the

[74] Here I disagree with D. Bates, 'Rouen from 900 to 1204', p. 4: 'After 1066, William does not seem to have been an especially frequent visitor to Rouen.'

[75] Richard is recorded as having entertained both King Swein and King Æthelred II at Rouen (Jumièges, ii. 16, 18), and met his Scandinavian allies there (Jumièges, ii. 26). A later story would suggest that Bernard the Philosopher found him there, too (Jumièges, ii. 30). Count Hugh was to make satisfaction to Richard at Rouen (Jumièges, ii. 38). Richard III returned to Rouen after defeating his brother at Falaise (Jumièges, ii. 46). In addition, like Dudo, Jumièges wrote of the dukes returning to the city (Jumièges, ii. 100, 102–4, 120–2, 124–6, 128–30, 144, 150, 152).

[76] Poitiers, p. 70. Although it should be noted that Poitiers does not otherwise remark upon Rouen or the periods that Duke William spent there (Hicks, 'Through the city streets', p. 128).

[77] Orderic, iv. 220; vi. 222. Orderic also used the word *metropolis* to refer to Canterbury (ii. 244; iv. 176) and Myra (in the sense of 'chief city': iv. 56). *Metropolita* or *metropolim* was often used for archbishops (for example, Orderic, iii. 22, 94, 282; iv. 6, 170).

legend 'Metropolis ... Rotomagus', which might also constitute further evidence that Rouen was widely regarded as the capital of Normandy.[78]

Orderic's relatively detailed record of Henry's movements during the rebellion of 1118–19 reveals not only just how quickly the duke might move in times of emergency, but also how he would return to Rouen between strikes. He was at Rouen in June or July 1117 when he ordered the arrest of the count of Eu and Hugh of Gournay.[79] On 3 September 1118, Henry set out to L'Aigle from Rouen, but having reached Livet a false rumour sent him back to the city. At an unknown date he moved east into Bray, attacking La Ferté-en-Bray before moving west to attack La Neubourg. He had completed this stage of the campaign by 7 October, by which date he was back at Rouen and presiding over a church council.[80] In the second week of November he moved to L'Aigle, and in December marched against Alençon, possibly having based himself at Falaise in the interval.[81] He returned to Rouen after the pacification of Glos and Lyre in 1119 and he took Eustace of Breteuil back to the city with him after he had surrendered.[82] He was also at Rouen in the days before the rebellion of 1123, and judged the rebels there in 1124.[83] In around November 1128 Henry was at Rouen and summoned a council to be held there in the presence of the papal legate.[84] In contrast, Henry is recorded at other centres such as Bonneville-sur-Touques, Caen, Falaise, and Lisieux much more rarely.[85]

Narratives, place-dates, the behaviour of beneficiaries, and the size and connections of the city itself all permit the conclusion that Rouen was the place where the dukes stayed most often and for long periods of time. Indeed, the city was so closely associated with the dukes that when Rouen fell to Geoffrey of Anjou in 1144, the duchy was seen to fall to him with it, and probably not just by Robert of Torigni.[86]

---

[78] L. Musset, 'Réflexions sur les moyens de payment en Normandie aux XIe et XIIe siècles', in *Aspects de la société et de l'économie dans la Normandie medieval (X^e–XIIIe siècles)*, ed. L. Musset, J.-M. Bouvris, and V. Gazeau, Cahiers des Annales de Normandie, 22 (1989), 79. Bates dated these coins *c*. 1150 in an article published four years later, but he took his information from an article by J. Pilet-Lemière that was published, before Musset's, in 1985: Bates, 'Rouen from 900 to 1204', p. 5 and n. 53, p. 10. The dating of Norman coins is so difficult, however, that either conclusion could be correct.

[79] Orderic, vi. 190–2; Hollister, *Henry*, p. 248.

[80] Orderic, vi. 198–202.

[81] Orderic, vi. 204–8. He was at Falaise when Reginald of Bailleul defied him (Orderic, vi. 214).

[82] Orderic, vi. 250, 278.

[83] Orderic, vi. 334, 352.

[84] Orderic, vi. 388.

[85] Orderic, vi. 178 (Bonneville); 92, 136 (Falaise); 92, 138, 142, 224 (Lisieux).

[86] RT, s.a. 1144; Delisle, i. 233; Howlett, p. 148.

We may therefore fairly conclude that when in Normandy the dukes preferred to reside at, and govern from, Rouen. That is not to say that they might not choose to move, but rather that it *was* a choice. The conditions that seem to have driven other rulers to a state of semi-perpetual motion did not apply in the duchy. Some of those conditions were summarized by Stephanie Mooers Christelow in 1996:

> modern historians have recognized that itineration was fundamental to medieval kingship and that it was crucial to the governance of a geographically disparate realm, as kings divided their time between historically separate regions. Itineration was a practical device in the absence of fully-developed governmental institutions as well as an economic necessity, for in partially monetarized economies, it was not always possible to move goods from county districts to main centres of power.[87]

The governmental institutions of Normandy were sufficient for the needs of the time. The duke's presence at Rouen acted like a magnet, attracting petitioners from across the duchy. Messengers might be dispatched either on the duke's initiative or as the result of a petition that had been brought before him.[88] Under Henry I, writs might be issued, sealed with the royal duke's seal, and transported to their recipient by the beneficiary. Moreover, the presence of *ministri*, *prévôts*, and *vicomtes* across the duchy meant that ducal government continued to function even in the duke's physical absence. There is no reason to suppose that there was a need for itineration in addition to the existing structures to make the duke's government effective.

There is equally no reason to suppose that movement was necessary to feed the duke and his court, or to consume the produce grown on the duke's demesne. The ducal demesne was concentrated in Upper Normandy, particularly in the Pays de Caux and along the Seine. The produce could be easily transported to Rouen for consumption there. Indeed, the lack of a sufficient concentration of demesne vills around other centres, with the probable exception of Caen, is another reason for thinking that the duke remained at Rouen most of the time he was in the duchy.[89] It is unlikely that the supplies provided by the demesne and the dukes' forests ever came close to exhaustion, not least because the dukes' courts were not comparable in size to those maintained by the Carolingian kings and emperors, which had

---

[87] Mooers Christelow, 'A moveable feast?', 187.

[88] See below, *infra*, pp. 527-30 and Table 9.

[89] It might also be noted, in this respect, that under the Carolingians 'the largest concentration of royal lands were organized around … residences, or places' (Nelson, 'Kingship and royal government', p. 386).

sometimes made a degree of movement necessary for them to maintain supply.[90]
The witness lists, and the size of William's hall at Caen, would suggest a court
composed usually of fewer than one hundred persons.[91] Furthermore, should
supplies have faltered, Normandy had a monetarized economy by the beginning
of the eleventh century, and probably from its inception.[92] Food and drink and
other supplies could be purchased if necessary, for the markets of Rouen were
fed from far afield. One of the miracles found in the *Inventio et miracula sancti
Vulfrani*, for example, reveals that grain might be shipped to the city from the
Orne.[93] In any event, the supply of food to Rouen was clearly not a problem.
Despite the fact that it was home not just to the duke and his household but also
to the archbishop and cathedral canons, the monks of two large abbeys (Trinité-
du-Mont and Saint-Ouen), the nuns of an important convent (Saint-Amand),
the inmates of a number of dependencies (Saint-Paul, Saint-Gervase, and Notre-
Dame-du-Pré), and several thousands of people all year round, we do not hear of
shortages or famine in any of our sources.

And so, as noted at the outset of this discussion, for the most part the dukes
moved from Rouen for specific reasons, principally to defend the duchy or to
take part in significant public occasions such as the dedications of the cathedrals
or major abbey churches of Normandy in a manner that is not dissimilar to the
present queen's presence at ship launchings or the opening of new public buildings. And just as the crowds turn out to see the reigning monarch and other
royals, wave flags, and hope for a word or two in the UK today, so a duke's arrival
at a city or monastery might be punctuated by the performance of an *aduentus*,
a ritualized public manifestation of loyalty and respect, orchestrated by the local
bishop, abbot, or corporation.[94]

Such celebrations were ultimately inherited from the formal entry of the
Roman emperors into the great cities of their empire, although also inspired by

---

[90]   The Astronomer said that Louis the Pious rotated his winter quarters between four
centres (Doué, Chasseneuil, Angeac, and Ebreuil) for reasons of supply when king of
Aquitaine, but even at that stage in his career his household may be supposed to have
been much larger than that maintained by the dukes (*Son of Charlemagne*, pp. 38–9). It
has been calculated that Otto I's court required, on a daily basis, 1,000 pigs and sheep,
ten wagon-loads each of wine and beer, 1,000 measures of grain, eight head of cattle,
chickens, pigs, fish, eggs, and vegetables. The cost of provisioning on this scale is calculated at 30 *livres* of silver every day (Steane, *The Archaeology of Power*, p. 29). The Salian
court is thought to have consisted of some 300–1,000 persons, rising to a maximum of
1,600 (Bernhardt, *Itinerant Kingship*, p. 58).

[91]   See above, Chapter 7, pp. 370-2, 375-7, 386-7 in particular.

[92]   See below, Chapter 10, pp. 572–4.

[93]   *Inventio*, p. 85, noted (in a different context) in Bates, *Normandy*, p. 96.

[94]   See also Hicks, 'Through the city streets', pp. 140–3.

a biblical model: 'in greeting their lord with such ceremony, his people were said to welcome him as Christ had been welcomed to Jerusalem. The *aduentus*, then, was yet another ritual designed to celebrate a lordship uniquely sanctioned by God.'[95] Such welcomes were usually portrayed as spontaneous shows of love or grief, demonstrating sincere affection for the king, duke, or count. The reality might have been different, however. In 1004, or thereabouts, Count Theobald of Chartres sent a letter to the monks of Saint-Père instructing them 'that he was to be received into the monastery with a procession'.[96] It is plausible that the dukes of the Normans did likewise. It would not have done, after all, for such a public display of affection to be omitted.[97]

The tradition of the *aduentus* in Normandy might have begun early in the duchy's history. Dudo tells us that in 942 William Longsword returned from Laon, where he had stood as godfather to Louis IV's son Lothair.

> When swift rumour of the longed-for return of Duke William reached the Normans of a sudden, and warned them that their most resplendent leader was at hand. The whole city of Rouen was overjoyed and rushed out to meet him with a sudden procession, and went questing down the various side roads in order to catch sight of him. The female sex stood on the battlements of the wall, the old-aged commoners at the road junctions, and the young and middle-aged plebeians ran out to meet him; and the waiting clergy received him at the gates of the city, exultant, along with the veneration of the monastic order.[98]

Dudo described another *aduentus* which occurred when the young Richard I, recently freed from the tutelage of King Louis, was conducted to Rouen, which apparently shared a number of the same elements.[99] William of Jumièges

---

[95]   Koziol, *Begging Pardon*, p. 133.

[96]   Fulbert, *Letters*, no. 1, p. 6.

[97]   Roger II of Sicily enjoyed an *adventus* when he arrived at Telese in 1135 (Alexander of Telese, 'History of the Most Serene Roger', p. 117). But such celebrations could annoy rather than appease an angry king. In 1133, the citizens of Troia in Apulia, which had rebelled against him, greeted King Roger II with an *aduentus*. They went out in procession, singing *laudes*, 'thinking, as we have heard, to soothe his ferocious spirit by carrying before him the bodies of the saints so as to honour him'. But Roger, who was furious, put an end to the procession. '"I do not want," he said, "honours of this sort, but if life is granted to me I shall destroy everything and exile everyone." The clergy and the people who had gone out to meet him were put to flight, and everybody fled as best they could' (Falco of Benevento, 'Chronicle', in *Roger II and the Creation of the Kingdom of Sicily*, trans. G. A. Loud (Manchester, 2012), p. 206).

[98]   *Dudo*, p. 76.

[99]   *Dudo*, p. 121.

recorded these same events, but a little differently, suggesting that he was describing the form of the processions held in his own day. So, Jumièges wrote that when Longsword returned from Laon,

> the clergy of Rouen knowing of his arrival, walked in procession singing hymns to meet the duke at the city gates, and the citizens of both sexes called from the ramparts: 'Blessed is he that cometh in the name of the Lord.' Accompanied by the harmonious voices of the clergy and the people, the duke was led into the church of Mary, mother of God, where he poured out his prayers to God. Thereafter he quickly returned home to enjoy a banquet, surrounded by many retainers.[100]

Jumièges used the same words when reporting Louis IV's arrival at Rouen, which was marked by a banquet, too, which again suggests that this was how such things were done c. 1057.[101] His words can thus supplement William of Poitiers's report of the *aduentus* that celebrated William the Bastard's return to Normandy in 1067: 'When he entered his metropolitan city of Rouen, old men, boys, matrons and all the citizens came out to see him; they shouted out to welcome his return, so that you could have thought the whole city was cheering, as did Rome formerly when it joyfully applauded Pompey.'[102] A similar but more solemn scene greeted William's corpse when it arrived at Caen in 1087: 'Then Dom Gilbert the abbot came out reverently in procession with all his monks to meet the bier, and with them came a great multitude of clergy and laity, weeping and praying.'[103] When Henry I went to Normandy in 1104 he 'visited Domfront and other fortresses under his control in great state. He was honourably received by his magnates and entertained in royal fashion with lavish gifts.' Although not made explicit, such a reception sounds like a series of *aduenti*.[104] Two years later, the clergy and people of Rouen issued from the city to greet with all due honour some hairs of the Virgin Mary which a certain Ilgyrus had given to the cathedral, the abbey of St Ouen, and others.[105]

Those who played host to the dukes during their visits most likely saw it as an honour. Their closeness to the duke was publicly flaunted and observed as a result.

---

[100] Jumièges, i. 84. The passage is almost certainly from Mark, 11:9, which as might be expected from Koziol's comments above, recounts Christ's entry into Jerusalem, rather than Psalm 118:26.

[101] Jumièges, i. 106–8.

[102] Poitiers, p. 176.

[103] Orderic, iv. 104.

[104] Orderic, vi. 56.

[105] Eadmer, *HN*, pp. 180–1; trans. Bosanquet, pp. 192–3.

Local lords were presented with a chance to gain access to the court, and perhaps a greater opportunity to impress the duke than would have been the case at Rouen. The dukes might give something back to their lesser subjects, too, in the hope of gaining their affection, while also increasing their own prestige. If Ralph Tortarius is to be believed, when William the Bastard visited Caen in some unknown year after 1066, he provided the citizens with a wild animal show involving lions, leopards, lynxes, camels, and ostriches.[106] If this description reflects reality, it may be how Henry gained his love of exotic animals – and the fact that he did have a menagerie including some of these same creatures suggests that Ralph's words might contain some truth.[107] There was also the boost to the local economy that a ducal visit might provide. But visits and tours did have to be properly planned, or instead of helping the duke to develop and consolidate his authority outside the immediate vicinity of Rouen, and giving his subjects a chance to demonstrate their loyalty, such movements might undermine affection for the duke as an unrestrained court might cause the devastation of the lands through which it moved.[108] Henry I issued legislation restraining the behaviour of his courtiers in England in 1108, but did not apparently do so for Normandy. That perhaps indicates that the problem was not so serious in the duchy – we certainly do not hear about it – and one reason for that would be the infrequent movement of the duke's court out of Rouen.

Far from being 'on the move every week or two', then, it is both possible and plausible that the dukes remained at Rouen for much of the time they spent in the duchy, moving away from the city only for specific reasons and for a limited period of time.[109] It seems that they were unconcerned to visit the remoter parts of Normandy at all often, and while acts might have been made at staging posts, the dukes stayed at only a small number of centres – Bonneville-sur-Touques, Caen, Falaise, Fécamp, and Argentan being the most conspicuous. Like the Lombard kings or Alphonso II of Asturias, then, the dukes 'made prolonged stays at a few

---

[106] Rodulf Tortarius, *Carmina*, p. 325.

[107] Malmesbury, *GR*, i. 372. The menagerie included lions, lynxes, camels, and, famously, a porcupine.

[108] Eadmer wrote that 'a great number of those who attended the court had made a practice of plundering and destroying everything; and, there being no discipline to restrain them, laid waste all the territory through which the king passed … Consequently when it became known that the king was coming, all the inhabitants would flee from their houses anxious to do the best they could for themselves and their families by taking refuge in the woods or other places where they hoped to be able to protect themselves' (Eadmer, *HN*, pp. 192–3; trans. Bosanquet, pp. 205–6). See also *ASChr*, 'E', s.a. 1097; trans. Garmonsway, pp. 233–4.

[109] Green, *Henry*, p. 298. Mooers Christelow wrote of the dukes' 'incessant travel', too ('A moveable feast?', 193).

places',[110] even in Henry I's reign. That was in part because Normandy was not very big. In time of crisis, a duke could ride from one end to the other of his duchy in a couple of days.[111] When he *could* be so immediately present, itineration was not a necessity. The presence of ducal officials in the provinces of Normandy, the counts, *vicomtes*, *prévôts*, even to some extent the bishops, also manifested and entrenched the dukes' rule. But it is also clear that most of the dukes' subjects acknowledged the dukes' power most of the time and did what they were told without the need for the dukes to be present.

Messengers

Even had the dukes itinerated around their duchy, attendance at court and face-to-face meetings could not by themselves have resulted in effective government. The dukes thus needed to find ways to communicate with their subjects as and when the need arose, and they had to be sure that what they commanded would be acted on. The most obvious way to do this, and one that would have been used by every other lord of the period, too, was to dispatch messengers to transmit their orders and prohibitions to their *fideles* or officials.

A duke needed to have complete confidence in his messengers, just as those who received them needed to be able to trust that what they told them was reliable. As such, messengers tended to be members of a duke's household.[112] The use of household knights or chaplains as messengers also overcame the difficulties in finding a suitable messenger with which lesser lords seem to have struggled.

---

[110]   Nelson, 'Kingship and royal government', p. 386.

[111]   Poitiers, p. 36 gives an impression of the speed with which the dukes might move. In 1173, Henry II moved from Rouen to Dol in two days (W. L. Warren, *Henry II* (London, 1973), p. 128.

[112]   See Table 9 below. As other lords faced the same problems, it is not at all surprising that most rulers used members of their households for this purpose. According to Ann Williams, writing of late Anglo-Saxon England, 'such evidence as there is implies that the duties of the stallers were not fixed but various, and were performed as and when the king had need of them' (A. Williams, *The World Before Domesday: The English Aristocracy, 900–1066* (London, 2008), p. 32. She discussed the status and duties of the stallers at pp. 26–32, and see also p. 72). Although the stallers appeared in the king's household only during Cnut's reign, men seem to have performed the same function under a different name in the tenth century. Alfred's household warriors followed him to Athelney, but feasted with him in better days, and were used as messengers and ambassadors when necessary (Abels, 'Household men, mercenaries, and Vikings', p. 150). Similarly, *c*. 1017, St Olaf of Norway sent Bjorn the Marshal – his name reveals him to have been a household official – as a messenger to the king of Sweden, told him what to say, paid him in advance with a richly decorated sword, and gave him a finger ring as a token to prove his authority to Olaf's ally, Earl Rognvald (*Heimskringla*, pp. 299–300).

Some tenants held their land in return for performing such service, as was the case with two of the tenants of the monks of Troarn,[113] but there may often have been something of a Hobson's choice for even the greatest of lords. For example, Archbishop Lanfranc told Archbishop John of Rouen that even when he was able to find the time to write letters, 'there are no messengers, or the men available are individuals of such status that they think it beneath their dignity to carry a letter'.[114] Anselm, while still abbot of Le Bec, complained in a similar vein: 'For even if many Normans cross over to England, there are very few who do so to my knowledge; among these very few there is scarcely anyone to whom I would entrust our commission and who would carry it out conscientiously and without delay.'[115] Both men did, however, use the monks of their houses to carry their messages, and if making a response might use the same messenger who had carried the initial petition.[116] In other cases, men carried letters that they had themselves petitioned for. One of Lanfranc's letters to Abbot Baldwin of Bury St Edmunds begins: 'The man who brings you this letter says that he has incurred your anger and so has left his home, where he was born and brought up, and his family and friends. Because he thought that for me you would do much, he begged me to write to you, father, on his behalf. May our intercession move you in your goodness to show him mercy.'[117] One of Anselm's letters was carried to Abbot William of Caen by a certain Odo, who had importuned him to intervene with the abbot on his son's behalf: 'Odo, the bearer of this letter, has persistently asked me by many supplications that our fidelity entreat your holiness on behalf of his son, whom you have excluded from your service.'[118]

As trust was fundamental to the successful delivery of a message, if the recipient could not be sure that the messenger truly represented his principal, then his words might fall on deaf ears. One such wasted journey was made in 1165, when Owain Gwynedd sent a messenger to Louis VII. The French king refused to believe that the letter he carried was actually from Owain because he did not

---

[113] Ctl. Troarn, fo. 64v; Tabuteau, *Transfers*, p. 58.

[114] *Letters of Lanfranc*, no. 15 and see also no. 17 on the problems of finding messengers and also for the identities of some of those who carried letters between Lanfranc and his correspondents.

[115] *Letters of Saint Anselm*, no. 43. See also G. Constable, 'Letters and Letter Collections', *Typologie des Sources du Moyen Age Occidental*, 17 (Turnhout, 1976), 53–4.

[116] For example, *Letters of St Anselm*, nos. 5, 30, 66, 70, 71, 74, 89. No. 22, however, seems to have been carried by a member of the Crispin family. Lupus of Ferrières complained about the quality of messengers, too: 'messages relayed by couriers are not reliable for they are often noticeably marred by falsehoods' ('Letters of Lupus of Ferrières', in Dutton, *Carolingian Civilization*, p. 467, no. 12).

[117] *Letters of Lanfranc*, no. 22.

[118] *Letters of Saint Anselm*, no. 18.

recognize the man who carried it. As Huw Pryce noted, 'this implies that the question of authenticity turned on the identity of the messenger … rather than on any internal or external features of the letter itself, such as a seal'.[119] That conclusion might need some small qualification, however, in that similar problems might arise when the messenger was of insufficient status to perform his function adequately, and had not been provided with additional authorities such as a seal. In around 1078, for example, Anselm of Le Bec received a letter from Abbot Henry informing him that his kinsman, Fulcerald, was thinking of becoming a monk at Le Bec. Anselm did not believe the message, writing to Abbot Henry that, 'since I see neither your letter nor your seal, which is a reliable witness to a document, I do not entirely trust your messenger'.[120] He went on: 'a letter confirmed by your seal should show me your undoubted will.' The real reasons for Anselm's objections, however, are clearly expressed in a related letter that he sent to Fulcerald at the same time as this reply to the abbot. In it, he expressed his annoyance that his orders had not been obeyed: 'you should have insisted that he inform me of this by his letter and seal, as I ordered … It is not fitting for me to initiate such an action merely on the word of such an unimportant fellow.'[121] In other words, where a messenger was of insufficient social standing, written instructions had to be included as well, and the weight of a command or request, even if not the question of authenticity, might turn on the presence of a seal. This passage is crucial in understanding the importance of the sealed writ that increasingly appeared in Normandy after 1106.

The status of the messenger, then, was important – at least if the message was of a sensitive nature or if the sender was seeking a favour. The lack of messengers complained of by Lanfranc and Anselm might have been the result of the need to find someone of appropriate stature to carry the message concerned.[122] Thus, in 945, the chief Normans sent 'knights of the nobler and richer sort' to a King Harold of the Danes, then supposedly in exile in Normandy, to ask for

[119] Pryce, 'Owain Gwynedd and Louis VII', 18.
[120] *Letters of Saint Anselm*, no. 110.
[121] *Letters of Saint Anselm*, no. 111.
[122] In the earlier eleventh century, Bernard of Angers made clear his distrust of 'the common people' (preface to the *Liber miraculorum Sancte Fidis*, in *The Book of Sainte Foy*, trans. P. Sheingorn (Philadepphia,1995), p. 39). Around 150 years later, William of Canterbury wrote, when recording the miracles attributed to Thomas Becket, that 'just as we conclude that beggars are liars, so we do not at all assume the same of nobles who win divine favour by making a pilgrimage' (William of Canterbury, *Miraculorum gloriosi martyris Thomae, Cantuariensis archiepiscopi*, Bk. 6, no. 140, in *Materials for the History of Thomas Becket, Archbishop of Canterbury*, ed. J. C. Robertson and J. B. Sheppard, Rolls Series (London, 1875–83), i. 524). That attitude underlies the concerns addressed here.

assistance against King Louis.[123] Messengers might have to look the part, too. Henry of Huntingdon noted that 'envoys remarkable for their massive physique and magnificent apparel were sent by Henry, the Roman emperor, to ask for the king's daughter in marriage with their lord'.[124] When Thomas Becket was sent to Paris on behalf of Henry II in 1158, he arrived splendidly attired and with an enormous quantity of presents for the recipients of his embassy and beer enough for everyone in Paris, 'so that before all men and in all things the person of the sender might be honoured in the one sent'.[125]

It may consequently be supposed that the dukes' messengers were selected with some care throughout the period under consideration. When we know the identities of those sent as messengers (see Table 9), it is often clear that this was indeed the case. If King Henry across the Rhine was on familiar, even if not intimate, terms with William Longsword, it is likely that he would have recognized Tetger, the chief of the young warriors of the household. His pre-eminent position among Longsword's followers certainly made him an obvious choice of messenger. Rainald of Bayeux, Bernard fitz Ospac, and Robert Bloet were all William the Bastard's chaplains and would have been frequently at court. Bernard and Robert would thus have been well-known to Queen Matilda and Archbishop Lanfranc who received William's orders from their mouths or hands. Rainald's toponym suggests that he would have been well known in Bayeux, as well as at court, making him an appropriate observer of the ordeal that was held in the city in 1080 × 1084. Earl William of Warenne was probably chosen to negotiate with Stephen of Aumale and Count Charles of Flanders not just because of his comital status, but also because of his position as an Upper Norman lord and a close confidant of the royal duke. Why Fulk, 'prior of Saint-Evroult, who later became abbot of Saint-Pierre-sur-Dives, was sent by William the Bastard, king of the English, to Countess Bertha at Brie on private business' is less clear, however, but it is unlikely that he was selected at random.

In addition to those named messengers, whose work is listed in Table 9, unnamed messengers were sent on a number of missions. It is worth listing these, if only to give a wider sense of the types of business that messengers were used for. Thus, 'Rollo sent his envoys to him [Æthelstan] without delay, having told them beforehand what to say'.[126] Before 1008, 'when the duke became anxious about offspring to succeed him, he sent messengers to Geoffrey, count of the Bretons, to ask

[123] *Dudo*, p. 114.

[124] Huntingdon, p. 456.

[125] William fitz Stephen, *Vita*, in *Materials for the History of Thomas Becket, Archbishop of Canterbury*, iii. 29–31; *The Lives of Thomas Becket*, trans. M. Staunton (Manchester, 2001), pp. 55–6.

[126] *Dudo*, p. 30.

Table 9 Ducal messengers, 911–1144

Name(s)	Sent by	Sent to	Business	Date	Reference
Young knights of the household (*tirones suae domus*)	Rollo	Gisla and the Frankish knights staying with her	To arrest the Frankish knights	*c.* 920	*Dudo*, p. 53
Tetger, chief of the *tiros* of the household (*tyronem domus suae principem*)	William Longsword	Henry, king across the Rhine	To come to the aid of King Louis	942	*Dudo*, p. 71
Duke Cono	William Longsword	Norman army	To command them to cease fighting the Saxons (succeeds only when he displays Longsword's sword)	942	*Dudo*, pp. 73–4
Household retainers in the duke's confidence (*domigenas secreti sui conscios*)	William Longsword	Richard I and his guardians	To fetch Richard to Quevilly in secret	*c.* 942	*Dudo*, p. 96
Distinguished envoys from his household (*praecipuos suae domus legatos*)	Richard I	The Danes	To ask for help against Count Theobald of Chartres and the Franks	*c.* 960	*Dudo*, p. 150
Herfast, Gunnor's brother	Richard II	King Robert the Pious and other lords	Various matters, perhaps including the heresy of *c.* 1022	*c.* 1020	*Ctl. Saint-Père*, i. 109
William fitz Osbern and Roger II of Montgommery	William the Bastard	Geoffrey Martel	To fix a date for battle	1052	Poitiers, p. 26
Ralph of Tosny	William the Bastard	King Henry I of the French	To announce French defeat at Mortemer	1054	Jumièges, ii. 144
Turold	William the Bastard	Count Guy of Ponthieu	To demand the release of Harold Godwinson into William's custody	*c.* 1064	Bayeux Tapestry, scene 11
Monk of Fécamp	William the Bastard	King Harold of the English	To announce William's demands	1066	Poitiers, p. 120

Rainald the clerk of Bayeux	William the Bastard	Bayeux	Witness ordeal	1080 × 1084	*Regesta: William*, no. 162
Earl Roger of Shrewsbury, William of Breteuil, Roger of Beaumont	William the Bastard	Le Bec	To confirm the manner of the election of Anselm as abbot	1077	*On the Liberty of the Abbey of Le Bec*, p. 134
Bernard fitz Ospac	William the Bastard	Normandy	Command restitution of property to the monks of Marmoutier	1080	*Regesta: William*, no. 200
Fulk, prior of Saint-Evroult	William the Bastard	Countess Bertha at Brie	Private business	1066 × 1078[a]	Orderic, iii. 336
Robert Bloet, chaplain	William the Bastard	Lanfranc	To deliver William the Bastard's letter commanding the archbishop to crown Rufus	1087	Orderic, v. 202
Arnulf the chancellor, William of Breteuil, William fitz Richard	Robert Curthose	Archbishop of Rouen	Command the archbishop to bless Abbot William of Le Bec without a profession	1093	*On the Liberty of the Abbey of Le Bec*, pp. 138–9
John, bishop of Lisieux	Henry I	Henry's officials at Argentan	To liberate provisions for the monks of Saint-Evroult	1113	Orderic, vi. 176
William of Warenne	Henry I	Stephen of Aumale and Count Charles of Flanders	To bring them to terms and thus prevent an invasion of the duchy	1119	Hyde, p. 82
Prior of Notre-Dame-du-Pré	Henry I	Abbot Boso of Le Bec	Summon him to Henry	1124	*On the Liberty of the Abbey of Le Bec*, p. 141
Robert de Sigillo	Henry I	Archbishop Geoffrey of Rouen	Forbid him to take profession from the newly elected Abbot Boso of Le Bec	1124	*On the Liberty of the Abbey of Le Bec*, p. 142

Note

[a] Fulk left Saint-Evroult to become abbot of Saint-Pierre-sur-Dives c. 1078, which thus provides the last possible year for his embassy (Gazeau, *Normannia monastica*, ii. 300).

to marry a sister of his named Judith'.[127] Around 1055, William the Bastard 'issued a command ordering the captains of his knights to be ready to enter the territory of the Angevin, Martel, to build the castle of Ambrières; and he sent messengers to tell Martel what day he had fixed for its commencement.'[128] When Harold seized the throne in January 1066, William sent messengers to him in England urging him 'to renounce this act of folly and with worthy submission keep the faith which he had pledged with an oath'.[129] In 1067, William 'sent out heralds (*praeconis*) to proclaim peace for all men, denizens and foreigners alike, and threatened thieves, rebels, and all disturbers of the peace with severe but just punishments'.[130] In 1090, 'Duke Robert … sent envoys to his lord, Philip, the French king, caused him to come to Normandy, and together with Philip he besieged one of the castles defended by his brother's knights'.[131] Henry I importuned Louis VI on behalf of his ally the count of Blois: 'long did the messengers on our king's behalf toil to and fro to persuade Louis to accept satisfaction from Theobald.'[132] In 1118, 'King Henry came to Alençon and sent out messengers (*missi*) to summon military contingents from the whole of Normandy to battle'.[133] There is no suggestion of written letters or writs being sent with these men, although it is the case that William the Bastard had used writs for this purpose, no doubt in addition to messengers.[134]

Letters were used, though, as noted above, and when they were it was often to give extra emphasis or weight to the message that the messenger delivered orally. Indeed, the writs issued by the dukes after 1066, along with their seal, may have been seen as carrying his persona to the addressees despite his physical absence.[135] Towards the beginning of the eleventh century, Fulbert of Chartres wrote to one of his clerks, identified only by an initial letter 'G': 'I have already made two complaints to you by messenger; now I am sending a third in writing.'[136] This is

---

[127] Jumièges, ii. 28.

[128] Poitiers, p. 50.

[129] Jumièges, ii. 160.

[130] Orderic, ii. 208. And see similarly Orderic, ii. 198; iv. 208; v. 90, 114, 164, 176; vi. 472.

[131] Worcester, iii. 56.

[132] Malmesbury, *GR*, i. 732.

[133] Orderic, vi. 194.

[134] *Regesta: William*, no. 54. It is unlikely that lack of time resulted in a lack of writs. In November 1188, the future Richard I left a conference with his father at Bonsmoulins in anger. As he headed south, he spent a night at Amboise where 'he had had drawn up / at least two hundred sets of letters or more' (*History of William Marshal*, ll. 8248–9, ed. A. J. Holden, trans. S. Gregory, and notes by. D. Crouch, Anglo-Norman Text Society, Vol. 1 (London, 2002), pp. 418–19).

[135] For a discussion see, M. Clanchy, *From Memory to Written Record: England 1066–1307*, second edition (Oxford, 1993), pp. 311–13.

[136] Fulbert, *Letters*, no. 16, pp. 32–3.

perhaps similar to the statement in Lanfranc's third letter to Roger of Hereford: 'I have sent messengers, I have sent letters not once but for a second time inviting you to come to me.'[137] When the garrison of Le Mans sent to King William for help in 1099, they also sent a letter. Gaimar dramatized its reception at the court: 'Take this writ (*bref*), [dear] Lord King!' The king took it, immediately broke [the seal], handed the writ to Ranulf Flambard. Everything that the messenger had said, the knights sent by the writ: they awaited help in the city.'[138] Here again, then, the letter reinforced the oral report, apparently emphasizing the seriousness of the crisis.

Gaimar's words also constitute a reminder that the Norman dukes and kings were most likely unable to read the letters that they were sent. The narrative *On the Liberty of the Abbey of Le Bec* includes a similar passage: 'Then the messenger who had brought the letter [from Anselm] handed it to Baudry the prior and the prior offered it to the duke. Immediately, the duke bade his chancellor, Arnulf, read the letter to all present, and when it had been read the duke addressed them pleasantly …'[139] It may be supposed that Arnulf translated into Norman French as he read, although that is not made clear. Henry I, in contrast, was no crowned ass: 'The king, who was literate, read the letter.'[140]

It should be noted that the reception of news and letters provided another opportunity for the sort of political theatre discussed above.[141] Good news might be greeted with a cheerful face, bad news with anger. Archbishop's Lanfranc's letters were certainly not always welcomed by their recipients, and as there was no need to worry about *maiestas* when dealing with a bishop, his letters could be treated with contempt and he himself might be publicly reviled without fear of serious punishment. One of Lanfranc's letters to Bishop Peter of Chester makes it clear that this had happened and, moreover, that he had been told about it: 'I wrote to you a few days ago. You were unwilling to accept my letter, scorned to read it, and very disdainfully, as I am told, threw it onto a bench. Now I am sending another, instructing and directing you in the king's name and my own to desist completely from all the harassment which you are said to be practising on the monastery of Coventry.'[142] A second example, this time sent to Bishop Herfast of Thetford, dates

---

[137] *Letters of Lanfranc*, no. 33A.
[138] Gaimar, p. 314, my translation.
[139] 'On the Liberty of the Abbey of Le Bec', trans. S. N. Vaughn, *The Abbey of Le Bec and the Anglo-Norman State* (Woodbridge, 1981), p. 138.
[140] Orderic, vi. 50. Giles Constable noted that most laymen had letters read to them. In the eleventh century, the ability of Count Palatine Frederick to read and to understand a letter was regarded as exceptional (Constable, 'Letters', p. 54).
[141] See above, Chapter 7, pp. 422–32.
[142] *Letters of Lanfranc*, no. 27.

from 1070 × 1081: 'Abbot Baldwin's clerk and servant Berard brought you our letter about his affairs. As he himself affirmed to me later, you made a coarse joke about it; you uttered cheap and unworthy remarks about me in the hearing of many; and you declared with many an oath that you would give me no assistance in that matter.'[143] In contrast, Henry I received Anselm's messengers with 'unruffled good humour' in 1109, despite the unwelcome content of their message.[144] As remarked above, a studied lack of emotional response, an ability to remain unruffled, was one way that a king or a duke might choose to respond to unwelcome news.[145]

William's writs, and those of later dukes, had a seal attached to them as additional evidence of authenticity. Others used seals, too, although before 1144 their use was probably not yet so widespread as it would become in the second half of the century.[146] As noted above, in his letter to Abbot Henry Anselm referred to the lack of a seal that would have given the messenger's words greater credibility. That remark implies that it was possible to use tokens, such as seals, or perhaps code words, to support the testimony of the messenger, particularly if he was himself unknown to the recipient or if he was known as the man of a different lord. Two episodes from Dudo's *De moribus* provide further evidence that this happened. When Norman troops began to fight against the Franks during the meeting of the king of the Franks and the king beyond the Rhine at Visé, William Longsword's command to his men to cease fighting, delivered by Duke Cono, was at first ignored by his troops simply because they did not know him and did not trust him. As a result, 'William gave Cono a sword … to bear it away as a signal for dismissal and present it to the legion occupying the houses and still damaging houses. And when Cono again hurried up to confront them, and displayed to them the sword of Duke William, flashing with gold and precious stones, they not only fell silent at once, but bowed towards the sword with downcast gaze.'[147] Here, then, it was the sword rather than Cono that carried the duke's authority. In the second case, the issue of trust was dealt with in advance by the use of a code word or other secret sign. When Bernard of Senlis and Bernard the Dane secretly met to

---

143 *Letters of Lanfranc*, no. 47.

144 Eadmer, *HN*, p. 220. The letter concerned the dispute between Canterbury and York.

145 See above, Chapter 7, pp. 426–8, 430–2.

146 As is well known, the *Chronicle of Battle Abbey* notes the dismissive comment of Richard of Lucé: '"It was not the custom in the past", he said, "for every petty knight to have a seal. They are appropriate for kings and great men only"' (*The Chronicle of Battle Abbey*, ed. and trans, E. Searle (Oxford, 1980), p. 214. See also Nieus, 'Early aristocratic seals', 97–123.

147 *Dudo*, p. 74. Leah Shopkow interpreted this story as revealing Longsword's monastic dislike of display, but the story can be read as revealing the reality of William's authority, despite his lack of ostentation, against the French king's lack of authority (see above, Chapter 7, p. 396).

plan their campaign, after they had learned that Richard I had been liberated from his confinement and was being kept safe at Coucy, they realized that if they met again King Louis might learn of it and thus divine their intentions. The conclusion they reached was that the two would from now on have to communicate through a messenger. And so they agreed that Bernard the Dane would 'trust whatever word I send you, when the envoy gives the sign agreed to between you and me'.[148]

But it was also recognized that messengers were not always an appropriate way to communicate. Count William of Poitou came to meet with William Longsword at Lyons-la-Forêt to ask for his sister's hand in marriage, because, 'as you are so worthy a count, I was unwilling to send envoys to you and have chosen to negotiate as my own envoy'.[149] That seems to have been unusual. More often, messengers were involved in preliminary negotiations and then stepped aside. Messengers and ambassadors had negotiated a peace between Richard I and King Lothair, for example, but that peace was made by the rulers in person: 'When the time of the longed-for meeting had come, King Lothair arrived on the stream of the Epte, with the Franks, and pledged to Duke Richard his promise of unbreakable peace … And when the peacemaking assembly had been concluded and the king and Duke Richard had been allied, and each had been copiously enriched by gifts from the other, each rode home to his own country in safety.'[150] In 1094, 'Robert, duke of the Normans, told his brother King William the Younger through envoys (*per legatos*) that he would no longer keep the peace which they had both agreed'.[151] As a result, the king went to Normandy to confer in person with his brother. Similarly, Archbishop Anselm of Canterbury wrote to Archbishop Gerard of York regarding the publication of a defamatory letter, but added that 'if this answer is not satisfactory, I hope that speaking to you personally will satisfy you that I am not guilty in this case, nor has any untruth been introduced by our messengers'.[152] Indeed, this might sometimes have been a real problem – or could be presented as one. In 1101, Henry I claimed that the noble envoys shuttling between him and his brother had 'twisted words and sowed seeds of dispute', and so demanded to speak to Curthose face to face. The two reached an agreement in short order, perhaps because Henry could clear the soured air by claiming that he had been misrepresented.[153]

---

[148] *Dudo*, p. 108.

[149] *Dudo*, p. 69.

[150] *Dudo*, p. 162.

[151] Worcester, iii. 68. Similarly, Hubert of Sainte-Suzanne negotiated a truce with King William through envoys before securing a safe conduct to cross the Channel to see the king face to face (Orderic, iv. 52).

[152] *Letters of Saint Anselm*, no. 253.

[153] Orderic, v. 318. Something similar could happen even when communication had been

The use of writs in Normandy

The use of letters to add weight to a messenger's words has already been mentioned. But during the first decades of the twelfth century, so far as the administration of Normandy is concerned, the written word would all but replace the oral reports or instructions delivered by word of mouth by messengers – or so it seems. Instructions and prohibitions were then delivered in sealed writs, obtained and delivered by the beneficiary. Writs had been found in England before the Norman Conquest, and while they might have been occasionally employed in Normandy during the Conqueror's reign, they were only sent round the duchy routinely during that of Henry I.[154]

The increasing use of writs does mark a change from the way that the the duchy was governed previously, but the line was not quite as sharp as it might at first sight appear. Letters had been sent and received by the dukes and other French lords, too, for many years before 25 December 1066. Those letters might convey greetings or news, but they might also convey orders. For example, Pope Alexander sent a letter to Bishop John of Avranches concerning his transfer to the archbishopric of Rouen: 'we wish and command on your charity, in accordance with apostolic authority, that you do not resist that which divine will has provided, and that you show yourself obedient by accepting your election.'[155] Lanfranc later commented that Alexander II had 'issued a written directive' calling for the question of the primacy to be judged in England.[156] In April 1102, the pope commanded Bishop Osbern of Exeter to allow the monks of Battle at St Nicholas in Exeter to have a

---

in writing. It seems that Anselm had asked a certain Ralph to return some books that he had borrowed from Le Bec. The manner of his asking, however, caused offence, and Ralph seems to have expressed his displeasure to Anselm in a letter. He then attempted to calm the troubled waters by writing: 'the letter sent to you about the return of the books I neither ordered to be written that way, nor did I know until the report of those who brought the books back that it had been done that way' (*Letters of St Anselm*, no. 12).

[154] Writs may be defined as comprising a command or mandate, or, more rarely, a notification or instruction. A writ can be addressed to a variety of persons: private individuals; ducal officers; a local court; or even to a generality of officers and men. It is not the address that makes a writ, but its purpose. All writs, even when they look like notifications, require their addressee to take some action; to do something or to desist from doing it. See also R. C. van Caenegem, *Royal Writs in England from the Conquest to Glanville: Studies in the Early History of the Common Law*, Selden Society 77 (1959), pp. 108–10; Sharpe, 'The use of writs in the eleventh century', 249; and Hagger, 'The earliest Norman writs revisited', 181–205.

[155] *AAbps*, pp. 40–1, 54.

[156] *Letters of Lanfranc*, p. 50. He mentions another papal directive sent to the archbishop of Reims in no. 25.

cemetery for their dead ('command and prohibit you to forbid the said monks any longer to have a cemetery for burying their dead').[157]

The pope was not the only churchman to use letters to make commands. Archbishop Lanfranc commanded Bishop Wulfstan of Worcester to consecrate a new bishop for the Orkneys, with the note that the messenger would give the bishop the place and time.[158] He also sent written commands to Bishop Stigand of Chichester and to Abbot Odo of Chertsey.[159] His successor Anselm did similarly. In 1102, for example, he wrote to the abbess and nuns of Romsey commanding them to desist from venerating a dead man – Waltheof – as a saint. He had previously commanded the archdeacon of Winchester to prevent it.[160]

In Normandy, the dukes received missives from churchmen such as Fulbert of Chartres. However, although it is clear that letters were composed in the names of Duke William V of Aquitaine, Count Odo II of Chartres, and Count Fulk of Anjou, there is no evidence that letters, as distinct from diplomata, were issued in the duke's name before 1066.[161] After 1066, perhaps because letters were required more frequently now that the duke was more often absent, or because William was now also a king, or because he was writing to more eminent persons, a handful survive. For example, William wrote to Pope Gregory VII regarding the doing of fealty for England and the payment of Peter's Pence.[162] His letter to Abbot John of Fécamp, regarding the transfer of Vitalis from Bernay to Westminster, also survives.[163] In addition, there is a command sent to Queen Matilda, apparently drafted by the monks of Marmoutier rather than royal scribes, commanding her to take particular action.[164] Moreover, as Haskins and Bates both noted, a writ was issued for the abbey of Montebourg.[165] William Rufus was also given a letter

[157] *Letters of Saint Anselm*, no. 226. The letter also contains what is effectively a *nisi feceris* clause: see above, Chapter 8, pp. 480–3.

[158] *Letters of Lanfranc*, no. 13.

[159] *Letters of Lanfranc*, nos. 30, 48.

[160] *Letters of Saint Anselm*, nos. 237, 236.

[161] Fulbert, *Letters*, nos. 86, 96, 103, 104, 107, 111, 113, 116.

[162] *Letters of Lanfranc*, no. 39.

[163] *Regesta: William*, no. 139.

[164] *Regesta: William*, no 202. David Bates had originally thought this a forgery, then a beneficiary production, but now inclines to the view that it was drafted by the writing office (Bates, 'The origin of the justiciarship', 7–8; Bates, 'The earliest Norman writs', *EHR*, 100 (1985), 268–9; note to *Regesta: William*, no. 202). The comparison Bates originally made with an act of Henry I for Fontevraud in *charte-mandement* form (P. Chaplais, 'Une charte originale de Guillaume le Conquérant pour l'abbaye de Fécamp, pp. 97–8) suggests that his view that it is a beneficiary production is to be preferred.

[165] *Regesta: William*, no. 209. There is, however, some uncertainty as to whether this is a writ of William I or William II.

sealed with the royal seal to take to Lanfranc, in which William instructed the
archbishop to crown his son king.[166]

By William's post-Conquest reign, then, there is evidence of letters being used
to convey his orders to or in Normandy. These might be drafted by the beneficiary as well as by the king's scribes. It is also likely that they were sealed, and
so could have been carried by the beneficiary rather than by a royal or ducal
messenger. That seal, incidentally, seems to have been an original product of
William's goldsmiths. It was double-sided. The majesty side was probably taken
from earlier Ottonian, French, or English precedents, although given its production in England it is likely that Edward the Confessor's seal provided the model.
The obverse, however, showed the royal duke as a mounted knight carrying a gon-
falon. This was novel. The image might have been suggested by the iconography
of warrior saints such as St George, or even by historiated capitals or manuscript
illuminations. Whatever the origin of this equestrian portrait, however, it gave
rise to a whole host of imitations not just in the Anglo-Norman *regnum* but across
western Europe.[167]

Writs seem not to have become much more popular in Normandy in the years
that immediately followed William the Bastard's death. There is one Norman writ
of King William II for the monks of Le Bec,[168] and one of Robert Curthose for the
monks of Montebourg.[169] There are, in addition, three lost writs from before 1106:
one of William I and two of Robert Curthose. Two of these three were remarked
by David Bates.[170] The third, the second of the lost writs of Robert Curthose, is
referred to in the *Ecclesiastical History* of Orderic Vitalis. Recounting the election of Roger of Le Sap in 1091, Orderic noted that when the abbot elect finally
appeared before Curthose and his brother, William Rufus, in England, Curthose
sent letters (*apices*) to the bishop of Lisieux instructing him to admit Abbot Roger
fully in accordance with the canons.[171] That this was a writ is suggested by the
context and function. The letter 'instructed (*mandauit*)' the bishop of Lisieux to
give Roger seisin of the abbey and its possessions in a manner that is analogous
to the later writ-charter of Henry I that gave Roger's successor, Warin, the abbey

---

[166] Orderic, iv. 96.
[167] See Nieus, 'Early aristocratic seals', cited at n. 146 above.
[168] *NI*, p. 82.
[169] Ctl. Montebourg, p. 63, no. 136; J.-M. Bouvris, 'Un bref inédit de Robert Court-Heuse,
duc de Normandie, relatif à l'abbaye de Montebourg, au diocèse de Coutances', in
Actes du congrès national des sociétés savants (Caen, 1980), section de philologie et
d'histoire jusqu'à 1610 (Paris, 1984), 150.
[170] Bates, 'Norman writs', 269.
[171] Orderic, iv. 254.

in December 1122,[172] as well as to English writs and writ-charters of appointment dating from the reigns of William II and Henry I.[173]

It seems only to have been in Henry I's reign as duke that writs became routinely used in Normandy.[174] There are forty-two authentic Norman writs and fourteen Norman writ-charters of Henry I. These fifty-six acts are scattered among the archives of various Norman beneficiaries, with the single largest surviving collection found in the archive of the abbey at Montebourg (Manche). As has been noted already, the records preserved by the monks of Montebourg also include what may be the only surviving Norman writ (as opposed to *charte-mandement*) of William the Bastard, as well as the sole surviving text of a writ issued by Robert Curthose. In addition, ten Norman writs and one writ-charter of King Henry I were either retained as originals or copied into the abbey's cartularies (with two more English ones), so that the archive contains approximately 20 per cent of Henry's surviving Norman writs.[175]

In comparison with the number of acts surviving from England, the overall number of surviving Norman writs and writ-charters is small. There are fifty-six against just over one thousand surviving English examples. David Bates used these numbers to raise 'statistical objections' to the conclusions reached by both Haskins and Le Patourel that writs were used as frequently in the duchy as in England.[176] But we simply do not have the evidence on which to ground those objections because we do not know *why* there are so few, relatively speaking. Nor do we know the answer to a question posed by Laurent Morelle: 'Does the view conveyed by the sources simply show a reduction of what was once there, or is it a distortion?'[177] But although the evidential basis needed to answer these questions is absent, the scarcity of surviving Norman writs is symptomatic of a lack of Norman acts generally, and not just of writs and writ-charters. If the lack of Norman writs reveals that they were not as frequently issued as in England, then can we also maintain – as we must if the argument is to be consistent – that the

---

[172] Orderic, vi. 324 (*Regesta*, ii. no. 1337).

[173] *Regesta*, i. 293 and 304 (William II); Regesta, ii. nos. 493, 512, 607, 881, 885, 1027, 1048, 1057, 1063, 1091, 1101, 1203, 1242, 1243, 1259, 1424, 1425, 1426, 1483, 1641, 1724 (Henry I).

[174] For much of what follows see Hagger, 'The earliest Norman writs revisited', 181–205.

[175] Eight of the ten are found in Ctl. Montebourg, pp. 7–8 (nos. 8–15). A further writ is in London, BL, Add. MS 15605 (s. xv, fragment of a second Montebourg cartulary), fo. 16r (*Regesta*, ii. no. 1682). The original survived in the Archives départementales de la Manche until 1944. A transcript by Léchaudé d'Anisy is in PRO transcripts PRO31/8/140/B.ii, 178 (*Regesta*, ii. no. 1155).

[176] Bates, 'Norman writs', 267.

[177] L. Morelle, 'The metamorphosis of three monastic charter collections in the eleventh century (Saint-Amand, Saint-Riquier, Montier-en-Der)', in *Charters and the Use of the Written Word in Medieval Society*, ed. K. Heidecker (Turnhout, 2000), p. 171.

same is true of charters and diplomata? The problem, then, is a broad one. It is a question of why fewer acts – not just writs – from the eleventh and twelfth centuries have survived in Normandy than in England.

Specific examples should also act as a warning against rushing to conclude that writs were less frequently used in the duchy than England just because few of them survive. The abbey of Montebourg, mentioned above, has an obscure history, but nothing suggests that it was in any way remarkable. That being the case, the fact that there survive ten writs and one writ-charter of Henry I for the abbey – almost all of them found in just one manuscript – is extremely interesting as this is more than survive for the English Benedictine abbeys at Chertsey (Surrey) and St Albans (Hertfordshire), or at the Augustinian St Frideswide's in Oxford, as well as for a host of other English beneficiaries. Writs, then, were routinely obtained by the abbots of Montebourg, and there is no good reason to think that the abbots or priors of other Norman houses were any less keen to gain these documents.

Although diplomas and charters might be drafted by a beneficiary, so far as we can tell from the surviving originals, with one exception Henry's Norman writs and writ-charters were drafted by the scribes of the royal writing office. Of the six Norman writs that survive as originals, five are in the hands of identified royal scribes.[178] The remaining writ was issued for Archbishop Geoffrey of Rouen and concerned the restoration of the manor of Douvrend. The act does not seem to be in a 'Chancery' hand and employs abnormal contractions, but the royal style and formulae employed are those that would be expected. It might be that the act was written while Henry was on campaign against Amaury of Montfort in 1118 or 1119 so that there were no writing-office scribes available to draft the act.[179] In addition, four original writ-charters survive, or survived until the mid twentieth century. Three of the four are the work of identified writing-office scribes,[180] while the fourth original, for Savigny, was destroyed in the bombing of the Archives Départementales de la Manche in June 1944 before T. A. M. Bishop conducted his survey.[181]

Although Henry I's writs apparently reveal differences between England and

---

[178] *Regesta*, ii. nos. 842 (probably scribe viii), 1229 (scribe iv), 1919 (scribe xiv), 1931 (scribe xiii), 1932 (scribe x).

[179] *Regesta*, ii. no. 1234. Omitted from Bishop, *Scriptores Regis*. The act looks like a later copy of an authentic act of Henry I, even to the extent that the tag for the seal and the tie have been replicated. It may, however, be contemporary, as the hand seems to have some similarities with one that drafted a charter for the abbey of Saint-Etienne of Caen during Henry's reign.

[180] *Regesta*, ii. nos. 1200 (scribe v), 1946 (scribe xiv), 1964 (scribe xiv).

[181] *Regesta*, ii. no. 1433.

Normandy in the competences of the officials who put the royal duke's commands into effect, the actual subject matter of the writs issued on either side of the Channel is not noticeably different.[182] The vast majority of English writs take the form of instructions to hold a plea, to reseise the disseised, to allow beneficiaries to hold lands as they had been granted to them or as their predecessors held them, to respect hunting rights, to exempt property from tolls or other exactions, to return fugitives, and to put land in the king's protection. These are the matters dealt with in the Norman writs, too.[183] That is not to say that the English writs do not concern a plethora of other business; they do. But the survival of a relatively small number of English writs that cover matters which are not dealt with in the surviving Norman corpus cannot detract from the overall picture.

That writs were used for the same sorts of business on both sides of the Channel is best illustrated with reference to writs of exemption from toll, passage, and custom. During the reign of Henry I, these writs took on a quasi-standard form. A writ for the bishop of Evreux can be used as an exemplar:

> Henry king of the English to all *vicomtes* and his officials of the whole of England and Normandy and the ports of the sea greeting. I command that the household stuff and all possessions of the bishop of Evreux which his men are able to swear to be his demesne possessions shall be quit of toll and passage and all custom. And no one shall unjustly disturb them or their \<possessions\> upon 10 *livres* forfeiture.[184]

The writs for both English and Norman beneficiaries, then, state what goods are exempt (those which the bishop's men can swear belong to his demesne), what they are exempt from (toll, passage, and all custom), and the penalty for failing to act on the writ (10 *livres*). This form was employed on both sides of the Channel and in acts that were addressed to the officials of England or the officials of Normandy. The address of this act, however, also provides solid evidence that it was to be effective on both sides of the sea. Like most others issued for Norman or French beneficiaries, it is addressed to 'all sheriffs/*vicomtes* and his officials of the whole of England *and* Normandy and the ports of the sea'. That does not

---

[182] For the differences in responsibilities, particularly vis-à-vis sheriffs and *vicomtes* and justices, see above, Chapter 8, pp. 487–9 and below, *infra*, pp. 542–50.

[183] Although there are no writs commanding that a recognition be made, as David Bates pointed out, an act of William I reveals that men – here Richard Goz and Abbot William of Caen – might be commissioned to make a recognition, and it may be conjectured that a writ or mandate commanding them to do so once existed (*Regesta: William*, no. 149).

[184] *Regesta*, ii. 1555.

mean that the procedures employed were necessarily the same in Normandy and England, or even that the fine would have had the same value on both sides of the Channel, but at the end of the day money had to change hands and opportunities for redress and collection of the fine had to be available.

King Henry's Norman administration, then, used writs. As Haskins and Le Patourel had it, 'the writ came to be used ... just as regularly in Normandy as in England, certainly in Henry [I]'s reign'.[185] By the time King Henry took Normandy from his brother, he had been king of the English for six years. He would have had plenty of time to have become familiar with the English use of writs, and to have become aware of their usefulness as an instrument of government. Even before he conquered Normandy in 1106, King Henry was concerned about the lack of effective administration in the duchy, and his first actions after Tinchebray had been to hold councils at which he commanded that peace and order should be restored.[186] It is hardly surprising, then, that the writ, which, it must be supposed, had already served him well in England, was brought into routine use in the duchy as well.

What the increasing use of writs does not suggest, however, is that Henry was dissatisfied with the underlying customs and mechanisms that would operate to put his will into effect in the duchy. They had ceased to work properly because of the failure of Robert Curthose to maintain them, not because they were themselves inadequate. Nor is there evidence to suggest that Henry was trying to assimilate the administrations of the two parts of his realm – indeed the fact that the justices, one of Henry's innovations, had different functions on both sides of the Channel is clear evidence against it. His aim was simply to make the machinery work efficiently and effectively.

To an extent the use of writs would have achieved this. But we should not push the argument for increased administrative efficiency too far. The instructions contained in a writ could have been transmitted by a messenger, and were often just as transitory. Writs did not give the administration a greater and more reliable memory, as there is no evidence that office copies were kept.[187] What the use of writs did do was, first, save the duke the inconvenience of sending one of his own household to convey a command or attest to the veracity of a letter. Instead beneficiaries themselves now carried their own writs and had them published in the relevant forum, and could do so as there could be no argument with a document that carried an impression of the royal duke's seal. It was the increasing use of,

---

[185]   Le Patourel, *Norman Empire*, pp. 244–5. Quoted in Bates, 'Norman writs', 267, where his view was rejected.

[186]   Orderic, vi. 86, 92–4, 136–8.

[187]   Clanchy, *From Memory to Written Record*, pp. 90–1. It is odd, though, that writers such as Anselm did keep copies and then chose to preserve some but not others.

and familiarity with, the seal that provided perhaps the second important result of the routine use of writs in Normandy. Particularly because the Norman coinage did not bear a portrait of the prince, the use of the seal in Normandy allowed a 'routinization of charisma', which might in turn have helped to strengthen the duke's authority.[188]

In contrast, it is not clear that Norman beneficiaries saw many advantages to the writ to begin with. The tiny number of known Norman writs from before 1106 suggests that until that point Norman beneficiaries were reluctant to ask for or to accept them. It is possible that they began to change their minds as a result of their experiences in England, where they could see the utility of such documents at first hand. Equally, as the dukes and their officials became increasingly concerned to maximize the revenues produced by the demesne and by tolls and other dues, so writs evidencing exemptions from such payments probably became more important and more desirable, especially as they needed to be produced regularly. It is even possible that the duke's officials were told not to recognize such rights in the absence of a writ and a seal. Their attractiveness would have continued to grow as beneficiaries began to take the initiative in developing new formulae that would be of benefit to them. By the 1120s, wording had been developed that would permit swifter justice should ducal or seigniorial officials refuse to recognize the rights or exemptions evidenced by writs. This was the *nisi feceris* clause, which is likely to have been a development demanded by beneficiaries – and not just from the dukes but from the popes, too, as we have seen already.[189]

Over time, then, the writ caught on in Normandy. The result was that Norman lords began to issue their own Norman writs in a form that mirrored the royal style, presumably for practical as well as symbolic reasons. The earliest date from the last years of the eleventh century, although the practice only seems to have taken off during the course of Henry's reign. Thus Roger of Montgommery sent a writ to his son, Robert of Bellême, which must date to before Roger's death in 1094.[190] Amaury of Montfort, count of Evreux, sent at least one writ to his officials sometime after his inheritance of the county in 1119.[191] So too did Robert of La Haye-du-Puits, a man who was prominent in Henry I's Norman administration.[192] There are also two writs of Count Waleran of Meulan, dating from the 1120s, in the cartulary of the abbey of Tiron,[193] while the rediscovered cartulary

---

[188] See Clanchy, *From Memory to Written Record*, p. 67, albeit there with reference to Henry II.
[189] See above, Chapter 8, pp. 480–3.
[190] Ctl. Sées, fo. 95r.
[191] AD Calvados, H 7761.
[192] Ctl. Montebourg, p. 113 (no. 307).
[193] *Ctl. Tiron*, ed. M. L. Merlet, vol. 1 (Chartres, 1883), pp. 76–7 (nos. lv and lvi).

of Saint-Etienne in Caen includes a writ of Stephen of Blois, styled *consul* of Mortain, concerning the continued validity of the grants made to the abbey by Count Robert of Mortain.[194] Moreover, writ-form drafting was adopted by lords outside, but with links to, the Anglo-Norman *regnum*. Count Theobald of Blois was a close ally of Henry, and brother of King Stephen, and *c.* 1140 he issued an act in writ form for the abbey of Saint-Jean-en-Vallée of Chartres, which survives as an original.[195] A small number of acts that exhibit characteristics of the writ were also issued by King Roger II of Sicily (1130–54) and by his son King William I (1154–66), and grandson King William II (1166–89).[196]

The dukes' vicomtes

By the first decades of the eleventh century, Normandy was administered by a variety of officials who acted in the duke's name and in his interests. The most important of these officials were the *vicomtes*. We can trace them and their territories in the ducal *acta*, but their functions and responsibilities never become entirely clear, even during the reign of Henry I when the royal duke's writs provide an extremely useful new body of evidence. Moreover, we know nothing at all about the ducal *vicomtes* during the tenth century. Indeed, it is entirely possible that they did not exist. With the ducal demesne concentrated along the Seine and the coast of the Pays de Caux, and the duke himself based at Rouen, Richard I might well have relied on stewards who had been charged to look after individual, or small groups of, vills. The ducal demesne that lay further afield was conquered only from the 960s, with Bayeux falling to the duke *c.* 989. In such circumstances, *vicomtes* would have been surplus to requirements until almost the end of Richard I's reign.

That was because the *vicomtes*' most important job was to administer the ducal demesne in their *vicomtés* – an established if mutable territory often coterminous

---

[194] Ctl. Caen, fo. 23r. David Bates has noted that there is also an original writ of Stephen as count of Mortain in the archives départementales de l'Orne, but under the definitions followed here that act is in fact a charter (AD Eure, H 10).

[195] AD Eure-et-Loir, H 3093; *Cartulaire de l'abbaye de Saint-Jean-en-Vallée de Chartres*, ed. R. Merlet (Chartres, 1906), p. 31 no. 51.

[196] *Rogerii II Regis Diplomata Latina*, ed. C. Brühl, Codex Diplomaticus Regni Siciliae: II.1 (Böhlau, Verlag, Köln, Wien, 1987), no. 17; *Guillelmi I Regis Diplomata*, ed. H. Enzensberger, Codex Diplomaticus Regni Siciliae: III (Böhlau, Verlag, Köln, Weimar, Wien, 1996), nos. 3, 26. Graham Loud briefly noted the use of mandates in the Norman kingdom of Sicily, but did not discuss their form or their similarity to Anglo-Norman writs (G. Loud, 'The chancery and charters of the kings of Sicily, 1130–1212', *EHR*, 124 (2009), 779–810).

with the *pagi*.[197] Ducal *acta* produced from the 1020s indicate that they oversaw the collection of the revenues it produced, and organized their transportation to wherever the duke wanted them sent. They seem to have assisted, too, with the administration of justice in their *vicomtés*, and they might have acted to preserve the peace in times of emergency. Their functions, then, were similar but not identical to those of the Carolingian official on which they were apparently modelled.[198]

Aside from collecting the revenues produced by the duke's demesne, which is considered in detail in the following chapter, the *vicomtes* also kept track of the grants that the dukes made out of it, and also of the additions made to it through forfeiture or wardship. At least, they performed these functions from the end of the eleventh century, even if we want to conjecture that they had such responsibilities from a much earlier date. As a result, if a *vicomte* did not know that a grant had been made, he would refuse to recognize that it had been. Thus, in 1080, Robert Bertram, *vicomte* of the Cotentin, unaware of a grant of the customs of Héauville to the monks of Marmoutier, refused to release the money to them.[199]

A writ of Robert Curthose dating from 1092 reveals that the *vicomtes* would also put a beneficiary into seisin if a grant was made out of the ducal demesne: 'Count Robert to Eudo the *vicomte* greeting. I command you that you seise Abbot Roger of the land of Neuilly and of the land of *Rosce* since I gave to the abbey of St Mary of Montebourg the said land in alms for the soul of my father and my mother and for the souls of my brothers and for my soul and those of my relatives.'[200] A writ-charter issued by Henry I in 1107 × 1109 for the monks of Jumièges provides a second example: 'Henry king of the English to William archbishop of Rouen and Robert of Candos and all his sworn men of the Roumois greeting. Know that I

---

[197] Probably the earliest appearance of a *vicomte* whose title was attached to a geographical area, namely Goscelin, *vicomte* of Rouen, is found in an act for the abbey of La Trinité-du-Mont, just outside Rouen, which dates from 1030 × 1035 (*RADN*, no. 83). That men attested simply as *uicecomes* rather than as the *uicecomes* of a certain place was, however, probably just diplomatic practice. It should not be taken as meaning that a man could be a *vicomte* without a territory. Thus even during the reign of Henry I, when it is certain that *vicomtes* had authority over a county, we have an attestation by Ranulf le Meschin, the *vicomte*, in 1120 (*Regesta ii.* no. 1102); Anselm the *vicomte* in the period 1120–35 (*Regesta ii.* nos. 1921, 1697); and Robert the *vicomte* in 1114 × 1135 and *c.* 1116 × 1135 (*Regesta ii.* nos. 1577, 1963). In this respect it may also be noted that counts usually attested simply as 'count' and not as, for example, count of Arques or count of Mortain. Only bishops were regularly named as bishops of a particular diocese rather than appearing simply as 'bishop' (see for example, *RADN*, nos. 133, 141, 148).

[198] F. L. Ganshof, *Frankish Institutions under Charlemagne*, trans. B. Lyon and M. Lyon (New York, 1968), 28–33 and see also Hagger, 'The Norman *vicomte*', 65–83.

[199] *Regesta: William*, no. 200.

[200] Bouvris, 'Un bref inédit', 150.

have given and granted to the abbey of Jumièges the land of the forest of Roumare that is called Duclair and it shall hold it in peace and in perpetuity. And you, Robert, shall seise it of it.'[201]

The very fact that this second grant appears in a writ-charter addressed to the archbishop of Rouen, the *vicomte*, and the county community of the Roumois indicates that, at least during the reign of Henry I, the *vicomte* would preside over the county court. Henry's fourteen surviving Norman writ-charters provide almost the only evidence that such courts existed during his reign, but as the address clauses fail to make sense if there were not such a court, their testimony is compelling.[202] In addition, it is likely that a diploma for the monks of Marmoutier records William Crispin, *vicomte* of the Vexin, presiding over what looks to have been a county court during the reign of Robert Curthose. The act relates that Robert of La Faillie had claimed the property that his brothers, Ralph and Roger, had given to the abbey in Noyers-en-Vexin, and that a settlement had subsequently been reached 'in the court of Robert, count of the Normans, at the castle of Neaufles, before William Crispin, of that land *vicomte*'.[203] That the *vicomtes* presided over these gatherings, in the company of the bishop, is consistent with their management of the duke's rights, and in particular with the duke's right to expect his will to be put into effect. Thus the slight evidence that we have indicates that the county court was where grants, gifts, and the results of lawsuits were published, and that it might provide a forum for the public settlement of disputes by the parties concerned. There is no evidence, however, that the county court acted as a forum in which lawsuits were heard and decided as a matter of course.[204]

As well as putting into effect subtractions from the demesne, the *vicomtes* might also make additions to it. After Helias of Saint-Saëns fled Normandy with William Clito *c*. 1110, the *vicomte* of Arques, Robert of Beauchamp, took Helias's castle and county into the king's hand.[205] The same Robert was also given custody of the lands of Walter of Auffay after his death sometime during Henry's reign. Presumably this, too, was in his capacity as *vicomte*, as the estates were subsequently purchased by Jordan of Sauqueville, a transaction that suggests Robert had not fined for them himself.[206]

---

[201] *Chs. Jumièges*, i. 136–7 (no. 49) = *Regesta*, ii. no. 912.

[202] See Hagger, 'The earliest Norman writs revisited', 190–4.

[203] L. Delisle and L. Passy, *Memoires et notes de M. Auguste Le Prevost pour servir a l'histoire du département de l'Eure*, vol. 2 (Evreux, 1864), p. 506.

[204] See above, Chapter 8, p. 492.

[205] Orderic, vi. 162–4. Hollister suggested either 1110 or 1111 (Hollister, *Henry*, p. 227), while David Crouch plumped for 1110 (Crouch, *The Normans*, p. 185). Judith Green also implicitly favoured 1110 (Green, *Henry*, p. 122).

[206] Orderic, iii. 258.

In some cases the honours, or parts of honours, that fell to the duke were converted into *vicomtés* while they remained in their possession. For example, Ivry was taken from Bishop Hugh of Bayeux by Duke Robert the Magnificent and remained part of the ducal demesne throughout the reign of William the Bastard and into that of Robert Curthose. Before Curthose granted it to William of Breteuil *c.* 1090, Ivry and its appurtenant honour had become a *vicomté*.[207] Similarly, Moulins-la-Marche had been held by William of Moulins and his sons since the mid eleventh century.[208] Simon of Moulins died between 1118, when he is noticed supporting King Henry at the siege of Evreux, and Michaelmas 1130, when Robert of Vern (Vere) fined for the English lands of his wife – that is Simon's widow – in the pipe roll.[209] On Simon's death his Norman honour of Moulins-la-Marche devolved to the duke, presumably because he lacked heirs. By 1135, and probably before, the honour had been integrated into the ducal demesne and placed in the hands of a *vicomte*. This is revealed by an act of 1130 × 1135 that granted to the monks of Saint-Père of Chartres the tithes of any new acquisitions they obtained in Moulins-la-Marche and Bonsmoulins. The act was addressed to Normandy generally, but also to the *vicomte* of these two places, for while the honour was held by the duke he needed to know what was given to whom.[210] The *vicomté* would have been extinguished in 1137 when King Stephen gave Moulins-la-Marche to Count Rotrou of the Perche and Bonsmoulins to Richer of L'Aigle.[211] Thirdly, the *vicomté* of Conteville, which appears unambiguously for the first time only in an act of Henry I for the abbey of Saint-Georges at Boscherville,[212] was probably created after Count William of Mortain forfeited his estates in 1106.

In addition to their administration of the duke's demesne, the *vicomtes* also seem to have acted to enforce the duke's peace, although the evidence for this function is slight indeed and again dates only from the end of the eleventh century. On 4 August 1073, there was a riot at Rouen as a result of the actions of Archbishop John. The *vicomte* of Rouen, 'having heard that the archbishop was

---

[207] Jumièges, ii. 226–8 and notes.

[208] E. Tabuteau, 'The family of Moulins-la-Marche in the eleventh century', *Medieval Prosopography* 13 (1992), 37.

[209] Orderic, vi. 230; *PR 31 Henry I*, 64. Adeliza, Simon's widow, is not identified in the pipe roll, but Robert is known to have married her from acts for Monk Horton priory (J. R. Scott, 'Charters of Monk Horton Priory', *Archaeologia Cantiana*, 10 (1876), 270, no. 3; 271, no. 4), which name his wife as Adeliza the daughter of Hugh of Montfort. The pipe roll entry, then, may be supposed to relate to this marriage.

[210] *Ctl Saint-Père*, ii. 640–641 (no. 25) = *Regesta*, ii. no. 1932. The abbreviation *uic'*, found in the original (BnF MS lat. 9221, no. 8), which is the standard abbreviation of *uicecomes* or *uicecomitibus*, was expanded incorrectly to *uicariis* by Guérard.

[211] Orderic, vi. 484.

[212] *Regesta*, ii. 353 (no. clxxvi) (with errors) = *Regesta*, ii. no. 1440.

encircled on all sides, and fearing that he would be the target of an ill-considered act, and would himself be accused of a crime, gathered a gang of soldiers, all of whom he placed under the royal *ban*, hastened to help, and with no one resisting … removed the danger'.[213] Here, then, at a time of civil unrest, the *vicomte* acted to save the archbishop and to restore order. While it is possible that the *vicomte*'s response was ad hoc and owing to his presence at the scene, it does seem clear that the *vicomtes* had some role in enforcing order in their counties. The first of the canons of the Council of Lillebonne of 1080 provides that in the last resort the duke's *vicomte* should act to enforce the Truce of God, by compelling an offender to submit himself to the bishop, presumably by arrest or distraint.[214] He would, therefore, act in order to enforce the peace, even if retrospectively.

Where justice was concerned, however, and despite earlier arguments to the contrary, the *vicomtes*' role was limited.[215] As discussed above, they helped to facilitate the doing of justice by apprehending and holding malefactors or taking distraint, but apparently did not have jurisdiction over certain pleas as the English sheriff did.[216] This interpretation of the *vicomtes*' function – that they had no role in the actual exercise of justice – is supported by the address clauses of the Norman writs of King Henry I. While some of Henry's English writs command sheriffs to hold pleas, none of his Norman writs instruct *vicomtes* to do likewise.[217] In Henry I's Normandy, writs commanding the holding of pleas were addressed to justices or to lords with jurisdiction over their men, such as the bishop of Bayeux.[218] That continued to be the case under Geoffrey of Anjou.[219] The *vicomtes*' role in the

---

[213] *AAbps*, pp. 43, 57. For a detailed discussion of this event see A. Alexander, 'Riots, reform, and rivalry: religious life in Rouen, c. 1073–c. 1092', *ANS*, 33 (2011), 23–40.

[214] Orderic, iii. 26.

[215] For the contrasting view see, for example, Valin, *Le duc et sa cour*, p. 96; *NI*, pp. 46–7; Douglas, *William the Conqueror*, p. 140; Yver, 'Premières institutions', 328; Le Patourel, *Norman Empire*, p. 258; Bauduin, *Première Normandie*, p. 277.

[216] *Historia Ecclesie Abbendonensis*, ed. and trans. Hudson, ii. 170–2; *English Lawsuits from William I to Richard I*, ed. and trans. R. van Caenegem, Selden Society, 107 (1991), 197 (no. 232); 261–18 (no. 254); *Monasticon*, vi.2, pp. 992–3. For the previous discussion, see above, Chapter 8, pp. 487–9.

[217] *English Lawsuits*, 567–9 (no. 517) = *Regesta*, ii. no. 600; *Historia Ecclesie Abbendonensis*, ed. and trans. J. Hudson, vol. 2, Oxford 2002, 134–6 = *Regesta*, ii. no. 815; Galbraith 'Royal charters to Winchester', 392 (no. xxvii) = *Regesta*, ii. no. 1185.

[218] See above, Chapter 8, pp. 477–8, 481.

[219] For example, *Regesta*, iii. nos. 53, 54, 55, 57. In addition, the *Etat de l'Avranchin*, dating from the end of the twelfth century, notes that the *vicomte* of Avranches 'has all the trespasses and he has the customs of the burgesses of Genêts who buy or sell in Avranches', meaning that the *vicomte* had the right to the fines accruing, not the right to hear these pleas (*Recueil Henri II*, i. 345). Likewise, the statement that 'the *vicomte* pleads three times each year at Ardevon and in Genets to obtain his customs from the abbot and

enforcement of judgements was also limited. In England it was the sheriffs who were commanded to reseise institutions or individuals with possessions they had recovered, but the Norman writs reveal that in Henry I's Normandy this job fell to the justices.[220]

Equally, and again despite a long-held view to the contrary, the office of *vicomte* did not apparently encompass the role of military commander or custodian of ducal castles.[221] The story that has been most often cited to support the opposite view is William of Jumièges's tale of how Nigel of the Cotentin defeated a force of English soldiers that Æthelred II had sent to Normandy to 'inflict shame and harm' on Duke Richard II by devastating the land and bringing the duke himself back to England as a prisoner. Nigel, he tells us, 'gathered the knights of the Cotentin together with a multitude of common people' and defeated the English raiders.[222] This raid occurred *c.* 1008. There is no evidence that Nigel had been appointed *vicomte* of the Cotentin by this date, and Jumièges did not suggest that he was acting in that capacity when he saw off the English invaders. He was simply the greatest of the local lords, who happened to be on the spot when the English troops landed, and who could use his position to launch a counter-attack. Instead, where ducal troops were mobilized as part of a planned military campaign, they were led by members of the duke's military household.

Thus, in around 1106, it was Robert of Étoutteville (Stutteville) who 'was in charge of [the duke's] household knights and castles in the region of Caux'.[223] He is not known to have acted as *vicomte* at any stage in his career. In 1105, it was Gunter of Aunay, castellan of Bayeux, who led the duke's household knights, and

take them away (*Vicecomes placitat ter in anno in Ardeuun et Genez de consuetudinibus suis absportatis et procurator ab abbate*)' (*Recueil Henry II*, i. 346) is not about holding pleas but obtaining the fines and forfeitures that had resulted from guilty verdicts found in the abbot's court.

[220] *Chronica Abbatiae Ramesiensis*, ed. W. D. Macray, Rolls Series (London, 1886), p. 217 = *Regesta*, ii. no. 574; *Chronica Abbatiae Ramesiensis*, p. 217 = *Regesta*, ii. no. 582; *English Lawsuits*, 156 (no. 187b) = *Regesta*, ii. no. 997; *Historia Ecclesie Abbendonensis*, ed. and trans. Hudson, ii. 108–10 = *Regesta*, ii. no. 1133. Justices are never addressed in such acts. For Normandy see: *Livre Noir*, i. 43–4 (no. 37) = *Regesta*, ii. no. 1898; *NI*, p. 102 (no. 14) = *Regesta*, ii. no. 1952. Robert Curthose's writ for Montebourg commanded Eudo the *vicomte* to give seisin to the abbey of the possessions that the duke had granted it (Bouvris, 'Un bref inédit', 150). In other words, to put his grant into effect. Clearly, this is not the same as restoring seisin after a plea.

[221] For this earlier view see, for example: Valin, *Le duc et sa cour*, p. 96; *NI*, pp. 46–7; Douglas, *William the Conqueror*, pp. 140–1; Yver, 'Premières institutions', 327–31; Le Patourel, *Norman Empire*, p. 258; Bates, *Normandy*, p. 158 (although more reluctantly); Bauduin, *Première Normandie*, pp. 277 and 234, n. 316.

[222] Jumièges, ii. 10–12.

[223] Orderic, vi. 73.

it was Gunter again who was leading the men of Caen and Bayeux when they captured Henry I's ally, Robert fitz Haimo, at Secqueville-en-Bessin.[224] The *vicomte* of the Bessin at the time was, of course, Ranulf le Meschin. At Tinchebray in 1106, the three divisions of Henry's army were led by Count Robert of Meulan, Henry's most trusted adviser, Ranulf le Meschin, and William of Warenne. Of these three, only Ranulf was a *vicomte*, but his office was irrelevant. He was put in charge of a division because he was a member of Henry's household.[225] At Brémule in 1119 the royal knights were led by Rualon of Avranches and Ralph the Red of Pont d'Echanfray, both trusted members of the household.[226]

As was probably also the case with the English sheriff, then, *vicomtes* did not generally lead the military levies produced by their shires.[227] The *vicomtes* were not generally entrusted with the custody of the ducal castles located within their *vicomtés*, either, even though they might have used them as their base of operations.[228] In 1077, the castle at Rouen was in the custody of Roger of Ivry, the king's butler.[229] The *vicomte* of Rouen at this time was almost certainly called Ansfrid, named as such in an act for the abbey of Saint-Pierre at Préaux, dating from between March and August 1078.[230] The castle of Rouen was subsequently held by Count Henry of the Cotentin, the future Henry I, in 1090, and by Hugh of Nonant in 1106, neither of whom, so far as we can tell, was ever *vicomte* of Rouen.[231] Similarly, the castle at Exmes was held by Gilbert fitz Engenulf of L'Aigle in 1090 and not by the *vicomte* of the Hiémois, Robert of Bellême,[232] while the castle at Caen was held by Robert fitz Haimo and later by Earl Robert of Gloucester and not by the *vicomtes* of the Bessin.[233]

There were naturally exceptions to this general rule. William I Crispin was both granted the castle at Neaufles (although this was not strictly speaking a ducal castle) and, at the same time, made *vicomte* of the Vexin, although he did not hold

---

[224] Orderic, vi. 60–2, 78; Wace, 214, 216.

[225] J. O. Prestwich, 'The military household of the Norman kings', *EHR*, 96 (1981), 1–35, especially 15–17.

[226] Orderic, vi. 246.

[227] Green, *English Sheriffs*, p. 11.

[228] This was also the case in England (Green, *English Sheriffs*, p. 11). Annie Renoux's work at Fécamp has revealed that the ducal palace and *vicomte*'s office comprised two separate buildings, facing each other across the courtyard (Renoux, *Fécamp: du palais ducal*, pp. 446–7). The castle at Caen was certainly large enough for a similar arrangement to have existed there.

[229] Orderic, ii. 358.

[230] *Ctl. Préaux*, no. A139.

[231] Malmesbury, *GR*, i. 712 (Henry); Orderic, vi. 62 (Hugh).

[232] Orderic, iv. 200.

[233] Wace, p. 218; Orderic, vi. 516.

other ducal castles in his county such as those at Neuf-Marché or Gisors. The *vicomtes* of Arques seem to have had custody of the fortress at Arques, albeit not necessarily those at Bures-en-Bray and Neufchâtel. The castle at Falaise was held by Thurstan Goz while he was *vicomte* of the Hiémois *c*. 1040–*c*. 1043, although we do not know if he also held Argentan and Exmes.[234] Custody of the castle at Saint-James-de-Beuvron was given to Richard Goz, *vicomte* of Avranches, by Duke William when it was built in 1064, although he and his successors might not have held that at Avranches until later.[235] Robert of Torigni noted that 'Robert count of Meulan was castellan of the stronghold (Ivry), while he was *vicomte* in the town' (note *while* he was *vicomte*, not *because* he was *vicomte*).[236] Wigan the marshal, too, most likely held ducal castles while in post. Orderic tells us that after Henry I's death he handed over to the Empress Matilda 'Argentan and Exmes and Domfront and other fortified towns (*oppida*) which he governed as *vicomte* by the king's command', and while the word Orderic used is ambiguous, he certainly implied that the castles were surrendered with the towns.[237] But in these cases, and others like them, the *vicomtes* only held ducal castles within their counties because they enjoyed the confidence and favour of the duke. If that confidence were lost, then the castles might be given to others, even if the *vicomtes* themselves remained in post. That the dukes could do this is another indication that the custody of the castles did not pertain as of right to the office. Castellans were instead chosen by the duke and held their charges at his pleasure, at least until Henry I's reign. As Abbot Anselm of Le Bec said to Count Robert of Meulan, who was not the relevant *vicomte*: 'This castle (Brionne) is not part of your inheritance, but the gift of your lord prince, who, at any time he wants, may take back his own property.'[238]

Vicomtes, then, were, by and large, administrators. For the most part they did not lead troops or defend castles, and even when they did it was not as a result of their office. And yet despite the rather unglamorous appearance of their work, men sought the office. And not just middle-ranking men, but members of some of the greatest families of the duchy. That is because to be the *vicomte* conferred prestige on the holder. The title indicated that he stood in the duke's place, and so his local standing was enhanced and his value as a patron increased. Equally, the administrator of the duke's demesne could obtain a variety of perks and offer

---

[234] Jumièges, ii. 100–2.

[235] Jumièges, ii. 208. William of Poitiers confirmed the date (Poitiers, p. 72). Orderic implied that Hugh of Chester did not hold Avranches during Henry's term as count of the Cotentin (Orderic, iv. 120, 220).

[236] Jumièges, ii. 226.

[237] Orderic, vi. 454. Orderic's use of the word *oppida*, however, might mean simply that he held only the towns and not the castles within them.

[238] *On the Liberty of the Abbey of Le Bec*, p. 136

a degree of patronage to his own followers, just as English sheriffs did across the Channel.[239] Lesser officials were perhaps appointed at the *vicomte*'s recommendation and might be willing to pay for it, too. Domesday Book suggests that 100s. was the going rate for such shrieval favour in England.[240] Favoured men might otherwise be given additional time to pay their taxes, or might even find the sum demanded of them reduced. To provide an English example, Abbot Ingulf of Abingdon was 'long accustomed to give 100s. annually to the sheriff of Berkshire to treat the abbey's men more leniently and help them in pleas and hundreds'.[241] The Norman *vicomte* might not have been able to help with regard to pleas to the same extent, but there were other things that he might or might not do in order to assist his clients. The office of *vicomte*, then, almost certainly gave its holder the chance to feather his own nest, reward friends, or hurt enemies under cover of bureaucracy and red tape, as well as to bask in their relationship with the duke and their presidency of the county court.

The office was thus something worth having, so it is perhaps not surprising that those who held it attempted to keep it. That many of the Norman *vicomtés* became the hereditary possessions of their families is well known and often repeated. The move from office to property can be seen in the cases of the *vicomtés* of the Avranchin, the Cotentin, the Bessin, the Vexin, and to a lesser extent the Hiémois and Arques-Talou. But a general statement does not do justice to the various and particular processes that saw each of these counties become part of a family's inheritance. Equally, it should not be assumed that the dukes intended that the *vicomtés* should become heritable when the first appointments were made, and it should perhaps be remembered that during the first half of the eleventh century there was less expectation that offices and benefices should be heritable, too.

This is not the place for a full survey of the descents of the Norman *vicomtés*, but an examination of the descents of the counties of the Cotentin and Vexin, even though they are necessarily idiosyncratic, can nonetheless reveal some of the wider trends that affected the inheritance of the *vicomtés* and indeed of offices generally during the later eleventh century.

The appointment of William Crispin to the *vicomté* of the Vexin at some time between 1035 and 1054, perhaps 1052–54,[242] was almost certainly not made in the

---

[239] On the behaviour of the English sheriffs of the late eleventh century see S. Harvey, *Domesday Book of Judgement* (Oxford, 2014), pp. 246, 251, 253–5.

[240] Harvey, *Domesday*, p. 246.

[241] *Historia Ecclesie Abbendonensis*, ed. and trans. Hudson, ii. 314, quoted in Harvey, *Domesday*, pp. 251–2.

[242] *RADN*, nos. 66, 67; Green, 'Lords of the Norman Vexin', pp 49–50; Bauduin, *Première Normandie*, p. 276. Bauduin suggested the narrower date range. The duke's action

expectation that the office should be inherited by William's children, despite the twelfth-century assertion of Milo Crispin.[243] William I died during the reign of Robert Curthose, and it was he who permitted William II to succeed to his father's lands and office, perhaps in the hope that he would consequently retain a firm supporter on this difficult frontier. That began the chain of descent from father to son, and established a precedent or custom that was firmly established when William II died c. 1100 and William III was allowed to inherit in turn. As a result of these unopposed successions, reinforced by developing ideas about inheritance more generally, by the time Henry I took control of the duchy, William III was so firmly entrenched that Henry could not eject him from either lands or office despite the fact that Crispin attempted to injure or kill Henry at the battle of Brémule in 1119 (most likely as a result of suffering exile between 1106 and 1113).[244] And so even though Henry banished him from the duchy, there is no evidence that the duke recovered his county, and it may be supposed that in his absence the *vicomté* was administered by members of Crispin's household or family on his behalf.

The *vicomté* of the Cotentin was another that became hereditary, but here the descent of the county was less clear-cut until Henry I's reign. The first known *vicomte* of the Cotentin was Nigel I, who passed the office to his son Nigel II c. 1042. Probably because the hereditary principle had not become adequately established by the time Nigel revolted in 1046–47, William the Bastard was able to recover the office and pass it to one of the men he had settled on part of Nigel's honour, Robert Bertram.

Robert held the office down to his death c. 1080.[245] He was not, however, succeeded by his son, William, but by Eudo Haldup, lord of Créances, co-founder of Lessay abbey, and by then related to Duke William through marriage.[246] Eudo made a donation to the monks of Marmoutier with the style 'vicomte of the county of the Cotentin' in 1081, and also attested two acts for the monks of Saint-Etienne of Caen as *vicomte* at about the same time.[247]

One of those acts was also witnessed by a Nigel the *vicomte*. Although Nigel II had continued to be styled *vicomte* during his period in exile, it seems unlikely that the monks of a Norman ducal abbey would have given him the title unless he really had been *vicomte* at the time. If that was the case, it appears at first sight as if

---

might suggest the expected deterioration in the relationship between William and Malger in the build up to, or aftermath of, Count William of Arques's rebellion.

[243] Milo Crispin, *Miraculum quo B. Maria subuenit Guillelmo Crispino Seniori*, in *PL*, 150, col. 737; translation in van Houts, *Normans*, pp. 85–6.

[244] *Letters of St Anselm*, no. 401 and Orderic, vi. 91 n. 3; Orderic, vi. 180, 238–40.

[245] *Regesta: William*, nos. 200 (for his actions as *vicomte*); 49 (for his death).

[246] *Regesta: William*, no. 201.

[247] Delisle, *Sires de Saint-Sauveur*, pp. 44–5 (no. 40); *Regesta: William*, nos. 48, 49.

we have two men holding office at the same time. This is possible. Specific *vicomtés* are not named. Eudo might have been *vicomte* of Coutances and Nigel *vicomte* of the Cotentin. A better explanation might be to suppose that the joint attestation of Eudo and Nigel 'the *vicomte*' is actually an example of the monks' practice of collecting *signa* over time. That would then indicate that Eudo had been replaced by Nigel II for a period during (most likely) the last years of William the Bastard's reign.[248] This is also suggested by Duke William's confirmation of Nigel's gifts to the monks of his foundation at Saint-Sauveur-le-Vicomte, made between 1080 and 1085, in which Nigel is also styled *vicomte*.[249]

After 1087, the question of who should hold the *vicomté* might have been pushed into the background as the future Henry I took over the county of the Cotentin, turning the local *vicomtes* into his officers rather than the duke's. Between Henry's exile in 1091 and his return around a year later, however, Robert Curthose sent a writ to Eudo the *vicomte*. His identity is uncertain. It might have been Eudo Haldup, who lived until *c.* 1105, but it is perhaps more likely to have been Eudo, the brother of Nigel II of Saint-Sauveur, who was certainly in possession of the office in 1104.[250] Eudo was perhaps allowed to succeed his brother by Count Henry, as he needed to win the friendship of the Montbray family and might have hoped to make a good impression by returning the office to Bishop Geoffrey's kinsman.[251] After that date, however, we know little about the succession to the *vicomté* until the 1130s when Roger was acting as *vicomte*.[252] He was the brother of Nigel III, who seems to have acted as *vicomte* immediately before him, although their relationship to Nigel II and Eudo is not so clear.[253] Roger remained in office under Stephen until his murder in 1138 by supporters of the Empress Matilda.[254] The title then passed by right of inheritance to Jordan Taisson, a right based presumably on this second period of family office-holding that had begun in the late 1080s and which was continued under Curthose and Henry I.

---

[248] *Regesta: William*, no. 48. For the practices of the monks of Saint-Etienne see the discussion at *Regesta: William*, p. 225.

[249] *Regesta: William*, no. 260.

[250] Bouvris, 'Un bref inédit', 150 (quoted above, *infra*, p. 543); Delisle, *Sires de Saint-Sauveur*, pp. 55–8 (no. 46), which act also establishes the family relationship between Eudo and Nigel.

[251] The *De statu* remarks the kinship between Geoffrey and Nigel II, and thus Eudo (*GC*, xi. Instr. col. 222).

[252] Roger attested the *Emptiones Eudonis* of 1129 × 1131 as Roger the *vicomte* (AD Calvados, H 1834; Chanteux, *Recueil*, no. 79). He is also ambiguously styled Roger the *vicomte* of Saint-Sauveur in the Inquisition of 1133 (*Inquisition*, p. 16).

[253] Delisle, *Sires de Saint-Sauveur*, pp. (no. 47). The lack of clarity regarding the relationship to Nigel II was noted by Delisle, *Sires de Saint-Sauveur*, p. 27.

[254] Orderic, vi. 512.

By the end of the second decade of the twelfth century, then, a number of *vicomtés* had become hereditary and were no longer 'revocable and entirely dependent on the goodwill of the duke'.[255] That was perhaps because Curthose, and perhaps Henry, too, was compelled to make concessions to their *vicomtes* in order to retain their loyalty, or to give them the necessary strength and investment to stand against their enemies. Curthose was unfortunate here. Such demands for the recognition of a hereditary right to lands and offices would almost certainly have become louder during his reign no matter how strong his leadership, simply because of the strengthening of inheritance customs, and tightening of ideas of lordship, at about this time.[256] Thus, as Lucien Valin noted, little by little, most of the *vicomtés* fell to the law that converted offices into fiefs, thereby undermining the dukes' ability to appoint men of their own choosing to the office.[257] There was little that the dukes could do about this. Even Henry I was powerless to hold back that tide. But it is tempting to think that he found a way to minimize the problem that having hereditary *vicomtes* like William III Crispin and Robert of Bellême might cause. The multifarious farms that can be seen in the Norman pipe roll of 1180 relate to assets that might at one time have belonged to the *vicomté*. If so, we may conjecture that it was Henry who had first hived off and farmed these assets to officials other than the *vicomte* in order to limit the damage that malcontent but unsackable *vicomtes* might do to a duke's finances and to his power in the localities. They might also have had the advantage of reducing a *vicomte*'s ability to build local support through patronage.

That said, there is no evidence to suggest that the dukes were generally unhappy with their loss of control over the *vicomtés*. Indeed, successive dukes tried and failed permanently to alienate the county of Arques-Talou from the demesne. The *vicomté* was passed from Goscelin fitz Heddo to his son-in-law Godfrey, the son of Osbern of Bolbec and Gunnor's sister Wevia,[258] *c.* 1035, shortly after Goscelin had taken over the *vicomté* of Rouen. But this first attempt to turn the *vicomté* into

---

[255] J.-M. Bouvris, 'Une famille de vassaux des vicomtes de Bayeux au XIe siècle: les Broc', *Revue de la département de la Manche*, 19 (1977), 6–7.

[256] The strength of inheritance customs can be seen in Orderic's narrative, which at least reflects the situation in the 1130s when he was writing, and can also be seen in the *Leges Henrici Primi* (*LHP*, p. 224, paras. 70.18–70.23). For more recent discussions see, for example: R. DeAragon, 'The growth of secure inheritance in Anglo-Norman England', *JMH*, 8 (1982), 381–91; Tabuteau, *Transfers*, p. 102; Hudson, *Land, Law, and Lordship*, pp. 71–85. Strengthening lordship is perhaps reflected in the lists of losses sustained by the nuns of Holy Trinity, Caen, as well as by Orderic's complaints about unjust exactions (*Chs. Caen*, pp. 125–8 (no. 15); Orderic, iv. 296; vi. 46, 196, 206, 272, 330. This suggestion derives from Power, *The Norman Frontier*, pp. 367–8).

[257] Valin, *Le duc et sa cour*, pp. 97–8.

[258] Jumièges, ii. 268.

a hereditary possession was cut short when William the Bastard made his uncle, William, count of Arques *c.* 1037.[259] Although Count William had a son, his rebellion and forfeiture ensured that the second attempt to alienate the county would also fail. Then, in 1090, at a time when he was losing control of Upper Normandy to his brother, 'Duke Robert, to put up a barrier against his numerous enemies, gave his daughter by a concubine in marriage to Helias, the son of Lambert of Saint-Saëns, and provided Arques and Bures and the adjoining province as her marriage portion, so that Helias would resist his enemies and defend the county of Talou'. Helias might not have been made count of Arques by Curthose, but it does look as though he was intended to act at least as the hereditary *vicomte*, making this grant the third attempt permanently to alienate Arques from the ducal demesne.[260] Helias held the castles and county until *c.* 1110 when Henry I made his failed attempt to arrest William Clito and Helias fled Normandy with his charge. Incidentally, the attempted arrest was made by the man who had already apparently been appointed *vicomte* of Arques, despite Helias's claims to the county: Robert of Beauchamp.[261]

In all the counties so far discussed, there was only a very limited amount of ducal demesne. That might have been why the dukes appear to have been reasonably relaxed about allowing the *vicomtes* to become the hereditary possession of their holders. That was not the case with the Caux or Roumois, however. There was a great deal of demesne in those counties, and neither of those posts became a hereditary office.[262]

---

[259] Bouvris, 'Contribution', 155; Bauduin, *Première Normandie*, p. 291.

[260] Orderic, iv. 182; vi. 92.

[261] Orderic, vi. 162-4.

[262] The first known *vicomte* of the Roumois was Richard fitz Tescelin, who held office *c.* 1015-*c.* 1030 (*RADN*, nos. 10, 43; Bouvris, 'Contribution', pp. 155-9; Jumièges, ii. 274). Despite the argument made by Bouvris, Richard seems to have been succeeded by Goscelin fitz Heddo *c.* 1030. He retired *c.* 1045 and was probably immediately succeeded as *vicomte* by Roger of Beaumont, who certainly held that office *c.* 1050 (*Ctl. Préaux*, A162), at a time when the duke needed steadfast and powerful supporters to hold Rouen and the surrounding country for him. Roger had been replaced by 1078 by Ansfrid, whose background is unknown, but who was to continue in office until 1081 (*Ctl. Préaux*, A139; *Regesta: William*, no. 143. Also *RADN*, no. 211. Bouvris, 'Contribution', pp. 160-1). There follows a period of about twenty years for which we have no information as to the identity of the *vicomte*, but by 1106 × 1109 Robert II of Candos apparently held the office (*Chs. Jumièges*, i. 136 = *Regesta*, ii. no. 912). The next known *vicomte* was a man called Oin, who attested an act of Henry I for Robert fitz Richard at Sainte-Vaubourg (*Cartae Antiquae Roll*, no. 182 = *Regesta*, ii. no. 1222). We know nothing of him aside from his name. He had been replaced by Anselm the *vicomte* by June 1123, and he remained in post until at least 1130 (*NI*, p. 306 = *Regesta*, ii. no. 1921; Lot, *Saint-Wandrille*, p. 118 = *Regesta*, ii. no. 1697; *PR 31 Henry I*, p. 97.). He had previ-

But even where the *vicomtes* did not hold their office in inheritance, the dukes seem to have retained individuals in office for long periods of time. For example, Goscelin served as *vicomte* of Rouen for fifteen years or thereabouts (*c.* 1030–*c.* 1045); Robert Bertram seems to have served as *vicomte* of the Cotentin for about twenty years (*c.* 1060–*c.* 1080); and Robert of Beauchamp was apparently *vicomte* of Arques under Henry I for about twenty-five years (*c.* 1110–35). They were probably maintained in office for so long because it took time to gain the experience that made a *vicomte* efficient and effective and which would thereby allow him to increase the revenues accruing from his county. Once that experience had been won, the dukes were reluctant to lose the benefit of it. The picture was similar on the other side of the Channel at least until *c.* 1120. There, Urse of Abbetôt held office 1069–1108 and Picot of Cambridge from *c.* 1071 until at least 1086, while William of Pont de l'Arche seems to have served as sheriff of Hampshire for more than thirty years under Henry I.[263]

Experience counted when the duke needed his officials to maximize revenues, which was particularly the case when they paid all the (identified) revenue that had accrued from their counties into his coffers.[264] Once English sheriffs began to pay fixed farms for their counties from the end of the eleventh century, experience became less important, and they tended to hold their office for shorter periods of time, perhaps for only five years or so. Judith Green suggested that one reason for this was increasing competition for the office.[265] That increasing competition was the result of this same introduction of farms, which made experience less important and a profit more likely. But even then, some sheriffs were permitted to continue in office for long periods, and were even allowed to have their sons succeed them, especially if they had a good track record when it came to paying farms in full.[266] Farms seem to have developed later in Normandy, perhaps not

ously served as sheriff of Berkshire and also farmed Bosham (*PR 31 Henry I*, pp. 56–7, 96–7 and see also Green, *Government*, p. 213). The situation is much more obscure in the county of Caux. Jean-Michel Bouvris uncovered two *vicomtes* of Fécamp, who might have been ducal *vicomtes* operating in the county, but who might equally have been officials appointed by the abbot of Fécamp. That is perhaps suggested by the fact that there was in 1121 × 1129 a *vicomté* of Lillebonne which, the wording of the act in question indicates, had existed during the reign of William the Bastard (*Regesta*, ii. 353 (no. clxxvi) = no. 1440). A few years later, 1126 × 1135, the *vicomte* of the Caux (perhaps identical with Lillebonne) was almost certainly Rabel of Tancarville, although there is nothing to suggest that his father had held the office before him (Lot, *Saint-Wandrille*, no. 65 = *Regesta*, ii. no. 1971).

[263] Green, *Government*, p. 198–9; Green, *English Sheriffs*, p. 29.
[264] See below, Chapter 10, pp. 593–601.
[265] Green, *Government*, pp. 201–3; Green, *English Sheriffs*, pp. 13–14.
[266] Green, *Government*, p. 206.

until the 1130s,[267] but without an equivalent of the pipe roll of Michaelmas 1130 and with far fewer writs and writ-charters for the duchy than England, it is simply not possible to tell if the Norman *vicomtes* also served for shorter terms towards the end of Henry's reign or if there was more competition for the office.

It used once to be thought that in England the baronial sheriff, who held lands in the county he administered, gave way to the curial sheriff, who was an experienced administrator but a stranger to his shire, during Henry I's reign. Judith Green picked out a number of flaws in this argument in 1986. She noted that both before and after 1100 sheriffs were not necessarily members of major baronial families. The difference that earlier historians, principally Morris, had perceived was actually the result of a different trend: that the opportunities to make a fortune in royal service diminished after 1100. Green also dismissed the idea of the curial sheriff, at least as it had been framed by Morris. Instead, English sheriffs might be both *curiales* and barons. These two properties were not mutually exclusive.[268]

Some of the Norman *vicomtes* appointed before 1100 were significant figures in their localities. Nigel of the Cotentin, appointed *vicomte c.* 1020, looks to have been the most important lord in the north of the peninsula. Roger of Montgommery, appointed *vicomte c.* 1027, seems to have been of equal significance in the south of the Lieuvin. Others seem to have come from the next rung or two down the social ladder. Ansketil of Briquessart, for example, seems not to have numbered among the greatest lords in the Bessin. Indeed, it is not at all clear why he was selected to serve as *vicomte*. It is possible that it had something to do with his relationship with Bishop Hugh of Bayeux. An act of Bishop Odo and the inquisition of 1133 reveal that the *vicomtes* held a significant honour from the bishops, and if this had also been the case in Duke Robert's reign then Bishop Hugh might have played a key role in nominating Ansketil for the office.[269] It was after all unlikely that the duke's *vicomte* would have been able to perform his functions in the Bessin in the face of Bishop Hugh's opposition. Richard Goz, parachuted into the Avranchin *c.* 1054, seems not to have been of the highest rank when he took office, either, although he was perhaps related to the lords of Creully. Furthermore, like his contemporaries and colleagues, William Crispin and Robert Bertram, he seems not to have held lands in the *vicomté* to which he was appointed before his appointment.[270]

There was not so much change after 1100, principally because of the acceptance of hereditary claims to the office in the preceding years. The *vicomté* of

[267] See below, Chapter 10, pp. 596–603.
[268] Green, *Government*, pp. 206–10.
[269] *Livre Noir*, i. 95–7 (no. 76); *CDF*, no. 1435; *Inquisition*, pp. 16, 21–2.
[270] L. Musset, 'Saint-Sever', pp. 357–73; Musset, 'Une famille vicomtale', pp. 94–8.

the Cotentin might have changed hands, but all those who held it were all sig-nificant lords in that county. The *vicomtes* of the Bessin and Avranchin under Henry I were great lords, too, by then made all the greater by their lands in England. In Upper Normandy, Robert II of Candos, appointed *vicomte* of the Roumois, held lands in that county as well as the lordship of Caerleon across the Channel, and was wealthy enough to establish an abbey at Beaumont-le-Perreux (later moved to Mortemer) towards the end of his life *c.* 1130.[271] Anselm *vicomte* of Roumois held estates in England in at least seven counties, and received exemptions on Danegeld totalling £7 14s. 6d.[272] He hoped to augment these lands by succession to the property held of the bishop of Winchester by Thomas of Saint-Jean-le-Thomas, for which he paid half a gold mark (60s.) in full.[273] This suggests that Anselm, too, was of baronial status, even if we know nothing of the location or extent of his property in Normandy – although it has been suggested by Judith Green that he was related to Emma the *uicecomitissa* who appears during the reign of Henry II and who appears to have been a woman of some substance.[274]

That is not to say that *all* the Norman *vicomtes*, both before and after 1100, were of baronial status. We do not have the information to know if that was the case. But some, at least, were. That does not, however, lead to the conclusion that the distinction between baronial and curial *vicomtes* is any more relevant for Normandy than it is for England. Indeed, it quite clearly is not.[275] The mightiest Norman lords were generally *curiales*, too. Nigel I, *vicomte* of the Cotentin, was, as noted, perhaps the greatest lord in the peninsula, but he was also a frequent witness of ducal acts and acted as custodian of ducal castles outside his *vicomté*. Goscelin, *vicomte* of Rouen and Arques, seems to have been an important figure in the county of Talou, perhaps related to Papia's family, but he was also appar-ently regularly at court, revealed not just by the number of ducal acts he attested

[271] Orderic, vi. 342–4 and 342 n. 2; *Monasticon*, vi.II. 1022, no. 1; *RHGF*, xiiii. 509–14; Loyd, *Origins*, pp. 26–7.

[272] *PR 31 Henry I*, pp. 5, 12, 18, 32, 81, 86, 99. This would make an estate of some 120 hides, which we might guess, using the Domesday account of Berkshire as the basis for a very rough and ready calculation, as equivalent to say twenty manors and a revenue of £80.

[273] *PR 31 Henry I*, p. 97.

[274] Green, *Government*, p. 213; L. Musset, 'Une arisocratie d'affaires anglo-normande après la conquête', in *Etudes Normandes*, 3 (1986), 9–12; M. Six, 'De la vicomtesse Emma et de son entourage', in *Les Femmes et les actes, Tabularia: Etudes*, 4 (2004), 79–103 available online at < http://www.unicaen.fr/mrsh/craham/revue/tabularia/femmesetactes.html> accessed 25 January 2016.

[275] The question was simply redundant for John Le Patourel, who thought that *all* the Norman *vicomtes* were of baronial rank and wealth (Le Patourel, *Norman Empire*, p. 258).

but also by Duke Robert's unusual generosity to his monastic foundations.[276] Roger II of Montgommery was the greatest lord of the southern Lieuvin and Hiémois during William the Bastard's reign, but he was also almost constantly at the duke's side. Ranulf le Meschin, the best known of the *vicomtes* of the Bessin, was an important lord in the Bessin and in England, too, but also a royal official and a commander of Henry I's household knights.[277]

All of this goes some way to undermining Orderic's famous assertion that Henry I relied on the services of men 'raised from the dust' in his administration.[278] To begin with, the thrust of Orderic's comment is somewhat reduced by the fact that earlier dukes had raised their own men from the dust, too. The Goz and Bertram families only came to the fore during William the Bastard's reign, but rose to great things as a result of their service. The same is also true of a host of others who were not *vicomtes* but held some other office under Duke William, such as Hugh of Grandmesnil, Richard of Courcy, Hugh of Montfort, and Hugh and Roger of Ivry. Of course, not everyone rose quite so high. Ansfrid the *vicomte*'s unknown origins suggest that he should be classed as one of William's 'new men', too, but he seems not to have been able effectively to reap the rewards of his term of office. Moreover, as should already have become clear, even if some men and families emerged from obscurity during his reign, Henry I relied heavily on members of well-established and important families: Hugh and Richard Goz; Ranulf le Meschin; William of Warenne; and William of Tancarville, for example.[279]

Although we do not have the necessary information to establish the social standing of all of Henry I's *vicomtes*, or even the names of all of them who served in the duchy during his reign, it was probably easier for men of lesser social standing to make a career through office-holding in Normandy than it was in England. When we can see the value of the county farms in the Norman pipe rolls, they were considerably lower than those charged in England. For example, in 1180, the farm due for the *vicomté* of Vire, which first appears in Henry I's reign, was 20 *livres* (£5 sterling); that from the *vicomté* of the Cotentin was 70 *livres* (£17 10s. sterling); that of the Bessin was 140 *livres* (£35 sterling); and that of Arques was 423 *livres* 10 *sous* 2 *deniers* (around £106 sterling).[280] In England in the same year, the honours of Berkhamsted and Eye were farmed for £120 and £336, respectively, while the farms for Worcestershire, Northamptonshire, and Northumberland

---

[276]   For Robert's patronage see *RADN*, nos. 61.
[277]   Orderic, vi. 88, 346–52 and see below, Chapter 11, pp. 631, 634, 644.
[278]   Orderic, vi. 16.
[279]   Also noted by Hollister and Baldwin, 'Administrative kingship', 889–90.
[280]   *Norman pipe rolls*, pp. 21, 27, 29, 47, respectively. Note, however, that it is possible, although on balance unlikely, that the introduction of Norman *baillies* and *bailliages* after 1144 significantly reduced the farms.

were £219 17s. 8d, £232 3s., and £206 19s., respectively.[281] The difference in values
was to some extent owing to the fact that the large towns of the duchy formed
prévôtés which were farmed separately, and occasionally the fairs, forests, and
tolls, multure, and ovens were also farmed as a separate account. The only really
sizeable farm in Normandy was due from the city of Rouen, amounting to 3000
livres in 1180 (£750 sterling). That meant that Anselm the *vicomte* probably owed
an even larger sum for his Norman *vicomté* than he had for Berkshire.[282]

The evidence for the work, origins, and status of the Norman *vicomtes* is thus
both uncertain and incomplete. We know nothing about these officials throughout the tenth century, and might even question whether the office even existed
until the last decade or so of that century. From what we can see after c. 1020, it
seems reasonably certain that the *vicomte* was a civilian official who oversaw the
administration of the ducal demesne in his county, including the collection of
the revenues produced by both the land and the men who lived there, and who
might also act as a policeman when occasion demanded. He did not, however,
have regular military responsibilities – at least not as part of his job description.
Where the origins and status of the various men who acted as *vicomtes* is concerned, however, it seems that few generalizations are possible. Over the period
as a whole, some *vicomtes* were from great families, while the origins of others
are entirely obscure, although all those identified were laymen. Some held land
in their *vicomtés* before they took up office, but others did not. Many, at least by
Henry I's reign, held their offices by hereditary right, although the *vicomtés* of the
two Norman counties where most of the ducal demesne was located, the Roumois
and the Caux, did not. Finally, while some Norman *vicomtes* seem to have held
their offices for long periods of time, giving them the experience they needed to
maximize their revenues, the evidence is not adequate to be certain that this was
always the case.

The Norman counts

In England, the writ-charters that were publicized in the shire courts were regularly addressed to the bishops and to the sheriffs of the relevant shire or shires.
That was also the case in Normandy, where the surviving writ-charters are most
frequently addressed to the bishop and *vicomte* of the county to which they
related.[283] In England, writ-charters were also addressed to the earls who, with

---

[281] *Pipe Roll 26 Henry II*, pp. 8 (Berkhamsted), 24 (Eye), 77 (Worcs), 81 (Northants), 141
(Northumb).
[282] *Norman Pipe Rolls*, p. 50.
[283] See above, *infra*, p. 544.

the bishops, acted as presidents of the shire court and representatives of God and king. That did *not* happen in Normandy. This difference raises questions about the role of the count in Normandy.[284]

The first Norman count, Rodulf, was more likely than not count of Bayeux.[285] His honour did not outlive him, however, perhaps because most or all of his estates in the Bessin passed to his son, who had become bishop *c.* 1011. But there were three permanent Norman counties that endured from their creation *c.* 1000 until after 1144. These were, from east to west, Eu, Evreux, and Mortain. They have been discussed at various points above, but a little of their history and transmission should be recapped here.

Eu first appears *c.* 1000. The first count was Richard II's half-brother Godfrey. The county passed from Godfrey to his brother William *c.* 1017,[286] from William to Godfrey's son Gilbert,[287] and from Gilbert back to William's two sons, William Busac and Robert, in turn.[288] Only after this period of family ping-pong did the county become heritable from father to son, descending from Robert to his son William (d. *c.* 1095), grandson Henry (d. 1140), and great-grandson John (d. 1170). David Douglas wrote that 'the county of Eu was situated in the extreme east of Normandy', meaning the compact territory around Eu itself mapped by Suzanne Deck,[289] but there was probably more to the county than this. Count William also held land in the Lieuvin from his appointment *c.* 1017, and while at least some of these possessions were transferred to the monks of Saint-Pierre-sur-Dives when Count William I's wife founded the abbey there *c.* 1046, the remainder might have continued to comprise part of the county.

The first count of Evreux was Archbishop Robert of Rouen, Richard II's brother, who was given the county by that duke *c.* 1015.[290] On his death in 1037

---

[284] 'There appears to have lingered in Normandy longer than elsewhere in northern Gaul the older notion that the count was in some sense a *palatinus*, an emissary of the reigning household' (Douglas, 'The earliest Norman counts', 152). Others have been less certain about the role of the count, with David Crouch a particularly notable (and correctly) dissenting voice: see below, *infra*, p. 568.

[285] Orderic, ii. 200; iv. 290 and see also above, Chapter 1, pp. 71–2.

[286] Jumièges, ii. 10 and see also Bauduin, *Première Normandie*, pp. 193–4, 297 (for the date of *c.* 1017 see Louise, *Bellême*, i. 144. Douglas in contrast suggested *c.* 1015: 'The earliest Norman counts', 140).

[287] *Ctl. Trinité-du-Mont*, p. 457.

[288] Jumièges, ii. 128. David Crouch thought that William Busac rebelled in 1046–47 rather than in 1053 (Crouch, *The Normans*, pp. 65–6); Douglas, 'The earliest Norman counts', 139–40 and Note A, pp. 154–6. The succession of William Busac and then Robert in that order is also suggested by Deck, 'Comté d'Eu', 101; Searle, *PK*, p. 135; and others.

[289] Deck, 'Comté de l'Eu', between pp. 112 and 113.

[290] For the county of Evreux see Bauduin, *Première Normandie*, pp. 194–5 and Annexe 1, pp. 325–61 as well as above, Chapter 2, pp. 85–6 and Chapter 3, pp. 96–7, 157–8, 166,

it passed intact to his eldest son Richard, and on Richard's death in 1067 to his son William. Archbishop Robert had married Herleva, the daughter of Thurstan the Rich, and that marriage brought him and his heirs lands and forests from the meander of the Seine by Jumièges to the valley of Lillebonne, including the forests of Le Trait, Gauville, Caudebec, and Gravenchon, this last being the site of the count's principal castle in the Caux.[291] The acquisition of these estates led to the development of a close, if at times uneasy, relationship with the monks of Saint-Wandrille where Counts Richard and William were buried.[292] Archbishop Robert had also given his son Richard the archiepiscopal estate of Douvrend, and that was joined to the county until the reign of Henry I.[293] Other estates were added later at Noyon-sur-Andelle, Gacé, Bavent, and Varaville.[294] When Count William died in 1118, he left as his heir a nephew, Amaury of Montfort-l'Amaury. His succession was initially opposed for political reasons by Bishop Ouen of Evreux and Henry I, but his rebellion in 1118–19 was effective enough to convince Henry to change his mind and to allow him to inherit the county, even if Henry retained the castles in his own hand.

The composition and descent of the county of Mortain is perhaps the most complicated of the three. The first count, Robert, was another of Richard II's half-brothers and had been established as count by c. 1015. He was succeeded by a younger son, Richard, who had spent some time as a monk at Saint-Benoit-sur-Loire.[295] Richard entered into his inheritance without first seeking Duke Richard

---

172–4, 175–6. In contrast, Valin thought that Archbishop Robert had been given the county by his brother, probably on the basis of the foundation deed for the abbey of Saint-Sauveur at Evreux (Valin, *Le duc et sa cour*, p. 49; *RADN*, no. 208. See also Bauduin, *Première Normandie*, pp. 326–7).

[291] See Bauduin, *Première Normandie*, p. 344. The castle at Gravechon has been excavated: J. Le Maho, *L'enceinte fortifiée de Notre-Dame-de-Gravenchon (Seine-Maritime) XIe–XIIIe siècle: Le site de la Fontaine-Saint-Denis, des fouilles archéologiques aux travaux de restauration (1979–2001)* (Notre-Dame-de-Gravenchon, 2001); J. Le Maho, 'Remarques sur la construction de bois en haute-normandie aux XIe et XIIe siècles', in *L'architecture normande au moyen age*, ed. M. Baylé, second edition, 2 vols (Caen, 2001), i. 243–68; A. M. Flambard Héricher, 'Fortifications de terre et residences en Normandie (XIe–XIIIe siècles)', *Château Gaillard*, 20 (Caen, 2002), 89–90.

[292] See, for example, *Regesta: William*, no. 262; Orderic, vi. 148; Bauduin, *Première Normandie*, p. 328.

[293] *RADN*, no. 10; *Regesta*, ii. 337 (no. cxxiv) = no. 1234; Bauduin, *Première Normandie*, p. 345, n. 127.

[294] Bauduin, *Première Normandie*, pp. 345–6.

[295] André de Fleury, *Vie de Gauzlin*, pp. 48–51. See also J. Boussard, 'Le comté de Mortain', 253–79; D. Bates, 'Notes sur l'aristocratie Normande', 21–38; B. Golding, 'Robert of Mortain', *ANS*, 13 (1991), 119–44; C. Potts, 'The earliest Norman counts revisited: the lords of Mortain', *HSJ*, 4 (1993), 23–35.

II's consent, however, and was subsequently accused of conspiring to murder the duke and forfeited. His successor was William Werlenc, the son of yet another of Richard II's half-brothers, Malger, who was by that time count of Corbeil. Werlenc was removed on uncertain grounds by William the Bastard between 1047 and 1054, and his erstwhile county was curtailed. Avranches and the other estates in the Avranchin were retained by the duke, but Mortain and its vale and some additional estates in the Cotentin including Cérences and La Haye-du-Puits were given to William's half-brother Robert. Robert was succeeded in 1095 by his son, William, who was captured by Henry I at Tinchebray in September 1106, imprisoned, forfeited, and blinded. Mortain was then trimmed again – Vire and La Haye-du-Puits, for example, were detached from it – before it was granted to Stephen of Blois c. 1113.[296] He seems to have retained control of the county until Geoffrey of Anjou conquered it in 1142, although it was subject to the attacks of Matilda's supporters from c. 1136 and Matilda herself issued an act addressed to the foresters of Tinchebray 1135 × 1139.[297]

As with Eu and Evreux, the county of Mortain did not comprise a discrete cluster of estates. Rather, around 1082 there were three principal groups of property (excluding Count Robert's possessions in the Lieuvin around Conteville that he had inherited from his father). The most significant of these consisted of a large and compact lordship centred on Mortain itself, more or less contained within the area between Saint-Hilaire-du-Harcouët, Saint-Pois, Tinchebray, and Le Teilleul, with outriders to the north and north-east at Talevende, Saint-Pierre-d'Entremonte, Condé-sur-Noireau, and Proussy. It is likely that these possessions at least had been held by the earliest counts. The second loose group comprised a scattering of three vills in the Cotentin to the south of the river Sienne, at Equilly, Cérences, and Lingreville. Jacques Boussard placed a fourth vill, Montsurvent, with this group, but it could just as easily go with the third and final group of vills which were loosely clustered around the castle and vill of La Haye-du-Puits and which included at least part of Helleville and Houtteville which Count Robert gave to the monks of Marmoutier and Saint-Etienne of Caen, respectively.[298]

In addition to Rodulf's county of Bayeux and these three long-lived counties, there was a small number of much more short-lived ones. Count William I of Eu had originally been given the county of the Hiémois, although as we do not know if he was also given the title of count he could have acted as the ducal *vicomte*

[296] King, *King Stephen*, pp. 11–12.
[297] RT, s.a. 1043; Delisle, i. 226–7; Howlett, p. 143; *Regesta*, iii. no. 805; King, *King Stephen*, p. 23; Dutton, 'Geoffrey', p. 53; and above, Chapter 3, p. 181.
[298] *Regesta: William*, no. 215; Boussard, 'Le comté de Mortain', 258–72, with a map at p. 270.

there. In any event, if a county had been created it did not survive William's rebellion *c.* 1000, even though he retained his lands in the Lieuvin.[299] In 1026, Richard II created his younger son, Robert, count of the Hiémois.[300] The county was extinguished when Robert succeeded his brother as duke in 1027 at which point it became a *vicomté* instead. At some date between 1035 and 1046, the young William the Bastard apparently created his cousin, Guy, count of Brionne. He was given the castle there, probably the surrounding *banlieu*, too, and also the castle at Vernon. But he rebelled in 1046–47 and left Normandy after a period of house arrest. His county was extinguished, and the castles and land were recovered to the demesne.[301] Then, *c.* 1037, William gave his uncle, William of Arques, a county that seems to have included that part of the *pagus* of Talou not within the county of Eu and the eastern part of the *pagus* of Caux. The county did not survive Count William's rebellion and exile in 1053, and the castle at Arques and the rest of the demesne that had been given to William then reverted back to the duke.[302] It was probably William the Bastard, too, who made Herluin, the knight who married his mother Herleva, the count of Conteville, a county which was to last only for his lifetime.[303] Finally, in around 1087, Robert Curthose sold or leased the Cotentin and Avranchin to his youngest brother Henry.[304] This probably seemed like a very good deal to the new duke. The ducal demesne in the Cotentin and Avranchin was limited. In 1180, the farms it produced, as well as the income from pleas and taxes, amounted to just over £459 sterling.[305] On that basis, which will suffice as a rough-and-ready figure, and if Orderic is right about how much Henry paid, Curthose received a sum equivalent to more than six years' revenues. In addition to the demesne, Henry seems also to have been given a comital title. He certainly attested at least one act as count during Curthose's reign and was given the title by Orderic, too.[306]

In each case, it seems that the ducal demesne within the established bounds of a county was transferred to the new count. That is especially clear in the cases of Evreux, which was clearly a ducal possession during the tenth century and at the beginning of the eleventh; Arques, which was described as a 'certain seat of ours'

---

[299] Jumièges, ii. 8–10, and see above, Chapter 2, pp. 79–80 and Chapter 6, pp. 324–5.

[300] Jumièges, ii. 40, and see above, Chapter 6, pp. 317, 325.

[301] Jumièges, ii. 120–2; Poitiers, pp. 8–12, and see above, Chapter 2, pp. 107–9 and Chapter 6, p. 326.

[302] Jumièges, ii. 102–4; Poitiers, pp. 32–42, and see above, Chapter 2, pp. 122–5 and Chapter 6, pp. 326–7.

[303] Golding, 'Robert of Mortain', 119.

[304] Orderic, iv. 120 and see above, Chapter 3, p. 143.

[305] *Norman Pipe Rolls*, pp. 8–10, 22, 27–8, 36.

[306] Orderic, iv. 148; Delisle, *Sires de Saint-Sauveur*, no. 45.

by Robert the Magnificent; and the Cotentin, where Henry held the erstwhile ducal castles at Cherbourg, Coutances, Gavray, and Avranches.[307] Count William of Arques described his lands as a 'benefice', which is a further indication that he had been given them by the duke.

The counts, then, were endowed out of the ducal demesne. It might originally have been intended that these lands, like those given to Carolingian counts and Anglo-Saxon earls, should change hands as the office changed hands.[308] Unlike a number of the *vicomtes*, and with the exception of Count William of Arques, the Norman counts seem not to have held estates of their own within the area of their county beforehand or, indeed, anywhere else. We do not know if the counties were granted with hereditary right, and the early transmission of Eu suggests that they were not, but as a count's sons would be landless if this were not the case, there was a strong incentive for the counts to treat them as hereditary property even if the dukes themselves might be reluctant to do so. As the vills had been granted to their holder *with* the title of count, and as they were held *because* their holder was count, the office and title may be supposed to have been seen as necessarily hereditary, too.

Aside from land, it seems that the Norman counts enjoyed a wide-ranging jurisdiction. As discussed above, there is only clear evidence for this in the case of the counts of Eu, but the fact that the counts of Evreux and Mortain had established their own justices in their counties by the last decade or so of Henry I's reign is a strong indication that they, too, enjoyed great franchises that are otherwise unevidenced.[309] Just as important were the exemptions from, and grants of, the taxes and customs that elsewhere belonged to the dukes. A diploma of Richard II for the monks of Jumièges of 1025 notes that Archbishop Robert had given the monks 'all the customs which belong to the county (*omnes consuetudines que ad comitatum pertinent*) which he possessed from our right'.[310] After 1040, Count Richard of Evreux gave the monks of Saint-Taurin the customs of justice, *septenage*, and toll.[311] A diploma for the monks of Saint-Wandrille notes that Count Richard of Evreux had given them the count's custom (*consuetudinem*

---

[307] *Flodoard*, p.38; *RADN*, no. 5; *Dudo*, p. 103 (Evreux); *RADN*, no. 69 (Arques); Orderic, iv. 220 (Cotentin), and see above, Chapter 3, pp. 143, 144–5.

[308] Nelson, 'Kingship and royal government', p. 412; S. Baxter, *The Earls of Mercia: Lordship and Power in Late Anglo-Saxon England* (Oxford, 2007), pp. 141–2.

[309] *Regesta: William*, no. 215. The act includes interpolations from the times of Count William and Count Stephen, and it is likely that the reference to comital justices belongs to Stephen's time as count, and thus after the introduction of the name for this office during the reign of Henry I (see *Regesta: William*, p. 680 and also above, Chapter 8, pp. 475–86).

[310] *RADN*, no. 36.

[311] The act is edited by Bauduin, *Première Normandie*, pp. 370–1, no. 5.

... *comitisiam*) in all his woods.[312] At least some of the customs would presumably have been found among the *consuetudines uicecomitatus* that Duke William granted to the monks of Préaux *c.* 1050, which included the fines and profits arising from, '*hamfara* (attacks on houses), *ullac* (probably the harbouring of outlaws), rape, arson, bernage (the tax for the duke's hunting dogs), and making war'.[313] Certainly, the count of Eu held his land on the Dives free from 'all exactions and secular customs and also of all *grauarium* and bernage and services' and by the end of the twelfth century the counts of Evreux also collected bernage on their own account.[314] Indeed, it is likely that the Norman counts had the right to all the revenues produced by their counties. The Norman pipe roll of 1180, for example, reveals that the county of Eu rendered nothing to the duke, while the county of Evreux produced revenue for the dukes only when the count was a minor.[315] No wonder, then, that Count Amaury of Evreux was irritated by the actions of ducal collectors of *grauarium* and beadles in his county.[316] They were probably not supposed to operate there at all.

The Norman counts thus seem to have retained for themselves all the revenues produced within their titular counties. But they might also have enjoyed such rights over the other lands they held, even if not all of them had previously been ducal demesne. Count William of Eu certainly seems also to have enjoyed comital powers in the Lieuvin, as revealed by his widow's grants to the monks of Saint-Pierre-sur-Dives.[317] It is not clear that the powers and rights he held in each area were the same, and it is not clear whether his rights in the Lieuvin accrued to him because he had once held the county of the Hiémois or because he was then count of Eu. If the latter was the case, then his comital rights covered all his lands, not just those that lay within his titular county. If the former, he had retained comital rights without being count. This is not very much to go on, but it is worth noting that some of the Carolingian counties established east of the Rhine 'were not always discrete territorial units, but were interspersed with areas of others' jurisdiction',[318] and it is possible that the comital rights of the Norman counts were also rather more geographically dispersed than has previously been thought.

What now remains to be considered is why these counties were created, and what functions and duties the counts had vis-à-vis the duke. Carolingian counts

---

[312] *RADN*, no. 234.

[313] *RADN*, no. 121; *Ctl. Préaux*, A161 and A163. The first act in the cartulary lists the customs, the second refers to them as the *consuetudines uicecomitatus*.

[314] *Chs. Jumièges*, no. 129; Bauduin, *Première Normandie*, p. 350.

[315] Noted by Power, *The Norman Frontier*, p. 57.

[316] Orderic, vi. 330.

[317] AD Calvados, H 7031(5) = *Regesta*, ii. no. 1569.

[318] J. Nelson, 'Kingship and royal government', p. 411.

seem to have had three main functions: 'first, to keep social order in their localities, presiding over local courts to "do justice" between local landowners, and repressing crime; second, to look after royal estates in their localities; third, to summon men to the host when the king campaigned.'[319] The ealdormen of Wessex and Mercia were also provincial commanders, responsible for particular regions from which they received dues and services, and that they were also responsible for enforcing justice in these regions.[320] The earls said to have been established in Norway by Harald Fairhair had similar functions. Snorri Sturluson asserted that Harald placed an earl over every province 'whose duty it was to administer the law and justice and to collect fines and taxes. And the earl was to have a third of the taxes and penalties for his maintenance and other expenses. Every earl was to have under him four or more *hersar* ... Every earl was to furnish the king sixty soldiers for his army, and every *hersir* twenty.'[321]

The Norman counts look rather different. It will have become apparent from what has been said above that they did not administer the ducal demesne or collect revenues for the dukes. Instead, the dukes' demesne and their rights had passed wholesale to the counts who took what they produced for themselves. There was consequently no need for an institution equivalent to the English 'third penny' which was 'intended to give the earls an incentive to ensure the collection of royal revenue derived from towns, trade, and the profits of justice', as the Norman counts had the right to all the pennies produced in these ways.[322] It is also possible that the counts gained control over the county courts, whatever form these took in Normandy, as Henry I seems to have been obliged to communicate with his subjects in the Evrecin through the bishop's court as a result of the count's appropriation of the usual forum.[323] We do not know what happened in Eu or Mortain.

As to the military role, it has often been remarked that the earliest counts held counties located on the frontiers of the duchy. That was also the case with the later county of the Cotentin held by the future Henry I. The counties of Arques

---

[319] Nelson, 'Kingship', p. 411. See also McKitterick, *The Frankish Kingdoms*, pp. 87–91; Costambeys, Innes, and MacLean, *The Carolingian World*, p. 179.

[320] Williams, *Kingship and Government in Pre-Conquest England*, pp. 52–6; C. P. Lewis, 'The early earls of Norman England', *ANS*, 13 (1991), 209.

[321] *Heimskringla*, p. 63. Snorri's claims might be anachronistic, of course, although the cohorts required look plausible, not least because they look as though they comprised ships' crews (see also below, Chapter 11, p. 667 for the similar obligation of the archbishops of Canterbury).

[322] Baxter, *The Earls of Mercia*, p. 142.

[323] L. Delisle and L. Passy, *Memoires et notes de M. Auguste Le Prevost pour servir a l'histoire du département de l'Eure*, 3 vols (Evreux, 1862–69), ii. 41 = *Regesta*, ii. no. 1578. Previously noted in Hagger, 'The earliest Norman writs revisited', 191.

and Brionne, in contrast, were well within the borders of the duchy when they were created in the middle of the eleventh century, but Count William of Arques was clearly involved across the border in Ponthieu, while Count Guy's castle at Vernon guarded the frontier with the French Vexin.[324] All of this suggests that the Norman counts were intended to have a military function, organizing the defence of their section of the frontier against enemy incursions.[325] The number of knights who already surrounded Count Robert I of Avranches-Mortain c. 1015, as well as his construction of a castle at Mortain by 1026, would certainly suggest that he was concerned with the defence of his county and, perhaps, the duchy more generally.[326] Likewise, Robert of Mortain had expanded his county to Gorron in Maine by 1082, alongside, but perhaps independently of, Duke William's advance to Ambrières.[327] Similarly, Count Gilbert of Eu led a campaign against Count Enguerrand of Ponthieu during Robert the Magnificent's reign, perhaps on his own initiative as the peace apparently agreed by the two counts seems not to have included the duke.[328]

There are thus grounds for concluding, with Pierre Bauduin, that the military character of the counties remained important until at least the end of the eleventh century.[329] But even so, it could hardly be maintained that the Norman counties were exceptional in this respect. The Crispin *vicomtes* of the Vexin fought against Count Walter of Amiens-Vexin, while Hugh of Grandmesnil defended the Norman border from the later attacks launched by Count Ralph from his castle at Neuf-Marché.[330] The lords of Breteuil and Tillières also saw off incursions launched against their lordships.[331] On the western frontier, the counts of Mortain were joined in their battles against the Bretons by Alured the Giant and Nigel of the Cotentin, custodians of Chéruel in the time of Robert the Magnificent, as well as by the *vicomtes* of the Avranchin.[332] The role of the members of the dukes' households in leading troops has also been noted above, and will be considered in the final chapter, too.[333] It would consequently be difficult to classify military

---

[324] For William of Arques see above, Chapter 2, pp. 122–3.

[325] See also Bauduin, *Première Normandie*, p. 193.

[326] *RADN*, nos. 16, 49.

[327] *Regesta: William*, no. 215.

[328] Orderic, ii. 10–12; *RHGF*, xxiii. 718; Bauduin, *Première Normandie*, p. 298.

[329] Bauduin, *Première Normandie*, p.335.

[330] For the Crispins see, Milo Crispin, *Miraculum quo B. Maria subuenit Guillelmo Crispino Seniori*, in *PL*, 150, col. 737; translation in van Houts, *Normans*, pp. 85–6. The record of Hugh of Grandmesnil's defence of the Vexin frontier is at Orderic, ii. 130–2.

[331] Jumièges, ii. 22–4, 100; Orderic, vi. 248 (Tillières); Jumièges, ii. 146; Orderic, vi. 246–8 (Breteuil).

[332] Jumièges, ii. 56–8 (Chéruel); Jumièges, ii. 208 (for the *vicomtes*).

[333] See below, Chapter 11, pp. 634–7, 643–4.

leadership or the defence of the frontier as a specifically, or an especially, comital function.

In fact, there is no reason to think that any particular responsibility fell to the Norman counts as a result of their office. As David Crouch commented: 'Norman counts had no known formal powers ... They were no more than barons who happened to have a hereditary and prestigious title and who had control over a *ciuitas* or major fortress which gave them something of an antique air of quasi-public authority.'[334] The absence of any discernible official function leads to the conclusion that it was the prestigious title and control over prestigious property that was the point. Just as all the sons of the counts of the Bretons might be styled counts, so the Norman dukes seem to have developed a tradition whereby their close kinsmen were given the same dignity.[335] Indeed, Dudo more or less made this very point. When Richard I was arranging his succession, Dudo had Count Rodulf ask what should be done with the duke's other children. Richard answered: 'When they have been made my son Richard's faithful men by an oath of fealty, and their hands have been given into his hands as a pledge of their hearts, let him bestow the land which I shall show you, so that they may be able to live honourably.'[336] Thus a duke's closest male relatives were set apart from, and above, the other great lords of the duchy, bringing increased prestige to the ducal line at the same time. As a title had, in contemporary understanding, to be accompanied by appropriate power, the Norman counts were given a portion of the demesne and the associated ducal rights to rule as a discrete territory in a quasi-autonomous manner.[337]

Nonetheless, although the title was prestigious, it did take some time before it became hereditary. Succession to the counties was probably kept insecure for as long as possible. As noted above, Eu passed between brothers and cousins until *c.* 1095 when it passed from father to son for the first time, while Mortain changed hands on a number of occasions. Although the county of Evreux seems generally to provide a more straightforward case of inheritance from father to son, it is noteworthy that Count Richard, Archbishop Robert's son, declared that he had been 'elected and established as count of the city of Evreux' (*Ebroicae ciuitatis comes electus et constitutus*) in an act of 1038.[338] 'Elected' does not suggest an automatic right to inherit, and the choice of wording apparently indicated a recognition that a duke had the right to choose or veto a count's successor at that point in time.

William the Bastard's reign seems to form the watershed here, a generation

---

[334] Crouch, *Image of Aristocracy*, pp. 55–6.
[335] Crouch, *Image of Aristocracy*, p. 54.
[336] *Dudo*, p. 171.
[337] See on this Douglas, 'The earliest Norman counts', 151.
[338] *RADN*, no. 208.

earlier than was the case with the *vicomtés*, probably because the counties had been created a generation earlier than most of the *vicomtés*, too. At the beginning of his reign, sons could be denied succession to their father's office with relative ease. By *c.* 1050, however, the counties were beginning to become heritable. The county of Eu descended to the children of Count Robert, who had been established as count *c.* 1052. When Duke William sought to depose William Werlenc as count of Mortain *c.* 1054 he did so on what looks suspiciously like a trumped-up charge, suggesting that there was no other way to remove him from the office.[339] When Count Richard of Evreux died *c.* 1067, his son William seems to have inherited his county without comment or question. When Roger of Hereford succeeded to his father's English lands in 1071, he expected to inherit not just the property but also the title of earl and the rights that went with it.[340] That had not been the case in pre-Conquest England, and only five years after the Conquest it is unlikely that Roger's attitude was influenced by English practices. If he expected to inherit his father's earldom and rights it was because that was how it would have been in Normandy. By the reign of Henry I, the right to inherit was so firmly established that Henry was unable to prevent Amaury of Montfort from inheriting the county of Evreux, and the title of count, as his uncle's nearest heir. Henry's attempts to recover the county into his own hands caused a rebellion and ended in failure, despite his victory at Brémule.[341] All that Henry could do was trim the county of estates that could with justice be said to belong to another, as was the case with the complex centred on Douvrend, and garrison the count's castles.[342] In other words, Henry could do no more about the inheritance and control of the Norman counties than he could with any other lord's honour.

* * * * * *

The analysis of ducal acts and the narratives at the outset of this chapter leads to the conclusion that the Norman dukes operated a palace-style government, which saw them based for most of the time they spent in the duchy at Rouen. When they moved out of the city they did so for a variety of reasons: war; high-profile public and religious events; and leisure, for example. These movements related to their office, and to the promotion of their authority. The dukes were obliged to protect their subjects against their enemies, and wanted visibly to lead the religious celebrations that took place in their duchy. Moreover, they could make

---

[339] Jumièges, ii. 126; see above, Chapter 2, p. 117 and *infra*, p. 562.

[340] Indicated by *Letters of Lanfranc,* no. 31.

[341] Orderic, vi. 188, 204, 220, 236–42, 278. He would later issue a writ as count in favour of the monks of Troarn: AD Calvados, H 7761(1).

[342] See above, Chapter 3, pp. 173–4 and *infra*, p. 538.

their travels work for their own benefit, by requiring the bishop, lord, or corporation to welcome them to their town, castle, or church with elaborate honour in the form of an *aduentus*. But although these tours did have a role to play in government and in the promotion of the duke's authority, if only by building up local good will, they were no more essential for the efficient working of ducal government than are the movements of the reigning British monarch between Windsor, London, Sandringham, and Balmoral or the appearances of members of the royal family at ship launchings or at the opening of public buildings.

Instead, those who needed the duke went to find him. Those whom the duke wanted to see were summoned to court. Messengers plied to and fro, although it is difficult to gain a sense of the scale of messenger traffic. In any event, the duke could communicate easily with his subjects when he required, having a pool of household knights or chaplains whom he could call on to take his messages orally or in writing to recipients within or without the duchy. Nonetheless, there was only a finite number of possible messengers at court, and their dispatch on a beneficiary's business meant that the duke could not use their services again until they returned. The introduction of the writ, then, while it did not give government a longer or more accurate memory (because copies were not kept), did tend to preserve the reservoir of manpower available at court for the duke's own use. It probably saved money, too, assuming that messengers were paid an allowance for his time out of court on the duke's business.

The routine use of the writ under Henry I is unlikely to have transformed the reach or effect of the duke's power, but they did change its appearance . Now the beneficiary produced the writ with its seal in the relevant forum. The seal in particular manifested the duke's person and authority.[343] There was no longer a spoken command and severe glance from an emissary sent especially from the ducal court. It might have taken Norman petitioners some time to get used to putting their trust in a wax medallion, despite the presence of local ducal officials to whom they could turn should a writ not be obeyed, and there is some slight evidence from the abbey of Saint-Amand in Rouen that the nuns there were a little uncomfortable with the form of the document they obtained from Henry's clerks.[344] But the writ was to become *the* instrument of executive power in the

---

[343]   As with Carolingian seals: Koziol, *Politics of Memory and Identity*, p. 36.

[344]   AD Seine-Maritime, 55 H 8; AN, JJ 49, fo. 26r (no. 46) = *Regesta*, ii. no. 1221; Hagger, 'The earliest Norman writs revisited', 188–9. The modified document is in some ways comparable with a writ-charter of King William II for Peterborough, which survives as an authentic original at Burghley House (facsimile in *Facsimiles of English Royal Writs to A.D. 1100*, ed. T. A. M. Bishop and P. Chaplais (Oxford, 1957), no. 20, plates 19–20). The act was written by a royal scribe in normal 'chancery' style except for the fact that after the witness list come the *signa* of the king (who is not among the witnesses) and

duchy, and beneficiaries would come both to embrace it and to find ways to shape the formulae employed in these documents for their own benefit. As ever, ducal power was mediated by the requirements of those who benefited from it.

Writs were sent to the lords of the duchy, instructing them to do something, or prohibiting them from doing it. They were also addressed to the variety of ducal officials who administered the demesne and collected taxes and tolls and other revenues. The counts did not number among those officials. Indeed, they apparently had no public role to play that was not also played by their untitled peers. They were simply a particularly conspicuous tier of lords, whose title marked them out as (increasingly distant) kinsmen of the reigning duke, and who probably enjoyed unusually wide-ranging jurisdiction over offences across all their lands. Instead, the greatest of the dukes' officials was the *vicomte*. But while the *vicomtes'* part in the administration of the demesne has been established in this chapter, much more needs to be said about how that role was performed in practice, the revenues that were collected under *vicomtal* supervision, and the other officials who were supervised by, or at least accounted to, the *vicomtes* in the course of their own duties. The next chapter considers these essential activities in some detail.

four of the witnesses. Why the act was drawn up in this way cannot now be explained, but Abbot Turold, who was not remembered for his tolerance of English practices, might have insisted that something more akin to Norman diplomatic forms than the usual English writ-charter be drawn up as testimony to the grant.

CHAPTER 10

Accounting for Power: Ducal Finance

The demesne vills and towns, the people living in them, those travelling through them, or along public highways more generally, and those selling and buying in the markets and fairs established in them, all produced revenues for the dukes' coffers. Those revenues were spent on the castles and palaces that provided the backdrop for the dukes' display of majesty and power, which has been discussed in Chapter 7. Wealth, then, was essential to all civilian aspects of ducal rule. But contemporaries associated wealth in particular with power and military might. Thus the dukes' income was also used to purchase the munitions that allowed their castles to stand against their enemies, and the arms and horses necessary to equip their knights, and to pay the salaries of the members of their household knights and the wages of their mercenaries.

The mechanisms that developed to allow the dukes to collect their revenues were no doubt imperfect, but they were certainly adequate, for the dukes of the Normans were renowned for their wealth – even more so after they became kings of the English. William of Jumièges wrote that Richard II 'kept the count (Geoffrey of the Bretons) with him for a while through his enormous wealth revealing to the count the greatness of his might as he choose',[1] while Orderic, writing of William Clito, noted that 'his uncle's arm was long and powerful and formidable to him, for Henry's might and reputation for wealth and power were known far and wide from the west to the east.[2] And even if not all of that wealth was liquid, they had access to as much coin as they needed. Normandy had a money economy, and it is likely that even the lowest orders of society used coins to some extent.[3] As David Bates noted, this is particularly evident in the multifarious grants of

---

[1] Jumièges, ii. 14.

[2] Orderic, vi. 358.

[3] As discussed below, the tenants of Holy Trinity, Caen, paid their rents in cash as well as in kind. In contrast to the situation in eighth- and ninth-century England, however, the miracle collections produced in Normandy do not provide references to, or inferences of, the use of coins at the lowest social levels. For example, they lack accounts of peasants going to markets or making offerings of a penny or two (for England see R. Naismith, *Money and Power in Anglo-Saxon England: The Southern English Kingdoms, 757–865* (Cambridge, 2012), pp. 280–4).

tolls or disbursements of money found in ducal and seigniorial *acta*, as well as
by the discovery of the Fécamp hoard with its 8,000 or so coins.[4] Indeed, as
Lucien Musset discussed, the diversity of coins circulating within the borders of
the duchy reveals how important money was. A hoard found at Sébécourt, for
example, contained coins from Rouen, Dreux, Vendôme, Le Mans, and Angers.[5]
It is likely that they could all be used in transactions within the duchy; Musset
noted that *acta* rarely state the type of coins that rents or purchases were paid in,
implying that they were all equally acceptable. Indeed, as Norman issues seem not
to have been recalled and recoined, there were several different types of Norman
pennies in circulation at the same time, too.[6] Musset did, however, note that the
circulation of these 'foreign' coins reflected local interests. Thus, the money of Le
Mans was widely used in the Avranchin and the county of Mortain, as well as in
the lands ruled by the Montgommery-Bellême family, while the coins of Chartres
and Dreux could be found in the Evrecin – the former probably as a result of
the Beaumont possession of the county of Meulan.[7]

The availability of coin is perhaps best illustrated for the second half of the
eleventh century and first decade or so of the twelfth century by the records of the
purchases of the abbots of Fécamp and Caen, which seem to have been made in
cash. Those made by the abbots of Fécamp have been discussed by Musset, who
remarked that the sums spent might rise to a little over 300 *livres*.[8] The records
of the purchases made by the abbots of Caen reveal that Abbot Lanfranc (1063–70)
spent 96 *livres* 4 *sous* on acquiring new possessions for his abbey. His successor,
Abbot William (1070–79), spent 183 *livres* 1 *sou*, and his successor, Abbot Gilbert
(1079–1101), spent some 135 *livres* 5 *sous* down to 1083. That, at least, is the situation reported in the *Emptiones* confirmed by William the Bastard in that year.[9]
King Henry I's acts for the same monks, as well as the deeds on which his *acta*
were based, reveal that the abbots continued to spend large sums down to 1135.
Abbot Gilbert spent almost another 327 *livres* on property between 1083 and 1101,
including the immense sum of 250 *livres* on the purchase of Baupte from Rainald
of Orval. Abbot Eudo (1107–44) continued to add to the endowment of his house

[4] F. Dumas-Dubourg, *Le trésor de Fécamp et le monnayage en Francie occidentale pendant
    la seconde moitié du Xᵉ siècle* (Paris, 1971); Bates, *Normandy*, pp. 96–7. It should perhaps
    be remarked that these 8,000 or so pennies made up a sum of around only 35 *livres*.
[5] L. Musset, 'Réflexions sur les moyens de payment en Normandie', p. 77. Françoise
    Dumas mentioned the hoard, but was concerned only with the Norman coins in it:
    Dumas, 'Les monnaies Normandes', 121 (no. 54).
[6] As revealed by the lists of finds in Dumas, 'Les monnaies Normandes', 116–36.
[7] Musset, 'Réflexions sur les moyens de payment en Normandie', pp. 80–4.
[8] L. Musset, 'A-t-il existé en Normandie au XIᵉ siècle une aristocratie d'argent?', *Annales
    de Normandie*, 9 (1959), 285–6.
[9] *Regesta: William*, no. 53.

and spent around 184 *livres*, one ounce of gold, three horses, one palfrey, three sesters of grain, one sester of barley, two pieces of fustian (*fustania*), and a bacon when doing so.[10] His purchases thus constitute a useful reminder that, although the duchy had a strong money economy, payments were also made in kind, not just to lords but also to vendors. This continued to be the case down to *c.* 1125.[11]

Ducal finance

Despite their fundamental importance to the dukes' ability to rule, Norman revenues and their collection have been remarkably understudied. This lacuna in the scholarship is almost certainly owing to the sparse and intractable nature of the evidence. There are no equivalents to Domesday Book or the pipe roll of Michaelmas 1130 which give a sense of royal income in England. It is consequently impossible to discuss Norman revenues in anything like the detail with which Judith Green, among others, has been able to discuss Henry I's revenues and government there. Indeed, so unpromising does the Norman evidence appear, that no historian has been tempted to investigate this topic in the round since Haskins published his *Norman Institutions* in 1918.

Haskins spent only a few pages examining ducal revenues.[12] In his opening chapter on 'Normandy under William the Conqueror', Haskins noted that the sources of income found in the late-twelfth- and early-thirteenth-century Norman pipe rolls were already in existence by William's reign. He mentioned the evidence for a *census*, but warned that 'it would be rash to attempt to define too closely the content of the *census* and the customs, but the *census* must at least have covered the returns from the demesne and forests'.[13] He inferred that the farms of the *vicomtés* were in existence before 1087.[14] And he concluded that 'in order to make grants of tithes of fixed amounts, the duke must have been in the habit of dealing with these local areas as fiscal wholes and not as mere aggregates of scattered sources of income; the unit was the *vicomté* or *prévôté*, and not the individual domain.'[15] His chapter on Henry I then went on to discuss the advent

---

[10]   AD Calvados, H 1834 (*Emptiones Eudonis*). The reference to fustian cloth is unusual, but supported by two uses of the word by Orderic in his *Ecclesiastical History*. In both instances, the cloth was used as a counter-gift (Orderic, iii. 190, 204). For comparison with England see Naismith, *Money and Power in Anglo-Saxon England*, pp. 267–73.

[11]   Musset, 'Réflexions sur les moyens de payment en Normandie', pp. 66–71.

[12]   *NI*, pp. 39–45, 105–10.

[13]   *NI*, p. 41.

[14]   *NI*, pp. 43–4.

[15]   *NI*, p. 44. It should be noted that, while his general argument is sound, Haskins was mistaken in that William did not make grants of fixed amounts of tithes.

of the exchequer, and to frame an 'ingenious' argument as to the identity of the earliest Norman treasurers.

Much of what Haskins wrote depended on later twelfth-century practices, making his conclusions unsafe. Work carried out on the English royal estates in the last thirty years or so suggests that the tidy picture of sheriffs paying a set farm for their shire did not exist before the reign of Henry I.[16] There is no reason to suppose that it was found in William's Normandy, either. Indeed, even in 1180 it is clear that the *vicomte* was not – in contrast to the English sheriff – always responsible for all the ducal possessions found in his county. Nor did all sources of revenue necessarily become incorporated into the farms. It may well have been the case, as a result, that the *vicomte* was not the only figure from each *vicomté* who turned up at the Norman exchequer to make an account. The roll of 1180 certainly suggests a far greater lack of structure than its English counterpart, with entries for revenues or places in one region separated by apparently random accounts for places elsewhere. Indeed, the very appearance of the 1180 roll is more confused and confusing than its English equivalent.[17]

More recent anglophone work has touched on ducal revenues in passing, but has not tried to develop our understanding of the composition of the dukes' income, how it was collected and accounted for, and the personnel involved. David Douglas was prepared to believe that there was both a system of accounting and a body of officials dedicated to this work during the reign of William the Bastard, 'but the progress towards anything that might be legitimately termed a finance bureau seems to have been very limited before 1066'.[18] John Le Patourel discussed ducal finance over seven pages of his *The Norman Empire*, but did little more than summarize and update the work of Haskins.[19] He remarked on the various types of revenue that might flow into the royal dukes' treasury: those produced by the demesne lands; the forests; markets and fairs; the coinage; the *fouage*; and some other revenues or taxes of Carolingian origin such as tolls. He noted that regular revenues were farmed by the *vicomtes*, while taxes were paid directly into the camera (as they did not constitute regular income). There was an itinerant treasury, the chamber, before 1066 as well as some system of record keeping, although he saw the development of treasuries at Rouen and Falaise, and treasurers with them, as post-Conquest developments. The exchequer was the product of Henry I's reign. David Bates's discussion of ducal finance was equally

---

[16] See below, *infra*, pp. 596–603.

[17] In contrast, Vincent Moss stressed the similarities between the two sets of rolls (V. Moss, 'Normandy and the Angevin Empire: A Study of the Norman Exchequer Rolls 1180–1204' (unpublished Ph.D. thesis, University of Wales, Cardiff, 1996), pp. 14–15).

[18] Douglas, *William the Conqueror*, p. 150.

[19] Le Patourel, *Norman Empire*, pp. 146–53.

summary in form. He noted the existence of two taxes, bernage (according to him analogous with the earlier *fodrum*) and *grauarium*. He briefly discussed the chamber, noting that it might make 'simple payments out of the revenues, such as a tenth of the profits of coinage' by the end of Richard II's reign, although he added that 'the precision with which these payments are recorded may suggest a system of record keeping of which all trace has been lost'.[20] He noted, too, the *vicomtes*' role in the collection of the dukes' revenues.[21]

The footnotes to these books reveal that the advances that have been made in the area of ducal finance and revenues since 1918 are principally the result of work of Lucien Musset. He considered topics such as the development of tolls, the ports and the revenues that they produced, markets and fairs, public taxation, and the various means of payment to be found in Normandy in the ducal period.[22] These articles are full of details: where the markets were found, the ports identified around the Normandy coast, how much fairs were farmed for, the types of coin to be found circulating in the duchy, and so on. But they were not synthesized by Musset to construct an overarching discussion about ducal finances or how they were collected. There are some issues with, and lacunae in, his arguments, too. Farms, for example, were treated by Musset – as by Haskins – as though they had always existed. The means of collection was suggested but not investigated.

Despite most historians' reluctance to explore these topics, there are more clues about the various types of income and the ways in which it was collected in the surviving *acta*, whether individually or in combination, than have previously been recognized, even if we cannot come close to a sense of the dukes' income as a whole, or what proportion of it derived from the demesne, rights such as tolls, the profits of justice, and so on. The following diploma provides an example of the material at our disposal. It yields some information about ducal finances, but it also raises a number of questions that other *acta* help us to answer.

I William duke of the Normans, studying to increase the abbey of Cerisy established by my father in honour of St Vigor, for the remedy of my soul and also his, gave to the same place the tithe of all my pennies of the *vicomté*

---

[20] Bates, *Normandy*, pp. 153–4.

[21] Bates, *Normandy*, pp. 157–8.

[22] L. Musset, 'Aristocratie d'argent', 285–99; L. Musset, 'Que peut-on savoir de la fiscalité publique en Normandie à l'époque ducale ?', *Revue historique de droit français et étranger*, fourth series, 38 (1960), 483–4; L. Musset, 'Recherches sur quelques survivances de la fiscalité ducal', *BSAN*, 55 (1961), 317–25, 420–35, 525–30; L. Musset, 'Recherches sur le tonlieu en Normandie à l'époque ducale' and 'Les ports en Normandie du XIe au XIIIe siècle: equisse d'histoire institutionelle', both in *Autour du pouvoir ducal normand Xe–XIIe siècles* (Caen, 1985), 61–76 and 113–28, respectively.

of the Cotentin and the tithe of the *vicomté* of Coutances and the tithe of the *vicomté* of Gavray in mills, in the grove, and of all my returns. And in my woods, namely in the wood of Montebourg and in the wood of Brix and in the wood of Rabey and in the wood of Cherbourg and in the wood of Valdecie and in the wood of Luthumière and of the meadows I gave to the same church the tithe of the pannage, the pleas, cows, pigs, and hunting. In Valognes, the tithe of my harvest and one *hôte* free from all custom. In Quettehou, I gave one *hôte* with his land free from all custom. I also gave the church of Rauville and one alod-holder in that vill. And in Sotteville the third part of the church and an alod-holder. And on the island of Jersey two free churches, namely the church of St Mary of Arsmoutier and Saint-Martin-le-Vieux with their lands and also the share of the grain. Also I gave a fourth part of the whole of *Withulle*, namely the land which Wigot the bearded held in alod, freely and absolved from all custom belonging to me. I also gave one alod-holder in Emondeville quit from all custom. And on top of these things I added Littry with all its appurtenances, with the church, with the woods, with the mills, with the waters, with the meadows, freely and absolved from all customs, both ecclesiastical and secular. I also granted the Bois de la Queue from the source of the Ruisseau Morel as far as Montfréard, with all the customs which it had previously. This little charter I, William, duke of the Normans, confirm by my authority and grant to be free and absolved of all customs. And whosoever shall presume to violate any of these things he shall be anathema. This is enacted in the year from the incarnation of the lord 1042, 12 kalends of May, during the reign of Henry, king of the Franks.[23]

The act, then, notes several revenues: tolls; the customs due from alod-holders and *hôtes*; tithes; woods; mills; waters; meadows; and the 'pennies' of the *vicomtés*.[24] It suggests something of the units of account: individual income streams; vills; and *vicomtés*. The very existence of the diploma informs us about revenue collection, too, for there must have been systems in place that would allow each of the items granted to be identified and released to the monks. And so, in the absence of pipe rolls or other financial records, this examination of ducal finances will seek to understand, as precisely as possible, how this document and others like it might have been put into effect by attempting to perceive the

---

[23] *RADN*, no. 99.

[24] An act of Count Richard of Evreux for Saint-Sauveur of Evreux dating from 1055 × 1066 includes a grant of the 'tithe of the toll, *census*, and all the rents of (or 'in') pennies' (*RADN*, no. 208). It seems plausible that the 'pennies' of the *vicomtés* were similarly comprised of rents or issues paid in cash.

structures that lay behind the written words that allowed the dukes to collect and distribute their revenues.

Types of revenue

The revenues of the dukes of the Normans were, of course, composed of a number of different elements. Our information about these various sources of revenue comes almost entirely from the ducal *acta*, and is consequently incomplete. In particular, there is as ever almost no information whatsoever about the situation as it was in the tenth century. Nonetheless, there is material enough to provide at least some clues as to the various sorts of income that the dukes might enjoy, as well as how it was accounted for, and by whom.

The demesne estates produced rents, which took the form of cash payments as well as of payments in kind (for example, in grain, hens, and eggs). These rents would probably count among the 'customs' of the *hôtes* (also known as *coloni* and *villani*) and alod-holders granted to the monks of Cerisy. In the absence of polyptychs for the dukes' demesne, there is little evidence for the value or make-up of these rents. There is, however, a series of surveys for the nuns of Holy Trinity of Caen that provide a sense of what the dukes might have expected from their own tenants, not least because Ouistreham, which was one of the vills surveyed, had been ducal demesne before part of it was granted to the nuns in 1082.[25] In *c.* 1113, the nuns recorded that:

> In Ouistreham we have 29 full villans, and half of the land of Serlo. Each of them returns 4 and a half *sous* per year, and three quarters of wheat, and 5 pounds of malt, and 2 capons at Christmas, and 20 eggs at Easter. And they plough an acre of land each year, half of it before Christmas and half of it after Christmas. And they harrow and sow our seed. And also of one of their pigs, 1 *denier* each year … We have six men there who the vulgar call alod-holders; each of them holds his garden (*ortus*) and they do service at nearby manors and they return each year 16 *deniers* and four pounds of oats.[26]

From their share of the vill, then, the nuns received 6 *livres* 18 *sous* in cash, an unknown amount of pennies for the pigs, 87 quarters of wheat, 145 lb of malt, 58 capons at Christmas, 580 eggs at Easter, and 24 lbs of oats. Similar rents can also be seen on other of the nuns' properties, and there is other evidence to show that such rents and services were owed elsewhere both before and after these surveys

[25] *Regesta: William*, no. 59.
[26] *Chs. Caen*, p. 53.

were drawn up. Thus an act of 1017 × 1026, by which Richard II confirmed the grant of Autigny by a certain Mainard to the monks of Saint-Ouen, noted that 'the dues that are paid by the cultivators of this land every year are 12 *deniers*, and from Gauzelin 2 *sous* and from the others 4 *sous*, and 16 sesters of oats ready for making good drink; at Christmas 2 sesters of wheat and 12 hens; and at the feast of St Rémi 8 *deniers* and 4 cart-loads of wood.'[27] Similarly, in 1125 × 1146, the monks of Préaux were given the service of one *hôte* which comprised a rent of three *sous*, four capons, four loaves, and forty eggs and two loaves at Easter.[28]

In addition to such rents, lords would also have had the produce of their own demesne that the villans and others had been ploughing, sowing, and harrowing, surpluses of which might be sold in return for cash. Grants of tithes provide the best available evidence for the types of commodities produced by the dukes' demesne, and so we may surmise that the dukes' vills were stocked with various types of livestock, most notably cows, pigs, sheep, and horses. There was hay from the meadows. Some vills had fisheries. There might be wood for building or burning, or salt from salt pans as at Bouteilles near Dieppe or around the estuary of the Dives.[29] There were mills and ovens, too, both of which produced revenues.[30]

In addition to the produce of the demesne and the payments in cash and kind, there is clear evidence that both ducal and seigniorial estates in Normandy might produce another type of annual rent known as a *census*.[31] *Census* is not

[27] *RADN*, no. 45.
[28] *Ctl. Préaux*, A146.
[29] *RADN*, no. 231; *Regesta: William*, nos. 95, 282, 284; *Regesta*, ii. 353–4 (no clxxvii) = no. 1441; 362–3 (no. ccxii) = no. 1577; 374 (no. cclv) = no. 1706. The count of Evreux's vill at Varaville also produced salt (Bauduin, *Première Normandie*, pp. 391–2).
[30] For example, *RADN*, nos. 101, 139, 144, 222, 224; *Regesta: William*, nos. 149, 158, 162, 166, 198, 205, 215, 238, 252, 260, 280, 281; *Regesta*, ii. 331 (no. xcii) = no. 1085; 353–4 (clxxvii) = no. 1441 (for multure); *RADN*, nos. 120, 122; *Regesta: William*, nos. 59, 62, 166, 196, 215, 251, 252, 281 (II and III); *Regesta*, ii. nos. 1019, 1553, 1554, 1700, 1742, 1764; Chanteux, *Recueil*, no. 13 (for ovens).
[31] The *census* in Normandy was probably inherited from Carolingian *Francia*. The Annals of Saint-Bertin, for example, record that a *census* amounting to 50 *livres* of silver was delivered to Charles the Bald from Brittany in 864. There is no sense that Charles had demanded this tribute. It was a voluntary offering in (temporary) recognition of Frankish overlordship. The annal for 877 then records the arrangements for the collection of a tribute from that part of Francia which Charles had held before Lothair's death and from Burgundy, stating that every free manse was obliged to produce 4 *deniers* from the lord's rent (*census*) and 4 *deniers* from the tenant's assets (*The Annals of Saint-Bertin*, trans. Nelson, pp. 118, 200). These annals thus illustrate the ambiguity of the word, which could shade from 'tribute' to 'rent' with the actual meaning dependent on context. In both cases, however, the word also implied a lack of compulsion and thus a sense of bilateral agreement. This can be seen elsewhere. Robert Guiscard promised to pay the pope a *census* in recognition of his overlordship in 1059, that *census* thus being

a word that is commonly found in ducal *acta*. It appears just nine times in the Norman (as opposed to Manceaux) acts collected in Marie Fauroux's *Recueil*;[32] in ten Norman acts of William I after 1066;[33] one of Curthose; and just two of the Norman *acta* of Henry I (one of them repeating a gift made by his father).[34] While a payment described as a *census* might be a payment made voluntarily as tribute, the word also described a payment that took the form of a rent, the level of which was either fixed by *bilateral* agreement or which would vary depending on the actual revenue produced in any given period. Thus, in 1006 × 1017, Richard II subscribed an act by which a certain Drogo gave to the abbey of Saint-Ouen outside Rouen some land and vines at Bailleul. He also left the abbey two mills, which were to be held during their lifetimes by his two brothers. In the meantime those brothers were to pay a *census* each year to the abbey for those mills.[35] In 1027 × 1035, Roger of Montgommery agreed to pay the monks of Jumièges a *census* of

a sum agreed to by both parties (G. A. Loud, 'Coinage, wealth and plunder in the age of Robert Guiscard', *EHR*, 114 (1999), 823). The Treaty of Benevento of 1156 also provided for the payment of a *census* to the pope. Ian Robinson noted that such payments had been made since the eighth century, and that they were 'fixed arbitrarily without reference to its relative wealth (apparently by the benefactor who gave the monastery to the Roman church)'. They were also paid by those who were papal vassals or who had sought papal protection (Robinson, *The Papacy*, pp. 271–4). In such cases, the meaning of *census* is closer to 'tribute' than 'rent', but again without any hint of coercion. A similar use of the word can be found in an act of William I for the bishop of Exeter (*Regesta: William*, no. 138). Lyon and Verhulst, writing of a document dating from 1233, suggest that *census* might mean both a quit-rent or a fixed-term rent (B. Lyon and A. Verhulst, *Medieval Finance: A Comparison of Financial Institutions in Northwestern Europe* (Bruges, 1967), p. 31). Baldwin defined 'census' as a fixed rent (J. W. Baldwin, *The Government of Philip Augustus: Foundations of French Royal Power in the Middle Ages* (Berkeley, Los Angeles, and Oxford, 1986), p. 45), although Richard fitz Nigel in his near-contemporary *Dialogue of the Exchequer* wrote that a cess-rent (*census*) varied from year to year as it related to the actual sums produced by the property in question and so was not fixed as farms were (*Dialogue*, p. 46). None of these sources remark the bilateral nature of such rents suggested here, although their definitions do not exclude it. Finally, while Geoffrey Koziol would seem to have found an exception to the rule, his translation has distorted the meaning of the document in question. He wrote of a *census* being ordained for a potential tenant/claimant, but the Latin (*aut talem ille censum inde persoluat, qualis et fuerit constitutio*) does not bear that meaning (Koziol, *Begging Pardon*, p. 395, n. 15).

[32] *RADN*, nos. 19, 34, 61, 74, 83, 98, 120, 186, 208. In addition, no. 165 concerns property in le Mans.

[33] *Regesta: William*, nos. 52, 59, 149, 162, 166, 196, 215, 243, 271, 281(III). In addition, no. 172 concerns property in Maine.

[34] Chanteux, *Recueil*, no. 95 = *Regesta*, ii. no. 1927 (Saint-Etienne, Caen); Chanteux, *Recueil*, no. 13 (Lyre).

[35] *RADN*, no. 19.

3 *livres* each year so that he might hold a market at Montgommery, just down the road from the monks' pre-existing market at Vimoutiers.[36] In 1042 × 1066, a grant made by Roger the son of Bishop Hugh of Coutances to the nuns of Saint-Amand of Rouen mentions a *census* of 15 *sous* for a fishery that was paid to the monks of Saint-Denis.[37] There was a *census* 'of the villans' at Pîtres and Romilly, which William fitz Osbern granted to the monks of Lyre, and which may be supposed, on the basis of their status, to have been a variable sum reflecting the actual value produced by their land.[38] The surveys on the lands of the nuns of the Holy Trinity of Caen further suggest that the *census* might be owed only by certain individuals known as *censarii*, who were probably among the free tenants of the nuns' manors.[39]

The use of the word in these acts suggests, as indicated above, that the *census* was not a unilaterally imposed rent for land or for things planted or built on land, but rather the result either of a bilateral agreement between, for example, landlord and tenant, or else of an understanding that the sum in question was variable. The voluntary nature of a *census*, either as a tribute or as a rent, is also suggested by the wording of a diploma of Duke Richard II for the monks of Fécamp dating from 1025, in which he confirmed grants including the tithe of the duke's money, and of the chamber, 'namely of whatever is given to me, in the service of any business, namely the purchase of lands or of other transactions or any other business or gifts freely given except the *census* of the *fisc* and except those things which are from old times called customs'.[40] It would seem that the *census* was numbered among those gifts freely given – in other words that it was paid by agreement. Furthermore, the idea of a *census* of the *fisc* hints that such payments might not only constitute money handed over in return for particular pieces of property, but also payments for whole blocks of territory – a point to which we will return shortly.

Aside from the income generated by the demesne and those tenants who lived on it, the dukes gained income from a variety of customs and taxes that were levied across the duchy. According to the *Liber de reuelatione* of the abbey of Fécamp, when Richard II approached Abbot Mayeul of Cluny for the monks he needed to turn his father's college of canons into an abbey, Mayeul is said to have demanded the custom of *pasnagium*, or pannage, which Richard collected across

---

[36] *RADN*, no. 74.

[37] *RADN*, no. 186.

[38] *RADN*, no. 120.

[39] *Chs. Caen*, pp. 57, 58. On the *censarii* found in Domesday Book, similarly thought to be among the free tenants of the manors, see H. Ellis, *A General Introduction to Domesday Book* (London, 1833), p. 88.

[40] *RADN*, no. 34.

582   NORMAN RULE IN NORMANDY 911–1144

his duchy in return.[41] There is some evidence for the custom in the Norman pipe roll of 1180, which contains an account for 63 *sous* and 5 *deniers* of pannage arising from the forests of the Passais, but it may be that the revenues produced from this custom were more usually accounted for in the general accounts for the forest regards.[42] In some cases, exemptions might be granted, but otherwise it seems that those allowing their pigs to roam in the dukes' forests in the autumn were liable to pay a charge for the privilege.

When remarking on this passage, Cassandra Potts suggested that the custom of pannage was actually a 'pasture tax'. While that is not right, there does seem to have been a custom amounting to a pasture tax in the duchy as a 'custom of pasture' is found at Bavent and Hotot in an act of William I for the monks of Caen.[43] There was also a custom, perhaps paid in both money and kind, for the use of the dukes' meadows.[44] In addition, there were customary fees for the (compulsory) grinding of grain at ducal mills (multure) and the baking of bread in the dukes' ovens.[45] There was a custom due on wine stored in warehouses.[46] Tolls were levied on sales and purchases at markets and fairs, including on wine and salt,[47] and on goods being brought to market. An act of Robert Curthose for the monks of Caen reveals that in one vill at least – Vains in the Avranchin – these tolls were paid not just by merchants going to and from markets, but also by those who lived in the vill.[48] Other tolls were paid for passage over bridges and along roads – especially perhaps the public highways occasionally mentioned in

---

[41] *Neustria Pia*, p. 210. J.-F. Lemarignier, *Privileges*, pp. 30–1 (who translated the passage correctly); Potts, *Monastic Revival*, pp. 27–8. Lords might also have the right to collect pannage in their forests: for example, *Regesta: William*, nos. 262, 266.

[42] *Norman Pipe Rolls*, p. 20. The foresters were notified of the right of the monks of Envermeu to put their pigs out to pannage by Henry I, which suggests that they had responsibility for collection (*Regesta*, ii. 315 (no. xliv) = no. 794).

[43] *Regesta: William*, no. 49. The act of Ralph fitz Herfred granting the monks the custom at Bavent, later incorporated into King William's act, is found in Ctl. Caen, fos. 12v, 47v–48r. It is possible that this custom was based on a grazing tax found in the Carolingian period and noted in, for example, the polyptych of Saint-Germain-des-Près (quoted in A. Verhulst, *The Carolingian Economy* (Cambridge, 2002), p. 39). The count of Mortain also had a custom of pasture in the Forêt de Lande-Pourrie (*Regesta: William*, no. 215)

[44] See on this, L. Musset, 'Les prés et le foin du seigneur roi', in *Autour du pouvoir ducal normand, X^e–XIIe siècles*, ed. L. Musset, J.-M. Bouvris, and J.-M. Maillefer (Caen, 1985), pp. 77–93.

[45] See above, n. 30.

[46] *Les actes de Guillaume le Conquérant et de la reine Mathilde pour les abbayes Caennaises*, ed. L. Musset, MSAN, 37 (1967), p. 92 (no. 10).

[47] Musset, 'Recherches dur le tonlieu', p. 71.

[48] *NI*, Appendix E, no. 1; Musset, 'Recherches dur le tonlieu', p. 72.

ducal *acta*. There were charges for licences for navigation and mooring fees, too.[49] Perhaps there was also a landing tax, such as was found in Norway, which foreigners paid on arrival and departure (rather like a modern visa).[50]

Although they were collected in individual vills such as Vains or Cheux, revenues from tolls would have flowed in above all from the cities and towns of the duchy, and from Rouen in particular.[51] Unfortunately, there are few contemporary records that suggest how much profit might accrue from markets, fairs, and other tolls and charges. We do know, however, that Roger of Montgommery gave the monks of Sées '40 *sous* from the tithe of the toll of Sées', suggesting that the annual income from that toll was more than 20 *livres*.[52] The college at Beaumont-le-Roger had 6 *livres* of the toll of Neubourg from Roger of Beaumont before 1087.[53] The *De statu huius ecclesiae* ('this church' being, it will be remembered, the cathedral at Coutances) famously notes that after Bishop Geoffrey of Montbray built a mill and a stone bridge over the Vire at Saint-Lô, the toll of the *bourg* rose from 15 *livres* to 220 *livres*.[54] The grants that Henry I made from the income from tolls also provide some indication of the minimum revenue they generated. Thus the canons of Sées were given 'fifteen *livres* of the money of Rouen each year, which I gave on the dedication of that church, namely seven *livres* and ten *sous* from my toll of Falaise and seven *livres* and ten *sous* from my toll of Exmes'. Another 60 *sous* 10 *deniers* had been given from the toll of Exmes to the canons by King William previously.[55]

It is worth looking at the evidence of the Norman pipe roll of 1180 to supplement this sparse information, even if it is not certain that the sums produced then would also have accrued before 1144. For illustrative purposes only, then, the 'farm of the tolls and ovens and mills of Mortain' was set at 160 *livres*. The tithe of the

---

[49] *RADN*, no. 90. See also L. Musset, 'Les ports en Normandie', pp. 122–4. The customs of Chester, set out in Domesday Book, reveal the existence of charges there, too (GDB, fo. 262c; Chester, §§ C.15–17). See also S. Kelly, 'Trading privileges from eighth-century England', *Early Medieval Europe*, 1 (1992), 16–22, who noted that in Carolingian Francia *teloneum* was a charge on the circulation of merchandise as well as an indirect tax on sales, and noticed, too, the existence of *portaticum* (a charge on entry into a port) and the *ripatium* (probably a landing fee).

[50] *Heimskringla*, p. 277.

[51] Musset suggested that they were collected on a county or town basis, but the link he made between toll and county is not convincing (Musset, 'Recherches sur le tonlieu', pp. 64–5, 68). There seems also to have been an elision here between collection and accounting.

[52] Ctl. Sées, fo. 2r; Musset, 'Recherches sur le tonlieu', p. 73.

[53] *Ctl. Beaumont*, p. 5; Musset, 'Recherches sur le tonlieu', p. 74.

[54] *GC*, xi. Instr. Col. 219.

[55] *NI*, pp. 300–2 (no. 11).

ovens was worth 2 *livres*, suggesting a total income of 20 *livres* from that source, while the tithe of the two fairs can be multiplied to give a figure of 6 *livres*. The revenue of the mills and tolls at Varreville and Poupeville in the Cotentin was 6 *livres* (again based on the tithe), and the mills at Sainte-Mère-Eglise seem to have produced some 48 *livres*.[56] The fair at Montmartin (in the *vicomté* of Vire) was held at farm for 300 *livres*, while the farm of the fair held at Argentan at Pentecost was 15 *livres*, and the farm of the fair field at Caen was 100 *livres*.[57] Moreover, the tithe of the toll of Caen amounted to 80 *livres* in the roll of 1198, suggesting a total sum of 800 *livres*.[58] The income produced from these charges, then, might be significant.

It may be that there were additional one-off payments as a result of these tolls and other charges or gifts, too. For so long as the right to grant a market remained a ducal monopoly,[59] and it is not clear that Musset was right to argue that this had already ceased to be the case *c.* 1000,[60] if a lord desired to establish a market in one of his vills and thus enjoy the tolls that it would produce, he would most likely have had to pay the duke for the grant. Markets that were established without a licence would be shut down by the local *vicomte*, acting here to protect the dukes' rights. Fairs, too, also required the duke's licence, and it may be deduced from the address clauses of the two Norman writs concerning grants of fairs that *vicomtes* might act to close down unlicensed ones, or seize the revenues they had produced.[61] It is clear that there was also a desire for exemptions from payments of

[56] *Norman Pipe Rolls*, pp. 6, 28, 71, respectively.
[57] *Norman Pipe Rolls*, pp. 22, 28, 41, respectively. See, for some other figures, Musset, 'Recherches sur le tonlieu', p. 75.
[58] Noted in Musset, 'Recherches sur le tonlieu', p. 75.
[59] This would then be a right inherited from the Carolingians, as Charles the Bald had claimed this monopoly in the Edict of Pîtres (Nelson, 'Kingship and royal government', p. 397).
[60] L. Musset, 'Foires et marchés en Normandie à l'époque ducale', *Annales de Normandie*, 26 (1976), 15. The example of Vimoutiers, if correctly interpreted here, argues against it. There is no evidence that the duke held any demesne in the vill, but Richard II had still created a market there (*RADN*, no. 25). William the Bastard likewise granted 'a certain market and fairs' to the monks of Baeumont-lès-Tours in 1066 (*RADN*, no. 227), apparently in vills that did not comprise part of his demesne. Furthermore, while Duclair had been granted in its entirety to the monks of Jumièges by 1025 (*RADN*, no. 36), Richard I granted the monks a market there on 28 August 1197 (Ctl. Jumièges, p. 175, no. 191). Equally, while Hugh of La Ferté-en-Bray did grant the church of Boissay to the monks of Saint-Ouen along with three fairs (*RADN*, no. 103), as Musset noted, there is no evidence that the fairs originated with this donation. They could well have been in existence already as the result of a ducal grant.
[61] *Regesta*, ii. 331 (no. xciii) = no. 1086; *NI*, p. 101 (no. 10) = *Regesta*, ii. no. 1708. In contrast, a writ-charter granting Bishop Ouen of Evreux half of the proceeds of the fair at Nonancourt-sur-Avre was not addressed to the *vicomte*, but rather to Henry's adminis-

toll, passage, and custom, with the dukes granting them to a number of religious houses, which included in their number 'foreign' abbeys such as Flay, Pontigny, and Saint-Père of Chartres.[62]

There are two other taxes that deserve to be discussed, bernage and *grauarium*, which were both levied across the duchy including from alods outside the demesne.[63] These seem to have been based on Carolingian taxes,[64] but that does not necessarily mean that Bates was right when he opined that they had been collected for many years before they appeared by name during the reign of William the Bastard.[65] Their appearance during William's reign, Bates argued, was indicative of greater exploitation of such resources now that the demesne had been so much reduced in extent, and this is possible. And by explicitly naming particular customs in their grants, thereby implicitly excluding others, the dukes were limiting what they were giving away to beneficiaries in a way that they had not done previously.

Bernage – paid in oats or coin – appears *c.*1050 among the *consuetudines uicecomitatus* granted to the monks of Saint-Pierre of Préaux (the customs here being sums of money accruing from such customs, rather than the actual right per se).[66] The monks of Cerisy, Saint-Etienne of Caen, Grestain, and Saint-Pierre-sur-Dives, as well as the cathedral at Rouen, were given exemptions from payment of bernage, and sometimes *grauarium* too, by William the Bastard and his sons.[67] Only two acts, however, provide information about the collection and value of this tax. In 1096 × 1099, William Rufus issued a writ concerning the collection of bernage on one of the vills belonging to the monks of le Bec:

> William king of the English to F. the fewterer and Isembard the berner and all his serjeants collecting this custom greeting. Know that I quitclaim the land of St Mary at Surcy of bernage until I shall learn how the custom was in my father's time.[68]

Frank Barlow thought that these men were the officials in charge of the greyhounds and harriers respectively, and that the address might be interpreted

trators and to the generality of Normandy (*Regesta*, ii. 347 (no. clviia) = no. 1356). This may be because the act was not a writ.
[62] See n. 99 below.
[63] The alod of Ansfrid of Poussy was quitted from payment of these two taxes in 1081 × 1082 (*Regesta: William*, no. 50).
[64] Musset, 'Recherches sur le tonlieu', p. 61.
[65] Bates, *Normandy*, p. 153.
[66] *Ctl. Préaux*, A161, A163; *RADN*, no. 121.
[67] *RADN*, nos. 169, 196 (Cerisy); *Regesta: William*, nos. 50 (Caen), 158 (Grestain); AD Calvados, H 7031(5) (Saint-Pierre-sur-Dives); *NI*, p. 70 (Rouen).
[68] *NI*, p. 82.

as revealing that the king's own kennel-men collected the tax from the audit, with their sergeants collecting the tax on the ground and bringing the money to the audit.[69] As King William sought to establish the custom of his father's time, it would seem that the amount owing was fixed. Whether the amounts due remained fixed at the same rate until 1180 is another question, but it may be that the Norman pipe roll of that year can shed at least some light on the value of the bernage for the period before 1144. In that roll, there are accounts for 4 *livres* 11 *sous* 10 *deniers* of bernage due from the *baillia* (probably the earlier *vicomtés*) of Argentan and Exmes, 26 *livres* 18 *sous* and 4 *deniers* from the Cotentin, 11 *livres* 12 *deniers* from the Hiémois, and 6 *livres* from the *vicomté* of Arques, among others.[70] The separate accounts for bernage suggest that it was not considered part of the farm, even after farms were established, perhaps because it was a payment that could be made in kind.

Less still is known about *grauarium*. Although when it appears it is usually twinned with bernage – as in William the Bastard's acts for Cerisy and Henry I's act for Saint-Pierre-sur-Dives – it appears less frequently than that tax. Musset noted the existence of four or five known collectors of *grauarium*, but suggested that they were not of great interest. He did remark, though, that it was possible to trace the family of Herbert *grauerenc* – who himself appears in an act of 1051 × 1066 for la Trinité-du-Mont outside Rouen – through the cartulary of that house.[71] In Henry I's reign, Amaury of Montfort had to suffer the work of *grava-ringos* (collectors of *grauarium*) on his lands, and this was one of the reasons why he rebelled for a second time against the royal duke in 1123.[72] It looks, then, as if some effort was put into its collection. The amount of revenue produced by the tax is extremely unclear, however, and the sums collected seem to be concealed in

---

[69] Barlow, *William Rufus*, pp. 126–9 for hunting with dogs, and p. 127, n. 133 for a brief discussion of the writ.

[70] *Norman Pipe Rolls*, pp. 15, 28, 35, 66, respectively. Other accounts may be found at pp. 50 (Bonneville), 51–2 (Vesly), 57 (Pavilly and *Scura* in the Roumois), 59 (between Risle and Seine), 65 (Lieuvin), 69 (Auge), 71 (Sainte-Mère-Eglise). Moss calculated that income from bernage, added to that produced by *regardum*, fines for selling wine above the established price (this is *vinum super venditum*, which Moss sees as 'a fiscal source based on the extensive wine trade' (V. Moss, 'Normandy and England in 1180: the pipe roll evidence', in *England and Normandy in the Middle Ages*, ed. D. Bates and A. Curry (London, 1994), p. 192) rather than a fine), and fines for taking fat fish or whales without licence, amounted to 1,028 *livres* 5 *sous* 10 *deniers Angevins* in the incomplete roll of 1180 – or 3.8 per cent of total income (Moss, 'Normandy and England in 1180: the pipe roll evidence', p. 192).

[71] *RADN*, no. 202; Musset, 'Aristocratie d'argent', 289.

[72] Orderic, vi. 330. They almost certainly had no right to be there in the first place: see above, Chapter 3, p. 175 and Chapter 9, pp. 564–5.

the farms in the Norman pipe rolls so that they do not help. But there is an act of the Empress Matilda that reads as follows: 'Know that I have granted and given in perpetual alms to God and the monks of Saint-André-en-Gouffern next to Falaise … 46 *sous* and 6 *deniers* of Rouen which the *vicomtes* of Argentan are accustomed to return annually of *grauarium* of *Mons Guarulfi* from their own land that they held there.'[73]

Even allowing for the relatively low value of Norman pennies, a sum of 46 *sous*, or just under 12 shillings, in tax from the *vicomte*'s demesne in one manor would seem to compare favourably with the sums brought in by the Danegeld in England, charged at a rate of 2 shillings per hide. This one act, then, suggests that the *grauarium* was a lucrative source of income, but without more information, we cannot be sure.

Thomas Bisson suggested, with suitable qualification, that another tax, the *monetagium* (which he identified with the *fouage*), was collected in Normandy from the end of the eleventh century.[74] David Bates hesitated to accept his argument, and Daniel Power is more convincing in arguing that it was only introduced after 1144.[75] As such, this tax need not be considered here.

There may have been other, more arbitrary forms of taxation, too. The *Anglo-Saxon Chronicle* notes that both Normandy and England were taxed in 1117, and uses the same word 'geld (*gyld*)' for both levies.[76] This is unexpected, and as there was no tradition of Danegeld in Normandy, this report may be misleading. However, an act for the monks of Caen of 1081 × 1082 includes a grant that the abbey's men in Rots and Cheux should be free from 'service in the army, carriage, and geld'.[77] This statement indicates that this tax constituted a charge on the general population, but as there is no further indication of irregular taxation in Normandy, the matter must be left unresolved.

It is, however, clear that some lords did arbitrarily demand money and services from their men. Another charter for the monks of Caen records Ingelran fitz Ilbert's gift of the tithe of the 'boon-works and corvées (*precationum et*

---

[73] *Regesta*, iii. no.748. The editors confused the reference to *grauarium* for a place name.

[74] T. N. Bisson, *Conservation of Coinage: Monetary Exploitation and its restraint in France, Catalonia and Aragon, c. 1000–1225AD* (Oxford, 1979), pp. 14–28. It will be recalled that three years later Bates equated the *fouage* with bernage. The link between the *fouage* and either of these other taxes, however, is unconvincing.

[75] Power, *The Norman Frontier*, pp. 35–8.

[76] *ASChr*, 'E', sa. 1117; trans. Garmonsway, p. 247. The Old English text is: 'Normandig wearð swiða gedreht, ægðer ge þurh gyld ge þurh fyrde þ se cing Henri þærongean gaderode' (*The Anglo-Saxon Chronicle: A Collaborative Edition, 7 MS E*, ed. S. Irvine (Cambridge, 2004), p. 119.

[77] *Regesta: William*, no. 50. The word is missing from the original, but survives in the cartulary copy (fo. 6r).

corvetarum)' of Aunay-sur-Odon.[78] Orderic noted that Robert of Bellême had oppressed the monks of Troarn and Sées with unjust 'exactiones',[79] and also that unaccustomed charges (*insolitas exactiones*) were levied on the citizens of Alençon by Stephen of Blois and on the county of Evreux by Henry's officials.[80] Those levied by Stephen were also described by Orderic as 'angariis et exactionibus'.[81] The first of these, also inflicted by Bellême, did not comprise revenue but rather the exaction of forced labour.[82] The differentiation might suggest that 'exactiones' took the form of demands for money. It is possible that these 'exactiones' over-lapped with the later tallages, which also seem to have existed in Normandy before 1144,[83] but it is impossible to be sure because even the word 'exactiones' is unusual in (apparently) authentic Anglo-Norman *acta* before the reign of Henry I and remains rare until after 1135.[84] Orderic similarly employed it only from Book 7 of his *Ecclesiastical History*, which he wrote 1130–33.[85] Such forms of taxation, then, may have been unusual in the eleventh century, and became widespread, even if still rarely levied, only during the course of the twelfth century. The imposition of such charges was clearly unpopular, but the dukes no doubt felt the additional revenue was worth the grumbling it caused. The Norman Pipe Roll of 1198 records the effect of such a tax, in this case a tallage. It brought in around 48,000 *livres angevin*, which was just under half of the revenue recorded in the roll for that year. In contrast, the farms brought in just 13 per cent of that year's revenue.[86]

Aside from customs, regular taxation, and one-off payments for grants or

---

[78] *Regesta: William*, no. 48. The grant is repeated in no. 49. The context suggests that *corveta* should be translated as corvée. That form of the word seems to be unusual and is not found, for example, in the *Dictionary of Medieval Latin from British Sources*. If the translation is correct, this would be very early evidence of the existence of that right in the duchy. A gift of customs including *corvaria* is also found in an act for the monks of St Vincent of Le Mans (*Regesta: William*, no. 173).

[79] Orderic, iv. 296; vi. 46.

[80] Orderic, vi. 206 (Alençon), 330 (Evreux).

[81] Orderic, vi. 196.

[82] Orderic, iv. 296.

[83] Tallages are noted only very rarely in Norman documents from before 1144. I have found only two references, one in *Ctl. Mont-Saint-Michel*, p. 94 (no. 16), which notes that Thomas of Saint-Jean-le-Thomas acknowledged that the abbot had the right to the multure, tolls, tallages (*taillas*), aids, and other services of his men, and the second in Ctl. Troarn, fo. 182v. For a discussion of the use of tallages in Normandy as revealed by the Norman Pipe Rolls at the end of the twelfth century and beginning of the thirteenth century see Moss, 'Normandy and the Angevin Empire', pp. 65, 70–3.

[84] *RADN*, nos. 61, 199, 214, 222; *Regesta: William*, nos. 27, 264; *Regesta*, ii. nos. 1434, 1569 (authentic original), 1589, 1680, 1742 (authentic original), 1764 (authentic original).

[85] Orderic, iv. xix.

[86] Moss, 'Normandy and the Angevin Empire', p. 65.

exactions, there were also profits from justice. We may infer that the dukes derived income – even if we have no idea how much – from the fines that were described as *consuetudines uicecomitatus* in around 1050, which comprised 'hamfara (assault within a house), *ullac* (either the harbouring of outlaws or forfeitures resulting from exile), rape, arson, … making war'.[87] The *consuetudines et iusticie* of 1091 or 1096 reveal that the duke would also gain fines from attacks made on men going to court or serving in the army of Normandy, as well as for breaches of the other customs established there, for example, the construction of an unlicensed castle, attacks on merchants or pilgrims, or the minting of counterfeit coins.[88]

Something of the scale of these fines can be seen in two acts of Henry I. Firstly, in 1129 × 1133, the royal duke issued the following charter for the monks of Fécamp:

> Know that by the judgment and consideration of my court by the privilege of Fécamp from the gift and grant of my predecessors there remain to Abbot Roger of Fécamp and the convent of Fécamp 21 *livres* of the plea of a certain arson and 20 *livres* of a plea of a certain homicide done in the land of the Holy Trinity of Fécamp, from where my justice had pleaded and had held a duel, about the arson, in my court.[89]

Just two cases, then, raised over 40 *livres*. Secondly, in 1134, Henry granted wide-ranging jurisdiction to the monks of Le Bec. The act explicitly set out the fines to be levied in cases of assault and related offences:

> if one of the men of the church of Le Bec strikes someone within the parish of Le Bec without premeditation and not on account of an old hatred he shall pay a fine of 18 sous to the abbot and the monks. If, truly, he did this as the result of an old hatred, he shall be convicted and pay a fine of 60 sous. If a stranger in a sudden anger should strike someone within the parish, if he is captured and retained, he shall be deraigned about it in the abbot's court and according to the judgment of that court he shall pay a fine. If anyone in the vill of Le Bec or outside the vill in the parish shall assault someone in a premeditated manner he shall pay a fine of 60 sous. And if the abbot's men see something like this done outside the church and the park, and if they should not make a public announcement about it, and unless in the abbot's court they show that

---

[87] *Ctl. Préaux*, A161 and A163; *RADN*, no. 121. The first act lists the customs; the second refers to them as the *consuetudines uicecomitatus*.

[88] *NI*, Appendix D, pp. 281–4.

[89] *NI*, p. 90 = *Regesta*, ii. no. 1579.

they could not keep (*retinere*) him, each of them shall pay a fine of 18 sous. We also forbid and establish (*statuimus*) that none of the abbot's men of the vill of Le Bec shall either by day or night be armed within the vill of Le Bec. Thus if anyone carries arms he shall be seized, unless he has to go far outside the vill for his work, and he shall pay a fine of 18 sous.[90]

It may be supposed that the royal duke collected similar fines himself, even if it is not clear that they were set at the same level. In addition, there is mention of the right of wreck in an act of 1115 × 1129,[91] while the Norman pipe rolls record fines for a breach of the customs concerning the sale of wine or the taking of fat fish or whales, and the income from the sale of the chattels of fugitives from ducal justice.

Collection and account

The capitulary *De uillis*, which dates from *c.* 800, set out Charlemagne's expectations about the stocking and maintenance of his demesne estates, as well as the collection of the income that they produced.[92] Among the various provisions it makes for the collection, recording, and delivery of income and produce, Chapter 62 reads:

> Each steward shall make an annual statement of all our income … of the rents (*de censis*), of the obligations and fines, of the game taken in our forests without our permission, of the various payments, of the mills, of the forest, of the fields, of the bridges, and ships; of the free men and the hundreds who are under obligations to our treasury; of markets, vineyards, and those who owe wine to us … of the people giving tribute; of the colts and fillies. They shall make all these known to us, set forth separately and in order, at Christmas, in order that we may know how much we have of each thing.[93]

In Charlemagne's day, then, stewards were responsible for collecting the revenues produced by, or due from, their vill. Thus they did not pay a fixed rent, but rather a variable *census* comprised of, or reflecting in cash terms, everything that they

---

[90]   BnF, MS lat. 13905, fol. 9r–v; Porée, *Histoire de l'Abbaye du Bec*, i. 658 (with errors, but with a French translation at, i. 377–8) = *Regesta*, ii. no. 1900. The authenticity of this document is open to question, even though it cannot be condemned outright.

[91]   *Regesta*, ii. pp. 365–6 (no. 219).

[92]   On the capitulary see D. Campbell, 'The *capitulaire de uillis*, the *Brevium exempla*, and the Carolingian court at Aachen', *EME*, 18 (2010), 243–64.

[93]   *MGH, capitularia regum Francorum*, ii. 88, with the English translation in *Carolingian Civilization*, ed. Dutton, pp. 87–8.

had collected. Moreover, everything was itemized in writing. Such officials, and such accounting, almost certainly existed in ducal Normandy, too, although they have left little trace.

There were also foresters who were responsible for the ducal forests. Those forests produced revenues in the form of, among other things, timber, pannage, venison, furs, and (most likely) honey, and we have reference to tallies being used as receipts in order to exempt particular items from the account.[94] Thus an act of Henry I for the monks of Montebourg was sent to William of Brix, commanding that the justices of the Cotentin, William, and his foresters should 'permit the monks of Montebourg to have as many trees in Brix for their fire as there are weeks in the year and timber for their building and their pannage quit and all their customs free and quit and the foresters shall be quit in my pleadings for as many trees as the monks acknowledge by their tallies'.[95] The writ appears to constitute a fairly comprehensive statement of the responsibilities of the foresters, which are also implied by Henry I's grant to the monks at Envermeu of a wood and of the right to graze their pigs and other animals there, which was addressed to the custodians and officials of the forests of Arques and Aliermonte.[96] The foresters, then, were responsible for the trees, the wood, and the undergrowth on which the beasts of the forest would feed. Their permission was required before living wood was taken for building or for the fire, and receipts would be kept for when the forest pleas were held. Pannage, too, was carefully policed, as was the right to graze animals in the forest, for these domesticated animals would compete for nourishment with the duke's deer and boars. As the monks of Saint-Martin-du-Bosc were granted the right to honey and bees in the forests,[97] it may be supposed that these too came under the purview of the foresters.

---

[94] Grants of pannage (i.e. exemption from pannage) are found in just two ducal acts from before 1066: *RADN*, nos. 64, 99 (both for Cerisy-la-Forêt), and also in *Regesta: William*, nos. 175, 205, 215, 258, 260, 266, 271, 281; and, for example, the acts calendared at *Regesta*, ii. nos. 877, 1012, 1019, 1569, 1921. The account for timber/trees is revealed by *NI*, p. 102 = *Regesta*, ii. no. 1951. For furs, see L. Delisle, *Cartulaire Normand*, no. 2 = *Regesta*, ii. no. 1087. There is mention of the production of honey in *RADN*, no. 208, which is an act of the count of Evreux confirmed by William the Bastard, and in an act purportedly issued by William after 1066, but probably a confection of the 1140s: *Regesta : William*, no. 258. This last act notes in addition woodland tithes of wild animals, birds, sales of wood, assarts, and pannage. See also F. Neveux, *La Normandie des ducs aux rois Xe–XIIe siècle* (Rennes, 1998), p. 197 and for the situation in England the articles collected in Langton and G. Jones (ed.), *Forests and Chases of Medieval England and Wales c. 1000–c. 1500: Towards a Survey and Analysis* (Oxford, 2010).

[95] *NI*, p. 102.

[96] *Regesta*, ii. 315 (no. xliv) = no. 794.

[97] *Regesta*, ii. 320–21 (no. lviii) = no. 877.

Other income, not directly produced by the demesne, was collected by other officials who had particular responsibility at a local level for collecting it. We have already come across collectors of bernage and *grauarium*. In addition, an act for Saint-Etienne, Caen, of 1083 reveals that there was a toll keeper based in the monks' *bourg* at Caen, who had a post where he collected tolls.[98] It is likely that ducal toll-collectors (*thelonarii*) worked in the same way, and they may be supposed to have been the *ministri* addressed in Henry I's writs granting exemption from such charges.[99] There were in addition men who acted as custodians of meadows or parks, and collected the dues arising from them at grass roots.[100] As with the foresters, they may be supposed to have kept a record of, and given receipts for, the sums collected.

At the top of the local hierarchy of officials stood the *vicomte* and the *prévôt*. As discussed in the previous chapter, despite the long-held view that the *vicomte* was a military leader as much as an administrator, the evidence suggests that this official was primarily responsible for the administration of the demesne in his county, including publicizing transfers of lands and rights and the results of lawsuits in the county court.[101] The *prévôt* seems to have had a similar function to the *vicomte*, but limited to a single vill or town.[102] Thus, Henry I informed the *prévôt* of Argentan of a grant of land 'in the ditch between the bourg and the causeway' that he had made to his armour-makers (*loricarii*).[103] If the *prévôt* was informed of grants out of the demesne in his jurisdiction, then it seems likely that he administered it. That administration may have included ensuring the vills were

---

[98] *Regesta: William*, no. 54.

[99] Abbé M. Desroches, 'Analyse des titres et chartes de l'abbaye de Savigny', *Memoires de la Société des Antiquaires de Normandie*, second series 10 (1853), 256 (with editorial changes) = *Regesta*, ii. no. 1003; *Ctl. Tiron*, i. 75 (no. liv) = *Regesta*, ii. no. 1169; *Regesta*, ii. 361 (no. ccix) = no. 1555; *CCR*, iv. 157 = *Regesta*, ii. no. 1682; *NI*, p. 308 (no. 23) = *Regesta*, ii. no. 1919; *NI*, p. 306 (no. 20) = *Regesta*, ii. no. 1941; *Le Premier cartulaire de l'abbaye cistercienne*, ed. Garrigues, p. 86 (no. 3); *Cartulaire de la Léproserie de Grand-Beaulieu*, eds. Merlet and Jusselin, p. 2 (no. 2); D. Lohrmann, 'St-Germer-de-Flay und das Anglo-Normannische Reich', *Francia* 1, 1973, 228. See also Musset, 'Aristocratie d'argent', 290; Musset, 'Recherches sur le tonlieu', pp. 63, 65–6.

[100] *Regesta: William*, nos. 45, 53, 54 (*pratarius*); Chanteux, *Recueil*, no. 95; *Regesta*, ii. no. 1927; *Recueil Henri II*, i. 304 (no. 173) (*parcarius*).

[101] See Hagger, 'The Norman *vicomte*', 65–83.

[102] Likewise in Capetian France, *prévôts* might be responsible for large towns to small rural hamlets (Baldwin, *The Government of Philip Augustus*, p. 44). Not everything might be lodged and inventoried at these depots. Some products might have been taken directly to the court, as was the case with the wine, beer, and soap, among other things, produced on the imperial Carolingian estates (Campbell, 'The *capitulaire de uillis*', p. 245).

[103] *NI*, pp. 306–7 (no. 21).

adequately stocked with animals and furnishings – along the lines of the responsibilities of the stewards set out in detail in *De uillis*.

Although there is no evidence that *vicomtes* held particular estates in right of their office, there is some slight evidence that particular pieces of land were associated with the holding of a *prévôté*. An act for the monks of Caen dating from 1080 × 1083 remarks that Abbot William 'recovered two *iugera* of meadow, once of Odo of Carpiquet, of the fee of the *prévôté* of Cheux (*de foedio prepositure Ceusii*)'.[104] In this case, then, it seems that part of the erstwhile ducal demesne in Cheux was held by the *prévôt* who administered it for the abbot in right of his office. It may be supposed that the *prévôt* who had replaced Odo had not taken kindly to the diminution of that estate, and had attempted to wrest possession of the alienated land back from the monks. That Odo had been able to alienate part of his *prevot's* fee in the first place, however, suggests that he saw the land as his. His view is most likely to have resulted from his inheritance of the office – although this is conjecture. But such offices might become hereditary. In 1170, Henry II notified his subjects that Rualen of Genêts had forsworn the *prévôté* of Genêts (a possession of the monks of Mont-Saint-Michel) which he had held by inheritance.[105]

At least some of the money and produce collected by the various lesser officials would periodically have been taken to an estate centre or depot and handed over to the *vicomte* or *prévôt*. The existence of these centres is implied by a very small number of ducal *acta*.[106] Thus, an act of 1015 × 1025 for the monks of Saint-Père at Chartres notes that Breteuil (formerly *Rescolium*) 'is so-called from the former collection of money: for there the property of the fisc was collected or assembled (*supradictus viculus a rebus colligendis Rescolius olim quidem dicebatur: ibi enim res fisci colligebantur uel congregabantur*)'.[107] It may be supposed that the cash collected there, at least, would have been taken to the duke. Further evidence for these depots is probably found in the act by which Richard III settled dower on

---

[104] *Regesta: William*, no. 53.

[105] *CDF*, no. 748.

[106] Such centres were known in the Carolingian period. Further, the Trelleborg fortresses constructed by Harald Bluetooth across Denmark might also have acted as collection points (Roesdahl, *The Vikings*, pp. 139–40, although Christiansen, *Norsemen in the Viking Age*, pp. 84–6 is less certain). In addition, *c.* 1118 × 1124 the monks of Saint-Pierre of Préaux had a tithe-collector with a house and grange where Saint-Pierre's tithes were gathered together. This seems to have been located at Pont-Audemer (*Ctl. Préaux*, A70).

[107] *RADN*, no. 29. Le Patourel thought the place functioned as a treasury, rather than a depot (*Norman Empire*, p. 147, n. 4). The two need not be mutually exclusive. It should be noted that local depots also existed in Flanders at about this time: Lyon and Verhulst, *Medieval Finance*, pp. 20–5.

Adela in 1026. This makes mention of several *curtes* – estate centres – across the Cotentin at Ver, Cérences, Agon, Percy, Moyon, Hambye, and Valognes, all of which appear to have had dependent *pagi*.[108] The unusual wording of the act has been remarked on in the past,[109] but it was most likely the result of the draftsman's resort to obsolete Carolingian terminology to describe what he saw as the similar organizational structures that existed in his day. There is one further piece of evidence for the existence of the depot at Valognes in one of William the Conqueror's grants to the monks of Marmoutier. In it, the monks resident at the abbey's priory at Héauville were given the whole tongue of one whale each year in the county of the Cotentin, 'at Valognes'.[110] Even the most disorientated of whales could not have beached in Valognes, and so human agency must have been required to transport the whale there, before its tongue was released to the monks. If whales, or parts of whales, were being taken to Valognes, it is likely that other revenues were collected together there, too. The existence of such depots is also suggested by the collection of the duke's hay, which, according to Lucien Musset, was deposited in centres at Caen, Le Vaudreuil, Rouen, Avranches, and Bonneville-sur-Touques.[111] Such depots almost certainly existed across the duchy – it seems likely that there was at least one for every *vicomté* and *prévôté* – and might have been the origin of some of the treasuries which seem to have existed at various locations in Normandy during Henry I's reign.

The various sums and produce lodged with the *vicomtes* or *prévôts* at these centres would have been inventoried or accounted for in detail. It may be supposed that the various collectors were given receipts in the form of tallies and that the sums collected were labelled or enrolled (or both) so that they could be easily identified, as with later exchequer practice.[112] That must have been the case, because it would otherwise have been impossible to put many of the gifts made by the dukes into effect. Those gifts included dues accruing from the use of seigniorial ovens, of multure from the mills, tolls from roads, fairs, and markets, and so on. As these items are listed separately in ducal *acta*, they may be supposed to have comprised discrete and identifiable items of account.

By way of illustration, we can return to the act for the monks of Cerisy-la-Forêt quoted towards the beginning of this chapter. That act names, among other things, the tithe of the pennies of the *vicomté* of the Cotentin, the tithes of the mills, groves, and returns of the *vicomtés* of Coutances and Gavray; the tithe of

---

[108] *RADN*, no. 58.
[109] Musset, 'Les domaines de l'époque franque', 18.
[110] *RADN*, no. 160.
[111] Musset, 'Les prés et le foin du seigneur roi', p. 375.
[112] Indicated by *Dialogue*, pp. 12, 32–4.

the pannage, pleas, cows, pigs, and hunting in the forests of Montebourg, Brix, Rabey, Cherbourg, Valdecie, and Luthumière; and the tithe of the harvest and one *hôte* in Valognes. For the act to take effect, it must have been possible to establish the value of the items listed, which were not given a set value. For that to happen there must have been detailed records listing the income from each of the revenue streams concerned. That, incidentally, implies that there was an awful lot of writing in government that has now been lost, and that was produced well before the inception of Norman pipe rolls and writs. Furthermore, the tithe of the pennies of the *vicomté* of the Cotentin or the returns of the *vicomtés* of Coutances and Gavray could not have been obtained from the individual collectors, but only after all the revenues had been gathered together at the relevant estate centre. So the monks either obtained their tithes there (like the monks of Héauville did their whale tongue), or else from the officers of the duke's chamber or treasury.

A second example can be used to reinforce those conclusions:

I William king of the English grant what Maurice bishop of London gave to Saint-Amand of Rouen: the tithes which he had in the forests of Aliermont and Eawy as much in assarts as in pennies, and the tithe of the pennies of Barfleur and the tithe of Saint-James-de-Beuvron. And I command and affirm that Saint-Amand shall have all these well, just as Bishop Maurice best had them.[113]

Again, this act says nothing explicitly about the existence of estate centres or the chamber in Normandy before 1087, and nor does it provide any express information about the collection of revenues in the duchy during William's reign. But it does once again imply a great deal about such matters. Some, perhaps all, of the tithes granted to Maurice would have taken the form of money. Again, they were not liquidated sums, so in order to establish the value of the tithes in question, all the income would have to have been collected together first by the foresters or *prévôts* or other local officials and a record kept of its origin. Someone must have known precisely what the tithe of the pennies of the forests was in order to pass the due sum on to Maurice.

While the monks of Cerisy, based as they were in the west of the Bessin, might have found it easier to collect their revenues from the relevant estate centres in the Cotentin, it is likely that Maurice preferred to collect his income from the chamber officials after the money, or tallies representing the sums due, had been brought to Rouen. That option was certainly available to the monks of Cluny in

[113] *Regesta: William*, no. 242.

Henry I's England (substituting the exchequer for the chamber), as an act for the monks dating from 1131 reveals:

> Know that I have given and granted to God and to the church of the blessed Peter of Cluny one hundred marks of rent each year in England, namely sixty marks of my rents of London of the farm of the city and forty marks of the farm of the city of Lincoln so that my officials of those cities who hold my farms shall each offer this money to my exchequer at the feast of St Michael and there it shall be released to the messenger of St Peter. Truly, if this is not done my justice of the exchequer shall do justice to them concerning it.

The existence of estate centres under the control of the *vicomtes* further explains why those officials were addressed in writs of exemption from toll, passage, and custom. As has been seen, tolls were collected on the ground by toll-keepers (*thelonarii* or simply *ministri*). Writs of exemption were thus addressed to the dukes' 'officials', and might be shown to them by those transporting goods on behalf of their beneficiary. But such writs were also addressed to the *vicomtes*. Indeed, no fewer than nine of Henry I's Norman writs command the *vicomtes*, among others, that their beneficiaries' demesne possessions should be so quit.[114] As the *vicomtes* did not collect the tolls themselves, such an address would have been meaningless unless it was intended to allow beneficiaries to approach them after the event, when the tolls had been collected together and a record made of their origin, so that money taken in error might be returned – presumably on the production of a valid receipt.

Farms

The *vicomtés* did not remain stable. As discussed above,[115] they divided or combined as the dukes acquired land or divested themselves of it, or else for political reasons. William the Bastard seems to have divided the *vicomté* of the Cotentin into smaller units by 1042, most likely to reduce the power of Nigel of the Cotentin and to provide offices with which to reward his other supporters in the region. Henry I *might* have broken up the *vicomté* of the Hiémois into three new counties (Falaise, Argentan, and Exmes). If he did so, it could have been because he had seen how a powerful *vicomte* – Robert of Bellême – could deprive him of the revenue from the county. It is more likely, however, that Henry divided the Hiémois because his forfeiture of Bellême and his son, William Talvas, between

---

[114] See n. 99 above.
[115] Chapter 9, p. 545, 553.

1113 and 1119 augmented his possessions in the region to such an extent that a single *vicomte* was no longer sufficient to administer them all.[116] It might be that the division was also linked to the ongoing growth of the three towns that formed the new centres: Exmes, Falaise, and Argentan. Orderic tells us that Henry had enlarged the town of Exmes shortly before his death, building a new town there, a new town that was burned by Gilbert of Clare in 1136.[117] Similarly, the forfeiture of Count William of Mortain in 1106 resulted in the creation of the *vicomté* of Vire – revealed by the mention of a 'Ralph the *vicomte* of the castle of Vire' in an act for the monks of Troarn dating from *c*. 1120.[118] The *vicomté* of Conteville, which appears ambiguously in a single act of Henry I for the monks of Saint-Georges at Boscherville, was probably another new creation resulting from Count William's forfeiture.[119] In addition, King Henry's acts also reveal apparently new *vicomtés* based on Lillebonne and Le Vaudreuil, although the reasons for their creation are entirely unclear.[120]

This restructuring of the Norman *vicomtés* suggests that the farms paid for some of them, at least, could only have been established for the first time in Henry I's reign.[121] This stands against the argument advanced a century ago by Charles Haskins. He noted the deduction of sums in 'established alms' from the farms recorded in the Norman pipe roll of 1180 and, as some of these payments could

---

[116] Orderic, vi. 178, 454. Henry addressed an act to the men of the Hiémois in 1108 × 1118, and probably between 1113 and 1118 when he was withholding Robert of Bellême's lands from his heir, William Talvas (*NI*, p. 90 (no. 2) = *Regesta*, ii. no. 1200). Orderic's description of three *vicomtés*, then, most likely relates to a period subsequent to November 1112, although possibly from before 1118. It is less likely that this break-up of the Hiémois only occurred after September 1135, when Talvas lost his lands for a second time (Orderic, vi. 446).

[117] Orderic, vi. 462.

[118] Ctl. Troarn, fos. 65v–66r = *Regesta*, ii, nos. 1023, 1023a and 1088. The *vicomté* is referred to as that of the Val-du-Vire in 1180 (*Norman Pipe Rolls*, p. 21).

[119] *Regesta*, ii. 353 (no. clxxvi) (with errors) = no. 1440. There may not have been a *vicomté* here at all, as the usual contractions make it uncertain whether the act was addressed to a *vicomte* of Lillebonne or *vicomtes* of Lillebonne and Conteville. It is possible that there were only 'officials' at Conteville. David Bates, incidentally, believed that this Conteville was near Neufchâtel (D. Bates and V. Gazeau, 'L'abbaye de Grestain et la famille d'Herluin de Contevile', *Annales de Normandie*, 40 (1990), 23), but it seems more likely to have been Conteville near Grestain, now in Henry I's hands after the forfeiture of Count William of Mortain.

[120] *Regesta*, ii.353 (no. clxxvi) = no. 1440 (Lillebonne); *NI*, p. 295 (no. 4) = *Regesta*, ii. no. 1221 (Le Vaudreuil).

[121] A 'farm' existed when 'the grantor rented land to a tenant … either for a fixed annual sum or a lump payment, in return for which the farmer received the dues from the estate' (A. Williams, 'How land was held before and after the Norman conquest', in *Domesday Book Studies*, ed. R. W. H. Erskine and A. Williams (London, 1987), p. 38).

be traced back to donations made by William I, he concluded that the farms had existed before 1087. Haskins was mistaken here, however, as can be seen if reference is made to the counties and *prévôtés* located within the bounds of the old county of Mortain. Various payments in established alms that appear in the roll of 1180 under the accounts for Mortain, Teilleul, Gorron, Tinchebray, and Cérences originated in grants made by Counts Robert and William before 28 September 1106.[122] As the county of Mortain only came into Henry I's hand after that date, the creation of the farms that were paid to Henry and his successors for these places must post-date those grants. Nonetheless, the alms in question were subtracted from the farms. Thus the deduction of payments in alms from the Norman farms provides no indication of when those farms were created.

Although we have only a handful of acts issued by Robert Curthose, one of them might shed some light on a developing situation. In around 1087, Curthose confirmed his father's gift to the monks of Saint-Etienne, Caen, of the manor of Vains, which William had made during his last illness, 'retaining, however, in my hand towards the *census* of my *vicomté* the toll of the same manor'.[123] As discussed above, a *census* might have been either the payment of a variable sum or a rent that had been agreed between the two parties. The *census* of a *vicomté*, then, was *not* a farm by a different name. It was only later that the duke would become dissatisfied with a situation where he did not know what his income over the coming year would be, and so moved to establish a fixed rent, or farm, instead, giving up the increased revenue of a good year in favour of certainty. It is likely that the farm was based on an estimate of the annual income made by jurors living in each county or perhaps even in each vill.[124]

At the very beginning of Curthose's reign, then, the *vicomtes* either simply agreed to pay over the sum of the produce of their counties at the end of the year, or else agreed to pay a higher sum of money for the office than their competitors. The ambiguity of the word *census* allows for either possibility. And that William the Bastard *had* been used to leasing the demesne to the highest bidder in this way before the conquest of 1066 is suggested by the words of the Anglo-Saxon Chronicler who wrote that: 'the king granted his land on the hardest terms and at the highest possible price. If another buyer came and offered more than the first had given, the king would let it go to the man who offered him more. If a third came and offered still more, the king would make it over to the man who offered

---

[122] *Norman Pipe Rolls*, pp. 6, 7, 10, 17, 38; *Regesta: William*, no. 215.

[123] *NI*, Appendix E, no. 1. Musset equates the toll of 'those remaining' with the 'theoloneum cotidianum' mentioned in an act for Saint-Wandrille (Lot, *Saint-Wandrille*, no. 42, p. 96) in 'Recheches sur le tonlieu', 72.

[124] See below, *infra*, p. 600.

him most of all. He did not care at all how very wrongfully reeves got possession of it from wretched men.'[125] It is possible that William was here simply disposing of demesne estates in accordance with established Norman tradition. Moreover, while the fragmented nature of Norman farms in the pipe roll of 1180 might have been the result of a desire to limit the power and patronage of the *vicomtes*, it is also possible that they were the legacy of just this sort of horse-trading. Those who collected revenues from the forests or fairs might have had a better idea of the amount of money they produced, and of the opportunities to supplement that sum, than did those who had acted as *vicomtes* or *prévôts*. In such cases, it may be that these local officials approached the duke and outbid the *vicomte* on those items, leading them to be established as separate items, accounted for outside the county farm. There is no way to prove this, of course, but it would provide another explanation of why the Norman *prévôté* and county farms excluded so many items in 1180 and 1184.[126]

The fact that the word *census* could be used to mean the sum total of the produce of whatever was being leased, a bilaterally agreed rent, or a voluntarily rendered tribute might obscure an earlier development. As noted above, an act of 1025 makes mention of a '*census* of the *fisc*'. If this is taken as a reference to accounting for all the revenues produced or to an agreed rent for parts of the ducal demesne, then such payments were no novelty even in William the Bastard's day.[127] It is, however, perhaps more plausible to think of these payments – or at least some of them – as rather closer to tribute. Richard II had brought the Hiémois, the Séois, parts of the Bessin, and the Cotentin under his power, but his influence there was probably reliant on the great lords and chiefs who were much better established in those regions. For example, Richard II's rule in the north of

[125] *ASChr*, 'E', s.a. 1086; trans Garmonsway, p. 218.
[126] For example, the farm of Falaise excluded the mills which were accounted for separately (*Norman Pipe Rolls*, p. 36), even though they were farmed by the same man. The fair at Montmartin was excluded from the account for Vire (*Norman Pipe Rolls*, p. 22). The meadows of Bonneville were excluded from the farm of Bonneville (*Norman Pipe Rolls*, p. 49), as was the mill at *Adevill* (*Norman Pipe Rolls*, p. 50). The farm of the *prévôte* of Lyons-la-Forêt did not include the mills or the forest (*Norman Pipe Rolls*, p. 53). The farm of Exmes, on the other hand, was expressly said to include 'the *census* and tolls and fairs and mills and the proportional rent (*campartum* or *champart*) of the demesne lands' (*Norman Pipe Rolls*, p. 75. *Champart* is defined by Baldwin, *The Government of Philip Augustus*, p. 45). These should almost certainly not be seen as increments to the farm. Judith Green has noted that in eleventh-century England the sheriff might not farm all the royal demesne in his shire, providing further evidence that the shire farms were a later development (Green, *Government*, p. 64). See also above, Chapter 9, pp. 542–5, 553.
[127] *RADN*, no. 34.

the Cotentin most likely relied on Nigel of the Cotentin. Nigel might have been prepared to call himself *vicomte* by 1020, but it is not clear that Richard would have been able to extort a rent from him in return for insecure possession of the ducal demesne in the peninsula. It seems equally unlikely that Nigel would have been prepared to watch over a variety of ducal officials collecting tolls and taxes. The conclusion to be drawn, then, is that Nigel, among others, paid a tribute (*census*) in recognition of Richard's authority rather than a rent in any form (*census*). The word should probably be given that meaning, at least across Lower Normandy, during Richard II's reign and perhaps even into the 1040s.

Emily Zack Tabuteau was of the view that no Norman farm could be dated earlier than *c.* 1080, although she did suggest that it was only the term that was novel rather than the practice of holding land on a short-term lease at a fixed rent.[128] The word does not appear in authentic ducal *acta* until the 1130s, however, when two of Henry I's Norman acts make mention of farms, with the more authoritative of the two being a surviving original charter for the Grand-Beaulieu outside Chartres:

> Know that I gave and granted in perpetual alms to God and St Mary Magdalene in Beaulieu and the infirm there serving God for the soul of my father and my relatives and for the remission of my sins and the state and security of my kingdom of England and my duchy of Normandy every year 10 *livres* of Rouen from my treasure. And always they shall have these at the feast of St Michael when my farms and money (*firme et pecunia mea*) are collected.[129]

From the wording of this act, it would seem that farms had by then been imposed across the duchy, although it may be that the process still remained incomplete at that date.[130] Indeed, it is possible that Henry made a decision to keep some vills directly under his own control. The archbishops of Rouen had certainly taken that decision. An agreement made between Archbishop Walter of Coutances and the canons of Rouen of 1198 provided that where vills had been retained in the archbishops' hands and not put out at farm, a jury of four lawful men from those vills would be empanelled to declare the sum of all the returns they produced.[131]

---

[128] Tabuteau, *Transfers*, pp. 71–2.
[129] *NI*, pp. 106–7 (no. 17) = *Regesta*, ii. no. 1917.
[130] There is some evidence in the Norman pipe roll of 1180 to suggest that a *census* rather than a farm was still agreed for property that had come into the duke's possession only temporarily or recently (for example, *Norman Pipe Rolls*, pp. 8, 17).
[131] Ctl. Rouen, fos. 66r–v (no. 88). A longer version of the same agreement is at fos. 79v–80v (no. 121).

This might also provide some indication of how the farms of the ducal demesne vills had been calculated in the first place.

Where farms had been imposed, the *vicomtes* and *prévôts* and other officials would have paid a fixed sum for their territories or offices. Although that was to the duke's advantage, in that it gave him the security of a predictable income, it is also likely to have given the *vicomtes* and *prévôts* more of an opportunity to make a profit.[132] There were, then, advantages for both sides in making this administrative change. What the duke might expect to get on an annual basis might perhaps be indicated by the farms recorded in the Norman pipe roll of 1180. While we cannot of course be sure that the farms paid there reflected those paid before Henry I's death, it might nonetheless be noted that in that year the Lieuvin was farmed for 35 *livres*, the Bessin for 140 *livres*, the *uicecomitatus* of Arques for 1,000 *livres*, and that of Rouen for 3,000 *livres*.[133] The total revenue from the Norman farms in 1180 was 16,642 *livres*, or £4,160 sterling.

The introduction of farms in Normandy *might* have been linked to similar developments in England. Judith Green noted the lack of established shire farms in England in 1086:

> In a few counties in 1086 sheriffs may already have been making payments similar to the later county farm. In other counties, however, the sheriff was only one of a number of officials who held royal manors at farm, and there is no indication that the latter were subletting from the sheriff ... The county farms may, therefore, only have been generally introduced after 1086 – possibly as part of the measures described in the *Dialogue*.[134]

Those measures were apparently as follows:

> According to our ancestors, as things stood in the kingdom right after the Conquest, the kings did not receive any quantities of gold or silver from their

---

[132] Hollister and Baldwin suggested that farms were set low to allow for a profit (Hollister and Baldwin, 'Administrative kingship', 893).

[133] *Norman Pipe Rolls*, pp. 62, 29, 66, and 50 respectively. The agreement between Henry II and Margaret, sister of King Philip II of France, as to Margaret's dower established that 13s. 4d. sterling was equivalent to 54 *sous* angevin (*CDF*, no. 1084). This makes the Norman farms much smaller than they at first sight appear; on this calculation, the 1,100 *livres* farm for the *vicomté* of Arques was equivalent to just £270 sterling.

[134] Green, *Government*, pp. 63–4. In support of this argument, it might be noted that the word 'farm' is rarely found in royal *acta* or even in Domesday Book: *Regesta: William*, no. 216 and see, for example, GDB, fos. 162a (Gloucester, § G.4), 163b (Gloucester, § 1.21), 269b (Chester, § G.1).

estates, but only victuals, from which the daily needs of the royal household were met, and the officials in charge of this matter knew how much each estate produced … During the whole time of King William I, then, this arrangement continued, until the time of King Henry his son, so that I myself have known people who saw victuals brought from the king's estates to the court at appointed times … But as time went on, and as King Henry was grimly waging war to pacify lands overseas or in remote regions, coined money became very important to him in these ventures. Meanwhile crowds of farmers kept coming to court to complain … For they were burdened by innumerable troubles because of the victuals they were transporting from their own lands to all parts of the realm. Therefore, hearing their complaints, the king consulted his barons and sent out into the kingdom persons whom he knew to be prudent and discrete in his matter. These individuals travelled around … and when they had estimated the goods that each estate owed, each debt was converted into coin. They decided that the sheriff should be bound to pay at the exchequer the total amounts arising from all the estates in his county, and that he should pay on a fixed scale.[135]

We do not need to believe all the details of this account, but it does suggest that in England Henry I was remembered as the king who had fundamentally reformed the royal finances due to his need for ready money.

For similar reasons, it is noteworthy that King Henry's act for the Grand Beaulieu reveals not just the existence of farms by 1135, but of one established accounting date, namely Michaelmas. That development affected only those who had to account directly to the duke, chiefly the *vicomtes* and *prévôts*, although even then they might well have paid money into the treasury or chamber at other times during the year and simply handed over the receipts when it came to the audit. The *ministri*, *thelonarii*, *gravarii*, foresters, and peasants would have continued as before, though, paying their rents and dues at intervals throughout the year or on the traditional dates. Those dates, incidentally, might vary: an act for the monks of Saint-Ouen of 1017 × 1026 notes that the tenants at Autigny paid two sesters of what and twelve chickens at Christmas, and 8 *deniers* and four wagon-loads of wood at 1 October (the feast of St Rémy);[136] although it concerns lands in Maine, an act for the monks of Marmoutier records that *census* payments were made on 13 December, 22 February, and 24 June;[137] the canons of Cherbourg

---

[135] *Dialogue*, p. 62–4. The passage is criticized by Barlow, *William Rufus*, p. 227, ns. 43 and 44 and by Green, *Government*, pp. 62–4.

[136] *RADN*, no. 45.

[137] *RADN*, no. 165.

received two pigs worth 5 *sous* at Christmas and 20 *sous* at Easter;[138] the monks of Caen received rents at Easter and during 'the fair in the meadow';[139] and the nuns of Caen received dues at Christmas and Easter or on 30 October.[140]

The importance of this reform, then, lies in what it tells us about Henry's thinking more generally. It seems likely that Henry had reorganized the dates at which payments were due to ensure that the Norman audit would take place at the same time as its English equivalent, thereby allowing officials easily to communicate with each other should they need to account for debts as they moved across the Channel. Indeed, there is some evidence that this happened – or at least that it had been agreed in advance that it should.[141]

Chamber and treasury

It may be supposed that at some point or points during the year the duke's revenues would be taken from the various estate centres to Rouen or a local treasury. One agreement preserved in the cartulary of Saint-Etienne of Caen saw Abbot Gilbert of Caen grant William Bendengel 'the whole land from the road along which the coffers (*arcas*) are taken',[142] and it may be that this is a reference to such shipments of the duke's revenues from one place to another. It also seems likely that even in the eleventh century the *vicomte* would have presented a single amalgamated account to the duke and his counsellors when he deposited money with them, even if he had not been solely responsible for the collection of its various elements. That would explain why the dukes were able to conceive of revenues coming from particular *vicomtés* as well as from individual bourgs or vills. Thus, for example, Saint-Taurin at Evreux was given the 'tithe of the toll of the city and *vicomté* of Evreux' by its founder, Duke Richard I,[143] while Richard II gave the tithes of the tolls of the *vicomté* of Bayeux to Jumièges;[144] and William the Bastard gave the nuns of Montivilliers 100 *sous* from the rents of the *prévôté* of Caen each year.[145]

It may be supposed that the *vicomtes* or *prévôts* were themselves responsible for paying the sum agreed as their *census* or their farm. The revenues that were included within that *census* were almost certainly itemized in a written account,

[138] *RADN*, no. 224.
[139] Ctl. Caen, fos. 50v–51r.
[140] *Chs. Caen*, pp. 53–4.
[141] *PR 31 Henry I*, pp. 6, 11, 30, 96, 114.
[142] Ctl. Caen, fos. 39v–40r.
[143] *RADN*, no. 5.
[144] *RADN*, no. 36.
[145] *RADN*, no. 172.

but if the income actually received had been greater than the agreed *census*, if they were not simply accounting for everything, the *vicomte* or *prévôt* concerned presumably kept the difference. It may be that the *thelonarii* and others also paid a *census* for their offices, and took the risk of losing money on the deal. Alternatively, they may have been required to account for every penny that they took, in which case it may be supposed to have been the perks of the job – a stipend or a parcel of land or exemptions – that made the role attractive.[146]

The body to which the *vicomtes* and *prévôts* made their account is obscure. There is no evidence of either a treasury – at least by that name – or a treasurer in Normandy before the last year or so of Henry I's reign. Instead, there was a chamber and chamberlains. In Richard II's reign, when it first appears, the chamber seems to have taken receipt of both regular and irregular income. Thus the monks of Fécamp received from Duke Richard II the tithe of 'whatever is given to me, in the service of any business, namely the purchase of lands or of other transactions or whatever other business or gifts ... except the *census* of the *fisc* and except those things which are from old times called customs'.[147] There is no suggestion that this regular income was paid into some other office; in other words there was as yet no distinction between chamber and treasury. All revenues, then, were paid directly into the chamber, regardless of their nature.

Those revenues and other payments, as well as the gifts given to the duke, comprised the treasure, made up of valuable objects as well as coins. The sorts of objects that might be found in the treasure are occasionally described in narrative and documentary sources. Duke Richard I is said to have rewarded the two knights who warned him of an attempt to kidnap him with 'a sword gleaming with four pounds of gold on the hilt, and to the other he gave an arm-ring, wrought of as many pounds of purest gold'.[148] Helgaud of Fleury recorded that Duke Richard II had given Robert the Pious 'a statue of a deer made from solid silver ... Attached to this ornament was a horn cup through which wine was poured for the celebration of Mass.'[149] The recollections of Abbot Isembert of La Trinité-du-Mont provide a further indication of some of the other sorts of objects that might be presented to the duke.

> We must certainly note here how generous the venerable Duke Robert was ... For if he began to make gifts to someone early in the morning he would

---

[146] See above, Chapter 9, pp. 549–50.

[147] *RADN*, no. 34.

[148] *Dudo*, p. 142.

[149] Helgaud de Fleury, *Vie de Robert le Pieux*, ed. R. H. Bautier and G. Labory (Paris, 1935), pp. 92–3; translation in van Houts, *Normans*, p. 194.

handover whatever came into his hand during that day to the same person whom he had thought worthy of reward early that morning. One day a certain smith from Beauvais came to see him and offered him two knives as a gift. The duke, unwilling to give the impression that he despised such a small present from a poor man accepted them joyfully, and ordered his chamberlains to give the smith one hundred pounds of the money of Rouen in return. The smith had hardly received them in full, when immediately some of the magnates presented two strong horses of exceptional strength to the duke, who again ordered them to be given to the smith ... That evening, when any gifts were brought to Duke Robert, he gave orders likewise to hand them over to the smith.[150]

We also know of a gift of jewels by Henry I to Theobald of Blois, which later found their way into the hands of Abbot Suger of Saint-Denis, and that the jewels had themselves once been part of the great vessels placed before him at crown-wearings. There were also silver basins given to William of Tancarville, a golden cup that Henry gave to Juhel of Mayenne, and enamelled candlesticks that had found their way into the treasury of Rouen cathedral by 1183.[151] Unspecified treasures of gold and silver were also given to Hugh of Payens in 1128.[152] The purchase or transfer of lands can certainly be seen to have provided the duke with irregular income, and to have passed into the chamber. For example, sometime before his retirement to the monastery c. 1046, Nigel 'the old' had made a grant to Mont-Saint-Michel, for which he had paid 150 *livres* to Duke William which Ralph his chamberlain had accepted.[153] Orderic noted, in addition, that when Bishop Serlo of Sées died in 1123, his property was unceremoniously added to the king's: 'When the king's retainers heard of Bishop Serlo's sudden death, as I have described, they flew to the spot from the castle they were occupying like vultures to a corpse. They appropriated the treasure and everything that was found in the bishop's palace for the king's *fisc* (*in fiscum regis omnia transtulerunt*), giving nothing to the churches or the poor.'[154] Other one-off receipts might include treasure trove – an act of Richard I reveals that the duke had the right to things that had been found (*pro inventa re*) and this was still the case in 1121 × 1128 when Henry I noted in an act for the monks of Saint-Pierre-sur-Dives that 'if gold or silver or copper or lead or anything else pertaining to money is found under the ground it shall be mine'.[155]

---

[150] Jumièges, ii. 58.
[151] Green, *Henry I*, p. 295 and n. 67.
[152] ASChr, 'E', s.a. 1128; trans. Garmonsway, p. 259.
[153] *Ctl. Mont-Saint-Michel*, p. 181 (no. 115); Tabuteau, *Transfers*, p. 117.
[154] Orderic, vi. 340. Chibnall translates 'fisc' as 'Exchequer', which is perhaps deceptive.
[155] *RADN*, no. 3; Caen, AD Calvados, H 7031(5) printed in R. N. Sauvage, 'Les diplômes

In the absence of any other financial office, money must also have been disbursed from the chamber, too. We are poorly informed about such payments. An act of Robert the Magnificent, however, notes that William of Volpiano had been obliged to give the church of Longchamp to Atto le Fou in mortgage for 100 *livres*. Robert's father, Richard II, had subsequently repaid the money to Atto from his chamber, and thus restored the churches to the abbey.[156]

As the chamber was the only finance bureau before the end of the reign of Henry I, it may be supposed that the principal financial official was the chamberlain. Individuals bearing this style appear from Richard II's reign.[157] Berengar the chamberlain attested an act of September 1014 for the canons of Chartres, some ten years before the first appearance of the chamber.[158] He seems to have been succeeded by 1024 at the latest by a Rotselin the chamberlain.[159] Rotselin had earlier been sent to Abbot Gerard of Crépy by Richard II to invite him to become abbot of Saint-Wandrille, but although styled as 'chamberlain' in the *Inventio et miracula sancti Vulfrani*, it seems unlikely that he held the office at the time (1008).[160] A third figure, Ralph the chamberlain, emerges for the first time in 1035. He can be identified as Ralph of Tancarville and he remained in office for more than thirty years.[161] Ralph was succeeded by his son William,[162] who attested three acts of William the Conqueror,[163] and continued to hold the office until his death in 1128.[164] William was succeeded in turn by his son Rabel.

At some point in time, the Tancarville chamberlains may have become distanced from the day-to-day workings of the chamber – at least there is no evidence at all for their involvement in revenue collection or audit – even though Ralph and William were virtually the only men labelled 'chamberlain' in Normandy. It is possible that this development was signified by the end of Henry I's reign

---

de Henri pour l'abbaye de St-Pierre-sur-Dive', *Société de la Histoire de Normandie, Mélanges*, douxième series = *Regesta*, ii. no. 1569.

[156] *RADN*, no. 86.

[157] The count of Corbeil had one by 1006 (Telma, no. 2064).

[158] *RADN*, no. 15.

[159] *RADN*, nos. 44, 55.

[160] *Inventio*, pp. 31–2 (119). See also E. M. C. van Houts, 'Historiography and hagiography at Saint-Wandrille: the "Inventio et miracula sancti Vulfrani"', *ANS*, 12 (1990), 245.

[161] Ralph (whose name is sometimes given as Rodulf) attests *RADN*, nos. 89, 123, 131, 134, 137, 138, 141, 142, 148, 191, 197 (this is William's confirmation of the endowment given to Ralph's foundation of Saint-Georges), 198, 219, 220, 227, 231, 233. He was still alive in 1079: *Regesta: William*, no. 164.

[162] *Regesta: William*, no. 45 makes the relationship explicit.

[163] *Regesta: William*, nos. 48, 59, 95.

[164] *NI*, Appendix E, pp. 286–7, no. 3; *Regesta*, ii. nos. 842, 911, 1012, 1074, 1099, 1127, 1270, 1496, 1559, 1596, 1860b.

by the adoption of the title 'master chamberlain'.[165] Their apparent retreat from the practicalities of collection and disbursement might have begun around the time of the Conquest. A Humfrey the chamberlain appears in 1066, although he might not have been a ducal official, and a Rainald the chamberlain appears in the 1080s. Both would have served William the Bastard at the same time as Ralph.[166] There was also a Walkelin the chamberlain, who appears in an act for the monks of Montebourg dating from 1107 × 1120 and who might have been succeeded by William of Glastonbury c. 1130.[167] Other chamberlains working in Normandy are likely to have included Nigel the nephew of the bishop, Osbert of Pont de l'Arche, and Geoffrey of Glympton, as all of them seem to have received payments made into the treasury in Normandy in 1130.[168] William Mauduit, too, was a chamberlain, according to an act for the canons of Sées of 1131 as well as an act of Henry I in his favour, perhaps dating from the same year. Indeed, he was singled out in the *Constitutio domus regis*, perhaps because he had a special position as the receiver of revenue at the chamber – he is noted as having received the sole payment recorded as having been made directly into the chamber in the pipe roll of Michaelmas 1130.[169] Walter of Houghton was described as the king's chamberlain in an act for the monks of Ramsey issued at Falaise in 1133 × 1135.[170] Finally, Warren Hollister suggested that William fitz Odo also served as a chamberlain in the duchy, although he was styled constable, not chamberlain, in two of Henry's acts as well as in the *Constitutio domus regis*.[171]

The role of the chamberlains at the exchequer sessions during Henry II's reign suggests that the exchequer and the treasury both grew out of the chamber. They seem to have done so only late in the reign of Henry I, however. Certainly, no mention can be found of a Norman treasurer or a treasury until 1130. Even in the

---

[165] *Constitutio*, p. 206. The same seems to have been true of the grand chamberlains of France by the reign of Philip Augustus (Baldwin, *The Government of Philip Augustus*, p. 55).

[166] *RADN*, no. 231; *Regesta: William*, no. 49. Master chamberlains are discussed by Green, *Government*, pp. 31–2 with regard to England.

[167] *Regesta*, ii. 327 (no. lxxvii) = no. 1018; *PR 31 Henry I*, p. 11. The editors of the *Regesta* stated that the pipe roll described Walkelin as 'chamberlain of Normandy', but that is not the case. Indeed, it is only supposition that makes Walkelin the chamberlain William of Glastonbury's uncle, as the pipe roll described him only as Walkelin without any reference to the nature of his office. Warren Hollister was nonetheless apparently convinced that William of Glastonbury was a chamberlain (Hollister, *Henry*, p. 362).

[168] *Pipe Roll 31 Henry I*, pp. 29 (Geoffrey); 43, 49 (Nigel nephew of the bishop); 49 (Osbert). The wording for all three men is not so clear as it might be, however.

[169] *NI*, pp. 300–2 (no. 11) = *Regesta*, ii. no. 1698; *Regesta*, ii. 375 (no. cclx) = no. 1719; *PR 31 Henry I*, p. 106; Green, *Government*, pp. 27, 33.

[170] *Regesta*, ii. no. 1915.

[171] Hollister, *Henry*, p. 362 and n. 3; *Regesta*, ii. nos. 1693, 1698; *Constitutio*, p. 208.

previous decade, the monks of the abbey of Saint-Pierre-sur-Dives had written of pleas about money being heard in the abbot's court and concluded at the *archam moneta* – 'the money chest' – rather than 'at the treasury' or even 'at the exchequer'.[172] It is not clear if 'the treasure chest' in this diploma refers to a place or an occasion, nor is it clear if this were a court or a reference to a treasury, but the absence of the word 'treasury' is probably telling. Equally, Orderic's note that King Henry took his treasure with him when he crossed to England in November 1120 (although it was lost in the wreck of the *White Ship*) has nothing to do with any established Norman treasury, but was almost certainly a reference to the contents of the chamber.[173]

The treasury certainly existed by 1130, however. The pipe roll of that year refers to payments made into 'the treasury of Normandy (*in th(es)auro Normannie*)'.[174] In 1135, Henry I addressed his act for the Grand-Beaulieu to his treasurers, among others, and commanded 'those treasurers of mine' to release the sums granted to the lepers every year at the nominated terms without any disturbance and excuse.

A treasury needed a treasurer. Around 1130, Nigel the nephew of the bishop was appointed treasurer in England, and at this same time, Gilbert of Evreux may have been appointed treasurer in Normandy.[175] It was Charles Haskins who first identified him as treasurer under Henry I, picking up on clues found in the Norman pipe roll of 1180 and King Stephen's act for Sainte-Barbe-en-Auge of 1137. Stephen's diploma mentions 'the tithe of the *vicomté* of the Lieuvin and Auge, which are of my chaplaincy, which Gilbert of Evreux and Robert his son, the chaplains of King Henry and of me, gave and granted to the same church'.[176] It is the later *Chronicle of the abbey of Sainte-Barbe* that then goes on to explain that 'there was in the days of the elder Henry, king of the English, a certain clerk in the city of Rouen called Gilbert, from a family of clerks and knights. This man was the precentor of the church of Rouen, and the treasurer of the said king.'[177] He was succeeded, we are told, by the eldest of his five sons, William, and he by his younger brother, Robert, who lived into Stephen's reign. Although

---

[172] AD Caen, H 7031(5). Du Cange unwarrantedly translated this as 'treasury', which is understandable but overlooks the lack of any evidence for an officially constituted treasury in Normandy to this point. Isidore of Seville defined 'arca' as a strongbox (*Etymologies*, p. 307).

[173] Orderic, vi. 296. It should be noted that the distinction between mobile treasure and the royal treasury can still be found in the *Dialogue*, p. 134.

[174] *Pipe Roll 31 Henry I*, pp. 43, 49.

[175] Green, *Government*, p. 34 suggested that Nigel nephew of the bishop had been treasurer in Normandy before his move to England, but as discussed above there is no evidence for a Norman treasury before 1130.

[176] *Regesta*, iii. no. 749 (p. 277).

[177] *NI*, pp. 108–9.

Haskins' reconstruction was criticized by Geoffrey White in 1926,[178] it was not fatally undermined, and it still seems more likely than not that Gilbert of Evreux acted as Henry's treasurer.

The exchequer appears in England in 1110, at which point it was a body that dealt with finance and accounts.[179] At around the same time, it appears as a forum for lawsuits.[180] The panel of justices presided over by Bishop John of Lisieux in three of the records comprising the *Emptiones Eudonis*, who look more like the English exchequer court than any other body known to have been active in the duchy, is not described as such in the records in question. Consequently, there is no evidence for an exchequer in Normandy until 1129 × 1130. J. H. Round discussed that evidence in his article on Bernard the Scribe.[181] Among the documents Round cited was an act that recorded how Bernard had deraigned against Serlo the dumb a thicket and adjacent land at Maton in the presence of Robert of Courcy, steward of Normandy, William fitz Odo, Henry of Pommeraye, William of Glastonbury, Wigan the Marshal, Robert the chaplain of the bishop of Lisieux, Robert of Evreux (the treasurer), and Martin the scribe of the chapel. Serlo was there fined by the barons of the exchequer for tilling land of which Bernard was seised, and which he had earlier deraigned before Bishop John of Lisieux, Robert of La Haye-du-Puits, and others at the Norman exchequer. They testified to this by their letters (*per breuia sua*) since neither could be present when this plea was heard.

That there was no exchequer in Normandy until some years after it had developed in England is by now received wisdom. But it seems to have been England rather than Normandy that was out of step. The Capetians, for example, had no central audit until after 1190. Until then, the French kings seem to have presided over local audits as they moved around their demesne.[182] Lower down the social hierarchy, the Beaumonts had created their own exchequer in England, but made do without one in Normandy – apparently reflecting the arrangements of their king and duke.[183] That Normandy did not have an exchequer is not the real issue, then. The surprise is that one developed there so early.

The reasons for this development, however, are frustratingly obscure. Although

[178]   G. H. White, 'Treasurers in Normandy under Henry I', *Notes and Queries*, 150 (1926), 59–60.

[179]   *Regesta*, ii. no. 963, also nos. 1514, 1741.

[180]   *Regesta*, ii. nos. 1538 (1108 × 1127), 1879 (1121 × 1133).

[181]   J. H. Round, 'Bernard, the King's scribe', *EHR*, 14 (1899), 417–30.

[182]   Baldwin, *The Government of Philip Augustus*, pp. 144–5.

[183]   Crouch, *Beaumont Twins*, p. 166. Both Baldwin's and Crouch's observations are noted during the discussion of this subject in J. A. Green, 'Unity and disunity in the Anglo-Norman state', *Historical Research*, 62 (1989), 118–23.

Henry had gained the Bellême lands in the Hiémois and Bessin between 1113 and 1118, and the county of Evreux in 1118, those gains were temporary, and had been lost long before the financial reforms apparently took place. So, the expansion of the demesne seems not to have been relevant. Vincent Moss suggested that the collection of the 'gyld' of 1117 could have provided the stimulus for change,[184] but customs such as bernage and *grauarium* had been collected across the duchy for decades before then, so that systems appropriate for the collection and audit of a national tax may be supposed to have been in place already. More likely, the developments represent a desire more closely to supervise the *vicomtes* and *prévôts*, thereby to squeeze as much money out of them as possible. That is suggested both by the fact that the farms seem to have been set at a (too) high level in England *c.* 1130, as well as by the fact that only a small sum of the money was pardoned in the pipe roll of that year.[185] The development of the pipe rolls, too, suggests a desire to maximise revenue. As Frank Barlow noted, the pipe rolls provide no total sums, and thus on an individual basis do not look much like a step forward.[186] However, if the pipe rolls are thought of collectively, they can be seen to have provided a one-stop shop for the compilation of the following year's summons, and should – in theory at least – have ensured that no debt was forgotten.[187] It might further be the case that the development of a Norman treasury, exchequer, and pipe rolls (on the assumption that they existed in Normandy in this period) was the work not of Henry himself but of his administrators. They were the ones who had to work the machinery, and they were consequently the ones who would have been aware of its weaknesses and what needed to be done to correct them.

* * * * * *

The collection of the ducal revenues was a sophisticated, multi-layered process. Collection at grass-roots most likely remained more or less the same throughout the whole period under discussion. Dues could be taken directly from peasants in the individual manors. Those paying tolls would be stopped and the money would change hands. The receipts would periodically have been brought together at a local depot, where they might be disbursed to the beneficiaries of ducal grants, or reclaimed if taken against the duke's grant of exemption, or sent to the chamber or treasuries by the relevant *vicomte* or *prévôt*.

While the principle change at this most basic level seems to have been the

---

[184] Moss, 'Normandy and the Angevin Empire', pp. 96–7.

[185] Green, *Government*, pp. 67–8, 91–2, 223–5.

[186] Barlow, *William Rufus*, p. 216.

[187] For an examination of the reality behind the theory see M. Hagger, 'Theory and practice in the making of twelfth-century pipe rolls' in *Records, Administration and Aristocratic Society in the Anglo-Norman Realm*, ed. N. Vincent (Woodbridge, 2009), 45–74.

imposition of new imposts during the twelfth century, which could have increased ducal revenue drastically, there seem to have been more developments with regard to the interface between *vicomtes* and *prévôts* and the officials of the chamber and treasury. To begin with there were the changes in the way that these officials obtained their office. At first, they handed over a *census* in the form of a voluntary tribute. Later they handed over a *census* in the form of an agreed rent. Finally, they paid a unilaterally imposed farm, which might not have been of any greater value but which was imposed by the duke. Those developments may be supposed to say something about the changing balance of power between the duke and the more peripheral lords of Normandy, once almost autonomous Viking chiefs, who were now assimilated into the administrative structures of the duchy. Our sources make it clear that wealth was equated with power, but if this is right then it might also be the case that the way that wealth was collected could say something about power, too. Equally, from *c.* 1130 Henry and/or his administrators put in place an annual audit, which was perhaps only a viable proposition after the farms had been established. At least, during Henry II's reign, the county farms were the essential item for the audit of each shire, and the adversarial tone of the interviews remarked by Richard fitz Nigel could only have come about if the duke's officials knew what they were demanding.

Cash was vital to the dukes, perhaps especially to Henry I, and it may be supposed that all the modifications that were introduced were intended to increase income, to make that income as predictable as possible, and to make revenue collection as efficient as possible. As efficiency might be increased with uniformity, there might also have been an attempt, at the highest level of operations, to establish just such a uniformity between the audits that were held on both sides of the Channel. The pipe roll of Michaelmas 1130 certainly reveals that the officials of the English and Norman treasuries liaised with each other, and that debts owed in England might be paid in Normandy and vice versa. At the same time, it should be remembered that there is no evidence at all to demonstrate that the Norman exchequer worked in the same way as its English equivalent at this time, just as superficially similar English and Norman writs were not put into effect in the same way on both sides of the Channel. Indeed, given the state of the evidence, one may wonder if the sole English writer to use the word exchequer for a Norman court simply used the word as a convenient shorthand for a body that he saw as the equivalent of the English exchequer. We do not know that the Norman audit employed a table covered with a black, chequered cloth. And such is the lack of evidence about the Norman exchequer, that even doubts such as this should not be dismissed out of hand.

CHAPTER 11

Strength in Depth: The Dukes and their Knights, Castles, and Armies

Rollo, like all Scandinavian chiefs, gathered a band of warriors around him.[1] They crewed his ship and fought for him in his early campaigns in Francia. Later they lived in his hall at Rouen and were rewarded for their services from the revenues the city produced and with the lands now at Rollo's disposal. His successors, too, surrounded themselves with young *tiros*, as Dudo called them, ambitious for fame and reward. In the early eleventh century, when Dudo wrote of them, this body of men and warriors comprised the duke's *domus* or household. By the first decades of the twelfth century, however, the household had split into two parts: the *domus regis* and the *familia regis*. By then, the *domus regis* was composed of the chancellor, chaplains, bakers, kitchen-staff, and huntsmen while the *familia* comprised a wider body that included retained knights and their commanders, not all of whom were necessarily present at court permanently and not all of whom were retained, as such. But there was still some overlap between the *domus* and the *familia*, as J. O. Prestwich observed in 1981, for the leaders of the *familia* were also salaried members of the *domus*, with the offices of the master marshal and the constables, and their stipends, recorded in the *Constitutio domus regis*.[2]

These two terms, *domus regis* and *familia regis*, are most simply translated as 'the king's house' and 'the king's family', but the emphasis in the narratives on the use of the knights of the *familia* as garrisons, as shock troops, and as the backbone of ducal armies has led historians to prefer to translate *familia regis* as 'military household'. This is somewhat deceptive. Even in the twelfth century,

---

[1] Indicated, perhaps, by *Dudo*, pp. 32, 36, and suggested, too, by the retention of household warriors by men of broadly equivalent status. For example, in the eighth century, Ibn Fadlān came across a band of Rus on the Volga and wrote that a king of the Rus might have a household of 400 companions: 'these are the men who die when he dies, and allow themselves to be killed for him' (Ibn Fadlān, *Ibn Fadlān and the Land of Darkness: Arab Travellers in the Far North*, trans. P. Lunde and C. Stone (London, 2012), p. 54). Danish kings and chiefs also had households (Christiansen, *Norsemen in the Viking Age*, p. 53 and also p. 169; see also Roesdahl, *The Vikings*, p. 67). Indeed, it was when Harald Bluetooth lost control of his military household that he had to flee to the Slavs (Christiansen, *The Norsemen*, p. 150).

[2] Prestwich, 'Military household', 1–37; *Constitutio*, pp. 208–10.

the *familia regis* was not a military institution per se.[3] Although it included a shifting and assorted collection of young knights hoping to make their name, they did not just fight for the dukes, but might also act as messengers or hunting companions. Their function was not, then, necessarily military. Moreover, the attempt to equate the *familia* with the household is erroneous, as it suggests that the knights of the *familia* slept in the duke's hall at Rouen or followed him when he moved around the duchy. That was not the case. Some members of the *familia*, particularly the greater lords who might lead divisions of household knights, resided away from the court, in their own castles, unless they were summoned to join particular campaigns. As such, this discussion will talk of the household knights and the *familia*, but will eschew the modern, unwarranted, and deceptive 'military household'.

While all men of any status had a household of some kind, not all lords retained knights.[4] Equally, the number of knights retained depended on a number of interlocking factors. Among the most important of these were the character and position of the lord in question. The first section of this chapter therefore briefly considers the character and abilities of the dukes down to 1144, as portrayed in the narratives that tell us of their rule. The aim here is to provide a flavour of what sorts of behaviour knights might find attractive and what might bring them to question joining or remaining in any given household. The survey does not aim at completeness. There is no attempt to examine every duke's reign in turn. To begin with, the narratives do not permit such an exercise, but it is also the case that the same or similar characteristics are repeatedly highlighted so that one or two examples are sufficient to make more general points. That is itself a reminder that the various portraits we have were the constructions of the churchmen who wrote them and, as such, reflect the intentions, agenda, and education of their authors. In the narratives, the dukes are puppets on their strings, their actions the result of artifice and tropes. Nonetheless, although we cannot hope to understand the personalities of individual dukes from the evidence at our disposal, it is likely that the chroniclers did reflect contemporary views and understandings about the relative importance of military successes and, for example, a predictable temperament, a disciplined use of patronage, and the keeping of promises when recruiting and retaining knights or, indeed, supporters more generally.

Knights, whether lords of great honours or retained by a stipend, served the

---

[3] Hollister, *Henry*, pp. 258–60.
[4] In 1091, the future Henry I was allowed to retain one knight, one clerk, and three attendants (Orderic, iv. 352). In the later twelfth century, Walter Map had a small household, he tells us, although none of his servants appear to have been knights, over whom he was unable to exercise control or restraint (Walter Map, *De Nugis Curialium*, pp. 16–24).

duke in the expectation of reward. The second section of this chapter considers both the identities of those who served in a duke's *familia* and why they did so. The discussion focuses on men who were knights (*milites*), albeit with a quick glance at those who served as chaplains, too.[5] But the knights who served in the household were not simply young men hoping to make a reputation for themselves, or kicking their heels while awaiting their inheritances. Some of them represented the highest echelons of Norman society, even if they were only resident for a short time and even if they were only there because they had been summoned by the duke.[6] The result was that throughout the period covered by this study, the household knights were at the centre of the dukes' military and coercive power. Members of the household – although not exclusively household knights – would act as messengers for the dukes (as discussed above),[7] garrison their castles in peace and war, fight for them in the field, and provide counsel and the support of their own households and *fideles*. The *familia*, then, was more than just a force. It was an organ of government.

Often, or so it seems, the dukes' war-band or household knights were sufficient of themselves to deal with the forces put in the field by enemies or rebels. When a larger army was required, a duke's war-band might be combined with those that had coalesced around his supporters, and the smaller war-bands of his enemies

---

[5] I have assumed that the guests or *hôtes* (*hospites*) who appear in Norman acts were all representatives of a class of free tenant that can be found in north and central France (see, for example, Telma, nos. 249, 251, 368, 391, 401, 2393, 3132, 4899; L. Delisle, *Études sur la condition de la classe agricole et l'état de l'agriculture en Normandie, au moyen âge* (Evreux, 1851), pp. 13–14; G. A. Hodgett, *A Social and Economic History of Medieval Europe* (London, 1972), p. 177; Neveux, *A Brief History of the Normans*, pp. 103–4). This is certainly the case with an act for the monks of Fécamp of 1006, which states that 'guests' were also called 'settlers' or 'farmers' (*colonos*) and with an act whereby Achard the priest gave three 'guests, whom we call famers (*agricolas*)' in Fresne to the monks of the same abbey (*RADN*, nos. 9, 38). It is, however, just possible that some of these references were actually to figures equivalent to the 'guests' (*gestir* in Norwegian, translated as *hospites* in Latin) who were found in the households of St Olaf and Olaf the Gentle, kings of Norway (*Heimskringla*, pp. 289 and n. 1, 666). They could still be found in the king's household as late as the third decade of the twelfth century (*Heimskringla*, p. 720). It seems from the inadequate sources that these 'guests' were of lesser rank than the men who comprised the king's bodyguard, the *hird*, and that they acted not just as soldiers but also as policemen and undercover agents (*Heimskringla*, pp. 291–2, 294–5). If such warriors were found in the household of the Norman dukes, and it is at least worth questioning the assumption that 'hospites' always meant the same thing whenever it was used in ducal *acta*, they would have looked more Scandinavian than is usually thought.

[6] *Constitutio*, pp. 198, 208–10; Map, *De Nugis Curialium*, p. 470. Stenton remarked that housecarls, too, need not have been resident in the king's hall (F. M. Stenton, *Anglo-Saxon England*, third edition (Oxford, 1971), p. 582).

[7] See above, Chapter 9, pp. 524–30, and 528–9, Table 9.

would be brought to heel.[8] Richard Abels has painted a similar picture for England in the seventh and eighth centuries.[9] But sometimes even that was not enough. Richard I and Richard II were obliged to call on Scandinavian auxiliaries for help against the counts of Chartres *c.* 960 and *c.* 1013. During the uncertain minority of William the Bastard, and the uncertain majority of Robert Curthose, the duke might turn to the king of the French as his lord for help. In later years, William Rufus and Henry I would use their wealth to employ mercenaries, on occasion enlarging the numbers of troops under their command by several thousand in the process. The penultimate section of this chapter explores the use of these allies and mercenaries in the dukes' armies.

The last section of the chapter considers the recruitment of the composite force known as the 'army of Normandy'. This force first appears in Dudo's narrative *c.* 1015. It might have been assembled on occasion during the reigns of Richard II and Robert the Magnificent. Certainly, the force assembled by Robert the Magnificent in 1033, apparently with the intention of conquering England for Edward the Confessor, the report of which provides the first indication of an offensive capability sufficient – or so it must have been thought – to defeat a foreign foe in open battle, comprised of more than the duke's own household. This army need not have existed only in the imagination of William of Jumièges, as its subsequent success against the Channel Islands and Brittany, revealed by ducal *acta*, provides some support for his account of the scale of the force.[10] Orderic's *Ecclesiastical History* indicates that the 'army of Normandy' was used with more frequency from the 1090s, perhaps because Curthose could not afford to augment his own dwindling household with the mercenaries purchased in numbers by his rivals (and brothers), William Rufus and Henry I. While the intention here is to explore how this army was raised, it must be admitted that the evidence for the various aspects of this examination is both slight and ambiguous. It has also been mulled over on a number of previous occasions, without firm conclusions being reached. Nonetheless, while it is not possible to go very much further than previous commentators have gone, we can discern something of the obligations

---

[8] For this suggestion, see Searle, *PK*, pp. 48, 68–9, 121, 149–50, 204. Others did the same: *c.* 1013, Odo of Chartres 'called to his aid the counts Hugh of Maine and Waleran of Meulan with the forces of their knights (*copiis militum*)' (Jumièges, ii. 22).

[9] R. Abels, *Lordship and Military Obligation in Anglo-Saxon England* (Berkeley and London, 1988), pp. 11–37.

[10] Jumièges, ii. 78; *RADN*, nos. 73, 76, 85, 111. *RADN*, no. 73 was dated by Fauroux 1027 × 1035, but it was probably related to the campaign of 1033 and thus dates from 1033 × 1035; Keynes, 'The Æthelings in Normandy', 186–94 discusses the proposed campaign and the evidence for it, including the various acts and witness lists found in the *pancarte* for the monks of Mont-Saint-Michel act (*RADN*, nos. 73 and 111).

that impacted the army's recruitment, and one or two pieces of evidence that have been overlooked in the past perhaps help to establish more clearly when certain important developments took place and, indeed, what those developments meant in practical terms.

Reputation and recruitment

'A war-leader's military reputation and his political skills assured him of a growing following, and thus of growing powers.'[11] It might consequently be expected that the narratives recounting the politics and trickery that strengthened or threatened the dukes' hold on their duchy, and the battles that they fought to defend their position, would highlight their eloquence, foresightedness, courage, ferocity, and martial ability. And yet the Norman narratives, because they were written by churchmen who had agendas of their own and because they were not necessarily written for a lay audience, often downplayed the dukes' abilities as war leaders, preferring to portray them as idealized Christian rulers and even, in the case of Dudo of Saint-Quentin, as saints. Dudo's agenda placed a distinct strain on his credibility, but he was not alone in manipulating the dukes' characters and abilities for his own ends. Norman and Anglo-Norman writers were well aware that both good and bad dukes had to be portrayed in a certain way in order for their audiences to receive the right messages. That use of idealized or stock figures of course prevents us from perceiving anything of a duke's actual personality or character. But these portraits might still reveal something of what their supporters would have found attractive, and which would therefore have helped them to recruit men into their household forces, although that would in part depend on whether the behaviour of a good ruler was also the behaviour of a good employer. It is not clear that this was the case. On the other hand, the depictions of bad rulers – and in particular Orderic's portrait of Curthose, which amounts almost to a parody of a bad prince – *might* suggest the sort of behaviour that would make knights think twice about serving under a particular lord, not least because some of the great lords of Normandy whom Curthose slowly alienated had also numbered among the captains of his household.

A good military reputation was probably important, although perhaps not essential, for the recruitment of household knights. This was most explicitly spelt out by William of Poitiers in his *Gesta Guillelmi*. Poitiers had been a knight before he became a churchman and something of a soldier's sympathies and interests can be seen in his account of William the Bastard's reign. He certainly did not resist the temptation to record those martial characteristics that he found attractive or

---

[11] Searle, *PK*, p. 69.

praiseworthy in his subject, presumably because he thought that others would find them attractive and praiseworthy, too. And so, in contrast to William of Jumièges, whose agenda ensured that no duke should stand out from another and that they should share the glory of their successes with their subjects,[12] Poitiers placed Duke William at the centre of events throughout his work. For example, when suppressing the rebellion of Count William of Arques, the duke was portrayed as dynamic, and as responding with unusual speed to the threat posed by his uncle. His men were depicted as uncertain, but he was confident. He led his men from the front, and encouraged them by his own valour and confidence. He was courageous, but also merciful to those he had defeated.

When it came to the siege of Mayenne, Jumièges had provided only a very brief notice of the duke's successful capture of the castle. William had besieged the place for some time until finally he took it by throwing fire inside its walls and thus putting it to flames.[13] William of Poitiers wrote at much greater length and again highlighted the personal courage of Duke William and the importance of his conviction and encouragement to the successful outcome:

> all marvel at the confidence of the duke in the face of such a formidable enterprise. Almost all think that such great forces of mounted and foot soldiers will be worn out in vain; many complain; no hope rises in their breasts, except that perhaps, in a year or more, the defenders may be starved into capitulation. Indeed with swords, lances and missiles nothing can be done; there is no hope of achieving anything ... But the mettlesome leader, William, urges on the enterprise, gives orders, encourages, strengthens the faint-hearted, and promises a happy outcome. Their doubts do not remain for long. Behold, by their leader's clever plan, flames are thrown which set fire to the castle ... The garrison, who had fled into the citadel, surrendered the next day, convinced that no defence could prevail against the skill and courage of William.[14]

Poitiers thus built up the part played by the duke. The siege would have failed without his determination, encouragement, and imagination. His plan was clever, it worked, and his followers were rewarded for their trust by the plunder available to them when they took the castle.

There can be no doubt that William of Poitiers was well aware from his own experience of the benefits that accrued to a leader who developed a reputation for personal bravery, success, and the reward of his followers. And the conclusions

---

[12] See above, Introduction, pp. 14–15.
[13] Jumièges, ii. 150.
[14] Poitiers, p. 66.

that he had reached as a result of his experience compelled him to make plain, more than once, just how success led to prestige, how prestige attracted men into the duke's orbit, and how that recruitment in turn led to further success. After his discussion of the campaign led by King Henry against the Angevin castle at Mouliherne, for example, Poitiers stated that

> Geoffrey Martel enjoyed giving his opinion that there was no knight or warrior under the sun equal to the count of the Normans. From Gascony and Auvergne powerful men sent or took to him thoroughbred horses known by their regional name. Likewise Spanish kings sought his friendship with these gifts among others. And this friendship was sought and cultivated by the best and most powerful men. This was only right for there was in him something that *won the love of his household* (*domisticis*), his neighbours, and those far away.[15]

And then, to make sure that the point could not be missed, he added a further passage revealing the rewards that such a reputation might bring:

> Already none of his neighbours in Normandy dared attempt anything. All tumult of external war, as of revolt, was quelled. The bishops and counts of Francia, Burgundy, and of even more distant provinces frequented the court of the lord of Normandy; some to receive advice, *others in search of benefices*, most to bask in his favour. His friendship was aptly called a haven and a refuge, admitting and relieving many. Strangers, seeing that in our country horsemen go to and fro unarmed, and that the road is safe for every traveller, have often wished to have a similar blessing in their regions; this is the peace and distinction that the virtue of William has bestowed on his country.[16]

Poitiers here set out at unusual length – all the better to laud William – not just the foundations of William's reputation, which was attractive because knights would follow and obey a proven commander more willingly than an inexperienced or unsuccessful one, but also what that reputation meant in terms of fame, recruitment, and authority. What Poitiers did not say, and did not have to because William had more strings to his bow than martial ability alone, was that a reputation won in war but not supported by other characteristics would not remain untarnished. There was no plunder in peacetime, so other forms of rewarding knights and officials had to be found and nurtured, and that required other skills.

---

[15] Poitiers, p. 16 (my italics) and see also p. 30.
[16] Poitiers, p. 96 (my italics).

This was vital, as while a good ruler had to exercise political wisdom, keep the peace, and do justice, the narratives suggest that a good employer had to do little more than ensure that his knights received appropriate remuneration for their services – a view reinforced by the content of Bertran of Born's lament on the death of Henry the Young King in 1183.[17] To recruit household knights, then, a duke had to show that he would be able to keep them properly fed and had the resources to reward them with prizes or stipends. Dudo of Saint-Quentin wrote that Richard I 'spurred on the young warriors of his household (*suae domus*) with prizes and gifts; the older ones he enriched abundantly with benefices.'[18] Dudo also remarked that Richard I rewarded two French knights who, when he was travelling to meet with Archbishop Bruno of Cologne, had warned him that he was walking into an ambush and declared themselves to be his men: 'Richard thanked them and bade them farewell, and rewarded them handsomely in private. For he gave one of them a sword gleaming with four pounds of gold on the hilt, and to the other he gave an arm-ring, wrought of as many pounds of purest gold.'[19] This demonstration of his ability to reward men richly for their help was not just a reward, but an advert. Richard could and would enrich those who served his interests.

According to Isembert, chaplain of Duke Robert the Magnificent and later abbot of Sainte-Trinité-du-Mont outside Rouen, whose stories were incorporated into the *Gesta Normannorum ducum*, Duke Robert was so generous that 'if he began to make gifts to someone early in the morning he would hand over whatever came to his hand during that day to the same person whom he had thought worthy of reward early that morning'. Isembert then went on to recount the story of the smith of Beauvais, who was so awed by the duke's generosity towards him that he fled the court, but was so impressed, too, that the next year,

the same smith ... returned to Normandy together with his two sons who were well-instructed in military skills. He was allowed into the duke's presence and addressed him thus: 'Lord, do you recognize your servant?' 'No', said the duke. Then the smith said, 'I am the person to whom of your generosity you gave so many presents last year. Therefore I have come with my two sons to offer our faithful service if your excellency does not refuse it.'[20]

[17] Bertran of Born, *Planh for the Young English King*, in R. Kehew (ed.), *The Lark in the Morning: The Verses of the Troubadours, a Bilingual Edition*, trans. E. Pound, W. D. Snodgrass, and R. Kehew (Chicago and London, 2005), pp. 164–5.
[18] Dudo, p. 269; *Dudo*, p. 143.
[19] *Dudo*, pp. 141–2.
[20] Jumièges, ii. 58–60, and see also above, Chapter 10, pp. 604–5.

On another occasion, the same duke gave one of his knights a large sum of money so that he might make a gift at the altar. The knight gave the whole sum to the Church and was rewarded with double the initial amount. 'And so ... by this and similar deeds he won the love of many people and inspired them to take service with him.'[21] Orderic added that 'Robert duke of Normandy lavishly distributed the wealth he possessed among his knights, and gathered around himself a crowd of young knights greedy for gain, who were attracted by his promises'.[22] Here, then, gift-giving, maintaining the honour of the knights in their service, and keeping promises were expressly linked to the recruitment of more knights. Rufus acted in much the same way, and his ostentatious generosity resulted in swarms of knights joining his household who could then be rewarded only by the enormous outlay of money.[23]

In contrast, the portraits of poor rulers and weak lords might reveal qualities that would – or so it may be supposed – discourage knights from joining a particular household. Again, these portraits are artificial. Orderic's depiction of Robert Curthose, which constitutes the best example of inadequate leadership in a Norman context, was probably not an accurate portrait of the man or his rule. While Curthose clearly did lose the support of a number of his leading subjects, they did not necessarily desert him for the reasons Orderic proposed. Nonetheless, simply because the monk was explaining why Curthose lost the support of lord after lord, individual after individual, there seems to be more of a connection between his grand narrative and the duke's attractiveness as an employer than is the case with the altogether more positive but generic portraits of William the Bastard and Henry I.

No one could deny Curthose's military abilities. He had bested his father outside the castle of Gerberoy in 1079, and went on to carve out a mighty reputation for himself while on the First Crusade. Geoffrey Gaimar wrote that

> there was none nobler, none braver in all the world than he – and he was duke of Normandy ... This was a duke of Normandy who accomplished deeds of valour on many occasions, who made great display of his knightly accomplishments, and who performed many singular feats of bravery and many a fine act of chivalry ... He captured and liberated the fair city of Jerusalem from the pagans and became renowned amongst the Christians. The duke killed Kerbogha, and this caused him to be held in such high esteem that [the crusaders] were ready to elect him king.[24]

[21] Jumièges, ii. 60.
[22] Orderic, iv. 118.
[23] Malmesbury, *GR*, i. 558.
[24] Gaimar, pp. 310–12.

That reputation was a problem for Henry I when he was seeking to undermine Curthose's rule. Such a champion of God might expect to be defended by Him whose holy places he had so vigorously helped to liberate from the Muslims. Henry's chances of success were diminished accordingly. And so it may be that in 1105 King Henry attempted to undermine Curthose by suggesting that his failure to protect the Church in Normandy had made him as repellent to God as those Saracens he had fought in the Holy Land.[25] Indeed, Robert's military reputation was such that when he was defeated by Henry I at Tinchebray in 1106 some chroniclers felt obliged to explain how this mighty warrior for God had been beaten by his less experienced younger brother. Henry of Huntingdon blamed the defeat on Curthose's refusal to accept the throne of Jerusalem: 'The Lord repaid Duke Robert because, when He had allowed him to be glorious in the exploits at Jerusalem, he had refused the kingdom of Jerusalem when it was offered to him. He had chosen rather to devote himself to quietness and inactivity in Normandy than to toil for the Lord of kings in the holy city. So God condemned him to everlasting inactivity and perpetual imprisonment.'[26]

Military panache was all very well, then, but it would not help a man if God turned against him as a result of his moral failings or inability to live up to the requirements of Christian rulership. Curthose failed in these fundamental tasks:

All men knew that Duke Robert was weak and indolent; therefore trouble-makers despised him and stirred up loathsome factions when and where they chose. For although the duke was bold and daring, praiseworthy for his knightly prowess and eloquent in speech, he exercised no discipline over either himself or his men. He was prodigal in distributing his bounty and lavish in his promises, but so thoughtless and inconstant that they were utterly unreliable. Being merciful to suppliants he was too weak and pliable to pass judgement on wrongdoers; unable to pursue any plan consistently he was far too affable and obliging in all his relationships, and so he earned the contempt of corrupt and foolish men.[27]

Orderic provided examples of the duke's flaws. He wrote of his failure to prosecute a campaign against Robert of Bellême; his foolishness in relinquishing the

---

[25] The suggestion that Orderic utilized Henry's propaganda when composing this passage was suggested by Aird, *Robert Curthose*, pp. 229–30.

[26] Huntingdon, p. 51.

[27] Orderic, iv. 114. Malmesbury provided a example, remarking that Curthose had allowed his brother, Henry, to replenish the supply of water at Mont-Saint-Michel even while he besieged it, and commenting on the duke's 'softheartedness' and 'mild temper' in the process (Malmesbury, *GR*, i. 552).

fortresses at Ivry, Brionne, and Alençon; his loss of the fidelity of his greatest lords; and the indiscipline of his household. Orderic was not alone in portraying Curthose as a failure, although others were kinder when they did so. Eadmer wrote that 'Robert, duke of Normandy, brother of King Henry, had at that time sunk so low in the general estimation that there was scarcely anyone willing to do for him any such service as among all nations it is usual to do for the sovereign of a country. Piety and an almost total absence of any desire for worldly wealth, both of which qualities were prominent in Robert's character, had produced this estimation of him.'[28] These portraits are supported, to an extent, by the lists of injustices compiled during his reign, as well as the apparent reluctance to seek his judgement in lawsuits.[29] It is possible that, as a result of his experiences on crusade, Robert Curthose, like Dudo's William Longsword before him, had begun to long for the life of a monk rather than that of a monarch.[30] But in any event, these unflattering descriptions help to explain why Curthose lost the support of his *fideles* and at the same time cast a moral judgement on his rule and legitimized the conquest of the duchy by Henry I who, although 'not too well loved', was altogether more adept at the political games rulers had to play and who was both willing and able to reward those who were loyal to him.[31]

To potential recruits to the household, a lack of desire for worldly wealth was just as bad as indiscriminate prodigality and poverty – although it is difficult to see how a man who retained Rouen, Caen, and Bayeux could have been quite as poor as the chroniclers made out. Service in the household was, after all, a business arrangement. Knights served in return for pay and in the hope of greater rewards should they deserve them. As the duke was the most prestigious employer in Normandy, so service in his household was naturally attractive. But men wanted to know that they would be rewarded in a way that was commensurate with their service. They wanted to know that the duke would keep his promises to them. They wanted consistency not caprice, fairness not favouritism, prudence not prodigality.[32] Most dukes ruled according to these values but, at least in Orderic's depiction of him, Curthose did not. His actions made the wider political community of Normandy, those lords who had once been captains of the household knights, concerned about their prospects, just as a run of bad results can give investors in the stock market jitters. Comparing Normandy to a modern business might seem

---

[28] Eadmer, *HN*, p. 165; trans. Bosanquet, p. 176
[29] See above, Chapter 8, pp. 445–8, 489–90, 496, Table 8, 502.
[30] A similar suggestion may be found in Aird, *Robert Curthose*, p. 198.
[31] Quotation from Eadmer, *HN*, p. 166; trans. Bosanquet, p. 177.
[32] As Malmesbury noted: 'We ought, therefore, to be generous, but carefully and in moderation, for many men by inconsiderate generosity have poured away their patrimony' (Malmesbury, *GR*, i. 556).

trite, but Orderic was attempting to undermine Curthose's reputation, and reputation remains of enormous importance in City institutions, while the fragility of
modern financial markets and the volatility of economic forces in some ways echo
the precariousness of political success in the north of Francia at the end of the eleventh century. Seen in this way, the manner in which Curthose managed the family
business did not give those investing in it the sense of security they needed. The
duke's stock plummeted as hostile rivals circled. Investors pulled out one by one,
saving what they could while they could. Potential employees could see the way the
wind was blowing and looked for employment elsewhere. Regional competitors
eroded the duke's dominant position within Normandy, and eventually the whole
business was subject to a hostile takeover by a much wealthier foreign concern.

Curthose, then, was a failure and so he was given the failings and flaws of an
unsuccessful ruler or lord. As they comprise a stereotype, it is not surprising that
the same flaws were highlighted in the speeches that Henry of Huntingdon put
into the mouths of the protagonists who faced each other outside Lincoln on 2
February 1141. The commanders of the opposing armies told their troops why they
should not be afraid of advancing into battle, and in doing so they naturally highlighted personality traits that knights in search of employment would have found
unattractive. Earl Robert of Gloucester disparaged his opponents in his speech,
which was reported first, as follows:

> Now consider who your opponents in this battle are. Alan, duke of the Bretons,
> appears in arms against you – indeed, against God. He is an abominable man,
> stained with every kind of crime, not acknowledging an equal in evil, whose
> impulses are unfailingly harmful, who regards it as the one supreme disgrace
> not to be incomparable in cruelty. There also appears against you the count of
> Meulan, an expert in deceit, a master of trickery, who was born with wicked-
> ness in his blood, falsehood in his mouth, sloth in his deeds, a braggart by
> nature, stout-hearted in talk, faint-hearted in deed, the last to muster, the first
> to decamp, slow to attack, quick to retreat. … Simon, earl of Northampton,
> appears, whose action is only talk, whose gift is mere promise: he talks as if he
> has acted and promises as if he has given.[33]

Robert of Gloucester in turn, and those who fought with him, too, were disparaged in a similar manner by Stephen's spokesman, Baldwin fitz Gilbert of Clare:

> The power of Duke (*dux*) Robert [of Gloucester] is well known. He, indeed,
> usually threatens much and does little, with the mouth of a lion and the heart

---

[33] Huntingdon, pp. 728–30.

of a rabbit, famous for his eloquence, notorious for his idleness. The earl of Chester has nothing for which he ought to be feared, for he is a man of reckless daring, ready for conspiracy, unreliable in performance, impetuous in battle, careless of danger, with designs beyond his powers, panting for the impossible, having few steady followers, collecting together a ragged troop of outcasts.[34]

These characterizations were clearly untrue, and as a result they once again highlight those traits that contemporaries saw as unattractive. The greatest flaw, so far as Huntingdon was concerned, certainly the one that he repeated time and again, was that a man should be a talker.[35] Those singled out in his harangues were men who promised much but failed to deliver anything. Huntingdon's account also reveals that such traits opened a man to ridicule, which was something else that would be unattractive to those looking for a place in a noble's household. Knights, with their concern for honour and status, would hardly seek to be retained by a man who was derided by his peers.

As a postscript, and to highlight once again the artificiality of these portraits, it may be noted that because Orderic did not like the Angevins at all, he did not tar Stephen with the brush with which he had so liberally coated Robert Curthose. Instead, he suggested that Stephen's rule over Normandy was ineffective and disturbed because he was personally absent. Those absences left Normandy 'without a protector' so that 'the people were bewildered and, having no leader, did not know what to do'.[36] Orderic did not blame Stephen for these absences, however. Indeed, he was excused for them. An expedition planned for 1136 failed to materialize, Orderic wrote, because Stephen was distracted by an unfounded report of Roger of Salisbury's demise. Even Stephen's unsuccessful campaign in 1137 was blamed on divisions among the Normans which meant that Stephen could not place any trust in his own forces.[37] It was only in his reaction to the news of Stephen's treatment of Matilda at Arundel in 1139 that Orderic finally vented his frustration. After noting that Stephen had given Matilda licence to leave Arundel and join her supporters in the west, he commented:

---

[34] Huntingdon, p. 734.
[35] At the end of the twelfth century, Walter Map reported a similar comment that he had heard from the lips of King Louis VII: 'the emperor of Constantinople and the king of Sicily boast themselves in golden and silken webs, but they have no men who can do anything but talk, for in war-like matters they are useless' (Walter Map, *De Nugis Curialium*, p. 450).
[36] Orderic, vi. 456 (and similarly 478, 528), 458.
[37] Orderic, vi. 486.

in granting this licence the king showed himself either very guileless or very foolish, and prudent men must deplore his lack of regard for both his own safety and the security of the kingdom. He could easily have stamped out the flames of terrible evil that were being kindled if he had acted with the foresight characteristic of wise men and had immediately driven off the wolf from the entrance to the sheepfold, and if … he had nipped the malevolence of trouble-makers in the bud, and had struck down with the sword of justice, after the fashion of his ancestors, the pestilential strength of those who desired rapine and slaughter and the devastation of their country.[38]

Finally, then, Stephen was seen to be without wisdom – one of the trinity of characteristics essential for good rule. For William of Malmesbury, in contrast, his weaknesses had become apparent much sooner, not least perhaps because he was writing for Matilda's half-brother, Robert of Gloucester: 'He was a man of energy but lacking in judgement, active in war, of extraordinary spirit in undertaking difficult tasks, lenient to his enemies and easily appeased, courteous to all: though you admired his kindness in promising, still you felt his words lacked truth and his promises fulfilment.' A little later, he noted that he was a spendthrift.[39] Here, then, is the stock image of the poor ruler – militarily able but lacking in political wisdom, unreliable, and undiscriminating in dispensing money and patronage – a man doomed to weakness and failure as a result of his flaws, just as Curthose had been.

The rewards of service

While the previous discussion has suggested that there were a number of characteristics that might attract men to, or repel them from, the household of a particular duke (or lord), the narratives only make explicit the importance of reputation, generosity, and wealth. Those things were important, of course, as knights wanted to be rewarded for their services, although it was not necessarily the case that they all wanted to be rewarded in the same way.

Anselm of Le Bec, quoted with approval by Marjorie Chibnall, remarked that 'a prince has different kinds of soldiers at his court. He has some who are active in his service in return for the lands which they hold from him. He has others who bear arms and toil on his behalf for stipends (*pro stipendiis*). And he has yet others who labour with unbroken fortitude to obey his will for the sake of receiving back again an inheritance of which they bewail the loss through their parents' fault.'[40]

[38] Orderic, vi. 534.
[39] Malmesbury *HN*, pp. 28, 32.
[40] Eadmer, *Vita Anselmi*, ed. and trans. R. W. Southern (Oxford, 1962), p. 94; M. Chibnall,

For Anselm, then, there were three bases for service in the household. We can begin by looking at the second of them: service in return for a stipend or other form of remuneration.

Part of the stipend of the household knights was paid in kind, as they were both fed and housed by the dukes. The ability of any duke to provide suitable sustenance and conditions for the knights he retained was a matter of honour, not least because these were factors that would have affected recruitment and retention. According to Dudo of Saint-Quentin, Duke Richard I threw off the tutelage of Ralph Torta, imposed on his household by Louis IV, principally because Ralph had allowed only 18 *deniers* a day to Richard and each of his knights so that 'his retainers in the household were humiliated and disgracefully pinched with hunger'.[41] Ralph was punished by banishment. It is likely that the dukes continued to feed their households throughout the eleventh century as in Henry I's day the *milites* of the *familia regis* were still maintained at their lord's expense. Before the battle of Bourgthéroulde, Odo Borleng urged his troops to fight. If they refused to do so, he said, 'we shall deserve to forfeit both our wages and our honour; and, in my opinion, we shall never again be entitled to eat the king's bread'.[42]

Aside from sustenance, Borleng's words reveal that by Henry I's day the household knights might be paid a stipend, too. Henry was here continuing a tradition found in England under his brother, and which likely dated back at least to the reign of Cnut.[43] According to the late testimony of Walter Map, he paid each of his knights at least £5 per year and 'whenever it happened that he was sent for

'Mercenaries and the *familia Regis* under Henry I', *History*, 62 (1977), 15. Anders Winroth, in his recent work on the conversion of Scandinavia, identified a rather different set of incentives and rewards: 'Every ambitious chieftain faced the same problem: how was he to recruit and keep warriors in his retinue? His retainers, not simple mercenaries that fought for wages, were free men whose sense of honour would not have tolerated that kind of venal relationship. Instead, the chieftain needed to engage his warriors in close personal relationships. If they were not biological kin, they might create kinship through, for example, rituals of brotherhood, marriage alliances, and friendship formalized by drinking together in the chieftain's hall. Whatever their relationship, it was constantly reasserted through the exchange of gifts' (Winroth, *Conversion of Scandinavia*, p. 45). It is not clear that many of these considerations held true for Normandy, however, and the supposed abhorrence of serving in return for payment was certainly not found there.

[41]   *Dudo*, p. 122 and see also above, Chapter 6, pp. 338–9.

[42]   Orderic, vi. 348–50.

[43]   Gaimar, pp. 316–17 (for Rufus); R. Abels, *Lordship and Military Obligation*, pp. 167–8 (for Cnut). In contrast to the situation in England, there is no evidence for the payment of stipends to household knights in Normandy before the Conquest. Dudo noted only the award of prizes and gifts (*Dudo*, p. 143) and pre-Conquest ducal *acta* do not make mention of *stipendiarii*.

by that man, he received at his coming one shilling for every day after he left his residence'.[44] When William of Jumièges reduced the sum of money allowed to Richard I from the 18 *deniers* found in Dudo's story to 12 *deniers* per day, he might have done so because it was the daily payment due to a knight for every day that he served in the *familia* under William the Bastard.[45] Such payments do not make the household knights equivalent to mercenaries. They were not swords for hire, but men who loyally served their sovereign and were maintained in return, just like the soldiers of today.[46] That difference was reflected by the fact that by 1101 at the latest, Henry I's household knights were also compensated for any losses sustained while in his service, as is revealed by the treaty made with Count Robert of Flanders in 1101.[47]

Payment of the sums due, and in good time, was a matter of honour to the dukes. Just as Richard I banished Ralph Torta because of his shaming treatment of his household, so Henry reacted to the injury done to his own reputation when the money with which he paid his knights was found to be debased in 1124: 'Infuriated by the insult inflicted upon his knights (*militum suorum*), but even more by the violation of justice, the king announced a sentence ... that all the moneyers (*nummularii*) who could justly be accused of this crime should be punished by having their right hand and genitals cut off.'[48] Henry also ensured that the good reputation he enjoyed with his household knights should continue beyond the grave. As he lay on his deathbed at Lyons-la-Forêt, 'he commanded his son Robert, who had charge of his treasure at Falaise, to take sixty thousand pounds and pay out wages and largess for members of his household and his stipendiary soldiers'.[49]

Gifts and stipends allowed men to make a living out of their service, but there would come a time when they could no longer fight for the duke. When, or before,

---

[44] Walter Map, *De Nugis Curialium*, p. 470. The pipe rolls of 1172–73 and 1173–74 also suggest that knights were generally (although not always) paid 1s. per day at that time (*Great Roll of the Pipe for the Nineteenth Year of the Reign of King Henry the Second, AD 1172–3*, Publications of the Pipe Roll Society, 19 (1895), p. 33; *Great Roll of the Pipe for the Twentieth Year of the Reign of King Henry the Second, AD 1172–3*, Publications of the Pipe Roll Society, 21 (1896), pp. 51, 63, 139).

[45] Jumièges, i. 114, and see below.

[46] The point is well made by S. B. D. Brown, 'The mercenary and his master: military service and monetary reward in the eleventh and twelfth centuries', *History*, 74 (1989), 21–7, and the question is also discussed in a number of the articles found in *Mercenaries and Paid Men: The Mercenary Identity in the Middle Ages*, ed. J. France (Leiden, 2008).

[47] See below, *infra*, pp. 653–4.

[48] Jumièges, ii. 238.

[49] Orderic, vi. 448. Similarly, King Alfred left £200 cash to his household in his will, and each man was to be given the same sum that he had given them the previous Easter (noted in Abels, 'Household men, mercenaries and Vikings', p. 152 and Abels, *Lordship and Military Obligation*, p. 168).

that time came they would hope to be rewarded with land sufficient to maintain them for the rest of their days in a fitting manner. Not all would be so rewarded, however. Fulbert of Chartres advised Duke William of Aquitaine that 'the vassal should avoid injuring his lord … but this does not entitle him to a fief (*casamentum*). For it is not enough to abstain from evil, it is also necessary to do good. So it remains for him to give his lord faithful counsel and aid … if he wishes to be considered worthy of his benefice.'[50] Dudo's comments, noted earlier, reflected the need for knights to earn their benefice, too. It was only the older members of the household that Richard had 'enriched abundantly with benefices'. The younger, as yet underserving warriors, were rewarded instead with 'prizes and gifts'. Orderic similarly reported that 'King Henry, who had now, after tremendous toil, settled affairs admirably in Normandy, decided to cross the Channel, pay generous wages to the young champions and distinguished knights who had fought hard and loyally, and raise the status of some by giving them extensive honours in England'.[51]

The appearance of property described as *beneficia* in ducal *acta* may reveal something of the rewards of service. An act of Richard II for the monks of Jumièges of 1025 suggests that this was the case: 'It is also pleasing to write below those things which our *fideles* have granted from their benefices *which are ours by right* or from their paternal inheritances.'[52] His words suggest the temporary nature of the grants made to household knights. In theory, a benefice was held for life and would then return to the duke's demesne. That is why they remained 'ours by right'. An act of 1037 × 1046 records that, before his death in 1035, 'Robert the most noble duke of the Normans, the son of the most pious *princeps* Richard, gave the vic of Le Croix-Avranchin which is situated between Saint-James-de-Beuvron and Mont-Saint-Michel as a benefice to a certain one of his knights called Adelelm'.[53] This was demesne, but Robert's need to reward his followers, or to establish them in strategic locations, also caused him to alienate property to knights that was not his to give – if only in the days of his unruly youth. Thus, Robert, 'while a young man, depraved by the counsel of perverse men', took Ticheville on the river Touques away from the monks of Saint-Wandrille and gave

---

[50] Fulbert, *Letters*, no. 51.

[51] Orderic, vi. 294.

[52] *RADN*, no. 36. Two of the other acts apparently produced in August 1025 (*RADN*, nos. 34, 53) have near identical wording. See also Tabuteau, *Transfers*, pp. 96–7 and Bates, *Normandy*, pp. 122–4. In addition, it is worth noting that during a dispute between Count Odo of Chartres and King Robert the Pious, Count Odo stated that the land the king was claiming was not a benefice held from the king's right (*de tuo fisco*) but inherited property (Fulbert, *Letters*, no. 86; Reynolds, *Fiefs*, pp. 134–5)

[53] *RADN*, no. 110.

it to a knight called Haimo. William the Bastard was prevailed upon, while still in his minority, to promise to return it, although he did earn a delay: 'in such a way that within three years he should give his vassal a safe exchange and should give us back all our land and, if not before, then immediately at the end of three years' even if he still had nothing to give his knight in exchange.[54] The controversy, and others like it, reveals how the expectations of the dukes' knights, and the dukes' need to meet them, might outstrip the resources at their disposal.[55] A final, and particularly explicit example of the rewards of service, and the continuing obligations imposed on those rewarded with a grant of land, dates from 1046 × 1066 when Gilbert Crispin gave his benefice of Hauville to the monks of Jumièges. This benefice, he added, 'I hold from my said lord for fighting (*militans obtineo*)'.[56]

Such rewards were not just for the military members of the household, of course. Those serving the duke in other capacities expected to be rewarded for their work, too. They included the duke's chaplains who

> waited on the royal court out of covetousness for high office and, to the great discredit of their cloth, shamelessly pandered to the king. Like young *tiros* who receive wages from their officers for their service in war, some of these tonsured clerks accepted from laymen, as a reward for their service at court, bishoprics and abbeys … and other ecclesiastical offices and honours.[57]

Dudo of Saint-Quentin was granted two churches by Richard II.[58] William the Bastard gave Maurice, later made bishop of London, various tithes in some of his forests and vills.[59] It is likely that the 'tithes and goods' that Roger of Salisbury

---

[54] *RADN*, no. 95.

[55] Noted by Bates, *Normandy*, p. 196; Chibnall, 'Military service in Normandy', 68–9. Robert's actions also suggest that he saw Church property as his to give to his knights, as had been the case under the Carolingians (see above, Chapter 2, pp. 97–8 and Chapter 7, pp. 408–10).

[56] *RADN*, no. 188. Bates and Chibnall wrote that he had done his fighting in order to earn the benefice (Bates, *Normandy*, p. 123; Chibnall, 'Military service in Normandy', 67). Tabuteau suggested that he held in return for continuing to fight for the duke (Tabuteau, *Transfers*, p. 57). The wording of the act seems better to support the latter view. Similarly, in the county of Maine, Bishop Avesgaudus endowed a *miles* called Hebrannus with some property in the 1020s so that he 'might help him bring war against the count' – in other words in return for military service. Whether this service was to be performed regularly is not clear, however (the land might have been a bribe like Guy of Burgundy's grant of Le Homme to Nigel of the Cotentin): Barton, *Maine*, p. 125.

[57] Orderic, ii. 268

[58] *RADN*, no. 18.

[59] *Regesta: William*, no. 242 and see above, Chapter 10, p. 595.

held in Normandy at Valognes, Saint-Marcouf, Varreville, and Pouppeville had been given to him by Henry I towards the beginning of his career when Roger was in charge of his household.[60] He, like Maurice, would later be rewarded with a bishopric.

While some served to gain property and thus security for their old age, others may have served principally to gain justice or restitution – Anselm's third reason for service in the household. Dudo of Saint-Quentin suggested that King Louis IV numbered among such hopefuls, reporting that he became a temporary member of William Longsword's household while he awaited a chance to recover his inheritance: 'William was moved with pity for the afflicted king, and led him to his seat at Rouen. Many a time did he give him honourable entertainment there, along with all his men. For the king stayed in the house of Duke William as a member of the household (*domigena*) and a page-boy (*uernula*), and he waited for his assistance as a petitioner.'[61] When Helias of Maine was released from prison in 1098, following William Rufus's conquest of Maine, he appeared before the king at Rouen and asked that he 'receive me in your household (*tua ... familia*) with the title of my former rank, and I will repay you with worthy service. I do not ask to have the city of Le Mans or the castles of Maine until by some appropriate service I may deserve to receive them back from your royal hand. Until that day my desire is to be counted among the members of your household (*familiares*) and to enjoy your kingly favour.' Orderic thought that Rufus would have agreed, but that he was dissuaded by Count Robert of Meulan who 'was chief among the king's counsellors and justices, and therefore feared to admit an equal or superior into the royal council chamber'.[62] It is worth repeating Prestwich's point about this tale: 'Orderic's story shows that the military household was more than a fighting force: its leaders enjoyed the confidence of the king, shared in his counsels and judgements and stood at the centre of power, jealously guarding their privileges and opportunities.'[63] Henry I also had men in his household serving him in the hope of receiving inheritances or recovering lost lands. Geoffrey and Engenulf of L'Aigle were active in his household in 1118 and expected to receive their father's English honour as a result.[64] It is likely that the sons of Ivo of Grandmesnil and William of Rhuddlan, who were casualties of the wreck of the *White Ship*, had also served in the hope of recovering their fathers' estates.[65]

Aside from these hopefuls, there were elder sons making a career and hoping

---

[60] 'Cartulaire de l'abbaye de Saint-Lô', in *Cartulaire de la Manche* (1878), pp. 4–5 (no. 3).

[61] Dudo, p. 194; *Dudo*, p. 71.

[62] Orderic, v. 248.

[63] Prestwich, 'Military household', p. 108.

[64] Orderic, vi. 196.

[65] Orderic, vi. 304.

to gain experience and a reputation for themselves while they waited to inherit their fathers' lands, or even younger sons who simply wanted to make a name for themselves. Walter Map recalled that when Henry I heard of any young man living north of the Alps who wanted to gain a good reputation to help them make a start in life, he would appoint him to the *familia*.[66]

We know nothing of the great majority of those who served in the household who have disappeared without historical trace, but the careers of those few remarked by the chroniclers suggest a meritocracy in which capable men could do very well for themselves. Henry of Pommeraye was one of them. He was heir to Joscelin, lord of Berry Pomeroy in Devon, whose honour would later be assessed at thirty-two knights' fees. Neither his father nor his grandfather attest surviving royal acts, and it may be that Henry entered the royal duke's service in an attempt to raise his family's stock. If that was his aim, he seems to have achieved it. Henry attested seven of Henry I's acts.[67] Furthermore, he rose through his service, which saw him fighting among the household troops at Bourgthéroulde, to become a royal constable – a post he held long after his father's death between 1125 and 1130.[68]

Anselm had also noted the presence in the duke's *familia* of men who were 'active in his service in return for the lands which they hold from him'. Among these figures, perhaps, were some of the greatest lords of Normandy. By no means all of the great men found around the dukes were explicitly described as having been members of the *familia*, but those who were included luminaries such as William I and William II of Warenne, Ranulf Le Meschin, and Count Robert of Meulan.[69] Men described as captains of the household knights, who *might* thus have been (temporary) members of the household themselves, included Ralph of Gacé, Robert of Bellême, Count William of Evreux, Earl Hugh of Chester, Walter Giffard, the future Henry I, while still count of the Cotentin, and Gilbert of L'Aigle.[70] It is likely that men such as William fitz Osbern, Roger II of

[66] Walter Map, *De Nugis Curialium*, p. 470.

[67] Calendared at *Regesta*, ii. nos. 1292, 1339, 1464, 1465, 1468, 1693, 1764.

[68] *Constitutio*, pp. 208–10; Sanders, *English Baronies*, p. 106; Chibnall, 'Mercenaries and the *familia regis*', 17–18; Green, *Government*, pp. 266–7. Kathleen Thompson noted, almost certainly correctly, that Henry's wife Rohais was not an illegitimate daughter of Henry I as is often thought (Thompson, 'Affairs of state', 149).

[69] Prestwich, 'Military household', 13–18, 23–6.

[70] Jumièges, ii. 102; Orderic, v. 214, 216. Morillo followed Prestwich in maintaining that 'any military leader of any importance retained by William I, Rufus, or Henry became a member of that king's military household, the *familia regis*' (S. Morillo, *Warfare under the Anglo-Norman Kings 1066–1135* (Woodbridge, 1994), pp. 43–4, quotation at p. 44). Hollister, in contrast, thought that the men named as captains should not be assumed to have been members of the household at all (Hollister, *Henry*, p. 259). His comments,

Montgommery, and Roger of Beaumont were members of the *familia*, too, even though they are not named as such. They certainly acted on occasions in a capacity that implies their membership of that body, as when Montgommery and fitz Osbern were sent as messengers to Count Geoffrey of Anjou.[71]

None of these men are likely to have served in the household solely for material reward. While they might have been there simply because they had been summoned to serve in a particular campaign,[72] it is more likely that they served to increase their honour, for the opportunity to marry well and to inherit lands, and for access to the duke's ear. They needed such access to the duke's patronage because they maintained their own lordships to some extent by their ability to divert jobs, heiresses, wardships, and other benefits to their own men, thereby demonstrating their enjoyment of the duke's favour and their ability to reward their followers to their peers and actual or potential members of their households. As J. E. Lally put it in 1976, when writing of the court of Henry II, 'each of the leading members of the court had his circle of dependants who hoped through their relationship or association with the great to obtain access to the sources of royal patronage'.[73] The opportunity to enjoy such favour lay at the heart of William Longsword's offer to the rebel Riulf: 'If you are ready and willing to serve me, you will enjoy within my household (*in domo mea*) my constant favour, and the rewards of active service. I will accept from your mouth advice on how I should govern … Whomsoever you order to raise up, I will mightily exalt; whom to cast down I will dreadfully humiliate.'[74] Likewise, the men of the Cotentin were promised a greater place in William's household if they stormed the castle at Montreuil.[75] Dudo, then, readily equated a place in the household with influence over political decisions and the opportunity to grab patronage, and implied that greater access to the duke's favour was an incentive to more enthusiastic service.

---

however, lose some force when it is recalled that the household was not an established body but rather one that might expand and shrink according to circumstances. His view also failed to take into account the possibility that men might be summoned to join the household (by analogy with Map's words, cited above, and the agreement made by the monks of Mont-Saint-Michel and William Paynel in 1070 × 1081: *Ctl. Mont-Saint-Michel*, no. 90; *CDF*, no. 714; Tabuteau, *Transfers*, pp. 56–7).

[71] Poitiers, p. 26.

[72] A possibility suggested by the terms of William Paynel's agreement with the abbot of Mont-Saint-Michel by which Hugh of Bricqueville might be summoned to join William's *familia* (see above, n. 70).

[73] J. E. Lally, 'Secular patronage at the court of Henry II', *Bulletin of the Institute of Historical Research*, 49 (1976), 169.

[74] *Dudo*, p.65.

[75] *Dudo*, p. 80, and see below.

The influence and rewards that might come the way of the greatest members of the *familia* are revealed by the career of Count Robert of Meulan.[76] He developed a towering reputation for wisdom as a result of his experience and influence, particularly from *c.* 1100. He was adviser to three successive dukes, and used his shrewdness to his own advantage, too, abandoning Curthose shortly after 1090 and becoming a firm supporter of Henry I on both sides of the Channel *c.* 1100. Indeed, he and his brother together ensured that Henry would be crowned king in August 1100.[77] Eadmer wrote that 'King Henry himself in all matters affecting the kingdom trusted his judgement and followed his advice more than that of any other of his counsellors',[78] and Malmesbury that 'his opinion was regarded as the utterance of an oracle',[79] while Henry of Huntingdon thought him 'in secular business the wisest man of all living between here and Jerusalem, and King Henry's counsellor'.[80] This last writer went on to note that he was 'celebrated for his knowledge, persuasive in speech, shrewd and astute, sagaciously far-sighted, cunningly intelligent, unfailingly prudent, profound in his counsel, great in wisdom. Accordingly, by means of these qualities, he had acquired great and varied possessions.'[81] These possessions included the estates of Ivo of Grandmesnil, which gave Robert extensive property in Leicestershire and laid the foundations for his elevation to the earldom of Leicester in 1107.[82] It is likely that Henry also confirmed him in his possession of the castle at Brionne, and continued to recognize it as a Beaumont possession even after the rebellion of 1123–24 (although he placed his own garrison in it). But he also allowed Robert to bask in the prestige of his reputation and position which meant that it was thought that 'at his will French and English kings would at one time be peacefully allied and at another violently embattled. Anyone he attacked would be humbled and broken. Anyone upon whom he wished to confer benefit would be gloriously elevated.'[83] There are clear echoes of Longsword's promises to Riulf here. Count Robert of Meulan thus exemplifies why great lords would serve in the king's household.

---

[76] As has been noted previously by Prestwich, 'Military household', 16–17 and see also Crouch, 'Robert of Beaumont', pp. 91–9.

[77] Malmesbury noted only the efforts of Henry of Warwick, however: Malmesbury, *GR*, i. 714. Orderic recorded the opposition of William of Breteuil, although he also reported that Robert of Meulan accompanied Henry to Westminster (Orderic, v. 290, 294).

[78] Eadmer, *HN*, p. 191; trans. Bosanquet, p. 205.

[79] Malmesbury, *GR*, i. 736.

[80] Huntingdon, p. 462 and see also pp. 596–8. His counsel also mentioned by Orderic, vi. 174.

[81] Huntingdon, p. 598.

[82] David Crouch noted that his seal styled him count of Meulan on one side and earl of Leicester on the other (Crouch, 'Robert of Beaumont', p. 95).

[83] Huntingdon, p. 598.

Their 'regular participation in giving counsel, knowledge of royal secrets, being "in the know", reinforced the solidarity of the small but extremely powerful group around the king and helped to define its members against outsiders'.[84]

Castles and garrisons

The knights of the household did not always serve in a military capacity. As discussed above, they might be dispatched as messengers.[85] They might also serve as escorts and hunting companions. The greatest of them might be asked for counsel. But the majority of household knights would have performed those services that reflected their training and expectations as warriors. In peace and war alike, they garrisoned a duke's demesne castles, as well as those which he had taken over for the time being. For example, William the Bastard had built a siege castle in the valley of Beugy against Sainte-Suzanne and a great body of knights was posted in it: 'the king's household knights (*familia regis*), who were commanded by a Breton count, Alan the Red, were well provided with supplies, horses and war equipment; but the troops in the castle equalled them in courage and numbers.'[86] Orderic wrote that William Rufus 'commanded Count Stephen and Gerard of Gournay and the other tribunes and centurions who commanded his household knights (*familiis eius*) in Normandy' to assist Ralph of Conches and provision and garrison his castles.[87] Ralph can later be found leading these knights of the *familia regis* in a sally against his enemies.[88] Henry I placed his own men in Le Plessis in 1118 under Robert and William fitz Amaury,[89] and at Noyon-sur-Andelle in 1119 under William fitz Thierry.[90] Orderic also reported that in the winter of 1123, the king, 'placed his household troops (*familias suas*) under chosen leaders in the castles, and charged them to protect the country people against raiders. He stationed Ranulf of Bayeux in the tower of Evreux, Henry the son of Joscelin of La Pommeraye at Pont-Authou, Odo Borleng in charge of the castle of Bernay,

---

[84] J. Hudson, 'Henry I and Counsel', in *The Medieval State: Essays presented to James Campbell*, ed. J. R. Maddicott and D. M. Palliser (London, 2000), pp. 124–5.

[85] See above, Chapter 7, pp. 524–5, 527–30, and 528–9, Table 9.

[86] Orderic, iv. 48.

[87] Orderic, iv. 214. The use of Roman terms might have been intended to suggest that the force was well organized and well led, although it need not suggest familiarity with anything other than Isidore's *Etymologies*. It does seem to have been the case, from Orderic's own description of the use of household garrisons under Henry I, that the troops were divided into units of one hundred, which would explain the reference to centurions (*Etymologies*, p. 201).

[88] Orderic, iv. 216.

[89] Orderic, vi. 192.

[90] Orderic, vi. 218.

and other valiant athletes in other places to protect the region against enemy incursions.'[91]

Orderic and some other writers occasionally provided figures for the garrisons put into castles held by the dukes in the period from *c.* 1063 to 1144, and these can be found in Table 10. Although Orderic provided figures for knights alone, it is likely that the garrisons were composed of archers and other soldiers, too. Gilbert of L'Aigle, for example, is said to have brought a force of men-at-arms to garrison the castle at Exmes, while John of Worcester expands significantly on the figure of 700 knights in the garrison at Argentan in 1094 that is provided by the *Anglo-Saxon Chronicle*. As a result, the figures provided are often unlikely to represent the full strength of the garrisons of the castles concerned.[92]

These were sizeable contingents, especially given the likely size of any attacking army,[93] but once a garrison had become trapped within a castle, it could not hold out indefinitely if outside help was not forthcoming. Orderic reported how in 1118 Count Fulk of Anjou arrived at La Motte-Gautier-de-Clinchamp, which had been garrisoned by King Henry I, and laid siege to it. Although Henry I responded to the threat by commanding that his army should muster,

> the Angevins wore down the Normans by repeated assaults, and battered the castle with heavy showers of stones. In this way a hundred and forty knights, whose leaders Roger of Saint-Jean and John his brother had been hand-picked by the king, were forced to surrender without suffering injuries or loss of arms. The Angevins razed the fortress to the ground on 1 August and returned home victorious and rejoicing. The garrison, lamenting their misfortune, came to Alençon. When the king grew angry at the surrender they blushed with shame, but defended their failure on the reasonable grounds that though they had waited long and had repeatedly sent urgent messages he had delayed too long in bringing the help they needed, and they had been shut in under a ceaseless bombardment from the besiegers.[94]

The garrison might have been large, but it was still seriously outnumbered by the attacking forces who were also very determined. Had Fulk simply attempted to starve the garrison out, he would most likely have been forced to withdraw as

---

[91] Orderic, vi. 346. There is only an implication that there was a castle at Pont-Authou here.

[92] For a full discussion of this topic see Moore, 'Anglo-Norman garrisons', 205–59. According to Moore, the average garrison in wartime between 1047 and 1159 was 197 (p. 218) while in peacetime in the same period it was just sixteen (p. 217).

[93] See below, *infra*, pp 657–8.

[94] Orderic, vi. 194–6.

Table 10 Garrisons of ducal castles in Normandy to 1144

Castle	Year and garrison	Source
Echauffour	c. 1063. Garrison of 60 knights.	Orderic, ii. 92
Exmes	1090. Gilbert of L'Aigle brings 80 men-at-arms to Exmes, who probably comprise a ducal garrison.	Orderic, iv. 200
Argentan	1094. Held by 700 knights of King William against Duke Robert. John of Worcester says, in more detail, that there were '700 royal knights and 1400 squires, as well as the garrison in the castle'.	ASChr, 'E', s.a. 1094; trans. Garmonsway, p. 229; Worcester, iii. 70–2
Saint-Pierre-sur-Dives	1106. Held by 140 knights under Reginald of Warenne and Robert of Etoutteville. Castle was stormed by Henry's troop of 700 knights.	Orderic, vi. 80–2
La Motte-Gautier-de-Clinchamp	c. 1112 Garrison of 140 knights under Roger and John of Saint-Jean-le-Thomas. Garrison failed to hold the castle which was attacked and stormed.	Orderic, vi. 194–6
Noyon-sur-Andelle	1119. Garrison of 100 knights under William fitz Thierry. Castle not attacked.	Orderic, vi. 218
Le Sap	1119. Garrison of 30 knights. Castle not attacked.	Orderic, vi. 220
Orbec	1119. Garrison of 30 knights. Castle not attacked.	Orderic, vi. 220
Pont-Authou	1124. Garrison of 100 knights under Henry of Pommeraye. Castle – if there was one – not attacked.	Orderic, vi. 346–8
Bernay	1124. Garrison of 100 knights under Odo Borleng. Castle not attacked.	Orderic, vi. 346–8
Caen	1139. Garrison of 140 knights.[a]	Orderic, vi. 516
Cherbourg	1143. Garrison of '200 and more' knights. The castle eventually surrendered to Geoffrey, perhaps because of the imminent close of the campaigning season.	Chroniques d'Anjou, ed. P. Marchegay and A. Salmon, i. 229–30

Note
[a] Orderic says that Earl Robert remained in the castle with 100 knights, but that forty knights rode out. John Moore took this to mean that forty of the 100 knights rode out (J. S. Moore, 'Anglo-Norman garrisons', ANS, 22 (2000), 230). I think that Orderic meant that 100 knights remained in the castle and that the 'only forty knights' who rode out against Count Geoffrey's force were in addition to that number.

he would have given Henry's army the time to gather and advance on him. His decision to attack was no doubt made on that basis. And it was certainly the case that an inadequate garrison could not hold a castle against any attacker, even if it might hold them up for a time.[95] In 1090, as noted above, the castle at Brionne was held against Robert Curthose by just six knights. In November 1139, the rebel garrison at Pont-Echanfray comprised just eight knights, who surrendered to Count

[95] Moore, 'Anglo-Norman garrisons', 207.

Rotrou of the Perche without putting up any resistance.[96] Defending castles properly, then, was both an important and an expensive business. They might not be able to stop an opponent, but they could slow one down, giving the dukes the time they needed to muster their forces and fight back.

The dukes' use of household knights as garrison troops became increasingly important as castles began to proliferate within the duchy from the first decade or so of the eleventh century. These fortifications were not only residences and the setting for the dukes' courts, they were also vehicles by which territory was taken and held, constant reminders of ducal rule, and secure bases from which the ducal garrisons could deter defiance, patrol the roads, and sally forth to punish misdemeanours or defend the country from attack.[97] Thus, around 1013, during his war with Count Odo of Chartres, Richard II 'made a foray to the river Avre and built a stronghold there called Tillières. He collected much food from Odo's county and abundantly provisioned the fortress which he left in the care of Nigel of the Cotentin, Ralph of Tosny and his son Roger, and their soldiers.'[98] When Count Odo and his allies attacked soon afterwards, Nigel and Ralph 'left guards within the fortress and made a rapid sally from the stronghold with their men to join battle with the enemy. With God's help the duke's garrison overthrew the enemy so that many died, many were wounded, and all the others fled by the by-ways, wandering hither and thither, seeking the dark hiding places of the forests.'[99] Similarly, in around 1030, Robert the Magnificent 'moved out against [Count Alan of the Bretons] with a large army and built a stronghold not far from the river Couesnon, called Chéruel, in order to fortify the Norman frontier and to curb the arrogance of this most presumptuous man'.[100] This castle did its job, but only because the garrison under Nigel and Alured the Giant could lead their troops against the count as he invaded the Avranchin.[101] William of Poitiers wrote that William the Bastard 'established a castle called Saint-James at the frontier between them (the Bretons and the Normans), so that hungry predators would not harm defenceless churches or the common people in the remotest parts of his land by their pillaging raids'.[102] An act for the monks of Saint-Benoit-sur-Loire

---

[96] Orderic, vi. 534. The swift surrender of strong castles held by small garrisons was also a feature of the Great War of 1173–74, when Appleby and Brough were defended by very small numbers (Fantosme, ll. 1455–62, 1477–1505, ed. Johnston, pp. 108–9, 110–13).

[97] Morillo has highlighted the need for castle garrisons to remain mobile to do their job properly (Morillo, *Warfare*, pp. 94–7). On the use of castles in display and as symbols of power see above, Chapter 7, pp. 382–94.

[98] Jumièges, ii. 22 and see above, Chapter 2, pp. 84–5.

[99] Jumièges, ii. 22–4.

[100] Jumièges, ii. 56 and see above, Chapter 2, p. 101.

[101] Jumièges, ii. 58.

[102] Poitiers, p. 72.

reveals how the environment around the castle was developed to service the needs of the garrison.[103]

A particularly good example of the importance of castles in war in Normandy is provided by Orderic's account of the rebellion of 1118–19.[104] The campaigns and victories of that revolt were marked, with the exception of the battle of Brémule itself, by the taking or loss of castles, twenty-nine of them in total. In chronological order, they were: Saint-Clair-sur-Epte; Gasny; Arques; Bures-en-Bray; Le Plessis; Gournay; La Ferté-en-Bray; Gaillefontaine; Saint-Céneri-le-Gérei; La Motte-Gautier-de-Clinchamp; L'Aigle; Neubourg; Evreux; Alençon; Ivry; Lyre; Glos; Pont-Saint-Pierre; Pacy; Breteuil; Le Renouard; Andely; Noyon-sur-Andelle; Anceins; La Ferté-Frênel; Dangu; Châteauneuf-sur-Epte; Tillières; 'Old Rouen'.[105] In addition Orderic noted that eighteen 'castellans' were passively frozen in treachery,[106] and that the men of Courcy, Montpinçon, and Grandmesnil (all of which had castles) were pondering rebellion.[107] As to actions unrelated to castle warfare, we hear only of one raid into the Vexin by Norman knights and one raid by the French, which was intercepted by the Normans,[108] as well as the movements that led to Brémule.

It was probably because castles were so important a foundation of the duke's power that Orderic criticized the manner in which Curthose had disposed of the castles at Ivry and Brionne – not least because the ownership of these castles was disputed so that peace could be maintained only by denying them to all claimants.[109] In contrast, his brother, Henry I,

---

[103] *Regesta: William*, no. 251. On the military function of castles see also, for example, Suger, *Deeds of Louis the Fat*, p. 112; Orderic, ii. 218; *A Medieval Prince of Wales: The Life of Gruffydd ap Cynan*, trans. D. S. Evans, p. 70; *The Song of Dermot and the Earl*, ed. and trans. Orpen, ll. 3202–7.

[104] See above, Chapter 3, pp. 169–74.

[105] Orderic, vi. 184 (Saint-Clair-sur-Epte); 184–6 (Gasny); 190 (Arques and Bures-en-Bray); 192 (Le Plessis); 192 (Gournay, Gaillefontaine); 192, 200 (La Ferté-en-Bray); 194 (Saint-Céneri-le-Gérei, La Motte-Gautier-de-Clinchamp); 198–200, 204 (L'Aigle); 200 (Neubourg); 204, 228–30, 276–8 (Evreux); 206–8 (Alençon); 210–12, 228 (Ivry); 212–14 (Pacy); 212, 250 (Lire, Glos); 212, 226, 250 (Pont-Saint-Pierre); 212–14, 246 (Breteuil); 214–16 (Le Renouard); 216–18 (Andely); 218 (Noyon-sur-Andelle); 218 (Anceins); 222 (La Ferté-Frênel); 232 (Dangu, Châteauneuf-sur-Epte); 248 (Tillières); 280 (Old Rouen). For more general discussion of the importance of castles in the warfare of this period see, among others, M. Strickland, *War and Chivalry: The Conduct and Perception of War in England and Normandy, 1066–1217* (Cambridge, 1996), pp. 204–29 and Bradbury, *The Medieval Siege*, pp. 48–92.

[106] Orderic, vi. 194.

[107] Orderic, vi. 216.

[108] Orderic, vi. 220–2.

[109] See above, Chapter 3, pp. 149–50.

had all his own castles very well guarded by loyal garrisons shrewdly stationed there, so that all the wiles of the enemy never succeeded in forcing a way into them. As regards Rouen, the capital city, and Bayeux, Coutances and Avranches, Sées and Arques, Nonancourt and Illiers, Caen and Falaise, Exmes and Fécamp and Lillebonne, Vernon and Argentan, and other fortified cities which were directly subject to the royal control alone, he would never allow them to be wrested from his just dominion by specious arguments.[110]

Orderic's list provides an indication of the geographical coverage of the dukes' demesne castles. Not all of the fortifications that he listed had started off as ducal castles, however, and some others were to pass out of the duke's hands. Map 6 illustrates their locations.

The risk to the security of the duchy and to ducal rule that castles posed ensured that the dukes would attempt to gain oversight of the construction of castles by their subjects, and to obtain the right of entry into every seigniorial fortification on demand. That such rights were recognized as accruing to the duke by the political community of the duchy indicates that they, too, could see the threat posed by seigniorial fortifications. Thus, by 1087 at the latest, the dukes had gained their subjects' acknowledgement that castles could not be built without their licence. Even earlier, by 1053, the dukes had won the right to enter and garrison their subjects' castles with their own troops at will. As discussed above, these rights had been enjoyed by the Carolingian kings of West Francia, and had continued to be enforced by the dukes and counts and bishops who succeeded to their authority during the tenth century. In 1091 or 1096, these rights were among those acknowledged by the Norman bishops and secular lords assembled at Caen, and so were preserved in the document known as the *Consuetudines et iusticie*.[111]

The earliest example of the right of entry being claimed dates from around 1053, when Duke William demanded that the castle at Arques should be rendered up to him. William of Poitiers wrote that Count William of Arques 'had promoted many disturbances, endeavouring to increase his own lands against the might of his lord, whom he had attempted to *bar from entry*, not only *to the castle at Arques*, but to all the adjacent part of Normandy on this side of the river Seine'.[112] The count was ultimately unsuccessful. Poitiers continued: 'the duke ... seized the fortifications of the lofty refuge where he thought himself most secure, and put in

[110] Orderic, vi. 222.
[111] *NI*, Appendix D, pp. 281–4 at p. 282. The *Consuetudines* are discussed more fully above, Chapter 8, pp. 441–5.
[112] Poitiers, p. 34 (my italics).

a guard, but in no other way diminished his right.'[113] Ducal garrisons were present
in a number of seigniorial castles in 1087, too, perhaps as a result of the ongoing
war with King Philip of France. We know this because Orderic reported that they
were thrown out as soon as the news of William the Bastard's death reached their
lords:

> Robert of Bellême was hastening to the king's court to speak with him on
> important matters when, coming to the gates of Brionne, he heard that the
> king was dead. Instantly, wheeling round his horse, he galloped to Alençon,
> caught the king's men off their guard, and drove them out of the stronghold.
> He did the same at Bellême and in all his other castles ... In like manner
> William, count of Evreux, drove the king's watchmen out of the keep [of
> Evreux], and William of Breteuil, Ralph of Conches, and others gained control
> of all the castles in their domains ... So the magnates of Normandy expelled
> the king's garrisons from their castles and, plundering each other's lands with
> their own men at arms, they stripped the rich country of its wealth.[114]

Although Curthose seems to have been unable to reassert his right to enter his
subjects' castles – which may explain why it was enshrined in the *Consuetudines*
– Henry I was certainly able to enter seigniorial castles at will.[115] At first glance,
Robert of Torigni seems to have suggested that the exercise of this right led to
complaints: 'The king, however, can be reproached for only one thing, a just
reproach according to some. When he had seized some fortresses of his magnates
as well as some of his neighbours on the frontiers of the duchy, so that the former
would lack the latter's support to disturb the peace of his realm, he often fortified
the places as if they were his own by surrounding them with walls and towers.'[116]
Torigni was here writing about rendability, even if it is not entirely clear that he
realized it himself, but the complaints he noted were not due to Henry's demands
to garrison his subjects' castles, but rather to the fact that he fortified them as
though they were his own. Torigni might have been thinking in particular about

---

[113] Poitiers, p. 34. William of Poitiers's words are a useful reminder that rendability did
not have any effect on inheritance. 'The lord-castellan's right was in no way diminished or impugned by temporary delivery of his fortress for his lord's use' (Coulson,
'Rendability and castellation', pp. 61–2). Thus Orderic was able to write of castles being
inherited, and of lords enjoying, or fighting for, their right to particular fortresses.
For Count William's rebellion see also above, Chapter 2, pp. 122–5 and Chapter 6,
pp. 326–7.

[114] Orderic, iv. 112–14.

[115] See above, Chapter 8, pp. 442, 447–8.

[116] Jumièges, ii. 252.

the royal duke's construction of a new tower at the castle of Evreux in 1112, which had so offended Count William and Countess Helwise that they demolished it.[117] Suger of Saint-Denis provided further (general) evidence for Henry's ability to enforce his right of entry: 'The words "at the roar of the lion of justice the Gallic towers and dragons of the island will tremble" accord with King Henry's action in overturning nearly all the towers and strongest castles in Normandy, which is part of Gaul. He introduced his own men and maintained them from his own treasury.'[118] Orderic provided some specific examples, noting inter alia Henry's garrisoning of the seigniorial castles at Alençon, Evreux, and Conches.[119]

Service in the field

As the household ate, drank, and were entertained together, so their sense of loyalty to the duke and their sense of camaraderie grew. And on those relatively rare occasions when the chips went down, this friendship, loyalty, and sense of common purpose would have strengthened the resolve of the warriors of the household as they prepared to fight alongside their duke. That sense of loyalty and community can be seen in Dudo's depiction of Richard I fighting with his household knights at the ford of the Béthune, where he was attacked by King Lothair's army c. 960. 'While they were there, fighting with those warriors, Duke Richard recognized one who was his henchman, called Walter, and he ran to him unafraid with his household followers (*cum domigenis*), and pulled him away; and the rest of the enemy were routed and slain.'[120] The same sort of thing can be seen in the *Gesta Guillelmi*. Duke William went on a reconnaissance mission with twenty-five knights. 'When he returned on foot because of the difficulty of the path (not without laughter, though the reader may laugh), he deserved genuine praise, for he carried on his own shoulders both his own *lorica* and that of one of his followers, William fitz Osbern, renowned for his bodily strength and courage, who he had relieved of this iron burden.'[121] The reader might laugh, as this was a joke at fitz Osbern's expense, but it was also a joke that drew on the genuine camaraderie and friendship within this group of men. A final example illustrates how this same sense of community could exist between men of the same class

---

[117] Orderic, vi. 148. Henry also built a tower in the castle at Alençon, which belonged to William Talvas (RT, s. a. 1135; Delisle, i. 197; Howlett, p. 126)

[118] Suger, *The Deeds of Louis the Fat*, p. 70.

[119] See Orderic, vi. 214 (Le Renouard), 224 (Talvas's castles at Alençon, Almenèches, Vignats, and elsewhere), 278 (Evreux), 334 (Montfort-sur-Risle), 444 (Conches); Jumièges, ii. 230 (Breteuil).

[120] Dudo, p. 272; *Dudo*, p. 146.

[121] Poitiers, p. 116.

who, on this occasion, happened to be enemies, but who had got to know each other well over a long period of time. Orderic reported on the siege of Le Mans in 1100. 'Daily the two sides held parleys and threatened each other, but jokes were often mixed with the threats ... Besieged and besiegers alike passed their time in jocular abuse and played many tricks on each other in a far from malevolent spirit.'[122]

One reason for the maintenance of a pool of household knights was that they could be put in the field quickly, under the command of their more senior members. William of Jumièges wrote that William Longsword could mobilize 300 knights to fight against Riulf on the war field,[123] and that may give a sense of how many knights were maintained in the household of William the Bastard in the 1050s when he was writing. The numbers of knights retained, however, might vary dramatically. Gaimar's account of the events of 1099, when William Rufus and his household rushed to the relief of the garrison (composed of others of William's household troops) at Le Mans, gives a sense of the possible scale of the *familia* – and not necessarily just during times of crisis. Gaimar related that Count Helias had recommenced the hostilities that had ended only the previous year, entered Le Mans, and besieged William's men in the fortresses.[124] As soon as news of the desperate situation reached him, the king hurried to Southampton.

> With his household retinue he arrived at the seashore, and [prepared to] cross the Channel despite the fact that the winds were unfavourable ... They set course for Barfleur, where they eventually landed, having rowed across the whole way. The king's domestic household (*priv[e] meisn[e]*), which numbered seventeen hundred on this occasion, consisted exclusively of powerfully armed knights, and you can be sure that the king held them in special affection. He lost no time in recompensing those knights whom he retained in his service; they were all well paid and highly equipped, and poverty was unknown within their ranks. The king's arrival was a truly splendid affair, as befitted a worthy and courtly monarch. As for the mercenaries whom he had summoned, there were more than enough of these – 3,000, according to the official royal record. I am not sure why he retained so many, for he was not engaged in any war and went in fear of no one; he had brought such a powerful force with him as a display of his great personal nobility.[125]

---

[122] Orderic, v. 302.

[123] Jumièges, i. 78.

[124] See Barlow, *William Rufus*, pp. 402–6 for a synthesis of the campaign.

[125] Gaimar, pp. 316–17. It is worth noting that Gaimar made a distinction between retained and compensated household knights on the one hand and mercenaries on the other. That distinction is also discussed by Abels, *Lordship and Military Obligation*, pp. 168–9.

Gaimar's words make it clear that this was a force that could be mobilized quickly, that it was highly trained and well-equipped, and that the knights were rewarded for their service. He provided, too, an indication of the size of the military household and, equally, of the fact that this might vary. He also made the point that the size of the household reflected the king's nobility, wealth, and power.

Gaimar's description of Rufus's response to the threat to Le Mans provides one example of how quickly the household could be mobilized. Orderic provided others. In 1105, Abbot Robert of Saint-Pierre-sur-Dives treacherously offered to hand his fortified abbey to Henry I. 'When the king had shown his agreement, he said, "It is not necessary to bring a large army now, for the noise of a great multitude might be heard and our plan thwarted. There are only a few insignificant dependants inside, and they obey me implicitly". The king therefore rose at nightfall and rode all night with seven hundred knights, arriving just outside the place at dawn.'[126] These knights, then, were mobilized in the space of a few hours. When Reginald of Bailleul refused to surrender his castle of Le Renouard to Henry, the king reacted swiftly. 'As soon as Reginald had withdrawn the king summoned his knights and arrived at his castle that evening almost as soon as he did.'[127] In 1119, Amaury of Montfort urged King Louis VI to continue his war against King Henry, despite his defeat at Brémule. The king led an army against the frontier castle of Breteuil. Ralph of Gael, the lord of Breteuil, met Louis and his army as they advanced and attempted to delay their approach. 'When the king learned that the French were again in Normandy he sent his son Richard with two hundred knights to help Ralph of Gael and appointed Ralph the Red and Rualon of Avranches, who were bold and active men, as their captains. So the king's household troops (*regalis familia*) arrived while the fighting was at its height, and at the sight of them the French force, already weakened, began to waver.'[128] It was only later that 'the king of England followed his son Richard and the rest of his advance troops with a huge force, to fight once more against the French thousands, if he should find them in his lands'.[129] A final example dates from 1123. Hugh of Montfort, who had planned to rebel against King Henry, was surprised by the king's command to surrender his castle at Montfort to royal custodians. As he was riding to the castle, he outwitted his escort, commanded his wife and his retainers (*clientes*) to hold the castle against the king, and galloped off to warn his co-conspirators that their plot had been discovered. When the escort returned, bewailing that they had been outwitted by Hugh's trick, 'the

---

[126] Orderic, vi. 80.
[127] Orderic, vi. 214–16.
[128] Orderic, vi. 246.
[129] Orderic, vi. 248.

angry king quickly called his knights to arms to attack the garrison while it was unprepared'.[130]

The household knights, then, might be used as shock troops. They could be deployed quickly and thus gain a tactical advantage for the duke. But these knights might also fight for the duke on their own initiative. During Robert the Magnificent's wars with William of Bellême, 'some of the duke's household (*domus*), roused to action ... fought a bloody battle at Blavou'.[131] William Rufus's household troop (*familia*) plundered around Chaumont in 1098, apparently in the king's absence.[132] It seems that Henry I left members of his household to continue attacking Robert Curthose in Normandy when he returned to England in 1104. They did not do well, however. Robert Curthose's own household troops attacked them in turn and imprisoned them. 'Gunter of Aunay who was guarding Bayeux, Reginald of Warenne who favoured the duke's side, and other retainers of the duke, breaking the treaty of peace, captured Robert fitz Haimo and several other members of the king's household troops (*familia regis*) and kept them in close imprisonment for a long time.'[133] In 1124, Ranulf of the Bessin, an earl and *vicomte*, but also perhaps a member of the king's household at least for so long as the emergency lasted, had been put in charge of the castle at Evreux. He heard that Waleran of Meulan and the other rebels were in the area of the forest of Brotonne, and alerted other members of the household, who had also been left as custodians of castles, to their presence. One of these lieutenants, Odo Borleng, then assembled the troops that had been left to garrison three of the castles – amounting to 300 knights, most if not all of them members of the household – and attacked and defeated Waleran and his supporters as they emerged from the forest at Bourgthéroulde.[134] Henry was at Caen at the time, and rejoiced in a victory won in his absence and of which he had no prior knowledge.

Allies and mercenaries

The captains and knights of the household, then, like the *vicomtes*, *prévôts*, and other ducal officials, did their job whether the duke was supervising them or not, acted on their initiative to further their lord's interests, and so maintained his authority and position. But although the household was vital to the dukes, there

[130] Orderic, vi. 334.
[131] Jumièges, ii. 50.
[132] Orderic, v. 216.
[133] Orderic, vi. 60. Wace, p. 216 gives the story at greater length.
[134] Orderic, vi. 348–52.

were times when the household was simply too small for the crisis at hand, and occasions when the duke could not trust even those who stood closest to him. In such circumstances, ways had to be found to increase the size of his forces. This might be achieved by recruiting allies, using contacts with friendly rulers to gain use of a body of additional warriors for the duration of the emergency, or else by paying mercenaries to fight.

Just such an occasion seems to have arisen in 945 when the Normans of Rouen allied with the Normans based at Bayeux, who then comprised an independent chieftainship. These men were ruled by a chief called Harald. Dudo wrote that

> with a view to deceiving the king with a subtle stroke of policy, the chief Normans sent knights of the nobler and richer sort to Harald, king of Dacia, to ask him to come quickly to the assistance of his kinsman Richard, the son of the great Duke William, since the king of the Frankish nation was claiming the whole government of Normandy for himself and was taking away all respect for the boy Richard, who had, indeed, been dragged off in chains. And Harald, the magnanimous king of Dacia, received the envoys with honour on account of his love for his relation Richard; and when he had built ships, and these had been laden with supplies and warriors, he came with all possible speed, accompanied by an unbelievable number of young braves, to the coast by the salt-works at Cabourg ... And when they heard of the arrival of King Harald, the men of Coutances and Bayeux came to serve him, for love of the boy Richard.[135]

Harald was no king of the Danes in exile. Dudo was here attempting to conceal the fact, expressly reported by Flodoard of Reims, that Harald was the chief in command at Bayeux.[136] For now, however, the two groups of Northmen made common cause against their common enemy, Louis IV. Flodoard reported that:

> Harald ... sent a mandate to the king, stating that he himself would come to meet with the king at a time and place that was agreeable. The king came to the place with only a few men, but Harald arrived armed, with a large number of Northmen. They attacked the king's companions and killed almost all of them. Only the king escaped through flight, followed by a certain Norman who was his *fidelis*. The king came to Rouen and was captured by other Normans whom he had thought to be faithful to him.[137]

---

[135] *Dudo*, p. 114.
[136] *Flodoard*, p. 42.
[137] *Flodoard*, p. 42.

In its essential details, the story told by Dudo of Saint-Quentin is the same, although he made the Normans of Rouen out to be the masterminds behind the scheme in a way that Flodoard did not.[138] But the one point made clearly in both accounts is that groups of Scandinavians struggling to survive in the face of hostile Franks would combine against that common threat, even when they acknowledged different chiefs, and even though the Normans of Bayeux would continue to refuse to acknowledge Richard as their ruler until *c*. 989.[139]

According to Dudo, Richard I, now ruling in his own right, felt the need to augment his forces with Scandinavian allies again during a war with Theobald of Chartres that took place *c*. 962–65.[140] At that time, or so we are told, Theobald was in possession of Evreux, which had been taken from Richard with the help of King Lothair. Theobald was driven back by Norman forces while raiding along the left bank of the Seine – most likely the event recorded by Flodoard – but although he had apparently defeated his enemy in the field, Richard seems not to have had the forces he needed to prosecute the war. As Richard's relationship with the Northmen at Bayeux had almost certainly broken down by this time, when he dispatched envoys from his household to make the appeal they were sent to Denmark rather than to the Bessin. They were well-received, perhaps because Harald Bluetooth's enforced conversion of the Danes to Christianity had alienated many of his subjects who now hoped to gain a new livelihood elsewhere: 'and the Dacians are delighted by these embassies, and when they have rapidly fitted out ships and loaded them, they make for Rouen without delay. And when the most constant duke beheld the chiefs of so great a multitude, and sought of his own rage and indignation to take vengeance on the malevolence shown him, he ordered them to make for Jeufosse and lay waste all that belonged to Theobald and the king.'[141] This they did, Dudo tells us, for the next five years.

The omission of any report of the ravaging of France from Flodoard's *Annals* cannot but raise questions about Dudo's accuracy here, and while Ferdinand Lot was content to uphold Dudo's version of events, Lot's interpretation of some of the evidence he used to support Dudo's narrative is sometimes questionable itself.[142] Dudo certainly had reason to invent or exaggerate this episode if Richard II had subsequently used, or threatened to use, Scandinavian adventurers against Odo II

---

[138] *Dudo*, pp. 117–18.

[139] For the recovery of Bayeux see above, Chapter 1, p. 75.

[140] Flodoard noted that Theobald was defeated by the Northmen in 962 (*Flodoard*, p. 66). For the context of this war see above, Chapter 1, pp. 63–4.

[141] *Dudo*, pp. 150–1. Jumièges, in contrast, sent Richard's messengers to the Danish king (Jumièges, i. 126).

[142] F. Lot, *Les derniers Carolingians: Lothaire, Louis V, Charles de Lorraine (954–991)* (Paris, 1851), Appendix 8, pp. 346–57.

of Chartres *c.* 1013. Assuming Dudo *was* reporting past history here, his narrative highlights some of the risks that using such troops entailed. To begin with, it is not clear that Richard retained much control of these warriors as they plundered and burned the Chartrain. They were allies, not members of his household. They took no oath of fidelity to Richard – it seems simply to have been assumed that they would work towards a common objective – and they formed a number of discrete companies under different leaders which must have tangled the chain of command. And so when Richard attempted to put the dogs of war that he had let loose back on their leash, he was obliged to enter into a series of negotiations rather than simply being able to command his allies to stop fighting.[143] It was only after one of Dudo's set pieces, which saw the clever and eloquent duke sow dissension within the ranks of the Northmen by promising their leaders land in return for conversion, that peace could prevail: 'Let the elders and the more powerful be gathered together more privately, in the evening of the night to come, and let us blind them with the very biggest gifts, and a huge grant of lands, if they should happen to look with favour on our prayers and wishes.'[144] Richard's duchy was, of course, greatly strengthened by this new influx of Danes and Norwegians who had pledged their loyalty to him, and who held their lands as a result of his grant. They also strengthened the Scandinavian character of Normandy, reflected in the trajectory of Dudo's work. Nonetheless, Richard's control of his allies, and thus his ability to shape events to his own advantage, had been shown to be precarious.

Around 1013, Richard II turned to Norwegians and Swedes during a war with Count Odo II of Chartres over Dreux – perhaps now that the Danes had been firmly converted to Christianity they were less willing to ravage Christian lands, or perhaps they were too busy attacking Æthelred II's England at the time. According to William of Jumièges, whose account is rather confused, 'when the duke perceived the extent of Count Odo's folly he sent messengers to ask for help from two kings of lands overseas, Olaf of the Norsemen and Lacman of the Swedes, with a host of pagans'.[145] In William's narrative, however, these troops did not engage against Count Odo at all, but rather they fought against the Bretons, who until this point in the story had been portrayed as Richard's allies. Jumièges seems to have got his facts muddled here, and he might even have misremembered and elided the passages found in Book Two of Ralph Glaber's *Histories* which reported, first, on Duke Richard's ability to call on support from Scandinavia and, secondly, on a war between the Bretons and Count Fulk of Anjou which included a report of how the Bretons dug a trench across the battlefield to bring down the Angevin

---

[143] *Dudo*, pp. 156–7.
[144] *Dudo*, pp. 157–62, with the quotation at p. 157.
[145] Jumièges, ii. 24.

cavalry.[146] Jumièges then related how the two kings had sailed to Rouen, where the threat they posed was sufficient to cause King Robert the Pious to make peace between Richard and Odo at Coudres.[147] Nonetheless, despite their lack of action, the Norse and Swedes were rewarded with gifts 'fitting or kings' and given permission to return home.

Although there is no evidence that the Norman dukes called on Scandinavian allies for help after the war against Count Odo, the memory of the threat they had posed to the Normans' neighbours lived on. The treaty that Richard II made with King Swein and the marriage proposed between Robert the Magnificent and Cnut's sister must also have reminded the Franks of the continuing threat that the Normans' Scandinavian connections posed. Ralph Glaber remarked the close relationship that existed between Richard II and the recently established King Cnut, too, and his words usefully sum up the advantages that the Normans gained as a result of those continuing links with their Scandinavia kinsmen: 'whenever the necessity of war pressed upon him, the duke of the men of Rouen was able to call to his aid a great army from the islands across the seas. So it was that for a long time the Normans and the people of the islands enjoyed sure and certain peace, and far from the other nations terrorizing them, the fear they inspired terrified foreign peoples.'[148]

In England and Francia, Viking warriors might be employed as mercenaries.[149] In Normandy, they were allies. That alone helps to explain why it was that the dukes seem not to have employed mercenaries in the duchy before 1078. It is likely, too, that the dukes generally had sufficient manpower of their own to deal with those enemies they had to face in that period. In the duchy itself, rebels such as William of the Hiémois, the future Robert the Magnificent, Bishop Hugh of Bayeux, and Count William of Arques could not hope to command forces to match those that could be fielded by the dukes. Indeed, William of Jumièges stated that Bishop Hugh hired mercenaries in France to bring to Normandy *c.* 1030 in order to redress the balance, and Count William of Arques's appeal to King Henry of the French for aid reveals that he was in similar straits.[150] External enemies, too, with the exception of the kings of France and counts of Chartres and Anjou, are unlikely to have been able to field many more men than the dukes. Thus Robert

---

[146]   Glaber, pp. 56–60 and see Jumièges, ii. 24–5, n. 3. The Latin of the two accounts is dissimilar, suggesting that if this is what happened, it was a result of faulty memory rather than a faulty manuscript.

[147]   Jumièges, ii. 26. The lack of military action would also explain Snorri Sturluson's spare account of Olaf's visit to Normandy (*Heimskringla*, p. 259).

[148]   Glaber, p. 56.

[149]   Abels, *Lordship and Military Obligation*, pp. 152–8.

[150]   Jumièges, ii. 52, 102–4.

the Magnificent most likely fought against William of Bellême on even terms, and while he might have needed a larger army to bring to bear against the Bretons, Normandy could still supply adequate troops if the duke called up his knights and drew on the support, and thus the households, of his *fideles*.

As such, aside from the wars with Theobald and Odo of Chartres, the only time when a duke seems to have felt himself at a disadvantage before 1066 was during the rebellion of 1046–47, when the young William the Bastard called on the help of King Henry I of the French.[151] In this case, there were factors that might have prevented any other response. William might have been unable to mobilize his forces effectively, as the rebels seem to have been strong enough in Lower Normandy to attack those who openly sided with the duke, and Guy of Burgundy might also have been able to cut communications between Lower Normandy and Rouen as a result of his possession of the castles at Vernon and Brionne. With his position in the balance, and by analogy with the delicate situation faced by Henry I in 1118–19, Duke William might not have been able to rely on the support of members of his household. It is also unlikely that he could collect the revenues from much of his duchy, which might have prevented him from employing mercenaries. Faced with such problems, William had little alternative but to call on King Henry for help, apparently basing his petition on the assistance extended to Henry by his father, Duke Robert, in 1033 as much as on his position as Henry's vassal.[152] King Henry might have taken some convincing, but in the end he responded favourably to William's request, and the duke's forces were thus augmented to the extent that he was able to emerge victorious, defeating his enemies in battle at Val-ès-Dunes in 1047.

In 1094, Robert Curthose was similarly to ask the French king, now Philip I, for help. In this instance, Curthose needed aid not against a rebel, but against his own brother, William II, king of the English. Already by 1089, many of the lords of Upper Normandy had renounced their fealty to the duke and openly supported Rufus. John of Worcester suggested that the first to defect were Walter of Saint-Valéry-en-Caux and the castellan of Aumale.[153] Orderic provided more detail and more names:

> Stephen of Aumale, the son of Count Odo of Champagne, was the first of the Normans to support the king, and he fortified his castle on the river Bresle

---

[151] Jumièges, ii. 120.

[152] See above, Chapter 2, p. 109 and Chapter 5, pp. 262–3.

[153] Worcester, iii. 56 (s.a. 1090). Odo of Champagne was also count of Aumale from 1069 until his death in 1115. It was, however, his son Stephen who was in control of the castle at Aumale in 1090. This is made explicit by Orderic, but it also explains why Worcester was not as precise as might be expected, referring only to the castle of Odo of Aumale, rather than stating that Count Odo was himself involved.

at the king's expense, and established a strong garrison of the king's men to hold it against the duke. Gerard of Gournay soon followed suit. Handing over his castles of Gournay and la Ferté-en-Bray and Gaillefontaine to the king, he tried to win his neighbours to the king's side. Then Robert, count of Eu, and Walter Giffard and Ralph of Mortemer and almost all the lords between the Seine and the sea joined the English and received large sums of money from the king's resources to provide arms and men for the defence of their homes.[154]

Although peace was made between the brothers at Rouen in 1091, that treaty acknowledged the loss of the fidelity of these Upper Norman lords to Rufus. Moreover, the agreement was short-lived, and by 1094 Rufus was back in the duchy. In that year he attacked and took the ducal castle at Bures-en-Bray. Throughout, Curthose was outmatched. His household knights, even when supplemented by the knights of those lords who remained loyal to him, were outnumbered by the forces that Rufus could put in the field. King William was also by far the wealthier of the two, and even if Curthose could have afforded to recruit mercenaries, Rufus could have paid for more of them. As a result, 'forced by extreme need, Robert brought his lord, Philip, king of the Franks, with an army into Normandy. Philip besieged the castle of Argentan, and on the very first day of the siege, he took captive without the spilling of blood 700 royal knights and 1400 squires, as well as the garrison in the castle.' Curthose himself took the castle at 'Houlme'.[155] According to the Anglo-Saxon Chronicler, Curthose and Philip marched on Eu in the same year, but the king returned to Paris before seeing action.[156]

It is likely that calling on the French king for help was seen as an indication of a lack of support and money – a sign of weakness rather than evidence of friendship with potent allies and thus the last resort of a prince who should have been able to defend his own interests. Henry I might have bargained with Louis VI for recognition as duke in the period to 1113, and again over the succession before 1120, but he had no need to petition for his support to retain his hold on Normandy, even when the legitimacy of his rule was still open to question. Indeed, Henry fought against Louis in 1119 and against Louis's allies and schemes still more frequently. He won every time because, as Louis ruefully noted, Henry was richer than he was in both friends and coin.[157] In 1106, Henry fought at Tinchebray not just with 'all the nobility of Normandy', but also 'the flower of England, Anjou, and

---

[154] Orderic, iv. 182. See also Jumièges, ii. 206.
[155] Worcester, iii. 70–2.
[156] ASChr, 'E', s.a. 1094; trans. Garmonsway, p. 229. See also above, Chapter 3, pp. 150–1.
[157] Orderic, vi. 368.

Brittany'.[158] Henry had allies such as Theobald of Blois and Rotrou of the Perche as a result of family ties and their personal ambition. He neutralized the threat posed by the count of Flanders to his ambitions by treaties made in 1101 and 1110. And when his household knights and his web of *fideles* and allies could not produce a large enough force, he recruited mercenaries.

Mercenaries were, it seems, first employed by a duke *c.* 1078, during Curthose's first rebellion. Robert, after his failed attempt to take the castle at Rouen, had gone to Hugh of Châteauneuf-en-Thymerais. 'With misguided daring these deserters embarked on a wicked enterprise, leaving their towns and rich estates for vain hopes and worthless promises. The king replied by confiscating their estates, and using the revenues to pay mercenaries (*stipendiarios*) to fight against them.'[159] This measure allowed William to resist his son's incursions without any expense to himself, and it likely gave him some grim amusement to use the rebels' own revenues against them. It also meant that he did not have to rely on the support of his lords, a number of whom pressed him to make peace with his son and so might have been considered unreliable.[160] But William probably did not *need* to use mercenaries to fight his son and there is no evidence that he used mercenaries in Normandy again – although he did recruit them in Normandy for use in England in 1066 and 1085.[161]

William Rufus seems to have employed mercenaries much more routinely when fighting in Normandy. Suger of Saint-Denis wrote of the wars between Rufus and Louis VI and noted, rather ruefully, that 'the one, being wealthy, squandered the treasures of the English, hiring and paying knights splendidly; the other lacked estates and used the resources of his father's realm sparingly.'[162] Suger also reported that 'King William, concerned at his need to hire more knights, quickly ransomed the English prisoners, while the French wasted away during lengthy captivity, and there was only one way to get free: they had to undertake knightly service for the king of England, bind themselves to him by homage, and swear an oath to attack and make trouble for the kingdom and the king.'[163] Money, then, could do more than simply hire mercenaries if a duke had enough imagination. Other chroniclers report specific occasions when such troops were used. John of Worcester noted that, in 1094, William Rufus 'collected

---

[158] Huntingdon, pp. 452–4.
[159] Orderic, ii. 358. Those who left with Curthose at this time included Robert of Bellême and William of Breteuil. The latter at least had estates that William might confiscate (Orderic, iii. 100–2).
[160] Orderic, iii. 110–12.
[161] Malmesbury, *GR*, i. 446, 482.
[162] Suger, *Deeds of Louis the Fat*, p. 26.
[163] Suger, *Deeds of Louis the Fat*, pp. 26–7.

mercenaries from everywhere' to use against Curthose.[164] Orderic reported that messengers were sent to summon Rufus's subjects and neighbours to the army for his campaign against Helias of Maine of 1098–99, and that 'Frenchmen and Burgundians, Flemings and Bretons, and other neighbouring peoples flocked to the open-handed prince'.[165] In 1099, when returning to the county to relieve the siege of Le Mans, Rufus employed mercenary troops to the number of some 3,000 men, or so Gaimar claimed.[166]

As Suger remarked, Rufus could afford to recruit mercenaries in numbers because he had access to the wealth of England, and he needed their services because he was fighting in both the Vexin and Maine. After 1100, Henry I was to use the same wealth for the same purpose. In 1111, he seems to have used mercenaries against Fulk of Anjou, not just because, as Orderic noted, he 'was both prudent and wealthy and could rely on a very powerful army', but also because he could then sweep away his enemies' plans without shedding the blood of his own men.

The royal duke employed mercenaries again in 1118, but for a different reason: 'The king, acting cautiously, fortified Bures-en-Bray and, because he regarded many of the Normans with suspicion, placed there Breton and English mercenaries with ample supplies.'[167] John of Hexham reported that in 1124 Henry had employed Breton mercenaries whom he used at the siege of Pont-Audemer.[168] Henry 'may well have had to rely on mercenaries because of the extent and duration of his wars in Normandy, involving challenges to his rule there which would have made it difficult for him to rely on feudal obligations'.[169] Those challenges included a conspiracy at the very heart of is household, involving 'H' – probably Herbert – his chamberlain.[170] When a duke could not trust the men of his own household, mercenaries became very attractive, for they were men who sold their swords to the highest bidder and who remained loyal to their paymaster if only because disloyalty would bring their profession into disrepute.[171]

William of Malmesbury made explicit what the other chroniclers merely noted, remarking on Henry's employment of Bretons as mercenaries in his armies:

---

[164] Worcester, iii. 70.

[165] Orderic, v. 240.

[166] Gaimar, pp. 316–17, noted above; Orderic v. 234 reports the use of mercenaries on this campaign, too.

[167] Orderic, vi. 190.

[168] Simeon of Durham, *Symeonis monachi opera omnia*, ii. 274 (although they are not called mercenaries in the text but rather 'knights whom the king had led from Brittany').

[169] Green, *Government*, p. 25.

[170] See Hollister, *Henry*, p. 256; R. Sharpe, 'The last years of Herbert the chamberlain: Weaverthorpe church and hall', *Historical Research*, 83 (2010), 591–2.

[171] The point was made by the *stipendarii* who had been employed by Robert of Bellême to garrison Bridgnorth in 1101 (Orderic, vi. 28)

The Bretons, whom as a young man he had had as his neighbours in the castles of Domfront and Mont-Saint-Michel, he used to bring into his service for money. As a race they are penniless at home, and happy to earn the rewards of a laborious life elsewhere at the expense of strangers. Pay them, and they will throw justice and kinship to the winds, and not refuse to fight even in a civil war; and the more you give, the readier they will be to follow wherever you lead. Henry knew this habit of theirs, and if he ever needed mercenary troops (*stipendariis militibus*), spent a great deal on Bretons, taking short lease of that faithless people's faith in return for coin.[172]

In contrast, while Henry used Flemings as settlers, effectively as a permanent garrison, in Wales,[173] there is no evidence that he used them as mercenaries on the continent. He might, however, have envisioned doing so. In 1101, Henry re-established an agreement with the count of Flanders, first made by his father, which gave him the use of 1,000 knights in return for an annual premium of £500 sterling.[174] The treaty begins with the count's obligation to send 1,000 mounted knights to England. It then turns to the continent:

> And if King Henry wishes to have Count Robert's support in Normandy or Maine and if he summons him there, the count will go there with 1,000 knights and shall help him in faith as a friend and as one from whom he holds a fief … That should King Henry wish to take Count Robert as his ally with him in Normandy, and summons him by letters or messengers, the count shall come to him with 1,000 knights who for the first 8 days in Normandy shall live at Count Robert's expense. And should the king wish to retain them longer, they shall stay 8 more days with the king at his expense for those 8 days, and he shall restore any losses suffered over those 8 days to them as is his custom with regard to his *familia*. And if during that time King Philip invades Normandy against King Henry, Count Robert shall come to King Philip with 20 knights, and the other knights shall remain with King Henry in his faithful service. The same Count Robert shall come to King Henry in Normandy as has been prescribed above unless he is forced to stay [in Flanders] on account of severe illness of body or loss of his land or is on an expedition of the king of France or an expedition of the emperor of the Romans, as set out above. And

---

[172] Malmesbury, *GR*, i. 728.

[173] Malmesbury, *GR*, i. 726; *Brut y Tywysogion*, pp. 27–8 (s.a. 1108); Gerald of Wales, *Journey through Wales*, trans. Thorpe, pp. 141–2.

[174] It was Malmesbury who remarked upon William the Bastard's arrangement with Baldwin of Flanders; *GR*, i. 728.

if for this reason he has to stay, he will send, as we have set out, 1,000 knights into Normandy in the king's service.[175]

As Renée Nip has pointed out, 'the stipulations concerning the support of Count Robert II for King Henry in Normandy and Maine are remarkable'.[176] Indeed, their inclusion in the treaty indicates that Henry already intended to take Normandy from his brother and was primarily concerned to ensure that Count Robert should remain neutral in any ensuing conflict, while leaving open the possibility of gaining additional manpower if it should become necessary. If that was the primary intention – and the fact that the service of these 1,000 knights would be provided for only sixteen days in total suggests that it was – then the treaty was a success, because the count remained neutral while Henry conquered and subdued the duchy, despite at least one approach from Curthose.[177] When the treaty was reaffirmed in 1110, the terms of service remained the same, except that Henry felt secure enough to reduce the number of knights required by half. The payment due to the count was reduced accordingly to 400 marks (£266 sterling). It might have become apparent that the count could not hope to provide 1,000 mounted knights on demand, and had sought to reduce the number to a more reasonable level,[178] while Henry might not have wanted to continue to pay the count the original premium now that Normandy was his. Confirming the treaty did, however, implicitly acknowledge and legitimize Henry's rule in Normandy, and that might have provided a further benefit of the agreement. Indeed, as there is evidence that the treaty was reaffirmed shortly after the accession of both Charles the Good (c. 1119) and Thierry of Alsace (c. 1128), it may be that the counts of Flanders could see the diplomatic benefit provided by the treaty in this respect, too.[179]

Aside from rendering the counts of Flanders temporarily inactive, there is no evidence that Henry I gained any military advantage from the treaties of 1101 and 1110. Moreover, they could not be relied upon once the relationship between King Henry and Count Robert soured. Despite the treaty of 1110, Count Robert

---

[175] The translation here is based on that found in E. M. C. van Houts, 'The Anglo-Flemish treaty of 1101', *ANS*, 21 (1999), pp. 171–2 with some minor changes; part only is translated in Van Houts, *Normans*, p. 222. The treaty is also discussed in R. Nip, 'The political relations between England and Flanders, 1066–1128', *ANS*, 21 (1999), 159–63 and E. Oksanen, *Flanders and the Anglo-Norman World, 1066–1216* (Cambridge, 2012), pp. 60–8.

[176] Nip, 'England and Flanders', 161.

[177] Malmesbury, *GR*, i, 706; Oksanen, *Flanders*, p. 22.

[178] The numbers are discussed by E. Oksanen, 'The Anglo-Flemish treaties and Flemish soldiers in England 1101–1163', in *Mercenaries and Paid Men: The Mercenary Identity in the Middle Ages*, ed. J. France (Leiden, 2008), pp. 263–4.

[179] Orderic, vi. 378 and n. 4; Oksanen, 'The Anglo-Flemish treaties', pp. 266–7, 269–70.

occasionally supported Louis VI against Henry.[180] His successor, Count Baldwin, attacked the castles at Arques and Bures-en-Bray on behalf of William Clito in 1118, although he was wounded in the fighting and died soon afterwards.[181] Perhaps as a result of this deteriorating relationship, Flemish troops – not necessarily mercenaries – only appear in the pay of a duke during Stephen's reign. Stephen employed them in Normandy during his campaign of 1137, although this turned out to be a mistake. Orderic reported that Stephen 'greatly esteemed William of Ypres and other Flemings and placed exceptional reliance upon them. Because of this, the magnates of Normandy were much incensed, craftily withdrew their support from the king and, out of envy of the Flemings, hatched all kinds of plots against them.' Things came to a head as Stephen marched his army towards Count Geoffrey and the Angevin forces at Argentan. 'Stephen then intended to enter the land of the count of Anjou, but a great dispute now broke out in his army at Livarot, occasioned by the robbery of a barrel of wine which a certain Fleming carried off from an esquire of Hugh of Gournay. Hence arose a fierce feud between the Normans and Flemings, which compelled the king to return without having accomplished anything.'[182] The employment of mercenaries in ducal armies, then, did not always have the intended effect. They did not necessarily strengthen the duke's forces. Instead, they might weaken them, by creating internal divisions that might become so serious that they caused the army to break up.[183]

It was the wealth that the royal dukes had access to that gave them the cash they needed to hire mercenaries should the need arise. But their wealth could be put to other uses, too. In particular, it might be used to bribe would-be opponents to go home rather than to fight.[184] In 1089, for example, Rufus secured the towns of Saint-Valéry and Aumale 'by bribing the men in charge'.[185] When Curthose asked King Philip for aid in 1090, Rufus bribed him, too: 'On hearing this, William secretly dispatched a large sum of money to Philip, and earnestly sought and accomplished Philip's abandonment of the siege and his return home.'[186] By 1090, 'the power of the English king was effective almost everywhere in Normandy, and since the Norman magnates supported him because of his wealth he laid hands on

---

[180] The changing relationship is discussed by Oksanen, *Flanders*, pp. 23–4.

[181] Orderic. vi. 190.

[182] Torigni, s.a. 1137; Delisle, i. 207; Howlett, p. 132 and see also the briefer account at Orderic, vi. 484.

[183] See below, *infra*, pp. 680–3.

[184] Malmesbury noted among other aspects of the Norman character that 'they charge the enemy with spirit, and if force has not succeeded are equally ready to corrupt him with craft and coin' (Malmesbury, *GR*, i. 460).

[185] Malmesbury, *GR*, i. 548.

[186] Worcester, iii. 56 and see also Malmesbury, *GR*, i. 548. That is also the suggestion in the *Anglo-Saxon Chronicle*: *ASChr*, 'E' s.a. 1090, trans. Garmonsway, p. 225.

the province, neglected by the duke. Even the citizens of Rouen, won over by the king's gifts and promises, considered the possibility of changing their ruler, and decided to betray both the chief city of Normandy and the slumbering duke to the king.'[187] In 1094, King Philip was again dissuaded from attacking William at Eu: 'Then Duke Robert brought with him Philip, the French king, and a well-supplied army to besiege King William at Eu. But through King William's intrigue and cash, the French king was turned back, and thus the whole army disappeared, obscured by dark clouds of money.'[188] John of Worcester remarked, in the same vein, that 'to some of the chief men of Normandy he gave, and to others he promised, gold, silver, and land so that they would defect from his brother and place themselves and their castles under his jurisdiction'.[189]

Henry I, who succeeded to Rufus's kingdom and wealth, occasionally employed the same tactics and the same precious commodities. As early as 1101, faced by his brother's invasion of England, Robert of Meulan had urged Henry I to gain support by making promises: 'speak to all your knights with moderation; coax them as a father would his sons; placate every one with promises; grant whatever they ask; and in this way draw all men assiduously to your cause.'[190] In 1105, Henry invaded Normandy. 'On his arrival, almost all of the Norman nobles abandoned their count and lord, and the fealty they owed him, and rushed over to the gold and silver the king had brought with him and handed castles over to him and fortified cities and towns.'[191] In 1118, Richer of L'Aigle was promised the lands he claimed, and consequently abandoned his co-conspirators, as the result of advice given to Henry by Rotrou of the Perche. After Henry's victory at Brémule the following year, William of Malmesbury suggested that bribery was again used to smooth the way to peace: 'all things are subject to change, and coin can alleviate any wrong with its persuasive power getting its own way.'[192] The Hyde (Warenne) chronicler was equally alert to the use of money to subvert men who had promised to support Henry's enemy and rival for the duchy, William Clito: '"O sacred hunger for gold, what do you not compel mortal breasts to do?" Those who had claimed with ineffable oaths that they never would have peace with king Henry and never would abandon William, son of Count Robert, overcome by greed, these perjurers established a false peace and they abandoned this same young man. And so King Henry restored annual rents from England to the count of

[187] Orderic, iv. 220.
[188] Huntingdon, pp. 418–20.
[189] Worcester, iii. 70.
[190] Orderic, v. 316.
[191] Worcester, iii. 106.
[192] Malmesbury, *GR*, i. 734.

Flanders and all land to Stephen of Aumale.'[193] Thus, Clito saw his supporters 'conquered by avarice' while Henry 'restored peace with much diligence and money'.[194] In 1124, Henry's money again obstructed William Clito's plans. Fulk of Anjou had betrothed his daughter Sibyl to William, 'but King Henry with great pertinacity defeated the plan and broke off the intended marriage, making use of threats and pleas and an enormous quantity of gold and silver and other valuables'.[195] In 1127, Henry used money to win a war yet again, albeit indirectly on this occasion. Following William Clito's succession to the county of Flanders, Henry might have prohibited the export of wool to Flemish cities and more certainly charged tolls and customs from which the merchants of the county had previously enjoyed an exemption. His actions might have led to the revolts at Bruges and Saint-Omer and the consequent election of a rival count.[196]

The wealthy royal dukes, then, could win battles and cities without having to lead an army into the field, for while there was strength in iron and steel, it was found in gold and silver, too. The dukes could pay for mercenaries to fight for them, and they could pay their opponents' allies to go back home. The association of wealth and power could hardly be clearer.

The army of Normandy

The preceding discussion has suggested that the core of the duke's army was comprised of his household knights, and that the dukes seem not to have resorted to hiring mercenaries until the 1070s because they could raise sufficient troops to fight on at least equal terms against both the rebels and the neighbours they faced, such as the lords of Bellême and the counts of Rennes/Brittany. This is made all the less surprising if the scale of fighting is taken into consideration. The numbers of knights involved in particular engagements reported by Jumièges, Orderic, and some other writers – if not necessarily those provided by Poitiers – appear realistic, and are certainly consistent.[197] William of Jumièges thought that a force

---

[193] Hyde, pp. 82–4.

[194] Hyde, p. 84.

[195] Orderic, vi. 164–6.

[196] Noted by J. O. Prestwich, 'War and finance in the Anglo-Norman state', *Transactions of the Royal Historical Society*, fifth series 4 (1954), 31. For those using Ross's translation of Galbert of Bruges's work, it should be noted that the conjecture is not supported by his narrative, but rather is implied by an act of William Clito in favour of the men of Saint-Omer which promised that should William conquer his uncle's land or reach an agreement with him, the men of the town would recover their lost freedom from tolls and customs (*Actes des comtes de Flandre, 1071–1128*, ed. F. Vercauteren (Brussels, 1938), no. 127, ch. 7).

[197] Prestwich and John Moore were both of the opinion that Orderic's later figures were

of 300 men had seen off Riulf and his confederates *c.* 932.[198] Richer of Reims thought that Louis IV had fought against the pagan Turmold at Rouen in 943 with an army of 800 men.[199] The garrisons of the castles at Tillières and Chéruel, which most likely numbered in the hundreds, could repulse attacks by external foes during the reigns of Richard II and Robert the Magnificent.[200] William Rufus sent 300 knights under Reginald of Warenne to support his ally Conan at Rouen in 1090.[201] He sent another 300 knights as the garrison for the castle at Ballon in 1098,[202] while in 1099 Robert of Montfort was placed in command of an advance guard that numbered 500 knights.[203] In 1105, Henry I took 700 knights to Saint-Pierre-sur-Dives to fight a garrison of 140.[204] In 1118, Eustace of Breteuil, Richer of L'Aigle, and William of La Ferté-Frênel could muster 300 knights between them to attack Verneusses and some other vills in the district of Ouche.[205] Orderic thought that there were 900 knights in total at Brémule, 500 of them fighting with King Henry.[206] Two hundred household knights were apparently enough to see off the French when they attacked Breteuil later the same year,[207] while 200 French knights attempted to attack Tillières soon after.[208] Orderic stated that the royal duke's army at Bourgthéroulde in 1124 comprised 300 knights.[209] In 1137, Geoffrey of Anjou invaded Normandy with an army of 400 knights.[210] Even if the dukes sometimes needed to build an army that was composed of more than their household knights alone, these figures would suggest that the *familia* probably remained the most important and most numerous element in any Norman army, especially if Gaimar was right in saying that it might comprise 1,700 knights.[211]

Occasionally, however, a larger force was required. This army was termed the 'army of Normandy'. Whether the 'army of Normandy' referred to by Dudo of Saint-Quentin was the same as the 'army of Normandy' remarked by Orderic

reliable, too (Prestwich, 'The military household of the Norman kings', 11 (qualifying his earlier statement on p. 10); Moore, 'Anglo-Norman garrisons', 220).

[198] Jumièges, i. 78.
[199] Richer, i. 242 (ch. 35).
[200] Jumièges, ii. 22–4, 58, respectively.
[201] Orderic, iv. 222.
[202] Orderic, v. 242.
[203] Orderic, v. 258.
[204] Orderic, vi. 80–2.
[205] Orderic, vi. 220.
[206] Orderic, vi. 236, 240.
[207] Orderic, vi. 246.
[208] Orderic, vi. 248.
[209] Orderic, vi. 348.
[210] Orderic, vi. 482.
[211] I agree here with Morillo, *Warfare*, p. 57. He noted, too, that armies in this period numbered between 300 and 3,000 men (p. 58).

Vitalis, however, is not clear. The composition of this force is not set out in detail by any chronicler, and probably varied from occasion to occasion between *c.* 1000 and 1144.

Dudo reported on the 'army of Normandy' assembled to recover the castle at Montreuil for Count Herluin:

> William [Longsword] immediately summoned the whole army of Brittany and Normandy ... And when he came near the castle of Montreuil and inspected it from above, he called to him the men from the Cotentin and said to them: 'If you wish to be the first to win my thanks, and the reward of combat; if you wish to enjoy the greater and more egregious honour within my household; then you will not take long to bring me the timbers from the stockade of Montreuil castle, and you will lead back to me in captivity the men holding the castle against us.'[212]

Dudo, then, thought that this army included in its ranks men from Brittany and the Cotentin, and these men are likely to have been lords who had become Longsword's *fideles* and who now sought to rank among the movers and shakers of the duchy, although they might equally have included some men who held benefices from the duke. As discussed above, lords of both kinds would have been encouraged to greater exertion by the prospect of a greater standing in the duke's *familia.*[213]

Orderic was equally unclear about the composition of the army of Normandy, although he did report that, in 1118, when Henry I heard that Count Fulk of Anjou had taken his castle at La Motte-Gautier-de-Clinchamp, 'the king came to Alençon and sent out messengers to summon military contingents from the whole of Normandy to battle'.[214] If this was a summons of the army of Normandy, as seems likely, it would have been composed of units recruited from across the duchy. The name that Orderic used for the army certainly suggests that this was the case.

It should also be remarked that while we do not know precisely how the dukes mustered the army of Normandy, we are given some idea about what it was used for. According to Orderic, Duke William summoned the army of Normandy to Saint-Céneri-le-Gérei in 1060. The castle there had been built for Robert fitz Giroie by Geoffrey of Mayenne, who now found himself 'involved in the great conflicts between the Normans and Angevins' and, indeed, had

---

[212] *Dudo*, p. 80.
[213] See above, *infra*, pp. 631–4.
[214] Orderic, vi. 194.

garrisoned the castle with Angevin support.[215] In 1083 William the Bastard used the army of Normandy to attack Sainte-Suzanne in Maine.[216] In 1098, when Rufus decided to recover the county of Maine, he was urged to 'issue a summons to the whole Norman army' for the purpose of conquering it.[217] In 1113, after he had arrested Robert of Bellême and after William Talvas, Bellême's son, had rebelled against him as a result, 'King Henry ... mustered the army of all Normandy, besieged Bellême on 1 May, and succeeded beyond his hopes'.[218]

In all these reports, Orderic had the army of Normandy used against external foes. It is therefore instructive that Orderic also reported that the army of Normandy was levied on more than one occasion against Robert of Bellême – and not only against his possessions located outside the duchy. For example, in 1102, 'the duke ... summoned the army of Normandy and laid siege to the castle of Vignats, which was defended by Girard of Saint-Hilaire'.[219] Later the same year, 'Duke Robert came to Exmes with the army of Normandy and ought to have helped his supporters'.[220] The term Orderic used for the force mustered by Curthose indicates that Bellême's possessions in the Hiémois had moved beyond the duke's control. The use of the army of Normandy against Robert of Bellême within the usual borders of the duchy thus constitutes additional evidence for viewing him as a foreign enemy, as an expansionist lord of Bellême, rather than as a Norman rebel.[221]

It seems likely that the army included both those who had commended themselves to the duke and those who had acknowledged that they owed military service to him in return for their lands. The balance between the two may have swung in favour of the latter over the period as a whole, but so far as the period up to the middle of the eleventh century is concerned, David Bates was probably right when he wrote in 1982 that Norman 'feudalism' was characterized by bonds of obligation between individuals which were personal.[222] It was, in other words, the oaths of fidelity made to the duke, rather than the nature of land-holding, that established the obligation to fight for the duke in times of conflict. This is certainly suggested by Dudo's words, written c. 1015, that 'the chiefs of the Bretons and the Norman magnates most freely gave their hands, in lieu of their hearts, to Richard

---

[215] Orderic, ii. 28 and n. 2, 78–80.
[216] Orderic, iv. 48.
[217] Orderic, v. 240.
[218] Orderic, vi. 182.
[219] Orderic, vi. 22.
[220] Orderic, vi. 34.
[221] See above, Chapter 3, pp. 146–7.
[222] Bates, *Normandy*, p. 168.

... and with an oath of the most loyal and Christian integrity made a promise ... of hosting, aid and service'.[223] Such oaths of fidelity continued to cement the duchy together into the middle of the eleventh century. Thus William of Jumièges remarked that, in 1046, Guy of Burgundy 'detached [Nigel of the Cotentin] and many others from the service they owed by sworn oaths to the choicest of princes'.[224] There is nothing in these words to suggest that fidelity was connected to land-holding, even though Nigel at least held property from the duke.[225]

That military service depended principally on oaths of fidelity and commendation rather than land-holding was the result of both contemporary practices and the way that Normandy was created. The dukes had expanded the reach of their authority piecemeal, winning (and sometimes losing again) the commendations of lords both great and small in the decades between c. 940 and c. 1040, but without making any claim to their lands in the process. The consequent belief that a great deal of land in Normandy was owned outright rather than held from the duke might be reflected in the use of the word 'alod (*alodum*)' in a large number of ducal and seigniorial *acta*. Although the word might be used as a synonym for inheritance, it had a connotation of absolute ownership that seems not to have been diluted over the years.[226] Where men owned their land, the dukes had no right to demand service in return for it, so they had to negotiate

---

[223] *Dudo*, p. 121. Equally, in England by the end of the tenth century, individual lords recognized a personal obligation: 'those thegns personally commended to the king were expected to attend him on campaign if so ordered' (Abels, *Lordship and Military Obligation*, p. 116). Similarly, William of Jumièges could write that Hugh Capet 'took up arms against Arnulf of Flanders who refused him military service' (Jumièges, i. 132).

[224] Jumièges, ii. 120.

[225] On this see Hagger, 'How the west was won', 33–4.

[226] Perhaps the premier example of the use of the word in this way is Dudo of Saint-Quentin's description of Normandy as an *alodum et fundum* when recounting the events of 911(Dudo, p. 168; *Dudo*, p. 49). The best discussion of the use of alod, and other terms denoting different types of ownership or land-holding, is found in Tabuteau, *Transfers*, pp. 96–110, and particularly pp. 101–6, although see also Bates, *Normandy*, pp. 123–6 and Reynolds, *Fiefs*, pp. 145–7. One additional reason for the continuing distinction between alods and fees found in later eleventh-century acts can be suggested: that alods would not be forfeited to the duke, or to a man's lord, if he failed to render due service or if he rebelled against their authority. Herluin of Conteville, for example, had twenty knights in his service after he had withdrawn from the court of Count Gilbert, although it is not entirely clear that he had forfeited any lands he held from the count at that stage (Gilbert Crispin, *Life of Lord Herluin*, pp. 68–71, and see Chibnall, 'Military service in Normandy', 74 and n. 52). With regard to the meaning of the word, it is perhaps notable that even as late as 1259 and 1294 English negotiators claimed that the duchy of Gascony was an alod of the English king, rather than held from the king of France (see M. Vale, *The Angevin Legacy and the Hundred Years War (1250–1340)* (Oxford, 1990), pp. 59–60).

for its performance, albeit with both carrot and stick to hand. The oath of fidelity was undoubtedly one of the main ways that the dukes obtained such service, as it obliged a man to support his lord and the most obvious way to do that was by fighting in the dukes' armies with his own household knights. In addition, swearing fealty might also have opened up the possibility of forfeiture – if the duke were strong enough to do it – when a man failed to answer the call to arms.[227]

But as an alod was only an alod if its holder could defend his land and the nature of his land-holding, those who lived in the Roumois or the Pays de Caux might have found that their rights were eroded as the duke decided that the fidelity of his smaller and weaker neighbours was no longer sufficient. Such a development might be reflected in the fact that the brothers of Richard II's second wife, Papia, acknowledged that they held their alods in the Pays de Talou from him and so, presumably, would also have acknowledged that they owed him services, including military service, in return.[228] Those who held alods in regions dominated by other lords might find themselves brought equally firmly within their *mouvance*. The eleventh century, as David Bates remarked, saw 'the extension of the lordship of well-established stronger families over equally well-established lesser ones'.[229] For example, when a *fidelis* of Roger II of Montgommery called Goisfred wanted to become a monk at Jumièges in 1043 × 1048, Roger made a grant to the monks of the abbey at his request. This reads, in part:

> This Goisfred possessed an alod in the vill which is called Fontaine, and did service to me for it (*et inde michi seruiebat pro eo*) since that alod was within my dominion (*in mea ditione manebat*). This alod I, at the request and prayer of that man, granted, absolved and quit, to God and to St Peter in the monastery at Jumièges where he had been made a monk. And for this gift I accepted from the abbot of that place, Godefrid by name, and from that same Goisfred, a horse worth 30 *livres* and a hauberk worth 7 *livres*.[230]

Goisfred might have held an alod, but the reality of power in his region meant that he had acknowledged that he held that alod from Roger. Moreover, when Goisfred became a monk Roger lost a *fidelis* who was, in all probability, his knight. As compensation, he was given the means to make good the loss of his services in the form of the essential trappings of a knight: an enormously expensive horse and a hauberk. The link between the grant and counter-gift could not be clearer,

[227] Suggested by Reynolds, *Fiefs*, p. 164.
[228] *RADN*, no. 46.
[229] Bates, *Normandy*, p. 126.
[230] *RADN*, no. 113.

and it almost certainly reveals the nature of the service that Goisfred had per-formed to Roger in return for his land. The case might be unusual. Roger might have made a legally spurious claim so that the monks would make him a valuable counter-gift – it would not have been out of character. But if this act reflects the reality on the ground, Montgommery had unilaterally undermined both right and custom, so that Goisfred now served the duke indirectly, fighting among those soldiers provided for him by Montgommery, in return for land that he had once owned but which he now held from him.

While the dukes had usually to win the fidelity and service of alod-holders, or else to undermine their rights, they were also in a position occasionally to make grants out of their demesne. When they transferred property to another, it is likely that the transfer was made on restricted terms and in return for service, includ-ing military service, as was the case elsewhere.[231] In or around 911, for example, regardless of what Dudo said, Rollo was granted Rouen and the surrounding districts in return for his service. He would act to protect the region from further Viking incursions. Thus an act of Charles the Simple states that the monks of Saint-Germain-des-Pres should have the abbey of La-Croix-Saint-Leufroy and its lands, 'except that part of the abbey that we acceded to the Normans of the Seine, that is to Rollo and his companions, for the protection of the kingdom (*pro tutela regni*)'.[232] Within the duchy, the Norman counts had been established on lands that the dukes had once claimed as demesne. The counts of Evreux, for example, could trace the origin of their office- and land-holding back to a grant to Archbishop Robert of Rouen made, most likely, by Duke Richard II.[233] The dukes intervened to manipulate succession to the counties of Eu and Mortain, making the tenurial link between count and duke even clearer (if not always stronger). Further down the social ladder, Odo Stigand, lord of Mézidon, acknowledged that he had received (and therefore presumably held) his honour from William the Bastard.[234] Gerard Fleitel had held his lands in the Hiémois as a result of a grant most likely made by Robert the Magnificent.[235] Even lords such as Humfrey of

---

[231] Reynolds, *Fiefs*, p. 131.

[232] Telma, no. 2049; *Recueil des actes de Charles III* , ed. P. H. Lauer, 2 vols (Paris, 1940), i. 209–12 (no. 92).

[233] See Douglas, 'The earliest Norman counts', 132–3; Bauduin, *Première Normandie*, p. 144; and above, Chapter 9, pp. 560–4.

[234] *RADN*, no. 222.

[235] Gerard can be found holding Chambois, which had previously been given to Count Drogo of the Vexin by Richard II (RT, s.a. 1024; Delisle, i. 33; Howlett, p. 24; Van Houts, 'Edward and Normandy', pp. 65–6). Gerard's subsequent possession of the place may therefore be interpreted as the result of ducal patronage – perhaps received during the pilgrimage to Jerusalem undertaken by Robert the Magnificent, Count Drogo, and Gerard Fleitel, during which both Count Drogo and Duke Robert died (this attractive

Vieilles and Roger of Montgommery, who seem to have held most of their estates as alods, apparently had a share in some demesne vills which may be supposed to have come to their families as dowry or gifts, and this might have given the dukes some leverage when it came to obliging Humfrey and Roger and their successors to provide them with military service when demanded.[236]

It is likely, then, that many lords in Normandy would have acknowledged that they held at least some of their lands from the dukes. They would also have acknowledged that they owed service in return for that land. But we know surprisingly little about what those services were.[237] Orderic's story of the treatment meted out to the Bocquencé brothers *c.* 1059 suggests that it varied from lord to lord: the monks of Saint-Evroult demanded relatively little, including military service, but got less, while Arnold of Echauffour demanded rather more and forced his tenants to perform it all.[238] But there was probably a widely held expectation that those who held a benefice or a fief from any lord, including from the duke, would perform military service when required. As discussed above, Goisfred may be supposed to have owed military service to Roger of Montgommery for his alod in the 1040s and Gilbert Crispin implied that he owed military service to the duke in his act for the monks of Jumièges of 1046 × 1066.[239] The Penitential Ordinance, promulgated in 1067 or 1070, was aimed, among others, at those who had given William the Bastard 'military service as their duty'.[240] That expectation was also grounded in long-standing custom. In 807, a capitulary relating to the

suggestion is made by Van Houts, 'Edward and Normandy', p. 67). In addition, he was probably granted Ecouché, Fel, and Gacé by Richard II or, more likely, Robert the Magnificent, which explains the later claims advanced by William the Bastard and William of Evreux (Orderic, iv. 184 and see also above, Chapter 2, p. 99 and Chapter 3, p. 148).

[236] See above, Chapter 1, p. 70 and Chapter 2, pp. 80–1.

[237] As noted by, for example, Bates, *Normandy*, pp. 122, 168–9; Chibnall, 'Military service in Normandy', 66, 68, 72–6; Tabuteau, *Transfers*, pp. 51–2, 57–8; Reynolds, *Fiefs*, pp. 152–7, 168–9. This work has now thoroughly undermined the idea that Normandy was a thoroughly feudalized duchy before 1066 put forward by Haskins in 1918 and which is also found in Hollister, *The Military Organization of Norman England* (Oxford, 1965), pp. 16–17, 76–7.

[238] Orderic, ii. 80–2. Marjorie Chibnall was inclined to see Orderic's account of the services owed by the Bocquencé brothers as reflecting the situation in the 1130s (Chibnall, 'Military service in Normandy', 69–70), but the apparent differences in the services demanded of them, the evidence of the acts for Goisfred and Gilbert Crispin, as well as the well-known agreement between William Paynel and the monks of Mont-Saint-Michel which could have been written as early as 1070, suggests that Orderic's story accurately reflects the situation as it was under Abbot Robert before his exile *c.* 1059.

[239] *RADN*, no. 113; *RADN*, no. 188.

[240] Bessin, *Concilia*, pp. 50–1; English translation in *English Historical Documents*, pp. 606–7. This point was also noted by Van Houts, 'The ship list of William the Conqueror', 164.

recruitment of the army in western Gaul was promulgated. One chapter of this capitulary stated simply that all men who held a benefice were expected to muster when the army was called up.[241] Nor should the obligation necessarily be seen as an imposition. Given that one whole section of society, those who increasingly styled themselves *milites*, were defined, and defined themselves, as 'those who fight', there is a strong likelihood both that the services they performed for those to whom they had commended themselves, and from whom they increasingly acknowledged that they held their lands, included military service, and that such service was willingly given.

Although the evidence is not as explicit as it might be, the view that when land was held from a lord it was held in return for military service, whether in France in general or Normandy in particular, is uncontentious and almost certainly right. It is harder to find a consensus about when the move from service based on fidelity to service based on land-holding occurred.[242] Still more vexed is the question of the development of knights' fees and the quotas of service owed by lords for their honours as a whole. For Normandy, there are indications that it was during the 1050s and 1060s that lords and their men began to take the view that a certain amount of land was required to support one knight, and that the grant of a large parcel of land could therefore result in an obligation to provide the service of a number of knights. Around the year 1000, Richard II gave the county of the Hiémois to his half-brother, William. William of Jumièges, whose report of this grant dates from the 1050s, stated that the land was given 'as a gift, so that from it he could provide him with the established military service (*ut inde ei milicie exhiberet statuta*)'.[243] The phrase is remarkable at such an early date, and suggests that Jumièges was among those who believed that when larger parcels of land were granted, the beneficiary was obliged to provide the services of an agreed – or perhaps imposed – number of warriors in return. This might not have been carried out with any degree of uniformity across the duchy, but it is difficult to escape the conclusion that what we have here is a quota for service of the sort that can be more commonly seen from the turn of the twelfth century.[244]

While the import of Jumièges's words seems not to have received much comment previously, in part perhaps because it was once thought that he wrote

---

[241] Dutton, *Carolingian Civilization*, pp. 80–1.
[242] See, for example, Reynolds, *Fiefs*, pp. 131, 169.
[243] Jumièges, ii. 8.
[244] This example consequently stands against the conclusion reached by Susan Reynolds in 1996: 'in Normandy, despite much search and argument, historians have failed to find precedents for the kind of fixed quotas of service that were imposed on England after the conquest' (Reynolds, *Fiefs*, p. 155).

them some years later than is now believed to have been the case,[245] the same cannot be said of a grant made by Bishop John of Avranches in the summer of 1066. At that time, John transferred half of the forest of Vièvre, which he had inherited from his father Count Rodulf, to the cathedral of Avranches, although he would continue to hold the land in question for the rest of his life. No sooner had the gift been made when,

> Robert, the son of Richard of Beaufou and nephew of Bishop John, claimed it, saying that he had received as a gift in inheritance the said land from a certain uncle of his, namely Bishop John. But this claim was completely destroyed, in the presence of William *princeps* of the Normans and Roger of Beaumont, and Robert known as Bigot, by the largess of divine grace, and the granting to Robert of a gift of ten pounds and the commendation of five knights. Such was made a condition of the granting of the knights: that their land after the death of Bishop John would be held of the bishops of the church of Avranches in fee (*fevium*).[246]

The apparent conflict between commendation and land-holding found here was the result of the less-than-straightforward relationship between service and land brought into being – on a temporary basis – by the agreement. The service to be performed by the five knights was *owed* from their land, which was held in fee according to the mid-twelfth-century copy of the act that has come down to us. That land remained with John, and would pass to the bishops of Avranches on his death. But their service was *performed* for the man to whom they were commended – here voluntarily relinquished to another. Robert of Beaufou would thus enjoy the service of these knights while they remained his commended men, despite the fact that their obligation to perform it arose from land now held from another. Without the written agreement, Beaufou would perhaps have later claimed the land as well as the service of these five knights. It is likely that such claims were made frequently, and were the way by which alod-holders who commended themselves to lords found themselves holding their lands from those same lords some years down the line. This might have happened to Goisfred.

In addition, Bishop John's agreement with his nephew provides further evidence for the existence of the idea of a quota – a certain number of knights due from a particular piece of land – in Normandy (just) before the conquest of England. And in this case, once it had been established that the land would provide the service of five knights, that assessment became fixed. In 1172, the bishop of

---

[245] See the discussion in the Introduction, above, p. 9.
[246] *RADN*, no. 229.

Avranches acknowledged that he owed the duke the service of five knights from this same parcel of land, then known as the honour of Saint-Philbert.[247] We do not have the evidence to establish if other later twelfth-century quotas originated in mid-eleventh-century Normandy, but it is possible that they did. And the same is true for England. Nicholas Brooks has recently suggested that when Archbishop Ælfric of Canterbury 'bequeathed to his lord his best ship and the sailing tackle with it, and sixty helmets and sixty coats of mail' he intended to reflect his obligation, as archbishop, to provide the king with a longboat crewed by fully armoured warriors. Brooks then went on to suggest that the quota of sixty knights owed by Christ Church Canterbury in 1166 reflected the evolution of this service in the years after 1066. The Anglo-Saxon amphibious warriors turned into horse-riding knights but the number owed stayed the same.[248]

The nature of the services to be rendered in return for land, as well as the concept of the knight's fee, which had formed in Normandy before the Conquest, continued to develop after 1066. Whether these developments were driven by a deepening knowledge of English practices is unclear. Indeed, the influence of English customs on Normandy, or of Norman ones on England, is difficult to discern, not least because on both sides of the Channel before 1066 developments seem independently to have been taking the same sort of shape at the same time. Comparison with other trends, such as the use of writs in the duchy, however, would suggest that there was little obvious English influence on Normandy before the reign of Henry I, and so it is likely that those developments that appear during the reign of William the Bastard and Robert Curthose were home-grown attempts to work out how military service ought to be performed in practice.

Thus in 1066 × 1083, Guy of Saint-Quentin, 'adopting the habit of a monk, gave to God and St Vigor of Cerisy the land which I held in le Mesnil-Sicard with the third part of one mill, and in Couvains the land of one knight and half of the tithe of the said vill'.[249] Here, then, we have a further indication of the development of the knight's fee, although that term was still not employed.[250] Then, at some

---

[247] *The Red Book of the Exchequer*, ed. H. Hall, Rolls Series, 3 vols (London, 1896), ii. 624; Chibnall, 'Military service in Normandy', 36.

[248] *Anglo-Saxon Wills*, trans. D. Whitelock (Cambridge, 1930), pp. 52–3; N. Brooks, 'The archbishop of Canterbury and the so-called introduction of knight-service into England', *ANS*, 34 (2012), 49.

[249] *Regesta: William*, no. 93.

[250] The word *feodum/feudum/fevium* rarely appears in pre-Conquest ducal *acta*, and never does so in an authentic original. Even where the word is found in later copies, the earliest use need not date from before 1066 (*RADN*, nos. 208 (the text of which comes from a very late witness), 229). In some cases, we can see that it was added at a later date. For example, the word was added to a twelfth-century copy of an act of Richard II, but is not found in the original (*RADN*, no. 13).

point between 1068 and 1080, King William confirmed 'the gift which Humfrey of Bohon made to God and St Martin of Marmoutier of the church of Saint-Georges which is at Bohon, that is of the benefice of four canons and of the fee (*feudum*) of one knight, namely Serlo, that the brothers of the said monastery purchased'.[251] If David Bates was right about the tradition of this text, this might have been the earliest use of the word 'feudum' in Normandy. There is even evidence from before William the Bastard's death in 1087 of an apparently new precision in the period of, and gradations in, the types of service that might be owed. An agreement of 1070 × 1081 stipulated that Hugh of Bricqueville owed William Paynel 'forty days of watch and ward' with seven horsemen and that 'if William should summon Hugh, he will have him in his household (*familia*) with two knights at his own cost'.[252] An act that was issued for the nuns of Saint-Amand of Rouen between 1066 and 1087, which survives in a fourteenth-century copy of a most likely late-eleventh-century *pancarte*, and which appears to be authentic, set out the way in which the military service due in return for land had to be performed:

> I Baldric, with the consent of lord William king of the English and duke of the Normans, quitclaim to the nuns of Saint-Amand of Rouen the service of two knights which they owe for forty days each year from the fee of Bacqueville-en-Caux, until I or my heirs return the 30 *livres* of Rouen which I owe to St Amand and the nuns … Before this mortgage the said knights were prepared for service thus, one of them with full arms and the other with plain arms.[253]

Service with plain arms was defined in the 1133 inquisition of the bishopric of Bayeux, which recorded that 'all the vavassors of the bishop who hold freely fifty acres of land or sixty or more owe service to the lord of Normandy in his armies which are summoned to do battle with horses and plain arms, namely with lances, shields and swords'.[254] Those doing service with plain arms, then, were unarmoured horsemen or sergeants. Those performing service with full arms were presumably knights of the sort that Anselm of Le Bec had in mind when he wrote that besides his horse a knight would have a hauberk, helmet, and shield for defence, and a sword and lance for attack.[255]

---

[251]   *Regesta: William*, no. 199.

[252]   *Ctl. Mont-Saint-Michel*, no. 90; *CDF*, no. 714; Tabuteau, *Transfers*, pp. 56–7. Similarly, in the 1080s in the county of Maine, Richard the Baker received the fief of Mont-Griffier in return for serving the canons of Saint-Pierre-de-la-Cour with his horse and weapons for a month each year (Barton, *Maine* p. 200).

[253]   *Regesta: William*, no. 241.

[254]   *Inquisition*, p. 19.

[255]   Anselm of Canterbury, *Memorials of St Anselm*, ed. R. W. Southern and F. S. Schmitt

The surviving texts of these documents date from the twelfth century, which should give us pause before we accept them at face value. But even if we can have confidence in their wording, they can only hint that Norman lords and Norman knights were working out the practicalities of their relationship with each other, and give a fleeting sense of the issues that were up for negotiation. The nature of the service to be rendered was clearly among the priorities – what equipment should be provided, what services were to be provided, how long were those services to be performed for – but while some of these acts might hint at an established level of service for a particular parcel of land, it is the Bayeux Inquisition of 1133 that provides the first evidence for the systematic assessment of service and arrangements for its performance across an entire Norman honour.

The survey begins by making an important distinction between the service owed by the bishop's knights to the duke of the Normans and that due to the bishop. It is only the former that concerns us here: 'These sworn men said that the bishop of Bayeux owed to the lord of Normandy ten knights for the service of the king of the French, so that ten knights of the bishopric did this service through one knight for forty days. They also said that the same bishop owed the service of twenty knights in the marches of Normandy for forty days, wherever the king wished, so that one knight did this service for [every] five knights.'[256]

The jurors referred to the duke in two different ways when giving their testimony. The service of ten knights owed to the French king was performed for 'the lord of Normandy'. That style was usually, although not exclusively, used when the duchy was, or might be, in the hands of someone who was not also the duke.[257] This limits the likely date of the arrangement to a point between 1091, when the treaty of Rouen recognized Rufus as Curthose's heir, and 1113, when Henry I was acknowledged as duke of the Normans by Louis VI. As it was Louis VI who was the first of the Capetians to demand such concessions from his greater lords, and as Henry was in a relatively weak position when negotiating for recognition following his victory at Tinchebray, the most likely time for such an agreement to have been made was between 1108 and 1113.[258] The agreement seems subsequently to have been put into effect, too, as Suger of Saint-Denis stated that Henry I sent

---

(Oxford, 1991), pp. 97–102, and noted in M. Chibnall, *The World of Orderic Vitalis: Norman Monks and Norman Knights* (Woodbridge, 1984), pp. 142–3.

[256] *Inquisition*, pp. 14–15. There is no reason to believe, as Haskins did, that the jurors were pronouncing on the services owed during the pontificate of Bishop Odo, even though some of the events of his day (such as the restoration of the honour of Le Plessis-Grimoult) were noted now and again (*NI*, pp. 15–16).

[257] See above, Chapter 5, pp. 286–7.

[258] See above, Chapter 5, pp. 296–8, 300. Dunbabin, *France*, pp. 257, 261–4; Hallam and Everard, *Capetian France*, pp. 152–5, 214–20.

troops for Louis VI's Auvergne campaign of 1126.[259] In contrast, the service owed in the march of Normandy was performed for 'the king'. This king could have been William I, William II, or, and most likely, Henry I, but the different style suggests that the jurors had inspected a different agreement before pronouncing on this obligation – although Earl Robert of Gloucester apparently misremembered the correct formulations when he gave his oral account.[260]

This opening part of the inquisition also suggests how the bishop's knights shared the burden of service among themselves. The assessment seems to have been made on the basis that there were 100 knights on the bishop's lands, although the inquisition reveals that the bishop actually had the service of 119.5 knights, or 123.75 knights if the vavassors who owed knight service are added to the total.[261] The reasons for the discrepancy are unclear. Perhaps new knights' fees had been created in the interval, or perhaps there was a misunderstanding whereby when the jurors swore that the bishop had enfeoffed 100 knights they meant 120, according to one Scandinavian system of counting, while the royal duke's officials assumed that they meant 100 according to the Roman system of counting.[262] In any event, out of these 100 knights, one in ten of them was sent to serve in a French army. It is likely that the other nine knights who made up each unit of ten provided the cash needed to support their colleague who went to join the French muster. Equally, one in five knights joined the duke's army in the march for a period of forty days, and it is likely that this knight was maintained by a cash contribution from the four of his peers who did not go.[263]

---

[259] Suger, *Deeds of Louis the Fat*, p. 135.

[260] He declared that he performed his service in the march for the lord of Normandy (*Inquisition*, p. 15).

[261] The bishops of Bayeux were not the only lords to take military service from their vavassors. The cartulary of Saint-Pierre of Preaux has mention of a 'Ralph, a *miles* from the Pays de Caux, came to Preaux along with William Malet, the man for whom he performed his military duties (*cui idem miles militabat*), and gave to St Peter his land, namely the land of a vavassor' (*Ctl. Préaux*, A189[1]; noted in Bates, *Normandy*, p. 110).

[262] Given the relatively high level of Scandinavian settlement in the Bessin, this is possible, although Navel dismissed Haskins's similar suggestion that the figure was an Anglo-Saxon long-hundred (*NI*, p. 16; *Inquisition*, p. 45). Examples of this form of counting can be found in *Heimskringla*, pp. 274, 278, 281, 310, 312, and it is discussed under 'Numerals' in, P. Pulsiano (ed.), *Medieval Scandinavia: An Encyclopaedia* (London, 1993), pp. 440–1. Navel and Hollister suggested that it was possible that the additional twenty fees had been created after the assessment was made, while Navel added the further suggestion that the bishop and royal duke had simply agreed to round 120 down to 100 when making the assessment (*Inquisition*, p. 45; Hollister, *Military Organization*, p. 78, n. 4).

[263] Hollister was perhaps a little more certain than the evidence permits that this was the case, although the service was organized on that basis in the thirteenth century (Hollister, *Military Organization*, p. 78; *Inquisition*, pp. 47, 57).

So, the inquisition reveals that service was for a set period of forty days, which had already been seen in Paynel's agreement with the monks of Mont-Saint-Michel. It also reveals that the royal duke was willing to accept a discounted level of service from one of his greatest lords by 1133, *although* only in certain stated situations. But the inquisition is anomalous. It survived because it was appended, with some additions, to the 1172 survey commissioned by Henry II. No other earlier inquisition found its way into the portfolio. There may not have been any. No other lord offered a quota of knights for service in a French army in 1172.[264] Moreover, what was meant by service 'in the march' is not clear, as will be discussed more fully shortly. There is no evidence for a discounted quota on any other Norman honour in the years covered by this study. The level of discount found in the inquisition was not replicated across the duchy in 1172. In fact, the level of discount varied widely between honours. One in three was the average, or so the tally presented at the end of the survey suggests, although, broadly speaking, individual lords offered contingents of between one in three and one in five of the total number of knights enfeoffed on their lands.[265] All of this suggests that it might be very unwise to suppose that the inquisition of 1133 reveals obligations that applied anywhere other than the bishopric of Bayeux.

The lack of any other evidence for quotas of discounted service in Normandy before 1144 seems most likely to reflect the absence of such quotas before that point. Their absence might be explained by the usually small scale of any fighting, where ad hoc arrangements with individual friends and *fideles* about the numbers of troops to be supplied were sufficient. The negotiations concerning the provision of ships for the Hastings campaign of 1066 might provide an analogy. William of Malmesbury reported that Duke William, in council with his magnates, 'levied a demand on all of them for ships in proportion to their possessions'.[266] Four lords also offered to provide a certain number of troops as part of those same negotiations. Hugh of Montfort offered sixty knights, Remigius, almoner of Fécamp, offered twenty, and Abbot Nicholas of Saint-Ouen and Walter Giffard both offered 100. With the exception of Walter Giffard's contingent, all these offers were above the total number of knights enfeoffed on the honours in question in 1172 and well above the quotas that had been established by then.

In Normandy, such negotiations probably remained the norm into the twelfth century, even if the number of troops provided on previous occasions acted as a benchmark or created an expectation about future levels of service. There is

---

[264] See above, Chapter 5, pp. 301–2.

[265] *Red Book of the Exchequer*, ii. 624–47; *RHGF*, xxiii. 693–9. Discussed briefly by Douglas, *William the Conqueror*, pp. 282–3.

[266] Malmesbury, *GR*, i. 448. For the ship list see van Houts, 'Ship list', 159–74.

certainly no evidence for the creation of quotas for service across the duchy during the reign of Henry I. In England, on the other hand, the greater number of knights available, and the three decades of peace that the kingdom enjoyed under his rule, might have given Henry the sense of security he needed to relax his demands on his *fideles* and to agree a discounted quota as a *minimum* level of service. The move to such quotas would also have been encouraged by the development of scutage, which would have given both king and lords a need to know the level of service that was expected without the need for further negotiation. Scutage is first reliably mentioned *c.* 1127, in a writ for the abbey of Ely, and was certainly in place by 1129 when an altogether trustworthy original act for Westminster makes mention of it.[267] There is no mention of scutage in Normandy, however, which would remove that consideration from the equation so far as the duchy is concerned.

The Bayeux Inquisition also reveals that the quota of twenty knights for service in the duke's army in the march did not always apply. The introductory section that deals with the services owed to the duke goes on to set out one more provision: 'If truly the lord of Normandy summoned his army for battle, he [i.e. the bishop] would not be able to raise his *ban*, nor would anyone who held a knight's fee keep it unless he went to the army or, if he had a just excuse, sent a knight in his place.' When the duke summoned his army for battle, then, every knight who held a fee from the bishop would serve in the duke's army or else risk forfeiture, even though they did not hold their fees from the duke directly. This right may have comprised a part of the duke's jurisdiction over pleas of the army, other aspects of which were recorded in clause 2 of the *Consuetudines et iusticie* and from which the monks of Saint-Pierre-sur-Dives were specifically not exempted by Henry I.[268] Geoffrey V of Anjou might have had a similar jurisdiction, too, as he reserved the right to deal summarily with those men of the monks of Saint-Florent of Saumur who refused to join the count's army when summoned by the *prévôt*.[269]

But if the duke was owed the service of all of the bishop's knights if a battle was envisaged, what was the quota of twenty knights for? The answer to that question is dependent on both the meaning of 'service … in the marches of Normandy' and when an army might be summoned 'for battle'. To take the second point first, Orderic gives the impression that the army of Normandy was always summoned to do battle.[270] If he is reliable here, then discounted quotas would never have

---

[267]   *Regesta*, ii. 1499 (Ely) and 1882 (Westminster). See the discussion in F. M. Stenton, *The First Century of English Feudalism, 1066–1166, being the Ford Lectures delivered in the University of Oxford in Hilary Term 1929* (Oxford, 1932), pp. 179–82.

[268]   *NI*, Appendix D, p. 282; Caen, AD Calvados, H 7031(5) = *Regesta*, ii. no. 1569.

[269]   Dutton, 'Geoffrey', p. 79.

[270]   Orderic, iv. 48, 150–4, 294; vi. 22, 34, 182, 194, and probably 334.

applied to a muster of that army. Indeed, the survey of 1172 tends to support that view: 'The bishop of Avranches owes the service of 5 knights from the Avranchin and 5 knights from the honour of Saint-Philbert; the bishop of Coutances the service of 5 knights, and to his service 13 knights (that is he ought to take the service of 13 knights to the army (*exercitus*), and similarly for the others).'[271] Those words appear to suggest that the discounted quotas listed there only applied when the army (of Normandy) had not been summoned. The evidence provided by Orderic also suggests that it did not matter if the battle in question were a defensive one or an offensive one, and the survey of 1172 provides no evidence against that view.

If this conclusion is correct, then the discounted quotas necessarily related to situations other than the muster of the army of Normandy. In 1172, the quotas of service produced a body of 581 knights. This was not a large force. It was considerably smaller than the number of household knights that might be retained by the dukes. Indeed, it is tempting to see the twenty knights who would be sent by the bishop of Bayeux as a contribution to the duke's own *familia*. That suggestion is based on the terms of William Paynel's agreement with the monks of Mont-Saint-Michel whereby if Hugh of Bricqueville were summoned by William, 'he will have him in his household (*familia*) with two knights at his own cost'.[272] If this is right, then the obligation to provide a limited number of men for service in the march looks like a requirement to contribute to the number of a duke's household knights. It may be supposed that such service was due when the duke went to parley with the French king or the count of Anjou. In 1109, for example, Louis VI and Henry I parleyed with each other from opposite banks of the river Epte at Neaufles-Saint-Martin. Suger of Saint-Denis wrote that the two kings 'gathered together their best knights in order to display both pride and wrath at their meeting'. The number of knights he gives is clearly unreliable, but the assembly of a large number of bishops and secular lords was intended both to threaten and to impress, and the discounted quotas established by 1172 would have informed the lords of Normandy just how many men they needed to bring with them to such encounters.[273] Alternatively or additionally, this service in the march might have been related to Henry's maintenance of 'many centuries of soldiers in various places near his enemies, who by force of

---

[271] *Red Book of the Exchequer*, ii. 624–5 and n. 2 which adds the words in parentheses that are found only in one manuscript of the survey; *RHGF*, xxiii. 693–4.

[272] *Ctl. Mont-Saint-Michel*, no. 90; *CDF*, no. 714; Tabuteau, *Transfers*, pp. 56–7. Similarly, in the 1080s in the county of Maine, Richard the Baker received the fief of Mont-Griffier in return for serving the canons of Saint-Pierre-de-la-Cour with his horse and weapons for a month each year (Barton *Maine* p. 200).

[273] Suger, *Deeds of Louis the Fat*, pp. 71–2.

arms prevented these people from robbing churches and the poor', as reported by Robert of Torigni.[274]

Quotas, then, did not apply when the army of Normandy was mustered. Instead, Norman lords continued to be expected to provide the services of all their knights when the duke led his army to attack his foes or to defend his lands. Indeed, the obligation to serve in the army of Normandy was not limited to knights alone. In the inquisition of 1133, vavassors formed a rank of men below the knights (although some served for a fraction of a knight's fee), but, nonetheless, 'all the vavassors of the bishop who hold freely fifty acres of land or sixty or more owe service to the lord of Normandy, in his armies which are summoned to do battle'.[275] Whether vavassors from other honours also served in the army of Normandy is not known, but it seems likely.

Moreover, it seems that there was also a duty on all free men to serve in the army in such circumstances. It is possible that the Norman dukes here inherited obligations found in western Europe since the days of the Roman empire and which were 'entirely disassociated from fiefs and tenures, and rest[ed] on the ancient public duty of a nation in arms'.[276] These obligations had continued under the Carolingians and they could have survived the Norman settlement, too, with their memory preserved at Rouen and in the Evrecin and Hiémois where the population remained mostly Frankish and where Norman penetration was slow. David Bates certainly saw this 'universal levy of freemen' as revealing the maintenance of this Carolingian obligation.[277] Olivier Guillot and Bernard Bachrach observed the survival of this duty in Anjou, too.[278] And while Richard Abels has attempted to refute the existence of an English fyrd composed of free men in times

---

[274] Jumièges, ii. 236.

[275] *Inquisition*, p. 19. The property qualification did not apply to those vavassors who held fees or fractions of fees from the bishop (*Inquisition*, p. 15).

[276] Hollister, *Military Organization*, p. 77. The questions about service raised by the Bayeux Inquisition are discussed at length by Hollister at pp. 75-81. St Ambrose had written at the end of the fourth century to the Emperor Valentinian that 'Since all men, who are under the dominion of Rome, owe military service to you, to the generals and to the princes of the lands, so you too must be a soldier for omnipotent God and the holy faith (*Cum omnes homines, qui sub ditione Romana sunt, vobis militent imperatoribus, terrarum atque principibus, tum ipsi vos omnipotenti Deo et sacrae fidei militatis*)' (Ambrose, *Epistola* 17). Ambrose's words gave ecclesiastical sanction to a secular obligation that was subsequently imposed by the Franks on their subjects from at least the time of Clovis, and which continued under the Carolingians. It should be noted that there was a similar public obligation in Denmark and Norway, too (Reosdahl, *The Vikings*, p. 71).

[277] Bates, *Normandy*, p. 171.

[278] O. Guillot, *Le comte d'Anjou et son entourage au XIᵉ siècle*, 2 vols (Paris, 1972), i. 384-91; B. S. Bachrach, 'The Angevin economy, 960-1060: ancient or feudal?', *Studies in Medieval and Renaissance History*, new series, 10 (1988), 9; Dutton, 'Geoffrey', pp. 78-9.

of emergency, his reading of the sources here is too inflexible and too narrow entirely to convince.[279]

Besides, the evidence for the service of free men in Normandy is, for once, better than that for England. Dudo of Saint-Quentin noted that when King Otto besieged Rouen, he saw 'the country people of that district come to the city from the other side' and despaired of achieving his objective.[280] The men of the Rouennais, who had defended the city against King Otto, subsequently pursued their enemies as they fled.[281] Dudo was here apparently describing the local population taking to arms in time of emergency. Similarly, William of Jumièges imagined the people of the Cotentin defending their country against the men of King Æthelred II: 'As soon as Nigel was told by his scouts about the invasion, he gathered the knights of the Cotentin together with a multitude of common people, launched an unexpected attack upon the English, and slaughtered so many of them that hardly anyone survived.' The disappointed English king was informed that the Norman force 'consisted not only of fierce male soldiers but also of female warriors who crushed the heads of their boldest enemies with the carrying-poles of their water-jugs'.[282] In both cases, it may be that we are seeing an ad hoc response to an emergency rather than evidence of any obligation on all free men to serve in the duke's armies. Nonetheless, it does suggest that there was a belief that men (and women) should act to protect their country when it was under attack, and that they were willing to do so. Clearer evidence of an obligation to serve comes from an act of 1085 by which Gulbert of Auffay gave the vill of Notre-Dame-du-Parc to the monks of Saint-Evroult, and freed the men residing there 'entirely from every service they might owe him, except the duty of

---

[279] Abels, *Lordship and Military Obligation*, pp. 143–4, 175–9. Abels thought that the argu-
     ment for such a levy was based on an 'assumption that in early Germanic societies all
     able-bodied free men were obliged by their status to defend the homeland' (p. 175). His
     attempt to refute it was not entirely convincing, however. His arguments against the
     statements found in the *Anglo-Saxon Chronicle* are unusually unimaginative. We do
     not have to denude the countryside of labourers to allow for a general levy of free men
     (*ASChr*, 'D' and 'E' s.a. 1016; trans. Garmonsway, p. 147; Abels, *Lordship and Military
     Obligation*, p. 177), and the wording of the annal for 1006 is not equivalent to that of
     1015/16 (trans. Garmonsway, pp. 136, 146–7). Abels was also resistant to the idea that
     the freemen that Domesday Book recorded as having died at Hastings reveal a fyrd
     composed of peasants. He might have been right, but what the deaths of *liberi homines*
     such as Breme, a free man of King Edward in Suffolk, or Eadric the Deacon, or a name-
     less free man who held from Bury St Edmunds do suggest is an army swollen in number
     by the recruitment of able-bodied free men to deal with the emergency that had arisen
     (Abels, *Lordship and Military Obligation*, pp. 143–4).
[280] *Dudo*, p. 130.
[281] *Dudo*, pp. 135–6.
[282] Jumièges, ii. 12–14.

obeying a general summons of the duke of Normandy (*nisi in generalem principis Normanniae expeditionem*)'.[283] Henry I gave a similar exemption to the monks of Montebourg: 'I will and firmly command that the men of the vill of Montebourg are free and quit from all army and campaign, except those that are summoned in the name of war (*excepta illa que sub nomine belli summouetur*).'[284]

This evidence seems convincing: all free men were obliged to serve in an army raised to campaign against an enemy and/or to defend Normandy from attack. But there is more. An act of William the Bastard for the monks of Caen, dating from 1081 × 1087, includes the following grant:

> And the men, indeed, of the said two vills, namely Cheux and Rots, who do not hold free land (*qui francam terram non tenent*), I grant to the service of the church and monks altogether free and quit, so that they shall not neglect their service at any time through any summons to the army or any other matter, unless I through myself or through my writ shall summon the abbot in order that he shall send them to me, and this only within the borders of Normandy and especially only through the necessity of imminent war against a foreign people (*pro necessitate belli ab extranea gente imminentis*).[285]

If this single witness is to be believed, in Normandy the obligation to fight descended even to men holding unfree land (who were not necessarily unfree themselves, of course), and not only those resident on the dukes' demense. The dukes, then, could mobilize all the knights and free men living in Normandy in time of war, although whether there was a property qualification or whether the duke took only a certain proportion of free and unfree men is unknown. Carolingian precedents suggest that either could have applied.[286]

---

[283] Orderic, iii. 246–8 and also iii. 250 for a similar exemption.

[284] *CalCh*, iv. 157–8 = *Regesta*, ii. no. 825.

[285] *Regesta: William*, no. 54.

[286] In 807, service in the army of western Gaul was conditional on a property qualification: 'Each free man who seems to hold five *mansi* shall likewise come to the army; and he who holds four *mansi* shall do the same, and he who seems to have three shall likewise go. Moreover, when two have been found of whom each seems to hold two *mansi* one shall equip the other, and the one of them who shall be better able shall come to the army. And where two shall have been found of whom one has two *mansi* and the other has one *mansus*, they shall join together in the same way and one shall equip the other, and the one who shall be better able shall come to the army … Of those who have half a *mansus*, five shall equip the sixth. And of those who shall have been found so poor that they have neither serfs nor their own property in lands, and yet have personal property to the value of [100] *solidi*, five shall prepare a sixth … And to each of those who go in the army five *solidi* shall be paid by the aforesaid poorer ones who seem to

Let us sum up. Although the evidence is far from conclusive, the previous discussion has suggested, firstly, that commended men served in the duke's army as a result of their oath of fidelity; secondly, that from *c.* 1040 men might be expected to fight in return for their land, although it is unlikely that this idea had completely displaced the obligation based on the oath of fidelity before the end of the eleventh century; thirdly, that from *c.* 1050 the service owed for large parcels of land might be established when the transfer was made, which means that the idea of a form of quota (although not a discounted one) was in existence from that date; fourthly, that *c.* 1113 the dukes had in one case at least agreed that when they went to parley in the marches a lord need provide only a proportion of his knights when summoned to do service; and, finally, that it is likely that all knights, all vavassors with a certain amount of property, all free men (with or without a similar property qualification),[287] and perhaps unfree men, too, would serve in an army that was raised to do battle against a foreign enemy.

Divisions in the ranks

Such is one interpretation of the less-than-full evidence that tells us about how the dukes raised their armies. While it is impossible to be certain that this interpretation is correct, one thing that is abundantly clear from all the narratives is that the dukes *were* able to raise effective armies to repel invasions and defeat their foes – even if they did not always achieve their objectives. Those armies equally clearly were an amalgam of contingents that included the dukes' *familia*, knights who had been enfeoffed on the dukes' demesne or who otherwise owed them military service, and mercenaries, as well as the household knights of the dukes' *fideles*, and those such as Montgommery's knight Goisfred, or William Paynel's knight Hugh of Bricqueville, who owed military service to them.[288] Richard Abels

have no property in land' (Dutton, *Carolingian Civilization*, pp. 80–1). Later capitularies dispensed with this landed basis for the obligation, however, and demanded instead the service of one free man for every six or seven, while ninth-century capitularies demanded that *all* free men fight in the defence of their country (Dutton, *Carolingian Civilization*, pp. 81–3 and see also Costambeys, Innes, and MacLean, *The Carolingian World*, pp. 248–50).

[287] Howden remarked an assize of arms made at Le Mans in 1181 which, like the English equivalent, made the equipment to be furnished by a soldier dependent on a property qualification. When they heard of the edict, Philip II of the French and the count of Flanders issued similar commands (*Gesta Henrici*, i. 269–70; *NI*, p. 23). That might suggest that a property qualification had existed before 1144, too, although it might equally mean that the rules varied from time to time, as had been the case under the Carolingians.

[288] Another example, provided by Orderic, comes from 1124. Then, Nigel of Aubigny and

perceived the same approach in England, and supposed as a result that retainers believed 'the warriors of the king's host would fight at the side of their own lords, to whom they would be accountable for their behaviour', so that the tactical units 'may very well have resembled the *conrois* of the later Middle Ages'.[289]

The composite structure of the army of Normandy can be seen in Dudo's singling-out of the men of the Cotentin and Bessin in his narrative. It is hinted at, too, by an act of 1060 that reveals that, during his final war against Henry I of France, Duke William had with him on the frontier at Courdemanche a number of lords including William fitz Osbern, Walter Giffard, Fulk of Aunou, Hubert of Ryes, Robert Bertram, William Marmion, William fitz Corbucion; Raber and William of Vernon, and Richard of Reviers and his brothers.[290] It may be supposed that these men, who were variously lords in the Cotentin, Cinglais, Pays de Caux, and elsewhere, had brought at least some of their knights with them. When reporting of the events of 1099, Geoffrey Gaimar reported that Robert of Bellême brought 1,000 knights to William Rufus at Barfleur, and that other contingents were brought to the muster by the counts of Eu and Evreux, Walter Giffard, and others.[291] Gaimar might have exaggerated the numbers involved, but it seems clear that each of these lords brought with them a large number of knights. Indeed, Bellême brought so many warriors with him that his support for Rufus almost comprised a threat to his power, too. A duke who was not also a king might well have grown concerned at the size of the force he could put into the field.

The lords who brought their units to the muster were demonstrating their loyalty and their power to the duke and their peers. But as a failure to appear would have been tantamount to defiance or rebellion, it cannot be assumed that a lord's presence also revealed a sense of common purpose, or support for the duke's operational objectives. There were, then, latent divisions within this composite force which had to be suppressed or managed.

A lord of Normandy would therefore have been well advised to gain a consensus among his greatest lords before deciding to launch any major campaign. William the Bastard was obliged to do this in 1066, before launching his campaign to gain the English throne. Rufus similarly attempted to gain support for an invasion of Maine in 1096, but failed to win it. Orderic reported that Count Helias had come before the king as he took over control of the duchy from his brother

---

Robert of Gloucester led men 'from the Cotentin and other provinces' – probably their own men – to serve in Henry's army (Orderic, vi. 334). These men would be the equivalents of Abels's 'B thegns' (Abels, *Lordship and Military Obligation*, pp. 121–6.

[289] Abels, *Lordship and Military Obligation*, pp. 149, 184, respectively.
[290] *RADN*, no. 147.
[291] Gaimar, pp. 318–21.

and asked him to respect his possession of the county so that he could go on the crusade. Rufus refused, stating that he was determined to hold everything that his father had held. But although he threatened Count Helias's possession of his county, he could not put those threats into action because his nobles 'were in sympathy with the distinguished count who argued his case so resolutely'.[292] Two years later, Robert of Bellême captured Count Helias in an ambush and brought him to Rufus at Rouen. This put a new complexion on the situation. According to Orderic, Rufus assembled his barons and asked them whether he should now claim his paternal inheritance, portraying the capture of Helias as the judgement of God on his unjust retention of Maine. 'The magnates, after conferring together, replied, "by common counsel, lord king, we propose that you should issue a summons to the whole Norman army and we will all accompany it and willingly to conquer the province of Maine".'[293] Rufus, then, recognized that he could only act if he had the support of his lords, and he was prepared to wait until the circumstances would allow him to get it. Once the decision had been made, however, and also because of the success of the following campaign, Rufus's lords remained solidly behind him. In 1099, when his gains were under threat, Rufus's charisma and competence, and the Normans' sense of common purpose, kept the army together.

Politics, counsel, consent, and an effective military capability thus went hand in hand. They had to because the duke's own *familia* included the greatest lords of his duchy and their sons, so that even a relatively small army could be divided by political considerations. Henry I was to discover that for himself during the divisive rebellion, or civil war, of 1118–19, which aimed to replace the royal duke with Curthose's son, William Clito, but which broke out principally because Henry had denied the county of Evreux to Amaury of Montfort, the nephew and closest heir of the deceased Count William.[294]

Many of the rebels rose against Henry not necessarily because they favoured Clito's cause but because of what they saw as a lack of justice over their claims to land. In some cases, those seeking justice were able to bring their own supporters or friends or associates over with them. For example,

> William Pointel, to whom the king had committed the charge of the citadel of Evreux, reflected on his former association with Amaury [of Monfort] in Count William's court, and made up his own mind that this great man had been unjustly deprived of his ancestral inheritance. Unexpectedly he intro-

---

duced trustworthy accomplices into the citadel where he was and, heedless of the general peace of the whole community, deserted the king and went over to Amaury.[295]

Here, Henry was unlucky. He had appointed the wrong man as custodian of Evreux, and Pointel's possession of the castle gave him the opportunity to shape events in line with his own, rather than the royal duke's, sense of justice. But he was not alone. The lords of the Hiémois rose against Henry almost certainly because of his refusal to allow Robert of Bellême's son, William Talvas, to inherit his father's extensive Norman honours: 'the men of Exmes were considering an insurrection. For the men of Courcy and other garrisons in the neighbourhood, hearing that almost all the Normans had deserted the king and taken up his nephew's cause, themselves resolved to act likewise.'[296]

Orderic's words reveal how news of significant desertions could cause still more men to waver in their loyalty. Some resolved to rebel. Others adopted a wait-and-see approach, hesitating to support either side until they could discern the ultimate winner. This policy was not without danger, however, as inaction might be interpreted as treachery. As Orderic noted, 'at that time eighteen castellans of Normandy, magnates who far exceeded the rest in eminence and power, remained *passively frozen in their treachery*, favoured the supporters of the exiled William, and looked with satisfaction at the weakening of the king's cause'.[297]

In such situations, as with Rufus in 1096, a duke might hesitate to muster the army of Normandy or, indeed, even a smaller force, for fear of revealing all too clearly to their enemies and those of wavering loyalty their lack of support and strength. If they ploughed on regardless, the result could be disastrous. In 1102, Curthose's campaign against Robert of Bellême fell foul of such divisions in his army. Robert of Montfort and others who sympathized with Bellême set fire to their own army's camp during the siege of Vignats, which created such panic that the duke's army lifted the siege and fled before the castle was taken.[298] The result was that 'from that time, having little to fear, they [Bellême and his supporters] waged cruel war all over the Hiémois'.[299]

Orderic reported even more serious divisions within the army raised by King Stephen during his disastrous Norman campaign of 1137, some of which also look to have been caused by a lack of agreement about the objective of the campaign:

---

[295] Orderic, vi. 204.
[296] Orderic, vi. 214 and see above, Chapter 3, pp. 169–171.
[297] Orderic, vi. 194 (my italics).
[298] Orderic, vi. 22–4.
[299] Orderic, vi. 24.

In June King Stephen came to Lisieux and mustered a large army with the intention of besieging Argentan or some other fortress where they might find Geoffrey of Anjou, whom he hoped to engage in close conflict. His magnates, however, *were opposed to a battle of this kind* and resolutely dissuaded the king from fighting. During that campaign *a serious quarrel broke out between the Normans and Flemings* and men on both sides were violently slain. As a result the whole army was in a ferment and most of the leaders went off without taking leave of the king, each one followed by *his own troops of dependents*.[300]

Here, then, there were disagreements over the objective of the campaign, as well as serious friction between contingents within the army's ranks, so that Norman lords simply packed up and went home, taking their men with them. And although Stephen might have raged against the perfidy of his *fideles*, he could not put his army back together. 'Since for various reasons he judged them unreliable, he did not risk leading them back to battle but, acting on better counsel as some thought, he agreed to a two-year truce with the enemy.'[301]

A divided army, then, was a liability. Its use might openly reveal the duke's lack of support and military strength. It might even give troops the opportunity to defect to the enemy. In around 1053, the leaders of William the Bastard's knights had been unable to intercept supplies being taken to the castle at Arques by the forces of Count William because 'when they learned that very large armed forces were assembled there … they feared that even those who had come with them would go over to the company of William of Arques before the next day dawned (as they had been warned by information received in secret from friends)'.[302] In this case, William declared that men would remain loyal if he joined the siege in person, and was apparently proved right. The strength of his personality thus seems to have won the day.[303] Henry I, apparently aware of similar divisions in his own army, had been equally unable to bring his force to bear at the beginning of the rebellion of 1118–19. As Orderic explained,

King Henry could not support a long siege, because in the general confusion that always occurs in conflicts between kinsmen he was unable to trust his own men. Men who ate with him favoured the cause of his nephew and his other enemies and, by prying into his secrets, greatly helped these men. This

---

[300] Orderic, vi. 484–6 (my italics).
[301] Orderic, vi. 486.
[302] Poitiers, p. 36.
[303] See on this subject Strickland, 'Against the Lord's anointed', pp. 56–79.

was indeed a more than civil war,[304] and ties of blood bound together brothers and friends and kinsmen who were fighting on both sides, so that neither wished to harm the other. Many in Normandy then imitated Achitophel and Shimei, and other turncoats, and committed deeds like those of the men who, deserting the king divinely ordained by Samuel, joined Absalom, the parricide.[305]

Henry had no opportunity to agree a truce with his enemies, so he relied on the support of his remaining *fideles* and increased his strength by employing mercenaries. As noted above, Breton and English mercenaries garrisoned the ducal castle at Bures-en-Bray in 1118 because Henry 'regarded many of the Normans with suspicion'.[306] Uncertainty about the loyalty of his greater lords was the reason why William the Bastard turned to King Henry of the French in 1046–47, and probably also explains his decision to employ mercenaries against his son *c.* 1078.[307] Those who stood outside domestic politics were naturally more reliable in such situations than those with a vested interest in the outcome of civil wars and rebellions.

On occasion, however, the divisions within the army worked in its leader's favour. One well-known English example dates from 1102, just before Henry I's victory over Robert of Bellême. The greatest lords began secretly to withdraw their support from the king, and to think of ways to halt the campaign before Bellême had been crushed completely. As Orderic had it, they were motivated by the threat to their own self-interest. But their arguments had an unexpected effect.

> The earls and magnates of the kingdom met together and discussed fully how to reconcile the rebel with his lord. For, as they said, 'If the king defeats a mighty earl by force and carries his enmity to the point of disinheriting him, as he is now striving to do, he will from that moment trample on us like helpless slave-girls. Let us make every effort to reconcile them, so securing the advantage of our lord and our peer alike within the law, and at the same time, by quelling the disturbance, we will put both parties in our debt.' So on a chosen day they all attended on the king and, in an open field, seriously discussed the question of peace, using many arguments in an attempt to soften the stern king. At that time three thousand country knights, were standing by

---

[304] Chibnall here cited Lucan's *Pharsalia*, which is indeed where the phrase comes from, but it is also to be found in Isidore's *Etymologies*, where it is given the specific definition of a civil war that more than dividing a nation divides families (*Etymologies*, p. 359).
[305] Orderic, vi. 200.
[306] Orderic, vi. 190.
[307] See above, Chapter 2, p. 109, Chapter 5, pp. 262–3, and *infra*, p. 649.

on a near-by hill and, having a shrewd idea of the magnates' intentions, they shouted out loudly to the king, 'Henry, lord king, don't trust these traitors. They are out to deceive you and undermine your royal justice. Why do you listen to men who urge you to spare a traitor and let a conspiracy against your life go unpunished? See now, we all stand loyally by you and are ready to obey your least command. Storm the fortress, press the traitor relentlessly from all sides, and make no peace with him until you have him in your hands, alive or dead.'[308]

Henry was encouraged by these words and pressed home his advantage regardless of the opposition of his greater lords. The result was that Bellême was defeated and driven from England, and the country remained at peace for the rest of Henry's reign.

Apparently similar social divisions, although this time not within the army itself, gave Henry I a quick victory at Breteuil in 1118. Henry arrived with an army to besiege a castle fortified against him by his son-in-law Eustace of Breteuil and left in the care of his wife, and Henry's daughter, Juliana.

> The burgesses, however, being loyal to the king, had no wish to provoke his anger. Knowing that Juliana's arrival would be injurious to many of them, they immediately sent to urge the king to hurry to Breteuil. The provident king ... on receiving the messages of the burgesses came hot-foot to Breteuil and, since the doors were readily opened for him, entered the town. He thanked the loyal inhabitants for the fealty they had shown, and forbade his knights to take any plunder there.[309]

Henry went on to take the castle with relatively little resistance, despite Juliana's attempt on his life. And when the fighting was over, 'the king summoned the burgesses, praised them for preserving their fealty, rewarded them with gifts, promised more, and handed over the castle of Breteuil to their care' – although only for a short time.[310]

The English country knights of 1102 and the burgesses of Breteuil of 1118 were men of the same standing as the monks of Orderic's abbey of Saint-Evroult in that they were vulnerable to the oppressions of the greater lords of the duchy or kingdom. As such, they recognized the need for a strong duke or king who could protect their own interests, doing justice on those who took advantage of their

---

[308] Orderic, vi. 26.
[309] Orderic, vi. 212.
[310] Orderic, vi. 214.

position and relative strength to demand onerous services or exactions. They acted to defend themselves, and strengthened their rulers in the process, which increased those rulers' authority and thus allowed those same subjects to enjoy even greater security. In 1102, the country knights cut the ground from under the feet of the politicking lords, and gave Henry his victory. In 1118, the burgesses of Breteuil handed Henry one of his first victories over the rebels, helping to restore his prestige and shifting the balance in his favour.

The greater lords of the duchy, then, might bring their household knights and levies to a muster, but they did not necessarily have the final word about who should win and who should lose. If country knights and burgesses supported the duke's cause, the greatest of lords could find their opposition brought to nothing. If a duke had enough money, purchasing the services of mercenaries gave him an independence of action and a renewed strength that could, again, turn the tide in his favour. And if he was known to have wealth, then he might equally prise his enemies apart one by one through the judicious use of patronage and bribes.[311] The size of the army a duke could raise, then, was not the only guide to his military strength – even though it might be used to advertise his power to neighbours and potential rivals.[312] It was also found in gold and silver, in promises, and in reputation. We are back, then, to issues discussed towards the beginning of this chapter which thus affected not just the recruitment and retention of knights, but their performance, too.

* * * * * *

Although the mechanics of the operation are obscure, the dukes of the Normans could muster large armies when they needed to, composed of their household knights, their *fideles*, their allies, mercenaries, and at least a proportion of the peasants of Normandy. But the need to assemble such a force seems to have arisen quite rarely. For the most part, the dukes depended on a smaller army comprised of their *familia*, the household knights of their greater lords, and mercenaries. But no matter the size of the army, there was a need for consensus. Norman lords had to support the duke's objectives if the army was to be an effective force, for dissension or friction within the ranks of the army or even of the household had to be avoided.

That consensus was achieved by counsel and, when fidelity alone was not enough, by aligning lords' interests with those of the duke through bribery and patronage. To a considerable extent, then, the strength of the dukes depended

---

[311] See above, *infra*, pp. 655–7.

[312] As Poitiers seems to have thought with regard to the Norman contingent brought to the Mouliherne campaign (Poitiers, p. 14).

on their wealth, which they used to shore up their support and to develop a reputation for generosity that was known throughout Europe. That wealth also allowed the dukes to pay stipends to their household knights and wages to their mercenaries. That wealth was itself increased as a result of the wars that the dukes fought with the help of their knights. Those wars increased the reach of the dukes' power, gave them the opportunity to increase their demesne, and brought more men under their lordship. And as the dukes extended their *mouvance*, so they could also call on more men to fight in their armies. Wealth, power, and military strength were thus related to each other.

But no matter how powerful an army, it could not be maintained in the field indefinitely. There had to be more than military force, then, if a duke were to conquer, consolidate, and rule – as Lothair III and Innocent discovered when they attacked the kingdom of Sicily in 1137.[313] Moreover, some lords were too strong to defeat in battle, especially during the tenth century when the duchy was still being formed, when chiefs such as the Harald who ruled at Bayeux could even resist the power of Richard's ally Hugh the Great. Harald and others like him – the chiefs or lords who ruled at Coutances or Montgommery, for example – were well established on lands that were remote enough from Rouen to make them a real obstacle to a duke's ambitions. Fighting might grind them down, as perhaps happened at Bayeux, but when a duke came up against such individuals they could more easily achieve their objective by making alliances through marriages and patronage rather than risk making enemies by fighting.

Once those alliances were made, the dukes gained overlordship over the lands of their new allies, and gained the help of these lords' own households knights and commended men. With this increased strength, they might go on to establish their lordship over men who had previously recognized still stronger rivals such as the lords of Bellême or counts of Chartres. Indeed, as the dukes' power grew, so those external rivals might seek their friendship rather than face the political risks of unsettled frontiers, and the dukes might seek to consolidate their territory by making pacts with them. Sometimes this had the desired effect, but sometimes it did not. And that, of course, takes us back to the exploration of the duchy's origins and growth with which this study began.

---

[313] See, for example, J. J. Norwich, *The Normans in Sicily* (London, 1992), pp. 417–18; Houben, *Roger II of Sicily*, pp. 67–9.

Conclusion

THIS book has put forward an explanation of how it was that the dukes of the Normans came to take and then hold the territory that became known as Normandy from the 1020s and won and maintained the fidelity of the lords and lesser men living on it.

To dominate their neighbours and to turn at least some of them into their subjects, as well as to gain a degree of control over them, the dukes needed wealth – or at least the promise of it – and a good reputation for leadership, success in war, generosity, and justice. These attributes attracted warriors and others seeking to make a career through service to a lord. Thus, or so it may be supposed, Rollo had demonstrated his right to rule those Vikings who had come with him to Francia. His successes ensured that his warriors remained with him, his leadership saw Rouen fall to him, and the reputation he gained as a result of his successes, military, diplomatic, and economic, brought King Charles to the negotiating table, so that *c.* 911 he legitimized Rollo's de facto possession of Rouen by granting it to him along with the surrounding district.

King Charles's grant *c.* 911, as well as the grants of 924 and 933 did not mean that the dukes immediately gained power over the whole of the territory concerned. They did not map out a ready-made territory of Normandy. Equally, the establishment over ducal power across what would come to be Normandy did not follow a smooth trajectory. There were defeats and reverses. The assassination of William Longsword threw the future of Rollo's line into doubt. It seems that Rouen was almost lost to the Franks, just three years or so after the Loire Vikings had lost Nantes to the Bretons. Indeed, it is possible that the Vikings of the Seine only retained their hold on Rouen because the remaining Vikings of the Loire, who had perhaps taken shelter in the Cotentin and Bessin, could come to their aid. But even though the Normans survived the turmoil of the period between 942 and 945, still Richard I had to survive the attacks of King Lothair and Count Theobald of Chartres. His successors continued to struggle against hostile kings of the French and the counts of Chartres and Rennes, and Anjou, as well as against their own rebellious kinsmen and reluctant subjects. The internal divisions of William the Bastard's minority further threatened the unity of the duchy, and so, too, did the machinations of Robert Curthose's rule. It was consequently only during the reign of Henry I that Normandy finally reached its eventual limits with the recovery, or capture, of Verneuil-sur-Avre *c.* 1120. Henry's achievement on his southern border seems generally to have gone under the radar, but it needs to be acknowledged because it has an effect on how we see Henry I's wars on the Avre frontier, particularly the rebellion/war of 1123–24.

The slow construction of the duchy also reveals that while the ecclesiastical province of Rouen provided one possible frontier for ducal power, there was no guarantee that the dukes would establish their control over that area. The bishopric of Sées, and even part of Evreux, were outside the dukes' control until the second half of the eleventh century and second decade of the twelfth century, respectively. While the bishops of all seven dioceses of the province were mentioned in an act of 990, that does not constitute proof that the dukes had gained authority over their bishoprics, merely that they continued to recognize the overarching ecclesiastical authority of their metropolitan, Archbishop Robert of Rouen. Indeed, the border of the dioceses of Lisieux and Sées seems to have been redrawn *c.* 1020 as a result of the respective spheres of influence of Richard II and William of Bellême, while William the Bastard's campaigns on his southern frontier brought parts of the diocese of Le Mans within his duchy (which the bishop was probably only allowed to retain because Maine itself fell to the Normans so soon afterwards).

What is true of ecclesiastical units is also true of secular ones. Just because the duchy came to cover the whole of some Carolingian *pagi* does not mean that this was the inevitable outcome of the three grants, nor that such administrative units had anything to do with the growth of the duke's authority. A duke might think in terms of counties after they had been won, but the establishment of their power was about winning over the hearts and minds of those lords and men living on the land. Normandy was won, and lost, lordship by lordship, lord by lord. Administrative areas had very little to do with it until after the event, and might be redrawn accordingly. Thus those parts of the county of Maine that had been conquered before Robert Curthose's succeeded to it remained part of Normandy, and while the diocesan boundaries were not in this case redrawn, the secular county ones were.

The redrawing of both ecclesiastical and secular administrative boundaries was a result of the dukes' desire to admit no rivals into their duchy. And so while Rollo might have held Rouen by royal grant, and seems also to have remained loyal to Charles the Simple, his successors would claim that they held the duchy as an alod, free from any obligation to do homage or provide services to the kings of the French. The claim was first made and justified in Dudo's *De moribus*, but there seems to have been some truth in it. It seems certainly to have been the case that the beneficiaries of ducal acts saw no point in obtaining royal confirmation of the properties that they held within the duchy, while Henry I's surrender to

Louis VI's demands for both homage and service for the duchy apparently led to a renewed interest in Dudo's story and the claims to autonomy enshrined in it. Yet even though Henry agreed to provide homage and service for his duchy, still the kings of the French gained no influence within Normandy. Henry remained the supreme authority there, suffering no rival to his power, no doubt in the knowledge that a rival could only weaken his position.

For the same reason, the popes and their legates were also kept at arm's length by Henry, and their ability to intervene in Norman affairs was carefully controlled. The supranational reformed orders, too, were all but barred from the duchy. Here, again, Henry was the fortunate legatee of his predecessors' refusal to admit any superior to their authority in the duchy. Control over Christianity had been won only with difficulty. Doubts about the Normans' religious convictions seem to have been widely held, even into the eleventh century, but their promotion of Christianity, albeit for their own ends, coupled with their desire to be seen as the protectors of the Church in their duchy, meant that the popes, even so ferocious a pontiff as Gregory VII, would command their legates to respect the dukes' rights rather than risk a rift.

The dukes were able to expand the reach of their authority, albeit experiencing setbacks, because of their possession of Rouen and its hinterland. While the city's infrastructure and trade seem to have been in a poor state *c.* 911, Rollo and his successors would turn the city into a Viking emporium that enjoyed trading links with England, Ireland, and elsewhere – witness Dudo's perhaps overenthusiastic description of the peoples who thronged to the city.[1] With trade came traders, artisans, and residents and thus rents, tolls, mooring fees, licences for navigation, customs, warehousing charges, fees for pasture and fodder, and so on. And then there were the crops and revenues produced from the vast concentration of ducal demesne vills clustered along the Seine and in the pays de Caux which fed the duke and his household but might well also have provided a surplus for sale. By the middle of the eleventh century, Rouen had been joined by the new *bourg* at Caen, first developed by Richard II but taken to a higher level by the industry of William the Bastard, who needed a ducal centre in Lower Normandy – and one which was not shared with a powerful bishop. But while the new town attracted foreign merchants and generated healthy revenues for the dukes' chamber, and also constitutes evidence of their economic nous, it was never able to equal Rouen on its great river.

By the beginning of the eleventh century, if not before, Rouen was recognized as the dukes' capital. It was their chief seat, the place where they seem to have almost constantly resided, and which consequently came to be identified with

[1] *Dudo*, pp. 100, 112, and see above, Chapter 1, pp. 48–9.

the dynasty and duchy. Thus the coins of Richard I proclaimed the equivalence between Richard and Rouen. This coinage also constituted one of the symbols of authority that the dukes used to promote their power. Another symbol of their authority was the famous tower they built within their capital city, which seems to have awed those who saw it, and was no doubt intended to do so. In it they held some of the formal courts during which they sought to dazzle their *fideles* with rich dress, furnishings, plate, and food. If wealth was power, that wealth had to be displayed, and the dukes' buildings and courts provided the venue and stage for such heavenly ostentation. But the dukes might also display their power at these courts by parading their political prisoners or aristocratic petitioners to the assembled throng, or by the public grant or confirmation of gifts to churches, or the judgement of lawsuits or offenders. Such actions revealed their lordship and their subjects' demand for it. That did not mean that the dukes sought to confirm every donation or to do justice over every dispute that arose in their duchy, even though both William the Bastard and Henry I do seem to have attempted to enlarge their jurisdiction in different ways. Instead, they sought to ensure that the confirmations they made and the justice they did were effective. Indeed, such was the power of Henry I's reputation as an enforcer of justice that Peter of Saint-Hilaire-de-Harcouët who had agreed to an unfair settlement with the monks of Mont-Saint-Michel would nonetheless keep it while Henry lived.[2]

Rouen generated much of the wealth the dukes displayed, and which they used to pay for the military campaigns that had to be led now and again against reluctant subjects, rivals, or rebels. But that wealth did not simply fall into a duke's lap. It had to be channelled and collected. The dukes consequently ensured that their demesne was well managed, according to the tenor of the day. Officials were established, almost certainly in each vill, to oversee whatever labour services were due and the harvesting of the crops, and to collect the rents at the established times of the year and tolls and other fees as occasion demanded. It may be supposed that they were established from an early date, too, for such officials existed across much of early medieval Europe. At some point, certainly by the beginning of the eleventh century, the officials responsible for each vill accounted to, and took orders from, a *vicomte*. The use of *vicomtes* was suggested by the Carolingian administration, which may be supposed to have been remembered by the archbishops as much as by the Frankish communities who found themselves under the dukes' authority, and so the office either continued without much of a break after 911 or, more likely, was revived as the dukes' authority took hold over an ever-larger area. In any event, there were practical advantages to employing such a figure. Where there was a *vicomte*, the dukes needed to deal directly with only

---

[2]   *Ctl. Mont-Saint-Michel*, no. 116, and see above, Chapter 8, pp. 496–7.

one individual, and his appointment might also be used as a form of patronage for the duke and a source of prestige and influence for the recipient.

The ducal acts, both diplomas and writs, reveal something of the *vicomtes'* competences as well as the day-to-day running of the demesne in his county. Importantly, some of these acts reveal that receipts must have been given for money handed over as tolls or fees; that the *vicomtes* kept accounts of the sums they received from each revenue stream; and that crops, goods, and money were stockpiled at one or more depots in each *vicomté*. What that means, as has been suggested above, is that writing was much more commonly used in the duchy during the eleventh century than has previously been thought. The terms of many of the grants made by the dukes to the monasteries or men of their duchy could only have been put into practice if there was a precise record of the sums involved. Even tallies had to be labelled in some way. It follows from this that there was not so much a move from memory to written record during Henry I's reign as a movement away from the treatment of records as disposable to one where they were preserved. This move was perhaps related to an intensification of lordship and a desire on the part of both lord and man to know precisely what was owed and when and what had been granted or waived. The increasingly common preservation of documents probably led to changes in the way they were written, too. The formulation and introduction of new terms and phrases tend to suggest that the dukes had created new officials and new procedures for the more efficient administration of their duchy, but it is just as likely that they were actually diplomatic innovations rather than administrative ones, and were the result of their beneficiaries' desire not to return to court if the order they evidenced was ignored or to use these documents in the future as much as in their present. Administrative and diplomatic change, then, was driven from both the top down and the bottom up.

As the dukes expanded their authority across the Lieuvin and Bessin and Hiémois, and so on, so they took the opportunity to grab more demesne, and to reward their followers at their victims' expense. But for the most part they seem not to have been able either to take or to retain large numbers of demesne vills. This lack of a large reservoir of demesne with which to reward supporters made a duke's ability to take still more territory, gain control of heiresses, or defeat and forfeit rebels all the more important. Such actions gave them the land they needed to reward their loyal followers and to build them up so that they overshadowed those whose loyalties were less assured, or else to replace those who had openly rebelled. William the Bastard's actions in the years up to the mid 1060s indicate just how much a duke could do to reshape the pattern of land-holding and office-holding in Normandy – given the right combination of circumstances. So great was William's reorganization that by the mid 1060s no region of the duchy had been left untouched. The rebellions he faced and survived gave him the chance to act to replace established figures, using their forfeited lands to endow his own chosen supporters – although of course those rebellions were in part the result of William's choice of counsellors and the pique that it had caused among those who found themselves excluded.

William's conquest of England in 1066 would change the parameters of the game entirely. England gave William access to undreamed of resources, which he distributed to a very wide body of Norman lords. A few – Geoffrey of Montbray, Hugh of Chester, Roger of Montgommery, William of Warenne and Odo of Bayeux, for example – were enriched on a stupendous scale, such were the rewards due to those who had served in the ruling clique from the 1040s. But many, many more Normans were made the equals of their neighbours in the duchy, while at the same time being given a vested interest in the maintenance of William's regime on both sides of the Channel. William thus used England to organize and secure his regime in the duchy, and to that extent seems to have seen England as a useful annex to Normandy, to be used to help with Norman affairs. The complaints found in the *Anglo-Saxon Chronicle*, in part addressed by William of Poitiers, would support that view, albeit that those complaints focused on the treatment of ecclesiastical property.

Henry I would use English lands to equally good effect, making grants of English manors to Norman and French lords in order to construct a party to use against his brother and his continental enemies even before he had taken Normandy for himself. Henry's possession of England coupled with a powerful cross-Channel aristocracy – already reshaped before 1106 as a result of the forfeitures of Robert of Bellême and Count William of Mortain – gave him advantages over all his rivals. And this continued to be the case after Henry's victory at Tinchebray and the reunification of England and Normandy under one ruler. The identities of the rebels of 1118–19 in particular demonstrate the importance of Henry's possession of England to the success of his regime in Normandy. Almost without exception, no rebel held lands in England, and that was because their continued possession of those English lands and their public support for Clito's claim to Normandy were mutually exclusive. The dukes, then, did not need the support of all their *fideles*, just enough of them to win when trouble arose.

The advance of the dukes' power (in both Normandy and England) was not achieved only through, or by the threat of, force. If a ruler was seen to provide peace and security to his people by those living across the frontier, they might be tempted to become his men, too. It seems that even the greatest lords could not prevent their men from swearing fidelity to the dukes. William of Bellême encouraged Giroie to do so in the 1020s, perhaps saving political face himself as a result. William Talvas, in contrast, attempted violently to prevent Giroie's son from placing that portion of his lordship south of the Sarthe into Normandy, too. His actions led directly to civil war in Bellême and the end of his regime. Where lords could see that their power was being undermined, then, they might simply surrender with good grace to the inevitable and salvage what they could from the wreck of their independence. It was in their interests to do so. Where lords were in a stronger position, the dukes might have to try harder to win their fidelity or their acceptance of Norman power across their threatened borders. In many cases, they, or those rivals, played the marriage card to achieve this. Thus matches were made with the houses of Vermandois, Aquitaine, Chartres, England, Rennes, Flanders, Blois, and Anjou. They were also made with some of the greatest Norman lords. The houses of Beaumont, Montgommery, Giffard, Warenne, Tancarville, and others counted themselves kinsmen of the dukes through the marriages of Gunnor's sisters and nieces. In addition, it is tempting to think of Henry I's liaisons with his mistresses as being similar to marriages *more Danico*. Adam of Bremen wrote that in Sweden, at least, princes might have an unlimited number of such wives,[3] so the number of Henry's partners is probably not an obstacle to that interpretation. This would explain why aristocratic fathers such as Count Robert of Meulan and Reginald of Dunstanville were apparently prepared to allow their daughters to sleep with the royal duke – although there are other interpretations as to what might have happened which would lead to somewhat different conclusions.[4] In any event, the fact that Henry's illegitimate offspring were accepted as wives by powerful lords, including counts of the Perche and Rennes, suggests that they were at least of good birth. These liaisons, then, *might* also have been a way or forging closer links with their families as well as with their spouses.

The kinship with the ducal dynasty that resulted from these marriages was remembered, even though it was not always affective or effective in maintaining alliances.[5] Indeed, it is all too easy to overstate the importance of kinship in

---

[3] Adam of Bremen, *History of the Archbishops of Hamburg-Bremen*, p. 203 and see above Ch. 6, pp. 313–17.

[4] For Henry's liaison with Count Robert's daughter, Isabel, see Jumièges, ii. 250. David Crouch has suggested, in contrast to the hypothesis presented here, that the liaison was a quid pro quo for Waleran's release from Henry's custody in 1129 (*Beaumont Twins*, p. 25). This argument was perhaps based in part on Torigni's report that the couple's daughter, also Isabel, was still unmarried at the time he wrote Book VIII of the *Gesta Normannorum ducum*, that is *c.* 1139 (Jumièges, i. lxxviii–lxxx). As that was only around twenty years after their liaison, however, it is possible that it took place towards the end of Count Robert's life. The question would be easier to settle if we knew the date of the elder Isabel's birth.

[5] It might be noted in this respect that, when writing of the rebellion of the three earls in 1075, the 'D' and 'E' versions of the *Anglo-Saxon Chronicle* describe Roger of Hereford as King William's kinsman (trans. Garmonsway, p. 211), while William of Malmesbury

Norman politics simply because the marriage strategies pursued by the earlier dukes meant that by the reign of William the Bastard a great many of the *principes* of Normandy were also his kinsmen. Despite this, in the absence of explicit evidence, we cannot point to an individual's kinship with the duke and conclude that it was necessarily more important than their liking of, or friendship with, or fidelity to, their leader, or of their sense of common purpose, or the patronage that the duke ensured came their way in one form or another on a more or less regular basis.[6] It also means that we cannot point to kinship as the cause for such favour, because it was shared by so many great lords. By the middle of the eleventh century, then, kinship was everywhere and (as a result) nowhere at the same time.

The dukes thus worked hard to attract and retain the loyalty of those lords whose lordships were encompassed within their overarching authority. And many of the sources at our disposal, certainly those produced at or close to the political centre (to all intents and purposes the dukes' court), appear to reveal the dukes' success in achieving their aim. The narratives (or most of them and most of the time), the records of lawsuits, and the witness lists of ducal *acta* all conspire to show us a duke whose authority apparently stretched evenly across the whole of his duchy, and who could attract bishops and counts and other lords from across Normandy, and indeed beyond it, to his court.

But there is more to the story than that, and among the conclusions reached by this study of ducal power in Normandy is that, in fact, the dukes' power was more limited and more fragmented than many of the sources at first sight suggest. For example, if we look for absence from, rather than presence at, the dukes' courts, it is hard to escape the conclusion that those who most frequently petitioned the dukes for confirmations and justice were the monks of their own abbeys (including here those of La Trinité-du-Mont outside Rouen and Le Bec who seem to have looked to the dukes as their advocate once their founders had died), or those from outside the duchy who also naturally looked to the duke as their patron. Much more seldom seen were the monks of the seigniorial abbeys. Indeed, the monks of Marmoutier at Bellême were expressly prohibited from taking their pleas anywhere other than the court of Robert of Bellême,[7] and it is possible that the monks of Sées and Troarn received similar orders. It was certainly the case that both seem to have brought their pleas and settlements before Roger of Montgommery or

---

remarked that Earl Ralph was betrothed 'to a kinswoman of the king (*cognata regis*), a daughter of William fitz Osbern' (Malmesbury, *GR*, i. 472).

[6] Such a view of course runs counter to the main thrust of Eleanor Searle's *Predatory Kinship*. See also the criticism offered by D. Bates' review of E. Searle, *Predatory Kinship and the Formation of Norman Power* (Berkeley and London, 1988) in *Speculum*, 65 (1990), 1047.

[7] AD Orne, H2152; *Ctl. Perche*, pp. 23–6 (no. 13).

Robert of Bellême rather than the duke before November 1112.[8] But there is also very little evidence of engagement with the dukes from the monks of, for example, Lessay, Saint-Sauveur-le-Vicomte, Saint-Sever-Calvados, Fontenay, Grestain, Saint-Pierre-de-Préaux, Cormeilles, Lyre, Conches, and Eu, among others, albeit that the extent to which this reveals archival destruction or actual behaviour is not entirely clear in most cases.

Moreover, the way Norman lords behaved in their lordships indicates the precedence they gave to their own ambitions and priorities, which were not always the same as the dukes'. Thus, as suggested above, Roger of Montgommery preferred to further his own interests south of Alençon rather than support the arrangements that Duke William had made. The counts of Evreux built up a network of allies and kinsmen along both sides of the river Avre, which made the Norman border almost an irrelevance so far as they were concerned, and which acted to challenge the rule of Henry I in that area. Further west, the counts of Mortain were so remote from the duke and his court that they seem to have barely been part of Normandy until William the Bastard ejected William Werlenc and established his half-brother as count in his place. Even the Bessin, because it was so much under the sway of the bishop of Bayeux until the very end of the eleventh century, was a place apart, which had to be tied more closely to the duke through the development of Caen.[9] The conflicts that broke out between rival lords, particularly at times when the duke was weak, also reveal something of how they put their own interests before the unity and security of the duchy as a political whole.

The dukes, then, had to ensure that their authority was recognized by such lords, and the timing of these private wars generally suggests that they did. But that acknowledgement was won and retained not just by the dukes' wealth, display, emotional manipulation, or the military might that they could bring to bear, but also by their dispensing of patronage and the fact that even the greatest lord gained prestige, enhanced protection, and the expectation of improving their own situation more generally by doing so. In short, the dukes had to be able to give their greater *fideles* more than they would be able to get (and keep) by themselves.

Those further down the social scale were unlikely to benefit directly from the dukes' patronage in the same way, but then their ambitions were also more limited. What they wanted was the peace and protection that a strong duke could offer. They might not have witnessed it at first hand, but it is likely that those living in, for example, Foulbec, Vimoutiers, or Auberville-sur-Mer during the eleventh century could tell when there was a strong duke ruling over the duchy and when

---

[8] See Ctl. Sées, fos. 9r–v, 35r, 61v–62r; Ctl. Troarn, fos. 180r–v, 182v.

[9] For a more detailed study of the manner in which local issues and concerns affected the political community of the Vexin see Green, 'Lords of the Norman Vexin', pp. 47–61.

there was not.[10] The threat posed to those who inhabited the second rank of the Norman aristocracy, including most of the abbots, and those still further below, including most burgesses, by the regional magnates, whose ability to coerce and damage was almost unchecked, meant that they were probably the most enthusiastic about strong ducal government. Only a strong duke had the strength to keep those greatest lords in check. And so they supported him. Thus the self-interest of the magnates during the English rebellion of 1102 was brought to nothing by the determination of the 'country knights' that the king should see the business through to the end, while the burgesses of Breteuil opened their gates to Henry I in 1118, thwarting the revolt of their lord and lady.[11]

It might therefore not be a coincidence that so much of the evidence that promoted strong ducal government, and also reveals the demand for it, was produced by men and women who stood at this social level. The appeal made by William of Jumièges for the reconciliation of the Normans to their duke and vice versa was probably born of the desire for a strong duke, as well as a united Norman polity. As his work implicitly argued that the Norman lords should support their duke, it must have been useful to William the Bastard, even if Jumièges also reminded the duke of *his* obligation to reconcile with erstwhile rebels. The petitions of would-be beneficiaries and their presence at the dukes' courts, even if they did not represent every monastery or constituency in the duchy, also promoted the dukes' power, simply through their acknowledgement that it was sufficient to protect their property – even if they might also resort to anathema clauses, remind the dukes of their obligation to protect the grants made or confirmed by their predecessors, and reprimand them for their failures to live up to the appropriate standards. They also praised the dukes through the titles they gave them – and sometimes one was not enough to encompass the full range of their functions and responsibilities – in the use of *Dei gratia* formulations, and by the fact that those who held lands in Normandy went to no higher authority than the duke when seeking confirmation of them. They then returned home with a body of witnesses who could testify to the magnificence of the duke's palace at Rouen, and the fine robes and furs he wore, and the golden cups he drank from, and the number of lords and knights who danced attendance on him. Their diploma or writ might be read out in a court held in the duke's name, perhaps in one of his (empty) residences, by one of his officials. After 1106, the assembly would also have looked upon the great seal that from then on provided a still more impressive visual reminder of a

---

[10]   Foulbec and Auberville are listed among the properties of the nuns of Caen that were despoiled during Curthose's reign (*Chs. Caen*, ii. 125–8). The market of the monks of Jumièges at Vimoutiers was temporarily destroyed by Roger I of Montgommery *c.* 1030.

[11]   Orderic, vi. 26, 212.

duke who was also a king, and might have acted as a vehicle for the transmission of ducal charisma into every corner of the duchy.

It was the dukes' subjects, too, in the form of the bishops and barons sitting at Caen, who decided that the dukes should have the right to act against the greatest lords of the duchy in the event that they refused to provide service when asked for it, or built castles without licence, or acted in a way likely detrimentally to affect the economy of the duchy. Unlike pleas over property, the duke had a near universal jurisdiction over important offences such as these which could have threatened the existence, certainly the unity, of the duchy. Such rights, then, were not imposed from the top, but proffered by the Normans to the lord of Normandy. The dukes' subjects thus gave the dukes the powers they needed to do their job properly. And they judged them on the basis of their success or failure to live up to those ideals. Orderic wrote about good kings bringing peace and security to their people, protecting the Church, and doing justice and, as suggested above, one way he framed his arguments was to make implicit reference to the rights found in the *Consuetudines et iusticie*.

The dukes, then, might have asserted their authority, but they were given it by their subjects, too. The power they exercised was theirs by consensus, not just by coercion – which perhaps means that it should not be termed 'power' at all. If a duke could not protect his subjects, or if they felt that they could get more by going it alone or acknowledging the rule of another, that duke's authority would weaken. The Normans could make a duke's power, but they could break it, too. And so while Geoffrey of Anjou met strong resistance to his claim to Normandy during his first campaigns, he made great inroads immediately after the capture of Stephen of Blois at the battle of Lincoln on 2 February 1141. Initially, it was the lack of any alternative ruler that helped Geoffrey to make progress. But even after Stephen was released later the same year the Angevin conquest continued apace – its success now driven by Stephen's inability to fight back, Geoffrey's political acumen, and the growing sense among the Normans that their interests were now best furthered by supporting the count of the Angevins. And so while we might write of an Angevin conquest of Normandy, and although Geoffrey was clearly obliged to take power on more than one occasion, he was handed it, too. The political consensus between the Normans and their duke continued after 1144 just as it had done before; it was simply under new management.

Timeline

Duke	Year	Event
Rollo (c. 911–c. 927)	c. 911	Charles the Simple and Rollo make an agreement at Saint-Clair-sur-Epte.
	918	An act of Charles the Simple for Saint-Germain-des-Prés confirms the presence of Rollo at Rouen.
	923	Charles the Simple appeals to Rollo for aid against his Frankish enemies. The Normans raid across the Oise, while King Ralph and Count Herbert of the Vermandois ravage the *pagus* of Rouen.
	924	Rollo is granted Maine and the Bessin.
	925	The Franks attack the Normans in a camp on the Seine. Rollo subsequently attacks the *pagi* of Beauvais and Amiens. The men of the Bessin rise against the Normans, while Hugh the Great raids the *pagus* of Rouen, and Count Herbert of the Vermandois leads a successful attack on the Norman fort at Eu.
	926	The Normans almost capture King Ralph and then raid into Francia as far as the *pagus* of Porcien.
	c. 927	Rollo retires.
William Longsword (c. 927–942)	933	William Longsword swears fidelity to King Ralph and is granted the Cotentin and Avranchin.
	c. 933	Longsword's sister, Gerloc, marries Count William of Poitou. Longsword is probably baptized at the same time, taking the name William from his new brother-in-law.
	937	Alan Wrybeard drives Normans from Dol and Saint-Brieuc.
	c. 933–939	Longsword marries Liégeard, the daughter of Herbert of the Vermandois, and endows her with lands on the Seine and in the Evrecin. These subsequently fall into the hands of Count Theobald of Chartres and his Frankish successors.
	940	Longsword commits himself to Louis IV, but later in the year allies himself with Hugh the Great and Herbert of the Vermandois against the king.
	942	Louis IV visits Rouen, and Longsword commends himself to the king again. His new alliance with the king threatens Hugh and Herbert and they, with Count Arnulf of Flanders, plan his assassination. In December, Longsword is murdered at Picquigny by Arnulf's men.
Richard I (942–996)	943	Louis defeats an invasion of Rouen by King Sihtric and Turmold and, with the help of Hugh the Great, puts down a pagan rising at Evreux. Richard is taken to Laon.

Duke	Year	Event
	945	A skirmish on the banks of the river Dives sees the Frankish forces of Louis IV defeated by Scandinavians led by a chief called Harald. Louis is subsequently captured by the Normans of Rouen and surrendered to Hugh the Great.
	946	Louis attacks Hugh the Great as well as the lands of his Norman allies.
	948	Normans fight alongside Hugh the great at Soissons and Roucy.
	949	Normans fight with Hugh at Laon and at Soissons.
	954	Hugh attacks Harald the Northman in the Cotentin, probably on Richard's behalf.
	960	Richard marries Hugh the Great's daughter, Emma. Louis IV attempts to ambush and capture Richard at a meeting on the river Eaulne, but Richard escapes.
	961	Richard attempts to disrupt a meeting at Soissons but is defeated by the king's bodyguard.
	962	Count Theobald of Chartres attacks Saint-Sever, across the Seine from Rouen, but is defeated by Richard's forces and flees. Richard recruits pagan allies from Scandinavia who attack the Chartrain and neighbouring areas of Francia.
	c. 965	Richard makes peace with Louis IV and Count Theobald. The Frankish king acknowledges that Richard holds Normandy free from any obligation to perform service.
	966	Richard appears before Mont-Saint-Michel and establishes a community of monks there.
	c. 970	Richard begins his liaison with Gunnor, whose family are powerful in the Cotentin.
	c. 989	Richard takes Bayeux. His liaison with Gunnor becomes a marriage in accordance with the Christian rite. His second son with Gunnor, Robert, becomes archbishop of Rouen.
	990	Richard founds a college of canons at Fécamp.
	991	Richard fights with Louis IV against Count Odo of Chartres at Melun. Richard receives the papal chancellor and some representatives of King Æthelred II at Rouen and makes a treaty with the latter.
	c. 991	Count Odo's son, the future Odo II, marries Richard's daughter, Matilda.
	996	Richard dies and is buried at Fécamp.
Richard II (996–1026)	996 × 1008	Richard II marries Judith, the daughter of Count Geoffrey of Rennes.
	c. 1000	Richard is faced by a 'peasants' revolt', which is put down by Count Rodulf, as well as the rebellion of his half-brother, William, who had been given the county of the Hiémois. William is captured and imprisoned for five years. He then escapes and is reconciled with his brother.
	1002	King Æthelred II of the English marries Richard's sister, Emma.
	1003	Richard campaigns with King Robert against Auxerre, and will do so again c. 1005.

Duke	Year	Event
	1006	King Robert the Pious visits Rouen. Richard campaigns with the king against Flanders.
	1008	Count Geoffrey of Rennes dies. Richard becomes the guardian of his heirs and his county. Æthelred II (perhaps) launches a raid on the Cotentin with the intention of capturing Duke Richard. It is thwarted by Nigel of the Cotentin.
	1009	Richard confirms the resignation of Abbot Mainard of Mont-Saint-Michel.
	1013	Richard provides refuge to Æthelred II, Emma, and their children.
	c. 1013	Count Odo II of Chartres attacks Normandy. Richard takes Tillières-sur-Avre in the fighting and builds a castle there. He seeks to recruit pagan troops from Scandinavia, but peace is restored before they can be put in the field.
	c. 1015	Dudo of Saint-Quentin completes his *De moribus*. Archbishop Robert of Rouen is made (first) count of Evreux.
	1017	Judith dies.
	c. 1020	Richard campaigns in the Hiémois, taking Almenèches, Argentan, Ecouché, and Alençon (this last was subsequently granted back to William of Bellême). Radbod Fleitel is made bishop of Sées.
	1024	Richard marries Papia. They have two sons: William and Malger.
	c. 1024	Richard marries his niece, Godgifu, to Count Drogo of the Vexin.
	1025	A great court is held in August, during which Richard II issues lengthy diplomas for the monks of Fécamp, Bernay, Jumièges, and Saint-Ouen.
	1026	Richard II dies.
Richard III (1026–1027)	1027	Richard defeats his brother, Robert, who had rebelled against him in the Hiémois. Richard dies shortly afterwards.
Robert the Magnificent (1027–1035)	1027	Robert is elected duke in succession to his brother, despite the claim of Richard III's young illegitimate son, Nicholas.
	c. 1028	Robert besieges his uncle, Archbishop Robert of Rouen at Evreux. The archbishop flees to France and places Normandy under an interdict. They are reconciled soon afterwards.
	c. 1029	Robert launches a campaign against William of Bellême. At about this same time, Bishop Hugh of Bayeux rebels against the duke, and fortifies his castle at Ivry-la-Bataille. He is defeated and loses the county of Ivry and much of his influence.
	c. 1030	Robert launches a campaign against the Bretons, constructing a castle at Chéruel to defend the Norman border. At about the same time, Count Baldwin IV of Flanders seeks refuge at Robert's court. Robert helps him to recover his county from his son, leading an army to Flanders and destroying the castle at Chocques.
	c. 1032	Robert launches an expedition to place the future Edward the Confessor on the English throne. The fleet is blown off course.

Duke	Year	Event
		Robert establishes his authority over the Channel Islands and threatens the Bretons. Probably at this same time, he founds an abbey at Cerisy-la-Forêt.
	1033	Robert provides refuge to King Henry of the French. Robert is apparently instrumental in his restoration.
	1035	Robert founds the abbey at Montivilliers and makes his aunt the first abbess. He leaves on pilgrimage for Jerusalem, and dies at Nicaea on the return leg.
William the Bastard (1035–1087)	1037	Archbishop Robert of Rouen dies.
	c. 1041	William's guardian, Count Gilbert, dies as a result of a feud with the Giroie family.
	c. 1042	King Henry attacks Tillières-sur-Avre and Argentan.
	c. 1043	Thustan Goz recognizes King Henry's authority in the Hiémois but is then defeated and exiled by Norman forces led by the duke. At about this same time, William achieves his majority.
	1046	Guy of Burgundy rebels against Duke William. Nigel of the Cotentin, Haimo Dentatus of Creully, and Ranulf of Briquessart join the rebellion.
	1047	The rebels are defeated by Duke William and King Henry of the French at Val-ès-Dunes. Guy is subsequently besieged at Brionne. Nigel of the Cotentin goes into exile and his estates are taken and divided.
	1048	Duke William campaigns with the French king against the Angevin castle at Mouliherne.
	1049	William's half-brother, Odo, is appointed Bishop of Bayeux.
	c. 1049	William marries Matilda of Flanders, daughter of Baldwin V.
	1050	Members of the Grandmesnil and Giroie families found the abbey at Saint-Evroult.
	c. 1052	William attacks and captures Domfront and Alençon, which had been occupied by Count Geoffrey of Anjou. William retains Domfront, but gives Alençon to Roger of Montgommery, who around this same time marries Mabel, the daughter of William of Bellême and, ultimately, heiress to the whole lordship of Bellême. Montgommery begins to assert his own authority in the region.
	c. 1053	Count William of Arques, Duke William's uncle and contemporary, rebels. Despite French help, he is defeated and exiled.
	1054	French forces are defeated by Norman troops at the battle of Mortemer. Archbishop Malger of Rouen is deposed and replaced by a monk called Maurillius. Around this same time, William Werlenc, count of Mortain, is exiled and forfeited.
	1057	William defeats the rearguard of a French army led by King Henry and Count Geoffrey of Anjou at Varaville on the river Dives.
	1058	William takes the castle at Thimert in France and is besieged by King Henry.

Duke	Year	Event
	c. 1059	Robert fitz Giroie rebels at Saint-Céneri-le-Gérei, probably as a result of the ambitions of Roger of Montgommery and Duke William's failure to hold them in check.
	1060	King Henry dies, without having taken Thimert. Count Geoffrey of Anjou dies later the same year. Around this time, Nigel of the Cotentin is permitted to return to Normandy.
	1063	William conquers Maine in the name of his eldest son, Robert Cuthose. Lanfranc is appointed first abbot of the monastery of Saint-Etienne at Caen.
	c. 1064	William leads an army into Brittany against Count Conan.
	1066	The abbey of Saint-Trinité at Caen is dedicated in June. William collects an army over the summer and embarks on his campaign to take the English throne at the end of September. The men of Normandy almost certainly swear fidelity to Robert Curthose in anticipation of his succession as duke – just in case.
	1076	William besieges Ralph of Gael (who had rebelled against him in England the previous year) at Dol, but is obliged to lift the siege when King Philip of the French brings an army against him.
	1077	King Philip seizes the French Vexin when Count Simon retires to a monastery.
	c. 1077	Mabel of Bellême is murdered. Robert of Bellême inherits his mother's lordship, apparently in his own right.
	c. 1079	Robert Curthose rebels against his father. He is supported by Robert of Bellême and William of Breteuil and given aid by William's French enemies: the lords of Châteauneuf-en-Thymerais, the count of Flanders, and King Philip. William is unhorsed by his son outside the castle at Gerberoy.
	1080	William presides over the council of Lillebonne.
	c. 1083	William's daughter, Adela, marries Count Stephen of Blois. Bishop Odo of Bayeux is arrested. Robert Curthose rebels for a second time.
	1087	William attacks Mantes in the Vexin. He is injured when his horse shies during the fighting, and dies at Rouen on 9 September. On his death, Normandy passes to Robert Curthose, England to William Rufus. Ducal garrisons are ousted from seigniorial castles.
Robert Curthose (1087–1106)	c. 1087	Robert grants the Avranchin and Cotentin to his brother Henry.
	1088	Robert attacks the lands of Robert of Bellême and takes the castles at Ballon and Saint-Céneri-le-Gérei.
	1089	Rufus begins to construct a party of Norman supporters, including Count Robert of Eu, Walter Giffard, and Ralph of Mortemer. Curthose successfully besieges the castle at Eu and then strengthens his hold on Upper Normandy through the marriage of his daughter to Helias of Saint-Saëns. Helias receives the ducal castles at Arques and Bures-en-Bray as well

Duke	Year	Event
		as the county of Talou. Around the same time, Robert hands the castle at Ivry-la-Bataille to William of Breteuil.
	1090	As a direct result of the grant of Ivry to William of Breteuil, Robert grants Brionne to Roger of Beaumont and the honour of Le Hommet to Robert of Meulles. Some of the citizens of Rouen riot in favour of Rufus. Their rebellion is defeated and the rebel leader executed. Robert of Bellême attacks the duke's castle at Exmes. When defeated, he constructs unlicensed fortifications at Château-Gontier and Fourches.
	1091	Robert Curthose supports Bellême at the siege of Courcy, which is lifted only when news arrives that William Rufus has landed in the duchy. Curthose and Rufus agree the Treaty of Rouen, which establishes Rufus as Robert's heir and vice versa. Robert and William Rufus march against their brother Henry, who is besieged at Mont-Saint-Michel and driven into exile.
	1092	The citizens of Domfront, dissatisfied with the lordship of Robert of Bellême, hand control of their town and castle to Henry. He swiftly recovers control of much of the Cotentin.
	1094	Rufus is found to have broken the terms of the Treaty of Rouen. He retires in anger to Eu and takes the castle at Bures-en-Bray. Curthose appeals to King Philip for aid, which is given.
	1095	Robert takes the cross.
	1096	Curthose leaves on crusade, with Bishop Odo of Bayeux and others. Rufus takes over the rule of Normandy. Henry retains the Cotentin and is now also given control over the Bessin, except for Caen and Bayeux.
	c. 1097	Rufus appoints Turold of Envermeu as bishop of Bayeux. His election is opposed by the canons and burgesses of Bayeux.
	1100	Rufus is killed in a hunting accident on 3 August. On 5 August, his brother Henry is crowned Henry I. Curthose returns from crusade and resumes control of Normandy.
	1101	Curthose invades England, but is brought to terms. The Treaty of Alton, which makes each the heir of the other, sees Henry surrender his Norman possessions, except Domfront, but also obliges Curthose to pursue Henry's enemies in the duchy. The bishopric of Lisiux is handed to unsuitable relatives of Ranulf Flambard, bishop of Durham.
	1102	Robert of Bellême rebels in England. He is defeated by Henry, exiled, and forfeited. Curthose is obliged to attack Bellême's lordships in Normandy as a result of the Treaty of Alton, but divisions within his army mean that the siege of Vignats is abandoned.
	1103	Henry sends Robert of Meulan to Normandy to settle the dispute over the right to inherit the lordship of Breteuil.
	1104	Curthose makes peace with Bellême. Henry tours Normandy, and summons Curthose to his court to answer for his incompetent rule.

Duke	Year	Event
	1105	Ivo of Chartres informs the pope of the uncanonical elections to the bishopric of Lisieux, and urges Count Robert of Meulan to encourage Henry I to invade the duchy. Henry lands in the Cotentin and takes Bayeux and Caen.
	1106	Henry campaigns against Count William of Mortain. Curthose and his allies are defeated at the battle of Tinchebray on 28 September. Curthose is imprisoned in England. His son, William Clito, is taken and given into the custody of Helias of Saint-Saëns. Henry henceforth rules Normandy, but does not take the ducal title until *c.* 1115.
Henry I (1106–1135)	1107	Ranulf Flambard's son is deposed as bishop of Lisieux and John of Sées is elected in his place. Turold of Envermeu resigns the bishopric of Bayeux. Henry issues his earliest surviving Norman writ.
	1109	Henry recovers the castle at Gisors from King Louis VI. His daughter, Matilda, is betrothed to King (and later Emperor) Henry V of the Germans.
	c. 1110	Henry orders the arrest of William Clito. He escapes and flees into exile with Helias of Saint-Saëns.
	1111	Henry makes an alliance with his nephew, Count Theobald of Blois, who attacks the French royal demesne. Henry strengthens his southern frontier, building a tower within the castle at Evreux, and exiling the count and countess when they demolish it.
	1112	Henry takes Nonancourt-sur-Avre and Illiers-l'Evêque in the Evrecin from their French lords. Robert of Bellême is arrested in November, probably while acting as an envoy for Louis VI on behalf of Gervase of Châteauneuf-en-Thymerais, erstwhile lord of Nonancourt. Henry confiscates Bellême's Norman estates and grants some of them to his nephews, Theobald and Stephen of Blois.
	1113	Henry makes peace with Fulk of Anjou and then King Louis. He is recognized as lord of Bellême, Maine, and Brittany, and thus implicitly as duke of the Normans. He officially adopts the ducal title (on his 'fourth seal') a year or two afterwards. Henry grants Bellême to Count Rotrou of the Perche. Henry's son, William, is betrothed to Fulk's daughter, Matilda.
	1114	Matilda marries Henry V.
	1115	The Normans do fealty to Henry's son, William, in anticipation of his succession.
	1118	Arnulf of Montgommery occupies Alençon. Reginald of Bailleul rebels against Henry, almost certainly in favour of William Talvas, the son of Robert of Bellême, who claims his father's Norman estates. Amaury of Montfort-l'Amaury raises a rebellion, ostensibly in favour of Clito's claim to the duchy, as a result of Henry's refusal to allow him to inherit the county of Evreux. Other rebels include Eustace of Breteuil and Hugh of Gournay. Louis VI adds his support.

Duke	Year	Event
	1119	Count Fulk of Anjou brokers a settlement with Henry, whereby Talvas is restored to his Norman patrimony. Henry's son, William, marries Matilda. Louis VI is defeated by Henry at the battle of Brémule. After a further failed attack on Breteuil, the rebellion against Henry collapses. Amaury is allowed to succeed to the county of Evreux. Henry defends his treatment of Clito, and his poor relationship with Louis VI, in an interview with Pope Calixtus II.
	1120	Henry's son, William, performs homage for Normandy to Louis VI. He dies in the wreck of the *White Ship* on 25 November.
	c. 1120	Henry seizes Verneuil-sur-Avre.
	1123	Waleran of Meulan leads a rebellion against Henry, probably provoked by the taking of Verneuil-sur-Avre. The rebels also include Amaury of Montfort, who is unhappy about ducal interventions within his county of Evreux. Henry besieges and takes the rebels' castles at Montfort-sur-Risle and Pont-Audemer.
	1124	The rebel leaders are defeated at the battle of Bourgthéroulde by Henry's household knights. Waleran of Meulan is captured and imprisoned. King Louis is diverted by a threatened invasion of France by the Emperor Henry V.
	1125	The Emperor Henry V dies. Matilda is summoned back to Normandy.
	1126	Norman troops fight in the army that Louis VI leads to the Auvergne.
	1127	William Clito is established as count of Flanders by Louis VI. Henry revokes Flemish trading privileges in English ports and backs the Flemish rebellion against Clito. Matilda is betrothed to Geoffrey V of Anjou. The Anglo-Norman lords swear to support her succession if Henry dies without a male heir.
	1128	Geoffrey marries Matilda on 17 June. Clito dies at the siege of Aalst at the end of July.
	1131	Henry meets with Pope Innocent II at Chartres and Rouen. A second oath is sworn to support Matilda's succession.
	1135	Relations with Geoffrey and Matilda become strained as a result of Henry's refusal to release her dowry castles. Fighting breaks out. Henry grows suspicious of Roger of Tosny and William Talvas. He places a garrison in the former's castle at Tosny, while Talvas flees Normandy rather than attend Henry's court. His lands are taken into Henry's hands. Henry dies on 1 December at Lyons-la-Forêt.
Stephen / Matilda / Geoffrey (1135–1144)	1135	Stephen becomes king of the English and is consequently recognized as duke of the Normans. But Wigan the Marshal surrenders the ducal castles at Argentan, Exmes, and Domfront to Matilda, and she also gains possession of the castles at Châtillon-sur-Colmont, Gorron, and Ambrières. William Talvas is restored to his Norman possessions by Geoffrey of Anjou, apparently without any effective opposition.

Duke	Year	Event
	1136	Stephen grants Moulins-la-Marche and Bonsmoulins to Rotrou of the Perche and Richer of L'Aigle, respectively. He also gives the castle at Montfort-sur-Risle to Waleran of Meulan. In September Geoffrey raids into Normandy, reaching as far north as Lisieux.
	1137	Geoffrey raids into the Bessin. Stephen visits Normandy. He puts down a rebellion by Rabel of Tancarville, but his army breaks up in confusion at Livarot as it is marching against Geoffrey of Anjou.
	1138	Robert of Gloucester breaks with Stephen and allies with Matilda and Geoffrey of Anjou.
	1139	Matilda lands in England.
	1141	Stephen is captured at the battle of Lincoln on 2 February. Verneuil and Nonancourt surrender to Geoffrey. Lisieux falls to Geoffrey in April. Waleran of Meulan defects to the Angevin side. The men of the Roumois recognize Geoffrey's authority.
	1142	Geoffrey takes the counties of Mortain, Avranches, and the Cotentin, with the exception of Cherbourg.
	1143	Cherbourg falls to Geoffrey, who now takes the Evrecin and much of the region south and south-east of Rouen.
	1144	Geoffrey besieges Rouen in January. The castle surrenders when supplies run out and Geoffrey becomes duke of the Normans. The castles at Neufchâtel-en-Bray and Lyons-la-Forêt fall to Geoffrey soon afterwards.
	1145	The castle at Arques-la-Bataille surrenders to Geoffrey when its constable is killed during the siege.

Bibliography

Key Original Primary Sources

Archives Départementales

Calvados
2 D 11 (Copy *pancarte* of Henry I for Sainte-Barbe-en-Auge)
2 D 12 (Original *pancarte* of King Stephen for Sainte-Barbe-en-Auge)
H 1833(I) (Confirmation of King Henry I for Saint-Etienne of Caen)
H 1834 (*Emptiones Eudonis*)
H 6510 (Ctl. Saint-André-en-Gouffern)
H 7031(5) (Original act of Henry I for Saint-Pierre-sur-Dives)
H 7750 (Original *pancarte* for Troarn)
H 7752 (Original writ-charter of Henry I for Troarn)
H 7760 (Original act of Count William of Evreux for Troarn)
H 7761(1) (Original writ of Amaury of Montfort for Troarn)
Villers-Canivet, non-coté, carton 159(1) (Original writ of Henry I)
1 J 41 (Ctl. Saint-Etienne of Caen)

Eure
G6 (Ctl. Bishopric of Evreux)
G122 (Ctl. Canons of Evreux)
H 10 (Original charter of Count Stephen of Blois for Le Bec)
H 28 (Original act of Henry I for Le Bec)
H 91 (Ctl. Le Bec)
H 438(1) (Original *pancarte* for Lyre)
H 793 (Ctl. Saint-Taurin)
H 794 (Ctl. Saint-Taurin)
J.-L. Lenoir, Collection du Marquis de Mathan, MS 23 (transcripts of acts for the monks of Lyre)

Orne
H 2152(1) (Original act of Robert of Bellême for the church of Saint--Léonard of Bellême)
H 2152(2) (Original act of Robert of Bellême for the church of Saint-Léonard of Bellême)
H 2157 (Original settlement of 1117 over the rights of Saint-Léonard of Bellême)
H 2159(3) (Agreement regarding the church of Saint-Léonard of Bellême of 1127)

H 2159 (11) (Original act of the papal legate Gerard for the church of Saint-Léonard of Bellême of 1127)

Seine-Maritime
G 939 (Original writ of Henry I regarding Douvrend)
G 1115 (Confirmation of Innocent II of the possessions of the archdiocese of Rouen)
G 1116 (Letter of Innocent II concerning abuses within the province of Rouen)
7 H 12 (Original acts of Henry I for Fécamp)
9 H 29 (Original act of William the Bastard for Jumièges)
9 H 30 (Original act of Robert the Magnificent and William the Bastard for Jumièges)
9 H 906 (Original act of Richard II for Jumièges)
9 H 1224(2) (Original writ of Henry I for Jumièges)
13 H 8 (Original act of Henry I for Boscherville)
13 H 15 (Original act of William of Tancarville for Boscherville)
14 H 145 (Original act of William the Bastard for Saint-Ouen)
14 H 175 (Original act of Richard II for Saint-Ouen)
14 H 189 (Original act of William the Bastard for Saint-Ouen)
14 H 232 (Original act of Richard II for Saint-Ouen)
14 H 279 (Original act of Richard II for Saint-Ouen)
14 H 327 (Original act of William the Bastard for Saint-Ouen)
14 H 404 (Original act of Richard II for Saint-Ouen)
14 H 448 (Original act of Richard II for Saint-Ouen)
14 H 570 (Original act of Richard II and William the Bastard for Saint-Ouen)
14 H 774 (Original act of William the Bastard for Saint-Ouen)
14 H 797 (Original act of William the Bastard for Saint-Ouen)
14 H 829 (Original act of William the Bastard for Saint-Ouen)
14 H 915, 915A and 915B (Original acts of Richard II and William the Bastard for Saint-Ouen)
14 H 916 (Original act of Richard II for Saint-Ouen)
14 H 917 (Original act of Richard II for Saint-Ouen)
16 H 14 (Cartulary of Saint-Wandrille)
20 HP 5 (Original acts of Robert Curthose and Henry I for Le Bec/Notre-Dame-du-Pré)
55 H 7 (Ctl. St-Amand)
55 H 8 (Original *pancarte* of Saint-Amand)

Archives Diocésaines, Sées
Non-coté, Ctl. Saint-Martin of Sées

Archives Nationale, Paris
Paris, AN, J655, no. 4 (Original act of Henry I for Roland of Oissel)

Bibliothèques Municipale

Avranches
MS 210 (Ctl. Mont-Saint-Michel)

Lisieux
MS 5 (Ctl. Bishopric of Lisieux)

Rouen
MS 1193 (Ctl. Rouen Cathedral)
MS 1207 (Ctl. Fécamp)
MS 1233 (Ctl. Boscherville)

Bibliothèque Nationale de France, Paris
lat. 5650 (Ctl. La Trinité, Caen)
lat. 9221 (collection of original acts for Saint-Père of Chartres)
lat. 10086 (Ctl. Troarn)
lat. 10087 (Ctl. Montebourg)
lat. 11055 (Ctl. Saint-Evroult)
lat. 11056 (Ctl. Saint-Evroult)
lat. 12878 (Transcripts by Dom. Martène relating to Marmoutier)
lat. 12880 (Transcripts by Dom. Martène relating to Marmoutier)
lat. 12884 (Collection by Bénigne Thibault relating to Le Bec)
lat. 13905 (Collection by Dom., Jacques Jouvelin relating to Le Bec)
lat. 17137 (Ctl. Saint-Sauveur-le-Vicomte)
nouv. acq. lat. 1022 (Transcript of the cartulary of Savigny by Léopold Delisle)
nouv.acq. francais 21659 (Transcript of the cartulary of Cerisy-la-Foret by
    Léopold Delisle)

British Library, London
Add. Ch. 15281 (Pancarte of Roger the vicomte for the monks of
    Saint-Sauveur-le-Vicomte)
Add. Ch. 75743 (Original act for Chartres cathedral)
Add. MS 15605 (s. xv, fragment of a cartulary of Montebourg abbey)

Morgan Library, New York
MA1217 (Original act of Henry I for Saint-Etienne, Caen)

Printed Primary Sources

Abbo of Saint-Germain-des-Prés, *Bella parisiacae urbis*, ed. and trans. N. Dass
    (Paris, Lieuvin, Dudley MA, 2007)
Acta Archiepiscoporum Rotomagensium: a study and edition, ed. and trans. R.
    Allen, Tabularia, 'Documents', 9 (2009), 1–66
Acta pontificum Romanorum inedita, ed. J. von Pflugk-Harttung, 3 vols
    (Tübingen and Stuttgart, 1881–86)
Actes des comtes de Flandre, 1071–1128, ed. F. Vercauteren (Brussels, 1938)

Les actes de Guillaume le Conquérant et de la reine Mathilde pour les abbayes Caennaises, ed. L. Musset, MSAN, 37 (1967)

Adam of Bremen, *History of the Archbishops of Hamburg-Bremen*, trans. F. J. Tschan with a new introduction and selected bibliography by T. Reuter (New York, 2002)

Adémar de Chabannes, *Chronique*, ed. J. Chavanon (Paris, 1897)

Alcuin, *De uirtutibus et vitiis liber ad Widonem comitem*, PL, 101, cols. 613–38

Alcuin, *Epistolae*, ed. E. Dümmler, *MGH, Epistolae*, 4 (*Karolini aevi* 2) (Berlin, 1895)

Alexander II (pope), 'Epistolae et diplomata Alexandri II papae', PL, 146, cols. 1279–1430

Alexander of Telese, 'The History of the Most Serene Roger, First King of Sicily', in *Roger II and the Creation of the Kingdom of Sicily*, ed. and trans. G. A. Loud (Manchester, 2012), pp. 63–129

Amatus of Montecassino, *The History of the Normans by Amatus of Montecassino*, trans. P. N. Dunbar and revised by G. A. Loud (Woodbridge, 2004)

St Ambrose, *The Letters of Saint Ambrose, Bishop of Milan*, trans. H. Walford (Oxford, 1881)

L'ancienne coutume de Normandie, ed. W. L. de Grunchy (St Helier, 1881)

André de Fleury, *Vie de Gauzlin, Abbé de Fleury: Vita Gauzelini abbatis Floriacensis monasterii*, ed. R.-H. Bautier and G. Labory (Paris, 1969)

Anglo-Latin Satirical Poets and Epigrammatists of the Twelfth Century: 2. Minor Anglo-Latin Satirists and Epigrammatists of the Twelfth Century, ed. T. Wright, Rolls Series (London, 1872)

The Anglo-Saxon Chronicle, trans. D. Whitelock (London, 1961)

The Anglo-Saxon Chronicle, trans. G. N. Garmonsway (London, 1972)

The Anglo-Saxon Chronicle: A Collaborative Edition, 7 MS E, ed. S. Irvine (Cambridge, 2004)

Anglo-Saxon Wills, trans. D. Whitelock (Cambridge, 1930)

Anna Comnena, *The Alexiad of Anna Comnena*, trans. E. R. A. Sewter, (Harmondsworth, 1969)

Annales Gemmeticensis, ed. J. Laporte (1954)

Annales Nivernenses, ed. J. Heller and G. Waitz, *MGH, Scriptores* 13 (Hanover, 1881)

Annales regni francorum unde ab. a. 741 usque ad a. 829, qui dicuntur Annales laurissenses maiores et Einhardi, ed. F. Kurze, *MGH, Scriptores Rerum Germanicarum* 6 (Hanover, 1895)

'Ex annalibus Normannicis', ed. O. Holder-Egger, *MGH, Scriptores* 26 (Hanover, 1882), 488–500

The Annals of Saint-Bertin, trans. J. L. Nelson (Manchester, 1991)

Anselm of Canterbury, *The Letters of St Anselm of Canterbury*, trans. W. Frölich, 3 vols (Kalamazoo, 1990–94)

—— *Proslogion*, in *The Prayers and Meditations of St Anselm with the Proslogion*, trans. B. Ward (London, 1973)

—— *Memorials of St Anselm*, ed. R. W. Southern and F. S. Schmitt (Oxford, 1991)

Antiquus cartularius ecclesiæ Baiocensis (Livre Noir), ed. V. Bourienne, 2 vols (Rouen, 1902–03)

Asser, *Alfred the Great: Asser's Life of King Alfred and other Contemporary Sources*, trans. S. Keynes and M. Lapidge (Harmondsworth, 1983)

St Augustine, *The City of God against the Pagans*, ed. R. W. Dyson (Cambridge, 1998)

—— *Letters*, in *Political Writings*, ed. E. M. Atkins and R. J. Dodaro, Cambridge Texts in the History of Political Thought (Cambridge, 2001)

Bede, *Bede's Ecclesiastical History of the English People*, ed. and trans. B. Colgrave and R. A. B. Mynors, revised edition (Oxford, 1992)

—— *The Ecclesiastical History of the English People*, trans. L. Shirley-Price, revised by L. E. Latham, with the translation of the minor works, new introduction, and notes by D. H. Farmer (London, 1990)

The Benedictional of Archbishop Robert, ed. H. A. Wilson, Henry Bradshaw Society 24 (1903)

Benedict of Sainte-Maure, *Chronique des ducs de Normandie*, ed. F. Michel, 3 vols (Paris, 1836–43)

G. Bessin, *Concilia Rotomagensis Provincia*, 2 vols (Rouen, 1717)

The Bible, Authorized King James Version with Apocrypha, with an Introduction and Notes by R. Carroll and S. Prickett (Oxford, 1997)

The Book of Sainte Foy, trans. P. Sheingorn (Philadepphia,1995)

'The Breuis relatio de Guillemo nobilissimo comite Normannorum, written by a monk of Battle Abbey', ed. E. M. C. van Houts, *Camden Society Miscellany*, 34 (1997), 1–48; with a translation provided in E. M. C. van Houts, *History and Family Traditions in England and the Continent, 1000–1200* (Aldershot, 1999), ch. 7, pp. 25a–48.

Brut y Tywysogion or The Chronicle of the Princes, Peniarth MS 20 Version, ed. T. Jones (Cardiff, 1955)

Calendar of the Charter Rolls, 6 vols (London, 1903–1927)

Calendar of Documents Preserved in France, 918–1206, ed. J. H. Round (London, 1899)

Capitularia Regum Francorum 1, ed. A. Boreti, *Monumenta Germanae Historica, Leges* (Hanover, 1883)

Capitularia Regum Francorum, 2, ed. A Boreti and V. Krause, *Monumenta Germanae Historica, Leges* (Hanover, 1897)

Cartae Antiquae Rolls: 1–10, ed. L. Landon, Pipe Roll Society, new series 17 (1939)

Le Cartulaire de l'abbaye bénédictine de Saint-Pierre-de-Préaux (1034–1227), ed. Dominique Rouet, Editions du Comité des travaux historiques et scientifiques (Paris, 2005)

Cartulaire de l'abbaye cardinale de la Trinité du Vendôme, ed. C. Métais, 5 vols (Paris, 1893–1904)

Le cartulaire de l'abbaye de Marmoutier pour la Perche, ed. P. Barret (Mortagne, 1894)

Cartulaire de l'abbaye de Saint-Jean-en-Vallée de Chartres, ed. R. Merlet (Chartres, 1906)

'Cartulaire de l'abbaye de Saint-Lô', in *Cartulaire de la Manche* (1878)

Cartulaire de l'abbaye de Saint-Père de Chartres, ed. B. Guérard, 2 vols (Paris, 1840)

Les cartulaires de la baronnie de Bricquebec, ed. L. Delisle (Saint-Lô, 1894)

Cartulaire de l'église de la Sainte-Trinité de Beaumont-le-Roger, ed. E. Deville (Paris, 1912)

Cartulaire de la léproserie du Grand-Beaulieu, eds. R. Merlet and M. Jusselin (Chartres, 1909)

Cartulaire de Saint-Aubin d'Angers, ed. Le Comte B. de Brousillon, 3 vols (Paris, 1903)

Cartulaire de l'abbaye de la Sainte-Trinité de Tiron, ed. M. L. Merlet, vol. 1 (Chartres, 1883)

Cartulaire de la Sainte-Trinité-du-Mont, ed. A. Deville, in *Cartulaire de Saint-Bertin*, ed. B. Guérard (Paris, 1840), 403–87

Cartulaire de Louviers: documents historiques originaux du Xᵉ au XVIIIᵉ siècle, la plupart inédits, extraits des chroniques, et des manuscrits des bibliothèques et des archives publiques de la France et d'Angleterre, ed. T. Bonnin, vol. 1 (Evreux, 1870)

Cartulaire de Saint-Vincent de Mâcon: connu sous le nom de Livre enchaîné, ed. M. C. Ragut (Mâcon, 1864)

Cartulaire de Saint-Vincent du Mans, ed. R. Charles and S. Memjot d'Elbenne (Mamers-Le Mans, 1886–1913)

Cartulaires de Saint-Ymer-en-Auge et de Bricquebec, publiés avec notices par Charles Bréard (Rouen, 1908)

Le cartulaire du chaiptre cathédral de Coutances, ed. J. Fontanel (Saint-Lô, 2003)

Cartulaire Normand de Philippe-Auguste, Louis VIII, Saint Louis et Philippe-le-Hardi, ed. L. Delisle (Caen, 1882)

The Cartulary of the abbey of Mont-Saint-Michel, ed. K. S. B. Keats-Rohan (Donington, 2006)

The Cartulary of Tutbury Priory, ed. A. Saltman, Historical Manuscripts Commission (London, 1962)

Catalogue des actes d'Henri I, roi de France, ed. F. Soehnée (Paris, 1907)

'Catalogus librorum abbatiae Beccensis circa saeculum duodecimum', *PL*, 150, cols. 769–82

Charters and Custumals of the Abbey of Holy Trinity, Caen: Part 2. The French Estates, ed. J. Walmsley, Records of Social and Economic History, new series 22 (Oxford, 1994)

The Charters of David I: The Written Acts of David I King of Scots, 1124–53, and of His Son Henry, Earl of Northumberland, 1139–52, ed. G. W. S. Barrow (Woodbridge, 1999)

Charters of the Honour of Mowbray 1107–1191, ed. D. Greenway, Records of Social and Economic History, new series 1 (London, 1972)

Charters of the Redvers Family and the Earldom of Devon 1090–1217, ed. R. Bearman (Exeter, 1994)

Chartes de l'abbaye de Jumièges, ed. J. J. Vernier, 2 vols (Rouen, 1916)

Chartes du prieuré de Longueville, ed. P. Le Cacheux (Rouen, 1934)

Chartes Normandes de l'abbaye de Saint-Florent près Saumur de 710 à 1200 environ, ed. M. P. Marchegay, MSAN, 30 (1880)

'The Chartulary of the Priory of Boxgrove', ed. L. Fleming, Sussex Record Society, 59 (1901)

Chronica Abbatiae Ramesiensis, ed. W. D. Macray, Rolls Series (London, 1886)

The Chronicle of Battle Abbey, ed. and trans, E. Searle (Oxford, 1980)

'Ex Chronico Rotomagensi', *RHGF*, xii. 784–6

Chronique de l'abbaye de Saint-Bénigne de Dijon suivi de la chronique de Saint-Pierre de Béze, ed. E. Bougaud and J. Garnier (Dijon, 1875)

La Chronique de Morigny (1095–1152), ed. L. Mirot, second edition (Paris, 1912)

La Chronique de Nantes (570–1049), ed. R. Merlet (Paris, 1896)

La Chronique de Sainte-Barbe-en-Auge, ed. R. N. Sauvage, Mémoires de l'académie nationale des sciences, arts, et belles-lettres de Caen (1906)

Cicero, *The Republic and The Laws*, trans. N. Rudd (Oxford, 1998)

—— *On Obligations*, trans. P. G. Walsh (Oxford, 2000)

Diplomata, ed. H. Enzensberger (Böhlau, Verlag, Köln, Weimar, Wien, 1996)

Corpus Iuris Ciuilis, ed. T. Mommsen et al., 3 vols (1872–95)

Coutumiers de Normandie: textes critiques, ed. Ernest-Joseph Tardif, vol 1 (Rouen, 1881)

Domesday Book: Text and Translation, ed. J. Morris, 38 vols (Chichester, 1975–86)

D. C. Douglas, *Feudal Documents from the Abbey of Bury St Edmunds* (Oxford, 1932)

Dudo of Saint-Quentin, *De moribus et actis primorum Normanniae ducum*, ed. J. Lair, MSAN, 23 (1865)

—— *History of the Normans: Translation with Introduction and Notes*, trans. E. Christiansen (Woodbridge, 1998)

W. Dugdale and R. Dodsworth, *Monasticon Anglicanum*, ed. J. Caley et al., 8 vols (London, 1817–30)

P. E. Dutton (ed. and trans.), *Carolingian Civilization: A Reader* (Peterborough, Ontario, and Plymouth, 2004)

Eadmer of Canterbury, *Historia novorum*, ed. M. Rule, Rolls Series (London, 1884)

—— *Eadmer's History of Recent Events in England: Historia Novorum in Anglia*, trans. G. Bosanquet (London, 1964)

—— *Vita Anselmi*, ed. and trans. R. W. Southern (Oxford, 1962)

Earldom of Gloucester Chartres: The Charters and Scribes of the Earls and Countesses of Gloucester, to AD 1217, ed. R. B. Patterson (Oxford, 1973)

Early Charters of the Cathedral Church of St Paul, London, ed. M. Gibbs, Camden Society, third series, 58 (1939)

Early Yorkshire Charters, ed. C. T. Clay, vols 4–10, Yorkshire Archaeological Society, Record Series, extra series (1935–55)

Ebo and Herbordus, *The Life of Otto the Apostle of Pomerania, 1060–1139*, trans. C. H. Robinson (London, 1920)

Encomium Emmae Reginae, ed. A. Campbell with a supplementary introduction by S. Keynes (Cambridge, 1998)

English Historical Documents I, c. 500–1042, ed. and trans. D. Whitelock (London, 1955)

English Historical Documents II, 1042–1189, ed. and trans. D. C. Douglas and G. W. Greenaway (London, 1953)

English Lawsuits from William I to Richard I, ed. and trans. R. van Caenegem, Selden Society, 107 (1991)

Facsimiles of English Royal Writs to A.D. 1100, ed. T. A. M. Bishop and P. Chaplais (Oxford, 1957)

Falco of Benevento, 'Chronicle', in *Roger II and the Creation of the Kingdom of Sicily*, trans. G. A Loud (Manchester, 2012), pp. 130–249

Fleta, ed. and trans. G. O. Sayles, vol. 4, Selden Society, 99 (1984)

Flodoard of Reims, Les annales de Flodoard, ed. P. Lauer (Paris, 1905)

—— *The annals of Flodoard of Reims 919–966*, ed. and trans. S. Fanning and B. Bachrach (Peterborough, Ontario and Plymouth, 2004)

—— *Flodoardi historia Remensis ecclesiæ*, ed. J. Heller and G. Waitz, *MGH, Scriptores* 13 (Hanover, 1881), 405–599

Fulbert of Chartres, *The Letters and Poems of Fulbert of Chartres*, ed. and trans. F. Behrends (Oxford, 1976)

Galbert of Bruges, *The Murder of Charles the Good*, trans. J. B. Ross (New York and Chichester, 1959, reprinted 2005)

Gallia Christiana in provincias ecclesiasticas distributa.: XI. De provincia Rotomagensi, ed. D. Sammarthani et al. (Paris, 1759)

Geffrei Gaimar, *Estoire des Engleis/History of the English*, ed. and trans. I. Short (Oxford, 2009)

Geoffrey Grossus, *The Life of Blessed Bernard of Tiron*, trans. R. H. Cline (Washington, DC, 2009)

Geoffrey Malaterra, *The Deeds of Count Roger of Calabria and Sicily and of his Brother Duke Robert Guiscard*, trans. K. B. Wolf (Ann Arbor, 2005)

Gerald of Wales, *Giraldi Cambresensis Opera*, ed. J. S. Brewer, J. F. Dimock, and G. F. Warner, Rolls Series, 8 vols (London, 1861–91)

—— *The Journey through Wales and The Description of Wales,* trans. L. Thorpe (London, 1978)

Gesta pontificum Camaracensium, ed. L. C. Bethmann, in *MGH, Scriptores 7* (Hanover, 1846), pp. 393–489

Gesta Regis Henrici Secundi Benedicti Abbatis, ed. W. Stubbs, Rolls Series, 2 vols (London, 1867)

Gesta Stephani, ed. and trans. K. R. Potter with a new introduction and notes by R. H. C. Davis (Oxford, 1976)

Gilbert Crispin, *Life of Lord Herluin, Abbot of Bec*, trans. S. N. Vaughn, in *The Abbey of Bec and the Anglo-Norman State* (Woodbridge, 1981), pp. 67–86

Le grand cartulaire de Conches et sa copie: transcription et analyse, ed. C. de Haas (Le Mesnil-sur-l'Estrée, 2005)

Gregory the Great, *Morals in the Book of Job*, trans. J. H. Parker, 3 vols (London, 1844–50)

Guibert of Nogent, *A Monk's Confession: The Memoirs of Guibert of Nogent*, trans. P. J. Archambault (Philadelphia, 1996)

Guillelmi I Regis Diplomata, ed. H. Enzensberger, Codex Diplomaticus Regni Siciliae: III (Böhlau, Verlag, Köln, Weimar, Wien, 1996)

H. Guillotel, *Actes des ducs de Bretagne (944–1148)*, ed. P. Charon, P. Guigon, C. Henry, M. Jones, K. Keats-Rohan, and J.-C. Meuret (Rennes, 2014)

Guy of Amiens, *The* Carmen de Hastingae Proelio *of Guy Bishop of Amiens*, ed. and trans. F. Barlow (Oxford, 1999)

Haimon of Saint-Pierre-sur-Dives, 'Lettre de l'abbé Haimon sur la construction de l'église de Saint-Pierre-sur-Dive en 1145', ed. L. Delisle, *Bulletin de l'Ecole des Chartes*, 21 (1860), 113–39

Hariulf, *Chronique de l'abbaye de Saint-Riquier (Ve siècle au 1104)*, ed. F. Lot (Paris, 1894)

Helgaud de Fleury, *Vie de Robert le Pieux*, ed. R. H. Bautier and G. Labory (Paris, 1935)

Henry of Huntingdon, *Historia Anglorum*, ed. and trans. D. Greenway (Oxford, 1996)

Herman of Tournai, *The Restoration of the Monastery of Saint-Martin of Tournai*, trans. L. H. Nelson (Washington, DC, 1996)

Hincmar of Reims, 'Coronatio Caroli Calui', *PL*, 125, cols. 803–8

Historia Ecclesie Abbendonensis: The History of the Church of Abingdon, ed. and trans. J. Hudson, 2 vols (Oxford, 2002–07)

History of William Marshal, ll. 8248–9, ed. A. J. Holden, trans. S. Gregory, and notes by. D. Crouch, Anglo-Norman Text Society, Vol. 1 (London, 2002)

Hugh the Chanter, *The History of the Church of York 1066–1127*, ed. and trans. C. Johnson revised by M. Brett, C. N. L. Brooke, and M. Winterbottom (Oxford, 1990)

Hugh of Flavigny, *Chronicon*, in *Monumenta Germaniæ Historica, Scriptores* 8, ed. G. H. Pertz (Hanover, 1848), pp. 280–502

Ibn Fadlān, *Ibn Fadlān and the Land of Darkness: Arab Travellers in the Far North*, trans. P. Lunde and C. Stone (London, 2012)

Innocent II (pope), 'Epistolae variorum ad Innocentium', *PL*, 179, cols. 657–674.

Introductio monachorum, in *Chroniques latines du Mont-Saint-Michel (IXe–XIIe siècle)*, ed. P. Bouet and O. Desbordes (Caen, 2009), pp. 149–225

Inventio et miracula sancti Vulfranni, ed. J. Laporte, Société de l'histoire de Normandie, Mélanges 14 (1938)

Isidore of Seville, *The Etymologies of Isidore of Seville*, trans. S. A. Barney, W. J. Lewis, J. A. Beach, and O. Berghof (Cambridge, 2006)

Ivo of Chartres, 'Epistolae', *PL*, 162, cols. 11–504

John of Fécamp, 'Epistolae', *PL*, 147, cols. 463–76

John of Marmoutier, 'Historia Gaufredi ducis Normannorum et comitis Andegavorum', *Chroniques des comtes d'Anjou et des seigneurs d'Amboise*, ed. L. Halphen and R. Poupardin (Paris, 1913)

John of Salisbury, *Historia pontificalis*, ed. and trans. M. Chibnall (Oxford, 1956)

—— *The Letters of John of Salisbury, Vol 1. The Early Letters (1153–1161)*, ed. and trans. W. J. Millor, H. E. Butler, and C. N. L. Brooke (Oxford, 1986)

The Letters of John of Salibsury, Vol 2. The Later Letters (1163–1180), ed. and trans. W. J. Millor and C. N. L. Brooke (Oxford, 1979)

—— *Policraticus: Of the Frivolities of Courtiers and the Footprints of Philosophers*, ed. and trans. C. J. Nederman (Cambridge, 1990)

Jordan Fantosme, *Jordan Fantosme's Chronicle*, ed. and trans. R. C. Johnston (Oxford, 1981)

R. Kehew (ed.) *The Lark in the Morning: The Verses of the Troubadours, a Bilingual Edition*, trans. E. Pound, W. D. Snodgrass, and R. Kehew (trans.) (Chicago and London, 2005)

Lambert, bishop of Arras, 'Epistolae', *PL*, 162, cols. 647–702

Leges Henrici Primi, ed. and trans. L. J. Downer (Oxford, 1972)

The Letters of Lanfranc, Archbishop of Canterbury, ed. and trans. H. M. Clover and M. Gibson (Oxford, 1979)

Liber Eliensis: A History of the Isle of Ely from the Seventh Century to the Twelfth, trans. J. Fairweather (Woodbridge, 2005)

'De libertate Beccensis monasterii', in *Annales Ordinis Sancti Benedicti*, ed. J. Mabillon, vol. 5 (Paris, 1703), Appendix, pp. 635–40;

'On the liberty of the abbey of Le Bec', trans. S. N. Vaughn, *The Abbey of Le Bec and the Anglo-Norman State* (Woodbridge, 1981), pp. 134–43

The Lives of Thomas Becket, trans. M. Staunton (Manchester, 2001)

F. Lot, *Études critiques sur l'abbaye de Saint-Wandrille* (Paris, 1913)

Lucan, *Civil War*, trans. S. H. Braund (Oxford, 1992)

Martin of Braga, *Formula vitae honestae*, Latin text available online at <http://www.thelatinlibrary.com/martinbraga/formula.shtml> (accessed 2 January 2016)

Materials for the History of Thomas Becket, Archbishop of Canterbury, ed. J. C. Robertson and J. B. Sheppard, 7 vols, Rolls Series (London, 1875–85)

Milo Crispin, '*Life* of Lanfranc', *PL*, 150, cols. 29–58; trans. S. N. Vaughn, *The Abbey of Bec and the Anglo-Norman State* (Woodbridge, 1981), pp. 87–111

—— 'The *Lives* of Abbots William and Boso of Le Bec', *PL*, 150, cols. 713–34; trans. S. N. Vaughn, *The Abbey of Bec and the Anglo-Norman State* (Woodbridge, 1981), pp. 117–33

—— *Miraculum quo B. Maria subuenit Guillelmo Crispino Seniori*, in *PL*, 150, cols. 735–44

Des miracles advenus en l'église de Fécamp, ed. R.-N. Sauvage, Société de l'histoire de Normandie, Mélanges (1893), 9–49

'Miracula ecclesiae Constantiensis', in E. A. Pigeon, *Histoire de la cathèdrale de Coutances* (Coutances, 1876), pp. 367–83

'Miracula Audoini episcopi Rotomagensis II', in *Acta Sanctorum* 38 (August IV) (Paris, 1867), cols. 837–40

Miracula sancti Michaelis, in *Chroniques latines du Mont-Saint-Michel (IXe–XIIe siècle)*, ed. P. Bouet and O. Desbordes (Caen, 2009), pp. 259–367

H. Navel, 'L'enquête de 1133 sur les fiefs de l'evêché de Bayeux', *BSAN*, 42 (1934), 5–80

Neustria pia, seu de omnibus et singulis abbatis et prioratibus totiis Normanniae, ed. A du Monstier (1663)

Njal's Saga, trans. R. Cook (London, 2001)

Norman Charters from English Sources, ed. N. Vincent, Pipe Roll Society, new series 59 (2013)

Nouveau Coutumier Géneral, ed. C. Bourdot de Richebourg, 4 vols in 8 (Paris, 1724)

Oddr Snorrason, *The Saga of Olaf Tryggvason*, trans. T. M. Andersson (Ithaca, NY, 2003)

Orderic Vitalis, *Historia ecclesiastica*, ed. and trans. M. Chibnall, 6 vols (Oxford, 1969–80)

Orderici Vitalis ecclesiasticae historiae libri tredecim, ed. A. le Prévost, Société de l'Histoire de France, vol. 5 (Paris, 1855)

Papsturkunden in Frankreich. II. Normandie, ed. J. Ramackers (Göttingen, 1937)

Patrologiae Latinae cursus completes, series Latina, ed. J.-P. Migne, 221 vols (1844–1855)

Pipe Roll 31 Henry I, ed. and trans. J. Green, The Publications of the Pipe Roll Society, new series 57 (2012)

The Pipe Rolls of the exchequer of Normandy for the reign of Henry II, 1180 and 1184, ed. V. Moss, The Publications of the Pipe Roll Society, new series 53 (2004)

Plato, *The Republic*, trans. D. Lee with an Introduction by M. Lane, second edition (London, 2007)

Le premier cartulaire de l'abbaye cistercienne de Pontigny (XIIe–XIIIe siècles), ed. M. Garrigues (Paris, 1981)

A Medieval Prince of Wales: The Life of Gruffydd ap Cynan, trans. D. S. Evans (Llanerch, 1990)

Pseudo-Dionysius: The Complete Works, trans. C. Luibheid (New York and Mahwah, 1987)

Quintilian, *Institutio Oratoria*, ed. and trans. H. E. Butler (London, 1969)

Reading Abbey Cartularies: I. General Documents and those relating to English Counties other than Berkshire, ed. B. R. Kemp, Camden Society, fourth series 31 (London, 1986)

Recueil des actes de Charles III (le Simple), ed. P. Lauer, 2 vols (Paris, 1940–49)

Recueil des actes d'Henri II roi d'Angleterre et duc de Normandie concernant les provinces Françaises et les affaires de France, ed. E. Berger and L. Delisle, 3 vols and introduction (Paris, 1909–27)

Recueil des actes de Lothair et de Louis V, rois de France, ed. L. Halphen (Paris, 1908)

Recueil des actes de Louis VI roi de France (1108–1137), ed. R.-H. Bautier and J. Dufour, 4 vols (Paris, 1992–4)

Recueil des actes de Philippe Ier roi de France (1059–1108), ed. M. Prou (Paris, 1907)

Recueil des actes des ducs de Normandie de 911 à 1066, ed. M. Fauroux, MSAN, 36 (Caen, 1961)

Recueil des historiens des Gaules et de la France, ed. Dom. M. Bouquet, new edition published under the direction of L. Delisle, 24 vols (Paris, 1738–1904)

The Red Book of the Exchequer, ed. H. Hall, Rolls Series, 3 vols (London, 1896)

Regesta pontificum Romanorum, ed. P. Jaffé and G. Wattenbach (Leipzig, 1885–88)

Regesta regum Anglo-Normannorum 1066–1154 : I. Regesta Willemi Conquestoris et Willelmi Rufi 1066–1100, ed. H. W. C. Davis (Oxford, 1913)

Regesta Regum Anglo-Normannorum 1066–1154: II. Regesta Henrici Primi, 1100–1135, ed. C. Johnson and H. A. Cronne (Oxford, 1956)

Regesta regum Anglo-Normannorum, 1066–1154: III. Regesta regis Stephani ac Mathildis imperatricis ac Gaufridi et Henrici ducum Normannorum 1135–1154, ed. H. A. Cronne and R. H. C. Davis (Oxford, 1968)

Regesta regum Anglo-Normannorum: the acta of William I (1066–1087), ed. D. Bates (Oxford, 1998)

The Register of Pope Gregory VII 1073–1085. An English Translation, trans. H. E. J. Cowdrey (Oxford, 2002)

Registres du Trésor des Chartes, tome II: *Règnes des fils de Philippe le Bel. Première partie: règnes de Louis X le Hutin et de Philippe V le Long*, ed. J. Gueroult under the direction of R. Fawtier (Paris, 1966)

Richard of Poitiers, 'Ex chronico Richardi Pictaviensis', *RHGF*, ed. L. Delisle, vol. 12 (Paris, 1877), pp. 411–417

Richer of Saint-Rémi, *Histories*, ed. and trans. J. Lake, 2 vols (Cambridge, MA and London, 2011)

Rimbert, *Anskar: The Apostle of the North. 801–865. Translated from the Vita Anskarii by Bishop Rimbert, his Fellow Missionary and Successor*, trans. C. H. Robinson (London, 1921)

Robert of Torigni, 'The Chronicle of Robert of Torigni, Abbot of the Monastery of St. Michael in Peril of the Sea', in *Chronicles of the Reigns of Stephen, Henry II and Richard I*, ed. Richard Howlett, vol. 4 (London, 1889)

—— *Chronique de Robert de Torigni, abbé de Mont-Saint-Michel*, ed. L. Delisle, 2 vols (Rouen, 1872–73)

Robert of Tumbalena, *Epistola ad monachos sancti Michaeli de Monte de quodam monacho epileptico a leuitate conuerso*, PL, 150, cols. 1369–78

Robert the Monk's History of the First Crusade: Historia Iherosolimitana, trans. C. Sweetenham, Crusade Texts in Translation, 11 (Aldershot, 2005)

Rodulfus Glaber, *Opera*, ed. and trans. J. France (Oxford, 1989)

Rodulfus Tortarius, *Carmina*, ed. M. B. Ogle and D. M. Schullian (Rome, 1933)

Roger of Howden, *Chronica magistri Rogeri de Houedene*, ed. W. Stubbs, 4 vols (London, 1868–70)

Rogerii II Regis Diplomata Latina, ed. C. Brühl, Codex Diplomaticus Regni Siciliae: II.1 (Böhlau, Verlag, Köln, Wien, 1987)

Sallust, *Cataline's War, The Jugurthine War, Histories*, trans. with an introduction and notes by A. J. Woodman, Penguin Classics (London, 2007)

R.-N. Sauvage, *L'abbaye Saint-Martin de Troarn*, MSAN, 34 (1911)

J. R. Scott, 'Charters of Monk Horton Priory', *Archaeologia Cantiana*, 10 (1876)

Serlo of Bayeux, 'The Capture of Bayeux', ed. and trans. M. Arbabzadah in E. van Houts, 'The fate of priests' sons in Normandy with special reference to Serlo of Bayeux' *HSJ*, 25 (2014), 86–105

Sigibert of Gembloux, *Chronica*, ed. L. C. Bethmann, in *Monumenta Germanae Historica, Scriptores* 6, (Hanover, 1844), pp. 268–374

Simeon of Durham, *Symeonis monachi opera omnia*, ed. T. Arnold, Rolls Series, 2 vols (London, 1882–5)

Snorri Sturluson, *Heimskringla: A History of the Kings of Norway*, trans. L. M. Hollander (Austin, 1964)

Son of Charlemagne: A Contemporary Life of Louis the Pious, trans. A. Cabaniss (Clinton, MA, 1961)

The Song of Dermot and the Earl: An Old French Poem from the Carew Manuscript No. 596 in the Archiepiscopal Library at Lambeth Palace, ed. and trans. G. H. Orpen (Oxford, 1892)

W. Stubbs, *Select Charters and other Illustrations of English Constitutional History from the Earliest Times to the Reign of Edward the First*, ninth edition (Oxford, 1913)

Suetonius, *The Twelve Caesars*, trans. R. Graves revised by J. B. Rives (London, 2007)

Suger of Saint-Denis, *Suger: the Deeds of Louis the Fat*, trans. R. Cusimano and J. Moorhead (Washington, DC, 1992)

Thomas of Walsingham, *Gesta abbatum monasterii sancti Albani*, ed. H. T. Riley, Rolls Series, vol. 1 (London, 1867)

De translatione et miraculis beati Autberti, in *Chroniques Latines du Mont-Saint-Michel (IXᵉ–XIIᵉ siècle)*, ed. P. Bouet and O. Desbordes (Caen, 2009), pp. 229–55

The Treatise on the Laws and Customs of the Realm of England Commonly called Glanvill, ed. and trans. G. D. G. Hall, second edition (Oxford, 1993)

E. M. C. van Houts (ed. and trans.), *The Normans in Europe* (Manchester, 2000)

Wace, *The History of the Norman People: Wace's Roman de Rou*, trans. Glyn S. Burgess (Woodbridge, 2004)

Walter Map, *De nugis curialium: Courtiers' Trifles*, ed. and trans. M. R. James, revised by C. N. L. Brooke and R. A. B. Mynors (Oxford, 1983)

The Warenne (Hyde) Chronicle, ed. and trans. E. M. C. van Houts and R. Love (Oxford, 2013)

Warin, bishop of Beauvais, 'Peace oath proposed by Bishop Warin of Beauvais to King Robert the Pious (1023)', trans. R. Landes, in *The Peace of God: Social Violence and Religious Response in France around the Year 1000*, ed. T. Head and R. Landes (Ithaca and London, 1992), pp. 332–4

Warner of Rouen, *Moriuht*, ed. and trans. C. J. McDonough (Ontario, 1995)

William of Apulia, *La Geste de Robert Guiscard*, ed. M. Mathieu (Palermo, 1961)

William of Jumièges, Orderic Vitalis and Robert of Torigni, *The Gesta Normannorum Ducum of William of Jumièges, Orderic Vitalis, and Robert of Torigni*, ed. and trans. E. M. C. van Houts, 2 vols (Oxford, 1992–95)

William of Malmesbury, *Historia Novella*, ed. and trans. E. King and K. R. Potter (Oxford, 1998)

William of Malmesbury, *William of Malmesbury: Gesta Regum Anglorum*, ed. and trans. R. A. B. Mynors, R. M. Thomson, and M. Winterbotton, vol. 1 (Oxford, 1998)

William of Malmesbury, *Gesta Pontificum*, ed. and trans. M. Winterbottom, vol. 1 (Oxford, 2007)

William of Poitiers, *Gesta Guillelmi*, ed. and trans. R. H. C. Davis and M. Chibnall (Oxford, 1998)

Secondary Sources

R. Abels, *Lordship and Military Obligation in Anglo-Saxon England* (Berkeley and London, 1988)

—— 'Household men, mercenaries and Vikings in Anglo-Saxon England', in *Mercenaries and Paid Men: The Mercenary Identity in the Middle Ages*, ed. J. France (Leiden, 2008), pp. 143–65

L. Abrams, 'Conversion and assimilation', in *Cultures in Contact: Scandinavian Settlement in England in the Ninth and Tenth Centuries*, ed. D. M. Hadley and J. D. Richards (Turnhout, 2000), pp. 135–53

—— 'Early Normandy', *ANS*, 35 (2013), 45–64

W. M. Aird, *Robert Curthose, Duke of Normandy (c. 1050–1134)* (Woodbridge, 2008)

S. Airlie, 'The palace of memory: the Carolingian court as political centre', in *Courts and Regions in Medieval Europe*, ed. S. Rees Jones, R. Marks, and A. J. Minnis (York, 2000), pp. 1–20

—— 'The history of emotions and emotional history', *EME*, 10 (2001), 235–41

E. Albu, *The Normans in their Histories: Propaganda, Myth and Subversion* (Woodbridge, 2001)

A. Alexander, 'Riots, reform, and rivalry: religious life in Rouen, c. 1073–c. 1092', *ANS*, 33 (2011), 23–40

R. Allen, '"A proud and headstrong man": John of Ivry, bishop of Avranches and archbishop of Rouen, 1060–79', *Historical Research*, 83 (2010), 1–39

G. Althoff, '*Ira regis*: prolegomena to a history of royal anger', in *Anger's Past: Social Uses of an Emotion in the Middle Ages*, ed. B. H. Rosenwein (Ithaca, NY and London, 1998), pp. 59–74

—— *Otto III*, trans. P. G. Jestice (Pennsylvania, 2003)

—— *Family, Friends and Followers: Political and Social Bonds in Early Medieval Europe*, trans. C. Carroll (Cambridge, 2004)

M. M. Archibald, 'Anglo-Saxon coinage, Alfred to the Conquest', in *The Golden Age of Anglo-Saxon Art*, ed. J. Backhouse, D. H. Turner, and L. Webster (London, 1984), pp. 170–91

M. Arnoux, 'Before the *Gesta Normannorum* and beyond Dudo; some evidence on early Norman historiography', *ANS*, 22 (1999), 29–48

—— 'Border, trade route, or market? The Channel and the medieval European economy from the twelfth to the fifteenth century', *ANS*, 36 (2014), 39–52

L. Ashe, *Fiction and History in England, 1066–1200* (Cambridge, 2007)

M. Aurell, *The Plantagenet Empire, 1154–1224*, trans. D. Crouch (London, 2007)

B. S. Bachrach, 'The Angevin economy, 960–1060: ancient or feudal?', *Studies in Medieval and Renaissance History*, new series, 10 (1988), 3–55

—— *Fulk Nerra the Neo-Roman Consul, 987–1040: A Political Biography of the Angevin count* (Berkeley and London, 1993)

—— 'Writing Latin history for a lay audience c. 1000: Dudo of Saint-Quentin at the Norman court', *HSJ*, 20 (2009), 58–77

S. Bagge, *Kings, Politics, and the Right Order of the World in German Historiography, c. 950–1150* (Leiden, 2002)

—— *From Viking Stronghold to Christian Kingdom: State Formation in Norway, c. 900–1350* (Copenhagen, 2010)

H. Bainton, 'Literate sociability and historical writing in later twelfth-century England', *ANS*, 34 (2012), 23–39

J. W. Baldwin, *The Government of Philip Augustus: Foundations of French Royal Power in the Middle Ages* (Berkeley, Los Angeles, and Oxford, 1986)

A. Ballard, 'The Law of Breteuil', *EHR*, 30 (1915), 646–58

F. Barlow, *Edward the Confessor* (London, 1970)

—— *The English Church 1066–1154* (London, 1979)

—— *William Rufus* (London, 1988)

R. Barroux, 'L'anniversaire de la mort de Dagobert à Saint-Denis au XIIᵉ siècle', *Bulletin philologique et historique du comité des travaux historiques et scientifiques* (1942–43), 131–51

R. Bartlett, 'The conversion of a pagan society', *History*, 70 (1985), 185–201

—— *Trial by Fire and Water: The Medieval Judicial Ordeal* (Oxford, 1986)

—— *The Making of Europe: Conquest, Colonization and Cultural Change 950–1350* (London, 1993)

—— '"Mortal Enmities": The Legal Aspect of Hostility in the Middle Ages', T. Jones Pierce Lecture (Aberystwyth, 1998)

—— *England under the Norman and Angevin Kings, 1075–1225* (Oxford, 2000)

—— *Why Can the Dead Do Such Great Things? Saints and Worshippers from the Martyrs to the Reformation* (Princeton and Woodstock, 2013)

R. E. Barton, '"Zealous anger" and the renegotiation of aristocratic relationships in eleventh- and twelfth-century France', in *Anger's Past: The Social Uses of an Emotion in the Middle Ages*, ed. B. H. Rosenwein (Ithaca, NY, 1998), pp. 153–70

—— *Lordship in the County of Maine, c. 890–1160* (Woodbridge, 2004)

'Henry I, Count Helias of Maine, and the battle of Tinchebray', in *Henry I and the Anglo-Norman World: Studies in Memory of C. Warren Hollister*, ed. D. Fleming and J. M. Pope (Woodbridge, 2007), 63–90

—— 'Emotions and power in Orderic Vitalis', *ANS*, 33 (2011), 41–59

—— *Why Can the Dead Do Such Great Things? Saints and Worshippers from the Martyrs to the Reformation* (Princeton and Woodstock, 2013)

D. Bates, 'Notes sur l'aristocratie Normande', *Annales de Normandie*, 23 (1973), 7–38

—— 'The character and career of Odo, bishop of Bayeux (1049/50–1097)', *Speculum*, 50 (1975), 1–20

—— 'The origins of the justiciarship', *ANS*, 4 (1982), 1–12

—— *Normandy before 1066* (London, 1982)

—— 'The earliest Norman writs', *EHR*, 100 (1985), 266–84

—— 'Lord Sudeley's ancestors: the family of the counts of Amiens, Valois and the Vexin in France and England during the 11th century', in *The Sudeley – Lords of Toddington* (Thetford, 1987), pp. 34–48

—— *William the Conqueror* (London, 1989)

—— 'Normandy and England after 1066', *EHR*, 104 (1989), 851–80

—— [Review of] E. Searle, *Predatory Kinship and the Formation of Norman Power* (Berkeley and London, 1988) in *Speculum*, 65 (1990)

—— 'Rouen from 900 to 1204: from Scandinavian settlement to Angevin "capital"', in *Medieval Art, Architecture, and Archaeology at Rouen*, ed. J. Stratford, The British Archaeological Association Conference Transactions for the Year 1986 (1993), pp. 1–11

—— 'The rise and fall of Normandy, c. 911–1204', in *England and Normandy in the Middle Ages*, ed. D. Bates and A. Curry (London, 1994), pp. 19–35

—— 'Le rôle des évêques dans l'élaboration des actes ducaux et royaux entre 1066 et 1087', in *Les évêques normands du XIe siècle*, ed. P. Bouet and F. Neveux (Caen, 1995), pp. 103–15

—— 'The prosopographical study of Anglo-Norman royal charters', in *Family Trees and the Roots of Politics: The Prosopography of Britain and France from the Tenth to the Twelfth Century*, ed. K. S. B. Keats-Rohan (Woodbridge, 1997), pp. 89–102

—— 'West Francia: the northern principalities', in *The New Cambridge Medieval History III, c. 900–c. 1024*, ed. T. Reuter (Cambridge, 1999), pp. 398–419

—— 'Re-Ordering the Past and Negotiating the Present in Stenton's *First Century*', The Stenton Lecture 1999 (Reading, 2000)

—— 'The Conqueror's adolescence', *ANS*, 25 (2003), 1–18

—— 'The Conqueror's earliest historians and the writing of his biography', in *Writing Medieval Biography 750–1250: Essays in Honour of Professor Frank Barlow*, ed. D. Bates, J. Crick, and S. Hamilton (Woodbridge, 2006), pp. 129–41

—— 'The representation of queens and queenship in Anglo-Norman royal charters', in *Frankland: The Franks and the World of the Early Middle Ages. Essays in Honour of Dame Jinty Nelson*, ed. P. Fouracre and D. Ganz (Manchester, 2008), pp. 285–303

—— *The Normans and Empire: The Ford Lectures delivered in the University of Oxford during Hilary Term 2010* (Oxford, 2013)

D. Bates and P. Bauduin, 'Autour de l'année 1047: un acte de Guillaume, comte d'Arques, pour Fécamp (18 Juillet 1047)', in *De part et d'autre de la normandie médiévale: recueil d'études en hommage à François Neveux*, ed. P. Bouet, C. Bougy, B. Garnuier, and C. Maneuvrier (Caen, 2009), pp. 43–52

D. Bates and V. Gazeau, 'L'abbaye de Grestain et la famille d'Herluin de Conteville', *Annales de Normandie*, 40 (1990), 5–30

M. Bateson, 'The Laws of Breteuil', *EHR*, 15 (1900), 73–8, 302–18, 496–523, 754–7; 16 (1901), 92–110, 332–45

M.-P. Baudry, 'La politique de fortification des Plantagenêts en Poitou, 1154–1242', *ANS*, 24 (2002), 43–69

P. Bauduin, 'Une famille châtelaine sur les confins normanno-manceaux: les Géré (Xᵉ–XIIIᵉ s.)', *Archéologie Médiévale*, 22 (1992), 309–56

—— 'Du bon usage de la dos dans la Normandie ducale (Xᵉ–début XIIᵉ siècle)', in *Dots et douaires dans le haut Moyen Age*, ed. F. Bougard, L. Feller, and R. Le Jan (Rome, 2002), pp. 429–65

—— *La première Normandie (Xᵉ–XIᵉ siècles). Sur les frontières de la Haute Normandie: Identité et construction d'une principauté* (Caen, 2004)

—— 'Les fondations Scandinaves en occident et les débuts du duché de Normandie', in *Les fondations Scandinaves en occident et les débuts du duché de Normandie*, ed. P. Bauduin (Caen, 2005), pp. 3–9

—— 'Chefs Normands et élites Franques, fin IXᵉ–début Xe siècle', in *Les fondations Scandinaves en occident et les débuts du duché de Normandie*, ed. P. Bauduin (Caen, 2005), pp. 181–94

—— 'Autour d'un rituel discuté: le baisement du pied de Charles le Simple au moment du traité de Saint-Clair-sur-Epte', in *Des châteaux et des sources: archéologie et histoire dans la Normandie médiévale. Mélanges en l'honneur d'Anne-Marie Flambard Héricher*, ed. E. Lalou, B. Lepeuple, and J.-L. Roch (Rouen, 2008), pp. 29–47

S. Baxter, *The Earls of Mercia: Lordship and Power in Late Anglo-Saxon England* (Oxford, 2007)

M. Baylé, 'Le décor sculpté de Saint-Georges-de-Boscherville: quelques questions de style et d'iconographie', *ANS*, 8 (1986), 27–45

—— 'Jumièges: abbatial Notre-Dame', in *L'architecture normande au Moyen Age*, ed. M. Baylé, 2 vols (Caen, 2001), ii. 32–6

—— 'Bayeux: cathédrale Notre-Dame', in *L'architecture normande au Moyen Age*, ed. M. Baylé, 2 vols (Caen, 2001), ii. 37–42

F. de Beaurepaire, 'La diffusion de la toponymie scandinave dans la Normandie ducale', *Tabularia 'Études'*, 2 (2002), 47–56

J. Beckerman, 'Succession in Normandy, 1087, and in England, 1066: the role of testamentary custom', *Speculum*, 47 (1972), 258–60

G. Beech, 'The participation of Aquitainians in the conquest of England, 1066–1100', *ANS*, 9 (1987), 1–24

I. P. Bejczy, 'Law and ethics: twelfth-century jurists on the virtue of justice', *Viator*, 36 (2005), 197–216

J. W. Bernhardt, *Itinerant Kingship and Royal Monasteries in Early Medieval Germany, c. 936–1075* (Cambridge, 1993)

M. Biddle, 'Seasonal festivals and residence: Winchester, Westminster and Gloucester in the tenth to twelfth centuries', *ANS*, 8 (1986), 51–72

T. A. M. Bishop, *Scriptores Regis: Facsimiles to Identify the Hands of Royal Scribes in Original Charters of Henry I, Stephen and Henry II* (Oxford, 1961)

T. N. Bisson, *Conservation of Coinage: Monetary Exploitation and its Restraint in France, Catalonia and Aragon, c. 1000–1225AD* (Oxford, 1979)

—— 'The "annuary" of Abbot Robert de Torigni (1155–1159)', *ANS*, 33 (2011), 61–73

M. Bloch, *The Historians' Craft*, trans. P. Putman with a preface by Peter Burke (Manchester, 1954 and 1992)

—— *Feudal Society*, 2 vols, trans. L. A. Manyon (London, 1961)

J. Boorman, '*Nisi feceris* under Henry II', *ANS*, 24 (2002), 85–97

M. de Boüard, 'De la Neustrie carolingienne a la Normandie féodale: continuité ou discontinuité?', *Bulletin of the Institute of Historical Research*, 28 (1955), 1–14

—— 'La duché de Normandie', in *Histoire des institutions françaises au Moyen Age: I. Institutions seigneuriales. Les droits du roi exercés par les grands vassaux*, ed. F. Lot and R. Fawtier (Paris, 1957), pp. 1–33

—— 'Sur les origines de la trêve de Dieu en Normandie', *Annales de Normandie* 9 (1959), 169–89

—— 'Notes et hypothèses sur Maurille, moine de Fécamp', in *L'abbaye bénédictine de Fécamp. Ouvrage scientifique du XIIIe centenaire (658–1958)*, 4 vols (Fécamp, 1959), i. 81–92

—— 'La salle dite de l'Echiquier, au château de Caen', *Medieval Archaeology*, 9 (1965), 64–81

—— *Le Château de Caen* (Caen, 1979)

C. B. Bouchard, 'Family structure and family consciousness among the aristocracy in the ninth to eleventh centuries', *Francia*, 14 (1986), 639–58

—— *Strong of Body, Brave and Noble: Chivalry and Society in Medieval France* (London, 1998)

—— *Those of My Blood: Constructing Noble Families in Medieval Francia* (Philadelphia, 2001)

P. Bouet, 'Dudon de Saint-Quentin et le martyre de Guillaume Longue-Epée', in *Les saints dans la Normandie médiévale*, ed. P. Bouet and F. Neveux (Caen, 2000), pp. 237–58.

—— 'Le Mont-Saint-Michel entre Bretagne et Normandie de 960 à 1060', in *Bretons et Normans au moyen âge: rivalités, malentendus, convergences*, ed. J. Quaghebeur and B. Merdrignac (Rennes, 2008), pp. 165–200

P. Bouet and M. Dosdat, 'Les évêques normands de 985 à 1150', in *Les évêques normands du XIe siècle*, ed. P. Bouet and F. Neveux (Caen, 1995), 19–37

J. Boussard, 'Le comté de Mortain au XIe siècle', *Moyen Age*, 58 (1952), 253–79

J.-M. Bouvris, 'Une famille de vassaux des vicomtes de Bayeux au XIe siècle: Les Broc', *Revue du Département de la Manche*, 19 (1977)

—— 'Un bref inédit de Robert Courte-Heuse, duc de Normandie, relatif à l'abbaye de Montebourg, au diocèse de Coutances', in *Actes du cent cinquième congrès national des sociétés savants (Caen, 1980), section de philologie et d'histoire jusqu'à 1610* (Paris, 1984), pp. 125–50

—— 'Contribution à une étude de l'institution vicomtale en Normandie au XIe siècle. L'exemple de la partie orientale du duché: les vicomtes de Rouen et de Fécamp', in *Autour du pouvoir ducal normand, Xe–XIIe siècles*, ed. L. Musset, J.-M. Bouvris, and J.-M. Maillefer (Caen, 1985), pp. 149–74

'Aux origines du prieuré de Vains', *Revue de l'Avranchin et du pays de Granville*, 64 (1987), 3–21, 67–90

—— *Dans la marais du Cotentin à la fin du XIe siècle. Autour de la fondation du prieuré de Baupte, dépendance de l'abbaye de Saint-Etienne de Caen*, MSAN, 43 (2009)

E. Bozoky, 'The sanctity and canonization of Edward the Confessor', in *Edward the Confessor: The Man and the Legend*, ed. R. Mortimer (Woodbridge, 2009), pp. 173–86

J. Bradbury, *The Medieval Siege* (Woodbridge, 1992)

L. W. Breese, 'The persistence of Scandinavian connections in Normandy in the tenth and early eleventh centuries', *Viator*, 8 (1977), 47–61

M. Brett, *The English Church under Henry I* (Oxford, 1975)

K. Brockhaus, *L'abbatiale de la Trinité de Fécamp et l'architecture normande au Moyen Age*, MSAN, 44 (Caen, 2009)

C. N. L. Brooke, 'Princes and kings as patrons of monasteries', *Il monachesmo e la riforma ecclesiastica (1049–1122)*, Miscellanea del Centro di Studi Medioevali, 6 (Milan, 1971), pp. 125–44

N. Brooks, 'The archbishop of Canterbury and the so-called introduction of knight-service into England', *ANS*, 34 (2012), 41–62

P. Brown, *The Cult of the Saints: Its Rise and Function in Latin Christianity* (Chicago, 1981)

R. A. Brown, *The Normans* (Woodbridge, 1984)

—— 'Some observations on Norman and Anglo-Norman charters', in *Tradition and Change: Essays in Honour of Marjorie Chibnall*, ed. D. Greenway, C. Holdsworth, and J. Sayers (Cambridge, 1985), pp. 145–63

S. B. D. Brown, 'The mercenary and his master: military service and monetary reward in the eleventh and twelfth centuries', *History*, 74 (1989), 20–38

—— 'Leavetaking: lordship and mobility in England and Normandy in the twelfth century', *History*, 79 (1994), 199–215

S. B. D. Brown, 'The mercenary and his master: military service and monetary reward in the eleventh and twelfth centuries', *History*, 74 (1989), 20–38

—— 'Leavetaking: lordship and mobility in England and Normandy in the twelfth century', *History*, 79 (1994), 199–215

W. Brown, 'Charters as weapons: on the role played by early medieval dispute records in the disputes they record', *JMH*, 28 (2002), 227–48

G. Bührer-Thierry, '"Just anger" or "vengeful anger"? The punishment of blinding in the early medieval west', in *Anger's Past: Social Uses of an Emotion in the Middle Ages*, ed. B. H. Rosenwein (Ithaca, NY and London, 1998), pp. 75–91

M. Bur, *La formation du comté de Champagne v. 950–v. 1150* (Nancy, 1977)

R. C. van Caenegem, *Royal Writs in England from the Conquest to Glanville: Studies in the Early History of the Common Law*, Selden Society 77 (1959)

—— 'Public Prosecution of Crime in Twelfth-Century England', in *Church and Government in the Middle Ages: Essays presented to C. R. Cheney on his 70th Birthday*, ed. Christopher N. L. Brooke, D. E. Luscombe, G. H. Martin, and D. Owen (Cambridge, 1976), pp. 41–76

J. Callas, 'A Thor's hammer found in Normandy', in *Viking Trade and Settlement in Continental Western Europe*, ed. I. S. Klæsøe (Copenhagen, 2010), pp. 145–7

D. Campbell, 'The *capitulaire de uillis*, the *Breuium exempla*, and the Carolingian court at Aachen', *EME*, 18 (2010), 243–64

J. Canning, *A History of Medieval Political Thought 300–1450* (London, 1996)

D. Carpenter, *The Minority of Henry III* (London, 1990)

N. Cazauran, 'Richard sans peur: un personnage en quête d'auteur', *Travaux de Littérature*, 4 (1991), 21–43

P. Chaplais, 'The seals and original charters of Henry I', *EHR*, 75 (1960), 260–75

—— 'The Anglo-Saxon chancery: from the diploma to the writ', *Journal of the Society of Archivists*, 3 (1965–9), 160–76, reprinted in *Prisca Munimenta: Studies in Archival and Administrative History presented to Dr A. E. J. Hollaender*, ed. F. Ranger (London, 1973), pp. 43–62

I. Chave, C. Corvisier, and J. Desloges, 'Le château d'Argentan (XIᵉ–XVᵉ siècle): du castrum Roman à la residence princière', in *Argentan et ses environs au Moyen Age: approche historique et archéologique*, ed. M.-A. Moulin et al. (Caen, 2008), pp. 115–206

P. Chesnel, *Le Cotentin et l'Avranchin (département de la Manche) sous les ducs de Normandie (911–1204): institutions et état social de la Normandie* (Caen, 1912)

M. Chibnall, 'Mercenaries and the *familia Regis* under Henry I', *History*, 62 (1977), 15–23

—— 'Military service in Normandy before 1066', *ANS*, 5 (1983), pp. 65–77

—— *The World of Orderic Vitalis: Norman Monks and Norman Knights* (Woodbridge, 1984)

—— 'Anglo-French relations in the work of Orderic Vitalis', in *Documenting the Past: Essays in Medieval History presented to George Peddy Cuttino*, ed. J. S. Hamilton and P. J. Bradley (Woodbridge, 1989), pp. 5–19

—— 'Orderic Vitalis on castles', in *Studies in Medieval History Presented to R. Allen Brown*, ed. C. Harper-Bill et al. (Woodbridge, 1989), pp. 43–56

—— *The Empress Matilda: Queen Consort, Queen Mother, and Lady of the English* (Oxford, 1991)

E. Christiansen, *The Norsemen in the Viking Age* (Oxford, 2002)

M. Clanchy, *From Memory to Written Record: England 1066–1307*, second edition (Oxford, 1993)

K. Conant, *Carolingian and Romanesque Architecture 800–1200*, second integrated edition (London, 1978)

G. Constable, 'Letters and letter collections', *Typologie des Sources du Moyen Age Occidental*, 17 (Turnhout, 1976)

S. Corcoran, 'Before Constantine', in *The Cambridge Companion to the Age of Constantine*, ed. N. Lenski (Cambridge, 2005), pp. 35–58

M. Costambeys, M. Innes, and S. MacLean, *The Carolingian World* (Cambridge, 2011)

L. H. Cottineau, *Répertoire topo-bibliographique des abbayes et prieurés*, 2 vols (Maçon, 1935–1937)

C. L. H. Coulson, 'Rendability and castellation in medieval France', *Château Gaillard*, 6 (1973), 59–69

—— 'Fortress-policy in Capetian tradition and Angevin practice: aspects of the conquest of Normandy by Philip II', *ANS*, 6 (1984), 13–38

—— 'Cultural realities and reappraisals in English castle-study', *JMH*, 22 (1996), 171–208

—— 'Peaceable power in English castles', *ANS*, 23 (2001), 69–95

S. Coupland, 'From poachers to gamekeepers: Scandinavian warlords and Carolingian kings', *EME*, 7 (1998), 85–114

—— 'Trading places: Quentovich and Dorestad reassessed', *EME*, 11 (2002), 209–32

L. Couppey, *Notes historiques sur le prieuré conventuel d'Héauville de la Hague* (Evreux, 1898)

—— *Encore Héauville! Supplément aux notes historiques sur le prieur, conventuel d'Héauville la Hague*, Revue catholique de Normandie, 10 (1900–01)

S. Coviaux, 'Baptême et conversion des chefs scandinaves du IXe au XIe siècle', in *Les fondations Scandinaves en occident et les duts du duché de Normandie*, ed. P. Bauduin (Caen, 2005), pp. 67–80

H. E. J. Cowdrey, 'The Peace and the Truce of God in the eleventh century', *Past and Present* 46 (1970), 42–67

—— *Pope Gregory VII, 1073–1085* (Oxford, 1998)

—— *Lanfranc: Scholar, Monk, and Archbishop* (Oxford, 2003)

O. Creighton, *Early European Castles: Aristocracy and Authority, AD800–1200* (London, 2012)

D. Crouch, *The Beaumont Twins: The Roots and Branches of Power in the Twelfth Century* (Cambridge, 1986)

—— *William Marshal: Court, Career and Chivalry in the Angevin Empire* (Harlow, 1990)

—— *The Image of Aristocracy in Britain, 1000–1300* (London, 1992)

—— *The Normans: The History of a Dynasty* (London, 2002)

—— 'Robert, earl of Gloucester', *Oxford Dictionary of National Biography*, vol. 47 (Oxford, 2003)

—— *The Birth of Nobility* (Harlow, 2005)

—— 'Robert of Beaumont, count of Meulan and Leicester: his lands, his acts, and his self-image', in *Henry I and the Anglo-Norman World: Studies in Memory of C. Warren Hollister*, ed. D. F. Fleming and J. M. Pope (Woodbridge, 2007), pp. 91–116

—— *The English Aristocracy, 1066–1272: A Social Transformation* (New Haven, CT and London, 2011)

C. Cubitt, 'Sites and sanctity: revisiting the cult of murdered and martyred Anglo-Saxon royal saints', *EME*, 9 (2000), 53–83

P. Dalton, *Conquest, Anarchy and Lordship: Yorkshire 1066–1154* (Cambridge, 1994)

—— 'Allegiance and intelligence in King Stephen's reign', in *King Stephen's Reign (1135–54)*, ed. P. Dalton and G. J. White (Woodbridge, 2008), pp. 80–97

C. W. David, *Robert Curthose, Duke of Normandy* (Cambridge MA, 1920)

K. Davies, 'The count of the Cotentin: western Normandy, William of Mortain, and the career of Henry I', *HSJ*, 22 (2012), 123–40

R. H. C. Davis, 'William of Jumièges, Robert Curthose and the Norman succession', *EHR*, 95 (1980), 597–606

G. Davy, *Le duc et la loi: héritages, images et expressions du pouvoir normatif dans la duché de Normandie, des origins à la mort du Conquérant (fin du IXe siècle-1087)* (Paris, 2004)

R. DeAragon, 'The Growth of Secure Inheritance in Anglo-Norman England', *JMH*, 8 (1982), 381–91

J. Decaëns, 'Le motte d'Olivet à Grimbosq (Calvados): résidence seigneriale du XIe siècle, *Archéologie Médiévale*, 11 (1981), 167–201

—— 'Le Patrimoine des Grentemesnil en Normandie, en Angleterre et en Italie aux XIe et XIIe siècles', in *Les Normands en Méditerranée dans le sillages des Tancrède*, ed. P. Bouet and F. Neveux, (Caen, 1994), pp. 123–40

—— 'Le premier château, de Guillaume le Conquérant à Richard Cœur de Lion (XIe–XIIe siècles)', in *Mémoires du Château de Caen*, ed. J.-Y. Marin and J.-M. Levesque (Caen, 2000), pp. 15–21

—— 'Le château de Domfront', in *L'Architecture normande au moyen age: 2. Les étapes de la création*, ed. M. Baylé, second edition (Caen, 2001), pp. 288–90

S. Deck, 'Le comté d'Eu sous les ducs', *Annales de Normandie*, 4 (1954), 99–116

M. DeJong, 'Power and humility in Carolingian society: the public penance of Louis the Pious', *EME*, 1 (1992), 29–52

—— *The Penitential State: Authority and Atonement in the Age of Louis the Pious, 814–840* (Cambridge, 2009)

F. Delacampagne, 'Seigneurs, fiefs et mottes du Cotentin (X^e–XIIe siècles): étude historique et topographique', *Archéologie Médiévale*, 12 (1982)

G.-A. de la Roque, *Histoire généalogique de la maison de Harcourt*, 4 vols (Paris, 1662)

L. Delisle, *Études sur la condition de la classe agricole et l'état de l'agriculture en Normandie, au moyen âge* (Evreux, 1851)

—— *Histoire du château et des sires de Saint-Sauveur-le-Vicomte, suivi des pièces justificatives* (Paris, 1867)

L. Delisle and L. Passy, *Memoires et notes de M. Auguste Le Prevost pour servir a l'histoire du département de l'Eure*, 3 vols (Evreux, 1862–69)

Abbé M. Desroches, 'Analyse des titres et chartes de l'abbaye de Savigny', MSAN, second series 10 (1853), 252–78

M. Dietler, 'Feasts and commensal politics in the political economy: food, power and status in prehistoric Europe', in *Food and the Status Quest: An Interdisciplinary Perspective*, ed. P. Wiessner and W. Schiefenhövel (Oxford, 1996), pp. 87–125

P. Dixon, 'Design in castle-building: the controlling of access to the lord', *Château Gaillard*, 18 (1998), 47–57

—— 'The myth of the keep', in *The Seigneurial Residence in Western Europe AD c.800–1600*, ed. G. Meirion-Jones, E. Impey, and M. Jones, BAR International Series (Oxford, 2002), pp. 9–13

—— 'The influence of the White Tower on the great towers of the twelfth century', in *The White Tower*, ed. E. Impey (New Haven, CT and London, 2008), pp. 243–75

P. Dixon and P. Marshall, 'Norwich castle and its analogues', in *The Seigneurial Residence in Western Europe AD c.800–1600*, ed. G. Meirion-Jones, E. Impey, and M. Jones, BAR International Series (Oxford, 2002), pp. 235–43

H. Doherty, 'La bataille de Tinchebray et les actes d'Henri Ier', in *Tinchebray 1106–2006: actes du colloque de Tinchebray (28–30 Septembre 2006)*, ed. V. Gazeau and J. Green (Flers, 2009), pp. 167–87

M. Dolley and J. Yvon, 'A group of tenth-century coins found at Mont-Saint-Michel', *British Numismatic Journal*, 40 (1971), 1–16

D. C. Douglas, 'Rollo of Normandy', *EHR*, 57 (1942), 417–36

—— 'The ancestors of William fitz Osbern', *EHR*, 59 (1944), 62–79

—— 'The earliest Norman counts' *EHR*, 61 (1946), 129–56

—— *William the Conqueror* (London, 1964)

G. Duby, *The Chivalrous Society*, trans. C. Postan (London, 1977)

—— *Medieval Marriage: Two Models from Twelfth-Century France*, trans. E. Forster (London, 1978)

—— *France in the Middle Ages 987–1460: from Hugh Capet to Joan of Arc*, trans. J. Vale (Oxford, 1991)

—— *Love and Marriage in the Middle Ages*, trans. J. Dunnett (Cambridge, 1994)

W. Duczko, 'Danes and Swedes in written and archaeological sources at the end of the 9th century', in *Wulfstan's Voyage: The Baltic Sea Region in the Early Viking Age as seen from Shipboard*, ed. A. Englert and A. Trakadas, Maritime Culture of the North, 2 (Roskilde, 2009), pp. 58–71

F. Dumas, 'Les monnaies Normandes (X^e–XIIe siècles) avec un répertoire des trouvailles', *Révue Numismatique*, 21 (1979), 84–140

—— 'Un denier normand au nom de Robert, comte', *Bulletin de la société françoise de numismatique*, 35 (1980), 669–70

F. Dumas-Dubourg, *Le trésor de Fécamp et le monnayage en Francie occidentale pendant la seconde moitié du Xe siècle* (Paris, 1971)

F. Dumas and J. Pilet-Lemière, 'La monnaie normand – X^e–Xe siècles: Le point de la recherche en 1987', in *Les mondes normands (VIIIe–XIIe siècles)* (Caen, 1989), pp. 125–31

J. Dunbabin, *France in the Making 843–1180* (Oxford, 1991)

K. Dutton, 'Angevin scribes and collaborative charter production, *c.* 1109–1151', paper read at the Leeds International Medieval Congress, 8 July 2014

E. Eames, 'Mariage et concubinage légal en Norvège à l'époque des Vikings', *Annales de Normandie*, 2 (1952), 195–208

H. Ellis, *A General Introduction to Domesday Book* (London, 1833)

H. Enzensberger, 'Chanceries, charters and administration in Norman Italy', in *The Society of Norman Italy*, ed. G. A. Loud and A. Metcalfe (Leiden, 2002), pp.117–50

J. Everard and J. C. Holt, *Jersey 1204: The Forging of an Island Community* (London, 2004)

D. H. Farmer, *The Oxford Dictionary of Saints*, third edition (Oxford, 1992)

W. Farrer, 'An outline itinerary of King Henry I', *EHR*, 34 (1919), 303–82, 505–79

—— *Honors and Knights Fees. Volume 3: Arundel, Eudes the Sewer, Warenne* (Manchester, 1925)

G. Fellows-Jensen, 'Les relations entre la Normandie et les colonies scandinaves', in *Les fondations Scandinaves en occident et les débuts du duché de Normandie*, ed. P. Bauduin (Caen, 2005), pp. 225–39

F. Fichet de Clairfontaine, J. Mastrolorenzo, and R. Brown, 'Le château de Falaise (Calvados): état des connaissances sur l'évolution du site castral du dixième au treizième siècles', in *Castles and the Anglo-Norman World: Proceedings of a Conference held at Norwich Castle in 2012*, ed. J. A. Davies, A. Riley, J.-M. Levesque, and C. Lapiche (Oxford, 2016), pp. 231–55

A. M. Flambard Héricher, 'Fortifications de terre et residences en Normandie (XIe–XIIIe siècles)', *Château Gaillard*, 20 (Caen, 2002)

R. Fleming, 'Christ Church Canterbury's Anglo-Norman cartulary', in *Anglo-Norman Political Culture and the Twelfth-Century Renaissance*, ed. C. W. Hollister (Woodbridge, 1997), pp. 83–156

—— *Domesday Book and the Law: Society and Legal Custom in Early Medieval History* (Cambridge, 1998)

—— 'The new wealth, the new rich, and the new political style', *ANS*, 23 (2001), 1–22

R. Fletcher, *Bloodfeud: Murder and Revenge in Anglo-Saxon England* (London, 2003)

R. Foreville, 'Aux origines de la renaissance juridique. Concepts juridiques et influences romanisantes chez Guillaume de Poitiers, biographe du Conquérant', *La Moyen Age*, 58 (1952), 43–83

—— 'The synod of the province of Rouen in the eleventh and twelfth centuries', in *Church and Government in the Middle Ages*, ed. C. N. L. Brooke, D. E. Luscombe, G. H. Martin, and D. Owen (Cambridge, 1976), pp. 19–39

H. de Formeville, *Histoire de l'ancien évêché-comté de Lisieux* (Lisieux, 1873)

E. A. Freeman, *The History of the Norman Conquest of England, its Causes and its Results*, vol. 1 (Oxford, 1873)

V. H. Galbraith 'Royal charters to Winchester', *EHR*, 35 (1920), 383–400

F. L. Ganshof, *Frankish Institutions under Charlemagne*, trans. B. Lyon and M. Lyon (New York, 1968)

D. Ganz, 'Humour as history in Notker's *Gesta Karoli Magni*' in *Monks, Nuns and Friars in Medieval Society*, ed. E. B. King, J. T. Schaefer, and W. B. Wadley (Sewanee, TN, 1989), pp. 171–83

I. H. Garipzanov, 'Communication of authority in Carolingian titles', *Viator*, 36 (2005), 41–82

G. Garnett, '"Ducal" succession in early Normandy', in *Law and Government in Medieval England and Normandy: Essays in Honour of Sir James Holt*, ed. G. Garnett and J. Hudson (Cambridge, 1994), pp. 80–110

—— *Conquered England: Kingship, Succession, and Tenure 1066–1166* (Oxford, 2007)

—— 'Robert Curthose: the duke who lost his trousers', *ANS*, 35 (2013), 213–43

B. Gauthiez, 'Hypothèses sur la fortification de Rouen au onzième siècle: le donjon, la tour de Richard II et l'enceinte de Guillaume', *ANS*, 14 (1992), 61–76

—— 'The urban development of Rouen, 989–1345', in *Society and Culture in Medieval Rouen, 911–1300*, ed. L. V. Hicks and E. Brenner (Turnhout, 2013), pp. 17–64

V. Gazeau, 'Le patrimoine d'Hughes de Bayeux (*c.* 1011–1049)', in *Les éveques normands du XIe siècle*, ed. P. Bouet and F. Neveux (Caen, 1995), pp. 139–47

—— *Normannia monastica: prosopographie des abbés bénédictins (X^e–XIIe siècle)*, 2 vols (Caen, 2007)

—— 'Femmes en religion, personnes d'autorité: les abbesses normandes (XIe–XIIIe siècles)', *ANS*, 35 (2013), 17–33

R. Génestal, 'La formation et le dévelopment de la coutume de normandie', *Travaux de la Semaine d'histoire du droit normand tenue à Guernesey du 26 au 30 Mai, 1927* (1928), 37–58

C. de Gerville, 'Mémoire sur les anciens châteaux du département de la Manche', MSAN, 1 (1825)

M. T. Gibson, *Lanfranc of Bec* (Oxford, 1978)

J. Gillingham, 'The introduction of knight service into England', *ANS*, 4 (1982), 53–64

—— 'William the Bastard at war', in *Studies in Medieval History Presented to R. Allen Brown*, ed. C. Harper-Bill et al. (Woodbridge, 1989), pp. 141–58

—— 'Doing homage to the king of France', in *Henry II: New Interpretations*, ed. C. Harper-Bill and N. Vincent (Woodbridge, 2007), pp. 63–84

J. R. Ginther, 'Between *plena caritas* and *plenitudo legis*: the ecclesiology of the Norman Anonymous', *HSJ*, 22 (2012), 141–62

S. E. Gleason, *An Ecclesiastical Barony of the Middle Ages: The Bishopric of Bayeux, 1066–1204* (Cambridge, MA, 1936)

J. Glenn, *Politics and History in the Tenth Century: The Work and World of Richer of Reims* (Cambridge, 2004)

M. Godden, 'Money, power and morality in late Anglo-Saxon England', *Anglo-Saxon England*, 19 (1990), 41–65

B. Golding, 'Robert of Mortain', *ANS*, 13 (1991), 119–44

B. Gowers, '996 and all that: the Norman peasants' revolt reconsidered', *EME*, 21 (2013), 71–98

A. Gransden, *Historical Writing in England, c. 550–c. 1327* (London, 1974)

L. Grant, 'Suger and the Anglo-Norman world', *ANS*, 19 (1997), 51–68

—— *Abbot Suger of Saint-Denis: Church and State in Early Twelfth-Century France* (London, 1998)

—— *Architecture and Society in Normandy 1120–1270* (New Haven, CT and London, 2005)

W. Grape, *The Bayeux Tapestry* (Munich, London, and New York, 1994)

J. Green, 'William Rufus, Henry I and the royal demesne', *History*, 64 (1979)

—— 'The sheriffs of William the Conqueror', *ANS*, 5 (1983), 129–45

—— 'Lords of the Norman Vexin', in *War and Government in the Middle Ages: Essays in Honour of J. O. Prestwich*, ed. J. Gillingham and J. C. Holt (Woodbridge, 1984), pp. 47–61

—— *The Government of England under Henry I* (Cambridge, 1986)

—— 'Unity and disunity in the Anglo-Norman state', *Historical Research*, 62 (1989), 114–34

—— *English Sheriffs to 1154* (London, 1990)

—— *The Aristocracy of Norman England* (Cambridge, 1997)

—— 'Robert Curthose reassessed', *ANS*, 20 (2000), 95–116

—— 'King Henry I and northern England', *Transactions of the Royal Historical Society*, 17 (2007)

'Henry I and the origins of the civil war', in *King Stephen's Reign 1135–1154*, ed. P. Dalton and G. J. White (Woodbridge, 2008), pp. 11–26

—— *Henry I King of England and Duke of Normandy* (Cambridge, 2006)

—— 'Duchesses of Normandy in the eleventh and twelfth centuries', in *Normandy and its Neighbours, 900–1250: Essays for David Bates*, ed. D. Crouch and K. Thompson (Turnhout, 2011), pp. 43–59

P. Grierson, 'The monetary system under William I', in *Domesday Book Studies*, ed. R. W. H. Erskine and A. Williams (London, 1987), pp. 75–9

O. Guillot, *Le comte d'Anjou et son entourage au XIe siècle*, 2 vols (Paris, 1972)

—— 'La conversion des Normands peu après 911: des refets contemporains à l'historiographie ultiérieure (X^e–XIe siècles)', *Cahiers de civilsation médiévale*, 24 (1981), 181–219

M. Guilmin, 'Un exemple de réseau relationnel de l'aristocratie anglo-normande, les Paynel et leur entourage (milieu du XIe siècle–début du XIIe siècle', in *Tinchebray 1106–2006: actes du colloque de Tinchebray (28–30 Septembre 2006)*, ed. V. Gazeau and J. Green (Flers, 2009), pp. 221–34.

D. M. Hadley, *The Northern Danelaw: Its Social Structure, c. 800–1100* (London, 2000)

—— '"Hamlet and the princes of Denmark": lordship in the Danelaw, c. 860–954', in *Cultures in Contact: Scandinavian Settlement in England in the Ninth and Tenth Centuries*, ed. D. M. Hadley and J. D. Richards (Turnhout, 2000), pp. 107–32

—— *The Vikings in England: Settlement, Society and Culture* (Manchester, 2006)

M. Hagger, 'Kinship and identity in eleventh-century Normandy: the case of Hugh de Grandmesnil, c. 1040–1098', *JMH*, 32 (2006), 212–30

—— 'The Norman *vicomte* c. 1035–1135: what did he do?', *ANS*, 29 (2007), 65–83

—— 'A pipe roll for 25 Henry I', *EHR*, 122 (2007), 133–140

—— 'The earliest Norman writs revisited', *Historical Research*, 82 (2009), 181–205

—— 'Theory and practice in the making of twelfth-century pipe rolls' in *Records, Administration and Aristocratic Society in the Anglo-Norman Realm*, ed. N. Vincent (Woodbridge, 2009), 45–74

—— 'Secular law and custom in ducal Normandy, c. 1000–1144', *Speculum*, 85 (2010), 827–67

—— 'How the west was won: the Norman dukes and the Cotentin, c. 987–c. 1087', *JMH*, 38 (2012), 20–55

—— 'Lordship and lunching: interpretations of eating and food in the Anglo-Norman world, 1050–1200, with reference to the Bayeux Tapestry', in *The English and Their Legacy, 900-1200. Essays in Honour of Ann Williams*, ed. D. Roffe (Woodbridge, 2012), pp. 229–44

—— *William: King and Conqueror* (London, 2012)

—— 'Le gouvernement *in absentia*: la Normandie sous Henri Beauclerc, 1106–1135', in *Penser les mondes normandes médiévaux (911–2011)*, ed. D. Bates and P. Bauduin (Caen, 2017)

E. M. Hallam, 'The kings and the princes in eleventh-century France', *Bulletin of the Institute of Historical Research*, 53 (1980), 143–56

E. M. Hallam and J. Everard, *Capetian France 987–1328*, second edition (London, 2001)

L. Halphen, *Le comté d'Anjou au XIᵉ Siècle* (Paris, 1906)

G. Halsall (ed.), *Humour, History and Politics in Late Antiquity and the Early Middle Ages* (Cambridge, 2002)

C. Hart, 'The Bayeux Tapestry and schools of illumination at Canterbury', *ANS*, 22 (2000), 117–67

S. Harvey, *Domesday Book of Judgement* (Oxford, 2014)

C. H. Haskins, 'The administration of Normandy under Henry I', *EHR*, 24 (1909), 209–31

—— *Norman Institutions* (Cambridge, MA, 1918)

T. Head and R. Landes (ed.), *The Peace of God: Social Violence and Religious Response in France around the Year 1000* (Ithaca, NY and London, 1992)

P. Healy, *The Chronicle of Hugh of Flavigny: Reform and the Investiture Contest in the Late Eleventh Century* (Aldershot, 2006)

P. Heather, *Empires and Barbarians: Migration, Development and the Birth of Europe* (London, 2010)

R. Helmerichs, '*Princeps, comes, dux Normannorum*: early Rollonid designators and their significance', *HSJ*, 9 (2001), 57–77

J. Hemming, '*Sellan gestare*: saddle-bearing punishments of medieval Europe and the case of Rhinnon', *Viator*, 28 (1997), 45–64

S. Herrick, *Imagining the Sacred Past: Hagiography and Power in Early Normandy* (Cambridge, MA and London, 2007)

R. Herval, 'L'abbaye de Lessay', in *La Normandie bénédictine au temps de Guillaume le Conquérant (XIᵉ siècle)*, ed. D. Gaillard and J. Daoust (Lille, 1967), pp. 287–303

L. V. Hicks, *Religious Life in Normandy, 1050–1300: Space, Gender and Social Pressure* (Woodbridge, 2007)

—— 'Magnificent entrances and undignified exits: chronicling the symbolism of castle space in Normandy', *JMH*, 35 (2009), 52–69

—— 'Through the city streets: movement and space in Rouen as seen by the Norman chroniclers', in *Society and Culture in Medieval Rouen, 911–1300*, ed. L. V. Hicks and E. Brenner (Turnhout, 2013), pp.125–49

A. J. Hingst, *The Written World: Past and Place in the Work of Orderic Vitalis* (Notre-Dame, 2009)

G. A. Hodgett, *A Social and Economic History of Medieval Europe* (London, 1972)

C. W. Hollister, *The Military Organization of Norman England* (Oxford, 1965)

—— 'Normandy, France and the Anglo-Norman *regnum*', *Speculum*, 51 (1976), 202–42, reprinted in *MMI*, pp. 17–57

—— 'The taming of a turbulent earl: Henry I and William of Warenne', *Réflexions Historiques*, 3 (1976), 83–91, reprinted in *MMI*, pp. 137–44

—— *Henry I* (New Haven, CT and London, 2001)

C. W. Hollister and J. W. Baldwin, 'The rise of administrative kingship', *American Historical Review*, 83 (1978), 868–91, reprinted in *MMI*, pp. 223–45

J. C. Holt, 'Feudal society and the family in early Medieval England: I. The revolution of 1066', *Transactions of the Royal Historical Society*, fifth series 32 (1982), 193–212

—— 'What's in a name?', Stenton Lecture (Reading, 1982)

—— 'Feudal society and the family in early Medieval England: II. Notions of patrimony', *Transactions of the Royal Historical Society*, fifth series 33 (1983), 193–220

—— 'The introduction of knight service in England', *ANS*, 6 (1984), 89–106

—— 'Feudal society and the family in early Medieval England: III. Patronage and politics', *Transactions of the Royal Historical Society*, fifth series 34 (1984), 1–25

—— 'Feudal society and the family in early Medieval England: IV. The heiress and the alien', *Transactions of the Royal Historical Society*, fifth series 35 (1985), 1–28

H. Houben, *Roger II of Sicily: A Ruler between East and West*, trans. G. A. Loud and D. Milburn (Cambridge, 2002)

N. Howe, *Writing the Map of Anglo-Saxon England: Essays in Cultural Geography* (New Haven, CT and London, 2008)

E. M. C. van Houts, 'The ship list of William the Conqueror', *ANS*, 10 (1988), 159–83

—— 'Robert of Torigni as genealogist', in *Studies in Medieval History presented to R. Allen Brown*, ed. C. Harper-Bill, C. J. Holdsworth, and J. L. Nelson (Woodbridge, 1989), 215–33

—— 'Latin poetry and the Anglo-Norman court 1066–1135: the *Carmen de Hastingae Proelio*', *JMH*, 15 (1989), 39–62

—— 'Historiography and hagiography at Saint-Wandrille: the "Inventio et miracula sancti Vulfranni"', *ANS*, 12 (1990), 233–51

—— 'Countess Gunnor of Normandy (*c.* 950–1031)', *Collegium Médiévale*, 12 (1999), 7–24

—— 'The Anglo-Flemish treaty of 1101', *ANS*, 21 (1999), pp. 169–74

—— 'Les femmes dans l'histoire du duché de Normandie', *Tabularia: sources écrites de la Normandie médiévale: Études*, 2 (2002), available online at <http://www.unicaen.fr/mrsh/craham/revue/tabularia/dossier2/textes/03vanhouts.pdf> (accessed 7 April 2016)

—— 'Une hypothèse sur l'identification de *Willelmus notarius* comme l'historien Guillaume de Jumièges', *Tabularia 'Études'*, 2 (2002), available online at <http://www.unicaen.fr/mrsh/craham/revue/tabularia/print.php?dossier=dossier1&contribDebat=true&file=04vanhouts.xml> (accessed 7 April 2016)

—— 'Edward and Normandy', in *Edward the Confessor: The Man and the Legend*, ed. R. Mortimer (Woodbridge, 2009), pp. 63–76

—— 'Rouen as another Rome in the twelfth century', in *Society and Culture in Medieval Rouen, 911–1300*, ed. L. V. Hicks and E. Brenner (Turnhout, 2013), 101–24

—— 'The *planctus* on the death of William Longsword (943) as a source for tenth-century culture in Normandy and Aquitaine', *ANS*, 36 (2014), 1–22

—— 'The fate of priest's sons in Normandy with special reference to Serlo of Bayeux', *HSJ*, 25 (2014), 57–105

J. Hudson, *Land, Law, and Lordship in Anglo-Norman England* (Oxford, 1994)

—— *The Formation of the English Common Law: Law and Society in England from the Norman Conquest to Magna Carta* (London, 1996)

—— 'Henry I and Counsel', in *The Medieval State: Essays presented to James Campbell*, ed. J. R. Maddicott and D. M. Palliser (London, 2000), pp. 109–26

—— 'Court Cases and Legal Arguments in England, *c.* 1066–1166', *Transactions of the Royal Historical Society*, sixth series 10 (2000), 91–116

—— [Review of] *Robert Curthose, Duke of Normandy (c. 1050–1134)* by William. M. Aird (Woodbridge, 2008) in *History*, 95 (2010)

T. P. Hudson, 'Bramber Rape', in *A History of the County of Sussex, Vol VI, Part 1: Bramber Rape (Southern Part)*, ed. T. P. Hudson (London, 1980), pp. 1–7

L. L. Huneycutt, *Matilda of Scotland: A Study in Medieval Queenship* (Woodbridge, 2003)

P. R. Hyams, 'Feud in Medieval England', *HSJ*, 3 (1991), 1–21

—— *Rancor and Reconciliation in Medieval England* (Ithaca, NY and London, 2003)

E. Impey, 'La demeure seigneuriale en Normandie entre 1125 et 1225 et la tradition Anglo-Normande', in *L'Architecture Normande au moyen age*, ed. M. Baylé, 2 vols (Caen, 2001), i. 219–41

—— 'The *turris famosa* at Ivry-la-Bataille, Normandy', in *The Seigneurial Residence in Western Europe AD c.800–1600*, ed. G. Meiron-Jones, E. Impey, and M. Jones (Oxford, 2002), pp. 189–210

—— 'The ancestry of the White Tower', in *The White Tower*, ed. E. Impey (New Haven, CT and London, 2008), 227–41,

M. Innes, 'Danelaw identities: ethnicity, regionalism, and political allegiance', in *Cultures in Contact: Scandinavian Settlement in England in the Ninth and Tenth Centuries*, ed. D. M. Hadley and J. D. Richards (Turnhout, 2000), pp. 65–88

—— 'People, places and power in Carolingian society', in *Topographies of Power in the Early Middle Ages*, ed. M de Jong and F. Theuws with C. van Rhijn (Leiden, 2001), pp. 397–437

—— '"He never even allowed his white teeth to be bared in laughter": the politics of humour in the Carolingian renaissance', in *Humour, History and Politics in Late Antiquity and the Early Middle Ages*, ed. G. Halsall (Cambridge, 2002), pp. 131–56

C. Insley, 'Where did all the charters go? Anglo-Saxon charters and the new politics of the eleventh century', *ANS*, 24 (2002), 109–27

C. S. Jaeger, *The Origins of Courtliness: Civilizing Trends and the Formation of Courtly Ideals, 939–1210* (Philadelphia, 1985)

W. S. Jesse, *Robert the Burgundian and the Counts of Anjou, ca. 1025–1098* (Washington DC, 2000)

M. Johnson, *Behind the Castle Gate: From Medieval to Renaissance* (London, 2002)

V. B. Jordan, 'The role of kingship in tenth-century Normandy: hagiography of Dudo of Saint-Quentin', *HSJ*, 3 (1991), 53–62

N. Karn, 'Nigel, bishop of Ely, and the restoration of the exchequer after the 'anarchy' of King Stephen's reign', *Historical Research*, 80 (2007), 299–314

—— 'Robert de Sigillo: an unruly head of the royal scriptorium in the 1120s and 1130s', *EHR*, 123 (2008), 539–53

E. J. Kealey, *Roger of Salisbury, Viceroy of England* (Berkeley, Los Angeles, and London, 1972)

K. S. B. Keats-Rohan, 'William I and the Breton contingent in the non-Norman Conquest 1060–1087', *ANS*, 13 (1991), 157–72

—— *Domesday Descendants: A Prosopography of Persons occurring in English Documents 1066–1166: II. Pipe Rolls to* Cartae Baronum (Woodbridge, 2002)

T. Keefe, 'Counting those who count: a computer-assisted analysis of charter witness lists and the itinerant court in the first year of the reign of King Richard I', *HSJ*, 1 (1989), 135–45

—— 'Place-date distribution of royal charters and the historical geography of patronage strategies at the court of King Henry II Plantagenet', *HSJ*, 2 (1990), 179–88

S. Kelly, 'Trading privileges from eighth-century England', *Early Medieval Europe*, 1 (1992), 3–28

P. Kershaw, 'The Alfred-Guthrum treaty: scripting accomodation and interaction in Viking-age England', in *Cultures in Contact: Scandinavian Settlement in England in the Ninth and Tenth Centuries*, ed. D. M. Hadley and J. D. Richards (Turnhout, 2000), pp. 43–64

—— *Peaceful Kings: Peace, Power, and the Early Medieval Political Imagination* (Oxford, 2011)

S. Keynes, *The Diplomas of King Æthelred 'the Unready' 978–1016: A Study in Their Use as Historical Evidence* (Cambridge, 1980)

—— 'The Æthelings in Normandy', *ANS*, 13 (1991), 173–205

E. King, 'The accession of Henry II', in *Henry II: New Interpretations*, ed. C. Harper-Bill and N. Vincent (Woodbridge, 2007), pp. 24–46

—— *King Stephen* (New Haven, CT and London, 2010)

D. Knowles, C. N. L. Brooke, and V. London (ed.), *The Heads of Religious Houses England and Wales, 940–1216* (Cambridge, 1972)

G. Koziol, *Begging Pardon and Favor: Ritual and Political Order in Early Medieval France* (Ithaca, NY and London, 1992)

—— *The Politics of Memory and Identity in Carolingian Royal Diplomas: The West Frankish Kingdom (840–987)* (Turnhout, 2012)

K. Lack, 'Robert Curthose: ineffectual duke or victim of spin?', *HSJ*, 20 (2009), 110–40

J. Lake, *Richer of Saint-Rémi: The Methods and Mentality of a Tenth-Century Historian* (Washington, DC, 2013)

J. E. Lally, 'Secular patronage at the court of Henry II', *Bulletin of the Institute of Historical Research*, 49 (1976), 159–84

T. B. Lambert, 'Introduction: some approaches to peace and protection', in *Peace and Protection in the Middle Ages*, ed. T. B. Lambert and D. Rollason (Toronto, 2009), pp. 1–16

—— 'Theft, homicide and crime in late Anglo-Saxon law', *Past and Present*, 214 (2012), 3–43

J. Langton and G. Jones (ed.), *Forests and Chases of Medieval England and Wales c. 1000–c. 1500: Towards a Survey and Analysis* (Oxford, 2010)

C. Larrington, 'The psychology of emotion and study of the medieval period', *EME*, 10 (2001), 251–6

R. Lavelle, *Alfred's Wars: Sources and Interpretations of Anglo-Saxon Warfare in the Viking Age* (Woodbridge, 2010)

K. K. Lawson, *Cnut: the Danes in England in the Early Eleventh Century* (Harlow, 1993), reprinted as *Cnut: England's Viking King 1016–35* (Stroud, 2011)

F. S. Lear, '*Crimen laesae maiestatis* in the *Lex Romana Wisigothorum*', *Speculum*, 4 (1929), 73–87

J.-F. Lemarignier, *Etude sur les privileges d'exemption et de jurisdiction ecclésiastique des abbayes normandes depuis les origins jusqu'en 1140* (Paris, 1937)

—— *Recherches sur l'hommage en marche et les frontières féodales* (Lille, 1945)

B. Lemesle, *Conflits et justice au Moyen Age: normes, loi et résolution des conflits en Anjou aux Xe et XIIe siècles* (Paris, 2008)

A. Lemoine-Descourtieux, *Le frontière Normande de l'Avre: de la foundation de la Normandie à sa réunion au domaine royal (911–1204)* (Mont-Saint-Aignan, 2011)

R. Lepelley, *Dictionnaire étymologique des noms de communes de Normandie* (Caen, 2003)

A. W. Lewis, 'Anticipatory association of the heir in early Capetian France', *American Historical Review*, 83 (1978), 906–27

C. P. Lewis, 'The early earls of Norman England', *ANS*, 13 (1991), 207–23

'Warenne, William (I) de, first earl of Surrey', *Oxford Dictionary of National Biography*, vol. 57 (Oxford, 2003)

R. Liddiard, 'Castle Rising, Norfolk: a "landscape of lordship"?' *ANS*, 22 (2000), 169–86

F. Lifshitz, *The Norman Conquest of Pious Neustria: Historiographic Discourse and Saintly Relics 684–1080* (Toronto, 1995)

—— 'La Normandie Carolingienne: essai sur la continuité, avec utilisation de sources négligées', *Annales de Normandie*, 48 (1998), 505–24

—— 'Translating "feudal" vocabulary: Dudo of Saint-Quentin', *HSJ*, 9 (2001), 39–56

—— [Review of] 'Pohl, Benjamin. *Dudo of Saint-Quentin's* Historia Normannorum: *Tradition, Innovation and Memory*', *The Medieval Review*, 16 January 2015, available online at <http://scholarworks.iu.edu/journals/index.php/tmr/article/view/20857/26863> (accessed 6 February 2016)

L. K. Little, *Benedictine Maledictions: Liturgical Cursing in Romanesque France* (Ithaca, NY and London, 1993)

D. Lohrmann, 'St-Germer-de-Flay und das Anglo-Normannische Reich', *Francia* 1, (1973), 193–256

K. Loprete, *Adela of Blois: Countess and Lord (c. 1067–1137)* (Dublin, 2006)

F. Lot, *Les derniers Carolingians: Lothaire, Louis V, Charles de Lorraine (954–991)* (Paris, 1851)

—— *Fidèles ou vassaux? Essai sur la nature juridique du lien qui unissait les grands vassaux à la royauté depuis le milieu du IXe siècle jusqu'a l fin du XIIe siècle* (Paris, 1904)

G. A. Loud, 'The *gens Normannorum* – myth or reality?', *ANS*, 4 (1982), 104–16

—— 'Coinage, wealth and plunder in the age of Robert Guiscard', *EHR*, 114 (1999), 815–43

—— *The Age of Robert Guiscard: Southern Italy and the Norman Conquest* (Harlow, 2000)

—— 'The chancery and charters of the kings of Sicily, 1130–1212', *EHR*, 124 (2009), 779–810

G. Louise, *La seigneurie de Bellême X^e–XIIe siècles: devolution des pouvoirs territoriaux et construction d'une seigneurie de frontière aux confins de la Normandie et du Maine de la charnière de l'an mil*, La Pays Bas-Normand, 2 vols, 3 and 4 (1990) and 1 and 2 (1991)

L. C. Loyd, 'The origins of the family of Aubigny of Cainhoe', *Bedfordshire Historical Record Society*, 19 (1937), 101–12

—— *The Origins of Some Anglo-Norman Families*, Publications of the Harleian Society, 103 (Leeds, 1951)

N. Lund, 'Scandinavia, c. 700–1066', in *The New Cambridge Medieval History: II. c. 700–c. 900*, ed. R. McKitterick (Cambridge, 1995), pp. 202–27

M. Lupoi, *The Origins of the European Legal Order* (Cambridge, 2000)

B. Lyon and A. Verhulst, *Medieval Finance: A Comparison of Financial Institutions in Northwestern Europe* (Bruges, 1967)

R. McKitterick, *The Frankish Kingdoms under the Carolingians, 751–987* (London, 1983)

—— *Charlemagne: The Formation of a European Identity* (Cambridge, 2008)

S. MacLean, 'Making a difference in tenth-century politics: Athelstan's sisters and Frankish queenship', in *Frankland: the Franks and the world of the early middle ages. Essays in honour of Dame Jinty Nelson*, ed. P. Fouracre and D. Ganz (Manchester, 2008), pp. 167–90

F. McNair, 'The politics of being Norman in the reign of Richard the Fearless, duke of Normandy (r. 942–996)', *EME*, 23 (2015), 308–28

J. Le Maho, 'Rouen à l'époque des incursions vikings (841–911)', *Bulletin de la commission des antiquités de la Seine-Maritime*, 42 (1995), 143–202

—— 'Un exode de reliques dans le pays de la Bas Seine à la fin du IXe siècle', *Bulletin de la commission départementale des antiquités de la Seine-Maritime*, 46 (1998), 136–88

—— *L'enceinte fortifiée de Notre-Dame-de-Gravenchon (Seine-Maritime) XIe–XIIIe siècle: Le site de la Fontaine-Saint-Denis, des fouilles archéologiques aux travaux de restauration (1979–2001)* (Notre-Dame-de-Gravenchon, 2001)

—— 'Remarques sur la construction de bois en haute-normandie aux XIe et XIIe siècles', in *L'architecture normande au moyen age*, ed. M. Baylé, second edition, 2 vols (Caen, 2001), i. 243–68

—— 'Les premières installations normandes dans la basse vallée de la Seine (fin du IX siècle)', in *La progression des Vikings; des raids à la colonisation*, ed. A.-M. Flambard-Héricher (Rouen, 2003), 153–69

—— 'Les normands de la Seine à la fin du IXe siècle', in *Les fondations Scandinaves en occident et les débuts du duché de Normandie*, ed. P. Bauduin (Caen, 2005), pp. 161–79

—— 'Fortifications et déplacements de populations en France au temps des invasions normandes (IXe–Xe siècle)', *Château Gaillard*, 22 (2006), pp. 223–36

J.-M. Maillefer, 'Une famille aristocratique aux confins de la Normandie: les Géré au XIe siècle', *Autour du pouvoir ducal Normand X^e–XIIe Siècles*, Cahier des Annales de Normandie, 17 (Caen, 1985), 175–206

S. Marritt, 'Prayers for the king and royal titles in Anglo-Norman charters', *ANS*, 32 (2010), 184–202

P. Marshall, 'The ceremonial function of the donjon in the twelfth century', *Château Gaillard*, 20 (2000), 141–51

—— 'The great tower as residence', in *The Seigneurial Residence in Western Europe AD c.800–1600*, ed. G. Meiron-Jones, E. Impey, and M. Jones (Oxford, 2002), pp. 27–44

J. Martindale, 'Succession and politics in the Romance-speaking world, c. 1000–1140', in *England and Her Neighbours 1066–1453: Essays in Honour of Pierre Chaplais*, ed. M. Jones and M. Vale (London, 1989), pp. 19–41

—— '"His Special Friend"? The Settlement of Disputes and Political Power in the Kingdom of the French (Tenth to Mid-Twelfth Century)', *Transactions of the Royal Historical Society*, sixth series 5 (1995), 21–57

L. Mazet-Harhoff, 'The incursion of the Vikings into the natural and cultural landscape of upper Normandy', in *Viking Trade and Settlement in Continental Western Europe*, ed. I. S. Klæsøe (Copenhagen, 2010), pp. 81–122

Mémoires du château de Caen, ed. J.-V. Marin and J.-M. Levesque (Caen, 2000)

J. Mesqui, *Le château de Lillebonne des ducs de Normandie aux ducs d'Harcourt*, MSAN, 42 (Caen, 2008)

M. Meyer, 'Women's estates in later Anglo-Saxon England: the politics of possession', *HSJ*, 3 (1992 for 1991), 111–29

W. I. Miller, 'Ordeal in Iceland', *Scandinavian Studies*, 60 (1988), 189–218

—— *Bloodtaking and Peacemaking: Feud, Law, and Society in Saga Iceland* (Chicago and London, 1990)

J. C. Moesgaard, 'A survey of coin production and currency in Normandy, 864–945', in *Silver Economy in the Viking Age*, ed. J. Graham-Campbell and G. Williams (Walnut Creek CA, 2007), pp. 99–121

S. L. Mooers Christelow, '"Backers and stabbers": problems of loyalty in Robert Curthose's entourage', *Journal of British Studies*, 21 (1981), 1–17

—— 'A moveable feast? Itineration and the centralization of government under Henry I', *Albion*, 28 (1996), 187–228

J. S. Moore, 'Anglo-Norman garrisons', *ANS*, 22 (2000), 205–59

L. Morelle, 'The metamorphosis of three monastic charter collections in the eleventh century (Saint-Amand, Saint-Riquier, Montier-en-Der)', in *Charters and the Use of the Written Word in Medieval Society*, ed. K. Heidecker (Turnhout, 2000), pp. 171–204

S. Morillo, *Warfare under the Anglo-Norman Kings 1066–1135* (Woodbridge, 1994)

L. B. Mortensen, 'Stylistic choice in a reborn genre: the national histories of Widukind of Corvey and Dudo of Saint-Quentin', in *Dudone di San Quintino*, ed. P. Gatti and A. Degl'Innocenti (Trent, 1995), pp. 77–102

R. Mortimer, 'Anglo-Norman lay charters, 1066–*c.* 1100: a diplomatic approach', *ANS*, 25 (2002), 153–75

—— 'Edward the Confessor: the man and the legend', in *Edward the Confessor: The Man and the Legend*, ed. R. Mortimer (Woodbridge, 2009), pp. 1–40

V. Moss, 'Normandy and England in 1180: the pipe roll evidence', in *England and Normandy in the Middle Ages*, ed. D. Bates and A. Curry (London, 1994), pp. 185–95

L. Musset, 'Les domaines de l'époque franque et les destinées du regime domanial du IXe au XIe siècle', *BSAN*, 49 (1942–45), 7–97

—— 'Actes inedits du XIe siècle I. Les plus anciennes chartes du prieuré de Saint-Gabriel (Calvados)', *BSAN*, 52 (1952–54), 117–53

—— 'Les relations extérieures de la Normandie du IXe au XIe siècle', *Annales de Normandie*, 4 (1954), 31–8; reprinted in L. Musset, *Nordica et Normannica: Recueil d'études sur la Scandinavie ancienne et médiévale, les expéditions des Vikings et la fondation de la Normandie* (Paris, 1997), pp. 297–306

—— 'Les destins de la propriété monastique durant les invasions normandes (IXe au XIe siècles). L'exemple de Jumièges', in *Jumièges. Congrès scientifique du XIIIe centenaire*, vol. 1 (Rouen, 1955), pp. 49–55; reprinted in L. Musset, *Nordica et Normannica: Recueil d'études sur la Scandinavie ancienne et médiévale, les expéditions des Vikings et la fondation de la Normandie* (Paris, 1997), pp. 351–9

—— 'Actes inédits du XIe siècle III. Les plus anciens chartes normandes de l'abbaye de Bourgueil', *BSAN*, 54 (1957–58), 15–54

—— 'A-t-il existé en Normandie au XIe siècle une aristocratie d'argent? (Une enquête sommaire sur l'argent comme moyen d'ascension sociale)', *Annales de Normandie*, 9 (1959), 285–99

—— 'Que peut-on savoir de la fiscalité publique en Normandie à l'époque ducale ?', *Revue historique de droit français et étranger*, fourth series 38 (1960), 483–4

—— 'Recherches sur quelques survivances de la fiscalité ducal', *BSAN*, 55 (1961), 317–25, 420–35, 525–30

—— 'Actes inédits du XIe siècle: V. Autour des origines de Saint-Etienne de Fontenay', *BSAN*, 56 (1963), 11–41

—— 'Les origines et le patrimoine de l'abbaye de Saint-Sever', in *La Normandie Bénédictine au temps de Guillaume le Conquérant (Xe siècle)* (Lille, 1967), pp. 357–73

—— 'La Seine normande et le commerce maritime du IIIe au XIe siècle', *Revue des sociétés savantes de Haute Normandie*, 53 (1970), 3–14; reprinted in L. Musset, *Nordica et Normannica: Recueil d'études sur la Scandinavie ancienne et médiévale, les expéditions des Vikings et la fondation de la Normandie* (Paris, 1997), pp. 337–49

—— 'Naissance de la Normandie' in *L'Histoire de la Normandie*, ed. M. de Boüard (Toulouse, 1970), pp. 75–129

—— 'Une famille vicomtale: les Goz', *Documents de l'histoire de Normandie* (Toulouse, 1972), pp. 94–8

—— 'Foires et marchés en Normandie à l'époque ducale', *Annales de Normandie*, 26 (1976), 3–23

—— 'L'aristocratie Normande au XIe siècle' in *La Noblesse au Moyen Age XIe–XVe siècles: Essais à la Mémoire de Robert Boutruche*, ed. P. Contamine (Paris, 1976), pp. 71–96

—— 'Aux origines d'une classe dirigeante: Les Tosny, grands barons Normands du Xe au XIIIe siècle', *Francia*, 5 (1977), 45–80

—— 'Participation de Vikings venus des pays celtes à la colonisation scandinave de la Normandie', *Cahiers du Centre de recherches sur les pays du Nord et du Nord Ouest*, 1 (1979), 107–17, reprinted in L. Musset, *Nordica et Normannica: Recueil d'études sur la Scandinavie ancienne et médiévale, les expéditions des Vikings et la fondation de la Normandie* (Paris, 1997), pp. 279–96

—— 'Sur la datation des actes par le nom du prince en Normandie (XIe–XIIe siècles), in *Autour du pouvoir ducal normand, X^e–XIIe siècles*, ed. L. Musset, J.-M. Bouvris, and J.-M. Maillefer (Caen, 1985), pp. 5–17

—— 'Autour des modalités juridiques de l'expansion normande au XIe siècle: le droit d'exil', in *Autour du pouvoir ducal normand, X^e–XIIe siècles*, ed. L. Musset, J.-M. Bouvris, and J.-M. Maillefer (Caen, 1985), pp. 45–59

—— 'Recherches sur le tonlieu en Normandie à l'époque ducale', in *Autour du pouvoir ducal normand X^e–XIIe siècles*, ed. L. Musset, J.-M. Bouvris, and J.-M. Maillefer (Caen, 1985), pp. 61–76

—— 'Voie publique et chemin du roi en Normandie du XIe au XIIIe siècle', in *Autour du pouvoir ducal normand X^e–XIIe siècles*, ed. L. Musset, J.-M. Bouvris, and J.-M. Maillefer (Caen, 1985), pp. 95–111

—— 'Les ports en Normandie du XIe au XIIIe siècle: esquisse d'histoire institutionelle, in *Autour du pouvoir ducal normand X^e–XIIe siècles*, ed. L. Musset, J.–M. Bouvris, and J.-M. Maillefer (Caen, 1985), pp. 113–28

—— 'Les prés et le foin du seigneur roi', in *Autour du pouvoir ducal normand, X^e–XIIe siècles*, ed. L. Musset, J.-M. Bouvris, and J.-M. Maillefer (Caen, 1985), pp. 77–93

—— 'Administration et justice dans une grande baronnie normande au XIe siècle: les terres des Bellême sous Roger II et Robert', in *Autour du pouvoir ducal normand X^e–XIIe siècles*, ed. L. Musset, J.-M. Bouvris, and J.-M. Maillefer (Caen, 1985), pp. 129–48

—— 'Une arisocratie d'affaires anglo-normande après la conquête', in *Etudes Normandes*, 3 (1986), 7–20

—— 'Réflexions sur les moyens de payment en Normandie aux XIe et XIIe siècles', in *Aspects de la société et de l'économie dans la Normandie medieval (X^e–XIIIe siècles)*, ed. L. Musset, J.-M. Bouvris, and V. Gazeau (Caen, 1988), pp. 65–89

—— 'Ce qu'enseigne l'histoire d'un patrimoine monastique: Saint-Ouen de Rouen du IXe au XIe siècle', in *Aspects de la société et de l'économie dans la Normandie medieval (X^e–XIIIe siècles)*, ed. L. Musset, J.-M. Bouvris, and V. Gazeau (Caen, 1988), pp. 115–29

—— 'Considérations sur la genèse et la trace des frontiers de la Normandie', in *Media in Francia: recueil des mélanges offert à Karl Ferdinand Werner à l'occasion de son 65e anniversaire par ses amis et collègues français* (Paris, 1989), pp. 309–18; reprinted in L. Musset, *Nordica et Normannica: Recueil d'études sur la Scandinavie ancienne et médiévale, les expéditions des Vikings et la fondation de la Normandie* (Paris, 1997), pp. 403–13

—— 'Les scandinaves et l'ouest du contintent européen', in *Les Vikings: Les Scandinaves et l'Europe 800–1200*, ed. E. Roesdahl, J.-P. Mohen, and F.-X. Dillman (Paris, 1992), pp. 88–95

—— 'Les évêques normands envisagés dans le cadre européen (X^e–XIIe siècles)', in *Les évêques normands du XIe siècle*, ed. P. Bouet and F. Neveux (Caen, 1995), pp. 53–65

—— 'Les translations de reliques en Normandie (IXe–XIIe siècles)', in *Les Saints dans la Normandie Médiévale*, ed. P. Bouet and F. Neveux (Caen, 2000), pp. 97–108

R. Naismith, *Money and Power in Anglo-Saxon England: The Southern English Kingdoms, 757–865* (Cambridge, 2012)

H. Navel, 'L'enquête de 1133 sur les fiefs de l'evêché de Bayeux', *BSAN*, 42 (1934), 5–80

J. L. Nelson, 'Dispute settlement in Carolingian West Francia', in *The Settlement of Disputes in Early Medieval Europe*, ed. W. Davies and P. Fouracre (Cambridge, 1986), pp. 45–64

—— 'The Lord's anointed and the people's choice: Carolingian royal ritual', in *Ritual and Royalty: Power and Ceremonial in Traditional Societies*, ed. D. Cannadine and S. Price (Cambridge, 1987), pp. 137–80

—— 'Kingship and royal government', in *The New Cambridge Medieval History: II. c. 700–c. 900*, ed. R. McKitterick (Cambridge, 1995), pp. 383–430

—— 'Aachen as a place of power', in *Topographies of Power in the Early Middle Ages*, ed. M de Jong and F. Theuws with C. van Rhijn (Leiden, 2001), pp. 217–41

—— 'Normandy's early history since *Normandy before 1066*', in *Normandy and its Neighbours, 900–1250: Essays for David Bates*, ed. D. Crouch and K. Thompson (Turnhout, 2011), pp. 3–15

F. Neveux, *La Normandie des ducs aux rois X^e–XIIe siècle* (Rennes, 1998)

—— *A Brief History of the Normans: The Conquests that Changed the Face of Europe*, trans. H. Curtis (London, 2008)

R. Newhauser, *The Treatise on Vices and Virtues in Latin and the Vernacular* (Turnhout, 1993)

J.-F. Nieus, 'Early aristocratic seals: an Anglo-Norman success story', *ANS*, 38 (2016), 97–123

R. Nip, 'The political relations between England and Flanders, 1066–1128', *ANS*, 21 (1999), 145–67

A. Nissen-Jaubert, 'Le château de Domfront e la fin du XIe siècle au milieu du XIIe siècle. Les vestiges archéologiques et leur contexte historique', in *Tinchebray 1106–2006: actes du colloque de Tinchebray (28–30 Septembre 2006)*, ed. V. Gazeau and J. Green (Flers, 2009), pp. 139–55

G. Nortier, *Les bibliothèques médiévales des abbayes bénédictines de Normandie:*
Fécamp, le Bec, le Mont Saint-Michel, Saint-Evroul, Lyre, Jumièges, Saint-Wandrille, Saint-Ouen (Paris, 1971)

J. J. Norwich, *The Normans in Sicily* (London, 1992)

B. R. O'Brien, *God's Peace and King's Peace: The Laws of Edward the Confessor* (Philadelphia, 1999)

F. Oakley, *Kingship: The Politics of Enchantment* (Oxford, 2006)

E. Oksanen, 'The Anglo-Flemish treaties and Flemish soldiers in England 1101–1163', in *Mercenaries and Paid Men: The Mercenary Identity in the Middle Ages*, ed. J. France (Leiden, 2008), pp. 261–74

—— *Flanders and the Anglo-Norman World, 1066–1216* (Cambridge, 2012)

L. Oliver, 'Protecting the body in early medieval law', in *Peace and Protection in the Middle Ages*, ed. T. B. Lambert and D. Rollason (Toronto, 2009), pp. 60–77

G. Owen-Crocker, 'Stylistic Variation and Roman Influence in the Bayeux Tapestry', *Peregrinations*, 9 (2009), 51–96

The Oxford Dictionary of National Biography, ed. H. C. G. Matthew and B. Harrison, 60 vols (Oxford,2004)

E. C. Pastan, 'Building stories: the representation of architecture in the Bayeux embroidery', *ANS*, 33 (2011), 150–85

J. Le Patourel, 'Geoffrey of Montbray, bishop of Coutances, 1049–93', *EHR*, 59 (1944), 129–61

—— 'The Norman succession 996–1135', *EHR*, 86 (1971), 225–50

—— *The Norman Empire* (Oxford, 1976)

—— 'Norman kings or Norman "king-dukes"?', in *Droit privé et institutions régionales: études historiques offertes à Jean Yver* (Paris, 1976), pp. 469–79

A. Pedersen, 'Power and aristocracy', in *Vikings: Life and Legend*, ed. G. Williams, P. Pentz, and M. Wemhoff (London, 2014), 122–55

B. Pohl, *Dudo of Saint-Quentin's Historia Normannorum: Tradition, Innovation and Memory* (York, 2015)

—— 'The illustrated archetype of the Historia Normannorum: did Dudo write a "chronicon pictum"?', *ANS*, 37 (2015), 221–51

A. A. Porée, *Histoire de l'abbaye du Bec*, 2 vols (Evreux, 1901)

C. Potts, 'The early Norman charters: a new perspective on an old debate', in *England in the Eleventh Century*, ed. C. Hicks (Stamford, 1992), pp. 25–40

—— 'The earliest Norman counts revisited: the lords of Mortain', *HSJ*, 4 (1993), 23–35

—— *Monastic Revival and Regional Identity in Early Normandy* (Woodbridge, 1997)

—— 'Normandy 911–1144', in *A Companion to the Anglo-Norman World*, ed. C. Harper-Bill and E. van Houts (Woodbridge, 2002), pp. 19–42

D. Power, *The Norman Frontier in the Twelfth and Early Thirteenth Centuries* (Cambridge, 2004)

H. Prentout, *Essai sur les origines et fondation du duché de normandie* (Paris, 1911)

J. O. Prestwich, 'War and finance in the Anglo-Norman state', *Transactions of the Royal Historical Society*, fifth series 4 (1954), pp. 19–43, reprinted in *Anglo-Norman Warfare*, ed. M. Strickland (Woodbridge, 1992), pp. 59–83 at p. 76

—— 'The military household of the Norman kings', *EHR*, 96 (1981), 1–37

N. S. Price, *The Vikings in Brittany* (London, 1989)

H. Pryce, 'Owain Gwynedd and Louis VII: the Franco-Welsh diplomacy of the first prince of Wales', *The Welsh History Review*, 19 (1998), 1–28

—— 'Lawbooks and literacy in medieval Wales', *Speculum*, 75 (2000), 29–67

P. Pulsiano (ed.), *Medieval Scandinavia: An Encyclopaedia* (London, 1993)

J. Quaghebeur, 'Havoise, Constance et Mathilde, princesses de Normandie et duchesses de Bretagne', in *Bretons et Normans au moyen âge: rivalités, malentendus, convergences*, ed. J. Quaghebeur and B. Merdrignac (Rennes, 2008), pp. 145–63

M. Rampton, 'The significance of the banquet scene in the Bayeux Tapestry', *Medievalia et Humanistica*, new series 21 (1994), 33–53

K. Randsborg, *The Viking Age in Denmark: The Formation of a State* (London, 1980)

A. Renoux, 'Fouilles sur le site du château ducal de Fécamp (X^e–XIIe siècle)', *Proceedings of the Battle Conference on Anglo-Norman Studies*, 4 (1982), 133–52

—— 'Châteaux et residences fortifiées des ducs de Normandie aux Xe et XIe siècles', in *Les Mondes Normands (XIIIe–XIIe siècle)*, ed. H. Galinié (Caen, 1989), pp. 113–24

—— *Fécamp: du palais ducal au palaise de dieu* (Paris, 1991)

—— 'Les fondements architecturaux du pouvoir princier en France (fin IXe–début XIIIe siècle)', in *Les princes et le pouvoir au Moyen Age*, ed. M. Balard (Paris, 1993), pp. 167–94

—— Résidences et châteaux ducaux Normans au XIIe siècle', in *L'Architecture Normande au moyen age*, ed. M. Baylé, 2 vols (Caen, 2001), i. 197–217

—— '*Palatium* et *castrum* en France du Nord (fin IXe–début XIIIe siècle)', in *The Seigneurial Residence in Western Europe AD c.800–1600*, ed. G. Meiron-Jones, E. Impey, and M. Jones (Oxford, 2002), pp. 15–25

T. Reuter, *Germany in the Early Middle Ages, c. 800–1056* (London, 1991)

—— 'Nobles and others: the social and cultural expression of power relations in the Middle Ages', in *Nobles and Nobility in the Middle Ages*, ed. A. Duggan (Woodbridge, 2000), pp. 85–98, reprinted in *Medieval Polities and Modern Mentalities*, ed. J. L. Nelson (Cambridge, 2006), pp. 111–26

—— 'Whose race, whose ethnicity? Recent medievalists' discussions of identity', in *Medieval Polities and Modern Mentalities*, ed. J. L. Nelson (Cambridge, 2006), pp. 100–8

S. Reynolds, 'Medieval *origines gentium* and the community of the realm', *History*, 68 (1983), 375–90

—— *Kingdoms and Communities in Western Europe 900–1300* (Oxford, 1984)

—— *Fiefs and Vassals: The Medieval Evidence Reinterpreted* (Oxford, 1994)

S. J. Ridyard, *The Royal Saints of Anglo-Saxon England* (Cambridge, 1988)

L. Roach, 'Public rites and public wrongs: ritual aspects of diplomas in tenth- and eleventh-century England', *Early Medieval Europe*, 19 (2011), 182–203

—— 'Penitential discourse in the diplomas of King Æthelred "the Unready"', *Journal of Ecclesiastical History*, 64 (2013), 258–76

I. Robinson, *The Papacy 1073–1198: Continuity and Innovation* (Cambridge, 1990)

—— *Henry IV of Germany, 1056–1106* (Cambridge, 1999)

T. Roche, 'Les notices de conflit dans la Normandie ducale (milieu du XIᵉ–milieu du XIIᵉ siècle environ)', *Tabularia: 'Études'*, 7 (2007), 51–73

E. Roesdahl, *The Vikings*, trans. S. M. Margeson and K. Williams, second edition (London, 1998)

D. W. Rollason, 'Cults of murdered royal saints', *Anglo-Saxon England*, 11 (1982), 1–22

—— 'Protection and the mead-hall', in *Peace and Protection in the Middle Ages*, ed. T. B. Lambert and D. Rollason (Toronto, 2009), pp. 19–35

B. H. Rosenwein, 'Writing without fear about early medieval emotions', *EME*, 10 (2001), 229–34

—— *Emotional Communities in the Early Middle Ages* (Ithaca, NY and London, 2006)

C. Ross, *Edward IV* (London, 1974)

J. H. Round, 'Bernard, the King's scribe', *EHR*, 14 (1899), 417–30

J. Sabapathy, *Officers and Accountability in Medieval England, 1170–1300* (Oxford, 2014)

I. J. Sanders, *English Baronies: A Study of their Origin and Descent, 1086–1327* (Oxford, 1960)

G. Santini, 'Administration publique et droit romain dans la Normandie de Guillaume le Conquérant', *Revue historique de droit Français et Etranger*, 73 (1995), 23–40

Y. Sassier, *Hugues Capet* (Paris, 1987)

K. Schmid, 'The structure of the nobility in the earlier Middle Ages', in *The Medieval Nobility*, ed. and trans. T. Reuter (Amsterdam, 1978), pp. 37–59

C. P. Schriber, *The Dilemma of Arnulf of Lisieux: New Ideas versus Old Ideals* (Bloomington and Indianapolis, 1990)

E. Searle, 'Fact and pattern in heroic history: Dudo of Saint-Quentin', *Viator*, 15 (1984), 119–37

—— *Predatory Kinship and the Formation of Norman Power* (Berkeley and London, 1988)

R. Sharpe, 'The use of writs in the eleventh century: a hypothesis based on the archive of Bury St Edmunds', *Anglo-Saxon England*, 32 (2003), 247–91

—— 'Address and delivery in Anglo-Norman royal charters', in *Charters and Charter Scholarship in Britain and Ireland*, ed. M. T. Flanagan and J. A. Green (Basingstoke, 2005), pp. 32–52

—— *Norman rule in Cumbria*, Cumberland and Westmorland Antiquarian and Archaeological Society, Tract Series 21 (2006)

—— 'The last years of Herbert the chamberlain: Weaverthorpe church and hall', *Historical Research*, 83 (2010), 588–601

—— 'Peoples and languages in eleventh- and twelfth-century Britain and Ireland: reading the charter evidence', in *The Reality Behind Charter Diplomatic in Anglo-Norman Britain: Studies by Dauvit Broun, John Reuben Davies, Richard Sharpe and Alice Taylor*, ed. D. Broun (Glasgow, 2011), pp. 1–119

K. L. Shirley, *The Secular Jurisdiction of Monasteries in Anglo-Norman and Angevin England* (Woodbridge, 2004)

L. Shopkow, 'The Carolingian world of Dudo of Saint-Quentin', *JMH*, 15 (1989), 19–37

—— *History and Community: Norman Historical Writing in the Eleventh and Twelfth Centuries* (Washington, DC, 1997)

M. Six, 'Le prieuré de Saint-Gabriel I. La fondation et l'exploitation rurale, XIᵉ–XVᵉ siècles', *Annales de Normandie*, 52 (2002), 99–127

—— 'De la vicomtesse Emma et de son entourage', in *Les Femmes et les actes*, *Tabularia: Études*, 4 (2004), 79–103

R. Southern, *Saint Anselm: A Portrait in a Landscape* (Cambridge, 1990)

D. S. Spear, *The Personnel of the Norman Cathedrals during the Ducal Period, 911–1204* (London, 2006)

—— 'The double display of St Romanus of Rouen in 1124', in *Henry I and the Anglo-Norman World: Studies in Memory of C. Warren Hollister*, ed. D. F. Fleming and J. M. Pope (Woodbridge, 2007), pp. 117–32

P. Stafford, *Queen Emma and Queen Edith: Queenship and Women's Power in Eleventh-Century England* (Oxford, 1997)

—— 'Political ideas in late tenth-century England: charters as evidence', in *Law, Laity and Solidarities: Essays in Honour of Susan Reynolds*, ed. P. Stafford, J. L Nelson, and J. Martindale (Manchester, 2001), pp. 68–82

—— 'King and kin, lord and community: England in the tenth and eleventh centuries', in P. Stafford, *Gender, Family and the Legitimation of Power: England from the Ninth to Early Twelfth Century* (Aldershot, 2006), VIII, pp. 1–33

R. Stalley, *Early Medieval Architecture* (Oxford, 1999)

J. M. Steane, *The Archaeology of Power: England and Northern Europe AD800–1600* (Stroud, 2001)

F. M. Stenton, *The First Century of English Feudalism, 1066–1166, being the Ford Lectures delivered in the University of Oxford in Hilary Term 1929* (Oxford, 1932)

—— *Anglo-Saxon England*, third edition (Oxford, 1971)

M. Strickland, 'Arms and the men: war, loyalty and lordship in Jordan Fantosme's Chronicle', *Medieval Knighthood IV. Papers from the Fifth Strawberry Hill Conference*, ed. C. Harper-Bill and R. Harvey (Woodbridge, 1992), pp. 187–220

—— 'Against the Lord's anointed: aspects of warfare and baronial rebellion in England and Normandy, 1075–1265', in *Law and Government in Medieval England and Normandy: Essays in Honour of Sir James Holt*, ed. G. Garnett and J. Hudson (Cambridge, 1994), pp. 56–79

—— *War and Chivalry: The Conduct and Perception of War in England and Normandy, 1066–1217* (Cambridge, 1996)

W. Stubbs, *The Constitutional History of England in its Origin and Development*, vol. 1, sixth edition (Oxford, 1913)

E. Z. Tabuteau, *Transfers of Property in Eleventh-Century Norman Law* (Chapel Hill, NC and London, 1988)

—— 'The role of law in the succession to Normandy and England, 1087', *HSJ*, 3 (1991), 141–69

—— 'The family of Moulins-la-Marche in the eleventh century', *Medieval Prosopography*, 13 (1992), 29–65

—— 'Punishments in Eleventh-Century Normandy', in *Conflict in Medieval Europe: Changing Perspectives on Society and Culture*, ed. W. C. Brown and P. Górecki (Aldershot, 2003), pp. 131–49

H. Tanner, *Families, Friends and Allies: Boulogne and Politics in Northern France and England c. 879–1160* (Leiden, 2004)

—— 'Henry I's administrative legacy: the significance of place-date distribution in the *acta* of King Stephen, in *Henry I and the Anglo-Norman World: Studies in Memory of C. Warren Hollister*, ed. D. F. Fleming and J. M. Pope (Woodbridge, 2007), pp. 183–99

A. Taylor, 'Crime without punishment: medieval Scottish law in comparative perspective, *ANS*, 35 (2013), 287–304

H. Teunis, *The Appeal to the Original Status: Social Justice in Anjou in the Eleventh Century* (Hilversum, 2006)

K. Thompson, 'Family and influence to the south of Normandy in the eleventh century: the lordship of Bellême', *JMH*, 11 (1985), 215–26

—— 'The Norman aristocracy before 1066: the example of the Montgomerys', *Historical Research*, 60 (1987), 251–63

—— 'Robert of Bellême reconsidered', *ANS*, 13 (1991), 263–86

—— 'William Talvas, count of Ponthieu, and the politics of the Anglo-Norman realm', in *England and Normandy in the Middle Ages*, ed. D. Bates and A. Curry (London, 1994), pp. 169–84.

—— 'The lords of Laigle: ambition and insecurity on the borders of Normandy', *ANS*, 18 (1996), 177–99

—— *Power and Border Lordship in Medieval France: The County of the Perche, 1000–1226* (Woodbridge, 2002)

—— 'Affairs of state: the illegitimate children of Henry I', *JMH*, 29 (2003), 129–51

—— 'Being the ducal sister: the role of Adelaide of Aumale', in *Normandy and its Neighbours, 900–1250: Essays for David Bates*, ed. D. Crouch and K. Thompson (Turnhout, 2011), pp. 61–76

M. W. Thomson, *The Rise of the Castle* (Cambridge, 1991)

R. M. Thomson, *William of Malmesbury*, revised edition (Woodbridge, 2003)

B.-M. Tock, 'Les chartes originales de l'abbaye de Jumièges jusqu'en 1120', *Tabularia 'Études'*, 2 (2002), available online at <http://www.unicaen.fr/mrsh/craham/revue/tabularia/print.php?dossier=dossier1&file=04tock.xml> (accessed 7 April 2016)

E. van Torhoudt, 'Les sieges du pouvoir des Néels, vicomtes dans le Cotentin', in *Les lieux de pouvoir au Moyen Age en Normandie et sur ses marges*, A.-M. Flambard Héricher (Caen, 2006), pp. 15–24

—— 'L'écrit et la justice au Mont-Saint-Michel: les notices narratives (vers 1060–1150), *Tabularia*, Études, 7 (2007), 107–37

—— 'Henri beauclerc, comte du Cotentin reconsidéré (1088–1101)', in *Tinchebray 1106–2006: actes du colloque de Tinchebray (28–30 Septembre 2006)*, ed. V. Gazeau and J. Green (Flers, 2009), pp. 101–21

—— 'L' "énigme" des origines de l'abbaye de Montebourg: une question de méthode?', in *De part et d'autre de la Normandie medieval: recueil d'études en homage à François Neveux*, ed. P. Bouet, C. Bougy, B. Garnier, and C. Maneuvrier (Caen, 2009), pp. 331–46

E. M. Tyler, '"The eyes of the beholders were dazzled": treasure and artifice in the *Encomium Emmae Reginae*', *EME*, 8 (1999), 247–70

—— 'Talking about history in eleventh-century England: the *Encomium Emmae Reginae* and the court of Harthacnut', *EME*, 13 (2005), 359–83

—— 'The *Vita Ædwardi*: the politics of poetry at Wilton abbey', *ANS*, 31 (2009), 135–56

C. Urbanski, 'Apology, protest, and suppression: interpreting the surrender of Caen (1105), *HSJ*, 19 (2008), 137–53

—— *Writing History for the King: Henry II and the Politics of Vernacular Historiography* (Ithaca, NY and London, 2013)

L. Valin, *Le duc de Normandie et sa cour (912–1204): étude d'histoire juridique* (Paris, 1910)

E. Vacandard, 'Un essai d'histoire des archevêques de Rouen au XIe siècle', *Revue catholique de Normandie*, 3 (1893), 117–27

M. Vale, *The Angevin Legacy and the Hundred Years War (1250–1340)* (Oxford, 1990)

S. N. Vaughn, *The Abbey of Bec and the Anglo-Norman State 1034–1136* (Woodbridge, 1981)

B. L. Venarde, *Women's Monasticism and Medieval Society: Nunneries in France and England, 890–1215* (Ithaca, NY and London, 1997)

A. Verhulst, *The Carolingian Economy* (Cambridge, 2002)

N. Vincent, 'Warin and Henry fitz Gerald, the king's chamberlains: the origins of the FitzGeralds revisited', *ANS*, 21 (1999), 233–60

—— 'Regional variations in the charters of King Henry II', in *Charters and Charter Scholarship in Britain and Ireland*, ed. M. T. Flanagan and J. A. Green (Basingstoke, 2005), pp. 70–106

A. K. H. Wagner, 'Les noms de lieux issus de l'implantation Scandinave en Normandie: le case des noms en "-tuit"', in *Les fondations Scandinaves en occident et les débuts du duché de Normandie*, ed. P. Bauduin (Caen, 2005), pp. 241–52

W. L. Warren, *Henry II* (London, 1973)

—— *The Governance of Norman and Angevin England 1086–1272* (London, 1987)

N. Webber, *The Evolution of Norman Identity, 911–1154* (Woodbridge, 2005)

O. K. Werkmeister, 'The Political Ideology of the Bayeux Tapestry', *Studi Medievali*, third series, 17 (1976), 535–95

K.-F. Werner, 'Quelques observations au sujets des débuts du "duché" de normandie', in *Droit privé et institutions régionales: etudes historiques offertes à Jean Yver* (Paris, 1976), pp. 691–709

C. West, 'Count Hugh of Troyes and the territorial principality in early twelfth-century western Europe', *English Historical Review*, 127 (2012), 523–48

F. West, *The Justiciarship in England 1066–1232* (Cambridge, 1966)

G. H. White, 'Treasurers in Normandy under Henry I', *Notes and Queries*, 150 (1926), 59–60

—— 'The first house of Bellême', *Transactions of the Royal Historical Society*, 22 (1940), 68–80

G. J. White, *Restoration and Reform 1153–1165: Recovery from Civil War in England* (Cambridge, 2000)

S. D. White, '"*Pactum … legem uincit et amor iudicium*": the settlement of disputes by compromise in eleventh-century France', *American Journal of Legal History*, 22 (1978), 281–308, reprinted in S. D. White, *Feuding and Peace-Making in Eleventh-Century France* (Aldershot, 2005), ch. 5

—— 'Feuding and peace-making in the Touraine around the year 1100', *Traditio*, 42 (1986), 195–263

—— *Custom, Kinship and Gifts to Saints: The* Laudatio Parentum *in Western France, 1050–1150* (Chapel Hill, NC, 1988)

—— 'Proposing the ordeal and avoiding it: strategy and power in Western French litigation, 1050–1110', in *Cultures of Power: Lordship, Status, and Process in Twelfth-Century Europe*, ed. T. N. Bisson (Philadelphia, 1995), pp. 89–123

—— 'The politics of anger', in *Anger's Past: Social Uses of an Emotion in the Middle Ages*, ed. B. H. Rosenwein (Ithaca, NY and London, 1998), pp. 127–52

A. Williams, 'How land was held before and after the Norman conquest', in *Domesday Book Studies*, ed. R. W. H. Erskine and A. Williams (London, 1987), pp. 37–8

—— *The English and the Norman Conquest* (Woodbridge, 1995)

—— *Kingship and Government in Pre-Conquest England, c. 500–1066* (Basingstoke, 1999)

—— *Æthelred the Unready: The Ill-Counselled King* (London, 2003)

—— *The World Before Domesday: The English Aristocracy, 900–1066* (London, 2008)

G. Williams, *The Norman Anonymous: Towards the Identification and Evaluation of the So-Called Anonymous of York* (Cambridge MA, 1951)

E. A. Winkler, 'The Norman conquest of the classical past: William of Poitiers, language, and history', *JMH*, 42 (2016), 456–78

A. Winroth, *The Conversion of Scandinavia: Vikings, Merchants and Missionaries in the Remaking of Northern Europe* (New Haven, CT and London, 2012)

P. Wormald, '*Lex scripta* and *uerbum regis*: legislation and Germanic kingship from Euric to Cnut', in *Early Medieval Kingship*, ed. P. H. Sawyer and I. N. Wood (Leeds, 1977), pp. 105–38.

—— 'Charters, law and the settlement of disputes in Anglo-Saxon England', in *The Settlement of Disputes in Early Medieval Europe*, ed. W. Davies and P. Fouracre (Cambridge, 1986), pp. 149–68

—— 'Domesday Lawsuits: A provisional list and preliminary comment', in *England in the Eleventh Century: Proceedings of the 1990 Harlaxton Symposium*, ed. C. Hicks (Stamford, 1992), 61–102

—— *The Making of English Law: King Alfred to the Twelfth Century. Volume I Legislation and its Limits* (London, 1999)

—— 'Frederic William Maitland and the Earliest English law', in P. Wormald, *Legal Culture in the Early Medieval West: Law as Text, Image and Experience* (London, 1999), pp. 45–69

J. Yver, 'Les caractères originaux du groupe de coutumes de l'ouest de la France', *Revue d'Histoire du Droit Français et Etrangers*, fourth series 30 (1952), 18–79

—— 'Les caractères originaux de la coutume de Normandie', *Mémoires de l'academie nationale de sciences, arts et belles-lettres de Caen*, new series 12 (1952), 307–56

—— 'Les châteaux forts en Normandie jusqu'au milieu du XIIᵉ siècles', *BSAN*, 53 (1955), 28–121

—— 'Contribution à l'étude du développement de la compétence ducale en Normandie', *Annales de Normandie*, 8 (1958), 139–83

—— 'Les premières institutions du duché de Normandie', *I Normanni e la loro espansione in Europa*. Settimane di studio del centro Italiano sull'alto medioevo 16 (Spoleto, 1969), 295–366 and 589–98

—— 'Le "Très Ancien Coutumier" de Normandie: Miroir de la législation ducale?: Contribution á l'étude de l'ordre publique normand á la fin du XIIe siècle', *Tijdschrift voor Rechtsgeschiedenis* 39 (1971), 333–74

—— '"Vavassor". Note sur les premiers employs du terme', *Annales de Normandie*, 40 (1990), 31–48

E. Zadora-Rio, 'L'enceinte fortifiée du Plessis-Grimoult (Calvados). Contribution à l'étude historique et archéologique de l'habitat seigneurial au XIᵉ siècle', *Archéologie Médiévale*, 3–4 (1973–4), 111–243

Unpublished theses

R. Allen, 'The Norman episcopate 989–1110' (unpublished Ph.D. thesis, University of Glasgow, 2009)

J. Bickford-Smith, 'Orderic Vitalis and Norman society c. 1035–1087' (unpublished D.Phil thesis, Oxford University, 2006)

H. Chanteux, 'Recueil des actes d'Henri Beauclerc, duc de Normandie' (thèse inédite de l'Ecole des Chartes, 1932)

K. A. Dutton, 'Geoffrey, Count of Anjou and Duke of Normandy, 1129–51' (unpublished Ph.D. thesis, University of Glasgow, 2011)

C. Hammond, 'Family conflict in Ducal Normandy, c. 1025–1135' (unpublished Ph.D. thesis, University of St Andrews, 2013)

V. Moss, 'Normandy and the Angevin Empire: a study of the Norman Exchequer Rolls 1180–1204' (unpublished Ph.D. thesis, University of Wales, Cardiff, 1996)

Index of People and Places

Note: At the beginning of 2016 and 2017, a number of places in Normandy were merged into new communes. That is inconsistently reflected in this index, depending on whether I needed to check the département of the place in question. More consistent is the provision of regnal dates for kings, dukes, counts, and Norman bishops, which are given for ease of reference. For the same reason, I have also added (sometimes rather rough) dates for *some* members of the Norman aristocracy, where the successions can be confusing or difficult to establish.

Index of Subjects

9 781783 272143